Endorsements

Gilbert Lembree, retired IT Program Manager for a
manufacturing execution software, and a major U.

MW00675817

Mr. Ellis has written an excellent and monumental guide on how to protect yourself in the Internet. It is well written and contains detailed instructions for everything that you can do, which includes hardware, encryption, OS systems, software, email, social media, as well as online banking and other sensitive transactions. There is a gold mine of information in this book. You should read this book if you are interested in protecting yourself from identity theft and from being spied upon. I highly recommend it.

Yuri Signori, CIAP – President and Founder of I-PingU, LLC - providing IT Security and Data Forensic Services and Adjunct Professor of Computer Information Systems, University of Detroit, Mercy.

I think this is a first-class and all-encompassing book that is a great reference for people who are starting out and for experts alike! Kirk's writings on the subject matter are truly panoptic and will be a welcome contribution to the study of all information security and data assurance. His personal interpretations and experiences make the dry material engrossing and yet he manages to stay aligned with the facts.

The chapter pages are logically consonant in format. The book provides meaningful introductions, definitions to new words and concepts, presents the data clearly and concisely, gives related stories that the author has experienced or researched, and summarizes information neatly and intelligibly. As the book reads on, it evolves with the user's knowledge providing more in depth technical materials and examples.

To say that this book should be on the shelf of anybody responsible for data security should not be treated as a hackneyed phrase. The author's coverage of real world issues, home networking, business security tactics, meeting and creating security standards, outsourcing vs. purchasing/doing it yourself, data encryption, useful data security tools, mobile security including cellphones, common misconceptions, and an array of other topics, saves readers time from having to harvest the basis of what they need to know from volumes of information and from separate authors.

Jim Marano, Corporate Marketing Director, Percepta, LLC:

Kirk Ellis offers development and substantive writing attending to issues such as technical security for personal or commercial use captured in this book. Finding a person with insight, integrity on technical security that is also educated and worked in the ever changing technical environment captures real issues we face in business day to day is measurable.

If knowledge of technical security is what you seek or if you, your organization has concerns and is in need of a low cost fix to your technical security issues, I would encourage you to make a small investment of this book purchase.

Open Source, Donationware, and Freeware Projects Coverered in this Book

This book covers a vast array of freeware, donationware and open source software. Below are a few software projects that are covered, some in great detail, later in this book:

7-Zip 9.2, AbiWord 3.0.1, Adblock Plus 2.6.3 add-on, Alacarte, Anjuta software development studio, Amarok, aMule peer-to-peer, Apache OpenOffice 4.1.x, Audacious, Avidemux multi-purpose video editing & processing, Banshee Multimedia Management & Player, Belarc Advisor , Better Privacy add-on, BitTorrents, BleachBit 1.0, Bluefish Web Design Tool for Websites, Boot-Up Manager (BUM), BoxCryptor v2.0, BugMeNot plug-in, Calibre complete e-library solution, CCleaner 4.1x, Chocolatey Windows software downloader, Clonezilla, Darik's Boot And Nuke, Defraggler 2.18, Disconect.me add-on, DoNotTrackMe add-on, Dragon Naturally Speaking , Easeus Todo Backup, Empathy multi-protocol chat and call client, Evolution integrated mail--calendar--address book--to-do/task list and memo tool, Fedora 20 Linux OS, File Eraser, File Shredder, FileZilla 3.9.0.x is a cross-platform--multithreaded FTP--FTPS--and SFTP client, Firefox 33, Foxit Reader 6.2.2, Freemake, Ghostery 5.3.2 add-on, GNOME Desktop, GnuCash 2.6.3, GNU Image Manipulation Program (GIMP), GnuPG 2.0, GParted GNOME Partition Editor, Google Chrome, Gpg4win 2.2.2, GVim 7.3, Gwibber GNOME microblogging client, HiJackThis, HTTPS-Everywhere 3.5.5, HTTPS Finder 0.91, InfraRecorder 0.53, Inkscape is a SVG based vector image manipulation program/graphics editor, John the Ripper Password Cracking Tool, Lazarus Form Recovery 3.2, Kali Linux 1.0.9, Linux KDE Desktop, KeePass 2.25, Kingsoft Office Suite, KMyMoney 4.6.4, LibreOffice 4.3.3, Lightscribe, Linphone Voice Over IP phone (VOIP), Lubuntu 14.04.1/14.10 Linux OS, Lynis--Linux security & system audit tool, Mint Debian 201403, Kubuntu 14.04.1/14.10 Linux OS, Mint Cinnamon, Mate & KDE 17.1 Linux OS, Malwarebytes 2.0.x, Mate Desktop, Medusa Login Brute-Forcer, Memtest86+, Micorsoft Bitlocker, Microsoft MapPoint, Microsoft Process Explorer, NMap multi-platform security auditor, NoScript 2.6.8, Notepad++ 6.6.8, Opera secure Web Browser/Internet Suite, PrivacyFix add-on, OpenSSH 6.6, OpenSUSE 13.2 Linux OS, ophcrack, Password Safe, Privacy Badger 0.2.3, PuTTy 0.63, Quicken, Redo Backup and Recovery, Revo Uninstaller 1.95, Rootkit Hunter (RKHunter), Scribus desktop publishing application, Seagate Diskwizard, Seamonkey Internet Suite 2.3, Secunia Personal Inspector, SpiderOak 5.1.x, Spybot-Search and Destory 2.4, Tails Linux 1.2, Time and Chaos contact and time management Windows software, Thunderbird 31.2.x email client, Linux Tomboy desktop note-taking, Tor Browser Bundle 4.0.x for Linux and Windows, Totem Linux Video Player, Windows TrueCrypt 7.1a (don't trust versions after 7.1a), Ubuntu 14.04.1/14.10 Linux, VLC 2.1.5 multimedia player and streamer, VMware Player Desktop Virtualization 6.0.4, VirtualBox 4.3.20 Desktop Virtualization, , Web of Trust browser add-on, Whonix Linux anonymity solution, Windows 7, Windows Explorer, Linux Wine Windows compatibility layer, Linux XFCE Desktop, Xubuntu 14.10 Linux OS, USB YUMI-2.0.1.x tool, and much more.

Table of Contents

VI-----Contents

CHAPTER 8 – PREVENT CORPORATIONS FROM STALKING YOU – HOW TO USE THE TOR NETWORK, A PROXY, OR JONDONYM TO CLOAK YOUR BROWSER ACTIVITY (SURF ANONYMOUSLY) IN A VIRTUAL OS — 551

CHAPTER 9 – HARDENING SECURITY USING YOUR MOBIL DEVICES BY SETTING UP AND USING AN SSH SERVER ON YOUR REMOTE SECURE NETWORK — 606

About the Author

To briefly summarize my life, career and credentials; I have either contracted or worked directly for the: National Security Agency (NSA), U.S. Naval Air Systems Command (NAVAIR), U.S. Naval Sea Systems Command (NAVSEA), Naval Research Laboratory (NRL), United States Marine Corps (USMC), United States Marine Corps Reserve (USMCR), Cruise Missile Project (CMP), United States Air Force (USAF), United States Air National Guard (USANG), United States Army National Guard (USARNG), Tultex Corporation, GE Nuclear, Ford Motor, Lear Corporation, and JPMorgan Chase Bank. Of all these jobs and the many uniforms I have worn in life, I will always look back and remember that less than $1/10^{th}$ of 1 percent of U.S. citizens have ever worn the uniform of the U.S. Marine Corps, and as an old man, I wish I had stuck with that career. That figure is becoming less as the Corps slims it's active-duty roster to a mere 174,000 active duty Marines by the start of fiscal 2017, according to Semper-Fi magazine. However, I did not and instead moved on to work in Information Technology (IT) for these various industries and government/military organizations. My scope of work included: project management, leading development teams, software engineering, programming, software version control, administration and backing up many system's data, installing and cabling computers, switches, routers and other hardware in large data centers, and so much more. I have worked in almost every facet of large-entity data centers and have gained a great deal of my skill and expertise in these fields of general computer knowledge and IT security from my experiences in the corporate, military, manufacturing and financial sectors.

I am unique in that I have served in three branches of the U.S. Military and have worked for many agencies of the U.S. government as a contractor in many government agencies in Washington DC, that gives me a distinct perspective on the Internet and our current U.S. government. I know the inner workings of so many things that have I found disturbing, especially in how U.S. tax dollars are wasted spying on the American public. I have not met anyone that has my viewpoint or that has written about cyber security from a small business, corporate, military and multi-U.S. government agency perspective. If you wish to learn more refer down to <u>About the Author Continued-This Author's Survival Story in War, from Cancer, and Life. Never Give Up! Never Surrender!</u>

| **Story**  | After I came back from the Iraqi Freedom war, the corporation that that I was working for gave me plaque honoring my service. I quickly learned this meant nothing and I am sorry I allowed myself to be exploited as propaganda for their benefit. I hope that reading this book you now understand that I had many military unique talents to travel to and help the victims of Hurricane Katrina and during other U.S. events. I presented them to the Red Cross, which they desperately wanted my help. After Katrina I quickly requested one month off for leave without pay to travel down to Mississippi to help with the situation. I was capable of surviving on foot with backpack for over a month or two with my $4,000 in supplies and equipment to help the victims of that tragedy. The Corporation I worked for denied this request and I was told I would lose my job if I chose to help the Katrina victims in any way. Eventually that Corporation laid me off because I became a disgruntled employee traveling long distances to my work office and not understanding how they could deny the American people needed support. |

Acknowledgements

I have not attempted to name all of the authorities and sources that I have used in writing this book and in the context in which they were used. To do so would have distracted from the material presented and added many pages to this book. The list includes many universities, departments of the U.S. federal government, libraries, corporations, periodicals, websites, books, wikis and many individual blogs. Whenever cited, I tried to give them full credit by referencing their web pages or extolling their benefit to the production of this book.

There was no need to include in this book, a *credits* section, as is required in most computer books of this length and scope. As a disabled veteran, for years my family has been living on less than one fifth of my previous income while I battled cancer caused during war, and later tried to find gainful work, which I gave up on as an American long term unemployed disabled veteran. My family has been dependent upon Social Security Disability, a fund to which I paid into all 28 years of my civilian working life and military service, so I don't consider this funding as a handout as right-wing talk radio might suggest but with the publication of this book a hand up. The federal government applies a tax rate of 15% to these SSD payments and my family has faithfully paid those taxes quarterly and painfully. Under these limitations I could not afford to pay a multitude of artists, designers, editors, formatters, lawyers, marketers, managers, indexers, literary agents, proofreaders, project coordinators, publishers, website developers, or pay for things like expensive copyrighted corporate copyrighted artwork to help with this book. Therefore, I used my family's limited disability income to pay acquaintances, veterans, college students, lawyer friends, hired tax professionals, and family to experiment upon, and help review/refine this work as best I could. Some of them have worked for free, others I paid nominal amounts, compared to their usual per hour rate to review and edit my material. I owe them all my gratitude, respect and hopeful future compensation. I have made many mistakes paying relatives, law firms and tax preparing businesses that have ripped my family off but even with those losses I have kept costs within our SSD book budget, barely. Also, some of the advice from people who appeared to be knowledgeable but proved not to be professionals in their fields of expertise that has proven technically incorrect has cost me many hours to correct in this book. So please understand I have done the best I could with the honest resources I had on hand. In the end I managed to pay for final editing and to run a first few books off the press for promotional purposes. If you are reading this I assume the media to whom I sent my sample books actually gave it a moments notice. I have always expected a divorce at any time from my wife while writing this book. Consider this book a **freaking miracle** that it was ever published on my very limited budget and support![16][17] *What you are reading was never meant to exist and undoubtedly, the entities exploiting the infected Internet certainly never expected and for sure did not want to ever exist.* This book has come out of left field for them and I hope we all can enjoy the irony in that!

Judy Ellis - My loving wife and confidant in this endeavor. She never complained when I was sleeping as she left for work and was still in bed upon her return. The chemotherapy ravaged my body and even now, requires 10 to 12 hours of sleep after the exercise mandated by my doctor. She has watched me struggle these past years, first trying to survive cancer twice, then with all of the new IT technology, and ultimately with this book. She has patiently listened to me complain about my health, how the technological world has left me behind and how I had to catch up. She supported my decision to write this "crazy book", and encouraged me when I felt I that didn't have the energy to continue. Judy didn't complain about the substantial financial investment this book required on our very limited budget, and only raised her eyebrows when the Internet purchases arrived and we were surrounded by boxes of computer parts and software. Through it all, she has stood by my side and my hope is that this book will be successful enough to make her sacrifices while being our sole working income provider worthwhile. We recently adopted a dog and he has added much joy to our lives. If we are to travel the country promoting this book,we will enjoy his companionship as he has already shown himself to be the best road trip dog ever.

Jacob Emerte - Freelance artist, filmmaker and musician. Jacob is a proud student of Western Michigan University who took on the vague task that was assigned to him of depicting insecurity on the Internet. He has been involved in the arts since the age of four when he won the Christmas Greetings Cover design for Oakwood Hospital in Dearborn Michigan. He has won Scholastic awards for his artwork at the state level in high school and continues to utilize his talents for the good of mankind. Jacob is an up-and-coming graphics artist that any employer would dream of having. He hopes that his visual depictions used in this book not only aided the author, but also has valued the reader.

Jill Alecci - A long time veteran of the business world, assisted me with the editing of this book. She attained great insight, knowledge and experience, as well as competency in computer software, hardware, and data security programs through her commitment as an executive office manager and bookkeeper for several multi-million dollar U.S. corporations. Through the many legal contracts and accounting practices, she acquired a pronounced attention to detail. Owning and operating her own home-based business as a virtual assistant, she was able to gain entrepreneurial experience as well as update and maintain her skills. She relayed to me that her eyes were opened unbelievably so and that she considers the editing of this book a much needed learning experience; one that everyone should have. I consider her much more than an editor as she was my coach, confidant, and sometimes sole cheerleader keeping me going in writing this book. This book would not exist without her support and hard work.

Hunter Barrett - Social Studies teacher, basketball coach. Hunter is a two-time graduate from the University of North Carolina at Chapel Hill. He received a Bachelor of Arts in American History in 2011 and also a Master of Arts in Teaching in 2012. He has been studying history since middle school which inspired him to become a teacher to share his love of learning with students. He currently teaches World History at David W. Butler High School in Matthews, NC and hopes to eventually move on to teaching/working at the university level. He revised some of the historical references in the book for accuracy and consistency.

University of Detroit Mercy - They admitted me into their Master's Information Assurance program and allowed me to do volunteer work with their master's students in their advanced Homeland Defense Lab. These special projects opened my eyes and brought me up-to-date in many modern computing technologies. Those projects gave me my ideas for this book. Without their support and help, I would have never known the existence of much of what I am now presenting. My only regret is that I did not get the National Security Agency scholarship to pay for my masters in their Cyber Security Master's program for which I had applied. I consider this ironic as with no opportunity for further education or employment opportunities this brought about the creation of this book.

Eastern Michigan University - Eastern Michigan University admitted me to their Master's of Information Assurance program, which I could not take advantage of for financial reasons. I could not write the book, do research, look for a job, fight the VA, SSD, many other battles and seek aid to start their program at the same time. Their Master's program is great and I hope to perhaps attend someday after the publication of this book.

Henry Ford Community College - My thanks to Henry Ford Community College for allowing me to take a class in openSUSE Linux class and bypassing some pre-requisites thus enabling me to advance from my UNIX background into modern day Linux. That class opened my eyes as to how advanced the various flavors of Linux have become. I have used that class to spearhead my chapter on presenting four flavors of Linux in Chapter 7 on Virtualization in this book.

Michigan Rehabilitation Services - After surviving cancer twice, they supported my studies to get a Linux+ certification. That certification aided in my projects in small business and home computer security detailed in this book. They purchased my practice tests and paid for the certification test, which I greatly appreciate. These studies were all meant to aid me in getting a job. I applied for the various jobs that they presented and was rejected, so I gave myself a job to help the American people and perhaps someday, help MRS to gain the support that it needs to, once again, help the needy. Unfortunately, MRS remains underfunded by the State of Michigan and cannot support such things as continued education for the unemployed for Michigan citizens who need it.

American Legion - In order to make corrections and feedback from readers and editors on this book (which I felt is a critical necessity), I camped in many free, rustic Michigan areas and National Forest campgrounds. I received a lot of support from the veterans' facilities located nearby. One example is Manistee's American Legion Post 10, which allowed me to use their facilities and recharge the batteries on my laptop while camping free in the National forest. Without their help, along with the peace and quiet of my campsite, I don't know how I would have gotten through the arduous task of editing this book many times over. Writing and research are interesting, editing is awful! I camped in the most rustic, unpopulated campgrounds that I could find in order to edit this book. As I worked, all I wanted to see and hear were the forest and scurrying of the wildlife. My Dearborn MI post, to which I belong to, also funded the trimming of a tree in our backyard thus keeping the children next door safe. This is what helping others all is about!

Social Security Disability - For giving me back some of the money of which I had paid into the fund for many years. It has kept my family's bills paid while I wrote this book (since no one would give this disabled veteran who has limitations a job). That money has given me the time that I needed to show the world that I still have a contribution to make. My cancer was incurred during my service in Operation Iraqi Freedom and was acknowledged by the U.S. government as a disability caused during the war. I'm hoping that sacrifice will now have some further meaning to the world. However, they continuously harassed me many times with paperwork to cut off their funding as I worked on this book.

My Parents - I had the best parents on the planet as a child growing up. Unlike today's NANNY STATE, my brother and I were granted freedom to be stupid and possibly kill ourselves while doing many stupid things. We were loved and watched after as best as my parents could while they both worked for our future. They went into debt to make sure we experienced the best things in life. Someday I hope to see today's youth riding around without helmets when possible, playing tackle football in the backyard, riding skateboards on dangerous ramps, doing flips off of diving boards, playing with fireworks and so much more that we enjoyed. I realize that all these activities are all dangerous, but our youth today are deprived of these fun things for frivolous legal reasons. I regret in writing this book that my father has advanced in age such that this book holds no interest to him and my incredibly intelligent mother also has never read more than a few pages. I so wanted them to be proud of me but computer technology had passed them by, much like how I now struggle with smartphone technology. Maybe in their afterlife my parents will come to understand and appreciate my work on this difficult endeavor to protect individual Internet privacy and instruct our youth and the world as to how their lives and privacy are being invaded.

Lastly, in remembrance of friends lost, as I miss my best friend Christian McKinley Hutter and confidant Tom Bartos, both of whom were only a phone call away while writing this book. They both always offered encouragement and humor when I despaired while authoring this book. They are both in God's hands now among others I depended upon in the military.

Preface — Background Information and Preparation

*This book is my statement that I will/did not go gently into that good night. God allowed me to not bow down or admit defeat from the many physical setbacks in life that came due to service to my country. As a result, I set out to prove that any person with limitations can still contribute to, and change the world, even though the world they knew may reject their newfound limitations, and to prove that the pen is still mightier than the sword. This book is my testimony that we can all survive, endure adversity, and still triumph over the many obstacles placed in our path. My road has been a very difficult one to follow, and one I pray that no other person ever has to endure. Everyone in this world has value and I hope that the corporations, governments, and the insanely wealthy (plutocracy) who are invading our privacy, destroying our environment and exploiting our lives will someday realize these facts. I followed my heart, as this book is about the remembrance of my time spent with my military comrades in war, our U.S. history of individual liberty and our world's rapidly eroding digital freedom, which has been bathed in many U.S. heroes' blood, lost both in war and supposed peace, as U.S. soldiers have fought and continue to fight many undisclosed battles around the world. In this testimony, I state for the record there are many other heroes in war and illness whom I worship. I have been privileged to witness in my life extraordinary events, in the military, and while battling cancer with other malignancy victims who did not survive. These are the people who need to become the symbols of everybody's joint fight for their personal liberty and access to health care. Our youth must awaken to the privacy threats they now face when using the infected Internet, and choose liberty over security and convenience as western nations head down a path that their parents allowed but did not understand. Redemption, not condemnation, regret, despair or repentance, is necessary in our fight to right the wrongs of our clearly defined infected Internet past. I now bring all of my experience, my past knowledge, and my research to the page for posterity, in hope for realizing a free, fair and future democratic world or revitalized U.S republic and establish a free Internet. The pendulum has shifted way too far in favor of invading our supposed free Internet/digital privacy and it is this book's intent to address that shift as well as provide solutions that will, hopefully, bring our now infected Internet world back to an equilibrium position. With this book's introduction to the world we now have it within our power to begin to change the infected Internet realm that we all live in and now this book is here to begin the indispensable **war** that we all need to engage in addressing this attack on our individual liberty and privacy.*

I have faced a lot of opposition as I worked on this book to help educate you about the corruption that is taking place as you use the infected Internet. Known activists and whistleblowers have been suppressed, became fugitives or arrested in the past for presenting what I now can in this book, due to their public revelations and sacrifice. My dream is that this book will one day help produce a world in which we will achieve a future liberated Internet (communication medium) separate from the one that is being misused to gain information about people everywhere. Representative western governments worldwide have not amended their constitutions or passed the appropriate laws to protect individual Internet privacy.

We expect this activity from dictatorships, but supposedly free western citizens worldwide need to understand that their governments are also invading their own citizen's privacy, and they all need to stand against this assault with their votes and righteous indignation. This book is about helping you realize just what is taking place as you use the infected Internet and then aid you to employ how-to techniques that should make it much more difficult for you to be spied upon, cracked or tracked. *True Internet freedom is not possible until proper laws are passed by free representative governments worldwide*. By stating representative governments, I assume that free citizens elect officials that represent their fundamental principles of personal freedom and privacy, which seems to be increasingly rare in today's world. Until everyone understands that these fundamental rights are necessary and important to their individual freedom, and are now being exploited on a monumental scale, no change can be made. Most governments and large corporations are abusing the Internet and ignoring their country's citizens' privacy rights and the world's citizens' misuse of the Internet to make a document, such as the sacred U.S. Constitution I was sworn to protect, a joke. My goal in writing this book is that we can try to make exploiting your Internet use as difficult as possible for the hackers/crackers, criminals, scorned lovers, identity thieves, corporations, governments and any other entities that are victimizing us online. Knowing this, we need to try to change the laws and judicial systems that are allowing them to invade our privacy (e.g. U.S. citizens need to amend or repeal *The Patriot Act* and review the *U.S. Espionage Act* to allow whistleblowers to come forward unprosecuted).

How and Why this Book came into Existence

Federal, state, corporate and local services would not support my efforts at trying to get a part time job where I could use my IT skills or become self-employed as a writer or IT employee. They required many things such as constantly filling out useless employment applications, mailing resumes, and attending useless job fairs, establishing an LinkedIn account, all of which were ignored by the U.S. government and corporations in today's high-unemployment environment after the economic crash of 2008. With so many applicants clamoring for each precious position that became available, I quickly learned that there was no place for a four-time honorably discharged veteran who is a two time cancer survivor with many health work restrictions, a questionable survival status, and who has not held a steady job in six years after all this cancer carnage. This became the new reality in my life which placed my family in a position that seemed unattainable.

After my last stem cell cancer treatment, I was given a 40% chance of living, so this and my previous medical condition kept me out of work. Understand that the US government and insurance companies want to say that cancer remission is cured so they don't have to help the cancer victims. However, that is not true, as often the cancer comes back. If it does I will be given a 20% survival rating (assuming I choose to undergo the next round of treatments), so why would these institutions bother with giving me employment? The U.S. Affordable Care Act now seemed like a great thing since no health insurance company would even consider me as I worked to develop my cyber security small business. In the words of a recruiter, this makes me a *dinosaur* and completely unemployable in the field of corporate or government IT technology. I rapidly realized that I was a high cancer risk, an aged war veteran, and a perceived *dinosaur* in the corporate and government IT world that no one would want to take a risk on. This was a very humbling place to be in life when I used to demand very well paid salaries and respect. As a result, I view the constant advertisements about how corporations and government support veterans as self-aggrandizing.

Subsequently, I set out to write this book, even though I could not afford to pay the usual legions of employees that large companies making computer books can. Some computer books involve 20 or 30 people who participate in bringing them to market. I have replaced those unlimited resources with my 28 years of IT experience in the government, corporations, military, with volunteer work and by seeking out the very best unrecognized talent among college students and recent college Masters' graduates, friends, neighbors and recommended talent. I have paid my experienced friends, who had been let go by U.S. corporations, to help with marketing, photography, PowerPoint presentations and other things. These old "dinosaurs" proved useful in making this book happen. The people that I have hired on my very limited disability salary helped to create this book have taught me a lot about how to produce excellent artwork and editing. They were amazing in their talents and are acknowledged in this book.

I knew from the beginning that I would have to self-publish this work[16][17], so I took classes and read books on how to do so, properly and professionally. While trying to survive cancer I was abandoned by the corporate, military, and government institutions that I had served in the past. Upon the remission of my cancer (which insurance companies view as cured to profit them, *it is called remission for a reason*), I requested aid from various government and insurance agencies for this book and was rejected. You might think that their lack of support diminishes the content of this book. On the contrary, I feel that what I am presenting is far superior because I was not restrained or constrained by their bureaucracy or limitations, which is what the authors, who are employees of the government and corporate institutions, must endure when signing away their artistic freedom. The old adage about too many hands and legal limits in the mix holds true with this book. I have no *for-profit* motive by a corporate, periodical or Internet source to advertise my product as many other computer books do. Plus, I admit I have a chip on my shoulder to show them what a rejected cancer surviving **DINOSAUR** can produce. So consequently, the truth is that their day-in-and-day-out dismissal has driven me to make this book all it can be.

I thank our Holy Father for allowing me to write this book, and feel he has compelled me to write and publish it at all costs (which were enormous considering my family's very limited disability budget)[16][17]. I love a good book, but other than this one, I haven't had the time to read one in over eight years unless it was related to cyber security. The U.S. government, state institutions and insurance companies wasted my time with many fruitless endeavors and paperwork while writing this book; I wanted to give up countless times and many people suggested that I do so (including acquaintances, family, friends and previous co-workers). Nonetheless, every day I continued on my crusade toward this goal of publishing this book, against their protestations. While writing this book I have also survived bloodletting accidents that I should not have survived.

I have had many close encounters with crippling injuries and death, just by the nature of my life. This was due to my military service; accidents, cancer, war, PTSD and I hate to admit, being a little reckless (delinquent) as a young person. There are many examples in my life where I survived and others did not. I feel guilt over that, as I think any veteran does, and I often ask, "why me?" I am very grateful to still be alive and writing this book. I love my life and the free world. My prayer is that civilians, military heroes and their families, and oppressed freedom-loving dissidents around the world, will have more freedom using the Internet by the reading of this book. This is my acknowledgement and testament to their sacrifices. God has granted me the allowance of continued survival, against all odds, to write and publish this book. In dedication to his gift, I have worked non-stop every moment that I could. I cherish these values much more than my given experiences. I see this book as a continuation of my military service to establishing a free world and as a fulfillment of my promise to my many comrades who have died. I think that any veteran wants their service to stand for the cause of freedom and righteousness around the world. However, the current political goals of my government seem to stray from the causes for which I fought. For example, why were many forces withdrawn after the 21 day Iraq invasion ended when history demonstrated that we would need so many more soldiers than that (e.g. it took one million soldiers to occupy Germany after the war).

Quotation Publius Flavius Vegetius Renatus 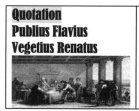	In Latin, "*Si vis pacem, para bellum*" translated as "*If you want peace, prepare for war.*" But if you dig deeper you also have "*Si vis bellum para pacem*" which roughly means "*if you are planning a war show the world you are cultivating peace.*" (See: https://en.wikipedia.org/wiki/Si_vis_pacem,_para_bellum)

According to https://en.wikipedia.org/wiki/2003_invasion_of_Iraq, "*General Eric Shinseki, U.S. Army Chief of Staff, recommended "several hundred thousand" troops be used to maintain post-war order, but then Secretary of Defense Donald Rumsfeld – and especially his deputy, civilian Paul Wolfowitz – strongly disagreed. General Abizaid later said General Shinseki had been right.*" The real question is why the war in Iraq was and VA underfunded to help those returning soldiers? After 9-11 Americans everywhere would have gladly purchased war bonds or perhaps suffered a temporary tax increase to fund the war. Moreover, why did the U.S. fight in Afghanistan for 15 years before bringing it to a close? General Eric K. Shinseki was appointed as Secretary of Veterans Affairs and was later discredited by the U.S. political community for mismanagement of the underfunded U.S Veterans Administration. I view this as a government asking him to fall on his sword and he was made to take the blame for years of their disparaging veterans in health care. (See: https://en.wikipedia.org/wiki/Eric_Shinseki)

In this book, I have tried to demonstrate how to use your Internet devices and still remain free and somewhat private on the Internet by applying the techniques that I present. I swore an oath in a prayer while flying overseas to war: "*If I survive this war I will honor and help the families of the men and women who died in Iraq, Afghanistan and Kuwait, when/if I return by whatever means I find possible.*" I have been unable to do so because of my individual struggle just to survive cancer. However, while sick, I started work on this project in the hope of fulfilling that commitment to my fellow service men and women, albeit in somewhat of a different fashion than I had ever imagined. Against all odds, God has granted me that opportunity and for the past nine years I have dedicated every waking moment of my life, my family's resources and my soul to this book. As one PhD put it, in a college venue, my work on this book would/should constitute a PhD thesis. I have not had much interaction with my parents, friends, relatives, strangers or even my wife as I battled cancer and worked on this "crazy book" as most everyone I know calls it. This book is the end result of what I hope God intended for my continued life and love of this planet, our United States, freedom loving dissidents around the world, my wife, family, friends, and the soldiers who did not survive in war where as I did. **I dedicate this book to all of you and the fallen veterans!**

There Comes a Time in History for Every Revolutionary Book

We have never seen a moment such as today, where a pivotal instant is taking place in our human technological story. We are conducting an incredibly important technological narrative on ourselves that has to be addressed. We have made, and are continuing to make, huge advances in computer/mobile hardware, software, applications, surveillance, and spyware technology, that not only tracks our every physical movement, but also our use of the Internet, GPS locations, and so much more. There are thousands of apps for smartphones and other mobile devices that we all use blindly to simplify our lives without considering that there are many hidden agendas concealed behind this software. Parents are installing applications on their children's smartphones to track their every move. Those tracking applications are getting cracked and have many back doors allowing others to track those smartphones as well. There are many other advanced technological choices that are just now coming into existence for Small Business Owners and Home Computer Users (SBO/HCU). In the last nine years of writing this book and blogging without profit and much attention, I have witnessed revolutions in camera and surveillance technology that we all now need to step back and consider carefully their use and safeguards for our privacy protection, which are very limited. This book covers how to use some of this technology, as well as how to circumvent some of its use.

Our governments and corporations have utilized this technology for many years, but it is just now becoming mainstreamed to the SBO/HCU. How far do we want to go with this equipment/technology? Thus far, we have been complacent in allowing this invasion into our privacy by our governments and corporations; but now anyone can afford to utilize much of this equipment. Do we really want to employ the use of this equipment on ourselves? We need to come to the understanding that the use of these devices and cloud services now open up new doors into our day-to-day activities for crackers*, corporations and governments who continue to further exploit these devices and our Internet activity, with and without our knowledge. Consider the fact that often foreign, for-profit businesses had a hand in the design and manufacturing of the devices that we use. We have to carefully examine these technological devices, their corporation and country of origin, and ponder their other possible other motives. Nevertheless, most of us just purchase this equipment without considering these important questions. We are all too busy to take in the bigger picture and depend on our governments to provide information about this technology, and that is not happening for the SBO/HCU. There are few, if any, "do-not-buy" recommendations from the British or United States governments about this equipment that I have found during my research on this topic. Ask yourself, why is that?

When we install hidden cameras and listening devices in our homes, spy equipment and software on computers, or mobile apps on smartphones and/or smart TVs, we are opening ourselves up to backdoors for "the man*", thieves, crackers*, foreign governments and corporations to tap into them as well. Do you really believe that something designed, engineered, manufactured and produced for you to purchase for your own security does not have some sort of override, U.S. or foreign government crack, or backdoor mechanism?

Can we all be so naive as to assume otherwise, especially without binding legal and privacy statements that have severe penalties to the contrary, which are rarely enforced or even exist. When was the last time that you heard of a corporation being brought to trial for spying on an individual citizen, or an admission from any government that it has gone too far with this type of invasion into our privacy or spying on our day-to-day lives? When the last time was a western (U.S) government was accused or pursued justice in the international courts as the Chinese, Russian or other criminal organizations in their countries blatantly crack their government, corporate, or SBO/HCU computers? We hear about how our governments meet and discuss these topics, but hear nothing about the outcome. These invasions into our Internet devices are quickly covered up and not exposed in today's media. Our governments have yet to provide proof to the public that these activities are not actually sponsored by foreign governments and continually downplay the magnitude of what is really taking place. The passage of the December 2012, U.S. Foreign Intelligence Surveillance Act (FISA) Legislation, while American citizens were distracted by their governments' make-believe fiscal crisis, proves that the U.S. government is much more interested in its individual citizens' use of the Internet rather than the exploitation of the Internet by foreign entities.

On the side of worldwide individual freedom, there are technologies like the Linux operating systems that exist for everyone's use. The advent of individual virtualization (guest operating systems), open source solutions, and donationware*/freeware* products, whose use as installations have become vastly simplified, can be used to combat this assault. These free open source solutions are now plug-and-play, like purchased alternatives. In the years that I have spent writing this book, these technologies have evolved such that it has allowed me to add new topics and present solutions that are even more advanced. I have reworked my exercises and my writing many hundreds of times in the last eight years, sometimes eliminating or altering entire chapters as more advanced solutions have presented themselves. For example, back in 2010 setting up a multiboot USB drive was a long chapter of this book, which required many weeks of experimentation on my part to produce. Now, as the open source* community progresses, it is so easy to do, that setting up a multiboot USB drive is now just a short chapter of this book. Three years ago, most Small Business and Home Computer users would have been overwhelmed with what I was attempting to present. However, because the open source* community has continued to develop their operating systems and software, they now have many advanced and easy-to-implement solutions to our everyday needs. These Linux Operating Systems (OSs) are now innovative "plug and play" and recognize all of my PC hardware as well. I continue to be amazed at how things progress and I have worked continually to keep this book current as new donationware*/freeware* and open source* solutions became available, which has not been easy. The answers presented in this book are up to date as of August 2014. Other computer books you read will never make that statement for fear of quickly becoming outdated. This book boldly makes that statement in anticipation of future revisions. My goal is to help the SBO/HCU stand on the leading edge of technology with this wonderful, inexpensive and advanced open source* technology, as well as use these solutions to keep ourselves safe from crackers*, corporations, governments, scorned lovers, thieves and anyone else who would want to invade our privacy.

WARNING	Be careful how far you want to go down the rabbit hole of learning about the infected Internet. This knowledge may affect your thinking about the world you and your children live in and for that I apologize. The world we live in is not one of my making and my hope is that this knowledge will not affect your sleep at night as it does mine. All I can tell you is that I was much happier years ago in my eight to five IT job and going-to-the-gym life, when I did not know or care about what was really taking place in the infected Internet world. I will always miss the innocence of those bygone working days. Please ask yourself, before reading further, if you really want to learn about these things.

In the remainder of this book, any terms, like open source and cracker followed by a "*", is defined in the context in which it is used. If it is a prominent term used throughout the rest of this book, future uses of the term will not include an "*". If a term is used rarely, it is defined in the Glossary of this book and an "*" follows it throughout the book.

Definition Open Source Software 	**Open source** is a way for people to collaborate on software legally. Developers are no longer encumbered by laws that protect proprietary intellectual property. It is a pragmatic methodology that promotes the free redistribution of wonderful software projects for you to use freely. For example, getting this book published required the use of a law firm to copyright all of my artwork and get rights to all artwork that I paid my artist to create. With open source software, you don't have to negotiate contracts, have many lawyers involved, or suffer the expense of having a group of people work on a creative software solution or project that you need for your home or business. (See: https://en.wikipedia.org/wiki/Open_source).
Definition Cracker	A cracker is a computer enthusiast, or computerphile, is one who gains or attempts to gain unauthorized access to computers or computer networks and tamper with operating systems, application programs, and databases. A cracker (black hat) knows they are intentionally breaking the law; a hacker (white hat) can be a computer security expert or a novice who does not know the law. (See: https://en.wikipedia.org/wiki/Hacker_(computer_security)).

Everyone is Spying on your Internet Activity and Storing it Permanently for your Lifetime

As I stated before, governments around the world expend *vast* resources to spy upon and exploit their citizens' Internet use to attack anyone not in their self-interests. In oppressive countries, using the infected Internet incorrectly can result in severe repercussions, torture, and even death. My hope is that freedom-loving dissidents, living under dictatorships, can get a copy of my book into their countries to help achieve some sort of limited Internet freedom, which western countries' citizens seem to take for granted. In no way do I want to present this book as an answer to your/their need for Internet privacy but I view it as the second battle after Edward Snowden's revelations waged in our continuing privacy war.

We all have to understand that the Internet has become *the* medium of communication and social interaction between individuals everywhere around the world. Things like Twitter, Facebook, LinkedIn, Google, YouTube, and Email quickly go viral with pictures and videos of what used to be impossible things to reveal about what is actually going on in the world.

The early Internet seemed to be a free, wonderful, and somewhat safe place to benefit the world with its roots presenting it to be a new and secure way of conducting online banking, e-commerce, doing research and gathering information. It is estimated that 85% of America is now online in some fashion every day. That free web paradigm has swiftly shifted and now, in all countries, by all citizens, must be viewed as a public forum. The Internet is **NOT** a wonderful medium that preserves and protects personal individual freedoms any longer. Governments, corporations, hackers (with the evil ones among them which we will call crackers), identity thieves, cyber criminals and scorned lovers (which my artwork depicts thanks to my wonderful artist) have corrupted our use of the Internet to invade our personal privacy and steal our freedom.

Quotation Albert Einstein	The world is a dangerous place not because of those who do evil but because of those who look on and do nothing.
Quotation Kirk Ellis	The Internet is a dangerous place not because of those spying on everything we do using it but because we are looking on and doing little about it.

Our use of the Internet is not only being exploited for ill-gotten gain and profit, but is also being used to spy on our day-to-day activity. In the United States, as technology and frivolous laws advance, the original intentions of our forefathers have been ignored as our new U.S. Republics security laws take effect concerning our governments treatment of the Internet in regards to privacy (e.g. **FICA legislation and the Patriot Act**). For example, the U.S. NSA has completed a massive facility to spy on U.S. citizens that house **billions of dollars** in computer equipment while their homeless veterans and citizens starve. Where is the outrage and why is their media not reporting on this daily? Other democratic/republic nations also have to consider their trends toward violating their citizens' individual privacy and use of the Internet. My dream is that one day the human race will make strides to judiciously protect their digital freedom in their continuing free use of the Internet, as we are now in the Internet information age of our worldwide civilization's existence. Instead of everyone working to suppress and/or exploit the use of the Internet, why can't we all work together to expand and safeguard its use, which is the purpose, hope and dream, as well as the focus of this book. This book provides solutions that use modern day technology to protect your privacy. I have worked eight years to produce the dedicated projects that are meant to help keep your Internet and daily life free, safe and secure as possible. The exercises in this book are an essential use of your time. If you have no interest in this author, or the validity of my work, please skip the following descriptions of myself and get on with the core of this book. Still, remember that until laws exist to protect you from your governments, none of what I have produced will help stop their surveillance and monitoring. It is ultimately up to you to demand Internet freedom and privacy.

We are all overwhelmed with day-to-day details and matters and do not want to or cannot take the time to figure out how to secure our Internet devices. We also do not want to, or cannot afford to pay experts to do this for us. However, we cannot trust anti-software and file cleaning software to do the job alone without taking other precautions and countermeasures. If we do so, we are exposing our devices to malware by not keeping them up-to-date with the many advances that crackers are making in malware and technology. Our front-line solution appears to be new hardware, or an expensive OS, or various anti-software purchases.

With so many responsibilities such as a job, family, cooking, cleaning, maintenance and/or repair, and a plethora of other duties in the picture, the computer has become an overused and neglected appliance. Unfortunately, the computer cannot be ignored like a coffee maker, stove, toaster, washer, or a microwave until it breaks, though this is how it is often treated. The truth is that most people would rather work around the house than face a computer problem. Incredibly, many users do not even recognize the threats to their home or small business computers. Crackers—those unethical black, or sometimes grey hat hackers, rely on the average SBO/HCU's inability or unwillingness to keep the computer s/he uses on a daily basis safe, secure, updated and in good working order. We will soon discuss the goals and achievements of these unethical hackers.

Crackers focus on breaking into systems by using available cracking programs, and exploiting well-known vulnerabilities in systems to uncover sensitive information for personal gain or to inflict damage on the target system or network. This book will show you that securing your network, computers and personal information is not as time-consuming, nor as difficult to do as you may think. Securing your computers is possible, even for novice users, and it is very important to do so.

My goal with this book was to abuse everyone's view and thinking about the Internet world in which they live. I have sought to show how both the left and the right extremist views are wrong, in my effort to help save our planet and make it one in which we all need to now co-exist with rights and privacy. I hope this book offends everyone in some way thus sparking a debate that needs to take place about how some self-interest are destroying our privacy, our freedom and our world. I know that we all want our children to grow up in a better world, but we must face the fact that the future we are building for them, based on our own self-interests and materialism, is not one that is better for them but one that has become much worse. We cannot kick these world-encompassing decisions down the road any further. We have to rise up beyond this misguided thinking and sacrifice ourselves, our time, our intellect, our wealth, and work for a private and free Internet future. Our world and privacy are dying, and unless we all make a stand for mankind, we will suffer in a manner never foreseen by our children, who will hate us for our lack of sacrifice as we all stood by and allowed this to happen. Yes, that means the super wealthy as well as the super poor must work together. I hope this book will make that notion clear that we are all in this battle to save our infected Internet world together. As I stated before, we have reached a pivotal moment in human history. The future of our planet and freedom is at stake and it is up to you change our future, which I hope my book depicts.

The U.S. Digital Fourth Amendment We All Need!

When the Bill of Rights was written over 200 years ago, the U.S. was largely agrarian, so communication depended on a few hand delivered newsletters and face-to-face communication. As society progressed, the Supreme Court was challenged to determine what it is that constitutes an unreasonable search or seizure and has ruled on the side of U.S. citizens' privacy. The first instance was to determine if a letter that was being handled by the U.S. Postal Service needed a warrant to be opened. The second came with the invention of the telephone and government wiretapping of phone conversations. In both cases, the Court determined that citizens could reasonably expect their communications to remain private and should not be subject to government surveillance without a warrant.

However, in this ruling, the Supreme Court created a **gaping hole** that allowed the U.S. government and corporations access to record, recover and view information that a citizen had turned over to a third party. As the digital age rapidly progressed, this hole effectively nullified the Fourth Amendment. A warrant in the U.S. has become a thing of the past in the digital age for just about all communication and data since just about anything we do while using the infected Internet is shared with a third party. Anything we do when using smartphones, text messages, email, social media and cloud computing can be shared with everyone, and is.

| **Factoid**  | The U.S. now ranks below many third world countries, worse than Cuba, Czech Republic, Egypt, Haiti, Iran, Iraq, Libya, Mexico, Nigeria, North Korea, Pakistan, Russia, Syria, Uganda, and so on. The level of income equality that U.S. citizens endure will hit critical mass as this disproportionate distribution of income places us behind 162 other countries in income equity. Wages for the average U.S. worker have not risen since the late 1970s. Our middle class has all but disappeared as less than one half of one percent of our population acquires all of the U.S. nation's wealth. (See: https://en.wikipedia.org/wiki/List_of_countries_by_income_equality , https://secure.huffingtonpost.com/2013/01/22/global-income-inequality-globalpost_n_2526425.html and the documentary "Inequality for All" by Jacob Kornbluth) |

Congress attempted to address digital privacy with the passage of the Electronic Communications Privacy Act in 1986 but as the digital age progressed, this law became moot, which we will discuss in Chapter 1. The current U.S. Fourth Amendment reads, **"The right of the people to be secure in their persons, houses, papers, and effects, against unreasonable searches and seizures, shall not be violated, and no Warrants shall issue, but upon probable cause, supported by Oath or affirmation, and particularly describing the place to be searched, and the persons or things to be seized."**

It is my belief that there is no law that can be passed that will take back the privacy rights that have been surrendered in our new U.S. digital age. The time has come to call a **Convention of the States** to return the U.S. to the original vision of the U.S. Founders, which was a limited Federal Government that respects the privacy of its citizens; we need nothing less than a *Digital Fourth Amendment* added to the U.S. Constitution. There are two methods to amend the U.S. Constitution:

1. Two-thirds of each House of Congress agrees to propose a particular amendment.
2. Two-thirds of the state legislatures pass applications for a convention for the purpose of proposing amendments on the same subject.

Our U.S. country's founders knew that the day might come when a bloated Federal Government drunk with the abuses of power and controlled by a plutocracy* and unforeseen future corporations may need to be reined in by changing or amending the U.S. Constitution. The current situation of uncontrolled corporate and government spying, out-of-control spending, irresponsible centralized government, a massively expanding gap in income distribution favoring less than 1% of the U.S. population and so much more; we must have a restoration of privacy, liberty and an American Renaissance. This can only happen if we mobilize, organize and energize everyone as to how these issues are important to their everyday lives, continued existence and future individual wealth, which has disappeared for middle income Americans. This is my paraphrased, proposed Digital Fourth Amendment to the U.S. Constitution:

"The right of the people to be secure in their digital communication, devices and data, against collection, dissemination by/to third parties or government, shall not be violated, and no Warrants shall issue, but upon probable cause, supported by Oath or affirmation, and particularly describing the device to be searched, the data being seized, and the persons or property affected." Join me by signing my petition at https://petitions.whitehouse.gov to get this Amendment enacted.

Warning -- Disclaimer

The intention of this book is to provide superior solutions than have ever before been presented to the SBO or HCU. This book was written solely by the author who made every effort to ensure that the solutions presented are as complete, accurate and up-to-date as possible. Every project (chapter) presented has been performed many and sometimes hundreds of times from multiple computers and is well documented. However, given the large volume and advanced nature of the security techniques covered there may be mistakes, both typographical and in content. I have worked very hard to give credit to my thousands of sources and have tried to cite them without plagiarism. If I made any mistakes and did not mention someone properly please bring that to my attention I will post a retraction on my blog and correct them in the second edition of this book.

I present in this book, many years and many thousands of hours of research (8 years of my life) in reading books, many thousands of web pages on the Internet, periodicals and books. I drew everything I could from my 28+ years of experience in Information Technology (IT) and poured that experience into this undertaking. Individually I cannot exhaustively test the tools, utilities, operating systems, and the techniques described in this book. Use them at your own benefit/risk. For example, I have not studied the mathematical algorithms used in the encryption software presented in this book. I trust in the fact that the software actually employs strong, documented encryption techniques that would make you much more secure than you would be if you were not using them. The open source, free programs and software presented in this book may have other hidden agendas, which would require study of the source code. The anti-software and references I have used and studied say otherwise. I have to assume the anti-malware companies are hard at work making sure this software is safe. All utilities, tools and software that I employ were scanned by using multiple anti-malware programs.

I have not deliberated upon the details on how the protocols that make up many of the solutions that I have presented in this book actually work so use them at your own risk and do your own study. I did my best to research these solutions and present them based as trusted, reliable sources. I vetted those sources for your benefit as best as I could and present them to you throughout the book. I detail arguments both for and against many of the solutions that I support. The Internet is a **very** vulnerable place to be! I believe this book will make it much less so.

Various websites claim that the U.S. government views anyone "overly concerned about privacy" or attempting to "shield the screen from the view of others" should be considered suspicious and potentially engaged in terrorist activities. (See https://en.wikipedia.org/wiki/Privacy) The use of anonymizers, portals, or other means to shield an IP address, could be viewed as a sign that a person could be engaged in or is supporting terrorist activity. The use of encryption is also listed as a suspicious activity. The use of GPG, SSH, VPN*, Tor, or any of the many other advanced technologies presented in this book for anonymity are also reportable activities. Use these tools only as an honest citizen protecting yourself from internet crackers and criminals. Corporations, which are considered individuals by law, use these techniques with impunity and the SBO/HCU should be able to do so as well. In fact, the ruling, Citizens United verses Federal Election Commission in 2010, upheld the right of corporations to make political contributions under the First Amendment. (See: https://en.wikipedia.org/wiki/Corporate_personhood, https://en.wikipedia.org/wiki/Citizens_United_v._Federal_Election_Commission)

If the U.S. government stands against your use of these tools for honest purposes, then it also has to take away the use of these tools from corporations. It would also mean that my 11+ years of military service stands for nothing. It is argued that the U.S. Constitution does not implicitly grant you the right to privacy against government intrusion. I beg to differ with that statement. Ask any soldier what they are fighting for, in any war, and they will tell you that it is freedom and a better way of life for the people they fight for and love. According to https://en.wikipedia.org/wiki/List_of_countries_by_number_of_military_and_paramilitary_pers onnel, the US troop size is 2,291,910, which by 2017 will only include 174,000 Marines and the U.S. population is 317,503,384 according to http://www.census.gov/main/www/popclock.html. This means that only 0.72% of the U.S. is in uniform are sworn to fight for the U.S. Constitution and of that number .00054% are Marines. Soldiers and veterans cannot fight this battle alone. *We must all work to keep the Internet from becoming a perversion of our liberty and instead make it an extension of our freedom!*

Otherwise all is lost, and our God-given right of free choice, which is guaranteed in the U.S. Constitution, will be gone. That is what this book is about. We have to prevent corporations and governments from perverting our use of the Internet into something for their exploitation of spying on everything we do, and keep it free and safe for small business and individual use. However, we all now know that the NSA has made this ideal otherwise, but following the techniques in this book should make you safer.

In this book, I used quotations extensively from Wikipedia to whom I have contributed to for their beneficial information to this book. Wikis are collaborative websites allowing people to update the information based on their personal experience and research. Their listings remain current and are becoming ever-evolving databases of information. Because wikis allow anyone, regardless of credentials, to suggest changes, the academic world does not regard them as reliable sources of data. The wikis were used in this book because:

1. Wikipedia is the world's largest and most popular encyclopedia, with content generated by users from experts to hobbyists. Wikipedia has a self-correcting mechanism that eliminates inaccuracies when they are found and corrected by knowledgeable readers.
2. Wikis can be quoted by adhering to their Creative Commons license, http://creativecommons.org/licenses/by/3.0/us, by giving full credit to the sources used without first garnering permission.
3. Wikis gives permission to use their information which duplicates the material found in many copyrighted sources.
4. The content of this book is time sensitive in nature. Technology is rapidly advancing as do the techniques to keep computer users secure. As soon as the final draft depicting my security solutions was up-to-date and with the latest versions of tools discussed, this book had to be published as quickly as possible. Waiting to receive permission from copyrighted sources dated the time-sensitive nature of this book.
5. To keep this book as credible as possible, I cross-referenced what was documented on the wikis with other "considered" reliable sources, when and where they could be found. Some of the material presented is on the leading edge of technology and had few, if any, other references.

My website http://thatcybersecurityguy.com and my blog at http://thatcybersecurityguy.blogspot.com will offer you technological solutions from my past and your future. However, if my cancer comes back or there is some other unforeseen event, updates will **not** be forthcoming. Your purchase of this book does not guarantee further correspondence on cyber security, even though that is my intention. I am planning to incorporate these updates into the next revision of this book. Because of my limited resources, I give no timeline or schedule as to when or what updates will be provided. I'm hoping to perhaps someday have a newsletter or some other mechanism of keeping you updated and if I do I will take very strict safeguards to protect any personal information you provide, such as your email address. Sometimes, for-profit corporations and bookmaking companies do not make this statement to protect your privacy of which you need to be very wary. In no way do I want to collect any information about you or profit from your Internet activity as these are the very principles upon which this book stands against. Any information provided for correspondence will never be used for profit or sold to any third parties. You need to understand that many businesses you give this information to will sell it to others for profit. My book is about how to prevent this activity from taking place!

Who Should Read This Book?

Anyone who connects to the Internet faces threats from crackers (malicious hackers) spies, corporations and governments, criminals and identity thieves, as discussed in this book. Anyone who wishes to protect themselves from those threats without paying for consultants and IT specialists to set up business or home networks, should read and benefit from this book. The latest U.S. government's strategic plan to Combat Identity Theft http://www.idtheft.gov which this sad dated 2007 material points out is that many small businesses (SB) using Information Technology (IT) and the Internet do not have basic security measures in place. Their 2005 survey gives us some startling numbers:

- nearly 20% did not use virus scans for email, a basic information security safeguard that does not reveal 20% of the malware infecting their devices
- over 60% did not protect their wireless networks with even the simplest of encryption solutions

However, Symantec Corporation released a 2012 survey, which is much more relevant than the 7 year old data that the U.S. government provides. These recent statistics are even more startling. Below is a brief summary of their findings:

- 83% of Small Businesses have no formal cyber security plan, but 77% say their company is safe from cyber threats such as hackers, viruses, malware or a cyber security breach
- six out of 10 (59%) do not have a contingency plan outlining procedures for responding and reporting data breach loses
- 40% of the over one billion cyber attacks Symantec prevented in the first three months of 2012 targeted companies with less than 500 employees
- the majority of U.S. small businesses believe their information is protected but admit they have no policies or protective measures in place; 69% of SBs do not even have an informal Internet security policy
- 70% of SBs do not have policies for employee social media use
- Visa Inc. reports small businesses represent more than 90% of the payment data breaches reported to the company
- 60% of SBs says they do not have a privacy policy that employees must comply with when they handle customer or employee information
- One in ten (11%) SBOs say that no one is responsible for cyber security at their business

- As fraud victims increase, small business retailers are dramatically impacted as some 15% of consumers change shopping behaviors after fraud to avoid those retailers

(See: https://www.symantec.com/about/news/release/article.jsp?prid=20121015_01, http://www.staysafeonline.org/download/datasets/4393/2012_ncsa_symantec_small_business_study_fact_sheet.pdf)

The survey also found that 47% of SBOs felt that if their business suffered a data breach this would prove to be an isolated incident and have little impact. However, the August 12, 2013 PCWorld article by Robert Strohmeyer titled "Hackers put a bull's-eye on small business" http://www.pcworld.com/article/2046300/hackers-put-a-bulls-eye-on-small-business.html#tk.nl_secur states "*According to the National Cyber Security Alliance, one in five small businesses falls victim to cybercrime each year. And of those, some 60 percent go out of business within six months after an attack. You've got a 20 percent chance of being hacked, and if it happens there's a good chance your business is finished. Smaller companies are increasingly attractive targets for attackers, too. Symantec's latest annual Internet Security Threat Report found that companies with fewer than 250 employees constituted a staggering 31 percent of targeted attacks in 2012—a massive jump from 18 percent the year before.*"

Whether you use your PC at home, at work or in public, and either for personal use or for your small business, you will find this book useful and easy to follow, assuming that you have some basic knowledge of computer use. On that note, this book also assumes that you have a basic working knowledge of the Windows Operating System and hopefully, Linux. This book presents solutions in Linux, but detailed knowledge of Linux is not necessary to grasp all of the solutions presented.

The examples and screenshots in this book are taken from the products listed on the copyright page of this book. Later versions of the products, applications, and OSs may appear differently than what is depicted in this book's step-by-step directions presented to the reader. Knowledge of how to perform the following tasks should make this book easily applicable for any computer user. Hopefully, you:

- can download a file from a website
- are no longer running Microsoft Windows XP SP3 operating system (According to http://windows.microsoft.com/en-US/windows/products/lifecycle mainstream support ended April 14, 2009, extended support will end April 8, 2014). Without mainstream support there will be no bug fixes or other patches unless you pay for it, though you still will receive security updates. We will use XP as a virtual environment in Chapter 7
- are no longer running Windows Vista SP2 (mainstream support ended April 10, 2012, extended support will end April 11, 2017)
- have a somewhat modern computer (see: What you will need to employ the techniques described in this book)
- understand what Windows Explorer is and how to navigate it to manage files and folders on your computers (e.g. find and create files and folders on your computer, store a download in a folder, move or copy a file or folder) (not to be confused with Internet Explorer which is used to browse the web)
- know how to unzip (extract) files from an archive (or zip file)

- know how to use Windows Explorer to get to an extracted archive and run the portable or installation executable in that folder
- know how to enter a Uniform Resource Locator (URL) in your browser window to surf to a website
- know how to use a Windows text editor such as http://notepad-plus-plus.org or in Linux, the VI or VIM editors

Some skills that would prove helpful to get the most benefit from this book, but are not completely necessary, include

- knowledge that Linux exists and can be useful to the techniques described in this book
- knowledge of how to open a terminal window in Linux and run a command from the command line; we will cover how to do this in Chapter 7
- ability to open an https://en.wikipedia.org/wiki/Windows_command_line https://en.wikipedia.org/wiki/Windows_command_line using **Start** > **Run...** > **cmd** to open a window and type commands from the Windows command line.

If you have some of these basic skills, then the instructions and tutorials in this book should prove very useful. Following the tips and suggestions offered here will help you to protect your business/family from predators on the Internet. If you aren't sure about whether you have the above-mentioned knowledge or skills, you might consider taking a community college, continuing education class or hiring someone you know that is skilled in (IT) to help you. They could briefly explain the rudimentary concepts that will make computer use clear and easy for you, after which, I'm hoping you will find that this do-it-yourself guide, of some seemingly complex processes, much simpler. You might be surprised how cheap that labor can be. You will find that peace of mind is worth the cost of securing your privacy, your finances, and your identity, all of which becomes vulnerable when you use an unsecured network or computer/device connected to the Internet--*a very vulnerable place to be!*

What You Will Need to Employ the Techniques Described in This Book

You will need a somewhat modern computer, with at least 4GB of RAM to use some of the techniques presented in this book. To see if your computer can employ the techniques described in this book, you will need to check your computer's Windows Experience Index (WEI), to see if you need to upgrade your hardware. With the release of Windows Vista and Windows 7, Microsoft wisely provided a tool that measure, from https://en.wikipedia.org/wiki/Windows_Experience_Index, "*performance characteristics and capabilities of the hardware it is running on and reports them as a WEI score*". (See: http://windows.microsoft.com/en-us/windows/what-is-windows-experience-index#What-is-windows-experience-index=windows-7) The WEI includes five scores numbering from 1.0 to 7.9 in Windows 7 for the Processor, Memory (RAM), Graphics, Gaming graphics, and Primary hard disk.

The good news is that the Virtualization and other software you choose do not need a super powerful computer setup. For example, one of my custom-built towers is over six years old, has a Windows Experience Index (WEI) of 5.9, and runs everything that I present in this book just fine. Vendors don't even sell my Motherboard anymore. My inexpensive laptop is about five years old, and the same holds true for that hardware as well. Every Parallels, VMware Player or VirtualBox virtual OS (discussed later) that you should install and use will chew up disk space. As you will go through disk space rapidly, depending on the number of virtual OSs you install, I am recommending at a minimum two or three. Buy the maximum hard disk space your laptop or computer(s) will support on the, now inferior, SATA hard disk platform. This extra SATA disk space can be purchased at minimal cost. For example, a top-of-the-line SATA 6.0GB/3.5 Seagate Barracuda 4 Terabyte hard drive can be purchased for a mere $169, which is remarkable as compared to a few short years ago. There are multiple methods to get to the Windows WEI screen to see if your hardware will support virtualization.

To check your WEI in Windows 7, click on <u>Start</u> > <u>All Programs</u> > select <u>Control Panel</u> on the right > in the upper right change <u>View by:</u> to <u>Large</u> or <u>Small icons</u> > select the <u>Performance Information or Tools</u> icon > if the test has been performed before the overall score will appear on the right > check the date it was performed on the lower left. If it is old, or you have added new hardware select <u>Re-run the assessment</u> on the lower right corner. This 5-point assessment shows you how the applications that you use, or want to use on your devices, will perform. Another method to evaluate your hardware is:

Add the <u>Computer</u> Icon to your desktop by right clicking on the desktop > select <u>Personalize</u> > click on <u>Change desktop icons</u> > add them all. Later we will make use of these desktop icons for various things later. Check your WEI in Windows 7 by ***right clicking on the <u>Computer</u> Icon > scroll down to select <u>Properties</u> > you will see a <u>Windows Experience Index</u> link with either no overall score or a previous rating > click on the <u>Rate and improve your computer's performance</u> screen, click on the link <u>Run/Re-run the assessment</u> in the lower right corner > A dialog box will pop up saying <u>This might take a few minutes.</u>*** When done this assessment will show you where you may want to upgrade your hardware. To use Windows 7 with virtualization you will need a "base score" of at least 4.0 or more in most categories. Don't worry if one or two fall below this baseline, but consider how you might address that lack in performance. This is the fastest way I know of to access your hardware and enter the world of virtualization.

Rate and improve your computer's performance

The Windows Experience Index assesses key system components on a scale of 1.0 to 7.9.

Component	What is rated	Subscore	Base score
Processor:	Calculations per second	5.6	
Memory (RAM):	Memory operations per second	5.6	
Graphics:	Desktop performance for Windows Aero	4.1	**3.4**
Gaming graphics:	3D business and gaming graphics performance	3.4	Determined by lowest subscore
Primary hard disk:	Disk data transfer rate	5.9	

NOTE If all the scores are basically the same or below 4.0, then there is little you can do with your current hardware and the purchase of a more modern computer is necessary. If some scores are high and some low, purchasing new hardware (e.g. more RAM) could raise that score to an acceptable level. HINT: WEI is also a good way to benchmark off-the-shelf computers before purchasing them.

As an experiment, I attempted to get Lubuntu (Lite Ubuntu) working in VirtualBox on an old computer with 1GB of RAM and a benchmark of 3.3. With a benchmark that low, virtualization proved to be impossible. If your computer components have less than a 4.0 score, then you are in luck by reading this book. Don't throw away that old computer. You can use your old computer setup to keep your mobile devices secure, which we will cover in Chapter 9. In Chapter 3 we will discuss how to put together a new computer using your old computer components that did not meet the 4.0 score. At best, WEI is a rudimentary tool for benchmarking a PC's performance. If you really want an accurate assessment of your hardware use Futuremark's PCMark 7, which tests the CPU, GPU, RAM and storage. PCMark Basic is a free benchmarking tool that will help establish a minimum score for the minimum hardware needed for this book. (See: http://www.futuremark.com) Their website is also a good place to compare hardware and see Futuremark's score for PC components.

Conventions Used in This Book

This book is full of hyperlinks to websites that are used as reference. URL's are fully quantified for my paperback readers. This book will eventually be published in e-book format where embedded links will prove useful.

- Commands typed on a command line are highlighted in grey and the output of that command is displayed in SimHei font:
  # pgrep bash   # Show the Process ID of the bash process
  1967
- Parts of prompts and commands typed on a command line that can vary are embedded in greater-than and less-than signs (e.g. C:\users\<UserID>\ifconfig /all or # userdel -r <UserID>).
- For long variable paths "..." was substituted to show the path was deep in the directory hierarchy (e.g. C:\...\netstat -b).
- Command line arguments are sometimes separated by two spaces to provide clear separation between them. In actual scripts and on the command line only one space is needed.
- Step-by-step directions with ***menu items***, ***buttons***, and ***checkboxes*** embedded in the text are presented in the Rockwell font are underlined, **Bolded** and in *Italics*.
- When directions are presented in table format, the step-by-step directions are presented in the Rockwell font. Window/screen *titles*, selected *menu items*, *checkboxes*, and ticks are underlined and presented in *Italics*.
- Quotations from books, periodicals, websites and wikis are contained within "double quotes", presented in the Franklin Gothic Book font, in *Italics*, and for e-book readers in a dark brown color to contrast them from other text.
- Scripts and configuration file changes are displayed in the Kaiti font.
- Usernames, groups, and other operating system IDs are enclosed in 'single quotes'.
- Abbreviations are introduced once in a chapter and then used throughout. For example, Small Business Owner/Home Computer User (SBO/HCU) will be referred to as, SBO/HCU throughout the remainder of the chapter.
- Words with definitions in the Glossary are followed by an "*".

NOTE	Something useful and interesting but may not pertinent to the information being presented. Something the reader may need to know.
Definition	Computer terms and lingo that exist in the world of Information Technology, or that I created writing this book.
$	An observation or experience based on research and/or implementation of technology in the past or present that should result in financial savings by employing practical solutions to today's requirements.
Tip	A tip is something that is not intuitive or easy to apply but will save you time and effort investigating on your own. This could be a work around or how to use a feature.
Story	Something I have encountered, which I have found amusing and informative, many times at my own expense. I like to laugh at myself. However, sometimes I want to convey a lifetime story that only I witnessed.
WARNING	Something that needs to be heeded to prevent damage to or exploitation of your identity, your health, a mobile device, computer or network.

Tip	To open up a website in a browser window, *hover the mouse pointer over the link, press down on the **Ctrl** key on your keyboard and click on the link using your mouse.* This will open up a browser window to the website. You can also *right click on the link and select **Open hyperlink***.

	Historical Reference – What a historical event is teaching us about hardening security techniques

In each chapter, I try to relate what it is that I am teaching about computer security to historical examples that have occurred in military history and my own personal experiences. Having served my country and seen how history was ignored in the war planning, I find that the past is often the best guide toward future lessons learned and what is taking place in our thinking about cyber security. These topics are often ignored in the cyber security debate. I try to show how catastrophic historical examples can result in huge losses in human life or freedom.

Introduction – Why You Need to Read This Book

The Internet is infected and *is* stalking you! It is a minefield that we must navigate as carefully as possible. It is also a wonderful, but **very dangerous** place to be. It offers convenience, information, networking, social media, communications and many other uses that have become routine to us. We are lured into using the Internet because of the ease with which we can perform everyday tasks such as banking, business activity, chatting, shopping, and anything else we can imagine. New mobile technology has the Internet woven into our everyday lives more so than at any previous time in human history. Used judiciously, the Internet saves us time and money. Ordering something online saves us a trip to the store, processing a transaction saves us a trip to the bank, using GPS to navigate to a location is wonderful, the Internet's benefits are too numerous to list. Even though we are familiar with the many benefits, we need to become acutely aware of its abundant risks and become very guarded. Often times, the SBO/HCU does not understand how vulnerable we all are using a resource such as the infected Internet. Just as we protect ourselves by installing a home security system we must take measures to protect ourselves from predators on the Internet. If you are using the Internet, you will need the many extra layers of security presented in this book to lessen your exposure to those threats. Otherwise as a SBO/HCU, you are vulnerable to exploitation from crackers, identity thieves, cyber criminals, corporations, neighbors, scorned lovers, and governments.

Factoid  	In various articles on the Internet, it is stated that an estimated 48 to 59 percent of the PC's worldwide have been hit by malware. There are over two billion computers in the world and that number is increasing. Therefore, potentially we have over one billion people worldwide using their Internet devices and revealing everything that they doing to crackers, criminals, and scorned lovers, corporations, not to mention their governments. These numbers do not take into account programs by various governments intercepting hardware and installing backdoors into Internet devices. (See: http://press.pandasecurity.com/news/in-january-50-percent-of-computers-worldwide-were-infected-with-some-type-of-computer-threat, http://www.infoworld.com/t/cyber-crime/malware-infects-30-percent-of-computers-in-us-199598)

What you reveal about yourself, knowingly or unknowingly, is being used by employers to make hiring and firing decisions. Internet data is also appearing in a growing number of court cases. Marketing lists compiled by companies are being used by con artists to target elderly and vulnerable investors. Even your medical data is not safe as there have been instances of con artists targeting individuals with "Mental Health Problems" and were found using cracked medical lists. Visit any local doctor's office and you may find them still using the deprecated Windows XP operating system which is rapidly changing twenty four years after the OS release. My experience with the medical world has shown that they are more focused on digitizing your personal data and care little about securing it as laws and regulations do not make them do so.

In a social setting, a friend who does hiring and firing for a mid-sized company told me how he is required to monitor his employees' Facebook pages. When one employee was found posting derogatory statements about the company, he was fired. Another factoid about Facebook: 2013 news reports outlined their exploitation of people clicking on their "likes". It turns out that some parents, who had posted their child's pictures on Facebook, have been clicking away on what they like, Facebook decided to use this for advertising purposes by sending the child's picture along with a product advertisement to all the parent's Facebook friends saying, "Buy this product because your "Friend" likes it." There is a lawsuit pending on this, but do we really expect anything to come out of it to protect our online privacy given recent political trends? Our politicians and justices seem to be bought and paid for by large and midsized corporations. At least, that has been the pattern of recent bills and court rulings. It is best to boycott these social media sites, and if that is not possible, assume everything posted there is shared and is there for all time to be exploited. Parents must lecture and prevent their children from posting things that may be used years later against them.

The U.S. Fourth Circuit of Appeals stated that "liking" was the "Internet equivalent of displaying a political sign in one's front yard, which the Supreme Court has held is substantive speech." A Facebook 'Like' is protected by the First Amendment but the Constitution does not distinguish between 'liking' something on Facebook and something publicly supported. There are instances of people being fired because of their likes, which have been upheld by U.S. courts.

Story  	While writing this book I often encountered situations/things that I have found amazing. One law firm that I was working with while writing this book was actively engaged in attending important government cyber security meetings and conferences making many hundreds of thousands of dollars discussing these cyber security topics. What I found amazing was they were still using an insecure FTP server to exchange data with their partners, including me. Of course I offered my services to help them set up a secure encrypted SSH server but I was unable to make them understand why they needed to do that. On March 25, 2013 Palo Alto Networks Research states, *"FTP is a highly-effective method for introducing malware to a network. 95 percent of malware delivered via FTP went undetected by antivirus solutions for more than 30 days."* (See: http://investors.paloaltonetworks.com/phoenix.zhtml?c=251350&p=irol-newsArticle&ID=1799887&highlight, http://www.paloaltonetworks.com/mmr)

Why I Wrote This Book about Using the Infected Internet

I have spent all my adult life serving the U.S. government, the U.S. military, working in and learning about the computer industry. Eight years ago I embarked on this task of researching and writing this book. I did this because after working for five large corporations, six government agencies, and serving in three U.S. military branches, I felt it was time to give something back to humankind when I was dying from cancer. I have been shot at, almost blown up numerous times, had faced many near fatal car accidents, and have had many missiles launched against my base of operations while serving in the military. I have also survived many juvenile delinquent activities and later, against all odds, two serious battles with cancer that the doctors gave me very limited odds of surviving. I reveal these facts freely in this book because I want our youth to understand that our medical and digital lives are being recorded and scrutinized for all time. All the stupid things we do and experience in life and our medical issues are being recorded forever, which we must stop. These mistakes and unfortunate events in life do not define who we are and who we may become, and this mass monitoring and lifetime digital trails are not a part of a world we want to live in! I find this disturbing Internet future very sad for our youth, as my generation was granted the privilege of moving past such events earlier in our lives. That is no longer possible, and if this book is successful, some people may try to find facts about my past to discredit this book. Can you see how the digital nightmare we are all living is wrong?

Quotation Sophocles	There is no witness so terrible and no accuser as powerful as conscience which dwells within us. -- (Greek Dramatist 495BC - 406BC)
Quotation Kirk A Ellis	To paraphrase from the quotation above, "*There is no accuser so terrible to our nightmares as the conscience that dwells within a good person as they move on with their life remembering their contribution to history's past and their future resolve to correct the mistakes of that prior life.*"

I feel that my miraculous continued existence is a message from our Holy Father or the holy spirit that we all possess within us, to do something important with our continued life when we are granted it against all logic. My diverse computer and Internet background should not be wasted no matter how stupid I could be from time to time. I came to terms with the fact that I must use my continued miraculous lifespan to draw from my experience and knowledge about computer safety to help the SBO/HCU, rather than carry on using my talents to profit corrupt corporations, and to serve militaries and governments who do not appear to be looking out for their citizen's Internet privacy, safety and freedom. I was compelled daily to write about how to change the infected Internet world we all now live in.

Using the Internet safely on your HCO/SBO's limited budget is about the time you spend studying this book. Big corporations can throw infinite amounts of cash at any security problem, SBO/HCU have been left to fend for themselves on limited budgets, and against threats to their personal information -- including personal email, photos, browsing habits, as well as to their very identities. There are many excellent products for large entities with big pockets, but the SBO/HCU typically does not have the vast resources that larger entities have to spend on their computer security. Many SBO/HCU believe that the best that they can do is to install free or improved, paid-for versions of antivirus and anti-spyware software and hope for the best. ***This book is now here to amend that thinking!*** This type of rationale is misguided for SBO/HCU. Front line antivirus and anti–spyware software are not the answer to your computer security, as you have been led to believe by your media, governments and for-profit corporations. You now need to study this book's step-by-step directions to protect your computers and business/home networks from spies, crackers, thieves and criminals that are everywhere. The design of this book is to make your computer use private and secure, and to make computer security affordable to any user, following the do-it-yourself projects outlined in this book. My goal is to enable everyone to be able to use the Internet more safely. However, you must come to the understanding that the whole world is striving to make the words "**Internet safety and privacy**" a forgotten paradigm. Everything we have done and experienced in life often blocks out what we can become with the wisdom to see past the confines engineered to keep us inside the limited Internet box. This book is meant to inspire you to strive to think outside this box of life's confines which may possibly make you happy, secure and successful.

I also want to help the open source and donationware* communities and their dedicated developers, who get too little credit and support. They give us wonderful solutions to our computing needs using the Internet with little or no help. Many of these projects are not in the public eye and do not get the financial support they deserve. I am hoping this book will change that, and keep the open source movement free and alive. If you find their solutions useful, please contribute to their project's continued development. I present many of their dedicated solutions to your needs in the various operating systems presented this book in the hopes that you will find them useful and donate to their projects. We must support the rapid technological innovation by the projects to counter how the Internet is being corrupted. We must allow these open source solutions to push the confines of our imagination and provide us with useful software solutions.

I have come to believe that the movie, media and other entertainment industries are designed to desensitize us to the mass surveillance that is taking place. I know that as I watch block buster films where comic book heroes rescue us all from *the man** observing all that we do they make us feel there is someone out there who will correct this ill behavior. I'm sorry to help you realize these Hollywood movies are not make believe and you have to live in the reality that you have surrendered your privacy to governments and corporations around the world as you use the infected Internet.

A Quick Review of the Usual, Inadequate Methods for Securing Your Internet Activity That We Hear About Daily

While writing this book, I have constantly listened to many TV and talk radio shows, read many periodicals, blogs, and web pages that inadequately present the information that we all need to know to be able to protect our small business or home networks, computers, laptops and mobile devices. These sources regurgitate the same old front line techniques, which are insufficient to the task of protecting our advanced devices from exposure to the Internet. These media people spend too much time promoting their sponsors and too little time looking into the real technical answers that we all need to protect our privacy. Much of the time the advice they are giving is intended to profit corporations and put money in their own or others' pockets. I have read and heard many interviews of so-called experts and knowledgeable sources who list all the things we all should do, but with little or no explanation of how to do it. They also state techniques and facts over, and over again, that we all should surely know by now. They seem to want us to purchase products, learn very little about what we have purchased, and profit corporations with little understanding of how our money was spent, or even what these products do. Many times off-the-shelf computer products come with preinstalled software, or the user inadvertently installs software, with what computer professionals call bloatware*. Listening to these media shows I find that these interviewed people present little or nothing new about how the SBO/HCU can protect themselves against the infected Internet.

 Story	Have you ever noticed how the media is much more likely to include an officer (most often a General who has retired many years ago) in their conversation rather than an active enlisted combat soldier, who is much more closely connected to the ground combat situation? An interview with an enlisted active duty or retired Sergeant Major, Marine Corps Recon, Navy Seal or any other enlisted soldier would be a more relevant person to be interviewed. That seasoned combat veteran is much more pertinent to the discussion of what is happening in any combat zone than a retired General. How many times have we seen a multi-tour Sergeant Major back from Afghanistan, give their assessment on TV as to how the war was going? How many times have the front line soldiers been interviewed as to their suggestions on how to conduct the war? Doesn't this seem strange to you?

The story above relates to my thinking about Internet security. Rarely do I hear or see a computer professional, hacker or true geek that has spent their life securing computers, engage in a conversation with the media. Usually it is a well-spoken, well dressed, polished commentator who regurgitates a few simple steps that we all know we have to do. They are hired because they look good on camera and are well spoken on TV. Almost anyone who looks good on camera is passed off these days as a cyber security or military expert.

So let's now quickly **make fun** of these well-dressed, polished commentators that regurgitate the ***deficient, lack-of-direction, cyber security action items*** that we hear over, and over again, reiterated by our media, for-profit talk radio, for-profit corporations and the secretive spying governments and bring you to what I am presenting later in this book. *The man** does not seem to want, or does not consider you capable of moving beyond these minor tidbits of information you are often fed. As you read this section of this book, think about how many times you have seen and heard these facts retold as if your media and these polished spokespeople are giving you important information. This will all start to ring a bell in your head as you realize how little material you are really given from media sources that have little information, or are suppressed and controlled. A free and independent media is becoming a forgotten paradigm in today's world. Once you have scanned these *very basic* precautions to using the **infected Internet** that you constantly hear about, you can move on to the core of this book, which is what my in-depth tutorials for securing your SBO/HCU network, computers, and mobile devices provide:

1. Use anti-software. Install, use and regularly update your anti-malware software and definitions. Run your anti-software often. Never install more than one antivirus product on your device/computer. If you believe you have a virus and your anti-software is not up to the task of wiping it out, you can go to other antivirus vendors and create a bootable CD or USB drive to scan your computer with their free software. I will teach you how to do that later in this book. Scanning for malware as a security tactic is a reactive approach to security, and this book is about being proactive. Signature based anti-software is the most common method used to identify viruses and other malware. However, it is estimated that this technique is incapable of detecting as much as 20% of the malware that exists on the Internet today. Signature based antivirus software compares the contents of a file to a dictionary of known virus signatures. Anti-software developers are working hard to combine a heuristic approach (meaning a method with which to detect an unknown virus before it can do harm) but

this technology is in its infancy and is imprecise. For example, in an IDG News Service article by Loek Essers, titled "Finland Says Government Communications Hacked" malware operated behind Finnish government networks for two to three years before being discovered. (See: http://news.idg.no/cw/art.cfm?id=CB8AA148-06AF-86C2-F7971F79E5A6C32F) In military terms, we know the enemy is up to no good and we are taking measures to counter their offensive, but how to eradicate it before the enemy can implement their plan, takes time, knowledge and study. (See: http://www.scmagazine.com/why-should-anti-virus-products-employ-heuristic-detection/article/31561, https://en.wikipedia.org/wiki/Anti-virus_software) , http://securitywatch.pcmag.com/none/309586-antivirus-better-at-detecting-email-malware-than-web-threats)

WARNING 	If you think you are safe using anti-software think again. We also have to fear logic bombs*. Because this type of malicious software may target a specific computer it is undetectable by anti-software. This malware is often triggered by an event such as a date, a message from its programmer, a file or home directory being deleted and so on. It can even be triggered by a non-event such as if its creator has not logged in for the past month. This could be created by an employee who knew they were on the chopping block as their form of retribution. There is also what is known as zero-day vulnerabilities for which no software fixes are available as the Veteran of Foreign Wars website found out. An attack believed to have been initiated in China may have been trying to spy on U.S. military members. According to the PCWorld article by Jeremy Kirk titled "Attack on U.S. Veterans Website May Have Been Aimed at Military Members," he states *"The attackers compromised the VFW's website and placed a hidden iframe on the site that delivered an exploit from the attacker's server, FireEye wrote in a blog post. If successful, the attack deposits a backdoor called "ZxShell," which can steal files from a user's computer."* Since the VFW has 1.4 million members, which includes 75,000 on active duty, so many former and current military Internet devices could have been compromised. The attack was found by the company FireEye, which scans the Internet for new attacks. Since zero-day attacks exploit unknown vulnerabilities, these attack vectors can exist for an average of 10 months according to one estimate on wiki. Because these attacks are unknown to anti-software, victims have no indication their Internet devices have been compromised. (See: http://www.pcworld.com/article/2098100/attack-on-us-veterans-website-may-have-been-aimed-at-military-members.html#tk.nl_secur, https://en.wikipedia.org/wiki/Zero-Day_Attack)

2. Use a software firewall. A software firewall is a set of related programs that prevents outsiders from accessing data on your private network. Install and maintain firewalls between your internal network and the Internet. Install firewalls on all devices that communicate with the Internet. Chapter 2 of this book will show you how to set up and secure a *hardware* firewall for your network (cabled and Wi-Fi) properly. Chapter 9 will

briefly cover setting up some software firewall rules, and how to communicate securely from behind your firewall.

3. Keep software up-to-date and download and install software updates for your operating systems (OS) and applications as they become available. For example, regularly run "Windows and Adobe Update". Every month, in the periodicals that I read, there are articles about new methods that crackers are using to attack your Internet devices and how software vendors and the open source software community are countering them. According to 60 Minutes, one in four American households owning an Internet device has had malware related problems.[1] According to the May 23, 2012 PCWorld article "*Malware Threat Level Hits 4-Year High*" by John P. Mello Jr, (See: https://www.pcworld.com/article/256051/malware_threat_level_hits_4_year_high.html) "*In first three months of the year, malware circulating in cyberspace reached a four-year high and is on a pace to reach 100 million samples by year's end, McAfee says in its quarterly threats report. "In the first quarter of 2012, we have already detected 8 million new malware samples, showing that malware authors are continuing their unrelenting development of new malware," Vincent Weafer, senior vice president of McAfee Labs, said in a statement. "The same skills and techniques that were sharpened on the PC platform are increasingly being extended to other platforms, such as mobile and Mac," he added.*"

4. Regularly change passwords and protect them. Never use the same password for multiple sites. Chapter 11 of this book covers this topic in detail to make this easy and manageable for you. Just changing passwords is not enough.

5. I often see **"Use password protected features included in your installed software applications"** as a recommendation. While a good idea, some of these password protected documents may still be scanned with software to read some of their content even if you password protect them. If a password protected document is emailed it will bounce from email server to email server where a cracker can make a copy of it. They can then spend an infinite amount of computer time cracking the password to your document, which is often very weak. We will discuss strong passwords in Chapter 11.

6. Know who you are dealing with. CBS's 60 Minutes says that 1 in 100 search links offered by Google will install, or attempt to install, malware on your Internet device.[1] That search engine click that took you to an ad or offer that looks so good, may just be a scam. Just because the web page looks professional and legit does not mean you are dealing with a reputable website. Typing a URL incorrectly often takes you to a malicious or targeted website to attack your Internet device.

7. If you are shopping or banking online, only use the sites that use encryption (https) which will protect your information as it travels over the Internet from your computer to their server. In addition, make sure once you are logged in to a site, that every page you visit remains (https) encrypted. In an article in the May 2012 PCWorld by Tony Bradley titled "Watch Out for Malicious Web Apps", he points out that "*a malicious Web app may be able to access information across tabs from within the same browser session.*" So if you are accessing a HTTPS secured site, don't open up another tab with same browser on an unsecured HTTP page.

8. Many websites offer both unsecured and secured versions of their web page content. When given the choice, always opt for the secure version of Internet content. I will show you how to do this automatically via browser plugins in Chapter 6.

9. Don't open an attachment or blindly click on links in an email, even if you know whom it is from. Many of your friends' and family's computers (1 in 4)[1] have been cracked and criminals are using their email to lure you into installing malware on your computer as well. You will often see email coming from them, which will include link(s) to websites that make no sense. *They have been cracked*. Weeks later you may get a follow-up email from them apologizing for being cracked, and not to click on the link(s) provided by their cracked computer. What constantly surprises me is how long this activity is allowed to progress without their knowledge.

10. Jokes disguised as links are a great way to take your browser to a malicious website. Once again, your friends' and relatives' computers have been cracked, and someone is watching everything they do and type, but they don't seem to care.

11. Block pop-ups and never click on them. Scammers like to put up a flashy pop-up that tells about how they have detected a virus on your computer. If you click on their pop-up to remove the virus that never existed, they will install malware on your computer and then you will then become infected. I will show you browser plug-ins that will block this activity.

12. Check your browser's security settings. For example, in Windows Internet Explorer <u>Medium</u> is the lowest setting you should use. This book recommends raising that setting to <u>Medium-high</u>. Microsoft explains what these settings will do when set, and we will talk about them in <u>Chapter 6</u>. I also show you how to secure Mozilla Firefox and Internet Explorer.

13. The Internet offers up all sorts of FREE software, a lot of which is presented in this book. Malware can install from any free game, screen saver, toolbar, open source, donationware*, or free anti-software. When you download software make sure you are using a website you know and trust, and scan that download with your anti-malware software before loading it. Even reputable sites will add bloatware* to free donationware* downloads to make money. Use other anti-software to scan it before installing, if you have it. You should also check the signature or checksum of the downloaded file, which I will teach you how to do in <u>Chapter 5</u> of this book. Performing this added step will ensure the file you downloaded is not corrupt and is legitimate.

14. Stories abound about phishing attacks on NPR and talk radio. The millions of dollars that corrupt organizations gain by using these attacks are hard to fathom. I admit, I had somewhat dismissed the success of these types of ploys as an exaggeration by our media. However, NPR and news stations continue to describe these attacks and warn people not to fall for these seemingly crazy phishing schemes. One example of a phishing attack that I listened to on NPR was a phone call from someone claiming to be from Microsoft saying they have found a virus on your computer that needs to be removed. To remove it the victim gives the caller some personal information, helps them log into their computer and then uses a credit card number to pay the attacker to fix a problem that did not even exist. What the attacker does is take their money and install malware on their computer. While I find it hard to believe that people would fall for this, my own personal experience says otherwise. My parents are aging and falling for some predators' advances (maybe not in this fashion, but others) that are occasionally talking them into spending money on expensive and/or questionable items they really could do without. And, for the record, I too was fleeced, many years ago, by the Charles J. Givens organization, which swindled me out of thousands before they went bankrupt.

Who hasn't been scammed once or twice in their life? We cannot dwell on these experiences, but just move on. I'm hoping to keep this from happening to you.   So let's state this for the record, there are no people overseas that you can help by sending them cash in some means or fashion to make everyone rich. If you feel they will make you rich, then contact your lawyer or someone who can advise you. 99.9% of the time there is no prince, king, queen or investment opportunity that is going to change your future. If there were, they would not be asking you for money, or to click on a link! Another example of a spamming scam is an email that can come from trusted friends' or relatives' email account asking you for money or to click on a link. That link will install malware on your computer. A different email scam from your friend or relative usually goes something like this: your friend is stranded overseas with no wallet or money because everything was stolen while they were on vacation. So they are asking you to wire them some money so they can purchase papers or to help them get back home. The reality is that your friend's computer has been cracked; using malware, a cracker has control of their computer, their email account and possibly other accounts as well.

15. Given the above phishing attacks, adopt the simple policy that if you did make the phone call, never give out any sort of personal or financial information. If they called you, tell them you will call them back and discuss whatever it is about which they called you. For example, I sometimes receive calls from my financial institutions about what they assume to be questionable activity on my account. I have their call back numbers programmed into my cellphone, so I call them back on those preprogrammed phone numbers and tell them to quit pestering me about my less than $1,000 purchases. I check my accounts weekly so there is no need for this low cash level of monitoring.

16. There is also the spear phishing attack where the attacker creates an official-looking email to lure the victim to a fake website to trick them into revealing personal information. This type of attack requires some inside information that is obtained by hacking into your organization's or your personal computer. This information can also be obtained through other websites, blogs, and social networking sites. The cracker then ends the email to the target group offering all sorts of urgent and legitimate-sounding reasons that the victim needs to reveal their personal data. (See: https://www.fbi.gov/news/stories/2009/april/spearphishing_040109).

17. Spammers send unsolicited email indiscriminately to multiple mailing lists, individuals, or newsgroups. These emails contain advertisements, viruses, and hoaxes. As much as 90.4% of the spam you receive will direct you to spam sites or malicious websites. Social networking sites can also redirect you to malicious sites. Report spam to the FTC at uce@ftc.gov.

18. If your computer has a virus or spyware and someone wants your money, read this book, or for $75 to $200, take your computer to Best Buy for repair. Don't provide anyone on the Internet personal information, or access to your computer to repair it. I have not found these paid online services that offer to fix your computer reputable. In my opinion, it is far better and cheaper to reload or rollback your operating system, which you can learn how to do by reading this book.

19. Be very wary of shoulder surfing. From https://en.wikipedia.org/wiki/Shoulder_surfing_computer_security, shoulder surfing *"refers to using direct observation techniques, such as looking over someone's shoulder, to*

get information." I'm afraid that with modern technology, this form of attack has become much more insidious. The federal government should be warning the public (SBO) about this technique, but visiting their cyber security advice web pages reveals little information about this threat. The attacker can use advanced binoculars or miniature cameras concealed in ceilings, walls, or fixtures to observe what you type on your keyboard and what appears on your computer monitor, or PIN numbers at an ATM or place of business. Because they know this, the Federal Government and large corporations have taken precautions. Nevertheless, imagine if you will, for example, an SBO with a disgruntled employee. That employee can visit his or her local spy store, place a miniature camera somewhere in the office and record every key stroke that someone is typing. By watching the monitor and what is typed on the keyboard, they can obtain the passwords to your accounts. Envision the damage that they could do to your business after that! Moreover, how many SBO/HCU sweep their offices for this type of surveillance equipment, or have a clue on how to even look for it? How many SBO/HCU users work with an unblinded window and in easy view of their monitor screen? The enemy is out there and they are smart! Most of us just want to enjoy a nice window view of the outside while we work. Special windows are needed to prevent easy voice and video surveillance from the outside. Government agencies and large corporations have already learned about this and are taking, or have taken, countermeasures, but how many SBO/HCU have done so? If you are a multi-million dollar SBO, how many government officials have banged on your door to warn you about this? Crackers are now moving on to easier victims (lower hanging fruit). Your multimillion/thousand dollar small business will prove a bonanza for them. We will discuss how to protect against this form of attack when we cover Identity Theft in Chapter 11.

20. Install a Video Surveillance system with motion detection. While not as effective as preventing thieves from stealing your equipment in the first place, it may help law enforcement catch the bad guys later, and maybe, get some of your belongings back.

21. Secure your equipment. Make sure that unauthorized users cannot gain access to your hardware. Laptops, smartphones, and tablets are subject to theft, so make sure they are locked up when not in use.

22. Be wary of using ATM's and gas card readers. Look to see if a suspicious front-end device is attached. Crackers have devised ways of installing front-end devices that will transmit your card number and pin back to themselves later after charging your credit cards and draining your bank accounts.

23. Backup your data on every computer. In the days of cheap USB drives and FREE cloud computing there is not any excuse not to have all of your computers' data backed up. Microsoft used to offer 25GB of free storage, http://explore.live.com/skydrive (which is grandfathered in to longstanding users), but now only offers 7 GB of free online storage that can sync to every Windows device you have.

24. If you have a small business, visit http://www.fcc.gov/cyberforsmallbiz. This is the U.S. Government's Cyber Security Resources for Small Business, which can help. Establish a clear set of rules and policies for employees using the Internet. Make sure they are trained in how to protect your data and your customer's data.

25. In the same vein, don't trust your employee's online activity. They must be trained in the techniques described in this book or curtailed by using strict firewall practices. If

they don't need services such as JAVA or Adobe Flash Player then don't install it, disable it or uninstall this software.

26. Limit employee access to only the information they need to do their job. We call this need-to-know in the military. If they have to share devices, make sure that everyone has separate accounts and only with the privileges that they need.

27. Many backing and investment institutions now provide security and fraud alerts on your accounts. When your personal or security information changes or thresholds are crossed, you can have your provider call or send you a text message or email. Some institutions will also report suspicious financial activity.

28. Never send or reveal confidential information of any sort in an unencrypted email, voice conversation or voice mail, or text message. This includes credit or debit card information, Social Security numbers or other personal information, for example.   I will teach you about encryption in Chapter 5. The policy must be adhered to, of personally visiting your financial institution, logging into their HTTPS website, or other form of communication.

Let's now look at Internet security beyond this usual inadequate advice that you have heard repeatedly on talk radio regurgitated by uneducated media sources who really know very little about cyber security. The time has come for SBO/HCU's to move on from this *fluff* with a new conversation and truly achieve some real/true Internet security and anonymity. As we will soon discuss U.S. NSA, FBI and others have almost limitless capabilities and hardware to spy on the Internet, which the American people have funded with infinite amounts of their tax payer dollars without protest. In doing any sort of business within or outside the U.S. or Great Britain you have to know it is now being recorded in redundant corporate and U.S. government databases. However, there are measures western citizens can take against this technology and the rest of the un-free world trying to invade everyone's Internet activity.

I'm fed up with seeing and hearing these same old mainstream media type recommendations for home security that all spying crackers, corporations and governments know. As stated earlier, those articles shamelessly promote corporate vendors wanting to sell you costly product solutions that you do not need, or that are produced to profit from your lack of computer knowledge. This book, my website, and my blog do not do that, and you need to think outside the box and go further than others, by reading this book, to enhance your Internet security. This book is about teaching you how to do that, and is not about selling corporate products, books and frivolous matter or material that will waste your time, money, and introduce other potential threats to your household. If corporations prove the benefit and value of their cyber security products to me after this book is published, I will post them on my website and blog for you to evaluate. (See: http://thatcybersecurityguy.com, http://thatcybersecurityguy.blogspot.com, https://twitter.com/ThatCyberSecGuy) In the meantime, understand that I will profit from none of the information presented in this book other than on my book sales. I only present a few for profit products that I feel have proven value and that I feel are important to your cyber security, computing needs or general welfare.

I have no sponsors, corporate affiliations, government connections or any other influences associated with this book. We briefly discussed the reasons I was cut off from those authorities/organizations that were a part of my livelihood. If you want this author's full story skip to the end of the book the read the rest of the story. As a result, I am no longer guided or dependent upon them, which has granted me the freedom to write this book as I have seen fit. This has granted me the autonomy and perspective to present information in this book about your Internet security material that no one else with my years and experience in the Information Technology field, could or would ever reveal to you.

To reinforce what I mean about the Internet threats that you face, view all of the Microsoft Update History on your computer. *Click on **Start** > **Control Panel** > click on **Windows Update** icon > and on the left pane select **View update history** > this will show you how many patches and updates have been provided by Microsoft to repair their OS and continuously plug holes in their security that crackers have found to exploit. Another way to view your update history grouped by category is click on **Start** > **Control Panel** > **Programs** > **Programs and Features** > and click on **Installed Updates**. **Let's add to this conversation, now that the same old tips you have heard over, and over, again, have been stated**.*

We are going to move beyond the masses that are doing the bare minimum (1 - 28 listed above) to protect their exposure to the Internet, which is a very unsafe place to be. **They have not read this book!**

What This Book Aims to Do for the Reader

Given these facts, marketing deceptions, and invasions into our privacy, we must come to realize that it is vital to secure and protect our Internet devices from the threats that loom while accessing the Internet. We need the Internet to make many things easier in our lives not invade and steal our identity. As a result, we have to be very careful about the information we are providing and ruses that are occurring in our day-to-day lives.

I have discovered also, that most users are not only unaware of how serious these threats can be, they don't even think that they are capable of combatting those threats on their own. I aim to show the average SBO/HCU—and that includes almost everybody—how to protect yourself and your devices, and how to do it yourself. Computer language is not intuitive; there are many of us, who have never learned how to understand or use the language of the PC or mobile devices. Consequently, many people feel that they are not equipped to understand computers or mobile devices, so they are reluctant to attempt to do anything beyond logging in, using the Internet, and logging out. Performing any task or process that seems complex can easily turn users off, even if performing those tasks and processes is in their best interest. I have written this book with these facts--these users--in mind, making the instructions as thorough and as simply written as possible, so that those who may have been intimidated before will feel welcomed to follow the instructions herein, and feel perfectly capable of managing the safety and security of their own networks.

A lot of what I will show you in this book should make life more difficult for those who have been able to easily access your Internet devices and network equipment for selfish or malicious purposes in the past, while helping to protect you in the future. Much of this book is not just about SBO/HCU security; it is also about general SBO/HCU computing knowledge-- meant to make computing time more productive and aid you with your job, network setup, as well as overall computer security. It will also help you stay secure on the road, an increasingly important aspect to an increasingly mobile population. For example, surfing the net at the nearest hotspot, (e.g. airport, coffee or sandwich shop, airport, hotel, etc.), without an encrypted connection to a secure work or home computer network is like inviting anyone to watch your every keystroke. (See: Wiki read on public Wi-Fi Internet connection points, https://en.wikipedia.org/wiki/Hotspot_(Wi-Fi))

The information highway is a two-way street. Everything you do on the Internet is reaching out and also has many people, governments, organizations and corporations reaching in. If you don't harden your home and business security, the reality is that many people are looking at your every keystroke, every website you visit, and everything you do on the Internet. Even if you don't use your computer for anything confidential, the thought of some botnet using your computer to send spam and to spy on others is an injustice that, were most users more aware of it, most of us would not tolerate. Let's do what we can to counteract these exploitative practices of hired crackers and other malicious entities in our own homes, small businesses, on our own networks and computers and let's protect ourselves from these attacks in the future, ***starting right now!***

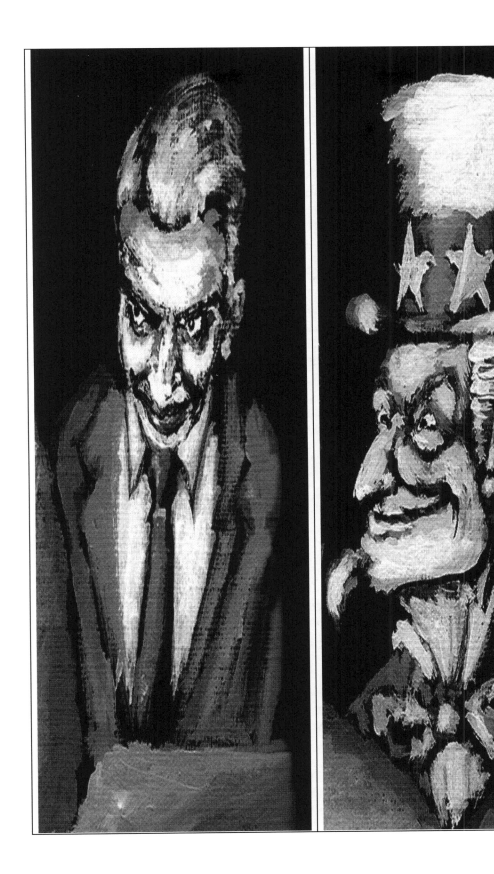

Chapter 1 – Government and Corporate Efforts to Stifle Internet Freedom, Invade Your Privacy and Destroy Your Health

While it is the intentions of this book to help people worldwide achieve a greater degree of Internet privacy and freedom, I cannot know or exhaustively write about how much governments are spying on their citizens. Since I am a citizen of the United States, I chose to use the U.S. government as my example of how expansive and well-funded these apparatuses have become in conducting Internet spying on your online activity. In my country, the communicable trust between citizens worldwide and the U.S. government has been grossly violated on a monumental scale. For example, the U.S. National Security State* has gone much too far in its collection of U.S. citizens' and our friendly foreign neighbors' private data. I don't understand how U.S. veterans and our younger generation can ignore this penetration into their privacy, but it is my hope and dream that they will someday wake up and object to it. We have to consider the fact that 21 western governments and their media now recognize these threats and have requested that this monitoring cease. The world also discovered that the U.S. NSA, the largest taxpayer funded intelligence agency on earth, was monitoring the calls of over 35 world leaders as well, which has done immense harm to U.S. relations with its allies. From the article "*NSA monitored calls of 35 world leaders after US official handed over contacts*" by James Ball at the Guardian, Friday 25, October, 2013, "*The revelation is set to add to mounting diplomatic tensions between the US and its allies, after the German chancellor Angela Merkel on Wednesday accused the US of tapping her mobile phone.*

After Merkel's allegations became public, White House press secretary Jay Carney issued a statement that said the US "is not monitoring and will not monitor" the German chancellor's communications. But that failed to quell the row, as officials in Berlin quickly pointed out that the US did not deny monitoring the phone in the past.

Arriving in Brussels for an EU summit Merkel accused the US of a breach of trust. "We need to have trust in our allies and partners, and this must now be established once again. I repeat that spying among friends is not at all acceptable against anyone, and that goes for every citizen in Germany." (See: http://www.theguardian.com/world/2013/oct/24/nsa-surveillance-world-leaders-calls) This electronic surveillance will continue due to a lack of U.S. laws to enforce or pronounce this activity as criminal due to forceful disputed foreign outrage and U.S. citizens' lack of attention or care as to this ignominy. American citizens appear to have grown bored with values such as privacy, due process of law and the rise of power in the uber-executive branch of the U.S. government.

Before Edward Snowden revealed the extent to which the NSA apparatus had expanded to spy on the Internet Directory of National Intelligence, James Clapper testified to the U.S. Congress that the NSA was not collecting data on millions of U.S. citizens and Internet users worldwide. (See: https://en.wikipedia.org/wiki/James_R._Clapper) Lying to Congress in the U.S used to be considered perjury, a federal offense, but Clapper remains unscathed for committing this crime. Clapper later said that he offered Congress the least untruthful statement he could think of. What is amazing is how the U.S. Congress and U.S. President seemed to look the other way as Clapper remained in his position of NSA power and faced no prosecution or consequences for the commission of this offense. The Obama administration refused to investigate Clapper, fire, or punish him in any fashion. Ask yourself, why is that? Is he the next J. Edgar Hoover, with dirt on every politician so that he can remain in power? It certainly seems so, as he unquestionably has the NSA apparatus, funding and a shiny new three billion dollar Utah Data Center facility located 25 miles from the Salt Lake City International airport.

To buffet all of this bad publicity, the Obama administration cited 22 separate briefings or meetings with members of Congress informing them of the details on the PRISM program. In articles and media releases by members of Congress, they admit that they were briefed on Section 702 of FISA, but some of them confessed that they did not understand the intricacies of the program or how broad in scope it was in collecting U.S. citizens' Internet activity/data.

Mr. Snowden later dispelled Clapper's earlier testimony when he revealed the details about the existence of the clandestine mass surveillance and data mining program called PRISM. The PRISM program was launched in 2007 to collect stored Internet communications from the servers and Internet backbones (fiber-optic cables) of technology giants such as Apple, AOL, Facebook, Google, Microsoft, Paltalk, Skype, Verizon, Yahoo, YouTube, and others. This massive tracking and monitoring program collects emails, file transfers, notifications of target activity - logins, etc., photos, telephone, social media, videos, video conferencing, and voice-over-IP chats, and is touted as "the number one source of raw intelligence used for NSA analytic reports". This data includes the locations and unique device signatures of the individuals that they target.

The PRISM program is estimated to cost U.S. taxpayers $20 million per year. What is most disturbing is, who has access to this data and how few, if any, legal challenges to which the NSA or IRS employees must adhere to look at this data. According to Wiki, "*According to The Guardian's Glenn Greenwald, even low-level NSA analysts are allowed to search and listen to the communications of Americans and other people without court approval and supervision. Greenwald said low level Analysts can, via systems like PRISM, "listen to whatever emails they want, whatever telephone calls, browsing histories, Microsoft Word documents. And it's all done with no need to go to a court, with no need to even get supervisor approval on the part of the analyst.*" (See: https://en.wikipedia.org/wiki/PRISM_(surveillance_program), http://online.wsj.com/public/resources/documents/prismfactsheet0608.pdf, http://www.washingtonpost.com/wp-srv/special/politics/prism-collection-documents, http://www.huffingtonpost.com/2013/06/10/prism-program-obama_n_3416973.html, http://www.usatoday.com/story/news/nation/2013/06/08/dni-declassifies-prism-data-collection-nsa-secret-program-obama/2403999)

The data gathering by the NSA was found to go much further when Edward Snowden revealed that the NSA and the British Government Communications Headquarters (GCHQ) were also tapping into fiber backbones operated overseas by Google and Yahoo, decrypting all of the digital traffic before it gets into their private clouds, storing copies, and then re-encrypting it before sending it on its way. This is an entirely different program from the PRISM program and known in NSA jargon as "Muscular", of which executives at Yahoo and Google denied any knowledge. The MUSCULAR surveillance program is jointly operated by GCHQ and the NSA but GCHQ is the primary operator of the program. We have to wonder about US corporate denials of their knowledge of this since these U.S. companies willingly allowed the NSA "direct access" to their networks without the world knowing about it; but yet they have vehemently denied any knowledge of this added surveillance that was taking place. Because of these revelations, the union representing German journalists advised its members to avoid the Google and Yahoo search engines, or even using them for digital communication of any sort. The Germans are extremely sensitive to maintaining their citizens' privacy because of the eavesdropping by the Stazi secret police in former communist East Germany. The German company Deutsche Telekom even launched privacy initiatives to protect their users' email and local Internet traffic from foreign intelligence services. The Germans have some of strictest privacy policies in the world. (See: http://www.washingtonpost.com/world/national-security/nsa-infiltrates-links-to-yahoo-google-data-centers-worldwide-snowden-documents-say/2013/10/30/e51d661e-4166-11e3-8b74-d89d714ca4dd_story.html, https://en.wikipedia.org/wiki/MUSCULAR_(surveillance_program))

In response to these continuing startling revelations, on April 2, 2014 Yahoo posted a blog entry detailing the security measures they say they have taken in response to all of this. The blog entry states:

- *"Traffic moving between Yahoo data centers is fully encrypted as of March 31.*
- *In January, we made Yahoo Mail more secure by making browsing over HTTPS the default. In the last month, we enabled encryption of mail between our servers and other mail providers that support the SMTPTLS standard.*
- *The Yahoo Homepage and all search queries that run on the Yahoo Homepage and most Yahoo properties also have HTTPS encryption enabled by default.*
- *We implemented the latest in security best-practices, including supporting TLS 1.2, Perfect Forward Secrecy and a 2048-bit RSA key for many of our global properties such as Homepage, Mail and Digital Magazines. We are currently working to bring all Yahoo sites up to this standard.*
- *Users can initiate an encrypted session for Yahoo News, Yahoo Sports, Yahoo Finance, and Good Morning America on Yahoo (gma.yahoo.com) by typing "https" before the site URL in their web browser.*
- *A new, encrypted, version of Yahoo Messenger will be deployed in coming months."*

(See: http://yahoo.tumblr.com/post/81529518520/status-update-encryption-at-yahoo)

In the Dec 30, 2013 PCWorld article titled "*Report: NSA intercepts computer deliveries to plant spyware*" by Jeremy Kirk, there is a special unit at the NSA that intercepts computers en-route to their destination to plant spyware. We will discuss how a modern computer equipment and a fresh set of Windows install DVDs can circumvent malware forms of software attack but does nothing against installed spying hardware. The article states "*The method, called "interdiction," is one of the most successful operations conducted by the NSA's Office of Tailored Access Operations (TAO), which specializes in infiltrating computers, wrote the publication, citing a top-secret document. "If a target person, agency or company orders a new computer or related accessories, for example, TAO can divert the shipping delivery to its own secret workshops," Der Spiegel wrote. The workshops, called "load stations," install malware or hardware components that give the NSA access to the computer, it wrote.*" (See: https://www.pcworld.com/article/2083300/report-nsa-intercepts-computer-deliveries-to-plant-spyware.html, http://www.forbes.com/sites/erikkain/2013/12/29/report-nsa-intercepting-laptops-ordered-online-installing-spyware)

The articles also described an NSA's ANT division (Advanced or Access Network Technology) which is said to have a specialized set of tools engineered by the NSA, with the cooperation of

U.S. corporations that give them easy access to products from Juniper Networks, networking giants Cisco Systems and Huawei Technologies, and Dell. Another report showed that NSA has access to crash reports sent by computers to Microsoft, which we will turn off in coming chapters. The NSA partners with private U.S. telecommunications and ISP's to intercept routers, server and other network equipment being shipped overseas, installs back-door surveillance bugs, rewraps the packages with factory seals, and sends them on their way, thereby ensuring that the agency will have clandestine access to all information that passes through them. (See: http://www.pcworld.com/article/2083300/report-nsa-intercepts-computer-deliveries-to-plant-spyware.html#tk.nl_secur, http://www.spiegel.de/international/world/the-nsa-uses-powerful-toolbox-in-effort-to-spy-on-global-networks-a-940969-druck.html, http://www.washingtonpost.com/opinions/no-place-to-hide-by-glenn-greenwald-on-the-nsas-sweeping-efforts-to-know-it-all/2014/05/12/dfa45dee-d628-11e3-8a78-8fe50322a72c_story.html, http://leaksource.info/2013/12/30/nsas-ant-division-catalog-of-exploits-for-nearly-every-major-software-hardware-firmware, https://en.wikipedia.org/wiki/NSA_ANT_catalog)

Story  	It came as an ironic twist to most Americans that Senator Dianne Feinstein was spied on by the CIA. Americans who called in to radio talk shows labeled it as poetic justice and said "welcome to our world" since she was one of the most outspoken defenders of the intelligence communities need to spy on every American and the whole Internet world. She seemed to take a sudden about face when she found out the CIA was attempting to hide a classified 6,000-page report that detailed possibly criminal CIA interrogation techniques authorized by the Bush administration. She even accused the CIA of trying to intimidate Congress and stated they may have broken the law by spying on Senate staffers. She stated this smacked of an attempt to bully civilians responsible for checking agency abuses, trying to group herself among the Internet masses being spied upon. The dispute went on further, as there were allegations that the CIA was hacking into Senate computers which, listening to NPR and other news agencies, most people felt her vice punished. She seemed to want to assuage her soul by publishing and talking about her committees report about CIA torture around excesses after 9/11 which detailed the excesses that the Bush administration went about in the torture its victims.

On May 12, 2014 Glenn Greenwald came forward to promote his new book "No Place to Hide" based on the revelations of Edward Snowden. In an interview with Stephen Colbert on Comedy Central Greenwald stated, "The NSA described its "*collection posture*" as "*Collect it All*," "*Process it All*," "*Exploit it All*," "*Partner it All*," "*Sniff it All*" and, ultimately, "*Know it All*." In his book, he goes on to show, "*In a one-month period last year, for example, a single unit of the NSA, the Global Access Operations unit, collected data on more than 97 billion emails and 124 billion phone calls from around the world; more than 3 billion of those calls and emails were collected as they passed through the United States. As of 2012, the agency was processing more than 20 billion telecommunications per day. In a single month in 2011, the NSA collected 71 million calls and emails from Poland alone.*" In response to all the debate about whistleblowers and the information they have revealed, I include the following quote.

Quotation **M. Scott** **Peck**	The whole course of human history may depend on a change of heart in one solitary and even humble individual - for it is the solitary mind and soul of the individual that the battle between good and evil is waged and ultimately won or lost.

Given what we learned above, I chose to write the next section of this book from a third person perspective as a foreign journalist after an epiphany during my long walks while listening to National Public Radio (NPR) and other media sources on revelations about Internet spying by the NSA. There was no other way that I could think of to effectively present my argument against this mass monitoring of U.S. citizens and worldwide Internet use that western citizens are allowing to take place. During my long walks required by doctors, I listened to many people calling in to talk radio to argue **for** this type of invasion into their privacy to ensure their safety. Therefore, I decided to write the following as a make-believe foreign reporter looking in on what is taking place in the United States, and to the same degree in Great Britain, in regards to their citizens' digital privacy. This presentation format seemed to be a much more effective way of presenting this sad story about everyone's loss of privacy, due process, freedom and their citizens' complacency as they go along with it. For example, I knew my argument for privacy was in desperate trouble when my 78-year-old, totally government-trusting mother decried to me **"our government needs to spy on everyone to prevent another 9-11!"**

It also occurred to me putting together this argument that free Western European nation's citizens who experienced the devastation that took place during WWII, and then the occupation afterward by the Soviets would have a totally different perspective on the privacy freedoms that U.S. citizens are willingly giving up and funding to spy on the Internet world. I felt this perspective was paramount to making my argument that we cannot all allow this travesty to happen again to mankind. If I could have included an interview with one of them I would have. Someone from one of those nations has a very different perspective on the erosion of personal digital privacy than other western citizens who are ready and willing to allow what is taking place in the guise of protecting their personal safety. This false argument and citizens' apathy to protect their freedom has been used throughout history to rob what we call "the commoners" of their liberty, their ability to provide for themselves, their personal freedom and eventually their lives. It is only when this type of tyranny hits critical mass that changes can happen. Before there is blood in the streets and oppression rules, I'm hoping this book will help roll back these invasions into our privacy, and it may help establish the Digital Fourth Amendment to the United States Constitution, which I proposed earlier.

I am not alone in this battle, as Senator Rand Paul proposed that we need to extend Fourth Amendment guarantees to digital communications such as email, which should require specific warrants to monitor. Senator Paul's amendment failed in a Senate vote 79 to 12, so we can see that there is little or no will in Washington to protect U.S. citizens' privacy in any way. We can clearly see that a majority of the U.S. Senate wants to abandon the Fourth Amendment and probably wish it never existed. Then, on January 3, 2014, the top-secret Foreign Intelligence Surveillance Court reauthorized the National Security Agency's program to collect phone records of all U.S. citizens. This came as no big surprise since it has been authorized 36 times over the past seven years, with little or no debate or outcry by U.S citizens. This comes after a federal judge in December 2013 called the NSA's surveillance program "almost Orwellian" and unconstitutional.

Some Western European citizens who experienced the Great Wars now greatly value the required transparency of their governments and their ability to question what their governments are doing. Ironically, they objected much more loudly to the recently revealed NSA's spying on everything in the digital world than did the U.S. media or U.S. citizens. WWII soldiers saw and reported back to U.S. citizens about the horrors of those wars, but much of that history is becoming lost, which this book attempts to amend with some historical references related to war and cyber security. For example, I tried to get my parents to agree with my views that recent events showed how U.S. citizens' privacy is being invaded by our government and with little public outcry. These revelations were met with stiff resistance from both my mother and father in their total trust in the U.S. government, even after all the NSA spying revelations. If my mother and father, along with what statistics show, over half of the U.S. population, want to give up their privacy for imagined state security due to a supposed terrorism threat without a fight, I had to contemplate how could I effectively argue against these misguided beliefs? There was no way I could do this from a U.S. citizens' perspective, but only as a foreigner who recently regained these freedoms after the horrific tragic losses of past wars, witnessing the loss of millions of lives.

Arguing these values and rights with a third-person perspective would only enhance my argument about how these inalienable rights were granted to U.S. citizens **by their forefathers, the world and God**. These rights that were laid down and established now seem to be forgotten by a nation of people and veterans who fought for these rights against all odds over 237 years ago. In the U.S. country's many wars since then, we seem to have lost how something established and placed into law by such a valuable document such as the U.S. Constitution, which was/is so important to future generations of U.S. soldiers, U.S citizens and the world but now becoming a forgotten or forsaken document. Our forefather's accomplishments and wisdom to establish our freedoms and privacy is now being circumvented or relegated into tyranny by the infected Internet's digital age that is now being allowed to progress unchecked. Our bought and paid for politicians do little to change this, and veterans and U.S. citizens look the other way, thinking that privacy, due process and an imperial presidency, can be overridden by media coverage reporting about such things as gay marriage, abortion, flag burning, building monuments or dedicating roads, bridges, rest stops and highways to veterans' sacrifices. We all have to have to find our cause to fight for so I hope we all can and will choose wisely to do the right thing that does the most good for mankind.

For the sake of argument, picture me as a make-believe German reporter rescued from NAZI imperialism after WWII and living in a world being rebuilt by the United States. I am writing many years later about what I see happening in the supposedly free U.S. republic, which I learned about in school and admired. This U.S. republic is one that I viewed as a model for the world, with checks and balances written into their laws and founding constitutional documents, that spelled out the limitations of their citizens' governmental system. I have studied extensively how their historical group of very knowledgeable and intelligent founding fathers, who risked their lives fighting to create the original United States, conducting an experiment in personal freedom creating a republic, and have revered them. Shortly after the

U.S. Constitutional Convention of 1787 Elizabeth Powell asked Benjamin Franklin, "*Well doctor, what have we got, a republic or a monarchy?*" To which Franklin replied, "*A republic, Madam, if you can keep it.*" So let us now begin that foreign reporter's story, which is far from history's complete story that began back in 1913 with the establishment of the U.S. Federal Reserve, which you should someday read about and study. **Let us begin...**

From the Perspective of a Make Believe Post WWII German Reporter Who I Now Am!

Most of my life I have respected the power, freedom and privacy that U.S. citizens have experienced. However, reporting from afar, I have observed how the checks and balances, which their U.S. forefathers so wisely wrote into their U.S. Constitution, have been eroded in the pretense of protecting their personal safety, national security, corporate greed, and compliance with their other "supposed" national security interests. Their republic appears to be headed down a path of self-destruction due to their mass hysteria about supposed terrorism, thus allowing greater and greater unchecked surveillance by their government and other entities. They seem to think that unchecked presidential power in their rising security state* will keep them safe. The system designed by their forefathers and as Alexander Hamilton wrote in "Federalist No. 1" is "*establishing good government from reflection and choice*" seems to be lost. Hamilton warned the American people that the alternative was "*to depend for the political constitutions on accident and force.*"

I see this erosion of their freedom impacting the rest of the free world who have looked up to and prized a U.S. citizen's personal freedom and privacy. Many of us whose parents have experienced what it is like to live under a totalitarian government have worshiped the freedom that U.S. citizens seem to be taking for granted and are giving away without a fight. We are all dismayed by this and our own personal fight to keep these freedoms, which may be sacrificed as a result, without this bright beacon in which to view our world. The fight we must now undertake is how to make the American people aware of what is happening to them and how important it is to them. As U.S. citizens are distracted and deceived into giving up their freedom consider the following quotations by their forefathers who shaped their current constitutional system.

Quotation Benjamin Franklin	"*They, who would give up essential Liberty, to purchase a little temporary Safety, deserve neither Liberty nor Safety.*" Benjamin Franklin's warning to future generations of U.S. citizens about concentrating power in the hands of a president creating an imperial presidency thus becoming tyrannical and then go on to create a massive infected Internet surveillance tool of such monumental scale such that the world has never seen or witnessed in human history.
Quotation James Madison	"*If Tyranny and Oppression come to this land, it will be in the guise of fighting a foreign enemy.*" James Madison who was prophetic in his warnings about today's events and the Iraqi and Afghanistan protracted wars. Just as we thought the Iraq war was at an end President Obama has continued the war with an air campaign costing U.S. taxpayers many billions more.
Quotation James Madison	In Federalist No. 14, "*In a democracy the people meet and exercise the government in person: in a republic, they assemble and administer in by their representatives and agents.*" In Federalist 55, a representative body would help "*avoid the confusion and intemperance of a multitude.*"

The U.S. Foreign Intelligence Surveillance Act
https://en.wikipedia.org/wiki/Foreign_Intelligence_Surveillance_Act was a huge battle-axe granting their federal government broad-reaching powers contradictory to their constitution.

That act was signed into law under the *Democratic* administration of Jimmy Carter back in 1978. Their government passed that law under the pretext of making it easier to gather intelligence on *foreign powers* and *agents of foreign powers*. However, unknown to most U.S. citizens, it also states, *which may include American citizens, violating U.S. law on territory under United States control*. U.S. citizens suspected of being involved with nefarious foreign activities were included in the broad reaching power of this legislation as well. This circumvented their government's need to obtain warrants or follow the checks and balances their forefathers granted as irrefutable rights, wisely written into their wonderful U.S. Constitution by their forefathers. Still, this infringement on their rights did not go far enough. After 9/11, the *Republican* Bush Administration pushed through huge changes to the American law, called The U.S. PATRIOT Act. That legislation had a much broader definition of terrorism that further circumvented their U.S. Constitution and was later used to eavesdrop on U.S. citizens in ways never before done in U.S. or world history. Among other powers, this legislation vastly expanded their government's ability to spy on its own citizens' use of the Internet without warrants or review by their judicial branch of government. Specifically, it allows for unwarranted wire taps, Internet monitoring, and many other forms of domestic intelligence gathering. In just a few short years the safeguards wisely setup by their forefathers and in place for hundreds of years, had been effectively circumvented. The few American whistle-blowing heroes who have tried to fight this new-found governmental power have had their lives turned into a living hell, prosecuted to the fullest extent of American rewritten law, and/or have chosen to live in exile. We have to view these events as the beginning of the end to U.S. citizens' 230+ years of personal freedom and personal privacy.

This unique experiment that was founded and established on the principles of a constitution, that no other nation in the history of mankind has ever witnessed or experienced, appears to be coming to an end. The U.S. experiment in human individual liberty and privacy that their revolution produced in the 1700's seems to be lost. It is the hope of this reporter that with our help they will regain their greatness and become a leader in personal freedom and privacy again but that may take a second American revolution. The BBC, Al Jazeera (See experiment in personal privacy, civil liberty and the rule of law appears have outlasted: http://www.bbc.co.uk, http://www.aljazeera.com) and other worldwide news agencies still provide the American people with untainted worldwide news, which their own local news agencies no longer do. American citizens are being trained to choose the illusion of national security over individual liberty. The U.S. entertainment media is focused on frivolous individual murder trials, a disappearing plane that occupied every moment of U.S. media attention for months of speculation about what happened and where it went, gay marriage, and many other social issues that seems to be designed to intentionally distract U.S. citizens from other important events that are happening in their governments political chambers and in the world around them.

Most U.S. citizens do not know or care that unknown U.S. courts now meet in secret to approve search warrants and rubber stamp ever expansive, extensive and expensive surveillance on them. According to http://topics.nytimes.com/top/reference/timestopics/subjects/f/foreign_intelligence_surveillance_act_fisa/index.html, "*In September 2012 the House voted, 301 to 118, to extend the FISA Amendments Act for five years. It was set to expire without new legislation at the end of 2012.*" However, in December 2012 came the final outrage (**that should have been to U.S.**

citizens) and was not debated or objected to by their now *Democratic* Obama administration, who campaigned to do so. Their Senate approved (https://en.wikipedia.org/wiki/Foreign_Intelligence_Surveillance_Act_of_1978_Amendments_Act_of_2008) by a vote of 73 to 23, to extend the FISA Amendments Act for five more years to 2017 after a very short debate, while the American people were distracted by a make-believe fiscal crisis, the holidays, and other things important to their everyday lives.

American citizens should be asking themselves why this legislation passed so rapidly at a time when they were distracted, but there seems to be little interest or knowledge about this within their country. There were some proposals pending that had the American entertainment media brought them to U.S. public's attention might have been debated. These amendments would have given the American people back some of their civil liberties, but most Americans had no idea their elected officials were renewing FISA. For example, from http://www.npr.org/blogs/thetwo-way/2012/12/28/168220266/congress-extends-fisa-wiretapping-act-to-2017-awaits-obamas-signature, Senator Ron Wyden D-Oregon sought to require the director of national intelligence to share information about telephone and email surveillance--how many American have been monitored, or whether communications between Americans is reviewed. The amendment was rejected by a 52 to 43 in a bipartisan vote. A similar measure, introduced by Senator Jeff Merkley (D-Oregon), sought to require the Attorney Genter to disclose some of the decisions and orders issued by the Foreign Intelligence Surveillance Court, whose records are secret was defeated 54 to 37. Another amendment, offered by Senator Rand Paul (R-Kentucky), sought "to ensure adequate protection of the rights under the U.S. Fourth Amendment" was also quickly defeated, 79 to 12.

While their Congress appeared willing to throw the U.S. back to the dark ages in locked controversy over a false government-made fiscal crisis that the media portrayed and reported extensively on, this surveillance legislation was pushed through in just days with little or no U.S. media coverage. Observing all this, we have to wonder why legislation, that should have proven controversial to their public, took place in just days with so little media coverage. We have to assume that the U.S. media is now largely controlled by their government and will no longer report on important events about civil liberties that U.S. citizens should be concerned and told about. This legislation was passed quickly at a time of the year when their citizens were celebrating Christmas and eating turkey and ham.

My belief is most U.S. citizens who pay little attention to these events certainly will not recall hearing anything about this major event, or even considers it important. As a result, this legislation was passed without even a whimper of protest by the American public. Their President Obama ran on a platform saying that he would push for rolling back this invasion into their privacy by the Bush administration, but in a matter of days this bill, unmodified and un-debated, was signed into law. U.S. citizens hoped that when he was elected he would roll back many of the policies embraced by the unilateral Bush administration that had offended so many people in their country and around the world.   Both of the U.S. republic's political parties, known as *Republicans* and *Democrats*, seem to be in total agreement on making sure that their Patriot Act law remains intact to allow their federal government to retain broad reaching power to spy unchecked on American citizens and the world in their correspondence, phone conversations and much more. There appear to be no limits -- ethical, legal, or political

-- as to how far their citizens will allow this invasion into their own privacy as their government claims to act in the name of 'terrorism'.

The result of the renewed passage of the Patriot Act became evident in June 2013, when a U.S. federal judge ruled that without a warrant, Google must release customer data to the FBI without a warrant. The U.S. government Federal Bureau of Investigation was shown to be secretly forcing Internet, telecommunication companies, and U.S. banks to reveal any information about anyone housed in their databases. This proved to be very alarming because this data included individual transactions as well. The multibillion dollar worldwide Google Corporation was ordered to turn over all their data despite Google's arguments that these secret demands are illegal. The FBI can now perform warrantless electronic data-gathering without even having to seek a judge's approval. Anyone using Google to conduct Internet searches, send email or use any of their services must refrain from doing so. However, these revelations proved far less severe than the truth about what the American citizens have allowed their government to survey. The United States is not a country with which to do business or conduct any sort of personal or private interaction. (See: http://www.usatoday.com/story/tech/2013/05/31/judge-google-fbi/2378799)

On June 5, 2013, the Guardian British newspaper in London exploded a story that revealed that an analyst working for the U.S. National Security Agency had presented evidence that the U.S. NSA was conducting widespread, domestic data gathering on millions of Americans. This individual gave them and "The Washington Post" a 41-point PowerPoint presentation exposing that a secret U.S. court had now coerced large U.S. Internet companies into allowing the U.S. NSA to tap directly into the servers of nine U.S. Internet service companies. These 41 slides exposed that all U.S. citizens' and foreign voice mail, email, VOIP, and all Internet activity are being monitored by the U.S. government. The news agencies originally only published four, and soon after, five of the PowerPoint slides given to them because they feared the power and reach of the mighty and now unchecked U.S. government's invasion into their citizens' privacy! According to the report, this presentation revealed, "*it gives the FBI and NSA access to "audio, video, photographs, emails, documents and connection logs" from the central servers of Microsoft, Yahoo, Google, Facebook, PalTalk, AOL, Skype, YouTube and Apple. Another program called BLARNEY sniffs up metadata as it streams past "choke points" on the Internet, continuing the theme of bulk scooping of data most would think is private.*" There was also talk that some of the cloud storage providers, such as Dropbox, may also be required to offer up Americans' data stored on their servers to the U.S. government.

As this story continues, we found out that Dropbox named U.S. Secretary of State Condoleezza Rice to their board. As she was a major proponent of wireless wiretapping, we have to wonder about the files of the over 275 million users that company holds. In 2005 Rice not only spoke in favor of the Bush Administration mass warrantless spying on everyone, she also authorized the illegal, warrantless wiretapping of UN Security Council members. Edward Snowden identified Dropbox as a surveillance target and that they automatically scan user files for abhorrent activity. Many privacy advocates appealed to Dropbox to reconsider this appointment to their board but the company appointed her anyway. Any Operation Iraqi War Veteran should find this appointment very offensive as she spoke in support of the war that they all found out later to be illegally justified by Iraqi WMD programs that did not exist, but with that said as a foreign reporter I supported the war. However, in the aftermath I knew the occupation was misguided and would result many thousands of U.S. soldiers deaths unnecessarily. This became especially apparent as not only were there insufficient numbers of U.S. soldiers to secure the country what few were there were diverted to securing the Iraqi oil reserves allowing the country to descend into chaos.

Reporting on this we saw U.S. General Shinseki retired (perhaps forcibly) who said publically "*Something on the order of several hundred thousand soldiers are probably, you know, a figure that would be required*" to stabilize Iraq after an invasion. "*We're talking about post-hostilities control over a piece of geography that's fairly significant, with the kinds of ethnic tensions that could lead to other problems. And so it takes a significant ground force presence to maintain a safe and secure environment, to ensure that people are fed, that water is distributed, and all the normal responsibilities that go along with administering a situation like this.*" General Abizaid later stated publically that General Shinseki had been correct in his assessment. Then to make matters worse after the war the Iraqi Army was disbanded which led to the insurgency and a destabilized Iraq. (See: http://www.drop-dropbox.com, https://en.wikipedia.org/wiki/2003_invasion_of_Iraq)

Even the Chinese have posted warnings to their citizens that when using U.S. company search engines, data storage, or even conducting business with U.S. companies, it is likely that they are being spied upon and recorded by the U.S. government. After all these startling revelations, the public outcry in the U.S. has been minimal, with many Americans agreeing to turn over all of their data about themselves for the promise of added security provided by their government. Now every citizen or business in U.S. has to assume that any communication or information they share with any business or citizen anywhere in the world is being spied upon and recorded.

These wonderful Americans who have proved to be the bastions in preventing tyranny everywhere in the world are now becoming the very things against which they fought. We must all take extraordinary measures to protect our data from the American NSA and doing business in their country. In fact, it is the opinion of this reporter that no secret, innovation, invention or discovery made by the citizens of any free country be communicated electronically with any citizen or business of the United States without German encryption software as U.S. corporate encryption solutions have NSA installed backdoors. We must revert to dealing with them personally or not at all. What the Americans fail to understand is that these programs being depicted as put in place to protect them were never about terrorism and represent the greatest threat to privacy that has ever existed in human history. Their Internet has become the Stazi (State Security) machine that we all experienced during the Russian occupation, and we can only hope they will wake up and become the country their ancestors fought for during WWII.

Whistleblower Edward Snowden Reveals He Ratted on the NSA

The **whistleblower personal privacy advocate Edward Snowden** revealed his identity shortly after showing the American public just how widespread their U.S. government NSA spying machine had become. One would have thought that Snowden would have been hailed as a hero but instead he was fired from his defense-contracting job at Booz Allen Hamilton and had to flee to Hong Kong in fear for his life. Former U.S. Vice President Dick Cheney and

House speaker John A. Boehner quickly labeled Mr. Snowden a traitor and it appears that in principle, and at the time a slim majority of Americans agreed with this charge in principle. Sen. Dianne Feinstein, D-Calif., chairwoman of the Senate Intelligence Committee, defended the programs and has proven to be the one of the biggest supporters of spying on the American public. The USA Today newspaper article on June 13, 2013 by Rick Hampson stated, "*In a Pew Research Center/Washington Post survey released Monday, 56% of those polled said the National Security Agency's tracking of Americans' phone calls to investigate terrorism is acceptable; 41% said it isn't. A slim majority — 52%-45% — said the government should not be able to monitor people's email to thwart possible terrorism.*" (See: http://www.usatoday.com/story/news/nation/2013/06/10/snowden-leaks-nsa-privacy-terrorist/2408803)   Others, such as radio talk show host Glenn Beck, moviemaker Michael Moore, former whistleblower Daniel Ellsburg, and a buzz feed at Twitter, called Snowden a hero by 30 to 1. Ironically, even the semi-totalitarian Chinese government hailed Edward Snowden as a hero. The existence of the PRISM system he revealed certainly debunked the U.S. high-profile accusations of Chinese hacking being the worst thing that Americans have to fear. China took the high ground with statements such as, "*We have the right to ask the US government to issue explanations on, for example, whether Prism is being applied to the US's business negotiation with the Chinese government and corporations.*")

 **Historical Reference – Leaker Daniel Ellsberg, his road from traitor to hero**

Before Edward Snowden, Daniel Ellsberg was known as the greatest leaker in U.S. history. Ellsberg was an insider, a man who worked for the RAND Corporation and the Pentagon before deciding that he could no longer tolerate what he saw as the lies of the American government in Vietnam, and used the media to get his message out. On June 13, 1971 Daniel leaked 7,000 pages that came to be known as "The Pentagon Papers" to the New York Times. The top-secret document revealed that senior U.S. leaders, including three U.S. Presidents, knew that Vietnam was an unwinnable quagmire. The papers further revealed that the executive branch had been lying to Congress and the U.S. public about the progress of the war.

Ellsberg surrendered himself to authorities who labeled him a traitor and then charged him as being a spy. He stood trial for espionage, and U.S. citizens did not know how to react. He was later vindicated when it was revealed that Richard Nixon's crew had been conducting illegal wiretaps and had broken into his psychiatrist's office in an effort to discredit the former intelligence contractor. Daniel Ellsberg was later labeled a hero by most U.S. citizens and was acquitted by the judge who was trying his espionage case.

In a CNN interview Ellsberg stated that Snowden was a hero who had done more for human privacy and for the protection of the First and Fourth U.S. Constitutional amendments than any man in history. On January 14, 2014, it was announced that Snowden was joining the Freedom of the Press Foundation board of directors. Ellsberg said that the public needed to know what it was that Edward Snowden leaked and that Snowden's actions have led to about a half a dozen proposals for reigning in the NSA. (See: https://pressfreedomfoundation.org)

The Nixon administration vilified Ellsburg for his abuse of the law using the U.S. Espionage Act* that originated in 1917, and has been amended numerous times since, to bring a criminal case against him. However, his use of these powers pales in comparison to the Obama administration that has brought twice as many criminal cases against whistleblowers as all other presidents combined. Nixon was later accused of putting a few reporters under surveillance and impeached for this and other crimes. However, the Obama administration has admitted to putting associated press reporters, as well as a Fox reporter under surveillance without any repercussions what-so-ever so we have to wonder is freedom of the press still alive in today's western world?

The U.S. NSA has an unlimited budget funded by the American people to spy on the whole Internet world and when **Edward Snowden** revealed that they were spying on their very own American citizens and how widespread and insidious this U.S. government spying had become, he was branded a traitor by some and a hero by others. Snowden stated that he revealed the widespread gathering of email, phone calls, etc. by NSA to the citizens of the U.S. because he felt they needed to know what information that they were unwittingly sharing with their government. I applaud his sacrifice and view him as a hero in many ways. I understand his actions to evade prosecution by fleeing to Hong Kong and eventually ending up in Russia given the history of how vehemently the Obama administration has pursued and has prosecuted whistleblowers in the past. The U.S. government's focus is on throwing whistleblowers in jail and not on what they reveal to the U.S public. Let's take the example of Bradley Manning who was sentenced to 136 years in prison for blowing the whistle on a massacre and the killing of Iraqi civilians. Manning's release of information to the media was excessive and it was argued by government officials that it placed government sources in danger, which may be correct but he had no other place to go to assuage his conscience.

 Historical Reference -- Bradley Manning was sentenced to 136 years in prison for his leaking of 700,000 U.S. government documents to WikiLeaks

Bradley Manning's faith in the United States was shaken after an attack on a convoy with his comrades. A roadside bomb exploded beneath a car full of civilians that had pulled aside to let the military vehicles pass. Members of his 305th Military Intelligence Battalion were not hurt but at least one civilian was killed. Coombs, Manning's attorney stated, "*That changed Manning's outlook on the war, he struggled.*" Then a 2007 video shot from an Apache helicopter crossed Manning's desk that showed an Apache attack in Iraq in which U.S. soldiers fired on civilians and killed 12. According to https://en.wikipedia.org/wiki/Bradley_Manning, "*one of the men was a journalist, and two other men were Reuter's employees carrying cameras that the pilots mistook for an anti-tank grenade launcher (RPG-7). The helicopter also fired on a van that stopped to help the injured members of the first group; two children in the van were wounded and their father killed.*" According to Manning's attorney, this and some other atrocities he was privy to was the catalyst that provoked him into bringing these events to the public's attention, which were all but ignored.

The Apache video shown in court proved to be quite graphic as it showed Reuters' Saeed Chmagh had survived the initial strafing by the helicopter, but apparently died when it opened fire again on the people that were attempting to get him off the sidewalk from where he lay and trying to get him into a van. In another video released by Bradley Manning, which vanished according to wiki was "the Granai airstrike". The airstrike occurred on May 4, 2009, in the village of Granai, Afghanistan, killing 86–147 Afghan civilians. In March 2013, Julian

Assange said that Wikileaks had received the video from Manning and described the airstrike as a "war crime," but said it was lost when Daniel Domscheit Berg left the organization."

In another incident, Manning discovered that 15 detainees had been arrested by the Iraqi Federal Police for printing anti-Iraqi literature. He was ordered by Army commander to find out who the "bad guys" were; he discovered that the detainees were the result of a corruption trail within the Iraqi cabinet. Manning says he reported this to his commanding officer, who said "he didn't want to hear any of it"; the officer told him to help the Iraqi police find more detainees. Manning realized he was actively involved in something that he was completely against.

The young PFC was very disturbed by all this and struggled with what should be done as his conscience weighed heavily upon him. Manning stated for the record that he tried to be selective and did not understand that releasing the material he did could harm the U.S. in any way; he only wanted to raise public awareness as to what was happening. However, the release of more than 700,000 State Department cables, terrorism detainee assessments, combat logs and videos, which constituted the largest breach of classified secrets in U.S. history seemed excessive to assuage his soul. I think God will judge him better than the U.S. government did.

The media has questioned why a PFC was given access to this level of classified data. My answer, from my experience as a soldier and working under wartime stress, is the long hours, sometimes 12 to 14 hours a day seven days a week, numb you to what is going on around you. You stop caring about anything other than surviving the next day. Imagine a civilian job where you only sleep in cat naps each day and constantly have your survival threatened.

As we can see from the above example, governments, corporations, small businesses and even families need a mechanism for whistleblowing to reach someone in authority who can make a difference. If Manning could have approached his congressional representative with impunity for revealing his information he might not now be facing life in jail and Wikileaks might not be posting all his information on their websites. However, the U.S. system is one of intolerance that has left men and women of conscience with little or no recourse other than to face the full brunt of the rewritten law system or worse, which thus limits their only course of action to local or foreign media. Sometimes they may be misguided in some ways, but there appears to be no other way to reach the U.S. public who seem to be unwilling to listen to something other than their U.S. government and their corporate controlled media. Let us hope that U.S. citizens wake up to how their media is being manipulated and watch foreign journalism to find out about what is really going on around the world. U.S. citizen's original constitution has been circumvented as they are no longer provided meaningful information upon which to make decisions. I'm not condoning Manning's actions and have not reviewed the material he released but I understand his need to expunge his soul to the American public who condemned him to *136 years* in prison. This sentence pales in comparison to the lesser sentences of many U.S. violent criminals and we have to ask why that is? The message here is clear; do not rat on the U.S. government in any way or you will be prosecuted to the full extent of the law. What has the U.S. become?

Snowden's escape from prosecution for his chosen actions allowed media commentators and government officials to try and discredit what he tried to accomplish for western civilization's privacy. However, evidence of U.S. government's intolerance to whistleblowers, he had no choice but to flee. The U.S. Espionage Act* and the Obama's liberal use of it to squelch all opposition to it's polices guarantees that Edward Snowden would be in jail for a very long time. Given the media spectacle surrounding his case I hope he will one day be able to return and face a jury of his peers. The media also questioned his choice of Hong Kong and subsequently Russia, especially if he was carrying other intelligence information that he may have copied. The right-wing media used this to discredit what he sought out to accomplish, which he said was to educate everyone on how their privacy and other freedoms were unknowingly, being violated.

In an American Legion article titled "A Question of Power" by Jonathan Turley the Shapiro Professor of Public Interest Law at George Washington University sums up why Snowden had to flee the country, "*We have learned of a massive surveillance program in which every citizen has had telephonic and email data captured by the government. Every citizen has been warned that the president may kill them on his own authority without a change, let alone a conviction. We have a secret court that approves thousands of secret searches every year and a federal court system that increasingly allows the use of secret evidence. We have a new Obama-ear law, the National Defense Authorization Act that allows indefinite detention of people by the government and, while exempted from mandatory detention, allows for such detention of citizens. We still have a detention center at Guantanamo Bay, established by George W. Bush just over our border to avoid jurisdiction of U.S. courts. It allows the president to choose who gets a real trial, or who gets a legally dubious military tribunal, or who gets no trial at all. While seeking to close the facility, Obama has continued to assert the right to send people to military tribunals on his sole authority - thereby stripping them of core legal protections.*" It appears the citizens of the United States may allow their nation become the next dictatorial nation to threaten the whole world.

In the same article he reveals what the rest of the world thinks of the erosion of freedoms that American is allowing without protest. "*The United States in now widely viewed as a hypocrite on the subject of human rights and civil liberties. This year, our nation fell to 46th in the world on press freedoms (behind the former Soviet republics of Latvia as well as Romania, Poland, Czechoslovakia, Ghana, South Africa and El Salvador), according to a recent study by Reporters Without Borders. Another study this year counts the United States as an "enemy of Internet freedom" with countries such as Iran, China and North Korea.*" (See: http://www.jonathanturley.org, https://en.wikipedia.org/wiki/Freedom_of_the_press, http://rsf.org/index2014/en-index2014.php)

	Historical Reference – Before Edward Snowden there was William Binney, a whistleblowing former NSA Technical Director

On July 11, 2014 in an interview with the Guardian, William Binney, a 30-year veteran of the intelligence community stated the following as fact; "*At least 80% of all audio calls, not just metadata, are recorded and stored in the US... At least 80% of fiber-optic cables globally go via the US... This is no accident and allows the US to view all communication coming in... The NSA lies about what it stores... The ultimate goal of the NSA is total population control...*" William Binney resigned from the NSA on October 31, 2001 because he was disgusted by Washington's move towards mass surveillance. The difference between Binney and Snowden was his high rank and that he did not take any documents as proof with him. From that time forward, he has been an outspoken critic of the NSA's unnecessary mass surveillance stating, "*it's better than anything that the KGB, the Stasi, or the Gestapo and SS ever had!*" He likes to mock the NSA by pointing out such things as how the NSA's mass gathering of data did not stop 9/11, missed Russia's intervention in Ukraine, the Islamic States' take-over of Iraq and has stopped zero terror attacks inside the US. Because of his vocal criticism he has been persecuted with investigations, had his home raided by the FBI who also took his computer and backup disks, had his security clearance revoked, which forced him to close a profitable $300,000 a year business and spend $7,000 on legal fees. In his Guardian interview he laid down the gauntlet by saying, "*There are no other views for the judges to consider. There have been at least 15-20 trillion constitutional violations for US domestic audiences and you can double that globally. I call people who are covering up NSA crimes traitors.*" Binney expressed publically on CBN in July 2014 that *the ultimate goal of the NSA is total population control.* He also stated that Internal Revenue Service has "direct access" to the NSA's domestic spying data and was likely using it to target the tea party. (See: http://www.theguardian.com/commentisfree/2014/jul/11/the-ultimate-goal-of-the-nsa-is-total-population-control, http://www.cbn.com/cbnnews/us/2014/August/Whistleblower-NSA-Goal-Is-Total-Population-Control)

In comparison, Great Britain who also spied on the Internet and has no constitution protecting the freedom of the press only fell to 33. Further revelations or even the power points slides that Snowden gave to the media that they chose not to publish at first and later did, may have caused some harm to U.S. intelligence, which would make his actions questionable. However, nothing else has come out to substantiate about that accusation except even more information how the NSA is invading the privacy of everyone in the world. Right or wrong, one has to admire the extraordinary safeguards he used to get that PowerPoint slide presentation via encrypted tunnels into the naive media's hands (prior to Snowden they did not know a lot about how everything they do is monitored). His careful steps, caution and sacrifice ultimately resulted in only a few, very scared and intimated western media papers publishing only five of the 48 NSA PowerPoint slide presentations that Snowden had provided them. Later a much more revealing sixth slide was released by the Guardian. I imagine he was dismayed by this but after my experiences during the 2nd Iraq war, if we had met I could have told him this would happen. I applaud his choice of the Guardian, but Al Jazeera would have been a better second choice than the Washington Post. However, both reporting agencies revealed further information months after the initial story broke.

Al Jazeera reporting during the Iraq war was the best information a U.S. soldiers could get. In reading this book, I hope you will come to learn that some of the skills that Snowden used are not rocket science. Once he had accomplished his mission of informing the public, it could be argued he should have made a stand and considered *Seppuku*, which is a gruesome form of Japanese ritual suicide originally reserved for samurai. Because of the media and government spin, Snowden may be viewed by some as a misguided young man who seemed to want to do the right thing but caused more damage than good.

Governments seem to be able to concentrate their citizen's focus on the individual whistleblowers and not what they revealed or accomplished. However, let's look how the NSA has violated American privacy thousands of times. In the Washington Post article "NSA broke privacy rules thousands of times per year, audit finds" by Barton Gellman, Published: August

16, 2013, "*The National Security Agency has broken privacy rules or overstepped its legal authority thousands of times each year since Congress granted the agency broad new powers in 2008, according to an internal audit and other top-secret documents.*

Most of the infractions involve unauthorized surveillance of Americans or foreign intelligence targets in the United States, both of which are restricted by statute and executive order. They range from significant violations of law to typographical errors that resulted in unintended interception of U.S. emails and telephone calls." While we want to think that U.S. elected administrations (whichever party) will alter these invasions into their citizen's privacy but the Obama administration has provided almost no public information about the NSA's compliance record and Obama has stated publically that he supports the NSA spying on U.S. citizens. This suggests that democratic and republican administrations, are in total agreement with NSA's spying on the entire Internet world. As much as the U.S. government tries to discredit Snowden, the debate he has sparked that is taking place about western civilization's fight for privacy and is one me must all take very seriously.

Some rightwing radio hosts have questioned why Snowden fled to Russia, which was actually not his intention. His passport was revoked on his way to Cuba and eventual sanctuary in South America stranding him in the transit zone of a Moscow airport. Since he was only granted asylum for one year this indicates that he was not spying for them. In an interview with NBC news titled "Inside the Mind of Edward Snowden," he stated that he destroyed the material he had copied from NSA before transit through Russia. Soon after this the second startling revelation of an XKeyscore spying program was eventually revealed by the Guardian. My supposition is that even the Russians were surprised at how far reaching NSA's capabilities had become and wanted to reward Snowden for his revelations.

Turns out the XKeyscore program allows NSA to go beyond what we imagined was spying to home invasion. XKeyscore has practically boundless access to monitor nearly everything U.S. citizens do on the Internet. If U.S. citizens thought before that the collection of phone messages and email was an invasion of their privacy, they now knew that was just the tip of iceberg. In the Guardian article titled "XKeyscore: NSA tool collects 'nearly everything a user does on the Internet'" by Glenn Greenwald, http://www.theguardian.com/world/2013/jul/31/nsa-top-secret-program-online-data, the files shed light on one of Snowden's most controversial statements made in his first video interview published by the Guardian published on June 10. These new revelations lend validity to Snowden's disparaged claim that "*I, sitting at my desk could wiretap anyone, from you or your accountant, to a federal judge or even the president, if I had a personal email*".

The article states, "*XKeyscore, the documents boast, is the NSA's "widest reaching" system developing intelligence from computer networks – what the agency calls Digital Network Intelligence (DNI). One presentation claims the program covers "nearly everything a typical user does on the Internet", including the content of emails, websites visited and searches, as well as their metadata. XKeyscore provides the technological capability, if not the legal authority, to target even US persons for extensive electronic surveillance without a warrant provided that some identifying information, such as their email or IP address, is known to the analyst.*"

Analysts can also use XKeyscore and other NSA systems to obtain ongoing "real-time" interception of an individual's Internet activity. Take note of the fact that it was **not** the

Washington Post who was given the same information that revealed this information. U.S. media sources seem to be curtailed in what they can present to U.S. citizens as I discovered during the 2003 Iraqi war. The Guardian states that with little more than an email address, NSA can search things such as email addresses seen in a session, phone numbers seen in a session, chat activity that includes information as a username, chat list, cookies, and much more. This invasion also included web pages and documents, To, From, CC and BCC, email addresses as well as the body of the email. This technology gives the NSA the ability to rummage through social media data such as Facebook chats with no warrant. We can only hope that free western civilization citizens everywhere will wake up to how this mass monitoring of the Internet has become more pervasive than we all could possibly fathom.

Then came another revelation about the program titled "Boundless Informant", which was another NSA program targeting U.S. citizens to gather intelligence about them. The Guardian first revealed public information about this program on June 8, 2013. This program was all about the worldwide heat map summarizing data records from many sources. According to Wiki, "*As this map shows that almost 3 billion data elements from inside the United States were captured by the NSA over a 30-day period ending in March 2013, Snowden stated that this tool was collecting more information on Americans located within the United States than on Russians in Russia. Snowden stated that he raised concerns with two superiors in the Hawaii regional base of the NSA Threat Operations Center and two superiors in the Technology Directorate of the NSA beginning in October 2012, and therefore that counted as using internal dissent channels in the NSA.*" (See: https://en.wikipedia.org/wiki/Boundless_Informant)

Just like whistleblowers other men of conscience in the U.S. are also being victimized. Major Jason Wright was assigned to represent Khalid Sheikh Mohammed, who was water boarded by the Bush administration into admitting many crimes. Major Wright was removed from the case because the military said he needed to attend a graduate course. In a stand against the military removing him from the defense team Major Wright chose to resign from the U.S. Army so that he could represent his client as long as possible. In his words, "*I had to make a legal and ethical decision as to what I was going to do in the best interest of my client, and I chose the option which 100 percent of all defense lawyers would chose,*" Wright told The Huffington Post. "*It's one of these law school scenarios; it's just being played out in real life.*" This whole fiasco is another indication of how the military tribunal process is broken.

The Huffington Post article also stated that Zeke Johnson of Amnesty International said "*I wish the government would care as much about the rules and fundamental principles of a fair trial as it does about a bureaucratic process for determining when a military defense attorney assigned to one of the most important cases in U.S. history – a death penalty case at that – should take a class. The government's actions will further erode the attorney-client relationship, a fundamental aspect of a fair trial, and further delay the proceedings – already dragging at a snail's pace. It's more evidence, as if any were needed, that the Guantanamo experiment is a failure. The 9/11 case should be moved to federal court, where it would be faster and fairer.*"
  (See: http://www.huffingtonpost.com/2014/04/21/jason-wright-guantanamo-ksm_n_5175707.html)

How the American Stazi State Security* System is Costing Their Taxpayers Many Billions to Spy on the Whole World

It has been suggested that the combined storage capacity of the U.S. NSA is now into the yottabyte category. To put that in perspective, a yottabyte = 1,000 zettabytes = 1,000,000 exabytes = 1 billion petabytes = 1 trillion terabytes. These numbers are completely mind blowing and hard for you or even any IT professional to understand just what they mean. To try to put this in perspective for you let's examine the fully funded, one million square foot NSA Utah facility, which was completed 2013. Upon investigation, I found the Forbes article titled, *"Blueprints Of NSA's Ridiculously Expensive Data Center In Utah Suggest It Holds Less Info Than Thought"* by Kashmir Hill, http://www.forbes.com/sites/kashmirhill/2013/07/24/blueprints-of-nsa-data-center-in-utah-suggest-its-storage-capacity-is-less-impressive-than-thought and Fox News *"Inside the NSA's secret Utah data center"*. According to the Fox News article by John Brandon published June 11, 2013, some reports have suggested that the NSA Utah data center could hold up to 5 zettabytes, who Charles King, principal analyst at data center consulting firm Pund-IT called *"an astronomical sum equivalent to 62 billion stacked iPhone 5s. King called that number "difficult, if not impossible to conceive. That would mean deploying about 5 million storage systems running roughly 1.25 billion, 4-terabyte hard drives,"* he said." In other estimates it is said this data center can store a yottabyte of data which is the equivalent of 16 trillion personal computers. As a 28 year IT veteran I had never heard the teams used to refer to storage capacity before now in any facility. One Exabyte is 250 million DVDs! (See: http://www.npr.org/programs/ted-radio-hour/?&showDate=2014-09-26 , http://www.foxnews.com/tech/2013/06/11/inside-nsas-secret-utah-data-center)

Former Google head Eric Schmidt once argued that you could house the entire amount of human knowledge from the beginning of man's existence until 2003 in only five exabytes. In a country with a debt of $18,084,000,000,000 and rising rapidly (See: http://www.usdebtclock.org), we have to wonder about the need for this mammoth two billion+ dollar data center, which will allow the NSA to store much more information about its own country's citizens, world Internet use, and for much longer periods. This is all being done under the guise of protecting U.S. citizens from foreign terrorists. U.S. citizens appear willing to give up their privacy rights granted, for hundreds of years by their forefathers, to prevent a few possible isolated terrorist attacks. Please refer back to "The Elephant in the Room Lets Crunch the Numbers on what is Really Killing Western Civilizations Citizens!" to see how misguided this type of thinking is.

Factoid	In 2011, there were approximately 1,000 large corporate data centers in the United States. It is estimated that increasing power demands, by the year 2020, the world's computer servers will match or exceed the carbon emissions of the airline industry. For example, according to Wiki, a Tier 4 data center is designed to host mission critical computer systems with fully redundant subsystems and compartmentalized security zones controlled by biometric access control methods. From my own experience, the physical environment of a data center is rigorously controlled as air conditioning is used to control the temperature and humidity in the data center. Backup power consists of thousands of uninterruptible power supplies, battery banks, and/or diesel/gas turbine generators. Energy use is an enormous issue for large data centers. The power draw for data centers ranges from a few kWh for a rack of servers in a closet to several tens of thousands of MW for large facilities. Some data centers have power densities of hundreds, if not

many thousands of times of a typical office building. By 2012, the cost of power for large data centers exceeded the cost of the original capital investment in most cases, which did not include personal, security and other operating costs. For example, Intel Corporation uses 3,102,050,000 kWh annually. In comparison, the U.S. Department of Energy uses 594,703,934 kWh annually. The city of Houston purchased 438,000,000 kWh for that city's municipal facilities. Boulder, CO purchases approximately 470,000 kWh annually to provide clean power for its municipal buildings.

We can only begin to imagine how much the U.S. taxpayer is willingly forfeiting to cover the operating costs of these massive NSA data centers used to spy on and record the whole world's Internet use for everyone's entire lifetimes. According to the U.S. Army Corp of Engineers, the Utah NSA center located outside of Buffdale (Buffdale is about 20 miles south of Salt Lake City) alone uses 65,000 kWh per day and has a series of back-up battery sites. It is manned by 150 to 200 employees. If we take the DTE Energy residential rate of 8.257 cents per additional kWh we have 65,000,000 x .08257 = $5,367,050 per day X 365 days = $1.959 billion of U.S. taxpayer money to just power this facility for one year. In other estimates speakers have stated that only 10s of millions is needed to power this 140,000 square meter facility. Next time you are at the largest Costco you have ever been in, picture in your mind five of them stacked side by side as this is the largest data center on the planet. (See: http://www.epa.gov/greenpower/toplists, http://energy.gov/savings/city-houston-green-power-purchasing, http://energy.gov/savings/city-boulder-green-power-purchasing, http://www.apcmedia.com/salestools/VAVR-5TDTEF/VAVR-5TDTEF_R1_EN.pdf, https://publicintelligence.net/u-s-army-corps-of-engineers-utah-data-center-udc-brief) Be advised that publicintelligence.net was flagged a malicious website by Malwarebytes when my editor visited it but Malwarebytes found no malicious software installed on my Windows computer after visiting this site.

Given these facts and the death toll numbers that I will soon present, should western civilization give up their privacy and taxpayer dollars for a few isolated terrorists attacks that account for less than 0.08% of the deaths worldwide? One has to wonder about why this is and what is happening with their government's mass spying on their citizen's and worldwide Internet usage. There seems to be an effort to dumb down the populous and especially western civilization's youth about how their constant use of Internet devices erodes their constitutionally guaranteed privacy freedoms under the guise of the convenience in the use of modern Internet devices.

No one is warning them about the dangers that these devices present to their future and loss of freedom! Because our older generation did not understand the use of these ever-advancing technologies, they are allowing their children to be spied upon with a scrutiny that Eric Arthur Blair who was known by his pen name George Orwell depicted so many years ago in the book *1984*. The book *1984* is a wonderful fictional read by the former English novelist and journalist (25 June 1903 – 21 January 1950). In his book governments and the super wealthy were pouring money and resources into departments much like todays U.S. NSA, whose function was to invade every facet of the common citizen's privacy, which we can now construe as the devices we use to connect to the infected Internet. His book portrayed a future, much like today's world, where a multibillion-trillion dollar minority illuminati were/are using their wealth to control the world, elect our politicians, and have our government observe us more and more. It is a vision of a world where a totalitarian bureaucratic nightmare exists, and individual freedom is no longer possible. It ranks amongst the most terrifying novels ever written and is today's reality. We must accept that the book *1984*, by George Orwell and published in 1949, has now proved to be a prophetic novel that depicts a powerful dystopian and warned of a future world where the state machine exerts complete control over social life and has now come to genuineness. Our loss of privacy and freedom has now progressed past the data gathering as described in George Orwell's depiction of lost freedom in his book *1984*, which I encourage you to read. The solution in his book was the awakening of the proletariats (common working people), which my book is now attempting to do. We all have to accept the fact that he was certainly inspired to provide this prophesy of mankind's future which is now our reality.

According to CNNMoney http://money.cnn.com/2013/06/07/news/economy/nsa-surveillance-cost/index.html June 7, 2013 *"What the NSA costs taxpayers"* by Jeanne Sahadi stated, *"The NSA is one of at least 15 intelligence agencies, and combined the total U.S. intelligence budget in 2012 was $75 billion, said Steve Aftergood, director of the government secrecy program at the Federation of American Scientists, a nonpartisan think tank that analyzes national and international security issues. After good estimates about 14% of the country's total intelligence budget – or about $10 billion – goes to the NSA."*

The VA 2013 budget is $61.342 billion according to http://veterans.house.gov/budget this includes VA medical care, construction, mental health services, medical and rehabilitation services for over 10 years of complex injuries of the 50,000 American military personnel wounded in Iraq and Afghanistan, medical support and compliance claims processing, medical facilities accounts of the veterans' health administration, national cemetery administration, VA entitlement programs such as disability compensation, pension, the GI Bill and more. These protracted wars, both the Gulf war and Operation Iraqi Freedom have cost the U.S. taxpayers greater than four trillion of new debt, and interest payments over the next 20-40 years will be almost 8 trillion. The oil is flowing in Iraq, which was the purpose of the war but as Iraq descends into chaos the U.S. is once again adding to their debt to keep the oil flowing. As of September 1, 2014 the U.S. had spent and additional $600,000 million in munitions bombing what westerners call the Islamic State in Iraq and Syria (ISIS). To put four trillion in perspective we could have covered the health care of every uninsured person for 25-30 years, not to mention the infrastructure or green energy improvements that could have been made winging the U.S. off of big oil. If you doubt the war was about big oil I encourage you to watch the Rachel Maddow documentary that shows how U.S. Armed forces were ordered to go through extraordinary lengths to secure and protect the Iraq's oil infrastructure while looting and the rest of Iraq descended into hell after the invasion. (See: http://www.msnbc.com/maddow-why-we-did-it)

In comparison to the VA budget we can look at the Department of State/USAID budget of $51.6 billion in the core 2013 budget. (See: http://www.state.gov/f/budget) I invite U.S. citizens to read about that budget and where their tax dollars are going. This budget almost equals what the U.S. Government spends on its veterans as beds go empty at Walter Reed hospital because the staff has been cut as we give governments such as Afghanistan 12 billion, Israel 4 billion, Iraq 2 billion, Pakistan 1.7 billion and the totalitarian Egyptian government 1 billion and so on. These numbers change constantly but I hope you get the picture as to how American citizens need to stand up against this travesty.

We also never know how the businesses and corporations that we deal with will go crazy selling our private information. Something as seemingly innocent as the information that we enter for a product, service or warranty card is sold for profit. This goes much further, as we try to be good citizens and the charity or organization we donate money to, ends up selling our personal information. Even though these may be causes that we believe in, we have to cut off all ties with them because of their information sharing practices as well as their constant harassment for money (solicitation). Our world has become one in which our information is sold for profit by almost everyone we deal with and it is being dispersed everywhere. This must be stopped and can be by demanding, and following up through research that our contributions are only to be used for the cause to which we have donated. If that information is not easily obtainable, then no longer support those charities.

Edward Snowden stated that he leaked the presentation because he felt that U.S. citizens, not a secret court operating behind closed doors, needed to decide what information they share with their government. That secret court was obviously rubber stamping whatever surveillance the U.S. NSA and FBI agencies wanted to conduct. Snowden's reply to being called a traitor was "*Ask yourself: if I were a Chinese spy, why wouldn't I have flown directly into Beijing? I could be living in a palace petting a phoenix by now. If an NSA, FBI, CIA, DIA, etc. analyst has access to query raw SIGINT databases, they can enter and get results for anything they want, phone number, email, user id, cell phone handset id (IMEI), and so on—it's all the same.*" When asked about national security concerns, Snowden stated, "*We managed to survive greater threats in our history... than a few disorganized terrorist groups and rogue states without resorting to these sorts of programs. It is not that I do not value intelligence, but that I oppose ... omniscient, automatic, mass surveillance ... That seems to me a greater threat to the institutions of free society than missed intelligence reports, and unworthy of the costs.*"

Later Mr. Snowden released an "open letter to the people of Brazil" in which he stated for the record, "*These programs were never about terrorism: they're about economic spying, social control, and diplomatic manipulation. They're about power.*" In that statement he is correct, as NSA started mass spying on Americans dates as far back as the Vietnam War 40 years ago. The documents show that NSA conducts widespread industrial espionage on U.S. allies, banks around the world, world leaders and the G20 summit. (See: http://www.washingtonsblog.com/2013/12/programs-never-terrorism-theyre-economic-spying-social-control-diplomatic-manipulation-theyre-power.html, http://www.alternet.org/edward-snowdens-open-letter-offers-help-brazil-over-us-spying-return-asylum, http://www.vanityfair.com/online/daily/2014/04/snowden-saga-10-key-questions-ben-wizner, https://www.aclu.org/what-difference-year-makes)

Historical Reference -- Brazilian president Dilma Rousseff's scathing speech to the UN general assembly labeling 'US surveillance a 'breach of international law'

Edward Snowdens revelations had fallout with countries that the many US citizens consider friendly to the US. Dilma Rousseff delivered an angry speech to the UN outlining how out of hand the NSA spying has become. In her words, "Personal data of citizens was intercepted indiscriminately. Corporate information -- often of high economic and even strategic value -- was at the center of espionage activity.

Also, Brazilian diplomatic missions, among them the permanent mission to the UN and the office of the president of the republic itself, had their communications intercepted. Tampering in such a manner in the affairs of other countries is a breach of international law and is an affront of the principles that must guide the relations among them, especially among friendly nations. A sovereign nation can never establish itself to the detriment of another sovereign nation. The right to safety of citizens of one country can never be guaranteed by violating fundamental human rights of citizens of another country."

While there was much more to the speech I felt her statement about why privacy is important summed up why US citizens need to be concerned.

"In the absence of the right to privacy, there can be no true freedom of expression and opinion, and therefore no effective democracy. In the absence of the respect for sovereignty, there is no basis for the relationship among nations. The time is ripe to create the conditions to prevent cyberspace from being used as a weapon of war, through espionage, sabotage and attacks against systems and infrastructure of other countries."

President Rousseff was imprisoned and tortured for her opposition to Brazil's military dictatorship in the 1970s so her words should hold true meaning as to why everyone should be concerned about their privacy. (See: http://www.theguardian.com/world/2013/sep/24/brazil-president-un-speech-nsa-surveillance)

Whether you want to brand him a traitor, spy or hero, he sparked a debate on how invasive American citizens have allowed or should allow their government to become. Enough so that a FISA amendment bill, which was crushed in a single day in December 2012, was resurrected by its original U.S. sponsor, Senator Jeff Merkley, D-Oregon, and a handful of co-sponsors, including Senator Mike Lee, R-Utah. This bill, if passed, would allow the U.S. Attorney General to declassify some opinions of the now totally secret FICA court. It is the hope and prayer of this reporter that the U.S. citizens will wake up and once again be a model of freedom and privacy for the world to admire! In May 2014, the House Judiciary and Intelligence Committees unanimously passed the USA Freedom Act, which is a watered down reform of NSA sweeping surveillance powers but any progress toward privacy is a good development. (See: http://epic.org/blog/2014/05/nsa-reforms-move-forward.html)

Further revelations about invasions into worldwide privacy continue to come out about what Edward provided the news agencies. Say what you will about him, he has stated for the record that he is eager to come back to the U.S. and testify before the U.S. Congress to lay the facts on the table and explain his actions, assuming that he is not locked up in some jail without a key. Allowing him to testify is something that we can rest assured that the U.S. government will never allow in their effort to crush individual privacy. We all have to ask the question once again, why is that? I hope I can someday meet this man and discover why he sacrificed his future in his slim Hail Mary hope that Americans might someday come to care about their digital privacy or fight to enact laws to protect them.

A few positive things have come out of Snowden's revelation, such as revelations by U.S. companies whom the U.S. government forced to release information. According to the PCWorld article titled "Court documents: NSA collected thousands of domestic communications in 2011" by Zach Miners, IDG News Service dated Aug 22, 2013, (See: http://www.pcworld.com/article/2047188/nsa-collected-thousands-of-domestic-communications-in-2011-court-document-shows.html#tk.nl_secur) an 86-page court assessment of the constitutionality of the agency's collection method revealed that "*NSA acquired roughly 2000 to 10,000 "multi-communication transactions," or MCTs, each year that contain at least one wholly domestic communication. An MCT refers to the capture of multiple different communications at once, such as emails within a single webmail service, one staff member at the Electronic Frontier Foundation said.*" For example, in the June 15, 2013 PCWorld article by Mark Hachman titled "Facebook, Microsoft disclose FISA requests, sort of, " *"For the six months ended December 31, 2012, Microsoft received between 6000 and 7000 criminal and national security warrants, subpoenas and orders affecting between 31,000 and 32,000 consumer accounts from U.S. governmental entities, the company said in a blog post. For its part, Facebook said that it had received 9,000 requests of the same nature during the same period."*"

This surveillance expanded in 2013, according to the PCWorld article titled "Facebook got 25,000 government requests about users in the first half of 2013" by Grant Gross, IDG New Service dated Aug 27, 2013. (See http://www.pcworld.com/article/2047550/facebook-got-25000-government-requests-about-users.html#tk.nl_secur) Then in the PCWorld article titled "Report: NSA broke into UN video teleconferencing system" by Lucian Constantin, IDG News Service reported that NSA cracked the encryption used by the video teleconferencing system and the United Nations headquarters in New York City. The August 26, 2013 article (see: http://www.pcworld.com/article/2047429/report-nsa-broke-into-un-video-teleconferencing-system.html#tk.nl_secur) states "*In June 2012 the NSA department responsible for collecting intelligence about the U.N. gained "new access to internal United Nations communication," German magazine Der Spiegel reported Monday based on information from secret NSA documents provided by former NSA contractor Edward Snowden.*

The NSA technicians were able to crack the encryption used by the U.N.'s internal video teleconferencing (VTC) system allowing VTC traffic to be decrypted. "This traffic is getting us internal UN VTCs (yay!)," one of the internal NSA documents said, according to Der Spiegel.

In less than three weeks, the number of U.N. communications that the NSA managed to intercept and decrypt rose from 12 to over 450. According to another NSA internal report from 2011, the agency caught the Chinese spying on the U.N. and managed to tap into their signals intelligence (SIGINT) collection to gain insight into high interest and high profile events at the time.

Media reports in June based on documents leaked by Snowden claimed that the European Union mission to the U.N. in New York and its delegation in Washington, D.C. have also been bugged by the NSA, prompting E.U. officials to demand answers from the U.S. government."

On January 17, 2014 President Barack Obama announced a few reforms to the U.S. surveillance programs, but these changes were like putting lipstick on a pig. The numbers and times of phone calls by all Americans will still be collected. Obama gave assurances that there will be no further spying on foreign leaders, but this privilege is only extended to a few dozen heads of state worldwide. As WikiLeaks founder Julian Assange put it, this speech was "embarrassing for a President to speak so long and say almost nothing."

What is wilder about this outrage is that the U.S. government is using U.S. citizens' taxpayer dollars to pay these Internet companies to provide this information about their very own U.S. citizens! American taxpayer dollars are financing their own loss of privacy, and big corporations are benefiting from their citizens identity theft. For example, AT&T admitted that they have 100 employees hired and dedicated to this task, which U.S. taxpayer dollars are financing. The amazing thing is that the American people are complacently going along with this mass surveillance at their own expense, as if this is the norm in the world, and do not even consider it a violation of their constitutional rights set up by their founding fathers! Their children are playing on iPads, Xboxes and PlayStations and not observing what is happening in the world around them, and their parents seem not to be willing to make a stand on these violations of their individual privacy. Where are the outrage and concern for this in their country? After a scathing speech by Brazil's president, Dilma Rousseff all Obama had to say was, "Just as we reviewed how we deploy our extraordinary military capabilities in a way that lives up to our ideals, we have begun to review the way that we gather intelligence, so as to properly balance the legitimate security concerns of our citizens and allies, with the privacy concerns that all people share."

We all have to wonder why news outlets such as http://america.aljazeera.com are kept out of the channel offerings that many U.S. cable companies provide. We have to assume that that the U.S. government wants this channel blocked as it would allow their citizens to view news of what is really happening in world that is not portrayed in a for-entertainment fashion. Who knows what might happen if U.S. citizens really learned what happening in the world around them.

We must assume that the U.S. is now a lost cause in the fight for privacy and individual freedom. U.S. veterans and their youths' need for privacy have lost their way in fighting for other noble causes, such as how to defend their flag from burning, building the next monument, dedicating highways and rest stops to veterans or even driving across their country to make a statement about a goal or cause they feel will establish the fact that they exist. The truth is, their citizens and government care little about the events documented above. We all must come to understand that the sad truth is attention and worry is not focused on the erosion of the freedoms for which their forefathers fought. We must assume they will continue to fund and allow their government to use the Internet to spy upon the whole world with no objection or protest. We can only hope that someday everyone in the U.S. will find the backbone to work on and correct this violation into their citizens' privacy and misuse of public funding. I dare say that this mammoth spying on the world's Internet use will not prevent ISIS from attacking the U.S. at will as their borders are so porous that thousands of children can cross it at will. There is also hundreds of U.S., British and French citizens fighting for and being trained by ISIS who could also attack these western countries. *Here ends my foreign commentary.*

Since the purpose of this book is to help you protect your business or family while using the infected Internet, I admire Edward Snowden's courage to put a stop to these mounting invasions into U.S. citizens' privacy. My hope is that the U.S. will someday reverse the trend of using the Internet for nefarious activities and instead try to make it a safe and private tool for all of us to use. Whistle-bowers like Snowden should be branded as heroes, not traitors, and given an avenue to bring these governments' snooping excesses to influential government officials, who could really make a difference in U.S. citizens' lives. Cries by individuals branding him a traitor, who should be hunted down and prosecuted to the full extent of the law, need to think about the laws to which they are referring. If we are referring to the U.S. Constitution and its safe-guards for personal privacy, which every U.S. soldier is sworn to uphold and protect, then we should be prosecuting judges and officials in the U.S. government as well. If we are referring to this unconstitutional interpretation of the Patriot Act, which was pushed through Congress after 9-11 and renewed into law in a single day in December 2012 with little or no debate, then Edward's whistle blowing may result in his death. Under these new laws the repercussions and persecution he would experience, should he ever attempt to return to the U.S., would be intense and could result in his death, torture or lifetime imprisonment without a trial, and we all have to consider-why this is? U.S. citizens have to determine which laws they prefer their children to live under, and I think Edward Snowden gave the world a new choice as to its digital freedom and a possible new, rewritten, digital Fourth Amendment.   Edward's revelations showed how the U.S. government was spying on German Chancellor Angela Merkel, and I imagine he felt some vindication as he offered to assist in a German probe on US spying while performing his new position in Moscow providing IT support for an unnamed Russian Internet company.

Edward Snowden's whistle-blowing also sparked a much needed debate on cloud computing. Alarmed Apple CEO Tim Cook, AT&T CEO Randall Stephenson, Google computer scientists and other technology executives met behind closed doors with President Obama to understand what the U.S. government is doing with their systems. They are hoping to assuage the concerns of their stakeholders as well as their customers. Snowden's disclosures showed how invasive the NSA has become as the U.S. government uses the Patriot Act to compel these tech giants to reveal everything that their customers store on their servers. Massive amounts of data has been turned over for NSA spying, which makes encrypting anything stored in the cloud essential, but no longer private. (See: http://www.usatoday.com/story/cybertruth/2013/08/09/tech-giants-meet-with-obama-to-save-cloud-computing/2635849)

In Obama's speech to the American public about reforms to the NSA spying, he pointed out that U.S. corporations were already collecting information about everything U.S. citizens are saying, clicking on, emailing and more while using the Internet. His argument was that allowing the U.S. government access to, or being able to make a copy of this information, is simply an extension of those practices that the American citizens are freely allowing. This argument is missing the mark on the fundamental problem, which is that U.S. citizens shouldn't or don't want corporations collecting this information, but there are no laws that allow them to opt-out of what should be an illegal activity. It is impossible to survive in today's technological world without using these corporations' products that require Americans to agree to their privacy agreements, which in reality, are actually *spying* agreements.

The problem becomes more complex when we consider the invention of data brokers (also known as the less objectionable name "lifestyle" companies). As we all now live in a constant state of surveillance there are, once again, no U.S. federal laws that give citizens the right or ability to learn what information is being collected, what is being held in databases about them, the duration that it is kept, or how to stop it. This data reveals loads of information about our day-to-day lives that we may not want the whole world to know, for example, if you are suffering from an illness or disease, have financial difficulties, and so on. These data brokers, who refer to themselves as Lifestyle Companies, claim that this data is anonymous, but no matter if it is held by your devices Media Access Control (MAC) address*, your name or IP address it is easily traceable back to you. These companies made $156 billion in 2012 spying on the American public, which shows how profitable this activity has become.

In a May 2014 article in Kiplinger's magazine titled "They Are Watching You" it revealed the following, "*The Government Accountability Office, which recently investigated data brokers, notes that no federal law gives consumers the right to learn what information is held about them for marketing purposes and who holds it, and often they have no legal right to control the collection or sharing of sensitive information.*" The data brokers claim to an unsuspecting U.S. Congress that this data is not traceable back to the individuals about whom it was collected about, but the reality is, as we discussed, it is easily traceable back to the individual. Data brokers are also maintaining lists of rape victims, alcoholics, drug addicts, bankruptcies, and so much more, that every U.S. citizen needs to be concerned about it.

The U.S. 4th Amendment no longer exists as we use the infected digital Internet, and we need the constitution amended because of that fact. As stated previously, in order to make a living in today's modern world, U.S. citizens have no choice but to use the invasive technologies that corporations provide and have to PAY for services, mobile apps and software to try to keep our information private. The reality is that U.S. corporations should be paying U.S. citizens for the information that they are willing to reveal about themselves, thereby helping their businesses rather than exploiting their customers by using privacy statement they do not have the time to read. The U.S. government views a computer using the Internet as having no 4th Amendment protection; hence these data brokers, corporations and the U.S. government can collect whatever they want.

Definition **Media Access Control Address (MAC)**	Media Access Control (MAC) address is a unique identifier assigned to all network devices usually by the devices manufacturer. Since the MAC address is stored along with everything you do and say using your infected Internet devices, everything is easily traceable back to the individual.

Your Digital Trail/Footprint—How You Are Being Tracked in Everything You Do Using the Infected Internet!

Another item being somewhat debated in the press is the sentiment of many people that we all knew corporations were collecting this information, so why not the government? They present these facts as if they are one in the same problem and that this is only a minor leap in the information being gathered about them. Both of these invasions into our privacy and liberty need to be decried by freedom-loving citizens and are certainly not related. *These privacy invasions are two entirely separate issues and must be addressed as such, but both must be stopped.*

1. We should not be allowing corporations to collect information about everything we do on the Internet, which is one of the focuses of this book. Legislation and safeguards need to be put in place by our governments to protect our Internet privacy. In a study of almost 200 companies on the Internet, more than 60 percent of their websites leaked personal information, such as usernames or email addresses, to other companies that track you. The options of Accept or Reject must be analyzed. How about a Digital Fourth Amendment stating we can select, **<u>Accept</u> gather all my personal information, <u>Accept but only allow certain information</u>, <u>Do not accept most information</u> but I will allow all the following to be collected for my Internet convenience, or how about, <u>Do no collect any of my Internet information</u> at all but let me use your service to survive!**

2. There is a distinct difference between the abuses of your data that a corporation can engage in and what a government can do. Governments have many vehicles and mechanisms to suppress dissent in their policies and actions. Intimidation can take many forms, such as harassment by the IRS (as the right-wing political groups found out), surveillance, and even being arrested on the many frivolous laws that exist. Governments can quickly and efficiently smash any dissent with their policies to make citizens go along with anything they want.

3. There is no way to prevent abuse of this data or these capabilities without checks and balances. The individuals that are given access to this data seem to be accountable to no one. This is a system begging for abuse and does not have sufficient oversight or transparency to the public or our elected officials in western democracies that are going along with this mass monitoring.

4. These U.S. NSA snooping programs are not a minor information-gathering violation that has been focused on a few thousand individuals of interest. This is a monstrous apparatus that threatens the private information of every American and every worldwide citizen, no matter how much they obey the flawed law. The potential for abuse is astounding and is reminiscent of the science fiction book *1984* previously discussed.

5. While the new Affordable Care Act can be viewed as a wonderful event for people without insurance or preexisting conditions, one has to wonder why everyone looking for health insurance has to give up all of their personal information to just view the few options that are available to them. This whole program is just another invasion into U.S. citizens' private information, which they do not even realize is happening. I wish this was otherwise, but the requirement to establish an account revealing everything about you without proper safeguards is lunacy. Healthcare shoppers should be allowed to view the policies available in anonymity without having to reveal anything about themselves. This program appears to be another U.S. government data gathering mechanism once again violating U.S. citizens' Fourth Amendment rights.

6. While we need laws to protect our Internet privacy, U.S. companies want to expand their data gathering on U.S. children. On February 4, 2014, in an article by the Associated Press titled "Obama Secures $750M in Pledges to Get Kids Online" Adelphi, Md. by Nedra Pickler, we learned that Apple, AT&T, Sprint, Verizon and Microsoft are

working to together put Wi-Fi in schools. We now know this will enable them to gather data about how these children use their assigned iPads, donated hardware and software that they use in class and at home. From the article, "*Beyond the promise of millions in donated hardware and software, the Federal Communications Commission also is setting aside $2 billion from service fees to connect 15,000 schools and 20 million students to high-speed Internet over two years.*"

7. Any massive surveillance program will persecute people who exist at the political margins. For example, Martin Luther King experienced the full force of government harassment, and there was a lot of pressure placed on members of the Civil Rights movement in the 1960's. What do you think people in power will do with something so much more invasive and powerful than J. Edgar Hoover ever had?

	Historical Reference – Dissent was impossible in Nazi Germany-it was the duty of the citizen to support their government no matter what!

A wondrous story about dissent and suppression of free speech in NAZI Germany is the story about Hans Scholl and his sister Sophie, along with their best friend, Christoph Probst, who were scheduled to be executed by Nazi officials on the afternoon of February 22, 1943. During the 1930's, they were enthusiastic members of the Hitler Youth and believed that Hitler was leading Germany on to a newfound greatness. However, their father, Robert Scholl, told his children that just the opposite was true; Hitler was leading their country down a path to ruin. While his arguments were ignored at first, eventually Hans and Sophie realized the truth of his words.

With a little help, and showing great courage, they authored a leaflet titled "The White Rose" about how the NAZI system was wrong and were imprisoning the German people. Coming in 1942 this was the first hint that their government was leading them down a path to eventual destruction. Many of the German people secretly agreed with the leaflet; it took on a life of its own as it was duplicated and widely distributed. The Gestapo was driven into a frenzy trying to suppress this free speech, but five more leaflets were created and distributed before Hans and Sophie were caught on February 18, 1943.

The trial was a farce, with a judge describing how they were a threat to the Fatherland and how their actions threatened the safety of all Germans. They were deemed to be irredeemable heretics who stood against everything their Fuehrer was doing to bring Germany to greatness. No one was allowed to speak a word in their defense as they were sentenced to death. Now, every German citizen knows the story of "The White Rose", there is a monument built to honor them, and they are national heroes. (See: http://www.jewishvirtuallibrary.org/jsource/Holocaust/rose.html)

You need to realize how invasive your digital trail using the infected Internet has become and how it can be used against you. From the NPR article, "Your Digital Trail, And How It Can Be Used Against You" by NPR STAFF dated Sep 30, 2013, and "Easily obtained subpoenas turn your personal information against you" by G.W. Schulz, Homeland Security Reporter, Daniel Zwerdling NPR (See: http://www.npr.org/blogs/alltechconsidered/2013/09/30/226835934/your-digital-trail-and-how-it-can-be-used-against-you, http://www.npr.org/blogs/alltechconsidered/2013/10/01/227776072/your-digital-trail-private-company-access, http://www.npr.org/blogs/alltechconsidered/2013/10/02/228134269/your-digital-trail-does-the-fourth-amendment-protect-us, http://www.npr.org/blogs/alltechconsidered/2013/10/04/228199021/your-digital-trail-data-fuels-political-and-legal-agendas, http://cironline.org/reports/easily-obtained-subpoenas-turn-your-personal-information-against-you-5104) they detail the following for you to consider:

- Law enforcement can create a map or timeline of a person's whereabouts by accessing data from license-plate scanners, toll-bridge crossings, and mobile phone carriers without much trouble, access records on your power consumption, purchasing habits and even snail mail. In 2012, Google reported that law enforcement demanded information from its users' accounts more than 21,000 times. Other big companies like Yahoo, Facebook and Microsoft say they get tens of thousands of requests from law enforcement, too. However, none of the companies have revealed exactly what kinds of information they surrender.
- When you log in with a username and password to sites like Gmail, Amazon or OKCupid, your behavior can be linked to your real name or email address. Software privacy specialist Ashkan Soltani said personal identifying information can also unintentionally "leak" to third parties, even if companies say they have no need for such data; it's not clear what happens to the information once it falls into their hands. Websites commonly allow many other companies to monitor what users are doing on their sites.
- Surveillance cameras in subway stations and on city buses watch you board and depart subways.
- To automatically identify celebrities and regular customers when they enter a store, some retailers reportedly are using another facial recognition technology originally developed in the U.K. for spotting terrorists and criminals. Those retailers' staffs then know the names of the customers from the moment they enter the door.   Facebook uses software to identify people from photos.
- Smart cards log when and where you travel using public transportation.
- Police departments in the San Francisco Bay Area and elsewhere around the country have used license-plate scanners to identify stolen cars and outstanding warrants. The devices are designed to photograph vehicles and record the location, date and time of everyone who passes by, without discriminating between criminals and innocent people.
- While many Americans are under the impression that their medical records are protected by privacy laws, investigators and private attorneys enjoy special access to those records.
- Often a simple form is all that's required to access prescription histories, credit card purchases, monthly banking statements, ATM withdrawals, wire transfers, tax returns and, perhaps most importantly, the rich digital portraits we keep on our smartphones.
- Smartphone apps, such as TuneIn and Pandora, will store data on their servers on which talk shows and music you enjoy.
- Dating activity and profile setup at dating websites can be easily subpoenaed or obtained by third-party advertisers and marketers, even if you use an alias.
- Movies and documentaries that you stream from companies such as Netflix are recorded and share information about your viewing habits.

- One of the most powerful sources of information is your mobile device, which creates a rough approximation of your whereabouts by checking in with nearby cell towers or even a more precise pinpoint when the GPS function is enabled. Your cellphone leaves behind a GPS trail, and collectively, the time, usage and GPS could prove significant in a criminal trial, divorce or just someone snooping.
- The U.S. government has interpreted the law titled "Electronic Communications Privacy Act of 1986" to mean that once your emails are opened or are older than 180 days, no warrant is required to view them.   All U.S. email metadata such as email address, IP locations, time stamps and more are stored in NSA databases and scanned for red-flag key words.
- Consumer-grade antivirus products are not up to the task of protecting Internet devices against well-funded malware created by nation-states. These entities with bulging budgets go through great lengths to avoid antivirus product detection by design. They meticulously go through and test their malicious code again all relevant antivirus products on the market to make sure their code cannot be detected. If should be very obvious that this is not a fair war that exists between the mammoth attackers and budgeted defenders especially when the attackers have access to all the defenders weapons.
- Car insurance companies are hoodwinking drivers into installing devices so they can obtain data from GPS and other devices to create what they call preferred pricing for good drivers. However, driving habits and data about the locations you visit speak volumes about your private life. Most drivers don't know what data is collected and how it is actually used. The National Highway Traffic Safety Administration has indicated that it even wants data recorders that can record driving habits such as speed, location and seat belt use installed on all cars.
- As you browse the web, companies can recognize and track your Internet activity as you move from site to site. Using the browser feature "Do Not Track" doesn't prevent companies from tracking you and is ignored by many companies. Contrary to popular belief, what you do online is NOT anonymous. It is easy for companies and law enforcement to determine a computer user's actual identity.
- A study by Jonathan Mayer and his Stanford colleagues of 200 companies on the Internet showed that more than 60 percent of those websites leaked personal information, such as usernames or email addresses to other companies that track you.

The Fourth Amendment states, **"The right of the people to be secure in their persons, houses, papers, and effects, against unreasonable searches and seizures, shall not be violated."** However, this amendment means very little in the digital age and is being all but ignored by the U.S. government, U.S. companies, law enforcement and western governments. From NPR, "Your Digital Trail: Does the Fourth Amendment Protect Us?" by Daniel Zwerdling October 2, 2013, he points out that it is even worse than what we had imagined. From the article, "*since the 1960s and 1970s, the Supreme Court and other courts have issued a series of rulings declaring that the government does not need a search warrant to obtain your personal documents if you have already shared them with somebody else. For instance, since you allow your bank and credit card company to know what you buy, and since you let your phone company know whom you call, you can't claim that information is private.*" As a result, almost everything you do, say, store, search for, visit, click on, and type can be easily viewed by almost anyone on the Internet. Government can monitor your email because you have shared that with your ISP, view your data because you have shared that with your cloud service provider, monitor your search engine activity and GPS activity because you have shared that information with Google, Yahoo or whatever search engine or service you are using. This pronouncement nullified applying the Fourth Amendment to your digital rights and is akin to being next to a tank firing down range in its ramifications.

| Story | The concussion from an M-60 tank firing downrange is amazing! Somehow, my squad managed to get our amphibious assault vehicle (track), the LVTP-7A1, (renamed to AAVP-7A1 in 1984), separated from our unit while installing some explosives to blow a breech in some concertina wire. (See: https://en.wikipedia.org/wiki/Assault_Amphibious_Vehicle) While we were working, the division advanced on ahead of us. The poor track driver was running around the desert looking for anyone who might have information as to where the rest of our unit was. I had the squad radio on my back, but the Sergeant (track commander) did not want to admit we were lost, so my radio remained silent. The track came to a stop, and the Sergeant ordered me to climb up and look out into the desert to see where we were. This order was obviously for the fun of the other troops in the track because the desert all looks the same to someone from the city. The track engine was running, which makes talking to anyone in the track very difficult. I was too short to reach the top, so the guys had to boost me up; I then wiggled my torso over the top, which the guys found humorous. With the AN/PRC-77 radio on my back, I probably looked like a turtle climbing a wall. (See: https://en.wikipedia.org/wiki/AN/PRC-77) I was all too happy to provide this entertainment just to get a breath fresh air out of the diesel fumes that we had been breathing for hours. Whatever idiot engineer who designed the track put the diesel exhaust outlet in the front of the vehicle. The result was that all the carbon dioxide blew back into the track because the top had to remain open. Tracks are not air conditioned, so in the heat of the desert, the troops inside would quickly be cooked by the high temperatures with the top closed. Turns out, we were smack dab in the middle of an M-60 tank formation. I turned my head to tell everyone that we were parked next to some M-60 tanks, when all at once the tanks opened fire down range. I cannot fathom how they did not know that we were right next door, and I will always believe that someone thought opening fire would be funny.

The concussion coming off the tank turret rocked our 29+ ton track, lifted me off the side of the track and blew me backwards through the air about eight feet to the other side of track, where my radio slammed into the wall of the track saving my back from injury. After hitting that wall, I dropped about 4 feet or so to land on top of my fellow marines, radio and all. All hell broke loose in our track as the tanks on both sides took turns blasting shells down range, thus rocking our track from side to side. The noise was deafening, and we were all trying to scream loud enough for the driver to hear our protestation to get us the hell out of there, which he could not hear over the engine noise and the tanks firing. Eventually the driver decided to move the track out from between this mayhem on his own. We were all deaf for a few hours after this experience, |

	and some of us probably had a few tank nightmares afterwards as well.

Just as I was blown across the track in the above example, this judicial conclusion is blowing away/nullifying your digital freedom and privacy rights, thus invalidating the rights granted to us by the Fourth Amendment of the U.S. Constitution. There is a flaw in this judicial conclusion and the power that it gives the U.S. Government, to violate the Fourth Amendment, which I hope you can see through. Citizens worldwide have a gun to their heads to adopt these corporate services and technologies in order to find jobs, make a living wage, pay bills and debts, communicate, get access to medical services, optimize travel via GPS, and so much more. To use these tools everyone must agree to the privacy policies of the companies that are providing them, which few people comprehend or have the time to read. If you did read one you will discover it is more of a spying policy than a privacy policy and should be labeled as such. All they know is that to conduct business and put bread on the table, they are required to use these invasive Internet tools, apps and services. Rarely are they offered the ability to opt-out of allowing companies to collect data about their use of these products, thus keeping their Internet use private. The result is a massive, unchecked privacy invasion taking place by corporations and western governments whose citizens do not grasp just how much information they are freely giving up about their day-to-day lives. We all have to come to grips with how this information can adversely affect our lives. For example, my wife called me about some medical issues she was having. She was going to tell me about them over a Samsung phone, which Google records, sells that conversation to her company and then will provide that chat to the NSA. I suggested that it would be better if the conversation waited until I could get home; these are the types of simple measures that we all need to all be taking now, as our privacy is being violated.

When you examine this privacy violation further, citizens worldwide should be required to grant corporations the ability to gather information about their Internet activity with the default being NOT to! If this were a court case, then I would agree with the judge that the information people willingly award their corporate partners to collect is public domain and subject to scrutiny by their governments. However, there is a "gun" to everyone's head in how we all need to make a living and that requires us to use the infected Internet. This technology requires citizens worldwide to use this technology and give up all their private information, which must be stopped! (See: The Harvard Law Review written December 15, 1890, Willes, J., in Millar v. Taylor, 4 Burr. 2303, 2312, http://faculty.pnc.edu/BBK/privacy.html) The U.S. needs to amend the Fourth Amendment and as well, other western governments need to include the Internet in their privacy protections.

In April 2014, the U.S. Supreme Court took up a few court cases to figure out how to fit data-packed smartphones into the contours of the broken U.S. Fourth Amendment, which in almost any fashion does not guarantee digital privacy. "*A modern smartphone,*" Stanford Law School professor Jeffrey Fisher noted in a briefing, "*is a portal into our most sensitive and confidential affairs. The digital contents of such a device should not be subject to a fishing expedition.*" Data carried on these devices could be seized without a warrant or subpoena simply because it is digitized; this includes photos, video, text messages, contacts, message and call logs, recorded phone conversations and so much more. The U.S. Fourth Amendment protects the "right of the people to be secure in their persons, houses, papers and effects." However, in the 21st century where many people store their "papers and effects" on a mobile device this had become a non-existent right of privacy by almost any U.S. citizen. In past rulings, the U.S. Supreme Court said that this invasion into privacy is necessary and lawful, but they provided for no checks and balances in their rulings because the U.S. founders set up nothing in the Fourth Amendment to address today's digital world.

Prior to June 15, 2014, U.S. law enforcement only needed an easily obtainable subpoena to track where you went, what you did or said with your cellphone because you are sharing that information with your cellphone company. If you were suspected of a crime and your smartphone was found or seen, the data on it could be downloaded and analyzed, revealing your life's history, and possibly involve you in another completely unrelated crime. As everything in the U.S. government seems to become more and more invasive into our privacy, an unprecedented privacy rights development occurred on June 25, 2014, against the protestation of the Obama Administration. The U.S. Supreme Court *unanimously* ruled that police may not search the cell phones of criminal suspects upon arrest without a warrant. This is first privacy limitation since 9-11 that we have seen placed on these infected Internet devices, as they have vast storage of information and capabilities. The ruling stated, *"The fact that technology now allows an individual to carry such information in his hand does not make the information any less worthy of the protection for which the Founders fought,"* the ruling said. *"Our answer to the question of what police must do before searching a cell phone seized incident to an arrest is accordingly simple — get a warrant."* Perhaps we are seeing the very beginning of rollback in the digital privacy invasion that has taken place. However, it is still best to limit the data you store on these devices and when you travel to carry a temporary cell phone that has no information about yourself on it.

How the Consumer Financial Protection Bureau Has Become the Second Most Well-Funded U.S. Government Agency to Invade the U.S. Citizens' Privacy Funded by U.S. Citizens

The U.S. NSA is not the only agency about which U.S. citizens and the world need to worry. The Consumer Financial Protection Bureau (CFPB) was created in 2011 under the Obama administration under in the guise of regulating consumer protection with regard to financial products and services. The Dodd-Frank Wall Street Reform and Consumer Protection Act which was passed in response to the great recession of 2008, was the catalyst that allowed this agency to come into existence.

This bureau exists outside the jurisdiction of the U.S. legislative or executive branches of U.S. government and answers/operates solely within the United States Federal Reserve. Its mission, who sounds benign, reads, *"promote fairness and transparency for mortgages, credit cards, and other consumer financial products and services. The central mission of the Consumer Financial Protection Bureau (CFPB) is to make markets for consumer financial products and services work for Americans—whether they are applying for a mortgage, choosing among credit cards, or using any number of other consumer financial products."*

The reality is that this has become another huge apparatus funded by U.S. taxpayers, which they must fear. The CFPB's program mines credit card account data maintained by 18 of the largest card issuers in the United States. CFPB is forking over 2.9 million in U.S. taxpayer dollars to obtain credit card data from at least nine credit card issuing companies. The combined data represents approximately 85-95 percent of U.S. citizen's outstanding credit card balances. The data collected includes, card-account identification reference number, ZIP code, monthly ending balance, borrower's income, FICO score, credit limit, monthly payment amount, and days past due.

The sad news is that U.S. citizens cannot even opt out of this type of surveillance. The leader of this U.S. agency, Duffy, went so far as to say in testimony to the U.S. Congress, "*The NSA does not ask Americans' permission to collect their phone records and emails and texts. The CFPB does not ask permission to collect information on America's financial consumers.*" It is estimated that the Angus Company contracted to collect this information will collect about 51 terabytes of data by spying on the U.S. public at their expense before this project is scheduled to conclude in March 2017. (See: https://en.wikipedia.org/wiki/Consumer_Financial_Protection_Bureau)

Future and Past Efforts by the U.S Government to Further Circumvent the U.S. Constitution and Erode U.S. and Worldwide Citizens' Freedom

Still, these examples above do not go far enough to outrage the U.S. citizens-why? The U.S. government wants its citizens to believe that The Federal Reserve, large U.S. banks, and politicians can solve Internet problems through additional legislation. Their out-of-control U.S. government has failed to invade U.S. citizens' privacy further with two other unsuccessful bills called the "Stop Online Piracy Act, H.R. 326", which was defeated in the House because of the public outcry, and in the Senate, the bill S. 968: Preventing Real Online Threats to Economic Creativity and Theft of Intellectual Property Act of 2011 (PIPA), which was also was defeated. From https://en.wikipedia.org/wiki/Protect_IP_Act and https://en.wikipedia.org/wiki/Stop_Online_Piracy_Act, *these bills would have expanded the ability of U.S. law enforcement and copyright holders to fight online trafficking in copyrighted intellectual property and counterfeit goods.* If either of these bills had passed, they would have had the opposite effect of what they are intended to accomplish. But the U.S. government did not stop there. Congress's relentless pressure to invade their U.S. citizens' privacy continues. On April 18, 2013, for the second year in a row, the Republican-controlled House of Representatives passed the "Cyber Intelligence Sharing and Protection Act" (CISPA) 288-127, which is much like SOPA, but under a different name. (See: http://www.forbes.com/sites/erikkain/2012/04/24/as-cispa-nears-a-vote-can-the-controversial-cyber-security-legislation-be-stopped) Many large U.S. corporations and U.S citizens don't seem to care about domestic privacy laws and are pushing this legislation. However, many privacy organizations noted that this bill would have given the U.S. government even more unprecedented powers to snoop through U.S. citizens' private information (medical records, email, financial information, etc.) without the need for a warrant, or even proper oversight, with the few limits that still exist in the U.S. This legislation could be viewed as the final erosion of U.S. citizens' civil liberties, and probably the final nail in the coffin, ending anything that American citizens once knew as personal privacy.

Every time Congressional efforts to invade U.S. citizens' privacy further through legislation are defeated, Congress introduces a new more invasive bill that also must be continuously fought. In June 2014 Rep. Mike Rogers and Senator Dianne Feinstein introduced yet another bill to destroy any privacy protection that U.S. citizens had using the infected Internet. The bill called the "Cybersecurity Information Sharing Act of 2014" contains broad immunity clauses for companies, broad reaching spying powers, and vague definitions that would be subject to constant debate and interpretation. (See: https://www.eff.org/deeplinks/2014/06/zombie-bill-comes-back-look-senates-cybersecurity-information-sharing-act-2014)

One would think that after the outrage of the defeated bills above that Congress tried to pass, which would have invaded their privacy, that American citizens would storm Washington to express their outrage, as their politicians continue to push Cyber Intelligence agencies to invent new ways to invade their citizen's privacy further. This type of legislation would stifle the open source movement that is trying to fix the security holes that crackers, criminals and foreign governments are exploiting. It would shut down open source developers' efforts to offer Internet users FREE donationware* solutions, and FREE Linux operating systems to meet our Internet needs. Open source sites, where we get things like free anti-software, tools and utilities, would be shut down due to the endless litigation and frivolous law suits that would be brought against them.

We must all stand up against this sort of government intrusion into our lives, unless we want to live in a further government controlled society. We have seen instances of where this leads in the past century and are marching down a path to self-destruction. These types of bills will expose Internet users and free companies to undue liability, making lawyers everywhere rich. The best path to thwart piracy is by reading this book! Limiting freedom on the Internet and spying on everyone is not the answer. Educating corporations and the SBO/HCU on their security options is the real answer to online privacy.

Many Americans think that the laws that govern the health information that they provide to doctors, hospitals, health plans and their business associates will protect their privacy, but there is a lack of repercussions for when these entities allow themselves to be cracked. Crackers know that medical records are easy targets, and cyber-attacks against healthcare organizations are growing in frequency. The Ponemon Institute, which surveyed 80 healthcare organizations in the US found that 75% don't secure medical devices containing sensitive patient data, while in the last two years 94% have leaked data (mostly due to staff negligence). Cyber Security is not healthcare's job as they depend upon device providers and contracted IT departments to take care of that for them. However, they need to shift their thinking, as Ponemon calculates that the average cost to a breached organization will hit $2.4 million over the course of two years, up slightly from $2.2 million in 2011 and $2.1 million in 2010. (See: http://www2.idexpertscorp.com/ponemon2012) These same laws apply to financial institutions, but the problem is that it does not include the data that is free-floating on the web. For example, if you go online and search health sites or do financial research, everything you do is tracked and/or sold.

As reported in the December 6, 2013 Washington Post article titled "FBI's search for 'Mo,' suspect in bomb threats, highlights use of malware for surveillance", in serious investigations the FBI has the capability to install spy software that will give them access to a webcam.

Once in, they can turn on the webcam on to view and listen to anyone within range without triggering the light that indicates that the webcam is transmitting. This was reported to be revealed by Marcus Thomas, who was a former Assistant Director of the FBI's Operational Technology Division in Quantico. In another instance the FBI lured a Washington state high school student The Post reported that the FBI has hacked computers to download files, photographs and stored emails. The good news for privacy enthusiasts is that these hacks are described as a "traditional hack" where the user is lured into a phishing attack, and then the user has to click on a link in an email to install the malware on their computer. However, as Christopher Soghoian, who is the principal technologist for the American Civil Liberties Union, worries that the FBI is doing this without a serious public debate on this privacy invasion, and as non-tech-savvy judges are making rulings on this as well. (See: http://nypost.com/2013/12/08/fbi-can-turn-on-your-web-cam, http://www.washingtonpost.com/business/technology/2013/12/06/352ba174-5397-11e3-9e2c-e1d01116fd98_story_2.html)

The FBI's use of malware to attack Internet devices is not new. For example, in 2007 the U.S. FBI used spyware to catch a Washington state high school student who was emailing repeated bomb threats to his school. The FBI used malware they call "Computer & Internet Protocol Address Verifier" (CIPAV) which was installed on the student Josh's computer remotely. CIPAV, once installed, allowed the FBI to collect the machine's IP address, MAC address, list of running programs, operating system, Internet browser used, language used, the registered computer name, the currently logged-in username and more. Once this one time information was relayed to the FBI the malware would switch to what is called a "pen register" that records the routing and destination addressing for electronic communications. The FBI has been using what they call "network investigative technique," (NIT) since 2002 which is a full-featured backdoor program that gives them access to a user's files, location, web history and webcam. What could be a much broader possible abuse of power is when the FBI infects a computer server and it delivers a NIT to any computer that accesses that server. People in the computer industry refer to this as a "drive-by download" and it should be a violation of the U.S. Fourth Amendment. However, because this was a child porn case, U.S. judges are upholding the right of the FBI to use these blanked techniques to spy. The issuing of U.S. search warrants by the U.S. Justice Department will now start allowing the U.S. government to spy on their citizens' Internet activity without any public debate about the use of these techniques. (See: http://www.wired.co.uk/news/archive/2014-08/06/operation-torpedo-fbi)

Another new technology invading U.S. citizens' privacy is the government's use of drones in the United States. We have all heard about them flying over Afghanistan, Kenya, Mali, Pakistan, Somalia, Yemen and other counties. Americans citizens now need to ask themselves how they feel about these drones raining down death and destruction on them, like what is happening in other countries. These drones can be equipped with Hellfire missiles, Viper Strike glide weapons, laser-guided folding-fin rockets, grenade launchers, machine guns and other weapons. They have killed hundreds, if not thousands, around the world and the American people complacently go along with this program in the guise of protecting their national security. Western countries now have to come to terms with the fact that these drones are being employed on their home country's citizens with little resistance. Why is that? The U.S. drones contain high-powered day and night cameras and surveillance gear, motion detectors, a siren, and more that can transmit video and photos to those persons flying them.

In the American Legion September 2012 article written by Ben Barber titled "Robot Wars," he states that in February 2012 "*President Barrack Obama signed a law allowing wider use of drones inside the U.S. airspace, previously off-limits due to civil aviation safety concerns. Since Jan. 1, the FAA has granted more than 200 authorizations to federal, state and local government entities - as well as to law-enforcement agencies and academic institutions - to fly drones, the Government Accountability Office's Gerald Dillingham told the House Homeland Security Oversight Committee in July.*" He also states that "*The Federal Aviation Administration (FAA) estimates that 10,000 drones could be flying U.S. skies by 2017.*" Where is the U.S. public outcry or outrage on this? Why isn't the U.S. media reporting anything about this crime? The American people are really what we in the military called, "**mushrooms being kept the dark!**"

On the flip side, Americans do need their government to draft legislation that will protect their privacy while using the Internet. They need a legal framework that will address modern day threats and will allow everyone to avoid stifling laws that limit Internet technical innovation. In the May 2012 PCWorld, Mark Sullivan wrote an article titled "A Digital Consumer Bill of Rights," and he points out "*Consumers need a legal framework that imposes security responsibilities on cloud-storage companies as well as others that host sensitive data.*" I would add to that, "and all of the companies that are tracking your Internet activity". The article goes on to suggest to government officials actions that they could take to protect Internet users. In a company's privacy statement (written in legalese), you can find out if a company is collecting, storing and aggregating data about your use of their websites. However, just as on a cigarette carton, there should be something more obvious to the user, such as a warning on every web page that collects data about you, as well as a way to easily turn it off (I will teach you how to do that). I often hear about the benefits of cloud computing and storage to Small Businesses. Yet, as the article points out, what law is out there to protect you if your cloud company is selling your data for profit to web marketing and advertising firms or giving your data to governments worldwide? What about compensation for lost, stolen or misused data? What measures are these companies taking to keep your data safe and secure? We also need a legal framework that outlines just what is considered reasonable protection of our data, as well as stiff fines against companies that don't follow those guidelines. There are cloud companies that seem to take protection of your data seriously. They state that they use data encryption technology to protect a user's data. (See: http://www.vaultive.com)

If you think your cloud data is safe from Uncle Sam, *think again*. In the same PCWorld article by Mark Sullivan, he states; "*Currently law enforcement needs to obtain only a "D order"-named after subsection (d) of section 2703 of the Stored Communications Act-from a court to force an ISP to hand over the email, all Internet activity (IP addresses that a user communicates with), and the URLs of all the web pages the user visits.*" It gets more ominous as he goes on to say, "*Agencies can also use the D order to acquire information about a user's location over time from a wireless company, which keeps records of the cell towers that the user's phone contacts while the person is within range.*" Where is the outrage about this, and why are we not trying to limit the reach of the U.S. government to easily invade our privacy in this fashion?

As you can see from all of the above, there is abundant evidence the U.S. government is ready, willing, and able to pass laws that profit and make it easier for corporations to invade everyone's privacy, but they are unwilling to consider laws that compensate their citizens' cost of a company losing or allowing their personal data to be stolen. Where is that legislation and why aren't American citizens lobbying their government to correct this behavior? The PCWorld article by Mark Sullivan reveals the following alarming statistics, "*The Privacy Clearinghouse says at least 500 million sensitive records have been breached since 2005, with more than 22.4 million records lost or exposed in 2011.*" In a Fox news report interviewing Greg Evans (See: Cyber Security Expert Greg Evan-Fox and Friends promoting book), Fox stated that 2,500 corporations and governments had been cracked in the last 18 months, back in 2010. Greg stated that corporations and government hire IT managers to perform cyber security jobs that have little or no training in those fields. This is done while China and Russia are training children at a young age to be great hackers and perhaps become the next Bill Gates. It is no wonder that high paid western IT managers find themselves overwhelmed when placed in a role they know little or nothing about and have no education in this technology. Our western civilization trends to globalize IT and allows cronyism placement of high paid management to oversee low paid foreign employees. This has jeopardized every western citizen's privacy and freedom. Identity theft is rampant for a reason, and this is one of the primary causes. Until western citizens wake up to this problem and demand accountability from their governments and corporations, they will spend much of their lives trying get their identity back from a system designed to give it away without their knowledge and implicit consent. Until competent IT professionals are placed in charge of cyber security instead of political appointees or cronies who financed their political campaigns, *IT security will remain a joke in western cultures*.

Another program in place, which is completely separate from the NSA, is the requirement by the U.S. Justice department for financial institutions and local law enforcement agencies and others to file "Suspicious Activity Reports (SAR)" regarding suspicious or potentially suspicious activity. From https://en.wikipedia.org/wiki/Suspicious_activity_report, "*SARs include detailed information about transactions that are or appear to be suspicious. The goal of SAR filings is to help the Federal government identify individuals, groups and organizations involved in fraud, terrorist financing, money laundering, and other crimes.*" The problem with this law is that many people are being caught in this juggernaut of required reporting, and their privacy is being grossly violated. Many local law enforcement agencies, who do not fully understand these vague guidelines of this program, have refused to go along with this reporting for worry about individual privacy. For example, SARs requires that police officers report anything considered suspicious, such as using binoculars, taking measurements, taking pictures or video footage, taking notes, or individuals championing "extremist" views. If that does not go far enough, an SAR can also be filed by private sector organizations and foreign partners. Once an SAR is filed, it is considered a criminal offense to disclose that the SAR has been filed.

Thanks to Edward Snowden's revelations, we are now seeing the beginnings of a movement to reverse this mass monitoring of everyone's digital activity. Patriot Act author Representative Jim Sensenbrenner, Republican from Wisconsin, submitted a bipartisan bill called the "USA FREEDOM Act" to end the bulk collection of data and phone calls by the NSA. This legislation had 60 other cosponsors in the House. There are other bills and proposals coming from the U.S. Congress to reign in the mass surveillance, but until this type of surveillance is prevented by amending the Fourth Amendment of the U.S. Constitution to protect digital privacy, I'm afraid none of these stop gap measures will mean very much.

Also thanks to Edward Snowden, "The Washington Post" and "The Guardian" both won Pulitzer Prizes in the public service category for their reporting on the secretive global surveillance that the NSA was conducting. The Pulitzer jury credited both news organizations with helping the public understand the relationship between national security and personal privacy. Edward Snowden released the following statement about this development on April 14, 2014, *"Today's decision is a vindication for everyone who believes that the public has a role in government. We owe it to the efforts of the brave reporters and their colleagues who kept working in the face of extraordinary intimidation. This decision reminds us that what no individual conscience can change, a free press can. My efforts would have been meaningless without the dedication, passion, and skill of these newspapers, and they have my gratitude and respect for their extraordinary service to our society. Their work has given us a better future and a more accountable democracy."*

If identity and personal information theft were a disease, we would have an epidemic on our hands, and the Center for Disease Control and Prevention (See: http://www.cdc.gov) would have these companies in quarantine. Instead, the U.S. government has only politely asked corporations to examine their cyber security practices and try to improve them. There are websites like http://onguardonline.gov that the government maintains to help SBO/HCU research these threats. However, seeing how little time everyone has to do that, and how little emphasis has been placed on this important topic, one can assume the U.S. government does not mind the fact that the average SBO/HCU remains ignorant of the dangers that they face using Internet devices. In fact, they seem to encourage it. There certainly has been no consolidated advanced material written to help the SBO/HCU understand and use the Internet more wisely, **until now, with the introduction of this book**!

Examples of the Threats Corporations, SBO's and HCU's Face from the Internet

According to 60 Minutes, bank robbers are now stealing more money with computers via the Internet than they are with guns.[1] Crackers could potentially disable critical infrastructure, disrupt essential services, extort millions from public companies and even sabotage our weapons systems. It is feared that a cyber-attack could even do something catastrophic, as in bringing down the power grid in various sections of the United States. The facts are that cyber-war-defense is now a top national priority. 60 Minutes went on to point out that cyber-intruders have probed our electrical grid. [1] Cyber-terrorists may have plunged entire cities into darkness. This was suspected in Brazil when they experienced roaming blackouts. At the time when those cities went dark is consistent with when the warnings of this type started. U.S. banks have lost over 100 million dollars to crackers, mostly to organized crime units based in Russia and China. Crackers are wreaking havoc on government and corporate Internet devices. As government and corporations plug security holes, crackers are increasingly going after easier targets - like small business and home Internet devices.

Talented crackers are making many thousands of dollars, sometimes each day, from banks, corporations, small businesses and home computer users. In polls, 45% of Internet users prefer doing household chores to fixing a computer problem. In my own personal experience, I have been staggered by the number of SBO/HCUs who have been compromised by *crackers*, whose aim to it is steal their personal information, from their browsing history and habits, to personal and banking information--which are being used to extort information, perform malicious tasks under remote control, and steal data and identity information. The SBO/HCO victim's apathy toward this activity is amazing and very disturbing to me. I can't help people who don't realize they need help. Even talking about this problem in my social networks, I find little interest in a response, which is astonishing to me.

Story

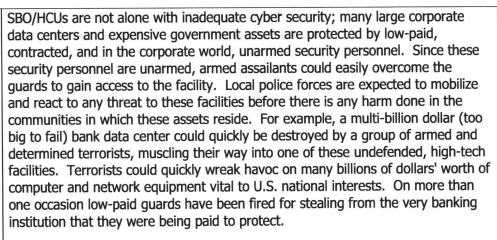

SBO/HCUs are not alone with inadequate cyber security; many large corporate data centers and expensive government assets are protected by low-paid, contracted, and in the corporate world, unarmed security personnel. Since these security personnel are unarmed, armed assailants could easily overcome the guards to gain access to the facility. Local police forces are expected to mobilize and react to any threat to these facilities before there is any harm done in the communities in which these assets reside. For example, a multi-billion dollar (too big to fail) bank data center could quickly be destroyed by a group of armed and determined terrorists, muscling their way into one of these undefended, high-tech facilities. Terrorists could quickly wreak havoc on many billions of dollars' worth of computer and network equipment vital to U.S. national interests. On more than one occasion low-paid guards have been fired for stealing from the very banking institution that they were being paid to protect.

Government, corporations and banks should consider hiring retired police officers and honorably discharged veterans (experienced in various weapons technology and warfare) to guard these important facilities. From my personal experience, major U.S. banks are only required to have three major redundant data center facilities. As stated above, these data centers house many billions of dollars' worth of computer and other equipment vital to the U.S. economy. Some of those facilities were reportedly destroyed in the 9-11 attacks. By reportedly, I mean I never personally visited or worked in more than one of those data centers. Imagine what a coordinated attack on all three physically unsecure data centers could do to a "too big to fail" bank, and after the 2008 crash, we have to question why do we still have "too big to fail" banks? The havoc wreaked on the United States financial system could be devastating. Yet, security audits make no mention of this.

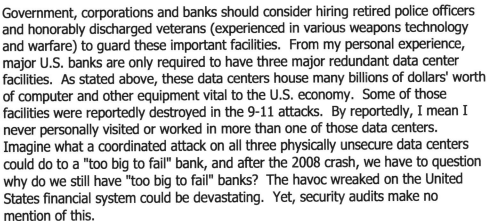

Take another example of a multi-billion dollar corporation in which I am familiar. There were two redundant data centers within 20 miles of each other and no armed protection for either data center. That corporation later retired one of those data centers, thus concentrating all their data into one place. In the IT world, this is called a single point of failure, and not for a device or computer, but for the entire corporation. Any disaster destroying that data center would put that multi-billion dollar U.S. corporation out of business. One would think that a multi-billion dollar business would not put its stock-holders in this type of jeopardy. However, stockholders don't seem to review this type of information, nor have I seen it revealed at a stock holders meeting or the corporate prospectus, ever.

Some companies go through a simple question and answer process to allow individuals to gain access to their data center. Due diligence (depth of questioning and verification) is not done. Access is granted to people who shouldn't be allowed to enter the data center. This can have catastrophic consequences as one

corporation that I worked for found out. Our data center was equipped with a safety kill switch in case something life threatening was taking place. A minimum wage, contracted security guard making his rounds thought the red button on the wall was to kill the lights and hit it on his way out of the data center. Instead, what he achieved was to kill all power to all of the computer equipment in that four billion dollar company's data center. The guard was unfairly fired, and the switch was encased in a plastic box with warnings that it only be pressed in the event of an emergency, which should have been done in the first place.

In another instance, at the same corporation, the data center lost power during the "Great Northeast Power Blackout of 2003" and the backup generators kicked in. As the power outage dragged on for days, the computer administrators (myself and others) called management to determine what was being done to refuel the generators, which had been running for over 24 hours. As data center administrators, we were wondering if we should start beginning a controlled shutdown of the data center. The answer was "don't worry about it, it is being taken care of," which was not the case. The diesel generators eventually ran out of fuel, and the entire data center **HARD crashed**. Once power was restored, days were lost bringing the data center back online. This down time lost the corporation millions. After this event, management decided to purchase a fueled (less than $100,000) diesel truck to keep this from ever happening again. None of the managers who allowed this to happen were disciplined or lost their jobs.

I present these stories to motivate you to protect your SBO/HCU setup and help you to understand that many times government and corporations also have vastly insufficient security measures in place. It always costs much more to recover from a disaster than it ever did in preparing for one. One million dollars, small change to a corporate executive, would be enough to pay **seven armed security guards** $16 an hour for an entire year to guard a major computer facility 24 hours a day! You do the math.

The examples above are meant to show how implementing some simple preventive security measures can result in enormous savings if there is a disaster. Corporations and large SBO's need to come the understanding that their IT departments are not an expense to be outsourced to the lowest bidder, who knows or cares little about their core business. The IT department should be an integral core part of their business model that is staffed by well-paid, highly-qualified, trained and loyal employees. The stories above also relate to the security of your Internet devices. We don't even realize how dependent we are on them until they are lost, stolen, invaded or damaged, resulting in a colossal waste of our time, possible loss of identity, or worse. A good site to visit, where the government has compiled a lot of information on Data Security, is the Bureau of Consumer Protection Business Center http://business.ftc.gov/privacy-and-security/data-security.

Physical security can be viewed as three things:

- Surveillance (these are the technical devices, cameras, and/or sensors that surround what we are trying to protect)

- Personnel (qualified, well paid, properly armed and situational-aware employees to backup and plug any gaps in our surveillance equipment)
- Procedure (patrol routes and frequency, alarm and courses of action in special situations)

Given the above examples, let's examine another form of attack that is being used by crackers to perform malicious tasks that may be unknown to you. We have all heard of Internet sites being attacked, or we have received an email from a friend, who later writes us as to how they have been cracked. What has happened is that computers around the world have been enslaved into what are called botnets. A botnet is a network of computers used for malicious purposes. The web page, https://en.wikipedia.org/wiki/Zombie_computer points out that hijacked home computers are responsible for 50% to 80% of the spam worldwide. The web page http://www.bbc.co.uk/news/technology-11531657 reports that crackers have hijacked entire botnets of business and home computers. Many of us don't know what a botnet is or that they even exist. Wiki, at https://en.wikipedia.org/wiki/Botnet, defines a botnet as "*a collection of comprised computers connected to the Internet.*" Once these computers are connected to a botnet they can be used for whatever malicious purpose the creator of the botnet wants. Wiki goes on to explain, "*Infected computers, or newly formed "bots", were then used to steal passwords, log keystrokes, and act as a proxy* server to conceal the attacker's identity. The bot herder can also 'rent out' the services of the botnet to third parties, usually for sending out spam messages or performing a denial of service attack against a remote target.*" These crackers enslave your computer to their will and use them to gather and distribute personal information for profit. Can you imagine 12 million computers enslaved into a botnet? Yes, it did happen! According to Wiki, "*The Dutch police found a 1.5 million node botnet and the Norwegian ISP Telenor disbanded a 10,000-node botnet. In July 2010, the FBI arrested a 23-year old Slovenian held responsible for the malicious software that integrated an estimated 12 million computers into a botnet. It has been estimated that up to one quarter of all personal computers connected to the Internet may be part of a botnet.*" On October 13, 2010, the BBC published in their NEWS Technology commentary an article titled "Two million US PCs recruited to botnets", reference http://news.bbc.co.uk/2/hi/technology/8010729.stm "*Almost two million PCs globally, including machines Inside the UK and US government departments, have been taken over by malicious hackers. Several PCs inside six UK government bodies were compromised by a botnet and traced back to a gang of cyber criminals in the Ukraine.*" From PCWorld, January 2013, "Malware Attacks Target Home Networks" by John R. Mello Jr., "*Some 2.2 million home networks worldwide are infected with malware controlled by the ZeroAccess botnet, the report estimated. "Cybercriminals are primarily using it to take over victim computers and conduct client fraud." Kevin McNamee, Kindsight security architect and director said in a statement.*" In his October 31, 2012 article titled "Malware infects 13 percent of North American home networks," he states that half of these networks have "serious" threats that turn them in to a spam-spewing zombie on a botnet or compromise everything the network owners do using the Internet such as Identity Theft and raiding their bank accounts. (See: http://www.pcworld.com/article/2013354/malware-infects-13-percent-of-north-american-home-networks.html)

In the Bloomberg BusinessWeek article titled "Iran Gets Flamed in a New Cyber-attack" by Jordan Robertson, Barrett Sheridan and Jeff Bliss titled, they point out that a virus known as FLAME has been active since 2007 and has been spreading for years. Because the virus is highly selective, it has remained hidden for years much of this time. Flame could even communicate wirelessly, thus enabling it to spread to devices that other software could not attack. From the article and edited, *"Flame can monitor keystrokes, steal passwords, turn on victims' microphones to record conversations, and take screenshots of Internet sessions. It's able to send the captured information to so-called "command-and-control" servers around the world and receive software updates from them. It's essentially a permanent desktop spy."* Later in the article, *"Dave Aisle, a former computer scientist with the National Security Agency and now CEO of the security firm Immunity Inc. states that "once a hacker gets into your system, it's almost impossible to get them out. They know everything about you. It's sort of like pulling an ex-wife out of your system."* (See: http://www.businessweek.com/articles/2012-05-30/iran-gets-flamed-in-a-new-cyberattack)

After Flame came Mask which has spent over six years stealing valuable intelligence from supposedly secure government and diplomatic computers around the world. The virus is more sophisticated than Flame and was almost certainly developed by some government to become the new gold standard in cyber-espionage. It was discovered by Russia's Kaspersky Labs and was found to be designed to steal files, keystrokes and encryption keys, and as we can see it was designed to operate for a long time undetected. (See: http://www.bloombergview.com/articles/2014-02-13/the-world-s-most-dangerous-software)

The "Syrian Electronic Army" has taken credit for hacking the websites of numerous newspapers and corporations. These attacks came as the Obama administration talked about military action in the face of Syrian use of chemical weapons on their own people. The "Syrian Electronic Army" warned that that the media is going down-and proved effective in accomplishing that task. By tampering with domain name servers they denied access to the New York Times website. They have taken credit for Web attacks on any website that appears sympathetic to Syria's rebels, including prior attacks on the Washington Post, Huffington Post UK, Agency France-Press, 60 Minutes, CBS News, National Public Radio, The Associated Press, Al-Jazeera English, Twitter, and the BBC. Now the Obama administration is helping keep the Syrian government in power by bombing ISIS at a cost of billions to American taxpayers, why is that?

Another example is the Conficker Worm. According to https://en.wikipedia.org/wiki/Conficker, *"The Conficker infected millions of computers including government, business and home computers in over 200 countries, making it the largest known computer worm infection since the 2003 Welchia."*

Story	I read that Windows 7 had addressed the Conficker worm, but I did not investigate as to how. We will cover virtual machines in Chapter 7, which are the only OSs you should expose to the Internet. I am guilty of not following my own advice and using my laptop core OS to do banking and investment research. Imagine my shock, when, during a routine security scan, Microsoft Security Essentials found the Conficker Worm on my laptop? This happened even with all of the latest security updates applied, and this worm was still able to strike through Microsoft's defenses. Evidently, Microsoft addressed the worm by being able to detect it during a full virus scan. Many users rarely do full scans because it drags down performance, so the worm could exist for weeks or months before it is found, if it ever is. Using VMs may seem like overkill, but I cannot stress how important they are.

Conficker paid me a visit, so let's pay Conficker a visit and learn a bit about it. When someone breaks into your house, you need to find out who they are, what they are capable of, what they may have compromised or stolen while they were there, and how to watch out for them in the future. Many computer users just view the fact that their anti-software removed this threat and move on with their lives. This is so far from the truth; I hope I can educate you on what you need to do.

Conficker is a complex piece of software that exploits multiple vulnerabilities and inputs vectors on Windows computers. It is believed to have originated in the Ukraine and must still have an active development team. Microsoft reports that about 1.7 million Windows computers are now infected with the worm, which they feel has remained a steady number, as new patches come out. Microsoft and Conficker are continuously playing a counter-to-counter strike game. This exemplifies how anti-software is reactive, which I have talked about. My laptop had the latest Microsoft patches applied, which may have blocked the newly revised worm; however, it could not detect its existence prior to these updates. Alternatively, the other possibility is that there is no patch to block this new threat, and the only way to detect it is with a full security scan. So the next question is, what might this nasty worm have done?

1. Some Windows services may have been disabled. That is actually a good thing in a small way. I recommend disabling automatic updates in Chapter 6 and doing them yourself.
2. It conducted a scan of my local network to infect other vulnerable computers. I'm not too concerned about that. But knowing this I conducted a full security scan of all my computers using the latest Security Essentials update definitions. No other problems were found.
3. The other possible problems such as congestion on my local network and websites related to antivirus and other sites becoming inaccessible did not manifest, and user accounts being locked out did not happen either.

Researching this further did not present much information on how a fully updated 2013 Windows 7 computer could become infected with a worm that Microsoft says was blocked by the latest updates back in 2009 (See: http://www.microsoft.com/security/pc-security/conficker.aspx). Nevertheless, we have to consider just what information was revealed to that criminal group in the Ukraine. At the very least, I have to set about changing all my passwords. Nonetheless, ask yourself, how many of your friends and neighbors have a fully patched version of Windows 7 or Linux running on their Internet devices? How many of them are unknowing victims of a worldwide botnet?

I have never encountered a PC running Windows Me, which had a very short shelf life and was considered by many a failure for Microsoft. (See: https://en.wikipedia.org/wiki/Windows_Me) However, Microsoft turned around and created the successful operating system Windows XP. Windows XP was the first operating system produced by Microsoft built on the NT kernel (See: https://en.wikipedia.org/wiki/Windows_XP). Many corporations, government agencies, doctor's offices, SBO/HCU, and charities that I have visited and worked for are still running the ancient Microsoft Windows XP operating system that was released August 24, 2001, but did not become generally available till December 31, 2001. We have to look at the history of

Windows to understand why everyone needs to get rid of XP. Windows 98, ME, and later, XP were designed to be a feature-rich, user-friendly environment before the Internet became enormously popular. There was not much time or effort spent by its developers worrying about security. To sell these OSs to a broad audience Microsoft designed them with all sorts of networking capabilities that many home users don't need. There were many superfluous components deeply integrated into the kernel that provided crackers many avenues to attack these OSs and the applications that run on them.

Microsoft also designed the OS to hide what is taking place in the background with many hidden processes and services that are difficult to turn off. Windows and the applications that run on it constantly reach out to the Internet in ways that were/are unknown to their users. Often times they do this in the guise of providing updates. This lack of transparency is something we will address in Chapter 6 on Windows 7.

WARNING	Windows XP is deprecated and receives no support from Microsoft. The XP OS is over 14 years old and when compared with modern Linux and MAC OSs, is vastly inferior. Because of this, crackers have/are discovering ways to exploit known/new weaknesses that they find in XP.

Running XP connected to the Internet is a feeding bonanza for criminals, governments and crackers everywhere. If you cannot afford to buy Windows 7/8, or your hardware is not capable of running Windows 7/8, consider installing a donationware* Linux operating system like Fedora, Linux Mint, openSUSE, Ubuntu or some other flavor. You can do everything in these modern open source OSs that you can in Windows. Linux also gives you an open source office suite called http://www.libreoffice.org or http://www.openoffice.org that you can use. There are many other flavors of Linux to choose from that that are far superior to Windows XP.

Factoid	To secure your SB/HC you must renew your technology often. A few thousand dollars a year invested in the solutions of tomorrow could save your business millions and thwart crackers everywhere. As we continually innovate, the crackers must keep up and develop new techniques. Please try to imagine how many exploits are available for a 2001 OS such as Windows XP.

Employees who access the Internet often also need training on cyber security, which is almost always neglected. It is estimated that 80% of successful attacks occur because of human-based exploits. Most network breaches occur due to employees bringing malware behind firewalls. It is sad that businesses give so little training in these important topics!

Another example of how pervasive the Internet has become would be what has been dubbed, Twitter's hash crash. In April 2013, hackers took control of the Associated Press news agency's Twitter feed and posted a tweet. The tweet suggested that the U.S. president had been injured or killed in an explosion at the White House. As a result the markets had a massive selloff. The fake news was corrected in minutes, but because of the hack Wall Street lost more than 100 points, which translated to $136 billion (105 billion euros). That is a phenomenal number that could have made 136,000 hackers millionaires in just a few minutes. Quite the incentive to hack for a living, don't you think?

WARNING	In 2013, the Library of Congress struck a deal with Twitter to collect and archive all public tweets on an ongoing basis. That means anything you've publicly tweeted since 2006 is in the possession of the U.S. government, even if you've deleted your account so carefully consider what you Tweet.

Even the biggest security minded U.S. banks can be hacked, as reported on Dec. 5 2013 in the BBC article "JP Morgan warns customers of possible data theft after cyber attack". (See: http://www.bbc.co.uk/news/business-25247490) As many as 465,000 holders of pre-paid cash cards issued by the bank may have had their personal information hacked. JP Morgan admitted that their network was hacked in July but it took until September to detect the breach. No money was stolen and only a small amount of data that did not include sensitive information such as SSN, birth dates and email addresses.

On October 22 and November 7, 2014 the U.S. Postal Service informed member of Congress that it had been hacked. Once again we see how a lack of cyber security leaked not only 800,000 employees' information but also people who called the post office's Customer Care center. Information that was stolen included names dates of birth, Social Security numbers, addresses, beginning and end dates of employment, emergency contact information and other data. These breaches are and epidemic and I'm hoping you can see the pattern developing.

Then, in December 2013, the major retailer Target admitted that they had a breach of credit and debit card data that may have affected as many as 70 million customers. While Target was busy collecting people's names, card data, social security codes, phone numbers, email addresses, home mailing addresses and more, this information was being sent to crackers overseas. This is another example of corporations collecting personal data for profit and then not having proper security measures in place to protect it. Over a two week period, the malware collected 11GB of data from Target's POS terminals and sent it to a hijacked U.S. server. That compromised server then forwarded the data to a server based in Russia. To put this in perspective, Target is the number two general retailer after Wal-Mart Stores, and from Nov. 27 to Dec. 15 all shopper transactions were recorded by a malicious entity before this hack was detected. As a result of this breach the thieves were empowered to withdraw cash from ATMs using counterfeit debit cards, as they had recorded PIN data from the Target transactions. This is nothing new for Target, as they were targeted back in 2006 when crackers gained access to at least 95 million domestic and international accounts, which held credit card, debit card, and check information. Maybe it is the bull's-eye on their logo that is attracting crackers everywhere!

The stolen information included card numbers, expiration dates, CVV codes and customer names. It is estimated that one in three victims of the Target crime became victims of identity theft in some fashion. To add to this insult, we quickly learned that Neiman Marcus and five other retailers also suffered major data breaches. On June 16, 2014, hackers cracked a Domino's Pizza database thus compromising the personal data of 650,000 trusting customers. The crackers demanded a ransom from the company to not release their customer's information so that identity thieves everywhere could use it. They even boldly posted the following letter online:

"Dear friends and foes,

Earlier this week, we hacked our way into the servers of Domino's Pizza France and Belgium, who happen to share the same vulnerable database. And boy, did we find some juicy stuff in there! We downloaded over 592,000 customer records (including passwords) from French customers and over 58,000 records from Belgian ones. That's over six hundred thousand records, which include the customers' full names, addresses, phone numbers, email addresses, passwords and delivery instructions. (Oh, and their favorite pizza topping as well, because why not)." I say why not indeed! Corporations everywhere want more and more personal information from their customers but have little regard for their customers' privacy. Their lack of regard for cyber security is appalling, ask yourself why that is?

The real question we have to ask ourselves is, what laws are there to protect the affected consumers, and why are credit card companies and corporation's lack of concern for cyber security tolerated? What is really sad is victims of corporate credit fraud are legally responsible for cleaning up this mess afterward. They are given a limited amount of time to report unauthorized purchases and fraudulent activity or their liability can become unlimited. We live in a world where everyone is told you should have been monitoring your accounts instead of one where the people responsible are held accountable. Suppose, after shopping at Target you went on a sabbatical with no access to mail, the Internet or your accounts? Target offered its customers free credit monitoring and repayment for any unauthorized charges but I think we are all missing the point on these breaches.

On May 21, 2014, auction giant eBay advised their users to change their passwords due to a cyber-attack that may have compromised a password database and obtained other non-financial data. EBay said that its database was compromised sometime between late February and early March. At that time the cyber crackers were able to access information that may have included eBay customers' names, encrypted passwords, email addresses, physical addresses, phone numbers and dates of birth (DOB). However, eBay stressed that this database did not contain financial information or other confidential personal information so we have to ask how DOB is not confidential? The company further added that the compromised employee login credentials were first detected in early May, so it took them months to discover and correct this. As with the Target cyber-attack, the eBay data breach involved a lot of data otherwise eBay would not have advised all its customers to change their passwords.

In September 2014, we discovered that Home Depot had been hit by cybercriminals. We found out about this after thousands of fresh credit and debit card numbers appeared on the carding site Rescator, which are websites where stolen credit card data is sold. This is very profitable to Eastern European crackers who are demanding up to $200 per card number. What was really amazing about this is that this massive crack affected 2,200 stores which topped the record-setting Target breach back in December by 400. Home Depot felt some pain as their shares dropped 2.6% but the stock rebounded fairly quickly and investors did not feel this would drive customers away from Home Depot even though it should have. At the same time hijacked computers with malware were used to steal data from JPMorgan and send it to Russia. The news stories I reviewed did not reveal what data was stolen from JPMorgan.

On October 11, 2014 we learned that Sears Holding Corporation Kmart retail chain was hacked compromising shoppers' credit and debit card numbers. This was once again an instance where anti-virus software proved to inadequate to the task of protecting a major retailer and shows it cannot be depended upon as this book presents.

1. Why isn't there a law in place to have corporations such as Dominos, eBay, Home Depot or Target compensate their customers in some meaningful fashion for the lost time and agony of dealing with a data breach when in today's hourly working world, time is money? This becomes especially true as one in three data breach victims suffer some form of identity theft on average.
2. Where are the laws to hold U.S. corporation's feet to the fire to implement better cyber security practices in the face of these massive events?
3. Lawyers and the government make money off of these incidents but most times the actual victims get nothing but having to deal with these nightmares themselves.

For example, in the U.K., Canada and Hong Kong they are using chip-based credit cards, which are considered more secure. These chip-and-PIN cards have an embedded microchip that requires you to put the card into a terminal and enter a PIN or sign your name. These Europay, MasterCard and Visa chip cards (EMV) have dramatically reduced fraud and counterfeit activities in the markets where they are used. The reason for this is, the magnetic strip technology that we are still using here in the U.S. is decades old, remains static, and crackers have many known techniques to exploit it such as "skimming". These EMV chip cards allow for the encryption of each transaction, thus making them unique. What this means is that even as crackers intercept these transactions, as occurred in the Target example, the impact would have been minimized. Chip cards use authentication technology and are more sophisticated and difficult for criminals to replicate. The sad truth is that some U.S. card issuers, such as Bank of America, Chase, Citibank, USAA and other U.S. banks, offer EMV cards to their customers, but retailers and merchants refuse to adopt this technology because of its added expense. Instead, they prefer to allow these breaches, leaving U.S. citizens holding the bag as they are ultimately held responsible for dealing with these crimes and the financial consequences.

Factoid	There were 26.2 billion credit card transactions in the U.S. in 2012, according to the Federal Reserve. That is about 50,000 purchases every minute.
Factoid	390 million credit card accounts are currently open in the United States. Each card weighs about 0.2 ounces. Putting all these cards together would weigh almost 5 million pounds.

On the bright side, in 2015, liability for fraudulent transactions may shift to retailers and merchants who have not adopted EMV technology by the end of 2015. The credit card manufacturers have devised a strategy to offload liability to their customers instead of sharing the burden of helping everyone convert over to this more secure technology. Moreover, expect nothing out of Washington, as there is a lack of political and/or corporate will to implement the necessary cyber security changes and practices to prevent these cybercrimes. The investment in new technologies and a few domestic, well-paid, IT experienced and proven effective cyber security professionals might prevent some of these offenses, but it appears that corporations would rather invest millions into their corporate executives. After all, if it was a simple credit card transaction and their consumers dealt with these crimes within thirty days, they would suffer no financial losses, but what happens if they don't know about this as they lay in a coma or are off on some adventure, what then? However, after all these disasters banks in the U.S. are finally slowly moving to chip-based debit and credit cards to make shopping in stores more secure. (See: https://en.wikipedia.org/wiki/EMV, http://www.nytimes.com/2014/10/08/your-money/credit-and-debit-cards/banks-in-us-moving-to-chip-based-debit-and-credit-cards.html?_r=0)

While the world's HCU/SBO's and corporations remain unmoved in their concern over using something as dangerous as the Internet, the U.S. government does not. On November 14, 2013, in a Washington Post article by Greg Miller, it was reported *"FBI Director James B. Comey testified that the risk of cyber-attacks is likely to exceed the danger posed by al-Qaeda and other terrorist networks as the top national security threat to the United States and will become the dominant focus of law enforcement and U.S. intelligence services."* (See: http://www.washingtonpost.com/world/national-security/fbi-director-warns-of-cyberattacks-other-security-chiefs-say-terrorism-threat-has-altered/2013/11/14/24f1b27a-4d53-11e3-9890-a1e0997fb0c0_story.html) Comey recognized the fact that the U.S., and soon the world, have connected or are connecting their personal, professional, national and financial lives to the Internet. As such, this is where the bad guys will go to invade people's privacy, steal identities, and perform cyber-terrorism, cyber-espionage and cyber-attacks, which pose the most significant threat that intelligence agencies will face in the coming Internet future. So ask yourself, how many other threats to do we face that the security firms and our government have not countered?

Don't Be a Sheep, Become a Shepherd, Stop Snail Mail and Change your Diet!

Some people argued against including this section of the book, but I felt we needed to examine what is happening in our day-to-day lives in order to figure out where valuable time in our lives is being lost. Every day we are assaulted by snail mail, which usually means nothing to us, from investment organizations, current and past employers, charities, U.S. government agencies, insurance companies, local businesses, and almost anyone else with whom we have had contact with. These advertisements, solicitations, surveys, and supposedly general information are a major distraction that consumes our valuable time. They often have personal information printed on them that is a threat to our security and must be shredded. You will have to waste your valuable time and take action to stop this activity! Skip down to Chapter 11 - Before You Are Cracked! There Are Many Preventive Measures You Can Take to Thwart Identity Theft! to get some general techniques to reduce unwanted and intrusive invasions into your valuable time.

Another assault **that is systemically related to what is happing in our individual lives**, which are as insidious as the Internet or snail mail, is occurring in our food supply. I admit including this information was quite a stretch for this cyber security book, so you might question what this information is doing here. Having worked as an IT professional most of my life, I felt this was all related to your welfare, and this came about because of my two-time bout with cancer. I wanted to prevent a third fatal dose of cancer in my life, so I had to go off the grid to find out how to prevent it from occurring again. IT professionals tend to eat processed diets that destroy their health. During my illness, what I found out is that western governments are making decisions that are not in the best interests of their citizens and these cancer issues are related to everyone's continued health. Our western food supply is another example of how our governments are letting down their citizens and serving their own political, and ultimately corporate-controlled puppeteer's self-interests. In the U.S., corporations are using crafty package labeling to mislead the public into buying products that are highly processed, very fattening, and have little or no nutritional value.

In Leah Zerbe's article titled, "11 Reasons to Ditch Processed Foods" Saturday, March 23, 2013 at http://www.rodale.com/processed-foods, *"Flavored noodle mixes, processed meats, packaged mac and cheese, soda, frozen dinners, other processed foods, and fast food are notorious for containing questionable levels of phosphate-laden ingredients that could promote kidney deterioration and weaker bones. Research shows both the phosphates and the genetically engineered ingredients are often added to processed foods and promote premature aging."* This U.S. FDA-allowed mislabeling is similar in how the government permits corporations to gather information on our use of the Internet without most people knowing it. Americans hear, sometimes on a daily basis, how obesity and diabetes have become an epidemic in the United States, or how cyber security has become a national priority, but their politicians are turning a blind eye to the root causes of these crises. These widespread problems are acknowledged by western media and their politicians, but there are no penalties for these abhorrent types of corporate behavior. Very little is being done to protect our children from this epidemic of processed food containing large amounts of sugar, harmful chemicals, antibiotics and many harmful artificial sweeteners. These processed foods contain many destructive engineered chemicals that are killing millions more people in the western world than drugs, alcohol, guns and car accidents combined. Yet, this fact is being ignored while misleading labels are put on products for consumers. As a U.S. citizen this fraud came to my attention when I was instructed by a knowledgeable cancer doctor to cut sucrose and high fructose corn syrup out of my diet and buy organic food after my second round of cancer. ***Sugar is a drug and high fructose corn syrup (HFCS) is sugar on speed***. (See: http://foodidentitytheft.com/culprits/high-fructose-corn-syrup)

| **WARNING**
 | From Leah Zerbe's article titled, "11 Reasons to Ditch Processed Foods," Saturday, March 23, 2013 at http://www.rodale.com/processed-foods, *"The Facts: Added sugars, specifically fructose from table sugar and the high-fructose corn syrup found in most processed foods, block the hormonal signal that tells your brain it's time to stop eating, according to obesity research by Robert Lustig, MD, a pediatric neuroendocrinologist at the University of California - San Francisco. The result? Never-ending hunger that leaves you fatter yet feeling unsatisfied. The Facts: Added sugar is the not-so-sweet trick the makers of processed foods use to get you hooked. In 2005, Princeton researchers found that eating sugar triggers the release of opioids, neurotransmitters that light up your brain's pleasure center. Addictive drugs like morphine and heroin stimulate those same pleasure pathways. Scary fact? After 21 days on a high-sugar diet, you could start showing signs of withdrawal–chattering teeth, anxiety, and depression–when sugar is taken away... The trans fats and sugar common in fast-food menu items trigger inflammation, an unhealthy condition tied to asthma. According to the American Heart Association, we down about 22 teaspoons of sugar a day; that's about 25 pounds more than people consumed annually just a few decades ago. Watch out for surprising hidden sources of added sugars, such as bread, crackers, bottled tea, frozen dinners, and sauces and marinades."* And the following slightly reworded, The Facts: Kids who eat fast food two to three times a |

week face a significantly higher risk of developing asthma, possibly due to the processed foods' ability to create inflammation in the body, which is an unhealthy condition tied to asthma. (See: http://www.bbc.co.uk/news/health-21082629)

I had no idea how difficult the task of removing sucrose, HFCS, corn syrup and foods loaded with sugar from my diet would be or how pervasive this challenge would become. Almost everything that I pulled off the shelf at my local grocery store contained sucrose, HFCS, corn syrup and/or sugar. I had to rethink my diet completely in order to follow my doctor's advice. Upon further study, I discovered that the billion dollar food conglomerates have hijacked our food supply and have added these chemicals, sugars and other fattening ingredients into about 80% of what we eat.

Story

To gather the data below I tried to use the Internet but after comparing what the websites presented to what was actually on the grocery store labels, I found discrepancies. So I spent days wandering around grocery stores with my reading glasses on and a pen and pad in hand pulling items off the shelves and writing down their ingredients. No one ever questioned what I was doing and I even had store managers walk right by me. While there is nothing wrong with this I would have thought at least one curious customer, employee or store manager would have asked what the heck I was doing and why!

Below is a just a sampling of the foods and other products that contain HFCS in ingredient order:

Arizona Green Tea: green tea & water, HFCS, honey	Brisk Iced Tea: water, HFCS, citric acid, lemon juice concentrate, sodium hexametaphosphate, natural flavor, tea powder, phosphoric acid, potassium sorrate
Campbell's Old Fashioned Tomato Rice Soup: tomato puree (water, tomato paste), water, rice, HRCS, wheat flour	Campbell's Pork & Beans: water, pee beans, HFCS, 2% or less of other ingredients
Campbell's Tomato Soup: tomato puree, wheat flower, water, HFCS	Campbell's Tomato with Roasted Garlic & Herb Soup: tomato puree, water, HFCS
Delsym Cough Suppressant: citric acid, edetate disodium, ethyl cellulose, FD&C Yellow 6, flavor, HFCS	French's Honey Mustard: distilled vinegar, water, HFCS, #1 grade mustard seed, sugar, corn syrup, salt
Kraft Hickory Smoke Barbeque Sauce: HFCS, water, vinegar, tomato paste, molasses, modified corn starch	Kraft Creamy French Dressing: soybean oil, HFCS, vinegar, tomato puree, skim milk
Kroger Apple Butter: apples, HFCS, corn syrup, spices, molasses	Kroger Coleslaw Dressing: soybean oil, vinegar, HFCS, sugar, egg yolk, water, salt
Kroger Cranberry Sauce, Jellied: cranberries, HFCS, water, corn syrup	Kroger Pork & Beans: white beans, water, cane syrup, tomato paste, HFCS, salt vinegar, pork
Kroger Sweet Orange Marmalade: HFCS, corn syrup, orange peel	Lipton Green Tea: water, HFCS, citric acid, natural flavor, sodium hexametaphosphate, green tea, ascorbic acid, potassium sorrate

Marzetti Chocolate Fruit Dip: HFCS, skim milk, corn syrup, sugar, chocolate liquor, cocoa	Marzetti Cream Cheese & Strawberry Cream Cheese: cream cheese, salt, lactic acid, locust bean gum, guar gum, sodium phosphate, carrageenan, natural flavors, HFCS
Minute Maid Premium Fruit Punch: water, HFCS, grape and pineapple juices from concentrate	Minute Maid Premium Lemonade: filtered water, HFCS, lemon juice from concentrate, lemon pulp, natural flavors, sugar
Miracle Whip: water, soybean oil, HFCS, vinegar, modified corn starch	Mt. Olive Sweet Petite: cucumbers, HFCS, vinegar, salt, calcium chloride
Mt. Olive Sweet Gherkins: cucumbers, HFCS, vinegar, water, salt	Mt. Olive Sweet Relish: cucumbers, corn syrup, HFCS, vinegar, salt, water
NyQuil: acesulfame potassium, alcohol, citric acid, D&C Yellow 10, FD&C Green 3, FD&C Yellow 6, flavor, HFCS	Olde Cape Cod Chipotle Ranch Dressing: soybean oil, distilled vinegar, water, corn syrup, HFCS, cultured buttermilk, salt
Open Pit Original Barbeque Sauce: HFCS, water, vinegar, tomato puree, salt, food starch-modified	Powerade: water, HFCS, lest that 2% of many other items
Slim-Fast: fat free milk, water, sugar, other ingredients, fructose 6th, HFCS 11th	Sweet Baby Ray's Barbeque Sauce: HFCS, distilled vinegar, tomato paste, modified food starch
Welch's Passion Fruit Juice: filtered water, white grape juice from concentrate, HFCS, granulated sugar, apple juice from concentrate, passion fruit	Welch's Concord Grape: filtered water, concord grape juice from concentrate, HFCS, grape juice, citric acid, ascorbic acid

Obvious candidates, such as soft drinks (Pepsi, Coke, Canada Dry Ginger Ale and others) contain large amounts of HFCS. However, other foods that you might not suspect such as breads, breakfast cereals, candy bars, cookies, cakes, cough syrups, crackers, dairy items, drink mixers, frozen pizzas, fruits, vegetables, ice creams, pastries, salad dressings, sauces, snacks, soups and so many more, also have HFCS added! As horrified as I was of HFCS, I quickly found out that there are other ingredients being added to our food supply about which we all need to worry.

Story

Subway announced it was removing a chemical that is used to produce plastic in yoga mats and shoe soles from their bread. The activist blogger Vani Hari had written extensively about this cancer causing agent, which the U.S. FDA has ignored. She collected 57,000 signatures from concerned citizens to petition Subway to remove this chemical, which is called Azodicarbonamide. It produces air within yoga mats and shoe soles, and is used in bread to make it look more palatable. When added to bread it acts as a bleaching agent to make the bread whiter and increases flour strength by improving the dough's ability to retain gas, thus making the bread more elastic.

The World Health Organization has linked this chemical to respiratory issues, allergies, skin sensitivities, asthma and other health problems. However, the U.S. and Canada still allow this chemical to be added to their citizens' food supply even though it is banned in Europe and Australia. I used to buy the premium Meijer Country Harvest 14 Grain, 10g Whole Grain bread, which touts

> itself as a good source of fiber. Out of curiosity, I studied the ingredients and what did I find but AZODICABRONAMIDE in my bread, so I threw the whole loaf out. Organic breads are not allowed to add this chemical to their product. (See: http://foodbabe.com/subway, http://abcnews.go.com/Health/subway-takes-chemical-sandwich-bread-protest/story?id=22373414)

After hearing about plastic in my bread, I decided to take a quick look at the breads we eat and found most of them are filled with HFCS, sugar, alcohol sugars, plastic, and other chemicals that poison our bodies. All of the following breads contain the cancer causing plastic Azodicarbonamide (AZOD), HFCS, as well as other sugars but their labeling makes them sound OH so healthy. Look at Aunt Millie's Cracked Wheat with Whole Grain (AZOD), Healthy Life Soft Style 100% Whole Grain Heart Healthy (AZOD), Aunt Millie's Light Whole Grain 35 Calorie Healthy Goodness (AZOD), Aunt Millie's Country Buttermilk Enriched Bread (AZOD), Kroger Round Top Harvest Grain Bread (AZOD), Kroger Whole Wheat Hamburger Buns (AZOD), Mother's Split Top Wheat Bread (HFCS)/(AZOD), Nature's Own 100% Whole Wheat (AZOD), Private Selection Golden Flax & Grain (AZOD), Private Selection Dark Rye Wide Pan Bread (AZOD), Roman Meal American Original Since 1912 (HFCS)/(AZOD), and so on.

Healthy sounding items that have loads of sugar:

You have to go beyond the advertising and labeling to understand the food that you are eating. Corporations label foods to make them sound "natural" or "pure" but really, they are full of sugar and other harmful ingredients. What is worse is that it often appears we have choices under different labels but upon closer examination, the same harmful ingredients are in all of the products. To demonstrate my point let's examine sweet peas, jelly and ketchup.

Del Monte Sweet Peas: peas, water, sugar, sea salt	Freshlike Tender Garden Peas: sweet peas, water, sugar, salt
Green Giant Sweet Peas: sweet peas, water, sugar, salt	Kroger Sweet Peas: peas, water sugar, salt
P$$T Sweet Peas: peas, water, sugar, salt	

Heinz Tomato Ketchup, tomato, vinegar, HFCS, corn syrup, salt	Hunts Tomato Ketchup: tomato, HFCS, vinegar, corn syrup, salt
Kroger Tomato Ketchup: tomato, HFCS, vinegar, corn syrup, salt, onion powder, spice, natural flavors	P$$T Tomato Ketchup: tomato concentrate, HFCS, vinegar, corn syrup, salt, onion powder

Kroger Concord Grape Jelly: grape juice, corn syrup, HFCS, fruit pectin	Kroger White Grape: white grape juice, corn syrup, HFCS, fruit pectin
P$$T Strawberry Spread: strawberries, corn syrup, HFCS, fruit pectin, citric acid	P$$T Grape Jelly: grape juice, HFCS, corn syrup, fruit pectin, citric acid, sodium citrate
Smucker's Blackberry Jam: blackberries, HFCS, corn syrup, fruit pectin, citric acid	Smucker's Strawberry Jam, strawberries, HFCS, corn syrup, sugar, fruit pectin, citric acid
Welch's Concord Grape: concord grapes, corn syrup, HFCS, fruit pectin, citric acid,	Welch's Strawberry Spread: strawberries, corn syrup, HFCS, sugar, fruit pectin, citric acid, sodium

| sodium citrate | citrate, red grape juice |
| WindStone Farms Blackberry Jam: blackberries, sugar, fruit pectin, citric acid | WindStone Farms Strawberry Jam: strawberries, sugar, fruit pectin, citric acid |

For example, see this brief list of the first few ingredients in these processed and modified foods:

Brianna's Rich Poppy Seed Dressing: canola oil, sugar, water, white vinegar, salt, apple cider vinegar, poppy seeds	Bush's Homestyle Baked Beans: white beans, water, brown sugar, sugar, tomato paste, bacon
Bush's Grillin Beans, prepared white beans: water, sugar or brown sugar	Campbell's Home Style Harvest Tomato with Basil Soup: water, sugar
Cascadian Farm Organic Vanilla Chip Chewy Granola Bars: granola, tapioca, syrup, sugar	Dannon Yogurt: milk, sugar, modified food starch, water
Del Monte Fruit Naturals Mandarin Oranges: mandarin oranges, water, sugar, ascorbic acid, citric acid, cellulose	Dole Mandarins In Orange Gel Fruit Bowls: water, mandarin oranges, sugar, carrageenan, also has yellow 6
Fiesta Style Corn with Red and Green Peppers: corn, water, red & green bell peppers, sugar, salt	Gatorade: water, sugar, 2% or less of other ingredients
Glaceau Vitamin Water: reverse osmosis water, crystalline fructose & cane sugar	Green Giant Niblets: golden whole kernel corn, water sugar, salt
Jif Creamy Peanut Butter: roasted peanuts, sugar	Ken's Steak House Apple Cider Vinaigrette: water, blend of veg-soy-canola oils, sugar
Kraft Classic Lite Ranch Dressing: water, corn syrup, soybeans oil, vinegar, egg yolks, modified food starch, salt, sugar	Kraft Thousand Island Dressing: soybean oil, tomato puree, vinegar, sugar, water, chopped pickles, egg yolks
Kraft Zesty Italian Dressing: vinegar, water, blend of veg-soy-canola oils, sugar	Kroger Cream Style (Golden or White) Corn: corn, water, sugar, modified corn starch, salt
Kroger Sweet Golden Corn: corn, water, sugar, salt	Kroger vacuum packed Golden Corn Whole Kernel: corn, water, sugar, salt
Kroger Peach Iced Tea: water, sugar, black tea powder	Kroger Sweet Hot Mustard: water, sugar, vinegar, mustard seed, salt
Low Calorie G2 Gatorade, water, sugar, citric acid, natural flavor, salt	Maple Grove Farms of Vermont Fat Free Poppyseed Dressing: water, sugar, cider vinegar, maltodextrin, concentrated lemon juice, poppy seeds, dried onion
Marzetti Slaw Dressing Lite: water, sugar, soybean oil, corn cider vinegar, egg yolk, salt	Marzetti Sweet & Sour Dressing with Celery Seeds: HFCS, soybean oil, corn-cider vinegar, water, sugar, salt
Nantucket Nectars Orange Mango Juice: water, cane sugar, orange juice concentrate	Ocean Spray Craisins Cranberry Fruit & Nut Trail Mix: dried cranberries, sugar, also contains Yellow 5 and Yellow 6
Ocean Spray Craisins Original: cranberries, sugar	Prego Italian Sauce Traditional: tomato puree, dried tomatoes in tomato juice, sugar, canola

	oil, salt
Progresso Heart Healthy Creamy Tomato with Basil Soup: tomato puree, water, sugar, cream	Progresso Traditional Creamy Tomato with Bacon & Cheese Soup: tomato puree, water, tomatoes, cream, sugar
Silk Pure Almond Milk Original: almondmilk, cane sugar, sea salt, locust bean gum, sun flower lecithin, gellan gum	Stubb's Sticky Sweet Bar-B-Q: water, brown sugar, sugar
Sunny D Lemonade: Grape & Orange, water, corn syrup	Sweet Leaf Green Tea: water, organic cane sugar, organic green tea, natural flavors
Read German Potato Salad: potatoes, water, sugar, vinegar, bacon cured, corn starch	Read Three Bean Salad: green beans, water, wax beans, kidney beans, sugar
Red Bull Energy Drink: carbonated water, sucrose, glucose, sodium citrate	Trappey's Tomatoes And Okra: tomatoes, okra, water, sugar, salt
Wickles Relish: cucumbers, sugar, water, vinegar, dehydrated garlic and red bell peppers, salt	Yoplait Low Fat Yogurt: low fat milk, sugar, modified corn starch, nonfat milk, kosher gelatin, natural flavor, tricalcium phosphate

Almost all instant oatmeal, most chips and most all cereals are loaded with sugar. What is most disgusting is that cereals with cartoon characters, which are targeting young kids, have the most added sugar. As you travel to friends' houses that have kids take notice how they have the worst cereals in their cubboards (Kellogg's Froot Loops Marshmallow, Kellogg's Apple Jacks With Marshmallows, Post Golden Crisp, Malt-O-Meal Golden Puffs, Kellogg's Honey Smacks) and so on.   Sugar or some other sweetener is being added to most everything we consume thus causing a health epidemic! (See: http://www.huffingtonpost.com/2014/05/15/most-sugary-cereals-2014_n_5317771.html)

Our cheap processed food diet is especially bad for people living paycheck to paycheck or who receive food stamps. Prior to this research, I wondered how someone who is poor or impoverished could become grossly obese. Since they have less to spend on food than people who do have large sums of money, one would assume that they would be buying and eating fewer calories.

However, just the opposite is true as they try to stretch their dollars as far as they can at the grocery store. Corporations are tricking them into purchasing cheap products with deceptive package labeling that makes them think that these processed products are somewhat healthy. After all, if you are stretch a dollar to feed a hungry family, a lot of something sounding *somewhat* healthy is better than a little of something we know is healthy.   Unfortunately, the reality is that this food is loaded with empty calories, sugar, unbeneficial fiber and other highly unhealthy and fattening ingredients.

"If the people let the government decide what foods they eat and what medicines they take, their bodies will soon be in as sorry a state as the souls of those who live under Tyranny." Thomas Jefferson, 1778.

The media is focused on gun killing incidents, where deranged or militant individuals kill innocent people. While these incidents are horrific, we are missing the bigger picture. There are **millions of U.S citizens with awful medical problems who are dying from obesity and diabetes because of the poisons that they are eating.** These threats to U.S citizens' health are much more relevant to their political discussion than most of the other threats that they face. The American public is constantly reminded by the media of isolated events such as gun violence, individual criminal trials, birth of a royal baby, the latest Ebola victim or the death of royal family member in England. However, they see very little publicity about how this harmful processed food is killing countless more people in their country and the world each day. Why is that? Shouldn't we all consider the U.S. government's lack of regard in protecting its citizens from the processed food industry, which keeps politicians in power, criminal? Where is the outrage and protest on this?

| **WARNING**  | From Leah Zerbe's article titled, "11 Reasons to Ditch Processed Foods" Saturday, March 23, 2013 at http://www.rodale.com/processed-foods, *"genetically engineered food has not received long term testing and we have to question this experiment on our food supply. If you eat processed foods you are an unknowing participant in a huge experiment. To date, more than 80,000 chemicals have been approved for use in the U.S., most of them used in processed foods. Unfortunately, only about 15 percent have been tested for long-term impacts on human health. Cereals that many parents feed to their children are high in sugars and low in nutritional content. What are worse residues of more than 70 pesticides have been found in individual boxes of cereal. Why? Many pesticides today, particularly the go-to chemical applied to genetically engineered crops, are systemic. That means the chemicals wind up inside of the food you're eating. Beware of "natural" cereals. Testing by the Cornucopia Institute found that "natural" cereals are often contaminated with crop pesticides, warehouse fumigation chemicals, and genetically modified ingredients (GMOs). Choose organic if you truly want to avoid toxic chemicals in your food."* |

The average American eating this processed food carries an extra 23 pounds of fat, and no less than 40% of Americans are considered obese. As we talk about this we should understand how drugs work. After all, the U.S. government spends many billions of dollars prosecuting and incarcerating individuals who exploit illicit drugs. Alcohol, prescription and illegal drugs hijack the circuits or receptors in the brain causing a feeling of euphoria and excitement. However, this same drug-like effect happens when you eat highly concentrated processed foods or foods containing HFCS. These foods are poisons, where the fiber, water and mineral content have been removed and sugars and fat are substituted in concentrated quantities. Why isn't the media reporting on this daily? If one gram of methamphetamine can put a person in jail for five years how about the possession of a thousand pounds of processed food containing sucrose or HFCS? The consumption of these processed poisons affects our health much more than legislation designed to protect us from ourselves (seatbelt and helmet laws). Where is the legislation to start throwing producers and consumers of processed food in jail? Let's take the example of the laws about methamphetamine. Methamphetamine is made out of pharmaceuticals for the most part, and someone manufacturing them gets a five year prison sentence for possession of one gram; can you imagine who lobbied for that law?

| **Quotation** | *"Let food be thy medicine."* Hippocrates. If you want to learn more about what you should be eating please read the dated New York Times 1990 article titled http://www.nytimes.com/1990/05/08/science/huge-study-of-diet-indicts-fat-and-meat.html "Huge Study Of Diet Indicts Fat And Meat" by Jane E. Brody. Then, do |

some research about what is happening as the Chinese adopt a western processed food diet. This study, financed by the National Cancer Institute, hired hundreds of trained workers to gather information from one region of China to another and cost $2.3 million plus 600 person-years of labor contributed by the Chinese Government.

The Elephant in the Room; Lets Crunch the Numbers on What Is Really Killing Western Civilizations' Citizens!

Our western media sensationalizes events such as marginal criminal trials, murders, car chases, drunken driving accidents, robberies, scandals, and a host of other things that are relevant to the victims affected, but they are not the elephant in the room that is affecting the majority of citizens in their everyday lives. This form of news for entertainment television keeps us focused on a few select cases of human misery while millions suffer and die from corporate and/or government policies and causes. To see how the media rarely reports on what is really important to western civilization you have to crunch the numbers on the causes of death and misery for people living in the western (so called civilized) world. Our forefathers did not want corporations and a few very wealthy people in control of our republic, and you have to know that gifts to corporate executives' greed certainly do not represent your everyday interests.

For example think about the Ebola virus epidemic in West Africa. The epidemic began in Guinea in December 2013 and was largely ignored until September 2014. The world did not take notice until it spread to Liberia, Sierra Leone, Nigeria and Senegal. Only when the human misery and suffering became monumental and the world was threatened was action taken. Reported deaths are 2,984 but many experts say this number substantially understates the real size of the outbreak which we are learning daily is spreading exponentially.

When we crunch the numbers about the things being reported on and debated on the most by our media we discover that these events hold little significance as to the leading causes of death in western civilization. Seemingly HUGE issues that western media present, such as isolated gun violence, alcohol related car accidents, drug abuse, terrorism, politics, abortion, criminal trials, racism, and so on, are just a minor blip in the actual causes of western civilizations' citizens' deaths. U.S. government statistics state that 89 people a day (32,485 a year) die in auto accidents and 30,470 die in gun related deaths a year. An article titled "Terrorist attacks soar, deaths down from 2007 peak: study" by Peter Apps on December 4, 2012 states *"Iraqis account for one third of terrorism deaths"*, which in 2011 was 4,564 terrorist incidents globally resulting in 7,473 deaths. (See: http://www.reuters.com/article/2012/12/04/us-security-attacks-idUSBRE8B306M20121204)

These truths become even more staggering as we take in the fact that in the 2010 U.S. National Vital Statistics Report states that 25,692 persons died of alcohol-induced and 40,393 of drug-induced causes. (See: http://www.cdc.gov/nchs/data/nvsr/nvsr61/nvsr61_04.pdf)

According to http://millionhearts.hhs.gov/abouthds/cost-consequences.html "About Heart Disease & Stroke," it says that *"Americans suffer 1.5 million heart attacks and strokes each year. Cardiovascular disease—including heart disease and stroke—is the leading cause of death in the United States. Every day, 2,200 people die from cardiovascular diseases—that's nearly 800,000*

Americans each year, or 1 in every 3 deaths. Together, heart disease and stroke are among the most widespread and costly health problems facing the nation today, accounting for more than $312.6 billion* in health care expenditures and lost productivity annually—and these costs are rising." This disease is certainly not gender specific, as the number above includes 460,000 women who are also dying from heart disease and stroke. Even a risky profession such as firefighting is not immune, as heart disease is the number one killer of fire fighters, who exercise regularly, which many of us do not. Looking at the statistic on firefighters, we have to arrive at the conclusion that there is some other underlying cause to their premature deaths. Over 500,000 Americans a year succumb to heart by-pass surgery costing $100,000 each, profiting the health industry immensely. These operations alone constitute nearly $50 billion in medical expenditures a year. Heart disease is the number one cause of death in the U.S.! In another article at Medical News Today, published 16 June 2013 titled "Too Much Sugar Can Cause Heart Failure," it states *"Researchers at the University of Texas Health Science Center at Houston (UTHealth), have revealed that consuming too much sugar can greatly increase the risk of heart failure.*

In fact, a previous study conducted by researchers at Emory University School of Medicine and the US Centers for Disease Control and Prevention (CDC), found that people who consume high levels of added sugar, such as in processed foods and beverages are much more likely to have higher heart disease risk factors." This article says that according to the Centers for Disease Control, *"more than 5 million people suffer from heart failure in the U.S. each year. Approximately half of people diagnosed with the condition die within a year of diagnosis and there are over half a million new cases of heart failure in the country every year."* Now we have tied together cause and effect, so why is it we are allowing the travesty to happen? (See: http://www.medicalnewstoday.com/articles/262014.php)

Another problem growing out of this corporate, processed food diet is that one out of three Americans will develop problems with diabetes. Diabetes is now number three on the cause of death scale behind malignant neoplasms (cancer). From http://www.diabetes.niddk.nih.gov/dm/pubs/statistics, *"Diabetes affects 25.8 million people of all ages, which is 8.3 percent of the U.S. population.*

- *Diabetes was the seventh leading cause of death based on U.S. death certificates in 2007. This ranking is based on the 71,382 death certificates in 2007 in which diabetes was the underlying cause of death. Diabetes was a contributing cause of death in an additional 160,022 death certificates for a total of 231,404 certificates in 2007 in which diabetes appeared as any-listed cause of death.*
- *Diabetes is likely to be underreported as a cause of death. Studies have found that about 35 to 40 percent of decedents with diabetes had it listed anywhere on the death certificate and about 10 to 15 percent had it listed as the underlying cause of death.*
- *Overall, the risk for death among people with diabetes is about twice that of people of similar age but without diabetes.*
- *Total direct and indirect costs of diabetes in 2007 were $174 billion."*
-

And from other sources:

- If trends continue, by 2020, half of all Americans will have diabetes or pre-diabetes. [4]
- The average American man's waist size was 32" in 1985, that is now 38".[4]

- 62% of Virginian's are at an unhealthy weight.[4]
-

To analyze this heart/cancer/diabetes/obesity epidemic, let's crunch some more statistics:

- The average burger, large fries and a medium soft drink have 1,300 calories.[4]
- 1 pound of fat = 3,500 calories = 14 miles of walking.[4]
- The average American sees 7,000 processed food commercials a year.[4]

Many of the numbers below were taken from the enlightening documentary "Forks over Knives" who got their numbers from other sources. I highly encourage you to view this and other documentaries that I used in my research, such as "Farmageddon, Food Matters, Food Fight, Food Incorporated, Frankensteer, Vegucated" and more. All of which are available on Netflix and other streaming video sources via the Internet. (See: http://www.organicauthority.com/foodie-buzz/17-must-see-food-documentaries.html)

- Prostate cancer is the most common form of cancer in American men, with 215,000 new cases a year.
- Parkinson's disease affects 1 million Americans today.
- About ½ of Americans are taking some form of prescription drug, with Lipitor being the most commonly prescribed drug in the world.
- 1 in 5 American four-year-olds are considered obese. These children are being set up to die young, and their parents are letting it happen.
- Every minute a person in the U.S. dies from a coronary event.
- 1,500 Americans die every day from cancer.
- In 2008, 4 out of 10 leading killers in the U.S. were food-related chronic diseases. That number is increasing rapidly.
- Americans spend $2.2 trillion a year on health care, five times more than on the U.S. defense budget, which a U.S. citizen so proudly keep funded and has been substantially reduced to fund their mismanagement of these programs.
- Americans spend more per person on health care than any other industrialized nation in the world.

WARNING 	While we have to commend these documentaries for giving us valuable information about our food supply, they are rapidly becoming illegal in the U.S. as state after state is passing laws to protect their agriculture industries so that they can poison U.S. citizens and inhumanely treat livestock with impunity. These laws make it illegal to photograph or film at a farm and distribute that content for public consumption if it shows inhumane treatment of animals. Laws have been or are currently being passed in Tennessee, Indiana, Iowa, Missouri, Utah and Wyoming that will make it nearly impossible to bring these types of animal abuses to light.

For example, in Tennessee and Wyoming undercover animal rights activists brought grotesque animal abuses to light using undercover video that showed horrors such as hens caged alongside rotting bird corpses, workers burning the ankles of walking horses with chemicals, and employees punching and kicking pigs and flinging piglets into the air. (See: http://www.nytimes.com/2013/04/07/us/taping-of-farm-cruelty-is-becoming-the-crime.html?pagewanted%253Dall&_r=0) These serious types of stories are rapidly being squelched in the U.S. in favor of their entertainment media.

In studying these statistics and facts, it quickly becomes obvious that the cause of most misery is likely the western, processed, corporate food diet, which is designed to make their citizens sick, and also to complete the circle; their multi-billion dollar pharmaceutical companies who are profiting by selling drugs and pills to control the problems caused by the huge western, corporate food conglomerates. These food conglomerates put things like MSG, chemicals, pesticides, HFCS, various sugars and other alcohol sugars into their citizens' food supply.

The number of U.S. citizens potentially dying from the processed food that for-profit industries are feeding them is a staggering **1,137,404** deaths, or more, each year! So when we compare that number to a combined death total of 95,928 each year resulting from *U.S. car accidents, gun related deaths, drug abuse and total global terrorist activity*, where do you think your government and media priorities should be focused? As we can see from these numbers, western civilization should not give up its privacy because of drugs, alcohol or fear of a few horrific, but isolated, incidents. Using those crimes as an excuse to conduct mass spying and incarceration is being accepted and is taking place as governments and media portray this as necessary for their citizens' security. As stated previously, my hope in writing this book is to bring about a Digital Fourth Amendment to the U.S. Constitution, protecting everyone from these invasions into their lives.

Ask yourself where the public's interest is best looked after -- an out of control U.S. government spending billions to spy on their own citizens and who allow corporations to poison their citizens food supply, or an investment into an agricultural shift back to organic plant-based foods that do not use chemicals or pesticides that kill their citizens by the millions. This effort would require educating farmers on known methods to naturally grow foods in known ways that don't require the use of known corporate poisons and a campaign to re-educate the populous away from animal-based grain fed foods. Bear in mind that the results from a minimal effort by governments to educate their farmers in a healthier food supply could possibly result in an astronomical loss of human suffering and lower the cost of medical care by billions of dollars. I hope my statistics above prove that as I now have another story for you.

Story My wife and I go on golf trips up North in Michigan. On one such trip we ate with a couple that enjoyed the trip with us. The boyfriend of the woman with us ordered a large steak and ate not only the lean mean but also the fat and gristle attached to the steak. I had never seen such a thing except in the movie "The Great Outdoors" with John Candy, who is now dead. Needless to say the boyfriend no longer plays golf and suffers from a variety of ailments, including **heart disease**. This is his God-given right, but wow.

We also have to consider the focus and immense expense of U.S. law enforcement and the budgets of the various western and U.S. government agencies. In Chapter 11 on Identity Theft we will briefly touch on those agencies' various budgets and when you compare the proposed 2014 $295.8 million FDA budget to those numbers, we will see how madly out of proportion (many billions versus millions) U.S. spending is on what the real threats truly are that U.S. citizens actually face. How many of the 2.2 million people incarcerated in the U.S. are sitting in jail for killing 95,928 of its citizens, which accounts for only 4.36% of the total American deaths each year? How many of those 2.2 million people are in jail for causing the other 1,137,404 deaths that die from their corporate processed food diet and pharmaceuticals? Why aren't these corporate criminals brought to trial for the mass suffering that they have induced from pushing their toxic products on the U.S. populous by using enticing advertisements, and where is the outrage that should see them being brought to trial and justice?

It should come as no big surprise that the misinformed and propagandized western civilization people are unknowingly fueling this profitable system because their bought-and-paid for elected representatives (politicians) are turning a blind eye to this nightmare. These food conglomerates and massive pharmaceutical companies make huge contributions to the political campaigns of politicians so that they will be friendly to their corporate agendas. I write about this because this situation is very similar in how politicians are not addressing the invasion into their constituent's privacy by large companies who are exploiting our use of the Internet by playing on people's fear. This book is about cyber security and not your general diet and health, but I hope you see how these examples help emphasize how little governments and corporations care about your food supply and/or Internet privacy and are sanctioning the exploitation of the data that you reveal about yourself daily. These two issues are **systemically related** and are symptoms of broader fundamental problems, which is what we now miss in a politician's "public service". The information that you are revealing about yourself is akin to currency to governments and corporations who keep pushing the envelope for you to reveal more and more about yourself. This constant gathering of information through your use of the Internet is a privacy issue that is not being addressed by western media or our governments. The fact is that almost everyone, with and without your knowledge, is gathering information about you.

Additionally, anyone that spends large amounts of time working behind a computer is susceptible to following a processed food diet to save time so that they can keep up with their overburdened computer IT workload. To exemplify these facts let's examine the exploitation that is taking place by looking at the facts below that describe how deceptive the food labeling practices have become in the U.S.:

- The word **"Organic"** on food labeling is worth buying at the added expense. The USDA organic label on poultry means that chickens are grown without antibiotics, had access to the outdoors, and are not genetically modified, irradiated or cloned. However, it does not mean they were humanely raised, as they could be housed in a three-foot area, or have their beaks broken off without anesthesia. For other products, the USDA organic label means that 95% or more of the ingredients must have been grown or processed without synthetic fertilizers or pesticides (among other standards). A label stating "made with organic ingredients" must have a minimum of 70% all ingredients that meet the standard.
- Look for the "Animal Welfare Approved" (AWA) logo on the packaging. AWA certifies farms that raise their animal humanely, outdoors on pasture or range. AWA standards are the most rigorous and progressive animal care requirements in the nation. If you

want good chicken look for both Organic and AWA on the label. (See: http://www.animalwelfareapproved.org).

- Look for the words **"Grass fed (USDA)"** on the packaging. This label means the animals were raised on a lifetime diet of 100% grass and forage, including legumes and cereal grain crops. The USDA label means that the U.S. Department of Agriculture verified this claim. (See: http://www.greenerchoices.org/eco-labels/label.cfm?LabelID=303).
- The word **"Natural"** or **"All Natural"** on a food label means nothing. These products may contain preservatives, be injected with sodium, have additives, be reconstituted and have HFCS, and can still be labeled all natural by the food industry. The FDA has not developed a definition for the use of the term natural or its derivatives. For example, the term natural could be put on a bag of sugar.
- The phrase **"Made With Whole Grains"**, **"Whole Grain"** or **"Multigrain"** means that there are trace amounts of whole grains and that the product most likely has large amounts of refined corn flower, which has a high glycemic index and isn't healthy. If the ingredients list **"Enriched Wheat Flour"** comes before **"Whole Wheat Flour"** there is not much whole grain in the product. Look for products that say 100% whole grain or 100% whole wheat in the ingredients.
- The FDA allows the phrases **"Free-Range"**, **"Cage-Free"** or **"Free-Roaming"** labels on a poultry, eggs or meat product if the animals had open-air access for a minimum of five minutes per day. These terms do not mean that the animals ever scampered around outside. There are also no requirements for what they are fed or their possible exposure to chemicals. These products can be no healthier that non-free-range foods.
- The phrase **"A Good Source of Fiber"** means that a packaged food contains a fiber additive, which is not as beneficial as the fiber found in organic foods. Products such as ice creams, yogurts, and juices boast about their fiber content even though it is gained from isolated fibers. The isolated fibers are derived from purified powders such as inulin, polydextrose, and maltodextrin that do not have the same health benefits as traditional intact fibers found in whole grains, beans, vegetables and fruits.

 From Leah Zerbe's article titled, "11 Reasons to Ditch Processed Foods" Saturday, March 23, 2013 at http://www.rodale.com/processed-foods, "*The Facts: Processed foods—even pickles, cake mixes, and "healthy" juices—often contain food dyes that make food appear fresher than they really are, in essence, tricking you, the consumer. Some berry juices contain 0 percent fruit juice, relying solely on artificial coloring. The problem? Some food dyes are tied to serious health problems like ADHD, asthma, allergies, and cancer. Stick with organic foods, since organic standards ban the use of artificial food dyes, so organics are colored with food sources like turmeric and beets.*"

- The phrase **"Made with Real Fruit"** means that there is a miniscule amount of fruit in the product that may not even be the same fruit that's advertised on the product. Even worse, these products may contain dye to make it look more like the fruit on packaging. The "real fruit" quantities in food products are not regulated by the FDA.

- The terms **"Lightly Sweetened"** or **"Low Sugar"** means that the product can have anywhere from 1-100 grams - or more - of sugar. The terms "lightly sweetened" and "low sugar" are not regulated by the FDA. An example is Kellogg's Frosted Mini-Wheat's that, despite being "lightly sweetened," actually contains 20% sugar by weight (12g per serving). The phrases **"No added sugar"**, **"Sugar Free"** and **"reduced"** are regulated by the FDA and may lead you to foods that will help cut your carb and calorie count. However, some of these products contain the highly processed additive maltodextrin, which is a carbohydrate that sweetens the product. Also, look out for sugar alcohols such as erythritol, Glycerol (also known as glycerin of glycerine), hydrogenated starch hydrolysates, isomalt, lactitol, maltitol, mannitol, sorbitol, or xylitol, which are used to sweeten "diet" food. The sugar alcohols' chemical makeup varies slightly from sucrose and differs in how the human body absorbs them. In small amounts they are not harmful to the human body. However, in larger amounts sugar alcohols can have a laxative effect, cause gastric symptoms, bloating, diarrhea, and weight gain, especially in children.
- Statements such as **"helps maintain a healthy heart"** or **"supports the immune system"** are NOT FDA approved and do not have any scientific basis. Instead, look for the FDA approved statements **"may help reduce the risk of heart disease"** or **"may reduce the risk of cancer"**.
- Food packaged with the phrase **"Zero trans-fat"** can actually contain up to 0.5 grams per serving. If the food product lists saturated fats or added sugars in the first five ingredients, or has any partially hydrogenated oils, don't buy it. If the ingredient list has hydrogenated oils or shortening, this means the product contains trans-fat even though the packaging may say zero trans-fat.
- The declaration **"omega-3"** on the packaging of a processed product can mean very little. Companies will sprinkle a little flax on their food products and then slap "omega-3" on the packaging. If you want omega-3, stick to fish and seaweed products. Foods rich in omega-3 fatty acids, such as organic eggs, wild-caught Alaskan salmon, and walnuts, help hydrate your skin, thus reducing wrinkles. If you buy a fish oil supplement, look for the amount of EPA and DHA in the product. Organic Tomatoes can help fight damaging sunburns, reduce skin roughness, and boost collagen.
- Ingredients such as **"autolyzed yeast extract"** or **"free glutamic acid"** means that the product is chemically enhanced with MSG in what could be a highly concentrated form, which will function as a neurotoxin.
- Store shelves offer us a variety of milk choices. Two percent milk sounds like a good thing, but what most people don't realize is that whole milk only contains 3.25% milk fat. The term **"low-fat"** or **"fat free"** when used on processed or organic products means that they have been stripped of conjugated linoleic acid (CLA), which is a healthy fat shown to fight weight gain and cancer. It also usually means that sugar or HFCS has been added to the product, which we have discussed. Grass fed, organic animal meat can contain up to 300 to 500 percent more CLA than animals fed a 50% hay and a silage, 50% grain diet. So enjoy your fatty, organic yogurt, whole milk, and non-lean hamburgers, and feel good about it!
- Nearly all soda or diet soda products should be avoided as they either have HFCS or Aspartame in them. HFCS is sugar on speed and can lead to cancer, will fatten you up, and eventually destroy your health. Aspartame will kill brain cells, eventually make you

stupid and may give you Alzheimer's disease. My family no longer purchases or consumes these products.

- Avoid food products with dyes and/or artificial coloring. These synthetic ingredients remain on the FDA's approved list even though some are banned in other countries. The food dyes include Blue No. 1, Blue No. 2, Green No. 3, Red No. 3, Red No. 40, Yellow No. 5 and Yellow No. 6. Yellow No. 5 and Yellow No. 6 are banned in the UK which forced Kraft to switch to using paprika and beta carotene in products such as their mac and cheese. In November 2013, Kraft also changed the recipe on some of their mac and cheese products after hundreds of thousands of concerned parents petitioned the company to produce healthier products. Other products that you would never suspect, such as over the counter drugs, also have these dyes. For example, Nyquil Cold & Flu has Yellow 10, Green 3, and HFCS; Dayquil Mucus Control has Yellow 10, Yellow 6 and HFCS.
- Be careful of products that contain caffeine. The FDA does not require food producers to disclose the amount of caffeine that is in their products. For example, a single serving of Dannon Coffee Yogurt contains 30mg of caffeine, 5 squares of Hershey's Special Dark Chocolate contains 31mg and energy drinks can contain anywhere from 160 to 280mg. This much intake of caffeine is reaching unhealthy levels.

You can make a difference in not only the diet of the people you love, but also by voting with your dollar to stand up against the processed food conglomerates. Don't underestimate the value of every dollar you spend. Every dollar you spend on organic foods (preferably plant-based foods) changes the food industry. Our consumer choices are our only way to get involved in changing the world we live in. We all have to take responsibility, demand the truth and learn about how corporations are poisoning our bodies and destroying so many lives. Don't get me wrong, when and where a company offers a healthy food product, I will support and purchase it. However, as I research and find out more about these processed empty calories that are destroying so many lives; I will write about this topic and stand against this destruction of our food supply!

Story 	When I drove 10 hours to visit my parents, I discovered their house full of unhealthy corporate processed food. My mom complained as I went grocery shopping at the local organic food stores to bring whole grain cereals and bread, organic vegetables and produce, organic chicken and beef for them (not me), alternatives to HFCS soda (pop), and basically, stock up for my stay with them. However, to my wonderment, I discovered the food that I purchased was disappearing, and their diets changing, albeit temporarily, with little complaint to eating this healthier diet. Your purchasing habits and the food you have readily available in the house can make a difference! I have also visited many friends' houses that put me up for a day or two and saw their diets. There were very little fresh vegetables or fruits and hordes of easy-to-fix processed foods in their diets.

As our processed food diet causes medical problems our big pharmaceutical drug companies clean up on the other side of the equation.

Consumer + processed food (profiting food conglomerates) = illness + drugs controlling medical conditions (profiting pharmaceutical drug companies).

Quotation	"*The government isn't your nanny. They're your dealer and they are subsidizing illness to line their pockets because they have to. To do otherwise is political suicide especially after the supreme court ruling that anyone can fund political campaigns in the United States anonymously and unlimitedly. There's too much money vested in the destruction of your health to stop this juggernaut. You see, there's no money in healthy people and there's no money in dead people. The money is in the middle, people who are alive (sort of) but with one or more chronic conditions that puts them in need of Celebrex, Nasalnex, Valtrex, or Lunesta. Fifty years ago, children didn't even get Type-2 diabetes. Now it's an emerging epidemic, as are a long list of ailments that used to be rare, and have now been...mainstreamed. Things like asthma, and autism, and acid reflux, and arthritis, allergies, adult acne, attention deficit disorder. And that's just the A's. Doesn't anybody wonder why we live with all this illness?*" (See: https://en.wikiquote.org/wiki/Real_Time_With_Bill_Maher)
 Bill Maher Sep 28, 2007	

According to the documentary, "Food Matters," 106,000 U.S. citizens die each year from adverse reactions to the pharmaceutical drugs that they are taking. Government data shows that drug overdoses has overtaken automobile crashes as the leading cause of accidental death in the United States. Most of the drug deaths, nearly three out of four, can be ascribed to overdoses involving prescription painkillers. Data from the National Institute on Drug Abuse (NIDA) shows that overdoses from perfectly legal drugs have tripled since 1990. The April 10, 2014 article titled "4 Shocking Facts About Prescription Drug Abuse in America" by Beth Buczynski reveals the following:

1. In the United States, drug overdose was the leading cause of injury death in 2010. Amongst people aged between 25 and 64 years old, drug overdose caused more deaths than motor vehicle traffic crashes. Perhaps most shocking is how quickly drug abuse is escalating among people in their fifties. "This is, at least in part, due to the aging of the baby boomers, whose rates of illicit drug use have historically been higher than those of previous cohorts," explains NIDA. But seniors aren't the only ones experimenting with prescription drugs. Every day in the United States, an average of 2,000 teenagers use prescription drugs without a doctor's guidance for the first time.

2. Almost any prescription drug can be abused, but these two are the big killers: Opioids and benzodiazepines. Opioids are psychoactive chemicals that resemble morphine or other opiates in its pharmacological effects, and are most commonly found in pain killers. Benzodiazepines have sedative, hypnotic (sleep-inducing), anxiolytic (anti-anxiety), euphoric, anticonvulsant, and muscle relaxant properties. Where are Americans getting these fatal drugs? Not from pharmacy thefts or black market drug dealers, but from doctors who look forward to the repeat business an addict provides. "Opioids are more readily being prescribed in the past decade than ever previously before by doctors to patients, often without consideration of the severity of their condition, their state of mental health, and alternative medications and options," reports Tufts University. The same thing holds true for Benzodiazepines.

3. Rampant prescription drug abuse is costing us big: "In the United States, prescription opioid abuse costs [alone] were about $55.7 billion in 2007. Of this amount, 46% was attributable to workplace costs (e.g., lost productivity), 45% to healthcare costs (e.g., abuse treatment), and 9% to criminal justice costs," reports the CDC.

4. Certain demographic groups are more inclined to the abuse of medical substances (and not the ones you think): Among those who died from drug overdose in 2010, men were nearly twice as likely as women to die; American Indians/Alaska Natives had the highest death rate, followed by whites and then blacks. The highest death rates were among people 45-49 years of age. Geography and socioeconomic status also play a role in risk, as the southwestern United States and the Appalachian regions have seen the greatest impact from prescription drug use, particularly in West Virginia and New Mexico.

The only time these prescription drug overdoses come to the attention of western entertainment media is when a famous celebrity dies. When there is coverage it about who was at fault and the parties involved in the tragedy. Rarely will the coverage talk about the overall problem of how they are killing thousands and you certainly will not hear how they compare to illegal drugs. After making these points, the article sums up what we all should be wondering, *"With all of this addiction, injury and death directly linked to the over-prescription of "medicines" you'd think the War on Drugs would include pharmaceutical companies, doctors and the health insurance industry. But it doesn't. Instead, the U.S. government forks over huge subsidies to these companies, who then price-gouge customers until their drugs go generic—then incentivize doctors to over-prescribe so they can continue to rake in the profits."*

Factoid	Johnson and Johnson were fined two billion dollars for their marketing of the schizophrenia drugs Risperdal and Invega, and the heart failure drug Natrecor for unapproved uses. J&J also paid "kickbacks" to doctors and nursing homes to recommend and use these drugs as treatment options on elderly dementia patients, for which they were not approved. The truth is that patients on the drug Risperdal were at increased risk for developing diabetes. While this seems to be a HUGE fine, it is a drop in the bucket for large corporations such as J&J, or for BP after they destroyed the Gulf. I found no evidence that any BP or J&J corporate executive ever served a day in jail for the deaths and misery caused by their criminal activities. In contrast, imagine the sentence if any of them had been busted for possession or use of an illicit drug such as one gram of methamphetamine, which would hurt no one but themselves?

Despite the evidence of the mayhem that prescription drugs are causing, the U.S. has been conducting a War on Drugs it deems illegal for numerous years thus costing their taxpayers many billions of dollars, incarcerating millions and bankrupting many of their citizens. These offenders are charged exorbitant fees and fines, which many of them cannot pay thereby landing them in jail for other sentences that have nothing to do with their original crime. The Obama administration requested $25.6 billion in 2013 to spend on the drug war. All of that money left the drug addiction rates unchanged and supported the keeping of 2.2 million Americans in prison or jail--a 500% increase over the past thirty years--the highest incarceration rate in the world according to Sentencing Project. The Bureau of Justice Statistics says that about half of those prisoners are incarcerated for drug crimes, 50 percent of whom are African American making this one the most racist government funded programs on earth. (See: http://www.drugabuse.gov/publications/drugfacts/nationwide-trends, http://www.cdc.gov/homeandrecreationalsafety/rxbrief, http://www.care2.com/causes/4-shocking-facts-about-prescription-drug-abuse-in-america.html#ixzz332MasZVD, https://secure.huffingtonpost.com/2013/04/08/drug-war-mass-incarceration_n_3034310.html, http://www.sentencingproject.org/template/page.cfm?id=107)

From this and the numbers estimated above, we have to contemplate the number of deaths caused by what is reported on most often by the western media and debated on constantly by western governments and their media. Who are the real criminal in this capitalist, for profit nightmare?

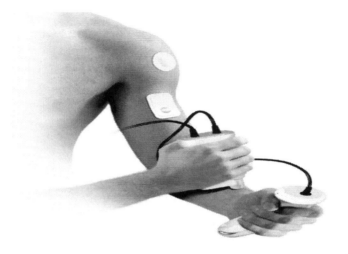

Hardening your Wired and Wireless Network

Chapter 2 -- Hardening your Network--Implementing Wireless Security Settings--Getting the Best Network and Internet Performance--Configuring Your Router to Support Your Mobile Devices

Nothing is more important in your home computer security than establishing a secure home base of operations. Having served in the armed forces for 11 years, fortifying your rear is paramount before beginning forward operations (*in our case, surfing and using an infected Internet*). Let's first study how the largest, and best equipped military force in the history of the world was defeated by not securing their rear operations and providing for resupply. The German Sixth Army was engineered to be the ultimate fighting machine. It succeeded in killing millions and achieving destruction on a massive scale, but was ultimately defeated by not securing their supply lines and rear defenses.

	Historical Reference -- Battle of Stalingrad in World War II -- arguably the bloodiest battle in human history with 1.5 million causalities, a staggering number

Probably the greatest example in human history of not having a secure home base or operations comes from the Battle of Stalingrad in WWII. The Germans rapidly advanced deep into Soviet territory before the Soviets forces counter-attacked in December 1941 and stopped the German drive toward their capital. Hitler insisted to his generals that there would be no need for winter gear. Surely the Sixth Army would take Moscow before winter set in. Not only did the Army not make it to Moscow in time, but Hitler's Generals were forced to stop the invasion due to the cold, which allowed the Soviet army to regroup and resupply itself. (See: http://www.newworldencyclopedia.org/entry/Battle_of_Stalingrad)

The Germans advanced without ensuring their supply lines were manageable, and were tired and ill equipped for winter warfare. The Germans waited till spring when the winter weather would no longer impede their mobility. Rather than perform a predictable advance on the Soviet capital, the Germans turned and moved on Stalingrad at Hitler's direction. Stalingrad was a huge industrial center for the Red Army, so this shift in tactics was an understandable and intelligent decision. Had Stalingrad fallen it would have severely weakened the Soviets.

Maybe evil attracts evil or dictators hate other dictators but Hitler's inflated ego was obsessed with defeating Stalin and taking the Stalingrad city, which was named after him. Against all sound advice, Hitler would not allow the Sixth Army to withdraw and ordered them to continue to fight and take the city at any cost. The rubble in the city impeded the German's use of their advanced mobility technology and there was close urban warfare benefiting the Soviets. Hitler remained so focused on the city that he denied all requests made by the German, Italian, Hungarian, and Romanian armies to withdraw and refocus their assets as they struggled to protect the Sixth Army's flanks. As a result, the Soviets were able to devise a strategy to exploit the known weak flanks and they surrounded the Germans. Hitler was delusional in believing his Luftwaffe air force could keep the massive army supplied under wartime conditions. To understand the scope of this decision, the Sixth Army was the largest unit of tanks, infantry, engineers, artillery, and ground-attack aircraft that has ever existed in the history or our world. Properly commanded, that military force should have been unstoppable by any force on earth. History now views the United States as a diminishing super power, but at that time in history the German Sixth Army's technology far advanced anything the world had ever seen. Had Hitler unleashed it on Europe the outcome of the war could have been far different. Britain may have fallen, which would have altered the outcome of World War II.

The Germans were not able to ensure their supply lines due to the bad weather and relentless Soviet attacks in close quarters on their immobile forces. The German commanders knew they needed to set up and keep a secure rear base of operations and withdraw. They repeatedly asked commanders for permission to withdraw, but luckily Hitler rejected their requests. The western world might not exist had Hitler listened to his generals' requests. Let us hope that our military leaders and NCOs in the field never succumb to this type of thinking and do the right thing in the face of wrong political decisions. Hitler's refusal to give up on Stalingrad resulted in a huge toll in German casualties. At the end of the campaign, 91,000 starving, exhausted, and ill Germans in the Sixth Army surrendered to the Red Army in early March 1943. Of the 91,000 only 6,000 survived captivity and returned home. Atrocities on both sides were horrendous throughout these battles and during the entire war. In addition, the eventual decimation of the Sixth Army allowed time for the Allies to start coordinating their invasion of France, which happened much later in the war during June 1944.

In computing technology this means your SBO/HCU network that operates behind Internet enemy lines has to be as secure as possible with today's rapidly changing technology. According to PCWorld, January 2013, "Malware Attacks Target Home Networks" article by John P. Mello Jr. "*Some 13 percent of home networks in North America are infected with malware, half of them with "serious" threats, according to cyber security firm Kindsight Security Labs in its third-quarter malware report.*" The article goes on to point out that these threats "*could turn a home computer into a spam-spewing zombie on a botnet or compromise a computer owner's back account.*" This chapter is about setting up and using your SBO/HCU network to protect your computers and other mobile devices (laptop, smartphone, etc.) anywhere in the world. If you have not secured your home base, then it, and the rest of your vulnerable devices, will be at risk of exploitation from predators that rely, primarily, on your taking too little precaution to protect yourself. In case some of the information in this chapter seems to go over your head, I have included links to articles that will help make things clearer regarding the threats you face.

Buying a router and not configuring it properly is akin to leaving the front door to your house wide open in a bad neighborhood. Unlike your dishwasher or microwave, your SBO/HCU network-router is going to require a few hours of your valuable time to set up securely. If you don't have that kind of time, you need to hire someone to set it up for you, but the goal here is to make this a project you feel comfortable doing yourself. Of course, there are some sections of this chapter that you may not need to address and that you can skip without risking your security. For example, if you don't stream video, skip the section on streaming, or if you don't have or want a home server that you need to use remotely, skip that setup also.

If you have a computer directly hooked up to a home DSL or Cable Modem then you *must* reconsider your network setup. Connecting a computer directly to the Internet is akin to inviting crackers and spies everywhere to watch your every keystroke unless you have correctly configured a software firewall. Windows 7 and Linux come with excellent software firewalls which we will learn about later. You are also deceiving yourself if, by relying on your antivirus software and anti-spyware applications, you believe you have protected your computers. They do a decent job at *reactive* protection with signature files that identify malware, but you cannot solely rely on them. In the introduction we briefly discussed heuristic detection, which is also being used. Antivirus and Antispyware should be viewed as your last line of defense. In the military we call this *final protective fire* https://en.wikipedia.org/wiki/Final_protective_fire. You have massed all your forces on the front line, and when that line is breached, your defensive position has been over-run.

WARNING	Connecting any mobile device directly to the Internet using a modem or Internet Service Provider (ISP) allows crackers access to your devices with no protection except your device's software limited firewall. There are numerous known and unknown methods that crackers can then use to try and find holes to exploit your OS security. The bad guys are constantly coming up with new and creative ways to attack your Internet equipment, and anti-software is playing catch-up.

In computer terms, this means the enemy (the cracker) has already breached every defense you have set up to keep them from overrunning your home network or computer, and you are now in a defensive position, trying to undo damage, rather than preventing it in the first place. This book is about computing and security, and I believe that the following two historic examples illustrate how important a secure home base is to support forward operations. They also show how defensive fortifications have been easily breached, time and time again, throughout history, by advancing technology. In order to secure your home computers you must be proactive and set up multiple lines of defense and adopt new technology as security holes are found. Don't wait until the enemy has a malicious hold on your computer and you are trying various means of eradicating the problem. This will waste many valuable hours, not to mention the damage done stealing your data, your account information, and possibly your identity.

Historical Examples of Advancing Technology Overwhelming Defenses

Bear in mind that trusting anti-anything software is reactionary for the most part. That means threats exist on the Internet for who knows how long before they are discovered and acted upon by software vendors and security companies. The latest website you visited, that 1 in 100 Google link you clicked on, or that email attachment or link from a trusted relative or friend you just clicked on installed some new malicious and (as yet) undiscovered software on your computer. Your Internet device is now cracked or slaved to some botnet (See: https://en.wikipedia.org/wiki/Botnet) or worse. Your one line of defense -- your anti-software -- has been breached by an as yet undiscovered threat. This book shows you how to prevent those threats. History is littered with instances of defensive fortifications breached by more effective advanced offensive weapons.

	Historical Reference – The French Maginot Line that France thought would stop the German advance
Just as the Battle of Stalingrad demonstrates how not securing your home base of operations is reckless, the building of the French Maginot Line shows us how important multiple lines of	

defense is to harden our security. Before WWII, the French built one massive line of defense measures that would have decimated any force attacking in a known frontal style WWI form. It was the ultimate example of generals fighting a pervious war which ignored the advances in technology being made. Mobile warfare was ignored in their fundamental doctrine. This repeated a mistake that allied commanders made during WWI, when both warring sides sent many hundreds of thousands of men to their deaths, charging fixed, well-armed machine gun and artillery fortifications. The expense of the Maginot Line kept investment in French armor and aircraft underfunded, so they did not have multiple lines of defense.

At the same time, Germany researched and made massive investments in the development or rapid mobile warfare techniques. This strategy allowed them to fight and win battles in days, versus months, as was previously known at that time. German armies and armor were able to quickly overwhelm the countries they invaded. This mobility enabled their army to quickly bypass the French and other countries' fixed fortifications. It was a new form of warfare that took the allies years to adapt to. From https://en.wikipedia.org/wiki/Maginot_Line, "*The French established the fortification to provide time for their army to mobilize in the event of attack, allowing French forces to move into Belgium for a decisive confrontation with German forces. The success of static, defensive combat in World War I was a key influence on French thinking. Military experts extolled the Maginot Line as a work of genius, believing it would prevent any further invasions from the east (notably, from Germany). The fortification system successfully dissuaded a direct attack. It was strategically ineffective, as the Germans indeed invaded Belgium, defeated the French army, flanked the Maginot Line, through the Ardennes forest and via the Low Countries, completely sweeping by the line and conquering France in days.*" The French thought they had created the ultimate solution to German aggression from their experiences in World War I.

Your computer and network security must be viewed like warfare. Your anti-software is your French Maginot Line and is one line of defense. The Germans, and later Allied forces, simply bypassed these fixed, one-line defenses. This is very similar to relying on your anti-software for all your defenses. If computer defenses get bypassed you must have other lines of defense to rely upon. On the flip side, one of the greatest examples in recent history of setting up multiple lines of defense and having secure bases of operations comes from the Battle of the Chosin Reservoir during the Korean War.

 Historical Reference – How Marine Corps General Smith Established Secure Bases of Operations and saved many men who would have otherwise died.

One of the unsung, greatest American wartime heroes was Major General Oliver P. Smith of the 1st Marine Division. During my Marine Corps Basic Training, I was taught about the Battle of Chosin Reservoir that took place in Korea during the 1950's. At that time it was required study by every Marine, which still holds true today. This engagement was probably one of greatest examples in history of U.S. Marine courage, endurance, and perseverance against an enemy of superior strength in numbers, hardware and fire power. The 1st Marines furthered their fame at that battle when Col. Lewis "Chesty" Puller famously said, "We're surrounded. That simplifies things." These men suffered greatly as they were poorly equipped for battle and cold weather. They were sent into a fight that they could not win. I lay much of what these men suffered at the feet of Douglas MacArthur's ego as he arrogantly telegraphed the battle plan to the Chinese by describing to the media exactly what the Allied plans in Korea were. In his arrogance, he saw an easy victory over the North Koreans and did not care about secrecy. He did not expect the Chinese to join the conflict. All the Chinese had to do to know the Allied plan of attack was to read the newspapers. I studied the battle and was disturbed to learn that the Marines, fighting their way back to the ships that would be their salvation, were written off as lost by their higher command. Luckily, the ships were still waiting when the exhausted, frostbitten Marines finally reached the coast. Many of them lost their lives and limbs as a result of this stupidity. From https://en.wikipedia.org/wiki/Battle_of_Chosin_Reservoir, *"General Douglas MacArthur ordered the Eighth Army to launch the Home-by-Christmas Offensive. To support the offensive, MacArthur ordered the X Corps to attack west from the Chosin Reservoir and to cut the vital Manpojin— Kanggye—Huichon supply line. As a response, Major General Edward M. Almond, commander of the US X Corps, formulated a plan on 21 November. It called for the US 1st Marine Division to advance west through Yudami-ni, while the US 7th Infantry Division would provide a regimental combat team to protect the right flank at Sinhung-ni."* But Major General Smith thought that Almond's strategy was rash. *"Smith believed that there were large numbers of Chinese forces in North Korea despite the fact that higher headquarters in Tokyo had said otherwise, while Almond felt Smith was overly cautious. The mutual distrust between the two commanders made Smith slow the 1st Marine Division's advance towards the Chosin Reservoir against Almond's instructions. Along the way Smith established supply points and airfields at Hagaru-ri and Koto-ri."* In other words, Smith was wisely setting up secure home bases of operations and allowing for resupply. To be fair, history has a way of rewriting itself. General Almond defends his decisions admirably (See: http://chosinreservoir.com/almondcomments.htm) where he points out many flaws in General Smith's decision making process. General Almond goes on to point out that the 3rd division of the U.S. Army was in a flanking position and provided the support that allowed the Marines to withdraw.

Regardless of whose version of history we believe, the bases and air fields that were wisely set up allowed for the evacuation of thousands of wounded and the resupply of the Marines. This made their withdrawal faster and was a factor in the Marines' ability to fend off eight poorly outfitted, but superior, Chinese divisions. However, this delay allowed Smith's forces to become completely surrounded. A reporter asked Smith about the coming retreat and Smith is attributed with one of the greatest quotations of all time. From Wiki, *"Faced with tough fighting between the blocking Chinese divisions and the withdrawing Marines, Smith remarked: "Retreat, hell! We're not retreating; we're just advancing in a different direction.""*

In my examples in this book, these *crackers* are going after soft targets. Our goal is to become a hard target, thus thwarting these crackers' malicious intent *in most instances*. Just as a burglar will choose the house next door that does not have an alarm system, in war and in our use of the Internet, attackers tend to choose the least protected target. Germany overran poorly defended countries at the beginning of WWII, and then moved on to more difficult targets only after total war was declared. Like warfare, crackers will go after your neighbors' or other businesses' networks if your defenses are better than theirs. Wars are fought over resources, and if yours are freely available and easy to obtain, then you have lost without a fight. *Just as aggressor nations will attack and overrun the defenses of other nations who do not protect themselves, sometimes exterminating their populations, and exploiting their resources, the cracker has the same thoughts in mind about your computer.* **I encourage everyone using the infected Internet to understand that you are on a total war footing using it.**

Complete security is a myth on the battlefield and off. No functioning device connected to the infected Internet in any fashion is completely secure. In war (and using the Internet) we must constantly *harden* our defenses by using multiple defense techniques:

- layered approach (using independent layers of security, such as multiple security products and the security & anonymity techniques described in this book)
- defense in depth (in military terms, shoring them up employing the latest weapons or technology), *in computer terms, buying a router using the latest encryption techniques; using multiple anti-malware products; using virtualization; and adding tracking blocking security browser add-ons and extensions*
- element of surprise (doing the unanticipated or unexpected, like employing virtualization to hide our core OS from the enemy, and using anonymity software), or booting into an anonymity Live OS solution
- redundancy (this would be your multiple online, USB, and other backups in case your defenses were breached or a natural disaster occurred)
- surveillance and intelligence (in computer terms this means monitoring your log files, auditing trails of system activity, and disclosing of vulnerabilities closing security holes as quickly as possible)

Knowing all this, I will refrain from using the word *secure* and use the more appropriate term *harden* in the remainder of this book. Sometimes computer/military books and other sources mistakenly throw about the words secure and security as if they really exist. I will not to do so, for the reality is they *do not exist*. This truth became much more so than ever before with the advent of our now "infected Internet".

You must have a hardware firewall between you and all the unscrupulous, highly intelligent crackers. Russia and China alone have many crackers scratching against your home computer / firewall to break into your home computer setup and slave it to a botnet or steal your private information. There are numerous articles you can read on the Internet by just typing *Chinese or Russian Hacker* in the search engine of your choice. A few quick examples are one from http://www.businessweek.com/news/2011-10-27/chinese-military-suspected-in-hacker-attacks-on-u-s-satellites.html on how the Chinese Military tried to hack U.S. Satellites or at http://www.guardian.co.uk/technology/2011/oct/27/chinese-hacking-us-satellites-suspected. These articles abound with hours of reading for you to understand the threats you face. You need a modern router (hardware firewall) between you and the Internet. Also, given the amount of cracking taking place, be sure you vet the company from which you are purchasing the router.

Just purchasing a router and hooking it up does very little. If millions of people are trying to break into U.S. satellites, how many are trying to exploit the unsuspecting SBO/HCU? Hopefully, this chapter will help you secure your router. If you can't follow along or don't have the time, find a friend or relative to help you do it, or hire someone to set up your router properly to reap the possible security and performance benefits it offers.

No network broadcasting radio transmission is totally secure. You must meet military grade wireless security specifications and upgrade regularly. No device connected to the Internet is totally secure, and technology continuously advances.

Let's harden our home network against all the unscrupulous people out there! In my travels I have been to the houses of friends and family where their wireless networks were running with no security at all! As stated above, some people connect directly through their cable modem. I try to explain the implications of this and tell them how crazy that practice is, but the care factor is minimal in most cases. I hope my book will make them and you think otherwise.

A serious mistake I see people making is buying a new router and using the default settings. Just because the wireless router is new and shiny, does not mean that the default settings are secure. The default settings are becoming more secure as technology advances, but you need at least a basic understanding of these devices. Older routers came with the factory default settings that crackers could look up by downloading the various router manuals. Crackers know to try those default usernames (admin, cisco) and passwords like (admin, password, superuser, 18268440, cisco) and they can easily find them on the Internet. (See http://www.routeripaddress.com, http://routerpasswords.com)

There are only a few competing companies manufacturing routers so the factory assigned Service Set Identifier (SSID) and password combinations could be quickly tried on your wireless network. The routers of 2012 come with a uniquely generated SSID and password. You have to record them to connect your Internet devices to the Internet, so why not log in and quickly change those settings. Who knows if the algorithm created by your router manufacturer to generate SSIDs and passwords has been compromised in some fashion by an employee who was either disgruntled or wants to make a profit by providing this information to crackers? Or consider the possibility that perhaps an inquisitive foreign government has cracked that company's algorithm with the purchase of a little inside help for a corporate employee! Your router must be locked down (configured) with a few simple changes and a few hours of work so that it protects your network from intrusion.

Users also blunder by setting the router password to something easily guessed and letting it sit for the next 10 years. I was just recently on a vacation with a friend who is accessing his neighbor's wireless network because they set the password to something easily guessed-their first name. He asked if his family can use that network to use the Internet, and I explained of course they can, but that it is illegal. But they lived in the country so the odds of them being detected were miniscule. Wardriving (also known as drive by download) and work by law enforcement is usually concentrated in large metropolitan areas and not in the rural areas. (See: https://en.wikipedia.org/wiki/War_driving)

 WARNING Using a wireless router with the default settings or using old wireless network equipment is a giant BILLBOARD ADVERTISMENT to every criminal, porn-surfing neighbor, or terrorist out there to *please use my home network and hack into everything I do. And please conduct all your porn/criminal/terrorist activities using my home network. It will look to the authorities as if you are the guilty party.*

Criminals, robbers, and terrorists don't just watch what you are doing; they use your open or broken wireless encryption for access to the Internet to do all sorts of unsavory things. Uncle Sam is watching, too. Imagine your surprise if Homeland Security were to show up knocking on your door, asking about your home Internet activity. Imagine your unscrupulous neighbor watching with binoculars through his living room window as you are interrogated and cuffed while he is free to continue his illicit activities without detection. This is another example of the ways that your unsecured computer can disrupt your life and lead to dreadful and very real life consequences.

As an experiment, I enabled the SSID broadcast on my router and watched to see if anyone would attempt to connect to my home network. I got three attempted connections in less than one hour. I assume they tried the default SSID / Login / password, but, of course, I had changed that.

Once again, if you don't know how to setup your home router, READ THIS CHAPTER, find a friend or relative to help you do it, or pay someone. If you do not, plan to spend hours/days/weeks of your valuable time fixing problems those crackers and identity thieves will create for you.

For example, I was at the bank yesterday and a woman was there with her statements showing transactions on her checking account that she did not initiate. Of course, I can't know for sure why this was happening to the woman, but she was in a situation that people often find themselves in, after the fact, when someone has hacked her home network or bank account password. Don't be a victim--***seek help; upgrade and/or replace your computer router now***.

Historical Reference and Story – Left at the Breach to Guide Traffic, Secure the Rear, and Dehydrate

When a breach is blown, two engineers are sometimes left behind to guide upcoming traffic through the breach. It so happens that another Marine and I were the ones left behind after our unit blew a hole through some concertina wire, also known as razor wire, to guide upcoming units through the narrow breach that we had produced. Ahead of us, the rest of the division advanced on with the promise that someone would come back to pick us up in a few hours. One would think that we would have been left with extra supplies of food, water and possibly shelter, but on an exercise, and without an enemy shooting back, everyone always assumes that everything will go according to plan. However, after eight hours, and having run out of water hours earlier, we were worried. I tried to reach someone on the radio, but to no avail. The desert's 140 degree ground temperature had drained the radio batteries to a very low level, and the division had moved forward beyond our ability to reach them.

We had obviously been forgotten, or someone would have long since been sent back to retrieve us from the breach. The other Marine and I had both arrived at the same conclusion; the only chance that we had was to get someone on the radio to let them know the breach we were stranded upon, which would be marked on most maps that anyone we might talk to may have. Without water and shelter we might not survive the night and another day, so rather than continue draining the radio batteries in further futile attempts, we came up with a plan.

We debated if climbing a mountain of rocks to get the radio to a higher location would be worth the effort, being without water. We decided that it would, and I climbed that mountain of rocks with the heavy radio on my back to the highest point in the area and used the whip antenna that I had already attached, which is a single straight flexible rod designed to give a radio receiver or transmitter maximum range, to try to contact anyone who might receive the signal. So as the sun was setting, I climbed for what seemed like hours, sweating out what little water remained in my body. I realized this might be my final gambit for survival because I was getting dizzy from dehydration. I had to pause often to keep from taking a fatal tumble down the rocks. When I got to the top, I said a prayer, and then pressed the mike to try to contact my unit or anyone else who might be listening on my frequency: "Tango-Delta-Yankee-X-ray, this is Victor-Lima-Bravo-Whiskey over... Tango-Delta-Yankee-X-ray this is Victor-Lima-Bravo-Whiskey..." Finally there was a faint voice coming through the radio, "this is T-D-Y-B, where in the hell are you guys... over." I wanted to pinch myself and dance the jig. "We are at Checkpoint Charlie, right where you left us, over." They responded as if it were our fault that we had been left in the middle of desert, saying "well stay right there, we are sending a vehicle to pick you up... out." I remember thinking at the time, "where the hell would we go?" and then dreading the climb back down the rocks. One thing I did not mention previously is that rocks offer shelter to all sorts of unsavory desert wildlife, so I was expecting a snake or something else to jump out of the crevasses, nooks and crannies at any time when climbing up and then back down again.

Your Router and Network Wi-Fi Equipment May Be More Vulnerable than you Thought

I have been to many households that are using old wireless routers running Wired Equivalent Privacy encryption or are using no encryption at all. They have no idea how big the threat is to their network and Internet security. Crackers band together and post online the locations of networks that can be used/cracked around the country. There is even a term for this online called *Wardriving*. Wardriving is someone driving around with an Internet device with the intent of finding wireless networks to break into and/or use. Online sites provide GPS coordinates of wireless networks found during Wardriving. From https://en.wikipedia.org/wiki/Wardriving *"software for wardriving is freely available on the Internet, notably NetStumbler, InSSIDer or Ekahau Heat Mapper for Windows; Kismet or SWScanner for Linux. Once a network is cracked criminal, cracker, or even hackers for fun use these networks."*

WARNING 	If you are using an old router, especially a wireless router with only Wired Equivalent Privacy (<u>WEP</u>), or Temporal Key Integrity Protocol (<u>WPA-TKIP</u>), which is based on <u>WEP</u> encryption, it is time to buy a modern router. Wiki read on Temporal Key Integrity Protocol. *"TKIP uses the same underlying mechanism as WEP, and consequently is vulnerable to a number of attacks."* There are many sources that outline the ineffectiveness of WEP encryption. For example: From https://en.wikipedia.org/wiki/Wireless_security *"this type of encryption is now being considered outdated and seriously flawed."* In the CompTIA Security+ Certification Student Edition[15], *"While WEP might sound like a good solution at first, it ironically isn't as secure as it should be. The problem stems from the way WEP produces the keys that are used to encrypt the data. Because of a flaw in the*

method, attackers could easily generate their own keys by using a wireless network capture tool, such as AirSnort, to capture and as little as 10 MB of data transferred through the air." From http://www.onguardonline.gov/articles/0013-securing-your-wireless-network "Some older routers use only WEP encryption, which may not protect you from some common hacking programs. Consider buying a new router with WPA2 capability." **If WEP was cracked before 2006, imagine what the cracker tools of 2012 can do**. (See: https://en.wikipedia.org/wiki/Wired_Equivalent_Privacy, https://en.wikipedia.org/wiki/Temporal_Key_Integrity_Protocol, http://www.smallnetbuilder.com/wireless/wireless-howto/30114-wep-crackingreloaded?start=1, https://help.ubuntu.com/community/WifiDocs/WiFiHowTo)

Let's look at quick analysis of how to hack WEP encrypted network. This is not intended to be a step-by-step tutorial, but a quick look into the hackers world, to let you know how easy all this really is. It is important to note that if your computer has both a Network Interface Controller (NIC) card and provides for wireless access, each will have its own unique hardware address. Your NIC is the hardware that connects your computer to a network. The web link http://www.net.princeton.edu/enetAddress.howto.html provides a good read on how this all fits together. The first thing we need to determine is do we have correct hardware to start hacking. If we travel to http://www.aircrack-ng.org/doku.php?id=getting_started and look at the getting started manual, we have to examine the chipset of our wireless card to make sure it is compatible. We have to be able to get low-level control over our card's chipset. Some manufacturers are not very forthcoming with their driver documentation for proprietary reasons. This can make it difficult to determine the wireless chipset manufacturer. Understand that the card manufacturer and the chipset manufacturers are usually different. *The easiest method to determine your wireless card and MAC address is to open a command prompt (which we will cover later) and type* getmac /v. *Another method you can use to determine the card is to click on* **Start** > **Control Panel** > **Device Manager** > *arrow down to* **Network adapters** > *hopefully your card name is the same as its adapter (e.g. Intel(R) Wi-Fi Link 5100 AGN) > you can then search the Internet for your card*. For my card, finding the chipset was not easy. I thought that looking at the PDF product brief from Intel would give all the technical specs. But finally the website http://linux-wless.passys.nl/query_alles.php provided the answer.

Then examine Aircracks compatibility list of chipsets at http://www.aircrack-ng.org/doku.php?id=compatibility_drivers. If you determine your chipset is not compatible, the website lists Wireless cards with chipsets that are. Be sure you read the comments at the bottom before you give up on your card. The next step is to visit Aircracks website and start studying their documentation. We can then setup some Linux VMs for hacking practice.

| **Tip**  | In experimenting with all of this to write about it, the wireless MAC address and devices were not visible in my VMs. It was not until I visited http://aircrack-ng.org/doku.php?id=install_aircrack#installing_vmware_image that the answer was revealed. From the link above, "*Virtualization solutions (VMware/VirtualBox/Virtual PC/...) only work with USB cards. Card that are PCI/MiniPCI/PCMCIA/CardBus/Express Card/PCI Express/PCI-X/MiniPCI Express* |

| | *won't work at all.*" An excellent link to search for a USB Wireless Adapter is http://linux-wless.passys.nl/query_hostif.php?hostif=USB. |

Aircrack comes installed in BackTrack now known as Kali Linux, which we will talk about in the virtualization chapter creating virtual machines (VMs). But perhaps you don't want to create an entire VM just to use Aircrack. We can also go to Aircrack's website and download the VMware image of their software (also covered in Chapter 6). Chapter 6 describes how to install Aircrack in other Linux Operating Systems' VMs as well. Once Aircrack is installed, we have to determine if it will work with our hardware. If it does, we then have to gather information to get to work breaking WEP encryption. A tool like inSSIDer (discussed later) will provide most of following information, which will be needed to use the Aircrack tool. The minimum is:

- Target Basic Service Set Identification (BSSID) (MAC address of the WEP Access Point (AP) you are hacking) provided by inSSIDer (See: https://en.wikipedia.org/wiki/Service_set_(802.11_network))
- Target (AP) Channel provided by inSSIDer
- Target MAC address / BSSID of a computer connected to the WEB encrypted network

Additional information you want:

- MAC address of your PC running or VM running the aircrack-ng suite.
- Your Extended Service Set Identification (ESSID) (Wireless network name (SSID) of the network you are using (your network) provided by inSSIDer
- Wireless interface (# ifconfig -a   # Inside a Linux Bridged VM or CD/USB boot)

Computer hardware you may want or need is:

- Target WEP router/network you are attacking
- Target notebook, laptop or desktop computer with wireless capacity (does not matter what wireless chipset or NIC the computer is using)
- An external antenna (the USB drive has a small antenna but you can get much more gain with a mobile patch antenna you can attach to your car windows)
- If using a VM, you will need a USB drive with wireless capacity; if you chose a wireless card make sure it comes with the *Atheros* chipset
- Attacking notebook, laptop or desktop with wireless capacity and hardware chipset that your software supports

If you are interested in hacking, see the citations that were among the many references used to write this book

| **Tip** | The USB drive recommended by Hacking Exposed, noted above, is the Ralink RT73/RT2770F. Ralink was bought out by MediaTek and the websites merged Feb 1, 2013. Looking at their website the latest USB that supports both 2.4/5 GHz (VERY IMPORTANT TO HAVE SUPPORT FOR BOTH) is the RT3572. I did not explore breaking WEP encryption further for three reasons: 1) I found no support for USB 3.0; 2) I found no USB support for the new 802.11ac standard; 3) Even |

 though BackTrack could be used from a bootable CD or USB drive, I saw no support by Aircrack for my wireless card. When/if a USB Wireless Adapter supports these standards it will be an excellent addition to my computer hardware. Modern routers only have four RJ-45 ports (which seems standard these days), and my lab needs more like seven or eight. So being able to connect PCs to the router wirelessly is a convenient solution when compared to constantly unplugging and plugging back in RJ-45 jacks. Buying a switch would also solve the problem but is not as versatile as wireless. I look forward to the day when I can locate desktop PCs in other places in the house using USB 3.0 Wireless Adapters. (See: http://www.mediatek.com, at the website *select __Connectivity__ > __Wi-Fi__ > __Home Networking__ > __USB__*).

If you want to try it, boot up BackTrack or Kali Linux off of your bootable media (e.g. multiboot USB drive) and type iwconfig at the command line to see if your WAN adapter has been recognized and loaded. Write down the logical name of your LAN (e.g. ath0, wlan0, wlan1, eth0, wi0, etc.). First make sure BackTrack or Kali recognized your Wi-Fi adapter by typing:

```
# iwconfig     # Make note of the name of your Wi-Fi connection
# airmon-ng     # Check the status of the Wi-Fi adapter
# airmon-ng stop wlan0     # Stop your normal Wi-Fi interface connection
# airmon-ng start wifi0     # Restart the Wi-Fi adapter in monitor mode
# iwconfig     # Check that monitor mode is enabled
```

To make this exercise worthwhile we will only look at a "zero knowledge" attack on the WEP encrypted network. This means we know nothing about the network and computers we are attacking and have to discover everything on our own. As we discussed, we need a WEP encrypted network with at least one client connected to attack it. The reason for this is we need network Internet activity to gather the information needed to break into the WEP network.

```
# airdump-ng --ivs --write capturefile wlan0     # Look at only the part of the network traffic
we need for WEP cracking
```

The command above causes *airdump-ng* to scan nearby networks on 2.4 GHz channels. Hopefully we will get a hit between the network and client accessing that network. The top panel shows all the networks you can try to hack. The bottom panel shows the devices connected to that network. We would need both to start hacking. We have gathered the information needed to start hacking our target network. Here ends our example on how easy it is to hack WEP encryption. There is much more information and other tools that can be used. I hope the exercises above demonstrate the need to replace a wireless device using WEP.

If you remember the Cold War, or learned about it at school, it is easy to understand that as we develop encryption methods and security measures, unscrupulous people and foreign governments are out there figuring out ways around them. What we SBO/HCUs can do is upgrade our hardware every few years, and then, either pay someone or learn everything we can about locking it down with the options the new hardware, firmware, and operating systems provide. We are good to go with a new modern router until Wi-Fi Protected Access 2 (WEP2) encryption is officially cracked as it may be.

WARNING   	We would all like to believe that setting up and enabling the latest Wi-Fi Protected Access 2 encryption is enough to protect our SBO/HCU network. But there are other vulnerabilities that hardware manufactures build into their equipment that can be exploited, essentially bypassing the WEP2 encryption. To make things convenient for customers most routers come with the Wi-Fi Protected Setup feature (WPS), which is designed to simplify connecting Wi-Fi equipment to the router. This feature is found in most routers made since 2007. Some routers, like the one provided to my parents by their ISP, assign an eight digit pin to the Wi-Fi that is printed on a sticker on the bottom of the device. Using this PIN number enabled my laptop to connect to their router. The other type of WPS allows the router owner to assign a PIN that is used to configure Wi-Fi devices to easily connect also. The problem is that many of these routers are not designed to combat brute force software that throws continuous strings of digits at the router eventually guessing the PIN. Think of the movies where the cracker puts a device on a door combination, and you see thousands of digits rolling, until suddenly, the door unlocks. The difference from the movies is an attacker has no time constraint to breaking into your system. They just have to be persistent trying multiple known methods to brute force their way into your network. Imagine if you will that your neighbor is a cracker, or you have a business competitor who does not play fair and knows a bit about cracking. They can place a device running 24x7 near your Wi-Fi network that will throw random strings of characters at your Wi-Fi device. They don't even have to be around, as their device eventually comes up with the code to crack yours. They just check the trap from time to time to see if they have caught anything. A good analogy is catching lobster, or in the old days, trapping beaver; sometimes the traps are full and sometimes empty. Almost all Wi-Fi networks are unshielded, and something as simple as a smartphone can be hidden near your network to crack it. Manufacturers can add enhancements to combat such attacks on their routers, but some of them haven't yet done so. If your router supports WPS, it's vulnerable to attack. Look for an eight-digit PIN printed on the bottom or a WPS logo on the router. If you don't see either one, run an https://duckduckgo.com search for your model number, and find its product description or data sheet online. If you still have the box, examine it. If your router supports WPS, log in to your router's Web-based configuration panel: From a computer that is connected to your network, open your Web browser and type in your router's IP address (e.g. 10.0.0.1, 10.1.1.1, 69.9.69.175, 192.168.0.1, 192.168.1.1, 192.168.1.10, 192.168.1.100, 192.168.123.254). Once logged, in disable WPS if that is possible. If WPS cannot be disabled, consider buying a new router that does not have the WPS feature. Your manufacturer may also release firmware that plugs this vulnerability, so keep your firmware up-to-date.

The modern D-Link DSL-2750B router had WPS enabled by default, http://www.dlink.com/products/?pid=803 . **To disable WPS in the D-Link router, click on the _Wireless_ tab on the top > click on the _Wireless_ sub-tab in the upper left > arrow down and next to WPS uncheck _Enabled_ > click on _OK_.**

If you have an older router you might want to replace your router's stock firmware with open source firmware to add some capabilities to it. To do this, clear the NVRAM and restore the factory defaults by pressing and holding the reset button on your router. Download the DD-WRT firmware for your router, and have it handy to be used as the firmware update for your router. The procedure for doing this is documented in your routers manual. (See: http://dd-wrt.com/site/index). Most router experts prefer the open source DD-WRT to the stock router firmware for older routers. See my blog at http://thatcybersecurityguy.blogspot.com where there is detailed commentary on DD-WRT.

Setting Up a Router and Repeater

When setting up a router for small businesses we don't hook them in a standard home configuration. To configure them, cut off your SBO/HCU router and cable modem. Most modern routers come with four RJ-45 ports that you can connect cables to. The other end of that cable connects to your computer's NIC. Hardwire a Cat 6a cable to/from your computers NIC to the RJ-45 port on your router. Make sure you insert the cable in a computer port on the router and not the Internet port. Once logged into the router, change the settings.

The first thing to look at setting up a router for a SBO is the Basic Settings. Make sure everything is set to get Automatically/Dynamically from ISP. We are not interested in optimizing the settings, but just making sure that everything works. The next thing to look at is the Wireless settings. Be sure to put together a text document on what you set these at. The Name (SSID): and the Passphrase have to be recorded for the SBO. Go ahead and "Enable SSID Broadcast" to make things easy when you deliver the equipment to their location. Click on the Set Up Access List button, and remove your "Wireless Card Access List" wireless devices.

If this is an old router be sure to delete any previous Address Reservations*. Under QoS Setup, if the customer wants streaming video, be sure to enable WWM for both the 2.4GHz and 5GHz settings and to turn QoS on. Under Port Forwarding / Port Triggering un-configure any ports you have forwarded. Click on the Dynamic DNS tab and remove your Dynamic DNS settings.

A wonderful tool for wireless computers that you can utilize to view neighboring wireless networks is **InSSIDer** which was a free Wi-Fi network scanner for Windows 7. (See: http://www.metageek.net/support/downloads, http://www.inssider.com) InSSIDer shows you a view of networks that are in detectable range of your wireless device, their signal strength, and what wireless encryption method they are using. This allows you to determine if interference from the neighbors' Wi-Fi networks are causing problems with your Wi-Fi network so you can troubleshoot those problems. After installing, **click on _Start_ > arrow up to _All Programs_ > click on _MetaGeek_ > click on _inSSIDer2.0_**. The tool showed me that both my parents and their neighbor were using WEP encryption on Channel 6, which was causing a conflict, something my parents' ISP had been unable to determine after many complaints and multiple technician visits. These intermittent outages had annoyed my parents for years. (See: Chapter 4)

InSSIDer is a wonderful tool, but crackers can also use this utility, and more sophisticated tools, to find unsecure networks that they can break into and use. For example, sitting at my desk writing this I see 12 networks broadcasting. One network is running with no encryption at all, three are using WEP encryption, three are running WPA-TKIP and the rest InSSIDer is showing as running WPA2-Personal. Since WEP and WPA-TKIP are broken wireless encryption methods, that makes seven networks that a cracker could break into easily. The WPA2-Personal routers are running at a Max Rate of 54, which tells me they are older routers using legacy mode for b/g networks. So those networks may by susceptible to a WPS attack or other brute force techniques. One network is broadcasting its SSID as *netgear*, so this indicates a default configuration, with possibly an easy password. Of the 12 there is only one network running ARRIS Group, Inc. at a Max Rate of 130, which would prove very difficult to attack.

WARNING	SSID broadcast enables crackers to easily pinpoint your router from its constant random broadcast seeking new connections and permitting any device to attack the encryption software. Crackers will attack your network by randomly cycling through possible MAC addresses and trying to crack your encryption key.

To write this chapter, I reset my router to the factory default settings. I turned my NETGEAR WNDR3700 router upside down and pressed the reset button, then logged in using the browser. This is also what you will have to do if you forget or lose the password to log into your router. Later on we will back up the router settings to a file on your computer, if your router permits that. We do this so that if you ever do lose your password or settings, and/or have to reset your router, it can be restored to the settings that we are going to take a few hours to configure.

I later revised this chapter by reworking the exercises using the NETGEAR Dual Band 11ac Wi-Fi Router R6300 and added a few things about the primitive ARRIS MG5225G. The manual that comes with your router will tell you the default username and password to use (*crackers know these settings on older hardware*). The router manufacturers are making the defaults harder to crack because the SSID and default Network Key on the NETGEAR R6300, and a D-Link 2750B were "Preset" with a unique SSID and Network Key that would not be easy to guess. The NETGEAR manual states, "*This product has a unique Wi-Fi network name (SSID) and network key (password). The default SSID and network key (password) are uniquely generated for every device, like a serial number, to protect and maximize security. Netgear recommends that you do not change these settings.*"

	Routers are just now making a huge leap in wireless speeds with the new AC standard. D-Link will soon release the DBL-5500, which will be an amazing router. It is advertised to deliver gigabit AC wireless speeds up to 1250 mbps and uses Qualcomm SteamBoost technology. Don't buy anything but an AC router.

Hopefully you have read the introduction and now know how much information has been compromised in banks, corporations, government, and the easiest targets, SBO/HCUs. I have already presented my argument for changing these default values. You should not trust these default settings to be secure, and you should change them. Even though the default settings are now unique and much more difficult to crack, some sort of algorithm was used to generate them. If that algorithm is compromised, as seems to happen, then your router is no longer secure.

NOTE	Depending on the complexity of your setup, record each setting that you configure in your router. Even though we will later save those settings to a binary configuration file, you will find yourself eventually setting up a new router. For example, my cable company offers a whole house solution in the ARRIS MG5225G. It is an inferior solution to my advanced cable modem and router, but I thought I would try it for the added media features, like recording 6 channels at the same time.

The first thing I noticed on the state-of-the-art NETGEAR R6300 was that the LAN cable packaged with the router was Cat 5e. The D-Link DSL-2750B was CAT 5, but since its connection speed is only 100 Mbps this is OK. We will discuss cabling quality and types in Chapter 4, but for now, surf to a cabling website such as https://www.monoprice.com and purchase a Cat 6a 500 MHz STP cable in the length that you need. A 7ft cable costs a mere $4.00. As you modernize your computers and network hardware, you don't want substandard cabling slowing things down. Many corporations use this substandard cabling to save money when the equipment they purchase is capable of much higher speeds. (See: https://en.wikipedia.org/wiki/Category_6_cable)

If you don't have your router manual, go to the website of your router manufacturer. From http://www.netgear.com **click on the _Support_ tab and then enter the model number of your router**. You can then read the manual to get the default login credentials.

If your cable modem is NEW, it cannot connect to the Internet without a call to your ISP to register the MAC address. My parents' DSL modem shipped from Verizon connected without this added step. They had what is called an unverified open DSL connection, which is something you would not want if you have a small business or just want to be more secure online. In Chapter 4 we will discuss the advantages and disadvantages of purchasing a top-of-the-line cable modem verses renting one from your ISP.

If you reset your router like I did, the router may not connect to the Internet through the modem without a few extra steps. The directions from this point forward refer specifically to the NETGEAR WNDR3700 router unless otherwise specified. The R6300 is similar enough that only a few footnotes about additional configuration items needed to be described. To test your connection, log into your router and click on **_Basic Settings_ > _Default or Use this MAC Address_ > _Test_** to see if the router will connect to your ISP on its own. If it does not, make sure that the connection light on the router indicates that the router and cable modem are talking. If they are communicating, below are a few steps you can try to get your router connected to the Internet through your modem:

1. Log into the router, *using the **Setup** menu click on **Basic Settings** > under **Internet IP Address** check **Get Dynamically from ISP** > click the **Test** button at the bottom to see if the router is connected.*

2. *On the WNDR3700 try under the **Maintenance** menu **Router Status** > click the **Connection Status** button at the bottom > select **Release/Renew**. When done renewing click on Basic Settings > Test button to see if the router is connected. On the R6300 click on the **Advanced** tab > select **Administration** on the left > click on **Router Status** > click on the Connection Status button on the right > in the **Connection Status** window click on **Release** > when done releasing click on **Renew**. If that did not work try clicking on **Reboot** to see if that works.*

3. Power down the router and cable modem, wait about 20 seconds, and power them back on. Login and see if you are connected.

4. ***Power down the router and your cable modem, > disconnect the power from both; and coaxial cable connection from the cable modem for at least 20 seconds > reconnect the coaxial using a small wrench, (finger tight is not tight enough) > reconnect the power to both devices.*** Login and see if you are connected.

5. *On the WNDR3700 go to the DNS screen and make sure a static IP is not configured and **Get Automatically from ISP** is checked. On the R6300 click on **Internet** on the left panel > on the right panel make sure **Get Dynamically from ISP** is ticked.*

6. The last resort is to call your ISP and have them help you troubleshoot the problem. They can tell you if the cable modem is communicating with ISP.

 Once you connect to a network you may have to remove it from your Windows 7 computer. ***Click on Start > Control Panel > click on the Network and Sharing Center icon > on the left panel select Manage wireless networks > click on the network you want to remove, on the top menu select Remove.***

Hardening the Basic Network and Wireless Router Settings

For your home computer setup, consider getting a power switch box and labeling all the switches. The ISP's favorite troubleshooting technique is power down everything. I can now do that from my chair while using the computer.

- Now that we are connected, update the firmware on the router. This is the default login screen with NETGEAR. ***Login and click on the Check button on the right. For D-Link DSL-2750B under System Information click on Upgrade.*** The link opened up a browser window on the D-Link website, which showed no updates were available.

- *From the **Maintenance** menu, click on **Router Upgrade** > and check the box **Check for new version upon login**.* If there is one device you want to keep the software up-to-date on at home, it is your router. All you have to do is log in occasionally to keep the software up-to-date.

- *Use the **Maintenance** menu to change the default login password by clicking on **Set Password**.* NETGEAR's router max password length was 30 characters. We will discuss how to generate, maintain, and understand the importance of a strong password in Chapter 11 on Identity Theft.

- Select the <u>Language</u> in the upper right corner: I changed it from ***<u>Auto</u>*** to ***<u>English</u>***. Any setting that a device does not have to figure out on its own is usually a faster path through the program logic.
- From the Setup menu to set up a Guest Network, ***click on <u>Guest Network b/g/n</u> > uncheck <u>Enable SSID Broadcast</u> and under <u>Security Option Profile 1</u> select <u>WPA2-PSK [AES]</u>***. We will discuss the purpose and use of guest networks later. Enter a 29 character generated passphrase and record it, which is covered in <u>Chapter 11</u>.
- From the Setup menu, ***select <u>Guest Network a/n</u>*** and do the same thing and enter a password.
- If you have not already done so you should ***add the <u>Network</u> icon*** to your desktop. In Windows 7, right click on the desktop, and select ***<u>Personalize</u> > <u>Change Desktop Icons</u> > check everything including <u>Network</u> > <u>OK</u>***. This will add all the system icons to your desktop. This is something that should be the default in Windows 7.
- **DO NOT disable Service Set Identifier (SSID) for now**. We will later disable SSID Broadcast on all wireless connections *after* they are configured. To make life easier, leave broadcast on to get everything connected for the first time. For example, try as I might to get Ubuntu connected without broadcast, I could not. The same held true for our Play Station®3. Once I allowed broadcast connection, it was as simple as entering the proper password.

From my NETGEAR routers' help, that displayed upon login:

Enable SSID Broadcast

"If this feature is enabled, the wireless router will broadcast its name (SSID) to all wireless stations (and, I might add, to criminals, neighbors, the man*, any device) *within broadcast range of your router. Stations that have no SSID (or a null value) can then adopt the correct SSID for connections to this access point."*

- If you have a Wireless laptop, right click on the desktop screen select ***<u>Personalize</u> > <u>Change Desktop Icons</u> > and enable all the desktop Icons, especially check <u>Network</u>. Now go to your desktop screen and right click on the <u>Network</u> icon and select <u>Properties</u> > you will see <u>Connect to a network</u> on the right bottom so select that***.

| WARNING  | Look at how many networks, broadcasting their SSID for the entire world to see there are to connect to. On my computer I have 12 nearby! Twelve networks announcing their names, practically inviting people to please attempt to crack my network and connect to me. There are crackers who look for your network, called wardriving, warbiking, warjogging, warwalking and even the old wardialing, which we will soon discuss with computers or battery-powered laptops, or other mobile devices looking for networks to use. Once a cracker is easily and covertly connected to a wireless network, think about what they have the potential to do. They could turn the owner of that network into a victim with potentially devastating consequences. |

- Under the Setup menu, change the ***Mode: Under Wire Network(2.4GHz b/g/n) to <u>Up to 300 Mbps</u>***. If your wireless devices were purchased in 2009 or later, they probably support Performance Mode, or 11a and 11n wireless stations. If you want to read about wireless protocols, go to <u>En.Wikipedia.org/wiki/IEEE 802.11</u>. The protocol 802.11n is a fairly new multi-streaming modulation technique that supports both 2.4GHz and 5GHz. In 2012 routers began appearing supporting the new 802.11ac, which is up to three times faster than 802.11n standard. One thing to consider is that your range may be shorted at 300 Mbps. If a device does not see the router, or will not connect, try changing the channel first, and then try changing it back to 130 Mbps. I had no problems with distance at 300 Mbps. (See: <u>https://en.wikipedia.org/wiki/IEEE 802.11</u>, <u>https://en.wikipedia.org/wiki/Long-range Wi-Fi</u>).

From my NETGEAR's routers' help:

Wireless Mode

"Select the desired wireless mode. The options are:

- *Up to 54 Mbps - Legacy Mode with maximum speed of up to 54 Mbps for b/g networks.*
- *Up to 130 Mbps - Neighbor Friendly Mode, with a speed up to 130 Mbps in presence of neighboring wireless networks.*
- *Up to 300 Mbps - Performance Mode - Maximum Wireless-N speeds up to 300 Mbps.*
- *The 2.4GHz (b/g/n) default is Up to 130Mbps, which allows all 11b and 11g and 11n wireless stations.*
- *The 5GHz (a/n) default is Up to 300Mbps, which allows all 11a and 11n wireless stations.*

The 2.4GHz (b/g/n) default is Up to 130Mbps, which allows all 11b and 11g and 11n wireless stations. The 5GHz (a/n) default is Up to 300Mbps, which allows all 11a and 11n wireless stations."

In the Setup menu, under Wireless settings set the security options to <u>WPA2-PSK [AES]</u>. Your router may present WPA-PSK [TKIP] as an added option letting your router present both protocols to the world, but WPA-PSK [TKIP] only operates at the legacy "Up to 54Mbps" rate, not N rate, *and WPA-TKIP is a broken (cracked) protocol*. WPA2-PSK [AES] gives full N support and should be used as your sole encryption protocol. Why present two encryption protocols for someone to hack into, when one better choice will suffice? D-Link DSL-2750B defaulted to WPA2 security. You can check on this by ***clicking on the <u>Wireless</u> tab on the top > click on the <u>Wireless</u> sub-tab in the upper left > arrow down to Security and to the right you should see WPA2 in the drop down > if you do not select WPA2 > click on OK***.

While you are on the D-Link Wireless screen, make note of SSID, the WPA, and the MAC address by cutting and pasting. We will use this later to connect wireless devices to the router. Since we will disable SSID broadcasting later, it is OK to use the MAC address SSID, which is the default. However, if you want to leave SSID broadcasting enabled, be sure to change the SSID so it is not revealing information that will help in an outside wireless attack, such as its MAC address. (See: <u>http://en.wikipedia.org/wiki/Wi-Fi Protected Access</u>, http://www.smallnetbuilder.com/wireless/wireless-howto/31914-how-to-crack-wpa-wpa2-2012)

- **_Change the Name (SSID):_ from the router default to something not easily guessed by a cracker like _<WebData-2.4G_ or _StreamVideo-2.4G>_ for the Wireless Network (2.4Ghz b/g/n); and _<WebData-5G_ and _StreamVideo-5G>_ for the (Wireless Network 5GHz a/n)**. I list both because my PS3 would only connect at 2.4GHz, and I used the 5GHz SSID for my laptop. These passwords are the only two passwords you may not want to generate. You will have to retype one of these passwords into all your wireless devices to allow them to connect to your router. It is painful selecting one character at a time with your streaming video device remote, but for peace of mind, hardening your security by using a password and not WPS, is worth it.

You probably noticed the names I picked were (**_WebData-xG_** and **_StreamVideo-xG_**) to imply a specific use for each connection. What you want to do (if you have family member(s) streaming video while you are using the computers) is connect your wireless laptop computers to one **_WebData-xG_** network, and connect your Streaming media, Voice over Internet Protocol (VoIP) or Skype VoIP proprietary protocol devices to the other network **_StreamVideo-xG_**. From PCWorld December 8, 2010 "How to Optimize Your Router for VoIP and Video" by Jon L. Jacobi, this will give you "*Simultaneous dual-band wireless: Concurrent wireless allows you to perform ad-hoc QoS by splitting traffic between two networks.*" I will talk about QoS later. (See: https://en.wikipedia.org/wiki/Streaming_media, https://en.wikipedia.org/wiki/VoIP, http://www.netgear.com/landing/dual-band.aspx and https://en.wikipedia.org/wiki/Skype_protocol)

- Also, if you separate the networks, you might be able to **_Enable Wireless Isolation_** for your wireless devices, unless you have a music library on your PC that you want to connect to from your video devices, or you share files with the laptop using Windows Homegroup, FTP, SFTP, etc. between home computers.

From my NETGEAR routers' help:

Enable Wireless Isolation

If checked, the wireless client under this SSID can only access Internet and it can't access other wireless clients even under the same SSID, Ethernet clients or this device. Other clients can't access the wireless client, either."

- Most of us are using streaming video these days. *Check the box _Enable Video Network_".*

From my NETGEAR routers' help:

Enable Video Network

(For 5GHz a/n network only) Select this check box if you will be streaming HD video. When this option is selected, the router uses Video reliability algorithms to reduce jitter and packet loss during video presentations. If you will not be streaming video, leave this check box unchecked.

- As previously discussed, using WPS to connect your devices is a security hole. If you are purchasing a new router, buy one that does not support WPS or allows you to disable this feature. If you live in a rural area where it is unlikely someone will try to break into your network, you might be tempted to use this feature as a simple approach to connecting your wireless devices. You can configure the router's wireless settings, or add a wireless client through WPS using the router's PIN only when the PIN is enabled. You can manually enable this function by clearing the check box and clicking the Apply button. To use WPS, refer to your routers' manual to determine where the button is located.

I did not find using WPS necessary for it was just as easy to go to the few wireless devices we own and configure them manually. From NETGEAR routers' help:

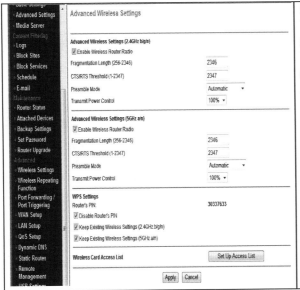

Router's PIN
This is the PIN number you use on a registrar (e.g., from Network Explorer on a Vista Windows PC) to configure the router's wireless settings through WPS. You can also find the PIN on the router's product label.

Disable Router's PIN
You can configure the router's wireless settings or add a wireless client through WPS using the router's PIN only when the PIN is enabled. The router's PIN can be disabled temporarily when the router detects suspicious attempts to break into the router's wireless settings by using the router's PIN through WPS. You can manually enable this function by clearing the check box and clicking the Apply button.

Hardening Wireless Access by Setting up a Wireless Card Access List (Also Known as MAC Filtering)

Setting up a Wireless Card Access List will give us another layer of security. This will restrict access to our wireless network to only the wireless devices that we have. Most households only have a few, so this is a quick and easy added layer of security.

From my NETGEAR routers' HELP:

Wireless Card Access List

"By default, any wireless PC that is configured with the correct SSID will be allowed access to your wireless network. For increased security, you can restrict access to the wireless network to allow only specific PCs based on their MAC addresses. On the Wireless Settings screen, click the Setup Access List button to display the Wireless Access List screen."

Now let's really lock things down. To make configuration easier, power on all the wireless devices that are going to be connected to the router so that the router sees them.

NOTE	To get the following to work I had to power the router off and back on. Simple things like this can consume valuable time if you don't know to try them.

From the Maintenance menu, select <u>*Attached Devices*</u> and look at all the Device Names and MAC addresses attached to your router. If you have DVD players or PS3s, the device name will be blank, requiring extra effort on your part.

Under the <u>*Advanced*</u> *menu, select* <u>*Wireless Settings*</u> *> Click on* <u>*Set Up Access List*</u> *button* and start adding devices. Adding the home wireless laptop(s) is/are easy. Just select them from the list, and the device name and MAC Address are added.

For the D-Link DSL-2750B click on the Wireless tab on the top > arrow down to <u>*MAC Filtering*</u> *and select* <u>*Allow*</u> *> the* <u>*New MAC Address*</u> *link will appear and you can start adding the wireless devices that you will allow to connect to the D-Link router. Once all your wireless devices are connected and MAC Addresses are entered, uncheck the* <u>*SSID Broadcast*</u> *box.*

The NETGEAR R6300 under <u>***Setup***</u> *>* <u>***WAN Setup***</u> *> the* <u>***Disable IGMP Proxying***</u> option is checked by default. Internet Group Management Protocol (IGMP) proxying allows a computer on the local area network (LAN) to receive the multicast traffic it is interested in from the Internet. It is used between IP hosts and their neighboring multicast agents to establish group memberships. IGMP supports one-to-many networking applications such as streaming video and gaming, and can be a more efficient use of resources for those applications. IGMP is a security risk and it should be disabled if it is not needed. (See: https://en.wikipedia.org/wiki/Internet_Group_Management_Protocol)

Once SSID broadcasting is disabled, adding other devices may no longer be possible. I had to connect them with SSID enabled, and then disable SSID broadcasting later.

- With SSID broadcasting enabled, on your laptop desktop, *right click on the* <u>*Network*</u> *icon and select* <u>*Properties,*</u> *go over to the right side and click on* <u>*Internet*</u> *>* <u>*Wireless Network Connection (networkname-5G)*</u> *> click on the* <u>*Wireless Properties*</u> *button > check the boxes labeled* <u>*Connect automatically when this network is in range,*</u> *and,* <u>*Connect even if the network is not broadcasting its name (SSID)*</u>.

- The PS3 and other devices are different. They don't have their device names listed on the router screen, so it is not easy to identify their MAC addresses from the list. I had to go to each device and work my way through the labyrinth.
- For example, on the PS3, to get Netflix streaming again, I had to log into the PlayStation Network (*the one that got cracked with all our information*), and then retype everything to login to Netflix. While I was at it, I updated both the PS3 box firmware ***Settings > System Update > arrow to the right and Accept the user agreement > check Turn Off System Automatically After Update to make sure a reboot happens*** and the PlayStation Network software. I then went to ***Settings > Systems Settings > System Information*** to look at the MAC address and the device name. The MAC address was listed on the router screen under the <u>Advanced</u> menu, select ***Wireless Settings > scroll down to the bottom and select the Set Up Access List*** button **> click the button beside the MAC address > select _Edit_** to add the PS3 device name. You could just cut them on and off one by one, but I like to see the MAC address in the device just to be 100% sure.
- If you have a streaming DVD Player, it also will probably not have a Device Name, so you will have to look at something like ***Setup > Network > Connection Settings***. This will show the MAC address, and then you can make up your own Device Name.

Hardening Router Visibility by Turning off SSID Broadcast – Backing up the Basic Router Settings

- It is now time to turn off your **network billboard advertisement SSID**. *Under the Setup menu, click on **Wireless Settings** and uncheck **Enable SSID broadcast*** for both the 2.4GHz b/g/n network and the 5GHz a/n network.

NOTE 	Once the SSID broadcast is turned off, if your laptop does not connect to the Internet, go back and check your settings to make sure ***Connect even if the network is not broadcasting its name (SSID)*** is checked. There is also another caveat to turning off the SSID. *"Because SSID is required to join the network, hiding it makes attacks slightly more difficult. An interesting note is that Microsoft actually recommends announcing your SSID because Windows Vista and later first look for these beacons before making an attempt to connect to the wireless network. This behavior protects the client, as it does not need to send out probe requests continuously when the network in unavailable, which opens up the client to Access Point impersonation, attacks."*[11] However, since your passphrase is required to connect to your network, I don't see how an AP attack could be done without the attacker knowing your passphrase. So broadcasting the SSID seems to be a bigger risk. Also, depending on the skill level of the cracker, programs like Kisment, which comes with BackTrack (covered in Chapter 6), are able to "decloak" access points by listening to traffic between the clients and the access point.

Make a backup of the router configuration so you have a copy of the default configuration if you ever want to restore it. ***Under the Maintenance menu, click on Backup Settings > select the Back Up button and save everything to a file.*** This backup is great to have in case you ever forget your router password and have to reset it, or have to reset it for some other reason. You can easily restore the settings we just configured--of course, not forgetting to change the password after you restore!

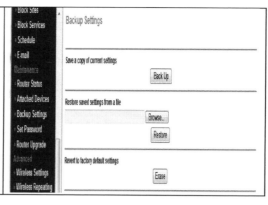

Backing up your router settings is enough to maintain your current router settings, but what happens when you purchase a new router? Even if you stay with the same manufacturer, upgrading your router usually will not allow you to import those settings. So record all your router settings to a text file or word document with your backup.

Hardening Network Access by Disabling Router Ports

As with our house, which has many windows and doors, there are many avenues a burglar can use to gain access to our computers. Take the analogy that for some households it is as simple as breaking a window, reaching an arm through the broken window, and unlocking the door to gain access. My parents changed this by adding a keyed deadbolt on both sides so the door could not be unlocked this easily. Unfortunately, the fire marshal decided that it was better for people to be robbed than protect themselves in this manner. It is illegal in many communities to have a duel key deadbolt. The thing this soldier finds shocking is how any home builder thought this was a good form of construction. Look at your own house. Do you have an obscured basement window that can easily be broken, allowing a thief access to your home? How about doors with a nice view outside that can have a window pane that can be broken out and the door easily unlocked? It is almost as if our homes are designed to be broken into, and laws are passed to keep it that way.

Securing your router can be viewed in much the same way as securing your home. If you leave easy avenues of access to your home, you may eventually be victimized. Just like if you leave easy access to your network, then a cracker may find a way to attack you. Take the example of where I set up an FTP inside my home network so I could move files easily between my home computers. It was just an experiment, but I left that door open. Suppose some cracker got into my network and saw that I had a computer listening to the FTP port 23. There are many known attack methods they could use to possibly exploit that vulnerability.

A port is a doorway that you can open up (like knocking a hole in your wall) that allows a specific process running on your computer to communicate or share a single physical connection to a packet-switched network like your local network or the Internet. Some of these ports and the applications that service them are well known. To gain access to a port, three things are needed--your IP address (usually advertised and easily obtained), a port number, and the protocol that it uses (most likely Transmission Control Protocol) or the User

Datagram Protocol (UDP). The applications that listen on these ports sometimes have vulnerabilities that crackers can use to break into your house.

Some people may feel it is overkill to block ports (build a wall) on your router, but doing so makes you a harder target. This is much like replacing the one-pane windows in your basement by putting in glass block windows. The robber will need a hammer rather than a rag wrapped around his fist to break in, making a lot more noise. Close down ports on your router that you do not use. In Chapter 9 on using SSH encryption, we will discuss what those ports are, and you can determine what you should block. Port blocking is also useful if you have a child or employee using Internet applications (like gaming software) that you don't want being used. *On the WNDR3700 router this is found on the left panel under Content Filtering > select Block Services > under Services Blocking make sure the Always radio button is ticked. On the R6300 select the ADVANCED tab at the top > expand the Security tab on the left > click on Block Services > in the right pane click on the +ADD button > start adding rules for blocking the services or ports you want blocked > under Services Blocking tick the Always choice.*

Now, my friend, breathe the free air, for the basic router security settings are done. However, to get the best performance and use out of your network, read on.

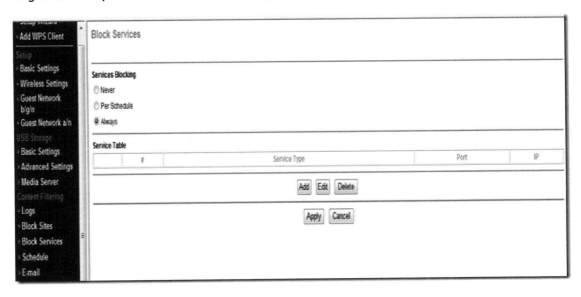

Block Services to Test SSH and VPN Tunnels

Later on we will cover how to encrypt your Internet activity to be more secure using hotspots. We can use a software firewall to block ports to test our success on a specific device using these SSH and tunnels. But if you are testing things like encrypted tunnels from multiple devices, you may find it easier to block ports from those devices in your router. This will all make much more sense later.

On the NETGEAR WNDR3700 router this is found on the left panel under Content Filtering > click on the Add button > Select Filter Services For > select Only this IP Address and enter the IP of your client > select Service Type, User Defined > enter the range (23-1024) to block most everything from the client/local computer. On the R6300 select the __ADVANCED__ tab at the top > expand the __Security__ tab on the left > click on __Block Services__ > in the right pane click on the __+ADD__ button > for __Service Type__: __User Defined__; for __Protocol__: __TCP__, for __Starting Port__: __23__; for __Ending Port__: __65535__; for __Service Type/User Defined__: type __All ports 23 up__; under __Services Blocking__ tick the __Always__ choice. To be thorough, block everything below 22 also, as this will make sure that browsers and other programs using any port above 22 will not have access to the Internet. If anything works, it will only work through your encrypted tunnel via port 22. Click Apply when done. Test your browser, and if it can go nowhere on the Internet, then you were successful. You have cut off your client/local computer from the Internet. NOTE: You may need a second computer to enable the ports again.

Hardening the Domain Name Service (DNS) Setup and Achieving Better DNS Performance

As with everything on the Internet, using your ISP or any other DNS resolver comes with security risks. From the Gibson Research Corporation website (See: http://www.grc.com/dns/configuring.htm):

- *DNS is used to convert all URL domain names into their public Internet IP addresses. This MUST be done so that your computer can connect to the services available at those domains because those domains are accessed and addressed by IP address.*
- *Any DNS resolver receiving your system's DNS queries also receives your system's or network's public IP address. It MUST receive your IP address since that's the only way for it to return the results of its DNS resolution to your computer or network on the Internet.*
- *The DNS resolver knows what DNS domain name you are asking it to resolve.*
- *Virtually all web queries carry both your IP address and persistent cookies, so tying the two together is the sort of thing that's probably already in someone's business plan.*
- *Imagine if that dictionary lookup process, of converting names to numbers, were deliberately corrupted. The attack is known as "Cache Poisoning", and although it has been understood to be a theoretical problem for many years, it was never believed to be a serious vulnerability until the inventor of this utility, Dan, discovered how to do it quickly and easily.*

Therefore, anyone providing your DNS services could easily build a huge and comprehensive log of all of the domain names looked up by everyone using their services. This might be done for various generally benign marketing and statistical reasons. But even so, any such service could be compelled to release their records to legal authorities.

Skip down to Chapter 4 where we will discuss things like OpenDNS and setting up an alternate DNS for greater speed and possibly enhanced security. **On the WNDR3700 to Setup > Basic Settings > Domain Name Server (DNS) Address > and click on Use these DNS Servers. On the R6300 under the BASIC tab click on the Internet button > in the right frame scroll down to the Domain Name Server (DNS) Address information**.

Setting up Dynamic DNS as a Permanent Domain to Use Your Home Network while Traveling with Your Mobile Devices

So now, if you are like I used to be, you are scratching your head saying, "What more could I possibly want from this never-ending router configuration chapter." Just think, we are doing a simple SBO/HCU router setup. Imagine what IT professionals trained in sophisticated corporate router and switch setup go through. It is no wonder that, on a regular basis, we read about security breaches in the government and at corporations. Those who do this for a living have thousands of devices to deal with.

If you never plan to use your **now secure home network to securely use your remote devices** in coffee shops, at school, in the local library, overseas, or at work, then you can skip this router configuration section. Personally, when I was using my laptop at the local community colleges and universities, I did not want anyone cracking my computer on a public connection, watching my every keystroke, so I created encrypted tunnels into my secure home network to do everything I needed to do remotely (view my email, sync up my encrypted sky drive, surf the Internet, look at my bank accounts, etc.). We will discuss how to do this in Chapter 9 but first we need to set up the router.

We must set up a permanent domain in the router configuration because of an ISP's roaming Dynamic Host Configuration Protocol (DHCP) IP address. Your ISP provider assigns an IP address to your cable modem that will change every so often. If you do not have a domain set up and an advanced router that can update that domain with your latest IP, you will not be able to connect to your secure home network using your remote devices.

You would not want to be in some far off place on the phone trying to direct family members on how to set up or determine the routers newly assigned IP address by your ISP to your SBO/HCU cable modem. Family members and employees only know that everything magically started working for every device in your small business or house (after all your hard work). There are providers that you can search for, that provide this service. For example, Dyn.com (formally DYNDNS.com) has a paid DNS service where you can create your own domain and point it to your home router. In May 2013, Dyn.com discontinued the creation and use of automated free accounts. They briefly grandfathered in previously free subscribers who had to manually revalidate their accounts every month. Paid-for accounts must be revalidated annually. There are other services that claim to be free that you can investigate. This comes in handy for things such as hosting your own website, SSH server, weblog/blog, etc., or at home, to access your computer remotely. (See: https://en.wikipedia.org/wiki/Dynamic_DNS, https://help.ubuntu.com/community/DynamicDNS)

1. Setup/register an account at http://dyn.com and log in. Using Internet Explorer, I was unable to sign in, but using Firefox, the website worked fine.
2. **Under _My Account_ click on _My Services_ > scroll down to _Host Services_ > click on _Add Hostname_** and add your domain name.

My website favorites are set up as tables of links with the description of the websites I need and find to be useful or of interest. They are my bookmarks, and much more, that I can access from anywhere in the world. I don't worry about syncing up bookmarks across various operating systems and computers using vendor's software that might be compromised. You can also use the Dyn.com paid service to map your website or blog to a different domain. For example, when the service was free I set up http://tcsg.dyndns.org to be redirected to my website, making it easy to remember and easier to use.

What this does, if your ISP changes your IP address, is allow you to configure your router to automatically update your http://dyn.com information to keep your domain name pointed at your router. So, if you are in a faraway place and your ISP changes your IP address on your SBO/HCU router, no problem. You have a domain name pointed at your server that will be automatically updated by your router communicating with http://dyn.com. The http://dyn.com/support/wizard web page explains very well how to set up an unchanging domain name and point it at your ever changing ISP cable modem IP address. It is really very straight forward. From the NETGEAR WNDR3700 router's help:

"*A Dynamic DNS (DDNS) service provides a central public database where information (such as email addresses, host names, and IP addresses) can be stored and retrieved. The Dynamic DNS server also stores password-protected information and accepts queries based on email addresses.*

If you want to use a DDNS service, you must register for it. The Dynamic DNS client service provider will give you a password or key."

IT sounds complex, but all you have to do is go to their website and create a domain. Then configure your router to keep http://dyn.com updated as to your router DHCP address. Below is a screenshot setting up a domain to point at your router no matter what happens to your IP address:

On the WNDR3700 you can test your setup under the _Advanced_ menu, click on _Dynamic DNS_ > _Show Status_ > and you should get a message like, _yourdomainname.dyndns.org_ / _x.x.x.x updated successfully at 04:49 pm, 02/05/2011_.

| **NOTE** | Once your domain is set up, it has to be broadcast to the DNS servers on the Internet, so it will not be immediately available. Give it a few minutes before using it. |

Setting up an Address Reservation for Your Home Printer and Assigning a Static (Unchanging) IP Address

A while back, I set up a static IP for my Printer. I did this because the family kept complaining to me about how the printer would suddenly stop working. It turned out my router was changing the DHCP address of the printer from time to time causing my home computers to not know where the printer was. To fix the problem I had to reconfigure all our home computers by deleting the printer from ***Devices and Printers*** and then reconfigure them to the new DHCP IP address every time it changed. This was a very painful and time consuming process. At that time, I had not played with my router settings to make an Address Reservation* for the printer as I am teaching you to do now.

When you specify a reserved IP address for a PC, device or printer on your LAN, that device will always receive the same IP address each time it accesses the DHCP server. Reserved IP addresses should be assigned to servers and network printers that require permanent IP settings. If you are going to remotely connect to a SSH or Virtual Private Network (VPN*) server, you cannot have your router assigning that server different IP addresses from time to time.

- The easiest way to get device (e.g. printers) information is to power them on and let them connect to the router. Then log into the router and from the <u>Maintenance</u> menu ***Select <u>Attached Devices</u>***, cut and paste the device name, MAC address and IP address from the router screen into something like <u>Notepad++</u>.
- Now that we have the DHCP address assigned to the printer, we need to reserve that in the router so that it won't keep changing. ***On the WNDR3700 the <u>Advanced</u> menu click on <u>LAN Setup</u> go down to <u>Address Reservation</u> > click on the <u>Add</u> button. Using the Netgear R6300 click on the <u>Advanced</u> tab > expand <u>Setup</u> > arrow down to select <u>LAN Setup</u> > and under <u>Address Reservation</u> click on the <u>Add</u> button.*** From there you can enter the IP Address, device name and MAC address of your printer that you cut and pasted to <u>Notepad++</u>.
- Then set up your printer to use this address as a static IP address. On my printer I pressed ***<u>Menu</u> > <u>Admin Menu</u> > <u>Wired Network</u> > <u>TCP/IP</u> > <u>IPv4</u>*** and set the IP / Subnet / Gateway. This is really easy to do, especially when you consider the alternative, spending time and effort changing the IP address every time your DHCP server assigns a new one to your printer.

From the NETGEAR's WNDR3700 routers help:

To reserve an IP address:

1. *Click the Add button.*
2. *Select the radio button of the computer you wish to add from the Address Reservation Table.*
3. *If the computer is not on the Address Reservation Table, enter the IP address, MAC address, and device name of the computer you wish to add.*
4. *Click the Add button when finished.*

Advanced
- Wireless Settings
- Wireless Repeating Function
- Port Forwarding / Port Triggering
- WAN Setup
- LAN Setup
- QoS Setup

Address Reservation

#	IP Address	Device Name	MAC Address

[Add] [Edit] [Delete]

[Apply] [Cancel]

 **TIP**	Sometimes we need to add a new wireless device to our router configuration. The easiest way to do this is to enable SSID broadcast and disable your Wireless Access Control List (WACL), and then configure the new device to connect to your router. Once the device is connected you can enable your WACL, disable SSID, and set up the Address Reservations and QoS if that is needed. From then on the device should connect until something changes.

Setting up Port Forwarding and Address Reservations for Your Home Servers to Use Them Remotely while Traveling

To use a home server of any kind you have to set up your router to forward the port that the server is looking for. You will also have to set up a Static IP address and make an address reservation* in the router for the server IP address. I covered that briefly in setting up your printer:

- *The easiest way to get your device or server information is to power them on and let them connect to the router > log into the router and from the Maintenance menu select Attached Devices > cut and paste the Device name, MAC and IP address from the router screen into something like Notepad++.*
- Now that we have the DHCP address assigned to the server we need to reserve that in the router so that it won't keep changing. *From the Advanced menu, click on LAN Setup go down to Address Reservation > click on the Add button.* From there you can enter the IP Address, device name and MAC address of your printer you cut and pasted to Notepad++.

The setup of a static IP address in the server will be outlined later in the book as I discuss setting up a home Apache Web server, and a home SSH server for secure remote access to your home network. If, against all odds (it happened to me), the computer you are using to configure the router address reservation* has the IP address of one of your static IPs, you will have to open a command prompt on that Windows computer and do a *ipconfig /release*, followed by *ipconfig /renew*.

- To set up *Port Forwarding* for your home Web, SSH, VPN* or other server--*From the routers Advanced menu, select Port Forwarding / Port Triggering > click on the Add Custom Service button for HTTPS, SSH and VPN*. The NETGEAR router did not offer HTTPS, SSH or VPN as selectable Service Names. In the custom configuration screen, you must also select the protocol. If you go to https://en.wikipedia.org/wiki/Transport_Layer_Security it states:

"Historically SSH has been used primarily with reliable transport protocols such as the Transmission Control Protocol (TCP). However, it has also been implemented with datagram-oriented transport protocols, such as the User Datagram Protocol (UDP) and the Datagram Congestion Control Protocol (DCCP), usage which has been standardized independently using the term Datagram Transport Layer Security (DTLS)."

- As we will cover later in <u>Chapter 9</u>, rather than allow two protocols access to your SSH server, set the router to ***TCP only***. For example, connect ability to my home SSH server with this setting was tested from my local community college by bypassing their proxy*. This allowed me to securely view my email and surf the web without the college proxy* keeping tabs on my Internet activity and blocking certain websites.
- ***On the D-Link DSL-2750B click on the <u>Firewall Settings</u> tab on the top > on the sub-menu select <u>Port Forwarding</u> > under <u>Local Host</u> select <u>New Entry</u> > when the <u>Add...</u> drop down appears select the SSH <u>Host Name</u> shown attached to the router > under <u>Protocol</u> select the <u>SSH</u> protocol.***
- For Apache Web server simply ***select the Service Name <u>HTTP</u> in the drop down and click on the <u>Add</u> button to forward port 80.***

WARNING	Once a port is forwarded to a server behind your router firewall, the task of checking your router logs becomes very important. As we know, obtaining your IP address is very easy for EVERYONE on the Internet to do. They will try to crack servers on your open ports. (e.g. I had my SSH server up for weeks while I exchanged data with my partners. I checked the router logs to find over 200 brute force attempts to log into my SSH server. I had to shut it down and change the weak passwords as a result).

Setting up Quality of Service in Your Router and Wireless Devices for Streaming Video and Gaming, Keeping the Family Happy

I mentioned QoS when we split the wireless networks. (See: http://technet.microsoft.com/en-us/network/bb530836, http://technet.microsoft.com/en-us/network/bb530836)

From the NETGEAR WNDR3700 router's help:

"QoS is an advanced feature that you can use to prioritize some Internet applications and online gaming, and to minimize the impact when the bandwidth is busy."

- ***Click on <u>QoS Setup</u> on the left menu. In the NETGEAR R6300 under Advanced > Setup click on QoS on the expanded Setup menu.*** If they are not enabled already (my router default was enabled), you should enable WWM (Wi-Fi multimedia) settings for 2.4GHz b/g/n and 5GHz a/n.

From the NETGEAR WNDR3700 routers help:

"WMM (Wireless Multimedia) is a subset of the 802.11e standard. WMM allows wireless traffic to have a range of priorities, depending on the kind of data. Time-dependent information, like video or

audio, has a higher priority than normal traffic. For WMM to function correctly, wireless clients must also support WMM."

Wireless Multimedia Extensions (WME) and Wi-Fi Multimedia (WMM) are two names for the same 802.11e wireless QoS service that you can setup in your router. You should enable WME or WMM if your router supports it. These settings help streamline applications that use voice and video, if your wireless devices support this feature. If your router supports these features, enable them to stream wireless video. In the QoS configuration section of your routers setup, if there are settings levels, raise them to the highest setting. There may be other proprietary video-streaming options or enhancements in your router; enable them.

I did a lot of research on WMM to determine its benefits. I finally found a dated but excellent article on WMM Basics and whether using Wi-Fi multimedia WWM really helps with streaming voice and video at http://www.smallnetbuilder.com/wireless/wireless-features/30833-does-wi-fi-multimedia-wmm-really-do-anything-part-1. This article was written by Tim Higgins, May 29, 2009. Excerpts from his article and research are summarized below.

The Wireless Multimedia Checklist for Gaming and Streaming Video

"To take advantage of WWM functionality in a Wi-Fi network, three requirements have to be met:

(1) The access point is Wi-Fi CERTIFIED for WMM and has WMM enabled;
(2) The client (device) that the application is running on must be Wi-Fi CERTIFIED for WMM; and
(3) The source application supports WMM.

As indicated in bold, it turns out that the third point is the weak link in the path to all the QoS goodness promised by WMM.

WMM defines four access categories (ACs) derived from 802.1d, which correspond to priority levels (Table information below taken from *http://www.smallnetbuilder.com/wireless/wireless-features/30833-does-wi-fi-multimedia-wmm-really-do-anything-part-1*). *The 802.1d tags are also used by 802.1p."*

Access Category	Description	802.1.Tags
WMM Voice Priority	Highest priority - Allows multiple concurrent VoIP calls, with low latency and toll voice quality	7,6
WMM Video Priority	Prioritize video traffic above other data traffic	5,4
WMM Best Effort Priority	Traffic from legacy devices or traffic from applications or devices that lack QoS capabilities. Traffic less sensitive to latency, but affected by long delays, such as Internet surfing	0,3
WMM Background Priority	Low priority traffic (file downloads, print jobs) that does not have strict latency and throughput requirements	2,1

The 2009 Tim Higgins article goes on to show in graphs how WMM smoothed out the video signal when video was given priority over data. It showed how to set this WMM up in a D-Link router if that is what you are using. It describes how you have to enable *Ad Hoc QoS Mode* in windows. The article also shows how they tested everything.

Tim Higgins used Windows XP and Vista to produce the article, but the information is still relevant. I am only describing how to do this in Windows 7. For example, in XP, a registry hack was necessary to get everything working, and he enabled *Ad Hoc QoS Mode*. (See: http://technet.microsoft.com/en-us/magazine/2007.02.cableguy.aspx, http://technet.microsoft.com/en-us/library/dd919203(WS.10).aspx, http://www.biztechmagazine.com/article/2010/03/boost-network-performance-windows-7-qos)

To enable ***Ad Hoc QoS Mode*** in Windows 7 on your wireless computer/laptop, ***right click on Computer*** > ***select Properties*** > *in left menu Select **Device Manager*** > *in left menu select **Network Adapters*** > *right click on **Intel® WiFi Link 5100 AGN*** > ***Properties*** > ***Advanced Tab*** > *select **Ad Hoc QoS Mode*** *and change Value to **WMM Enabled*** > *click on **OK**.*

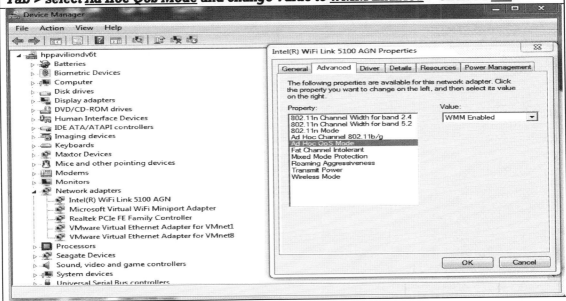

QoS Packet Tagging needs to be enabled for the Ethernet NIC. In XP this had to be manually enabled. Windows 7 has this enabled by default. If you want to check this yourself, ***right click on Network Icon*** > *click in the **Wireless Network Connection (WebData-xG)*** > *click on **Properties*** *button and you should see a check mark next to **QoS Packet Scheduler***. (See: http://www.smallnetbuilder.com/wireless/wireless-features/30833-does-wi-fi-multimedia-wmm-really-do-anything-part-1)

If you are a gamer, web host, or just the home user who wants to do downloads while your family watches streaming Netflix video on the TV, then there is more work to do. ***Click on QoS Setup*** *left menu* > ***QoS Priority Rule*** *button* settings.

From my NETGEAR WNDR3700 router's help:

Turn Internet Access QoS On

"*If this feature is enabled, the QoS function prioritizes Internet traffic. For applications, online gaming, an Ethernet LAN port, or a specified MAC address that already exists in the drop-down list;*

you can modify the priority level by clicking the Edit button. You can click the Delete button to erase the priority rule. You can also define the priority policy for each online game, application, LAN port, or the computer's MAC address by clicking the Add Priority Rule button.

For Applications or Online Gaming

To set up the priority for an application or online gaming:

1. Select Applications or Online Gaming from the Priority Category lists.
2. Select the Internet application or game you want to use from one of the relevant lists.
*3. Select the priority level: **Highest, High, Medium,** or **Low.***
4. You can also type the name in the QoS Policy for field for this rule.
5. Click Apply.

For an Ethernet LAN port

To set up the priority for computers connected to a LAN port:

1. Select the number of the LAN port for which you want to specify the priority level.
2. Select the priority level: Highest, High, Medium or Low.
3. You can also type the name in the QoS Policy for field for this rule.
4. Click Apply.

For a MAC address

To set up the priority for a specified computer through its MAC address:

1. Select the MAC address from the Priority Category list.
2. Click the Refresh button to update the list of those computers already connected to routers.
3. Select the entry's radio button in the table.
4. Modify the information in the MAC Address and Device Name fields.
5. Select the priority level: Highest, High, Normal, or Low.
6. You can also type the name in the QoS Policy for field for this rule.
7. Click the Edit button.
8. Click Apply.

To add the priority for a specified computer through its MAC address

1. Select MAC Address from the Priority Category list.
2. Enter the MAC address of the computer for which you want to define the priority.
3. You can also enter a name in the Device Name field.
4. Select the priority level: Highest, High, Normal, or Low.
5. You can also type the name in the QoS Policy for field for this rule.
6. Click the Add button.
7. Click Apply."

Block Services	QoS - Priority Rules	
Schedule		
E-mail	**Priority**	
Maintenance	QoS Policy for	DVDPlayer
Router Status	Priority Category	MAC Address ▼
Attached Devices		
Backup Settings		

The QoS setting allows you to customize how your router handles your network traffic. Think of it like a traffic light where you have a side road and a main thoroughfare coming together. The traffic light needs to stay green for the main thoroughfare a lot longer that it needs to for traffic entering from a side road. I tried streaming video the MAC address of my Blu-ray DVD Player at the *High* setting first, the next setting is *Highest*. You will see any connected computers listed as *Priority Normal*. My wife did some Netflix video streaming with the *High* settings and I rushed upstairs and kicked off some BIG downloads. I asked her to call me on the cellphone if streaming stopped flowing. This was a problem before I set up QoS – Priority Rules in the router. Picture streaming was unbroken, but when I went down later she complained that the picture quality was very poor, and it sure was grainy. Since I don't care how long a download takes, I changed the setting to *Highest* for my streaming video devices. The important thing was to keep household peace; I could now do downloads while the family gets to enjoy streaming video in the evenings. Life at home is good again! I can do downloads, and the family gets uninterrupted, non-grainy streaming video! Turn on all your devices that can stream video to make QoS set up easy.

*To setup QoS on the D-Link DSL-2750B select the **Services** tab on the top > under the **Services** table click on the **QoS** link on the left > read about each setting and select, or enter, the setting that fits your needs > for video streaming select **Triple Play User**.*

*To setup QoS on the R6300 click on the **ADVANCED** tab > expand the Setup menu > click on the QoS Setup link on the left > on the right panel click on Setup QoS rule button > at the bottom click on the +Add Priority Rule button > enter your QoS Policy name > change the priority category to MAC address > enter your device(s) information one by one.* When done you should see the rules appear at the bottom of your QoS rules list. When naming the rule I used the following conventions: For QoS Policy use something like "Pri_MAC_40A5DB", for Device Name try device and model "PS3690".

The last step, yes we are here at last, is to back up your configuration. ***On the WNDR3700 under Maintenance select Backup Settings > click on the Back Up button to save a copy of current settings. Name it something like NETGEAR3700FinalSettings.cfg. On the R6300 click on the Advanced tab > expand the Administration menu > click on Backup Settings > next to Save a copy of current settings click on the Back Up button.***

Setup a Guest Network for Meetings, Relatives and Visitors

Whether we are a business or home owner, we will likely have visitors, friends, relatives, customers, and others that will need to access the Internet. If we give them our trusted SSID and Passphrase, we have exposed our network devices. We need a separate SSID and a different Passphrase for them to do that. This can be done by configuring the Guest Network Settings in your router. Most wireless routers allow you to set up two or more networks; one is your trusted network, which we have discussed, and the second is a guest network. You can maintain a list of authorized devices for the trusted network, and limit visitors to the guest network, which gives access to the Internet but not your SBO/HCU network.

This project came about because a friend of mine has a cabin up North (as we like to call it in Michigan) where he wants wireless access. The campground where his trailer is parked has Internet and a router broadcasting wireless, but the signal does not reach his trailer. He asked me if I would set up a wireless repeater to extend the wireless network range. There are devices that can boost wireless signal strength that you can place between your router and your Internet device. The dilemma for me was what would work best?

Any users who connect to a guest network SSID can only access the Internet directly and other clients in the same SSID guest network. All clients in the SSID are not allowed to access router web Graphical User Interface (GUI), clients of other SSIDs, Ethernet network and other service of this Wireless Router.

The guest network can also be an added layer of security. All devices in your organization need not have access to your trusted network. Those gifted children or employees who might wreak havoc or bypass your security setup can be given guest access to protect your trusted devices and router setup. Granting visitors' guest access to the Internet is as simple as logging in to the router and doing the following:

- Check Enable Guest Network
- Check Enable SSID Broadcast (should be unchecked once all wireless devices are connected unless they change regularly)
- Check Enable Wireless Isolation (keep wireless stations from communicating with each other or with stations on the wired network)
- Change the Guest Wireless Network Name (SSID) from the default
- Under Security Options select WPA2-PSK [AES]
- Under Wireless Settings click on the Set Up Access List button and be sure to uncheck Turn Access Control On
- Enter a Passphrase

If visitors only need access to the Internet occasionally, when the visitors leave, log back in, and disable guest access. Add a wireless repeater to extend your range. These are things to look for in a repeater:

- Wireless Standards: b/g/n/ac (and in 2016 and beyond *ah, aj, ax*)
- Data Rate: Up to 450Mbps or more
- Frequency: Duel band support for 2.4 and 5.0 GHz
- Security: WPA2 and Access Control
- Ports: Five or more Gigabit Ports, Three RP-SMA Connectors

All these things can be found in the Hawking Technology Hi-Gain, Duel-Band Wireless-N Range Extender, HD45X. When you log into your wireless router, you will see two configurable Guest Networks (Guest Network b/g/n and Guest Network a/n). In my Netgear router the b/g/n Network was broadcasting at 2.4 GHz and the a/n network at 5.0 GHz. Since most devices support a/n, that was the network I chose to extend.

The first thing to do is update the firmware in both your router and the range extender. Don't hit the back button on the browser to log back in to the range extender after applying a firmware update. This will apply the same update again. Close the browser, and login with the default settings. When you see <u>Upgrade Accomplished</u>, close the browser and log in again.

NOTE	The Hawking repeater defaulted to setting its SSID to the same thing as my router. At first this seemed like a good idea until I began testing the repeater. While inSSIDer would show me which device was broadcasting, I had no way of knowing if my laptop was connecting to my repeater or my router as I walked away from my house with it, examining the screen. Without some sort of method to confirm I was connecting to the repeater, which was forwarding packets to my router, how could I know for sure if the repeater was truly extending my wireless network? So I configured the repeater to a different SSID and then connected the laptop to the repeater SSID. This proved that everything was working properly.

Following the above note, I could not get my laptop to show a connection to the Internet. The Quick Installation Guide included in the repeater box was failing. Included in the box was a CD with the FULL manual. Upon review of that manual, I found a section on Wireless Security. ***To get the Hawking setup properly, click on the <u>Security</u> tab at the top > select <u>Wireless Security</u> on the left > enable the <u>2.4 GHz Wireless Security Mode</u> and the <u>5 GHz Wireless Security Mode</u> for <u>WPA2(AES)</u> > for the <u>Pre-shared Key Format:</u> leave the <u>Passphrase</u> default selected > enter the <u>Pre-shared Key</u> for the network you are extending from the router and click on <u>Apply</u>***. This will join your laptop with the Internet through your repeater SSID thus proving you are using your wireless repeater to wireless router connection to modem to ISP to connect to the Internet successfully.

NOTE	Whatever device you are setting up for repeating, be sure to make note of all of your settings. Once your device is set up as a repeater the traditional method to login to your repeater will no longer work. For example, I set up my router as a repeater and connected it to my computer via CAT6e. I tried to surf to http://www.routerlogin.net to log in to the router and that browser address resulted in a "Server not found" message. What I had to do to turn off repeating in the router was to make sure that the router was connected to my Base Station (main router) and that it had a valid IP address assigned to it. I then accessed the router acting as a repeater using the IP address I configured as the repeater IP address.

So You Have Purchased a Shiny New 802.11ac Router – Now What?

Most router companies have come out with products supporting the new 802.11ac standard. In the December 2012 PCWorld article by Michael Brown, he listed few examples: Asus RT-AC66U, rated SUPERIOR; Netgear R6300, rated VERY GOOD; Buffalo WZR-D1800H, rated GOOD; D-Link DIR-865L, rated GOOD. Not listed in the article was the Linksys WUMC710 Wireless-AC Wi-Fi 5GHz Universal Media Controller Bridge with 4-Port Switch for extending an 802.11ac wireless network. Given the difference in the price between a five-year-old 802.11n

and a new 802.11ac router, there is no logic in the purchase of a
router/repeater/bridge/device that does not support the new 802.11ac standard.

If you are like me, the last time you looked at your home network was three to five years ago.
To write this book I had to try to stay on the leading edge of technology. I initially used my
2009 Netgear WNDR3700 as the example router for this book. But to keep things current, I
purchased the Netgear R6300 Wi-Fi 802.11ac Duel Band Gigabit Router and updated my
parents' D-Link Router. I then set about updating these setups to convert everything over
from the old routers to the new ones. In my case, my first thought was to back up the
settings from my Netgear WNDR3700 and then import them into the Netgear R6300. This
proved to not be possible according to Netgear support. So what I did was to physically
connect the new R6300 router to my laptop via RJ-45 Cat 6e cable, NOT THE INTERNET. I
could then switch between my wireless connection to my old router and the new router at will,
matching the configurations. The login address for both was http://www.routerlogin.net.
With the R6300, the Username was admin, and the Password was password. This was done
by physically turning off my laptop's connection to the old router by using the button on top of
my HP Pavilion laptop at the upper right that takes it offline. Once my wireless connection
was severed, I could physically login to the new router to the new route to configure it. I
developed a table of my old settings to update the new settings. Below is an example of what
I put together to port all my settings to the new router.

NOTE	The Netgear R6300 Wi-Fi Router is a significant improvement over the WNDR3700. Its USB support was flawless, whereas the WNDR3700 always had problems in my case. It revealed shares so I could play music anywhere in my house. I saw a difference in the wireless speed of devices around my house; this upgrade was worth the price.

Name (SSID):	yourssid-2.4G	Name (SSID):	yourssid-5G
Mode:	Up to 450 Mbps	Mode:	Up to 1300 Mbps
Primary DNS:	64.233.217.3	Secondary DNS:	208.59.247.45
Security Options:	WPA2-PSK [AES]	Passphrase:	yourpassphrase
Wireless Card Access List - On:	HPPAVILIONDV6T 00:1A:65:69:AD:04	PS3-670 A8:E4:EE:4D:9A:C2	LGDVDPlayer 00:43:08:78:91:7A
SAMSUNGBDE5900 30:14:8a:53:6e:e4	Port Forwarding:	Service Name SSH Port 22	Destination: 192.168.1.8
Port Forwarding:	Service Name HTTPS 192.168.1.6	Service Name: HTTPS, Port 443	Service Name: HTTP, Port 80
Address Reservation*	192.168.1.104	DELL40A5DB	08:00:37:40:A5:DB
Address Reservation*	192.168.1.6	Dell-Dimension-2350	00:0B:DB:0D:86:F5
QoS Setup	Enable WMM and Turn on QoS	Add QoS Priority Rules and give all streaming video devices highest priority.	Priority Category: MAC address
Dynamic DNS - On	Service Provider: www.DynDNS.org	yourdomainname.dyndns.org	yourusername yourpassword

Dirty Electricity: Do You Need to Be Concerned?

I listen to National Public Radio when I walk and travel. They aired a broadcast on "Dirty Electricity", which really opened my eyes to some of the potential problems in our relentless technological advances. Corporations and purchased politicians are making sure we don't slow down technology to examine what these advances are doing to our health. Samuel Milham, MD MPH, has been a voice in the wilderness about all this new wireless technology that we are allowing into our lives. He presents very strong arguments about the physical effects of this technology. I am an example of how correct his research is, being a two-time survivor of Lymphoma cancer, caused by exposure to strong electromagnetic fields during the war in Iraq. Here is what his 2010 edition of his book has to say from Amazon:

"Dirty Electricity tells the story of Dr. Samuel Milham, the scientist who first alerted the world about the frightening link between occupational exposure to electromagnetic fields and human disease. Milham takes readers through his early years and education, following the twisting path that led to his discovery that most of the twentieth century diseases of civilization, including cancer, cardiovascular disease, diabetes, and suicide, are caused by electromagnetic field exposure.

Dr. Milham warns that because of the recent proliferation of radio frequency radiation from cell phones and towers, terrestrial antennas, Wi-Fi and Wi-max systems, broadband Internet over power lines, and personal electronic equipment, we may be facing a looming epidemic of morbidity and mortality. In Dirty Electricity, he reveals the steps we must take, personally and as a society, to coexist with this marvelous but dangerous technology."

My advice is that when you are not using your Internet devices, cut off your router and do not allow it to broadcast wireless signals throughout your household. This is somewhat inconvenient, but could prove beneficial to your health! You can look for "Dirty Electricity: Electrification and the Diseases of Civilization, Second Edition by Samuel Milham at Amazon.

Fixing Difficult Wi-Fi Problems

Make sure your firmware is up-to-date by logging into the router occasionally and updating it. Not only can old firmware slow down your router, it can also be a security concern.

 **Story**	My wife took our laptop on the road, and when the computer returned home, it would not connect to the Internet. It turns out she had pressed the wireless button on the top that I never knew existed, next to the volume controls. It took me about an hour to figure out there is a button, that when pressed, will sever and reconnect all wireless communication.

From my HP wireless Laptop's help:

	*You can use the wireless button on your computer to control all of your integrated wireless devices in a single step. For example, on aircraft or in another restricted environment, you can use the wireless button to disable all wireless devices at once, and then enable them when you leave the restricted area.*

If you are having problems with your Wi-Fi range, try repositioning the router away from potential sources of interference. Microwave ovens, cordless phones, baby monitors, or your neighbors Wi-Fi network could be causing problems. You can test to see if the neighbor's Wi-Fi network is causing problems by using inSSIDer or Vistumbler, which are free Wi-Fi network scanners for Windows 7. (See: http://www.metageek.net, http://www.vistumbler.net) You can then try changing the channel (operating frequency) that is being used. Before you do so, know that on **Auto**, the router is supposed to figure out which channel is least crowded, but it never hurts to try manually setting it.

Under Setup select <u>Wireless Settings</u> > change Channel: from <u>Auto</u> to <u>01</u> through <u>13</u> and see if that clears things up. After buying the latest hardware in Netgear, our Internet connection became intermittent again. I wanted to blame the ISP. But after calling my ISP, they clued me in on to how to check my upload and download speeds, which after testing was obviously not my problem. So I had to look at my hardware or network settings at home as the culprit. It turns out a neighbor had spun up a wireless router operating on the same channel as mine. To get life back to normal I had to log into the Netgear router and change the configuration settings from Auto to Manual and reset the channel to one that was not being used. The new Netgear Genie software installed on my laptop allowed me to figure out this puzzle. Click on Wi-Fi Connection, and it will show you the Wi-Fi networks in your neighborhood on each Wi-Fi Channel.

If your wireless signal is too weak in a portion of the house you need to use (and you have tried all the normal solutions like repositioning the router), there are several ways to boost the signal.

1. Buy are third party antenna if your router lets you remove the original antenna or provides a jack. Vendors offer high-gain antennas that may support your router.
2. Buy a repeater to receive, amplify, and rebroadcast the original signal.
3. Buy a second router. Then configure your primary router as a Wireless Base Station and configure the new second router as a Wireless Repeater. Under <u>Advanced</u> ***select <u>Wireless Repeating Function</u> > check <u>Enable Wireless Repeating</u> and enter MAC Address of the Repeater Router***.
4. Use your home's electrical wiring to network your devices. You can add https://www.homeplug.org/home AV powerline-networking support to your Wi-Fi network. PCWorld recommended the <u>D-Link DHP-1320 WIRELESS N POWERLINE ROUTER</u> as another option. The Powerline router offers options, wireless connectivity and connectivity in all your electrical wiring.

You can read more about Wi-Fi problems at http://find.pcworld.com/71972. For additional details and product suggestions, go to http://find.pcworld.com/71971. To check on your security, you should look at your router logs from time to time. Under <u>Content Filtering</u>, *select* <u>***Logs***</u> and view the information provided by your router.

Summary - Physical Internet Communication Layer

For years in the Information Technology profession, IT professionals have been forced to memorize the Open Systems Interconnection mode OSI seven-layer model <u>https://en.wikipedia.org/wiki/OSI_model</u> which is an attempt to define what computer technology and software operate at what layer to show a system's outdated communications hierarchy. Each layer receives services from the layer below and above it. IT hardware and software creators have struggled for years designing and developing techniques for hardening security at each layer of the OSI Model. This book takes advantage of many of these advances in technology to layer/harden security. Putting a **properly configured** hardware firewall between our systems and the Internet is our first layer of security. We have hardened what I will refer to from this point forward at the *Physical Internet Communication Security Layer*. It is our rear supply line and what enables us to venture out and combat our enemies in the new world of the infected Internet.

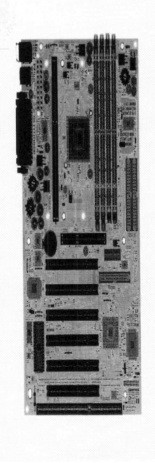

Computer Hardware -- Building a Computer Server

Chapter 3 -- Understanding the Computer Hardware Needed for Virtualization and Gaming -- Building Your Own Computer Server

You might be wondering why a chapter on computer hardware and building your own computer is in a cyber security book. This once again relates back to my military background.

	Historical Reference -- What Training US Marines Receive in Marksmanship to Wage War Effectively

Back in the early 80's when I was trained as a U.S. Marine at Paris Island, we were taught that our M16A1 rifle was the most important thing in our life. Drill Instructors constantly attempted to steal a rifle left unguarded or unlocked. You might ask how anyone knowing that fact would allow something so simple to take place. The answer lies in the fact that while in basic training you are constantly tested as to the physical limits of your endurance and then challenged as to your mental strength afterward when you are more vulnerable. If the Drill Instructors find a flaw in your armor, they will exploit it to see if you will break. Of the original 78 recruits in my flight that attempted to be Marines, only 32 graduated. I admit I would not have been one of them without the support of my father. Somehow he found a way onto Paris Island while I had only three weeks of training left. He did this because I had written home that the Marine Corps was not for me, and I had proven what I set out to do, which was to prove I had what it took to be a U.S. Marine. However, I had decided this military adventure needed to end, and I did not want a career in the military. My father met with me and strongly encouraged me to finish basic training. Those few hours with him and his words made me the man that I later became by becoming a U.S Marine honor graduate private first class.

As Marines, when in the field, we slept with the sling of our rifle wrapped around our leg and sometimes with our arms hugging it. We were required to learn to break down our rifle to the smallest component and put it back together, repeatedly, faster and faster. We memorized the name of every piece, its purpose, and all aspects of what our rifle was capable of (muzzle velocity, range, clearing jams, and much more). We were taught, "You can't shoot and kill the enemy without your weapon!" A Marine without his weapon, anywhere in the world, is a Marine out of uniform! We examined and cleaned our weapons, sometimes at the beginning, during and at the end of each day.

U.S. Marines receive the most advanced marksmanship training in the world. We learn multiple firing positions and proper sling tension on our arms and how to make the best shot, thus locking the weapon into its optimum firing position. A Marine in a proper firing position and sling tension can bring the weapon on target, close his eyes and then open them to see his rifles sights are still right on target with his natural point of aim. He does not anticipate the round traveling down range, which might jerk the rifle off target; he takes a deep breath, relaxes and slowly squeezes the trigger, which is a natural event for him. A Marine is taught how important breathing, as well as slow and smooth trigger movement, is to every shot fired at a target. Unlike in the movies, a Marine knows he does not have an unlimited supply of ammo to continuously fire at the enemy. Every shot fired is meant to kill an enemy target, otherwise, the trigger should not be pulled. There are exceptions to this such as a final defensive position where ammo is readily available; but out in the field every shot has to count. I hope this dispels your movies view of the world.

An expert Marine shooter can hit a silhouette from the waist up target (which is smaller than your 36 inch TV) at 500 yards with 10 out of 10 consecutive shots. Let's pause a moment to consider what 500 yards means. Most of us have visited football stadiums, where upwards of 100,000 people or more can surround a 100-yard field. Therefore, if you have ever sat in the goal post seats and could not see what was going on the other side of field, imagine adding 4 more football fields to your vision of the football field. Also, imagine how small the players would appear from four more stadiums away. Another analogy would be the next time you are on a golf course with a straight 500-yard par 5, try to make out the flag. At 500 yards a 3-foot silhouette target is hardly more than a tiny speck smaller than a tiny insect on the wall, but US Marines could hit it without special laser sights or scopes with their training. I can't speak for today's Marines, but I assume this standard of excellence is still being maintained. As a quotation by U.S. Army General Pershing who stated, "*The deadliest weapon in the world is a MARINE and his rifle!*" While there are far deadlier weapons in today's world, a MARINE and his/her rifle is certainly a very cost effective one.

What this story is meant to illustrate is that if you are going to venture out into enemy territory (the Internet) you need to have at least a basic understanding of the equipment with which you are employing to do so. You have to consider yourself at war with the Internet and everyone on it. This means learning a little bit about the hardware that you are loading operating systems onto, how to clean and protect that hardware, and in later chapters, learning how to use that hardware effectively against the enemy. Even if you never want to try to build a computer, learning about the components that go into a modern computer is valuable knowledge that you need for repairing and upgrading your Internet devices.

You may not consider yourself capable of building a computer yourself; I am hoping to change that perception about your computer knowledge with this chapter. It is really not as difficult as you might think. A custom-built system will outlast any off-the-shelf product you can purchase and at a sizeable cost advantage in the long run. The fact that I used my eight-year-old, custom-built computer to do many of the advanced exercises that I describe in this book is testimony to that. However, even if you don't want to build a computer system yourself, you should read this chapter to understand the technology you need to fulfill your needs. A custom-built computer will vastly increase the shelf life of your SBO/HCU desktop computer and give you versatility in the ability to add to your hardware. Ask yourself, how is your off-the-shelf system doing? Plus, if you enjoy searching for the latest gadget or the study of technology, this exercise can be FUN and provide many evenings of entertainment as you watch TV! Just like that do-it-yourself house project that you look back at with pride, every day that you use a computer that you designed and built yourself, you will enjoy also. In addition, with a custom-built system, you can run a Redundant Array of Independent Disks (RAID) at home, making your system much more bomb proof; I am going to teach you how to do that. Rarely are the off-the-shelf systems set up in such a fashion even if you paid a lot of money for them. More than likely you will have to hire an expensive computer professional to get a RAID system setup.

If you don't have the time or feel you don't have the skill necessary to build a computer, then buying a prebuilt desktop has a few drawbacks you need to consider:

- Many of the off-the-shelf computer setups are very limited in what they offer in component quality and options.
- Most pre-built computers come with an Original Equipment Manufacturer (OEM) copy of Windows 7/8.1/10 pre-loaded. This OS is loaded with tons of free trial (bloat ware*), demo and other software, which you will never use. The manufacturers do this to make selling their systems more profitable. This litters your OS with stuff no one wants, subsequently slowing down the OS performance and possibly broadcasting information about you to the Internet. You will have to explicitly go in, research the pre-installed trial or limited option bloatware*, and remove each application one-by-one, which many of us do not have the time to research or are not skilled enough to do. For example, a friend stopped by my house because her laptop was running slow, and I spent three hours with her removing tool-bars and bloatware* from their machine before it became *finally fast* (as seen on the TV commercial)!
- Many off-the-shelf computer providers do not provide the CDs/DVDs or downloads necessary to rebuild/reload a failed computer after hardware failure. Those DVDs can and should be purchased separately at nominal expense. This will allow a failed computer to be rebuilt from scratch. The alternative is hiring or finding a computer professional to try to solve your problems, which may be a huge waste of time and money. Writing this book, I kept going from system to system where the user wanted me to rescue them from oblivion. I always suggested that we just wipe (zero) the hard disk and reinstall their OS and their application software only to find out that they don't have any installation disks or even a system image backup. Their only alternative is to convert to a Linux OS, which no one seems willing to try, or to purchase a new OS and application software at tremendous expense. Sometimes their hardware was not capable of running Windows 7 or even a modern Linux OS, so I really could not help them.

 **WARNING**	Never purchase an off-the-shelf computer without also purchasing the installation media for all software that is installed on the computer. If the manufacturer will not allow you to purchase that media at a nominal price, buy or build a different computer.

- Many times, off-the-shelf systems are put together using cheap, inferior or poorly sized components tossed together by underpaid personnel to save money and increase their corporate profits. If you open up a pre-built, off-the-shelf system, you will likely discover your options to alter the hardware are very limited. These inferior components usually fail much sooner than well-researched, quality custom components.
- Computer standards are constantly changing, and off-the-shelf system use cheaper legacy components that only support old standards. This severely limits the shelf life of your computer. They do this because manufactures want to get rid of the components, as well as offer off-the-shelf builders huge discounts to move these parts.

While admitting my last server build was done in December 2011, I have tried to keep this chapter up-to-date until the publish date of this book. You want the most advanced hardware that embraces all the new technologies and has minimal legacy support for old standards such as a hard drive IDE bus or the outdated USB 2.0 ports. Any device with USB 2.0 ports should not be purchased for your SB/HC use.

The time frame for manufacturers to adopt the academic standards written by the standards experts is about five-years. If you go with an off-the-shelf computer, then you should compare the components in those computers with my custom-build recommendations. I think you will find this chapter's suggestions superior and cheaper than the off-the-shelf alternatives. There are many reasons for this, which I will discuss in this chapter. We must try to know our Internet devices as well as U.S. Marines know their rifle.

To use some of the techniques in this book to keep yourself secure, it is time to junk the old computer hardware running Microsoft Windows XP (discussed previously), *join the 21st century*, and buy computer hardware capable of running modern day OSs, and virtualization software, which we will discuss in Chapter 7. The good news is that the old XP machine and license will not go to waste. In Chapter 9 we are going to turn it into a modern Linux SSH server that we can use to tunnel into our home network and encrypt our communications from anywhere in the world using mobile devices like your smartphone, laptop, iPad 2, Notepad or any other device you own that uses the Internet.

Story  	While working for the Naval Research Laboratory as a contractor, my boss asked me to reverse-engineer a program for examining the data from our testing of chaff. Chaff is a radar countermeasure that our pilots use to keep enemy missiles from locking onto the plane and identifying the real target. (See: https://en.wikipedia.org/wiki/Chaff_(radar_countermeasure)) We would shoot the chaff up into the air and collect data like pressure curves, radar signature, etc. to make sure that the product that the private corporations were providing met the standards that the US Navy demanded. There were large amounts of money at stake, and if we condemned a chaff test, the contractor could lose millions. I reversed-engineered and duplicated the results that we were paying 15 to 20 government employees to process using some old Data General computers. However, what my boss did not tell me was the government supervisor in charge of the Data General computers and his staff of employees out-ranked my boss. My program would cause many of them to lose their jobs. I was, unknowingly, put in the middle of a political mess of which I had no knowledge. I was quickly laid off, and all of my work never saw the light of day. I loved that job, and eventually, those Data General computers went away when the boss of that staff was forcibly retired. You can fight technology, but eventually in the end, it will win.

As discussed in the Introduction, Microsoft has ended mainstream support for XP and Vista. Yet I find small businesses, charities and households still battling with old XP systems that take longer to boot than it takes to brew a pot coffee. In fact, that is a familiar theme I encounter, the users press the power button on the computer and go brew a pot of coffee while it boots. A good computer setup at home allows you to telecommute with technology that is many times vastly superior to the usual corporate desktop setup. It will make you more productive and shave many hours of frustration sitting behind hardware that was meant for a 15-year-old operating system. Having a superior setup at home may aid in convincing your company's management to allow you to work from home on an occasional or permanent basis, saving you time and money. While I admit this never worked for me, today's managers are beginning to realize the corporate savings that telecommuting provides (saving in costly office space, in capital purchases of hardware and furniture, in production, in utility and phone costs, in parking space, and much more). Study after study has shown that working from home, when possible, is often times a cost savings for the company and the employee.

Libraries with strained budgets are also still running XP, which is putting them and their users at risk. Windows XP should be viewed as a virus, spyware and bot infestation platform (at least this is what I find, especially on systems where the latest updates that Microsoft has issued have not been applied). XP is a *time bomb* running spyware, viruses and on bot-nets opening up libraries, businesses and homes to malicious intrusion by crackers and criminals to view anything they are doing on their computers. Windows 7, according to the Microsoft Security Intelligence Report http://www.microsoft.com/security/sir/keyfindings/default.aspx#!section_4_2 has been found to be five times less likely to be infected by malware. These XP systems must be replaced with a PC running a supported and maintained OS like Microsoft Windows 7, Macintosh, or a modern flavor of the Linux OS.

There are ways around this, using Clonezilla for example, to make a system image when you get the computer, but Clonezilla is not intuitive to many users. There are other imaging tools such as the system image tool in Windows 7, *click on Start > All Programs > Maintenance > Backup and Restore > on the left panel click on Create a system image*. The system image solution to backing up your system is great if your computer becomes corrupted or has a hard drive failure. However, what happens if you have some other hardware failure such as a smoked motherboard. When you fix a PC with newer and/or better components, will that system image lie down and work nicely on the new hardware? Windows has security measures that may prevent this from working; otherwise you could make images of their OS and load it on other computers. The Geeks at Best Buy have a "Tattoo" method of getting new hardware working with a failed hardware setup, but you will have to pay for that service. Sometimes having a current modern OS DVD around to reinstall the OS when the need arises and refresh everything, is a lot easier than working with system images.

Some SBO/HCUs believe that the software just magically came with the computer and it should run forever, even though their kids riddled it with spyware, viruses, bots, all sorts of malware and bloatware* that they have no idea about. Now it takes one minute per keystroke and five minutes to boot. Nonetheless, their computer is probably still a decent piece of hardware. If they wiped the hard drive and installed a flavor of a Linux OS they would have a usable computer again. Nevertheless, most everyone I have tried to help is adverse to that solution and would rather continue to fight with their XP's *blue screens of death*. All I could do is rescue their data and leave their computer in bad shape.

When it costs over $100 to fill an SUV gas tank at the pump, are you really worried about spending a few extra bucks to get a **great** or modern computer component, versus just a *good* or *outdated* computer component? You shouldn't be because you really ought to be buying a new computer about as often as you buy a new car, which for my family, is about every six years. Just as we don't want to get stuck driving a car we don't like for many years, we also do not want to be stuck operating a computer we hate for several years either. The same applies to a mobile device such as a smartphone, though users of these devices seem to expect to upgrade the latest and greatest every couple of years.

Savings 	Mobile device technology is emulating what the computer revolution did years ago by upgrading hardware frequently. However, cellphone companies devised a strategy to hook their customers into two-year contracts with upgrades to their hardware. Customers think they are getting a $600 smartphone for $200 or less but are actually paying for them many times over with contracts that include huge fines to cancel. In the long run, the cellphone companies are making thousands for a minor $400 upfront loss, whether or not the customer canceled their contract. They modeled this strategy after what in colonial times was called indentured servitude, which was a form of debt bondage, established in the early years of the American colonies and elsewhere. The unsuspecting victim is brought over on a paid contract to work as a slave for a number of years, usually ranging from one to seven years, after which they would be set free. Skip down to Chapter 12 on smartphones to see how you should use and purchase your mobile technology and avoid these contracts.

Seek out multiple reviews of the hardware that you are considering. Two good websites for commentary on some the latest technology are http://www.tomshardware.co.uk and http://www.legitreviews.com. However, in the http://www.overclock.net discussion forum titled "*Why not to trust Tom's Hardware (for PSUs at least),*" one person stated the following about Tom's Hardware, "*Nice how they gloss over the terrible +3.3V ripple on the CoolerMaster GX750. And don't mention the transient peaks on the +12V and +5V that exceed spec. That's not important at all, right? It's just exceeding the spec by huge margins for one of the most important areas of PSU performance. And then for the CoolerMaster Silent Pro Gold 700W they don't even mention the 58mV +3.3V peaks.*" Be sure you have an add-on that blocks trackers before visiting Tom's Hardware. The website had 17 trackers, which also indicates a for-profit motive. There were also many articles and forums that indicate Payola* has become a problem at many technology review sites. There are no laws preventing these websites from taking bribes to favor reviewing one product over another, or even going so far as to cast a favorable light on one product versus another. Your answer to this is to read many reviews, from many resources; the truth is out there, you just have to find it. We also need to lobby our governments for protection from this type of activity.

Story 	When I worked at Cruise Missile Project (CMP) many years ago, one of my responsibilities was maintaining all of their PCs. The manager in charge would call me into his office and watch me struggle to get his computer to boot (HE HATED THAT COMPUTER). After I failed to get it to boot by trying a few things, he would look at me with glee that I could not fix his computer, power on the computer and say "watch this," and give the PC a swift kick and that sucker would boot up. The moral of the story is that this is a man the taxpayers were paying the equivalent of $500,000 in today's dollars a year to, and CMP was wasting hours of his valuable time on a crappy PC. You do the math. How much is your time worth, and how much grief do you want to endure from your SBO/HCU PC?

Many of us spend more time on the computer than we do behind the wheel of our car. As telecommuting comes into vogue, the car sits parked in the driveway as we work behind the computer 8 to 10 hours a day. Most of us have a computer or mobile device with us everywhere we go. Even while camping in the peace and quiet of the forest, I'm guilty of carrying my laptop with me to get a few things done.

Virtualization technology has changed our hardware needs in a laptop or SBO/HCU PC. I blew through 1TB of disk space in no time loading many of the virtual versions of Linux and Windows XP for various uses that I will describe later. Eleven years ago, 1 TB of disk was unfathomable on a desktop PC. I noticed that my 2006 custom-built PC server running RAID 1 was getting slow, so I considered whether to upgrade some hardware or build a new server with 2012 technology. It was still a fine piece of hardware, and I was on a tight budget while writing this book, but I decided spending money on a computer that old did not make sense. Hence, I decided to take the next leap in technology and build a new computer and document it in this book. I was very glad about this decision later when, one day in June 2013, that server would no longer boot, and it took me over a month of hard word to fix it. At that time, I was faced with a choice, pay Best Buy $200 for a service contract for all my computers and hope they knew something I did not, or trust in my abilities and knowledge to determine if the computer was repairable. I tried all the usual suspects such as changing the motherboard battery, reseating the memory, unplugging and replugging the cards, and the trick that my old CMP boss used-kick it but-nothing worked. If you ever run into the problem where a computer powers up and does not boot, try these steps:

1. Test the monitor first before tearing the computer apart.
2. Make sure the PC has fully power-cycled by unplugging the power cord. Let the PC sit unpowered for at least 20 seconds to allow capacitors to discharge.
3. Try clearing the CMOS thus restoring the computer back to its default configuration. You will have to study your motherboard manual on how to do this. Removing the motherboard battery for a period of time usually works. If the computer boots add your Basic Input/Output System (BIOS) setting changes back in one at a time.
4. Check your power supply voltage switch to make sure it is set for your country (120V or 240V).
5. Take out all the cards/hardware you don't absolutely need and reseat everything in the computer, testing everything as you go along by powering on the computer after each change.
   a. Reseat all internal data and power cables
   b. Reseat the memory modules
   c. Reseat any expansion cards
   d. Try unplugging your keyboard and mouse

| Story | In my case with the server, I unplugged one of the hard drives from the RAID array and pressed the power button. Imagine my joy when I heard the BEEP indicating my server was booting up! I allowed the computer to boot with a degraded RAID array, backed everything up and then shutdown the server and reconnected the hard drive to the array. Go figure, I'm happy to say the server has been fine ever since. |

6. Make sure the Central Processing Unit (CPU) is seated properly. If the computer operated before, this is very unlikely to be the problem.

7. Look around inside the computer to see if there might be an electrical short. With the power on, wiggle wires and see if something lights up, sparks, etc.

8. Test or swap out the power supply. Even though fans may be spinning and lights lit up, a portion of your power supply may have failed. The easiest way to test a power supply is to spend around $40 to get a quality PSU tester. In my case I used an expensive multimeter I had left over from my time working in the Air Force. If any part of your PSU fails, buy a new one.

9. If you have spare parts lying around try swapping out parts from your computer with other parts testing each swap one at a time.

10. The last option rarely makes sense. You can take your computer to a repair shop, but depending on its age, that might be throwing away money that you should be using to purchase a new computer setup.

If you decide to read this chapter and consider a custom build, here are a few rules to help you pick out your components and do the right thing with your hardware:

· Evaluate any parts you can cannibalize off old computers. Your old DVD RW drive, power supply, case, hard drives, and more may be incorporated into your new system. This technology is not evolving as rapidly as it did in the past, so old components may be reusable.

· I have learned that in home computing technology, go where the gamers go. I don't game because I have never had the time for it, but I give gamers credit for scrutinizing every piece of hardware that goes into their home, custom-built systems. They take great pride in their hardware and gaming prowess. Gamers are wonderful people that rate and write about computer hardware from a performance perspective to which we all must pay attention to. The components they like usually have good reviews.

· The core components to any computer are the CPU and motherboard. Spare no expense on these components once they have proven themselves and been updated to the latest standards (never buy either when they are first released or have not been reviewed by the PC gamer community). See if a version two of the products is looming around the corner because of some problem discovered after their initial release. Technological advances sometimes take one step backwards before moving two steps forward. Everything else in the computer revolves around these core components.

· We have to narrow the playing field for each component by establishing the minimum standards that we will accept in our custom components. As new technologies develop, we have to embrace them. The fun thing is we can look at our previous setup and determine the things that annoyed us, or that we want to improve on, and do so. For example, years ago my computer had no front USB 2.0 ports. I later purchased a floppy drive that had a USB 2.0 port and have never regretted it. At a minimum, any new modern computer will build at least two USB 3.0 ports into the front computer case panel.

These requirements may seem trivial, but consider your last car purchase or lease. What was it about the vehicle that annoyed you the most that you wouldn't compromise on? In my case, my car has the best crash car safety ratings. However, after driving it a few weeks I found out why. The blind spots that were created in keeping the car safe in a crash put me at far greater risk because they have almost caused me to crash numerous times. I have to double/triple check before changing lanes and still sometimes have a horn beeped at me by an irate driver.

Researching things on the Internet is very dangerous as we have discussed. We will discuss (VMs) in Chapter 7 and using the Tor anonimizer in Chapter 8, both of which should be employed when conducting component research. You will find yourself clicking on hundreds of links to gather information about which components you want in your computer setup.

Precautions & Hardware 101 Tips to Building the Ultimate New Computer Server

Below are a few simple tips/precautions for building your ultimate home computer. Often these guidelines are ignored by computer professionals, both in government and corporations, who have infinite pockets and resources to demand new hardware from their suppliers. You need to employ these safety measures even if they do not.

1. Your hands are oily and can pass that oil to sensitive computer connections. For example, when pushing in the memory sticks, or gently dropping a CPU onto the motherboard, it is not a good idea to touch the metal connectors with your fingers. You should use latex gloves to do this type of work. Many times during my 27-year IT career, I have seen computer professionals ignore this.
2. Study in detail how to apply the Thermal Grease to the CPU. This is a very important! From https://en.wikipedia.org/wiki/Thermal_grease, "*Thermally conductive paste improves the efficiency of a heatsink by filling air gaps that occur when the imperfectly flat and smooth surface of a heat generating component is pressed against the similar surface of a heatsink, air being approximately 8000 times less efficient at conducting heat (see thermal conductivity) than, for example, aluminum (a common heatsink material).*" We will soon discuss how to apply the Thermal Paste in the CPU section of this chapter.
3. Electrostatic discharge can destroy any computer component. I have seen this ignored by military personnel and corporate IT professionals alike during my career. From https://en.wikipedia.org/wiki/Static_electricity, "*Potentials below 300 volts are not typically detectable by humans. Maximum potential commonly achieved on human body range between 1 and 10 kV, though in optimal conditions can reach as high as 20–25 kV can be reached. Low relative humidity increases the charge buildup; walking 20 feet (6.1 m) on vinyl floor at 15% relative humidity causes a buildup of voltage up to 12 kilovolts, while at 80% humidity the voltage is only 1.5 kV.*" 300 volts is more than enough voltage potential to destroy something as sensitive as a memory chip. The safest way to protect computer components is to wear an antistatic device such as a wristband. If you want to work with more risk, make sure to touch something metal, preferably connected to your home wiring, to discharge yourself, and then proceed with installing your computer's expensive motherboard components.
4. Make sure your computer has more than enough ventilation (fans). They are very cheap to buy and are so important to the life of your computer components. While we are on the subject, never operate your laptop or desktop in hot place (85+ degrees or more is my rule for shutting down all computer hardware). Doing so can/will overheat

the components. I ask my wife to try to keep the temperature below 78 degrees in the office. Buying a $300 dollar window air conditioner to protect your HCU/SBO costly computer equipment is well worth the expense.

5. Buy an Uninterrupted Power Supply (UPS) to protect your SBO/HCU setup. Your business or house may only be getting 100 volts if it is a long way from the nearest transformer. The US power grid is no longer stable and is becoming more intermittent as the infrastructure deteriorates, a trend that will continue in the foreseeable future. Just plug the two voltage leads into the outlet where your computer will be plugged in and check the voltage for yourself.

If you are experienced in electronics, you can measure what is coming into your location by using a multimeter to find out. The power supply coming into your home is unstable, and the voltages can vary. Contrary to what your power company and government may say, the power grid is becoming more unstable as it ages and is not upgraded. This is not conducive to keeping your home network / computer / electronic equipment safe and running. Many of the components in your computer operate at various very low and sensitive voltages that depend on a stable 110 volt power supply coming in. The reason for this is that a computer has many transformers converting the AC voltage into many low DC voltages, and they can only do that efficiently if the AC voltage coming from your utility company is not fluctuating. The United States power grid is many years old and in need of upgrade. There will be no upgrade due to lack of political will, the need for corporate profits, and a general apathy by American citizens until this problem affects the general basic needs in their homes. Expect things to become much worse in the future. A good UPS is mandatory in keeping your computer's health and will smooth out the voltages in a SBO/HCU setup to keep them protecting your computer equipment constantly. UPS's also protect your SBO/HCU setup from lighting strikes; the American Power Conversion Corporation (APC) even offers a replacement warranty if your computer equipment is damaged when these events occur from time to time and could corrupt your OS or destroy your computer. If you buy an APC Smart UPS you can rig it up to gently shutdown your SBO server(s) to keep it/them running 24/7 even if the power does not come back on in a certain amount of time. If you are, in any way, dependent on your SBO/HCU setup, this type of hardware is mandatory to your survival. (http://www.apc.com) A few of the Features Y Benefits of a UPS are:

➢ Lifetime data recovery warranty by professional data recovery services in the event data is lost due to the failure of the unit.
➢ Back up and protect your hardware and data during power outages, surges and spikes.
➢ Provides protection of connected equipment from power surges on the data lines.
➢ Protect secondary electronics from surges and spikes without reducing battery power used to run primary electronics during an outage.
➢ Gives higher application availability by correcting low and high voltage conditions without using the battery (option not available on all models).
➢ Adjust the voltage points (widen or tighten the range) where your UPS transfers to battery to maximize useful battery life and protect sensitive electronics.
➢ Provides temporary battery power when the utility power is out.

Story	One of my partners working on the book complained of delays because of power outages and thunderstorms. She wisely unplugs all her electronics

	during a storm. Since she depends on her computer for her job and contract work, and has read this book, I was very surprised she has not investigated and purchased a UPS.
Story 	Another friend of mine who has read my book sent me an email stating, "We had a bad thunderstorm a week ago, that hit my power grid. I lost my internet modem, wireless router, the network card in my laser printer (attached to the router) and my big screen TV!" I had to poke some fun at him and ask if he followed the directions in my book and had purchased a UPS, he had not.
Story 	I came home from my daily walk and discovered the dining room light would not work, nor did my entertainment center have any power at all. Even my glow-in-the-dark light switch was out. I ran down to the basement to reset the circuit breaker only to find that none of them had flipped. My wife said all she did was flip the switch to turn the light on and the bulb blew. This was weird, as other devices on the same circuit were working. I replaced the bulb and the light switch now glowed (who knew a working bulb was needed to make the light switch glow, it completed the circuit). I then pulled out the entertainment center to discover that the breaker on my entertainment center surge protector was flipped. The moral of this story is that if you think the power grid is stable, think again. Protect your expensive electrical devices (computers, entertainment centers, TVs, etc. with a UPS, or at the very least, a quality surge protector (preferably a protector that can kill your vampire energy draining devices, which I will describe later).
WARNING   	The U.S. has thus far refused to upgrade or protect their power grid against an electromagnetic pulse (EMP) event. It is estimated that should such an event occur up to 90% of the U.S. population could perish. What most Americans do not understand is that this cataclysmic effect could occur because of a natural phenomenon such as a massive solar storm. Such an event has occurred in past history such as during America's horse-and-buggy era when it did not matter but in today's world it would be devastating. Even a solitary nuke detonated above U.S. territory would be shocking and America's enemies have been probing U.S. defenses to see if they could make this happen. For example, North Korea tried to slip two ballistic missiles through the Panama canal to see if they would be detected. They have also been conducting low yield test below the ground and recently put up a low-orbit satellite. It is estimated that a figure as low as 1.5 billion spent on the power grid could save many millions, if not hundreds of millions of American lives should such an EMP event occur. It is also estimated that a well-planned terrorist attack on the U.S. power grid could wreak more havoc than Hurricane Sandy. There has been legislation proposed to address this threat but legislators such as the House Energy and Commerce Committee chairman Rep. Fred Upton (R-Mich) rigidly stand against these bills. What is ironic is that the many billions of dollars spent on massive data centers to spy on the worlds Internet use would become useless without massive amounts of power.

6. Your UPS or computer must have a good path to ground. Many old houses only have two wire systems. Plugging a three pronged device into a wall socket with an adapter for a two wire plug is not something that you should do. If you can't run a new wire to your breaker box with two paths to ground to where the UPS is located, buy a three prong outlet and replace the two pronged outlet by tying the common screw to the ground screw. Use a small piece of 12 gauge wire to do so, which will hold its position on the screw once bent around it. Using a 15 gauge wire can twist out from underneath the screw if you are not careful. The bend around the grounding screw will be backwards, which makes the 12 gauge wire a better choice. When you bend the 12 gauge wire, wrap it around the back of the outlet to keep it low on the screw so that you can fit a runner wire on top of the common screw if necessary. Then flip the breaker, killing power to that circuit, and replace the two prong outlet with a three prong outlet. That way your UPS plug has two paths to ground, even if your house wiring does not; this will help protect your computer equipment. A little more Electrical 101-the white wire is the common, which goes on the left three grounding screws where we tied the common to ground, and the black wire(s) goes on the two gold screws on the right side of the outlet. Make sure you bend any wires connecting to the outlet tightly around the screw in the same direction that you are tightening the screws. If your wiring system is REALLY old, the brown wrapped hot wire and common wire may look the same, but if you look more closely, the hot wire has strips of black mixed into the brown casing to distinguish it from your common wire.

WARNING	The above procedure gives the component plugged into the outlet two paths to ground but what happens if the outlet single common path is somehow severed? The hot wire is tied into the ground screw thus making the outlet a hot 120 volt hazard. In my career I have been hit by 120 volts a few times due to my carelessness and survived with a few shakes afterward. I feel the benefit of the component having two paths to ground outweigh the risk of the one common path being lost which some electricians will argue with.

7. If you are building a home computer, download all of the latest BIOS, drivers, software, documentation, etc. for all of your hardware to another computer before powering on the new computer. If there is a BIOS update for the computer motherboard, apply the BIOS update before doing anything else. It can save you a lot of grief later.

Test the new computer hardware with some diagnostics software. You can go to http://www.memtest.org and download their free software to test your RAM. Assuming your hard drive is a Western Digital http://support.wdc.com/product/download.asp?lang=en or Seagate http://origin-www.seagate.com/support/downloads, you can go their websites and download their latest and greatest software to test your hard drive(s).

The rest of this chapter is about my research on the computer components, some of which I used in my home system build. They may not be relevant to what you have in mind for your home computer. I have spent many hours of research on this, but technology keeps advancing, and this book is only up-to-date with its publishing date. There are new and better devices released constantly. I have included this information to give ideas on how to research a custom computer of your own.

 **Tip**	While working in a large bank data center we adhered to certain cable labeling practices. Your computer setup may get somewhat complex, so be sure you label all your cables at both ends to keep things organized. You can use masking tape and a pen or purchase a label printer. Establish a standard for what you put on each label, for example, Hostname-IP Address-MAC Address-Destination. For a low tech solution, route your cables through multiple paper towel or toilet paper tubes.

As a side note, PCWorld says buying those expensive cables for your new TV or computer (HDMI, Cat 6a, etc.) are not worth it. Go to an online alternative such as http://www.monoprice.com where I purchased a good HDMI cable for $3.00.

Case – Evaluating and Choosing

Since the computer case is our first part that we are researching, let us discuss how we go about picking the case we want. The case is the only part where size matters if we purchase a versatile case with extended ATX support. It is one of the most difficult components to pick for a desktop system because there are so many options from which to choose. Everyone wants different things from a computer case (e.g. gamers sometimes want flashy lights, glowing cables, and for the case to look cool; an SBO might want a cheap sturdy case that can house their computer components; an HCU may want something between the two extremes and that can hold up to some abuse. Depending on what you want you have to start narrowing the playing field by determining all the criteria you are looking for. We will repeat this procedure for every computer component from this point on.

Sample minimum requirements for your desktop computer case:

1. Dimensions that fit the ergonomic place you have chosen to house your computer setup. In my circumstance, the case had to stand less than 23 inches in height.
2. Less show and more air flow for cooling unless you are a gamer.
3. A minimum of two USB 3.0 ports on the front of the case and, preferably, all are USB 3.0 ports.
4. An internal USB 3.0 header for your motherboard.
5. Sturdy steel design with the least possible easily broken plastic (unless this is an SBO business server that is on 24/7 and will just sit in a corner).
6. Some simple case soundproofing to keep the computer operation quiet. It is shocking how loud a data center can be, and you will appreciate peace and quiet.
7. Filters for dust, which are easily cleaned and, preferably, removable.
8. External 5.25" drives that can slide into place by a locking latch mechanism making for easy drive installation and removal.
9. Enough room and length for two video cards (the new video cards can be quite long). Your case should have a spacious interior to ease component installation and to be able to house an *extended* ATX motherboard, tower CPUs and attached coolers, high-end

graphics cards, thick performance radiators or push-pull fan configurations, and more. Also, read reviews to find out how difficult cable management was for others.

10. Price range should be $100 to $300 dollars. Anything less than $100 will most likely have an abundance of easily broken plastic, or is designed for low-end components such as USB 2.0 ports.

Story	My 2006 mid-tower case, which is plastic, requires a pencil to hit the start button because the plastic power switch broke off years ago. Make sure you get a sturdy steel design. Imagine five years of this annoyance!

I did not want years of this type of grief in a future computer build. I also did not want to get into the complexity of a liquid-cooled system. When you think about what size case to get, bear in mind that today's full towers are close to the same size that mid-tower cases used to be, so don't rule them out as a possible solution to your needs.

Story 	Years ago I had a full tower in the office that was monstrously tall. Because of its large footprint, I had to put it in an awkward spot in my office just to roll out the keyboard under my desk. I finally downsized to a mid-tower and gave the steel full tower away. In another example, I purchased a short, cube-style computer case that forced me to buy special, expensive IDE disk cables because the disks were too far away from the motherboard and on the other side of the case. All those expensive IDE cables that I purchased years ago are now lying around going to waste, as IDE disks have become completely obsolete. Once the cube dies, I will have to recycle everything.

Every website you visit may reveal a few facts about the case that you are researching. As you find case candidates, put them in a spreadsheet or table. Some sites such as http://www.newegg.com allow you to compare case specifications side by side quickly. Most of the cases will not meet your minimum requirements and can soon be eliminated. However, as you keep going you will establish a list of cases to consider and compare. Gather information and commentary from various websites until you have narrowed the playing field. Establish a model computer case, and use that as your baseline case to compare against everything else. Compare cases until another rises to the top, and then use that as your baseline case until you have compared everything. Below is a quick list that I have researched that met or came close to meeting my requirements defined above. The massively narrowed list below shows how diverse the computer case market is and how to conduct this type of research. The first table is a list of cases of interest that warranted further research. The second table was my way of gathering details about the cases in which I had further interest.

I conducted some of this research back in December 2011 and chose the SilverStone Raven RV03B-W, which had superior motherboard compatibility options, good case material, dimensions that I needed, front ports that I needed, excellent fan support for a non-liquid cooled case, a weight of only 25.13 pounds, which is somewhat lighter that other cases in its category, and costs less than some of its competition.

I did another analysis in July 2013 and chose the Fractal Design Define XL R2 FD-CA-DEF-XL-R2-TI Titanium Grey Steel ATX Full Tower Computer Case. It weighs a whopping 36+ pounds but it is unbreakable steel and meets every requirement specified above. If cost is an issue, the $50 cheaper XION is also a great choice. You know your own needs, so below is an example analysis that you can conduct on your own. I spent a full week looking at cases and reading reviews before making my choices. Evaluating computer equipment is a hobby of mine and one I enjoy doing while watching TV sitting behind my laptop.

AZZA Fusion 3000 CSAZ-3000	AZZA Genesis 9000 CSAZ-9000W
Cooler Master Centurion 5	Cooler Master Elite 431 PLUS
Cooler Master Haf 922 Steel Mid Tower	Cooler Master Haf 932 ATX Full Tower
COOLER MASTER HAF X RC-942-KKN1 Black Steel/ Plastic	Corsair Obsidian 650D Mid Tower
Corsair Obsidian 800D Full Tower	Fractal Design Define XL FD-CA-DEF-XL-R2
NZXT Phantom 530	NZXT Switch 810
Rosewill Armor-EVO	Thermaltake Level 10 GT (VN10001W2N)
SilverStone RAVEN RV03B-W	XION Gaming Series XON-985-BK
XION Gaming Series XON-990-BK	

Antec's P280 Super Mid Tower, ComputerShopper Editors Choice&SilentPC Recommend. Winner of the first round case comparison at Tom's Hardware, December 2012.	Motherboards: XL-ATX, ATX, Micro ATX, Mini ITX; 3 x 5.25" tool-less drive bays External 5.25" Drive Bays; 6 x 3.5" / 2.5" drive trays Internal 3.5" Drive Bays; Front ports: 2 x USB 3.0, 2 x USB 2.0, Audio I/O. Dimensions: 22.1" x 9.1" x 20.7"; Weight 22.3 lbs. The Antec P280's dual-layer 0.8 mm SECC / polycarbonate side panels absorb noise for exceptional sound dampening.
AZZA Genesis 9000 CSAZ-9000W White 0.8mm SECC ATX Full Tower, editor's choice award by Neoseeker, bigger than my minimal dimensions but good for a SBO.	Motherboards: XL-ATX, E-ATX, Full ATX, Micro ATX; 2 x USB 3.0, 2 x USB 2.0, e-SATA, HD Audio, Mic Front Ports; 9 External 5.25" Drive Bays; 5+1 (up to 9) Internal 3.5" Drive Bays; 2x Easy Swap HDD trays (up to 5) allow easy, tool-less assembly of HDD; Dimensions: 25.1" x 9.8" x 23.2"; Weight 36 lbs.; Power supply can be located at the bottom of either the front or rear. Dual-power supply configuration is also supported to deliver robust energy for power-hungry system.
COOLER MASTER HAF X RC-942-KKN1 Black Steel/Plastic ATX Full Tower Computer Case, two X-Dock bays at the front that are compatible with up to two 3.5" or 2.5" drives.	Motherboards: Micro ATX / ATX / Extended ATX / XL-ATX; Front ports: USB 3.0 x 2, USB 2.0 x 2, Audio x 1, Mic x 1, e-SATA x 1, 1394a x 1; Dimensions: 23.20" x 9.10" x 21.70"; Weight 31.6 lbs.; The HAF X can handle up to four full-length graphics cards; A high airflow design strives to eliminate overheating with large 200 and 230mm fans that spin at lower RPMs to ensure high airflow without high noise; Limited 2-year warranty. 1,176 reviews at Newegg 5 egg positive.
Corsair Obsidian 650D Aluminum Mid Tower ATX Enthusiast Computer Case - Black CC650DW-1, Guru3D Best Hardware Award	Motherboards: Micro ATX / ATX Mid Tower. Front ports: USB 2.0 x 2, USB 3.0 x 2, IEEE 1394 x 1, Headphone x 1, Mic x 1, 4-channel Fan Controller. Steel structure with black brushed aluminum faceplate/bottom mounted PSU with room for extended PSU/ 4 x External 5.25" Drive Bays/ 3.5"/2.5" Drive x 6/ 8 expansion slots. Dimensions: 21.5" x 9" x 20.5". Boasting four tool-less 5.25" drive bays as well as six 3.5" SSD-ready

	drive bays (3.5"/2.5" Drive Caddies). The Corsair Obsidian Series 650D provides plenty of expansion, in addition to eight expansion slots that gives you tons of room for multiple graphics cards. There were many complaints about the awkward USB 3.0 support that comes from the back of the motherboard, but everything else was mostly positive. Limited 2-year warranty.
Fractal Design Define XL R2 FD-CA-DEF-XL-R2-TI Titanium Grey Steel ATX Full Tower Computer Case, and is a "Must Have Editor's Choice Award from Tweaktown with a 99% rating." Remove top cage to allow installation of video cards longer than 13" or 330mm. Golden Hardware Secrets Award.	Motherboards: ATX, Micro ATX, Mini ATX, E-ATX and XL-ATX; Front ports: 2 x USB 3.0, 2 x USB 2.0 and Audio I/O front panel ports; 4 External 5.25" Drive Bays, 8 Internal 3.5" Drive Bays. Noise reduction achieved with the dense bitumen used on the side panels. Up to seven fans can be installed (2 x 120/140 mm - front, 2 x 120/140mm - top, 1 x 140mm - back, 1 x 140 mm - side panel, and 1 x140 mm - bottom), with three silent series R2 140mm Hydraulic bearing fans pre-installed; Dimensions: 9.13" x 22" x 22.05"; Weight 36.2 lbs. High density noise-reducing material for an optimal silent case, bottom mounted power supply, limited 1-year warranty. (See: http://www.hardwaresecrets.com/article/Fractal-Design-Define-XL-R2-Case-Review/1733/4)
NZXT Phantom 530 CA-PH530-B1 Black Steel / Plastic ATX Full Tower	Motherboards: ITX, Micro-ATX, ATX, EATX (322x272mm); Front Ports: 1 x Audio / Mic, 2 x USB 3.0; 3 External 5.25" Drive Bays; 6 Internal 3.5" Drive Bays; Dimensions: 235mm/9 ¼" x 572mm/22 ½" x 543mm/21 ¾"; Weight 1.5 kg; bottom mount PSU; Limited 2-year warranty.
NZXT SWITCH 810 Black CA-SW810-B1 Steel / Plastic ATX HYBRID Full Tower, dual high-speed USB 3.0, hard drive dock along with a SD card reader	Motherboard: E-ATX, XL-ATX, ATX, Micro-ATX, Mini-ITX; Front ports: USB 2.0 x 2, USB 3.0 x 2, Audio, SD Card Reader; Dimensions: 9.25" x 23.43" x 23.03"; Removable HDD pull-out cages and large storage capacity for seven hard drives; 4 External 5.25" Drive Bays; 6 Internal 3.5" Drive Bays; Weight: 20.06 lbs.; limited 2-year warranty.
Rosewill ARMOR-EVO Gaming E-ATX Mid Tower Computer Case, support up to E-ATX, comes with six fans-2x front red LED 120mm, 2x top 120mm, 1x side 230mm, 1x Rear 120mm.	Motherboards: Micro ATX, ATX, E-ATX, SSI CEB, SSI EEB; Front ports: 2 x USB 3.0 (internal 20-pin connector to MB), 2 x USB 2.0, Audio In/Out(AC97, HD), LED switch of front fans (bottom); Dimensions: 8.62" x 18.58" x 22.40" (WxHxD); Weight: 21.6 lbs.; bottom mounted PSU; limited 1-year warranty.
SilverStone RAVEN Series RV03B-W Matte Black Steel / Plastic ATX Full Tower, includes two Air Penetrator 180mm fans for superb performance and quietness, graphics cards up to 13.58-inch long,	Motherboards: SSI EEB, SSI CEB, Extended ATX, ATX, Micro ATX; Front ports: USB 3.0 x 2, Audio x 1, MIC x 1. Dimensions: 22.44" x 9.25" x 20.55"; Weight: 25.13 lbs.; 7 External 5.25" Drive Bays; 10 (6 from 5.25" adapters) Internal 3.5" Drive Bays; Limited 1-year warranty. This steel tower has excellent cooling, quietness and quality; however, the face panel is held in place with eight screws in addition to snaps, and each of the bay adapter trios are also secured by eight screws. While most

Tweaktown 91% rating.	users can get away with a single 5.25" drive and the five bays behind the motherboard tray, access to the remaining front bays is unusually cumbersome. There were a few of complaints about how fragile the plastic components were.
Thermaltake Level 10 GT (VN10001W2N) Black SECC / Plastic ATX Full Tower Computer Case with Four Fans-1x 200mm Colorshift side fan, 1x 200mm top fan, 1x 200mm front fan and 1x 140mm rear fan	Motherboards: Micro ATX / ATX / Extended ATX; Front Ports: USB 3.0 x 2, USB 2.0 x 4, eSATA x 1, HD Audio x 1; Dimensions: 23" x 11.1" x 23.2"; Weight: 28 lbs.; With an EasySwap Pitstop X`X`5 every HDD/SDD has its own removable tray, EasySwap in hot-plug mode within seconds; space for up to 37 cm oversized cards; 3-year limited warranty, most expensive case at $250.
XION Gaming Series XON-990-BK Black with Blue LED Light Steel/ Plastic, Meshed Front Panel design. ATX Mid Tower Computer Case	Motherboards: Micro ATX / ATX / Extended ATX; USB3.0 x2, USB2.0x2, 7.1 Channel Audio x2. External 3.5" & 2.5" The hot-swappable front-loading HDD dock can accommodate 2.5"/3.5" SATA hard drive for fast, hassle-free data transfer without the fuss of opening case and groping inside. Dimensions 21.8" x8.3"x 20.5"; 4x 120mm fans or 1x 220mm fan, on top for 1x 120mm fan; Weight 19.5 lbs. features support for larger heat sinks, graphics cards. Easily removable dust-filters (front, bottom_front and bottom_rear). Bottom mounted PSU.

Case Fans -- Choosing and Installing

Case fans are cheap and very important to cooling the PC and sustaining it shelf life. A few usually come with the case, but in my experience, they are usually inadequate to the task of providing enough cooling capacity. In a personal incident, I cooked an expensive Gigabyte Motherboard (See: http://www.gigabyte.us) years ago due to inadequate cooling. That was an expensive lesson. I scoured the Internet for articles on fans and cooling PCs and came up with very little. The best method I could find for researching fans was to visit web-shopping sites such as http://www.newegg.com, where there are numerous user reviews of the cooling fan choices. During my research the best rated fans with superior speeds and ratings were:

Cooler Master 120mm Silent Blue LED Case Fan 2-in-1 Value Pack - (R4-L2S-122B-GP)	Cooler Master Computer Case Cooling R4-LUS-07AR-GP
Cooler Master R4-LUS-07AB-GP MegaFlow 200mm LED Case Fan (Blue); Scythe Gentle Typhoon D1225C12B5AP-15 - Case fan - 120 mm	ENERMAX UC-8EB 80mm Case Fan
MASSCOOL FD08025S1M4 80mm Case Fan	Scythe DFS123812-3000 "ULTRA KAZE" 120 x 38 mm Case Fan
Vantec Stealth SF8025L 80x80x25mm Double Ball Bearing Silent Case Fan (Black)	Vantec Tornado 80mm Double Ball Bearing High Air Flow Case Fan - Model TD8038H

CPU -- Choosing and Installing

Minimum requirements:

- Top of the line with an established reputation of proven reliability and performance over time. Often this is the second generation of a CPU which fixed a flaw in a revolutionary new initial release.
- Lower power requirements. No liquid cooling to keep things simpler.
- Price range $200 to $700.
- Support for SATA revision 3 6.0 GB/s RAID or Intel Rapid Storage.
- Quad or more cores.
- Intel Haswell or AMD Richland processor or AMD FM2+ socket CPU.

With processors operating at constantly higher clock speeds, the heat the processors create has become a difficult problem to deal with. Thermal dissipation is not only necessary but without a thermal solution properly installed you will destroy a CPU. Sometimes computer professionals have a difficult time convincing consumers to absorb the added cost of many case fans and implementing a superior CPU cooling solution. The most advanced solutions use liquid cooling that operates much like a car's radiator, but they are expensive.

The less expensive, non-liquid cooled, CPU kits sometimes include thermal paste (also known as thermal grease or thermal compound) that we can apply to increase thermal dissipation to the cooling unit from the processor. What you don't want to do is make a mistake applying the thermal paste to your CPU. When you purchase a CPU kit, it comes with a cooler (in our case a large fan). The thermal grease aids in the transfer of heat between the processor and the cooler. Think of it like this, if you are working on a car and you need a good seal on the headers, you cannot have an incorrectly fitting header gasket. You have to cut the gasket properly, center it over the ports, and then glue the gasket to the heads using a thick layer of high-temperature silicone seal (RTV). You then wipe a generous layer of the RTV on the outside of the gasket and let it dry completely. There is more to this process, but I think you get the point. Another analogy would be applying Vaseline to your hand and slapping it on top of a block of ice. The heat transfer between your hand and the ice should improve because there are no air gaps between your hand and the ice.

Just like the analogies above, thermal paste is designed to fill the gaps of air and improve the heat transfer between the processor and the cooler. Thermal paste has a higher conductibility coefficient than air, is cheap, and absolutely must be properly applied to the CPU. There are different varieties of thermal paste, and you may not want the one that comes with your CPU. What you do want is a **high-efficiency** thermal paste containing silver or ceramic that aids in thermal conduction. Carry your original compound to Best Buy and find the best geek, show them what came with your processor, and purchase the very best grease they can find for you. The compound will not be very expensive, and it will extend the life of, or save, your CPU!

Quality coolers have some material applied from the factory. Coolers that come with your CPU usually have thermal paste applied. The quality of this paste is usually good if it comes with an AMD or Intel processor; both companies recommend the use of those compounds. However, the use of this compound "from the factory" has some drawbacks.

Using compound "from the factory" is not as good a heat conductor as a high-efficiency thermal paste. It will also glue your CPU to your cooler, making it very difficult to separate the two. You should consider removing this compound and applying quality third-party thermal grease instead. You can use a razor blade to slowly and carefully scrape the compound off the cooler base. This takes a piece of cloth or gauze with isopropyl alcohol (isopropanol) to remove what is left of the compound. To remove the remaining thermal compound from the CPU, use a cotton swab with isopropyl alcohol (isopropanol). Also, some cheaper coolers come with graphite square or thermal tape similar to gum, which is a terrible heat transfer agent. This graphite square should be removed in the same manner, and quality thermal paste should be applied instead.

As with caulking a tub, you can apply too much thermal paste. A lot of paste will be less insulating as it will separate the CPU from the cooler by a thicker layer, making heat transfer more difficult. You only need as small drop of CPU grease before attaching the heat sink. You can try using a cotton swab to apply a small amount of the thermal paste to the CPU. Cover as much area (the pink part) as you can, but don't worry if you don't get it all because when the cooler is attached it will make it all uniform. Then carefully attach the cooler to the CPU. Be sure to study the manual, for your CPU/cooler combination for all installations differ slightly. Don't make the mistake of installing the cooler "inverted" by rotating it 180 degrees in relation to its correct position. This is prevented by design in some motherboards, but not in others. As the years pass, this type of mistake is becoming more and more idiot proof.

Savings 	Major redesigns of CPUs have followed a pattern of disappointment upon first release. The processors also tend to come down in price rapidly. Show patience in purchasing the new release of a CPU. For example, the new Intel i7-3970X 3.5GHz 5.0GT/s 15MB LGA2011 Processor costs $1,050 or more at discount online retailers. The established Core i7-3930K only costs $570 and is based on the advanced LGA 2011 socket architecture as well.

Intel's January 2011 release of the Sandy Bridge i7-2600 processor had to be halted because of a flaw in the Cougar Point Chipset on all 67-series motherboards. The issue affected the chipset's SATA-II ports and may have caused them to degrade and fail over time. It took until April 2011 to fix the problem and refund the customers. In a few short months after its release, the processor was no longer on the market. This was easily found out by looking at how the user community reacted to Intel's first attempt at the 2600 processor; there were very few reviews of it to be found and what was there was mostly negative. (See: https://en.wikipedia.org/wiki/Intel_Sandy_Bridge_(microarchitecture), https://en.wikipedia.org/wiki/Intel_Core_i7#Core_i7)

The September 2011 release of the Advanced Micro Devices (AMD) Bulldozer Zambezi CPU FX-8150 proved to be a disappointment when compared with the Intel Core i5 2500K at a lower price. AMD eventually addressed this with their 2nd generation CPU referred to as the Enhanced Bulldozer (Piledriver). The Zambezi matched up well against Intel's Sandy Bridge architecture, which was AMD's intention with this CPU release.

This later released Piledriver CPU core based AMD FX-8350 was priced at a mere $195, and the FX-8320 was priced at $170. These CPUs had clock speeds of up to 4.2GHz. The FX-8350 got up to 24% better frame rates in demanding games and was less expensive than the earlier FX-series Bulldozer technology. AMD now had a CPU that rivaled Intel's i7-3960X Extreme Edition, which was priced much higher, but were rapidly coming down in price.

 Unless you are really savvy with computers, make sure the heat sink and fan are included with the purchase of your CPU. If it is not, it may take many hours of research to find a good compatible fan for your CPU.

When searching for a CPU, do the same thing we did when searching for a computer case. Put together a spreadsheet and compare the various CPU options. The CPU that you choose is also dependent on your motherboard selection. I have found it is best to choose your CPU first, for this will narrow your motherboard selection process. There are only a few CPU manufacturers, however, there are many motherboard manufactures making that selection as difficult as choosing your computer case.

The rating factors for your CPU are the clock speed, shared cache, core count and thread support. Higher clock speeds don't necessarily translate into bigger gains in performance. The number of cores and the cache size has a larger impact on performance, but increasing the number of cores will escalate heat and fan noise, and on a laptop, reduce battery life.

Intel CPU	Core i7-4930K	Core i7-4790K	Core i7-4785T	Core i7-4770K
Model	BX80633i74930K	BX80646I74790K		BX80646I74770K
Core	Ivy Bridge-E 6-Core	Haswell Quad-Core	Haswell Quad-Core	Haswell Quad-Core
Frequency	3.4 GHz (3.9 GHz Turbo)	4 GHz (4.4 GHz Turbo)	2.2 GHz (3.2 GHz Turbo)	3.5 GHz (3.9 GHz Turbo)
Socket	FCLGA2011	FCLGA1150	FCLGA1150	FCLGA1150
Cores / Threads	6 / 12	4 / 8	4 / 8	4 / 8
MAX Memory Size	64 GB	32 GB	32 GB	32 GB
MAX Memory BW	59.7 GB/s	25.6 GB/s	25.6 GB/s	25.6 GB/s
PCI Express Revision	3.0	3.0 / Up to 1x16, 2x8, 1x8/2x4	3.0 / Up to 1x16, 2x8, 1x8/2x4	3.0 / Up to 1x16, 2x8, 1x8/2x4
Intel Virtual (VT-D)	Yes	Yes	Yes	No
Intel Smart L3 Cache / Mem Supp	12 MB	DDR3 1333/1600/1866	8 MB	DDR3 1333/1600	8 MB	DDR3 1333/1600	8 MB L3	DDR3 1600 / 1333
Power	130 W	88 W	35 W	84 W
Reviews/Cost	89 Newegg / $580	84 Newegg / $340	Not Found	633 Newegg / $320

Consider how the user community is reacting to any new processor. As you travel to tech shopping websites, note how many reviews there are, and the rating, and be sure to read what users are saying. For example, the 10 reviews of the Intel Core i7-3970X processor above would be too few for you to drop over a thousand dollars on this processor. This was far too little information with which to make a decision on to purchasing that expensive of a server processor. The Intel i7-3960X had about 73 more reviews and the Intel i7-3930K had 130 reviews, which told me that these processors have established reputations and may have been adopted by the gaming community. These three processors Haswell innovation is a huge development, but the processors above only support 32GB of 1333 RAM memory. Do your homework, and wait for a Haswell desktop processor that supports 64GB of 1066 RAM.

When shopping, another thing to make note of is what socket is necessary for the processor. Sometimes there are indications of a design flaw that you can pick up on. For example, the 2nd generation Intel Core i7 processors were NOT compatible with the Socket H LGA 1156 motherboards and were looking for a LGA 1155 socket. Motherboards supporting the LGA 1156 socket quickly became rare in the market. AMD released their Llano processor, which was based on their FM1 socket and was quickly replaced by the FM2 socket that has supported generations of CPU's. The FM1 socket motherboards were also quickly phased out.

The wattage a CPU uses is another important factor to consider. This value will affect your choice of power supply and your utility bill. In addition, purchasing a processor that includes a heat sink and fan included is usually a cost savings and presents much less research on your part as well.

 Historical Reference – Wait for Advancements in Technology So That You Can Get More for Less!

In 2010 and early 2011, the technological gap between Intel and AMD seemed to be something that AMD could not overcome. The Intel processors were superior and as cheap to purchase as the AMDs. Then on October 11, 2011, AMD made a huge technological leap over their previous processors with the Bulldozer CPU. The Bulldozer CPU was the first major redesign of AMD's processor architecture since 2003 and was a revolutionary advance in their CPU technology. Later releases showed that the Bulldozer processors matched up well against the Intel Core i7-2600K. In March 2012, AMD provided a BIOS update to motherboard manufacturers (Asus, Gigabyte Technology, MSI, and ASRock) that would fix some compatibility issues with their FX processors. So if you have not flashed your BIOS and have an AMD FX processor, you need to. (See: https://en.wikipedia.org/wiki/Bulldozer_(processor))

In January 2013, AMD officially introduced a new series of Accelerated Processing Units (APUs). The 3rd generation of retail APUs, known as *Richland*, was released at the beginning of June 2013. These processors offer improved graphical performance of 20 to 40 percent over the previous *Trinity* line of A-Series APUs. One excellent thing to note about the AMD *Richland A10-6800* and *A10-6700* is that they will fit and work in all AMD Socket *FM2* motherboards after a BIOS update. The series features six new APUs in total, two Piledriver modules operating at 4.1 GHz and 4.4 GHz in turbo mode, and an integrated GPU of 384 stream processors operating at 844 MHz and DDR3 2133 MHz memory support. Two other APUs, codenamed Temash and Kabini, are supposed to be the company's first true system-on-chip APUs. They are both scheduled to be released as the "industry's first quad-core x86 SoCs" in the first half of 2013. From personal experience, my 2012 server runs with a much older generation FX-8150 Bulldozer AMD processor, and I have been very impressed with its performance. However, AMD will be releasing a FM2+ processor in the near future, which will have a slightly different pin combination than their FM2 processors. (See: https://en.wikipedia.org/wiki/Accelerated_processing_unit, http://www.legitreviews.com/article/2209/1, https://en.wikipedia.org/wiki/Socket_FM2)

At the same time, Intel released their first round of Haswell processors, which are designed to replace the older Ivy Bridge processors. The Haswell changes the socket to an LGA 1150, and there were many inexpensive motherboards released in early June 2013 to support it. This once again leaped Intel over AMD's latest CPU. Intel is now on it 4th generation of the Core i7 Processor with five models release in the second quarter of 2014 selling for between $290 to $360, which is very affordable. However, these processors still only support DDR3 memory and still use the FCLGA1150 socket. (See: http://www.tomshardware.com/reviews/gaming-cpu-review-overclock,3106.html)

AMD and Intel have been dragging their heels to support the new DDR4 memory standard and create a new motherboard socket for their CPUs. However, expect that development by the end of 2014, so if you can hold out and wait the supporting motherboards and hardware have proven themselves in battle, you should. Intel has stated that is has 2014 processor that will use the new X99 chipset and DDR4 memory which is the successor the current x79 LGA2011/DDR3 motherboards. (See: http://www.forbes.com/sites/antonyleather/2014/03/19/intel-unveils-2014-roadmap-4-fantastic-new-processors-for-pc-enthusiasts)

WARNING	The CPU is one of the most easily damaged components on a PC. You must gently align the pins with the motherboard receptor and allow gravity to drop it into place. **NEVER press on it or handle it with your oily fingers**. You don't ever want to have to straighten the pins or pass your bodily contaminants onto this expensive component. The CPU will only align one way to fit the CPU socket. Once the CPU drops into place, lock the two ZIF levers that hold the CPU in place in the correct order. Be sure to read the manual to determine what that order is.

Hard Drive -- Selection, Technical Information and Installation

If you are running an old PATA (Parallel Advanced Technology Attachment), also known as IDE computer disk hardware, you may not be familiar with Serial Advanced Technology Attachment (SATA) or Solid State Drive (SSD) technology. IDE is a very old interface designed for mechanical hard and optical drives dating back to 1986. Support for IDE in computer hardware is practically non-existent. The Serial Advanced Technology Attachment (SATA) replaced IDE as the new disk standard in 2003 and rapidly advanced to faster and faster speeds and transfer rates. SATA is not being replaced by SSDs, and SSD/SATA hybrid drives are constantly improving in size and speed. These drives have taken over disk technology and have come down in price significantly as well. (See: https://en.wikipedia.org/wiki/Sata, https://secure.wikimedia.org/wikipedia/en/wiki/Solid-state_drive) Pure SSDs are quickly coming down in price and are an excellent choice for a Laptop or Ultrabook if the amount of storage needed by the user is limited. However, for virtualization, as covered in Chapter 7, a hybrid drive is necessary. For the average SBO/HCU, SATA only is a solid, cheaper drive alternative with more storage and will be around for a few years to come, but most custom computer builds come with strong arguments for using some sort of SSD. SATA hard drives consist of spinning disks and moving magnetic read/write heads. This mechanical activity makes them susceptible to failure and damage from both physical shocks and strong magnetic fields.

An SSD stores your programs and files in ultra-fast flash memory. They have no moving parts, so they're much less susceptible to damage from drops, bumps and magnets. An SSD delivers throughput about 100 times faster than which any SATA hard drive is capable. An SSD also consumes less power, which means your mobile device's battery will last longer. I'm not trying to sound like an advertisement, but if you want the ultimate in performance, productivity, and durability you should consider using an SSD. The only thing lacking on a SSD for my computer build was space but the SSD/SATA hybrid fixes that.

With virtualization technology readily available, huge amounts of disk space is needed to store data, music, videos and virtual operating systems. The minimum drive requirements of my target computer were:

- At least 2-4 TB+ or a RAID 10 using 1-2 terabyte drives
- SATA3 6 Gb/s interface
- Minimum 3-year limited warranty (on December 31, 2011 Seagate reduced its warranty from five to three, or one year, on many of their desktop and laptop drives. Western Digital reduced their warranties from three to two years)
- Minimum RAID 1 mirrored configuration with two hard drives

Advanced methods of safeguarding data for SBO/HCU have existed for years. Unfortunately, many store-bought systems do not employ or set up these techniques. The argument against implementing a RAID configuration is that this added measure of complexity or expense is not in the SBO/HCU's best interest. Based on my experience, I beg to differ with that disastrous philosophy. Most systems purchased are plugged in, and the owner starts using it. If something breaks, a quick and expensive trip to the local computer repair shop will take care of the problem. With that in mind, every custom built system should be set up with a Redundant Array of Independent (RAID), or Intel Rapid Storage hard disk configuration. The local computer repair shop (assuming it's reputable) will recognize that the computer is running RAID and will replace the faulty hard drive, then rebuild the RAID at a very nominal cost if you can't do it yourself. It would prove much more costly to have them recover data from a broken or failing hard drive that has no redundancy than to just install a new hard drive and rebuild the RAID. It is up to you to notice and act on the flashing (usually RED) warning on boot up, which is displayed on the monitor and indicates that a RAID drive has failed. Even with a drive failure, if the computer is needed before it can be repaired, it is still usable running a RAID 1+ configuration. The only down side to running RAID is tools, such as rescue CDs, cloning software, and CD malware scans may not work well with a RAID configuration, so be careful using them.

Periodicals will mention step-by-step measures to upgrade clone or replace a hard drive, although they rarely go into details about how to create an image backup or clone a hard drive for later restoration other than to mention you should do so. They state commonplace suggestions, for instance, make sure you have enough power and data cables to attach the new drive, which is almost never a problem, even if you are attaching the old drive as a secondary resource (after zeroing it and reformatting, which is not mentioned). The steps necessary to do this will be covered later.

There used to be many alternatives in hard disk manufacturers from which to choose, but over the years, like the airlines, the choices have narrowed. The familiar name Hitachi no longer exists except in older computer systems. On March 7, 2011, as revealed in a press release from Western Digital, it was announced that it had acquired Hitachi Global Storage Technologies for approximately 4.3 billion dollars in a cash and stock transaction. (See: http://www.wdc.com/en/company/pressroom/releases.aspx?release=ba433e4b-bff8-4d99-b60f-7f02aa42f444) Searching http://www.newegg.com Western Digital still markets a few Hitachi drive brand drives but most are just refurbished products; I presume to show competition, but the consumer is probably better off only purchasing the WDC name brand.

According to https://en.wikipedia.org/wiki/Seagate_Technology, "*Seagate acquired Maxtor in an all-stock deal worth $1.9 billion in 2006.*" Searching http://www.newegg.com Seagate is no longer marketing the Maxtor brand. It was only available as a refurbished product, but I would not recommend buying anything Maxtor. As with every other component, we have to put together a table of options from which to choose.

When purchasing any drives from any drive company (Western Digital, Seagate, Samsung, etc.), you may have hard drive failures and problems. In this category, I found no evidence that any manufacturer maintained an advantage over any other. The early motherboards and 6.0 GB/s hard drives had problems supporting this new standard, and some users complained that their RAID would only run at 3.0 GB/s, which for the most part are outdated. As things have advanced, most modern drives and motherboards are now capable of implementing 6.0 GB/s standard. The higher capacity drives come with dual actuator technology, so they are worth the extra money.

Some users complained that Windows 7 had problems with the 3TB drives, and when I tried to run RAID 10 with Windows 7 64-bit, it would not recognize all of the disk space upon installation. I did some research on this limitation, and it appears the OS will not install on volumes larger than 2.1TB. One way to get Windows 7 to recognize larger sizes as a single volume is to create multiple 2.1TB volumes then span them together as DYNAMIC drives. Another way to install Windows on a 2.1TB partition is as a "temporary/throw away" OS on a temporary hard drive; partition the system how you want with a boot with a GUID Partition Table (GPT) partition on your RAID, then remove the temporary hard drive and reinstall windows into the boot partition that you set up. From Windows website: "*Can Windows 7, Windows Vista, and Windows Server 2008 read, write, and boot from GPT disks? Yes, all versions can use GPT partitioned disks for data. Booting is only supported for 64-bit editions on a unified extensible firmware interface (UEFI) based system.*" (See: http://msdn.microsoft.com/en-us/windows/hardware/gg463525.aspx, http://technet.microsoft.com/library/cc725671.aspx). I did not experiment with the Unified Extensible Firmware Interface (UEFI) or extended disk space solutions described above that I found on various websites. The (UEFI) is the specification that is replacing the ages-old Basic Input/output System (BIOS) firmware interface. Don't buy a computer that does not support UFEI. (See: https://en.wikipedia.org/wiki/Unified_Extensible_Firmware_Interface)

If you are planning to run Linux as your core OS, as of the start of 2012, Seagate launched a new series of 3.5-inch drives, which they called the Barracuda 7200.14. These new drives have 1 TB platters, which was a new milestone for Seagate. These higher data-density drives meant more data per square centimeter, which yielded better performance, and the need for fewer platters meant lower prices for the drives.

This innovation made the Seagate Barracuda Green and the Barracuda XT obsolete. Seagate showed that the new 7200.14 were very energy-efficient because of the new platters, so therefore the company had no reason to maintain their separate Barracuda Green series. The Barracuda XT is also near end-of-life and due to be replaced with their hybrid HDD/SSD drives. Of course the question we all ask is what happed to the 7200.13? Was there a bit of superstition in the mix to make Seagate skip the unlucky 13 number? I don't know, but below is an example analysis of choosing which drives you may want for your new computer. (See: http://origin-www.seagate.com/internal-hard-drives/desktop-hard-drives/desktop-hdd)

Western Digital WD Black WD4001FAEX 4TB 7200 RPM 64MB Cache SATA 6.0Gb/s 3.5" Internal Hard Drive, 5 year limited warranty. Newegg $320, 4 egg rating with 13 reviews. Amazon $327, 4 ½ star rating with 14 reviews.	Western Digital WD Green WD30EZRX 3TB IntelliPower SATA 6.0 Gb/s 3.5" Internal Hard Drive, cache 64MB, 2-year limited warranty. Newegg $140, 3 egg rating with 204 reviews. A lot of Newegg reviewers had many failed drives to send back. Amazon $134, 4 star rating with 458 reviews.
Western Digital Black WD2002FAEX 2TB 7200 RPM 64MB Cache SATA 6.0Gb/s 3.5" Internal Hard Drive, cache 64MB, 5 year limited warranty. Newegg $175, 4 egg rating with 329 reviews. Amazon $178 free shipping, 4 stars rating with 32 reviews. Consumer Choice Award Winner.	Western Digital WD VelociRaptor WD1000DGTZ 1TB 10000RPM SATA 6.0Gb/s 3.5" Internal Hard Drive, cache 64MB, 5 year limited warranty. Newegg $230, 4 egg rating with 41 reviews. Amazon $219, 4 ½ star rating with 45 reviews.
Seagate ST4000DM000 Barracuda HDD.15 5900 RPM SATA 6.0Gb/s 3.5" Internal Hard Drive, Cache 64MB, Transfer Rate 600MB/s, Sustained Data Rate OD 180MB/s, Average Seek Time <8.5ms, Average Write Time <9.5ms. Newegg $210 with only one review. Amazon $205, 4 star rating with 938 reviews.	Seagate ST30000DM001 Barracuda 7200.14 3TB 7200 RPM SATA 6.0Gb/s 3.5" Internal Hard Drive, Cache 64MB, Transfer Rate 600MB/s, Sustained Data Rate OD 210MB/s, Average Seek Time <8.5ms, Average Write Time <9.5ms. Newegg $140, 3 egg rating with 581 reviews. Amazon $140, 4 star rating with 938 reviews.
Seagate ST2000DM001 Barracuda 7200.14 2TB 7200 RPM SATA 6 Gb/s, Cache 64 MB, Transfer Rate 600MB/s, Sustained Data Rate OD 210MB/s, average access time 8.5 ms, 2 year limited warranty. Newegg $105, 3 egg rating with 397 reviews. Amazon $97	Seagate ST1000DM003 Barracuda 7200.14 1TB 7200 RPM SATA 6.0 Gb/s, Cache 64 MB, Transfer Rate 600MB/s, Sustained Data Rate OD 210MB/s, Average Latency 4.16ms, 2 year limited warranty. Newegg $80, 4 egg rating with 423 reviews. Amazon $77, 4 star rating with 938 reviews.

with free shipping, a 4 star rating with 938 reviews.	

Zeroing Your Hard Drive to Install a New OS -- Recovering your Data

There multiple reasons to zero a hard drive. If you are upgrading or replacing a computer, you may want to get rid of an old hard drive. Before disposing of it, you need to sanitize it. Depending on the status of your hardware, your options may be limited in trying to zero the hard drive. Refer down to <u>Recycle your Failed Hard Drives, Old or Unusable CDs and DVDs to Save the Environment</u> to learn how to sanitize a hard drive when software cannot be used. Another reason is, if you are building a computer and want to make sure that the drive is fully operational, zeroing a hard drive is a thorough test that you can run, which will test all the components of the drive. If we are rebuilding a computer, we don't want an OS such as Windows or Linux making assumptions about trying to fit in/use existing partitions. You also don't want a fresh install to see previous software. It is best if an OS install proceeds in the default fashion for which the developers have programmed.

In the past, I have zeroed hard drives with the tools provided by the hard drive manufacturers to DOD standards of non-recovery. Most modern drives have a feature built into the firmware that allows you to choose a--Secure Erase--option. However, these tools, such as Seagate Max Blast, could not see through modern RAID configurations. (See: <u>http://origin-www.seagate.com</u>, <u>http://support.wdc.com/?wdc_lang=en</u>) The Mini Tool Partition Wizard Home Edition utility (See: <u>http://www.minitool.ca</u>) was a great, free tool that saw the drives through the RAID and had excellent drive erase options. Why bust a RAID apart and rebuild it if you don't have to? (See: <u>http://www.partitionwizard.com</u>) You can also go to Seagate or Western Digital and download their latest disk tools to work on their hard drives. However, Partition Wizard was a *one hat* that fits all sets of tools, so you don't even have to know your own disk hardware. In <u>Chapter 10</u> we will discuss other tools for a multiboot USB drive, such as Parted Magic, that you can also use.

For system hard drive recovery, I have tried many free partition recovery and data recovery software applications, such as Gparted, Parted Magic, Fedora File Manager, Ubuntu File Manager, Paragon Free, Partition File and Mount, Virtual Lab, Easeus Partition Master, Seagate Maxblast 5 (which did not even see through the RAID to show that there were disks in the computer), Backtrack, Seagate SeaTools, Ultimate Boot CD, System Rescue CD and Trinity Rescue. The only program that worked with my RAID setup was Partition Wizard Mini-Tool Power Data Recovery Demo, which was awesome. It somehow scoured the partition through my RAID setup and displayed the files that I wanted to restore; no other tool even came close to achieving these goals. Nevertheless, before you discount the other FREE, DEMO, PAID tools, remember that my situation was unique. Most SBO/HCU configurations may not be running a RAID 1 mirror and the other programs might work fine if you have a less complex setup.

The *Mini Tool Power Data Recover Demo* has the *Save Files* feature disabled. I had to go to <u>http://www.PowerDataRecovery.com/buy.html</u> to purchase the license key to actually be able to recover my files. I hate spending money on data recovery software when there are so many FREE options that usually work, but sometimes you have to ask yourself how much your time is worth. A trip with my computer to the *Geek Squad* may have cost more than the $70 that I paid for the software, and there would have been no guarantee that they would have had the correct software to recover my files; plus, then I would not now own this robust tool for later use. I did talk to one guy there, and he recommended some software that the store did not have on the shelf. In addition, I can see from the recovery tool that there is no repairing the drives to make them bootable again, so why bother if I can get my data myself.

After investigating many FREE options, nothing else matched Mini Tools product. Most of the other programs did not even see the RAID partition, or if they did, could only display a few files that were irrelevant. The Mini Tool even teased me more with a <u>File Preview</u> feature that showed what was in my files. My Action Pack key file alone had hours of work in it. So to recover the many hours of work I know/may not have backed up, I purchased the software.

 **Story**	I feel like an advertisement for them, but if you ever need a data recovery tool in a desperate hour of need, I know of nothing better than MiniTool's Power Data Recovery utility. (See: http://www.minitool.ca) From firsthand experience, about a year ago I tried everything I could think of to recover my data after a confluence of events that wiped out my data and USB backups. (I had experimented with many tools during my university volunteer work and those programs wiped out my USB backup drive and my RAID computer hard drives.) I then purchased the Mini Tools *Power Data Recovery* product and it succeeded where everything else had failed and I tried a LOT of other tools!

To completely rebuild my main office RAID computer, I had to come up with a plan of attack. The first step was recovering my data; Mini Tool Power Data Recover software did the job. All of the files I have examined are A-OK; this included my data, music and downloads. They were housed in three separate directories on the now broken tower.

Running RAID in Your SB/HC and Recovering from Hard Drive Failure

Let's continue to layer that SB/HC protection yet again. Now we need to layer our computer(s) against hardware failures, teenagers, hammers, earthquakes or anything else that might happen! Is running RAID at home worth the added cost? Unequivocally, YES! In these days of cheap hard drives and motherboards that support RAID, why risk an important home computer to hard drive failure? In all my years of home computing the component that fails most often in my custom built computers is the hard drive. It makes sense if you think about it. The hard drive is probably most mechanical device in the computer. It has spinning platters, read write heads moving around, data being written and read constantly, etc.

There is nothing worse than when a family member calls you in because there is a problem with the primary house computer. For example, my wife uses our computer to work from home and much of our household income is dependent on the successful operation of this computer. When you arrive on the scene and see the error message "Degraded NVIDEA Mirror" flashing in RED on the screen, what do you do? Everything had been purring along perfectly on this computer. What is going to happen to all of your data, not to mention your 10 Linux virtual environments that you have installed and updated (covered later in this book)? My wife has tasted what real computing power can mean when working from home, and she loves working on this computer.

The first step in fixing this problem is to pry the user away from the computer. A degraded array is nothing to mess around with, as the user can continue to work using the degraded array but anything could happen, possibly making it so that you cannot rebuild the RAID and/or perhaps corrupting another drive in the array.

You should always have a backup computer set up and ready to take over if your income is dependent on functioning computer hardware, or if the continuous operation of the tasks your computer provides are important. Your family or small business is dependent on this. In my example, it took me an entire evening to apply all of the OS and application software updates to the old backup computer due to some neglect, but the next morning my wife was off and running, and I could sleep on how to attack this latest computing disaster. A few days of downtime fixing the RAID is acceptable, a few weeks and thousands of dollars of lost income fixing a down computer system is not.

Be careful what you read out on the Internet. My Internet research revealed all kinds of questionable websites, so I used a virtual Operating Systems running Tor, to see what others had to say about this problem. I saw crazy solutions, from testing the RAM, to unplugging one drive at a time and rebooting. While testing memory is never a bad idea, randomly unplugging drives and rebooting is probably not a good idea. What happens to the RAID configuration in the scenario? It may get corrupted, and you could debase the one drive that has not yet failed. You don't want to RISK that. I suggest the following steps in the event of a RAID 1 hard drive failure:

1. Originally, if your computer is set up as a RAID 1 mirror, consider buying two cheap refurbished drives. If your mirror becomes degraded you should still be able to boot off of the drive(s) that is/are still working. If the computer boots, back up all your data and in Windows 7 create a system image to your backup device using, ***Start* > *Control Panel* > *Backup and Restore* > *Create a System Image***.

2. Next, download all the latest tools from your hard disk manufacturer. I had two refurbished Seagate Barracuda 750 GB drives in the mirror. Since the mirror was degraded, the problem had to be with one of the hard drives.

3. If you are adding hard drives to the array or changing the RAID, make sure that your power supply can handle the added load.

4. I installed Seagate SeaTools in Windows but it would not run. I burnt a copy of the latest bootable SeaTools DOS utilities to CD. If you don't use CD/DVD-RW disks you should consider them. They save a bit of money keeping up with all the latest releases from the hardware manufacturers. I have found that about every six months there are updates to the diagnostic bootable CD software to troubleshoot the latest PC hardware disasters.

5. Boot your tools disk CD and try to look at the hard drives. In my case, SeaTools was only displaying one hard drive. I wondered how I was going to figure out which drive had failed? I thought to take the computer apart and see if one of the drives was not spinning by feeling the drives during startup, but both drives were spinning, so this was a dead end.

6. I went back into SeaTools and, wonderfully, it was displaying both drives. I quickly tested both drives, and one drive failed all tests and eventually died completely... but not before I had written down the serial number from the SeaTools diagnostics. In hind sight, I could have just written down the serial number of the good drive and pulled the one that SeaTools could not see.
7. I carefully examined the hard drives serial numbers, and I pulled out the drive with the confirmed failed serial number and put it aside. I then went to Seagate's website to see if the drive was under warranty; it was not.
8. I ordered another refurbished drive from Newegg.com for a mere $40. The Seagate Barracuda 750GB drive comes with a 16MB cache or 32MB cache. Always get the bigger cache. Because I run a mirror, I did not purchase any sort of extended warranty. From my experience, refurbished drives are a roll of the dice. I've had pretty good luck with them lasting four years or more, which puts them just outside any sort of warranty that I could have purchased.
9. Upon arrival, I put the drive in the computer and used SeaTools to run diagnostic tests on the new drive.
10. I then rebuilt the mirror and booted up the computer to see it running as good as new.
11. I opened up the failed drive and sanded the platters to destroy my data on the old drive.
12. I then sent the drive off with some CDs and DVDs to be properly recycled. Skip down to <u>Recycle your Failed Hard Drives, Old or Unusable CDs and DVDs to Save the Environment</u>.

The moral of the story is that running a RAID 1 configuration may seem like overkill to most SBO/HSUs, but it is mandatory if you depend on your computer for banking, investing, or a living wage. A mirror can save you weeks of work rebuilding a computer, and since you are dealing with legacy components, most times you can obtain them at a nominal cost. You have to ask yourself, how much is your time and data worth? RUN RAID 1, 5 or 10 in your SB/HC! If you can afford it, RAID 10 is optimal (best of both worlds). It yields close to the performance of RAID 0 and has the benefits and the redundancy of RAID 1, without the performance hit of RAID 5. I called ASUS to see if their motherboards could run RAID 10 on two drives and did not get an answer (the technician had no idea what I was talking about). The standard RAID 10 configuration seems to take a minimum of four drives.

WARNING	Running RAID limits your recovery options that would otherwise be available on a system not running RAID. Many PC recovery tools are designed for systems running a non-RAID setup. From my experience on running an antivirus Rescue CD, it destroyed the system on disk running across a mirror RAID 1 setup. The data was recoverable by scanning each disk in the mirror. The system had to be rebuilt from scratch. So, RAID had its drawbacks with primitive PC tools.

There are books and websites that describe in detail all the various RAID levels. (See: https://secure.wikimedia.org/wikipedia/en/wiki/Standard_RAID_levels, https://secure.wikimedia.org/wikipedia/en/wiki/RAID_10#23RAID_10_.28RAID_1.2B0.29). I will briefly summarize the RAID levels supported by most modern SBO/HCU computing motherboards:

- RAID 0 (Data striping) strips the data over multiple hard drives. RAID 0 would be a good choice if you have two hard drives of different sizes. RAID 0 will give a minimal boost in the performance of the system. Bear in mind that a set of two disks is roughly half as reliable as a single disk.
- RAID 1 (Data mirroring) creates an exact copy (or mirror) of a set of data on two or more disks. To maximize performance benefits of RAID 1, independent disk controllers are recommended, one for each disk. RAID 1 should be implemented on two identical drives but does not have to be. When reading, both disks can be accessed independently, and requested sectors can be split evenly between the disks, but how the data is read is dependent on the controller. For the usual mirror of two disks, this would, in theory, double the transfer rate when reading. When writing, the array performs like a single disk, as all mirrors must be written with the data.
- RAID 5 uses block-level striping with parity data distributed across all member disks and has achieved popularity because of its low cost of redundancy. A minimum of three disks is required for a complete RAID 5 configuration. RAID 5 implementations suffer from poor performance when faced with a workload that includes many writes that are smaller than the capacity of a single stripe. This is because parity must be updated on each write, requiring read-modify-write sequences for both the data block and the parity block. The read performance of RAID 5 is almost as good as RAID 0 for the same number of disks. Except for the parity blocks, the distribution of data over the drives follows the same pattern as RAID 0. The reason RAID 5 is slightly slower is that the disks must skip over the parity blocks.
- RAID 10 is a combination for RAID 0 and RAID 1, or what is called a stripe of mirrors. As stated about RAID 0, striping is a method of storing data on multiple devices (hard drives) by interleaving it in a manner that allows for faster access to the data than just using a single hard drive. RAID 10 requires a minimum of four drives and gives us the advantages of both RAID 0 and 1. Linux "RAID 10" can be implemented via software with as few as two disks. In most cases RAID 10 provides better throughput and latency than all other RAID levels except RAID 0 (which wins in throughput). It is the preferable RAID level for I/O-intensive applications such as database, email and web servers, as well as for any other use requiring high disk performance. As in RAID 1, all but one drive from each RAID 1 set can fail without damaging the data. Consequently, in a four drive configuration, two drives can fail as long as they are not the mirror of the other. If a failed drive is not replaced, the single working hard drive in the set then becomes a single point of failure for the entire array. Some RAID 10 vendors address this problem by supporting a "hot spare" drive, which automatically replaces and rebuilds a failed drive in the array.

Recovering Hard Drive Data from a Computer That Will No Longer Boot

If you are part of the information age, there will come a day when your Internet device will cease to function. Hopefully, you have taken precautions to back up as much as possible, but as life marches on, data sometimes is needed from a failed computer or Internet device that was neglected, or was a backup in transition. Sometimes we think we have adequate backup processes in place only to be rudely awakened after a failure that our backup solution was inadequate.

A lot of this chapter came about because of my life's experiences. There will always be a confluence of events designed to conspire against you to produce the worst possible scenario with your Internet and computer equipment. In my example:

Story 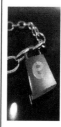	I had 25GB of my data comfortably backed up with Microsoft Live Mesh on the cloud, including my website. While I updated my favorite's website often at my ISP, it was comforting to have a second backup on the cloud. Microsoft announced in early 2013 that Mesh was going away and that I needed to convert over to their new SkyDrive technology, which only had 7 GB of storage. In the mean time I had discovered SpiderOak, which encrypts my data, so I transitioned 2GB of my confidential data to a SpiderOak SkyDrive (detailed later). During this confluence of events, my ISP locked me out of updating my website. I called them a few times, and their technical support suggested that somehow my computers were preventing me from updating my website. This attempted deflection by my ISP's untrained personnel was frustrating but typical in today's world. In the end, this was as far as I could get with my ISP's limited technical supports knowledge. Most of the people I talked to at my ISP did not even know they hosted websites, which I found amazing. They kept going on and on about my Internet speed and service, which were completely irrelevant to the discussion. I made a decision on the spot to move my website to my new domain http://thatcybersecurityguy.com. So I kept updating my website on my 7-year-old tower computer day-after-day in anticipation of transitioning everything to my new website. In the meantime, all this work was not being backed up. As events would have it, the tower died and would no longer boot, making all my work inaccessible. The moral of this story is, as life's events change, backup all your data daily!

Motherboard – Selection and Technical Information

Minimum requirements and technologies you want:

1. Maximum number of Thunderbolt connector's money can buy. Thunderbolt is twice as fast as USB 3.0 but cabling and devices are more expensive than USB 3.0. There is the new USB 3.1 standard so look for that in future motherboards, as it matches Thunderbolt speeds.
2. Maximum number of USB 3.0 ports money can buy. USB 3.0 offers transfer rates up to 5Gbps, which means users, may experience up to a 10x improvement over USB 2.0. Additionally, backwards compatibility with USB 2.0 assures long term use of legacy USB 2.0 devices.
3. True SATA revision 3.0 (SATA 6 GB/s) for RAID and/or Intel Rapid Storage support. (See: https://en.wikipedia.org/wiki/Serial_ATA)
4. Support for eight channel High Definition Audio with six ports. Most modern motherboards come with this support built in. Years ago, a separate sound card was required. You don't want or need Analog Surround Sound in your mother board. If you want sophisticated sound for you PC, all you need is speakers with an optical input.
5. Minimum of two USB 3.0 port on the front panel, and four or more on the back panel.

6. Data Double Rate Type Three (DDR3 2800 and below) synchronous dynamic random access memory support.
7. Unified Extensible Firmware Interface support which replaces the old BIOS standard.

Story 	My 6-year-old last tower computer build included no front USB ports. When USB drives became popular and important to our daily lives, I found myself often crawling around behind the computer to plug in USB drives. I found an answer to the problem by purchasing a floppy drive that included a USB port. This has saved my knees countless hours of misery ever since, until I wanted a multiboot USB drive. To use a multiboot USB you will need a second USB for your data. Hence at least two USB 3.0 ports are needed on the front of a computer.

8. Price range between $200 to $400 dollars.
9. Not to be on the bleeding edge of technology by being on the front line trying the motherboard before it has become established by objective reviews.
10. Intel Haswell socket 1150 or AMD socket FM2+.
11. Memory support for 32GB, preferably 64GB.
12. No PS/2 support which has been around since 1987. Most modern mice and keyboards connect via USB ports. The only reason they are still around is because corporations want to disable their employees' USB ports to prevent information theft. A noble goal, but it is time to toss in the towel and develop a better solution.
13. No support for eSATA. The eSATA ports cannot deliver power to an external device so it never caught on as something computer savvy users wanted.
14. No FireWire support, which was an Apple designed high-speed serial bus that never caught on. Few external hard drives support this standard.

Tip	We never know when a motherboard is going to die but usually they give some warning signs before going down permanently. A dying motherboard may have you repeat installing a device driver upon boot up, have difficulty booting your OS, or if you start getting the blue screen of death, take frequent backups.

Thunderbolt and USB 3.0 Devices and Connectors

If you have not already, you will start seeing the word Thunderbolt associated with devices like motherboard, hard drives, NAS, etc. The September 2012 issue of PCWorld included an article titled, "*How can Thunderbolt make my PC perform better?*" written by Alex Wawro, illustrations by Parke Polo. In the article, Alex tells us that "*Thunderbolt is a new high-speed interface designed by Intel. Thunderbolt ports are extremely fast at moving data between devices. Thunderbolt devices are blazingly fast and can transfer data at theoretical speeds of up to 10 gigabits per second. The Thunderbolt interface combines the high-speed PCI Express interface and the DisplayPort interface into a single interface supporting a serial data stream that is easy to transmit over long distances. Since Thunderbolt can transmit data, audio, video, and power over a single cable, hardware manufacturers can reduce the number of cables and ports that they must provide for connecting different devices.*" He goes on to explain that Thunderbolt devices can also be daisy-chained. This is much like my old days of using SCSI to daisy-chain hard drives, but simpler.

By developing this new standard, and not worrying about supporting older devices, Intel has leap-frogged the competition, which is proving to be effective. According to Alex Wawro, USB 3.0 data transfers have a theoretical maximum speed of 5 gigabits per second, which is far superior to the USB 2.0 theoretical maximum speed of 460 megabits. USB 3.0 also allows simultaneous data transfer in both directions, where USB 2.0 can only transfer data in one direction at a time. Looking at these statistics, USB 3.0 seems to be a revolution in data speed over USB 2.0. But Thunderbolt, with theoretical speeds up to 10 gigabits, is twice as fast as USB 3.0. This is a revolution within a revolution. Most advances of this magnitude come about because inventors put aside the past and develop something completely new, usually at great risk. This approach sometimes backfires, and many times new and better interfaces and standards do not beat out established technologies like USB. But in this case, there are many devices now using Thunderbolt, which indicates to me that this leap in technology is now successful.

However, all is not peaches and cream with Thunderbolt connections. USB 3.0 comes standard with most chipset from both AMD and Intel. USB 3.0 can almost be viewed as free, as this technology has been around many years, and cabling is cheap. In contrast, Thunderbolt chips and cables can get very expensive, which will come down in price. Until we see Thunderbolt technology for about the same price as USB 3.0, we will want chipsets and devices that support both standards. Also, USB 3.0 is widely supported and comes on a wide range of devices.

We all want to look back to the days of BETA versus VHS tapes. Many argued that BETA was a better format than VHS, therefore, BETA would become the new standard. But VHS won the battle with better marketing and shrewd business strategies. For a few years VHS dominated, but now they are both deprecated. This is much like the early days of Microsoft. Windows 3.1 was a disaster and there were better alternatives like DESQview (DV). But in the end, Microsoft's marketing and shrewd business strategies beat out the competition with an inferior product. In light of all this, I predict that in a few years we will also see USB become a dying standard in most modern devices, and Thunderbolt will become a shining star. (See: Go.pcworld.com/mybooktboltduo)

SATA Revision 3.0 (SATA 6 GB/s) and Intel Rapid Storage

There is a lot of confusion surrounding SATA specifications on devices. When observing specifications for hard drives and motherboards we will see things like SATA3-SATA 3.0 Gb/s; SATA3-SATA 6.0 Gb/s; SATA 3.0 Gb/s and so on. Looking at the specifications it is sometimes difficult to determine what standard and transfer speed is being used for things like "Just a Bunch of Drives" (JBOD), RAID and Intel Rapid Storage. (See: https://en.wikipedia.org/wiki/JBOD#JBOD)

What is Serial ATA Revision 3.0?

SATA Revision 3.0 is the latest specification, released May 2011, from the SATA International Organization (SATA-IO). SATA 3.0 stands for third-generation specification of the SATA standard. The SATA standard is meant to be a high-performance, low-cost interface for data streaming, better power management and a smaller footprint for optical and hard disk drives.

What Is the SATA 6Gb/s Standard?

SATA 6Gb/s is the transfer speed defined in SATA Revision 3.0, the latest evolution in SATA technology. The 6Gb/s transfer rate doubles the 3Gb/s transfer speed of the previous SATA Revision 2.6 specification.

What are the benefits of SATA 6Gb/s?

By doubling the transfer speed from 3Gb/s to 6Gb/s, SATA 6Gb/s will allow users to spend less time transferring data. SATA 6Gb/s will enable the movement of large amounts of data at a much faster rate. The higher transfer rate provides greater bandwidth for emerging high-performance storage solutions that directly utilize the increased transfer rates. RAID controllers also rely on the aggregated bandwidth of several hard disk drives to maximize the throughput advantages available through the faster bus. RAID cards which are designed for data redundancy and performance in particular are expected to benefit from the move to SATA 6Gb/s architectures. There are other benefits, like Serial ATA Native Command Queuing (NCQ) http://en.wikipedia.org/wiki/Native_command_queueing which accommodates isochronous data transfers, making SATA more suitable for audio/video applications, among other benefits.

The hard drive and motherboard manufacturers were quick to adopt the SATA3 standard and now-stable, inexpensive support for this hard drive technology. The adoption by chipset vendors has been rather slow, or anemic, when referring to Intel's RAID support. AMD featured a 6-port SATA Gb/s RAID controller as early as July 2010, and most AMD motherboards have full SATA3 RAID support.

What is Intel Rapid Storage?

The Intel Rapid Storage technology supported allows you to create a RAID 0 and RAID 1 set using only two identical hard disk drives. The Intel Rapid Storage technology creates two partitions on each hard disk drive to create a virtual RAID 0 and RAID 1 sets. This technology also allows you to change the hard disk drive partition size without losing any data.

RAID is a method of combining two or more disks drives into one logical unit. (See: http://en.wikipedia.org/wiki/RAID_10#RAID_10_.28RAID_1.2B0.29) When creating a RAID set, identical drives of the same model and capacity should be used. Above, we set our minimum disk standard as SATA3 6.0 Bb/s. Until recently, many motherboards only came with SATA 3Gb/s RAID support. The article http://www.hardocp.com/article/2010/02/20/sata_6gbs_on_your_new_motherboard provides a good comparison of various 6 Gb/s controllers with the Marvell 9128 doing well in burst speed testing. The ASUS Maximus IV Extreme-Z uses the Marvell PCIe 9182 controller. If you are going to use RAID there is no advantage on this type of architecture to running a RAID configuration on the SATA 6 Gb/s interface over the SATA 3 Gg/s interfaces. I verified this by calling ASUS and asking about their motherboard support for SATA3 6 Gb/s RAID support. Their technician pointed out this was a limitation of the Intel Z68, P67, P55 and H55 chipsets.

However on these motherboards, running a SATA 6 Gb/s drive outside of RAID will yield a performance improvement (double) over a SATA 3 Gb/s drive.

Intel took years to introduce a chipset with SATA3 RAID or Intel Rapid Storage, so an AMD solution was a better alternative for RAID. Running two (or more) 6 GB/s drives with RAID on a 2011 Intel motherboard actually yielded only a 3 GB/s (or less) transfer rate. In some tests with 6 GB/s drives on Intel motherboards the throughput was worse than running 3 GB/s drives in a RAID configuration. For years after Intel released the Sandy Bridge technology they did not support the new SATA revision 3.0 (SATA 6 Gb/s) standards for RAID. Even Intel's release of Intel X79 (Patsburg) chipset only included support for 2x Serial ATA (SATA) 3.0 (6 Gb/s) ports and 4 x SATA 2.0 (3 Gb/s) ports. I hope all this explains how this technology has improved and matured in a few short years.

Motherboard Selection How To Choose One

There are many good choices for motherboards but only a few great ones. Motherboard manufacturers embed in the specifications acronyms and abbreviations to make it look like some standards are being fully supported when, in fact, they are only partially implemented. For example, look at the RAID specification on any Intel motherboard. It was difficult to see that SATA revision 3 6.0 Gb/s RAID is not being fully supported.

	Sometimes you have to wait for technology to catch up and support a new standard. New technology for a new standard will last for many years (USB 2.0, IDE, and others lasted for many years). Patience = money well spent.

Story	In the 80's when I began my computer career contracting for the National Security Agency I convinced myself I needed a home computer to help with my job. At great expense I purchased an Intel 286 setup, which I felt I would need in my newfound IT career. Within a few months Intel released the 386 processor that was a revolutionary advancement over the 286. Within less than two years all I had was a very expensive paper weight that I was still paying the bank loan on. To make matters worse, I never used the machine for work and rarely used it for projects at home.

I have only created computers with ASUS, and Gigabyte motherboards. I have never owned an ASRock motherboard, but from all the reviews online this Japanese company is offering very solid motherboard solutions. (See: http://www.asrock.com/index.us.asp, http://www.asus.com/us, http://www.gigabyte.us) There are other motherboard manufacturers that you can investigate, but the field is narrowing as the demand for PC's declines. For example, Intel is planning to dissolve its motherboard-making unit by the end of 2016. Each motherboard comes with different Intel chipsets, which you should study before doing a motherboard analysis. This can narrow the playing field immensely when you begin to compare motherboards. For example, the Intel X79, code name Patsburg, was released November 14, 2011. The X58 chipset was released November 2008. So we can quickly narrow our Intel motherboard search to the X79 chipset. We can also narrow the search by only looking at motherboards based on the latest Intel Socket type of 2011, released 14 November, 2011, which supports Sandy Bridge-E processors. (See: https://en.wikipedia.org/wiki/Z68#5.2F6_Series_chipsets, https://en.wikipedia.org/wiki/LGA_2011). Based upon the minimum requirements, we will need to start comparing technology to see which vendor's product best meets our needs. There are many features, whistles and bells that you need to consider. Below is a brief example analysis that you can conduct to arrive at a motherboard solution, but there are many other features that you need to consider in your analysis:

ASROCK Fatal1ty X79 Champion	ASROCK Fatal1ty X79 Professional
TweakTown Editor's Choice Award	Techwarelabs Editor's Choice Award
Form Factor: Extended ATX, 12" x 10.5"	Form Factor: ATX 12" x 9.6"
Price: $360	Price: $265
CPU: Intel Core i7 (LGA2011)	CPU: Intel Core i7 (LGA2011)
Memory: Supports DDR3 2500+(OC)/2133(OC)/1866(OC)/1600/1333/1066 non-ECC, un-buffered memory Max RAM Memory: 64GB	Memory: Supports DDR3 2600+(OC)/2133(OC)/1866(OC)/1600/1333/1066 non-ECC, un-buffered memory Max RAM Memory: 64GB
Expansion slots: 5 x PCI Express 3.0 x16 slots (PCIE1/PCIE5: x16/16 mode; PCIE1/PCIE3/PCIE5: x16/8/8 mode; PCIE1/PCIE4/PCIE7: x16/8/8 mode; PCIE1/PCIE3/PCIE5/PCIE7: x16/8/8/8 mode) - 2 x PCI Express 2.0 x1 slots - Supports AMD Quad CrossFireX™, 4-Way CrossFireX™, 3-Way CrossFireX™ and CrossFireX™ - Supports NVIDIA® Quad SLI, 4-Way SLI, 3-Way SLI and SLI	Expansion slots: - 4 x PCI Express 3.0 x16 slots (PCIE1/PCIE2/PCIE4/PCIE5: x16/8/16/0 mode or x16/8/8/8 mode) - 1 x PCI Express 2.0 x1 slot - 2 x PCI slots - Supports AMD Quad CrossFireX™, 4-Way CrossFireX™, 3-Way CrossFireX™ and CrossFireX™ - Supports NVIDIA® Quad SLI™, 4-Way SLI™, 3-Way SLI™ and SLI™
Storage Devices: 2 x SATA3 6.0 Gb/s connectors by Intel® X79, support RAID (RAID 0, RAID 1, RAID 5, RAID 10 and Intel® Rapid Storage 3.0), NCQ, AHCI and Hot Plug functions - 4 x SATA3 6.0 Gb/s connectors by Marvell SE9230, support RAID (RAID 0, RAID 1 and RAID 10), NCQ, AHCI and Hot Plug functions	Storage Devices: - 2 x SATA3 6.0 Gb/s connectors by Intel® X79, support RAID (RAID 0, RAID 1, RAID 5, RAID 10 and Intel® Rapid Storage 3.0), NCQ, AHCI and Hot Plug functions - 4 x SATA3 6.0 Gb/s connectors by Marvell SE9172, support RAID (RAID 0 and RAID 1), NCQ, AHCI and Hot Plug functions
Audio: - 7.1 CH HD Audio - Creative Sound Core3D quad-core sound and voice processor - Supports CrystalVoice - Supports Scout Mode - Supports EAX1.0 to EAX5.0 - Premium Headset Amplifier (PHA)	Audio: - 7.1 CH HD Audio with Content Protection (Realtek ALC898 Audio Codec) - Premium Blu-ray audio support
USB Ports: - 8 x Rear USB 3.0 ports by TI, support USB 1.0/2.0/3.0 up to 5Gb/s - 2 x Front USB 3.0 headers (support 4 USB 3.0 ports) by TI, support USB 1.0/2.0/3.0 up	USB Ports: - 4 x Rear USB 3.0 ports by TI, support USB 1.0/2.0/3.0 up to 5Gb/s - 2 x Front USB 3.0 headers (support 4 USB 3.0 ports) by TI, support USB 1.0/2.0/3.0 up

to 5Gb/s	to 5Gb/s
Limited 3 year warranty	Limited 3 year warranty

ASRock X79 Extreme11	ASRock X79 Extreme9
AnandTech Editor's Choice Bronze Award	TweakTown Editor's Choice
Form Factor: Extended ATX, 12" x 10.5"	Form Factor: ATX
Price: $600	Price: $345
CPU: Intel Core i7 (LGA2011)	CPU: Intel Core i7 (LGA2011)
Memory: 8 x DDR3 DIMM slots, 2500+(OC)/2133(OC)/1866(OC)/1600/1333/1066 non-ECC, un-buffered memory Max RAM Memory: 64GB	Memory: 8 x DDR3 DIMM slots, 2400+(OC)/2133(OC)/1866(OC)/1600/1333/1066 non-ECC, un-buffered memory Max RAM Memory: 64GB
Expansion Slots: 7 x PCIe 3.0 x16 slots (2 x PLX PEX 8747 bridges), Support 4-Way SLI/CrossFireX in full x16 PCIe 3.0 speed	Expansion Slots: 5 x PCIe 3.0 x16 Slots, Supports AMD 3-Way CrossFireX™ and NVIDIA® 3-Way SLI
8 SAS2/SATA3 from LSI™ SAS 2308 PCIe 3.0 Controller	8 SAS2/SATA3 from LSI™ SAS 2308 PCIe 3.0 Controller
Audio: Creative Sound Core3D 7.1 CH, Supports Premium Headset Amplifier, THX TruStudio PRO	Audio: Creative Sound Core3D 7.1 CH, Supports THX TruStudio PRO
USB Ports: - 4 x Rear USB 3.0 ports by TI, support USB 1.0/2.0/3.0 up to 5Gb/s - 2 x Front USB 3.0 headers (support 4 USB 3.0 ports) by TI, support USB 1.0/2.0/3.0 up to 5Gb/s	USB Ports: - 4 x Rear USB 3.0 ports by TI, support USB 1.0/2.0/3.0 up to 5Gb/s - 2 x Front USB 3.0 headers (support 4 USB 3.0 ports) by TI, support USB 1.0/2.0/3.0 up to 5Gb/s
Storage Devices: - 2 x SATA3 6.0 Gb/s connectors by Intel® X79, support RAID (RAID 0, RAID 1, RAID 5, RAID 10 and Intel® Rapid Storage 3.0), NCQ, AHCI and "Hot Plug" functions - 8 x SAS2/SATA3 6.0 Gb/s connectors by LSI SAS2308 PCIe 3.0 controller, support RAID (RAID 0, RAID 1, RAID 1E and RAID 10), NCQ and "Hot Plug" functions	Storage Devices: - 2 x SATA3 6.0 Gb/s connectors by Intel® X79, support RAID (RAID 0, RAID 1, RAID 5, RAID 10 and Intel® Rapid Storage 3.0), NCQ, AHCI and "Hot Plug" functions - 8 x SAS2/SATA3 6.0 Gb/s connectors by LSI SAS2308 PCIe 3.0 controller, support RAID (RAID 0, RAID 1, RAID 1E and RAID 10), NCQ and "Hot Plug" functions
Limited 3 Year Warranty	Limited 3 Year Warranty

ASUS P9X79 PRO LGA 2011 Intel X79	GIGABYTE GA-X79-UP4 LGA 2011 Intel X79
Anadtech Editor's Choice Award	
Form Factor: ATX, 12.0" x 9.6"	Form Factor: ATX, 12.0" x 9.6"
Price: $320 NewEgg, $350 Amazon	Price: $260 NewEgg, $271 Amazon
Memory: 8×240pin DDR3 2400(O.C.) / 2133(O.C.) / 1866 / 1600 / 1333 / 1066	Memory: 8x1.5V DDR3 2133/1866/1600/1333/1066 MHz
Audio: 8 Channels, Realtek ALC898 codec	Audio: 8 Channels, Realtek ALC892 codec

Onboard LAN: Intel 82579V, 10/100/1000Mbps	Onboard LAN: Intel GbE LAN chip (10/100/1000 Mbit)
Expansion Slots: - 3 x PCIe 3.0/2.0 x16 (dual x16 or x16, x8, x8) - 1 x PCIe 3.0/2.0 x16 (x8 mode) - 2 x PCIe 2.0 x1	Expansion Slots: 2 x PCIe 2.0 x16 (PCIEX16_1, PCIEX16_2) 2 x PCIe 2.0 x8 (PCIEX8_1, PCIEX8_2) 2 x PCIe 2.0 x1 1 x PCI
USB Ports: ASMedia® USB 3.0 controller - 6 x USB 3.0 port(s) (4 at back panel, blue, 2 at mid-board) - 12 x USB 2.0 port(s) (6 at back panel, black+white, 6 at mid-board)	USB Ports: - Up to 14 2.0/1.1 ports (8 ports on the back panel, 6 ports available through the internal USB headers) 2 x Fresco FL1009 chips: Up to 4 USB 3.0/2.0 ports (2 ports on the back panel, 2 ports available through the internal USB header)
Storage Devices: - 4 x SATA 3Gb/s port(s), blue - 2 x SATA 6Gb/s port(s), white - SATA RAID: 0, 1, 5, 10 Marvell® PCIe 9128 controller : - 2 x SATA 6Gb/s port(s), white ASMedia® ASM1061 controller : - 2 x Power eSATA 6Gb/s port(s), green	Storage Devices: - 4 x SATA 3Gb/s ports - 6 x SATA 6Gb/s - SATA RAID: 2 x SATA 6Gb/s (SATA3 0/1) and 4 x SATA 3Gb/s (SATA2 2~5) Support for RAID 0, RAID 1, RAID 5, and RAID 10 4 x SATA 6Gb/s (SATA3 6~9) and 2 x eSATA 6Gb/s Support for RAID 0 and RAID 1
Limited 3 Year Warranty	5 Year Warranty

Gigabyte GA-990FXA-UD7 AMD3+	ASUS Crosshair V Formula-Z AMD3+
Editor's Choice Award at HITechLegion	PC Perspective Editor's Choice Award
	Price: $225
Model: GA-990FXA-UD7	Model: Cross V Formula
Form Factor: Extended ATX, 12" x 10.35"	Form Factor: ATX, 12" x 9.6"
Chipsets: AMD 990X/SB950	Chipsets: AMD 990FX/SB950
Audio:	Audio: 8 Channels, SupremeFX III
Memory: 4×240pin DDR3 2000(O.C.) / 1866 / 1600 / 1333 / 1066 Maximum: 32 GB	Memory: 4×240pin DDR3 2400(O.C.) / 2133(O.C.) / 2000(O.C.)/ 1800(O.C.) / 1600 / 1333 / 1066, Maximum: 32 GB
CPU: FX / Phenom II / AthlonII / Sempron	CPU: FX / Phenom II / Athlon II / Sempron
	Onboard LAN: Intel®, 1 x Gigabit LAN Controller(s)
Expansion Slots: 2 x PCIe 2.0 x16 (PCIEX16_1, PCIEX16_2) 2 x PCIe 2.0 x8 (PCIEX8_1, PCIEX8_2) 2 x PCIe 2.0 x4 (PCIEX4_1, PCIEX4_2) 1 x PCI	Expansion Slots: 3 x PCIe 2.0 x16 (dual x16 or x16, x8, x8) 1 x PCIe 2.0 x16 (x4 mode) 2 x PCIe 2.0 x1
Storage Devices:	Storage Devices:

- 6 x SATA 6Gb/s port(s), RAID 0,1,5,10,JBOD Marvell 88SE9172 chips: - 2 x SATA 6Gb/s connectors - 2 x eSATA 6Gb/s connectors (including 1 - eSATA/USB Combo connector) on the back panel supporting up to 2 SATA 6Gb/s devices - Support for RAID 0 and RAID 1	AMD SB950 controller: 6 x SATA 6Gb/s port(s), red Support Raid 0, 1, 5, 10 ASMedia® ASM1061 controller: 2 x SATA 6Gb/s port(s), red 2 x eSATA 6Gb/s port(s), red
USB Ports: 4 x USB 3.0 port(s) (2 at back panel, 2 internal) 14 x USB 2.0 port(s) (8 at back panel, 1 eSATA/USB Combo, 6 internal)	USB Ports: 6 x USB 3.0 port(s) (4 at back panel, blue, 2 at mid-board) 12 x USB 2.0 port(s) (8 at back panel, black+white, 4 at mid-board)
$216 Amazon; $204 Newegg	$333 Amazon; $280 NewEgg

Story 	I have purchased four ASUS motherboards over the many years of my career, and they have done well for the most part. One lasted nine years before failure. The one Gigabyte motherboard I purchased years ago failed a year out of warranty. At the time I did not know how to measure the temperature of the components, and I might have overheated the motherboard or CPU, putting it in the motherboard graveyard. I have had a lot of trouble with ASUS technical support in the past; hence my earlier foray into Gigabyte arena. If you do have a problem with an ASUS motherboard during warranty, it will require working your way through their long and involved RMA process before you can finally send it in to an ASUS repair shop for final resolution. For example, my second ASUS motherboard had problems which I had to RMA in to their shop, which found nothing wrong with it. It was not until a new BIOS release stabilized everything that I got use out of the motherboard. These types of things can cost you many hours of productivity.

	If you are worried about the temperatures within you system http://www.almico.com/speedfan.php, not for the faint of heart, is an advanced free tool used by PC technicians that will show you temperature, fan speeds, and other information about your computer.

Checking and Flashing the Computer BIOS

Before you begin anything with setting up your new (or old) computer, the motherboard BIOS should be flashed up to the latest version. The BIOS needs to be flashed up to the latest version to alleviate many headaches in setting up your computer. This becomes especially important if you have to seek technical support from the manufacturer, which many times happens when building a computer. The first thing the manufacturer's technician will ask you to do is update the BIOS and see if that fixes your problem (a legitimate suggestion). If you have already flashed the BIOS, it will save you another phone call, working through the labyrinth of prompts and waiting on hold until a qualified technician is reached again.

Sometimes this can very easily be done from a newly installed Windows OS just by downloading a BIOS executable and running it. Other times, things can prove more difficult. Let's take the easy example of my HP laptop first:

I flipped the laptop upside down and wrote down the MODEL and the Part Number (P/N). I then surfed to __DuckDuckGo.com__ and entered my laptop information, (e.g. HP Pavilion DV6T FV161AV drivers, or HP Pavilion DV6T-1200 BIOS). Many times the search engine will serve up the link to the driver's page for your laptop. If not, surf to your manufacturer's website and search for your make and model. In my case I clicked on the top link presented by the search engine for my HP laptop, clicked on __Software and Driver Downloads__ on the web page > selected my operating system, then clicked on the __Next__ button. If you were doing this under __Step two: Select a download__ click on __BIOS (1)__ > under __BIOS (1)__ click on __HP Notebook System BIOS Update (Intel Processors)__ download the BIOS update (e.g. __sp52884.exe__) > once downloaded double click on the executable to run it > accept the license agreement > save the files in folder __C:\HP\sp52884__ > click on the __Start__ button to flash the BIOS and reboot.

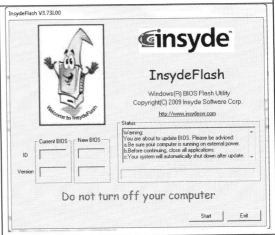

Back in the days of floppy drives coming with your computer setup, flashing BIOS was as simple as creating a bootable floppy. You would copy the BIOS update and flash software to the floppy, then reboot to run the flash update from the floppy disk. Modern computers no longer come with the outdated floppy drive technology. The BIOS update for a modern motherboard like the ASUS Crosshair V still has to be run as a DOS program. So flashing the BIOS is a bit more complicated than it used to be. PenDriveLinux http://www.pendrivelinux.com/boot-dos-from-usb offers Rufus from http://rufus.akeo.ie as an open source solution to this problem.

If your computer still has a floppy drive, right-clicking on the drive with a floppy installed will look much like Rufus on the right. Rufus will format your USB drive to boot into DOS. After you reformat your USB drive, copy the BIOS update files downloaded from your manufacturer's website (e.g. http://usa.asus.com/Motherboards/AMD_AM3Plus/Crosshair_V_Formula) to your USB and boot your computer from the USB drive. When the Crosshair BIOS update download was extracted, the BUPDATER.txt included instructions on how to run the BIOS update from the command line in DOS:

Usage

----

bupdater.exe /i<ROM filename> [/o<backup filename>] [/pc] [/g]

Copy the BIOS updater and BIOS file to the USB drive and boot from the USB drive. Upon reboot, pressing F8 on most computers will bring up the boot menu. Select your USB drive and upon boot type something like:

C:\>bupdater -i/crossh~1.rom

This will update your BIOS and finish with a message like "The BIOS Update is finished. Please restart your system." To get my computer to boot from the USB drive I had to move the first boot option in the BIOS ahead of the Blu-Ray DVD and hard disk options.

Once you have flashed BIOS to the latest version you should view your BIOS setup. Upon reboot, pressing a key like the DEL key, when your computer first starts booting will bring up the BIOS setup. Looking through the BIOS setup will quickly tell you if your motherboard is properly connected to all your computer components, what temperature they are operating at, and other useful information. For example, I quickly determined that one of my DDR3 RAM modules was not seated properly because the BIOS did not report it as being installed. While doing this, if you have not already updated your BIOS as suggested above, make note of the BIOS revision, and check to see if a later revision is available.

Power Supply Unit (PSU) – Choosing and Installing

Minimum requirements:

- 750 Watts or greater
- Platinum or Gold-Certified with 80 PLUS efficiency
- Favorable reviews by websites that reveal in detail their testing methodology

The Power Supply Unit (PSU) is the beating heart of your computer system as it converts AC link voltage to the various DC voltages needed by other computer components. When looking for a power supply, you have to estimate the power requirements of your custom built system before searching for a power supply. Based on that estimate, add 20% more power than you think you might need. The two components that consume the most power are your CPU and video card.

Story	During my days as a Combat Engineer in the Marine Corps, we were tasked with learning the demolitions lore. We used precalculated tables to determine the amount of explosive to use to accomplish the task at hand. Marines being Marines did not want to risk an obstacle being around after blowing it up the first time. So as a rule of thumb we would add 20% more explosive to the tables just to be sure. The truth is the tables already factored in more than enough explosive, but I could never convince my troops of that. As a result, some of the obstacles we blew up just vanished.

Like using explosives, it never hurts to buy an over-rated powerful power supply. A power supply is in many ways a mechanical device. It is the power engine of your computer. If it is operating at half capacity, then there is little or no strain on the power supply to meet your computers demands, but if it is operating at near, or exceeding, full power capacity, the power supply could quickly fail or even start a fire. We also want to be able to expand hardware in the future which may increase power requirements. Plus this is one component we can cannibalize for our next computer build. As computer components become more efficient, I expect power requirements to start coming down in the near future. This will buck the trend of the last 20 years.

Output and rating alone is not enough to rate a power supply. Be careful visiting sites that take a few pictures of a power supply, stick it in a computer, and then sing praises about it. They are more than likely Payola sites who will say anything for money. There are a few websites that discuss in detail how they test a power supply. Things to look for:

- Computer power supplies output multiple voltages. Measuring these outputs is a waste of time and is no indication of the quality of the power supply. Even low-end power supplies usually pass a voltage fluctuation test using a multimeter. Plus, with this test there is no way to measure the outputs all at the same time, unless you use five multimeters all calibrated the same, and can watch all five at the same time.
- One measurement is the noise levels at the power supply outputs. These can easily be measured using an Oscilloscope and reveals a lot about the quality of the power supply. The ATX12V specification states that the noise and ripple a power supply can present: 120 mV for the +12 V and -12 V outputs and 50 mV for the +5 V and 3.3 V outputs. HardwareSecrets states that we want to actually see outputs presenting one half or less in these values to consider a power supply "excellent". Another thing to consider is that high ripple and noise can damage the computer components over time.
- The reviewer should reveal how they did load testing. Inserting a power supply in a loaded computer is not a load test of the power supply. According to HardwareSecrets the only way you test load on a power supply is by connecting them to specialized active load testers, and only a few testing facilities have that type of equipment.
- Mean Time Between Failures (MTBF) measure the average time a PSU is expected to perform before failing. This figure, usually expressed in multiples of hours, is determined differently by various vendors making it hard to use for comparisons.

 **Tip**	Sometimes we fail to realize that a power supply is a mechanical device. As with any mechanical device, it will fail over time. This will result in the power supply not delivering enough voltage to the various components of your computer, which may result in random shutdowns. This can also occur if you install a power-hungry component in your computer that stretches your power supplies' capabilities. Also, a sure sign your power supply has failed is when you press the power button on your computer and nothing happens. This is a wonderful opportunity to justify to the wife and family the purchase of a good Multimeter so you can test your computer power supply outputs. Rather than give your local computer repair shop hundreds of dollars, you can test things on your own and have a shiny new Multimeter for testing electrical stuff around the house for the rest of your life.

HardwareSecrets.com also lists all the other facilities who host websites that they know of that do proper testing of power supplies at http://www.hardwaresecrets.com/article/522/7. (See: http://www.tomshardware.com, http://www.hardwaresecrets.com, http://www.hardwaresecrets.com/page/power, http://www.hardwaresecrets.com/article/Why-99-Percent-of-Power-Supply-Reviews-Are-Wrong/410/1, http://www.hardwaresecrets.com/article/Hardware-Secrets-Power-Supply-Test-Methodology/522/7). Because web links tend to change over time I decided to include the English links from HardwareSecrets so that you know where to go for good Power Supply reviews:

AnandTech (USA)	http://www.anandtech.com/show/2259
HardwareHeaven (UK)	http://www.hardwareheaven.com/reviews/948/pg4/enermax-modu87-gold-600w-power-supply-review-testing-methodology.html
Extreme Overclocking (USA)	http://www.extremeoverclocking.com/articles/guides/Power_Supply_Testing_1.html
[H]ard|OCP (USA)	http://enthusiast.hardocp.com/article/2007/02/25/hard_look_at_power_supplies
JonnyGURU (USA)	http://www.jonnyguru.com/modules.php?name=Testing_Methodology
Overclock3D (UK)	http://www.overclock3d.net/articles/power_supply/overclock3d_improves_its_psu_testing_equipment/1
PC Perspective (USA)	http://www.pcper.com/reviews
PCLinuxOS Magazine	http://pclosmag.com/html/Issues/201401/page03.html
SPCR (Canada)	http://www.silentpcreview.com/article683-page1.html
The Tech Report (USA)	http://techreport.com/review/13271/eleven-enthusiast-power-supplies-compared/4
VR-Zone (Singapore)	http://vr-zone.com/articles/behind-the-scenes-vr-zone-s-psu-testing-station-mark-ii/16485.html
X-bit labs (USA)	http://www.xbitlabs.com/articles/cases/display/psu-methodology2.html

You have to pay attention to the efficiency rating of your power supply. An 80% efficiency rating is not enough for a modern power supply. Higher efficiency is not only possible, the 80 plus revised the standard and added Bronze, Silver and Gold certifications for higher-efficiency power supplies. By October, 2009, 80 plus had to add a Platinum standard for power supplies with efficiency above 90%. (For a comprehensive list of power supply manufacturers see: http://www.tomshardware.com/reviews/power-supply-oem-manufacturer,2913.html). Calling retailers of power supplies to learn about the products is a waste of time also. As soon as you start asking questions about things such as what power supplies they sell with a Platinum rating, or what they might recommend for your hardware, you will quickly find you have lost the person on the other end of the line. With one company I called, the technician I got on the line actually steered me to power supplies with lower efficiency ratings than other power supplies listed on their website. Intel has a web page that might aid in the selection of power supplies at http://www.intel.com/reseller/psu_selector. You can also look at http://www.intel.com/support/processors/corei7/sb/CS-030866.htm. Although I have shown you many websites above, my favorite site is JonnyGURU. Not only does the author have a good sense of humor, I believe that OklahomaWolf (as the author calls themselves) does some pretty impressive testing on power supplies. Below is the beginning of research on power supplies that you will want to put together.   This example is meant to show you a good starting point to see how to gather and cross reference this data with review websites.

AZZA Platinum 750/850/1000 W, Hardware secrets silver award; internally identical to Kingwin Lazar Platinum number of connectors OK but more SATA would be good. Excellent voltage regulation, extremely low ripple and noise. http://azzatek.com	Corsair AX760i, 80+ Platinum, Hardware secrets recommend over the Rosewill Tachyon 750W. Golden Hardware secrets award; flawless noise ripple and voltage regulation. Self test button to make sure the supply and fan are OK. Lots of connectors but uses minimum gauge wire.
Corsair HX850 Gold, Jonny GURU Total Score 9.4.	Corsair AX860i, 80+ Platinum Efficiency, 7 Year Warranty, JonnyGURU Total Score 9.7
Corsair 1200i Digital ATX 1200W, 80+ Platinum Efficiency, 7 Year Warranty, JonnyGURU Total Score 9.6.	Enermax Maxrevo 1500W, 80+ Gold, JonnyGURU 9.6 Total Score.
Enermax Platimax 1200W, 80+ Platinum Efficiency, JonnyGURU Total Score 9.3.	Fractal Design Newton R3 800/1000 W, 80+ Platinum, Golden Hardware secrets Award; TweakTown Rating 89%. In the transient filtering stage, flawless. Outstanding voltage regulation, with all voltages within 2.2% on their nominal values. Low ripple and noise levels on all outputs. JonnyGURU 9.4 Total Score. Five year warranty. http://www.fractal-design.com
Kingwin Lazer Platinum 1000W, 80+ Platinum Efficiency, JonnyGURU Total Score 9.4. Illuminated connectors only difference from AZZA Platinum 750.	PC Power & Cooling Silencer Mk III 1200W, 80+ Platinum Efficiency, 7 year warranty, JonnyGURU Total Score 9.5.
Rosewill Tachyon 1000W, 80 Plus Platinum, JonnyGURU Total Score 9.1, Tweaktown rating 90%.	Seasonic Platinum Series 860/1000 W, 80+ Platinum, utilizes top quality components, such as gold-plated high current terminals and Japan-sourced 105°C aluminum electrolytic capacitors, full set of protections since even the rare OTP (Over Temperature Protection) is included, cooling fan

	features double ball bearings, the 24pin ATX uses 18AWG gauges which 16AWG gauges are preferred for smaller impedance. For $17 more than the XFX, you get a better fan, 7 year warranty and a few extras such as cable ties and a bag for the unused cables. JonnyGURU 9.7 Total Score.
XFX ProSeries 1250W, voltage regulation is outstanding, finishes about even with the Enermax Platimax 1200W, uses a 135mm Protechnic FDB fan, excellent build quality, good to very good DC output quality, good transient load test results, excellent efficiency, and is very quiet.	SilverStone Strider Gold Evolution 750W, HardwareSecrets recommend. JonnyGURU Total score 9.4. http://www.silverstonetek.com
XFX PRO 750/850/1000 Black Edition Full Modular, Hardware Secrets recommend. 80 Plus Gold certification. JonnyGURU Total Score 9. Used a 120mm Sanyo Denki BB fan, 5-year warranty, all of the cables are 60cm or more long that would be good for larger cases, both the two CPU and the three PCIe cables have a hugely satisfying wire cross-section (16 AWG). Eleven SATA and eight Molex connectors are more than enough to power any computer. Soldering quality is outstanding, XFX uses expensive Japanese capacitors from Nippon Chemi-Con and the PCB consists of epoxy resin and fiberglass. Again Infineon MOSFETs are one reason why this PSU is so efficient, and the regulation circuit also received some improvements.	EVGA SuperNOVA 1000 P2 80 PLUS PLATINUM Certified 1000W Active PFC ATX12V v2.31/EPS 12V v2.91 SLI Ready CrossFire Ready ECO Thermal Control Full Modular PSU 10 Year Warranty 220-P2-1000-XR Intel 4th G. JonnyGURU Total Score 9.7.

RAM Memory – Choosing and Installing

Minimum requirements:

- DDR3 or DDR4 standard support only
- Minimum kit size of 16GB with 32GB to 64GB preferred

Random Access Memory (RAM) has evolved from DDR1, DDR2, and DDR3 to the manufacture of DDR4 in 2014. Most all modern motherboards support DDR3, which has been around since 2007. DDR3 memory is much faster and uses 30% less power than DDR2. DDR3 has been around so long that older DDR2 memory modules are becoming rare and expensive relative to the price of DDR3 memory. RAM has followed a pattern of advancing about every five years, but the adoption of DDR4 memory support started in 2014. No computer or motherboard should ever be purchased if it does not support DDR3 or DDR4. It is estimated that 50% of all Internet devices will support DDR4 by the end of 2015. In 2014, the DDR4 memory have slim profit margins as desktop computer sales have diminished because of the rise in tablets and smartphones. As a result, manufacturers have been hesitant to tool up for DDR4 memory, but that is changing in 2014. If you are building a server, try hold off until the DDR4 devices are being produced. (See: https://en.wikipedia.org/wiki/DDR3_SDRAM, https://en.wikipedia.org/wiki/DDR4_SDRAM)

Story 	The old Pentium III that I custom built for a friend, who later gave it to me after I built him another more advanced computer, finally died. The computer had sentimental value as this was one of my first custom computer builds. Every time I tried to load an OS on the computer it would lock up. I used http://www.memtest.org Memtest86+ Advanced Memory Diagnostic Tool to test the RAM memory, and after running for about 20 minutes it locked up with a memory error. I went to http://www.crucial.com/index.aspx to price a new PC133 memory module, and the cost was $34.99 for a 256MB of SDRAM. Considering the fact that most OSs require a minimum of 1GB to 4GB this would be throwing money away. It was time to junk the old dinosaur that had been with me for so long. Plus, this made my wife happy as she questioned my need to have five computers in the office. I recycled the PC at Best Buy after taking the hard drive out and wiping it. Best Buy will not take a hard drive, but read on to find out how to recycle it.

Although the memory can be installed one module at a time, the best performance usually comes from using a matched pairs of modules. This is how most RAM memory is packaged and sold. If you have the choice, purchasing more memory at a clock rate less than the MAX available is sometimes a better deal than buying the MAX MHz at the highest price. However, before you buy, be sure to study up on possible motherboard limitations and determine what your motherboard will accept. For example, one ASUS motherboard description said, "*Due to CPU behavior, DDR3 2200/2000/1800 MHz memory module will run at DDR3 2133/1866/1600 MHz frequency as default.*" Any modern computer should never have less than 8 GB of RAM, and I would recommend 16 or 32 GB as the new minimum. Motherboards are allowing more and more RAM to be installed (modern motherboards up to 64 GB). A good rule of thumb is to make sure you install at least half as much RAM as your motherboard is capable of running in a size that will allow you to max out the RAM later if you so desire. For example, if your motherboard can handle up to 64GB of RAM, you would not want to buy a memory module of less than 8GB per memory module.

Finding the RAM for your hardware is easy because RAM dealers maintain databases of recommendations for your computer hardware. It can be as simple as surfing to http://www.crucial.com where the website will ask for your ***Select Manufacturer (e.g. Giga-Byte, ASUS, ASRock, etc.) > Select Product Line (e.g. ASRock Motherboards, ASUS Motherboards) > Select Manufacturer (e.g. X79 Extreme9, Crosshair V Formula, Maximus IV Extreme-Z)***. If you want to stick to a specific manufacturer http://www.kingston.com/us/ will also guide you to the correct RAM. Buying the most advanced/fastest RAM can drive up the price, but DDR3 has been around so long it is worth a few extra dollars to get the fastest RAM your motherboard will support. In June 2014, a 32GB kit of (8GBx4) memory was running from $300 to $350. However, what is the fastest DDR3 RAM and what do all the numbers mean? When you find the recommended RAM for your computer you will see something like:

Specs: DDR3 PC3-12800 • 8-8-8-24 • Unbuffered • NON-ECC • DDR3-1600 • 1.35V • 1024Meg x 64 • Low Profile

Crucial has a good description of what some of these numbers mean, and I will fill in the blanks on the rest below. The table below was taken from Crucial.com:

NON-ECC/Non-parity -- Most desktop and laptop computers take NON-ECC or Non-parity memory.
ECC/Parity -- ECC or parity modules look for errors in data and are most often found in servers and other mission-critical applications used by large networks and businesses.
Unbuffered -- Most PCs and workstations use unbuffered memory which is faster than registered memory.
Registered/Buffered -- Registered or buffered modules delay all information transferred to the module by one clock cycle. This type of memory is primarily used in servers.
Fully buffered -- Designed for next generation servers, features an advanced memory buffer.
CL -- CAS (column address strobe) latency, which is the number of clock cycles it takes before data starts to flow after a command is received. Lower CL is faster. Modules with different CL can be mixed on a system, but the system will only run at the highest (slowest) CL.
Component configuration -- (For example: 64Meg x 64) Indicates the size of the memory chip components on the module.
Voltage -- For example 2.6V, indicates the power used by the module. The lower the better.

The definitions above clarified a few things for me, but I was still hazy on what some of the specifications meant. PC3-14900 means that the Peak Transfer Rate is 14900 MB/s. Same for the PC3-12800 means the Peak Transfer Rate is 12800 MB/s. Each memory module displayed as compatible with your motherboard has a different Memory Clock Speed, Cycle Time, I/O bus clock, Data Rate, and Peak Transfer Rate. In this example, PC3-14900 is faster than PC3-12800 memory. If you want a more technical description, the PC3-14900 after the DDR3 is the module name and we want the highest number offered. The PC3-xxxx denotes theoretical bandwidth that can be rounded up or down, and is used to describe assembled DIMMs. With DDR3 there are a few different module names such as PC3-14900, PC3-12800, PC3-10600, PC3-8500, and now rarely PC3-6400. Bandwidth is calculated by taking transfers per second and multiplying by eight. This is because DDR3 memory modules transfer data is on a bus that is 64 data bits wide, and since a byte comprises 8 bits, this equates to 8 bytes of data per transfer.

So what does the number DDR3-1600 mean? In means the max speed at which this RAM can run is 1600MHz RAM. If your motherboard is rated at DDR3-2300+, then putting in DDR-1600 memory is limiting the capabilities of your hardware as you will not be running your RAM at your motherboard's rated speed. It is always a good idea to look at the RAM listed in the Qualified Vendors List (QVL) published by the manufacturer or EVGA.

How about the words *low profile* above; what do they mean? Simply put, *low profile* means the RAM memory sticks are thin and short, while high profile might be thicker or taller. They are designed to fit in tighter spaces. One of the main benefits of using LP RAM is that it creates more room for bulky CPU heat sinks that a computer builder may need to overclock their system. Smaller memory sticks also allow more air to pass through, though in most cases, it's probably a negligible benefit. Most modern motherboards use *low profile* RAM.

The last mystery when it comes to the numbers above is what does 8-8-8-24 mean? These numbers refer to the memory timings. From https://en.wikipedia.org/wiki/Memory_timings, *"Memory timings or RAM timings measure the performance of DRAM memory using four parameters: CL, tRCD, tRP, and tRAS in units of clock cycles; they are commonly written as four numbers separated with dashes, e.g. 7-8-8-24. The fourth (tRAS) is often omitted, and a fifth, the Command rate, sometimes added. These parameters specify the latencies (time delays) that affect speed of random access memory. Lower numbers imply faster performance."*

To summarize, the RAM you want is DDR3-(high number) • ?-?-?-?-(low number) • Unbuffered • NON-EEC • DDR3-(high number) • (low number)V • Size • Low profile

Tip

Choosing the RAM for your motherboard can be tricky. Websites that sell RAM usually give you an excellent recommendation for your motherboard that you should examine. For example, researching my book sample server computer below the website recommended: 32GB kit (8GBx4), Ballistix 240-pin DIMM, DDR3 PC3-12800 memory module for $288. However, I selected "show me all RAM memory options" and quickly saw 32GB kit (8GBx4), Ballistix 240-pin DIMM, DDR3 PC3-14900 memory module for $292. So for a mere $4 more I could get memory that could run faster but at the sacrifice of latencies.

RAM Memory -- Installing

Memory modules and your CPU are probably the most delicate components that you will install in your computer. They are especially sensitive to electrostatic discharge and the oil on your fingertips. NEVER handle your memory sticks by the gold-plated contacts. Preferably wear latex gloves for this type of work, and make sure you are properly grounded which we discussed previously. Before installing your memory modules, there may be obstructing items or cables that are in the way of the motherboard slots for your RAM memory modules. Be sure to manage your cables to make installing the memory as easy as possible, or put the sticks in before cabling up your computer.

Most memory sockets have two locking tabs on either side that flip down to release the memory modules for removal. Some motherboards may have a locking tab on only one side. If you are replacing old modules with new memory, unlatch the one tab, or both tabs when there are two, to release and lift out the memory module.

Before putting minimal pressure on the memory module to insert it, make sure it is orientated (not reversed) such that the key notch aligns with the corresponding ridge(s) in the memory socket. Also, make sure the locking tab(s) are fully open. Once you have the memory module orientated properly, push straight down into the socket until you feel the locking tabs snap into the fully closed position. The pressure you have to apply may seem excessive, but you sometimes have to push down hard to get the memory to click into place.

Before replacing the case cover and tying off all of your cable management neatly, replace the removed obstructions to inserting your memory modules and power up the system. If you hear multiple beeps, then one of the modules may not be seated properly. Reseat the module and try to boot again. If the beeps happen again you may have a defective memory module. Replace the module with your old memory and see what happens. If you don't have old memory, boot up on what you do have minus the memory module in question.

Upon boot run a memory test using the RAM memory test utility found at http://memtest.org. **Don't skip this step**! Memory problems can cause frustrating intermittent failures of your system that may cost you weeks of investigation and tons of cash. You can download the program and burn it to a CD or install it on a USB drive. The best thing you can do is support this project by purchasing a CD from their website. The CD is self-booting, automatically running the test software. Plan to walk away for a few hours to let the software thoroughly test your computer's RAM memory. I have had computers take an hour or more before the test software encounters a memory problem and reports the error (sometimes locking up afterward).

You also have to make note of your OSs maximum RAM limits. The RAM limit for all the 32-bit versions of Windows 7 is 4GB, except for the Starter Edition, which is 2GB. For the 64-bit edition the amount of RAM memory varies depending on which edition of Windows 7 you are running:

Windows 7 Ultimate: 4GB x86, 192GB x64	Windows 7 Enterprise: 4GB x86, 192GB x64
Windows 7 Professional: 4GB x86, 192GB x64	Windows 7 Home Premium: 4GB x86, 16GB x64
Windows 7 Home Basic: 4GB x86, 8GB x64	Windows 7 Starter: 2GB x86, N/A

(See: http://msdn.microsoft.com/en-us/library/windows/desktop/aa366778(v=vs.85).aspx#physical_memory_limits_windows_7)

Video Card – Choosing and Installing

Video card selection is almost as complex as motherboard selection. For your video card selection, if you are not a gamer, pretty much any good mid-level card will do. You have to dig around and read consumer reviews of the various card options that exist. Tom's Hardware points out that today's graphics cards handle all the new games with ease. They also don't expect any new major releases in the graphics technology. In my research these new cards are big, and some of them run pretty hot. Go to http://www.newegg.com and look up the card you are contemplating and read all the user reviews. You can also use the site to compare the specifications on the various card options. Even though technological change is slowing down, I try to keep the price of the card between the $200 to $450 ranges. You can always double up on the cards if you want better performance or more than two monitors.

The main thing is to make sure you get the ports you need for your current hardware and also plan for the future as hardware fails.

The slots for video cards have rapidly evolved over the last 15 years. I had some awesome AGP slot video cards that I had to recycle because I could not find a friend to give them to. I know a lot of people with old XP computers, but they bought them at a store, and even though old, those computers did not have an AGP slot. The 2004 motherboards came out with PCI Express slots that were twice as fast as the old AGP slot. AGP motherboards quickly ceased to exist after this advancement. PCIe has also evolved. Modern video cards have become power-hungry monsters that have their own cooling fans. They can take up two or three PCIe cards slots and can be quite long, measuring 10" or more in length. (See: https://en.wikipedia.org/wiki/Video_card)

NOTE	Modern video cards are quite long and will not fit in cheap PC cases, so if you are using an old case rather than one designed for these large video cards, you may run into problems. Plus, you want the added durability of a slightly more expensive case. Cheap cases can have annoying things like plastic power switches that break off. One of my custom servers that appeared to die and had to be resurrected, has had to be annoyingly powered on using a pencil for the past seven years after the power switch quickly broke off.

When you start searching for video cards, you will discover they come in all sorts of shapes and sizes and from various manufacturers at various prices. You will have to compare them, read the user reviews, and decide which one fits your needs. The way to narrow the field of choices is to put together a requirements list that will move some of the cards off the choice list. Below is a sample list of requirements for you to emulate that I put together to help you narrow the field of cards to pick from:

- Examine the video memory of the card. The difference in the price for double the RAM was sometimes in the $25 range. So the card will need the maximum memory you can get at a nominal increase in price for the RAM memory. Only consider cards with memory from 2GB to 8GB.
- Find out what version of OpenGL standard the card supports. From https://en.wikipedia.org/wiki/OpenGL, "*OpenGL (Open Graphics Library) is a standard specification defining a cross-language, cross-platform API for writing applications that produce 2D and 3D computer graphics.*" There are differences between the various OpenGL standards that you may want your card to support. The OpenGL 4.2 standards came out in August, 2011 and 4.3 in August 2012. So your video card needs to support OpenGL 4.2 or later.
- The *Core Clock* or *Graphical Processing Unit* (GPU) is the most important part of a video card. The GPU's strength is measured by its clock speed. With today's cards, we want that benchmark at 1000 MHz or more. On the 2GB cards there was not much difference in the price for a higher GPU clock speed.
- The Tech shopping site http://www.newegg.com has a very active geek community that rates the hardware. Any card with less than a four star rating has to be ruled out if the number of reviews is 20 or more.

- The Effective Memory Clock ranged from 1000MHz to 1300MHz so we will pick something higher than 1000MHz.
- Some of the Manufacturers sweeten the pot with free games and/or rebates. All things being equal, go with the sweetened pot.
- No VGA or DVI support. VGA has been around since 1987. The fact that this standard still exists at all is amazing. Any video card or motherboard that supports this standard must never be purchased. Digital Visual Interface was meant to replace VGA but the new DisplayPort technology, which allows multistreaming and daisy-chaining several monitors, had displaced this standard also.

Example analysis of a few modern video cards:

NVIDEA GeForce GTX 770	Radeon HD 7970
1536 Stream Processors	2048 Stream Processors, DirectX 11.1
Memory: 2GB 256-bit GDDR5	Memory: 3GB 384-bit GDDR5
PCI Express 3.0	PCI Express 3.0 x16
Core Clock: 1137MHz (Std 1046MHz)	Core Clock: 1100MHz
Effective Memory Clock: 7000MHz	Effective Memory Clock: 1500MHz (6.0Gbps)
Ports: 1 x HDMI, 1 x DisplayPort, 1 x DVI-I, 1 x DVI-D	1 x HDMI, 2 x Mini DisplayPort, 1 x DVI
Price: $400	Price: $450
Warranty: 3 years limited	GOLDEN HARDWARE Secrets Award

There are other worthy, older cards that can cost less if you are not a gamer and want to save some money on a work computer:

| NVIDIA GEFORCE GTX 680, Core Clock 1GHz, Memory Clock: 6 GHz, Memory Interface: 384-bit, Memory Transfer Rate: 288 GB/s, Memory: 3 GB GDDR5, Shaders: 2,048, DirectX: 11.1. January 2013 PCWorld says this card blends the high performance of the company's Kepler architecture with the terrific efficiency of its earlier Fermi design to deliver a well-balanced powerhouse that suited to both gaming and GPU-computer applications. | HIS IceQ X Turbo H695QNT2G2M Radeon HD 6950 2GB 256-bit GDDR5 PCI Express 2.1 x 16 HDCP Ready CrossFireX Support Video Card with Eyefinity. Effective Memory Clock 1280MHz (5.12Gbps); Core Clock 840 MHz; OpenGL 4.1; Dimensions 10.23" x 5.59" x 1.65"; 5 star user rating; $270 with Free Dirt3 game included. |
| GeForce GTX 670, Core Clock: 915 MHz/980 MHz, Shader Clock: NA, Memory Clock: 6,008 MHz, Memory Interface: 256-bit, Memory Transfer Rate: 192.3 GB/s, Memory: 2 GB GDDR5, Shaders: 1,344, DirectX 11. $440 Newegg, $443 TigerDirect, $460 Wal-Mart. | The GTX 580 received the GOLDEN HARDWARE Secrets award. A PC Builder called this card a power-sipping card that only requires two six-pin power connectors, which is unheard of in high-end graphics card. The 680 is faster than the Radeon |

GOLDEN HARDWARE Secrets AWARD.	7970 and has the ability to support four monitors.

Monitor – Choosing and Installing

Monitors are devices that you may want to share between computers. For example, once your SSH server is set up, which we will talk about in Chapter 9, you will rarely need to use a monitor with that computer again. To allow using a monitor with multiple computers we can use a KVM switch. But as technology changes, your expensive KVM switch may quickly become obsolete. Also, a KVM is usually limited to one type of connection port. For example, I had to recycle my old four port S-Video/VGA-KVM switch. (See: http://en.wikipedia.org/wiki/KVM_switch) KVM stands for "keyboard, video and mouse" and the switch does just that; you can use the same keyboard, mouse and monitors with multiple computers. You simply dial in whichever computer you want to work on with the switch. Unfortunately for me, but not for you, the monitor connection has evolved again to a new standard that is called DisplayPort. I have been using a digital KVM switch that cost me a lot, which is also soon to be obsolete with the new DisplayPort technology. If you are purchasing a new monitor, make sure it has a DisplayPort, which was introduced in 2008. My suggestion is to consider manually moving your monitor cables from computer to computer before purchasing a KVM switch. For those of us still using DVI, we must ask, what are the advantages and disadvantages of using a DisplayPort over DVI?

- The DisplayPort is an improvement over DVI. It can deliver data to your monitor in discrete packets instead of the steady stream that the old DVI and VGA standards required. Each data packet contains additional data like a time stamp that allows a DisplayPort monitor to assemble the data and display it better.
- The data-packet approach reduces distortion and image degradation, and it allows for future development of how data is transmitted and interpreted by the monitor.
- Audio data can also be transmitted about a DisplayPort connection. In the past, to have audio on a monitor required a separate cable.
- DisplayPort adapters are available to connect up an old VGA/DVI monitor.
- DisplayPort's are sturdier, smaller, easier to use, cheaper to cable, and a lot easier to work with. No more tiny little pins that might get bent trying to cable a monitor to a graphics port. No more thumbnail screws to tighten the cable into place.
- Most, if not all, monitor manufacturers are adopting DisplayPort standard and are phasing out the old DVI and the very old VGA connectors.

If you can wait or afford it, purchase an LED monitor, not an LCD that is rapidly being replaced. The difference between LED and LCD monitors is mainly in the backlighting technology. LED monitors are in fact LCD, or "Liquid Crystal Display" monitors, that use a more energy-efficient, "light emitting diode" technology to light the back of the monitor. They also can consume up to 40% less energy, and with no use of mercury, LED monitors are environmentally friendly as well. LED monitor are also easier on the eyes and clearer to view with more color contrast. They have come down in price, and a top of the line 29" monitor is now only running about $400 to $700. If you are spending the extra cash for an LED monitor, make sure it supports USB 3.0 and display port technology.

 **Tip**	If you have monitor problems, try a few things first before purchasing a new monitor. The first obvious solution is to reseat the cables and the monitor card in your computer. The next step is to try a different cable. For example, I was ready to recycle a monitor that I had given up hope on but when I used a new monitor cable everything worked fine. Another thing you can check is to make sure the cooling fans for your video card are dust free and operating properly. Then try using a different video port on your computer or another computer to make sure the video card is not the problem.

Monitors come in all shapes and sizes that people prefer, so I chose not to do an analysis of this. For example, I could never make due with a tablet, small laptop, or even a notebook. However, these devices are very popular which I admit, is a "go figure" moment for me. When I am watching TV or working on the computer, I want the biggest screen possible. If I could afford a new 70" LED TV, I would have one in my TV room! For a computer monitor I would consider the Dell UltraSharp U2713HM LED monitor with IPS panel. Given the diverse nature of monitors, I leave it up to you to decide what fits your needs, space and budget.

Blue Ray DVD Burner – Choosing and Installing

Most all DVD drives come with Blu-ray capability these days. Blu-ray drives superseded the old DVD optical storage medium. Blu-ray can support disks with a number of layers the latest format being quadruple layer (128GB) available for BD-XL re-writer drives. From wiki, "*the name Blu-ray Disc refers to the blue laser used to read the disc, which allows information to be stored at a greater density than is possible with the longer-wavelength red laser used for DVDs.*" Blu-ray and DVD burners come with a pitiful limited 1-year warranty but a 1-year extended warranty can be purchased for as little as $8.

Many of the old DVD drives also supported HP's LightScribe technology. This technology allowed the user to burn an image onto one side of the disk. This was convenient for making copies of software disks provided with your computer, downloaded and burned to DVD, or purchased. On the burned disk we could burn the name, the key and other relevant information about the software on the DVD. Lightscribe DVD drives only support up to DVD+R as its highest capacity. The drives are being phased out and as of June 2013, only LG is still manufacturing the drives. (See: https://en.wikipedia.org/wiki/Blu-ray_Disc, https://en.wikipedia.org/wiki/LightScribe)

Blu-ray drive burners are not really a necessary component for your computer. They have a great deal more capacity than DVD drives but are more expensive. They are good for recording HD video and playing Blu-ray Discs. An external drive will give you the most versatility but you have to make sure your computer hardware supports that. Blu-ray burners have come down significantly in price, and if you are building a computer, I see no reason to purchase a pure DVD drive. Another alternative is to purchase a drive capable of Blu-ray playback but only DVD burning for about a cheaper price. Pure DVD burners are dirt cheap if you don't need Blu-ray and are handy to have internally in your computer. However, if all you need is storage space, a USB drive is probably a better choice and is portable. Minimum drive requirements:

- Max 14X BD-R writing speed, Supports BDXL (128GB) discs
- 3D BLU-RAY title playback & M-DISC support, USB 3.0 if external
- 24X DVD+R 8X DVD+RW 12X DVD+R DL 24X DVD-R 6X DVD-RW 16X DVD-ROM 48X CD-R 32X CD-RW 48X
- 4MB Cache, BD-ROM Access Time 180ms, 1-year warranty

Internal 24X DVD+R 8X DVD+RW 12X DVD+R DL 24X DVD-R 6X DVD-RW 48X CD-R 24X CD-RW 16X DVD-ROM 48X CD-ROM, 1.5MB Cache, 53 positive reviews Newegg	LG Black 14X BD-R 2X BD-RE 16X DVD+R 5X DVD-RAM 12X BD-ROM 4MB Cache SATA BDXL Blu-Ray Burner with SW, 3D Play Back - BH14NS40, Max 14x BD-R writing speed Supports BDXL (128GB) discs 3D Blu-ray title playback & M-disc support CD-R/RW, DVD-R/-RW/-R DL/-RAM/+R/+RW/+R DL read and write compatible, CD Family, DVD-ROM(SL/DL), BD-ROM(SL/DL)/R(SL/DL/TL/QL)/RE (SL/DL/TL) read and write compatible 4MB Cache, 44 reviews Newegg

Backup – Solution Selection and Technical Information

Backup needs vary wildly between the HCU/SBO and the data they generate. I thought a 2 terabyte 2.0 USB drive would be the ultimate in backup technology when I purchased it. But once I took on the task of writing this book, my **slow** 2 TB USB 2.0 drive became grossly inadequate. The transfer speed was so slow with all the VMs I had to generate, all OSs I had to create, all the software and OSs I downloaded; I chewed thru 2 TB in a few short months as this book took eight years to write. This revelation was shocking given what this amount of storage used to cost just a few years ago. Imagine what a SBO may see in their backup requirements?

I have been asked by a few HCU/SBOs what they should purchase to backup their Internet devices. If you have multiple computers, you will have multiple "System Image" backups and multiple "System Repair Discs" that you will need to store on your backup device. If you refer down to Chapter 6 I have a few suggestions about where these backups need to be made during a Windows 7 installation and setup process.

For an HCU/SBO with only a need to backup data, my advice is to purchase the biggest Thunderbolt or 3.0 USB drive available. Other technologies are coming, but they will take a while longer. USB 2.0 is a legacy standard, which is rapidly being phased out with much faster technology and should not be considered. A USB 3.0 device can be hooked up to modern day 802.11ac router that can be shared among all your computers and Internet devices in your network. This solution may be adequate for most HCUs but some SBOs need more storage capacity. The company ioSafe http://iosafe.com/products-rugged-portable-overview makes some rugged portable hard drives that can survive some extreme environments. For example, this USB 3.0 drive offers crush protection up to 5,000 lbs., drop protection up to 20', immersion protection up to 30 feet for three days and more.

Consider skipping a USB backup solution, spend a little more money, and purchase a Network-Attached Storage solution (NAS) backup solution for your computers and mobile devices. An NAS is a smart storage device in which you can house multiple hard drives to backup your data. It can also run RAID, which protects you data from a single point of failure. It can be used both as a file server, for sharing files between multiple computers, and/or as backup device. An NAS has many advantages over using a USB drive. It is much faster than a USB drive because it has a CPU enabling it to operate in an efficient fashion as a computer. It is an optimized, stripped down computer connected to your network. An NAS used to be cost prohibitive to a SBO/HCU, but that has changed. It is now an excellent low-cost solution that every SBO/HCU should consider. USB 3.0 is already a dated technology, and USB 2.0 should not even be considered as a backup/file sharing solution.

Minimum requirements:

1. Thunderbolt and USB 3.0 support. Thunderbolt is slimmer than and twice as fast as USB 3.0.
2. RAID 5 and 10 support.

A few NAS manufactures where you can review and compare products are QNAP and Synology. (See: http://www.qnap.com/static/products/comparison/All_NAS.php, http://www.synology.com/us/index.php)

Keyboard and Mouse – Choosing and Configuring

This is really personal preference. Most of the keyboards and mice I looked at had good user ratings. The Logitech MK550 Black USB RF Wireless Ergonomic Wave Combo looks like a nice choice for non-gamers. BestBuy had it on sale for $60.00. I started with the keyboard and mouse combination. This was because I could try it out in my current home network/computer configuration without too much hassle. My wife and I chose the Logitech MK550 Combo because of its good reviews and its ergonomic design. I took my wife to Best Buy and had her try out all the keyboards and she liked the feel of the Logitech MK550 the best. It curves up slightly in the center, unlike some of the ergonomic keyboards that really curve up in the center, requiring some getting used to. This is a more natural position for the hands and should help prevent carpel tunnel syndrome.

The keyboard has a nice feel. It is padded in the front where you can rest your wrists. In the past my keyboards provided a cheap plastic piece for this purpose. There are also the usual extra keys that do all kinds of wonderful things, which you will have to learn about from the limited manual. Install the latest software from Logitech; don't use the disk provided with the combo. My SetPoint disk was at version 6.1. The software at Logitech was at version 6.3. Always surf to the manufacturer's website to get the latest and greatest drivers and software for any new device.

My problem was making the new keyboard work with my DVI switch so I could use the keyboard with all my computers. I could not figure out how to do this. The keyboard operates off of Logitech's Unifying technology. You plug a very small USB transmitter into a USB port and that transmitter sync's up with your keyboard and mouse. I tried moving the transmitter to other computers to no avail. It would only sync up on the original computer. I purchased more of the Unifying Receivers from Logitech with the thought of plugging them into my other computers and then using the keyboard and mouse combo with all my computers. This worked somewhat after many hours of experimentation. In hindsight, if you install Logitech's software on all your computers, then move the transmitter around as needed, syncing everything up you will be good to go without the added expense. In my case, having the extra transmitters plugged in ready to switch over with a few mouse clicks is better.

Tip	If your USB keyboard suddenly stops working, check the batteries and make sure you plug it into another USB port before condemning the keyboard and mouse to the junkyard.

The manual states that one keyboard/mouse combo will only work with one unifying receiver at a time. But what does that really mean? My hope was to cut one computer off, cut another computer on and have the keyboard/mouse combo work (sync up to the new receiver automatically). This did not happen. There is little help in the small manual provided and searching Logitech's website was not much help. ***Run the Logitech Unifying software click on Start > All Programs > Logitech > Unifying > Logitech Unifying Software on each computer you switch to that has a Unifying Receiver. The easiest way I found was to click on the Advanced... button and then the Un-pair button for the keyboard and mouse > click on Pair a New Device to re-sync the keyboard and mouse to the new receiver > sync up the combo by cutting off each device (keyboard and mouse, up to six devices) one at a time and cutting them back on***. While this is inconvenient, it is a solution. The problem is you will have to have another keyboard/mouse combo hooked to each computer to sync everything up so you can use the MX550.

Laser/InkJet Multifunction Printers – Choosing

If you want up-to-date, in-depth, full reviews of various laser printers, visit http://go.pcworld.com/laserMFP. The January 2013 and September 2012 PCWorld rated the Brother MFC-9970CDW http://find.pcworld.com/71935, http://go.pcworld.com/brother9970 as the Best Buy Laser Multifunction Printer. Other printers below $1800 that got VERY GOOD ratings are:

- Brother MFC-9970CDW (PCWorld January, 2013 and September 2012 Best Buy); print/copy/scan/fax; photo quality is middling; color scans can be overly dark); USB, wireless, and Ethernet connectivity; 300-sheet standard input, auto duplexing; average toner cost, per editorial research: 1.9 cpp black, 12.7 cpp four-colors
- Brother MFC-9560CDW (PCWorld January 2013 and September 2012); USB, wireless, and Ethernet connectivity; 300-sheet standard input, auto duplexing; average toner cost, per editorial research: 1.9 cpp black, 12.7 cpp four-colors
- Samsung CLX-6260FW (PCWorld January 3013) USB, wireless, and Ethernet connectivity; 300-sheet standard input, auto duplexing; lowest vendor-specified toner cost: 3 cpp black, 17.1 cpp four-colors
- HP Laser Jet Pro 400 Color MFP M475dw; (PCWorld January 2013 and September 2012); USB, wireless, and Ethernet connectivity; 300-sheet standard input, auto duplexing; lowest vendor-specified toner cost: 2.6 cpp black, 16.4 cpp four-color

- Lexmark X548dte (PCWorld January 2013 and September 2012), USB, wireless, and Ethernet connectivity; 900-sheet standard input, auto-duplexing; lowest vendor-specified toner cost: 17 cpp black, 11.9 cpp four-colors
- Canon Imageclass MF8380Cdw, good quality (PCWorld January, March, and September 2012 recommend); can print and scan both sides of the paper automatically; USB, wireless, and Ethernet connectivity; 300-sheet standard input; average toner cost per page, 3.7 cpp black, 16.4 cpp four-colors

If wireless connectivity is important, only the Lexmark listed above does not have wireless. The Canon Imageclass MF8380Cdw at the top of the GOOD rating also had wireless and was recommended in the March 2012 issue of PCWorld. The January 2012 issue included user feedback on customer satisfaction with reliability and service. Only Canon and Brother had a strong showing in both reliability and service. Some Inkjet choices to consider are:

- Epson WorkForce Pro WF-5690 Network Multifunction Color Printer with PCL/Adobe PS; PrecisionCore 4S print head 4-color, Max Print Resolution 4800x1200 dpi; Copy (Color/Black-and-White: Standard/Best), auto 2-sided, preview, resize, collate; Scan (Color flatbed / Automatic 2-sided ADF, 2400 dpi); Fax (Black-and-white and color, 33.6 Kdps, Memory Capacity 550 pages, PC Fax); USB 2.0, IEE 802.11 b/g/n; 45,000-page monthly duty cycle; three-year limited warranty.
- Epson WorkForce Pro WF-4640 All-in-One Printer; PrecisionCore 4S print head 4-color, Max Print Resolution 4800x1200 dpi; Copy (Color/Black-and-White: Standard/Best), auto 2-sided, preview, resize, collate; Scan (Color flatbed / Automatic 2-sided ADF, 2400 dpi); Fax (Black-and-white and color, 33.6 Kdps, Memory Capacity 550 pages, PC Fax); USB 2.0, IEE 802.11 b/g/n; 30,000-page monthly duty cycle; one-year limited warranty
- HP Officejet Pro 8600 Plus e-All-in-One Printer (PCWorld December 2012 VERY GOOD); supports legal-size paper throughput; Text quality: Very Good; Graphics quality: Good; USB, Ethernet and wireless connectivity; 250 sheet input, automatic duplexing; Lowest vendor-specified ink cost: 1.6 cpp black, 7.2 cpp four-colors
- Kodak Office Hero 6.1 All-in-One Printer (PCWorld December 2012 VERY GOOD); supports legal-size paper throughput; Text quality: Very Good; Graphics quality: Very Good; USB, Ethernet and wireless connectivity; 200 sheet input, automatic duplexing; Lowest vendor-specified ink cost: 2.2 cpp black, 7.1 cpp four-colors
- Cannon Pixma MG5320 (PCWorld December 2012 VERY GOOD); the ability to print CD/DVDs separates this low cost printer from the rest of competition; Text quality: Good; Graphics quality: Very Good; USB and wireless connectivity; 150 sheet input, automatic duplexing; Lowest vendor-specified ink cost: 5.1 cpp black, 14.2 cpp four-colors
- Brother MFCJ6910DW Professional Series Inkjet; 11-Inch x 17-Inch Duplex Printing and 11-Inch x 17 Inch Scan Glass; USB, Ethernet and wireless connectivity; 500-Sheet Input Capacity; 3-Year Limited Warranty.
- Brother MFC-J4610DW, the January PCWorld liked the Brother MFC-J45100W which has a wide printhead and the ink is cheap. Upon further investigation the new MVC-J4610DW has a better 400-sheet capacity for the same price and the same features. Low cost printing and up to 11" x 17; Dual Paper Trays, up to 400-sheet paper capacity; USB, Ethernet and wireless connectivity; 2-Year Limited warranty.

These ink-jet printers only have USB 2.0 and only support the Wireless 802.11 b/g/n standards. Someday there may be multi-function inkjet printers supporting the new USB 3.0 and 802.11ac standards.

| **Tip**

  | Both Adobe's PS and HP's PCL drivers are page description printer languages. The printer interprets the language that describes to the printer how to print every page. Each language has its own positive and negative qualities, and each is good for different things. This is much like spoken languages. In some spoken languages it is easy to convey certain concepts, ideas or emotions -- in others, it is difficult.

 PCL drivers do most of the rendering (figuring out how to print the page) on the local workstation, and then in essentially binary form, send information to the printer. Postscript drivers send a page description to the printer where it is rendered. Since local workstations are generally MUCH faster than the printers are, PCL printing can be much faster than Postscript and because it requires less printer memory, and some print jobs may only print if sent using the PCL drivers. However, PCL is a simpler language than Postscript, so it lacks many of the complex drawing and scaling functions that are available in Postscript. Therefore, if you are using a package that takes advantage of Postscript's capabilities (e.g. most Adobe products and some open source alternatives), you may get better quality output by using postscript drivers, as your complex print job may not print properly or at all using the PCL driver. On the flip side, if your print job is HUGE and you have nothing complex, PCL would print it faster without hogging all of your network printer's memory thus preventing other jobs from being submitted. You should install both and choose the one that best suits your needs. |

Troubleshooting Network Printers

As we talked about in <u>Chapter 2</u>, your network printer has to be set up as a static route or as an Address Reservation. If you do not, its DHCP address could change your printer's IP address rendering it unusable to the computers on your network. This happens because with some printers the Internet devices are set up to look for the printer at a specific IP address. When the IP address changes we can go around to all those network devices and reconfigure them, but that would be a waste of our valuable time. Below are a few steps to try to get your network printer working again if it suddenly stops printing or you have a hardware change in you HCU/SBO set up.

1. Make sure the printer IP address has not changed.
2. Log in to your router and make sure that it sees your printer.
3. Try pinging the network printer from a device on the network.
4. Surf your browser to the printer configuration page by entering the IP address of your printer as a URL.
5. If all the above items pass, then it is the devices themselves that are likely to be the problem. You can try deleting your printer and then add it back in. ***Try to delete any print jobs by clicking on <u>See what's printing</u> at the top menu > click on the print***

job > select the __Document__ menu > select __Cancel__ to try to cancel the print job. You usually cannot remove the device until you cancel all the print jobs, and you may not want to try to do so. When the print jobs are deleted *click on __Start__ > select __Devices and Printer__ > right click on your printer driver and select __Remove device__. If there are print jobs removing this device may appear impossible.* Try rebooting if this device will not go away; if that does not work, try booting into safe mode and then restarting. Keep trying to delete the print jobs and the device and hopefully the printer device will be removed.

6. When the device finally goes away, skip down to Chapter 6 that documents how to install a print driver in Windows, and Chapter 7 that covers how to do this in Linux.

Using Surge Protector Vampire Hunters to Lower Your Electric Bill & Protect Your Equipment

If you decide not to purchase an Uninterrupted Power Supply (UPS), you must have a quality surge protection device between your electronic equipment and the power grid. You may get complaints from family members about how unsightly your surge protector becomes with all the power cords plugged in, but it may save you many thousands of dollars. Eco-surge protectors also allow you to turn off all electrical vampire-sucking devices that are plugged into them, like the entertainment center and TV boxes, which are constantly adding to your utility bill. According to a Lawrence Berkeley National Laboratory report, "*A typical American home has forty products constantly drawing power. Together these amount to almost 10 percent of residential electricity use.*" You may meet resistance from family members who want to program DVRs to record their favorite shows but you can cut everything else off where you can. Before we get into some power strip solutions to consider let's examine some of those costs. (See: http://standby.lbl.gov/summary-table.html)

You leave your desktop on all the time. A desktop in idle mode consumes nearly the same amount of energy as it does in active mode because its memory, disc, and processor are all still running.	Conserve Smart AV	Vampire cost: $7 month
You never turn off your game console after play. Game consoles are like specialized PCs with the same type of components inside. Leaving your game console on is comparable to leaving your computer on.	Game Consoles	Vampire cost: $6 month
Plasma TVs are the most culpable when it comes to vampire power sucking. They consume about two times more energy than LCDs.	Plasma or LCD	Vampire cost: $5 per month
Your DVR--when not recording--still chugs large amounts of energy.	Cable (or Satellite) Box with HD DVR	Vampire cost: $3 per month
You forget to turn off your DVD player after watching a film, and it stays on the Menu page for days. Your DVD player never rests when left on the Menu as it is constantly reading material on the disc.	VCR/DVD Player	Vampire cost: $1 month

There are some very good power strips that you can purchase to protect your equipment and keep them from running up your electrical bills. For example, I purchased the cheap 10 outlet Belkin with remote control. It only has 1000 Joules of protection but I then plugged it into my existing surge protector, which has 3700 Joules of protection.

Monster GreenPower HDP 1400G has RF remote controlled outlets so that you can easily turn off vampire devices. It has 10 outlets that offer 4626 Joules of protection for your equipment. There is also the HDP 1850G to consider.	Available at Walmart, Newegg, Sears and many retail stores. It features filtering to remove electrical noise and interference. Disconnects your devices from live power lines (line and neutral), and only reconnects when power levels are safe.
Tripp Lite Eco-Surge Protectors offer a variety of products ranging from 6480 to 1080 joules of protection, 12 to 6 outlets.	The company offers a lifetime warranty and allows the user to switch off individual outlets manually and on some models via IR remote.
Belkin's Conserve Socket is a different approach to vampire devices. You can set a timer to shutoff standby power. This is handy for charging electronic devices such as lights, fans heaters, as well as drills or a cellphone.	Belkin also offers surge protectors with remotes, timers, smart USB charging stations, and their *Conserve Insight* product. Conserve Insight lets you find out how much energy your devices really use so you can determine where you can really save money.

(For Products see: http://www.tripplite.com/products/series/sid/866, http://www.belkin.com/us/Products/Power/c/WSPWRSP, http://www.amazon.com/Monster-GreenPower-HDP-1850G-PowerCenter/dp/B0034HQK5K) (For articles see: http://www.pcworld.com/article/203716/vampire_hunters_devices_reduce_energy_waste.html

http://www.pcworld.com/article/249074/vampire_power_reality_check_what_tech_gear_sucks_the_most.html#tk.nl_spx_t_topnews)

Laptops – Specifications – Changing the Hard Drive – Securing

Let's examine the minimal hardware requirements to replace an old laptop in 2014:

- Intel Core i7 CPU (any model) or an AMD Socket FM2 processor or later.
- 12 to 32GB of DDR3L/DDR4 MHz SDRAM RAM (4GB to 8GB is no longer the minimum needed)
- A wired RJ45 Ethernet 10/100/1000MB connection port
- Wireless 802.11a/b/g/n/ac. (802.11ac is the latest standard, which is up to 3 times faster than 802.11n. 802.11ac was also developed to be compatible with the next generation of Wi-Fi devices and is backwards compatible with 802.11n)
- SATA hard drive support of at least a 1-2TB (7200/10000 rpm) drive, or a Solid State Hybrid Drive of at least 1-2TB (Periodicals and other sources may recommend a SSD for your laptop. While these drives are fast and quiet, they lack the capacity for multiple virtual OSs, which you will need to conduct your Internet activity in. We will cover

Virtualization in Chapter 7. Virtualization consumes large amounts of disk space. Hard drive manufacturers are just now coming out with hybrid drives that are part SSD and part SATA, providing the benefits of both technologies. As this technology matures only purchase a laptop with a hybrid drive or SSD and SATA duel support.

- Super-Multi DVD Blu-Ray Optical Drive/Burner/Reader
- Flash memory card slot and Bluetooth 4.0 support
- Maximum USB 3.0 support and **NO** USB 2.0 ports. USB charging support for your smartphone while the laptop is sleeping.
- The Maximum Thunderbolt Ports money can buy. Modern laptops that have Thunderbolt ports hit the market years ago. Thunderbolt is twice as fast as USB 3.0 with data transfer rates of 10Gbps
- Screen Size 17" or larger with Full-HD support (you will hate staring all day at a smaller monitor that many laptops come with)
- HDMI port(s) for TV presentations as you travel and built-in speakers
- 1080p or better resolution on the monitor of at least 1920 by 1080 pixels
- 64-bit advanced Operating System (Window Ultimate comes with encryption techniques you may want)
- A set of re-installation DVDs for your OS (make sure you get this!)
- Price tag below $2,100.

If you have an older laptop that only supports 750GB or less, if your hard drive fails or you want a backup hard drive, consider the Seagate Momentus XT Hybrid 750GB 7200 RPM SATA 6.0Gb/s Solid State Hybrid Drive. It is a beautiful mix of the fast SSD technology upon which you can install your OS, with the capacity of a SATA drive, which you will need for Virtualization. If you are purchasing a new laptop, Seagate has the Solid State Hybrid 1TB 64MB Cache SATA 6.0Gb/s Laptop Hard Drive.

Users in the February 2013, issue of PCWorld rated most laptops on the market very reliable. Apple was on top; Asus, Lenovo, Sony, and Toshiba had slightly higher ratings than Dell and HP, but the numbers were very close. The article found that the easiest to use laptops were Apple, Lenovo and Samsung. PCWorld readers for top reliability rankings of laptops voted for: Apple, Samsung, Toshiba, Asus and Acer (in that order). For top customer support: Dell for Business; Toshiba, Dell and Acer for Home; Apple for both. For my own personal use, I own and use the HP Pavilion dv6t. I have found it very reliable and very easy to use. So these ranking are subject to personal opinion and may be skewed.

Above I listed a 17" screen and the *bare minimum* screen size for a laptop. A lot people view a bigger, heavier laptop as something they don't want to haul around. I would agree with that sentiment without the invention of laptop backpacks that you can purchase at your local office supply store. With my laptop backpack I can haul around external speakers, a 15' CAT 6a cable, a HDMI cable, books, magazines, extra charged batteries, you name it. Having a backpack for your laptop is as simple as grab and go. Some options are standard across similar priced laptops but depending on how much you want to spend, can decide what high-end components you need in your laptop. For example, the video card, memory and hard drive(s) can vary depending on your performance requirements. Below is a sample analysis you might perform while searching for a laptop to meet your requirements:

ASUS ROG G750JS-DS71 Gaming Notebook	DELL Alienware 18
Intel Core i7 4700HQ Quad Core 2.4GHz	Intel Core i7-4710MQ 3.5GHz, 6MB Cache
Chipset: Intel HM87 Express	Chipset: Intel HM87 Express
Video card: NVIDIA GeForce GTX 870M 3GB GDDR5 VRAM	Video card: Dual NVIDIA GeForce GTX 860M graphics with (2x 2GB) GDDR5
Display: 17.3" Auto FHD EWV LED Backlight Non-Glare LCD (1920 x 1080), matte	Display: 18.4" WLED FHD (1920 x 1080)
RAM Memory: DDR3L MHz SDRAM 32GB	Memory: DDR3L MHz SDRAM up to 32GB
Storage: 1TB 7200RPM SATA + 256G SSD, RAID0 Support	Hard Disk: 1TB 5400RPM SATA 6Gb/s + 256GB mSATA SSD
Optical Drive: Super-Multi DVD Blu-ray Writer, Blu-ray reader	Optical Drive: Super-Multi DVD, DVDR/RW
Networking: 802.11 a/b/g/n/ac (WiDi) Built-in Bluetooth V4.0	Networking: 802.11ac Dual Band 2x2 AC Wi-Fi + Bluetooth 4.0
Audio: Built-in Speakers And Array Microphone, Built-in subwoofer, MaxxAudio	Audio: Audio Powered by Klipsch
Webcam: HD Camera	Webcam: Has one (unknown if HD)
Card Reader: 2-in-1 card reader SD/MMC	Card Reader: 1 x 7-in-1 Media Card Reader
Interfaces: 1 x Microphone-in jack 1 x Headphone-out jack 1 x VGA port/Mini D-sub 15-pin 4 x USB 3.0 port(s) 1 x RJ45 LAN Jack for LAN insert 1 x HDMI 1 x mini Display Port 1 x Thunderbolt port (Optional) 1X AC adapter plug	Interfaces: 1 x Power/DC-in Jack 1 x RJ-45 Gigabit Ethernet IPv6 3 x SuperSpeed USB 3.0 Ports 1 x SuperSpeed USB 3.0 Port with PowerShare Technology 1 x Mini-Display Port 1 x HDMI 1.4 Output / 1.3 Input 2 x Audio Out 1/8" Ports (One compatible with inline mic headset) 1 x Line In Microphone 1/8" Port (retaskable for 5.1 analog audio output)
Dimensions: 16.1 x 12.5 x 0.7 (WxDxH)	Dimensions: 17.9 x 12.9 x 2.23
Weight: 9.9 lbs (with 8 cell battery)	Weight: 12.064 lbs with SSD
Security: Kensington lock, LoJack, Intel Anti-theft	Security: Kensington Lock port (cable and lock sold separately)
Windows 10 64-Bit	Windows 10 64-Bit
Limited Warranty period: 1 year	Limited Warranty period: 1 year

How to Swap the Hard Drive in Your Laptop

1. With the battery out and power unplugged, turn your laptop over and look for a compartment with two or more screws about the size of a 2 1/2 inch disk drive.
2. After unscrewing the screws, open up the compartment, ground yourself (dispel any built up electrostatic charge your body may be carrying) by touching something metal around you or by wearing a grounding strap. If you have a built up static electric charge, it will dispel into the metal in a spark.

3. The connector to the hard drive looks like two pieces but is really just one. Look at the back of the new hard drive to understand what I am talking about. The connector easily slides off. Be careful not to touch the pins on the back of the hard drive. The oil from your fingers is not good to spread on to sensitive computer connections. Latex gloves should be considered for this type of component work.

4. Label the old hard drive with the Windows 7 key from the bottom of your laptop that also describes what it is.

5. Just like on a desktop, there are two side-rails on the old hard drive that have to be moved to the new drive. Don't do this right away if you will be swapping drives back and forth while building your new computer.

6. Connect all the cables, including a Category 6e or 7 copper cables to your laptop and router's or cable modem's RJ-45 port. Sometimes you cannot do this wireless, and cabled connection to the router is faster for downloads and applying updates.

7. If your hard drive has a previous install on it, consider using the previously discussed free tool, Partition Wizard Home Edition from http://www.minitool.ca. Download and install the latest version to zero your hard drive. This is one of the greatest free tools for working on hard drives I have found. They also sell the Power Data Recovery tool to recover data from USB and hard drives. It succeeds where other products fail.

When Possible -- Lock Your Laptop

Theft of devices, such as laptops and, increasingly, tablets, remains the most common computer crime because it requires zero know-how to pull off. Tablets are popular because they are easily resold on the black market. A physical cable lock will help deter someone from swiping a laptop off your desk or out of a hotel room. At colleges and universities criminals have been daring enough to scale the outside wall of a dormitory to steal a laptop out of a student's room where the window was left open. The websites http://us.kensington.com and http://www.targus.com/us/index.aspx sell assorted products that attach to the lock port on your laptop. For PCs without a lock port, you can purchase a universal lock system that you can attach to the PC chassis. These products can be used to chain it to something that cannot be moved easily, or at http://www.targus.com/us/index.aspx they have a second level of security provided by the high decibel alarm that is triggered if the cable is severed or the motion sensor is activated.

| Story | I personally worked in a large corporate office building where a group of thieves walked right into the office building staffed with minimum-wage paid security workers, took an elevator up to the million-dollar executive floor, bagged all their executive laptops, and then brazenly walked right out the front door with them. I shudder to think of the data they obtained. Expense-related items like background checks are sometimes neglected in the name of profit. Most times the security guards are not armed, and sometimes even act as greeters to people entering the building. This is especially true in situations where multiple corporations share the same building, and the building manager is responsible for security. Had those computers had a physical lock, it might have stopped or slowed these criminals down, or even sounded an alarm. Nobody was terminated as a result of this incident, and everything continued with business as usual. Since this was a 4+ billion dollar company, who knows what was on those laptops, or what they sold |

them for on the black market. That same corporation eventually went through bankruptcy, then after litigation was over, issued a new stock offering with the same executives in charge, and resumed operations like nothing had happened. The only losers were the original stake/stock holders in the company. That same company spent 16 thousand dollars training me in various applications like PeopleSoft and UNIX applications which I greatly appreciated. But as is the trend with corporate America, I was eventually laid off and replaced by three workers from India. This formally bankrupt corporation's stock is now worth $39 a share, so go figure. I compare this experience to our governments many thousands of dollars investmented in each of our soldiers and then letting them go, or forcing them to leave service for various reasons that make little or no sense. We need to explore finding a middle ground to retaining these trained and expensive resources, rather than just trying the next cheapest thing available.

Sextortion, Put Tape over Your Laptop Webcam When You Are Not Using It

If you are not wary of using the Internet after all the ground we have covered thus far, you need to know about the cracker crime called *sextortion*. Almost all Laptops come with a built-in webcam. Most modern laptops come with a light that will show when the webcam is in operation. Most Internet devices are easily broken into by crackers, which gives them access to the device's webcam. Once the webcam is on, the cracker can record everything that is visible through it. Criminals have been convicted of spying on more than 200 women through their webcams, even blackmailing some of them. People don't know they are victims until their information is all over the Internet. If the thought of a cracker spying on your kids does not creep you out, I don't know what else will.

In another instance, server computer-rental companies used webcam images to extort past-due payments from their customers. One man arrested by the FBI may have coerced as many as 350 women to strip for him via webcam. He did so by breaking into email, Skype and Facebook accounts. He then stole information and photos the victims would not want made public. Of course, this crime goes both ways. Young men who engage in sextortion do not realize they will go to jail for a very long time when caught perpetrating these crimes. In no way am I condoning their actions, but society pays a price for parents allowing their childrens' misuse of Internet devices to permit many entities to spy on them. (See: https://en.wikipedia.org/wiki/Webcam)
.

The media has nicknamed this software creepware*, which is really just a remote administration tool (RAT) that is easy to use. Blackshades has been marketed as an actual product that could be purchased for about $40. When Miss Teen USA, Cassidy Wolf, approached the FBI after a former classmate she knew, Jared Abrahams, had installed the RAT on her computer, a worldwide sting operation ensued. In the end, about 700,000 computers worldwide were found to be hijacked by Blackshades and more than 90 people arrested in Germany, Denmark, Canada, the Netherlands and elsewhere. Wolf now campaigns to urge other young people to practice cyber security.

WARNING 	While I find this story very sad I am very happy that Miss Wolf is now campaigning for the cyber security her generation needs and deserves. However, I wonder where her parents were during this year long invasion. This is the flip side of the story that our media will never reveal. Parents provide their children Internet devices that they know little or nothing about, which is akin to equipping them with loaded guns with no safety measures. According to my reading, simple malware tools such as Malwarebytes and updated anti-virus would have picked up on this year-old hacking tool. Once again I revert back to my Marine training; if you are going to give a child a weapon, then you must train them in how to use it and safeguard its use. To do otherwise should be considered criminal in today's world. Miss Wolf's nude webcam pictures may now be on the infected Internet for all time, and her parents should be held accountable. Our media constantly wants to hold gun owners accountable so let's now start holding parents accountable for their negligence in giving their children infected Internet devices. I detail this horror to make fun of how far we can to go down the liability holes we seem to want to drill into our society about how everyone else is responsible.

People also refer to (RAT) as Remote Access Trojan's or Remote Access Tools. This software enables people to take full control of your computer or Internet access point. This software is used by cyber criminals to remotely monitor, review, alter the computer's functionality, change the overall function, and record your computer activities. We talked about botnets, and with an RAT your computer can be used to commit a crime or attack other computers. (See: http://blog.malwarebytes.org/intelligence/2012/06/you-dirty-rat-part-1-darkcomet, http://blog.malwarebytes.org/intelligence/2012/06/you-dirty-rat-part-2-blackshades-net) Simple steps you can take are to close your laptop when not in use or to put a piece of tape over the webcam when you are not using it.

Label Your Mobile Devices and Keep the Fans Open

Sometimes your mobile device will fall into the hands of someone with a conscience. You should (at a minimum) put some sort of contact information (not enough for ID theft) on your device. You can also use a service like http://boomerangit.com or http://stuffbak.com to attach a coded label to your device. The label encourages the finder to go to the BoomerangIt or StuffBak website and follow instructions to report your device as found. You can improve you the odds of your device being reported by putting a monetary reward on the label.

Mobile devices can overheat and destroy themselves. Some obvious things we all must do are never leave them in hot vehicle or in the hot sunlight where possible, and never operate them in extremely hot conditions. If they feel overheated, do not turn them on until they have cooled down. With laptops be careful not to block the fans by operating them on a pillow or in your lap. A hard surface is usually better, but I have used my laptop in my lap in a cool air conditioned room with no ill effects. Modern laptops are much better at cooling themselves than older laptops were.

Track Your Laptop

There are also options to track your laptop using Lojack for Laptops, http://www.lojack.com/Laptops and http://preyproject.com. Both options require installing software on your laptop and are rather invasive. The potential for misuse of this technology may make you hesitant to employ these security techniques. But Lojack could help law enforcement locate your PC or laptop. The software comes with a variety of features (GPS location, ability to lock your device, remotely wipe the hard drive, take a photo remotely using the built-in webcam, sound and alarm, and more). Lojack costs about $40 per year and Prey is free for up to three devices.

Extending Laptop Battery Life and Purchasing Extra Battery Life

Noticeably absent from our minimum laptop specifications was a minimum requirement for battery life. Evaluations of battery life sometimes don't mean much since your battery life is subject to how you use your laptop or smartphone. If you are gaming or viewing video, this will substantially reduce battery life compared to doing something such as just running office programs.

 **TIP**	When you purchase a laptop, often times the manufacturer will offer a larger battery pack as an accessory that you can purchase. **BUY IT** and you will never regret it. The small battery that came with my laptop burns out in 6 to 8 hours when using office applications. My second, much larger accessory battery lasts many more hours and was a life-saver in editing this book in the forest. The squirrels were amazed.

There is a lot of misinformation about how to extend the life of our laptop batteries. Let's dispel some of the myths you may have heard and apply some common sense tactics:

1. When I first got my laptop I left the battery in all the time even though I was primarily using AC power. This will constantly have your battery charging and discharging as you power the laptop on and off. Take the battery out if you are using AC, to preserve it. Make sure the battery is at least half-charged when you remove it. I only remove at 100% but I never know when I will need them.
2. Don't leave your battery out of the laptop for too long without putting it back in the laptop to recharge. A good rule of thumb is no longer than two months. Longer than that you run the risk of discharging it completely, which is bad for the battery.
3. It is OK to recharge your battery all the way.
4. This next warning seems to me like the signs we see over and over again stating, *Be careful when floor is wet,* -- don't remove or insert a battery when the laptop is running.
5. Make sure the laptop is well-ventilated and kept cool. Hot batteries shorten battery life. For example, setting your laptop on a pillow while working in the bed might be a bad idea! Clean the laptop vents with compressed air if they have collected dust.
6. Set your PC's power settings to sleep and hibernate to save battery power. ***Click on Start > open the Control Panel > click on the Power Options icon > in the left panel click on Choose when to turn off the display > adjust when to Put the Computer to sleep: > click on the Change advanced power settings link > expand the Sleep menu > expand the Hibernate after menu and adjust the settings.***

Sometimes these lithium batteries run out exceptionally fast or feed the OS disinformation as to their status. This can sometimes be corrected by completely discharging the battery a few times and completely recharging it. By default, Windows will not allow you to completely discharge a battery. The best advice I found on this topic was to allow Windows to drain your battery as far as it allows before shutting down. Then restart your computer and enter your laptop's setup by pressing ESC or F8, and leave that up until the laptop completely drains the battery. The directions for doing this differ from laptop to laptop.

Laptop Accessories

For a speaker solution, we need something compact but with good quality sound. The Phoenix Wireless Bluetooth Speaker is no bigger than a coffee mug and is easy to pair with a Bluetooth-enabled phone, laptop or tablet. The speaker has a rechargeable battery that allows the user to play tunes for up to eight hours. (See: http://www.beaconaudio.com/the-phoenix.html)

Caring for Your Computer, Laptop and Monitor

We talked about the importance of a good UPS to preserving your server's health. But what other things do we need to consider about caring for our computers? Below is a list of steps you should perform about every six months to a year.

1. We all know that any component you are trying to clean or work on should not have power coursing through it. However, computers are vampire devices that can have powered components even when the rest of computer is shutdown. Some power supplies have a switch to cut power to those components, but the best course of action is pulling the power plug and also removing the battery if it is a laptop.
2. Thoroughly vacuum around and under the computer from time to time. Never use the vacuum inside the computer as it can carry a static electric charge that could damage components. You can carefully vacuum the fans on the back of the computer keeping your hand between a plastic attachment and the fan. Never touch vacuum metal to a computer fan or any other part of the computer for fear of electric discharge.
3. Some computers I have worked on in people's homes go beyond the word "dusty" to the "filthy" category. In fact, I was shocked that those computers were still operating. Unless you want dust all over your house, take the computer outside and use compressed air to blow the dust out from the inside of the computer and off the fans. Hold the fans still, or insert something such as a pencil as you hit them with the compressed air so that they do not spin. If a fan is allowed to spin too fast it can damage the fan. When saying that, I got this picture in my head of Tim "The Tool Man" holding up a can of compressed air and telling his audience, "if this little baby, compressed-air canister can clean the dust out of a computer, imagine what this Binford 60-Gallon Two-Stage Pro Air Compressor can do!" The fans would spin so fast the computer might take flight!
4. It is not intuitive, but it is even more important to clean the fans in laptops, which you may not be comfortable with. Turn your laptop upside down and with a small screw driver, unscrew the panel covering your laptop's fan. In my case there was no easy

panel to unscrew. I had to remove practically the whole bottom panel to get to the fan to clean it. This might be something you would feel more comfortable paying the Geek Squad at Best Buy to do for you.

5. If taking the computer outside is not an option to limit dust blowing about your home, use slightly moist paper towels to pick up the dust off of the easy-to-reach surfaces being **very careful** not to swipe any sensitive components such as RAM, CPU or the motherboard. Then, with a vacuum running nearby to suck up the dust, blow out the inside of the computer with compressed air. What I do is, in the direction I am blowing the dust with the right hand, I have the vacuum nozzle catching the dust with the left (once again keeping the vacuum nozzle well away from the inside of the computer).

6. For hard-to-reach places in the computer, you can use alcohol soaked swabs to clean those surfaces. Gun kits have the ones with long wooden handles and a tightly wrapped tip, which is perfect for cleaning these surfaces. Never use water!

7. It is unrealistic to say "never eat or drink new a laptop or computer" even though that is what we all should do. However, we do have to be careful when eating or drinking around a computer. If you have a drink nearby make sure it is placed in a spot where if it is knocked over the liquid will not rain down onto your computer equipment or dump into your keyboard. I have gone so far as to keep the liquid safely placed on the floor.

Story	I eat and drink while working on my computers all the time. I usually have a cup of water nearby because computing is thirsty work. As luck would have it, the one time I placed the water near my wireless keyboard while working on computer equipment, I managed to knock it over, dumping pop (soda for down South speakers) right into the keyboard. In another instance a relative called me and said their cat knocked over a cup of water, dumping it right into their laptop keyboard. She dried it off as best she could and then tried to use it. It worked briefly and then died. I told her that applying power so soon may have killed it permanently. She gave the laptop a week to dry, at my advice and, amazingly, it worked again. I was not so lucky; my keyboard was never usable again.

8. Those of us who eat near our computers have to clean the keyboard a little more often. Turn the keyboard upside down outside, over a trash can or sink; tap it gently on the back and then play with the keys to get as much of the dirt out as possible. Next, use compressed air to blow out what remains stuck in the keyboard. If you have particularly stubborn debris in a mechanical keyboard, you can pop off the keys to remove that.

9. Using a clean, damp cloth, wipe down the outside of the computer.

10. Moisten a clean cloth with rubbing alcohol that will not deposit lint, as opposed to a paper towel, to wipe down the USB drives, your keyboards and mice. The keyboard and mouse can become quite germ-ridden, and using water does not alleviate that, nor will water remove the oil left behind from your handing of them. Be sure to flip the mouse over and make sure to rub optical sensors also. An alcohol-soaked Q-tip might come in handy for this as well.

11. Cable management is something that is cheap and easy to do. You can use masking tape to label both ends of every cable and power cord at both ends. Use twist ties to tie cables together and find tubes to provide routing channels in which to combine cable

runs. For example, using something as simple as a cardboard paper towel or toilet paper tube can be helpful.

12. If you have dogs, cats or smoke, try to keep them out of room that houses your computer equipment. Certainly don't allow pets to lie down, walk on, or eat near your computer equipment.

Story	I traveled to one house to repair a friend's computer. I immediately noticed the cat's feeding bowls on his desk where the computer and keyboard resided. While I was working the cats came up to eat out of the bowls, and I had to shoo them away to keep them off the keyboard. Cat hair was everywhere, and I was amazed the computer worked at all.

Sometimes our computer will have a mysterious problem that seems to be unexplainable. Three websites you can visit to troubleshoot these types of problems are http://www.cybertechhelp.com, http://www.suggest-a-fix.com, and http://www.techguy.org. There is a lot more ground we could cover on how to take care of your Internet devices, but there are books dedicated to those topics. I just wanted to highlight a few quick and easy things you can do to maintain your computer equipment.

Cleaning a LCD Monitor, HDTV, Phone and Camera Display

With old TV's, some Windex and paper towel sufficed to clean the dust from the screen. But with the new technology you could damage or destroy your screen using those cleaning methods.   In the January 2012 issue of PCWorld, in an article titled "*Clean Your Laptop or Desktop LCD Properly*" by Rick Broida, and a much older PCWorld article at https://www.pcworld.com/article/201388/the_proper_care_and_feeding_of_your_hdtv_phone _and_camera.html by Lincoln Spector, outlined how to care for your digital equipment.

To clean a dirty HDTV screen, phone screen, or a camera lens use a microfiber cloth—the same microfiber one you use on your glasses, except bigger for an HDTV or LCD/laptop screen. You can buy large microfiber cloths for a few dollars at camera stores, electronics stores, hardware stores, or online. Try to clean the screen with a dry microfiber cloth first. If that does not work, you will need to use a wet cloth.

Disconnect whichever screen you are cleaning from its power source. Just powering it down is not enough. Modern electronics have vampire voltages coursing through them running up your electric bill (which we discussed how to turn them off in Chapter 3). Never use any sort of wet cloth on a device connected to a power source. Make sure it is disconnected for at least 30 seconds to allow its capacitors to discharge.

Never use a glass-cleaning product like Windex, or a cleaning liquid that has alcohol or soap in it, on an LCD screen. Don't apply any liquid directly to the screen. Water is the safest liquid to use on an LCD screen. If that does not prove powerful enough, a 50/50 mix of distilled water and white viniger is the safest liquid to use on a LCD screen. This can clean as good as any commercial LCD-cleaning fluid, at less cost. Put the liquid into a spray bottle, and spray it onto the microfiber cloth. Gently wipe the display, and then wait until the screen is completely dry before plugging the device back in.

Recycle Your Old or Failed Tech Devices, Computer Equipment, and Batteries to Save the Environment

According to Wiki on computer recycling, disposing of a PC properly is a huge issue for the environment. I think we all want to do what is right for the environment and future generations, but we have not been instructed or encouraged to do so. From https://en.wikipedia.org/wiki/Computer_recycling, *"The U.S. Environmental Protection Agency, estimates 30 to 40 million surplus PCs, classified as "hazardous household waste", would be ready for end-of-life management in the next few years. The U.S. National Safety Council estimates that 75% of all personal computers ever sold are now surplus electronics."* For every SBO/HCU user your choices are to trash your used PC, try to sell it for little or nothing, donate it somewhere that may not want it, recycle it, or attempt reuse it for some purpose such as an SSH server. Many people are inclined to place it out with the garbage, but that is the worst thing you can do if it is still functional.

WARNING 	These devices fill up landfills and are incinerated and will pollute the atmosphere and underground aquifers with toxic substances. Circuit boards contain lead, mercury as well as chromium. Motherboards and connectors often contain beryllium. Cadmium can be found in chip resistors, semi-conductors, infrared detectors, stabilizers, cables and wires. Chromium and mercury can be found in switches and relays. Brominated flame retardants are used in many computer components, including circuit boards and plastic casings. Other toxins found in computers are polyvinyl chlorides, phthalates, and arsenic. According to the Electronics TakeBack Coalition (ETBC), the U.S. disposed of 423,000 computers and 595,000 monitors in 2010. Just 40 percent of computers and 33 percent of monitors were recycled; the rest were trashed. Un-recycled computers are poisoning American food, water and air; future generations will bear the brunt of what could have been an avoidable environmental disaster.

In some wise communities, dumping computer equipment into the garbage or landfills has been declared illegal and includes stiff fines for attempting to do so.

WARNING	E-waste, a popular term for electronic products that are at an end of their useful life, often times contains hazardous substances like lead and mercury. These should not be discarded in the regular trash or left on public property. Some progressive communities have laws against leaving things like TVs and computers on roadsides, open streets, and paved alleys. Some states such as California have made dumping illegal and enacted a statewide e-waste recovery program which collects a nominal fee to dispose of these items properly.

According to wiki, only 15% of electronic devices and equipment are recycled in the United States. We rarely repair broken electronics because there are few repair shops, and it is often cheaper and easier to replace it. We are all very busy poisoning our planet, but leaving our children to clean up this mess is not something we should be doing. There is also an even more positive side to recycling. An electronic device is a wealth of metals and plastics that can be recovered and reused to reduce the costs of manufacturing new technological systems.

Manufacturers of electronics also benefit from shorter and shorter life cycles for their equipment. Warranties are getting shorter and shorter, so users can't even send in broken items to be recycled or fixed. There is no incentive for them to do otherwise as they have no repercussions for those devices improper disposal. Some technology companies offer free recycling, and they use those recycling programs to keep legislation from being passed that gives incentives for the users and companies to recycle their equipment. This increases their profits as local governments struggle to deal with tech equipment filling up and poisoning our dumps, which in turn poison everything and everyone around them. According to the May 2013 PCWorld article "How Companies Get You to Keep Buying New Stuff" by Christina Desmarais, "*Environmental group E-Stewards estimates only 11 to 14 percent of e-waste goes to recyclers; the rest ends up in landfills or is burned, causing soil, water, and air pollution.*" Where is the outrage about this and why aren't citizens trying to correct this behavior?

I had equipment lying around, such as an old KVM switch, a failed keyboard and mouse, and some old Category 5e (Cat5e) cabling. (See: http://en.wikipedia.org/wiki/KVM_switch, http://en.wikipedia.org/wiki/Category_5_cable) I upgraded the connections to all my computers and network printer to Category 6 (Cat6), which reduces crosstalk, allows for faster data transfer and has twice the bandwidth of Cat5e. The website http://www.serverracksandcable.com/category-5e-category-6-questions-and-answers.php describes the differences between Cat 5e and Cat 6 cabling and why Cat 6 is a much better solution than Cat 5e. Since cabling my lab with Cat 6, the new Cat 6a (or Augmented Category 6) cabling has become standard. The new Cat 6a is characterized to 500 MHz, twice the frequencies of Cat 6, and has improved alien crosstalk characteristics. My recommendation is to buy Cat 6a for a mere 50 cents more. (See: https://en.wikipedia.org/wiki/Category_6_cable)

There are easy recycling options available, and if you type *computer recycling* in your favorite search engine, many options will be revealed. I hope this book will help you choose some of these easy alternatives. One website I found is http://www.computerhope.com/more.htm, which states they were founded in Salt Lake City, Utah, by Nathan Emberton, and they offer free technical support to everyone. Examining them at the Better Business Bureau shows no BBB Accreditation, but they have an A+ rating, reference http://www.bbb.org/us. Computer Hope and the EPA list many recycling options, some of which are presented in this book. (See: http://epa.gov/osw/conserve/materials/ecycling/donate.htm, http://www.epa.gov/epawaste/conserve/materials/ecycling/donate.htm, http://www.computerhope.com/disposal.htm).

Sometimes it requires a bit of effort to save the environment. For example, the county in which I reside offers free computer recycling twice a year. Visiting their website to find out when and where the next recycling event was going to be hosted proved to be a rabbit hole of wasted time. I finally found a web page on their website that described when and where the next recycling event would occur. The date listed was about a month prior to the month in which I was searching. My county, and perhaps yours, sometimes send out flyers informing residents when the next event will be hosted, so hold on to your equipment and watch for the next event. The great thing about hazardous waste disposal day in your local community is it gives you the opportunity to really feel good about yourself and prove how much you care about the environment. It is your opportunity to properly dispose of alkaline, dry cell, alarm system and automotive batteries; paints, stains, dyes, glue, carpet cleaner, furniture, and nail polish, bathroom cleaners, stain removers, solvents, pharmaceutical waste, fertilizer, lawn and garden chemicals, antifreeze, motor oil, CSL and florescent bulbs, fire extinguishers, smoke detectors, thermostats, computer monitors, CPUs, printers, keyboards, mice, scanners, cell phones, fax machines and televisions. I put hazardous waste disposal day on my calendar and start piling stuff up about two weeks prior.

Another more immediate alternative is to use http://www.bestbuy.com, which will recycle most of your old computer equipment, other tech devices, and *rechargeable* batteries for free. After talking to the Geek Squad at the local Best Buy, I dropped off my broken computer, keyboard and mouse, and the old KVM switch, which they accepted for recycling. There are also websites dedicated to helping you purchase environmentally responsible products, keep you informed on what political steps are taking place to protect the environment, and help them make the large retailers to be more environmentally responsible. Greenpeace even has an online guide to help you purchase greener electronics. (See: http://www.healthystuff.org, https://ww2.epeat.net, http://www.greenpeace.org/international/en/campaigns/toxics/electronics/how-the-companies-line-up)

The office supply chain Staples offers recycling programs for not only PCs, but also for office electronics such as copy machines, personal electronics, smartphones, digital cameras, inkjet-printer cartridges, and *rechargeable* batteries. If you have a laser printer, most manufacturers allow you to ship back your worn-out cartridge in the box your new cartridge came in for recycling. (See: http://www.staples.com/office/supplies/home)

Apple, Dell, Hewlett-Packard and Samsung offer comprehensive in-house recycling services. Some companies provide incentives for you to replace the donated machine or machines by purchasing from them. Apple gives their customers a gift card for old tech equipment. Dell provides over 2,000 physical drop-off recycle centers and has a mail-back recycle program for things such as spent print cartridges and other print supplies / hardware. Samsung will help you print a prepaid label to allow you to mail them an expired cellphone.

The one glitch to my *operation recycle* was that http://www.bestbuy.com would not take my hard drive for liability reasons. You will have to take that out of the computer or let them do it for you. After removing the hard drive myself, I did not want to just throw the hard drive in the trash for someone to steal my data off of, and I wanted to recycle it if that was possible. You can easily sanitize your hard drive and ship it to companies that will recycle it for you, which we will explore next.

Recycle Your Failed Hard Drives, Old or Unusable CDs and DVDs to Save the Environment

To recycle a failed hard drive, visit http://www.freeharddriverecycling.com home URL to use Back Thru The Future Technology Disposal services to recycle your failed hard drive. Their website states they will recycle a failed hard drive properly. They also accept CDs and DVDs for recycling. With this option available we don't have to feel guilty about all our obsolete CDs and DVDs piling up in the local dump polluting our world. The company is based out of

Franklin, NJ. To recycle your drive, box up the failed drive (*the box your new hard drive came in is an excellent choice*), write "*Free HD* or *Free CD*" somewhere on the box (in my case both), and send it to:

FREE HD FREE CD **Back Thru The Future** **1 Park Drive, Suite 9** **Franklin, NJ 07416**	Their website points out: Each hard drive contains approximately one pound of aluminum, the energy equivalent of 1.5 gallons of gasoline. Recycling one hard drive saves enough energy to: • light a 100 watt bulb for 134 hours • run your television for 102 hours

Recycling aluminum is 95% more energy efficient than producing aluminum from ore Recycling aluminum results in 95% less air pollution and 97% less water pollution than producing aluminum from ore. The following on CDs and DVDs:

- A CD/DVD is considered a class 7 recyclable plastic
- To manufacture a pound of plastic (30 CDs per pound), it requires 300 cubic feet of natural gas, 2 cups of crude oil and 24 gallons of water
- It is estimated that AOL alone has distributed more than 2 billion CDs. That is the natural gas equivalent of heating 200,000 homes for 1 year
- It is estimated that it will take over 1 million years for a CD to completely decompose in a landfill

---

Back Thru the Future Microcomputers is not Better Business Bureau Accredited and has no BBB rating. There are zero complaints registered against them in the last three years. I asked the company about that and their reply was, "*The National Association for Information Destruction Naidonline.org is the association we belong to that can vouch for the integrity of our company.*" (See: http://www.freeharddriverecycling.com, http://www.bbb.org/us)

There is also http://www.harddriveshredding.com where you can pay to have them maintain detailed, auditable records of your entire hard drive destruction process. In my case, I went the free route. Below is what their website has to say about the company:

"Founded in 1990, Back Thru the Future is one of the oldest computer recycling companies in the US. It was one of the first electronic recyclers to receive both US EPA and State DEP registration as a qualified electronic recycler and we were the first electronic recycling facility in the country to receive the National Association for Information Destruction (NAID) certification as an AAA certified secure destruction facility. We were a member of both the NAID and ARMA committees that established their industry guidelines for the destruction of electronic media. We were a member of the State of NJ stakeholder committee that helped develop NJ's new e-scrap regulations.

If you are 100% confident that your drives no longer contain sensitive data and you are looking to dispose of the drives in the most environmentally friendly fashion, look no further. The materials used in the manufacture of hard drives are valuable recyclable materials. We have developed a sophisticated materials sorting system that allows us to recapture 100% of the hard drives component materials.

Simply box your drives up, write "HD" on the container and ship to the address below. For quantities in excess of 1000 we will pay the cost of transportation."

The tricky question is what do we have to do prior to disposing of our hard drive to make sure a cracker or government can't get at the data? How can we be 100% confident our hard drive no longer contains any data? It is still possible for thieves to recover and steal your personal information. All the major disk manufacturer support websites have a utility that will "ZERO" a hard drive. Just look at the device drivers on your computer to get make and model and then download their utilities. You will then have to expand their software to an old floppy or more likely burn it to a CD. The utility/diagnostic will do a through an erase on the hard drive that probably only NSA can recover with their infinite hardware.

Normally this company provided software is enough to erase everything on the hard drive and allow it to be recycled. However, if your security is paramount it will take more than five full days to sanitize a 1 terabyte capacity hard drive using any DOD specification overwrite software. Some articles suggest that three passes zeroing the drive is sufficient. But in my example case the drive has completely failed. It cannot be sanitized that way. If we take a sledge hammer to the drive or drill holes in it, it becomes difficult to ship for recycling. So I decided to determine the recommended sanitization method for a hard drive so that it could no longer be read and recycled without worry.

I called Back Thru the Future and asked them the best way to sanitize a hard drive for a home user. They said that soaking a hard drive in water overnight will completely sanitize a hard drive; I had never heard of that. If you decide to use this method, I suggest using salt water for a week or two. So I continued my research in destroying hard drives by typing "can water destroy a hard drive" at my favorite search engine, and found many articles about how water will not render drive data as unrecoverable. There were also testimonies on forums about how "Drive Savers Data Recovery" recovered the data from laptops dropped into pools for brief periods of time. (See: http://www.drivesaversdatarecovery.com). DriverSavers, Inc. has been a Better Business Bureau accredited business since 01/01/2001 and has an A+ rating.

After reading everything I could find about physically destroying a hard drive, the only sure method that I could find was to physically destroy the hard drive platter surfaces. So I set about taking the drive apart and sanding down the platter surfaces. That proved more difficult than I ever imagined, and if you would rather not do it, I would understand. But please read on, for this is entertaining, and I hope you will change your mind. I tell this story so that you know that you are not alone in your frustrations with technology.

| **Story** | The screws holding the drive together are Torx head screws, which are characterized by a 6-point star pattern. No problem I thought, I have all kinds of bit sets in the house. I have been working on and building computers all my life. After examining all my bit sets, I found that the smallest Torx bit I could come up |

with was a T-10, which was too big to fit the drive screw. I went to the Black and Decker outlet and the smallest Torx they had was a T-10. I then went to Sears with the hard drive in hand and discovered that a Torx T-9 was the tool that was needed. I could have purchased one Torx T-9 screwdriver for $4.00 but I decided that the 10-piece Precision Craftsman Screwdriver set, which was on sale for $21.00, was a better option. I was very happy later when I had to use the Torx T-7 tool to take the circuit board off the back of the drive. Plus, they have the Craftsman lifetime guarantee, which would be helpful if you were to break one of screwdrivers in the set.

I took all the screws out, but the cover still would not come off. I went down to the basement and began pounding on the cover with a hammer and screw driver to no avail; I even used my carpenter wall deconstruction tools to get the cover off. It just would not come apart from the rest of the hard drive. It finally hit me; there might be more screws I had missed underneath the label. I removed some silver tabs with a razor blade, and sure enough, underneath I discovered the remaining screws I needed to remove. Man, these Seagate guys really don't want you getting into their hard drives, I said to myself.

WARNING	When handling all the hard drive parts and platters, use latex gloves. Hard drives are very toxic in the nature in which they are manufactured. All the more reason we don't what them ending up in our dumps for our children to deal with.
Story 	I then discovered the read/write head arm would not let me get the platters out for sanding. I finally turned the drive over and used the Torx T-7 to unscrew the circuit board on the bottom of the hard drive and there was the screw holding the read-write arm head in place and I removed that. It took a bit of effort but I got the platters out and sanded them at last. I put the drive back together and sent it in for recycling.

OK, I admit, the sledge hammer approach will also work but that would make packaging the failed hard drive in the same box your new hard drive arrived in, difficult or impossible. Remember, we are trying to save the environment, protect ourselves, and maybe this is more effort than you want to expend helping in that regard, but now that I have plowed the road, how much time will you really spend sanitizing your hard drive? I am guessing no more than an hour. I was not sure soaking the drive in salt water for a long period of time would work, so I wanted to present my sure fire solution.

If you care nothing for the environment, just smash the drive in to pieces and throw it in the trash, but I'm hoping you won't do that. Sending the hard drive to a recycle facility is also a good opportunity to package all the obsolete DVDs and CDs with the drive to also be recycled. Look around; you will be surprised at how many you have. I filled the entire box with CDs and DVDs to accompany my hard drive.

Smartphone Dropped in Water, Liquid Dumped on a Keyboard or Laptop— What Now?

I have had a few instances where people have consulted me about what they can do after soaking their Internet device with a liquid. If the liquid was just water, unplug the device immediately and position the device so that liquid can drain out. If it has a battery like a smartphone or laptop, remove that immediately. If it is a laptop, turn it upside down immediately and leave it that way. If it is a keyboard or mouse with batteries, turn it upside down and remove the batteries immediately. If you dropped your smartphone into water, remove the battery! Allow plenty of time (days, not hours) for any of these devices to dry before introducing a power source to test it. Place it near a fan, and allow unheated air to blow gently on the device. Liquids deep in the components can take a long time to dry.

If the liquid is something like pop or wine, you have no choice but to immediately turn it upside down, and while holding it upside down, use a cloth damp with water to try to clean the liquids off as best you can. Your odds of recovering the device just went way down! Some of that liquid may dry in your laptop or keyboard, but clean it as best you can. All the rules above still apply except you may want to go even longer than a few days (a week) before applying power.

If, after allowing your keyboard to dry, the keys stick, you can pop off the key and use a cotton, or preferably foam, swab doused in rubbing alcohol to clean the key hole and key. If a lot of keys are sticking I saw it suggested that you try putting the keyboard in a dishwasher on rinse only with no hot water or heated setting. It should be placed on the top rack only.

Summary – A Sample 2014 Computer Server Setup

Below is a modern computer setup to easily implement the security techniques illustrated in this book:

Motherboard	ASRock Z97 Extreme9 LGA 1150 Intel Z97 HDMI SATA 6Gb/s USB 3.0 ATX Intel Motherboard	$250
CPU	Intel Core i7-4790K Haswell Quad-Core 4.0GHz LGA 1150 88W Desktop Processor Intel HD Graphics BX80646I74790K	$350
Memory	2 x 16GB kit (8GBx2) DDR3 PC3-12800 Unbuffered NON-ECC 1.35V 1024Meg x 64 part #:CT5868242, 9-9-9-24 • DDR3-1600 • Low Profile	$352
Video card	GIGABYTE GV-N770OC-4GD GeForce GTX 770 4GB 256-Bit GDDR5 PCI Express 3.0 HDCP Ready WindForce 3X 450W Video Card	$379
Hard drives	2 Seagate Desktop HDD.15 ST4000DM000 4TB 64MB Cache SATA 6.0Gb/s 3.5" Internal Hard Drive	$300
DVD drive	LG Black 14X BD-R 2X BD-RE 16X DVD+R 5X DVD-RAM 12X BD-ROM 4MB Cache SATA BDXL Blu-Ray Burner with SW, 3D Play Back - BH14NS40	$80

Case	Fractal Design Define XL R2 FD-CA-DEF-XL-R2-TI Titanium Grey Steel ATX Full Tower	$128
Case fans	2 Additional 140MM Gaming Case Fans	$31.78
Power supply	SeaSonic Platinum-1000 1000W ATX12V / EPS12V 80 PLUS PLATINUM Certified Full Modular Power Supply New 4th Gen CPU Certified Haswell Ready	$240
Total		$2110.78

Dealing With Your Internet Service Provider

Chapter 4 -- Getting and Keeping Your Business/Home Continuously Connected to the Internet through an ISP

My wife started working from home a year or so ago. When working from home, it is amazing how dependent your life becomes on your Internet Service Provider (ISP). In the past we could live with an occasional home network outage, but now we need 24/7 ISP support, and an uninterrupted connection to the Internet is a necessity. I have been happy with my ISP, but a few years ago I went round and round with them while trying to solve an intermittent connection outage problem. I also had a similar experience solving my parents' DSL problems.

Working From Home -- How to Talk to Your ISP

If you are an employee working from home, be sure to make that fact known to the ISP every time you call them for support. Most home Internet users can live with the occasional outage and your ISP may think that this is the case for you. You must make it very clear to them that this interruption in service is extremely disruptive. Point out that an uninterrupted Internet connection is needed for your continued employment. If you are a small business owner or a company and your employee that is working from home is having problems with their Internet connection, consider making a phone call to their ISP to help them out. A business owner's or a company's representative's voice in an employee's ISP battle will hold a lot of weight spurring the ISP to action. The lone voice of your employee who is working from home will take much more time to get the problem resolved.

From past experience it seems as though employer contracted IT departments do not understand some of the mechanics behind Virtual Private Network (VPN*) connections into work networks, and the problems employees face when using them. This lack of IT departmental knowledge signals a reason to worry about the sensitive data they are protecting. In our case, the company's technical support had no clue as to why our VPN* connection could not pick up where it left off after a temporary loss of signal to our ISP. My wife would have to completely logout, close all open windows and reconnect from scratch (most times having to reboot the computer). Repeating these steps over, and over again during the day cost her many hours of valuable work time. Because of these disruptions, she had to make that time up in unpaid hours of overtime to replace the work that was not accomplished. The corporation's final response, after many helpdesk calls was, "*get the ISP to quit dropping your connection.*" What was needed from the corporation was two-fold: 1) An intervention from the corporation with the ISP to determine why the connection was being dropped. 2) An investigation into why a dropped VPN* connection would require a client/employee to have to reboot their home computer system. One would think that when the connection reestablished itself, the employee would be allowed to continue where they had left off without interruption, but this was not the way their VPN* tunnel worked.

TIP	Our home computer setup uses two monitors. The browser using VPN* would only display on one monitor at a time. The company IT support said that it was not possible to use multiple monitors with the VPN* client software. This is just an example in the frustration of dealing with corporate contracted IT departments. The statement from the IT department was flawed due to the fact that it is the OS that allows the use of multiple monitors, not the applications

running on top of the OS. For that company's IT department's benefit and yours, if you are using Jupiter Networks software for VPN* connections, *spread the VPN browser window across both monitors by clicking on the Windows Explorer middle icon in the upper right corner of your browser > move the window that is visible across both monitors > and then maximize the window again by clicking the middle icon in the upper right corner again.* If this does not work, use Windows or REVO UNINSTALL (covered later) to remove the Jupiter Networks software and reinstall it. The window should expand to cover both monitors. This technique assumes that your display settings in the Control Panel are set to use multiple monitors, which we will cover in <u>Chapter 6</u>.

Working From Home – Do You want to Use Your ISP's Provided Equipment and DNS?

The answer to the question above is usually NO! I have limited experience with some ISP's provided equipment, but so far all of those experiences have been bad. As for their DNS services, they have all been bad. From my parents' DSL modem, to my cable company's cable modem that I had to install to get technical support, both of these devices were old and very outdated technology. My parents' DSL modem was also a security threat using broken WEP encryption. I also recently tried some new hardware from my ISP that cost me days of work and had to be removed in favor of my own equipment, which we will soon discuss.

My wife was shopping at the local Walmart when she was approached by a Direct TV representative offering a special onetime deal on their service. It actually sounded pretty good and I was inclined to try it. While I am happy with my cable company's ISP service, I have been very unhappy with some of the restrictions and limitations I have when using their cable service. Direct TV promised to address those problems for a nominal monthly rate. Before making this change in our lives, I called the cable company to see if they had something to address those limitations and if we could work a deal.

They dealt and offered me their new ULTRA TV service at a cheaper price than what I was paying for my current service contract. I started asking questions like: Does your system support QoS? Can I set up a server behind my firewall using your equipment? Does your router have 802.11ac support? The sales people at these cable companies know nothing about these things, but you have to pressure them until they route your call to the backline support, which they did. Getting to backline support will have you on hold for a much longer period of time. Shockingly, I started asking the same questions of the backline support and they had no idea what I was talking about either. I don't know where cable companies are finding their personnel to employ, but many of them are not qualified to perform in the positions in which they have be cast. I was left with one choice, which was to allow them to dispatch a technician with their equipment and ask him about the equipment's limitations.

The technician arrived, so I asked him the same questions about what he was getting ready to install. His words were, "Dude I am just a contractor that installs this equipment and gets it all working; beyond that I can't help you." So I was out of options if I was going to try this solution for my household. I almost cried as I let him disconnect my state-of-the-art Netgear

R6300 Router and Motorola SB6120 cable modem. He replaced them with the ARRIS MG5225G that I admit, I had never heard of. From ARRIS's website, ARRIS is a global company that specializes in broadband solutions around the world. The device my cable company is pushing out is the ARRIS Media Gateway Family product. They promote this product as a Whole Home Solution, which it is, if you have no requirement other than watching cable TV. It is not a solution for streaming video or handling servers based behind Small Business firewalls. (See: https://arrisi.com/about_arris/index.asp)

Once I downloaded and read the manual NOT PROVIDED by my ISP on how to set up and configure the MG5225G, I quickly discovered the limitations of this device. I called the ISP back again trying to salvage the situation. After defining things like: Address Reservations, QoS priority video streaming, and so on, to a few cable company employees, I finally got someone on the phone who understood these technologies. It was my first FUN conversation with a cable company employee. The discussion progressed without the deer-in-the-headlights pauses that occurred while talking to other cable company employees. We discussed two options that I had come up with:

- Setting up a second IP to allow me to use my Internet equipment, and use the first IP with the ARRIS MG5225G for TV and streaming ($60 to $100 more per month)
- Setting up my Netgear router as a repeater

Neither solution proved practical. To put in perspective the limitation of the ARRIS Media Gateway, lets quickly outline them and wonder forever who at the cable company chose this solution to provide to their customers:

- No QoS support; this means you cannot give priority to streaming video or computer games that consume a lot of bandwidth.
- No simultaneous 5.0 GHz support. This means that we can't use dual-band wireless, which would allow us to perform ad-hoc QoS by splitting traffic between two networks. This is also bad because using the 5.0GHz devices are a noticeable performance improvement over older 2.4GHz equipment.
- Only 512MB of RAM. Computers dating back to the 1990's had more!
- I had no USB 3.0 support and I was not sure if the USB 2.0 port could be used for backups. There was no mention of that in the manual or specification sheet.
- No 802.11ac support. Modern ac routers are selling for as low as $170 (less than the cost of two cable bills). According to Wikipedia, over one billion devices installed worldwide will support this new wireless standard by 2015. In fact, wireless-n devices began appearing in 2008 making this router's technology over five years old!
- No Address Reservation support. Address Reservations* allow devices to receive static IPs within a DHCP network. This has many advantages as described in the Glossary.
- The Media Gateway only comes with a 500GB hard drive. A 500GB hard drive only costs $60 these days. This means that your bill for one month of cable service will more than pay for what was probably the most expensive component in this device. In comparison, a modern state-of-the-art 7200 6.0Gb/s 1TB hard drive only costs $80. Talk about pinching a penny!

I could go on, but my point has been made. Don't use your ISP's rented equipment unless it is absolutely necessary to use their services and you have no other alternative.

 There are many 802.11ac router options for you to consider before ever using your cable company's rented equipment. This equipment will remain current with technology for many years. Refer back to Chapter 2 on routers for examples of equipment choices you can purchase for $200 or less.

Alternatives to Your ISP's DNS for Better Speed and Security

Just like with the inferior equipment your ISP usually provides, you have to consider whether you want to use their Domain Name Servers (DNS). With recent legislation the trend is to have ISPs spy on more and more of your Internet activity. Using their DNS gives them the opportunity to gather more and more information about you. Another thing to consider is your Internet performance. Given the outdated state of the equipment that ISPs are providing to their customers, we have to consider that their servers may be subpar as well. Many Internet network gurus have stopped using their ISP's DNS after discovering they are slow and unreliable. You can investigate the use of the utilities and servers described below to improve on what your ISP is providing. However, after benchmarking my ISP's DNS server, they proved to have superior performance to any other nameserver involved in my testing for "Cached Name" and "Uncached Name". The only place my ISP was lacking is in the Tabular Data under DNS Benchmark. However, the "DotCom Lookup" of my ISP's DNS lagged behind the timings resolving to another nameserver's dot com's performance.

Gibson Research Corporation http://www.grc.com/dns/benchmark.htm provides a free utility, DNS Benchmark, (DNSBench) to analyze the best performing DNS servers within striking distance of your location. It also filters out DNS servers that can be spoofed*. You can add your ISP's DNS servers to compare them to what Gibson recommends. Gibson also provides a good read on public DNS servers in general.

Namebench, https://code.google.com/p/namebench is another free utility that will benchmark DNS servers. It provides reports on which DNS is the fastest, most secure, and more, to point out which DNS you should use. There can be amazing improvements in your Internet performance utilizing the top recommendations of these free programs as your primary DNS.

You can also consider using OpenDNS for your DNS service. This would require setting up your router to use OpenDNS instead of your ISP's default DNS. OpenDNS was a company formed in 2006 that says, "*OpenDNS is the leading provider of free security and infrastructure services that make the Internet safer through integrated Web content filtering, anti-phishing and DNS. OpenDNS services enable consumers and network administrators to secure their networks from online threats, reduce costs and enforce Internet-use policies.*" I figured I would give it a try, but when I went to the website, OpenDNS wanted me to register an account to do this. I don't know about you, but I am registered in too many places already, and if can get around registering, all the better. Internet shopping alone has my name registered all over the world. So I went to WIKI and found the DNS addresses. (See: http://www.opendns.com, https://en.wikipedia.org/wiki/OpenDNS) They are:

- 208.67.222.222 (resolver1.opendns.com)
- 208.67.220.220 (resolver2.opendns.com)

Everything free comes with a catch. By not registering with OpenDNS their resolvers will redirect users to a commercial "intercept page" that contains advertising, among other things. OpenDNS is in the business of making money but one expects a DNS to return an error message rather than an "intercept page" when an incorrect URL is entered. Hence, some computer professionals knowledgeable in DNS argue against using OpenDNS.

The IPs are also now prominently displayed on OpenDNS home page. Just enter one of these IP addresses in your router in place of your secondary DNS's automatic values and marvel at how fast your web surfing will become! OpenDNS also gives you web security you did not have before. Here is what Wikipedia has to say, "*OpenDNS offers DNS resolution for consumers and businesses as an alternative to using their Internet service provider's DNS servers. By placing company servers in strategic locations and employing a large cache of the domain names, OpenDNS usually processes queries much more quickly, thereby increasing page retrieval speed. The name OpenDNS refers to the DNS concept of being open, where queries from any source are accepted. It is not related to open source software; the service is based on closed-source software.*

Other features include a phishing filter, domain blocking and typo correction (for example, typing "example.og" instead of "example.org"). By collecting a list of malicious sites, OpenDNS blocks access to these sites when a user tries to access them through their service. OpenDNS also launched PhishTank.com, where users around the world can submit and review suspected phishing sites." PhishTank is a collaborative clearing house for data and information about phishing on the Internet.

Phishing is a fraudulent attempt, usually made through email, to steal your personal information. A common theme for this type of attack is the cracker will disguise an email as coming from a reputable source (your bank) that asks for your personal information like your account number, password and Social Security number.

After the Gibson analysis, consider opting for your best Internet speed and setting your primary DNS to Gibson's recommendation and maybe your secondary DNS to OpenDNS at 208.67.222.222.

Can Your ISP Technician Use the Advanced Technical Equipment Provided by Their Company?

Some ISP technicians appear to have minimal training and experience, and it could take multiple visits to solve your home device connection problems. The technician's test equipment, while expensive and effective, is inadequate without trained personnel to use it. Each technician that visits your small business/home may be better (or worse) at analyzing certain things than other technicians working for that same ISP.

Hopefully, you will get the one who is good at finding your particular problem and on the first visit. However, in my experience I've had to plan on many calls to my ISP, followed by multiple visits from untrained ISP technicians to solve my problems. In my latest occurrence, it took about twenty-five phone calls, three visits, and many hours of my valuable time escorting technicians around our house. In talking with friends and family, I am not alone in this experience.

 Historical Reference — My own experience with lack of training on expensive troubleshooting equipment

In the Cable Company's defense, it is an institutional tendency to undertrain troubleshooters and overpay for complex troubleshooting equipment. It was my own experience when working in the Air Force for years, and later for one of the top "too big to fail" US banks in one of their huge data centers. I had tons of expensive equipment to analyze problems in cabling, but little or no training on how to use it. In the Air Force, the old guard did not want to admit they could not use the Time Domain Reflectometer (TDR). (See: http://en.wikipedia.org/wiki/Time-domain_reflectometer) A TDR is used to pinpoint the exact location of faults in the airplane's metallic cables. More than once, I was instructed to change the end connectors by cutting the wire and re-splicing the cables, not even knowing for sure if that was the problem, or if it was somewhere else in the cable. This is very bad because in a plane, shortening a cable prematurely can cost Air Force personnel many weeks of work taking the plane apart to replace the cable before scheduled maintenance would do the same thing. For a home example, this is much like cutting a wire short that is coming into your home's breaker box. To extend a home's wiring properly would require tearing out the walls and replacing the entire electrical run. This is because of a splice's possible loss of voltage and current, its susceptibility to becoming loose due to continued vibrations, and the fact that it is an additional point of failure in the electrical path. I hope this is an example that you can relate to (FYI you should never cut existing house wiring especially in the breaker box where you may have to shift breakers! Some electricians don't know this and will cut those wires... DON'T LET THEM!). Conversely, consider the abuse that the wiring in a plane endures because of vibrations and the G-force turns a plane performs in its continuous training exercises. Splicing together a warplane's cabling (sometimes done) is absurd. The entire electrical run should be replaced to keep the pilot safe. In addition, it is also another point of failure you will have to examine if the circuit fails for some reason.

Instead, the Air Force would rather pay huge sums of taxpayer dollars to take apart planes prematurely and replace the cabling, rather than instructing personnel in the proper use of the expensive corporate equipment that your tax dollars have purchased. This equipment is readily available and is provided for the untrained Air Force personnel to use. In the soldier's defense, the Air Force technical school's education periods have been compressed in favor of students learning in the field. The use of complex corporate troubleshooting equipment is not covered in a technician's basic education. So if/when they get to their field assignment, and if the personnel in rank above them have not been trained in the use of that equipment, it will sit on the shelf benefiting no one. These technicians only know what the person in rank above them can teach or order them do.

As a Staff Sergeant, I argued more than once for use of the TDRs as a troubleshooting tool (which would sit back in the shop on the shelf) as we worked on the planes that were on the flight line. Since the shop chief has total authority (much like a corporate CEO), and whose knowledge may be somewhat outdated, if he doesn't want to admit that modern technology has improved on the old way of doing things, then the Air Force has to pay extra money and time to replace cut cabling ahead of time. This is essentially paying twice or more for each weeks-long maintenance project that would have been corrected during a plane's scheduled down time. This was the mindset I was working in, and I was powerless to change it.

I encountered the same type of thing in the civilian world. My experience at a major data center of a US bank had us leaving all of the advanced Fluke cable analysis equipment on the shelf and doing senseless things like pulling new cable and throwing out the old. Many times these were perfectly good cables, because we never determined what/where the real problem was. I eventually figured out how to use the equipment by reading the manuals, and then observing and questioning the vendors that were using the same equipment. My influence helped change that culture a bit, and eventually the data center personnel learned how to reference and use some of the equipment. But the bank paid huge sums of money to those contractors before we finally learned how to use the very same equipment that a few thousand dollars in training would have alleviated. It would have been far less expensive for the company to have paid to train its own personnel who were dedicated to their success. Therefore, seeing the cable company's lack of training in its personnel was not new to me. Apparently, having cheap, inexperienced, and untrained employees somehow makes more sense to management in today's technical world, both in corporate America and in the government.

Dial-up vs. DSL vs. Cable vs. Fiber

The number of people, how they will use the Internet, and the importance of uninterrupted service will dictate the ISP infrastructure needed by a home or small business. Different ISP's offer diverse types of Internet connections, solutions and cost structures. Within those connection types, ISP's offer different service plans to support a SBO/HCU's need for bandwidth when connecting to the Internet. From https://en.wikipedia.org/wiki/Bandwidth_(computing), *bandwidth defines the net bit rate or the maximum throughput of a logical or physical communication path in a digital communication system.* In plumbing terms, it is the size of the pipe that allows for a certain volume of liquid to flow past a single point in the pipe.

Dial-up: These days, when everyone seems to have high-speed Internet access, one might assume that the days of dial-up access are over. (See: https://en.wikipedia.org/wiki/Dial-up_Internet_access) Dial-up is still the only option for many rural or remote areas where broadband is not offered, due to low population density. Dial-up is also an excellent choice for users with limited budgets and/or limited Internet use. Some ISPs offer dial-up for free. A user who only checks their email occasionally, or banks online once or twice a month only needs dial-up. A modern V.92 modem can achieve transfer speeds as high as 56 kbit/s and can exceed that rate limit using compression. This is more than adequate for a user who has a limited need for the Internet. My parents had AOL dial-up for years, and after I upgraded their modem to a modern V.92, I was shocked at how fast the Internet web pages refreshed.

DSL: Digital Subscriber Line uses the existing phone lines simultaneously with the users wired phone services. This is possible by splitting the frequencies between voice and data, and filtering/modulating the transmitted and received carrier wave. DSL is usually the cheapest broadband connection type that can be made to the Internet and usually ranges from $30 to $90 per month. Speeds depend on the condition of the telephone wire and the distance between the SBO/HCU and the company's central office. DSL over copper wire only works within 18,000 feet (about three miles) of the central office facility. DSL can achieve speeds up to 15 mbps for downloads and 1 mbps for uploads, which is fast enough to support a dozen people or a point-of-sale system for a SBO. However, it is debated whether these speeds should continue to be categorized as broadband. Copper telephone cable was never designed for wide spectrum signals, unlike coaxial TV cable, which was.

Cable: Much like DSL, Cable uses the existing television cable lines to provide concurrent Internet, digital phone and television viewing. Cable ISPs offer bandwidth speeds of 50 to 100 mbps for downloads and streaming video; and 2 to 10 mbps for uploads. Those speeds can support up to 24 simultaneous users. Monthly prices vary widely and can range from $60 to over $300. Some cable companies are now offering speeds up to 200 or 300 Mbps.

Fiber: Fiber, unlike DSL and Cable, uses glass (or plastic) threads (fibers) to transmit data. One fiber optic cable can house many glass threads, each of which is capable of transmitting messages modulated onto light waves. Fiber has many advantages over metal cabling:

- much greater bandwidth
- thin and light to work with
- less susceptible to interference

The disadvantages of fiber are becoming less and less. Fiber used to be very expensive, fragile and difficult to repair. But costs have come down, and testing equipment can now easily determine and pinpoint problems. Fiber has become much less fragile allowing it to bend much more than used to be possible. Fiber permits download speeds of 15 to 150 mbps and upload speeds of 5 to 35 mbps. The price can range from $70 to $200 and can easily service 24 users with Internet, phone, and TV. Verizon is offering speeds up to 300 Mbps which is phenomenal.

Establish a Service Contract and Service Level Agreement with Your ISP

Before adopting an ISP, analyze and understand the ISP's contract. Similar to cell or cable service providers, signing the dotted line might tie you into an ISP's services for one to three years in order to get their special discounted bundle pricing. Also, examine your ISP's service-level agreement (SLA) that describes what services you can demand, how often, and what they will repair. The SLA will also quantify the ISP's guarantees for uptime, availability, performance, response time, and support availability. All these variables are very important to an SBO or an HCU working from home. Make sure that the ISP states what the penalties are (your compensation) for not meeting their SLA. If there are no penalties specified, what is an ISP's incentive to meet their SLA?

Determine how the SLA interacts with your investment in hardware. Many ISPs want you to rent the equipment necessary to connect to the Internet, watch TV or use a digital phone. Renting their equipment has the advantage of occasional upgrades when your ISP improves their equipment and smoother troubleshooting when dealing with ISP's technical support. But using rented equipment has the following drawbacks:

- Many times rented ISP equipment is not the latest advance in technology; sometimes it is shockingly old, insecure and unreliable. For example, my parents' DSL cable modem/router was using the WEP broken wireless technology, which we covered in Chapter 2. If you shop around you can also get network equipment that extends the capabilities of your network beyond that of which the rented equipment is capable.
- The equipment rental fees that ISPs charge add up quickly. Purchased routers and cable modems quickly pay for themselves, sometimes in less than a year or two. The top-of-the-line equipment that you purchase is often times more capable, reliable, secure and efficient than its rented counterpart. Most devices have limited warranties that will cover the equipment for at least a year, so even if the equipment fails you have lost nothing but your time.
- Quality purchased devices can remain current with advancing standards longer than rented equipment, saving you time and money. This more advanced equipment usually has more versatile configuration options that allow for things like prioritizing streaming video, guest networks and more.
- If your rented equipment suffers physical damage (e.g. liquid spilled on the device kills it) you are on the hook to pay the ISP for the damaged equipment, frequently at replacement costs and much more than it was worth.
- When you move, you are obligated to return the equipment to the ISP, either by paying for a technician visit, or driving the equipment to their office.
- When you purchase upgraded equipment you can sell, donate, or give the old equipment to a friend or relative. Donation=tax deduction.   Having an old router is better than connecting to the Internet without one at all.

Your SLA can change over time. For years, my ISP provided assistance free of charge, on any problems we had. I did not know that had changed, and when we were having service outages I initiated a service call. Our next bill from the cable company reflected a surprising $80.00 fee for the service call. Unless you pay a monthly service fee of around $3.00, your ISP may charge you for work on a "per technician visit" basis, whether they fix your problem or not. If you are working from home, as both my wife and I now are, your connection to the Internet is the bread line that is feeding your household. If you are having intermittent failures in your connectivity it may take many visits by technicians to determine your problem. Paying the service fee to include technicians' visits is, in my mind, worth the nominal fee.

Intermittent Outages to Cable Internet and Cable TV, What Can You Do?

If you are experiencing intermittent outages with your ISP, you may be required by your ISP to work through the same troubleshooting steps over and over again each time you call in on an outage, unless you are prepared in advance for their front line support. On a recent call to my parents' ISP, and after working through about five minutes of selecting phone options, then being on hold for about 20 minutes, I finally got a front line technician on the line. I was ready for the conversation by having a new and an old ISP router, multiple RJ-11 cables, and a proven connection to the Internet using the old router. I was ready for the usual troubleshooting steps, which I knew we were going to cover. I was able to get a new rental router sent to my parents' house in one phone call; this was a new record for me in dealing with an ISP. However, in the case of intermittent outages, your problem is not likely to be solvable over the telephone, or that easy. So here are my tips to expedite solving and moving the ISP juggernaut along:

1. Before calling your ISP, **unplug the power from your cable modem and router > wait 20 seconds and plug them back in > sometimes your connection will come back up.** This is the magic bullet that the cable technical support person is required to have you perform to fix all Internet connection problems. You don't need to waste an hour on the phone when five minutes may be all you need.

2. Note the color and which lights are lit or blinking on your cable modem and router. This may give you a clue to your problem prior to calling your ISP. Your manual will tell you what the lights mean. Your front line ISP support will eventually ask for this information if you do have to call them.

3. If the above advice did not work, prepare your equipment for a call to your ISP. Take your router and cable modem out of the accusation loop. If you own your cable modem and don't rent it, prior to calling your ISP, go to your nearest cable service provider office and rent one of their cable modems. My cable modem was of far superior quality to the rented ISP's cable modem technology, but the front line technician assumed that this modem and my router had to be the problem. Ruling them out can waste many hours of your time and multiple phone calls, to include being put on hold for long periods.

4. Have spare equipment like cables and additional computers ready to show the ISP front line that your hardware is not the problem. It is best to get all of that possible aggravation out of the way before even calling. All the front line ISP technical support personnel knows is a few simple checks of the rented cable modem and until those steps are performed; your case will languish with the front line. You will have to prove that devices like your computer Network Interface Controller (NIC), your router, or your cable modem are not the problem. So it is best to take away those pieces of the puzzle before engaging your ISP technical support in your problem.

5. Simplify things for them as much as possible. For example, the ISP front line had no way of troubleshooting and advancing my case with my state of the art router in the picture. I had to take my router out of the loop and connect my computer openly to the rented cable modem. If you can't call during every outage, record each loss of signal to the Internet using just the ISP cable modem. Then upon your next call, narrate to the front line all of your recorded results. You have to become a thorn in their side!

6. For an intermittent connection failure, powering things off and on may temporarily get you connected to the Internet, but it will not solve the underlying problem. Nonetheless, this fact will have to be proven to your ISP. Every time you call and perform this procedure with the front line, they will pronounce your problem as fixed and hang up. Make note of the time, date and the name of the person to whom you spoke. Then call back (on a speaker phone and with something else to do helps pass the 30 minutes on hold) *during* your next intermittent outage, describe your previous call, date and time, and request your ISP send a technician visit your SB/home, which will come at your time and expense. You may have to do this a few more times before getting your ISP to actually send a technician.

The first technician to arrive blamed the splitters in our basement, and some slightly loose cable connections to some of our TVs as the problem. While cheap splitters and loose connections can be a problem, I did not think this guy had a clue because I had a perfectly good Internet connection for years using those same splitters and connections. They were installed by the cable company many years prior to his visit. But on that note:

Tip 	If you need to split a cable connection, be careful of the splitter that you purchase, or one that a technician installs. Have the technician show you the dB loss, or gain, as each split is done. There is a statistical screen that the technician can bring up on your TV that shows this information. If you install a splitter yourself, you can call the ISP and get them to explain the procedure that will bring up that screen up, or visit your ISP's website and search for the procedure there. Cheap splitters usually have higher signal loss. The more outputs that are split, the higher the losses. Consequently, if you are using a three-way splitter to do a two-way split, you will have a higher dB loss of signal.

But what is dB? From https://en.wikipedia.org/wiki/Decibel, "*the decibel confers a number of advantages, such as the ability to conveniently represent very large or small numbers, and the ability to carry out multiplication of ratios by simple addition and subtraction.*" In our cable systems, dB is a ratio comparing the input level to the output level. This ratio is expressed as a logarithmic ratio of input to output. Your cable's dB losses are expressed as a negative dB and your cable's gains are expressed as a positive dB. The first technician did not show me this information after changing the splitters and running out the door to get to his next service call.

The second technician checked the noise on the lines. Cable TV/Internet is a closed network and all connections must be tight, and should be terminated. All open or unused ports on signal splitters, switches, etc. will result in a reduction in signal strength. Open cable ends (or connectors) can cause deterioration and degradation of your video signal. A loose connector on one TV or Internet device can affect other equipment that is in the same loop. Cable connectors on the TV or modem require more than a simple hand tight turn. I had noise on two of my connections, which the technician easily corrected with the turn of a wrench. He used his cable analyzer correctly and effectively, showing me the data he was looking at in trying to determine my problem.

Another argument I hear is it that indoor connections do not require silicon grease. Copper is very subject to corrosion, especially outdoors. Before you connect up a connector to equipment, coat the inner copper wire and outer copper braid with silicone grease. This will prevent any moisture and oxygen from causing corrosion over time. DO NOT work on a "live" cable that is connected to a powered device. (e.g. A satellite TV receiver supplies up to 18 volts to a LNB cable; this can short out the equipment if you are messing with the cabling).

Since the technician was using a regular wrench, this is another indication of how the cable companies are cutting corners. While it depends on the manufacturer, most type F connectors require 25 to 30 in-lbs of torque (versus finger tight, which is just 1 to possibly 5 in-lbs or torque). Every cable technician should be given a coaxial cable tool that will allow them to connect coax connectors to consumer electronic devices with the proper amount of torque recommend by the manufacturer. (See: https://en.wikipedia.org/wiki/F_connector) I have never seen this done!

Tip	Before you call the cable company about an intermittent TV picture or Internet connection problem, go around the house and tighten the connectors "finger tight". Then use and 1mm spanner to turn it a further 1/6 of a turn. You should not then be able to loosen the connector with your fingers. If you can loosen the connector, turn it another 1/6 turn. A loose connection at a splitter or device can cause snowy reception or intermittent play. Doing this only takes a few minutes and may save you hours of hassle and a visit by an untrained ISP technician.

A skilled ISP technician can bring up connection statistics like dB gain on your SB/Home computer monitor or TV. Have them do this when they first arrive, and make note of those values. Then when they are done "supposedly" fixing your problem, have them show you those values again. If the values have not improved, then they have not improved your signal or fixed your problem. Even if the values improve, the technician still may not have totally fixed your problem. Had I known to compare the dB gains, I might have been able to get the first technician to continue to troubleshoot the problem.

Tip  	As stated previously, cable has to be a closed system. If you have cable connectors un-terminated you will need to purchase 75-Ohm terminating plugs for all of your video ports or outlets that are not being used. This also applies to splitter outputs that are not being used. These terminators screw onto a standard F-connector, and present a "load" to the system, closing the loop. In technical terms, having unused outputs in a video/Internet system will result in reflection due to impedance mismatches, RF reflections and echoes. The unused outputs will also radiate or leak RF signals.
	This is much like how your plumbing works. If someone in the house is doing laundry, using a faucet, or flushing a toilet, your water pressure will drop. Imagine being in the shower when the water gets HOT! If you leave an un-terminated output you will have dB loss, which is like losing pressure in a closed water system.
	The 75 ohm terminating plugs are cheap, only costing about $0.40 each. Call your ISP and ask them where you can go to get 75 ohm terminating plugs and then once you have them, screw them onto your open outputs.

Unfortunately the journey continues. Noise was not the problem either; the intermittent outages continued. After many more calls to the ISP, a third technician was dispatched. This guy really and truly knew how to use the cable analysis equipment. He changed the splitters that the original technician replaced, showing me a dB gain.

He then went outside and tested the cabling from the box to the pole and quickly determined that the problem was the signal coming into the box from the pole. He drove his truck around to the alley behind my house and changed the cable traveling from the pole to the house. He showed me the cable that he replaced, and it was easy to see that squirrels had been chewing on the line. He explained that when the casing is breeched it will allow water into the line causing dB loss (the intermittent outages) as the wind blows. I now knew why so many calls to the ISP were ignored. By the time I got a front line technician on the line, our connection was OK, which made getting a technician dispatched difficult. The quick test that these front line technicians ran remotely indicated that nothing was wrong.

Together, the third technician and I viewed the dB strength on the TV for about five minutes and saw no variance in the dB signal. My connectivity-problem was finally fixed. Since his visit, we have had a flawless connection to the Internet. I wish I could have given him a beer, not appropriate in today's world! No more having to listen to my wife stomp on the floor, yelling down the stairs for me to get this fixed. I installed the Jupiter Networks VPN* software so my wife could work from home in bliss. Life at home was now good. Based on our experience, I'd say you will have to beat your ISP over the head about 20 times to get their top-level support. The sad thing is that due to their lack in training personnel and their practice of outsourcing their help desks, this is an expense to them and to us. This is the new reality in America!

TIP	Cable device providers (like DVD players) often times include coaxial cables for you to use. Many times these cables are of poor quality and should not be used. Resistance in coaxial cable produces the greatest amount of attenuation per unit length (loss of dB). Resistance is based on the cable materials, the frequency of the transported signal, the diameter of the conductors, and the ambient temperature. Use your cable company's cables or go purchase some of quality.

Intermittent Outages to DSL Internet, What Can You Do?

If your Internet connections use DSL and the phones are still working, more than likely you have either a hardware failure, a connection problem (bad cable or phone line), or with wireless, a signal channel conflict. In my sample case, the Verizon technicians installed the Westell A80-750015-07 modem, which had been experiencing intermittent failures for years. My parents were frustrated with this, and therefore used the computing technology that I had setup for them less and less because of the frustration in dealing with the outages. Technicians had been called in and they told them that there was no problem, or some craziness about how they were at the end of the line and their DSL signal was weak. If there was a weak signal, then a repeater was needed, or Verizon should not be offering DSL to that area. My parents accepted these explanations and endured intermittent outages for years while I battled and then recovered from cancer. When I came home to help them, I asked them to read this chapter to see if it made sense. Asking a 78-year-old to read your technical book is not a good idea. Their response was that if I had written a chapter on how to deal with an ISP, then I should be able to deal with their problem once and for all, following the advice in my book. They had a good point!

Examine your equipment and read your service contract. My parents were paying TOP DOLLAR to their ISP for a bundled package of TV, Internet, and phone, which included in-house support. With that kind of money and contract, you can hold your ISP's feet to the fire and demand new hardware when it becomes available. I examined my parents' Westell A80-750015-07 modem/router and discovered it was using WEP encryption with an assigned key, and sells for $15 at Amazon. I sure hope my parents were not paying rent on that cheap router. This sort of technology was outdated and insecure in 2006. Verizon should have been ashamed to allow their customers to continue to use this technology without warnings and alerts. Thus, I called Verizon and demanded something more advanced and explained the intermittent Internet outage problem that my parents were experiencing. To Verizon's credit, they quickly agreed (after keeping me on hold for ½ hour) to send a new, more advanced router.

I hooked up the D-Link DSL-2750B, tested everything, and thought I was done. The next day my dad was complaining that he could not check his email. I went into the office and sure enough, the DSL light was blinking RED indicating that the router could not communicate with the phone lines. Luckily, I still had the old router with the Channel 6 conflict found in Chapter 2, and I could prove to the technician that was on the phone line that the problem was in the new DSL modem/router, and I did so by hooking up the old router and have it connecting it to the Internet. We have already discussed how to lead front line support to the answer. So the second router arrived, I hooked it up and it worked; mission accomplished.

Your ISP Website May Be Separate from Your ISP Email & Account

For years I hosted my favorite's website at my ISP as my portal to the Internet. That way as I used alternate browsers, Internet devices and computers around the world I always had access to my favorites. But one day along came a spider, and I could no longer login to my website. I called my ISP, and the technicians there had no idea what the difference was from their email accounts and their web hosting accounts. In fact, they did not even know there were websites supported by their company. It took me many phone calls until I finally reached a technician who could explain it all to me. My ISP had gotten out of the website hosting business and had grandfathered those websites over to another company. The ISP had not offered web hosting to customers for years, so no one at the company knew websites like mine even existed.

Summary – ISP Infrastructure, Testing the Final Result

When you believe that your ISP's intermittent problems are solved, then switch back to your advanced modem and hardware firewall router for security. To summarize, here is my bullet point list for dealing with an ISP:

- Take your own possible problems out of the loop - tighten and terminate all cable connections; purchase quality cabling and replace what comes with your devices.
- Many modems provide diagnostic information on web pages that can be read at the IP address 192.168.100.1. Look at your downstream and upstream Signal to Noise Ratio (SNR) that shows the strength of the signal to your cable modem. SNR will show if there is noise on the line and its value should be higher than 30 dB. The higher the SNR value, the better. If the SNR decreases below 30 dB, then you will start to experience intermittent problems. If the SNR goes below 23.5, dB then your Internet connection will likely cease to function.
- Also look at the downstream and upstream power signal levels. Downstream shows the power of the signal your cable modem is receiving, where upstream shows the level from the modem to your ISP. Manufacturers say this signal level can range from -15 to

15 dB with 0 being the perfect value. However, websites I visited recommend that this value range from -8 to 8 dB. (See: http://www.speedguide.net/articles/cable-modem-signal-levels-1197)

- Check to make sure that the Send, Receive, and Online lights on the front of the Cable Modem are on or blinking. If the lights are off and do not blink, disconnect the power plug from the back of the modem and leave it powered off for at least 20 seconds. You can determine what these lights are by looking at your manual.
- Go get an ISP rental modem, and take your custom equipment out of the equation.
- Sign up for your ISP's service plan costing you $3.00 per month.
- Note every network outage; call your ISP at least twice daily, preferably *during* an outage.
- Take your router out of the loop and hook your computer's NIC directly to the rented cable modem before calling your ISP support.
- If front line support, says your computers NIC is the problem, and you have a second computer with an NIC, hook that second computer directly to the cable modem, and continue taking notes and talking to your ISP support technician.
- On each technician's visit, explain in detail what it was that the previous technician looked at, did, or changed. View the dB output with them for a few minutes on the TV and note the dB levels. If you have a problem later, phone support can help you display the dB levels on your TV again. Note the procedure for your cable equipment so that next time you don't have to call support to view your dB levels.
- Be patient with the technicians. It is not the fault of these technicians that they are not trained properly. Eventually you will get to the top dog!

My final thought for this chapter is to consider the most effective use of your time. If you have not gone around the house tightening all the connectors in the ten minutes it will take, do you really want to spend half a day following a cable technician around doing the same?

Most ISPs provide a URL where you can perform a speed test; test the total downstream and upstream capacity available on your Internet connection. For example, some WOW URL's are http://speed.nap.wideopenwest.com and http://speed.clv.wideopenwest.com. Surf to your ISP's speed test URL and run the test to make sure that your connection is performing as advertised. This is also a great way to figure out intermittent problems. Rather than wait on hold on the phone for 45 minutes, you can run these tests to determine if there is a problem with your connection to your ISP. If you want independent verification of your speed, http://speedtest.net by Ookla will also test your broadband capacity with tools that are freely available. http://speedtest.net "*measures the total downstream and upstream capacity available on an Internet connection, not just the amount of bandwidth that the browser visiting the site can use. It also gauges latency, or the amount of time it takes for a packet to travel from the user's system to the Internet and back.*"

| WARNING | Note how http://speedtest.net pinpointed your location. They also just gathered statistics about you that will be reported to the government for study purposes. We will address this type of information gathering later in this book. |

Using Encryption Software and Tools

Chapter 5 – Using Encryption Software and Tools to Protect Your USB Drives, Email, Files and Folders, and to Verify Your Downloads Is Mandatory for Data Exchange with SBO Partners

We have learned that anything that we post, email or do using our infected Internet must be encrypted if we want to keep it private. Everything we do and say is kept for all time on the infected Internet and even encrypting on the cloud, which may have backdoors will not protect our privacy. However, we must adopt the fundamental strategy of encrypting everything if we are planning to use our **"New World Order's"** infected Internet. The encryption technologies presented in this chapter are simple methods that you can employ to keep your exchange, communications and storage of data more secure. Whether that exchange of data is digital or otherwise, my intention is to help you learn to use these technologies. Prior to Edward Snowden's revelations, most people viewed encryption as something beyond their ability and not worth spending their time to learn about it. Encryption is simply a method of encoding information that makes it more difficult for someone to view if our files or messages are intercepted. Mankind has been employing, developing and using encryption for thousands of years, and it is time we all do so when using our infected Internet. Encryption seems like a lost art to the common person, but it need not be. This skill is mandatory to develop to be able to survive in today's digital world. If you want to keep the data that you exchange with your business partners or family secure, it is essential that you master this chapter.

I have heard news stories, read fear-mongering blogs, and have viewed various websites which imply that if you use encryption your government may target you as a person of interest. That may be true, but as more and more Internet users adopt and use encryption, we will change the nature of our infected Internet use from one that is designed to exploit us, to a potentially free digital world that might maintain some semblance of our privacy as we do our banking, communication and shopping. We must all try to change what is happening while we use the infected Internet, which is now an information gathering and exploitation tool, to something that is useful and private in our day-to-day lives. Understand that if you choose to live in fear of using the encryption technologies that are available to you, you are inviting everyone connected to the Internet into your life, and we have already discussed who they are.

Contrary to what our governments and media might portray, employing encryption is simply a philosophy of making sure that the information we want to keep private is kept that way with a confident degree of certainty. As modern day technology advances, this viewpoint of life's right to privacy is becoming lost to the common Internet user and today's youth. Hollywood seems to want to give the impression that encryption is something that only the super educated NSA or government intelligence spooks can do. For example, much of our youth who use smartphones and other Internet devices are only educated in the limited use of these invasive devices, which track and reveal everything they do while using the infected Internet for their entire lives. Parents often admire their children's expertise in the use of these devices with no knowledge or understanding of how they are being exploited by corporations or their own governments.

No one seems to want to come to terms with the fact that these technologies are being abused to watch and record everything we all do while using these infected devices. Parents need to become very frightened about what their children are revealing while using these devices, but instead ignore this incursion into their family's privacy. A familiar theme I hear is, "Let them track us because there is nothing interesting in our correspondence that would make us appear to be persons of interest". My response to this nonsense is "Are you really willing to accept this hypocrisy about yourself and your family?" This excuse has been handed down throughout mankind's history from many people who have seen their freedom taken away due to such thinking and lack of action. This is akin to dealing with the people we know who engage in self-destructive behavior and everyone including the victim dismiss this as nothing to worry about. This personal defense mechanism is one that is allowing western civilization to deny the fact that the "free world" we all think we live in has been violated and that these are things that need to change. It will take real effort on everyone's part to look beyond the feel-good aspect of supporting charities and other community activities to doing something that will really make a difference in protecting our children and their continued use of the infected Internet world that we all now live in.

If only we all could understand what it was like to live in East Germany after WWII. In that country, actions that their oppressed citizens took in life came back to haunt them in ways we can never fathom. Realize that our children, who are developing into mature adults, now have a permanent worldwide Internet digital trail following them. We can all now see the evidence of the invasive patterns of their Internet use is assaulting their privacy, but the modern western civilization seems to be turning a blind eye to this. Is this what we want in today's world or for the future of our children and our western civilization?

Everyone seems to have lost their sanity and the understanding that ancient society obfuscated their communications for their personal safety. Now we must double or triple their efforts in today's Internet massive surveillance world to survive. Rather than using the infected Internet blindly, where everyone (crackers, identity and cyber thieves, scorned lovers, corporations and governments) absorbs all of our Internet activity, parents need to educate themselves on the use of encryption technology, address the disconnect that exists between our youth's obsession with Internet devices and the lack of regard for their privacy, and teach our children how to use encryption in today's modern world. The paradigm that our ancestors had about the need for privacy seems to be lost in today's digital world. Video games and movies have desensitized our thinking as to what is really happening as this invasion into our solitude takes place. We all need to educate ourselves and our youth about how we are being exploited using these infected devices.   We need to learn about such things such as the ancient encryption technologies presented in this book.

Let's take the simple example of sending a letter in the mail. To protect our privacy we wrap that letter in an envelope so that only the recipient can read our correspondence. In the U.S., stiff laws and extreme measures have existed for centuries protecting citizens from anyone opening that letter except its recipient. Mail carriers in the past have put their lives at risk to deliver this mail. However, we should all now know that when we send unencrypted email we are allowing the whole world to view our correspondence. This data can/will be stored for many years in databases all around the world **by everyone**.

Encryption must be perceived as providing an "envelope" for our correspondences, just as we have been doing all of our lives through using the post office. It should be the rare exception that we send an unencrypted email; instead, most people send everything unencrypted. We see constant examples of where this unencrypted correspondence is resurrected from various databases to haunt the people that used unencrypted communication. Our society is encouraged to use unencrypted communication that is easily spied upon and logged for many years, while ignoring the implications of what it might mean to our future, jobs, and our family's lives.

 **Historical Reference – What the Christie Bridge Scandal email is trying to teach us, how unencrypted correspondence can come back to haunt us**

On September 9, 2013, the New Jersey Port Authority shut down lanes on the busy Washington Bridge for a "traffic study" that brought commuters to a standstill. There is a lot of speculation as to why this was done, from political retribution, to a tiff between New Jersey State Senate Democrats and the governor. In the investigation that followed there was nothing tying this back to Governor Christie's office until unencrypted emails and texts surfaced and revealed that a top aide had ordered the closings. One particular **unencrypted email** from Bridget Anne Kelley (a deputy chief of staff to Governor Christie) was sent to David Wildstien (a high school friend of the governor who worked at the Port Authority of New York and New Jersey, which runs the bridge) had devastating consequences. The smoking gun simply read, "Time for some traffic problems in Fort Lee." As a result, Ms. Kelly was fired, and Mr. Wildstein, along with Port Authority Deputy Executive Bill Baroni, who was Governor Christie's top appointed staff member at the Port Authority, resigned. Christie later fired his two-time campaign manager, Bill Stepien, because he did not like the tone of unencrypted emails he sent. In addition, Christina Genovese Rena, who was Christie's "Director of Departmental Relations", one of 17 people subpoenaed, also resigned. The scandal probably ruined Christie's pursuit of a 2016 bid for the White House. Had their correspondence been encrypted, this scandal may have never become known, and five very former powerful people would still have had their jobs.

We will soon discuss encrypting email by generating key pairs and exchanging them with our partners. In the example above, if encryption had been used, their correspondence would have remained private and credence may not have been added to this investigation. If you ever employ encryption at a work place or any other public venue, you should keep your private key on a portable device, such as an encrypted USB stick. When not in use, that stick should be kept in a separate and safe place so that it can be destroyed quickly or used on other Internet devices. This way, if your business or department comes under investigation and equipment is seized, your private key, and thus your correspondence, will remain secure. As long as your private key remains secure, it will take incredible amounts of computing power and expertise for anyone to read your email or text messages. This holds true for securing your correspondence at home as well. If someone gains access to the computer you are using for private encrypted email, all of your correspondences are compromised. We will discuss the need to use Virtual OSs in Chapter 7 and one of which should be used for all of your private email. You can encrypt and store your private key in your email Virtual Machine; both can be quickly deleted if necessary.

Another example of what we could employ would be the ancient encryption techniques that are completely lost in our modern-day school systems. This basic, fun knowledge of encryption education has been removed from our children's schools, which I find disturbing. I refer to the fun codes and ciphers that we learned and practiced in our youth, which provided simple forms of communication that obfuscated information between our friends and us. We practiced these techniques, having fun passing messages back and forth that our teachers and other students could not read. This art form has become totally lost as Smartphones and other Internet spying devices are taking over. Our youth knows nothing of these old forms of cryptography, and their parents are allowing modern day technology to invade every facet of their children's/family's lives. These simple forms of encryption between two parties, which have existed for centuries, need to be resurrected as they are becoming lost to our modern digital world. Modern techno devices are engineered with no form of privacy in mind and are taking over our youth's daily lives. Children depend on their parents to protect them from the modern world, but those same non-techno parents don't understand the technology that is needed to protect or even explain to their children how the world has changed since their youth. The world that their children are living in is now designed to spy on all their Internet and mobile activity, as well as record everything about their lives. Parents don't understand that taking them back to a non-digital encryption age may be in their children's best self-interest and health. For example, a single school violation or expulsion may follow your child for the rest of their life. Our children have no one in their lives explaining how they much they need cryptography or how it works.

Story	On one of my walks I was happy to see a bunch of teenagers gathered around a picnic table in a nearby park. Upon further observation, I saw they were totally absorved and all pecking away at their smartphones and no converstion was taking place. I was wondering why, if they were sitting around to supposedly enjoy each other's company, they would be ignoring each other and messing with their smartphones, and why their parents are allowing this?

I state this all again, if you follow the news at all, you now know that your children are being exploited by your governments, corporations, news agencies and crackers who are recording everything your children are doing when using their smartphones and other Internet devices, with little observation or objection by you as parents. Combine this with the lack of robust reporting by news agencies about these violations of your/their privacy, and we have this epidemic where privacy seems to be no longer possible in today's world. Their smartphone activity may affect them and your family for the rest of your lives.

However, Internet bullying seems to take an upfront focus in today's media as our youth commit suicide because of what is posted about them online. The information gathering that these entities are engaged in is being ignored by the SBO/HCU who does not know how to counter these threats or doesn't take the time to do so. We should also all know by now that we need to vote against and object to these privacy invasions by our supposed government representatives. The Internet has become everyone's worst nightmare. Most people don't even realize it, and free citizens around the world are doing nothing to prevent this invasion into their privacy!

When we encrypt and send information, we want the recipient to be able to quickly and easily decrypt and process it. The simple methods that our ancestors used seem to have been lost in all the mind-blowing movies about this technology, but they may be your best way to communicate privately. We all appear to have lost or forgotten the fun in teaching our kids codes that replace words, phrases, or sentences with groups of numbers or letters, or perhaps a cipher that rearranges letters or uses substitute symbols to disguise a message that they can exchange with their friends. Instead of teaching our children ways to maintain their privacy, the trend appears to be just the opposite, as parents are encouraged to spy on them more and more in the guise of keeping their kids safe. Not to mention the fact that parents are freely allowing corporations and governments to gather information about everything their children do online to market products to them. There has to be a balance in this maze of technology, and the pendulum has swung way too far to the side of allowing over-monitoring, exploitation, and online manipulation of our children's online behavior.

Where has the wonderment and fun that we all knew as kids using simple codes and ciphers gone, and why are we all letting our kids use mobile devices today that allow everything they do, everywhere they go, everything they post online to be spied upon? Think of how much fun they would have encrypting information that they send to a friend that is personal in nature to secure an online message in the knowledge that only their friend who could be taught to decrypt then could read the message? Our children don't need to become part of a world that is spying on everything they do in their lives if we teach them how to become more private in their use of the Internet and communicating privately outside of the infected Internet. Parents everywhere appear to be lost in the fact that modern day technology, computer games and corporations are now set up to control many aspects of their children's lives. We must work to scale back this type of virtual/digital existence and work to keep our children active in sports such as tennis, golf, baseball, soccer, football, racquetball and so much more. We must teach them how to communicate privately and not allow the Internet and modern-day technology to rule their lives. This post *1984* book world does not need to exist without due diligence.

In recent news, we have discovered that almost everything that we do using the now infected Internet is being observed by a cracker, criminal, corporation, and especially by your governments. There are massive criminal organizations and government databases recording your Internet activity that logs your email, your credit card activity, your purchases using debit and credit cards, what groceries you buy, what you click on, EVERYTHING YOU DO IN YOUR DIGITAL LIFE! I write this chapter having found little evidence of advancements in encryption algorithms for the HCU/SBO, so we must assume that our governments may have cracks available for most known corporate encryption software. You should not depend on these techniques to keep your data secure from your governments, who have expended vast resources to break through and put backdoors into these known encryption technologies. It seems strange that U.S. citizens are so willing to have their tax dollars spent in such enormous amounts to fund these massive programs and facilities to spy upon themselves. One would think noble programs such as Food Stamps, Social Security and possibly helping veterans would be more important to U.S. citizens. In the PCWorld article titled "Leaked U.S. spying budget reveals investments in 'groundbreaking' cryptanalysis" by Lucian Constantin, IDG News Service http://www.pcworld.com/article/2047902/leaked-u-s-spying-budget-reveals-investments-in-groundbreaking-cryptanalysis.html#tk.nl_secur dated August 30, 2013 "*The U.S. intelligence community is reportedly using a fifth of its $52.6 billion annual budget to fund cryptography-related programs and operations. Some of those funds are invested in finding weaknesses in cryptographic systems that would allow breaking encrypted communications* *collected from the Internet and elsewhere, according to a portion of a top-secret document published Thursday by The Washington Post and obtained from former National Security Agency contractor Edward Snowden. Cryptanalysis is the science of analyzing cryptographic systems in order to find weaknesses that would allow obtaining the contents of encrypted messages without advance knowledge of the encryption key. Some crypto experts believe that there is no reason to believe the NSA can crack strong encryption algorithms vetted by scientists, but others said that the feasibility of breaking widely used encryption protocols like SSL/TLS depends on various factors, like key size and other configurations."* Then on September 5, 2013, in an article titled "Leaks Show NSA is Working to Undermine Encrypted Communications, Here's How You Can Fight Back" by Dan Auerbach and Eva Galperin https://www.eff.org/deeplinks/2013/09/leaks-show-nsa-working-undermine-encrypted-communications-heres-how-you-can-fight *"In one of the most significant leaks to date regarding National Security Agency (NSA) spying, the New York Times, the Guardian, and ProPublica reported today that the NSA has gone to extraordinary lengths to secretly undermine our secure communications infrastructure, collaborating with GCHQ (Britain's NSA equivalent) and a select few intelligence organizations worldwide.*

These frightening revelations imply that the NSA has not only pursued an aggressive program of obtaining private encryption keys for commercial products—allowing the organization to decrypt vast amounts of Internet traffic that use these products—but that the agency has also attempted to put backdoors into cryptographic standards designed to secure users' communications. Additionally, the leaked documents make clear that companies have been complicit in allowing this unprecedented spying to take place, though the identities of cooperating companies remain unknown." Then in the September 6, 2013, PCWorld article by Brad Chacos titled "Here's how to best secure your data now that NSA can crack almost any encryption" we learned, *"The latest Snowden-supplied bombshell shook the technology world to its core on Thursday: The NSA can crack many of the encryption technologies in place today, using a mixture of backdoors baked into software at the government's behest, a $250 million per year budget to encourage commercial software vendors to make its security "exploitable," and sheer computer-cracking technological prowess."* (See: http://www.pcworld.com/article/2048248/heres-how-to-best-secure-your-data-now-that-the-nsa-can-crack-almost-any-encryption.html, http://www.technologyreview.com/news/519131/circumventing-encryption-frees-nsas-hands-online) Imagine how at a young age this man could come up with the following quotation.

Quotation Edward Snowden, March 2014	*"Employ whatever encryption tools you have at your disposal to make the National Security Agency's job a little bit harder. There's a policy response that needs to occur but there's also a technical response that needs to occur. It's the makers, thinkers, and the development communities that can help make sure we're safe. We need to think about encryption not as this arcane black art but as a basic protection, the defense against the black arts in the digital realm."*

While using encryption is far better than sending unencrypted data over the Internet, understand that governments, such as the United States and Great Britain, are developing the ability to break known encryption technologies and installing backdoors. There also seems to be a lack of innovation in the science behind Internet encryption technology for the individual but there has been much advancement in the ease of its use. We have to be cautious when choosing the encryption techniques that we choose to employ to try to keep our data safe. After all, it is far easier to spy on someone who thinks they have taken measures to protect themselves than to work to develop new methods to circumvent the latest encryption technology. With that said, some governments like Germany seem to want to provide some viable advanced encryption techniques to the world, and we all have to thank them for their investment. GunPG is an encryption project, covered later, that may be meeting our modern-day needs for encryption technology for the HCU/SBO. I no longer work for the U.S. government in any fashion, so I cannot attest to how the encryption techniques presented in this chapter may help keep you private from your governments. Suffice to say, that once upon a time I worked with these technologies that U.S. corporations used to find adequate. Edward Snowden showed how most of the encryption technologies that I was familiar with have been broken by the NSA and GCHQ, but some of what I'm showing you might protect you from crackers while using the Internet.

The perceived need for protection from those who might attack us has become more important than any desire for the protection of personal privacy. We have descended down the slippery slope, and the result is the rampant and constant spying that has been revealed. Our western "no longer free" governments seem to feel that they need to know everything that their citizens are doing in their self-deception of protecting their nations and their citizens from who knows what. This illogical premise that they have arrived on is disputed back in the introduction section of this book "The Elephant in the Room, Lets Crunch the Numbers on what is Really Killing Western Civilizations Citizens!" On the flip side, common citizens just want to be left alone and to be allowed to communicate privately with their friends, family and business partners. These two extremes conflict, and there have to be checks and balances, which are now vastly tilted in the favor of western government's Internet spying that is taking place. However, the need for personal privacy still exists, and we all have to make an attempt to protect our families and our businesses from this extreme governmental surveillance activity. Employing the techniques below should make you a harder target than your neighbor, who is freely opening up their digital activity on the Internet and potentially damaging themselves and their children.

A lost or stolen computer, a household visitor (house cleaner, party crasher, caregiver) can get all of your personal information and access to accounts if that information is unencrypted on your hard drive! A virus, spyware, key logger, etc. could also expose sensitive files to Internet hackers (thieves) while the computer is online. If you are a doctor, lawyer or business person, you have an ethical and perhaps legal responsibility to shield sensitive data. I even encrypt the encrypted KeePass database on my traveling laptop, which gives me double or triple the protection for my password file. Yes, my wife calls me paranoid.

Understand that using encryption does nothing to ensure your safety while using the infected Internet. We discussed physical security in the introduction, which you must practice. If you leave your Internet devices lying around, it is very simple for an attacker to install a hardware/software keylogger*, a bus-mastering device to capture your RAM memory, or some other form of malware to capture your encryption passwords and keys. This will allow them to decrypt files and data on your Internet device with ease, which your anti-software may not even flag as a problem. Simply watch TV and you will see many examples of how plugging in a USB device, installing a camera, or some other physical measure can bypass all of your security. Finally, there are government programs that install software or hardware before you receive your Internet device that will allow them to spy upon you.

The computer expertise of people I have paid and asked to review the material in this book has varied wildly. Encryption proved to be a difficult concept and skill to teach, and I often had to resort to using unencrypted email to converse. As a result of this experience, I worked very hard to make my coming directions about this technology as easy to follow as possible because I want you to use these encryption techniques to learn how unencrypted email and documents are very often (almost always) compromised. For example, I was not about to send my hundreds of hours of research and work on this book unencrypted over the Internet to anyone, so I taught my partners how to use encryption, which added volumes to what we are about to cover. There was too much potential for my writing to be stolen, exploited or shut down.

If you have malware installed by not carefully using the Internet and following the directions in this book, a cracker can use their malware/software to retrieve your keys, encrypted files, and passwords. We don't know if the computer programmers creating these encryption tools are trustworthy and have not included some sort of backdoor in their code, but I think we can trust the solutions coming out of Germany. Some of these encryption tools' source code still needs an independent review by knowledgeable experts in the art of computer programming. Now that the whole world knows that their governments are spying on them, these necessary, independent reviews are starting to occur.

Most crackers are not sophisticated enough to exploit the data on stolen devices that use encryption technologies. With that said, I would not want to throw down the gauntlet and challenge the ones who may be able to do so. As I keep emphasizing, there is no impenetrable defense and there are many unknown threats lurking about on the Internet. Even the multi-layered Internet defenses that we are developing in this book may not protect you completely. The attempt of this book is to make you a more difficult target so that crackers move on to easier prey. If your laptop or smartphone is stolen, the thief will likely look for things like password files and identity theft data, but if all that is encrypted, they will probably just wipe the device and sell the hardware on the black market.

You might ask why using encryption software is in Chapter 5. After all, if we have not installed a working OS on our shiny new laptop or desktop computer, why am I talking about encryption? The reason is almost all the utilities and software presented in this book are donationware*, open source, and freeware*. Many of the utilities have updated versions with other capabilities that you can purchase. When you download them (or anything off the Internet) you have to verify the integrity of what you have downloaded. All freeware that you download will post files on their website containing a MD5 hash, SHA-1 or SHA-2 hash or some other means of making sure what you download is correct. There are many scams on the Internet where websites pretend to offer you a download, but it is loaded with malicious software. We can use tools to generate an MD5, SHA-1 or SHA-2 hash or a detached GPG signature on the software you have downloaded to verify that it is from the original authors.

However, even these techniques are not totally foolproof. Checking the MD5 sum on a download is no longer a sure thing. According to https://en.wikipedia.org/wiki/MD5#Vulnerability "*MD5 is not suitable for applications like SSL certificates or digital signatures that rely on this property. In 1996, a flaw was found with the design of MD5, and while it was not a clearly fatal weakness, cryptographers began recommending*

the use of other algorithms, such as SHA-1–which has since been found to also be vulnerable."
The wiki goes on to say that the United States Computer Emergency Readiness Team, https://www.us-cert.gov says, *"MD5 should be considered cryptographically broken and unsuitable for further use."*

Despite these warnings, MD5 is still being used as an algorithm to verify data download integrity. From http://searchsecurity.techtarget.com *"MD5 is an algorithm that is used to verify data integrity through the creation of a 128-bit message digest from data input (which may be a message of any length) that is claimed to be as unique to that specific data as a fingerprint is to the specific individual. MD5, which was developed by Professor Ronald L. Rivest of MIT, is intended for use with digital signature applications, which require that large files must be compressed by a secure method before being encrypted with a secret key, under a public key cryptosystem. MD5 is currently a standard, Internet Engineering Task Force (IETF) Request for Comments (RFC) 1321."* If you do an MD5 search on the website, you will find many other articles discussing the security flaws in the algorithm.

You can take a generated MD5 value for a download and compare it to what is on the software website and you know with some confidence:

- The software downloaded correctly
- You have the correct program and not a bot/virus ridden version someone cracked

You don't have to do this; it is an added precaution for your protection. The two most common scenarios that come to mind as to why you want to do this:

- The generous people in the open source community have their hands full working on the free software they provide us. They don't have billions of dollars to spend keeping their websites secure. Consequently, it is possible a cracker might get a malicious file up on their website or put a phishing site to lure you in. How many times you have heard about crackers breaking into corporate websites and changing things to embarrass a company or government agency with deep pockets?
- Another reason is making sure there was no problem with the download. Perhaps it did not finish or got corrupted for some reason. I admit I have burnt ISO files I did not verify to disk that were corrupt, thus wasting DVDs and CDs. (Be green, recycle them! Chapter 3 covers recycling options available to you).

Travel to the Tactical Technology Collective who has built the guide to open source security software that your can trust, which will keep you communications private from surveillance. (See: https://tacticaltech.org, https://alternatives.tacticaltech.org)

Cryptography, What Is It, How Does It Work and Why Do You Need It?

Before we talk about cryptography, let's take a historical example about how important this technology is to our privacy and very existence.

	Historical Reference - The German Enigma is an example of how you have to upgrade your hardware and encrypt your communication

Let's go back to World War II for some examples of using old hardware and encryption techniques. The Germans used a portable machine called Enigma to encrypt their communications, which in the 1920s was thought to be unbreakable. The Enigma was a portable machine that consisted of a keyboard, a rotating disk, and a lamp. These rotors contained each of the 26 letters of the alphabet and would rotate with each key press. When a letter was typed, the output letter produced on the Enigma keyboard was a product of the positioning of these rotors. Depending on how the rotors lined up, the lamp would light a different letter. There were many different types of the Enigma machine with varying numbers of rotors, and there were even commercial versions as well. Although the Germans did modify the Enigma machines a few times by adding additional rotors, by 1945 nearly all German Enigma traffic could be translated in a day or two. The Germans still remained confident of its security and continued to transmit Enigma messages. This alerted the Allied Forces to the locations of the German Army and Navy and led to various surprise attacks that the Germans could not explain. Captured intelligence from the Enigma has been credited with ending the war as much as two years earlier than it would have. By sticking with the same technology for almost 30 years, the Germans exposed all of their communications to the Allies during the war. (See: https://en.wikipedia.org/wiki/Enigma_machine)

We will never know how many thousands of Germans soldiers lost their lives because of their high commands lack of attention paid to secure communications, but this example emphasizes the importance of practicing secure cryptography. There have been many intellectual books written on cryptography that are difficult to understand but do apply to our everyday lives using the Internet. Suffice to say that the technical details about this subject are a field best left to governments, college professors, mathematical geniuses and master's students and that does not fit in this book. As such, assume that most civilian cryptography techniques have been broken and may not protect you from the likes of agencies such as the NSA, GCHQ or other governments. However, in my reading, they will protect your privacy from a common cracker when encrypting your keys, if you employ large encryption numbers, which we will discuss. These techniques should work against most everyone who does not have unlimited resources and computing power funded by their country's willing citizens and backdoors built in.

Encryption methods described in this chapter use cryptologists Rivest, Shamir and Adleman (RSA) or cryptologists Daemen and Rijmen (DES) standards that were developed and/or leaked back in 2001 or earlier. The DES standard was quickly adopted and became the Advanced Encryption Standard (AES), which is presumed to be one of the most frequently used and most secure encryption algorithms available today. The https://www.boxcryptor.com/en/aes-and-rsa-encryption web page claims that no practical attack against AES exists, so perhaps the infinite computing power and intellectual knowledge of the NSA cannot break this 256 bit encryption unless you come up on their radar as a person of interest.

However, according to Boxcryptor, RSA is one of the best and most successful asymmetric encryption techniques that exist today. From their website, *"The security of RSA itself is mainly based on the mathematical problem of integer factorization. A message that is about to be encrypted is treated as one large number. When encrypting the message, it is raised to the power of the key, and divided with remainder by a fixed product of two primes. By repeating the process with the other key, the plaintext can be retrieved back. The best, currently known method to break the encryption requires factorizing the product used in the division. Currently, it is not possible to calculate these factors for numbers greater than 768 bits. None the less, modern cryptosystems use a minimum key length of 3072 bits."* Therefore, as you read this chapter, I recommend using a key size of no less than 4096 or greater for added protection.

Windows 7 – Adding Tools & Utilities to the System PATH

We will soon be installing various applications, tools and utilities in Windows. To make them easier to use and write scripts for, we will have to adjust the System PATH in Windows. To view your System PATH open a command line window and type "C:\...\echo %PATH%", and to determine if your tool is in the system PATH type "C:\...\where <executable>".

To view/edit your System PATH, go to your desktop and right click on the __Computer__ icon that we added earlier to the desktop earlier > scroll down to the bottom to select __Properties__ > click on __Advanced system settings__ in the left frame, this will bring up the __Systems Properties__ dialog with the __Advanced__ tab selected > click on the __Environment Variables...__ button near the bottom.

Another method you can use to add a utility directory to the System PATH, open the __Control Panel__ > with __View by: Large/Small icons__ selected upper right > click on the __System__ icon > on the left menu click on __Advanced system settings__ link > at the bottom click on the __Environment Variables...__ button.

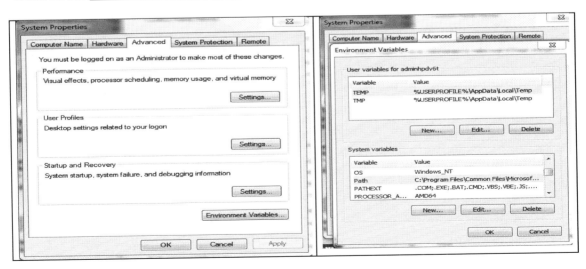

Under System variables in the bottom pane scroll down until you see the __Path__ system variable, click on it > click on the __Edit...__ button at the bottom-middle to change the System PATH.

| WARNING  | Changing the Windows 7 System PATH is something that must be done very carefully. If you accidentally alter the other directories in the path, or enter the installation directory incorrectly, you can break other application's ability to run on your computer or mobile device. *In the __Edit System Variable__ dialog next to Variable value: right click on the path displayed > arrow down to select __Copy__ and save your current path in a file using your favorite text editor. At the end of the Variable value: add a semi-colon and the path to directory where you installed the software*. Semi-colons must be maintained and are used to separate directories in the path. If you leave out these details, you will break things on your computer, and the applications, tools and utilities you use may no longer operate. |

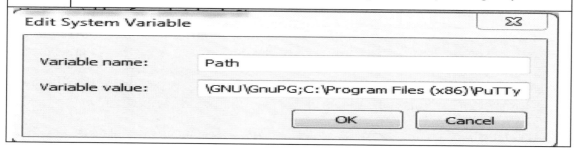

At the end of the Variable value--add a semi-colon and then the path to the directory where your software is installed. Many utilities we download are very small executables that do not need to have a path of their own. We will soon discuss Gpg4win and PuTTy, which upon installation are in our Windows system path. We should house our simple, related utilities in their executable directories thus not complicating our system path for a single executable file or two.

Windows 7 -- Verifying Downloads Before Installation

There are many free and open source options that can be used to verify downloads. The Windows 7 OS comes with no utility for calculating the MD5, SHA hash or signature value of a download, which one might wonder why it does not. The omission of this capability is unforgivable in our fight for privacy and against malware. You should find this disturbing because now you have to download something to verify a download, but what verifies the verifying software download? This is like the old, what came first, the chicken or the egg question. This means we need a second utility to verify the first utility. Microsoft does provide a free and unsupported command line utility called "File Checksum Integrity Verifier" that computes MD5 or SHA1 sums, but why not include it with the OS? In addition, as you will find out in Chapter 7, this utility is years old and needs to be updated to other methods of verifying downloads. A good place to extract the binary to is *C:\Program Files (x86)\GNU\GnuPG\pub*, which will be in your system path after installation of Gpg4win and a reboot. (See: http://support.microsoft.com/kb/841290, https://www.microsoft.com/download/en/details.aspx?displaylang=en&id=11533)

C:\Downloads\Linux\Mint>fciv linuxmint-17-kde-dvd-64bit.iso
// File Checksum Integrity Verifier version 2.05.
67357c88145115421dca869b26dad767 linuxmint-17-kde-dvd-64bit.iso

HashTab is another utility for Windows that you might consider. However, the website asks for your email address, which probably means they are making a record of it to market or sell. (See: http://implbits.com/HashTab/HashTabWindows.aspx) Using software that requires your email address is something you don't want to do.

Other tools to consider are DivHasher, MD5sums, FSUM from SlavaSoft, Quick Hash GUI, SHA256 Checksum Utility, File Checksum Tool, which are freeware* that you can download that support many formats. (See: http://soft.mydiv.net/DivHasher.html, http://www.pc-tools.net/win32/md5sums, http://www.slavasoft.com/fsum , http://quickhash.sourceforge.net , https://kanguru.zendesk.com/entries/21747773-SHA256-Checksum-Utility, http://www.krylack.com/file-checksum-tool) Scanning these alternatives with antimalware software showed all of them to be safe to use.

Another utility recommended by VMware is MD5, which from their website, "*MD5 is a command line utility usable on either Unix or MS-DOS/Windows, which generates and verifies message digests (digital signatures) using the MD5 algorithm. This program can be useful when developing shell scripts or Perl programs for software installation, file comparison, and detection of file corruption and tampering.*" (See: http://www.fourmilab.ch/md5)

C:\...\md5 -h   REM To get help, C:\...\md5 filename   # To calculate MD5

Congratulations, you have just verified your first download. You now have your very own checksum generator. You should put whatever utility you choose to use, such as MD5.exe, somewhere in your Windows System PATH. Adding a new directory to your System PATH for one executable file does not make sense. Copy the executable file to somewhere on the computer that's already in the path such as GnuPG discussed above. Linux comes preinstalled with utilities that you can use to perform these tasks:

sha256sum ISOFileName or, # md5sum ISOFileName

Boxcryptor — To Encrypt Individual Files for Syncing with the Cloud

Boxcryptor https://www.boxcryptor.com is a wonderful tool set that is designed for use with an OneDrive. You now know that we should never store data at a cloud service unless we don't mind it being compromised, invaded or shared with governments or corporations. Boxcryptor provides a fairly easy method of setting up a virtual disk that we can use in which to encrypt individual files. This has the advantage of, when our OneDrive syncs up with our local computer it is then storing our Boxcryptor encrypted files from our local computer. This added layer of encryption is mandatory to protect your data. This is the way all data should be stored on the cloud if we choose to use these services. Boxcryptor uses 256-bit Advanced Encryption Standard (AES) encryption, which is what all other civilian products offer. From a PCWorld, January 2013 article by Brad Chacos, titled "Encrypt Your Cloud-Storage Content for Free", "*Boxcryptor is basically a virtual hard disk that encrypts files on the fly using 256-bit AES encryption. Since Boxcryptor encrypts and decrypts files locally, and doesn't send your password to third parties, your files remain unreadable to out-siders even if hackers steal your password or otherwise breach your cloud storage provider's defenses.*"

When you travel, you should never travel with unencrypted data on a USB drive that you don't want criminals/crackers to look at. There are easy ways to encrypt all of your import documents using the software provided by Boxcryptor and TrueCrypt. The advantage of using these tools is that we can create a virtual disk of files that will be stored on the cloud just like storing individual files. The free version of Boxcryptor software allows us to access a single virtual folder, which is adequate for the few files, such as contact information and password files information, that we want to store encrypted on the cloud or a USB drive. If we combine this with SpiderOak or another cloud service that stores our data encrypted, we will achieve double encryption for our very sensitive data stored on that cloud.

With the revelations released by Edward Snowden, we now know that the NSA is able to decrypt, what was assumed, secure communications that use HTTPS, VPN, TLS and Voice-Over-IP. We also learned that U.S. companies have built backdoors into their software to allow the NSA to decrypt U.S. citizens' data. However, Boxcryptor is a German company located in Bavaria that takes your privacy very seriously. So much so that they released a statement as to how they do not cow down to the NSA by being a zero-knowledge provider, which means all data sent to their servers is secured before and during transmission. This also means that even if the NSA has broken HTTPS to capture your data during transmission, they would still have to decrypt your encrypted files, and that is next to impossible without your private RSA keys or non-retrievable password hash. (See: https://www.boxcryptor.com/en/blog/boxcryptor-and-latest-snowden-disclosure)

To get started using Boxcryptor, surf to https://www.boxcryptor.com/en/download and download the install program Boxcryptor_version_Setup.msi > double click on the MSI file and the click on the Run button > the Welcome to the Boxcryptor... screen will appear, Next > read the license agreement, check the I Accept the terms... box, Next > on the Destination Folder screen let Boxcryptor install where it wants, Next > Boxcryptor will need to install device driver software from EldoS Corporation, Next > click on Install button at the bottom and the Installing Boxcryptor... screen will appear, Finish. Boxcryptor may need the Microsoft .Net 4.0 frameworks that also had to be downloaded and installed, which requires a restart of your computer after everything is installed.

Upon reboot the Boxcryptor Login screen appears automatically, which implies that Boxcryptor has invaded your computer startup. Don't enter anything for username or password as they will be set later > you can sign up for their cloud services or click on the Use Boxcryptor with a local account link at the bottom > on the Create your Boxcryptor account screen click on the Local Account button at the bottom > on the Take care of your key file! screen check that you understand that you will manage your key file, Create > browse to the location that you want it stored in and enter a filename (e.g. C:\<UserID>\Boxcryptor\BoxcryptorKeyFile), Save > on the Set password screen enter your password in the Password and Confirm password boxes and check the agreements boxes, OK > when you confirm, Boxcryptor will create your local account that will be started upon startup > on the Choose plan screen click on OK.

Boxcryptor will allow you to work with whichever cloud service you use as it will create what they call a virtual drive on your computer. To the user, this is the drive letter that you drag and drop files into, like a folder on a USB drive, which will automatically prompt you to encrypt them. Within that drive letter and folder, you can view and access files from all of your cloud servers or subdirectories that you create as if they are just unencrypted folders on your computer. To encrypt your files or folders in the Boxcryptor that are not encrypted on the virtual drive, right click on them to encrypt them, which will change their color to green.

If you are using the free version of Boxcryptor, you can only have one folder set up for encrypted files at any given time. However, it is easy to use other folders to store encrypted data. **_Open up the Boxcryptor settings dialog and Disable the folder where your encrypted Boxcryptor files are stored by unchecking it > click on the Add button to specify a new location and enable it._** Boxcryptor, like many other applications, will constantly poll the Internet checking for updates. As we will do with many other applications, consider turning off this waste of resource and potential security hole.

WARNING	Automatic update can be turned off by **_right clicking on the Boxcryptor_** drive letter or shortcut in **_Windows Explorer_** > arrow down to highlight **_Boxcryptor_** and select **_Settings_** > in the **_Boxcryptor Settings_** dialog click on the **_Advanced_** tab > uncheck **_Check for updates_**. You can also get to the settings and other option by right clicking on Boxcryptor in the System Tray. There does not appear to be a way to easily update the Boxcryptor application manually, so every so often you will have to visit their website to download the latest version of their software.

If you lose or forget your password to Boxcryptor, you will lose all your encrypted data. However, to begin using the software again, simply remove the software using Revo Uninstaller and reinstall. This will allow you to set up a new password and start using the application again.

TrueCrypt – Encrypting USB Drives and Folders

TrueCrypt was/is a multipurpose encryption tool that has many uses and options, which should prove to be effective against crackers and many non-US-UK-governments spooks. TrueCrypt calls their encryption technique "on-the-fly" encryption, which means the data is automatically encrypted right before it is saved and decrypted right after it is loaded, without any user intervention. This means when that when you open a file with an application, the portion of the file that you are working on or viewing is automatically decrypted and loaded into Random Access Memory (RAM). You can then either work on or view that decrypted portion of data while the remainder of the file remains encrypted. This book only covers how to create a virtual encrypted disk within a file and mount it as a real disk, or encrypt an entire USB drive. There is much more to TrueCrypt than these simple exercises.

WARNING	TrueCrypt submitted itself to an independent audit by the security firm iSec who found 11 flaws but it passed the software as a security solution. Many cryptographers worried that TrueCrypt had backdoors built into this tool's encryption software. While iSec found 11 flaws, none of them was immediately exploitable and there was no evidence of backdoors or intentional flaws. Therefore, it came as quite a shock when the developers announced on May 28, 2014 that development on TrueCrypt was ending with directions on how to migrate to Microsoft BitLocker who, as Edward Snowden pointed out, has known

encryption backdoors. This sudden shutdown of their website and this outrageous recommendation of using BitLocker were highly suspicious. Some news agencies such as *The Register* are reporting that the most recent version 7.2 of the TrueCrypt software that their website redirects the customer to is compromised. (See: http://www.theregister.co.uk/2014/05/28/truecrypt_hack, http://www.pcworld.com/article/2241300/truecrypt-now-encouraging-users-to-use-microsofts-bitlocker.html#tk.nl_today) If you recall our discussion of Lavabit who was killed off by the U.S. government, it appears that the TrueCrypt programmers are being suppressed from updating their software and have abandoned this privacy solution to the world. Could it be that the U.S. Stazi state has continued to suppress encryption attempts for individual privacy?

TrueCrypt was/is the most versatile graphical encryption solution presented in this book that you could use. Using it could encrypt an entire operating system and even hide an encrypted OS within an OS. The same holds true for an encrypted folder or partition. Fleeing the U.S. Stazi security state they have relocated in Switzerland to avoid US legal issues. Therefore, TrueCrypt will probably live on once more and I expect this encryption solution to improve and remain a viable solution to your encryption needs above using a corporate compromised tool with backdoors such as BitLocker. (See: http://www.forbes.com/sites/jameslyne/2014/06/02/truecrypt-is-back-but-should-it-be/?ss=Security)

TrueCrypt was/is a sophisticated, well thought-out tool that addresses the worst possible security scenarios. For example, if you are being held at gunpoint to reveal your password, you can give the enemy your outer password, making them believe they have access to all of your encrypted data. However, the reality is that you have an inner encrypted folder that only decrypts to a different password. The same thing can be done with multiple OSs. This is the stuff of spy novels everywhere and you can read about how to do all of this at TrueCrypt's website. For our purposes, a few simple but effective examples using TrueCrypt is probably adequate. As you move around the file, the portion you need is decrypted on-the-fly. TrueCrypt has many options from which you can choose:

- The simplest and most versatile strategy is to create an invisible, password-protected, virtual encrypted disk (folder) on your computer or USB drive where you can store all your sensitive documents. This keeps you from having to encrypt your entire USB or hard drive, which you may not want to do. Because this container is treated as a file you can delete, move, or copy it wherever you want. The entire container is encrypted, which includes file names, folder names, the content of the files, free space, meta data, etc. To access the contents of the file container you have to mount the volume as a drive and enter a password. In Windows, that file container will appear as a drive letter and is used the same way as the known C: and D: drive letters are used. As with the folders on C: you can now access, modify, remove and add files and folders inside the encrypted file container by using the drive letter. ***Start TrueCrypt > click on the Create Volume button lower left > leave Create and encrypted file container ticked, Next > > under Volume Type leave Standard TrueCrypt volume ticked, Next > > under Volume Location select the file location and name, Save (e.g. E:\TrueCrypt), Next > > under Encryption Algorithm chose your algorithm, you*** *can read about the various choices at the TrueCrypt website documentation pages (e.g. Serpent-Twofish-AES), under Hash Algorithm (e.g. SHA-512), Next > > under Volume Size select your volume size for the file (NOTE: many USB drives are still FAT32 so the maximum TrueCrypt file size is 4095 MB), Next > > under Volume Password enter your password for the encrypted folder, Next > (consider using a keyfile see: http://www.truecrypt.org/docs/keyfiles) > move your mouse around for at least 30 seconds and click on Format > when done, select a drive letter and click on the Select File... button, navigate to your newly created TrueCrypt folder, Open > click on the Mount button lower left and enter your Password: > next to your drive letter you will see the volume mounted > minimize TrueCrypt and you are ready to access the folder's contents.*

- Alternatively, you can encrypt an entire device (USB drive, partition, etc.). For example, perhaps we want to encrypt our entire USB drive for travel. Performing these steps will erase everything on the USB drive. *Start TrueCrypt > click on the Create Volume button > tick Encrypt a non-system partition/drive, Next> > under Volume Type leave Standard TrueCrypt volume ticked, Next > > under Volume Location click on the Select Device... button > under Select a Partition or Device select your USB drive, Next> > leave Create encrypted volume and format it ticked, Next> > under Encryption Algorithm chose your algorithm, (same as above, listed at TrueCrypt's website), under Hash Algorithm (e.g. SHA-512), Next> > under Volume Size the entire USB drive will be selected, Next> > from this point forward the steps remain the same as above to encrypt the USB drive. To open the USB volume start TrueCrypt > select a drive letter > click on the Select Device... button > click on Mount > enter your password and then you can access the data on the drive.*

WARNING	Now that the USB drive is encrypted it can only be accessed by using TrueCrypt and mounting it on a different drive letter. Any attempt to access the drive under the drive letter assigned to the USB drive will prompt you to format it.

- My favorite and final option covered in this book is to encrypt the USB drive with a hidden folder to house my password database and other sensitive documents. That way if I am ever forced to reveal the password to my outer encrypted USB drive, I don't have to reveal the inner hidden volume password. The extortionist will think that they have access to all of my encrypted data. *Start TrueCrypt > click on the Create Volume button > tick Encrypt a non-system partition/drive, Next> > under Volume Type tick Hidden TrueCrypt volume, Next> > under Volume Creation Mode leave Normal Mode ticked > under Volume Location click on the Select Device... button > under Select a Partition or Device select your USB drive, OK, Next> > under Outer Volume, Next> > under Encryption Algorithm chose your algorithm, under Hash Algorithm choose your hash, Next> > under Outer Volume Size the entire USB drive will be selected, Next> > under Outer Volume Password enter your outer password, Next> > under Outer Volume Format move the mouse around for at least 30 seconds, click on Format > under Outer Volume Contents click on the Open Outer Volume button to copy some files to the outer volume, Next> > or perform the same steps for the Hidden Volume entering a different password when prompted.*

The hidden container is an excellent place to store your password file that has already been encrypted by using something such as KeePass or GnuPG, which will give you double encryption and hide your data. Then again, if you are really paranoid, encrypt your encrypted KeePass password file with GnuPG and then store that in a hidden encrypted TrueCrypt folder on your USB drive. So now if some cracker gets a hold of our laptop or USB drive they will have to break through three layers of encryption to get your most sensitive data. While this is feasible, it will take them massive amounts of time and expertise, giving you the opportunity to change all of your passwords if these devices are missing or stolen.

We will discuss virtualization in Chapter 7 in which we will install a guest Linux OS and cover how to use the command line. We want to be able to access our TrueCrypt USB drive from a virtual OS. Download and install TrueCrypt in your VM.

```
$ cd Downloads
$ tar zxvf truecrypt-7.1a-linux-x86.tar.gz
$ ./truecrypt-7.1a-setup-x86
```

Under Install options—Select 1 to install TrueCrypt. You will see:

```
Installing package...
[sudo] password for suroot:
usr/bin/truecrypt
usr/bin/truecrypt-uninstall.sh
usr/share/applications/truecrypt.desktop
usr/share/pixmaps/truecrypt.xpm
usr/share/truecrypt/doc/License.txt
usr/share/truecrypt/doc/TrueCrypt User Guide.pdf
```

In Mint, TrueCrypt was/is now available from the Menu. To be able to access the USB drive from a VM you have to unmount the TrueCrypt volume in your core OS and mount it in the VM. Make sure you have not made the USB safe to disconnect from the core OS. *In VMware Player, right click on the USB drive icon in the upper right > select Connect (Disconnect from host), OK > start TrueCrypt and click on the Select Device... button > on the Select a Partition or Device dialog look for your device (e.g. /dev/sdb1: 1.9 GB) and click on it, OK > choose a slot and click on the Mount button > enter your password for your outer or hidden (inner) encrypted USB storage area.* Your data is now available to the VM mounted under /media/truecrypt<slot> in Debian flavors of Linux.

Alternatively, you may decide that you want an encrypted folder in your Linux OS or VM. The steps to perform that task are almost identical to steps in Windows. *Start TrueCrypt > click on the Create Volume button > under TrueCrypt Volume Creation Wizard, leave the default Create an encrypted file container ticked, Next> > under Volume Type leave Standard TrueCrypt volume ticked, Next> > under Volume Location select or type your folder to use (e.g. /home/<username>/truecrypt), Next> > under Encryption Options select your Encryption Algorithm and Hash Algorithm, Next> > type in your Volume Size, Next> > type in your password, Next> > select your file system type (e.g. Linux Ext4) > under Cross-Platform Support choose your mount option (e.g. tick I will mount the volume only on Linux), Next> > under Volume Format create the encrypted file* *container, **Format**, **OK**, **Next>** > the Wizard then takes you back to create another volume, click on **Cancel**. To use the encrypted folder you have to mount the /home/<username>/truecrypt folder. Select the slot you want to mount, click on the **Mount** button > navigate to your TrueCrypt folder, **Open** > click on the **Mount** button and enter your password > you will see your folder mounted in TrueCrypt. The actual mount point in Linux, where you can copy files will be /media/truecrypt<slot>.*

(The old Truecrypt links such as http://www.truecrypt.org/downloads, http://www.truecrypt.org/docs now redirect you to http://truecrypt.sourceforge.net which suggests using Bitlocker, which I recommend against as it has a backdoor. See: https://en.wikipedia.org/wiki/TrueCrypt)

BitLocker – Encrypt Folders, Hard Drives and USB Drives

Before I describe BitLocker, you need to decide if you may just want to skip this section because BitLocker is only available in Windows 7 Ultimate and Enterprise, or Windows 8.1/10 Professional and Enterprise editions. We also now know that the NSA has paid corporations such as Microsoft vast sums of money to build backdoors into their encryption technology. Privacy buffs suggest that most all commercial U.S. encryption technology has been compromised in some fashion by the NSA. As such, presenting this solution is very limited for this book's presentation purposes. It is also assumed that readers of this book may not have these expensive OSs installed on all their SBO/HCU office and portable hardware. Still, if you are a Windows power user, this option is a choice to consider using. Much like the other encryption solutions presented in this chapter, BitLocker protects your data by encrypting it to a password or private/public key combination. The utility encrypts your data using a 128-bit AES algorithm with key plus an Elephant diffuser, which is a data-mixing algorithmic function that provides additional disk-related security features. BitLocker is also able to encrypt to a 256-bit AES key, which should be used on mildly advanced hardware. Microsoft BitLocker can be used to encrypt an OS Volume, folder, or a USB flash Drive. For a USB drive in Window 7/8 only, we would use the BitLocker To Go feature, which supports the encryption of externally attached portable devices.

*Connect your USB drive to a USB port and wait until a drive letter is assigned > open **File Explorer** > right click on the assigned USB drive letter > select **Turn on BitLocker** from the menu, or press the <Windows> key and search for 'BitLocker' > click on the **BitLocker Drive Encryption** utility > Windows will display the drives that can be encrypted using BitLocker, click on **Turn On BitLocker** next to the USB drive that you want to encrypt > you will see a **Starting BitLocker** screen and then BitLocker will prompt to see if you want to protect the drive with a password or use a smart card to unlock the drive > tick the box next to method you plan to use (e.g. **Use a password to unlock the drive**) and enter your password, **Next** > the next screen will prompt for whether you want to save your recovery key to a file or print it > I choose **Save the recovery key to a file** and saved the key to the default name, you should see the message "Your recovery key has been saved." message, **Next** > depending on what you have selected, encrypt only your data or the entire drive, **Next** > click on **Start Encrypting** > the Encrypting... dialog will appear showing the percentage complete as it encrypts the drive and will eventually show Encryption of F: is complete.*

*The next time you plug in your USB drive BitLocker will pop up a **This drive is protected by BitLocker Drive Encryption** dialog prompting you to enter your password, **Unlock**. From now on you can use the USB drive as an unencrypted drive. Later if you need to enable access to a drive, right click on a newly inserted drive and select **Unlock Drive**.*

To access a BitLocker drive for read only access in other versions/releases of the various Microsoft OSs, get the BitLocker To Go reader at http://go.pcworld.com/BLTGReader, which lets you open and view the content of portable drives protected by BitLocker. (See: http://technet.microsoft.com/en-us/library/cc732774.aspx, https://en.wikipedia.org/wiki/BitLocker_Drive_Encryption)

Microsoft Office – How To Password Protect & Unprotect Your Documents

Microsoft Office has undergone numerous variations since its original release many years ago. For example, the July 2012 release of Office Word 13 can do many things such as insert an online video, reuse the content of a PDF, make it easier to align pictures and diagrams, etc. The 2010 version of Office Word also had some fine nuances added, which were an improvement over its predecessor, Microsoft Word 2007. These included a better user interface, more user-friendly and extensive graphics and layouts. It is hard to trust these document encryption techniques though, as we now know backdoors have been built into them by direction of the U.S. NSA. These backdoors are easily leaked to foreign governments and crackers, so don't trust this form of encryption. Still, using Microsoft document encryption is much better than sending a document through the infected Internet unencrypted.

In these times, when all of our important documents of business use, as well as other personal material, are usually in the electronic format, it is important to keep them safe and secure. You do not want confidential documents/data falling into the wrong hands. Thus, it is imperative that you encrypt your documents and protect them with a password to ensure a sound sleep.

Microsoft Word, Excel and PowerPoint Office applications allow you to password protect your work. Before you do so, consider creating a copy of your unencrypted document and store it in a safe place. The procedure to password protect is almost identical in all three products. The Microsoft directions at http://office.microsoft.com/en-us/word-help/protect-your-document-workbook-or-presentation-with-passwords-permission-and-other-restrictions-HA010354324.aspx describes the process to password protect your files. *Open the document that needs to be encrypted > click on **File** upper left > on the drop down menu arrow down to select **Info** > arrow right to click on the (Protect Document, Protect Workbook, or Protect Presentation) icon > arrow down to select **Encrypt with Password** > when the **Encrypt Document** dialog pops up, enter the password you are going to use, twice > then save the file. If you repeat the steps above, when you click on **Info** below the **Permissions** heading you will see the words **A password is required to open this document**.* This is proof that you completed your encryption task successfully. The next time you open the file a Password dialog will pop up requiring the password you just entered. Microsoft states that your document will be unretrievable without the correct password if you do this, so store your password in a safe place.

Consequently, we see that the process of encrypting a document and applying a password is a very easy task and does not even require a much time to do, so we should employ this encryption technology to keep our work safe. Encrypting documents to a password is a good solution when users share the same Internet devices or shared disks. However, as we will talk about later, password protection can be one of the most insecure methods of protecting your data depending on the strength of the password that you use. If you ever send a sensitive data file attached to an unencrypted email over the Internet, the password needs to be very strong. Crackers can make a copy of that document as the email crosses their server and then spend an infinite amount of time trying to brute force their way into the correct password for the document. We will cover sending and receiving files securely in Chapter 9 using our own SSH server.

In order to remove a password from a protected document *open the document > when the Enter password to open file dialog pops up enter the document password, OK > click on the File menu and arrow down to select Info > click on the Protect Document button and arrow down to select Encrypt with Password > the Encrypt Document dialog will appear with the password hashed and already entered > delete the password leaving the area blank, OK, Save*. This will unencrypt and un-password-protect this document.

This makes working on an encrypted document easy if there is no reason to keep it secure. For example, suppose you sent the document attached to an email and it only needed to be protected in transit. There is no need to risk forgetting the password once the document is secure behind your firewall.

How Secure Is Microsoft Office Encryption?

Before the release of Microsoft Office 2007, the Office encryption was easily broken. The outdated Microsoft XP OS and the original Office products were designed with convenience and not security in mind. Office 2003 made a feeble attempt at allowing the user to encrypt the documents, but that encryption was/is easily broken. One might think that a 13-year-old product like Office 2003 would no longer be in use. However, I found just the opposite is true as I traveled around providing free technical support to write this book. Corporations, charities, non-profits, local governments and households are still using it.

Microsoft Office 2010 uses 128-bit AES strong encryption (See: http://office.microsoft.com/en-us/excel-help/password-protect-documents-workbooks-and-presentations-HA010148333.aspx, https://en.wikipedia.org/wiki/Advanced_Encryption_Standard) for password encryption. Taken from http://csrc.nist.gov/groups/ST/toolkit/documents/aes/CNSS15FS.pdf, "*The design and strength of all key lengths of the AES algorithm (i.e., 128, 192 and 256) are sufficient to protect classified information up to the SECRET level. TOP SECRET information will require use of either the 192 or 256 key lengths. The implementation of AES in products intended to protect national security systems and/or information must be reviewed and certified by NSA prior to their acquisition and use.*"

If you open a document created in an older version of Office 2003 in Office 2010 with the default encryption mode, the old 2003 encryption algorithm will be replaced with the strong 2010 128-bit encryption, but be careful, for the reverse is not true. You will have to remove encryption to save a document in the 2003 format.

This means that Word 2007 encryption can be used for secret information as far as the encryption algorithm is concerned, but the password strength is also just as important. Refer to Chapter 11 on passwords. In Chapter 10 on setting up USB drives I will cover a third command line method for encrypting files. Those exercises are going to require use of the command line and scripting, which will not be covered extensively until Chapter 7 on using virtualization.

Linux – Using GnuPG with SSH for Encryption Automation

GnuPG is a set of encryption tools, funded mostly by the German government that allows you to safely send messages and documents over the Internet. It does so by using a variety of methods, the most common of which uses a key pair methodology that you create. There are currently two variants of the gpg tool called gpg and gpg2. The difference between the two is gpg2 has a different architecture than gpg in that it splits up the functionally into several modules. The gpg command is smaller and does not depend on other modules at run and build time.

How the GunPG project software works is much akin to how your house or car keys work to unlock your house's front door or your car door. You have keys on your key chain that you use to gain access to your residence or vehicle. You hope that anyone without your keys will not be able to break into your car or house. How far you want to go in time and expense to protect these assets is up to you to determine. For example, you can add alarm systems, unbreakable glass, and keyed lug nuts on your tires, or pull down covers that conceal what is in the back of your SUV. GnuPG works much the same way in that you can exchange data with varying levels of security, such as denying crackers access to data without the proper keyfiles, passwords or passphrases. If you make a copy of the keys to your house or car at the local hardware store and give it to a trusted relative, friend or acquaintance, you have given them access to do what they may want with your assets. They can rob your house or steal your car with impunity. In GnuPG terms, this is called your digital private key, which should never be revealed or distributed except under the most trusting of circumstances. This is a very simplistic description of a somewhat complex tool, but I hope you can understand that the concepts behind this software are not all that difficult or different from your everyday life. Our entertainment industry seems to like to dramatize this technology into something of science fiction that only geeks, government spooks and crackers can understand. I'm hoping to show you that is not the case.

With GunPG, you would use $ gpg --gen-key command to generate a pair of keys consisting of a public key and a private key that is encrypted to a passphrase that only you know. Your private key is the newly installed locks on your house front door. The public key that you generated can now be distributed to your partners so that you can exchange data back and forth privately and securely. You can distribute your public key to the whole world through public key services or limit its distribution to a few select friends, relatives and/or business partners. The public key that you freely give out could be viewed much like what we see in the movies when the evil villain is trying to launch a nuclear missile to destroy a city. The movies depict the silo operators as two trusted officers with two separate and differing keys that must be turned at the same time for the missile launch to occur. If one of the keys were lost or stolen, it would be useless without the other key. This analogy is not perfect, but in our case we only have one private key to protect; the other public key we can freely distribute. Our private key is the only way that crackers can gain access to our encrypted data. If our private key is ever compromised, we can always generate a new key pair. This would be like changing the locks on your house doors because someone has a copy of your house key that presents a threat. Just as you should never give your new key to anyone that you don't fully trust, it is very important that your new digital private key be kept secure and never shared with anyone.

If/when you give others your public key(s), it is important that you verify that they have *your* public key. Some middleman may have intercepted your key in route and substituted one of their own. For example, someone intercepted (stole) a credit card application from your mailbox, changed the address on the application and is now using that credit card with impunity. Since you will never even see a bill and no one at the credit card company verified that you received the application that they sent to you, an Identity Thief can now do some REAL damage to your credit. I hope this example explains how important it is to verify an exchange of keys. This also shows how companies are not held accountable for setting you up to have your identity stolen. You will have to deal with the aftermath of this disaster, not the credit card company.

A key exchange is not as hard to do as it is in the movies where an armed escort is needed. It is done by examining what is called the 40-digit "fingerprint" of the keys that you generate and exchange. This fingerprint is unique to anywhere else in the world, i.e. no other person will have a certificate with the same fingerprint. Most times only 8 digits are needed to verify your public key, as it is quite unlikely that the same 8-digit sequence would occur twice anywhere in world. For this reason the key ID or fingerprint is often only displayed as the last 8 digits. This fingerprint identifies the identity of the certificate, which is much like how the fingerprint of a person uniquely identifies a person.

Any form of simple communication can be used between you and your public key holder to verify that they have your public key, such as a private phone call. Your partner should do the same with you and once you have your partner's public key, you can then add it to a file called your public keyring. Once keys are verified you need some sort of mechanism to show the extents to which you went through to verify the keys and prove you or they are who you say you are. This is a very important step in the process, sometimes skipped by corporate or government IT employees, but this is critical to the verification and signing of your digital keys.

Verifying and signing a public key is an added and necessary step to enable the safe exchange of data between you and your partners. This process allows you and your partners to keep track of all the keys that you have all verified. It also a way of establishing a "Web of Trust" so that others can verify their keys based on your recommendations. We will get into the technical details, importance and further description of this process soon.

To securely send data to your partners securely, you encrypt your data to your private key and your partner's public key and send the encrypted data to your partner. Because the document is encrypted to their public key, your partner can decrypt the document using their private key. When your partner sends you a document they will encrypt it to your public key and you will then use your private key to decrypt the document. When your partner gives you their public key you should sign the key on your personal keyrings to show that the key has been verified.

If the data is a document, there are varieties of protocols that can be used to transmit documents to and from your partners. In 2006, most U.S. corporations were still using the insecure FTP protocol to transfer files. In 2013, when working on setting up my small business I have had to interact with other small businesses while writing this this book. What I found is that these million/billion dollar business were amazingly still using archaic insecure third party software and the insecure FTP protocol to exchange sensitive data with their customers. FTP was invented in 1971 and received some security updates in 1998. It has passive mode communication connection, which is/was somewhat secure and which I scripted for in 2006, but you must move beyond this outdated technology. Any business partners such as legal firms, printing companies, etc. that require you to use this form of file transfer is not someone that you want to continue doing business with, for security reasons. You are putting all your data at risk. This is akin to using Windows XP, which we previously discussed, which we have to assume that a large percentage of the world is spying on all XP Internet interaction with your partners. As I write this there seems to be little investment in cyber security education by SBO or large entities in regards to training their IT personnel how they should be interacting with and using the infected Internet. I hope you now understand that you must include how seriously your partners take cyber security in your business decisions.

For example, when working with one partner, I suggested they set up an SSH server to replace their FTP server. We will cover SSH in <u>Chapter 9</u>. I'm sad to say I was met with indifference, which I found disturbing, so I limited my data exchanges and business with them. I even offered my services at a bargain in the hope of benefiting us both, but again was met with indifference. Unfortunately, I had to risk my work on this book by connecting to them via FTP to conduct business. Many SBOs also use paid third party services, who they think are employing proper security techniques, but the reality is they rarely do. The files I transferred were not even encrypted, which demonstrates how some HCUs/SBOs do not even have a very simple/basic understanding of cyber security.

Story	Back in 2006 while working for multi-billion dollar corporations, all of the partners that we interacted with still used the insecure FTP protocol to exchange data. I managed all levels of file encryption for a major corporation using FTP. Because FTP is an insecure file transfer protocol, I had to devise methods for keeping our corporation's encrypted data secure. I certainly did not want to be the person responsible for the stolen identities of thousands of employees' and corporate customers' identities being stolen.
	Imagine the liability I might face, as well as the guilt that I would feel, for not exploring and developing every means possible to make sure a data breach never

happened. This was a huge burden on my conscience and one that I took very seriously. The corporate answer back then was to encrypt files with PGP and then send them via FTP to our partner's computer servers. However, the company had me automate everything so we could cut back on staff. To accommodate management I invented some crazy scripts and algorithms in trying to protect their data and automate just about everything else. Although, in automating everything, someone could easily copy the scripts that I was using to communicate with our customers/partners, who could then compromise the corporation's data. Those scripts had the password to our private encryption key, thus giving anyone with access the power to unencrypt everything. This information could be worth millions to identity thieves. Even though it kept me employed for at least another year by automating everything, I didn't feel comfortable doing what they were asking me to do, which was to use an insecure unencrypted file transfer protocol and scripting encryption passwords. However, when you accept a paycheck, you do as you are told. Any cracker or corrupt corporate administrator gaining access to those automation scripts would have the keys to all of the corporations' data.

I also felt it might prove dangerous to bring in low-paid, un-vetted foreign workers into our payroll department that would handle all of our confidential data, thus giving them access to all of our sensitive corporate data, but that was not my call. I felt that these workers might have other agendas or be working for other entities that did not have the corporation's best interest in mind (spies). Corporate espionage is a known problem that gets very little attention in our courts or media. When/if you are placed in this position, you have to trust in your talent and abilities to move on to bigger, and better things; and I later did, so I documented everything as best I could for the new foreign workers who would later perform my job. Conversely, I knew that by doing so I might be sacrificing the private information of all the customers, employees, and affiliates of the corporation thus revealing all the data in of all our private corporate databases to people who probably should not have that access. Cyber espionage* is real and can impact corporations and their employees in painful ways.

I give this example not as self-aggrandizement but to show you how your private information is made public that you later have to deal with, as well as how there are no laws to penalize corporations for this cost-cutting activity that result in a lack of internal cyber security. Corporations seem to have lost the perspective that the lifeblood of any organization is the people who work for it. We all have to determine just how far we want to allow this privacy invasion to continue until proper laws are passed and cyber security is taken seriously. This is akin to how military cutbacks can affect the survivability of soldiers and their fellow troops, but there is nothing a soldier can do about it. After all, what are the legal consequences for allowing crackers around the world access to corporate data or a soldier to die on the battlefield? It is all about the bottom line in the corporate and government worlds. You and I have heard a lot about these massive breaches in their data servers resulting in stolen information, but little about the individuals being held accountable for this negligence or incompetence. At the very least, these breaches should result in some sort of change in management that might do better with the

> company's or government's cyber security requirements. For example, placing an experienced IT professional in charge rather that a crony or business graduate might make a difference. **The bottom line is that corporations should be punished for cutting costs at the expense of sacrificing their confidential data. We need accountability for these criminals that cost common citizens time and money to deal with the consequences!**

I give these stories for a reason and that is because there is abundant evidence of how these practices rebound on corporations and their customers. I very much encourage you to read the Price Waterhouse Global Economic Crime Survey at http://www.pwc.com/en_GX/gx/economic-crime-survey/assets/GECS_GLOBAL_REPORT.pdf. Cybercrime now ranks as one of the top four economic crimes as businesses face serious threats from cyber criminals. The report points out those four in ten respondents to their survey say that their organizations do not have the capability to prevent or detect cybercrime. The report has many other disturbing statistics and facts to support the story above, so let's just cover a few:

- 1 in 10 who reported fraud suffered losses of more than U.S. $5 million.
- 56% of respondents said the more serious fraud was an 'insider job'.
- 2 in 5 respondents had not received any cyber security training.
- A quarter of respondents said that there is no regular formal review of cybercrime threats by the CEO and the Board.
- The majority of respondents do not have, or are not aware of having, a cyber-crisis response plan in place.

From the report, "*It's not just about IT. It's about HR making sure employees understand the security policies, and recruiting people with the specialist skills to protect the organization from cyber-attacks. It's about legal and compliance making sure laws and regulations are respected. It's about physical security protecting sites and IT equipment. It's about marketing thinking about cyber security when they launch new products.*" The survey goes on to report, "*But our survey results suggest that the perception of cybercrime is changing, and that organizations are now recognizing the risk of cybercrime coming from inside. 53% of the respondents who said the cybercrime threat was an internal one believe that there is a risk from the information technology ('IT') department. It's not surprising that many respondents think this, because they expect IT personnel to have the necessary skills and opportunity to commit these crimes. In particular, IT personnel might have 'super user' access, which gives them extra administrative rights to access systems and the ability to delete audit trails, making it harder to detect their wrongdoing.*"

In Chapter 9 we will cover SSH, where we will discuss the exchange of public/private key pairs for the exchange of data. However, in my experience I have seen how unknowledgeable IT managers direct their staff to do some crazy things. Throughout my many years in IT, I have written many scripts that automate the exchange of data between your home/business and the partners with whom you are working. GnupG is a wonderful tool to use to encrypt and exchange data with your partners, but I doubt many of them know how to use it. I don't know of any schools or continuing education classes that you can send employees to that will teach them about this easy to use open source encryption technology. (See: http://www.ibm.com/developerworks/aix/library/au-gnupg,

http://gnupg.org/gph/en/manual.html#AEN136,
https://en.wikipedia.org/wiki/GNU_Privacy_Guard)

GnuPG -- Generating Key Pairs -- Verifying Pubic Keys for the Exchange of Encrypted Data and Email

In my latest Linux distribution, the version of GnuPG was at 1.4.16. However, at the open source website the latest version of this encryption software was at 1.4.18. You can check the version of GunPG by typing $ gpg --version at the command line to see what version your flavor of Linux is providing. You must do this before performing the following steps. To get the latest version or Linux GnuPG surf to https://www.gnupg.org/download/index.en.html and download the latest release of the software gunpg-1.4.18.tar.bz2 or gnupg-1.4.18.tar.gz When done downloading be sure to check the validity of the download by checking the SHA-1 checksum displayed on the web page by typing:

```
$ sha1sum gnupg-1.4.18.tar.gz
ea7d66c3de7aaf46de9e8678f4fc4a8c329400b2   gnupg-1.4.18.tar.gz


$ sha1sum gnupg-1.4.18.tar.bz2
41462d1a97f91abc16a0031b5deadc3095ce88ae   gnupg-1.4.18.tar.bz2
```

Once downloaded you can unzip, configure, make and install the latest version by performing the following steps:

```
$ tar jxvf gnupg-1.4.18.tar.bz2
$ cd gnupg-1.4.18
$ su      # change user to root
# cd gnupg-1.4.18
# ./configure
# make
# make install
```

So now you have multiple options of GPG to run on your Linux OS.

```
$ /usr/bin/gpg --version
gpg (GnuPG) 1.4.16
Copyright (C) 2013 Free Software Foundation, Inc.


$ /usr/local/bin/gpg --version
gpg (GnuPG) 1.4.18
Copyright (C) 2014 Free Software Foundation, Inc.
```

There is also a new GnuPG 2.0 modularized version of GnuPG supporting Open PGP and S/MIME, which their developers recommend. This will likely make three options available of GnuPG to run in you Linux OS. Installing this version becomes more complicated as there are also libraries that you need to first download and install. I found no other easy way to get this version of their software installed. The first step is to download the gnupg-2.0.x.tar.bz file from gnupg.org, expand the compressed file and view the README file.

```
$ sha1sum gnupg-2.0.25.tar.bz2
890d77d89f2d187382f95e83e386f2f7ba789436   gnupg-2.0.25.tar.bz2
$ tar jxvf gnupg-2.0.25.tar.bz2
$ cd gnupg-2.0.25  &&  vim README
```

In my case at the top of the README in the build instructions it stated that GnuPG 2.0 depends on the following packages:

libgpg-error   (ftp://ftp.gnupg.org/gcrypt/libgpg-error)
libgcrypt   (ftp://ftp.gnupg.org/gcrypt/libgcrypt)
libksba   (ftp://ftp.gnupg.org/gcrypt/libksba)
libassuan >= 2.0 (ftp://ftp.gnupg.org/gcrypt/libassuan)

You also need the Pinentry package for most of the GnuPG functions; however it is not a build requirement. Pinentry is available at ftp://ftp.gnupg.org/gcrypt/pinentry. You should get the latest versions of course, the GnuPG configure script complains if a version is not sufficient. After building and installing the above packages in the order as given above, you may now continue with GnuPG installation (you may also just try to build GnuPG to see whether your already installed versions are sufficient). As 'root':

```
# tar jxvf libgpg-error-1.13.tar.bz2
# cd libgpg-error-1.13  &&  ./configure  &&  make  && make install  &&  cd ..
# tar jxvf libgcrypt-1.6.1.tar.bz2
# cd  libgcrypt-1.6.1  &&  ./configure  &&  make  &&  make install  &&  cd ..
# tar jxvf libksba-1.3.0.tar.bz2
# cd  libksba-1.3.0  &&  ./configure  &&  make  &&  make install  &&  cd ..
# tar jxvf libassuan-2.1.1.tar.bz2
# cd libassuan-2.1.1  &&  ./configure  &&  make  &&  make install  &&  cd ..
# tar jxvf pinentry-0.8.3.tar.bz2
# cd pinentry-0.8.3  &&  ./configure  &&  cd ..
# tar jxvf gnupg-2.0.25.tar.bz2
# cd gnupg-2.0.25  &&  ./configure  &&  make  &&  make install && cd ...  &&  exit
# /usr/bin/gpg2 --version
gpg (GnuPG) 2.0.25
libgcrypt 1.6.1
Copyright (C) 2014 Free Software Foundation, Inc.
```

This will install a GnuPG binary in /usr/local/bin directory. So now you have three options of the software to choose to run. To get started using GnuPG we have to generate a key pair.

```
$ gpg  --gen-key
gpg: directory `/home/testuser/.gnupg' created
gpg: new configuration file `/home/testuser/.gnupg/gpg.conf' created
gpg: WARNING: options in `/home/testuser/.gnupg/gpg.conf' are not yet active during this run
gpg: keyring `/home/testuser/.gnupg/secring.gpg' created
```

```
gpg: keyring `/home/testuser/.gnupg/pubring.gpg' created
Please select what kind of key you want:
   (1) RSA and RSA (default)
   (2) DSA and Elgamal
   (3) DSA (sign only)
   (4) RSA (sign only)
Your selection? 1
RSA keys may be between 1024 and 4096 bits long.
What keysize do you want? (2048) 4096
Requested keysize is 4096 bits
Please specify how long the key should be valid.
         0 = key does not expire
      <n>  = key expires in n days
      <n>w = key expires in n weeks
      <n>m = key expires in n months
      <n>y = key expires in n years
Key is valid for? (0)
Key does not expire at all
Is this correct? (y/N) y
You need a user ID to identify your key; the software constructs the user ID
from the Real Name, Comment and Email Address in this form:
    "Heinrich Heine (Der Dichter) <heinrichh@duesseldorf.de>"


Real name: GPG User
Email address: gpguser@domain.com
Comment: GPG User ID for partner data exchange
Change (N)ame, (C)omment, (E)mail or (O)kay/(Q)uit? O


Enter passphrase:
Repeat passphrase:
```

Whenever a key pair is generated it is important that the revocation certificate be generated as well. The certificate is needed in the event that you forget your passphrase or your private key is lost or compromised. A revocation certificate is published to notify your partners that your public key should no longer be used.

```
$ gpg --output gpguser_revoke.asc --gen-revoke gpguser@domain.com
sec  4096R/11C12F2E 2013-08-14 GPG User (GPG User ID for partner data exchange) <gpguser@domain.com>


Create a revocation certificate for this key? (y/N) y
Please select the reason for the revocation:
  0 = No reason specified
  1 = Key has been compromised
  2 = Key is superseded
  3 = Key is no longer used
  Q = Cancel
(Probably you want to select 1 here)
Your decision? 1
Enter an optional description; end it with an empty line:
> This gpguser key is no longer valid, remove it.
```

Since our private key is so very important, let's make a backup copy of it and store it in a very safe place.

```
$ gpg --export-secret-keys > > <userid>-privkey.gpg
$ gpg --export-secret-keys --armor <youremailaddress> > <userid>-privkey.asc
```

We now need to exchange keys with our partners; this means you have to export your public key to a file then send it to and verify it with your partners. The GnuPG tools support keys in binary and ASCII format. The binary format is appropriate if you can safely exchange files with your partner. If this is not possible, you can post an ASCII version of your public key on your website or send it in an email to your partner. The fingerprint verification previously discussed will ensure that they received the correct key.

```
$ gpg --list-keys
/home/testuser/.gnupg/pubring.gpg
_____

pub   4096R/11C12F2E 2013-08-14
uid                  GPG User (GPG User ID for partner data exchange) <gpguser@domain.com>
sub   4096R/90317E49 2013-08-14
```

```
$ gpg --output gpguser.gpg --export gpguser@domain.com
$ gpg --armor --output gpguser.asc --export gpguser@domain.com
```

To keep things organized you may want to maintain all of your GPG files in the keyring directory.

```
$ ls /home/gpguser/.gnupg
gpg.conf        gpguser.gpg          pubring.gpg    random_seed   trustdb.gpg
gpguser.asc     gpguser_revoke.asc   pubring.gpg~   secring.gpg
```

We are now ready to exchange keys with our partners and start adding their public keys to our keyring. When we receive or retrieve their public key, we need to import it to our public keyring.

```
$ gpg --import partner_pub.gpg
gpg: key 66D4F240: public key "partner@domain.com (Test key) <partner@domain.com>"
imported
gpg: Total number processed: 1
gpg:               imported: 1  (RSA: 1)
```

```
$ gpg --list-keys
pub   4096R/11C12F2E 2013-08-14
uid                  GPG User (GPG User ID for partner data exchange) <gpguser@domain.com>
sub   4096R/90317E49 2013-08-14

pub   2048R/66D4F240 2013-08-08
uid                  partner@domain.com (Test key) <partner@domain.com>
sub   2048R/FD2E1B71 2013-08-08
```

Once the public key is added to our keyring we can view the fingerprint we need to verify with our partner.

```
$ gpg --fingerprint partner@domain.com
pub   2048R/66D4F240 2013-08-08
      Key fingerprint = 2F5E 359E C718 0CAF 746B  366B 567D 7831 66D4 F240
uid                   kellis2@hotmail.com (Test key) <kellis2@hotmail.com>
sub   2048R/FD2E1B71 2013-08-08
```

GunPG -- Signing and Assigning Trust Levels to Public Keys

Once the fingerprint has been verified to your level of satisfaction you should sign the key to show that it has been verified. When you sign a public key you are establishing a level of trust that you want to place on the key. If you are going to exchange the public key with others who trust you, be sure to *thoroughly vet the key*. Never sign a key where your partner has not provided their key length, key type, key id, creation date, expiration date if any, and their public key fingerprint. Your reputation and possible legal repercussions are on the line.

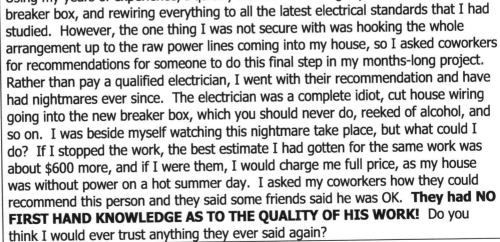

Story	
	As an Electronic Warfare technician, I learned a lot about dealing with all sorts of devices that handled a lot of lethal amounts of voltages, amperes and all facets of the dangers faced in the field of electricity that your average home electrician would never encounter. Upon my return from the Iraq 2003 war, I decided to study home electrical codes and methods and found out that there was a lot I did not know about simple 120-volt systems. In the military, we study and work on complicated Electronic Warfare equipment that we have to deal with on the war front. So when we come back home, it is weird learning about the elementary electrical equipment civilians deal with on a day-to-day basis. It is kind of like watching the show "Are You Smarter Than a Fifth Grader" and find out sometimes you are not. Using my years of experience, I quickly set about rewiring my house, building a new breaker box, and rewiring everything to all the latest electrical standards that I had studied. However, the one thing I was not secure with was hooking the whole arrangement up to the raw power lines coming into my house, so I asked coworkers for recommendations for someone to do this final step in my months-long project. Rather than pay a qualified electrician, I went with their recommendation and have had nightmares ever since. The electrician was a complete idiot, cut house wiring going into the new breaker box, which you should never do, reeked of alcohol, and so on. I was beside myself watching this nightmare take place, but what could I do? If I stopped the work, the best estimate I had gotten for the same work was about $600 more, and if I were them, I would charge me full price, as my house was without power on a hot summer day. I asked my coworkers how they could recommend this person and they said some friends said he was OK. **They had NO FIRST HAND KNOWLEDGE AS TO THE QUALITY OF HIS WORK!** Do you think I would ever trust anything they ever said again?

The moral of the story above is never assign a level of trust to a partner's public key without properly verifying and vetting it. Below are the guidelines that I use to assign the trust levels on crypto keys:

1   No opinion means you know nothing about the key or won't assign a level of trust to it for your own reasons.
2   Do not trust means that you don't trust the key, but you have to exchange data with the creator for some reason.
3   Limited or marginal trust means that you verified the fingerprint and email address over the phone and verified the business address (that they exist at the address listed). This can be done with a signature required letter at the post office. Signature confirmation provides shippers with the name of the recipient as well as the delivery date, time, and location; a copy of the recipient's signature will also be faxed, mailed, or emailed to you upon request. This should be kept in a file cabinet for legal purposes. This can also mean that you trust someone else's verification of the key, just be sure you trust in the fact that they vetted the key thoroughly.
4   Casual or fully, means that, in addition to all of the above, verifying the user ID against a copy of a hard to forge photo ID of the key owner, such as a driver's license or preferably, a passport.
5   Extensive or ultimately, means all of the above, except verification is done in person with original hard to forge multiple documents such as a passport or birth certificate. Be extremely pedantic with checking the person's identity, as your reputation is on the line. Verifying keys correctly is what signing PGP keys is all about. You should also look up their business at the Better Business Bureau or some other service such as Angie's List http://www.angieslist.com to see if there are any problems reported with their business reported. The remaining task prior to signing is to determine whether the other party has control over their email. To check this, send them a file such as a random number encrypted with their key. The task of your partner is to decrypt this file or random number and send it back to you encrypted to your public key. It is very important that your partner sign the message or file they send back so that you can verify their identity. If they are technically incapable of this task give their key a lesser rating.

Of course there are exceptions that you will have to determine for yourself. For example, if you are dealing with a large corporation you might give them a 3 after just a phone call and an exchange of email if you feel confident with that information. It is unlikely that you will reach a computer professional at a corporation willing or capable of establishing a level 5 key rating. The management at the multi-billion dollar corporations that I worked for did not even inquire, know or care if I verified the keys or not. I do not believe they even knew that this was an important step in the process of exchanging encrypted data. To sign the key, you can edit the key or just sign it from the command line. However, editing the key will allow you to establish the level of trust that you want to place on the key, which is much more important.

```
$ gpg --sign-key 11C12F2E
```

```
$ gpg --edit-key partner@domain.com
gpg (GnuPG) 1.4.11; Copyright (C) 2010 Free Software Foundation, Inc.
```

```
This is free software: you are free to change and redistribute it.
There is NO WARRANTY, to the extent permitted by law.

pub  2048R/66D4F240  created: 2013-08-08  expires: never       usage: SC
                     trust: unknown       validity: unknown
sub  2048R/FD2E1B71  created: 2013-08-08  expires: never       usage: E
[ unknown] (1). partner@domain.com (Test key) <partner@domain.com>
```

gpg> fpr

This will also show the fingerprint of the key being verified.

gpg> sign

You need a passphrase to unlock the secret key for
user: "GPG User (GPG User ID for partner data exchange) <gpguser@domain.com>"
4096-bit RSA key, ID 11C12F2E, created 2013-08-14

gpg> check

```
uid  partner@domain.com (Test key) <partner@domain.com>
sig!3       66D4F240 2013-08-08 [self-signature]
sig!        11C12F2E 2013-08-14 GPG User (GPG User ID for partner data exchange
```

gpg> trust
```
pub  2048R/66D4F240  created: 2013-08-08  expires: never       usage: SC
                     trust: unknown       validity: unknown
sub  2048R/FD2E1B71  created: 2013-08-08  expires: never       usage: E
[ unknown] (1). thatcybersecurityguy@outlook.com (Test key) <thatcybersecurityguy@outlook.com>

Please decide how far you trust this user to correctly verify other users' keys
(by looking at passports, checking fingerprints from different sources, etc.)

  1 = I don't know or won't say
  2 = I do NOT trust
  3 = I trust marginally
  4 = I trust fully
  5 = I trust ultimately
  m = back to the main menu

Your decision? 5
```

We can also view the trust status of a key from the command line.

$ gpg -kvv 66D4F240
```
gpg: using PGP trust model
gpg: checking the trustdb
gpg: 2 keys cached (5 signatures)
gpg: 2 keys processed (2 validity counts cleared)
gpg: 3 marginal(s) needed, 1 complete(s) needed, PGP trust model
gpg: depth: 0 valid:  2 signed:  0 trust: 0-, 0q, 0n, 0m, 0f, 2u
```

```
pub     2048R/66D4F240 2013-08-08
uid                    partner@domain.com (Test key) <partner@domain.com>
sig 3         66D4F240 2013-08-08  partner@domain.com (Test key) <partner@domain.com.com>
sig           11C12F2E 2013-08-14  GPG User (GPG User ID for partner data exchange)
<gpguser@domain.com>
sub     2048R/FD2E1B71 2013-08-08
sig           66D4F240 2013-08-08  partner@domain.com (Test key) <partner@domain.com>
```

Now that you have signed your partner's public key, you can now provide that key to your other partners creating what GnuPG calls your "Web of Trust". The way this works is that, you have expended time and effort to verify and sign someone's public key. Someone else you know or do business with needs to exchange data with you and the partner that you verified. Therefore, what you can do is export that partners signed public key and send it to your third party, who can then choose to trust your endorsement of the key or not. You will also want to provide your copy of the signed key to your partner so they can add your signature to their keyring. Once your partner adds your signature to their public key, they can then export their public key with your signature to provide to people with whom they correspond. GnuPG suggests having "key signing parties" where everyone gets together to verify, sign, export and import everyone else's public keys. You can then all exchange data within your group with a high degree of certainty and security. (See:
https://en.wikipedia.org/wiki/Key_signing_party,
http://www.cryptnet.net/fdp/crypto/keysigning_party/en/keysigning_party.html,
https://en.wikipedia.org/wiki/Linux_User_Group)

To put another way, you have a partner that expends at lot of time and effort managing and verifying their OpenPGP keys. You have verified, vetted and assigned a level of trust to your partner's key. Your partner has thoroughly investigated and verified another person's public key at a key signing party that you are adding to your public keyring so that you can exchange encrypted email with them. The person who directly owns the public key has also fully trusted the key they are managing.

The above scenario creates a "Web of Trust" or a trust path from you to the public key of the person you want to exchange encrypted email with. You can now trust that public key without having to depend on certificate authorities, which cost money. Understand that this method of key trust is not perfect as it depends on a network of direct human relationships and it is hard to find qualified personal at the businesses you exchange data with that are capable of using OpenPGP.

$ gpg --list-sig
```
/home/partner/.gnupg/pubring.gpg
--------------------------------
pub     2048R/66D4F240 2013-08-08
uid                    partner@domain.com (Test key) <partner@domain.com>
sig 3         66D4F240 2013-08-08  partner@domain.com (Test key) <partner@domain.com>
sub     2048R/FD2E1B71 2013-08-08
sig           66D4F240 2013-08-08  partner@domain.com (Test key) partner@domain.com
```

$ gpg --import /tmp/partner.gpg
```
gpg: key 66D4F240: "partnerl@domainl.com (Test key) <partner@domain.com>" 1 new signature
```

```
gpg: Total number processed: 1
gpg:           new signatures: 1
gpg: 3 marginal(s) needed, 1 complete(s) needed, PGP trust model
gpg: depth: 0  valid:  1  signed:  0  trust: 0-, 0q, 0n, 0m, 0f, 1u
```

$ gpg --list-sig
```
/home/partner/.gnupg/pubring.gpg
————————————————————————————————
pub   2048R/66D4F240 2013-08-08
uid                   partner@domain.com (Test key) <partner@domain.com>
sig 3       66D4F240 2013-08-08  partner@domain.com (Test key) <partner@domain.com>
sig         11C12F2E 2013-08-14  [User ID not found]
sub   2048R/FD2E1B71 2013-08-08
sig         66D4F240 2013-08-08  partner@domain.com (Test key) <partner@domain.com>
```

If you look above you see that User ID 11C12F2E has signed our public key. To see more information about whom they are import their public key.

$ gpg --import /tmp/gpguser.gpg
```
gpg: key 11C12F2E: public key "GPG User (GPG User ID for partner data exchange)
<gpguser@domain.com>" imported
gpg: Total number processed: 1
gpg:           imported: 1  (RSA: 1)
```

$ gpg --list-sig
```
/home/partner/.gnupg/pubring.gpg
————————————————————————————————
pub   2048R/66D4F240 2013-08-08
uid                   partner@domain.com (Test key) <partner@domain.com>
sig 3       66D4F240 2013-08-08  partner@domain.com (Test key) <partner@domain.com>
sig         11C12F2E 2013-08-14  GPG User (GPG User ID for partner data exchange)
<gpguser@domain.com>
```

Until you sign a key, GPG will question whether you want to use this added key to encrypt a file. Therefore, if you plan to automate processes through scripting or some other process, you should sign all of the public keys that you plan to automate using the public keyring. Below is an example of using an unsigned key:

$ gpg --encrypt --sign --yes --passphrase-file pass.txt -r 66D4F240 -r 11C12F2E <file>
```
Reading passphrase from file descriptor 3

You need a passphrase to unlock the secret key for
user: "gpguser@domain.com (Test key) <gpguser@domain.com>"
2048-bit RSA key, ID 66D4F240, created 2013-08-08

gpg: 90317E49: There is no assurance this key belongs to the named user

pub  4096R/90317E49 2013-08-14 GPG User (GPG User ID for partner data exchange) <gpguser@domain.com>
 Primary key fingerprint: 14B8 675B 7518 E745 19B6  D628 E478 9919 11C1 2F2E
   Subkey fingerprint: BF29 B994 CB06 0567 43D8  C00C 8931 60AD 9031 7E49
```

```
It is NOT certain that the key belongs to the person named
in the user ID.  If you *really* know what you are doing,
you may answer the next question with yes.

Use this key anyway? (y/N) y
```

Even after using the quiet option, you may get the warning "gpg: WARNING: message was not integrity protected". You will receive this warning if the original file was not encrypted with modification detection checking (MDC) enabled. This warning can be suppressed by issuing the --no-mdc-warning when decrypting the file. However, it is best to encrypt the file with MDC in place. MDC will force the use of encryption with a modification detection code, which is always used with new ciphers that have a block size greater than 64 bits.

```
$ gpg  --symmetric --force-mdc  --passphrase "thisistosavethis"  p.txt
$ gpg  --symmetric --armor  --force-mdc  --passphrase "thisistosavethis"  p.txt
```

To decrypt the file, use the following:

```
$ gpg  --passphrase "thisistosavethis"  --yes  p.txt.gpg
gpg: CAST5 encrypted data
gpg: gpg-agent is not available in this session
gpg: encrypted with 1 passphrase
$ gpg  --passphrase "thisistosavethis"  --yes  p.txt.asc
```
... same output as .gpg above.

As we discussed, there are levels of security for you to consider using encryption technologies such as GnuPG. The example above is one of encrypting a file to a simple passphrase. This is called symmetric key encryption because the same passphrase is used to both encrypt and decrypt a file. This is the simplest form of encryption that you can quickly employ to start exchanging encrypted data with your partners or protecting a few files on your computer. All that is needed is a working version of GnuPG and a known passphrase on one or both sides of the data exchange. In the example scripts in the next sections we will use this form of encryption to encrypt a file that houses our private key passphrase so that we can automate the decryption of data retrieved from our partners. We do this so that if a cracker or administrator gets access to our files, they would have to know which script we used to run to retrieve encrypted data and find the code in that script that encrypts and decrypts our passphrase file. This is not as easy as you might think, as corporations and governments may have many thousands of lines of scripting code running on their computers. No methodology is foolproof, but this method is better than having an unencrypted version of your passphrase lying around on your computer in easy to read text form. It is an added level of security that may keep a cracker from gaining access to your very private passphrase.

The GunPG web page http://www.gnupg.org also offers a less versatile, more sophisticated Windows GUI as a solution that we will discuss later. ***In the upper left click on Download > scroll down until you see GnuPG Binaries and next to Packages for MS-Windows are available at Gpg4win click on Gpg4win link.*** This will take you to http://www.gpg4win.org where you can download their encryption software. There is also an Apple Gnu Privacy Guard encryption solution which can be found at http://www.gpgtools.org. You can use Gpg4win to validate a public key also, but this software does not offer us the option of assigning different levels of authentication. (See: http://www.gpg4win.org/doc/en/gpg4win-compendium_16.html)

Another method you can use is to download a keyring where the public key you obtained is already signed by the keys of others that have already trusted the key. For example, you can download the keys of all Debian developers by installing the debian-keyring package. You can then verify the signatures Debian developers have made with their keys on other public keys you need to use and verify. Much of the following tutorial was taken from the Tails web page https://tails.boum.org/doc/get/trusting_tails_signing_key/index.en.html which describes various ways to verify a key signature.

apt-get install debian-keyring

To get a list of the signatures made by other people on the signing key you are verifying let's use the Tails signature and ISO file as an example:

```
$ gpg --keyid-format long --list-sigs <RSA key ID>
$ gpg --keyid-format long --list-sigs 1202821CBE2CD9C1
pub    4096R/1202821CBE2CD9C1 2010-10-07 [expires: 2012-10-06]
uid                          Tails developers (signing key) <tails@boum.org>
sig 3       1202821CBE2CD9C1 2011-04-16  Tails developers (signing key)
<tails@boum.org>
sig         BACE15D2A57498FF 2011-04-16  [User ID not found]
sig         CCD2ED94D21739E9 2011-06-12  [User ID not found]
uid                          T(A)ILS developers (signing key) <amnesia@boum.org>
sig 3       1202821CBE2CD9C1 2010-10-07  Tails developers (signing key)
<tails@boum.org>
sig         BACE15D2A57498FF 2010-10-07  [User ID not found]
```

The lines ending in [User ID not found] mean that these are signatures from public keys that you have not verified and added to your keyring. To learn more about them you can search the Debian keyring using the 16 digit code between the "sig" tag and the date.

```
$ gpg --keyring=/usr/share/keyrings/debian-keyring.gpg --list-key CCD2ED94D21739E9
pub    4096R/CCD2ED94D21739E9 2007-06-02 [expires: 2012-05-31]
uid                          Daniel Kahn Gillmor <dkg@fifthhorseman.net>
uid                          Daniel Kahn Gillmor <dkg@openflows.com>
uid                          [jpeg image of size 3515]
uid                          Daniel Kahn Gillmor <dkg@debian.org>
sub    4096R/C61BD3EC21484CFF 2007-06-02 [expires: 2012-05-31]
sub    2048R/125868EA4BFA08E4 2008-06-19 [expires: 2011-05-31]
```

We can now import a key from the Debain keyring that trusts the Tails public key to our own keyring:

$ gpg --keyring=/usr/share/keyrings/debian-keyring.gpg --export CCD2ED94D21739E9 | gpg --import

After import, we can verify the signature made by this new key on the Tails signing key by typing:

```
$ gpg --keyid-format long --check-sigs 1202821CBE2CD9C1
pub     4096R/1202821CBE2CD9C1 2010-10-07 [expires: 2012-10-06]
uid                            Tails developers (signing key) <tails@boum.org>
sig!3      1202821CBE2CD9C1 2011-04-16  Tails developers (signing key) <tails@boum.org>
sig!       CCD2ED94D21739E9 2011-06-12  Daniel Kahn Gillmor <dkg@fifthhorseman.net>
uid                            T(A)ILS developers (signing key) <amnesia@boum.org>
sig!3      1202821CBE2CD9C1 2010-10-07  Tails developers (signing key) <tails@boum.org>
sig!       CCD2ED94D21739E9 2010-12-29  Daniel Kahn Gillmor <dkg@fifthhorseman.net>

pub     4096R/1202821CBE2CD9C1 2010-10-07 [expires: 2012-10-06]
uid                            T(A)ILS developers (signing key) <amnesia@boum.org>
sig!3      1202821CBE2CD9C1 2010-10-07  T(A)ILS developers (signing key) <amnesia@boum.org>
sig!       CCD2ED94D21739E9 2010-12-29  Daniel Kahn Gillmor <dkg@fifthhorseman.net>

3 signatures not checked due to missing keys
```

From the Tails web page, "*On the output, the status of the verification is indicated by a flag directly following the "sig" tag. A "!" indicates that the signature has been successfully verified, a "-" denotes a bad signature and a "%" is used if an error occurred while checking the signature (e.g. a non supported algorithm).*" The above output shows that the signature of Daniel Kahn Gillmor on Tails signing key has been successfully verified.

If you are not comfortable using the command line to manage keys, there are graphical tools you can use in Linux that can help you. For example, in Fedora you can try "seahorse":

yum install seahorse

You can then manage key by typing $ seahorse to bring up the Password and Key management tool. In the KDE Desktop we can use kgpg to create a GPG key pair.

(See: https://fedoraproject.org/wiki/Cryptography,
https://fedoraproject.org/wiki/Creating_GPG_Keys,
https://help.ubuntu.com/community/GnuPrivacyGuardHowto)

GnuPG -- Digital Signatures and Why They Are Important

Wiki defines a digital signature as "*a mathematical scheme for demonstrating the authenticity of a digital message or document.*" A digital signature is an added measure of security that allows the recipient of a message or document to verify its integrity. By integrity, we mean it shows that the data was not altered in transit so that we know it was not tampered with or forged. Some schemes also associate a time stamp with when the data was signed thus showing the signature is valid. The signature is used to authenticate the sender of the document or message and to verify that it was not changed during transit.

It shows the recipient that the message or document was created by a known sender much like how we view a hand written signature. While "gpg" can be used to encrypt and decrypt files to send to your partners, it can also be used to sign those documents. Encryption can keep someone from understanding a message or deciphering a document; it does not prevent someone from altering the encrypted data. A signature allows the receiver to verify that the file or message has not been altered since the signature was assigned. For example, a cracker could apply a fake signature to a document encrypted to your public key, thus impersonating you, or perhaps a financial partner has to know that you cannot later deny having signed the transaction that you asked them to conduct, thus having legal significance. A digital signature can be applied to both encrypted and unencrypted messages to show that they have arrived intact and unaltered. Here is how this works:

1. You create and email a correspondence or document that your receiving party needs to know is unaltered upon receipt.
2. You use software such as GnuPG to obtain a hash, checksum, Cyclic Redundancy Check or some other means to "hash" the message thus creating a "message digest" so that upon receipt it can be proven to be authentic.
3. That same software uses your private key and your partner's public key to encrypt the "message digest" and appends or surrounds the document or message. This encrypted digest becomes your signature and is different for every message you send. Since this message digest is encrypted to your private key, which only you possess, it becomes your digital signature. Hopefully this shows how important protecting your digital private key is!
4. The GnuPG software then appends the encrypted message digest to the document or message, thus signing it.

Below is what a signed message looks like before being decrypted:

```
-----BEGIN PGP SIGNED MESSAGE-----
Hash: SHA1

What happens when I sign this...

-----BEGIN PGP SIGNATURE-----
Version: GnuPG v2.0.22 (MingW32)
Comment: Using GnuPG with Thunderbird - http://www.enigmail.net/

iQEcBAEBAgAGBQJSzNffAAoJEFU8OnvnBjsjITIH/36o3Fjj4XHzOaodEIeciTvY
ppT3LEq2KsnwOuz/eOHtVixyJ4dvKRdzEuTH/8S3NiQ4EkzcEDB2EbXhOykc6XjZ
WIcRXIrRM+hFbIWhniVj3oaViFMm1WchUIZ5rxotfuWvhI77NtBZWIGHhuzSTn4y
```

LEBzewxNO3kTP4rrPJUaSNGfmbngMvgzXP4eCOLgfOmtBjQnXArgEIB8+OKXIHE1
wph5yBxIrXBsHiIbyPdtB7efr4vvbSADmVhw5RmaaDLv5jqAmOPh49/7bdzYmQtk
UhwSt4o4WHZmI5UrDoVHHD28tcUx3VKb+jjq8pg80IjYenNub0bzpyy/boNz4pU=
=XFC5
-----END PGP SIGNATURE-----

When your partner receives your correspondence:

1. When your partner receives the data, they use their software to decrypt the signature using your public key and their private key, thus changing it back into a message digest. If your partner can decrypt your signature, this proves you sent the message since it was encrypted to your private key, which only you possess.
2. The GunPG software then makes a hash of your decrypted document or message to compare to the message digest that was attached as your signature, and if they match, your partner knows that the data has not been changed during transit.
3. The decryption software will tell your partner that this message contains a good signature from you, thus verifying the message or document.

This sounds somewhat complicated, but the software does everything for you. (See: https://en.wikipedia.org/wiki/Digital_signature)

GnuPG -- Scripting Encryption and File Transfer with Your Partners

Now that we have everything set up to exchange encrypted data with our partners, we have to create a low-cost infrastructure to do so efficiently and automatically. While we could assign an employee to perform the repetitive steps necessary to encrypt, decrypt, sign, send and receive encrypted data, this could become an ever-expanding process that would prove very painful and costly to have someone do day after day in your home or business. Odds are you don't have the resources to have someone who works for you trained and dedicated to this task. The answer for most SBOs as they conduct their core business is to pay an expensive service to handle these tasks for them, which is essentially the same thing as having an employee dedicated to this task.

Therefore, rather than present step-by-step directions and have you figure out how to incorporate encryption and file transfer to/from your SB/HC, I chose to show you some scripting that you can use to automate everything to exchange encrypted data with your partners. Odds are you know an experienced computer professional in your social sphere, or can temporarily employ a local college student who can use my example below to quickly adapt it to your business's needs. If the script below appears above your pay grade, it is not to individuals in the computer profession. You can hire an experienced Linux professional wanting some extra money to come into your small business and adapt the code below to exchange encrypted data with your business partners. While disabled, I dreamed of someone asking me to do this type of work.

I spent many years of my life scripting and automating encrypted file exchange to and from multi-billion dollar corporations with various other corporate and government partners. I could have written a book on this one topic alone, but I doubt many HCU/SBO users would have found a book dedicated to that topic very useful. I would have enjoyed presenting my technical work, constantly coding all of this, but that would have taken many pages and would be beyond the abilities of someone not skilled in writing scripts or computer software in all the various computer languages that I have worked in during my career. In addition, that book would have only landed me a job working for the government or corporations that I'm trying to help you understand are spying on everything you are doing in your Internet life. If I presented the limited information that highly paid corporate and government employees know, it would have defeated the purpose of this book.

Therefore, I chose to present the sample Linux BASH script below in the hopes that you can adapt it to your needs. Some of the original scripts and programs I wanted to present were over 5,000 to 14,000 lines in length. So, while the simple script below may seem overwhelming, it is a fraction of what I had running in the background at various corporations and government agencies. I tried to limit the script below to what I felt would benefit you the most. Perhaps, if this book is successful and you want further examples of coding, you can contact me via my website http://thatcybersecurityguy.com or my blog http://thatcybersecurityguy.blogspot.com, and I will get some scripts up or include them in my next revision of this book.

Before we get into the complexity of the script below, there are a few things that we want to set up for data exchange with our partner. In Chapter 9 we will discuss setting up an SSH server and the creation and use of partner SSH user IDs for the encrypted exchange of data. Once those IDs are created by both parties you have to mutually agree as to how the encrypted exchange of data will take place. Below are a few tips that I have used in the past to automate the exchange of data. Underneath the $HOME directory in Linux create the following directory tree:

```
$ mkdir -p <companyname>/in  && mkdir <companyname>/out
$ mkdir <companyname>/in/archive && mkdir <companyname>/out/archive
```

The "in" directory is where you both deposit files that you each need to process and the out directory is from where you both retrieve files. To automate things between you and your partner's SSH servers you will need to script getting a directory listing of the *out* directory on your partner's server to see if there are files to retrieve. If there are files there you can retrieve them to your SSH server and process them. Once the files are decrypted and processed, you probably want to archive them for possible reference later. There are many strategies that can be used to archive files, which are also covered in Chapter 11. The script below will use variables such as 'UserID', 'CompanyName', etc. as the script needs to be able to support multiple partners.

The SSH scripting in Chapter 9 will duplicate some of this code and I will show you a much more sophisticated requirements definitions about the automated exchange of data. In my attempt to present my many years of work on projects such as this, I had to break it and thousands of lines of scripting in these technologies down to be able to show you a few simple examples in this book that I hope will provide the most benefit to you. In defining these SBO/HCU requirements, I hope I am presenting an example you can expand upon and adapt to your purposes.

Requirements Definition for Automated Encrypted File Transfer and Decryption

After the manual setup of the infrastructure necessary to exchange encrypted files with our various partners, this script shall automate various processes for the exchange of that data.

1. The script shall scan for, analyze, retrieve, decrypt and archive any new 'in' data files that our partner places in their remote SSH server 'out' directory.
2. This script shall scan for, analyze, encrypt, send, and archive files placed in our SSH server partner's account 'out' directory to our partner's SSH servers 'in' directory.
3. The script shall provide the capability to transfer unencrypted files to/from both SSH servers.
4. The script shall provide the capability to archive and encrypt files placed in our SSH server's 'in' directory.

While this requirements definition sounds very simple, it is actually **very broad in scope**. This is an example of what IT professionals may face if an unknowledgeable manager without an IT background is placed in charge of an IT project. Some managers do not understand the value a well-thought-out *narrow* "Requirements Definition" is and how it can prevent scope creep during an IT development project. Their careers are on an entirely different path, and their IT staffs have to step up and demand limiting the projects to a tapered set of goals. However, this is akin to asking a business major to build a bridge or design a nuclear power plant. In most businesses this reflection does not happen often, and IT scope creep is often allowed to occur from a poor "Requirements Definition". We talked about whistleblowers previously, and from personal experience, if IT professionals object too loudly to the scope creep and course misdirection of an IT project, they are quickly ostracized as troublemakers and subject to removal. This occurs in all professions, but much more often during IT projects, to IT professionals. This science is very much misunderstood by most businesses that are not making a profit off their IT workers.

As stated above, the requirements definition above may sound simple but the scripting or coding to satisfy the needs of this project could become very **broad** in scope and could get very complex depending on how our requirements change. Unless things are narrowed down, this project could suffer some very serious scope creep. Scope creep is the allowance of uncontrolled changes or continuous growth in a project's scope that the unknowledgeable patrons holding the purse strings allow. Government contractors and corporations use this methodology to suck in billions of taxpayer dollars because sometimes the people running these projects do not understand the technology that they are managing. They are sometimes placed in charge of these projects as a political reward, crony favoritism or are just misadvised by the technical IT professionals that they are relying upon.

Take the example above and understand archiving alone could require months of work and thousands of lines of code depending on the government or business requirements and evolving requirements. For example, the statement "and archive files" could take on a life of its own resulting in thousands/million/billions of dollars. Archiving legal or clandestine information requirements that may be needed to house this data for years versus days or months imply the need for expensive backup solutions. The U.S. government needs the NSA's two billion dollar archive facility to record all Internet activity conducted by U.S. citizens. That data needs to be readily accessible for their sophisticated algorithms to peruse. For your SBO, there may be special naming requirements for archive files, such as the need to append a prefix or suffix to the archived files, attach a version number to the name of the file, change the owner or group the archive files belong to, attach a payroll run number to the file, compress the files, attach a date to the files, or in the case presented below, just rotate the archived files a defined number of times.

As we deal with partners, they will have their own processes setup. Some will post files on their server for us to process that coexist with files that we have already processed. Consequently, if we are automating things, we may have to script code to determine which files have been processed and which have not. Some partners will delete the files once they know we have successfully downloaded them. Some partners will want us to manage the files on their server, while others will not let us delete or move anything on their server. Some applications cannot distinguish between processed data and duplicate data. These are not simple tasks and in our business, coding to automate these tasks can vary from partner to partner, and application to application.

The script below is meant to be an example that satisfies the requirements above as simply as possible. I hope you can see how incredibly complex the automation of the exchange of encrypted data can become as each entity (corporation/government) we deal with may have differing requirements. These complications are why HCU/SBOs pay large sums of money to companies to handle these services for them. However, with this book I'm hoping to show how this type of automation is not out of the SBO/HCU's reach and give you some possible, in-house low-cost solutions. Doing these things on your own can save your business enormous sums of money, but I understand the need to concentrate on your core business and pay someone to perform these services for you. This works if you are vastly profitable, but perhaps you are like me, writing this book on a $22,000 a year budget. You may want to hire someone unemployed and skilled in Linux scripting to handle these tasks for you. God knows I would have taken this work and run with it while writing this book, but there were no offers. Once this initial infrastructure is in place, your systems will require minimal tweaks as requirements change or as you have to deal with new partners whom you can hire out to temporary workers or your local unemployed IT professional. By studying this book you now know what to look for in paid services, and that should help you find the best workers to fit your needs.

```
#!/bin/bash
# SCCS File %P%
# %Z% %M%:  %Q% Version %I%.
# Made on %G% at %U%.
#
# Script is best viewed with "set ts=4".
#
set -x
#================================================
#
# {Description}
# See Requirements Definition documentation.
#
# {Usage}
```

```
# See usage procedure below.
#
# {Description}
# The script uses Hungarian Notation prefixes as developed by Microsoft:
#
# strVar - string
# bVar   - boolean
# iVar   - integer
#
# GPG Notes:
#
# gpg —gen-key  -> Generate a new key pair.
#
# Generate a key revocation certificate for your public key in case
# your private key is ever lost or compromised:
# gpg —output <mykeyrevoke.asc> —gen-revoke mykey
#
# gpg —list-public-keys  # List all keys from the public keyrings.
# gpg —list-secret-keys  # List all keys from the secret keyrings.
# gpg —import <partnerpubkey>     # Import partners public key.
# gpg —delete-key <partnerpubkey> # Delete partners public key.
#
# How to encrypt files to public keys:
# gpg -e -r <YourPubKeyID> -r <CoPubKeyID> <file>
# gpg —encrypt —recipient <YourPubKeyID> —recipient <CoPubKeyID> <file>
#
# Create ASCII armored output:
# gpg -e -r <YourPubKeyID> -r <CoPubKeyID> —armor <file>
#
# Encrypt to public keys and write to 'outputfile.gpg':
# gpg -o <outputfile.gpg> -e -r <YourPubKeyID> -r <CoPubKeyID> <file>
#
# Decrypt the file given on the command line:
# gpg —decrypt <file>
#
# List all keys on the keyring and their fingerprints:
# gpg -kvc
# gpg —fingerprint
# gpg —fingerprint <CoPubKeyID> -> List the keys for the specified company
#
# gpg —output somepubkey.gpg —export name@domain.com  # Export public key
#       in binary format for name@domain.com.
# gpg —armor —export name@domain.com  # Export public key in ASCII format
#       for name@domain.com
# gpg —import somepubkey.gpg  # Import somepubkey.gpg that someone sent to
#       your public keyring.
# gpg —symmetric <text file>   # To encrypt to a passphrase.
# gpg —symmetric <text file> —passphrase <passphrase> -> To encrypt and
#       specify the passphrase on the command line.
# gpg —symmetric <text file> —passphrase-file <passphrasefile>  # To
#       encrypt and specify the passphrase file on the command line.
# gpg —passphrase-file <file> —yes <file>.gpg  # Decrypt symmetric file
#       with password file <file>.
```

```
#
# gpg —edit-key name@domain.com   # Command> fpr   -> To get fingerprint to
#       verify by phone with customer.
#       Command> sign  -> To sign their public key to validate it.
#
# To view the signature for keys on your keyring:
# gpg -kvv
# gpg —list-sig
# gpg —list-sig <partnerpubkey>
# gpg —verify <file>    # Verify a signed file.
#
# gpg —output file.gpg —encrypt —recipient someone@domain.com,me@domain.com file
#       Encrypts a file to an intended recipient and my public keys.
# gpg —output file —decrypt file.gpg  # Decrypt file.gpg to your private key.
# gpg —armor —export alice@cyb.org  # Exporting a public key to text file.
#
# $HOME/.gnupg/secring.skr —> contains the private portion of the key pair.
# $HOME/.gnupg/pubring.pkr —> contains the public key.
#
# Script static changing variables:
typeset -x strCryptedFiles    # Name(s) of the encrypted or decrypted files


#=================================================================
# Declare static CONSTANT variables.  They are declared here in the
# header for ease of change.
#
BREAK="————————————————————————————————————————————————————"
typeset -x strBaseName="`basename ${0}`"   # Get name of running script
typeset -x strOurGPGKeyID=0xFD2E1B71
typeset -x strPassDir=$HOME/.pass


#
#=================================================================
#
# Declare boolean and character command line static variables:
# Declare static company specific boolean and string variables (set in
# procedure procSetCompanyVars) or passed in via the command line:
#
typeset -x strCompany           # Command line company specified to be
                                # processed on our server
typeset -x strGPGFormat         # GPG Format to be used
typeset -x strUser              # Connection User ID
typeset -x strPass              # Connection Password
typeset -x strSubDir            # The subdirectory to process on our
                                # partners server
typeset -x strWorkingDir        # Directory we are getting or putting
                                # to/from on our company SSH server
typeset -x strCoGPGKeyID        # Company GPG Public Key ID
typeset -x strFilesToProcess    # List of file(s) being processed
typeset -x strSSHAddress        # SSH IP Address of remote host
typeset -x strLogsDir           # Script log file directory
typeset -x strLogFile           # Log of script actions
typeset -x strLSofDestDirFile   # On get we compare previous "ls" of incoming
```

```
typeset -x strTrajectory=get      # -t command line argument defaulted to
                                  #    to 'get' which means don't get or put
                                  #    the files being process to SSH server.
typeset -x strEmailList           # Application owners to be notified on our
                                  # local network or server
typeset -x bDebug=/bin/false      # -d command line argument
typeset -x bEnDeCrypt=/bin/false  # -e command line argument
typeset -x bTestMode=/bin/true    # -s command line argument
typeset -x bPutGet=/bin/false     # -p command line argument
typeset -x bFileSpecified=/bin/false # -f command line argument


#=============================================================
# Send an Email with subject $1 and Email addresses $2.  The current log
# file is concatenated into the Email.
#=============================================================
procSendEmail ()
{
if ${bDebug} ; then
    set -x
    echo "Entering procSendEmail" >> ${strLogFile}
fi
    strSub=$1
    strMList=$2
    strTmpMailFile=/var/tmp/mailfile.tmp
    strHost=`hostname`

    date +"%d%b%y (date +%H) $(date +%M)" > ${strTmpMailFile}
    cat ${strLogFile} >> ${strTmpMailFile}
    mailx -s "${strHost}-${strSub}" ${strMList} < ${strLogFile}
    rm -f ${strTmpMailFile}
}


#=============================================================
# Severity codes in $1 are as follows:
#  - 1 means log a warning and continue processing
#  - 2 means log a Fatal Error and exit 1
#  - 3 means log a Fatal Error, send an Email and exit 2
#=============================================================
procLogAbort ()
{
# set -x
    typeset -i iSeverity=$1
    strMsg="$2"

    if [[ ${iSeverity} -eq 3 ]]
    then
        printf "Fatal Error: ${strMsg}, aborting...\n" | tee -a ${strLogFile}
        printf "Finished processing of Company ${strCompany} on `date`\n" | tee -a ${strLogFile}
        procSendEmail "Fatal Error: ${strMsg}" ${strEmailList}
        exit 1

    elif [[ ${iSeverity} -eq 2 ]]
    then
```

```
            printf "Fatal Error: ${strMsg}, aborting...\n" | tee -a ${strLogFile}
            printf "Finished processing of Company ${strCompany} on `date`\n" | tee -a ${strLogFile}
            exit 1
        else
            printf "Warning: ${strMsg}\n" | tee -a ${strLogFile}
        fi
}


#
# Set the path to the GPG command.  Some flavors of Linux do not have
# the latest gpg binary in their repositories.
# NOTE: Must come after procedure procLogAbort.
#GPGCMD=`which gpg`      # Yields /usr/bin/gpg at version 1.4.11
GPGCMD=/usr/local/bin/gpg      # Downloaded from http://gnupg.org at version
                               # 1.4.14

if [ Y"$GPGCMD" = Y ]
then
    procLogAbort 3 "'gpg' not found, variables hard coded..."
fi


#================================================================
# Display the list of partner companies this script supports.
#================================================================
procDisplayCompanyHelp ()
{
    echo "Valid companies are:"
    echo
    echo "    lifeinsurance"
    echo "    legalservices"
    echo "    benefitservices"
    echo "    payrollservices"
    echo "    localsshserver"
    echo "    testcompany"
}


#================================================================
# Display the supported GPG crypt formats.
#================================================================
procDisplayGPGHelp ()
{
    echo "Valid GPG formats are:"
    echo
    echo "    ASCII"
    echo "    ASCIISigned"
    echo "    Binary"
    echo "    BinarySigned"
}


#================================================================
# Display script usage help.
#================================================================
Usage ()
{
```

```
        echo "Usage:"
        echo " $0 -c <company name>    Specify company to process, required!"
        procDisplayCompanyHelp
        echo
        echo "    -a <GPG Format> Specify the GPG format of the input or output File"
        procDisplayGPGHelp
        echo
        echo "    -d              Enable debug logging."
        echo "    -e              Enable file encryption or decryption."
        echo "    -f <filename>   Override default file to process with this file."
        echo "    -h              Display usage."
        echo "    -p              Enable SSH file transfer with partner."
        echo "    -s              Run in Production mode.  Default is Test."
        echo "    -t <trajectory> Specify SSH get or put, default is get."
}


#================================================================
# Get and process the command line arguments.
#================================================================
while getopts a:c:def:hpst: option
do
    case $option in
        a)
            strGPGFormat=$OPTARG
            echo "GPG Format set to ${strGPGFormat}..."
            ;;
        c)
            strCompany=$OPTARG
            echo "Company to process is ${strCompany}..."
            ;;
        d)
            bDebug=/bin/true
            echo "Debug logging enabled..."
            ;;
        e)
            bEnDeCrypt=/bin/true
            echo "Encrypt or Decrypt files enabled..."
            ;;
        f)
            bFileSpecified=/bin/true
            strFilesToProcess=$OPTARG
            echo "File to process is ${strFilesToProcess}..."
            ;;
        h)
            Usage
            exit
            ;;
        p)
            bPutGet=/bin/true
            echo "Send or receive files from partner enabled..."
            ;;
        s)
            bTestMode=/bin/false
```

```
            echo "Run in PROD mode enabled..."
            ;;
      t)
            strTrajectory=$OPTARG
            if [[ ${strTrajectory} != "get" && ${strTrajectory} != "put" ]]
            then
                procLogAbort 2 "Invalid trajectory ${strTrajectory} specified"
            fi
            echo "Trajectory for file transfer is ${strTrajectory}..."
            ;;
      *)
            Usage
            procLogAbort 2 "Invalid command line argument '$option' specified..."
            ;;
    esac
done

if [[ ! bEnDeCrypt && ! bPutGet ]]; then
    Usage
    procLogAbort 2 "Script not told to encrypt/decrypt files, or to retrieve/send files..."
fi


#————————————————————————————————————————————————————————
# Log variable values for company being processed.  This information is needed
# to determine how the script was run and what data was processed.
#————————————————————————————————————————————————————————
procLogVars()
{
if ${bDebug}; then
    set -x
    echo "Entering procLogVars()"
fi
    echo "Company being processed————————> ${strCompany}"             >> ${strLogFile}
    if ! ${bFileSpecified}
    then
    echo "File being processed————————> ${strFilesToProcess}" >> ${strLogFile}
    fi

    echo "Environment is————————————————> ${strEnvironment}"    >> ${strLogFile}
    echo "Company GPG Public Key ID————————> ${strCoGPGKeyID}"  >> ${strLogFile}
    echo "Encrypt or Decrypt Format————————> ${strGPGFormat}"   >> ${strLogFile}

    if [[ -n ${strSSHAddress} ]]; then
    echo "Company SSH Address————————————> ${strSSHAddress}"    >> ${strLogFile}
    echo "Company SSH User Name————————————> ${strUser}"        >> ${strLogFile}
    echo "Company SSH Password————————————> ${strPass}"         >> ${strLogFile}
    echo "Performing SSH————————————————> ${strTrajectory}"     >> ${strLogFile}
    fi

    if [[ ${strTrajectory} = "get" ]]; then
    echo "Inbound DIR for SSH get————————> ${strWorkingDir}"    >> ${strLogFile}
    elif [[ ${strTrajectory} = "put" ]]; then
    echo "Outbound DIR for SSH put————————> ${strWorkingDir}"   >> ${strLogFile}
```

```
        else
            echo "File will be en/decrypted only> ${strWorkingDir}"    >> $strLogFile}
        fi


        echo "${strBaseName} Logging DIR————————> ${strLogsDir}"    >> ${strLogFile}
        echo "${strBaseName} Logging To—————————> ${strLogFile}"   >> ${strLogFile}


        if [[ -n ${strLSofDestDirFile} ]]; then
            echo "${strBaseName} LS of Dest Log-> ${strLSofDestDirFile}" >> ${strLogFile}
        fi


        if [[ -n ${strSubDir} ]]; then
            echo "Company Subdirectory—————————> ${strSubDir}"    >> ${strLogFile}
        fi


        if [[ -n ${strEmailList} ]]; then
            echo "Error Notification list—————> ${strEmailList}"    >> ${strLogFile}
        fi
}


#————————————————————————————————————————————————————————————————
# If the file exists then
# - Move filename.2 to filename.3  and so on...
# - Move filename.1 to filename.2
# - Move filename.0 to filename.1
# - Move filename    to filename.0
#————————————————————————————————————————————————————————————————
function procStash
{
if ${bDebug}; then
#    set -x
    echo "Entering stash"
fi


#
# Sometimes routine is called with file names that don't exist.  If the
# file does not exist we ignore the request to stash.
if [[ ! -f ${1} ]]
then
    return 1
fi


typeset -i l k=20
while [ $k -gt 0 ];
do
    l=$k-1
    if [ -f ${1}.${l} ]; then
        mv -f ${1}.${l} ${1}.${k} 1>>${strLogFile} 2>&1
    fi
#    if [ ! -s ${1}.${k} ]; then
#        rm ${1}.${k}      # Remove zero byte files
#    fi
    k=$k-1
```

```
done

if [ -f ${1} ]; then
    mv -f ${1} ${1}.0 1>>${strLogFile} 2>&1
    chmod 660 ${1}.0 1>>${strLogFile} 2>&1
fi


return 0
}


#————————————————————————————————————————————————————————————————
# On all SSH puts we check for the existence of the file(s) being processed.
# If the file specified is not a file abort, if it is empty log a warning
# message.
#————————————————————————————————————————————————————————————————
procCheckFiles()
{
if ${bDebug}; then
    set -x
    echo "Entering procCheckFiles()" >> ${strLogFile}
fi
    typeset fFile=$1
    cd ${strWorkingDir}

    if [[ -z ${fFile} ]]; then
        fFile=${strFilesToProcess}
    fi

    for i in ${fFile}
    do
        if [[ ! -f ${i} ]]; then
            procLogAbort 3 "File ${strWorkingDir}/${i} not found."
        fi
        if [[ -z ${i} ]]; then
            procLogAbort 1 "File ${strWorkingDir}/${i} is empty."
        fi
    done
}


#————————————————————————————————————————————————————————————————
# On all SSH puts we check for the existence of the file(s) being processed.
#————————————————————————————————————————————————————————————————
procCheckForOneFile()
{
if ${bDebug}; then
    set -x
    echo "Entering procCheckForOneFile()" >> ${strLogFile}
fi
    typeset strFileDesc=$1
    typeset fFile=$2
    typeset -i iCnt=0

    if [[ -z ${fFile} ]]
```

```
    then
        printf "No file found at ${strWorkingDir}" | tee -a ${strLogFile}
        printf "containing string ${strFileDesc}" | tee -a ${strLogFile}
        procLogAbort 3 "Checking for NULL file string is not allowed"
    fi

    cd ${strWorkingDir}
    for i in ${fFile}
    do
        if [[ ! -f ${i} ]]
        then
            procLogAbort 3 "File ${strWorkingDir}/${i} not found"
        fi
        iCnt=$(( ${iCnt} + 1 ))
    done

    if [ ${iCnt} -gt 1 ]
    then
        printf "There is supposed to be only one file." | tee -a ${strLogFile}
        procLogAbort 3 "More that one ${fFile} found"
    fi
}


#————————————————————————————————————————————————————————————
# Move file specified in parameter 1 to the destination specified in
# parameter 2.
#————————————————————————————————————————————————————————————
procMoveFile()
{
if ${bDebug}; then
    set -x
    echo "Entering procMoveFile()" >> ${strLogFile}
fi
    typeset strFromFile=$1
    typeset strToFile=$2
    strBreak="_____"

    if [ ! -f ${strFromFile} ]
    then
        echo "Attempt to move a file that does not exist!" >> ${strLogFile}
        procLogAbort 3 "File `pwd`/${strFromFile} not found"
    fi
    mv -f ${strFromFile} ${strToFile} 1>>${strLogFile} 2>&1
    if [[ $? -ne 0 ]]     # Check the return status
    then
        echo ${strBreak} >> ${strLogFile}
        echo "ll listing of directory `pwd`" >> ${strLogFile}
        ls -al >> ${strLogFile}
        echo ${strBreak} >> ${strLogFile}
        procLogAbort 3 "'mv -f ${strFromFile} ${strToFile}' failed with status $?."
    fi
}
```

```
#-----------------------------------------------------------------------
# Remove all files named in the static variable "strFilesToProcess".
#-----------------------------------------------------------------------
procRemoveFiles ()
{
if ${bDebug} ; then
    set -x
    printf "Entering procRemoveFiles ()" >> ${strLogFile}
fi
    cd ${strWorkingDir} 1>>${strLogFile} 2>&1

    if [[ "" = "${strFilesToProcess}" ]]
    then
        procLogAbort 2 "No Files found to remove where files were expected..."
    else
        for i in ${strFilesToProcess}
        do
            rm -f ${i} 1>>${strLogFile} 2>&1
        done
    fi
}


#-----------------------------------------------------------------------
#-----------------------------------------------------------------------
procArchiveFiles ()
{
if ${bDebug} ; then
    set -x
    echo "Entering procArchiveFiles ()" >> ${strLogFile}
fi

    cd ${strWorkingDir} 1>>${strLogFile} 2>&1
    if [ ! -d archive ]; then
        echo "No archive directory found, executing 'mkdir archive'" >> ${strLogFile}
        mkdir archive 1>>${strLogFile} 2>&1
    fi

    for j in ${strFilesToProcess}
    do
        if [[ ! -f ${j} ]]; then
            procLogAbort 3 "Archive attempt on ${j} failed, file does not exist"
        fi

        echo "Archiving `ls -lF ${j}`" >> ${strLogFile}
        procMoveFile ${j} archive
    done
}


#-----------------------------------------------------------------------
# This function encrypts to the file (s) specified in the variable
# 'strFilesToProcess' to ours and our partners' public key in ASCII armor
# or BINARY format.
#-----------------------------------------------------------------------
```

```
procEncryptFiles()
{
if ${bDebug}; then
    set -x
    echo "Entering procEncryptFiles()" >> ${strLogFile}
fi
    typeset strTmp=""
    typeset -i iCnt=0

    if [[ ${strGPGFormat} = "ASCII" ]]
    then
        strExt=".asc"
        strOption="--armor"
    else    # The default is BINARY
        strExt=".gpg"
        strOption=""
    fi

    cd ${strWorkingDir} 1>>${strLogFile} 2>&1
    for j in ${strFilesToProcess}
    do
        if [ -f ${j}${strExt} ]
        then
            echo "${j}${strExt} already exists, removing..."
            rm -f ${j}${strExt}
        fi

        echo Encrypting: `ls -lF ${j}` >> ${strLogFile}
#        gpg -e -r ${strCoGPGKeyID} -r ${strOurGPGKeyID} ${strOption} ${j} 1>>${strLogFile} 2>&1
        echo "gpg -e -r ${strOurGPGKeyID} ${strOption} ${j} 1>>${strLogFile} 2>&1"
        gpg -e -r ${strOurGPGKeyID} ${strOption} ${j} 1>>${strLogFile} 2>&1
        if [[ ! -f ${j}${strExt} ]]
        then
            procLogAbort 3 "Unable to create ${strGPGFormat} GPG file ${j}${strExt}"
        fi
        echo Encryption file: `ls -lF ${j}${strExt}` >> ${strLogFile}

        iCnt=$(( ${iCnt} + 1 ))
        chmod 660 ${j}${strExt} 1>>${strLogFile} 2>&1
        strTmp="${j}${strExt} ${strTmp}"
    done

    if [[ iCnt -eq 1 ]]; then
        strCryptedFiles=${strFilesToProcess}${strExt}
    else
        strCryptedFiles=${strTmp}
    fi
}


#----------------------------------------------------------------------
# pgp -es <textfile> <Recipient KeyID> -u <your_userID> -> to sign a
#          plaintext file with your secret key and encrypt it with the
#          recipient's public key in binary format.
```

```
#------------------------------------------------------------------
procEncryptAndSign()
{
if ${bDebug}; then
    set -x
    echo "Entering procEncryptAndSign()" >> ${strLogFile}
fi
    typeset strTmp=""
    typeset -i iCnt=0

    if [[ ! -f ${strPassDir}/p.txt.gpg ]]; then
        procLogAbort 3 "Pass phrase file ${strPassDir}/p.txt.gpg not found"
    fi

    cd ${strPassDir} 1>>${strLogFile} 2>&1
    ${GPGCMD} —passphrase "thisistosavethis" —yes p.txt.gpg 1>>${strLogFile} 2>&1

    cd ${strWorkingDir} 1>>${strLogFile} 2>&1
    for j in ${strFilesToProcess}
    do
        if [ -f ${j}.gpg ]
        then
            echo "${j}.gpg already exists, removing..."
            rm -f ${j}.gpg
        fi
        echo Encrypting: `ls -lF ${j}` >> ${strLogFile}
        ${GPGCMD} —encrypt —sign —yes —passphrase-file ${strPassDir}/p.txt \
            -r ${strCoGPGKeyID} -r ${strYourGPGKeyID} ${j} 1>>${strLogFile} 2>&1
        if [[ ! -f ${j}.gpg ]]
        then
            cd ${strPassDir} 1>>${strLogFile} 2>&1
            ${GPGCMD} —yes —symmetric —passphrase "thisistosavethis" p.txt 1>>${strLogFile} 2>&1
            rm -f p.txt
            procLogAbort 3 "Unable to create GPG file ${j}.gpg"
        fi
        echo Encryption file: `ls -lF ${j}.gpg` >> ${strLogFile}

        iCnt=$(( ${iCnt} + 1 ))
        chmod 660 ${j}.gpg 1>>${strLogFile} 2>&1
        strTmp="${j}.gpg $strTmp"
    done

    cd ${strPassDir} 1>>${strLogFile} 2>&1
    ${GPGCMD} —yes —symmetric —passphrase "thisistosavethis" p.txt 1>>${strLogFile} 2>&1
    rm -f p.txt

    if [[ iCnt -eq 1 ]]; then
        strCryptedFiles=${strFilesToProcess}.gpg
    else
        strCryptedFiles=${strTmp}
    fi
}
```

```
#———————————————————————————————————————————————————
# Decrypt the Binary or ASCII GPG file.
#
# where input.txt contains:
# o passphrase (Eat my shorts)
# o an answer to the Question, "Output file 'filename' already exists,
#   overwrite (y/n)?
# o a new plaintext filename
#   or use FORCE to run PGP non-interactively.
# o When you decrypt a file that has a filename with the same name an
#   another in the directory, FORCE causes PGP to overwrite the original
#   file without prompting.
#———————————————————————————————————————————————————
procDecryptFiles()
{
if ${bDebug}; then
    set -x
    echo "Entering procDecryptFiles()" >> ${strLogFile}
fi
    strDestFile=$1
    typeset strTmp""
    typeset -i iCnt=0

    if [[ ! -f ${strPassDir}/p.txt.gpg ]]; then
        procLogAbort 3 "Pass phrase file ${strPassDir}/p.txt.gpg not found"
    fi

    cd ${strPassDir} 1>>${strLogFile} 2>&1
    ${GPGCMD} —passphrase "thisistosavethis" —yes p.txt.gpg 1>>${strLogFile} 2>&1
    cd ${strWorkingDir}
    for j in ${strFilesToProcess}
    do
        chmod 660 ${j} 1>>${strLogFile} 2>&1
        printf "Decrypting `ls -lF ${j}`" >> ${strLogFile}
        strOutFile=`echo ${j} | cut -d. -f1`      # Get the output filename

        if [[ -z ${strDestFile} ]]
        then
            ${GPGCMD} —output ${strOutFile} —decrypt —yes —passphrase-file \
                ${strPassDir}/p.txt ${j}
        fi

        if [[ ! -f ${strOutFile} ]]
        then
            cd ${strPassDir}
            ${GPGCMD} —symmetric —passphrase "thisistosavethis" —yes p.txt 1>>${strLogFile} 2>&1
            rm -f p.txt 1>>${strLogFile} 2>&1
            procLogAbort 3 "Unable to decrypt ${j}"
        fi
        iCnt=$(( ${iCnt} + 1 ))
        chmod 660 ${strOutFile} 1>>${strLogFile} 2>&1
        printf "Decrypted file at `pwd`:" >> ${strLogFile}
        ls -lF ${strOutFile} >> ${strLogFile}
```

```
            strTmp="${strOutFile} $strTmp"
        done

        cd ${strPassDir} 1>>${strLogFile} 2>&1
        ${GPGCMD} --symmetric --passphrase "thisistosavethis" --yes p.txt 1>>${strLogFile} 2>&1
        rm -f p.txt 1>>${strLogFile} 2>&1

        if [[ iCnt -eq 1 ]]; then
            strCryptedFiles=${strOutFile}
        else
            strCryptedFiles=${strTmp}
        fi
}


#===============================================================
# When retrieving files from partners' websites we have to see if there are any
# new files posted to process.
#===============================================================
procEchoNotFoundMessage ()
{
if ${bDebug}; then
    set -x
    echo "Entering procEchoNotFoundMessage" >> ${strLogFile}
fi

        echo "No files found to SSH ${strTrajectory} from ${strUser}@${strSSHAddress}." >> ${strLogFile}
        if [[ -f ${strLSofDestDirFile}.0 ]]; then
            echo "See previous log:" >> ${strLogFile}
            ls -lF ${strLSofDestDirFile}.0 >> ${strLogFile}
            echo "Which contains files '`cat ${strLSofDestDirFile}.0`'" >> ${strLogFile}
        fi
        echo "Finished processing of company ${strCompany} on `date`" >> ${strLogFile}
        exit
}


#===============================================================
# This routine is passed a string of files to 'get' or 'put' to a partner' SSH
# server.  It is assumed the code calling this procedure has processed and
# vetted the files to be transferred.  This procedure makes no decisions about
# which format these files are in or whether they should be transferred, it only
# attempts to do so to the data specified.
#
# The variables necessary to establish a connection to our partner's SSH server
# are checked to see if they have been set.  Other variables such as the
# working directory where the files to be transferred are housed are also
# checked and assumed to be set up prior to calling this procedure.
#===============================================================
procSSHFiles ()
{
if ${bDebug}; then
    set -x
    echo "Entering procSSHFiles()" >> ${strLogFile}
fi
```

```
strDestFile=$1     # Sometimes we may want to specify the name of the destination file

if [[ -z ${strFilesToProcess} ]]; then
    procEchoNotFoundMessage
else
    # Make sure the necessary SSH variables are set:
    if [[ -z ${strUser} ]]; then
        procLogAbort 3 "No SSH user ID specified for ${strCompany}"
    elif [[ -z ${strPass} ]]; then
        procLogAbort 3 "No SSH password specified for ${strCompany}"
    elif [[ -z ${strSSHAddress} ]]; then
        procLogAbort 3 "No SSH address specified for ${strCompany}"
    fi
fi

echo "Files being processed for ${strCompany} are ${strFilesToProcess}" >> ${strLogFile}

cd ${strWorkingDir}
if [[ ${strTrajectory} = "get" ]]; then
    # Use the SSH scp command to copy the files to our account
    #
    typeset -i j
    for i in ${strFilesToProcess}
    do
        (( j = j+1 ))
    done

    if [[ j -eq 1 ]]; then
    if [[ -z ${strDestFile} ]]
    then
        echo "${strTrajectory}ing file ${strFilesToProcess}" >> ${strLogFile}
        echo "From ${strUser}@${strSSHAddress}" >> ${strLogFile}
        echo "scp ${strUser}@${strSSHAddress}:${strCompany}/out/${strFilesToProcess} ." >>
${strLogFile}
        scp ${strUser}@${strSSHAddress}:${strCompany}/out/${strFilesToProcess} .
1>>${strLogFile} 2>&1

    else
        echo "${strTrajectory}ting file ${strDestFile}" >> ${strLogFile}
        echo "From ${strUser}@${strSSHAddress}" >> ${strLogFile}
        echo "scp ${strUser}@${strSSHAddress}:${strCompany}/out/${strDestFile} ${strDestFile}"
>> ${strLogFile}
        scp ${strUser}@${strSSHAddress}:${strCompany}/out/${strDestFile} ${strDestFile}
1>>${strLogFile} 2>&1
    fi

    else
        echo "${strTrajectory}ting file ${strDestFile}" >> ${strLogFile}
        echo "From ${strUser}@${strSSHAddress}" >> ${strLogFile}
        echo "scp ${strUser}@${strSSHAddress}:${strCompany}/out/* ." >>${strLogFile}
        scp ${strUser}@${strSSHAddress}:${strCompany}/out/* . 1>>${strLogFile} 2>&1
    fi
```

```
    elif [[ ${strTrajectory} = "put" ]]; then
            echo "${strTrajectory}ting file(s) ${strFilesToProcess}" >> ${strLogFile}
            echo "To ${strUser}@${strSSHAddress}" >> ${strLogFile}
            echo "scp ${strFilesToProcess} ${strUser}@${strSSHAddress}:${strSubDir}"
1>>${strLogFile} 2>&1
            scp ${strFilesToProcess} ${strUser}@${strSSHAddress}:${strSubDir} 1>>${strLogFile} 2>&1
    else
        procLogAbort 3 "Invalid trajectory specified as '${strTrajectory}' for ${strCompany}"
    fi

    cd ${strWorkingDir} 1>>${strLogFile} 2>&1
    for i in ${strFilesToProcess}
    do
        chmod 660 ${i} 1>>${strLogFile} 2>&1
        iRet=$?
        if [[ iRet -ne 0 ]]
        then # chmod failed
            if [[ ! -f ${i} ]]
            then
                procLogAbort 3 "${strWorkingDir}/${i} does not exist after 'ssh ${strTrajectory}'"
            else
                id >> ${strLogFile}
                ls -al . >> ${strLogFile}
                procLogAbort 3 "chmod 660 on ${strWorkingDir}/${i} failed."
            fi
        fi
    done
}


#==============================================================
# Get a directory listing of our partner's website.  We do this to see what,
# if any new files may have been posted on our clients SSH server.  We store
# this listing in a file to compare to a previous directory listing to see if
# there are any files we need to retrieve and process.
#==============================================================
procGetSSHLSofDest ()
{
if ${bDebug}; then
    set -x
    echo "Entering procGetSSHLSofDest()" >> ${strLogFile}
fi
    procStash ${strLSofDestDirFile}

#    strCmd=`echo "ssh ${strUser}@${strSSHAddress} ""ls ${strSubDir}"""`
#    strCmd=`echo "ssh ${strUser}@${strSSHAddress} ""find ${strSubDir} -maxdepth 1 -type f"""`
    strCmd=`echo "ssh ${strUser}@${strSSHAddress} ""ls -l ${strSubDir} | awk '{print \$9}'"""`
    echo "Executing '${strCmd}'" >> ${strLogFile}
    strFilesToProcess=`${strCmd}`

    echo ${strFilesToProcess} > ${strLSofDestDirFile}

    if [[ -z ${strFilesToProcess} ]]; then
        procEchoNotFoundMessage
```

```
    fi
}

#——————————————————————————————————————————————————————
# Call the appropriate procedure to decrypt or encrypt the file(s).
#——————————————————————————————————————————————————————
procProcessCryptFormat()
{
if ${bDebug} ; then
    set -x
    echo "Entering procProcessCryptFormat()" >> ${strLogFile}
fi
    strCrypt=$1

    case ${strCrypt} in
        encrypt)
            case ${strGPGFormat} in
                Binary)
                    procEncryptFiles
                    ;;
                BinarySigned)
                    procEncryptAndSign
                    ;;
                ASCII)
                    procEncryptFiles
                    ;;
                ASCIISigned)
                    procEncryptAndSign
                    ;;
                *)
                    procLogAbort 2 "Invalid GPG Format '${strGPGFormat}' specified..."
                    ;;
            esac
            ;;
        decrypt)
            case ${strGPGFormat} in
                Binary)
                    procDecryptFiles
                    ;;
                BinarySigned)
                    procDecryptFiles
                    ;;
                ASCII)
                    printf "${strGPGFormat} not supported for decryption." | tee -a ${strLogFile}
                    exit 0
                    ;;
                ASCIISigned)
                    printf "${strGPGFormat} not supported for decryption." | tee -a ${strLogFile}
                    exit 0
                    ;;
                *)
                    procLogAbort 2 "Invalid GPG Format '${strGPGFormat}' specified..."
                    ;;
```

```
            esac
            ;;
    *)
        procLogAbort 2 "Invalid Crypt directive '${strCrypt}' specified..."
        ;;
    esac
}


#===========================================================================
# Test Company is a make believe company that is used to test changes to this
# script.  It is an account setup on our HCU/SBO SSH server that we can connect
# to and test SSH and decryption automation.  This procedure will either download
# and decrypt files from our test company, or just decrypt files housed on our
# local SSH client in the 'strWorkingDir' directory.
#===========================================================================
procProcessTestCompanyGet ()
{
if ${bDebug}; then
    set -x
    echo "Entering procProcessTestCompanyGet ()" >> ${strLogFile}
fi

    cd ${strWorkingDir} 1>>${strLogFile} 2>&1

    if ${bPutGet}; then
        procGetSSHLSofDest
        if [[ -f ${strLSofDestDirFile}.0 ]]; then
            strFilesToProcess=`diff ${strLSofDestDirFile} ${strLSofDestDirFile}.0`
        fi
        procSSHFiles
    fi

    procArchiveFiles

    if ${bEnDeCrypt}; then # Decrypt files from partner website.
        strFilesToProcess=`find . -maxdepth 1 -type f | grep -e gpg -e asc`
        if [[ -z ${strFilesToProcess} ]]; then
            echo "No files found to decrypt at ${strWorkingDir}." >> ${strLogFile}
        fi
        echo "Company ${strCompany} files ${strFilesToProcess} will be decrypted." >> ${strLogFile}
        procProcessCryptFormat decrypt
    fi
}


#===========================================================================
# See if there are files in the working directory that need to be encrypted.
# If so, encrypt and move the original files to the archive directory for
# reference later if that becomes necessary.
#===========================================================================
procProcessTestCompanyPut ()
{
if ${bDebug}; then
    set -x
```

```
        echo "Entering procProcessTestCompanyPut()" >> ${strLogFile}
fi

    cd ${strWorkingDir} 1>>${strLogFile} 2>&1

    if ${bEnDeCrypt}; then
        if ! ${bFileSpecified}
        then
            strFilesToProcess=`find . -maxdepth 1 -type f | grep -v gpg | grep -v asc`
        fi
        if [[ -z ${strFilesToProcess} ]]; then
            procEchoNotFoundMessage
        fi
        printf "Company ${strCompany} files ${strFilesToProcess} being decrypted." >> ${strLogFile}
        procCheckFiles
        procProcessCryptFormat encrypt
        echo "Company ${strCompany} files encrypted." >> ${strLogFile}

        # Archive the orignal files that have been encrypted
        procArchiveFiles
    fi

    if ${bPutGet}; then
        # Files in 'out' directory need to be transferred to partner SSH server.
        if ! ${bFileSpecified}; then
            strFilesToProcess=`find . -maxdepth 1 -type f`
        fi
        procSSHFiles
    fi

    procRemoveFiles
}


#------------------------------------------------------------------------
# Set all company specific variables based on command line arguments.
#------------------------------------------------------------------------
procSetCompanyVars()
{
if ${bDebug}; then
    set -x
    printf "Entering procSetCompanyVars()" >> ${strLogFile}
fi

    if [[ -z ${strLogsDir} ]]; then
        strLogsDir=$HOME/logs
    fi

    if [ ! -d ${strLogsDir} ]; then
        procLogAbort 1 "Dir-> ${strLogsDir}\nDoes not exist, attempting to create."
        mkdir ${strLogsDir}
        if [[ $? -ne 0 ]]
        then
            procLogAbort 3 "Could not create:\nDir-> ${strLogsDir}."
```

```
        fi
        chmod 770 ${strLogsDir}
fi

case ${strCompany} in
    lifeinsurance)
        if ${bTestMode}
        then
            strEmailList="root@localhost"
        else
            strEmailList="admin1@domain.com, admin2@domain.com"
        fi
        strTrajectory=put
        strWorkingDir=${strPayOutDir}
        strCoGPGKeyID="0x8EEB4512"
        strUser=""
        strPass=""
        strGPGFormat="Binary"
        strSSHAddress=""
        strSubDir="."
        strLogFile="${strLogsDir}/life_${strBaseName}.log"
        strLSofDestDirFile=""
        ;;

    legalservices)
        if ${bTestMode}
        then
            strEmailList="root@localhost"
        else
            # On failure conditions send log to:
            strEmailList="admin1@domain.com, admin2@domain.com"
        fi
        strCoGPGKeyID="0x9A3291D5"
        strUser=sshlegal
        strPass="legalpass" # New password as of 10 Nov. 2005
        strSSHAddress="65.199.74.23"
        strGPGFormat="Binary"
        strSubDir="."
        case ${strTrajectory} in
            get)
                strSubDir="company"
                strWorkingDir=$HOME/legal/in
                strLogFile="${strLogsDir}/legal_get_${strBaseName}.log"
                strLSofDestDirFile="${strLogsDir}/legal_get_${strBaseName}_ls.log"
            ;;
            put)
                strWorkingDir=$HOME/legal/out
                if ${bTestMode}
                then
                    strSubDir="legaltest"
                else
                    strSubDir="mybusiness"
                fi
```

```
                    strLogFile="${strLogsDir}/legal_put_${strBaseName}.log"
                    strLSofDestDirFile=""
            ;;
            *)
                    procLogAbort 2 "Invalid Trajectory '$strTrajectory' specified..."
            ;;
        esac
        ;;

benefitservices)
        if ${bTestMode}
        then
            strEmailList="root@localhost"
            strSubDir="bentestdir"
        else
            strEmailList="admin1@domain.com,admin2@domain.com"
            strSubDir="bendir"
        fi
        strTrajectory=put
        strCoGPGKeyID="0x5EBB4182"
        strUser=sshyourcompany
        strPass="benefitpass"
        strSSHAddress="42.266.29.34"
        strGPGFormat="Binary"
        strWorkingDir=$HOME/benefits
        strLogFile="${strLogsDir}/benefits_${strBaseName}.log"
        strLSofDestDirFile="${strLogsDir}/benefits_${strBaseName}_ls.log"
        strSSHCMDFile="${strLogsDir}/benefits_${strBaseName}.ssh"
        ;;

payrollservices)
        if ${bTestMode}
        then
            strEmailList="root@localhost"
            strSubDir="paytestdir"
        else
            # Failure email list only
            strEmailList="admin1@domain.com,admin2@domain.com"
            strSubDir="paydir"
        fi
        strSSHAddress="SSH.BENEFITS.COM"  # 62.333.45.67
        strCoGPGKeyID="0x2B235675"
        strUser="payuser"
        strPass="paypass"
        strGPGFormat=Binary          # use -e to encrypt
        case ${strTrajectory} in
            get)
                    strSubDir="outgoing"
                    strWorkingDir=${strBenInDir}
                    strSSHCMDFile="${strLogsDir}/pay_get_${strBaseName}.ssh"
                    strLogFile="${strLogsDir}/pay_get_${strBaseName}.log"
                    strLSofDestDirFile="${strLogsDir}/pay_get_${strBaseName}_ls.log"
                    ;;
```

```
        put)
            if ${bTestMode}
            then
                strSubDir="incoming/mytest"
            else
                strSubDir="incoming"
            fi
            strWorkingDir=${strBenOutDir}
            strSSHCMDFile="${strLogsDir}/pay_put_${strBaseName}.ssh"
            strLogFile="${strLogsDir}/pay_put_${strBaseName}.log"
            strLSofDestDirFile=""
            ;;
        *)
            procLogAbort 2 "Invalid Trajectory '$strTrajectory' specified..."
        ;;
    esac
    ;;

localsshserver)
    if ${bTestMode}
    then
        strEmailList="root@localhost"
    else
        strEmailList="admin1@domain.com, admin2@domain.com"
    fi
    strCoGPGKeyID="0xE403569A"
    strSSHAddress="xxx"
    strUser=sshuser
    strPass=sshpass
    strWorkingDir=$HOME/ssh/in
    if [[ -z ${strGPGFormat} ]]; then
        strGPGFormat=Binary
    fi # Can be specified on command line
    strSubDir="."
    strLogFile="${strLogsDir}/ssh_get_${strBaseName}.log"
    strLSofDestDirFile="${strLogsDir}/ssh_get_${strBaseName}_ls.log"
    strSSHCMDFile="${strLogsDir}/ssh_get_${strBaseName}.ssh"
    strSSHLSFile="${strLogsDir}/ssh_get_${strBaseName}_ls.ssh"
    ;;

testcompany)
    strCoGPGKeyID="0x11C12F2E"   # Test Company public key
    strSSHAddress=thecaptainslatest.dyndns.org
    if [[ -z ${strGPGFormat} ]]; then
        strGPGFormat=Binary
    fi # Can be specified on command line
    strUser=testuser
    strPass=nopass        # Key validation only

    case ${strTrajectory} in
        get)
            strWorkingDir=${HOME}/ssh/in
            strSubDir="testcompany/out"
```

```
                        strLogFile="${strLogsDir}/ssh_get_${strBaseName}.log"
                        strLSofDestDirFile="${strLogsDir}/ssh_get_${strBaseName}_ls.log"
                        ;;
                put)
                        strWorkingDir=${HOME}/ssh/out
                        strSubDir="testcompany/in"      # Partner subdirectory
                        strLogFile="${strLogsDir}/ssh_put_${strBaseName}.log"
                        strLSofDestDirFile=""
                        ;;
                *)
                        procLogAbort 2 "Invalid Trajectory '$strTrajectory' specified..."
                ;;
            esac
            ;;

        *)
            Usage
            procLogAbort 2 "Invalid company name '${strCompany}' specified..."
            ;;
    esac

    if [ ! -d ${strLogsDir} ]; then
        procLogAbort 1 "Dir-> ${strLogsDir}\nDoes not exist, attempting to create."
        mkdir -p ${strLogsDir}
        if [[ $? -ne 0 ]]; then
            procLogAbort 3 "Could not create:\nDir-> ${strLogsDir}."
        fi
        chmod 770 ${strLogsDir}
    fi

    if [[ ! -d ${strWorkingDir} ]]; then
        procLogAbort 1 "Dir-> ${strWorkingDir}\nDoes not exist, attempting to create."
        mkdir -p ${strWorkingDir} 1>>${strLogFile} 2>&1
        if [[ $? -ne 0 ]]; then
            procLogAbort 3 "Could not create:\nDir-> ${strWorkingDir}."
        fi
        chmod 770 ${strWorkingDir} 1>>${strLogFile} 2>&1
    fi

    if [ ! -d ${strWorkingDir}/archive ]; then
        procLogAbort 1 "Dir-> ${strWorkingDir}/archive\nDoes not exist, attempting to create."
        mkdir ${strWorkingDir}/archive 1>>${strLogFile} 2>&1
        chmod 770 ${strWorkingDir}/archive
    fi
}


#==============================================================================
# MAIN PROGRAM:
# - Perform initial error checking
# - Setup company specific variables
# - Initialize log file
# - Determine process to perform on company being processed
#==============================================================================
```

```
#
# Check to see if number of parameters is correct... may be needed in
# future.
#
if [ "$#" -eq 0 ]
then
    Usage
    procLogAbort 2 "No Argument specified..."
fi


procSetCompanyVars

# It is assumed that files you are receiving from customers is known and
# should not be altered.
if [[ ${strTrajectory} = "get" ]]
then
    if ${bFileSpecified}
    then
        procLogAbort 2 "All file gets cannot have the files to be processed overridden."
    fi
fi

#procStash ${strLogFile}      # Stash the previous log and initialize a new log
if [[ -f ${strLogFile} ]]; then
    rm ${strLogFile}
fi
echo "Started processing of company ${strCompany} on `date`" > ${strLogFile}
procLogVars

case ${strCompany} in
    lifeinsurance)
        case ${strTrajectory} in
            get)
                procProcessLifeGet
            ;;
            put)
                procProcessLifePut
            ;;
            *)
                procLogAbort 2 "Invalid Trajectory '${strTrajectory}' specified..."
            ;;
        esac
        ;;
    legalservices)
        case ${strTrajectory} in
            get)
                procProcessBNYGet
            ;;
            put)
                procProcessBNYPut
            ;;
            *)
                procLogAbort 2 "Invalid Trajectory '${strTrajectory}' specified..."
```

```
                ;;
        esac
        ;;
    benefitservices)
        procProcessBenefitPut
        ;;
    payrollservices)
        procPayrollPut
        ;;
    localsshserver)
        case ${strTrajectory} in
            get)
                procProcessLocalGet
            ;;
            put)
                procProcessLocalPut
            ;;
            *)
                procLogAbort 2 "Invalid Trajectory '${strTrajectory}' specified..."
            ;;
        esac
        ;;
    testcompany)

        case ${strTrajectory} in
            get)
                procProcessTestCompanyGet
            ;;
            put)
                procProcessTestCompanyPut
            ;;
            *)
                procLogAbort 2 "Invalid Trajectory '${strTrajectory}' specified..."
            ;;
        esac
        ;;
    *)
        Usage
        procLogAbort 2 "Invalid company '${strCompany}' specified..."
esac

echo "Finished processing of Company ${strCompany} on `date`" >> ${strLogFile}
```

Encrypting Emails Before Sending Them over the Infected Internet – Don't Expose Your Correspondence to Crackers Everywhere

If you do not understand how email works, your transmission of an email bounces from Mail Transfer Agent (MTA) to MTA server until it reaches its final destination. An MTA is simply a computer server maintained by someone that relays your unencrypted email, which may be intercepted and read, manipulated, and/or exploited. Any documents attached may also receive the same treatment. This is similar to a "Man-in-the middle" attack. From, https://en.wikipedia.org/wiki/Email, "*Email privacy, without some security precautions, can be compromised because:*

- *Email messages are generally not encrypted.*
- *Email messages have to go through intermediate computers before reaching their destination, meaning it is relatively easy for others to intercept and read messages.*
- *Many Internet Service Providers (ISP) store copies of email messages on their mail servers before they are delivered. The backups of these can remain for up to several months on their server, despite deletion from the mailbox.*
- *The "Received:" fields and other information in the email can often identify the sender, preventing anonymous communication.*"... and from other sources:
- Hackers have stolen the login credentials from many Internet users and can access their email anytime.
- Leaked classified documents show that that NSA has direct access to encrypted emails stored on various U.S. Corporations servers, which they deny. The NSA also makes copies of those emails on their own servers for years of reference.
- The NSA has obtained direct access to the systems of Microsoft, Google, Facebook, Apple, Yahoo, AOL, YouTube, Skype and PalTalk, as well as other U.S. giants, which they also deny.

(See: http://en.wikipedia.org/wiki/Man-in-the-middle_attack, http://www.theguardian.com/world/2013/jun/06/us-tech-giants-nsa-data, http://news.softpedia.com/news/Microsoft-Offered-the-NSA-Direct-Access-to-Outlook-com-Skype-SkyDrive-Accounts-Report-367531.shtml)

You must encrypt or password-protect any email sent over the Internet, **PERIOD**. Think about it, would you put a letter in your post office mailbox without an envelope? Crackers scan and record unencrypted email, text messages, and attachments for things such as passwords and usernames. Crackers will steal this information and use it for their own gain. Corporations and governments will record this information for years, which may come back to haunt you. If you want to send a file, please get help from a friend or neighbor on how to, at the very least, password-protect or encrypt that file. These precautions are the bare minimum of protection that you should use for sending data on our infected Internet.

Every email you send unencrypted goes through multiple MTAs and are read going into and out of those servers. Crackers, your ISP, everyone will make a copy of your email message and your attachments on their server's hard drives. Some will go through everything that passed through their servers looking for things of value like usernames, passwords and things in attachments. They also collect email addresses and sell them to spammers everywhere. People everywhere send email unencrypted with valuable information that crackers, governments and others exploit. Assume that every email you sent unencrypted HAS BEEN READ by someone else and examined for exploitation.

So the answer is NEVER, EVER send anything of value in an unencrypted email! The traditional method of sending encrypted email requires that the person you're sending the email to, have everything set up to receive an encrypted email. This requires an exchange of public keys with the person to whom you are sending that encrypted email. You both will have to develop the skills necessary to generate, exchange keys, encrypt and decrypt your correspondence. This is not very complex, and with a few simple directions, you can make this happen, which we will soon cover.

- You want to send a friend an encrypted email. To do so you have to generate a public/private key pair and send your public key to your friend. You then have to instruct your friend on how to generate a public/private key pair and have them send you their public key.
- Once these keys have been exchanged, and in order to exchange encrypted messages, you both have to encrypt your data to your public keys, preferably using both at the same time so you can both decrypt the received and sent messages.

The above process is not complex, and you may have some business partners who resist learning how to do this. For example, I have tried to get friends and family to encrypt email and found little interest from them in learning how to do so. I have to be very careful with any correspondence with them as a result. However, if you are an SBO, you should not do business with a partner that will not learn how to encrypt their correspondence.

Encrypting Email with Outlook and Encipher.it

Outlook encryption is key-based encryption. The email account user has to generate a digital certificate and exchange that certificate via a digitally signed email message with the Outlook user whom they wish to correspond with and vice versa. The certificates are then used to automatically encrypt and decrypt email correspondence between the two recipients. To set this up, open Outlook and read http://office.microsoft.com/en-us/outlook-help/get-a-digital-id-HP010355070.aspx. Be careful using this form of email encryption, as there is abundant evidence that the NSA has backdoors in most U.S. corporate encrypted email.

Then in Outlook when sending an encrypted email click on Options > More Options > Security Settings > check the box Encrypt message contents and attachments.

Encipher.it boldly states they will protect your email from being read by hackers, eavesdroppers, NSA, your employer or your with. Their privacy policy is outstanding and says *"Any personal information received will only be used to fill your order. We will not sell or redistribute your information to anyone."* Encipher.it uses JavaScript in your browser to encrypt your message so no data leaves your browser in plain text protecting it from packet sniffing software.

Encipher.it is a website that will allow you to encrypt text to a password and send that encrypted message in an email. From their website to use their encryption:
1) Add a bookmark in Firefox or Google Chrome:

- Drag this link: https://encipher.it to your Bookmarks Bar

Internet Explorer:

- Right click: Encipher It and click on "Add to Favorites"

2) Encrypt the message

- Login to Google Mail, Facebook, or another site where you want to protect the text.
- Type your message and click the bookmark.
- Enter the password and click the "Encrypt" button.

3) Decrypt the message

- To decrypt the message on the page, just click bookmark again and reenter the same password.

What https://encipher.it does is encrypt your message to a password that you can send, phone, or text to the person to whom you send your email message to. The recipient of the message will have to visit the Encipher.it website or add the bookmark to be able to decrypt your message. According to an article written by Alex Wawro from PCWorld titled "https://encipher.it Encrypts Email for Free", July 2012, *"The bookmarklet runs all code locally on your PC, so there's no danger of Encipher.it staff or someone else listening in as you transmit messages to a server for encryption/decryption. The Encipher add-on will apply a 256-bit Advanced Encryption Standard (AES) algorithm, https://en.wikipedia.org/wiki/Advanced_Encryption_Standard that runs in real time; 256-bit encryption is the same kind of data protection that the websites of many banks and government services employ."*

To encrypt your email using a browser simply type the message in your text editor or word processor and paste it on the website to encrypt it. *Surf to https://encipher.it and copy your message to the clipboard > in the Type the message here to encrypt it box paste or type in your message > click on the Encipher It button and next to Encryption Password enter your encryption password > you can then click on Send to Gmail or Copy button to send it to another email service provider > when your recipient gets your message if they are using a web browser to view their email they can use the Encipher-it plug-in to decrypt it using the password you provide them > if they are using a local email server visit the website and cut and paste the message > click on the Encipher It link > then enter the password that you provided them to decrypt the message.*

To encrypt you email in Linux surf to and click on Download > choose the Linux button and download the encipher_2.3_amd64.deb file to your Downloads directory > become root and type the following on the command line in Debian Linux flavors:

```
# cd ~suroot/Downloads
# dpkg -i encipher_2.3_i386.deb
# dpkg -i encipher_2.3_amd64.deb
```

```
# apt-get update  &&  apt-get upgrade -y
```

To make all this work for any browser visit the https://encipher.it/email-encryption#install web page and **under _Bookmarklets_ on the left next to _Drag this link:_, drag the _Encipher It_ link to the _Bookmarks Bar_ in Firefox or Google Chome**. For Internet Explorer right click on the link and click Add to Favorites. Type in your message to your browser email and click on the Encipher It bookmark and a dialog box will appear asking you to Enter encryption key which is the passphrase you will need to provide to your message recipient.

Use Multiple Email Addresses for Your Correspondence

Don't allow advertising to brainwash you into believing that Google, Microsoft, ISPs and other big corporations that record every email you send and share with them and the NSA are your only choices for email. The truth is if you look around you can find FREE email providers that actually want to protect your privacy. We should use these services to safeguard all of the various facets of our lives online. We can use them to set up separate email addresses for all of the things we do in life. For years I have maintained a few different email addresses that I have used for various things. I have a Microsoft Hotmail address, which I have used since the Internet was born, which I log into, that allows all of the big spamming corporations and crackers to sell this email address and spam it constantly (I hope that spam costs Microsoft, crackers and the NSA many thousands in storage on their servers). Of course, as a U.S. citizen, these are my taxpayer dollars. My ancient Hotmail email address gets upward of 50 to 200 spam emails a day. Since we all now know that these U.S. corporations share everything we do on the Internet, I think we should record our Microsoft and Google Email address everywhere and allow everyone to spam and record everything we do, thus littering their servers with things we care nothing about. This is a definitive way that we can all fight back against this invasion into our privacy.

Something else for you to consider is when you use the email services from the major ISP providers, they keep all of your email for years, and in the USA, the NSA has been storing your Internet activity since 2001. U.S. citizens are just now coming to know these facts and are complacently going along with this mass monitoring of their Internet activity by corporations and their government, which I find astonishing. Additionally, their ISPs scan their emails to create profiles of their individual lives. This information is then freely available to anyone who wants to buy it. (E.g. An inflammatory email written 10 years ago can be used to investigate anyone communicating with a U.S. citizen, deny you or them of insurance, or even a job). This level of scrutiny does not seem to register with the average U.S. citizen as to how adversely it could affect their everyday lives. Nevertheless, there is little outcry from U.S. citizens about this invasion into their privacy, something generations of soldiers and myself fought to prevent.

Let's develop separate sets of email accounts, one for shopping logins, another for banking and investing, and at least a third for other things such as your social media accounts. A fourth could be used to develop a set of very private accounts only shared between a few trusted sources:

1. You want a very public email address that all the spammers, your ISP and government know about. Register this email address at every shopping or government site you use, and give this email address to friends and relatives that also send spam. For example, register with CDW, Domino's Pizza, Dell, Federal Student Aid, Linux Professional Institute, Pizzahut, Best Buy, NewEgg, GM, GroupGolfer, GolfNow, Honda, LastMinuteGolf, Logitech, RedHat, REI, Soaring Eagle Casino, TigerDirect, Travelocity, USGS Store, VMware, Walmart, etc.. Visit it every so often to flush it out and make it look like this is your very active primary email account. Never tie this email address to an HC/SB domain/website or blog for logins, never use or register this email account at any financial institution you do business with.

2. Create a job search or SBO email address and try to keep it as private as possible. Unfortunately, as you put it up on LinkedIn and post on job search websites, it will become a spam haven also. You also have to provide this email address on applications, resumes, business cards and employer websites who will spread your job search email address to third parties. Nevertheless, to exist in today's information-sharing world you have to allow this email address to be compromised. It goes without saying, use this email address as professionally as possible, never conduct personal or clandestine matters, never communicate with friends and family using this email address, and never register or use it with a financial institution.

3. There are people we trust in life for whom we should maintain a separate email address for unencrypted and/or encrypted email. This would be our very private email address that we only hand out to a few select individuals. The "Hide My Ass" and "Anonymouse" services, discussed in Chapter 8, offer free anonymous email accounts. There are also other notable, somewhat free email services with good privacy protections, which include Hushmail, Silentcircle and Unspyable. For example, Hushmail will give you a free email account, but you cannot configure an email client such as Thunderbird, and you must log in every three weeks to keep the account. POP & IMAP are available only to Hushmail Premium customers with Desktop Access and Hushmail Business with Desktop Access subscribers. (See: https://countermail.com, https://www.hushmail.com, https://riseup.net, https://silentcircle.com, http://unspyable.com, https://help.hushmail.com/entries/243624-thunderbird-3-imap)

4.

| **WARNING** | Hushmail promises "end-to-end" encryption, which means their keys can be used to decrypt your email. Refer forward to how Lavabit was shutdown as the U.S. government requested their private keys. True end-to-end encryption means that the service provider cannot look at your communications even if they wanted to. Riseup requests that you have cookies enabled, which is suspicious, so you have to question their email service as well. |
| ATTENTION ! ON VOUS ÉCOUTE OPGEPAST ! ZWIJGEN | |

5. Maintain a separate email account for financial matters that you check on often. This is the email account that we use to login at our credit unions, banks, legal firms, PayPal, investment firms and shopping sites that you allow to maintain financial data such as a registered credit card. There are two trains of thought on this account. You may want it as public as possible using Gmail, Outlook or Yahoo so that if your identity is stolen there are records of correspondence with your financial institutions that are kept by your ISP, email provider and the NSA, or perhaps you want a private email service such

as Hushmail to keep your financial correspondence as private as possible between you and your financial institutions. Realize that any email correspondence with your financial institutions is only private on your side of the fence and that your financial institution may keep your correspondence for their records.

6. You may want an encrypted email address that you can use to correspond with your business partners or people of like mind that feel your correspondence need not be read by everyone on the Internet. This might be one of the email addresses above, but I have found it easier to have a separate email address for encrypted email. You can also use this email account for your website/domain and blog, and perhaps social media sites if they are used for business purposes. For example, some Twitter handles have monetary value and have huge numbers of followers. Never use this email as a login to a financial institution or for unencrypted email.

7. You can also create a disposable email address at http://maildrop.cc. MailDrop offers up a quick disposable email address so that you can register at websites you want to access that want your personal information. There is no privacy protection using MailDrop, as anyone can read anything you send or receive, but sometimes that is not a concern. MailBox is by design a layer of obfuscation to using your real email addresses that get spammed constantly. While your email is stored for posterity and government viewing in a MailDrop, your Internet activity is not tracked by MailDrop. MailDrop is just another tool in your privacy arsenal to consider.

Historical Reference – Once upon a time there was Lavabit to protect the privacy of U.S. Internet users

Please visit http://lavabit.com, which was a private email service run by Ladar Levison, Owner and Operator of Lavabit, LLC. It now hosts his testimony as to how invasive the U.S. government surveillance system has become. His company was forced out of business by the U.S. government as the FBI relentlessly pursued Edward Snowden. Edward hosted his email account with Lavabit, and Lavabit was subsequently served with a U.S. national security letter in which the FBI demands information about a user, but the email service provider was prohibited to tell his users or anyone else about this request. Ladar tried to resist this and sent five, 2,560-character SSL encryption keys on an 11-page printout in what was more or less, an illegible 4-point type. To decrypt Snowden's emails, someone at the FBI would have had to type every character perfectly. However, a U.S. court ordered a $5,000-a-day fine on Lavabit LLC, and on Aug 7, 2013, Ladar handed over the digital copies of the keys. Ladar shutdown his business with a letter stating "*This experience has taught me one very important lesson: without congressional action or a strong judicial precedent, I would _strongly_ recommend against anyone trusting their private data to a company with physical ties to the United States.*" Among other things, I encourage you to read his full statement. Ladar was later found in contempt of court for resisting turning over his Secure Socket Layer key that was used to encrypt communications for his 400,000 users. This key would have allowed the U.S. government to access the communications of all of Lavabit's users, something that the U.S. Fourth Amendment used to protect.

After the U.S. government released Ladar Levison from a criminal sentence for silence order, he explained to his very angry email service users exactly why he had suddenly shutdown access to all of his Internet email users without allowing them to backup their email. If he had warned them that he was shutting down his email service, the U.S. Government had the right by their new invasive laws, to demand that he keep the site up and running while the U.S. government, who now had the encryption keys, could/would monitor/compromise all of their communications for all time. He could not, in good conscience, allow that to happen.

He has endured a lot of criticism and anger about this decision, but he said he would bring the site back up if the U.S. government ever allowed him to generate a new set of uncompromised keys that he does not have to share. I admire his stand, and I hope others will follow his example. However, that is not the trend that other U.S. companies are following. The data leaked by Edward Snowden indicates that the NSA is maintaining a database of encryption keys used by many online providers who say they secure your data. These keys are obtained via court orders, buying the keys with taxpayer dollars, or by hacking into corporate networks and servers. Once the NSA has these keys they can easily monitor all Internet traffic flowing to and from these corporations.

Ladar later appealed and lost this ruling so just try to fathom how far the U.S. government is willing to go to invade their citizens' privacy with this type of behavior. Who wants to do business with a country willing to take such extreme measures? On May 4, 2014, Ladar released a final statement which sums up how secretive and heavy handed the U.S. government has become to invade their citizens' privacy. I think that any business respecting privacy and Internet freedom will have to move to move their facilities to legal jurisdictions, such as Germany, that provide much better protections for privacy and security. If you visit http://lavabit.com you can read Mr. Larders final salvo in his cry for the American people to wake up and fight for their freedom. Below are a few paragraphs of what he had to say.

"*When the judge granted the contempt charge unopposed – ignoring my attorney's request to dispute the government's claims – he created a loophole. I was never given an opportunity to object, let alone provide a meaningful defense. An important point, since the contempt charge endorsed new legal claims – reversing what the court had previously indicated. Without an objection on the record, the appellate court would rule that my right to an appeal had been waived – since the charges hadn't been disputed in district court. Given the Supreme Court's tradition of declining to review cases decided on procedural grounds, I will likely be denied justice, forever.*

The most important question raised by my appeal was what constitutes a "search," i.e., whether law enforcement may demand the encryption keys of a business and use those keys to inspect the private communications of every customer, when they are only authorized to access information belonging to a select few.

The problem here is technological: until a communication has been decrypted and the contents parsed, it is impossible for a surveillance device to determine which network connections belong to the targeted accounts. The government argued that since the "inspection" would be carried out by a machine, they were exempt from the normal search-and-seizure protections of the fourth amendment.

More importantly, the prosecution argued the exemption was because my users had no expectation of privacy, even though the encryption they were trying to break was created specifically to ensure a users' privacy.

If my experience serves any purpose, it is to illustrate what most already know: our courts must not be allowed to consider matters of great importance in secret, lest we find ourselves summarily deprived of meaningful due process. If we allow our government to continue operating in secret, it is only a matter of time before you or a loved one find yourself in a position like I was – standing in a secret courtroom, alone, and without any of the unalienable rights that are supposed to protect us from an abuse of the state's authority.

Sincerely,
Ladar Levison
Owner and Operator, Lavabit LLC"

My advice is, if you want to try to keep your email somewhat private on the Internet, make sure you are dealing with a non-U.S. email service provider that I present in this book later, or encrypt your email yourself, which we will soon cover. You can use Microsoft, Google, Yahoo and others as your public email addresses, which we all now know freely provide information to the U.S. and British governments, or you can try Countermail, HushMail, Silentcircle, RiseUp and Unspyable for your more private correspondence. However, remember that email sent unencrypted is subject to observation by everyone connected to the Internet. However, the listed services above have greater privacy protection than the large U.S. corporations and ISPs. However, if you are a reader of forums and in tune with the IT buzz, many people suggest that the only true method of secure communication is to set up a GPG key exchange and encrypt email to you and your partner's public and private keys.

Windows 7 -- Using Gpg4win and Claws to Encrypt Emails & Files

As you now know, any email sent via any major email provider is screened automatically by intelligence services. Most people in the U.S. I have met say "so what, let them screen me because I have nothing to hide". This is because they and their ancestors never experienced the Stasi excesses during Communist rule. A common joke in Germany is "Why, despite all the shortages, is toilet paper in eastern Germany two-ply? Because they have to send a copy of everything they do to Russia." German courts are blocking the implementation of the EU Data Retention Directive, and they have ruled against Google's data gathering practices. As German Chancellor Angela Merkel stated "*These two values – freedom and security – to a certain extent are and always have been at odds with one another. The proper balance needs to be struck again and again by means of the law. The end does not justify the means. Not everything that is technically possible should also be permissible.*" Western citizens in the U.S. do not understand how violations in their privacy can be exploited or how providing this information can come back to haunt them.

Gpg4win is Windows encryption software supported by the German Federal Office for Information Security (BSI). Because of the expressed German outrage over the NSA scandal, we can have a high degree of certainty that there are no U.S. backdoors built into this open source software. However, the source code is freely available, and you can rest assured it has been studied and perhaps broken by some very smart NSA folks. Gpg4win is actually a suite of encryption utilities bundled together that will be installed on your Windows computer. From the Gpg4win website those utilities are:

- GnuPG - The core; this is the actual encryption tool.

- Kleopatra - A certificate manager for OpenPGP and X.509 (S/MIME) and common crypto dialogs. (See: http://docs.kde.org/stable/en/kdepim/kleopatra/kleopatra.pdf)
- GPA - An alternative certificate manager for OpenPGP and X.509 (S/MIME).
- GpGOL - A plugin for Microsoft Outlook 2003/2007/2010/2013 (email encryption).
- GpgEX - A plugin for Microsoft Explorer (file encryption).
- Claws Mail - A complete email application with crypto support.
- Gpg4win Compendium - The documentation (for beginner and advanced users), available in English and German.

The Gpg4win Compendium documentation is an excellent reference for learning about their software, how email message encryption works and much more. Their encryption software is designed to integrate well with Microsoft Outlook using their GpGOL plugin. However, using other email clients is a bit more difficult, but easily mastered. Since many of you are probably not using Outlook, I decided to only present a simple solution using the Gpg4win Claws Mail client. Rather than repeat what is in Gpg4win's documentation, the following example is intended as a quick step-by-step guide to get you started. I chose to present only OpenPGP message encryption in Gpg4win because by using this method you can practice generating key pairs exchanging your public key with Gpg4win's automated practice server. I have found that many people are intimidated by this technology, and having a tool where you can practice without repercussions should make things fun and easy. For example, posting a public key on a public key server or saying something incorrect on technical forum can invite some hostile criticism and attacks from knowledgeable computer professionals. I highly encourage you to read Gpg4win manual at http://www.gpg4win.org/doc/en/gpg4win-compendium.html, which details everything you need to know about encrypting messages, files, setting up certificates and much more. If you are a SBO you will need to study and pay close attention to the certificates portions of the manual. Setting up, registering and using certificates is a somewhat complex topic that I chose not to cover in this book. It is important to an SBO, but has little or no significance to an HCU. (See: https://en.wikipedia.org/wiki/Gpg4win)

As previously discussed about encrypting files, and as you will learn about in detail in Chapter 9, using the digital communication encryption technology SSH, encrypting messages is very similar. Once you master any one of these technologies you know how they all work. The only problem is getting your business partners, friends, relatives and anyone else that we communicate with to take a few minutes and learn about them as well. As you will see, setting up your computer to encrypt messages is easy and hopefully fun for you. It is certainly important to your privacy and worth a few minutes of your time.

Just like you have a key or digital code to gain entry to your house or business, we have to create a key pair to encrypt the email messages that we will send and receive to/from our partners. As we discussed previously, while encrypting files, one of the keys in that pair is a public key that we will provide to our partners with whom we want to exchange encrypted messages. We will backup the private key that we generate and will never share or allow it to be compromised. In other words, it should never be housed on a computer or virtual machine that you use to surf the Internet or read questionable email. To get started using Gpg4win *click on **Start** > **All Programs** > **Gpg4win** > select **Kleopatra** which we will now use to generate our key pair > click on the **File** menu upper left > select **New Certificate...** > choose **Create a personal OpenPGP key pair** > under **Enter Details** enter a bogus **Name:***

John Doe, for *Email:* a valid email address that you created earlier for spam, and next to *Comment: Test* , *Next* > review what you entered and click on the *Create Key* button > enter a simple Passphrase (we are just practicing), re-enter your passphrase, *OK* > type in your random keyboard information and the *Key Pair Successfully Created* screen will appear along with your public keys Fingerprint > cut and paste your Fingerprint text file and store it the same directory where you plan to backup your key pair > click on *Make a Backup Of Your Key Pair...* and save both a GPG binary copy and a ASC copy of your keys in the Fingerprint directory naming them after the email address you used, *Finish* > this is a good time to generate a public key certificate that we will exchange with the Adele email robot to practice correspondence. Select your certificate and click on the *File* menu > select *Export certificates...* and save your public key to the directory you want, save it in both the binary (.gpg) and ASCII (.asc) forms. The directory I chose to use for all of these files was on my backup USB drive because I have multiple computers from which I use to send encrypted email. Your OneDrive is also a good candidate for your public key so you can share it among your Internet devices. Since you will exchange these files with associates you want to share encrypted email with, consider naming you public key file after your public key's Fingerprint. This will emphasize to your partners how much they need to call and verify the fingerprint of your public key, which you will find they often ignore.

We have now generated and backed up our key pair. Now we have to configure Claws Mail to send and receive email. You can skip this step if you have Outlook or want to use another email client. For example, we will soon cover how to do this in Thunderbird, which is an alternative and perhaps superior email client to using Claws. To set up any email client you will need information from your email service provider, which you should have recorded when you originally setup your email account. I keep all this information in my Keepass Password Safe database, which we will talk about later. *Click on Start > All Programs > Gpg4win > Claws Mail and the Welcome to Claws Mail wizard will appear, Forward > enter Your name:, Your email address:, and Your organization: (e.g. That Cyber Security Guy), Forward > you have to be careful on the Receiving mail dialog as the default Server type: POP3 is presented.* Most email services will support POP3, which will download and delete all email from your email service provider. Try changing this setting to IMAP, as most email services such as Gmail or Outlook support leaving email on their servers. If your setup using IMAP does not work, change the setting to POP3, which works with older ISPs that do not support IMAP. *Enter your Server address:, Username: and Password:, Forward > on the Sending mail dialog enter your outgoing SMTP server address:, Forward > on Configuration finished, Save.* We are now ready to exchange public keys with the Gpg4win server robot and learn how to encrypt and decrypt email.

The Gpg4win project provides Adele, who is a very nice email robot with which you can set up and practice encrypted email correspondence. We must do this so that we don't embarrass ourselves trying to exchange keys with our partners or putting pubic keys on key servers before we know what we are doing. The Adele robot provides us the means to practice setting up and using email encryption technology. To set up an encrypted exchange of email or files, we have to exchange keys with our partners, or in this case, the Adele robot. Startup whichever email program you are using and in the subject type: "My Public OpenPGP Certificate" and either cut and paste your ASCII key in the email text body, or use the easier solution and just attach the <file>.gpg binary version of your public key that you generated.

Send this email to adele@gnupp.de from which you should receive a return email from Adele that will have Adele's public key, which you will have to process using Kleopatra.

The Adele robot will return its public key, which you should save to the same directory from which you exported and stored information about your generated key. Name the file something like AdelePublicKey.asc. You can now import the public key returned by Adele by cutting and pasting your email or from the file that we just created, and associate it with the adele@gnupp.de email address. The Gpg4win manual section titled "Importing a public certificate" describes in detail how to do this. ***Save Adele's public key to the file AdelePublicKey.asc > in Kleopatra click the Import Certificates... button upper left > navigate to the file containing the public key and select it, Open > the Detailed results of importing C:\...\AdelePublicKey.asc dialog should confirm that the certificate was processed and imported.*** The text you want to cut and paste into the file is the following:

```
-----BEGIN PGP PUBLIC KEY BLOCK-----
Version: GnuPG v1.4.10 (GNU/Linux)
All text down to the following...
-----END PGP PUBLIC KEY BLOCK-----
```

In the public key message returned by Adele, there is a message in German that when translated to English using http://translate.google.com states:

```
This is more than is normally the case for testing. Since can email addresses easily
fake and I by a stranger an excessive number of emails will bother, I would like to
take this opportunity make sure the address is correct. To make this confirm, please
send me a reply that the string `AD-DYZELXHIPLFEAXXA ' in the subject line contains.
In a normal response to this email, this should automatically happen.

ATTENTION! As long as I do not receive this confirmation, will NO I send more emails
to the specified address. As soon as I get the confirmation, you can think continue
to use service. More confirmations are then every 25 emails due.
```

While this translation is not perfect, we get the gist that after you get Adele's public key response you must reply with the string above in your email subject line before you can begin exchanging encrypted email with the Adele robot. If you do not do this, you will get a response from adele-abuse@gnupp.de stating:

```
The following email is rejected because the correctness of the address given has not
been confirmed yet.
```

The Gpg4win manual describes in detail how to encrypt your email in Outlook using their GpgOL utility. It is as simple as selecting ***Extras > Encrypt message*** in the menu of the message window. The lock button will appear stating encrypt message with GnuPG and then all you have to do is send the message. Gpg4win will automatically detect the OpenPGP protocol and the public key of your partner that you imported to Kleopatra.

To do this using Claws, Thunderbird or some other email client is somewhat more complex since we don't have the GpgOL utility to automate this task for us. In Claws, the first step is to load the PGP/Core, PGP/Inline and PGP/MIME plugins. The PGP/Core plugin provides the core components of the Claws Mail PGP system. The PGP/MIME plugin allows you to send encrypted messages as attachments and the PGP/Inline handles signed and/or encrypted email. *Click on the **Configuration** menu > at the bottom select **Plugins...** > in the **Plugins** dialog click on the **Load...** button > select **pgpcore.dll**, **Open** > Load... select **pgpinline.dll**, **Open** > **Load...** select **pgpmime.dll**, **Open** > **Close**.* Once the needed plugins are loaded we can now use the Configuration menu to setup our encryption preferences. *Click on **Configuration** > arrow down to select **Preferences...** > and decide which options you may want, such as checking **Automatically check signatures**.*

We are now ready to send an encrypted message to adele@gnupp.de by *clicking on the* **Options** *menu > arrow down to select* **Privacy System** *and select the encryption method you plan to use:*

- *None: Use no encryption*
- *PGP Inline: Encrypt your message inline*
- *PGP MIMI: Encrypt your message and add it as an attachment*

*Click on the **Options** menu again > arrow down to select **Encrypt** and consider also selecting **Sign** if you have certified/verified the public key in Kleopatra > click on **Send** to encrypt and send the message to the public key of your choosing, if you have more than one > you may see an Encryption warning dialog warning you that attachments and headers are not encrypted, **Continue** > enter your passphrase and the encrypted message will be sent.* To make sure everything worked *click on the **Get Mail** button upper left > select the Claws **Sent** folder and you should see a key next to the encrypted email that you just sent > view the message by double clicking on it, and only for the first time will you have to enter your passphrase.* This proves that the message was encrypted without having to call or experiment upon one of your partners. Adele will respond with an automatic unencrypted email showing that they received and decrypted your email. To prove that Adele received and decrypted your email, send them a decrypted email and look at the reply. It will just contain their encrypted pubic key showing that their automated server did not understand your unencrypted message.

Once you have practiced these steps and are confident in their use, you need to change your digital life and commit to using email message encryption technology. *When you generate your certificate for real using Kleopatra, click on **File** > **New Certificate...** > on the **Choose Certificate Format** dialog, click on **Create a personal OpenPGP key pair**, **Next** > on the **Enter Details** screen, click on the **Advanced Setting...** button lower right and under **Key Material** increase the RSA key length to 4096, which is the MAX currently offered by Kleopatra > check the **Authentication** box so that you can include the user IDs of other certificate holders who have confirmed the authenticity of your certificate, **OK** > Enter your **Name:**, **EMail:**, and **Comment:** details. By selecting the **Authentication** box you can establish a "Web of Trust" which will save your partner's time and effort authenticating your public key certificate as you share it. Consider setting an expiration date as there is no need to have these keys hanging around on the Internet forever.* Setting a lengthy expiration date is a courtesy to key servers' administrators and to your partners as it shows them when obsolete keys can be removed and possibly the need to be renewed at higher levels of encryption. For example, eight years is more than long enough for a key pair to exist as technology and encryption techniques advance. Remember, authentications are only relevant to OpenPGP certificates. Modern computers can process a 4096 key length with minimal effort for your added security. In eight years you may want 8192 or greater.

You also have to take a moment to plan where your keys will be stored, how and where you are going to back them up, and how you are going to use them. For example, if you are an SBO, you may want just one set of keys available to everyone that uses your computer(s) to allow the exchange of encrypted messages with your partners. However, if you are doing this just for yourself, then the defaults may be fine.

Section 18 of the Gpg4win describes very well how to sign and encrypt a file. Once again, sending an encrypting a file is very simple using GpgEX. *Using __Windows Explorer__ browse to the files or folders that you want to select and right click on the mouse to bring up the menu > arrow down to select __Sign and encrypt__ > on the __Sign/Encrypt Files__ dialog choose what you want to do*. From http://www.gpg4win.org/doc/en/gpg4win-compendium_24.html:

- You sign a file using your private certificate to ensure that the file cannot be modified.
- Then encrypt the file using a public certificate to prevent unauthorized persons from seeing it.

Please note these lessons are intended for email clients such as Claws that do not have GpgOL that will automatically sign and encrypt your attachments, which you can easily do in Windows Outlook. There are plenty of simple web pages on the Internet that will show you how to do this in Outlook.

The lessons above were meant to get you started and to show how easy it is to put your email in an encrypted envelope. It is up to you to take these lessons to heart, learn more and apply encryption to your digital use of email. I hope you can see how easy all of this is to protect your digital privacy. An example of a public key server is http://www.rossde.com/PGP/pgp_keyserv.html by David Ross--PGP Public Key Servers--Mozilla Firefox.

Thunderbird -- Using Enigmail to Encrypt Emails

Enigmail is a plug-in for the Thunderbird or Seamonkey email clients that allow them to interface easily with GnuPG. Mozilla Thunderbird is a versatile email client that is available for GNU Linux, Mac OS, Microsoft Windows and other OSs. To use Enigmail you will need to download the latest version of Thunderbird from their web page https://www.mozilla.org/en-US/thunderbird and install it. Once installed, you will have to configure Thunderbird to work with your email service providers. Thunderbird is very good at figuring out how to configure itself for most email service providers, so most likely all you will have to do is enter your username and password. Once you have set up your email accounts in Thunderbird, refer back to <u>Windows 7-Using Gpg4win to Encrypt Emails & Files</u> to install their project's encryption software. Once installed, we need to add the Enigmail add-on to be able to encrypt and decrypt email. To install the Enigmail add-on:

1. *At the top of Thunderbird right click on top bar and check <u>Menu Bar</u> to add the Menu Bar*.
2. *In Mozilla Thunderbird, click on the <u>Tools</u> menu > arrow down to select <u>Add-ons</u>*.
3. *In the search box upper right type <u>enigmail</u> and you should see <u>Enigmail 1.6</u> > click on the <u>Install</u> button on the right to install the add-on*.
4. *If your search does not find Enigmail download surf to <u>https://addons.mozilla.org/en-US/thunderbird/addon/enigmail</u> or <u>https://www.enigmail.net/home/index.php</u> and download the add-on which will work in Thunderbird > save the <u>enigmail-*.xpi</u> file to your hard drive*.
5. *From the option button next to the top-right add-on search field, select <u>Install Add-on From File...</u> and browse to the downloaded add-on file to install it*.

In the Gpg4win section of this chapter above we generated a <u>John Doe</u> key pair to practice using with the Adele robot using the Claws email client. We will again use that same key pair to practice encrypting email using Thunderbird/Enigmail before we venture out into the real world. Enigmail comes with a setup wizard that you can run any time by *clicking on the Thunderbird <u>OpenPGP</u> menu added when you installed the add-on > arrow down to select <u>Setup Wizard</u> > the <u>Welcome to OpenPGP Setup Wizard</u> should appear, leave <u>Yes, I would like the wizard to get me started</u> ticked, <u>Next ></u> > on the <u>Select Identities</u> dialog select the email accounts with which you plan to use to encrypt email, <u>Next ></u> > on the <u>Digitally Sign Your Outgoing Emails</u> screen tick <u>No, I want to create per-recipient rules for emails that need to be signed</u>, <u>Next ></u> > on the <u>Encrypt Your Outgoing Emails</u> screen tick <u>No, I will create per-recipient rules for those that sent me the public key</u>, <u>Next ></u> > on the <u>Change Your Email Settings To Make OpenPGP Work More Reliably</u> screen, allow Enigmail to change your defaults settings, leave <u>Yes</u> ticked, <u>Next ></u> > on the <u>Create A Key To Sign And Encrypt Email</u> select the <u>John Doe (Test)</u> key we created while studying Gpg4win, <u>Next ></u> > on the <u>Summary</u> screen confirm your choices, <u>Next ></u> and we are ready to practice sending encrypted emails using Enigmail*. (See also: <u>https://securityinabox.org/en/thunderbird_main</u>)

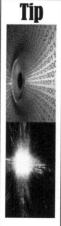

Tip

Most people you send email to care nothing about their privacy and drag you down that rabbit hole. They do not see the need to set up an OpenPGP-aware email program, and your signature will be displayed as an attachment or as text around the email messages you send. This will annoy and confuse them resulting in endless questions and explanations from yourself. In a perfect world, leaving <u>Yes, I want to sign all my email</u> ticked would be appropriate, and to know why, refer back to <u>Digital Signatures and Why they are Important</u> to understand their purpose. The same holds true with the next <u>Encrypt Your Outgoing Emails</u> screen where you can choose to encrypt all your email. Accidentally send one encrypted email to someone who knows nothing about encryption, and you will get grief about how you are sending gibberish, and most likely an accusation from them about how you must have a virus on your computer. Maintaining a separate email address for all of your encrypted communication is a wonderful solution that you should consider.

In the above settings when asked if we wanted to change a few default settings to make OpenPGP work better, we answered "Yes". By doing this the following changes were made to our Thunderbird configuration:

- Disable loading IMAP parts on demand
- Disable flowed text (RFC 2646)
- View message body as plain text (Enigmail does not work well with HTML)
- Use 8-bit encoding for message sending
- Do not compose HTML messages

The first step to test and learn about Enigmail is to sign a message and send it to Adele. This will allow Enigmail to sign your email and send it off to its lists. Only sign the email and do not encrypt it. *Click on the Inbox of the email account you are using > click on the Write icon to draft a message and put together a message to send to Adele > click on OpenPGP menu at the very top and arrow down to select Sign Message > then click on Send to deliver it to Adele.* Adele should respond with its public key, which you can import if you have not already done so. The next step is to send an encrypted email to Adele.

Click on the Inbox of the email account you are planning to use > click on the Write icon to draft a message and put together an email message to send to Adele > click on OpenPGP and arrow down to check Encrypt Message > you may be prompted to configure OpenPGP for this email identity click on Configure > check Enable OpenPGP support (Enigmail) for this identity > click on the Select Key... button and you may want to select your John Doe key that we created while learning about Gpg4win, OK > click on the Send button, enter your passphrase and wait for a response from Adele. It is not necessary to select your own key unless you want to review your sent encrypted emails later, as an SBO may want to do. What Adele sends back will be decrypted if everything is working OK. If the response from Adele comes back in German unencrypted with something like the following:

```
Hallo ThatCyberSecurityGuy,

hier ist die unverschlüsselte Antwort auf Ihre EMail.

Ich habe von Ihnen eine verschlüsselte Botschaft empfangen.
Allerdings finde ich keinen öffentlichen Schlüssel von Ihnen, sodass
ich Ihnen nicht verschlüsselt antworten kann. Da man verschlüsselte
Texte vertraulich behandeln, also nicht unverschlüsselt
weiterschicken soll, gehe ich in dieser Antwort nicht auf den Inhalt
Ihrer verschlüsselten EMail ein, sondern sage Ihnen hiermit nur, dass
ich sie entschlüsseln konnte.
```

Go to http://translate.google.com and you will see that Adele is telling you it received an encrypted email but could not find a public key from you. Open up Kleopatra to make sure Adele's public key has been imported and registered. OpenPGP should recognize the adele@gnupp.de email address and associate it with the proper public key when you send

your email. ***Click on OpenPGP > arrow down to select Default composition options >
arrow over to select Signing/Encryption Options... > make sure <u>Use email address of
this identity to identify OpenPGP key</u> is selected. If that does not work, send your <u>John
Doe public key to Adele</u> again to get the robot to reregister it***. Adele does not keep your
public key long for obvious reasons, and you have to confirm your pubic key with the string
Adele sent you in its public key every 25 emails. When you get an email response from Adele
looking like the following, you have mastered the novice level of using email encryption:

```
********* *BEGIN ENCRYPTED or SIGNED PART* *********

Hallo ThatCyberSecurityGuy,

hier ist die verschlüsselte Antwort auf Ihre EMail.

Ich schicke Ihnen Ihre Botschaft im Wortlaut zurück, damit Sie
sehen, dass ich sie erfolgreich entschlüsseln konnte.

> Test encrypted email to Adele public key...

Viele Grüße,
adele@gnupp.de

********** *END ENCRYPTED or SIGNED PART* **********
```

Which, when translated to English, means:
```
Here is the encrypted response to your email.  I'll send you back your message in
the text, so you see that I was able to decode successfully.
```

Windows 7 – Using GnuPG to Encrypt Files for Your OneDrive or Mobile Devices

Let's suppose you don't want the full blown Gpg4win implementation of GPG with its multiple
modules. You can just download the Windows command line version of GnuPG, which is the
free implementation of the OpenPGP standard as defined by RFC4880. GnuPG is a secure
email and file encryption tool. It comes installed in most versions of Linux, and Chapter 7 will
cover how to install it from various Linux repositories. However, for Windows you can
consider downloading and installing this useful encryption software if Gpg4win is not for you,
or if you prefer, you can purchase Symantec's commercial PGP software if you want to trust a
corporate encryption solution. (See: http://www.gnupg.org, http://www.pgp.com,
https://www.symantec.com/products-solutions/families/?fid=encryption) Using the command
line allows you to automate things on your computer using scripts. If you cannot find GnuPG
in your version of Linux, you can download the software from their website. Surf to
http://www.gnupg.org and on the left pane of the home page click on Download > this will
take you to the various download options and you can choose in which format and version you
want to download the software.

The Windows implementation of GnuPG was a bit more difficult to find but the latest version dated 6/23/2014 is at the GunPG FTP site ftp://ftp.gnupg.org/gcrypt/binary. You can also look through the GunPG mirrors binary directories at http://www.gnupg.org/mirrors.html. It is a good package to use as a Windows command line encryption solution. Download the executable gnupg-w32cli-1.4.18.exe file and double click on it to install it. The GnuPG command line tools will install in the directory C:\Program Files (x86)\GNU\GnuPG in a 64-bit OS. There is no GUI so don't plan to use it from the Windows *Start* > ***All Programs*** menu. Refer back to Windows 7-Adding Tools & Utilities to the System PATH to add C:\Program Files (x86)\GNU\GnuPG to the System PATH so you can use these tools from any directory on your computer.

NOTE	Gpg4win will also install in the C:\Program Files (x86)\GNU\GnuPG directory where you can use gpg2.exe to handle all your scripting needs. This easy install is more versatile solution to using just the GunPG command line tools.

If you don't want to add GNU to the System PATH, you can script the encrypting and decrypting of your confidential files by using the full path to the tools. Regardless, there are two ways of encrypting and decrypting files on your computer. You can use symmetric encryption by entering a password every time you encrypt and decrypt a file, or use asymmetric encryption to create a public/private key pair.   We will cover key pairs in detail in Chapter 9 on SSH, or you can read about them now at the http://gnupg.org website. Below is the command to use to create your initial Windows key pair:

C:\<UserID>\gpg --homedir c:\<userid>\gnupgrings --gen-key

"--homedir" specifies where you want your keyrings stored. Otherwise, gpg uses the default. From now on you will have to specify the "--homedir" to use the GnuPG commands that need the keyring, if you choose not to use the default. The 40-digit "fingerprint" of your newly generated OpenPGP certificate is displayed in the results text field which, as we discussed, should be recorded and verified when we share our public key. Below is a sample simple Windows CMD script that you can adapt to encrypt your sensitive data files. Microsoft has a new Powershell scripting language to which you can convert this. After you create a script for your files, put a shortcut to it on your desktop.

```
@echo off
set keyring=C:\Users\<YourUserName>\finance\gnupgrings

echo GnuPG keyring is located at %keyring%

rem Set the executable path for GnuPG based on 32 bit or 64 bit machine running
script:

if defined ProgramFiles(x86) (
    set gnupgdir="%ProgramFiles(x86)%\GNU\GnuPG"
    set gnupg="%ProgramFiles(x86)%\GNU\GnuPG\gpg"
    echo Running script on 64 bit machine..."
```

```
) ELSE (
  set gnupgdir="%ProgramFiles%\GNU\GnuPG"
  set gnupg="%ProgramFiles%\GNU\GnuPG\gpg"
  echo Running script on 32 bit machine...
  )


echo Running GnuPG executable at %gnupg%

set filedir1=C:\Users\<YourUserName>\<OneDrive>\finance
set file1=<keepassfilename>.kdbx
set filedir2=C:\Users\<YourUserName>\<OneDrive>\finance\Quicken2014
set file2=<quickenfilename>2014.QDF
set filedir3=C:\Users\<YourUserName>\<OneDrive>\TimeAndChaos
set file3=~phone.isd
set file4=~phone.ism


set errmsg1=missing, could not encrypt.


set /p en_or_de="Enter (E) to encrypt or (D) to decrypt file: "
if %en_or_de%==e set answer=E
if %en_or_de%==d set answer=D
if "%en_or_de%"=="v" set answer="V"


rem Check the download to make sure it matches the signature file:
if %answer%=="V" (
  echo Checking download signature at %gnupgdir%
  echo Checking file gnupg-w32cli-1.4.11.exe.sig
  cd %gnupgdir%
  gpg --verify gnupg-w32cli-1.4.16.exe.sig
  pause
  exit
)


cd %filedir1%
if %answer%=="E" (
  echo In directory %filedir1%
  if EXIST %file1% (
    echo Encrypting %file1% at %filedir1%
    move %file1%.gpg %file1%.gpg.safe
    %gnupg% --homedir %keyring% -r <YourEmailAddress> -e %file1%
    rem %gnupg% -c %file1%
    del %file1%
  ) ELSE (
    echo %file1% %errmsg1%
```

```
    )
)

cd %filedir2%
if %answer%=="E" (
  echo In directory %filedir2%
  if EXIST %file2% (
    echo Encrypting %file2% at %filedir2%
    move %file1%.gpg %file2%.gpg.safe
    %gnupg% --homedir %keyring% -r <YourEmailAddress> -e %file2%
    rem %gnupg% -c %file2%
    del %file2%
  ) ELSE (
    echo %file2% %errmsg1%
  )
)


cd %filedir3%
if %answer%=="E" (
  if EXIST %file3% (
    echo Encrypting %file3% at %filedir3%
    move %file4%.gpg %file3%.gpg.safe
    %gnupg% --homedir %keyring% -r <YourEmailAddress> -e %file3%
    rem %gnupg% -c %file3%
    del %file3%
  ) ELSE (
    echo %file3% %errmsg1%
  )
)


cd %filedir3%
 if %answer%=="E" (
   if EXIST %file4% (
     echo Encrypting %file4% at %filedir3%
     move %file5%.gpg %file4%.gpg.safe
     %gnupg% --homedir %keyring% -r <YourEmailAddress> -e %file4%
     rem %gnupg% -c %file4%
     del %file4%
   ) ELSE (
     echo %file4% %errmsg1%
   )
 )

 if %answer%=="D" (
```

```
  %gnupg% --homedir %keyring% --decrypt-files %filedir1%\%file1%.gpg
%filedir2%\%file2%.gpg %filedir3%\%file3%.gpg %filedir3%\%file4%.gpg
)


pause
exit
```

Save the script above as something such as en_de_crypt.cmd. Then for convenience, you can create a shortcut to this script on your desktop. The script above can be used to protect all of your important files, as in password files, contact and financial data. GnuPG can also be used to verify the detached GPG signature of any files that you download.

FreeOTFE Explorer -- A Deprecated Project to Create Encrypted Folders

FreeOTFE is a deprecated open source project that can produce on-the-fly encryption. From Wikipedia on FreeOTFE, "*It creates virtual drives, or disks, to which anything written is automatically encrypted before being stored on a computer's hard or USB drive. It is similar in function to other disk encryption programs including TrueCrypt and Microsoft's BitLocker.*" The software is compatible with Windows and Linux, allowing data encrypted under both to be read and written. The software can be run in a "portable mode" which allows it to be used under Microsoft Windows and Linux without installation of the complete program to *mount* and access the encrypted data through a virtual disk. This makes this software ideal for the travel. The software does not have great reviews and the website no longer exists. I cannot recommend this software for encryption, but to be thorough, I wanted you to know it exists for your consideration and use. Plus, these open source projects are sometimes resurrected from the ashes. (See: http://download.cnet.com/FreeOTFE/3000-2092_4-10656559.html, http://www.pcworld.com/article/233171/freeotfe.html, http://sourceforge.net/projects/freeotfe.mirror, https://en.wikipedia.org/wiki/FreeOTFE, http://web.archive.org/web/20130305192649/http://freeotfe.org/main_explorer_differences.html)

Androsa -- A Deprecated Graphical Tool to Encrypt Files

Androsa is a dated GUI solution that Windows users may find useful for encrypting files. I cannot recommend this as an encryption solution, but there are websites that still expunge this encryption solution such as CNET that still gives the dated Androsa project a 5-star rating and users have a 4-star rating. In my experimentation years ago, using Androsa in virtual Windows XP VM worked perfectly. Because we don't want to continuously litter our computers with installed software, you may find using the outdated portable version of Androsa preferable, and it was the only solution that worked in a 64-bit Windows 7 OS. The website for this project is gone, so I am not sure of the status of this project. From my research, the last update to this software was August 6, 2009, so this is a very dated project that has probably been discontinued and is no longer a viable encryption solution. (See: http://androsa-fileprotector.en.malavida.com, http://download.cnet.com/Androsa-FileProtector/3000-2092_4-10693806.html, http://androsa-fileprotector.en.softonic.com, http://www.pcworld.com/article/231493/androsa_fileprotector.html)

Widows 7 -- Loading, Configuring and Setting Up

Chapter 6 -- Windows 7 -- Loading, Configuring and Setting Up Free and Useful Applications, Tools and Utilities

Loading and configuring a new computer is a wonderful opportunity to clean up files and directories, to get all of the latest software and updates, and to get organized. We would also want to purchase the latest versions of the applications that we use such as "Dragon Naturally Speaking", "Microsoft Products", "Quicken", "Print Master", "MiniTool Data Recovery", and games. We must also clean up backups, downloads, multiple copies of data files, videos and music. You may have files on another desktop, laptop or on multiple USB drives, which can be confusing, for example. We should consider updating all of our computing platforms to the same software versions and configuration. This is a good opportunity to examine and consolidate everything onto your backup device(s). We need to download all utilities, drivers and free software first, as they will be needed to set up the new system. After that, we can then load and configure our data files and music as we install and configure the new OS.

When we re-install the OSs and software, we are fortifying our defenses while improving our strategies for what could be considered a battle: You vs. crackers, corporations, government agencies, or any others who might want access to your personal information and web use habits. A military that understands the enemies' strengths can stay ahead of its enemies by developing weapons and tactics that thwart the enemies at their best game, which is one that succeeds and sustains successes, while a military that relies on unchanging standard operations succumbs to those who were quick to adapt, change and advance. I offer one of the most famous, successful militaries in history as an example of continued success gained by continuous adaptation and improvement.

 **Historical Reference -- Roman Tools of War -- The Roman military continually improved on the tools of war which is what we are attempting to do!**

The Roman army improved upon and perfected the tools of war during their reign, almost conquering the world. Roman military success relied heavily on the technology of others. Much of their military equipment was based on designs adapted from their enemies. The Romans mass produced their armor and weaponry in order to make sure things were uniform across the empire and those new soldiers could get supplies quickly. They took tools like the Gladius (sword), the Pilum (spear), armor, shields, giant siege engines and among many other devices, perfected their deployment and use. As the nature of warfare and enemies changed, so did the Romans' tactics and weapons. They developed a clear-cut system of rank, and a way of dividing the army into a number of different divisions down to the basic unit. At one time each legion had about 5,500 men. The legion was subdivided into ten units called cohorts. The cohorts were subdivided into six "centuries" or *centuria*, of about 80 men each. There were nine cohorts of about 480 soldiers and one first cohort made up of five double-strength centuries, totaling 800 men. The Romans designed a layered approach to attacking the enemy. With all that said, Romans often fought against opponents (Germanic tribes, in Gaul) that did not have armor, so this gave them a huge advantage. However, it doesn't seem that Roman armor or weaponry was that much better than their adversaries if they did have it. Romans also experimented with things like elephants and camel troops once they began fighting farther in the east. The Roman military was organized by fighting skill and social class. The first ground troops sent in (hoplites) normally did not have heavy armor and were not as skilled in battle.

As soldiers gained ranks their armor got nicer and better crafted, and their skill in fighting went up as well. Our modern military rejects this model and relies on technology, which is a mistake. One would have thought that the opposition our ground troops faced in Iraq proved the value of what history taught us, and shows that the Roman model is the correct way to wage war and train soldiers. But given history's lessons, we continue to stray from educating and equipping the common fighting soldier (to be all that he/she can be) in favor of relying on technology. The Romans had Light Infantry, Infantry, Cavalry and Flankers. They then put together a playbook of various formations taking into account terrain, the type and strength of opponent's troops, and the type and strength of the Romans' troops. Keeping their troops in order allowed them to fight effectively against enemies who simply ordered their troops to rush wildly at the Romans. History is littered with later examples of Generals ordering wild charges at well-fortified and ordered defenses, resulting in devastating losses. History is a great teacher in all things. (See: https://en.wikipedia.org/wiki/Cohort_(military_unit)).

- The Scorpion (originally a Greek invention) worked like a fixed crossbow and threw large javelins. The Roman version was extremely accurate and powerful.
- The Pilum was a long spear or javelin (a Roman original). There were two types of these: thick and thin. The thin Pilum was about 2 meters long with a barbed point. The thick Pilum was of similar length but was attached to the shaft with a 5 cm wide tang. They later revised it so that the Pilum would bend upon impact, keeping the enemy from throwing them back. However, making a Pilum that would bend every time upon impact proved difficult to produce. Subsequently, the Romans added a wooden pin so that the Pilum would break upon impact. Usually, the Pilum was thrown before engaging the enemy with close order swords. The Pilum was eventually phased out because of the demands of border warfare.
- The Romans developed various forms of armor (derived from the Celtics); the helmet (Etruscan), once bronze, then iron and then bronze again, was used to protect the soldiers against projectiles like spears (Semite), javelins and arrows, and against hand-to-hand weapons like swords and daggers. The sanctum (shield) was a curved oval made from two sheets of wood glued together and covered with canvas and leather. Other facets of the Roman military, such as the Cavalry, were equipped in the Greek fashion, with a cuirass and round shield.
- The Gladius originated in Spain and was a short stabbing sword. The Romans modified the design to give the sword a sharp tip, parallel the sides, and make a shorter point. This gave the sword better balance and enabled the use of a slashing blow in addition to stabbing with the point (the preferred method of slaying an enemy).

To defeat their enemies and conquer much of the world, the Romans stayed current with technology and adapted as the world around them changed. Computer OSs, tools, utilities and applications also adapt and evolve rapidly. We only want to install the latest software versions because upgrading and/or removing applications in Windows 7 can leave traces of the software installations behind, effectively slowing down or eventually corrupting the system. Having the latest version of a product should also yield added capabilities and be more stable. From this chapter, you will learn how to update and improve your system. You will be guided through the following processes: Check online to see if you have all of the latest software. Download the firmware, drivers, applications, tools, utilities and updates for your APC, cable modem, disk drives, motherboard, Blu-Ray DVD drive, monitor, printer, router, sound card, video card and webcam. Copy them all to a backup device like a USB drive or a DVD so that we can install them on the new computer later. We want our system to serve us for many years with all its capabilities enabled. This is a time consuming but worthy project.

The above paragraph bears a little explanation. When you purchase a new computer or peripheral (device attached to your computer), or are reloading an OS onto an old computer, your hardware manufacturers have been hard at work correcting any problems in all of the software that controls the components that make up your setup (BIOS, CPU, DVD Drive, Keyboard, Mouse, Printer Touchpad, etc.), which you probably have not kept updated. Nobody has the time to continuously check the manufacturer's websites for all of our computers, peripherals and mobile devices. If your manufacturer has supplied your device with a preloaded OS, or if you install their software, they usually have installed background processes that continuously poll their websites for updates. These processes may also be providing them with information about your Internet activity and device use as well. When you find these processes running, turn them off to help your devices' performance and to protect your privacy. You are going to be taught how to look for these updates yourself.

Many times clicking on <u>Start</u> > <u>All Programs</u> > and selecting <u>Windows Update</u> to download all the Updates will keep other manufacturers software up-to-date. However, sometimes there are additional updates and software that Windows does not provide. Browse to your devices' manufacturer's website(s) (e.g. http://support.hp.com, https://support.dell.com, http://support.asus.com and so on), enter your devices' information such as part number, serial number or just the general name and download all of the latest drivers and software. You might be surprised at how many drivers and software there are on your vendor's site that did not install via Windows Update (e.g. Webcam Software, the Audio driver, the Graphic's driver and much more). For my laptop, there were 39 downloads in all to install; for desktops, it is usually much less. Sometimes these files will have generic and unidentifiable names, so stay organized. Create a desktop or laptop directory (e.g. VendorLaptopModel or VendorDesktopModel). Create subdirectories according to how the vendor presents the software for download (Bios, DriverAudio, DriverChipset, DriverGraphics, DriverLAN, Manuals, SoftwareMultimedia, SoftwareSecurity, DriverUSB, etc.). As you download each update, rename it or create a directory entry that describes it (e.g. sp0925HPSmartLiveTVSoftware, sp3456HPMediaSmartSmartMenu, etc.). As you install each download, create a directory in the sub directory (e.g. sp0925Installed110521, AllApplied5July2014) so that you know where you are in the installation process. Be selective in what you install and read the full descriptions of what your vendor is providing. Some of this software is bloatware or unnecessary for what you may need for your computing needs. Creating the directories are also handy to track the date the install took place, so that if you later check for updates, you will know whether there is a more recent update and/or software at the vendor site. Do the same for all of your other devices that are installed in or connected to your device (e.g. printer, router, monitor, etc.). Your vendor may also provide software such as Lightscribe for the computer's hardware. You are better off not installing these updates and going directly to the vendor's website, which we will soon cover.

When you purchase new software online for immediate download, here are a few things you should consider doing:

1. Create a separate folder for the product downloads, information, manual, etc.
2. Save the web page that details the purchase order in a word or text document.
3. Download all of the software purchased right away once you receive the confirmation email. There is usually a deadline as to how long the vendor will allow you to download. Backup the software to your backup device.
4. Create a text document, cut and paste the keys sent to you in an email or document by your software vendor, and save them in a safe place. You may need them again someday.
5. Check the MD5 hash, SHA-1 or GPG signature to make sure your download is correct and not corrupt. There are excellent FREE and easy-to-use open source applications covered in this book that you can use to do that. See Chapter 5-Verifying Downloads Before Installation.

Before you install your OS, cable your computer to the router and all peripherals (connect your router, monitor, printer, keyboard, mouse, etc.) and install all of the hardware (DVD drive, gaming devices, etc.) that you will use with the new computer. In Chapter 3 we tested all of our hardware and zeroed the hard drives. Trying to install an OS using wireless wastes time and can cause headaches. If you have any problems installing an OS, often times you will find online advice about disconnecting devices to get your OS installed. This can be bad advice, for later you may have to spend many hours researching how to get those devices working in your new setup. As Windows 7 loads, we want it to see all of the hardware and peripherals so it will load the drivers and software for those devices, if they are available from Microsoft. We never want to install an operating system onto a system that has been previously partitioned. Windows 7 and other OSs can make assumptions and try to fit in or use existing partitions, thus corrupting our installation. It is best to let any new OS, like Windows 7, partition and load the OS onto the hard drives the way that their developers designed it. We only build a system when our hardware fails or our previous system becomes obsolete. This is our one shot at making sure that all of the hardware is fully operational and optimized. We also don't want the install to see previously loaded operating systems or applications.

To load Windows 7 onto your computer, you may have to load drivers that allow Windows to see the hard drives. We downloaded those drivers from our Motherboard's manufacturer, expanded the compressed files and backed them up in Chapter 3. Insert the Windows 7 install DVD, and when Windows prompts for drivers, navigate to the directory where those drivers are and load the RAID or SATA drivers from your backup device. That directory can be unintuitive so following are some examples of the locations of the ASUS, SATA and RAID drivers, depending on your setup:

E:\Downloads\MotherboardCrosshairVFormula\SATA\AMD_RAIDAHCI_V32154092_121292XPVi staWin7\AMD\Driver\Disk\AHCI\Win7\x64
E:\Downloads\MotherboardCrosshairVFormula\SATA\AMD_RAIDAHCI_V32154092_121292XPVi staWin7\AMD\Driver\Disk\RAID\Vista_Win7\x64.

After Windows loads, it will reboot and ask you to <u>Type a user name (for example, John)</u>, which I consider to be a terrible suggestion. The user ID that you enter will be the ADMINISTRATOR on your Windows 7 machine. The only advantage I see to naming it something like "John" would be if a cracker breaks in to your computer and starts looking for your administrator IDs. However, if they have cracked your PC, they either already have admin rights or will quickly learn which user ID does. Therefore, I would suggest naming this user ID, 'admin'. Windows 7 then asks you to <u>Type a computer name:</u> and suggests <u>PC</u>. This would be another terrible choice. A better choice would be to name the computer something informative like the name of the computer or motherboard (e.g. asusa7n8xdeluxe, hppaviliondv6t, etc.). This works well for a Home Computer User (HCU) because we will rarely have the same motherboard in multiple computers, or own two of the same types of computers. We usually only purchase a computer about every six years or so, therefore, the hardware is usually different. A SBO may need a different naming convention, such as adding a numeral after the PC name. The important point is to make the computer name something that identifies its hardware and differentiates it from your other computers.

The next screen asks you to set a password. This is very important if you work in a place where multiple users you want to separate, need to use the same office computer. If you are in an HCU setting, this can be annoying, and if you install malicious software from the Internet, they will have a backdoor around your password anyway. Leave it blank if you can.

The next screen asks for the product key and has a checkbox titled "Automatically activate Windows when I'm online", which must be unchecked. We do this in case there is a problem loading Windows so that we don't burn a license ID. Microsoft and other software vendors are also offering their products in ISO format for you to burn to disk. I always write, or burn an image of the software key onto the Windows DVD. This way you don't have to go looking for the key every time you use the disk to load an OS.

Windows 7 -- After Loading the OS

Connect your USB drive to the computer and copy everything that downloaded from your hardware manufacturers to the C:\Downloads directory. To apply all of the latest Windows 7 updates, we have to get our computer talking to our router. In the motherboard manual, it should tell you the color coding on the LAN port. The ASUS Crosshair has Intel Ethernet Gigabit LAN, so we make note of the LAN port LED indicators:

Activity/Link	Speed LED	Common Description of Left NIC LED
OFF	OFF	Soft-on Mode
Yellow Blinking (Amber)	OFF	10 Mbps connection or suspend
Yellow Blinking (Amber)	Orange	100 Mbps connection
Yellow Blinking (Amber)	Green	1 Gbps connection

Activity/Link	Speed LED	Common Description of Right NIC LED
OFF	OFF	Indicates no connection, everything is dead
Flashing	Yellow (Amber)	Indicates collisions, more green less amber!
Flashing	Green	Indicates intermittent connectivity
Steady	Green	Indicates connectivity is present

The right LED should be green indicating a good connection to your router; the left light should be blinking yellow. In my case the left light was dark, showing no Internet activity at all. This indicated that the generic drivers that came with Windows 7 were not seeing the LAN port. *Open Windows Explorer > Navigate through the hierarchy down to the LAN driver directory > C:\Downloads\MotherboardCrosshairVFormula\LAN\Intel_Gigabit_V16500_XPVistaWin7 > double click on AsusSetup and install the LAN drives into Windows 7. The yellow light should start blinking and when the Set Network Location dialog box pops up > select the type of network Home Network if behind a hardware firewall > record the Homegroup password.*

If the yellow light is still not blinking, examine the device drivers. *Click on Start > Devices and Printers > double click on your motherboard > select Hardware tab > mouse down to you LAN drivers (Intel® 82583V Gigabit Network Connection) > click on Properties > the device status should read This device is working properly. As a last resort click on Start > Control Panel > View by: Large icons in the upper right corner > Administrative Tools > Computer Management > Device Manager > Network > try uninstalling and reinstalling the driver > if that does not work, try deleting the device (NOT the driver) > rebooting and allowing Windows to rediscover the NIC driver.*

A fresh install of Windows 7 on a very old ASUS A7N8X computer also did not recognize the LAN connection to my router. Updating that driver was somewhat different than it was on a modern motherboard, *Open up the Window Control Panel > in the upper right click on View by: Large or Small Icons > click on Device Manager > look at your Other devices and see what devices like Ethernet Controller may need to be updated > as previously discussed, we have downloaded all of the drivers needed from our motherboard's manufacturer before attempting to reload the OS > double click on Ethernet Controller which will have a yellow highlight next to it indicating Windows has no driver for the hardware > click on the Update Driver... button > select Browse my computer for driver software and navigate to the directory to where you expanded your driver software from your hardware's motherboard manufacturer (e.g. C:\Downloads\MotherboardASUSA7N8XDeluxe\DriverLAN\3com_90xv54\Disk1) > click on OK to install the expanded driver > right click on the Network icon added to the desktop (see Step 2 in the coming directions) and see if you are now connected to the Internet > select Home Network when prompted by Windows.*

Soon, we are soon going to apply ALL Windows Updates and then make sure everything is copacetic with our PC hardware. These updates will require multiple reboots of your computer and hours of your time. Still, **DO NOT Activate Windows**, because Microsoft has limited the number of times you can Activate Windows. We have to make sure Windows is working well with **all** of our hardware before we activate the OS. Sometimes, trying to get something working with Windows 7 will break the OS and we will have to reinstall the OS trying different things. So don't activate the license until you get everything working. Activations you do with Microsoft will decrement the license install limit you have purchased for Windows 7. It can be very annoying and a waste of your valuable time when this limit is reached. You could spend hours on the phone with Microsoft to increase the install count of your legally purchased license(s). In Microsoft's defense, the theft of their intellectual property around the world is so prevalent they have had to take these measures to protect their product.

1. *Once Windows 7 is installed > click on the <u>Start</u> button > click on <u>All Programs</u> > move the cursor up and select <u>Windows Update</u> which will bring up the <u>Windows Update</u> window > click on the <u>Check for updates</u> button, or <u>Check for updates</u> at the top of the left menu > if Windows finds updates, click on <u>Install updates</u> > once the updates are installed, restart the system > repeat this procedure over and over, until all of the updates have been applied and Windows says <u>No updates are currently selected</u>.*

Tip	It is a good idea to reboot after applying the recommended updates whether Window 7 asks for it or not. After the reboot, running Windows Update may turn up additional updates that would not have been there otherwise.

2. Install all of the other drivers, utilities, tools and software not updated by <u>Windows Update</u> that support all of your hardware, and then restart the computer repeatedly. Once the video card drivers and software are installed, adjust the display settings. For example, if you use two monitors, the primary display may not be correct. *Right click on the <u>Desktop</u> > select the bottom menu item <u>Personalize</u> > select <u>Display</u> on the lower left menu > select <u>Change display settings</u> in the upper mid left menu > make sure Multiple displays is set to <u>Extend these displays</u> > if the display you want as your main monitor is different than the default, click it to make that your main display numbered either 1 and 2 > check the box at the bottom <u>Make this my main display</u> > move the displays around as to how you plan to use your mouse. For example, I put 2 on the left and 1 on the right > practice where you position monitor 1 in relation to monitor 2 by sliding your mouse from one display to the other (you have to hit <u>Apply</u> prior to testing mouse movement).* You will notice that where you position the graphical monitors vertically in relation to each other affects where the mouse can be to slide back and forth from display to display, unless both of your monitors are both the same size.

3. Windows may not detect your printer automatically, so you may have to add it. *Click on <u>Start</u> > select <u>Devices and Printers</u>; or click on <u>Start</u> > <u>Control Panel</u> > in the upper right corner, select View by: <u>Large icons</u> > select <u>Devices and Printers</u> > select <u>Add a printer</u> > select <u>Add a network, wireless or Bluetooth printer</u> > under <u>Printer Name</u> your printer should pop up with its IP address (e.g. Color Laser 3110cn (Dell)), <u>Next</u> > my Dell printer was not listed as a selectable option in Windows 7 > clicking on the <u>Windows Update</u> button did not bring down the configuration for my Dell printer after a long wait > so I went to <u>https://support.dell.com</u> to download and expand my print driver to the directory C:\Downloads\Dell3110cnDriver\3110cn-Win-PCL & PS DRVR\Burgundy-Win-PS-42134_cat\64bit\English > click on <u>Have Disk...</u> > browse to the directory where your print drivers are and select the device driver file, <u>Open</u> > on the <u>Install from Disk</u> dialog click on <u>OK</u> > <u>Next</u> > under <u>Type a printer Name</u> accept the default or enter your own printer name, <u>Next</u> and the print driver should install > click on <u>Finish</u> > if prompted and if you are not setting the computer up as a print server select <u>Do not share this printer</u> > <u>Next</u>.* This should be done again for the Burgundy-WinPCL-42134_cat driver for the same printer also.

4. Windows may not automatically recognize other disks in the computer if they are not part of a RAID. (See: <u>Chapter 3</u>) *Click on <u>Control Panel</u> > select <u>Administrative Tools</u> >*

click on __Computer Management__ > on the left select __Disk Management__ > right click on any disk's volumes that are not recognized and select __Delete Volume...__ > after the volume has been deleted, right click on the __Unallocated__ space > select the option needed. In my case, I had three disks. Windows 7 was installed on the largest, which was zero; I wanted to use Disk 1 and 2 for my data. *I could have created two volumes by right clicking and selected __New Simple Volume...__ > __Next>__ > __Next>__ > assign drive letters or select __Do not assign a drive letter or drive path__ > __Next>__ > for Volume label: __Data1__ and __Data2__ > File system: __NTFS__, unchecked __Perform a quick format__ > then, when formatting was complete, I would have had two separate data volumes.*

Instead, I created a spanned volume out of disk 1 and 2 and assigned it drive letter E:. *To use drive letter E: I had to remove what windows was displaying as a pseudo drive > select pseudo drive E: select __Change Drive Letter and Paths...__ > click on the __Remove__ button > select __New Spanned Volume...__ __Next>__ > __Next>__ under __Available__ add __Disk 1__ on the left to the __Selected Disk 2__ on the right by clicking on the __Add >__ button in the middle, __Next>__ > Windows defaulted to __Assign the following drive letter E:__, __Next>__ > for __File system: NTFS__, __Volume Label: Data__, uncheck __Perform a quick format__, __Next>__ > and the volume will be created as one drive letter and partition > reopen the __Device Manager__ and disable E:\ as a Portable Device.*

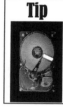 **Tip**	A spanned volume is a volume that spans more than one disk, but appears to the user as just one drive letter in Windows, the advantage being that we can store all of our data on one drive letter. This is convenient for scripting and use. We don't have data scattered about with multiple drive letters. The drawback is that we have a no-fault-tolerance situation. The failure of one data disk results in the loss of all our data. But since we backup our data constantly, this is not a concern.

5. On my rebuild of an old Asus A7N8X for this book, every time I powered off the computer it would lose its BIOS settings and the clock setting would revert to 2001. This indicates that the battery backup for the CMOS is dead. Open up your computer and replace the battery on the motherboard, which is usually a 3V CR2032 Lithium button cell. If you order them online, order them in quantity. It does not cost that much more, and in some computers, you will end up replacing this battery every few years anyway.
6. The next thing I ran into on the A7N8X was that the sound was not working. Long ago I cabled all the computers in my lab to the speakers. That told me that the Windows default drivers were not working. Using the Run... prompt and typing msinfo32 revealed the fact that I had forgotten that I had a Creative Audigy 2 sound card installed. I then went to Creative's website and downloaded the latest drivers, which superseded the Windows drivers and subsequently, fixed the sound on the computer.
7. *Run Internet Explorer > accept the common settings > add the Menu to Internet Explorer by right clicking on the top and select __Menu bar__.*
8. If you decide to install Windows Silverlight lock it down by *clicking on __Start__ > __All Programs__ > select __Microsoft Silverlight__ > double click on __Microsoft Silverlight__ > on the top select the __Application Storage__ tab > and examine the storage requirement on your computer > consider unchecking __Enable application storage__ if you don't extensively use Silverlight applications.*

 NOTE 	Microsoft may have abandoned trying to compete with flash players by further development of Silverlight. Silverlight will be supported until around 2021 but no further improvement is planned. It looks like Microsoft is embracing HTML5 instead of Silverlight.

9. Windows Live is a good application to use for viewing all your email accounts but Thunderbird may be better. ***Click on Windows Live Mail > select the down arrow in the upper left > mouse down to Options > select Email Accounts... > Add... > and start adding your email accounts***.

10. Microsoft offers an antivirus solution for use with Windows 7/8 in their releases of the Microsoft Security Essentials application. If you use other antivirus software, don't download and install Microsoft Security Essentials. Running two antivirus solutions is a hazard to your computer. If you decide to try Security Essentials, you can download and install it from http://windows.microsoft.com/en-us/windows/security-essentials-download. Paid solutions I have used in the past dragged down the performance of my computer, which Essentials has not done.

WARNING 	In an article by Barry Collins posted 19 Dec 2013 from PC PRO titled "Microsoft Security Essentials misses 39% of malware in Dennis test" states, "*While the other eight packages all achieved protection scores of 87% or higher - with five scoring 98% or 99% - Microsoft's free antivirus software protected against only 61% of the malware samples used in the test.* *Microsoft conceded last year that its security software was intended to offer only "baseline" performance, saying it wanted to "give customers a good reason to pay for their [security] products" because that would create greater diversity in the market and make life harder for malware writers.* *Norton Internet Security received the strongest protection rating in DTL's tests, detecting 99% of the malware used. Taking into account false positives against legitimate software, Kaspersky Internet Security 2014 provided the best overall level of protection.*" (See: http://www.pcpro.co.uk/news/security/386185/microsoft-security-essentials-misses-39-of-malware-in-dennis-test)

Alternatives to using Microsoft Security Essentials can be found at http://www.pcmag.com/reviews/antivirus. When finished, backup everything to your backup devices(s). If you don't like or trust Microsoft Security Essentials, below are a few popular products for anti-software:

- Avast, http://www.avast.com Internet Security and AntiVirus.
- Ad-Aware, http://lavasoft.com Ad-Aware Free Internet Security. PC Magazine Editor's choice for free Antivirus. Reviews say Ad-Aware runs unobtrusively in the background and does not conflict with other security software. Ad-Aware will co-exist with Microsoft Security Essentials. Ad-Aware has some invasive things that it may ask to do to your computer. Be sure to uncheck things like (Set my homepage and new tabs to Ad-Aware Safe Search in IE, Firefox & Google Chrome; Make Blekko my browser default search provider in IE, Firefox & Google Chrome) and any bloatware Ad-Aware offers.

Ad-Aware will run in the background polling for updates unless you disable this activity. **_Click on the bottom left icon to switch to Advanced Mode > select Settings > select Do not automatically check for updates_**.

- AVG AntiVirus Free and AVG Internet Security (See: http://www.avg.com, http://www.pcmag.com/article2/0,2817,2391931,00.asp, http://go.pcworld.com/avg2013)
- Avira Internet Security 2015 (See: http://us.avira.com, http://go.pcworld.com/avira2013)
- BitDefender, BitDefender Internet Security and/or Antivirus (See: http://www.bitdefender.com, http://go.pcworld.com/bitdefender2013)
- Comodo Cleaning Essentials (See: https://www.comodo.com, http://www.pcmag.com/article2/0,2817,2398834,00.asp)
- Coranti 2012 Multi-Engine AntiVirus & AntiSpyware (See: http://www.coranti.com, http://www.pcmag.com/article2/0,2817,2398691,00.asp)
- F-Secure Internet Security (See: http://www.f-secure.com, http://go.pcworld.com/fsecure2013)
- G Data Internet Security (See: http://www.gdatasoftware.com, http://www.pcmag.com/article2/0,2817,2385599,00.asp, http://go.pcworld.com/gdata2013)
- Kaspersky Internet Security 2015 (See: http://usa.kaspersky.com, PCMag.com/article2/0,2817,2390995,00.asp, http://go.pcworld.com/kaspersky2013).
- McAfee Internet Security or Total Protection (See: http://www.McAfee.com/us, http://www.pcmag.com/article2/0,2817,2390995,00.asp, http://go.pcworld.com/mcafee2013)
- Normon Security Suite PRO 9 (See: https://www.norman.com/index, http://www.pcmag.com/article2/0,2817,2398347,00.asp)
- Norton Internet Security (See: https://www.symantec.com, http://us.norton.com, http://www.PCMag.com/article2/0,2817,2368876,00.asp, http://go.pcworld.com/norton2013)
- Panda Internet Security 2015 (See: http://www.pandasecurity.com/usa)
- Trend Micro Titanium Internet Security (See: http://www.trendmicro.com, http://go.pcworld.com/trendmicro2013).
- ClamTk Virus Scanner A GUI front-end for ClamAV Linux antivirus protection (See: http://clamtk.sourceforge.net/faq.html, https://help.ubuntu.com/community/ClamAV, https://help.ubuntu.com/community/Antivirus)

NOTE	Comodo has a treasure trove of tools for cyber security. Their numerous products and team of 600 people help you authenticate individuals, business websites and content, secure your information, secure websites and ecommerce, secure and maintain your PCs, and a lot more! They even have a free secure browser and email certificate. (See: https://www.comodo.com/products/free-products.php)

11. ***Download and Install CCleaner, Defraggler, Recuba, and Speccy from*** ***https://www.piriform.com > uncheck Automatically check for updates to <Program>*** ***> uncheck Add 'Open <Program>...' option to Recycle Bin content menu > uncheck*** ***Add 'Run CCleaner' option to the Recycle Bin content menu > click on Next >*** ***uncheck Install the free Google Toolbar along with <Program> if it appears > click*** ***on the Install button.*** Alternatively, you can get CCleaner Portable for your PC or USB drives if you don't want to install it onto your computer. Run it and clean the disk and registry. Reboot when done. Since CCleaner may wipe out all of your cookies (unless you configure it not to), so some of your automatic logins will be removed.

Tip

CCleaner is one of the best free utilities for Windows users that I have ever known. CCleaner is the battle-axe to clean everything that you don't want hanging around on your PC. It is not anti-software per se, but it does protect your privacy online by eliminating malware posing as cookies or temporary files that browsers and other applications collect. It also allows you to keep importing cookies from certain sites (like your credit unions) if you want to configure it to do so. Using CCleaner's Tools you can also examine what is starting up in the background on your computer and put a stop to all those background processes. ***Click on Tools on the left > select Startup*** and examine what is starting up in the background on your computer. For example, on my computer the Microsoft deprecated Mesh daemon WLSync was still starting. While I recommended SuperAntiSpyware portable, the regular Windows install of this software had it starting in the background. Other software we all may use such as Adobe, TomTom HOME Visual Studio Merge Modules and others were constantly running in the background polling the Internet. The easiest way to prevent this is to remove these programs with REVO Uninstaller if you are no longer using them.

---

12. The Piriform Defraggler application offers more features than the Windows 7 defragmentation utility. PCWorld has recommended this software and this is a good addition to running the Windows 7 defragmentation utility. When installing the software, be careful of the options you choose. ***Uncheck Automatically check for updates to*** ***Defraggler if you will do that occasionally on your own > uncheck Replace Windows*** ***Disk Defragmenter, we want the option of using both > uncheck Add Defraggler*** ***menus to Windows Explorer, Windows Explorer is cluttered enough without adding*** ***more menus > uncheck Include Google Chrome, along with Defraggler > uncheck*** ***Make Google Chrome my default browser > click on the Install button > Run*** ***Defraggler on the hard drive by clicking on the Defrag button.***

13. The Piriform Recuva utility will help you recover accidentally deleted files and images! Piriform Recuva can be used to recover files deleted from your Windows computer, Recycle Bin, digital camera card, or MP3 player. Speccy is tool that will provide system information.

After running CCleaner, and perhaps before performing some of next steps to setting up Windows 7, it would be an advantageous time to take a system image backup of your system. We can use the second RAID or DATA partition to store a system image of our fully functional and completely updated OS. We also need to backup an image to your backup device.

To get the second RAID mirror working on my newly created RAID 1 server partition named <u>Data</u> I had to unplug all USB devices and click on <u>Start</u> > <u>Control Panel</u> > <u>Administrative Tools</u> > <u>Computer Management</u> > <u>Storage</u> > <u>Disk Management(Local)</u>. I got a dialog box that asked, <u>You must initialize a disk before Logical Disk Manager can access it.</u> Select <u>GPT (GUID Partition Table)</u> and click on <u>OK</u>. We will discuss the difference between MBR and GPT in <u>Chapter 7 - GParted-Manually Creating Partitions</u>. Right click on the <u>Unallocated Disk 1 space</u> and select <u>New Simple Volume...</u> Because we are running a hardware RAID 1 configuration that is transparent to the Windows OS, this is your only option > click on <u>Next</u> as the wizard helps you to create a simple volume on the physical RAID 1 > select the Maximum disk space > <u>Next</u> > on the <u>Format Partition</u> dialog, enter a Volume Label (e.g. DataVMRAID1) uncheck <u>Perform a quick format</u>, since a long format will be a better test to make sure that hardware is operating properly, and click on <u>Next</u> > click on <u>Finish</u>.

How to Configure and Load Up a Desktop or Laptop Computer with All the Tools and Utilities You Will Ever Need

If you purchase a license for Windows 7 or Windows 8.1/10, I strongly recommend against doing an upgrade of your current Windows OS. Since you are following the mantra of this book and have backed up all your data, music, pictures and downloaded files on a regular basis, you can zero your hard drive and start fresh. You can have a new desktop or laptop (computer) anytime for the cost of an inexpensive second hard drive. This will make it a close duplicate of your original hard drive, but it will be much better because you got rid of all of the excess baggage (e.g. software trials your vendor loaded, malware, applications you loaded but did not find useful, etc.), and now you will only load what you really want and need.

Story	The hard drive on a friend's laptop became corrupted. She took it to a technician, who told her she needed a new laptop, which my friend purchased at her great expense and profit for that company. My friend gave me the supposedly broken hard drive to recover their data. After a simple scan of the perfectly good drive, I told them it was fine. My friend donated the drive to me in return for my service, and I decided to make it a backup to my current laptop setup in case I had a drive failure.

Many circumstances result in the loss of use of a valuable computer. The most frequently occurring problems are theft, hardware drive failure, corruption due to malware, electrical surge, or an application install that went awry. These problems are not a signal that you need to buy a new computer or laptop, unless the hardware is outdated or you are rich. In <u>Chapter 3</u> we outlined how to build a top-of-the-line desktop computer and listed a few quality laptops to consider. Computer hardware is no longer advancing at the pace it was in the last decade. A modern desktop computer/laptop with quality components will last you many years.

Savings	Many of the computers I have worked on are not that old and are still nice pieces of hardware. Users who have littered their computers with malware have the inexpensive alternative of buying a new hard drive and rebuilding the computer. Buying a new computer or having it expensively repaired should be your choice of last resort. Buy or download a new OS and install it. I teach you how to do that.

For example, if you go to http://www.newegg.com and search for "Seagate Momentous," you will find many inexpensive drive models to choose from to replicate your current laptop hard drive.

WARNING 	A dangerous trend, which is fleecing consumers everywhere, is the selling of computers with pre-loaded OSs and not providing the re-installation media DVDs. Manufacturers count on the fact that users will eventually corrupt their systems and only have the recourse of going out and purchasing new computer hardware that they really don't need. There are many corporations that are making a profit trying to clean malware off these systems, which is usually a waste of time and money. Another problem is that often times these preloaded systems come with tons of bloatware* (free trials) that many times have processes running in the background, doing who knows what. This bloatware* also drags down the performance of the computer. If you have a preloaded OS and are reading this chapter, consider reinstalling the OS for a fresh start.

Computer professionals on the radio and in periodicals everywhere, are advising users to back-up their data, but do not advise how to make a clone of your OS disk and to store your data offsite, somewhere other than your house or place of business. They want you to use paid services in the cloud, which I think is a mistake. Many of these "cloud" corporations may have hidden agendas and may not protect your data.   Other corporations you deal with may reveal data about how you used their services to affiliates for profit.   You need to consider these things as you use these services, as well as social media.

As we use our desktops and laptops, we personalize them with things such as shortcuts, favorites, power settings, applications, and a plethora of other things. When we add these customizations to our computer, it becomes an extension of ourselves. All of our latest homework assignments, our tweaks, shortcuts, projects, taskbar items and much more, are all there, where and when we need them. Everything has become quick and easy over years of tips and tweaks. When disaster strikes, we may have a backup of our data, but we have lost years' worth of changes and tweaks that are now unrecoverable. This can result in weeks or months' worth of work because many times we have forgotten how we set these things up in the first place. That is how this chapter came about. Because of my experimenting with various products and security techniques, I found myself destroying computer OSs on a regular basis. This chapter is a set of directions to everyone on how to rebuild a computer from scratch after a disaster or purchase. However, if you have a clone of your OS at an opportune time, this chapter may not be necessary, except as a reference. You can have your old computer back in an hour or less.

Being able to bring up a presentation with a click of the mouse is not possible on a NEW computer. All of that customization we did for years will have to be set up the way we had it, to look professional in a meeting while doing a demonstration--or something else, which we took for granted in our old computer setup. Therefore, in addition to a data backup, we also need a computer OS backup. If you stand to lose a job, profitable contract, or credibility with a presentation tomorrow, you cannot afford to risk everything on a hard disk crash or a virus/spyware infestation. You can't just go out and buy a new computer and expect things to run along smoothly. You will run into many things that you forgot where you learned them when trying to get everything back the way you had your computer setup. This will cost you many valuable hours of your time and money, time and money better spent with your core business or family. From my own personal experience, these disasters have cost me family vacations, where my time, would have been much better spent otherwise.

My advice would be that, in addition to holding your USB data backup in a safety deposit box, you should also hold a duplicate laptop hard drive in there as well. It is very easy to do for a laptop because most times they only have one hard drive. This may not be practical for a desktop setup in where I recommend a RAID configuration with multiple drives. You can do this easily by cloning your current hard drive with an open source, donationware* application such as http://clonezilla.org/downloads.php, https://en.wikipedia.org/wiki/Clonezilla, or pay somebody to clone it for you. The problem with a clone is that we run the risk of bringing all the BAD garbage along for the ride with the good. So a clone should only be done when the computer is purchased, reloaded with a fresh OS, or has reached some milestone in customization and application installation that you can't do without.

An alternative to cloning is to create a new CLEAN computer build by downloading and installing all of the latest and greatest software and drivers onto a new hard drive until it is just as functional as, but better than your current setup. Then you can swap hard drives that are in a safety deposit box every so often to keep them both up-to-date with all the latest updates, configuration changes, software installs, data, etc. It is the same as having two fully functional computers in one computer. This practice also makes sure that you have all of your data and downloads (music, applications, etc.) backed up, for you will have to make sure all your data is duplicated on both of the hard drives. If you don't want to pay for a safety deposit box, keep your USB backup and hard drive at an off-site location, such as at a distant relative's house and swap them on visits. Another alternative is using a server farm, the cloud, or sky drive on the Internet. However, as we have read or heard about often in the news, corporate and government sites continuously get cracked, subpoenaed and may not be dedicated to keeping your data private. Consequently, if privacy is a concern, just like the bank in the Cayman Islands, you should consider managing your data on your own.

If you decide to do this for your single drive desktop or laptop, make sure that you buy the VERY BEST hard drive your computer is capable of running. The hard drive, CPU and RAM are your most important pieces of hardware in a laptop or desktop computer. The hard drive being the biggest bang for the buck. For example, I investigated and my laptop can only run a 750 GB hard drive. New laptops can run 1.5 terabytes or more. Refer back to Chapter 3 where we discuss modern computer hardware, laptops and how to build a server.

 Most modern laptops are capable of running Windows 7 64-bit. I once spent many hours loading and configuring a 32-bit OS on a laptop capable of running a 64-bit OS. Make sure you install the best/correct OS for your hardware.

Windows 7 -- 45 Steps Configuring, Customizing and Optimizing for Use

Below are many open source and donationware* solutions, and in many cases, these projects are funded solely by the donations from the people and will cease to exist without our support. If you use these solutions, please donate to their projects. The customizations and open source solutions will add many capabilities and shortcuts to your laptop or desktop computer. They will also enhance performance, will make you more productive, and keep you safer connecting to the Internet.

1. Turn off Windows Update if you will remember to manually keep your OS updated. I have had the setting <u>Install updates automatically (recommended)</u> reboot my computer right in the middle of my work. This setting is dangerous and we do not want Windows constantly polling the Internet. If you won't remember to install updates, choose the <u>Check for updates but let me choose whether to download and install them</u> which will warn you that updates are needed but allow you to control their impact on your work. ***Click on <u>Start</u> > select <u>Control Panel</u> > on the upper right make sure <u>Small</u> or <u>Large icons</u> is selected > select the <u>Windows Update</u> icon > in the left panel click on <u>Change settings</u> > under Important updates change the drop down to <u>Never check for updates (not recommended)</u>, <u>OK</u>.***

2. ***Add the <u>Network</u>, <u>Recent Items</u>, and <u>Run...</u> commands to the Start menu by right clicking on the bottom taskbar > scroll down to the bottom of the menu that pops up and select <u>Properties</u> > click on the <u>Start Menu</u> tab > select the <u>Customize...</u> button > scroll down and check the <u>Network</u>, <u>Recent Items</u>, and <u>Run command</u> boxes.***

3. Make sure that the computer is seeing all of the hardware installed and connected to it. ***View the system information by selecting <u>Start</u> > <u>Run...</u> > type <u>msinfo32</u> to examine the hardware that it shows.***

4. Microsoft turned off Windows Live Messenger support March 2013 worldwide with the exception of China. If you have a copy installed on your computer it will start automatically unless you turn it off. ***When the Messenger window pops up click on <u>Options</u> > uncheck the <u>Start Messenger when I log on to my computer</u> check box > <u>OK</u>.***

5. Reorganize the start menu. ***Click on <u>Start</u> > <u>All Programs</u> > Drag and drop the menu items to where you want them.*** For example, move all the Windows Live icons to the Windows Live folder, thus making your start menu less cluttered.

6. Go into the programs menu and send all of the icons that you use most to the desktop. ***Click on <u>Start</u> > <u>All Programs</u> > right click on the icons > arrow down to select <u>Send to</u> > arrow right to select <u>Desktop (create shortcut)</u>.*** Following are some applications to consider putting on the desktop: Calculator, Command Prompt, Internet Explorer, Internet Explorer (64 bit), Microsoft Security Essentials, Notepad, Snipping Tool, Windows Explorer, Windows Live Mail, Windows OneDrive, and Windows Live Writer if you have a blog, etc. When done, ***right click on the desktop > select Sort by > and select your favorite sorting method.*** (See: https://onedrive.live.com/about/en-us)

7. Send a second Command Prompt to the desktop to Run as Administrator. ***Right click on the Command Prompt icon > select <u>Rename</u> > type <u>Admin Command Prompt</u> > select <u>Properties</u> > click on the <u>Advanced...</u> button > check the <u>Run as administrator</u> box > click on <u>OK</u>.*** Windows 7 did not feel that the administrator user ID should have administrator command line privileges; this shortcut will override that.

8. We can now drag and drop the icons that are most used to the taskbar. ***Unpin any icons from the taskbar that you don't want by right clicking on the icon and selecting <u>Unpin this program from the taskbar</u>. Do the same for any shortcuts that are on your desktop by right clicking > select <u>Delete</u>.***

9. Add the Toolbars you want to the taskbar. *Right click on the taskbar > select **Toolbars** > and add the tool bars you want.* For example, add the desktop toolbar to the taskbar so that you can take advantage of all of your desktop shortcuts without having to go to the desktop. *Right click on the taskbar > click on the **Toolbars** menu item > check the **Desktop** box.*

10. *Auto-hide the taskbar by right clicking on it and unchecking **Lock the taskbar**.*

11. *Skip down to **Internet Explorer-Setup & Hardening your Browser Security** to configure your Internet Explorer browser.*

WARNING 	Windows 7 comes with a default service startup configuration that Microsoft feels represents the needs of the average SBO/HCU. Some of these services can be disabled to save valuable computing resources and prevent exploitation by a cracker. The website http://www.blackviper.com has a few service configurations that you should consider. This exercise may seem excessive but it is necessary to our layering or hardening security practices. *Click on **Start** > **Run...** > type **services.msc** > scroll down to the Service Name > right click and select **Properties** > change the **Startup type:** change it from **Automatic** to **Manual**, or **Manual** to **Disabled**.* Another useful tool you can download and install to manage programs, drivers and services, and windows features is Comodo Programs Manager. (See: https://www.comodo.com)

12. Consider disabling the Application Management service. According to Black Viper, this service processes installation, removal, and enumeration requests for software deployed through group policy and has no dependencies. This is consistent with the Microsoft description of this service which reads, "*Processes installation, removal, and enumeration requests for software deployed through Group Policy. If this service is disabled, users will be unable to install, remove, or enumerate software deployed through Group Policy.*" This is something that a home computer user will probably not engage in. It is set to Manual by default, and Status was *not* Started. (See: http://www.blackviper.com/windows-services/application-management)

13. If you see services BBUpdate and BingBar Service running, this means that you have installed the Microsoft Bing Bar. To disable these services run Revo Uninstaller and remove the Bing Bar application from your computer. The description that Microsoft provides for the BBUpdate service is ominous, "*Enables the detection, download and installation of up-to-date confirmation files for Bing Bar.*" If the description stopped there, just having it polling the Internet is cause enough to uninstall the Bing Bar, but the description goes on to say, "*Also provides server communication for the computer experience improvement program. Stopping or disabling this service may prevent you from getting the latest updates.*" So not only is this service polling the Internet, it is also providing metadata* on how you are using the Internet. The Bing Bar Service states "*Keeps Bing Bar up-to-date. Disabling this service might prevent updates and expose your computer to security vulnerabilities or functional flaws in Bing Bar.*" Rather than have a Bing Bar, which may have security vulnerabilities and is constantly polling the Internet, uninstall it!

14. If you have no use for external Bluetooth equipment with your computer such as mice, keyboards, phones, PDA or other devices, disable the Bluetooth Support Service. (See: http://www.blackviper.com/windows-services/bluetooth-support-service) It is set to Manual by default, and Status was *not* Started.

15. If you don't use or know what a smart card is, then disable the <u>Certificate Propagation</u> service. According to Black Viper this service "*copies user certificates and root certificates from smart cards into the current user's certificate store, detects when a smart card is inserted into a smart card reader, and, if needed, installs the smart card Plug and Play mini-driver.*" According to https://en.wikipedia.org/wiki/Smartcard, smart cards provide identifications, authentication, data storage and application processing. Smart cards (much like the new smartphones) can serve as credit or debit cards, fuel cards, mobile phone SIMs, authorization cards for pay television, household utility pre-payment cards, and much more. It is set to <u>Manual</u> by default, and <u>Status</u> was *not* <u>Started</u>.

16. Consider disabling the Windows <u>Distributed Link Tracking Client</u> service. Unless you plan to maintain links between New Technology File System (NTFS) files within a computer, across a domain, or to use AVG AntiVirus, this service is not necessary. (See: http://www.blackviper.com/windows-services/distributed-link-tracking-client) It is set to <u>Automatic</u> by default, and <u>Status</u> was <u>Started</u>.

17. If you have no use for them, consider disabling or changing to manual vendor services that may have come preinstalled on your computer. For example, <u>HP Quick Synchronization Service</u> http://h10025.www1.hp.com/ewfrf/wc/document?docname=c02066996&cc=us&dlc=en&lc=en. From the web page, "*You can use HP QuickSync to synchronize your personal files such as music, pictures, and documents with files on another computer, or syncable device, through a network connection. Syncable devices include phones, MP3 players, flashdrives, and external hard drives.*"

18. Disable <u>Microsoft ISCSI Initiator Service</u>. According to Black Viper this service "*manages Internet SCSI (iSCSI) sessions from this computer to remote iSCSI target devices*", and has no dependencies. (See: http://www.blackviper.com/windows-services/microsoft-iscsi-initiator-service) It is rare that a SBO/HCU needs access to an iSCSI target. The Microsoft description of this service reads, "*Manages Internet SCSI (iSCSI) sessions from this computer to remote iSCSI target devices. If this service is stopped, this computer will not be able to login or access iSCSI targets.*" It was set to <u>Manual</u> by default, and <u>Status</u> was *not* <u>Started</u>.

19. Disable the <u>Netlogon</u> service. This service is not needed for most HCU/SBO networks and is only required to login to a domain controller. (See: http://www.blackviper.com/windows-services/netlogon) The Microsoft description reads, "*Maintains a secure channel between this computer and the domain controller for authenticating users and services. If this service is stopped, the computer may not authenticate users and services and the domain controller cannot register DNS records.*" It was set to <u>Manual</u> by default, and <u>Status</u> was *not* <u>Started</u>.

20. If you are using a local, unmonitored network, disable the <u>Network Access Protection Agent (NAP)</u> service, which collects and manages health information for client computers on a Network. (See: http://www.blackviper.com/windows-services/network-access-protection-agent, http://wiki.blackviper.com/wiki/Network_Access_Protection_Agent) According to http://technet.microsoft.com/en-us/library/bb632818.aspx, "*Enabling the Network Access Protection client agent makes it possible for Configuration Manager 2007 clients that support Network Access Protection (NAP) and are assigned to this site to evaluate software updates for their statement of health. Configuration Manager 2007 can also monitor clients that are in remediation for any NAP policy defined on the Network Policy Server.*" The Windows service <u>Network Access Protection (NAP) agent</u> is probably valid for a SBO/HCU network. It was set to <u>Manual</u> by default, and <u>Status</u> was *not* <u>Started</u>.

21. Disable the Parental Controls service. From Microsoft, "*This service is a stub for Windows Parental Control functionality that existed in Vista. It is provided for backward compatibility only.*" If parental controls are needed, this can be done effectively by using your router to block websites. (See: http://www.blackviper.com/2010/12/17/black-vipers-windows-7-service-pack-1-service-configurations) It was set to Manual by default, and Status was *not* Started.

22. Disable Remote Procedure Call (RPC) Locater service. According to Black Viper and Microsoft, this service is left over from Windows 2003 that manages the RPC name service database. In Windows 7, it does not provide any functionality and is present for application compatibility. (See: http://www.blackviper.com/windows-services/remote-procedure-call-rpc-locator) It was set to Manual by default, and Status was *not* Started.

23. Disable Remote Registry Service. I can't imagine an instance where we would want to allow an external user to alter our PC registry. It is rare that an SBO/HCU user would need this service enabled. It was set to Manual by default, and Status was *not* Started.

24. If you have no need to access smart cards on your computer, disable the Smart Card and the Smart Card Removal Policy services. (See: http://www.blackviper.com/windows-services/smart-card) It does not make sense to have this process running in background consuming resources when it is there to support hardware you may not even own or use. They were set to Manual by default, and Status was *not* Started.

25. Go to http://www.blackviper.com to see if there are other services whose startup status you may want to change. Then take a few hours to review non-Microsoft services that are also running. Plug their names into your favorite search engine inside a Virtual Machine using Private Browsing mode. Click on the questionable links to try to find out what they are. ***Select Start > Run... > type services.msc and change the startup of any other services that may need it***. Analyzing the services on your computer is also a way to find software applications you might want to uninstall. For example, I noticed that the Maxtor Scheduler2 Service was being Automatically started. The Maxtor Scheduler2 Service is part of Seagate's Disk Wizard software. When building computers, I experimented with their software on my PC and forgot to uninstall it. If I ever need Seagate's tools again, I would want to download and install the latest version of their software.

26. Another tool for examining what is running in the background is msconfig. ***Select Start > Run... > type msconfig and click on the upper Startup tab***. Examine what is starting up and deselect that which you know you don't need every time your computer starts. The Tools tab is also a quick way to get at a lot of powerful Windows 7 Tools quickly. For example, running *msconfig* identified a lot of bloatware such as Adobe Reader and Acrobat Manager, DigitalPersona Pro, HP Adviser, HP Quick Launch Buttons, Intel(R) Common User Interface, Java(TM) Platform SE Auto Updater, KeePass, Maxtor MaxBlast, Maxtor Scheduler2 Service, Microsoft OneDrive, MUI StartMenu Application (if you don't use your webcam), NCPluginUpdater (checks for HP updates) and more, were all starting in the background on my laptop. For my use of the computer, there was no need to have any of these processes running in the background sucking down resources and possibly accessing the Internet.

27. Yet another utility to discover what is running in the background on Windows is Autoruns. Autoruns claims it is the most comprehensive tool for discovering and displaying what programs are configured to run during system boot up or login. The tool will also show you the order in which these processes are started. You can also configure the tool to show other hidden toolbars, browser helper objects and more that you may want to stop.

When you see all the things running in the background, you may find this disturbing. (See: http://technet.microsoft.com/en-us/sysinternals/bb963902.aspx)

> You will have to research what each background process is doing and whether you can do without them. For example, researching NetGEAR Genie showed that it was valuable to have this process running in the background. (See: http://netgear.com/landing/genie/faq.aspx) This process monitors network activity and will auto fix many network disconnection issues, among other things. It is also a good tool to use to see if there are any channel conflicts with your Wi-Fi Network.

28. Windows 7 comes with an annoyingly short power setting before the screen goes black. *To adjust this click on **Start** > **Control Panel** > make sure **Large** or **Small icons** are selected in the upper right combo box > select **Power Options** > under **Preferred plans** select **Balanced (recommended)** > on the right select **Change plan settings** > adjust **Turn off the display: 10 minutes; and Put the computer to sleep: 30 minutes** to something more preferable.* You should use the same series of steps to set your laptop to Power saver Mode when using the battery.

29. *Defrag the hard disk by clicking on **Start** > **All Programs** > Arrow up to select **Accessories** > arrow down to select **System Tools** > click on **Disk Defragmenter** > click on the **Defragment disk** button.* There is usually more than one way to accomplish a task, *open **Windows Explorer** > on the left click on **Computer** to expand the menu > right click on the drive letter you want to defragment > arrow down to select **Properties** > click on the **Tools** tab > click on the **Defragment now...** button > click on the **Defragment disk** button.*

30. Consider downloading and installing Microsoft's free Process Explorer as an alternative to Task Manager. This tool presents processes in a nice tree format and shows a lot more information than Task Manager, which includes process identifiers. (See: http://technet.microsoft.com/en-us/sysinternals/bb896653.aspx)

31. If you have installed the Windows Office software *click on **Start** > **Windows Update** to apply all the latest Office updates > click on **Start** > **All Programs** and send your often used Office applications to the desktop to create shortcuts > drag them down to the taskbar.*

32. *Open up Microsoft Word, Excel, and PowerPoint and click on the little down arrow in the upper left corner to **Customize the Quick Access Toolbar** > mouse down to **More Commands...** and start adding options like **Save As**, **New**, **Open**, **Open Recent File...**, **Cut**, **Copy**, **Paste**, **PasteMenu**, **Find**, **Spelling & Grammar** > **Print Preview and Print** in whichever order you prefer.*

33. Configure and optimize Windows 7 Explorer by referring to Windows 7 Explorer Demystified - How to open up the directories, files and programs you use the most with only a few clicks of the mouse!

34. Setup a GodMode directory to navigate the computer quickly by referring to Windows 7 - Using GodMode to quickly navigate to all your administrative needs.

35. Sort all your desktop icons by type. *Right click on the desktop > select **Sort by** then select **Item type**. Drag the icons from the desk top to the taskbar located at the bottom that you want on the taskbar.*

36. Unlock the taskbar, use small icons and allow it to Auto-hide. ***Right click on the <u>taskbar</u> > uncheck the <u>Lock the taskbar</u> > select <u>Properties</u> > check the <u>Auto-hide the taskbar</u> box and consider checking the <u>Use small icons box on a Laptop</u>.***

37. Add the Address Toolbar to the taskbar. ***Right click on the taskbar > select the <u>Toolbars</u> tab upper right > check the <u>Address</u> box.*** Any URL you type as an URL address in the toolbar will bring up your default browser to that URL address on the Internet.

38. If you have not already done so, change the desktop icons to add <u>Network,</u> <u>Computer</u> and <u>Control Panel</u>. ***Right click on an open area in the desktop > go to the bottom and select <u>Personalize</u> > click on <u>Change desktop icons</u> in upper left corner > check which icons you want on the desktop.***

39. If Windows is your favorite OS, consider setting up and using an https://onedrive.live.com/about/en-us. You can work on the same files from ANY *Windows* computer you own by just by powering on. Windows OneDrive can be used to sync up all your files with a Windows cloud server and can be particularly helpful if you are planning to use Microsoft Office 365 or buy Office 2013, which is integrated with OneDrive. In fact, purchasing these products will give you 20GB more of free storage. You can also upgrade to as much as 100GB or less for $20 to $50 a year. While writing this book I had to use five computers, which I had synced to my Mesh Drive. When I started my book I found out quickly I had to be able to work on any computer and start work in the book where I left off on anther computer.

WARNING	Microsoft does not encrypt your data on their OneDrive and, according to data leaked by Edward Snowden, they share your email and Skype conversations with the U.S. NSA. There have also been incidents where Microsoft has banned use based on the data stored on their OneDrive. How could Microsoft know there was pornography on their OneDrive unless they were spying on the data? (See: http://www.forbes.com/sites/kellyclay/2012/07/19/is-microsoft-spying-on-skydrive-users) There are encrypted skydrive alternatives such as SpiderOak. The alternative is to use a tool such as BoxCryptor to automatically encrypt your data prior to transfer to your OneDrive. (See: https://www.boxcryptor.com/en/microsoft-skydrive)

You have to carefully weigh the risks versus the time and convenience of using the cloud. I encourage all cloud services to adopt SpiderOak's model to keeping data secure by encrypting it. Always keep a local copy and/or backup in case your OneDrive ever gets confused or your OneDrive service is cut off or discontinued for some reason.

40. Update the Windows <u>Send to</u> Menu to include a shortcut to your OneDrive, other files and perhaps, open other applications. ***Open <u>Windows Explorer</u> > click on the address bar at the top in an empty area to the right > this will highlight the directory location you were residing in > type the following in the address bar, <u>%APPDATA%/Microsoft/Windows/SendTo</u>, hit <u>Enter</u> > the menu displaying the <u>Send to</u> options should now be displayed > start adding shortcuts, such as your SkyDrive or SpiderOak directories to the <u>Send to</u> options that are listed > to copy in these shortcuts, open a second Windows Explorer window and then start to copy and paste them in.***

41. Consider updating Windows to allow safe removal of USB drives without first having to click on <u>Safely Remove Hardware and Eject Media</u> in the system tray. *Plug in your USB drive > select <u>Start</u> > arrow right to select <u>Control Panel</u> > make sure <u>Small</u> or <u>Large icons</u> are selected upper right > click on <u>Device Manager</u> > expand <u>Disk Drives</u> on the left > right click on your USB device and arrow down to select <u>Properties</u> > click on the <u>Policies</u> tab at the top > under <u>Removal Policy</u> make sure <u>Quick removal (default)</u> is selected.* This means that as long as you are reading from or writing to your USB drive you can safely remove it without using the <u>Safely Remove Hardware and Eject Media</u> system tray icon on the taskbar. This allows us to unplug the USB device safely.

42. Consider copying in all your data files from backup prior to system imaging.

43. Add some unprivileged user accounts--*click on <u>Start</u> > <u>Control Panel</u> > click on <u>User Accounts</u> > on the right panel select <u>Manage another account</u> > click on <u>Create a new account</u> link near the bottom > under <u>This name will appear...</u> type in your <u>New account name</u> and make sure <u>Standard user</u> is ticked > click on the <u>Create Account</u> button at the bottom.* From now on, log in as this standard user for added security.

44. The Windows 7 core OS configuration is now complete. We should consider creating a system image on a USB drive and/or alternate formatted disk partition by *clicking on <u>Start</u> > <u>All Programs</u> > <u>Maintenance</u> > <u>Backup and Restore</u> > <u>Create a system image</u> on the left menu > select your backup device (e.g. DataVMRaid1) > click on <u>Next</u> > <u>Start Backup</u> when prompted. Also, create a System Repair CD, label it with your motherboard name/Win7 64-bit and date it before storing it in a safe location.* This will create a system image file on your second partition and/or USB drive from which Windows 7 can restore your computer. If you have a lot of data and/or downloads copied onto your computer hard drive, this file will be large. If your drives are from Western Digital, they are offering (Acronics True Image) software to clone your drive which is another option to consider for imaging your hard drive. .

45. Once system disk imaging is complete, move/copy all downloads and music from your backup device to the computer. If you have multiple users, (which was recommended) put them in a community directory such as (C:\Downloads, C:\Music) directories, then add a shortcut to them in the Windows Explorer Favorites for easy navigation to by all users.

Windows 7 -- 58 Donationware, Freeware and Open Source Software Solutions

1. Before we get into adding useful freeware*, donationware*, open source Tools and Utilities, we may want to download Chocolatey. Chocolatey can download, install and update software from the Windows command line (C:\> choco install <software>). This utility is intended for developers and system administrators to script/automate getting all of this useful software. Users familiar with Ubuntu flavors of Linux may have used the apt-get command. Chocolatey, http://chocolatey.org/packages operates in a very similar fashion.

2. *Download and consider running HiJackThis*. HiJackThis can identify many potential problems with your computer. HiJackThis provides a quick way to get a look at everything that is running in the background on your PC. Be careful using the software to fix anything unless you have done your homework first and are using an anonymous VM. For example, HiJackThis showed me that Seagate DiscWizard, some experimental software from a project long ago, was still running services in the background. (See: http://find.pcworld.com/64317, http://free.antivirus.com/us/#cleanup-and-prevention, http://sourceforge.net/projects/hjt/?source=directory)

3. Consider downloading and installing AbiWord, which their website describes as "*an award winning, small, fast, featureful and crossplatform word processor.*" AbiWord also boasts that it is tightly integrated with https://abicollab.net, which will allow you collaborate and write documents with your friends in real time. AbiWord works in both Windows and Linux and is a fairly active project, but has a lack of Windows developers with the latest version at 2.8.6 versus 3.0.1 for Linux. (See: http://www.abiword.org)

4. Copy your Microsoft installation files to your computer and the install Microsoft Office 2010 either from DVD or your copied files. If you don't have Windows Office, then download and install https://www.libreoffice.org, which is the continued open source alternative Windows, or look at Apache http://www.openoffice.org software, which is now hosted by the Apache Software Foundation. If you install LibreOffice, go to the desktop and delete the Installation files.

NOTE

On 1 June 2011, Oracle Corporation submitted the OpenOffice code base to "The Apache Software Foundation (ASF)". According to Oracle, this was done because of contractual obligations with IBM. There was a transition period after being submitted for OpenOffice, and many forums say that the project fell well behind the open source LibreOffice project. According to wiki, most of the development is now being done by IBM employees. All the Linux distributions covered in Chapter 6 have switched to LibreOffice. (See: https://en.wikipedia.org/wiki/OpenOffice, http://www.openoffice.org)

Conversely, at http://blogs.apache.org/foundation/entry/the_apache_software_foundation_announces35 on 18 October 2012, ASF "*announced that Apache Open Office has graduated from the Apache Incubator to become a Top-Level Project (TLP).*" With that announcement Apache OpenOffice became available and has experienced millions of downloads. They also stated "*During its development period in the Apache Incubator, the Apache OpenOffice project transitioned nearly 10 million lines of code, added numerous enhancements, and fixed dozens of user-reported bugs in the popular and free productivity suite. In addition, the software received five industry awards, ranging from individual component highlights to top download to best open source desktop office productivity application suite.*" ASF has continued to actively support OpenOffice with their 4.0.1 release in October 2013, a 4.1 release just around the corner, and a reported 85,000,000 downloads.

The Apache Software Foundation is a non-profit corporation that also develops open source software like the Apache Web Server. However, their license is different from the GNU General Public License (GPL) license. Apache software can be used in a GPL project, but the reverse is not possible. The Apache Group is an organization made up of volunteer developers, nonprofit and commercial organizations.

5. An alternative to the office solutions above is Kingsoft Office Suite, which has three modules: Writer, Spreadsheets, and Presentation. Kingsoft offers free, Standard and Professional editions. Kingsoft says their product is smaller, and faster than Microsoft. At $70 for the Professional version, this is significantly cheaper than Microsoft Office. (See:

http://find.pcworld.com/72746, http://kingsoftstore.com/windows/professional-office-difference.html)

6. Optional: Download and Install Firefox, which is the default browser in most Linux operating systems. Firefox is a versatile browser that has many plugins from which to choose. Refer down to <u>Firefox-Setup & Hardening your Browser Security</u> to configure Firefox for safer Internet use. (See: https://www.mozilla.org/en-US, https://en.wikipedia.org/wiki/Mozilla_Firefox, http://www.pcmag.com/article2/0,2817,2349494,00.asp)

7. Consider downloading and installing the open source system cleaner BleachBit, which can be used in a professional setting. BleachBit can hunt down and find trash files on your computer to remove, which CCleaner may miss. (See: http://bleachbit.sourceforge.net/download/windows)

8. Consider downloading and installing Linphone is an open source VOIP project, available on mobile and desktop environments (iOS, Android, Windows Phone 8, Linux, Windows Desktop, MAC OS X) and on web browsers. Their website says, "Linphone leverages the Session Initiation Protocol (SIP) to provide users the capability to make voice and video calls directly through web browsers. Linphone is well maintained and supports advanced features such as IPv6, most all webcams, multiple calls simultaneously with call management features, text instant messaging and much more. (See: https://www.linphone.org)

9. Consider an alternative to using Adobe Reader that is to download and install the Foxit Reader. This is a small, fast, and feature-rich PDF viewer, which allows you to open, view, and print any PDF file. Also, download the manual. Foxit has an A+ rating at the Better Business Bureau. (See: http://foxitsoftware.com/Secure_PDF_Reader, https://en.wikipedia.org/wiki/Foxit, https://www.bbb.org/us). Unlike other free PDF readers, Foxit Reader also includes easy to use collaboration features, like the ability to add annotations, fill out forms, and to share information with social networks. There are a number of add-ons, short cuts and preferences documented in the manual. ***Double click on the icon, <u>Next ></u> > <u>I accept...</u>, <u>Next ></u> > uncheck options like <u>Set Ask.com as my homepage</u>, <u>Next ></u> > <u>Next ></u>, <u>Next ></u> > I unchecked <u>Show PDF files in browsers</u>, I prefer to view PDF's in their own windows, <u>Next ></u> > leave <u>Enable Safe Reading Mode</u> checked, <u>Next ></u> > <u>Install</u>.*** The first element of surprise was that Foxit opened my PDF files in Full Screen mode. ***Hitting the <u>Esc</u> or <u>F11</u> key will exit Full Screen mode. You can also configure Full Screen mode by selecting <u>Tools</u> > <u>Preferences...</u> > mouse down to select <u>Full Screen</u> and select options like <u>Show Menu bar</u> and <u>Show Navigation Pane</u>***. The Full screen mode is very handy for viewing PDF files. There have been some user complaints that it won't open some PDF files that Adobe will, but every PDF that I have viewed has worked fine.

Tip	Foxit version 6.1 and later will also load what they call Foxit Cloud as a separate install. If you do not plan to use their 1GB of free cloud storage you should use Revo Uninstaller to remove this bloatware that will run services in the background on your computer. (See: http://www.foxitcloud.com)

10. If you decide not to try Foxit Reader, go to http://www.adobe.com and download the latest Reader, Flash Player and Shockwave Player. ***Uncheck any add-ons like <u>McAfee antivirus install add-on</u> or <u>Include Norton Internet Security</u>***. Adobe is invasive and will

constantly poll the Internet and run the <u>Adobe Acrobat Update Service</u> and the <u>Adobe Reader and Acrobat Manager</u> process in the background. If you plan to handle the Adobe updates on your own (recommended), run <u>Adobe Reader</u> and *select **Edit** > **Preferences** > under **Categories:** scroll to the bottom and click on **Updater** > tick the **Do not download or install updates automatically** option, **OK** > arrow up to select **Tracker** > uncheck **Show notification inside system tray***. One might think that by disabling automatic update this would stop the update service, but that is not the case. All we have done is to stop Adobe from installing automatic updates; we have not killed its background services and processes. ***Click on <u>Start</u> > <u>Run...</u> > type services.msc > right click on the <u>Adobe Acrobat Update Service</u> > arrow down to select Properties > beside <u>Startup type:</u> change <u>Automatic</u> to <u>Manual</u> > click on <u>Start</u> > <u>Run...</u> > type <u>msconfig</u> > uncheck <u>Adobe Reader and Acrobat Manager</u> > reboot.*** You will have to update Adobe yourself occasionally, but this is far better than having the updater polling the Internet with who knows what slowing down your computer constantly. It is very important to keep Adobe updated, so if you won't remember to update it manually, then *leave automatic updates enabled*. Depending on your needs for Adobe, there are a few security changes we can make to Adobe Reader to make its use safer. ***Click on <u>Edit</u> > arrow down to select <u>Preferences</u> > on the left pane select <u>Trust Manager</u> > uncheck the box <u>Allow opening of non-PDF file attachments with external applications</u> > arrow up on the left pane to select <u>JavaScript</u> > uncheck the box <u>Enable Acrobat JavaScript</u> > on the left pane select <u>Internet</u> > uncheck the box <u>Display PDF in browser</u> > OK.***

11. Consider changing the settings for Adobe Flash Player to keep it from constantly polling the Internet for updates. ***Click on <u>Start</u> > arrow right and up to select <u>Control Panel</u> > click on the <u>Flash Player</u> icon > under the <u>Storage</u> tab consider selecting <u>Block all sites from storing information on this computer</u> > click on the <u>Advanced</u> tab > under <u>Updates</u> click on the <u>Change Update Settings</u> button, <u>Yes</u> > tick <u>Never check for updates</u> (not recommended). If you do this you will have to manually check for updates by following the steps above. Under <u>Updates</u>, click on the <u>Check Now</u> button, which will show your flash player version and offer up a link to download the latest flash player > uncheck <u>Yes, install McAfee Security Scan Plus - optional</u> > click on the <u>Download now</u> button > open the downloaded file to run the update > when the <u>Update Flash Player Preferences</u> dialog appears tick <u>Never check for updates (not recommended)</u> again, <u>NEXT</u> > flash will install, <u>FINISH</u>. When installing a new flash player update always check <u>Never check for updates</u>.***

	Whenever I installed Flash Player updates the software prompted me if I wanted it to automatically check for updates. I always ticked <u>Never check for updates</u> which was completely ignored during startup. Sometimes within a month or two upon boot a dialog box would appear indicating that I needed to update my Adobe Flash Player. The only way this could happen is if the software was polling their corporate website upon boot up giving information about what I was doing using my computer. I hope this shows how without laws to protect you even saying no this invasive computer software does little to protect your Internet privacy.

12. Windows 7 comes with the ability to burn CD and DVD disks. The open source program http://infrarecorder.org comes with additional abilities that you may need to burn CDs and DVDs. Consider downloading and installing it. I have experienced problems using

Windows new CD/DVD Burn utility. Another FREE alternative I have used is the ISO burning software from http://imgburn.com. With it, I have successfully burned many CDs and DVDs on old hardware using their 1X speed. ImgBurn has to make money and comes loaded with baggage. Their website is a nightmare of advertising. If you want to try http://imgburn.com software, consider using http://download.cnet.com/windows to download the software. I scanned and installed the latest version 12/2/2011 and discovered two advertising cookies on my desktop. The install also wanted to add the http://www.ask.com toolbar to my browser (**say no**). After the install, delete the cookies from your desktop and then run CCleaner to make sure you have removed everything that ImgBurn created. After that, the software will succeed where others fail to burn CDs and DVDs. Either of these solutions may also succeed on old hardware.

13. If your DVD drive is capable of imaging LightScribe CDs and DVDs http://lightscribesoftware.org, one of your vendor updates may be to install the LightScribe Software, which you may not want to do. Lightscribe is invasive and will run on startup, and automatically start a service in the background. If you have other purchased or open source CD/DVD disk-burning software, those products usually support burning LightScribe disk images, pictures, and text to the back of your media.

14. If you don't have purchased software, LightScribe provides free programs and designs for that, which will also burn images, pictures, and text on the back of your CDs and DVDs. *Go to http://lightscribesoftware.org > look for Get the latest downloads > download the LightScribeSimpleLabeler, and LightScribe Template Labeler in that order.* On the original site there were label designs and they downloaded and installed one by one which still holds true on the ".org" site. Surf to http://lightscribesoftware.org/template-labeler-templates and download the installer files for the templates you need. Each Label design will show up as a separate install in Windows 7 *Control Panel > Programs and Features*, which is somewhat cumbersome.

15. LightScribe will run in the background unless you tell it not to. *Click on Start > All Programs > LightScribe Direct Disk Labeling > LightScribe Control Panel > uncheck Run this program when I log onto Windows > click on OK. Consider also Modifying contrast settings to This will make your labels darker, but you will experience a longer label time*.

16. Consider changing the LightScribe service to Manual only if you will be using the software occasionally. Doing this makes LightScribe unable to label disks until this service is started again. *Click on Start > Run... > type services.msc > and scrolls down to LightScribe Direct Disc Labeling Service > right click on the entry > Select Properties > change the Startup Type to Manual*.

Tip

The days of getting CDs and DVDs in the mail with your online purchase of a vendor software product solution are over. Most all of the vendors will supply any software downloads that you may need to burn to disk, backup and store somewhere secure. This is also true of many open source and donationware* solutions as well. When you burn an ISO image to a Lightscribe disk, take the added time to do a nice design for the top of disk. Be sure to include the complete name of the product, the key that unlocks the software for use, the date you burned the disk, as well as any other information like reference numbers, support phone numbers, purchase order number, etc., all on the cover of the disk. The disk itself then becomes your one-stop-shop for all of the information that

	you may need to contact support and install the software product.

17. Consider downloading and installing the latest Java 32-bit and 64-bit Runtime Environments if you plan to use both browser options at http://java.com/en. ***Click on the Free Java Download button > Agree and Start Free Download > Save file > install the Java software > uncheck any suggested bloatware such as Install the Ask Toolbar... if prompted, Next> > the Installing Java dialog should appear, when done installing click on Close. After installation click on Start > Control Panel > Java > General > click on the Settings... button > uncheck Keep temporary files on my computer > click on the Delete Files... button > click on OK > select the Advanced tab > expand the JRE Auto-Download menu > select Never Auto-Download > OK. If you want Java for Mozilla browsers click on Advanced > scroll down to Default Java for browsers > select Mozilla family.*** Enabling Java enhances your Internet experience but at a sacrifice to your Internet security. Java is also very persistent in that even if you tick Never Auto-Download the Java (TM) Platform SE Auto Updater will continue to run in the background. You will have to use the previously discussed *msconfig* utility to prevent this bloatware from running in the background.

18. After installing the latest version of Java, adjust the settings to your requirements and to enhance your security. ***Click on Start > arrow right and up to select Control Panel > in the Control Panel window click on the Java icon > with the General tab selected at the bottom under Temporary Internet Files click on the Settings... button > at the top uncheck Keep temporary files on my computer. > or, under Disk Space consider lowering the amount of space available for storing temporary files > click on the Delete Files... button at the bottom to remove the temporary files that may have already been placed on your computer.*** There are other settings that you may want to adjust under the Advanced tab. For example, ***under Security-General consider unchecking Use TLS 1.0 and checking Use TLS 1.2. Transport Layer Security (TLS) version 1.2, which is cryptographic protocol that provides communication security over the Internet.*** However, doing this may break some websites that only have TLS 1.0 support. TLS 1.0 is enabled by default in most browsers, and if your browser has TLS 1.2 support, it is usually disabled by default. According to Wikipedia, security holes have been discovered and exploited in the TLS 1.0 protocol making it is less secure than the 1.2 protocol. TLS 1.2 was defined back in August 2008 and was further refined in March 2011. (See: https://en.wikipedia.org/wiki/Transport_Layer_Security)

19. Consider Downloading and installing open source FileZilla, which supports FTP, FTP over SSL/TLS (FTPS) and SSH File Transfer Protocol (SFTP). FileZilla is a cross-platform, multithreaded FTP, FTPS, and SFTP client that has an intuitive GUI interface. It is fast and reliable, easy to use, and has many useful features. (See: http://filezilla-project.org)

20. Consider downloading and installing Freemake at http://www.freemake.com to use their free Video Converter, Video Downloader, Audio Converter and Free Music Box! Convert video free to AVI, MP4, WMV, MKV, FLV, 3GP, MPEG, DVD, Blu-ray, MP3, iPod, iPhone, iPad, PSP, Android, Nokia, Samsung, BlackBerry. Convert audio free to MP3, WMA, WAV, FLAC, AAC, M4A, OGG, convert audio to MP3 player, iPod, iPhone, iPad, PSP, and more.

21. Install your web development software. I use an old version of Microsoft Expression Web. A very dated open source solution that you can try at http://www.activestate.com is Komodo Edit. Activestate also sells a fully featured IDE development application.

22. Donationware* Spybot-Search and Destroy http://www.safer-networking.org version 2.4 includes a modern user interface that is more user friendly than older versions of their product. It has also been tested for compatibility with other third-party products. Safer-Networking Ltd has a very good privacy policy and boldly makes the statement, "*Safer-Networking Ltd. will not rent or sell potentially personally identifying or personally identifying information to anyone.*" The malware definitions are actively maintained.

23. Install Microsoft MapPoint 2010. Insert DVD and click on <u>Setup</u>. This will also install Access database engine and C++ Redistributable. ***Click on Start > All Programs > Right click on Microsoft MapPoint North America 2010 and Send to Desktop > drag the desktop icon to the taskbar***. If this is a backup OS disk, which you will store off-site, don't run and activate it. Make sure that the license key is in a text file on the disk.

24. Consider downloading and installing Malwarebyte's Anti-Malware software, definitions and updates from http://www.malwarebytes.org. Malwarebyte's free version of their product will not run processes in the background on your computer, so it has to be manually updated. This means that the free version does not come with any real time protection, making it useless for front line defense. Using this free version can be viewed as a **good thing** because background processes don't drag down your computer's performance. To install the free version, you must uncheck the <u>Enable free trial of Malwarebytes...</u> unless you are planning to upgrade and purchase the PRO version for $25 (which is not a bad idea!). Malwarebytes finds malware that other anti-software misses, so having it active in the background is not a bad idea. In addition, I have not heard of it conflicting with other anti-software like so much of the other anti-software does.

WARNING 	Backup your data before removing any malware that any anti-software identifies. Crackers put bombs in their software that will destroy your computer when programs such as Malwarebytes try to remove their malicious deeds. They do this to teach you the lesson that it is better to let them spy on and use your computer than to have to fix what they have done to spy on you. That way, the word spreads that someone who used Malwarebytes or some other anti-malware software had it destroy their computer, thus spreading false information, making it easier for the bad guys to operate unmolested. One friend ran Malwarebytes and rebooted after it removed some malware, only to have their computer take over ½ hour to recover.

So, what do I like about this? It is not another program running in the background doing who knows what. It adds another layer of defense that you can run and update, when you deem fit. I have used this software many times on my computers where it reported finding nothing. This indicates to me that this software is genuine in its intent to find malware. Otherwise, it would present the removal of malware to make you want to purchase it. A friend asked me to fix her slow-running laptop. I ran CCleaner to clean out most of the temporary files, which usually wipes out the majority of malware on most systems. The laptop was then scanned with an updated copy of Microsoft Security Essentials, which found nothing. I then ran Malwarebytes, which found **48 installations of malware** on my friend's laptop that her other anti-software had missed. On another friend's computer, it found and removed eight traces of a very malicious rootkit that Norton had ignored. (See: https://en.wikipedia.org/wiki/Malwarebytes_Anti-Malware)

NOTE 	A rootkit is an extremely nasty piece of malware that derives its name from the administrator account *root* in UNIX, BSD and Linux. A *root* user can do anything in Linux and has total control of the system. So a rootkit, by definition, gives the cracker total control of the system. The Window equivalent of *root* is the *administrator* and *system* accounts. A remote attacker had administrator privileges on that computer. If you go to http://www.malwarebytes.org/products/other_tools Malwarebytes now provides their Anti-Rootkit BETA software, which promises to remove the latest rootkits. Being BETA software means you use it at your own risk.

If Malwarebytes discovers malware like the serious threat above, you have to assume someone has been watching what you have been doing and attacking other devices on your network. You should change all your passwords and freeze your credit, which we will cover in the section of this book on Identity Theft. Malwarebytes is a worthy addition to your anti-malware arsenal that you should run and update on an occasional basis.

25. If you download and install SuperAntiSpyware Free Edition, it will run in the background using resources. Consider using the SuperAntiSpyware Portable Version at http://superantispyware.com, which does not run in the background and will scan your computer. This is not one of the best-rated products, but it is a good addition to an anti-spyware arsenal. The portable version will not update on its own, so every so often you will have to download the portable version to use it. If you download the portable application, place it on the desktop and then rename it to make running it easy to find. SuperAntiSpyware was acquired by Support.com in June 2011, who promptly improved this product. Their Privacy Policy does allow the collection, use and distribution of information about you. **Right click on the file > mouse down and select _Rename_ > type _SuperAntiSpyware_**.

26. Download and install Revo Uninstaller http://www.revouninstaller.com, a free or paid software uninstall/removal utility for Windows. The program does very a good job cleaning up files and the registry during removal. I have been using Revo Uninstaller for years. It seems to do a better job at removing unwanted applications than using the **_Control Panel_ > _Programs and Features_** tool that Windows provides. Revo also offers a Professional version of their software. You can view a comparison of the freeware* versus Professional versions at http://www.revouninstaller.com/revo_uninstaller_free_download.html. For example, the Pro version has full 64-bit compatibility, which was very important to my computers.

27. Consider downloading and installing 7-Zip. It is a file archiver that recognizes many formats and has a high compression ratio. It works in both Linux and Windows. If you are using a 64-bit OS, be sure to download the 64-bit version of the software. 7-Zip also gives you the ability to encrypt your files or an email to an AES password encrypted zip file. (See: http://7-zip.org)

28. Consider downloading and installing open source Pidgin, which is a graphical, multi-platform, instant messaging client. It supports various chat networks (AIM, Bonjour, Gadu-Gadu, Google Talk, Novell Groupwise, ICQ, IRC, Jabber/XMPP, MSN, MXit, MySpaceIM, SILC, SIMPLE, Sametime, XMPP, Yahoo!, and Zephyr). Pidgin integrates with the system tray on Windows, GNOME 2, KDE 3, and KDE 4. It has been suggested that Pidgin is not tracked by the NSA. (See: http://pidgin.im, http://www.pidgin.im/download/source)

29. For an easy to use source code and text editor that comes with many more added options than Windows 7 Notepad, consider downloading and installing the open source http://notepad-plus-plus.org. Uncheck the Auto-Updater option if you will maintain the software updates yourself.   Notepad++ boasts high execution speed and small size.

30. Windows comes with the Windows Media Player (WMP), which is an excellent and versatile media player. If you want to try alternate media players, Linux comes with a variety that you can read about in Chapter 7 on virtualization. Since we can run those media players in Linux, we should leave WMP as the default in Windows 7. There are alternatives to WMP, visit https://en.wikipedia.org/wiki/Comparison_of_audio_player_software or https://en.wikipedia.org/wiki/Comparison_of_video_player_software both of which have excellent comparisons of all of the various media playing options. A few of the more popular are J. River Media Jukebox http://jriver.com/mj, Songbird http://getsongbird.com, and Winamp http://www.winamp.com.

31. VLC is a multimedia player and streamer. The project page for VLC (initially VideoLAN Client) describes VLC as a highly portable multimedia player for various audio and video formats, including MPEG-1, MPEG-2, MPEG-4, DivX, MP3, and OGG, as well as for Audio CDs, DVDs, VCDs, and other various streaming protocols. It also can be used as a server for unicast or multicast streams in IPv4 or IPv6 on a high-bandwidth network. The browser plugin adds support for formats to web browsers. (See: http://www.videolan.org/vlc, https://en.wikipedia.org/wiki/VLC_media_player)

32. Consider downloading and installing Google Chrome https://encrypted.google.com/chrome or https://www.google.com/intl/en/chrome/browser, which is highly rated by PCWorld and PCMag, as an alternative to open source Firefox, introduced above if you would prefer both, or only Chrome. Software developers I have talked to tell me that web development is easier for Chrome than Firefox and that they really like Chrome. Be sure to examine Google's privacy policy at https://www.google.com/intl/en/chrome/browser/privacy prior to using Chrome. (See: http://www.pcmag.com/article2/0,2817,2365692,00.asp)

46. ***Consider downloading and installing Windows Live Essentials which has become dated by surfing to http://windows.microsoft.com/en-us/windows-live/essentials > click on the Download Now button > save and run, or just run the wlsetup-web.exe executable > install the Windows Live Essentials you may need (e.g. Messenger is deprecated, Mozilla Thunderbird is a superior email solution, you may not want an unencrypted OneDrive which Microsoft shares with NSA, and so on) > restart your computer > run Windows Update again > reboot the computer > repeat this process until Windows Update says No updates are currently selected***. The Live essentials install will pull down Microsoft Silverlight. Microsoft says, "*Silverlight delivers rich Internet applications and media experiences on the Web.*" You can still use the dated Windows Live Mail 2011 with all your email accounts but I think Thunderbird presented later is a better email client solution. ***Click on the Windows Live Mail icon > click on the down arrow in the upper left > select Options > select Email accounts... > click the Add... button and add your email accounts***.

47. Windows Live Mail does not use the signature that you have set up with Microsoft. As a result, you have to manually add a signature to every computer that uses Live Mail. Windows Live Mail allows you to use an HTML file as a signature, so you can get fancy if you want. If you have an OneDrive, you can maintain your email signatures there, in a directory like EMailSignatures. You can edit the signature(s) in Microsoft Word documents, then save the Word signature files as Web Page, Filtered, (*.htm, *.html) files, which

Windows Live Mail can read and attach to outgoing email messages. Sending a signature as HTML maintains the hypertext links and other advanced things that you might like in your signature. If you want to personalize a signature for each account that includes something such as your email address as part of the signature, you will need a different signature for all your email accounts. When you synced up to the OneDrive you automatically got all your signature files. All that is left is to configure is <u>Windows Live Mail</u> to use the signature files. ***Open <u>Windows Live Mail</u> > click on the down arrow in the upper left corner > scroll down to <u>Options</u> > select <u>Mail...</u> > click on the <u>Signatures</u> tab > click on the <u>New</u> button > rename the signature to something like <u>Hotmail Signature</u> > check the <u>File</u> box at the bottom > click on <u>Browse...</u> > click on the right button down arrow to select HTML Files (*.htm, *.html) > select the signature file from your synced OneDrive files > > associate the signature with the email account highlighting the signature > click on the <u>Advanced...</u> button > and check the box next to the <u>Account</u> > repeat the process for your other signatures.*** Refer back to OneDrive.

33. An excellent alternative to using Windows Live for your email is Mozilla Thunderbird. Download and install the latest version of Thunderbird from <u>https://www.mozilla.org/en-US/thunderbird</u>. Once the software is installed it will have to be configured to your email service provider. ***When the System Integration screen appears you will have to decide if you want Thunderbird as your default for Email, Newsgroups and Feeds. Set as Default > under <u>Would you like a new email address?</u> enter an existing or new email address. This is your chance to create a new email address, so under <u>Would you like a new email Account?</u> screen will appear you can click on <u>Create a new account:</u> or just choose to use an existing account.*** Thunderbird is very good at looking up your server information so all you should have to do is enter a username and email address and you are off and running. The next step is to add the personal information such as contacts and signature files.

34. Another excellent alternative to Window Live is the Seamonkey all in one Internet suite. Seamonkey comes packed with a Web-browser advanced e-mail, newsgroup and feed client, IRC chat, HTML editing. The suite appeals to advanced users, web developers and corporate users. (See: <u>http://www.seamonkey-project.org</u>)

35. Consider downloading and installing gVim, which is an extension of the VI editor for Windows that offers all the benefits of the UNIX/Linux VI editor, which will be covered in the chapter on Virtualization. It also has the cut and paste capabilities of text-based programs like Notepad. This is a must have for a UNIX/Linux person. Because it is a programming tool, it also shows which double quote matches another double quote, or which parenthesis matches another parenthesis, and so on, which is great for scripting when this is needed for coding. ***Remove the <u>gVim Read only 7.4</u> and the <u>gVim Easy 7.4</u> shortcuts from the desktop to keep it clean.*** If you need those options, they are available in the <u>Start</u> menu. (See: <u>http://www.vim.org</u>)

36. I don't agree with storing contact information at an ISP cloud site or on an ISP email website. There have been too many cases in which websites and corporations are being cracked or subpoenaed for the personal information that their customers have stored on their websites. I use the NOT Free software Time & Chaos at <u>http://www.chaossoftware.com</u>, which is now offering a free version of their software. Time & Chaos is a locally secure application that keeps all my appointments, calendar, contact, memo, notes, and task information in files on my local computers. (See: <u>http://www.chaossoftware.com/products.aspx</u>) This is advantageous because we don't

have to have an Internet connection to get to all of our contact, appointment, to-do, and calendar information. Time and Chaos also have a very small footprint on my computers. Years of data in its files only take up 30 Megabytes. ***Consider downloading all the other freebies that are provided by ChaosSoftware like Google Updater, National Holiday transportable records and the Technical word database for spell checking > to the C:\Program Files (x86)\Chaos Software\Chaos 8 directory > Run TimeandChaos and point the application to where its data files are located C:\Data\TimeAndChaos.*** Time and Chaos will not force you to upgrade or renew your license every few years. In all of the time that I have used it, I have only had to pay for one upgrade, which was not required if I wanted to continue to use a previous version. This longevity and upgrade support are the qualities that I look for in a good product. We can also encrypt and share the T&C data between all of our Internet devices using the cloud. Skip down to SpiderOak-Encrypting and Syncing up your Contacts, Finance, and Investment data to learn about how to do this. Then consider double encrypting the data with BoxCryptor encryption tool discussed in Chapter 5.

37. Download and install KeePass at http://KeePass.info, the free, open source, light-weight and easy-to-use password manager* that has erased hours of password frustration from my life! It is covered in detail in Chapters 7 and 11 of this book.

38. Password Safe is the open source twin of KeePass. It is also covered in Chapter 11. (See: http://pwsafe.org, http://passwordsafe.sourceforge.net)

39. GnuPG ftp://ftp.gnupg.org/gcrypt/binary is the free implementation of the OpenPGP standard as defined by RFC4880. This software is a scaled down command line version of GunPG version for Windows that you can use instead of software from the Gpg4win project. GnuPG is a secure email and file encryption tool. Consider downloading and installing this useful software. ***Click on Download in the left menu > Scroll down until you see under Binaries the text Packages for MS-Windows are available at Gpg4win > click on Gpg4win, which will take you to http://gpg4win.org***. Refer back to Chapter 5 for a more detailed description of this software and encryption technology.

40. Consider using the SpiderOak backup/sync service for your more sensitive data. Reference http://go.pcworld.com/spideroak, and https://spideroak.com to learn about their secure online backup/sync services. They provide 2GB free, and their product will work on Linux, Windows, and Mac. SpiderOak appears to take protecting your data seriously by encrypting it to keys that only you know. SpiderOak calls this its "zero-knowledge" privacy policy, which is rare or possibly unique among cloud service providers. Before I knew about SpiderOak, I was using many computers and mobile devices to write this book, so to keep my work up-to-date on all my Microsoft computers, I took the risk that my work might become compromised for the sake of the time savings. Moving my book and other sensitive documents to SpiderOak mitigates that risk. Now is the time to copy all of your sensitive data. To read about setting up a SpiderOak Sync between all of your computers and virtual environments, skip down to SpiderOak-Encrypting and Syncing up your Contacts, Finance, and Investment data.

41. Hopefully, you use some sort of home financial software. It automates many tasks such as downloading checking account transactions. I have been a Quicken http://quicken.intuit.com user for years. However, when you read Chapter 7 , your will see that I have switched to using an open source solution in a guest OS for all my banking. When using Quicken, I encrypted the Quicken database and kept a backup on my SkyDrive. If you install Quicken delete the added desktop Icons that Quicken might add,

such as <u>One Month Free – pay bills right from Quicken</u>, <u>Best Card for Quicken Users – Great NEW rewards</u> and <u>Free Credit Report and Score</u>. Let Quicken apply updates. Then update Quicken with latest financial data.

42. An alternative to using Quicken is the open source alternative KMyMoney-KDE or GNUCash-GNOME, which you can install into any virtual guest Linux OS. We will cover how to do that in the upcoming virtualization chapter.

43. Consider downloading and installing File Shredder at <u>http://fileshredder.org</u>, to shred confidential files. Windows delete only removes bits of information, making deleted files recoverable. If you need to delete a file in a fashion that is unrecoverable, File Shredder claims it is the tool for the job.

44. Consider downloading and installing Kernel File Shredder at <u>http://www.fileeraser.net</u>, which is another alternative to File Shredder. This is an alternative to just deleting a file in Windows and making sure it is unrecoverable.

45. Consider downloading and installing GNU Image Manipulation Program to edit your digital photos. GIMP is widely considered to be the main, donationware-functional drop-in replacement for Adobe Photoshop, with a similar feature set as well as a similar and complex user interface. (See: <u>http://www.gimp.org</u>, <u>https://en.wikipedia.org/wiki/GIMP</u>)

46. Consider downloading and installing Adaptable GIMP, which is a modified version of the GNU Image Manipulation Program. This makes it easy to create and share task-based interface customizations. (See: <u>http://adaptablegimp.blogspot.de</u>, <u>http://adaptablegimp.en.softonic.com</u>)

47. Install all of your other purchased software like Nuance Dragon Premium. Dragon Naturally Speaking is speech recognition software that will type what you say. The headset that comes with Dragon is plastic and breaks very easily, so consider purchasing a headset separately. I would consider using the Astro A50 Wireless Headset with Dragon, which has been touted to be the best wireless gaming headset. It is very comfortable to wear and works with PCs and gaming consoles. Nuance installs a service that will start automatically in the background that you should change to manual to save computer resources. When you run Dragon it starts the service, so why have it running in the background all of the time doing who knows what? I suppose they think it saves a second or two on application startup. (See: <u>http://www.nuance.com</u>)

48. Consider downloading and installing Easeus Todo Backup at <u>http://todo-backup.com</u>, which is a free and easy-to-use backup solution. The application can perform incremental and differential backups, image your system partition from within Windows, and browse to recover individual files and folders. The program has a 5-star rating at <u>http://download.cnet.com/windows</u> and was recommended by the March 2012 issue of <u>PCWorld.com</u>.

49. Consider downloading and installing Oracle's <u>https://www.virtualbox.org</u> at <u>https://www.virtualbox.org/wiki/Downloads</u> and Extension pack so that you can download and run virtual OSs on your computer. VirtualBox is covered fully in <u>Chapter 7</u> . For the individual home user it is the best free virtualization solution for your Guest OS needs.

50. Consider downloading and installing VMware Player so that you can download and run virtual OSs on your computer. VMWare Player is covered fully in <u>Chapter 7</u>. (See: <u>http://www.vmware.com</u>)

51. Consider downloading and installing Secunia Personal Software Inspector (PSI) that will scan the third-party software on your computer for vulnerabilities. It will identify programs that are in need of security updates and allow you to automatically apply the updates. As

we already covered, you were encouraged to turn off automatic updates for all of the software installed on your computer. Running PSI occasionally will allow you to keep everything up-to-date with one caveat. Secunia will run upon boot-up and keep polling its online database to see if updates are needed. (See: http://secunia.com/vulnerability_scanning/personal).

52. Consider downloading and installing Belarc Advisor, which can conduct a security analysis of your computer. This software is free for personal use and will detail many problems in your computer setup. The problems list will include links on how to fix any security issues it finds. One of the things this book recommends is turning off automatic updates for everything. Belarc will tell you when security updates for those applications become available. (See: http://belarc.com)

53. Set up all of your desktop shortcuts. *Click on Start > All Programs > Highlight the applications you use the most > Right click and pick Send to > Desktop (create shortcut)*. Examples of some shortcuts that we might want to send to the desktop are: Ad-Aware, Adobe Reader X, Calculator, CCleaner, Command Prompt, Admin Command Prompt, Computer, Control Panel, Dell Webcam Central, Dragon Naturally Speaking, Firefox, Foxit Reader, gVim 7.4, Internet Explorer, Internet Explorer 64bit, Keepass Password Safe, Lightscribe, Malwarebytes, Microsoft Access 2010, Microsoft Excel 2010, Microsoft Expression Web, Microsoft MapPoint 2010, Microsoft PowerPoint 2010, Microsoft Security Essentials, Microsoft Word 2010, Network, Oracle VM VirtualBox, Quicken, Recycle Bin, Revo Uninstaller, SuperAntiSpyware Portable file, PuTTY, Windows Explorer, Scripts we run often, Snipping Tool, Time And Chaos, SpiderOak, Windows Live Mail, Windows Live Writer, Yahoo Finance Web Link, VirtualBox, and/or VMware Player and so on.

54. Now that all of the software is installed, we should again check to see what is starting automatically on your computer to keep the performance fast and secure. *Click on Start > Run... > type msconfig > click on Software Environment > select Startup Programs > Examine what is starting up*. There may be some pesky programs that don't show up in msconfig that startup in windows, which you will also have to examine. *Click on Start > Run... > type regedit, and press <Enter> > in the left pane, expand the registry to HKEY_LOCAL_MACHINE\SOFTWARE\Microsoft\Shared Tools\MSConfig\startupreg*. You can export and then delete these startup keys to keep them from starting upon reboot.

55. Clean up your data files prior to imaging. Run CCleaner and defrag your hard drive prior to imaging. Move all downloads to your backup device. I leave my data files in place so that they will be part of the disk image file that I am about to create. CCleaner Tools can also be used to adjust what is starting up on your computer.

56. If you want more refined control on what is starting up on your computer, try using WinPatrol. It will show you what is starting up in the background. If you want to speed up the boot process, you can delay things starting in the background with the tool also. (See: http://www.winpatrol.com).

If you are not running RAID, consider downloading http://clonezilla.org, https://en.wikipedia.org/wiki/Clonezilla and burning it to a CD. If you have a bootable USB, you can run Clonezilla from that, as well as use it to image your hard drive to your backup device. The example to the right shows the use of a Lightscribe Template to burn an image onto a CD. At this point, with a clone of the system we can always recover the system, to a new hard drive from a catastrophic system failure.

57. Another option for backing up your computer is the Seagate Disk Wizard at http://origin-www.seagate.com/support/downloads/discwizard. From the Disk Wizard manual, "*It can backup the entire disc drive or selected partitions, including your operating system, applications, settings and all of your data. You can also use the software to securely delete any confidential data you no longer need.*" Seagate says you can quickly restore your computer from any backup that you may have made. What is really nice is the number of storage devices you can backup to using the software IDE, SCSI, FireWire (IEEE-1394), USB (1.0, 1.1 and 2.0) and PC Card, formerly called PCMCIA removable media drives, as well as CD-R/RW, DVD-R/RW, DVD+R/RW, magneto-optical, Iomega Zip and Jaz drives. Disk Wizard is also an excellent solution to clone a hard drive to a new hard drive.
58. The Windows 7 freeware*, donationware* and open source software OS installs are now complete. We should consider creating a system image on a USB drive and/or alternate formatted disk partition detailed as the last few steps in the previous section.

If you ever lose your software keys, a FREE program, Magical Jelly Bean Finder can be used to examine installed keys. (See: http://www.magicaljellybean.com/keyfinder)

SpiderOak – Encrypting and Syncing up Your Contacts, Finance, and Investment Data

There are many options for backing up data to the cloud or having easily accessible sky drives for you to use to sync your data to and from multiple computers. However, we have to consider that anything we put out on the cloud is public information. Companies, by U.S. law, can be made to turn over all of your data stored on the cloud very easily to government officials.

Cloud services that don't encrypt your data can be cracked, subpoenaed by government officials, or have an employee go rogue with your data. Dropbox and SugarSync are two more services you can use to house data on a SkyDrive. While they encrypt your traffic in route, they both hold the storage decryption keys, which mean that a rouge employee or the government can view your data at anytime. SpiderOak, in their privacy statement says that they do not. We will talk about data encryption keys in Chapter 9, but if you were using SpiderOak and someone tried to compromise your data, they would have to break SpiderOak's 256-bit AES encryption of your data. That is about as secure as we can be in the civilian world using front line encryption. SpiderOak also tries hard to be transparent. They provide an annual report that shows how many times the company complied with subpoenas to turn over information to the government. We will discuss later as to how to set up an encrypted SSH server that could house this type of information and be accessed from anywhere in the world, and from inside your local network. The SSH solution to keeping your devices updated is the most secure. But doing so is inconvenient, and things can get confusing as to what computer is updated with what. Plus, trying to teach family members or employees how to get the latest files from an SSH server is difficult. Files that are constantly changing, which include things such as appointment schedules, may just have to be just synced with the SpiderOak sky drive, where they are at the very least, encrypted to SpiderOak's privacy standards.

There are certain files that contain very sensitive data that we wouldn't want housed on the cloud, unencrypted, or at all. As discussed, the OneDrive that Microsoft offers houses your data unencrypted. My data list includes my book and its artwork, contacts, passwords, financial and investment information, as well as a few other items. This limited set of files can usually be stored easily inside the free SpiderOak 2GB limit. SpiderOak is a good compromise between security and convenience. The first thing that I worried about was how I had to allow SpiderOak access to my private network through the Windows 7 firewall. While this is scary, it is not as bad as setting up unencrypted SkyDrive's and giving them access. The Privacy statement https://spideroak.com/privacy_policy, to their credit, has many details about the measures they are taking to protect your data and privacy. This is very unlike the trend in other privacy statements which are long, confusing, and usually have many loopholes and caveats. Read these other privacy statements and come to your own conclusion. (See: https://en.wikipedia.org/wiki/SpiderOak)

WARNING	When a program is added to the list of allowed programs in your software firewall you are allowing that program to send and receive information to or from your computer via the Internet. That application can punch a hole in your firewall when it is running. This is not as bad as permanently opening a port, which you should only do with grave consideration.

The SpiderOak license agreement points out a few things that you need to understand about using SpiderOak. If you lose your password, you will not be able to access your data or reset your password; this is the price you pay for encryption that is somewhat secure. SpiderOak also does not offer any guarantees that your data will not become lost or compromised. This is pretty standard in the cloud world. For that reason, it is always best to backup your data in the old traditional fashion, which is to a local backup device, then swap that backup device with another device located offsite, perhaps a safety deposit box or at a friend's or relative's house.

Surf to https://SpiderOak.com/opendownload > at the top of the web page click on Downloads > under Supported Downloads find the download that you need for your OS and download SpiderOak's software for your OS platform. Install SpiderOak and click on the Finish button > if Launch SpiderOak on exit. is checked the application will open automatically > open the folder housing the downloaded software (e.g. C:\Downloads\SpiderOak) and run the installation software > on the Welcome to SpiderOak Setup Wizard screen, Next > click on I accept the terms of the License

Agreement, Next > click on Custom Setup SpiderOak defaults to installing everything on local hard drive, Next > under Ready to install SpiderOak, Install > once the software is installed click on Finish > if you leave Launch SpiderOak on exit checked, SpiderOak will launch to a signup dialog > enter your Username: and Password:, Next > select whether you are Adding a new device to my SpiderOak account or Reinstalling an Existing Device, Next > SpiderOak does not automatically figure out your computer's name, so go to the Desktop and right click on the Computer icon > arrow down to select Properties to view your computer name > under Please enter a name for this new computer: type your computer name into the text box, Next > Finish.

Windows Firewall will prompt you to allow SpiderOak access to communicate with your private network, click on the Allow access button with only Private networks checked. It is now time to sync up the sensitive data that you want SpiderOak to house on their server. *Wait until SpiderOak has finished syncing with any previous devices that you may have configured > to actually SYNC a folder, you first have to configure SpiderOak for Backup, the Backup tab is selected by default > to only Sync/Backup a specific directory click on the Advanced button on the upper right > this will present you with a list of folders to select from, navigate to the folder you want to Sync/Backup (e.g. C:\yourname\SpiderOak) and check that folder > click on the Save button at the top.*

We are now backing up the C:\yourname\SpiderOak directory to the cloud. To sync the directory with our other Internet devices and virtual machines *click on the SYNC tab > click on the New button > enter your Sync information (e.g. Sync Name: SpiderOakSync, Sync Description: Home sensitive cloud data that needs encryption.), Next > beside Browse Folder 1: click on the Browse button to browse to your SpiderOak folder you are planning to Sync (e.g. C:\yourname\SpiderOak), click on the Select button lower right.*

The steps above will automatically sync all of your other devices with folder(s) you have just configured. *Below Sync Folder 1 is Sync Folder 2, click on the Browse button to the right and browse it to its SpiderOak folder shown as a previously configured device and click on the Select button lower right > if there are more computers or devices click on the + symbol and repeat this process for each device that you want synced to this computers/device > when done, Next > Step 3 allows you to Exclude file(s) from your sync, Next > Step 4 allows you to verify your configuration, click on the Start Sync button lower right.*

When using SpiderOak, there are a few things of which to make note. The default Sync Schedule is set to follow your Backup schedule which is set to Automatic. *Open up SpiderOak > click on the Overview tab > Under BACK UP, SYNC or SHARE click on the Change button on the right and you will see your backup options in the Preferences window.* The default setting for how often SpiderOak scans your system for changes is automatic. This means that a directory watcher process is constantly running in the background, watching for changes made in the folder(s) you are backing up and possibly syncing.

SpiderOak has to be running in order to backup or sync your data. As we have seen, many programs that we install automatically start services and background programs without giving us the option to easily turn those things off. Many times, finding descriptions of what these background processes and services are doing is very difficult. SpiderOak gives us the option of having it automatically start, or not, which is a wonderful thing. This means that unlike other software and cloud sync services, SpiderOak can be configured to stop constantly polling the Internet. Having this ability to set these and other options is a testimony to the integrity of their product. With the deprecated Windows Live Mesh, double clicking on their Mesh icon did not even bring up a window. This behavior was very distributing and meant that you had to wonder how often Mesh was polling the Internet. Utilities like this need to be more transparent.

Programs that run in the background can also hold ports open to your computer. This is a security risk because these ports provide more abundant opportunities for crackers or malicious software to exploit, spread a worm, access your files or use your computer or spread malicious software to others. Because SpiderOak **can be configured to NOT run in the background**, the ports it uses are only open when you run the application. The "hole" is only open when SpiderOak needs it to communicate with it SkyDrive servers. A good analogy would be opening the door of your house to allow a visitor in and locking it upon their departure.

In the upper right of the SpiderOak window click on the word PREFERENCES to bring up the __Preferences__ dialog > if it is not already selected click on the __Interface__ tab > adjust the options how you see fit (e.g. uncheck __Launch SpiderOak at OS startup?__). There is no reason to have SpiderOak running all the time when backing up your data can be done anytime by just double clicking on the SpiderOak icon. Plus we don't want SpiderOak backing up when we use insecure hotspots.

We will discuss Requirements Definitions and their purpose in Chapter 9 on SSH, but for now let's introduce a Requirements Definition for your SBO/HCU that you must adhere to.

Requirements Definition 1 (RD1) which we will later build upon:
Sensitive data shall be shared between all of our Internet devices so that family members and employees can have access to the contacts, passwords, and financial and investment data that they may need from anywhere in the world that an Internet connection can be found. No confidential data (people's names, phone numbers, addresses, email address, SSN's, birth dates, pictures of, relationships, locations, financial data of any kind, passwords or password files, projects we are working on, or work related data, etc.) shall ever be put on the cloud/Internet unencrypted.

Given this requirement, the first problem was how to keep this information secure and share it between various Internet devices. My first solution was to write scripts using Gpg4win encryption software to encrypt this data and store it on my Microsoft OneDrive. While this kept the data encrypted and secure, it proved to be very difficult to keep current. When my wife added an appointment and did not let me know to update the OneDrive by running a script on my laptop, things got of sync very quickly. I found myself adding contacts, appointments, changing passwords and then forgetting to run the script to update the OneDrive. Since SpiderOak is encrypted, we might consider that this type of data only needs intermediate encryption, which is what I call SpiderOak. SpiderOak's encryption is more secure than just putting data on the cloud unencrypted, but we may want additional protection for data files with SSN's, account numbers, or for our intellectual work.

You will also quickly discover other sensitive data (e.g. your password file, contacts, intellectual property assets lists, etc.) that you will want to share and store at SpiderOak's cloud servers double encrypted. Fortunately, Linux provides the easy-to-script and use *gpg* tool with which to encrypt files.

Requirements Definition 2 to encrypt anything put out on the cloud:
Any sensitive data that we store on the cloud encrypted at SpiderOak shall be encrypted to an AES 256 local passphrase/password using additional local encryption technology. Refer back to Chapter 5 to encrypt the financial data file in $HOME/finance and copy $HOME/spideroak/finance. It would be very simple to modify this to handle any important files. Then we can share our financial data with any computer or VM running Linux or Windows.

I briefly introduced KeePass previously, which is an encrypted password file for your computer. If we store this file at SpiderOak, we in essence have double encryption of our passwords to use anywhere in the world. Keep in mind though we don't have that luxury with some of our other files such as our contacts. While RD1 does a lot for our Internet security, do we really want to trust unencrypted files to SpiderOak when we can easily go one-step further?

Privacyfix Add-On to Check Your Privacy Settings

Everywhere you go in the Internet you are tracked by many corporations. Websites I visited state that there are over 580 tracking technologies developed by 200 companies that follow your activity on the Internet to build up a detailed profile about what you read, like, click, and buy, to sell to advertisers. Just visiting a website page can send your data to 21 more corporations. Websites host many trackers for profit (e.g. 24/7 Media, AddThis, BloomReach, BlueKai, Chartbeat, ClickTale, Coremetrics, Criteo, DemandMedia, DoubleClick, DoubleClick Floodlight, Facebook Connect, Facebook Social Plugins, Gigya Socialize, Google +1, Google AdSense, Google AdWords Conversation, Google AJAX Search API, Google Tag Manager, Google Analytics, iCrossing, Krux Digital, LinkedIn Widgets, Monetate, MSN Ads, New Relic, NetRatings SiteCensus, Omniture, Optimizely, Outbrain, OwnerIQ, Pinterest, Reddit, ScoreCard Research Beacon, SimpleReach, Think Realtime, Turn, Twitter Button, Typekit by Adobe, Valueclick Mediaplex, Viglink and more!) I hope this short list reveals how data is collected about you and how you are tracked in everything you do on the Internet by many entities. We have an epidemic of tracking and direct marketing taking place on the Internet.   There are add-ons that you can add to your browser that will block most of these known trackers.

The Privacyfix add-on will show what the major online trackers are tracking about you. It will also show how much they are making from tracking you. From PCWorld, Jan 2013 *"Privacyfix Tracks the Data You Share"* by Alex Wawro, *"The first thing Privacyfix will do for you is show you which privacy features you've enabled on your Facebook and Google accounts. You can see at a glance whether your Facebook "Likes" are being used to advertise products, or whether Google is logging your search history and is using it to customize the ads you see."*

Privacyfix appears to be a very inconspicuous add-on that tries to guide the user in configuring Facebook and Google security settings to keep them from tracking you. It's also a very informative add-on as well; it reveals a lot about what is happening when you allow these companies to gather information about your Internet activity and sell it. It also helps you to understand what your browsing history is revealing about your Internet use to other companies' websites. Another feature of PrivcyFix is that it will let you know when policies change at the tracking sites. (See: https://privacyfix.com/start)

The only problem with this add-on, and I did not install and test it, is that you are depending on the honesty of these companies to do what they say they will when you enable and disable their tracking and privacy settings. This is much like the "Tell websites I do not want to be tracked" option that browsers have now. There is no law requiring corporations to honor this request. I prefer a more active solution to this epidemic of tracking all of our Internet activity.

Ghostery Add-On to Harden Browsing

Ghostery is a plug-in that you might want to use to block companies from gathering information about your Internet activity. Evidon, Inc., a technology company that allows businesses and end users to control data online, owns the add-on. For businesses and NGOs, Evidon provides the AdChoices icon which their website states, "*functions as a "tracking nutrition label" into ads, as well as reports on trackers and what they are doing on the web.*" Ghostery is the add-on provided to consumers. Evidon says their mission is to make the Internet more transparent for everyone. Ghostery asks that you opt-in to GhostRank. When a user does opt-in to GhostRank, Evidon will gather the following information:

- the tracker identified by Ghostery
- the blocking state of the tracker
- domains identified as serving trackers
- the time it takes for the page and the tracker to load
- the tracker's position on the page
- the browser in which Ghostery has been installed
- Ghostery version information

This data helps to make their server better, is used in studies by university students and privacy researchers, and as a source of the Better Business Bureau. Their privacy policy states that Ghostery does not collect any data unless you initiate it using the icon or enabling GhostRank, and what they do collect is kept anonymous.

From the May 23, 2010 PCWorld article titled "Good-Bye to Privacy" by Tom Spring http://www.pcworld.com/article/196787/good_bye_to_privacy.html?page=2, "Better advertising offers a browser plug in called *Ghostery* that can alert you to hidden trackers and block scripts from tracking you." From https://www.ghostery.com, "Ghostery is your window into the invisible web -- tags, web bugs, pixels and beacons that are included on web pages in order to get an idea of your online behavior. Ghostery tracks over 1,200 trackers and gives you a roll-call of the ad networks, behavioral data providers, web publishers, and other companies interested in your activity.

Ghostery boasts that it will keep you informed and give you control of what you reveal to companies using their websites. Companies gather information about your Internet activity so that they can trade your online behavioral data. Ghostery can help you to make these decisions about what you may or may not want to reveal. Ghostery supports Chrome, Firefox, Opera, Safari and Internet Explorer. Ghostery will put an icon on the top toolbar so that when you click on it, it shows you what it blocked on the web page you just visited. You can also Enable/Disable the add-on, edit the options, give them feedback, get help and share Ghostery.

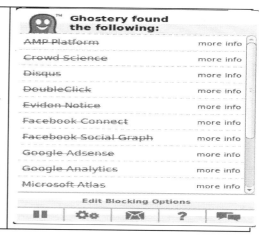

Disconnect.me Add-On to Harden Browsing

Disconnect at https://disconnect.me is very much like Ghostery. It works with Internet Explorer, Firefox, Chrome and Safari. It monitors the data that your browser exchanges with websites and selectively filters the traffic that websites would use to track you. You will still be able to use the services of websites like Facebook or Twitter, but they won't be able to track where you point and click.

To get and install this add-on, visit their website at https://disconnect.me and click on the blue "Get disconnect" button. Disconnect states right on their privacy policy, which is on their home page, "*We don't collect your IP address or any other personal info.*" They also state, "*Disconnect protects, not violates, your privacy!*"
We will discuss anonymity in Chapter 8 with the use of Tor, but if you add https://disconnect.me to your Tor browser, it should keep your Internet activity that much more private and anonymous.

Albine's "Do Not Track Me" to Block Cookies and Trackers

Albine's DoNotTrackMe plugin can be used with Chrome, Firefox, Internet Explorer, Opera and Safari. This is another option to block third-party tracking via cookies and other methods. Albine boasts that since its launch in 2011, it has blocked over one trillion attempts to track users. The plugin makes you feel good as it keeps a running total in your Web browser of the number tracking attempts on each site much like Ghostery does. Before you trust Albine, understand that they are a private, for-profit company and we have seen how just about all of them are exploiting your Internet activity in some fashion. We will discuss the other services provided by Albine in Chapter 11 on identity theft. (See: http://abine.com/donottrackme.html)

Internet Explorer – Setup & Hardening your Browser Security

In the upcoming virtualization chapter we will get to the core of this book and talk about using guest operating systems for all of your Internet activity. Using any browser from a core OS is an invitation to crackers everywhere. We can quickly and easily install a guest OS for browsing and surfing the Internet and for keeping our core OS secure. Although sometimes we may be required to use a core OS browser rather than use virtualization, so it is important to harden our security settings in Windows Internet Explorer browser for use on the Internet. We could also run an old copy of XP on top of Windows 7 as a guest OS, and these instructions should be used to harden that virtual browser as well.

Most browsers are offering the option of housing your favorites online. For example, Apple, Google and Microsoft offer the ability to sync your bookmarks, history, extensions and more, from PC to PC or mobile device. There are a few issues with this strategy. The user cannot sync the information across different browser applications, and you are providing these companies with more tracking information about how you use the Internet. Another option is Xmarks, which is a free cross-platform extension that works with Firefox, Internet Explorer, and Safari. (See: http://xmarks.com, https://en.wikipedia.org/wiki/Xmarks) Xmarks synchronizes bookmarks, passwords, open tabs, and browsing history in Firefox. It will also backup changes you make to your synced information and allow for multiple sync profiles. According to wiki, an Opera version of the add-on is anticipated soon.

A better choice might be to set up a simple website of your favorite links and upload the web pages to your ISP (e.g. see my favorite's website http://thatcybersecurityguy.com/favorites). This way your favorite links are always available from any browser, on any computer, VM or mobile device. No special setup or configuration is necessary to sync up your browsers. You are also spared having your history stored in the cloud and possibly tracked.

Run __Internet Explorer__ and configure the Internet options by clicking on __Tools__ Menu, or the Tools gear on the far right > __Internet options__, or select __Start__ > __Control Panel__ > __Internet Options__ > and customize the setting how you see fit. For example, some of the customizations that I prefer, is to change the home page to my favorite search engines (https://DuckDuckGo.com, https://startpage.com), and add another tab to my website of favorite links to the Internet at http://thatcybersecurityguy.com) > at the bottom under __Tabs__ change the settings by clicking on the __Settings__ button > check __Always open pop-ups in a new tab__ and __Always switch to new tabs when they are created__, __OK__ > click on the __Advanced__ tab and scroll down to the __Security__ options and check the __Empty Temporary Internet Files folder when browser is closed__ box, __OK__.

A somewhat safe method to surf the Internet is to use InPrivate Browsing. InPrivate Browsing is especially important if you are researching a topic using search engines. The links that you click on may take you to unsafe web pages. From URL about:InPrivate "*InPrivate Browsing helps prevent Internet Explorer from storing data about your browsing session. This includes cookies, temporary Internet files, history, and other data. Toolbars and extensions are disabled by default.*" To **temporarily** turn this on in Internet Explorer while surfing the Internet *Click the __Tools__ button upper right* ⚙ *> point to __Safety__ > click __InPrivacy Browsing__ and a browser window will pop up showing that InPrivate is turned on*. To permanently turn this on *click on __Tools__ > scroll down to the bottom and select __Internet options__ > click on the __Privacy__ tab > check __Never allow websites to request your physical location__ > at the top Select a setting for the Internet zone at the highest setting thus blocking all cookies*. Private browsing can be disruptive when you surf to sites that you trust. So temporarily enabling and disabling private browsing, which is easy to do, is a good way to harden security that will still allow you to use the Internet effectively.

WARNING	InPrivate Browsing has its limitations. It does not hide your IP address or prevent websites, advertisers, and ad networks from storing information about your browsing history. It also does not stop surveillance, keyloggers* or shoulder surfing. You will have to study the coming anonymity chapter to become somewhat anonymous on the Internet.

While on the Privacy tab, **under _Location_ tick _Never allow websites to request your physical location_ > under _Pop-up Blocker_ check _Turn on Pop-up Blocker_ > under _InPrivate_ check _Disable toolbars and extensions when InPrivate Browsing starts_**. You can also change how cookies are handled by **_clicking on Tools_ > _arrow down to select Internet options_ > _select the Privacy tab_ > _under Settings consider raising your setting for the Internet zone to a level you can tolerate like Medium High, then click OK_**.

These settings are not very annoying to your browsing activity and should be enabled. Another option, which is off by default, is to delete your browsing history, automatically. **_Select the General tab > under Browsing history > check Delete browsing history on exit_**.

Most modern web browsers offer an option called Tracking Protection that is amazingly off by default. The excuse given for not having it on by default is that many people appreciate having their Internet activity tracked so that corporations can target them with advertising relevant to their interests, thus enhancing their Internet use. Do-Not-Track allows users to opt-out of third-party web tracking and is of limited value. The reason is that the browser sends a special header that corporations may or may not honor at their own discretion. But according to http://ip-check.info/?lang=en it does no harm. So enabling this option might help eliminate a bit of the tracking that is being done.

In Chapter 7 we will go over how harmful allowing this tracking information to be collected is to your privacy. A Tracking Protection List (TPL) is like a _Do Not Call_ list for third-party content on a website. Adding TPLs will instruct Internet Explorer to block sending things such as, your IP address, the web page you are viewing, and more, to some third-party sites. When you visit websites that you need to go to, other companies gather information by providing content to the website that you are visiting. You can still visit the third-party site directly by clicking on a link or by typing its web address.

To turn Tracking Protection on, **right click on the menu bar at the top of Internet Explorer and select _Command Bar_ to display the menu Bar. About five or six items from the left you will see a _Safety_ drop down, click on that > arrow down to select _Tracking Protection..._ from the menu**. You can also bring this option up by **_clicking on the Tools_** ⚙ **button in the upper right corner of your browser window > arrow down to expand the _Safety_ menu > arrow left and click on select _Tracking Protection..._ > you will see _Your Personalized List_ with Status _Disabled_ > click on this and select the _Enable_ button on the lower right**, this will automatically generate a tracking protection list based on which websites you visit. This will help to prevent other websites from gathering information about you when you the visit websites that you need to use. Microsoft is rather vague on how this works. We can improve on our Tracking Protection by adding <u>Tracking Protection List(s)</u> online. The Internet Explorer Gallery of Tracking Protection Lists will help you to control what third party sites track about you while you're online. ***With Tracking Protection selected on the left in the <u>Manage Add-ons</u> dialog box click on <u>Get a Tracking Protection List online...</u> at the bottom > the link takes your browser to <u>http://www.iegallery.com/en-us/trackingprotectionlists</u> web page which is <u>The Internet Explorer 10 Gallery Tracking Protection Lists</u> > there were 11 lists to choose from and descriptions of each one > click on the <u>Add</u> button on the right to add the list(s) that you want to use > go back to the <u>View and manage your Internet Explorer Manage add-ons</u> screen > click on <u>Tracking Protection</u> on the left and you will see that the tracking lists you added are enabled.***

Turn on ActiveX Filtering to block ActiveX controls. According to Windows Help and Support, ActiveX controls and web browser add-ons are small programs that allow websites to provide content such as videos. They can also be used to collect information from your computer, damage information on your computer, install software on your computer without your consent, or allow someone else to control your computer remotely. Same as above, ***click the <u>Tools</u> button*** ⚙ ***> arrow down to <u>Safety</u> > click <u>ActiveX Filtering</u> and a check mark will appear beside this option, enabling ActiveX Filtering.***

	Enabling ActiveX Filtering affected Internet Explorer's ability to use my wife's work VPN* connection. I had to disable this option to allow her to login, even though I had the website set up as a trusted site.

Tracking Protection or ActiveX Filtering can be turned off for trusted sites to allow content. Open Internet Explorer and navigate to a website. If the address bar is green, it indicates that this site has an independently verified certificate issued by a trusted Certificate Authority, making it safe. Next, check the website by ***clicking on <u>Safety</u> > arrow down to <u>SmartScreen Filter</u> > select <u>Check this website</u> > a dialog box should appear stating <u>SmartScreen Filter checked this website and did not report any threats</u> indicating this site is safe for you to turn off filtering options.***

	***Click on the filter button in the Address bar next to the URL and certificate lock, a dialog box will appear stating something like <u>Some content is filtered on this site</u> > click on <u>Turn off all filtering</u> for the website.***

When you turn off filtering for a website, Windows 7 adds an entry to the registry at HKEY_CURRENT_USER\Software\Microsoft\Internet Explorer\Safety\ActiveXFilterExceptions for that site. There was no easy way using the GUI to add or remove individual entries. ***Windows provides a tool called <u>regedit</u> that you can run by clicking on <u>Start</u> > <u>Run...</u> > type <u>regedit</u> and then you can navigate to the registry entries and delete or add individual entries.*** Alternatively, you can use the Command Prompt, which will be covered in the next chapter by typing:

C:\Users\<UserID>> reg add "HKCU\Software\Microsoft\Internet Explorer\Safety\ActiveXFilterExceptions" /v usaa.com /t REG_DWORD /d 1

C:\Users\<UserID>> reg add "HKCU\Software\Microsoft\Internet Explorer\Safety\ActiveXFilterExceptions" /v usaa.com /t REG_DWORD /d 0
Where 1=on, and 0=off

Or delete the entry: C:\Users\<UserID>> reg delete "HKCU\Software\Microsoft\Internet Explorer\Safety\ActiveXFilterExceptions" /v usaa.com

WARNING	In order to turn ActiveX filtering back on for a selected site once all of the filtering is/has been turned off, using the browser, *select **Tools** > **Internet options** > under Browsing history click on the **Delete...** button at the bottom tick **ActiveX Filtering and Tracking Protection** data > **Delete**.* This battle-axe will delete all of the websites that you have enabled for filtering. Using the command line offers a better solution until Internet Explorer offers the ability to turn off ActiveX Filtering for a specific website.

If there are sites that you want your browser to trust (like your banks or investment sites) you can ***browse to the trusted website and copy the URL to the clip board > click on Tools > scroll down to the bottom and select Internet options > click on the Security tab > click on the Trusted Sites icon to highlight it > click on the Sites button which will bring up the Trusted sites dialog > click on the Add button***. By adding "Trusted sites" you are telling your computer that files you download or run from the website will not damage your computer or data, so consider very carefully what sites you add.

Enable Transport Layer Security (TLS) https://en.wikipedia.org/wiki/Transport_Layer_Security version 1.2, which is cryptographic protocol that provides communication security over the Internet. Internet Explorer has TLS 1.0 enabled by default. However, security holes have been discovered and exploited in TLS 1.0. ***Disable TLS 1.0 and enable TLS 1.2 by clicking on Tools > Internet options > select the Advanced tab > arrow down to the Security group click in the box next to Use TLS 1.2 to check it > uncheck Use TLS 1.0 if it is enabled***. Enabling TLS 1.2 may result in some secure websites being unable to load. This protocol has been established since August of 2008, and most reputable websites will have adopted this more secure standard by now. If a web page you need fails to load, try enabling TLS 1.1 and see if that solves the problem.

Consider blocking unsecured images with mixed content. Mixed content on a secure web page puts you at the risk of a man-in-the-middle attack. What happens is an attacker replaces an unprotected image on an otherwise secure HTTPS with a malware version. You will see what the attacker presents instead of what the website meant to show. This allows spoofing and information disclosure attacks to take place. ***Click on Tools > Internet options > select the Advanced tab > scroll down to the Security group > check Block unsecured images with other mixed content***.

Internet Explorer -- Add-ons to Harden Browsing

Another add-on often presented by periodicals and security-minded users is Web of Trust (WOT). Before installing WOT, read https://www.mywot.com/en/privacy/privacy_policy to see the personal information that they will collect about you. Because of WOT's tracking and installation of cookies on your computer, you might want to consider other options. WOT is covered because of its wide use by users of the Internet.

Web of Trust at http://www.mywot.com will cause a circle to pop up next to the links on the page that you are viewing. These circles indicate which links are OK by turning the traffic light red, orange or green; this indicates the rating that millions of other WOT users have assigned to the link. WOT users' rate web links for trustworthiness, vendor reliability, privacy, and child safety. From their website, "*WOT shows you which websites you can trust based on the experiences of millions of users around the world. WOT identifies online threats which automated security technologies miss: Bad customer experience, phishing and age-inappropriate content for children are examples of threats that require human input. WOT is easy-to-use, fast and completely free for Firefox, Google Chrome, Internet Explorer, Opera and Safari.*" **Installing the add-on will open a link prompting you to _Please select a protection setting suitable for you:_ > select your option, _Continue_ > WOT will ask you to _Register a new account_.**

Internet Explorer -- Get Rid of the Bloatware*

I recently worked on a friend's VERY slow running computer. I have never encountered so much bloatware* installed on a computer as I saw in this instance. I spent three hours updating the system to the latest malware definitions, irradiating malicious software, and most of all, uninstalling trial software. Whomever my friend had purchased this prebuilt system from had maxed out their profits with corporate America by installing every trial application software known to man. After all this work, when I kicked off Internet Explorer, it still took forever to come up, but when it did, I saw the problem. Somehow, my friend had been coaxed into installing, or the computer had come with, every toolbar and add-on in the universe installed in their Internet Explorer browser. These add-ons proved very troublesome to remove. **To remove them click on the _Tools_ menu, or the Tools gear on the far right > arrow down to select _Manage add-ons_ > under _Add-on Types_ on the left select _Toolbars and Extensions_ > on the right examine the add-ons that are installed in Internet Explorer and click on them one by one > in the lower right click on the _Disable_ button to stop them from loading into the browser > on the left click on _Search Providers_ > in the right pane right click on the now disabled toolbars and select _Remove_.** This only removes the toolbar from Internet Explorer, but not from your computer. There are still background processes running and the software still needs to be removed. To remove these insidious installations completely, I had to use Revo Uninstaller, which we have previously discussed. Once Revo or Windows Uninstaller removes the programs they are finally and truly gone. It may take more than one try and a reboot to eradicate them.

Story	On a personal note, as I was working I kept rambling on and on about the unprecedented state of my friend's laptop. I told her how she had added pages to my book. When we were done she grabbed her laptop ran out the door. It hit me afterwards that perhaps she thought I was making fun of her and the state of her computer, but just the opposite was true. I was appalled at how corporate America and crackers had taken advantage of an unsuspecting, unknowledgeable computer user. My hope is that all of my friends (everyone) read and benefit from this book!

Firefox -- Setup & Hardening your Browser Security

Firefox at https://www.mozilla.org/en-US/firefox/new is an open source Mozilla Browser with many features, has broad cross-platform support, and is fast. Firefox is very customizable even to novice users. There are many add-ons and extensions available for the Firefox browser. Having a second browser on your computer is also a good way to surf the Internet without revealing so much information about yourself. Configure it to not accept cookies or temporary files, and use things like In-Private browsing which will help keep you more secure on the Internet. If your computer is not powerful enough to support Virtualization this may be your best option.

1. Make sure the Firefox browser is updated to the latest version by clicking on *Help > arrow down to the bottom and select About Firefox > click on the Check for Updates button.*
2. One thing that is new to Firefox is an auto hide feature of the menu bar. This was enabled by default in Ubuntu. If you are like me and prefer having the menu visible all of the time, *open Firefox and arrow up to the top left until the menu bar appears > click on Tools > on the left click on Extensions > on the right you will see the Global Menu Bar integration add-on, click on the Disable button > Restart now, and the menu will be permanently enabled.*
3. In Mint the menu bar was not visible. *Arrow up to the top under Start Page - Linux Mint - Mozilla Firefox and right click on the grey area and check Menu Bar.*
4. There are many Add-ons we can add or disable. The Linux Mint OS comes with Mint Search Enhancer 1.0 add-on preinstalled in Firefox, which enhances the results given by Google. If it is disabled and you like using Google, *click on Tools > Add-ons > Extensions > Enable > Restart now to enable the Add-on.* If you don't use Google consider disabling or removing this add-on.
5. Linux Ubuntu comes with a few Ubuntu extensions you may not want. For example, read about and consider disabling Ubuntu Online Accounts, Unity Desktop Integration and Unity Websites integration.
6. Ubuntu comes loaded with some plugins and extensions installed by default that you may not want or need. Arrow up to the top menu (e.g. Ubuntu Online Accounts, iTunes Application Detector, Windows Media Player Plug-in 10 (compatible; Videos)).
7. Firefox, by default, will store downloads in a preconfigured location. If you prefer to pick the location for your downloads and make Firefox prompt you as to where to store the downloads, *click on Edit menu item > arrow down to select Preferences; or in Windows select Tools > arrow down to select Options > select the General icon and below Downloads check the Close it when all downloads are finished and Always ask me where to save files* and change the home page. I use my website on Internet favorites and a search engine as my home pages https://duckduckgo.com | https://startpage.com | https://ixquick.com | http://thatcybersecurityguy.com/favorites.
8. *Click on Tabs tab and consider checking When I open a link in a new tab, switch to it immediately > check Show tab previews in the Windows taskbar.*
9. *Click on the Content tab > make sure Block pop-up windows is checked and consider unchecking Enable JavaScript.*
10. *Click on the Privacy tab and check Tell websites I do not want to be tracked.*

11. Optional: *While still on the **Privacy** tab under **History** change the selection to Firefox will: **Never remember history** > in the lower center click on **clear all current history** links*. Setting "Never remember history" is the same as using ***Tools** > **Start Private Browsing***. If we set the selection to "Never remember history" Firefox will *not* be able pick up where it left off by using the General tab and changing Startup, when Firefox starts.

12. Another option to the nuclear option above, which blocks everything is *under **History** change it to Firefox will: **Use custom settings for history** > consider unchecking **Accept third-party cookies** and check **Clear history when Firefox closes** at a minimum. To get maximum protection check **Always use private browsing mode** > uncheck **Remember my browsing and download history**, **Remember search and form history**, **Accept cookies from sites***. Without doing the maximum settings, privacy scanning sites reported that cookies were still being allowed even with Private Browsing enabled.

13. If you have a need to store cookies and pick up your Internet browsing where you left off, consider manually enabling Private Browsing when you need it. *In Windows and Linux select **Tools** in the upper menu > arrow down to select **Start Private Browsing** > click on the **Start Private Browsing** button > then turn it off again by selecting **Tools** > arrow down to select **Stop Private Browsing***. To permanently have private browsing in windows *select **Tools** > arrow down to select **Options** > **Privacy** > and under **History** select **Never Remember History***. In Linux *click on **Edit** menu item > arrow down to select **Preferences** > click on **Privacy** icon > under **History** select Firefox will: **Never Remember History***. Using private browsing, according to http://www.online-tech-tips.com/computer-tips/firefox-private-browsing, the following information will no longer be remembered by the browser as history: Visited Pages, Form and Search Bar Entries, Passwords, Downloaded Files List, Cookies, Web Cache Files.

14. Many times, unless we are using Private Browsing, when we are done working we want to shut down our browser and pick up the next day where we left off. We want to do this without creating bookmarks or noting URLs. Configure your browser to open up the previous tabs and not your home page(s). Clicking on the Home icon will take you to your home page anyway. *Under the **General** icon > under **Startup** select **When Firefox starts: Show my windows and tabs from the last time***.

15. While on the Privacy tab we are tempted to tick: Tell sites that I do not want to be tracked. This is just another way for corporations to track your Internet activity as there are no laws that make them adhere to this request. Leave this setting at Do not tell sites anything about my tracking preferences. If you are NOT using an anonymity solution, you might try this to keep honest companies who honor this request at bay, but how many do you really think will without laws to protect you?

16. *Click on the **Security** icon > make sure **Warn me when sites try to install add-ons**, **Block reported attack sites**, **Block reported web forgeries** are checked > uncheck **Remember Passwords for sites***. Click on the Help button at the lower left to read about these options.

17. *Click on the **Advanced** icon and under **System Defaults** uncheck **Submit crash reports** or **Submit performance data** if checked > check the box **Warn me when websites try to redirect or reload the page** > click on **Close** or **OK** > in Windows 7 click on the **Update** tab and tick "**Never check for updates**", uncheck **Use a***

background service to install updates, unless you don't think you can keep Firefox up-to-date on your own. Keeping a Linux VM updated brings down the latest version of Firefox. *In Windows the simplest way to update Firefox is click on Help > arrow down to the bottom to select About Firefox > click on the Check for Updates button*.

18. *Click on the Data Choices tab and uncheck Enable Firefox Health Report and Enable Crash Reporter if you want to remain more anonymous*.

19. *While on the Update tab under Automatically update: uncheck Search Engines*. Leaving this checked causes Firefox to retrieve automatic updates to your search engines.

20. You can add some icons to whatever tool bar you want to make life easier. If you *right click on the top outside a toolbar you can enable other toolbars like Bookmarks Toolbar or Add-on Bar > tick on Add-on Bar to add it to the bottom of the browser window > click on Customize and start dragging icons to the Add-on Bar*. For example, I drag *(Print, Zoom Controls, Cut, Copy, Paste, New Window and Full Screen) > Done*.

21. While it is not recommended, Firefox will allow you to save passwords to websites. If you enjoy this feature, encrypt your saved passwords to a master password. When encryption is enabled you will have the annoyance of having to enter a master password once per browser session, but that is better that having someone steal or use your computer having unfettered access to your accounts. *Select Tools > Options > select the Security tab > check the Use a master password option*.

22. If you want to see your plugins that are enabled in Firefox, *type about:plugins* as the URL.

WARNING	Just as using InPrivate Browsing with Internet Explorer, Firefox private browsing has its limitations. It does not hide your IP address or prevent websites, advertisers, and ad networks from storing information about your browsing history. It also does not stop surveillance, keyloggers* or shoulder surfing. You will have to study the coming anonymity chapter to become somewhat anonymous using the infected Internet.

Firefox -- Add-Ons to Harden Browsing, Encrypt Web Activity and Protect You

A very moderately intrusive, but effective Firefox extension that you that should consider using with all core OS and virtual OS Firefox browsers is the Electronic Frontier Foundation's "HTTPS Everywhere" project https://www.eff.org/https-everywhere. From their website, "*HTTPS Everywhere is a Firefox extension produced as collaboration between The Tor Project and the Electronic Frontier Foundation. It encrypts your communications with a number of major websites.*" The extension rewrites requests for HTTP sites to HTTPS alternatives where available. It comes installed by default in the Tor Bundle for anonymous surfing described later in Chapter 7. Using this add-on will sometimes not allow the loading of an HTTP web page you need to visit. But if you click on the HTTPS Everywhere icon in the upper right of the Firefox browser, it can be easily disabled allowing the web page to load.

The Hypertext Transfer Protocol Secure (HTTPS) allows for encrypted communication with websites. From https://secure.wikimedia.org/wikipedia/en/wiki/HTTPS, "*HTTPS is a combination of the Hypertext Transfer Protocol with the SSL/TLS protocol to provide encrypted communication and secure identification of a network web server. HTTPS is a protocol that provides encrypted communication and secure identification of a network web server. HTTPS connections are often used for payment transactions on the World Wide Web and for sensitive transactions in corporate information systems."* HTTPS uses Secure Socket Layer (SSL) as a way of encrypting the information that is being passed back and forth between your computer and the site that you are visiting. Sensitive sites, such as your banking, brokerage, shopping and others, default to HTTPS. However, there are many other sites like Facebook, Gmail, Twitter and many other that give you the option of using either an unencrypted HTTP connection or a HTTPS connection. The main idea of HTTPS is to create a secure channel over an insecure network. This ensures reasonable protection from eavesdroppers and man-in-the-middle attacks, provided that adequate cipher suites are used and that the server certificate is verified and trusted. HTTPS should not be confused with <u>Secure HTTP</u> (S-HTTP) specified in <u>RFC 2660</u>.

S-HTTP only encrypts the data on web pages being sent back and forth between the server and client. This allows S-HTTP to be used concurrently with the unsecure HTTP protocol on the same port. HTTPS, on the other hand, wraps the web, the entire transmission, web page, and all data, in the cryptographic SSL protocol. Thus the entire communication process is encrypted. HTTPS was the protocol adopted by most popular browsers so it became the de facto standard, but S-HTTP is used by some products. When you visit a SSL website you will see a padlock somewhere on your browser window that you can click on to view their certificate. (See: <u>http://en.wikipedia.org/wiki/Secure_Hypertext_Transfer_Protocol</u> , <u>http://www.linktionary.com/s/shttp.html</u>, <u>http://tools.ietf.org/html/rfc2660</u>)

Using an encrypted connection to websites will also help to keep your Internet activity from being tracked. Your company, ISP, law enforcement, crackers and others may be using Deep Packet Inspection on unencrypted packets to monitor online activity. HTTPS encryption should make this much more difficult, if not impossible. However, according to Edward Snowden's PowerPoint presentation, the U.S. NSA can break HTTPS encryption.

Just encrypting your Internet traffic does not keep you secure when visiting websites. Malicious websites use SSL to show you the lock icon on your browser toolbar to deceive users into believing that they are safe.

 SSL does not make a web application secure. It only makes it more difficult for a cracker to eavesdrop on the traffic between the client and the server. (See: <u>http://en.wikipedia.org/wiki/Eavesdropping</u> ,)

Enter CERTIFICATES into the safety equation. While working for a large corporation, I was responsible for certificate generation and maintenance for some of their websites. The certificate process works by the website/certificate administrators using a tool like Pretty Good Privacy (PGP) to generate a certificate. Since anyone can generate a certificate, some sort of second party certificate verification authority is needed. Up sprang companies that provide that authority for a fee. The administrator gives the certificate to a certificate authority who verifies the certificate provider by examining the information in the certificate and signing it, thus confirming the certificate. There are different levels of verification that can be purchased for a certificate. (See: https://en.wikipedia.org/wiki/Public_key_certificate, https://en.wikipedia.org/wiki/Extended_Validation_Certificate)

 When you visit HTTPS websites, check to see if the URL or certificate turns green. In Internet Explorer the URL turns green; in Firefox, the certificate is displayed in green next to the URL. This means mutual authentication of a website has been achieved.

Green indicates those websites have paid for extended verification. At http://www.thawte.com/ssl/index.html, which is an independent certificate verification company, this implies visual verification. Visual verification means that there was documentation provided to the certificate authority that allowed them to cross-reference the domain name owner with the owner of the company that claims to operate the website.

But before you jump for joy, in the August 30, 2011 PCWorld's article http://www.pcworld.com/article/239136/google_one_of_many_victims_in_ssl_certificate_hack.html, "Google One of Many Victims in SSL Certificate Hack" by Jeremy Kirk, he revealed that the SSL Certificates of Google and several dozen other sites were issued fraudulent certificates by their certificate authority. Somehow, crackers breached Diginotar's infrastructure and created the certificates. How the crackers managed this is not known.

There are many methods of circumventing the certificate process. For example, all of the web browsers come with a list of trusted certificates, many of which are controlled by organizations unknown to the browser provider. In addition, governments can order websites to use certificates to aid them in tracking Internet activity, hence our continued layered approach to security. There was also the NSA project, Bullrun that Edward Snowden revealed that says SSL has been broken and that NSA can now monitor all SSL internet activity.

Tip  As an addition to HTTPS Everywhere is https://code.google.com/p/https-finder/ which, as stated by Google, "*automatically detects and enforces valid HTTPS connections as you browse, as well as automating the rule creation process for HTTPS-Everywhere (instead of having to manually type "https://" in the address bar to test, and writing your own XML rule for it). HTTPS Finder is most powerful when used side-by-side with HTTPS Everywhere to create rule sets tailored to your browsing habits.*" **Click on _Tools_ > select _Add-ons_ > in the Search box upper right type _https-finder_ > click on the hour glass to search > click on the _Install_ button next to HTTPS Finder > click on _Restart now_.**

Browse to the Electronic Frontier Foundation https://www.eff.org/https-everywhere and use HTTPS Everywhere in Firefox and **click on _Click here to install it!_ > click on the _Allow_ button > _Install Now_ button > _Restart Now_ button** to install the latest version. Once installed you should see **HTTPS-Everywhere version** when you click on **_Tools_ > _Add-ons_ > _Extensions_**.

NoScript is a somewhat intrusive add-on that provides protection against reflected Cross-Site Script Inclusion (XSSI). From the NoScript website at http://noscript.net, "*The NoScript Firefox extension provides extra protection for Firefox, Seamonkey and other Mozilla-based browsers: this* free, open source add-on allows JavaScript, Java, Flash and other plugins to be executed only by trusted websites of your choice (e.g. your online bank). NoScript also provides the most powerful anti-XSS and anti-Clickjacking protection ever available in a browser." (See: https://en.wikipedia.org/wiki/NoScript)

From the June 17, 2010 PCWorld article titled "*Cross-Site Scripting: An Old Problem Returns*" by Robert Vamosi, cross-site scripting (XSS) attacks on your computer are on the rise, "*The most common XSS attack method uses email: A criminal appends special characters, such as those of a foreign language, to an ordinary URL. These characters might tell a Web server to run a script that the crook has crafted. For example, say an attacker appends such a script to your bank's URL and e-mails it to you. If you click the link, believing that it's legitimate email from your bank, your browser sends the script to the Web server, which runs the malicious code and passes a browser cookie with your bank login details to the attacker, who can then log in to your online banking account.*" (See: http://www.pcworld.com/article/198805/cross_site_scripting.html) Another XSS attack can also occur when attackers put malicious content in a link or an image onto a legitimate Web page. When exploited, the script redirects the user to a malicious site where crackers can hide malicious data-stealing code in a Web application's security holes. Scripts are also used to report information about you to Internet advertisers and spam social networking accounts. NoScript should be used in Core OS browsers.

The NoScript extension provides extra protection for Firefox, Flock, Seamonkey and other Mozilla-based browsers. It allows JavaScript, Java, and Flash and other plugins to be executed only by websites of your choice. This prevents executable web content from installing malware on an Internet device. NoScript provides powerful Anti-XSS protection. ***Browse to http://noscript.net/ and click on INSTALL button > click on Allow button > click on the Install Now button > click on Restart Now button***. The NoScript website has a good video that you should watch. You can watch the video by ***clicking on Watch the YouTube video by CNet to learn about its features***. (See: https://www.youtube.com/watch?v=GzBqnLgOzwM)

Click on Tools > Add-ons > select Plugins > click on Check to see if your plugins are up to date. If you have installed/have a Flash Player and HTTPS Everywhere, you should see that nothing is in need of upgrade.

Another somewhat intrusive add-on to consider using is Adblock Plus, which recently decided to allow non-intrusive advertising (See: http://eyeo.com, http://adblockplus.org/en/firefox, https://en.wikipedia.org/wiki/Adblock_Plus, https://addons.mozilla.org/en-US/firefox/addon/adblock-plus). The extension for Firefox blocks advertising on websites, and the project is getting feedback from webmasters who claim that the add-on is destroying their only revenue stream. Since the feature will allow some of the less annoying advertising it can to be turned off, this seems like a good compromise to keep the project alive. If you miss all of the banners and ads that used to popup, you can click on the Adblock icon on the upper right and disable it completely or you can disable it just for certain websites. There is also a version available for Google Chrome https://adblockplus.org/en/chrome, called Chrome Adblock Plus.

Adblock is a very versatile add-on that can do many things in addition to blocking annoying ads. As an option Adblock has Typo Protection that will prevent your browser from directing you to websites that crackers put up to capture users who make a small mistype when typing in a URL in their browser. Tracking Protection can be configured to keep many companies from collecting data about everything you are doing on the infected Internet. Stanford University says that Adblock offers the most efficient protection against tracking of all available tracking protection solutions. Adblock Plus also has a Disable Malware Domains feature that can be configured to block domains that are known to have been spreading malware; it can also disable social media buttons on web pages all over the Internet of those who put the buttons on their websites for profit. Even if you don't click on these buttons, they will still send data back to the social media servers, which is used to create a profile about you based on your browsing habits. Adblock Plus says that they can block all social media buttons on every website. This will prevent your information from being reported back to social media sites. ***Click on Tools > Add-ons > search for Adblock > click on Install.***

From the https://eyeo.com website, *"With our tools to block unwanted tracking codes and social media integration users can gain control over the companies they are willing to share their private data with."* Adblock can be configured to block malicious codes on any web page, which enables the user to block any unwanted element before a website page is loaded. This makes it another good tool to increase security against malware attacks, thus making our use of the Internet safer and more private.

ShareMeNot/Privacy Badger, like AddBlock Plus, will interfere with the annoying sharing buttons from Facebook, LinkedIn, Google and others. This extension was part of a research project not targeted for general use. However, on July 20, 2014 the capability of the ShareMeNot standalone tool was incorporated into the Electronic Frontiers Foundation's Privacy Badger tool. (See: http://sharemenot.cs.washington.edu, https://www.eff.org/privacybadger) Privacy Badger does not share your data with anyone, including Privacy Badger. Third-party buttons allow your Internet activity to be tracked, even if you do not click on them. Privacy Badger is designed to prevent social media buttons from **automatically** reporting back to their parent servers without removing them from the web page you visit. However, if you click on them, your information will be reported back to social media servers. Privacy Badger relies on JavaScript to work and is designed to prevent non-consensual invasions of your privacy.

Antisocial for Google's Chrome browser will also keep these third-party buttons from loading. ***Click on the wrench at the upper right > scroll down to select Tools > click on Extensions > double click on the browse the gallery link in the center of the page > under Chrome web store type antisocial in the Search box > double click on the ADD TO CHROME and then Add button to add Antisocial and Adblock Plus (Beta) to Chrome.*** This plugin will only block social widgets on third-party sites. The extension will disable itself on the sites back to which the widgets report. The following widgets are blocked: (Add This, Digg, Facebook, Google Plus, LinkedIn, Meebo bar, Pinterest "Pin It" button, Po.st widgets, Reddit, ShareThis, StumbleUpon badge, Tumblr Button, Tweetmeme button, Twitter, Wibiya toolbar, VK widgets).

Click&Clean provides security and privacy software for Chrome and Firefox. You can use it to access the preferences, which we discussed, that you can use to protect your privacy. What is nice about this tool is you can define an external application, such as Bleach Bit or Computer Janitor, to launch immediately after the browser default cleaning is complete. The license for this is freeware, and this add-on was launched March 6, 2013. It makes setting up your browser for privacy and cleanliness easy. (See: http://www.hotcleaner.com/clickclean_firefox.html)

If you have a Flash plugin installed in your browser, Better Privacy is another add-on for Mozilla Firefox that, according to PCWorld, can be used to "*Remove or manage a new and uncommon kind of cookies, better known as LSO's. The BetterPrivacy safeguard offers various ways to handle Flash cookies set by Google, YouTube, EBay and others...*" Better Privacy is unique in the fact that it blocks flash cookies (super-cookies or Local Shared Objects, LSO) set by Google, YouTube, eBay and others. They are called Flash cookies because they are pieces of information placed on your computer by a Flash plugin. LSOs are also capable of many malicious acts, which include sending stored information to servers on the Internet and tracking user Internet activity. Furthermore, they are not visible as they access, store and broadcast personal and technical information about your Internet device and more. BetterPrivacy provides the following list of properties about LSOs:

> they are never expiring - staying on your computer for an unlimited time.
> by default they offer storage of 100 KB (compare: Usual cookies 4 KB).
> browsers are not fully aware of LSOs, they often cannot be displayed or managed by browsers.
> via Flash they can access and store highly specific personal and technical information (system, user name, files,...).
> ability to send the stored information to the appropriate server, without user's permission.
> Flash applications do not need to be visible so there is no easy way to tell which Flash cookie sites are tracking you.
> shared folders allow cross-browser tracking, LSOs work in every Flash-enabled application
> the Flash company doesn't provide a user-friendly way to manage LSOs, in fact it is incredibly cumbersome.
> many domains and tracking companies make extensive use of Flash cookies.

No clearly stated privacy policy could be found for this plugin, but the BetterPrivacy website states that no personal data is stored. If you selected "Clear history when Firefox closes", when we were setting our Firefox settings and checked Cookies, wiki says Firefox will treat LSOs the same way as HTTP cookies and purge them. However, at Mozilla.org I found nothing there that clearly states that is the case. Another alternative is to use CCleaner every now and then to purge all of your Flash cookies.

(See: http://www.pcworld.com/article/231458/betterprivacy.html,
https://addons.mozilla.org/en-US/firefox/addon/betterprivacy,
https://en.wikipedia.org/wiki/Local_Shared_Object,
http://www.wired.com/epicenter/2009/08/you-deleted-your-cookies-think-again,
https://support.mozilla.org/en-US/kb/remove-recent-browsing-search-and-download-
history?redirectlocale=en-US&redirectslug=Clear+Recent+History)

Consider adding BugMeNot as an add-on. In Chapter 8 we will talk about how to access and
use the Internet anonymously. However, when you log into a website with a username /
password combination, they can track everything you are doing regardless of whether you are
using an anonymizing proxy, software or service. BugMeNot tries to automatically log you in
to many websites by right clicking on username field. This will keep you more secure in
bypassing the compulsory registration and/or the collection of information about you by many
websites. ***Click on Tools > Add-ons > type bugmenot in the Search box > click on Install
> Accept and Install... > Restart now***. (See: http://bugmenot.com,
https://addons.mozilla.org/en-US/firefox/addon/bugmenot)

NOTE	I tried using this add-on at a few websites and had little luck. However, the website FAQ says BugMeNot has accounts on 469,207 websites, so you may have better luck. It is presented here as an option worth trying.

Another add-on for securing your data is donationware* Lazarus Form Recovery
http://getlazarus.com/download. If you find yourself filling out forms online or you are
sending a meticulously composed message typed into the browser, Lazarus will save you in
the event of a browser crash. There is also the situation where you click on the Next button
and because you did not check a box, or fill in a field, the form pops up an error message;
then, when you click on OK and your filled-in fields disappear, requiring you to start all over
again. The add-on is especially useful if you find yourself filling out many online applications
for jobs and then something happens. Simply right-click in one of the fields of the form and
select Recover form to have Lazarus save you from the pain of retyping the data.

There are add-ons and extensions that may appear in your browser. For example, Ubuntu
seems to have sold out to the big corporations and installed some of their plug-ins by default.
Below is a description of the Apple plugins:

iTunes Application Detector	This app can be used to listen to and organize digital media files on a PC. It can also be used to synchronize files and media between iPod, iPhone and PC; watch TV shows, movies and listen to audio books, pod casts, and more. If you do not use the iTunes app or use the Apple music store to browse, listen and buy music and other things, disable this add-on.
Apple	This plugin enables the user to play movies and other online media in a Firefox

QuickTime plugin	browser. The QuickTime player can handle the following formats (Audio: AIFF audio, uLaw/AU audio, MIDI, Wave audio; MPEG: MPEG media, MPEG audio, MPEG-4 media; MP3: MP3 audio). Tor, discussed in the anonymity chapter, blocks browser plugins such as QuickTime because it can be manipulated into revealing your IP address. Apple has a wide open privacy policy that allows them to collect data about your use of their products that you should read. (See: https://www.apple.com/privacy)

When you are done adding add-ons, you have to keep them up-to-date to keep security as tight as possible. Visit the web page https://www.mozilla.org/en-US/plugincheck, which will identify and any out-of-date plugins and help you update them.

Firefox -- Backing Up and Restoring Your Bookmarks

Backing up and restoring the Firefox Bookmarks is not intuitive, but it is easy. *Click on Bookmarks on the top menu > select Show All Bookmarks Ctrl+Shift+O at the top of the Bookmarks menu > At the top select the Import and Backup menu > select Backup... > and save your bookmarks to the directory of your choice to a filename like bookmarks-2012-10-06.json.*

To restore your bookmarks the procedure is very similar. *Click on Bookmarks on the top menu > select Show All Bookmarks Ctrl+Shift+O at the top of the Bookmarks menu > At the top select the Import and Backup menu > select Restore > arrow right to either select one of your backups, which may be displayed, or select Choose File... > browser to the directory where you stored your bookmarks file bookmarks-2012-10-06.json and select it > when prompted "This will replace all of your current bookmarks with the backup. Are you sure?" > click on OK.*

I included these steps because in anonymity chapter we will talk about using the Tor Browser. An easy way to apply the Tor updates in Linux is to delete the previous version of Tor. So I wanted a way to save all my Firefox bookmarks prior to deleting the previous version of Tor. Plus, it is not a bad idea to keep a backup of your bookmarks on your backup device just in case something happens to your system.

Browser Diagnostics if Add-Ons Conflict or Drag down Performance

As you add browser plugins they will drag down the performance of your browser and can have conflicts. This can result in a situation where some browser troubleshooting becomes necessary. Just like most operating systems, most browsers offer the user the ability to start in safe mode. *To start Explorer and Firefox in safe mode click on Start > Run... > for Chrome type chrome.exe --incognito > for Internet Explorer type iexplore --extoff > for Firefox click on Help > arrow down to select Restart with Add-ons Disabled....* Once started in safe mode you must begin the painstaking process of starting the add-ons one by one to see where the conflict(s) reside.

Windows 7 Explorer Demystified – How To Open up the Directories, Files and Programs You Use the Most with only a Few Clicks of the Mouse!

Story 	The great thing about being in the IT business is that you find out how much you didn't know that could have saved you hundreds of hours of time over the years, or that which you should have known, or in some cases, thought that you did not know, but found later, you knew already! I'm trying to be funny with that sentence. The IT business is unique in the fact that it rapidly evolves. It is not a profession for the faint of heart. In the Air Force I worked in Electronic Warfare, which has changed slowly over the last 67 years or so, but once you are an expert on the equipment you are not going to have to reinvent yourself every few years. An electron will remain an electron and a proton will remain a proton for your entire career.

Optimizing the navigation on your PC to quickly and easily reach everything you use can save you many hundreds of hours if you use your PC often at home or at work. Having all of our important files and downloads should never be more than three clicks of the mouse or a few keystrokes away. Some quick general configuration options for Windows Explorer are to add the menu bar. ***Open Windows Explorer > click on Organize upper left > arrow down to Layout and select Menu bar to enable it.***

WARNING	Microsoft hides things from users to make their OS appear friendlier. This practice makes this OS less secure as it allows users to be tricked into doing things they would not otherwise do. Windows hides file extensions by default, which allows Virus writers to disguise executable files as something more innocuous, such as text files. Enable Explorer to show file extensions by ***opening Windows Explorer > click on the Tools menu > arrow down to select Folder options... at the bottom > click on the View tab > under Files and Folders uncheck Hide extensions for known file types***.

Power users of UNIX and Linux make liberal use of something called *symbolic links* to make navigating the directory structure simple and quick. It is a method often employed in Linux, which makes moving around the many applications, files, and directories, quick and easy. Windows shortcuts are basically the same thing as a symbolic link in Linux. Unfortunately, Microsoft does not have the easy command line, text-based interface that UNIX and Linux have. Windows users use GUI-based explore.exe program to browse to files, directories and applications on the hard drive.

The "explore.exe" application can be set up to open to a different directory than the Windows default. In versions of Windows prior to Windows 7, this default place used to be deep in the directory structure, which could be many clicks/directories away from where your files/directories/programs actually reside. In the old XP OS, which many people are still unwisely using, it would take more than a few clicks of the mouse and perhaps some typing to get where we wanted to be on the hard disk. Then more clicks to get somewhere else, and so on. Windows 7 addressed this with the Libraries and Favorites so that you can set up your own directory structure. Also, not housing data in the default locations is another small obstacle a cracker has to overcome.

Story	As I was updating my parents' computer over a Thanksgiving holiday, I wanted to have my profile explore.exe open up to where my most used directories and files are. This desire sent me on an Internet quest to figure out how to do that. I have been using and working in Windows for over 15 years and have lived with the Explorer default opening up in directory far away from my intended destination on the hard drive. I don't know why I went years without researching how to change this default behavior. The next section is the fruits of my labor for our mutual benefit.

Windows 7 Explorer -- File Locations

We want to set up Windows as a multiuser operating system for security reasons. We should not be using the Administrator account to access the Internet. That usually means sharing files between the admin account and other user IDs. The default in Windows is to store files under C:\Users\<UserID>\(Desktop, Downloads, Favorites, Links, My Documents, My Music, My Pictures, and so on). If you plan to have multiple user IDs sharing the same data, this makes it difficult to share files between multiple user IDs. Instead, consider locating your files into a directory structure that is reached easily by all users' IDs on the computer. For example, consider any of the following: (C:\Data, C:\Data\SpiderOak, C:\Data\Shortcuts, C:\Data\SpiderOak\Shortcuts, C:\<Yourname>, C:\<Yourname>\OneDrive, C:\Downloads, C:\Music, and C:\Pictures). This also keeps your data location(s) consistent as you move from computer to computer, or <UserID> to <UserID>. You can also set up various user IDs with different privilege levels and point them all to these data files, keeping all of your users/family happy. Data files specific to a user ID should be stored under that user ID. Libraries were a new invention under Windows 7. Using Windows Explorer we can include a directory in a library by *right clicking on C:\Data > arrow down to highlight Include in library > arrow right to select the library Documents*.

Windows 7 Explorer -- Creating a Shortcut Home Directory & Adding Favorites

Create a directory on your computer that you want to use as a portal to all of the directories/files/programs that you navigate to most using explore.exe. *Open Windows Explorer > click on Local Disk (C:) on the left > double click on the directory C:\<your name> or C:\Data > select New Folder at the top > type Shortcuts > double click on Shortcuts to navigate to the empty directory*.

In the C:\<your name>\Shortcuts directory, start creating shortcuts > right click in the area to the right where it says This folder is empty. > arrow down to highlight the New menu > arrow right to select Shortcut > under Type the location of the item: you can either type or click on Browse... to navigate to the directory/file/program that you want to open/run as a shortcut > click on Next > type the name of the shortcut (Shortcut Name). Do this repeatedly for all of the directories/programs/files that you often navigate to using explore.exe. Keep in mind that this useful Shortcuts directory can house links to directories and to the **C:\Program Files\<Applications you use frequently>**. So you are no more than two clicks away from anything on your computer.

Suggested shortcuts include Chaos8, DVDRWDrive, LocalData, LocalFinance, LocalDownloads, LocalFinance, LocalJobs, LocalKeepass, LocalMusic, LocalQuicken, MSGodMode, HP Personal Media Drive, SpiderOakFinance, SpiderOakSync, USBDisk (F), USBDisk (G), USBDisk (H), among others. Store your shortcuts folder on your SkyDrive so that your shortcuts are consistent on all your Internet devices and don't have to be created over and over again. However, what do we do with directories that do not remain consistent from user to user, or computer to computer? For example, suppose you are like most users and all of your downloads are stored in the Windows default **C:\Users\<UserID>\Downloads** directory. Luckily, in Windows we can create a shortcut to a shortcut. That way the name and result of clicking on our LocalDownloads shortcut remains the same across all our computers for one user, usually the administrator. First we create a shortcut in a folder constant to all computers called **<UserID>Downloads** and point it at the folder **C:\Users\<UserID>\Downloads**. We create a shortcut called **LocalDownloads** and point it at **C:\<ConstantDir>\<UserID>Downloads**. That way, as the versions and accounts change in Windows from version to version, and install to install, the synced shortcut will always work without modification.

If you are thinking this is the long way around to keeping your shortcuts consistent, you're right. An alternative to consider is housing all of your downloads in a folder like **C:\Downloads**, and then create your SkyDrive shortcut to point to that directory, which will remain constant. The point is to have everything we use regularly no more than a few clicks away.

In the left pane of Windows Explorer you'll find a convenient and easy-to-use Favorites menu. We can navigate to directories on the computer and drag and drop them onto the Favorites menu. You can also *right click on __Favorites__ > mouse down to select __Add current location to Favorites__*. We can only add directories and shortcuts to directories to the Favorites menu. Set up properly, this makes any file on the computer no more than two clicks away.

Windows 7 Explorer -- Desktop Shortcuts Setup and Use

A fatal flaw I am seeing as OSs progress is the loss of the use of the desktop. OSs should allow users to continue to litter the screen they boot up to with shortcuts to everything on their computer. To the logical computer developer this sort of chaos seems illogical, but to the common user, who does not want to learn how to navigate through menus, it is essential. The desktop puts everything after boot up one click away. As we will cover in the virtualization chapter, GNOME (a popular Linux GUI/desktop) removed the ability for the user to litter their boot up desktop with icons and suffered much ridicule for doing so. The Windows 8.1/10 OS is designed to work with both touch controls and with a traditional mouse and keyboard. The start screen is loaded with applications that probably won't interest you at all, and much of the information presented is much too big. To accomplish this task, the desktop was sacrificed and is now treated just like another application. It is clear that OS developers are headed toward the touch market and abandoning the desktop.

In the long term this strategy may prove to be correct. But there are many millions of users that are used to having their desktop and will continue to use it for years to come. OS developers need to take a step back and realize how much users love and use their desktop as a portal to everything they use and do on their computer. I have met users that had mastered the use of their desktop, but could not find a file that was not displayed on their desktop. Hence, while this section of the book has been made dated by Windows 8.1/10, I wanted to include it to defend users everywhere who love using their desktop as a customized portal to everything on their computer.

Set up explore.exe shortcuts on the desktop. *Click on __Start__ > __All Programs__ > arrow up to expand __Accessories__ > right click on __Windows Explorer__ > arrow up to __Send to__ then arrow right to select __Desktop (create shortcut)__.*

You can set up the shortcut to operate however you want. For example, a useful setup is to have the Windows Explorer shortcut open up to your Shortcuts directory. This makes everything that you use in Windows only a few clicks away. Let's demystify explore.exe so you can choose how you want your shortcuts to operate. The article http://www.sevenforums.com/tutorials/2863-windows-explorer-taskbar-icon-change-open-target.html, is a good guide on how to customize Windows Explorer. From their website, *"Windows 7 forum also covers news and updates and has an extensive Windows 7 tutorial section that covers a wide range of tips and tricks."* (See: http://pcworld.about.net/magazine/2004p146id81988.htm, http://www.mydigitallife.info/command-line-switches-to-display-special-objects-or-folders-when-opening-windows-explorer and http://support.microsoft.com/kb/314853)

Option	Description
/n	Opens a new single-pane window for the default selection. This is usually the root of the drive that Windows is installed on. If the window is already open, a duplicate opens. Do not open the selected directory.
/e	Opens Windows Explorer in its default view. List (explorer) view, Show large icons if missing (Open view).
/root,<object>	Opens a window view with the specified folder, file or program selected. Sets the top level folder.
/select	Specifies that the directory should be selected without displaying its contents.
/idlist,%I	Expects an ID/handle. May help with caching. By itself, opens the desktop as icons.

Command Line Examples	Description
%windir%\explorer.exe	Windows 7 default, open to the Libraries.
%windir%\explorer.exe shell:MyComputerFolder	Open in the My Computer folder.
%windir%\explorer.exe ::(450D8FBA-AD25-11D0-98A8-0800361B1103)	Open in the My Documents folder.
%windir%\explorer.exe C:\	Open directory as a single pair of icons.
%windir%\explorer.exe /e,C:\	Explore drive as two lists - directories on left & files on right.
%windir%\explorer.exe /e,/root,c:\	Explore drive without showing other drives.

%windir%\explorer.exe /n,/e,/select	Opens showing only drives.
%windir%\explorer.exe /e,/idlist,%I,%L	From Folder\..\Explore in the registry %I - ID number %L - Long filename.
%windir%\explorer.exe /select,C:\TestDir\TestProg.exe	Opens a window view with TestProg selected.
%windir%\explorer.exe /e,/root,C:\TestDir\TestProg.exe	Opens Explorer with drive C expanded and TestProg selected.
%windir%\explorer.exe /root,\\TestSvr\TestShare	Opens a window view of the specified share.
%windir%\Explorer.exe d:\work (without the /e switch), or just d:\work	Opens a folder window with no tree pane.
%windir%\Explorer.exe /e,/root,\\<server name>	To open a Windows Explorer view to explore only objects on \\<server name>.
%windir%\explorer.exe /n,/e,ftp://username:password@ftp.web site.com/	To open Windows Explorer to a FTP site. Excellent if you have a website to maintain.
%windir%\Explorer.exe /n,/e,C:\Data\Shortcuts	To open your Shortcuts directory and expand it.
%windir%\explorer.exe /n,/e,/Select,C:\Data\Shortcuts\Directory .lnk	Opens the directory and selects the Shortcut link that you use most often. You have to add the ".lnk" extension for this to work.

Once you have determined from the table above how/where you want Windows Explorer to open up > right click on the Windows Explorer desktop shortcut > place the cursor in the Shortcut key: box > enter a shortcut key stroke combination for your new explore.exe shortcut like CTRL + ALT + S > test the desktop shortcut to make sure it opens and highlight your most used shortcut by pressing CTRL + ALT + S. Consider renaming the shortcut to something descriptive as to how/where you decided to have it open up. *Right click on the Windows Explorer shortcut > next to the bottom select Rename > type something like Windows Explorer ShortcutsDir.*

We can do the same thing to have multiple Windows Explorers open up where/how we want from the desktop. The work above sets up a desktop Icon for Windows Explorer, but the taskbar icon will open up to the default Libraries directory. We may want the taskbar icon to open up just like one of our desktop icons.

1. *If you want Windows Explorer on the taskbar icon to operate the same as the Desktop icon right click on the taskbar Windows Explorer icon > select Unpin this program from taskbar > drag the Windows Explorer ShortcutsDir icon to the taskbar > double click on it to test it.*
2. Add the folders you copied in to the default Libraries on Windows 7, or the libraries you create. *Open Windows Explorer > navigate to the directories you want in the libraries > click on the directory > click on the Include in library menu item at the top and click on the library you want.*
3. When you open Windows Explorer, you will see a Favorites Menu on the left. For convenience, we can add shortcuts and/or directories to the Windows Explorer Favorites menu. *Navigate to a directory, or to the directory that houses your*

shortcuts, grab a directory or shortcut with the mouse > drag it to the Favorites menu on the left.

If later you want to remove the location from the library open <u>Windows Explorer</u> > Navigate to the directory that you want to remove from the library in the LEFT pane > right click on the directory and choose <u>Remove location from library</u>. You can read about Windows libraries at http://windows.microsoft.com/en-US/windows7/Libraries-frequently-asked-questions if you want to know more.

Below are a few useful shortcuts' key combinations you can use in Windows 7. The complete list of shortcut keys can be found at http://windows.microsoft.com/en-US/windows7/Keyboard-shortcuts.

Key	Description
Alt+D	Select Windows Explorer address bar and show actual path
Alt-Enter	Displays the properties sheet for the selected objects
Alt-F4	Closes Explorer
Alt+Up	Navigate up 1 folder in Windows Explorer
Backspace	Takes you to the parent folder of the current folder
Ctrl-A	Selects all of the objects in the current folder
Ctrl-arrow	Key Scrolls up, down, left, or right (depending on the arrow key used) without losing the highlight on the currently selected objects
Ctrl-C	Copies the selected objects to the Clipboard
Ctrl-V	Pastes the most recently cut or copied objects from the Clipboard
Ctrl-X	Cuts the selected objects to the Clipboard
Ctrl-Z	Reverses the most recent action
Ctrl+Esc	Display Start Menu
Ctrl+Shift+ Esc	Bring up the Windows Task Manager
Ctrl+Shift+ N	Open Windows Explorer and create a New Folder
Delete	Sends the currently selected objects to the Recycle Bin
F2	Renames the selected object
F3	Displays the Find dialog box with the current folder as the default
F4	Opens the toolbar's *Go to a different folder* drop-down list
F5	Refreshes the Explorer window. This is handy if you've made changes to a folder via the command line or a DOS program and you want to update the Explorer window to display the changes
F6	Cycles the highlight among the Folder pane, the Contents pane, and the toolbar's *Go to a different folder* drop-down list. Tab does the same thing
Shift-Delete	Deletes the currently selected objects without sending them to the Recycle Bin
Shift-F10	Displays the context menu for the selected objects
Tab	Cycles the highlight among the Folder pane, the Contents pane, and the toolbar's, *Go to a different folder* drop-down list. F6 does the same thing
Win+M	Minimize all windows
Win+D	Show Desktop
Win+P	Alter display mode (Disconnect Projector, Duplicate Display, Extend Display, Projector Only)

Win+Space	Glance at the Desktop (release the space bar to resume)
Win+Up	Maximize
Win+Down	Restore / Minimize
Win+Left	Snap window to left
Win+Right	Snap window to right
Win+Shift+ Left	Jump window to left monitor
Win+Shift+ Right	Jump window to right monitor

Windows 7 – Problem Steps Recorder Tool

The Problem Steps Recorder (PSR) tool will automatically capture your actions on a computer; this includes a text description of everything you click on and a screenshot during each click. Everything captured can then be saved to a file. So if you have a friend, relative, know a computer professional or have technical support on the line, you can capture the problem steps and send them a video of your computer activity for them to review. This is also a good tool to use in putting together a tutorial, which you can send to someone in need, or you can use it to present something at a meeting or conference.

| Tip | To further highlight what you are recording *pressing <Ctrl><Mouse Wheel> or, <Ctrl><+> to zoom in and <Ctrl><-> to zoom out in most browsers and some applications*. |

Click on Start > Run... > type PSR. Also add a shortcut on the desktop.

Clicking on the "down" arrow on the right will allow you specify the Output location and the number of screenshots. Another menu item allows the user to run PSR as the administrator. PSR will not record any key strokes you type, but the menu also offers a comment feature so you can highlight/describe the problem you are having.

Windows 7 – Using GodMode to Quickly Navigate to all Your Administrative Needs

Windows 7 GodMode is not set up or included by default. In the PCWorld article posted on Feb 27, 2011, titled *"Windows 7 GodMode: Tips, Tricks, Tweaks,"* Tony Bradley caught my attention with the word "GodMode". (See: http://www.pcworld.com/article/220753/windows_7_god_mode_tips_tricks_tweaks.html#tk.nl_hox_t_cbintro) GodMode is your quick navigation view into the Windows 7 universe. Using just a few clicks in GodMode, you can quickly negotiate your way to almost everything you will ever need to do administratively on your computer. Adding these directories is very useful, and one has to question as to why Windows 7 chose not to include them in the core OS. If you don't want to spend time reading the article above, create a folder on your computer and add it to your Shortcuts folder and desktop. Then create a BAT or CMD file for Windows 7, using your favorite editor file in that folder with the following:

```
mkdir "God Mode.{ED7BA470-8E54-465E-825C-99712043E01C}
mkdir "Location Settings.{00C6D95F-329C-409a-81D7-C46C66EA7F33}
mkdir "Biometric Settings.{0142e4d0-fb7a-11dc-ba4a-000ffe7ab428}
mkdir "Power Settings.{025A5937-A6BE-4686-A844-36FE4BEC8B6D}
mkdir "Icons And Notifications.{05d7b0f4-2121-4eff-bf6b-ed3f69b894d9}
mkdir "Credentials and Logins.{1206F5F1-0569-412C-8FEC-3204630DFB70}
mkdir "Programs and Features.{15eae92e-f17a-4431-9f28-805e482dafd4}
mkdir "Default Programs.{17cd9488-1228-4b2f-88ce-4298e93e0966}
mkdir "All NET Frameworks and COM Libraries.{1D2680C9-0E2A-469d-B787-065558BC7D43}
mkdir "All Networks For Current Connection.{1FA9085F-25A2-489B-85D4-86326EEDCD87}
mkdir "Network.{208D2C60-3AEA-1069-A2D7-08002B30309D}
mkdir "My Computer.{20D04FE0-3AEA-1069-A2D8-08002B30309D}
mkdir "Printers.{2227A280-3AEA-1069-A2DE-08002B30309D}
mkdir "Application Connections.{241D7C96-F8BF-4F85-B01F-E2B043341A4B}
mkdir "Firewall and Security.{4026492F-2F69-46B8-B9BF-5654FC07E423}
mkdir "Performance.{78F3955E-3B90-4184-BD14-5397C15F1EFC}
```

Open up a command prompt and run the .BAT or .CMD file. It will create a bunch of shortcuts making tweaking anything in Windows 7 only two or three clicks away.

Windows 7 – Repair Device Drivers Using Safe Mode and Other Methods

If you come from the world of Windows XP, you know how the addition of a device or software can suddenly make Windows act strangely or not boot up at all. As with XP and Vista, Windows 7 has a Safe Mode to use to repair the computer. Before you run the PC to the Geek Squad, you can use Safe Mode to try to repair it.

Power on the computer > wait for startup to check the RAM and other hardware > just before the operating system begins to load hold down the <F8> key > if you were late in pressing <F8> and the OS begins to load, reboot and try again.
When the __Advanced Boot Options__ screen appear with __Repair Your Computer__ highlighted arrow down to select (__Safe Mode__, __Safe Mode with Networking__, or __Safe Mode with Command Prompt__), Enter > a __Loading Windows Files__ screen should appear and the PC should come up to a screen with __Safe Mode__ displayed in all four corners.
Uninstall the device that caused the problem, or if there is some other persistent problem try to repair it. If the problem proves unrepairable, follow the steps above to reinstall, reload or refresh the OS from a system image of the installation disk.

Sometimes, for an unknown reason, a device will stop working in Windows. For example, the sound on my wife's computer suddenly stopped working for no apparent reason. The first thing to try is to uninstall the device driver, reboot the PC, and allow Windows to rediscover the device. ***To delete a device driver click on <u>Start</u> > <u>Control Panel</u> > select the <u>Device Manager</u> icon > expand the menu for the device that is not working, in my case <u>Sound, video and game controllers</u> > right click on the failed device and select <u>Uninstall</u> > on the <u>Confirm Device Uninstall</u> dialog do not check the <u>Delete the driver software for this device.</u> box > click on <u>OK</u> > reboot the computer.*** Hopefully, the computer will rediscover the device and everything will work again.

Windows 7 -- FlashCookieView Utility to View Your Flash Cookies

Flash cookies are also a threat on your home computer. CCleaner is the battle-axe to clean these out, but if you want to just browse them and keep cookies from certain sites (such as your banks or credit unions), then the FlashCookieView utility is a good tool. (See: http://www.piriform.com/ccleaner/download, http://www.pcworld.com/article/231770/flashcookiesview.html) You can also configure CCleaner to permanently keep certain cookies. You should clean everything and then browse to your sensitive sites like your financial websites. Then configure CCleaner to keep the cookies you need.

Windows 7 -- How to Find and Kill a Runaway Process in Windows That Keeps Reappearing

If you have ever had runaway processes on a Windows PC, you will appreciate this tip. I have had runaway processes on my PC in years past, killing performance on my PC. I would kill it only to have it reappear and crush things again. These processes can appear to be almost impossible to eradicate. My only recourse was to reload the PC with a fresh install of Microsoft's latest software thus solving the problem. This solution is like taking a sledge hammer to drive a nail! This problem happened more often in Windows XP than it does in Windows 7, but you may still encounter this.

To get enough computing power to start with you have to kill the process, ***right click on the taskbar at the bottom > arrow up to select <u>Start Task Manager</u> > click on the <u>Processes</u> tab on the top > click on the <u>CPU</u> column heading to sort by CPU usage > this will cause the performance-hampering culprit to show up at the top of list > to kill the runaway process, select it and click on <u>End Process</u> button lower right > if the process continues to reappear, visit <u>http://runscanner.net</u> and/or <u>http://www.processlibrary.com</u> to discover more information about them and how to possibly terminate them forever!***

WARNING 	DON'T use either site's options for scanning your drive. Instead, enter the processes' name in the site's Search field. Once you've identified which process is launching the resource hog, check to see if there is an update or bug fix available that addresses the problem. If not, try using their utilities to see if they can identify your problem.

Using Virtualization in Windows 7 or Linux

Chapter 7 – Using Virtualization in Windows or Linux to Host Guest OSs to Harden and Layer Our Computer Defenses

The use of Virtualization to keep your small business or family computers and mobile devices secure is the core of this book. The day has come at last for the average SBO/HCU to employ virtualization just like the government and corporations have been doing for decades. Virtualization has been used on mainframes since the 1960s, appeared on midrange systems in the 1970s, and worked its way onto x86 systems in the 1990s. For example, VMware introduced virtualization in 1999 and has since advanced their software to handle the challenge x86 systems have presented. As a result, modern day desktops and laptops can run Virtual Machines (VMs) with ease.

You should do all your Internet activity (web surfing, finance, ecommerce/shopping) using a **virtual** (guest) OS running on your core OS. What does this mean? For many years, the government and corporations have employed powerful computing technology, such as IBM mainframes, to run separate *virtual* operating systems on the very same computer hardware. By utilization of what used to be massively expensive, thousands, to hundreds of thousands, to millions of dollars' worth of hardware, (manufactured by IBM, HP and other big corporations) they could divide their core OSs into separate environments in order to maximize the use of the same expensive hardware. Those separate environments could function independently and be used by multiple divisions of the government or departments of a corporation. The payroll department applications and data could be kept isolated from the benefit's department. This secured one division's applications and data from another, placing an impenetrable wall between OSs that used the same computer hardware virtually.

This same technology, now known as Desktop Virtualization, is now freely (or at least inexpensively) available to the SBO/HCU and will protect your core OS from the many threats that exist on the Internet. A virtual machine is simply a computer defined in software as you will be running a separate virtual PC OS on top of your current PC's core OS. Implementing virtualization (big word, easy to do) is a mandatory, added measure of protection that will insulate your PC core OS against cookies, spyware, viruses, and other malware that can get in through many ways. The most prevalent way is from email attachments and visiting questionable websites that search engines present, which users blindly click on with no regard for their PC's security. Virtualization software for an SBO/HCU can be obtained very easily. When compared with the time and energy you will expend repairing a core OS infested with malware, using virtualization is a blessing. Reading this chapter will alleviate the pain of repairing a core OS and save you the time and money that would otherwise be spent recovering your data and/or identity.

The computer world is also using/promoting sandboxing as a method of securing an OS from the applications running on it. (See: https://en.wikipedia.org/wiki/Sandbox_(computer_security)). Sandboxing is only useful to isolate applications. It separates running programs in an OS from the core OS and other applications. By doing this, the rest of the computer is protected from harm. We can view a sandbox as a jail in which software can run. It is a heavily restricted form of virtualization. This is very useful if you are using a server to serve up multiple virtual OSs for your business or home, much like the government or large corporations do. Those virtual OSs must remain just as secure as your core OS. The disadvantage is that the application has to be self-contained. The capabilities that the OS provides are cut off from the application(s) unless we provide access to them. Setting up and using a sandbox can be very complex, but it is necessary when/if we have to expose an important VM or core applications to the Internet.

Sandboxing, unlike a VM, is a fairly new invention that separates the running programs in a tightly controlled set of resources that are helping to protect your core/virtual computer OS against remote code execution by isolating your system from untrusted programs. Remote code execution occurs when a cracker exploits vulnerability in software that you're using, such as browsers, PDF readers, video or music players, etc., while you're online to accessing the Internet for its content. (See: https://en.wikipedia.org/wiki/Arbitrary_code_execution) The criminal/cracker uses that hole in your defenses to gain access to your core computer OS and install/run malware on it. Sandboxing isolates the running Internet applications in such a way that if attackers do exploit a security hole, the other software and processes are not infected. Running a virtual OS goes one step further. The attacker can attack the virtual OS and infect it, and your core OS will still remain clean. If an attacker gains access to your Guest Virtual OS and corrupts it, you will only have spent an hour or two recreating the virtual OS, thus keeping your core OS secure. Running a virtual OS isolates the entire VM from the core OS. Hence, if all you want is a platform to keep you and your employee's safe using the Internet, virtualization is far better form of Sandboxing, which adds many useful capabilities to your computer setup.

Much of this chapter is about general configuration and adding the tools and utilities to get things working in your VMs that your employees/family are used to using in a costly proprietary (purchased) core OS like Microsoft Windows 7/8.1. If your employees/family cannot understand how to run, login and use their virtual OS software that you set up to perform the tasks that they need to do, then they will revert back to exposing your core OS to do those tasks. They have a job to do and will cite all sorts of reasons for their behavior, but the real reason might be that you skipped some of the sections of this chapter and forgot or neglected to get some other capability working. They are used to having a versatile Flash Player or sound working so they can view YouTube videos or other things that a proprietary OS such as Windows 7/8/10 provides. Users and IT professionals prefer to stick with what they know, avoid change, and pursue the course of least resistance. We have to make the VM (Guest OS) as user-ready/friendly as possible (avoid change), configure it to resemble what the users are used to (what they know), and avoid any large investment in expense and training. Depending on your hardware, virtualization also allows a SBO/HCU to exploit the excess capacity in unused resources in their computers, CPU, memory, and storage to speed and keep capital expense in hardware much more productive.

Virtualization is very much like the techniques that we employ in the military. We are presenting the attacker with a ruse to deceive them into committing resources and expending ordinance on a target that is really of no value. This is the act or art of creating something artificial intended to mislead the enemy. This will deceive the enemy into believing something false to gain the upper hand elsewhere. In computer terms, we have given disinformation to the enemy (the cracker) to have them commit resources to a place of our design, so that we can outflank them. In Virtual OS terms, we are creating an artificial environment that we are presenting to the cracker to conceal our core OS from attack.

An historical example of a Military Deception was the great Patton deception of WWII, the Allied ruse that used Patton to convince the Germans that the invasion was coming from the south and not Normandy. From http://en.wikipedia.org/wiki/Military_deception, "*This had the desired effect of misleading the German High Command as to the location of the primary invasion, thus inducing them to keep reserves away from the actual landings.*" If a cracker is attacking a target (VM OS), they are expending time and effort on a target that we don't mind them attacking, thus preventing an assault on your core OS. They will attack your VM, thinking that they are breaking into your core computer, which this book presents as a Windows 7, modern Linux or Macintosh OS. VMs are possible on top of all these OSs.

Story	During the war, in Operation Iraqi Freedom 2003, I was tasked with working on the Electronic Warfare (EW) equipment on the A-10 Warthog close air support combat aircraft. Mounted under the wing of each was the ALQ-184 Electronic Warfare Countermeasure Pod from Raytheon Corporation. Most of the information about the POD is classified, but revealing some of it capabilities, such as masking a plane's radar signature making it almost invisible, is not. Our enemies' outdated equipment radar could only detect what it was that we chose to show them. The EW equipment takes in the transmitted radar waves, modifies them using a variety of techniques, and then sends them back to the originating enemy radar station.
	This enabled our pilots to deceive the enemy into thinking that they were looking at just one plane, or many, or he could relocate his plane to a different position in the air, or he could jam the enemies' radar, thus blinding the enemy, and much more. All of these techniques deceived the enemy as to what was coming their way. EW equipment can make any modern day attack aircraft impervious to the enemies' electronic detection methods, anti-aircraft missiles and ground defenses. Hence the designation, Electronic Warfare. The enemy was expending weapons on virtual targets that did not exist, saving our pilots and planes from harm.

Virtualization Solutions You Can Use on Your Core Operating System

There are many Desktop Virtualization solutions that are available to SBO/HCU computer users. A few of them to consider are:

Product	Cost	Version
http://bochs.sourceforge.net	Open Source	2.6.2 released, May 26, 2013
https://www.microsoft.com/windows/virtual-pc/default.aspx, http://www.microsoft.com/en-us/download/details.aspx?id=3702	Free with Ultimate	6.1 released Feb 14, 2011
http://windows.microsoft.com/en-us/windows-8/hyper-v-run-virtual-machines	Comes with 8.1/10	June 26, 2014
http://www.parallels.com/products/desktop Parallels Desktop 9 for Mac	$80 after 14 Day Free Trial	Version 9 released Sep 5, 2013

https://www.virtualbox.org a powerful AMD86/Intel64 product for enterprise as well as home use.	Free for HCU	4.3.14 released July 14th, 2014
http://www.vmlite.com Workstation	$199	3.2.6
http://www.vmware.com/products/player/overview.html https://www.vmware.com/support/pubs/player_pubs.html	Free	6.0.4, released 30 Oct, 2014

If you are running http://www.virtualbox.org for Windows 7 or 8.1/10, or the Linux package VirtualBox-ose, each will allow you to run other OSs as a guest OS. VirtualBox, as discussed previously, and is a FREE virtualization option supported by Oracle, which obtained the software when they purchased Sun Microsystems. It lets you run your old Windows desktop or Linux OS as a virtual machine under your core OSs desktop. VirtualBox is a feature-rich virtualization solution for hosting guest operating systems on your PC. VirtualBox does a normal install of many OSs, which allows you to customize the installation with repositories and software during the install. With VMware Player those steps have to be performed after the install. For example, VirtualBox loaded the GNOME 3 desktop in Linux Mint without a problem on some of my more advanced hardware. Early versions of VMware had to run GNOME 3 in fallback mode and without the 3D effects, but all of that was corrected in the 5.0.x release. We will discuss a few of the various Linux desktops that are available to Linux later.

For Windows users, we can run many free Linux OS virtually on top of Windows 7, such as http://fedoraproject.org, http://www.linuxmint.com, http://www.opensuse.org/en, http://www.ubuntu.com, or other flavors of Linux. You can also use an old Windows XP disk and install that as virtual environment. Having a virtual XP environment is an excellent place to install all that questionable FREE software that everyone loves to try, without potentially destroying a computer's performance. You will no longer need to pay companies boasting that a visit to their website and using their software will make your computer "finally fast" again. It is also nice for running the occasional old program/game that will no longer run on Windows 7 and give the kids a nice gaming playground. You should make your employees/family use these VMs for all their Internet activities, thus keeping your core OS safe and secure.

For Windows 8, 8.1 and 10 users, Windows comes with a Hyper-V solution that computer experts tell me run Linux OSs better that both VMware and VirtualBox. Hyper-V will only work on 64-bit versions of the Windows OS but if you have purchased a computer capable of running Windows 8+, you more than likely have a 64-bit OS. For the purposes of this book, I had to cut off technical research at some point so I did not experiment with Microsoft Windows 8.1/10 OSs or Hyper-V technology, but I encourage you to do so.

There are many other flavors of Linux, such as http://damnsmalllinux.org, http://www.debian.org, which are not included in this chapter. DamnSmallLinux is a flavor of Linux designed to have a very small footprint. It was still supported by the free Virtual installers but is becoming very dated and is a possible choice on old hardware as a virtual OS. From http://www.debian.org "Debian GNU/Linux provides more than a pure OS: it comes with over 29000 packages, precompiled software bundled up in a nice format for easy installation on your machine."

To cover other OSs would have required many pages repeatedly conveying the same concepts. The installation and configuration directions would only have differed slightly from Linux distribution to Linux distribution. Examples in Ubuntu and Mint (Debian based), as well as Fedora and openSUSE (RPM based) are enough to enable you to port these instructions into your favorite flavor of Linux. Linux Mint KDE was my favorite choice for a finance VM (discussed later). Any of these OSs is an excellent choice for your General Purpose (GP) VM. Review <u>Virtual Machine Name Standardization</u> to see what the proposed purpose and name is for your VMs.

If you are an HCU, set up a virtual OS for each grandparent or child, or create separate user ID(s) in an existing VM and then let them go crazy littering it with their personal choices. Whatever malware they unintentionally download and/or surf to will leave your core OS unaffected and uninfected! When a virtual OS or user environment becomes so corrupted that it can't be used anymore, just install or create a new one. An hour or two of work following my step-by-step procedures in this book is better than having to buy a new computer or spending days/weeks trying to get your computers working again. As an SBO, you can allow you employees to venture out onto the Internet to do research safely and without exposing your core business OS to attack.

The virtual solutions above are not, by any means, your only options. Included in almost any OS these days, especially Linux, are ways to install and run virtual solutions without reverting to third-party software. Since most of the people that I know use Windows, the FREE third party solutions seem best to present. If you are an SBO, the pricey commercial solutions that allow multiple OSs to run simultaneously might be a better choice.

I present MAC Parallels, VMware Player, and VirtualBox as virtualization solutions in this book, which should prove stable and sufficient to meet most of your needs. The Parallels product is the only non-open source paid-alternative, but it is an inexpensive option to consider for MAC with paid technical support. If you are an SBO, a PAID solution like VMware Workstation or Parallel Extreme with a support contract might be a better solution for your business. (See: <u>http://www.parallels.com/products/desktop/pd4wl</u>, <u>http://www.vmware.com/products/player/overview.html</u>, <u>https://www.virtualbox.org</u>)

Advantages and Disadvantages of the Various Virtualization Solutions

Each one of the three virtualization solutions presented has its advantages and disadvantages. Your needs and level of expertise/comfort with computers will dictate your virtualization choice. The MAC Parallels Workstation Advantages:

- Parallels has the best front-end, which made it easy to install the VMs to a permanent different disk or RAID that did not belong to an individual user. All future installs inherit the new location, which is convenient.
- The backup and relocation of a Parallels VM is as simple as cutting and pasting the VM to a new location.
- Parallels are a great virtual solution for MAC OS, upon which they chose to focus.

Parallels Workstation Disadvantages:

Since I don't own a MAC computer, I could not write about this. When they were trying to support Windows, I had many pages of this book dedicated to their product. The deprecated Windows Parallels product could not coexist on a computer with another virtualization solution installed.

VirtualBox Advantages:

- VirtualBox (VB) has the broadest multi-platform OS support and works best with all of the latest and greatest Linux OSs that are being released. VB also seems to come out with software releases more often than do its competitors.
- Even though experimental, VB had superior 3D support once their directions were followed for installing additional software and the VB Tools.
- VirtualBox does not start any automatic background services or processes. The VBoxSVC service process will always run in the background with the first VM that is started and exits a short time after the last client exits.
- VirtualBox allows you to test drive OSs by allowing you to install an OS the way they would install on a computer without virtualization or as a core OS. For example, with the radical change from Windows 7 to 8 you can install a trial version of Window 8 in VirtualBox to evaluate for your SB/HC. The trial period will end after 90 days, and you won't be able to keep the OS or any changes you made, but at least you can determine if an upgrade to Windows 8.1/10 is what you want.

VMware Player Advantages:

- VMware Player has the easiest front-end for installing VMs, with its automatic install of some OSs and automatic installs of their VMware Tools software in those OSs.

VMware Player Disadvantages:

- Automatic installation of an OS is actually a disadvantage since this will not allow the user to customize the OS during installation the way the OS builders do when users perform a normal install.
- VMware Player automatically starts as many as five background service processes, plus an additional background process, thus chewing up system resources even when there is not any VM running on the computer.

To use virtualization you will need a computer powerful enough to run any core OS applications that you need, as well as your virtual OSs and their software. (See "What you will need to employ the techniques in this book" for your minimum hardware requirements.) If your setup does not meet the minimum hardware requirements, see Chapter 3. Any home computer that was sold in the last six years and that was built with good components should be able to handle virtualization. Should be, that is, as long as it's not loaded up with malware, demos, and software you will never use--either pre-installed by hardware manufacturers for profit, or later by users who love to try software that continuously runs in the background, thus crushing the computer's performance.

We are adding security in layers. Your cable modem is assigned an IP address by your ISP, which is advertised all over the Internet when users *open surf*. We will cloak that IP, as well as discuss and define *open web surfing* in Chapter 8 when we discuss being anonymous on the Internet. In Chapter 2, we put a *hardened* hardware firewall between that billboard advertisement, asking to **crack me** (cable modem) and the Internet. In Chapter 6, we customized a Windows 7 install with updates, installed anti-software and installed many FREE and useful utilities. Now we are creating virtual OSs to do our Internet surfing, e-commerce and banking online to keep our core OS safe while using the Internet.

As we discovered in Chapter 2, we needed to suppress the information that our cable modem will broadcast to the Internet and to crackers everywhere (*here I am, give me an IP address*). Our home computers do the same to thing to our home wireless and wired router (*here I am give me an IP address*). Consequently, if someone breaks into our home network they can quickly scan for computers connected to our router or cable modem. We can now use Virtualization to insulate our network from a break-in using Parallels, VMware Player or VirualBox using NAT, or Network Address Translation (explained below) by default. (See: https://en.wikipedia.org/wiki/Network_address_translation) If a cracker breaks into a virtual OS, they have not yet made it to your SBO/HCU core OS where all of your valuable data is stored. Conducting all of your Internet activity using *virtual surfing* is another layer in hardening our computer defenses. Unlike your core OS, virtual guest OSs can come and go quickly, making a VM the perfect sandbox to handle all of your Internet activity. If a VM is compromised, it can be deleted and then quickly recreated.

Network Address Translation – Using NAT

We must use NAT for any virtual OS that is exposed to the Internet *for anything*. While Virtualization has been around since the 1960s, Network Address Translation (NAT) did not arrive until around 1994. NAT technology allows us to use guest OSs to share an artificially generated Internet address with the host OS's address. This insulates the VM from the host network making it virtually invisible. The router does not present NAT addresses for crackers upon which to view and use discovery methods. NAT should be used (when possible) for any virtual OS that is being exposed to the Internet *for anything*. NAT allows us to insulate our core computer's private information from what the VM is presenting to the Internet, which is subject to attack. Anything that runs in a virtual OS requiring Internet access will work as long as the VM initiates the network connection. On your SBO/HCU network computer IP to which the NAT host is connected, the VM appears to be the host itself; however, the VM uses your home computer's IP address for all requests to your home router. The VM can send and receive data using TCP/IP to or from any device on your home network. This is accomplished by setting up a map between the VM address on the private NAT network and your home computer's network address which was established on your home router. Conversely, the reverse address translation is not true, as the router has no knowledge of the VM's IP address. This is a layer of protection that every SBO/HCU user needs in order to venture out onto the Internet.

A connection attempted from any device on your home network to the VM is not possible. It is possible to configure *port forwarding* for your NAT VM, much like we did for our home server in the router configuration described in Chapter 2, so that packets can reach a program listening on a port in a VM. (See: http://www.vmware.com/support/ws55/doc/ws_net_nat_externalaccess.html). So in effect, your VM is invisible to the devices on your home network. If a cracker gets into your home network, you still have another hardened layer of security.

The following is from the VMware Workstation 6 User's Guide:

"On the external network to which the host is connected, any virtual machine on the NAT network appears to be the host itself, because its network traffic uses the host's IP address. The virtual machine can send and receive data using TCP/IP to any machine that is accessible from the host.

Before any communication can occur, the NAT device must set up a map between the virtual machine's address on the private NAT network and the host's network address on the external network.

When a virtual machine initiates a network connection with another network resource, this map is created automatically. The operation is transparent to the user of the virtual machine on the NAT network. No additional work needs to be done.

Network connections that are initiated from outside the NAT network to a virtual machine on the NAT network are not transparent. When a machine on the external network attempts to initiate a connection with a virtual machine on the NAT network, it cannot reach the virtual machine because the NAT device does not forward the request.

However, you can configure port forwarding manually on the NAT device so that network traffic destined for a certain port can still be forwarded automatically to a virtual machine on the NAT network."

Hacking – A Simple Exercise Using Nmap to Scan Home Networks and Computers

You might ask why I'm demonstrating a hacking tool/technique. To appreciate the depth and scope of this book, we have to scratch the surface of how a *white hat hacker** (an ethical person who practices and studies how to hack Internet connected devices to help people) tests networks and systems. Nmap is one (of many) tools that *white hats** use to examine network performance and determine how vulnerable they are to intrusion. This book is designed to help the average Internet user to be safer on the Internet and does not explore in detail how to find and exploit security flaws, only prevent them. If you are interested in learning about exploitation, examine the references in the citations of this book.

If security is very important to your business, you may want to hire a *white hat* to crack your systems by performing a costly security audit. These knowledgeable professionals have dedicated a lifetime to their study of the "black arts" to learn how we can counter known network and Internet device vulnerabilities. An easy-to-use penetration tool for scanning networks and computers is Nmap ("Network Mapper"). At their website, Nmap is described as *"an open source (license) utility for network exploration or security auditing."* (See: Nmap.org). Many systems and network administrators also find Nmap useful for tasks such as network inventory, managing service upgrade schedules, monitoring host or service uptime, and to examine computer vulnerabilities.

Nmap uses raw IP packets in novel ways to determine which hosts are available on the network, which services (application name and version) those hosts are offering, which operating systems (and OS versions) they are running, which type of packet filters/firewalls are in use, as well as dozens of other characteristics.

Years ago, Nmap was considered a simplistic tool that could be used to quickly access which ports were open on a computer. As with any other hacking tool, it too has evolved. Among other things, Nmap can identify Snow Leopard systems, Android Linux smartphones, Chumbies and other OSs, in addition to seeing whether your computer is serving up malware. From https://en.wikipedia.org/wiki/Nmap, "*Nmap has succeeded to extend its discovery capabilities beyond basic host being up/down or port being open/closed to being able to determine operating system of the target, names and versions of the listening services, estimate uptime, the type of device and presence of the firewall. Nmap runs on Linux, Microsoft Windows, Solaris, HP-UX and BSD variants (including Mac OS X), and also on AmigaOS and SGI IRIX. Linux is the most popular Nmap platform with Windows following it closely.*" Using Nmap on my computer at home correctly identified everything about the OS that I was running.

We can use Nmap to perform a brief hacking exercise-- *remember: we are not cracking*-- to learn how NAT addressing and virtualization helps to protect you from crackers, along with learning a little bit about ethical hacking. First, let's pretend a cracker has broken into our virtual NAT OS; then let's pretend a cracker broke into our core OS or bridged a VM OS and do a Host Discovery in both to see the difference in what this tool reveals. Let's have some fun hacking on our home network and quickly learn how vulnerable we are when exposed to the Internet (remember: layers of security)!

	Once into your PC, the cracker can easily determine which private IP address scheme your home network is using. He will likely have Nmap scripted to swiftly scan your home network using these IP addresses to find a computer to attack. I hope you are seeing how easy all of this is! These crackers are not rocket scientists--they are just taking advantage of your lack of time to learn about some basic SBO/HCU security measures, something you are learning about now!

The next step will be to quickly scan your home computer ports to see if they can easily be broken into.

With Network Address Translation (NAT)	Nmap Without NAT (your home computer)

Let's do a port scan and see if a cracker can break into your computer using any number of known broken protocols, like the deprecated WEP encryption, which we have already discussed. The cracker will quickly scan a computer on your home network using a command like # nmap -O 192.168.1.7/24 and look at what they will see!

A plethora of options and tools can be used to attack your home computer and make your devices a slave, or worse! Seeing what your computers are revealing about themselves should induce an "*Oh My God*" moment for you. The cracker has breached your open or broken WEP encrypted network and in seconds now knows of some vulnerability to exploit. The first thing he might target is an open *telnet* and/or *ftp* port. These protocols can be taken advantage of by an experienced cracker. Look at the other information a cracker would know about your home computers--your router's MAC address, your computer's MAC addresses, your IP addresses, the operating systems that you are running, which ports are open to exploit, and more. The cracker would then attack your Internet devices using much more sophisticated and freely available software.

Crackers are scanning for easy victims! There are much more sophisticated tools than Nmap being used to exploit every hole in your SBO/HCU security. But if I were a cracker, I would use Nmap to quickly determine how slack your SBO/HCU computer security is and then deploy the more sophisticated software to do my real dirty deeds. Imagine what is happening to your laptop while you're using it at a university, an airport, or a coffee shop hotspot? In Chapter 9, we will cover how to encrypt your Internet hotspot traffic using SSH, but people everywhere are using these hotspots openly.

Let's pretend we are the cracker and are attacking a hotspot or have just broken into one of the seven vulnerable (one completely open) wireless networks nearby my house, which I have identified using the tool inSSIDer from http://www.metageek.net/support/downloads. Once the cracker has easily broken into your outdated wireless network, they will set about exploiting the devices using your network by doing a *Host Discovery*. The cracker is already in your unprotected network, and now it is time to put some malicious software on your Internet device to exploit it. Your home router is restricted (in IPv4 networks) to a limited set of private IP addresses. You can quickly learn what they are at https://secure.wikimedia.org/wikipedia/en/wiki/Private_IP_address, or by reading most any computer book. They are 10.0.0.0 – 10.255.255.255, 172.16.0.0 – 172.31.255.255, and most common 192.168.0.0 – 192.168.255.255. Until the IPv6 standard is fully adopted, this limitation in IP addressing will exist for many more years, making scans easy for crackers. (See: http://inssider.com)

NOTE	From this point forward in the book, we will be using terminal windows, command lines, and editors to change configuration files and write scripts. Later in this chapter we will install some tools into our virtual Linux operating system(s) to make these exercises easier. I have tried to make these instructions as simple as *cut & paste* by working through them many times in the hope that it will make my directions easier to follow. There were many complex commands and configuration changes sacrificed to keep these exercises as straight forward and effective as possible. Even though the following sections present examples using the command line, I chose not to cover that topic until after I present how to create VMs. If you need immediate help using the command line, skip forward to <u>Command Line-Using it in Windows and Linux</u>.
Tip	To cut and paste from Windows 7 to/from a terminal window in a Linux OS running in VMware, simply highlight what it is that you want to copy/cut from Windows and put it on the clipboard, click in the Linux application (e.g. VIM, terminal window) and then click on the middle mouse button to paste in the text to wherever your cursor is located in Linux. VMware Tools interacts with Windows 7, just like any other app.

If you want to try this in Ubuntu as root (covered later), type # apt-get install nmap. In Fedora, type # yum install nmap. Some sample scans that you can do on your local network are:

# nmap -v -A -T0 192.168.1.x	# nmap -v -A -T4 192.168.1.x
# nmap -v -O 192.168.1.1/24	# nmap -v -sP 192.168.1.1/24
# nmap -v -sS 192.168.1.x	# nmap -v -sV 192.168.1.x

There are graphical front-ends to Nmap as well as other tools for examining networks, which will be covered later, that make looking at this type of information much simpler than by using the command line. Each flavor of Linux offers a different variety of front-ends to Nmap.

Story	While using Nmap, one thing I noticed right away was that my laptop was listening on port 21 for connections. A long time ago, I was playing with FTP to transfer files and had enabled the FTP server on my Windows 7 laptop. This is a security hole which, when I am using hotspots, could be exploited.

Unnecessary services opens up security holes and have to be disabled. **Select _Start_ > _Control Panel_ > View by: _Large_ or _Small icons_ in the upper right corner > _Programs and Features_ > on the left pane select _Turn Windows features on or off_ > and arrow down to the service that you need to turn on or off > in my case, expand _Internet Information Services_ > and deselect _FTP Server_.**

Hardening Your Financial, E-commerce, and General Internet Activity Using Virtualization

We will be working with four popular Linux OSs and Windows XP to create VMs. The Linux OSs are Fedora, LinuxMint, openSUSE and Ubuntu (FedoraProject.org, LinuxMint.com, openSUSE.org/en and Ubuntu.com). Exercises for creating VMs using these popular flavors of Linux are included in this chapter. As you get used to virtualization, you will find yourself setting up many OSs for the specific purposes in different Linux OSs. Depending on your needs, you may need multiple flavors of Linux to accomplish your goals, each of which has its advantages and disadvantages.

To maximize the hardening of our Internet safety we will need a minimum of two and possibly three or four VMs. We will want to separate our financial (banking, investing, brokerage, etc.) activity VM from all of our other Internet activity and tools, utilities and applications. Our finance VM gives us a safe OS from which to enjoy the convenience of performing financial transactions online. We will create a General Purpose VM in which we will install many applications, tools and utilities. Those tools, utilities and applications might be serving up security holes to malicious crackers on the Internet so they are kept separate from our finance VM. In Chapter 8, we will cover how to set up a virtual environment for surfing the Internet anonymously. Anonymous web surfing has its own set of security holes that can be exploited and will be covered later. The anonymous surfing VM is our search engine and research tool that we may accidentally expose to dangerous places on the Internet, by doing things like clicking on dangerous links that search engines present.

If you have employees or children, you should consider separate, general purpose VMs for them to use also. If they need to conduct finance or do research, train them in the use of your finance/banking/investment/shopping and anonymous surfing VMs.

The primary reason many of the projects presented in this book are done in multiple flavors of the Linux OS is that they are FREE donationware*, easy to use, secure, and robust. Crackers spend much more effort and expense hacking Microsoft OSs than Linux. Microsoft OSs can be used as VMs, but Microsoft records every virtual installation as a use of a proprietary computer license. So to use a Microsoft OS in a virtual environment you will burn a license key when you activate it. Once you exhaust your license activation limit, it is difficult (hours of work) to get Microsoft to allow more activations of your license for additional installations. We can create as many free virtual Linux operating systems as we want using them for various specific purposes with impunity. This is the wonderful thing about free and open source software. Please donate to their projects if you find them useful.

Linux Desktops, Applications, Software, Packages, Utilities and Tools

For the sake of ease, I have included descriptions of, and installation directions for, many applications that you may use in your Linux VMs. In order to get employees and/or family members to use a virtual OSs for surfing, shopping, banking and personal use, we have to give them incentive to do so. If someone can do things in your core OS that they can't do in Linux, they are going to litter your core OS with vampire applications that run in the background, dragging down your computers performance, and exposing your SBO/HCU system(s) to viruses and spyware. Linux comes with a lot of tools, applications, and games that will keep the kids busy for many hours as they point and click away, learning about Linux and its capabilities. As everyone learns to use the multitude of open source applications as alternatives to PAID applications, it will save you money. If you do find an open source application particularly useful, you really should donate to their project. If we use open source solutions and neglect to donate, these projects will disappear, as no one will maintain them. Most Linux distributions also include Read/Write support for NTFS partitions if you have them on the same computer or network. This gives you access to all of your Windows files from your Linux VMs.

Most of the applications can be installed from the default Linux repositories, which are provided for each distribution. If you want to, you can go to the websites, where they will provide a download for the software that can also be used. The website http://pkgs.org has an excellent list of all the tools and packages that are available. Originally, I planned to provide one list with the descriptions of the many software solutions that come with or can be obtained and installed in Linux. However, after working with the various Linux flavors and desktops, I have determined that it was better to include, often times redundant, descriptions with the software installations into the various Linux OSs. Without presenting the application descriptions redundantly for each Linux OS presented, I found myself continuously flipping back and forth to determine what it was that I was installing. Just like with our core Windows 7 OS, we have to be selective about what we install in our virtual Linux OS(s).

Some of the solutions presented in this chapter are not free and open source solutions. Be aware of the legal limitations of using mp3 and other patented for-purchase or for-profit formats. The Fedora legal page outlines the limitations very well. (See http://fedoraproject.org/wiki/Legal).

A desktop environment (DE) is a style of Graphical User Interface (GUI) that is presented to the user. (See: https://wiki.archlinux.org/index.php/Desktop_Environment). For the sake of brevity, only a few of the more popular Linux desktops are presented in this book. As Linux desktops evolve, as with the paid OSs, they may make changes that the user community may or may not like. By desktop, I am referring to how a Linux GUI presents the capabilities, utilities, gadgets, tools, applications, and customizations that can be made using/to a Linux OS. GUI developers never know what that public might like and hate. Open source OSs, just like a corporation, can come out with changes that may not seem intuitive at first. For example, various periodicals and blogs have deemed Windows 8 was a radical departure from

Windows 7 GUI. You might not find it easy to use at first. For another example, the classic Start button had been removed, but could be added by installing third-party utilities. Windows 8.1 addressed some of these flaws and I hear that Windows 10 combines the best of both worlds.

For Linux users there are multiple desktops to choose from, which will serve a variety of different purposes and needs. Some are heavy-weight projects that come packed with tools and utilities, and others are lightweight and made for less powerful Internet devices such as Tablets. The desktops covered in this book are Cinnamon, GNOME, KDE, LXDE, MATE, Unity, and XFCE. (See http://cinnamon.linuxmint.com, https://www.gnome.org, http://kde.org, http://lxde.org, https://unity.ubuntu.com, https://en.wikipedia.org/wiki/Unity_(user_interface), and http://www.xfce.org).

Windows 7 users would have found any of these desktops an easy transition and very intuitive to use. GNOME 2 was a Windows like desktop that focused on usability. GNOME 3 forked from GNOME 2 and focused on the GNOME shell. This broke from the traditional desktop metaphor and gave the user less control over the desktop environment. Mint developers were so dissatisfied with GNOME 3 that Mint forked the GNOME 2 shell and developed its own version of GNOME 2, which is now called the Cinnamon version of the GUI. The Mint project claims Cinnamon now reflects more than 800 changes from GNOME 3. (See http://www.zdnet.com/blog/open-source/linux-mints-cinnamon-a-gnome-3x-shell-fork/10056, https://en.wikipedia.org/wiki/Cinnamon_(user_interface)).

The same can be said of Ubuntu's fork to improve the user experience in GNOME with the creation of the Unity desktop. Unlike GNOME or KDE, Unity is not just a collection of applications, tools, and utilities; it is also designed to use existing software. If you like Ubuntu but not Unity, you can install the GNOME 3, KDE or Cinnamon desktop covered later in this chapter.

NOTE	Many Linux users don't like the GNOME 3 GUI desktop. It is not very Windows-like and many users wonder what they were thinking. For one thing, users can't litter the desktop with icons. Furthermore, once an application is added to the launcher bar in either fall back or classic mode, it could not be removed. In GNOME 2, you could just right click and select remove; that is no longer possible. Even Linus Torvalds, the founder of the original open source Linux Kernel, has publicly announced his disdain for the GNOME 3.x interface. If you have the option, consider using the KDE, MATE or LXDE desktops for a more user-friendly experience. (See https://en.wikipedia.org/wiki/GNOME , https://en.wikipedia.org/wiki/GNOME_Shell, and https://en.wikipedia.org/wiki/Controversy_over_GNOME_3).

The flavors of Linux covered in this book mostly use GNOME 3 or the KDE 4.x desktops. I prefer the KDE desktop, especially after the GNOME 3 desktop release, which I find difficult to use and not very customizable. Having come from a Windows background, I find KDE the most intuitive and versatile solution for Linux. KDE, like GNOME, comes packed with applications, tools and utilities, which have been tailored for these OSs. However, unlike GNOME 3, KDE has handy gadgets and panels that you can easily add to your desktop by

right clicking on either > highlight __Panel Options__ > select __Add Widgets...__ or __Add Panel__.
In both desktops these tools, applications and utilities integrate well with system components,
although in KDE they are easy to find, start and use just by the nature of its desktop
presentation. (See: http://kde.org, https://en.wikipedia.org/wiki/KDE,
https://fedoraproject.org/wiki/KDE, https://wiki.archlinux.org/index.php/KDE,
http://userbase.kde.org/Welcome_to_KDE_UserBase).

Linux Mint offers the MATE desktop, which is described by Mint as an intuitive and powerful
desktop. It is a continuation of the GNOME 2 desktop, which was abandoned by the GNOME
developers in favor of GNOME 3. The MATE-Desktop was developed due to the negative
reaction of the Linux community to the GNOME 3 desktop. Even Fedora has gotten onboard
with the MATE-Desktop and Fedora 18 is offering a version of the OS with MATE. From
Fedora's website Wiki on MATE, "*For the advanced user that doesn't want a cutting edge desktop
and just wants to keep it simple this is perfect for them.*" The latest release of MATE-Desktop
claims to have fixed many of the problems that were in GNOME 2 and provides new features
that were not available in GNOME 3. (See http://wiki.mate-desktop.org,
https://en.wikipedia.org/wiki/MATE_(desktop_environment),
https://fedoraproject.org/wiki/Features/MATE-Desktop)

If your computer, notebook or other Internet device hardware is limited in resources, the
Lightweight X11 Desktop Environment (LXDE) or the XFCE should be considered. They are
both designed to be lightweight desktop environments that are fast and low on using system
resources. They are Windows-like, and user-friendly. They are an excellent choice for virtual
machines to which you don't want to allocate a significant portion of your computer resources.
(See: https://en.wikipedia.org/wiki/Xfce, https://wiki.archlinux.org/index.php/Xfce,
https://en.wikipedia.org/wiki/LXDE, https://wiki.archlinux.org/index.php/LXDE).

 Later we will discuss adding the many tools, utilities and applications
to a Linux VM. It seems as though that software was often times
written with a specific desktop in mind. It is not recommended that
you install software written for GNOME in KDE and vice versa.

Virtual Machine Name Standardization

Because of the number of VMs (minimum of three is recommended), we need to standardize
on the VM names to enable identification of the VMs by OS, flavor, CPU, and purpose. We can
freely create Linux VMs, but Windows VMs will eventually transition into *notification mode*,
usually after 30 days. Product activation allows Microsoft to confirm that the software is
genuine and that its product key has not been illegally shared or compromised. When all we
had was a core OS running Windows it was a rare event that a user would ever reach these
limits. Law requires SBO/HCUs to purchase Retail, Volume, and/or OEM licenses. Once the
user activates Windows, Microsoft will decrement the activation limit for that license by one.
This applies to both physical and virtual OSs. If you have reached your activation limit, you
can contact Microsoft at https://www.microsoft.com/licensing/existing-customers/activation-
centers.aspx to determine how to increase the limit. Because of the limit, and XP's security
risks, we will only create one GP virtual XP environment, which can also be used for
anonymous surfing if you are not comfortable with using Linux (though Linux is

recommended). Vista can be considered safe for Finance and could be used as Finance and/or GP environment.

Most Linux distributions allow multiple desktop options to be installed. Linux Mint adopted the strategy of providing a separate OS release for each type of desktop. By doing so, the Mint developers could release very stable versions of their OS. We should consider adopting this strategy for all of the flavors of Linux, rather than trying to have multiple desktops coexist within the same VM. Installing multiple desktops can destabilize a Linux OS. If you do adopt the strategy of using separate VMs for a Linux OS with one desktop, the type of desktop (e.g. GNOME, KDE, XFCE, etc.) should be added to the VM Name and Hostname in the same fashion as is done for Mint below.

Finance only VM with minimal install for (Banking, Ecommerce and Investments)- Only use LTS OS versions		
32bit VM Name	**64bit VM Name**	**Hostname**
Fedora-Live-KDE-i686-21-5-Finance	Fedora-Live-KDE-x86_64-21-5-Finance	fedora21kde-32-finance fedora21kde-64-finance
linuxmint-17.1-cinnamon-dvd-32bit-finance	linuxmint-17.1-cinnamon-dvd-64bit-finance	mint171-cinn32-finance mint171-cinn64-finance
linuxmint-17-kde-dvd-32bit-finance	linuxmint-17.1-kde-dvd-64bit-finance	mint171-kde32-finance mint171-kde64-finance
linuxmint-17-xfce-dvd-32bit-finance	linuxmint-17.1-xfce-dvd-64bit-finance	mint171-xfce32-finance mint171-xfce64-finance
linuxmint-17.1-mate-dvd-32bit-finance	linuxmint-17.1-mate-dvd-64bit-finance	mint171-mate32-finance mint171-mate64-finance
openSUSE-13.2-DVD-i586-Finance	openSUSE-13.2-DVD-x86_64-Finance	suse132-32-finance suse132-64-finance
ubuntu-14.04.1-desktop-i386-Finance	ubuntu-14.04.1-desktop-amd64-Finance	ubuntu14041-32-finance ubuntu14041-64-finance
MSWin-Vista-32bit-Finance	MSWin-Vista-64bit-Finance	MSWINVISTA-32-FINANCE MSWINVISTA-64-FINANCE

General Purpose VM for general safe surfing; many useful applications, tools & utilities added		
32bit VM Name	**64bit VM Name**	**Hostname**
BT5R3-GNOME-32-GP	BT5R3-GNOME-64-GP	bt5r3-gnome32 bt5r3-gnome64
BT5R3-KDE-32-GP	BT5R3-KDE-64-GP	bt5r3-kde32, bt5r3-kde64
Fedora-Live-KDE-i686-21-5-gp	Fedora-Live-KDE-x86_64-21-5-gp	fedora21kde-32-gp fedora21kde-64-gp
Fedora-Live-Workstation-i686-21-5	Fedora-Live-Workstation-x86_64-21-5	fedora21-32-gp fedora21-64-gp
kali-linux-1.0.9a-i386-gp	kali-linux-1.0.9a-amd64-gp	kali109a-debi386-gp kali109a-deb64-gp
linuxmint-17.1-cinnamon-dvd-32bit-gp	linuxmint-17.1-cinnamon-dvd-64bit-gp	mint171-cinn32-gp mint171-cinn64-gp

linuxmint-17.1-kde-dvd-32bit-gp	linuxmint-17.1-kde-dvd-64bit-gp	mint171-kde32-gp mint171-kde64-gp
linuxmint-17.1-mate-dvd-32bit-gp	linuxmint-17.1-mate-dvd-64bit-gp	mint171-mate32-gp mint171-mate64-gp
linuxmint-17-xfce-dvd-32bit-gp	linuxmint-17.1-xfce-dvd-64bit-gp	mint171-xfce32-gp mint171-xfce64-gp
linuxmint-201403-cinnamon-dvd-32bit-gp	linuxmint-201403-cinnamon-dvd-32bit-gp	mintdeb201403-cinn32-gp mintdeb201403-cinn64-gp
linuxmint-201403-mate-dvd-32bit-gp	linuxmint-201403-mate-dvd-64bit-gp	mintdeb201403-mate32 mintdeb201403-mate64
linuxmint-17.1-cinnamon-dvd-32bit-gp	linuxmint-17.1-cinnamon-dvd-64bit	mint171-cinn32-gp mint171cinn64-gp
linuxmint-17.1-kde-dvd-32bit-gp	linuxmint-17.1-kde-dvd-64bit-gp	mint171-kde32-gp mint171-kde64-gp
linuxmint-17.1-mate-dvd-32bit-gp	linuxmint-17.1-mate-dvd-64bit-gp	mint171-mate32-gp mint171-mate64-gp
openSUSE-13.2-DVD-i586-GP	openSUSE-13.2-DVD-x86_64-GP	suse132-32-gp suse132-64-gp
lubuntu-14.04.1-desktop-i386-gp	lubuntu-14.04.1-desktop-amd64-gp	lubuntu14041-32-gp lubuntu14041-64-gp
ubuntu-14.04.1-desktop-i386-gp	ubuntu-14.04.1-desktop-amd64-gp	ubuntu14041-32-gp ubuntu14041-64-gp
ubuntu-14.10-desktop-i386-gp	ubuntu-14.10-desktop-amd64-gp	ubuntu1410-32-gp ubuntu1410-64-gp
MSWin-XP-Pro-32-GP	MSWin-XP-Pro-64-GP	MSWINXPPRO32GP MSWINXPPRO64GP
MSWin-Vista-Ultimate-32-GP	MSWin-Vista-Ultimate-64-GP	MSWINVISTA32GP MSWINVISTA64GP

WARNING	A General Purpose VM is created to make the employees more productive, to keep the kids happy playing with many applications, and to experiment with the many open source software alternatives that are available. This type of VM should be considered unsafe for Ecommerce, Financial, Investing or Banking activities.

Anonymous Surfing VM for use surfing to unknown websites and commercial search engine use (Tor, Vidalia with Polipo proxy*)		
32bit VM Name	**64bit VM Name**	**Hostname**
Fedora-21-i386-DVD-Tor	Fedora-21-x86_64-DVD-Tor	fedora21-32-tor fedora21-64-tor
linuxmint-17.1-cinnamon-dvd-32bit-tor	linuxmint-17.1-cinnamon-dvd-64bit-tor	mint171-cinnamon-32-tor mint171-cinnamon-64-tor
linuxmint-17.1-kde-dvd-32bit-tor	linuxmint-17.1-kde-dvd-64bit-tor	mint171-kde32-tor mint171-kde64-tor
linuxmint-17.1-xfce-dvd-32bit-tor	linuxmint-17.1-xfce-dvd-64bit-tor	mint171-xfce32-tor mint171-xfce64-tor
linuxmint-17.1-xfce-dvd-32bit-	linuxmint-17.1-xfce-dvd-64bit-	mint171-xfce32-tor

tor	tor	mint171-xfce64-tor
linuxmint-17.1-mate-dvd-32bit-tor	linuxmint-17.1-mate-dvd-64bit-tor	mint171-mate32-tor mint171-mate64-tor
openSUSE-13.2-DVD-i586-Tor	openSUSE-13.2-DVD-x86_64-Tor	suse132-32-tor suse132-64-tor
ubuntu-14.04.1-desktop-i386-tor	ubuntu-14.04.1-desktop-amd64-tor	ubuntu14041-32-tor ubuntu14041-64-tor

SSH Stand Alone Server or Bridged VM for use tunneling remote mobile devices Only use LTS OS versions		
32bit VM Name	**64bit VM Name**	**Hostname**
Fedora-21-i386-DVD-Tor-SSH	Fedora-21-x86_64-DVD-SSH	fedora21-32-ssh fedora21-64-ssh
linuxmint-17.1-cinnamon-dvd-32bit-ssh	linuxmint-17.1-cinnamon-dvd-64bit-ssh	mint171-cinn32-ssh mint171-cinn64-ssh
linuxmint-17.1-kde-dvd-32bit-ssh	linuxmint-17.1-kde-dvd-64bit-ssh	mint171-kde32-ssh mint171-kde64-ssh
openSUSE-13.2-DVD-i586-SSH	openSUSE-13.2-DVD-x86_64-SSH	suse132-32-ssh suse132-64-ssh
ubuntu-14.04.1-server-i386-ssh	ubuntu-14.04.1-server-amd64-ssh	ubuntu14041-32-servssh ubuntu14041-64-servssh

 Linux, like the OS UNIX from which it derives, is case sensitive. To make referencing the host from other devices on the network easier, it should be left as all CAPS or all lower case. Lower case is the convention most often used.

Parallels – Creating Virtual Guest Operating Systems

Parallels Workstation, http://www.parallels.com, is advertised as being a professional solution for the Mac-owning Small Business Owner. This product will allow an HCU/SBO to maximize the use of their computer hardware by running multiple guest OSs at the same time on a Mac. Parallels Workstation 6 for Windows was discontinued, but Parallels Desktop for Mac can be purchased for $80. Parallels will allow Mac users to run Windows applications with ease. I only experimented with Parallels for Windows, that offered a Preferences menu option, and could configure some global VM options to apply to all of the Parallels VMs, which was unique. MAC users I have talked to say Parallels is great for running Windows on a MAC. With Parallels and a MAC, you have the best of three worlds, MAC, Windows and Linux. Below are some historical notes that you might be able to use with your Mac setup using Parallels:

 *Turn on all hardware such as printers, scanners, etc. connected to your network so that the OS installation automatically detects the hardware and automatically installs the devices' drivers and configures them.*

Open Windows Explorer and surf to the directory of the distribution being installed > (e.g. E:\Linux\Fedora) > right click on the ISO filename and arrow down to select Rename, type <Ctrl-C> to copy the distribution name to the Clipboard.

Most of the Parallels default settings do not need to be changed, but you should examine them to make sure. Parallels did not recognize my video card, so I could not enable 3D support. **Under _Default folder for virtual machines: C:\Users\admin\Documents\My Parallels_, change that default to your second RAID or disk storage array if you have one (e.g. E:/ParallelsVMs) > instead of having Parallels polling the Internet for automatic updates, click on _Update_ and uncheck _Check for software updates_.** Unlike VirtualBox and VMware Player, which will require you to specify the VM location during installation, with Parallels this only has to be done once, and it will retain this configuration.

To start creating VMs **click on the _File_ menu upper left > select _New_, and the _New Virtual Machine Wizard_ will appear > on the _Select Operating System Type and Version_ screen select your OS _Version:_ (for Mint12-LXDE-XFCE-KDE-GNOME selecting _Ubuntu Linux_, or _More Linux-Other Linux kernel 3.x_ both worked), _Next_ > on the _Virtual Machine Type_ screen tick _Custom_, _Next_ > On the _Name and Location_ screen paste in the distribution name for _Virtual machine name:_ (copied earlier to the clipboard) refer back to _Virtual Machine Name Standardization_ to determine the VM's suffix that will define the purpose of the VM (e.g. VM-ISOName-Desktop-GP), _Next_ > on the _CPU and Memory Options_ screen beside CPUs, consider raising the number of processor cores depending on your CPU. Beside Main memory: if your computer has plenty of RAM give the VM more memory, ¼ of physical RAM is a good rule of thumb, _Next_ > on _Hard Disk Options_ tick _New image file_, _Next_ > on the _Hard Disk Options_ screen Parallels defaults to an _Expanding disk_, in other VM tools using a fixed (_Plain disk_) size yields better performance, _Next_ > on the _Networking Type_ screen we usually want to leave the default _Shared Network (Recommended)_ option ticked, _Next_ > on the _Optimization Options_ screen we usually want to leave the _Virtual machine (Recommended)_ option ticked, _Create_ >on the _Install Operating System_ screen beside Source: click on the down arrow, arrow down to select _Choose an image file..._ and navigate to the OS image file being created, _Open_ > click on _Start_ and the install will begin.**

VMware Player -- Creating Virtual Guest Operating Systems

VMware Player defaults to storing the Virtual Machine in the directory C:\Users\<UserID>\My Documents\Virtual Machines. This will make things difficult if you try to use the VMs from multiple user IDs on the same PC. If you have a second hard drive or RAID partition, the VMs should be stored there. If you only use one hard drive, store the VMs at a place such as C:\VMwareMachines\VMName. If you change the default directory, you will have to manually create a directory for each VM. Make it the same name as Virtual machine name.

VMware Player does not prompt for many things when creating a virtual OS container. The steps to creating a VM into a VMware Player container differ slightly when VMware recognizes the Linux distribution versus when it does not. BackTrack and Mint were the only OSs covered in this book that was not recognized.

Even though I am running 64 bit Windows 7 VMware on my laptop, the VMware virtualization solution did not recognize my Intel Core(TM) 2 Duo CPU-T6500 @ 2.10GHz Processor running the 64-bit Windows 7 OS. 32-bit flavors of Linux OSs installed and worked just fine. After installing many VMs, I have standardized on the following steps.

 *Turn on all hardware (printers, scanners, etc.) that are connected to your network so that the OS installation automatically detects the hardware and automatically installs the devices drivers and configures them.*

When VMware Player starts click on the <u>Home</u> icon at the top of the left pane > click on <u>Create a New Virtual Machine</u> on the right pane > tick <u>Installer disc image file (iso)</u>: click on the <u>Browse...</u> button > browse to select the OS distro/ISO file being used to install the OS from, right click on it and arrow down to select <u>Rename</u> > type <u>Ctrl-C</u> to copy the distribution name to the clipboard, with the distro ISO file selected click on the <u>Open</u> button at the bottom > click on the <u>Next ></u> button. Skip the next paragraph if VMware Player recognized the OS (e.g. Ubuntu 14.04, Fedora 20, openSUSE 13.2 detected) and the <u>Easy Install Information</u> screen appears.

 NOTE Sometimes a flavor of Linux will not install in VMware Player. As new versions of the open source application come out, most of these problems have been fixed. In working with VMs I find it best to wait for the next release of VMware Player which will likely correct these problems. Unless you are required to have that flavor and version of Linux for some technical or business reason, scouring the Internet for an answer is not a productive use of your time, especially with so many other virtual solutions available.

When VMware Player does not recognize the distribution, such as Linux Mint and BackTrack, *a message indicating that VMware "<u>Could not detect which operating system in this disk image.</u>" will appear on the <u>Welcome to the New Virtual Machine Wizard</u> screen > click on <u>Next ></u> > on the <u>Select a Guest Operating System</u> screen, select the distro ISO file that the OS is based upon if not automatically selected > click on the <u>Next ></u> button,* skip the next paragraph and continue the VM creation directions from there.

 Tip To install Backtrack http://www.backtrack-linux.org or Linux Mint http://linuxmint.com all flavors under <u>Guest operating system</u> tick <u>Linux</u>; under Version, select Ubuntu or Ubuntu 64-bit / <u>Other Linux 3.x kernel</u> or <u>Other Linux 3.x kernel 64-bit</u>. For Debian Mint flavors selecting Debian 6/Debian 6 64-bit or Debian 7/Debian 7 64-bit caused the install to hang midway through.

In a recognized VM, the <u>Easy Install Information</u> screen will appear, for <u>Full name:</u> In Ubuntu type '<u>sudoroot</u>' > for <u>User name:</u> type '<u>sudoroot</u>'. For <u>User name:</u> in <u>Mint</u>, Fedora and <u>openSUSE</u> type '<u>suroot</u>' and '<u>suroot</u>' > for the <u>Password:</u> and <u>Confirm:</u> use a simple, easy to type password and keep it the same for all of your VMs. This password is for both the 'suroot' and 'root' accounts, <u>Next ></u> continue with the next paragraph. From this point forward the install remains the same, whether the OS is recognized or not.

On the <u>Name the Virtual Machine</u> screen, paste in the distribution name for <u>Virtual machine name</u>; (copied earlier to the clipboard) refer back to <u>Virtual Machine Name Standardization</u> to determine the VMs suffix that will define the purpose of the VM (e.g. VM-ISO-Name-Finance, VM-ISO-Name-GP, VM-ISO-Name-Tor) > if you are not using the default location, under <u>Virtual machine name:</u> highlight and copy to the clipboard *the full name of the suffixed VM > under <u>Location:</u> click on the <u>Browse...</u> button on the right and on the left navigate to the directory that will contain the VM OS that you are creating > click on the <u>Make New Folder</u> button, paste in the Virtual Machine name > hit <u>ENTER</u> > click on <u>OK</u>, under Location: you should see the new directory in which your VM will be created (e.g. C:\VMwareMachines\Fedora-20-x86_64-DVD-GP, C:\VMwareMachines\linuxmint-17-kde-dvd-32bit-gp, C:\VMwareMachines\openSUSE-13.1-DVD-x86_64-GP, C:\VMwareMachines\ubuntu-14.04-desktop-amd64-gp), click on <u>Next ></u> > on the <u>Specify Disk Capacity</u> screen tick <u>Store virtual disk as a single file</u> for better performance > if creating a General Purpose VM increase the disk space to a size needed for your software and data requirements (20GB for most VMs, 30GB if this is a General Purpose VM), <u>Next ></u> > click on the <u>Customize Hardware...</u> button, see below.*

 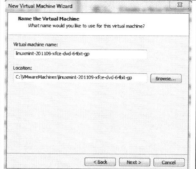 

You should determine whether you are going to use a NAT or Bridged IP prior to building your VM. Changing this setting after a VM is built occasionally presented problems.

NOTE

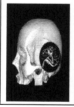

VMware Player 5.0.x enables 3D video by default. Version 5.0.0 of VMware Tools 3D support worked fine. With the 5.0.1 release 3D support had to be disabled to get some of the Linux OSs installed and working properly on my hardware. OpenSUSE 12.03, LinuxMint-KDE-14/13, and Ubuntu 12.04 with 3D graphics enabled were sometimes unstable using VMware Player 5.0.x. Rendering 3D graphics on my laptop and on an older PC sometimes required a reset of some of the VMs to get them to restart. Deselecting 3D graphics in the VM Settings enabled all of the VMs to install and work fine. I tried enabling 3D graphics in Ubuntu 13.04 after installation and applying updates, but this destabilized the VM, requiring it to need reinstallation. On my laptop, 3D graphics had to be deselected. Fedora 17-20 worked fine with 3D graphics enabled. Mint 14 was fine after a reset. So try 3D and see how it works for you.

As future releases come out we will to have to experiment with the various guest setup options. 3D support was considered experimental and may still have problems depending on your hardware. The software developers of the various virtual solutions are working out the kinks out in of all the VMs that I document in this book. Prior to VMware Player 5.0.x, 3D support was off by default, but now it must be disabled in the settings prior to the OS install if this causes problems. The VMware release notes describes the other options that we can pick and choose from. (See: https://www.vmware.com/products/beta/ws/releasenotes_ws65_beta.html).

On the last screen, we can customize the hardware by *clicking on the __Customize Hardware...__ button* > *under __Memory__, if your computer has plenty of RAM, give the VM more memory (¼ of physical RAM is a good rule of thumb)* > *under __Processors__ consider raising the number of processor cores depending on your CPU* > *under __Floppy__, in versions before 6.0.2 if the system has a floppy drive make sure __Connect at power on__ is checked; if it does not, make sure __Connect at power on__ is unchecked* > *under __Network Adapter__, if you want your VM visible to your local network, change the setting from __NAT: Used to share host's IP address__ to __Bridged: Connected directly to the physical network__ (BackTrack/Kali or a SSH Server VM have to be bridged)* > *under __USB Controller__ check __Show all USB input devices__* > *under __Printer__ make sure __Connect at power on__ is checked and your printer is powered on and connected to the network* > *under __Display__ check __Accelerate 3D graphics__ if your graphics card supports it (see NOTE above)* > *and so on if more settings need to be changed, select __Close__* > *click on the __Finish__ button and the install will begin in a recognized OS, or in the right panel click on __Play virtual machine__ if VMware Player does not recognize the OS or does not start immediately*.

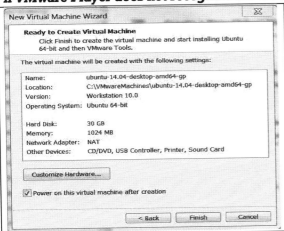
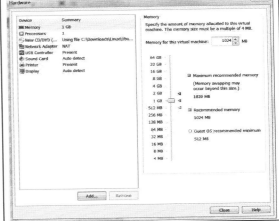

On the Network Adapter screen, if you are using Bridged, you may want to check the Replicate physical network connection state box select this option if the virtual machine uses a bridged network connection and if you use the virtual machine on a laptop or other mobile device. As you move from one wired or wireless network to another, the IP address is automatically renewed.

Tip

On an established computer that has VMware Player installed, you will have to upgrade from time to time. This can be done successfully, following the defaults presented by VMware Player and with a few reboots of the computer. When you run a virtual environment after the update, VMware then prompts you to update VMware Tools. This may have to be done manually for your existing virtual

 machines which are well documented by VMware. (See: VMware Player-Manual Installation of VMware Tools) The alternative is to create another virtual environment, which often times will load the tools automatically, depending on the Linux distribution. Version 6.0.x of VMware Player installed the tools automatically in most flavors of Linux simply by starting the VM. *Click on **Player** > **Manage** and you will see **Cancel VMware Tools Installation...** when the menu changes to **Reinstall VMware Tools...** the tools have been successfully installed*.

Once the OS is successfully installed, halt the VM and examine the VM settings. To use the CD/DVD in some Linux flavors, the settings have to be changed. *On the left select the VM that you want to edit > on the lower right or the pane on the right, select **Edit virtual machine settings** > select **Hardware** tab > arrow down to select **CD/DVD (SATA)** > make sure under **Device status** the **Connect at power on** box is check > under **Connection** make sure **Use Physical drive: Auto detect** is ticked. There are two tabs at the top left, **Hardware**, which we edited upon VM installation, and **Options** > select **Options**.* There are a number of options that you can adjust. For example, *under **General** select **Enhanced virtual keyboard** on the lower right and change it to **Use if available (recommended)** > if the VM is on a laptop, on the left click on **Power** and on the right check **Report battery information to guest** > on the left click on **VMware Tools** and on the right under **VMware Tools** updates tick **Update automatically** if it is not selected > check **Synchronize guest time with host** if you want that > **OK**.*

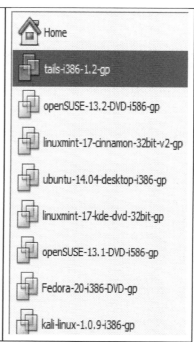

VMware Player sometimes prompted *"**The guest operating system has locked the CD-ROM door and is probably using the CD-ROM...**" to see if we wanted to close the CD-ROM door > click on **Yes** and the message **Installing VMware Tools. Please Wait...** will appear > give VMware about 4-5 minutes to install the tools automatically*.
If you see this error *open up the settings > click on CD/DVD > under **Connection** change the **Connection** from **Use ISO image file:** to **Use Physical drive: Auto detect**.*

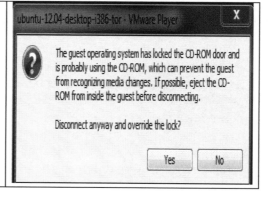

 As we load more and more virtual OSs, we will have to start cleaning things up. When removing an obsolete environment in VMware, *select **Delete VM from Disk**, which will completely remove the virtual OS from VMware and your disk.

VMware Player -- Manual Installation of VMware Tools

Linux flavors like Ubuntu, Fedora, and openSUSE install automatically in VMware Player, sometimes along with the VMware Tools. Any update released by VMware for their tools requires a manual installation of the tools into the existing VMs. Sometimes flavors such as BackTrack and Linux Mint will not install the tools by default. A few years ago VMware Player 4.0.4 required the manual installation of the tools in Fedora 16, and could not install Fedora 17. The 5.0.x release of VMware Player enabled the automatic installation of VMware Tools as well as the rendering of the 3D graphics correctly in all later versions of Fedora. The use of VMs on top of your core OS continues to improve and automate everything for you, as in the Fedora example above.

The steps below, performed as 'root', offer the easiest methods for manually installing VMware Tools, which differs from Linux distro-to-distro. VMware's method for manual installation is well documented. However, the directions below document installation in each version of Linux adding a little more detail. Earlier release installation directions are included in case future releases require similar steps.

NOTE 	In most cases, before installing the tools, (e.g. Mint-KDE required installation of the tools first) we want to apply all of the software updates and upgrades first so that installing the tools uses the latest compilers, linkers, and kernels available. When installing the tools, *if a dialog box appears stating "The guest operating system has locked the CD-ROM door and is probably using the CD-ROM..." > select No and refer back to VMware Player-Creating Virtual Guest Operating Systems to configure your VM settings.* Then repeat the steps that match your distro below. This problem appeared to be fixed after the 5.0.x release.

VMware Player – Navigating the Menu Structure to Install Tools Manually

In VMware Player 5.0.x/6.0.x > at the top left select the Player drop down menu > arrow down to highlight Manage > arrow right to select Install/Update VMware Tools.... Sometimes the OS install media is left mounted after the OS boots up. Before you can mount VMware Tools, this has to be unmounted. Right click on CD shown as an icon on the desktop and arrow down to select Eject.

Refer back to Navigating the Menu Structure to Install Tools Manually > the Nautilus file manager will pop up with the VMwareTools-version.tar.gz file > drag and drop the file VMwareTools-Version.tar.gz to the Downloads directory on the left, or, right click on the file > select Copy > click on Downloads > select Paste > close Nautilus, then as 'root' follow the command line procedure below.

In Mint-Cinnamon, refer back to Navigating the Menu Structure to Install Tools Manually if Nautilus does not start automatically click on the Files icon on the taskbar to start it > under Devices click on VMware Tools > drag and drop the VMwareTools-version.tar.gz file onto the 'suroot' Downloads directory shown under Bookmarks on the left panel > close Nautilus, and follow the command line procedure below.

In Debian Kali and Mint-201403-mate > refer back to <u>Navigating the Menu Structure to</u> <u>Install Tools Manually</u> > drag and drop VMwareTool-version onto the Desktop > then follow the command line procedure below.

In openSUSE-KDE and Mint-KDE, refer back to <u>Navigating the Menu Structure to Install</u> <u>Tools Manually</u> > an automatic window titled <u>Available Devices</u> pops up on lower right click on <u>Open with File Manager</u> > this brings <u>VMware Tools - Dolphin</u> file manager > drag and drop the VMwareTools-version.gz file in the 'suroot' or 'root' <u>Home</u> directory on the left (depending on the login user ID) > select <u>Copy Here</u> > close the <u>Dolphin</u> window > open a terminal window (Konsole) and as 'root' follow the procedure below without changing directory.

	In lUbuntu & kUbuntu, the *make* and *gcc* packages had to be installed prior to installing the VMware Tools. Perform the following: # apt-get install make gcc -y
Tip	In kUbuntu the manual install of VMware Tools failed with the message, "VMware Tools installation cannot be started manually while the easy install is in progress." 1) Power off the VM. 2) Go to VM > <u>Settings</u>, select <u>Floppy</u> & CD autoinst. Select <u>Use Physical drive</u>, and set the dropdown to <u>Auto detect</u>.

In Lubuntu or Ubuntu, after bringing up VMwareTools, when a window titled <u>VMware</u> <u>Tools</u> with <u>VMwareTools-version.tar.gz</u> file displays > drag and drop the <u>VMwareTools-</u> <u>Version.tar.gz</u> file onto the <u>Downloads</u> directory to the left > then follow the terminal window steps below to install the tools.

VMware Player -- Command Line Installation of VMware Tools

If the tools' file was copied to a directory under the Ubuntu "sudoroot" user; or in other Linux flavors the 'suroot' user, perform the following steps:

```
$ sudo su -    or,    su -    # This will be root's Home directory  or,
$ cd Downloads && su    # This is the 'suroot' directory
# cd ~sudoroot    or    cd ~suroot
# cd ~sudoroot/Desktop    or,    cd ~suroot/Desktop
# mv VMwareTools-9.6.2-*.tar.gz ../Downloads
# cd ~sudoroot/Downloads    or,    cd ~suroot/Downloads
# tar zxvf VMwareTools-9.6.2-*.tar.gz       # To uncompressed and extract the files
# cd vmware-tools-distrib
# ./vmware-install.pl
# service networking stop or, # /etc/init.d/networking stop
# rmmod pcnet32    # Remove module from Linux Kernel
# rmmod vmxnet
# modprobe vmxnet    # Add module to Linux Kernel
```

service networking start or, # /etc/init.d/networking start
shutdown -r now

If the tools were copied as 'root' to the Home, Desktop or Downloads directory:

```
# mv VMwareTools-9.6.2-*.tar.gz Downloads
# cd Desktop    or,    cd Downloads
# tar zxvf VMwareTools-9.6.2-*.tar.gz        # To uncompress and extract the files
# cd vmware-tools-distrib
# ./vmware-install.pl
```

In openSUSE, the tools are mounted "read only" under "/media/VMware Tools". If you don't want to use Dolphin, you can just copy the files to "/tmp" or "/home/suroot/Downloads":

```
# zypper install -t pattern devel_kernel
# cd "/media/VMware Tools"
# cp VMwareTools* /tmp    or,    cp VMwareTools* /home/suroot/Downloads
# cd /tmp    or,    cd ~suroot/Downloads
# tar zxvf VMwareTools-9.6.2-*.tar.gz        # To uncompress and extract the files
# cd vmware-tools-distrib
# ./vmware-install.pl
```

In BackTrack R2, after clicking on __Player__ upper left > arrow down to __Manage__ > arrow right to select __Install VMware Tools...__, open a terminal window and type the following:

```
# mount /dev/cdrom /media/cdrom
mount: block device /dev/sr0 is write-protected, mounting read-only
# cd /media/cdrom
# cp -ip VMwareTools* /tmp
# cd /tmp && tar zxvf VMwareTools*
# cd vmware-tools-distrib
# ./vmware-install.pl
```

In BackTrack R3 with VMwareTools-9.x, click on the __Install Tools__ button > or select __Player__ upper left and arrow down to __Manage__ and select __Install VMware Tools__ > wait for the File Manager to mount > drag and drop the __VMwareTools-version__ file onto the desktop > follow the procedure above.

Hit return quite a few times to accept most of the defaults. Be sure to read the questions and determine your answer. Some of the defaults are for VMware Workstation and Fusion and should be off in Player. *When prompted "The VMware FileSystem Sync Driver (vmsync) allows external third-party backup software that is integrated with vSphere to create backups of the virtual machine, type __no__ if it is not the default. When prompted "The VMware Host-Guest FileSystem allows for shared folders between the host OS and the guest OS in a Fusion or Workstation virtual environment."if you won't be sharing folders type __no__. When prompted "__Would you like to enable VMware automatic kernel__* _**modules?" consider typing yes**_. I have accepted the other defaults many times without any problems.

|
Tip | Originally, when I built VMs I would remove the VMware Tools file and directory. However, as future releases of the VMware Player Tools came out it was easy to lose track of which version of the tools was installed in the various VMs. To write this book I had to create many hundreds of VMs on numerous computers. I concluded quickly that keeping the tools' file in the <u>Downloads</u> directory for reference was better than the very minor increase in disk space gained by deleting them. If you need the disk space, you can delete these files after the installation by typing:

cd ~/Downloads; rm VMwareTools*
rm -rf vmware-tools-distrib |

shutdown -h now   # Reboot/halt the VM to enable the VMware Tools and adjust the VM settings.

VirtualBox – Creating Virtual Guest Operating Systems

The install of a Guest OS is basically the same for each flavor of Linux or Windows XP/Vista/7/8 into VirtualBox. The steps differ only when the actual installation of the OS into VirtualBox starts, which is documented in sections of this chapter later.

| | _**Turn on all hardware, for example printers, scanners, etc., that is connected to your network so that the OS installation automatically detects the hardware and automatically installs the device's drivers and configures them.**_ |

_The following step is only necessary if you are not using the VirtualBox default directory structure. If your computer has a second hard drive or RAID partition, consider housing the VMs there rather than using the default directories. Create a directory there called **VirtualBoxVMs**. Under the **VirtualBoxVMs** directory create the **Snapshots** directory under each VMs directory name. Refer back to **Virtual Machine Name Standardization** (e.g. E:\VirtualBoxVMs\Fedora-20-x86_64-GP\Snapshots, E:\VirtualBoxVMs\openSUSE-13.2-DVD-x86_64-GP, E:\VirtualVMs\ubuntu-14.04.1-desktop-amd64-gp, E:\VirtualBoxVMs\MSWin-Vista-Ultimate-64-GP, etc.)._

On the disk or partition where your VMs are being created, standardize on a directory structure where you will house all of the OS ISO image files (e.g. **E:\Linux**) > under **Linux** create directories for each distribution (**Debian**, **Fedora**, **Kali**, **Kubuntu**, **Lubuntu**, **Xubuntu**, **Mint**, **openSUSE**, **Tails**, **Ubuntu**, **Whonix**). This keeps things organized as new versions of these OSs are released. If you use the name of your distribution as the VM name, VirtualBox will automatically select the correct OS and Version. _**Open Windows Explorer** and browse to the directory housing the guest OS that is being installed > right click on the distro and arrow down to select **Rename** > type **Ctrl-C** to copy the distro name to the clipboard. You can also use a CD or DVD to install an OS (e.g. Microsoft Windows XP Pro 64-bit, Windows Vista Ultimate 64-bit)._

The minimum system resources you allocate to a VM depend on the OS and your hardware. Windows 8.1, if you have it, has the highest requirements at 25-30GB disk, 2-4GB RAM and 2 or more CPU cores. The other settings discussed below will also help optimize VirtualBox for Linux and Windows 7.

NOTE	Using the distribution as part of the VM name enables VirtualBox to select the correct Operating System and Version most of the time. Selecting Linux 2.6 (64 bit) worked with all unrecognized OSs. Still, you may have to experiment. Attempts to use Btrfs file system with Debian Mint would not allow the VM to boot. Use the ext4 file system instead. When VirtualBox does not recognize the distribution, often times selecting the platform upon which the OS is based will usually work. (e.g. BackTrack was not recognized, but could be installed as a <u>Debian</u>, <u>Ubuntu</u>, or as a <u>Linux 2.6</u> OS.) BackTrack and Kali should be attached to a Bridged Adapter, not NAT unlike other OSs installed as VMs. Some of the BackTrack and Kali tools, like Wireshark may need Promiscuous Mode in which to view all of the packets on the network.

*Run Oracle VM VirtualBox > click on **New** and the **Create Virtual Machine-Name and Operating System** Window will appear, on the screen paste the name of your VM, refer back to **Virtual Machine Name Standardization** to add the distribution suffix to identify its purpose, for "Operating System:" (e.g. **Linux**; Microsoft Windows; etc.) and for "Version:" make sure the flavor of Linux, Kernel, or Windows is selected along with the correct CPU type (e.g. Linux 2.6 / 3.x (64 bit); openSUSE (64 bit), Fedora (64 bit), Windows Vista (64bit), etc.), **Next** > on the **Memory size** screen a general rule of thumb is to increase the memory size to around ¼ of your system's RAM, **Next**.*

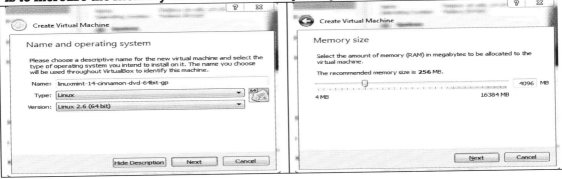

*On the **Hard Drive** screen leave the default **Create a virtual hard drive now** selected, click on the **Create** button at the bottom > on the **Hard drive file type** screen leave default file type **VDI (VirtualBox Disk Image)** selected, **Next** > on the **Storage on physical hard drive** screen choose **Fixed size** for better performance or **Dynamically allocated** if disk space is a concern, **Next** > on the **File location and size** screen, increase the size of the VM (20GB was the VMware default, which is adequate for most VMs unless you are creating a GP VM, which should have 30GB or more allocated, depending on your data and usage requirements), the disk space GB suffix is required > if you are not using the defaults, select the directory icon to the right of the **Location** box, then change the*

location of the VM to your second RAID or another hard drive by clicking on __Computer__, which is on the left > select the partition or disk where the VM will be created (e.g. __DataVMRAID1__) partition > click on the __VirtualBoxVMs__ directory > click on __Save__. The Virtual disk file location should change (e.g. E:\VirtualBoxVMs\Fedora-20-x86_64-GP.vdi) , E:\VirtualBoxVMs\openSUSE-13.1-DVD-x86_64-GP) > check your details and click on the __Create__ button > a dialog box stating __Creating fixed medium storage unit__ (e.g. 'E:\VirtualBoxVMs\Fedora-20-x86_64-GP.vdi' or "E:\VirtualBoxVMs\Fedora-20-x86_64-GP\Fedora-20-x86_64-GP.vdi') should pop up > when the storage unit is created we are ready to adjust the settings.

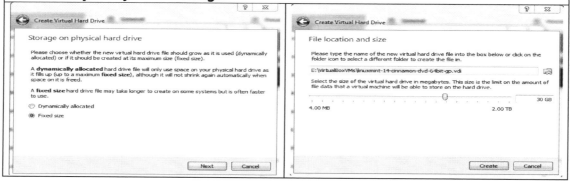

Before starting your VM to install the OS, the settings need to be customized to optimize the VMs creation and operation. Most of the options adjusted are self-explanatory, but a few options may need further research before you can consider selecting or adjusting them. Below is an explanation of some of the more advanced options from which to choose.

The Advanced Programmable Interrupt Controller (APIC) allows most modern motherboards to extend the number of IRQs available. (See: https://en.wikipedia.org/wiki/Advanced_Programmable_Interrupt_Controller) An Interrupt Request (IRQ) is a hardware interrupt request line that allows devices to send interrupt signals to the CPU. Devices use interrupts to stop the CPU from executing instructions and jump to a place in memory to handle the device request/instructions. (See: https://en.wikipedia.org/wiki/Interrupt_request, http://www.tldp.org/LDP/tlk/dd/interrupts.html)

According to Wikipedia, alternative firmware (EFI) is a specification that defines a software interface between an OS and the platform hardware. From the VirtualBox manual "*VirtualBox includes experimental support for the Extensible Firmware Interface (EFI), which is a new industry standard intended to eventually replace the legacy BIOS as the primary interface for bootstrapping computers and certain system services later. By default, VirtualBox uses the BIOS firmware for virtual machines.*" (See: https://en.wikipedia.org/wiki/Unified_Extensible_Firmware_Interface, or the VB manual at https://www.virtualbox.org/wiki/Downloads)

| WARNING | The VirtualBox manual states that the experimental EFI system option should work with Apple's Mac and some recent Linux OSs, but enabling EFI caused VirtualBox to stop responding during Fedora, Mint, openSUSE 13.1 and Ubuntu Linux OS installations. When this happened the VM storage unit had to be recreated. You can try this option in later versions of Linux as Mint recently said |

they support this technology. With OpenSUSE 13.1 there was a message "Secure boot not enabled", however the OS installed OK with EFI and PAE/NX selected.

Another option available in VirtualBox is Physical Address Extension (PAE), which is a feature that allows (32-bit) x86 processors to access a physical address space larger than 4 gigabytes. The VirtualBox manual states "*"Enable PAE/NX" setting determines whether the PAE and NX capabilities of the host CPU will be exposed to the virtual machine. PAE stands for "Physical Address Extension". Normally, if enabled and supported by the operating system, then even a 32-bit x86 CPU can access more than 4 GB of RAM. This is made possible by adding another 4 bits to memory addresses, so that with 36 bits, up to 64 GB can be addressed. Some operating systems (such as Ubuntu Server) require PAE support from the CPU and cannot be run in a virtual machine without it.*" Thus, we can see that this option is important to using Ubuntu server. (See: https://en.wikipedia.org/wiki/Physical_Address_Extension)

The VirtualBox settings should be adjusted to optimize your VM. **With your VM selected, click on the _Settings_ icon on the top > under _General_ select the _Advanced_ tab and consider changing the drop downs _Shared Clipboard:_ and _Drag 'n' Drop:_ to _Bidirectional_ > change the _Snapshot Folder:_ by selecting the down arrow on the right and selecting _Other..._ (e.g. _E:\ VirtualBoxVMs\Fedora-20-x86_64-GP\Snapshots_) > under _General_ select _Description_ refer back to _Virtual Machine Name Standardization_ for descriptions of the VM types > most systems no longer have a floppy drive, unless you want virtual floppy support under _System_ uncheck _Floppy_ and lower it in the _Boot Order_. Most modern motherboards support APIC, so tick the _Extended Features: Enable IO APIC_ if it is not already selected > if the VM is not Windows XP, try ticking _Enable EFI_ (trying this caused VirtualBox to stop responding during Linux startup, the install had to start from scratch) > still under _System_ click on the _Processor_ tab at the top > raise the number of CPU cores to a number less than what your CPU has as its physical maximum and then tick _Enable PAE/NX_ > under _Display_ check the _Extended Features: Enable 3D Acceleration_ box, if memory increases drag the bar to 128 or 256 MB of RAM memory > the _Display_ usually defaults to the very low setting of 12 MB, most video cards have 1 to 2 GB of RAM so raise this value to the MAX Video Memory offered, click on _OK_.** The rest of the settings can remain at the default settings most of the time unless you are installing a Kali penetration testing VM, in which case you will need to change the Network settings from NAT to Bridged Adapter.

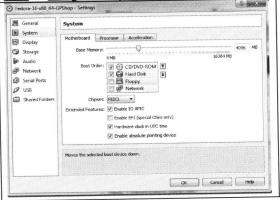
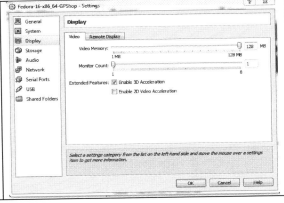

| Tip | Fedora 19/18 i386 and x86_64 appeared to install in VirtualBox (4.2.10, 4.2.12, 4.2.14, 4.2.16, 4.2.20 and 4.3.6 releases), but once installed, Fedora would reboot to the installation screen asking the user to install it over and over again. In researching this problem, I came across the web page http://www.wikihow.com/Install-Fedora-17-in-Virtualbox, which had a solution to this problem. ***Create a second VM (e.g. Fedora-19-x86_64-DVD-GPPtr, Fedora-19-x86_64-TorPtr) and when you reach <u>Hard drive</u> configuration screen, tick <u>Use an existing virtual hard drive file</u> instead of <u>Create a virtual hard drive now</u>, select your previously created Fedora 19 VDI file (e.g. Fedora-19-x86_64-DVD-GP.vdi), <u>Open</u> > click on the <u>Create</u> button at the bottom.*** Adjust your PTR VM settings to match the actual installed copy of Fedora. When we start this newly created PTR VM, Fedora will boot up to the <u>Welcome</u> screen for our final configuration setup. With the PTR VM store your snapshots under the actual VDI name (e.g. E:\VirtualBoxVMs\Fedora-19-x86_64-DVD-GP\Snapshots). This was no longer necessary with the release of Fedora 20. |

Following these instructions above, we have completed most of the steps for installing a guest OS on top of our core OS. In case you missed a step, the following may be needed:

- Halt the VM and click on <u>Settings</u> > <u>Display</u>
- Give the VM as much Video Memory as VirtualBox will allow
- Tick the checkbox <u>Enable 3D Acceleration</u>
- Choose the type on network adapter your VM will need on your local network

Consider whether to use the host I/O cache by ticking the <u>Use host I/O cache box</u>. The default setting by VirtualBox is disabled for SATA and enabled for IDE. From the VirtualBox manual, "*Starting with version 3.2, VirtualBox can optionally disable the I/O caching that the host operating system would otherwise perform on disk image files.*

1. *Delayed writing through the host OS cache is less secure. When the guest OS writes data, it considers the data written even though it has not yet arrived on a physical disk. If for some reason the write does not happen due to a power failure, or host crash, the likelihood of data loss increases.*
2. *Disk image files tend to be very large. Caching them can therefore quickly use up the entire host OS cache. Depending on the efficiency of the host OS caching, this may slow down the host immensely, especially if several VMs run at the same time. For example, on Linux hosts, host caching may result in Linux delaying all writes until the host cache is nearly full and then writing out all these changes at once, possibly stalling VM execution for minutes. This can result in I/O errors in the guest as I/O requests time out.*
3. *Physical memory is often wasted as guest operating systems typically have their own I/O caches, which may result in the data being cached twice (in both the guest and the host caches) for little effect.*

If you decide to disable host I/O caching for the above reasons, VirtualBox uses its own small cache to buffer writes, but no read caching since this is typically already performed by the guest OS. In addition, VirtualBox fully supports asynchronous I/O for its virtual SATA, SCSI and SAS controllers through multiple I/O threads."

Check your settings and click on the __Start__ button at the top, or double click the VM name > the __Select start-up disk__ screen defaults to the DVD drive. If installing from an ISO image, click on the icon to the right of __Host Drive 'D:'__ > browse to the location of the ISO file to be installed (e.g. __Fedora-20-x86_64-DVD.iso__, __ubuntu-13.10-desktop-amd64.iso__, __linuxmint-17.1-cinnamon-dvd-64bit.iso__, etc.) and select it, click on the __Open__ button and the selection box should change from __Host Drive 'D:'__ to the name of your ISO file, __Open__ > click on the __Start__ button at the bottom > depending on what the OS presents, double click an install desktop icon or menu item to install the guest OS (e.g. __Install Fedora 20__, __Install Linux Mint__, for openSUSE __Installation__, and Ubuntu __Install Ubuntu__) > follow the OS installation steps detailed later in this chapter for each OS.

WARNING	On modern computers with no IDE hardware, it seemed to make sense to remove the IDE controller. Before the OS install, doing this resulted in VirtualBox being unable to continue the OS installation. The IDE controller is also needed to mount the VBoxGuestAdditions.iso file in which to install the guest additions. By default, VirtualBox uses the SATA controller for the VM, which is faster and yields greater throughput than IDE. After installing the Guest Additions, the IDE controller can be removed, but I do not recommend doing so. ***Under __Settings__ click on __Storage__ > right click on __IDE Controller__ > select __Remove Controller Del__.***

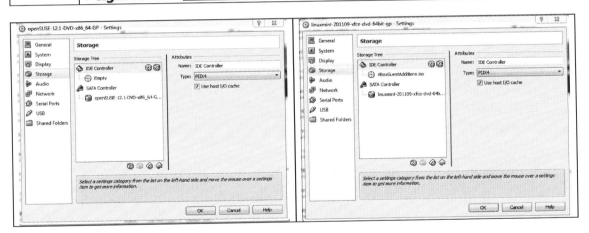

In many OSs VirtualBox will automatically install the guest additions. Sometimes the automatic install of the VirtualBox guest additions will get interrupted. Clicking on the <u>Force Unmount</u> button did nothing. If you want to attempt using the *GUI again shutdown the VM.* ***Select the VM and click on __Settings__ > select __Storage__ on the left > right click on __VBoxGuestAdditions.iso__ > click on __Remove Attachment__ > when the __Are you sure...__ dialog appears click on the __Remove__ button > click on the + to the right of the __IDE Controller__ > a "__You are about to add a new CD/DVD drive__" dialog box will appear, click on the __Leave empty__ button, __OK__ > restart the VM.***	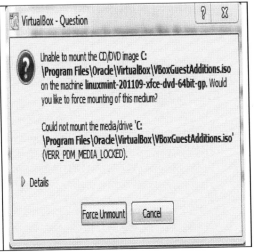

| Tip | Similar to the scenario above, sometimes after building a new VM, when you shutdown it does not shutdown cleanly, and you have to force the machine to power off. This may leave the linux.iso file mounted under <u>Controller: IDE</u>, and when you startup VirtualBox will want you to install the OS all over again. Simply cancel out of this, and using the procedure above, remove the attachment and then add an <u>Empty</u> entry. |

VirtualBox -- Installing the VirtualBox Guest Additions

From the VirtualBox manual, the VirtualBox kernel module is automatically installed on your system when you install VirtualBox. To maintain it with future kernel updates, for those Linux distributions that provide it, VirtualBox recommends installing Dynamic Kernel Module Support (DKMS). If DKMS is available and installed, the VirtualBox kernel module should always work automatically, and will be automatically rebuilt if your host kernel is updated. VirtualBox recommends using DKMS in the Linux Distribution, if it is available. DKMS should be installed prior to installing the VirtualBox Guest Additions. If DKMS is not available or is not installed, the guest kernel modules will need to be recreated manually.

You can switch VirtualBox back and forth between Scale mode and windowed mode. Scale mode will remove the VirtualBox menu and enlarge and shrink the windows that are open. Using scale mode may be good for those of us you are visually challenged or have small displays. Windowed mode is good for users used to working with Windows 7. When you hold down the right <Ctrl> key and press <C> you will see dialog box stating the following:

```
The virtual machine will be now switched to Scale mode.  You can go back to windowed
mode at any time by pressing Host+C.  Note that the Host key is defined as the Right
Ctrl key.  Note that the main menu bar is hidden in scale mode.  You can access it
by pressing Host+Home.
```

If you don't remember what this dialog is saying, you will not be able to bring up the main menu to do things such as adjust the settings, change the view, examine your devices, etc.. You might prefer to do as I do and just leave the menu enabled.

BackTrack/Kali/Mint/Ubuntu -- VirtualBox Guest Additions

Login as 'root', then open a terminal window and install the following:

```
$ su -    or,    sudo su -
# apt-get update  &&  apt-get upgrade -y  &&  apt-get install -y dkms
```

| NOTE | Sometimes when following the steps below, the install of Guest Additions is interrupted, or the VBOXADDITIONS_version file would not un-mount. The ISO file needs to be unmounted to install a new version or to follow the directions below. *Click on **Devices** > **CD/DVD Devices** > select **Remove disk from virtual drive**. If this does not work, shutdown the VM > select the VM > click on **Settings** > select **Storage** on the left > under the **IDE Controller** right click on **VBoxGuestAdditions.iso** > select **Remove Attachment** , click on the **Remove*** |

*button > click on the + sign next to **IDE Controller** and when prompted with the "**You are about to add a new CD/DVD drive to controller IDE Controller.**" dialog, choose the **Leave empty** button > **OK** > restart the VM and attempt to install the VBOX Guest Additions again following the directions below.*

*In BackTrack-GNOME, from the top menu click on **Devices** > scroll down to select **Install Guest Additions...** > when the **VBOXADDITIONS version** dialog appears with **Open Autorun Prompt** selected, click on **OK** > when prompted "**Would you like to run it?**" click on **Run** > once installed, press RETURN to close the window > right click on the **VBOXADDITIONS_versions** icon and select **Eject** > reboot the VM.*

Linux Mint-KDE and Cinnamon came with a prior version of the VirtualBox Guest Additions installed by default. Because of that you may get the message:

```
You appear to have a version of the VBoxGuestAdditions software on your system which
was installed from a different source or using a different type of installer.  If
you installed it from a package from your Linux distribution or if it is a default
part of the system then we strongly recommend that you cancel this installation and
remove it properly before installing this version.  If this is simply an older or a
damaged installation you may safely proceed.
```

If while trying to install the Guest Additions you get the message above, you need to purge those packages before installation to limit possible VM conflicts. Become 'root' and type the following:

```
# dpkg --list *virtualbox-guest*     # See is a prior version of the VirtualBox packages is
installed
# apt-get purge virtualbox-guest-*  &&  shutdown -r now     # If prior found
```

The next time you run Install Guest Additions... you will not be prompted to uninstall the prior version. Prior to installing the Guest Additions update your software:

```
# apt-get update  &&  apt-get upgrade -y  &&  shutdown -r now
```

To get the VBOADDITIONS* mounted under /media open up the Dolphin file manager and under Devices click on the virtual CD VBOXADDITIONS*. Then to install the Guest Additions open a terminal window and perform the following steps:

```
# cd /media/VBOXADDITIONS*  or,  cd /media/suroot/VBOXADDITIONS*
# ./VBoxLinuxAdditions.run  &&  exit
# exit
$ cd  &&  cd Downloads  &&  touch VBOXADDITIONS<tools-version>  # Future reference!
$ su -
# cd  &&  umount /media/VBOXADDITIONS* or,
# cd  &&  umount /media/suroot/VBOXADDITIONS*
```

```
# shutdown -r now
```

Sometimes the Guest Additions were mounted under media in your administration user directory. In that case:

```
# ls /media
suroot
# cd /media/suroot/VBOXADDITIONS*
# cd  &&  umount /media/suroot/VBOXADDITIONS_4.3.x
```

The touch command above creates a file so you can quickly determine which version of Guest Additions is installed. After reboot, eject/unmount the CD upon which we mounted the Guest Additions. If you prefer to use the GUI you can use the following directions in KDE and GNOME to install the Guest Additions in the various flavors of Linux.

In Mint-KDE, login as '__root__' > install the VirtualBox Guest Additions by clicking on __Devices__ in the upper left VirtualBox menu > arrow down to select __Install Guest Additions CD image...__ > when the __Available Devices__ window pops up select __Open with File Manager__ > double click on the __VBoxLinuxAdditions.run__ file > a window should pop up showing the progress of the install > when the install completes __Press Return__ to close the window > close the __Dolphin__ File Manager and reboot > after reboot in Mint-KDE activate the VirtualBox Guest Additions' Driver by right clicking on the __Menu__ icon lower left > up to select __Switch to Classic Menu Style__ > clicking on the __Menu__ icon lower left > arrow right to __Applications__ > arrow up to select __System__ > arrow right and then up to __Additional Drivers__ and click on it > click on the __Activate__ button lower right > a dialog will pop up stating __Downloading and installing driver...__ > when done, you will see the message __This driver is activated and currently in use.__, click on __Close__.

The terminal window steps above are also a quick work around if you get the Unable to insert the virtual optical disk C:... dialog, which indicates the Guest Additions' CD may be already mounted in the VM and all you have to do is open a terminal window and perform the steps above. However, sometimes the Guest Additions in Backtrack, Mint-KDE or Mint-XFCE will just create the device file */dev/disk/by-label/VirtualBox-4.3.x*, which you have to manually mount:

```
# cd /media  &&  mkdir cdrom
# mount  /dev/disk/by-label/VirtualBox-4.3.x  cdrom
# cd cdrom  &&  ./VBoxLinuxAdditions.run  &&  cd ..  &&  umount cdrom
```

In Mint-Cinnamon: from the top menu click on __Devices__ > arrow down to select __Install Guest Additions CD Image...__ > when the __VBOXADDITIONS version__ dialog appears click on the __Run__ button lower right > if not running as 'root', when the __Authentication is needed...__ dialog appears enter the 'root' password and click on the __Authenticate__ button lower right > this will bring up the __VirtualBox Guest Additions__ installation terminal window, if prompted __Do you wish to continue anyway?__ type __yes__ and this will remove the existing VirtualBox installation and reinstall the tools, otherwise VirtualBox will just upgrade the tools > when the tools finish installing press <RETURN> to close the window > right click on __VBOXADDITIONS version__ icon on the desktop > arrow down to the bottom of the menu and select __Eject__ > reboot the VM.

*In Mint-XFCE, from the top menu click on **Devices** > arrow down to select **Install Guest Additions...** > the **VBOXADDITIONS version** icon will appear on the desktop > right click on the icon and select **Mount Volume** > open a terminal window and perform the terminal window procedure above.*

In Ubuntu if you get the Unable to insert the virtual optical Disk C:... dialog follow the terminal window procedure above. Otherwise, ***with 3D graphics enabled from the top VirtualBox menu click on the Devices menu > scroll down to the bottom to select Install Guest Additions CD image... > a dialog box will appear asking " VBOXADDITIONS version" contains software intended to be automatically started. Would you like to run it? , click on Run button lower right > enter the root password, click on the Authenticate button > the VirtualBox Guest Additions will install > reboot the VM for the changes to take effect.***

If you are running the window in FULL screen mode, it may not come up maximized. ***Click on the Restore down icon upper-middle right > click on Maximize upper-middle right again and the graphics should render correctly.***

In Mint-Mate, I tried to Open Autorun Prompt, click on OK > on This medium contains software intended... and clicked on Run. This did not install the Guest Additions. It is better to follow the terminal window procedure above.

OpenSUSE -- VirtualBox Guest Additions

OpenSUSE comes with a version of the VirtualBox Guest Additions already installed. However, it was a release of the VirtualBox tools which was very outdated. The VM had to update to the latest tools release:

```
# zypper install -y kernel-devel kernel-headers
```

Click on Devices > scroll down to select Install Guest Additions... > if the dialog Unable to mount the CD/DVD image... appears refer back to VirtualBox-Creating Virtual Guest Operating Systems for the steps to fix this > select Open with File Manager from the lower right popup > double click on VBoxLinuxAdditions.run > if you receive a warning about replacing your OS version of VirtualBox tools type yes to replace them > the window will then show the progress of the install > when the install completes Press Return to close the window > close the Dolphin (File Manager) and reboot.

If you want to install the Guest Additions from a terminal window, after opening Dolphin and under Devices, click on VBOXADDITIONS* where you will find them mounted under the /var/run/media/suroot/VBOXADDITIONS* directory:

```
# cd /var/run/media/suroot/VBOXADDITIONS*  &&  ./VBoxLinuxAdditions.run
# cd  &&  umount /var/run/media/suroot/VBOXADDITIONS*
# exit
$ cd  &&  cd Downloads  &&  touch VBOXADDITIONS<tools-version>   # Future reference!
$ su -
# shutdown -r now
```

Another thing you can try to get the Guest Additions installed is OpenSUSE-KDE that may create the device file /dev/disk/by-label/VirtualBox*, which you can then manually mount:

```
# cd /media  &&  mkdir cdrom
# mount  /dev/disk/by-label/VirtualBox* cdrom
# cd cdrom  &&  ./VBoxLinuxAdditions.run  &&  cd ..  &&  umount cdrom
```

Fedora – VirtualBox Guest Additions

Make sure all the latest updates are installed along with the DKMS package:

```
$ su -
# yum update -y  &&  yum install dkms -y  &&  shutdown -r now
```

Often times when trying to install the Guest Additions after *clicking on Devices > **Install Guest Additions CD Image...*** I would encounter the <u>Unable to insert the virtual optical disk C:...</u> dialog. You can refer back to how to shutdown the VM and use the VirtualBox Settings to unmount the CD and use the GUI procedure below. Alternatively, you can use a terminal window to install the Guest Additions and look back at some additional steps you may want to follow. If you are not logged in as 'root' use Dolphin to determine the path to the VBOXADDITIONS_X such as */run/media/suroot/VBOXADDITIONS_X* and open a terminal window, become 'root' and type something such as the following:

```
# cd /run/media/suroot/VBOX*  &&  ./VBoxLinuxAdditions.run
# cd  &&  umount /run/media/suroot/VBOXADDITIONS*  &&  exit
$ cd  &&  cd Downloads  &&  touch VBOXADDITIONS<tools-version>   # Future reference!
$ su -
# shutdown -r now
```

To apply the VirtualBox Guest Additions in Fedora-GNOME GUI, *select **Devices** from the top VirtualBox menu > arrow down to the bottom and select **Install Guest Additions CD image...** > if the **Force Unmount** dialog appears refer back to Installing Guest Additions for the procedure to correct this > when the **VBOXADDITIONS** version dialog appears asking, "**This medium contains software intended to be automatically started. Would you like to run it?**" click on the **Run** button at the lower right > when the **Authentication Required** dialog appears enter the root password, click on the **Authenticate** button lower right > this will remove any previous version of the tools that may have been installed, and install the new version > when prompted **Press Return...** in the window hit **Return** > reboot the VM.*

*In Fedora-KDE, an **Available Devices** dialog appears at the lower right > select **Open with File Manager** > if you miss this rapidly disappeared dialog open up **Dolphin** and under **Devices** click on **VBOXADDITIONS_X** > double click on **VBoxLinuxAdditions.run** and a window should pop up showing the progress of the install > when the install completes **Press Return** to close the window > close the Dolphin (File Manager) and reboot. If a pop-up with **Open with File Manager** does not appear or if the pop-up disappears before you can select that menu item open up the "Dolphin File Manager" from the Classic menu. Click on the "F" icon at the lower left > arrow up to highlight **System** > arrow right and up to select **Dolphin (File Manager)** > on the left under **Devices** you should see **VBOXADDITIONS_version** mounted, click on that device > double click on **VBoxLinuxAdditions.run** > when the install completes **Press Return** to close the window > close the **Dolphin (File Manager)** and reboot.*

Windows Vista/XP -- VirtualBox Guest Additions

To enable Direct3D support, VirtualBox requires that XP be running in *Safe Mode*, **reboot the VM and press the <F8> key quickly as the system starts to come up > using the keyboard, arrow the cursor up and select *Safe Mode* > *Yes*.**

Install the VirtualBox Guest Additions by clicking on *Devices* in the upper VirtualBox menu > select *Install Guest Additions CD image...* > this may bring up the Oracle VM VirtualBox Guest Additions Setup *Next>* > leave the default Install Location, *Next>* > tick the *Direct3D Support (Experimental)* box > *Install* > trust the driver publisher > *Continue Anyway* multiple times > *Finish*. If the installer does not start install the Guest Additions from the drive (D:) the same as we did in Vista below. Based on the VirtualBox manual, this may fix your graphics rendering so that the resolution can be improved.

 This does **not** apply to the experimental WDDM Direct3D video driver available for Vista and Windows 7 guests shipped with VirtualBox 4.1 and later.

In Vista, to install the VirtualBox Guest Additions **click on *Devices* in the upper VirtualBox menu > select *Install Guest Additions CD image...* > this will automatically mount the Guest Additions on D: (NOTE: The VirtualBox manual suggests the Windows guest will automatically start the Guest Additions installer but that was not the case in my VM) > open Windows File Explorer where you will see CD Drive (D:) VirtualBox Guest Additions, click on this and run *VBoxWindowsAdditions*, which will bring up the Oracle VM VirtualBox Guest Additions 4.x.x Setup wizard, *Next>* > on *Choose Components* try out the Direct3D experimental support if this is a test install, *Install*. > went done leave *Reboot now* ticked, *Finish*.**

The WDDM interface supports the Windows Areo interface which will require some added configuration. On production systems, you probably only want Direct3D. The Aero theme is not enabled by default, to enable it in Vista right-click on the desktop > arrow down to select *Personalize* > on the *Personalize appearance and sounds* screen click on *Window Color and Appearance* > on the *Appearance Setting* screen under Color scheme: select *Windows Aero*, *OK*.

Command Line – Using It in Windows and Linux

Much of what I will show you in the remainder of this chapter will be implemented using the Linux command line in a terminal window. You can also use the GUIs and a Linux text editor, much like Windows Notepad, to do the same steps, which I will cover later. Still, using the command line is more efficient in many cases and is needed to master the techniques described in this book from this point forward.

Windows 7 does not come with the Run... command enabled by default. This command box is a shortcut to many useful Windows applications. If you have not already done so, add the Run... command to the Start menu: ***Right click on the taskbar > scroll down to select Properties > click on the Start Menu tab > select the Customize... button > scroll down and check the Run command box***.

To get to a Windows command line prompt click on ***Start > select Run... > type cmd***. You can also use ***Start > All Programs > select Accessories > select Command Prompt***.

Using the command line in Linux requires opening a terminal window and then using your editor of choice. The steps for opening a terminal window differ in Linux from flavor to flavor and version to version, so I will cover those as we build our virtual environments.

NOTE	Using the command line is a quick and easy way to apply updates and add software packages. This can also be easily done from the GUI. By using the command line it is a simple step to effortlessly create scripts that will quickly install updates and extra applications to a virtual OS. These scripts will come in very handy as we continuously upgrade to later Linux versions, and to create multiple virtual guest OSs.

Modern day operating systems are evolved pieces of software that ultimately interpret all the 1's and 0's to manage hardware resources and to provide an environment in which we can use our Internet devices. Everything on a computer needs an operating system to interact with the applications that everything else serves up to the user. An operating system provides a command interpreter, known as a shell, in Linux. We issue commands in a script or terminal window that the command interpreter passes along to the operating system. There are different command interpreters for Linux just like there are many programming languages and multiple OSs that we can run on our various devices. This book covers the BASH shell, which was a replacement for the Bourne shell back in 1989. (See:
https://www.gnu.org/software/bash/bash.html, https://www.gnu.org/software/bash/manual,
https://help.ubuntu.com/community/Beginners/BashScripting,
https://www.ibm.com/developerworks/linux/library/l-bash/index.html,
https://en.wikipedia.org/wiki/Bash_(Unix_shell))

The BASH shell *bashed together* (combined) many of the features of the Knon (ksh), C (csh), the Borne (sh) command processors and extended their capabilities. Consequently, to keep things simple, BASH is the only scripting/programming language covered in this book. There are more advanced programming languages, but I chose BASH, which is universal to most Linux OSs.

I have been using the VI editor for many years, which has been improved upon by VIM. VIM extends the VI's capabilities and does not change them, so learning VI for using VIM is completely relevant. Many other editors can be used in Linux. Several flavors of Linux default to *bash* command mode editing. I prefer to use VIM mode, which allows VI-like commands when at the *bash* prompt. When you are in VI mode, press the <ESC> key to enter command mode and enter VI commands. If you press <v>, your default editor will start up and your command will be visible to edit. Ubuntu defaults to the *Nano* editor.

To help you use the command line and create scripts, please try to take some time to read the VIM manual http://www.eandem.co.uk/mrw/vim/usr_doc/index.html, VI Reference, and my VIM Cheat Sheet in Appendix 5. If you take some time to study these sources, you will find out just how easy, powerful and wonderful VIM and the BASH shell are for performing the tasks of writing and using simple scripts, making configuration changes, and working from the command line. You will not regret your time spent educating yourself in this endeavor. It will certainly help as we cover some command line use and scripting later. (See: https://help.ubuntu.com/community/VimHowto, http://vimdoc.sourceforge.net, http://www.selectorweb.com/vi.html).

The http://www.vim.org site has all of the documentation and various flavors of VIM. *Vim-gnome*, or GVim, is the GUI version of the enhanced VI editor for GNOME, with Windows-like features built in, making it much friendlier to use. It is the best of both worlds: a GUI text editor with the power of VI. It is an intuitive tool for editing scripts and altering configuration files, which as you learn more, becomes a very quick and powerful text processing tool. The *vim-doc* package is the HTML documentation for VI Improved. Other packages you may want with Vim are *vim-gtk* (GUI version for GTK), vim-nox (version of VIM without the GUI), *vim-perl* (terminal version with Perl Programming Language bindings (see http://www.perl.org, http://learn.perl.org/ and https://en.wikipedia.org/wiki/Perl)), *vim-python* (terminal version with Python Programming Language bindings (see http://python.org, http://docs.python.org/2)), *vim-ruby* (terminal version with Ruby Programming Language bindings (see http://www.ruby-lang.org/en, https://en.wikipedia.org/wiki/Ruby_(programming_language), https://en.wikibooks.org/wiki/Ruby_Programming)), *vim-tiny* (is a lightweight, minimal version of VIM with a small subset of VIM features, good for lite versions of Linux), and *cscope* (an interactive text screen for browsing mostly C and C++ code). There are other packages we can use with VIM, which are presented later. We will also go over changing the command line mode once VIM is installed.

If you are strictly a GUI person, don't lose hope. The GEdit text editor, installed by default in the GNOME Desktop Environment, is an intuitive application that you will find easy to use. (See http://projects.gnome.org/gedit)

GEdit is a bit more sophisticated than Windows Notepad with basically the same functionality. You will still need to learn to use a terminal window to perform some of the exercises that are in the remainder of this book. For help using a terminal, see: http://en.opensuse.org/Terminal, which details the many advantages of using a terminal window, or view http://library.gnome.org/users/gnome-terminal/stable and http://docs.xfce.org/apps/terminal/start which are the GNOME and XFCE Terminal Manuals.

Soon we will be setting up our Linux environments and loading them up with many useful applications, tools and utilities. Many of these tasks can be performed using the GUI with searches, points and clicks. Using the command line to add software is as simple as the following:

Linux flavor	Application software installation command syntax
In BackTrack, Mint, and Ubuntu	# apt-get install -y <application/tool name/library>
In Fedora	# yum install -y <application/tool name/library>
In openSUSE	# zypper install -y <application/tool name/library>

Later, in our scripting we will use a few special parameters and tests to add some intelligence to the scripts presented. This is not a book on scripting, but we can cover a few of the parameters and tests used in this book to help you understand the scripts presented. When we run a script in Linux, the scripting language serves up useful command line arguments, variables, parameters and tests that we can use.

Special Parameters	Purpose
$0	Is the name of the script. echo The name of this script is $0
$1 ... $n	Are the actual command line arguments passed to the script. echo The first command line arg is $1 echo The second command line arg is $2
$#	Is the total number of command line arguments. echo There are a total of $# command line arguments
$*	Displays all the arguments passed to the script. printf "All args: %s\n" "$*"
$?	Exit status of the most recently executed command (foreground pipe).
$@	Expands the positional parameters, starting from one.

Compound Condition Tests	The result of the test
command1 && command2	The AND operator is used to execute one successful command after another. If the first command is successful (zero return value), command two is executed... and so on for the command tree. The first unsuccessful command executed terminates the command chain.
command1 || command2	The OR operator is used to execute the next command only if the previous command was unsuccessful. Upon the first successful completion of a command, the command chain terminates.
;	The semicolon allows us to put two or more commands on the same line. It is used it in this book to cut down on the whitespace.

"string"	This is used to preserve (from interpretation by BASH) most of the special characters in a string or command.
'string'	This is a stronger form of quoting than using double quotes in the BASH shell. It preserves all special characters within STRING.

There are many examples of scripts on the web. A wonderful website that has many examples of many useful scripts that you can pick and choose from can be found at http://www.intuitive.com/wicked/wicked-cool-shell-script-library.shtml.

Terminal Window -- Customizing the Linux Command Line to Make Life Easy

Not many years ago, the way a user interacted with a computer was by using something called a command prompt, terminal emulator, or terminal window. OSs did not have GUIs, which now conceal everything that is taking place when you click, expand, drag, point, speak, swipe, tap, type and more. To command a device to do something required typing in a text command to tell that device what to do. But now, advanced computer GUIs issue those commands to your operating system. The command line has not disappeared; it has been covered with flowery gardens (a GUI) so that common users do not know what is taking place on their Internet devices. This technology is both good and bad. GUIs opened up Internet devices to people who are not computer professionals, but at the same time it made the exploitation of your Internet activities much more possible. A terminal window allows you to issue commands to the operating system and know exactly what you are asking for in return. You can also give your Internet device tasks that you perform on a regular basis using scripting, which we will cover soon.

One of the first things that you will want to do to your Virtual OS is to make using a terminal window and the command line as easy as possible. This will save you time implementing your VM configuration and using the command line in the future. It is a bit backwards to describe how to customize our Linux command line environment before we have created a virtual OS, but we will want to do this in every Linux virtual OS that we create. If you will be creating additional user IDs in your virtual OS, you must also make these changes to the files in the **/etc/skel** directory, or set them globally for all users. Files in the **/etc/skel** directory contain the default environment files for the creation of new user IDs in Linux. Global settings apply to every user on the system at startup and cannot be modified by the users, whereas the files copied from **/etc/skel** can be modified by the user in their home directory. Providing your users with a good initial setup will make everyone on the system more productive and content. This is much like the way we customized Windows 7 to make ourselves more productive there.

Three files copied from **/etc/skel** have special meaning to the BASH shell, allowing the user to customize their terminal environment. When a user opens and closes a terminal (referred to as an *interactive shell*, that is, not a login shell), or is invoked by another BASH shell, one more of these initialization files are sourced thus executing the commands when a terminal window opens. A command file can also be sourced by typing either source <script> or typing ". <script>" at the command line, which will execute the lines of code in the file as if they were typed on the command line. Sometimes we have to tell a terminal window to open as a login shell to get it to source one of the files. Typing $ man bash will provide a more detailed explanation of the start and stop process, along with other configuration options. The <~> character below is shorthand for **$HOME**, which means the user's home directory and depending on the flavor of Linux which is described below, this can vary. These rules generally apply to the BASH shell command processor.

- **~/.bash_profile** - is a file read and executed when BASH is invoked as an interactive login shell and the file exists and is readable. It is also invoked when a user logs in to the system or root and executes a switch user command # su - <user ID> or $ bash -l (the - instructs BASH to source the configuration files as a login shell and switch to the users home directory). From the Linux (help) man page by typing $ man bash "*a login shell is one whose first character of argument zero is a -, or one started with the –login option.*" Without the '-', the **.bash_profile** is not sourced and **.bashrc** is.
- **~/.bashrc** - is read every time a terminal window is opened or a subshell is created. It is also sourced for non-login shells or when root or a user executes # su <user ID> to become another user. The **.bash_logout** will NOT be executed when the shell is exited.
- **~/.bash_logout** - is sourced when a login shell exits. Opening a terminal window is not considered a login shell. Invoking $ bash -l will make BASH act as a login shell and source **.bash_logout** upon exiting.

If we want a terminal window to open as a login shell in KDE, open a Konsole terminal window to allow the use of the command line, ***click on the Settings menu at the top > select Edit Current Profile... > select the General tab and add the -l option to Command: /bin/bash -l > change the terminal scrolling by clicking on the Scrolling tab and under Scrolling tick Unlimited scrollback > OK***.

If we want a terminal window to open a login shell in a GNOME or Unity Terminal, ***right click in the terminal or click on Edit if the menu is displayed > select Profile > Profile Preferences > select the Title and Command tab > under Command check Run command as a login shell > Close***. This will make the terminal window source the **$HOME/.profile** file, which usually sources the **$HOME/.bashrc** file if the user is using the BASH shell. In Ubuntu and openSUSE KDE, opening a terminal window sourced the **.bashrc** file without telling it to run as a login shell.

Two other files, which act as synonyms for **.bash_profile** file, are the **.bash_login** and **.profile** files. These files are derived or left over from the old C shell's file named **.login**, and from the old Bourne and Korn shell files named **.profile**. If **.bash_profile** isn't there, BASH will look for **.bash_login**. If both **.bash_login** and **.bash_profile** are missing then BASH will look for **.profile**, in that order. Only the first file found is sourced when a user logs in. The **.bash_profile** file is read and executed only when a user starts a login shell (that is, when you log in to the system). If they start a subshell (a new shell) by typing $ bash at the command prompt, it will read commands only from the **.bashrc** file. This allows the ability to separate commands needed at login from those needed when invoking a subshell.

Most Linux versions have one of the profile files above to source the user's **$HOME/.bashrc** file. This sets up the user's environment regardless of whether it is a login shell or a subshell. The startup process can differ slightly between Linux distributions.

To get information about a Linux command from a terminal window type:
apropos -e <command>   or,   man <command>

In Chapter 5 we talked about the Windows Problem Steps Recorder (PSR) command. Linux has the simple $ script command to make a typescript of everything you do or that is displayed using a terminal. This can come in very handy to show someone how to do something or as a record of how you have accomplished something. Script does not work well with interactive commands like VI, which manipulate the screen, so it is limited. Typing <CTRL-D> or exiting the shell will end what the "script" tool is recording. You can learn about the *script* command by typing $ man script or by visiting http://linux.about.com/library/cmd/blcmdl1_script.htm.

> **NOTE** The customization steps below are suggestions that I have found useful. This section is meant to show examples of a few changes that you can make, which might enhance your use of a terminal window and the command line.

Many of the tasks we will cover in Linux will require root privileges. The easiest way to work through the many configuration steps is to become 'root' and type these commands. There are several ways to become 'root' or to run 'root' commands in Ubuntu Linux using a terminal window:

$ sudo -s	Root shell with minimal environment, stay where you are
$ sudo -s -u <UserID>	Open a shell as <UserID>, don't source user environment
$ sudo su	More of the root's environment, stay where you are
$ sudo su -	Root login environment, cd to /root
$ sudo -H bash -l	Root login environment, stay where you are
$ gksudo	Visual sudo dialog to run commands as 'root' (GNOME)
$ kdesudo	Visual sudo dialog to run commands as 'root' (KDE)
$ sudo visudo	Edit the /etc/sudoers file
$ gksudo nautilus	Run a 'root' file manager in a GNOME desktop
$ kdesudo conqueror	Run a 'root' file manager in the KDE desktop

Before we begin making changes to the terminal window login configuration files enable some safety aliases for our systems user(s):

cd /etc/skel && vi .bash_aliases

```
# Safety 'sudoroot', 'suroot' or other common user aliases:

alias cp='cp -ip'      # Assign original date and prompt before overwrite
alias copy='cp -ip'    # Assign original date and prompt before overwrite
#alias rm='rm -i'      # Prompt before removing, can be annoying
#alias del='rm -i'     # Prompt before removing, can be annoying
alias move='mv -i'     # Prompt before overwriting an existing file
```

```
# Safety root aliases:

# In Fedora, as 'root' these are set by default:
alias cp='cp -i'        # Prompt before overwriting and existing file
alias rm='rm -i'        # Prompt before removing, can be annoying
alias mv='mv -i'        # Prompt before overwriting an existing file

alias cp='cp -ip'       # Assign original date and prompt before overwrite
alias copy='cp -ip'     # Assign original date and prompt before overwrite
alias del='rm -i'       # Prompt before removing, can be annoying
alias move='mv -i'      # Prompt before overwriting an existing file
```

When logged in as 'root' or 'suroot' $ type cd && cp -ip /etc/skel/.bash_aliases . to update the **.bash_aliases** in the home directory. The ending "." represents the current directory.

In Ubuntu, you can make an alias for your favorite method of becoming 'root' using the 'sudoroot' user ID by **double clicking on Terminal icon opening a terminal window** or by **typing <Ctrl><Alt><T>** and adding the above to your 'sudoroot' user account home directory **.bash_aliases** file:

```
$ cd && cp -ip /etc/skel/.bash_aliases .     # As user 'sudoroot'
$ vi .bash_aliases      # Add the following to end of file
# Add Ubuntu 'suduroot' alias for becoming 'root':
alias root1='sudo su -'
alias root2='sudo -H bash -l'
```

In Mint, openSUSE and Fedora:

$ su	(become root, do not source root environment, stay where you are)
$ su -	(root login environment, cd to /root)

The Ubuntu Help website is a good place to start learning about using a terminal command line window. (See: https://help.ubuntu.com/community/UsingTheTerminal) Most Linux flavors use the BASH (which stands for Bourne-Again Shell), that we talked about previously. BASH is a command processor that runs in a terminal window. It interprets what you type and script, and performs those commands to the OS accordingly. There are many examples on the Internet of BASH shell scripting and Linux commands that you can use. All Linux flavors covered in this book come with a package called bash-doc. This package provides documentation and scripting, which includes examples for customizing the BASH shell. This can help customizing your use of the command line in a terminal window. The package installs in the **/usr/share/doc/bash-doc** directory. The documentation and examples of using the BASH shell are located in the directory **/usr/share/doc/bash** and **/usr/share/doc/bash**. Whether you are new to Linux or a power user, you should consider installing this package:

```
# apt-get install bash-doc;  yum install bash-doc -y;  zypper install bash-doc;
```

By default, BASH uses the EMACS (the extensible, customizable, self-documenting, real-time display editor) key bindings. (See: https://en.wikipedia.org/wiki/Emacs) EMACS is a powerful text editor that provides many commands and customization capabilities via macros. Vim, described earlier, likewise can be used for command line editing mode instead. Vim has many supporting packages that can also be installed. Below is an example of using the *apt-cache* command to view them.

```
$ root1 or su -      # become root
```

In BackTrack, Mint, and Ubuntu:
```
# apt-cache search vim | grep -i vim     # View Vim packages that are available
# apt-get install vim vim-common vim-doc vim-gnome vim-scripts exuberant-ctags -y
```

BackTrack-Kali-Mint-Ubuntu-GNOME-KDE suggested packages:
```
# apt-get install cscope desktop-base glibc-doc gnome-mime-data graphviz graphviz-doc gvfs
gvfs-backends ispell libbonobo2-bin libgnomevfs2-bin libgnomevfs2-extra libtemplate-perl
libtemplate-perl-doc ri ri1.9.1 ruby-dev ruby1.9.1-dev ruby1.9.1-examples spell tcl-tclreadline
ttf-dejavu vim-addon-manager -y
```

 NOTE | The packages *perlsgml* and *ruby-switch* had no installation candidate. The packages *fam* and *gamin* had conflicts.

In Fedora:
```
# yum install vim-enhanced gvim vim-perl* -y
```

In openSUSE:
```
# zypper install -n vim-enhanced gvim vim-plugin-gnupg
```

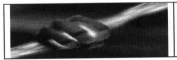 OpenSUSE comes with many plugins to enhance Vim for whichever application you are using. There is also yzis - which is a Vim Clone for KDE that claims to be as powerful as Vim.

There is an abundance of help online for Vim, which can be found with any search engine. Also installed with Vim is the command $ vimtutor, this is a lesson plan of exercises to help you with Vim. (See: http://simpletutorials.com/?path=tutorials/vim) When using the BASH shell on the command line or in scripts, anything prefixed by # is interpreted as a comment. When logged in as the root user, # is the default prompt. Some book reviewers found this confusing.

You might ask why I am using the ".orig" extension versus something like "file.bak". I learned early on performing system's administration that ".bak" becomes ".bak1, .bak2, and so on..." consequently, I quickly lost track of what the operating system developers had set up as the original configuration. So upon my first change to any original configuration file, I always name my first backup of a system configuration file "*.orig." After that, I use the ".bak," which later becomes ".bak1, .bak2", and so on.

Customize VIM for an individual user like 'suroot' and/or 'root' by editing **.vimrc** or for all users on the system by editing **/etc/vimrc** or **/usr/share/vim/vimrc**. These options are well documented in most books on VI and Vim (see http://vimdoc.sourceforge.net/htmldoc/options.html, https://en.wikibooks.org/wiki/Learning_the_vi_Editor/Vim/Enhancing_Vim, or the file **/usr/share/vim/vim74/vimrc_example.vim**). If you search the Internet, you can find many other options that can be set. Below is a sample configuration file with a few customizations that you may want to consider for your Vim editor defaults:

```
$ vi .vimrc; su -; vi .vimrc, or,
# cd /usr/share/vim && cp -ip vimrc vimrc.orig && vi vimrc   # In Debian flavors for all users
# cd /etc/vim  &&  vi vimrc    # In Mint KDE for all users
# cd /etc  &&  cp -ip vimrc vimrc.orig  &&  vi vimrc     # in Fedora & openSUSE
```

```
" Off by default in BackTrack, Fedora, Mint, Ubuntu, openSUSE
" Automatically write our contents of a changed buffer when :n(next)
" command to move to the next file to be edited, and before running a
" shell command with :!
set autowrite          " Automatically save before commands such as :next and :make

" Off by default in Mint-Cinnamon
set showcmd            " Show (partial) command in status line.

" Off by default in BackTrack, Fedora, Mint, openSUSE, Ubuntu
set ignorecase         " Ignore case in search patterns

set mouse=a            " Enable mouse usage (all modes)

" On by default in openSUSE, Off by default in BackTrack, Fedora, Mint & Ubuntu
set showmatch          " Show matching bracket if seen on screen

" Override the 'ignorecase' option if the search pattern contains upper
" case characters. Only used when the search pattern is typed and
" 'ignorecase' option is on.
set smartcase          " Do smart case matching

set expandtab          " Use spaces instead of tabs
set smarttab           " Be smart when using tabs
set shiftwidth=4       " 1 tab = 4 spaces
set tabstop=4          " 1 tab = 4 spaces

" The default dark blue color for comments was hard to see, try the following:
highlight Comment ctermfg=Green
"highlight Comment ctermfg=DarkGreen
" Change colorscheme from default to delek
"colorscheme delek
```

There are many *colorscheme* choices that you can experiment with for Vim. (See the files **/usr/share/vim/vim73/colors, /usr/share/vim-scripts/colors**) Typing :set all from inside VIM will show all of the options. Typing :set will show that options that have been changed or set, in either the .vimrc file or during your current session.

BackTrack, Ubuntu and Mint-KDE comes with a customized default ~username/.bashrc file that has many useful environment variables, settings and aliases. In Mint-KDE, the prompt is colored green by default as our 'suroot' user, and red as 'root'.

Any changes made to the .bashrc file can be made global in nature. We will go over that in the section on setting up aliases. BackTrack, Mint-KDE and Ubuntu all came with an extensive .bashrc file configuration.   Mint-Cinnamon did not have a home .bashrc file and had a minimal .profile; Fedora and openSUSE had limited .bashrc files. We can customize our terminal experience by editing these files.

Some general rules for where to set what in most flavors of Linux:

- ENVIRONMENT variables are inherited. If you need to set PATH or LD_LIBRARY_PATH for all of your shells or for all-user's shells, then put it in /etc/profile.d/localprofile.sh in some Linux flavors
- If you need to set a variable for YOUR account put it in ~/.bash_profile and export
- If you need to set a variable for ALL users put it in /etc/profile.d/localprofile.sh and export
- If you need to set an alias or shell function for YOUR account, put it in ~/.bashrc or ~/.bash_aliases sourced by ~/.bashrc
- If you need to set an alias or shell function for ALL users, it differs slightly from Linux flavor to flavor. See my examples below.

NOTE	As new releases of Linux come out, the default aliases can sometimes change. Before setting up the aliases, type # alias to see which aliases are already set up. Each user should control some aliases locally in their home account. The safety aliases that we set for 'root' likely are stricter than a standard or 'admin' group user. An individual user may want something less annoying and have a command execute without continuously prompting with a verify question. In addition, prompts and environments differ from distribution to distribution, so check those aliases before altering them.

We can setup aliases globally or locally in all flavors of Linux. In a VM, setting them up globally may be preferable to editing individual user environment profiles. As noted previously, the changes made in /etc/skel will be copied to new user accounts, so that is also an option to applying changes globally. The /etc/skel/.bashrc file in Ubuntu has many of these aliases set by default. If you want to add more, you should consider adding them to the user /etc/skel/.bashrc file rather than the global file. For convenience, we can set aliases globally. The most elegant way is to create a new file in the /etc/profile.d directory in Fedora, Mint-Cinnamon, Mint-KDE and Ubuntu:

$ root1; or, su -

```
# cd /etc/profile.d  &&  vim bash_aliases.sh
```

In openSUSE:
```
# cd /etc/profile.d  &&  cp -ip alias.bash alias.bash.orig && vi alias.bash
```

If creating the alias file in **/etc/profile.d** does not work, we can have the global BASH setup file run and set them:

```
# cd /etc  &&  cp -ip bash.bashrc bash.bashrc.orig
# vim bash.bashrc
```

Add the following, with comments, to the bottom of the **/etc/bash.bashrc** script file <shift-G><shift-A>:

```
# Add alias definitions.  We put them in a separate file instead of adding them
# here directly.  See /usr/share/doc/bash-doc/examples in the bash-doc package.
if [ -f /etc/bash_aliases ]; then
    . /etc/bash_aliases
fi
```

```
# cd /etc  &&  vim bash_aliases
```

```
# Enable color support of ls and also add some handy aliases.
# Many are set by default in most flavors of Linux.
# Type the "alias" command at the command prompt to see the default alias
# settings before adding these aliases.  See below for Fedora, Mint-KDE
# and Ubuntu additions.
if [ -x /usr/bin/dircolors ]; then
    test -r ~/.dircolors && eval "$(dircolors -b ~/.dircolors)" || eval "$(dircolors -b)"
    # Set up aliases for listing the contents of directories and environment.
    # Refer down to see want to set in Fedora.
    alias l='ls -CF --color=auto'
    alias l.='ls -d .* --color=auto'
    alias la='ls -A --color=auto'

    # List files with their inode numbers:
    alias li='ls -li --color=auto | sort -n | more'

    # Set as ll='ls -l --color=auto' in Fedora
    alias ll='ls -alF --color=auto'

    # Set by default in Mint-KDE-Cinnamon, refer down:
    #alias ls='ls --color=auto'
```

```
    alias ls-l='ls -l --color=auto'

    alias dir='dir --color=auto'   # or,
    #alias dir='ls -l --color=auto'
    #alias vdir='vdir --color=auto'

    # Set by default in Fedora and Mint-KDE, refer down
    # alias egrep='egrep --color=auto'
    # alias fgrep='fgrep --color=auto'

    # Set by default in Mint-Cinnamon
    # alias grep='grep --color=auto'
fi

# In Fedora, add the following:
if [ -x /usr/bin/dircolors ]; then
    test -r ~/.dircolors && eval "$(dircolors -b ~/.dircolors)" || eval "$(dircolors -b)"
    # Set up aliases for listing the contents of directories and environment
    alias la='ls -A --color=auto'

    # List files with their inode numbers:
    alias li='ls -li --color=auto | sort -n | more'
    # Set as ll='ls -l --color=auto' in Fedora
    alias ll='ls -alF --color=auto'

    alias ls-l='ls -l --color=auto'

    alias dir='dir --color=auto'
    alias vdir='vdir --color=auto'
fi

# In Mint-KDE, add the following:
if [ -x /usr/bin/dircolors ]; then
    test -r ~/.dircolors && eval "$(dircolors -b ~/.dircolors)" || eval "$(dircolors -b)"
    # Set up aliases for listing the contents of directories and environment
    alias li='ls -li $LS_OPTIONS | sort -n | more'  # List files with their inode numbers
    alias l.='ls -d .* --color=auto'
    alias ls-l='ls -l --color=auto'
    alias dir='dir $LS_OPTIONS'
    alias vdir='vdir $LS_OPTIONS'

    # If setting these globally then comment out in user home directories
    # and in the /etc/skel/.bashrc file.
    alias l='ls -CF $LS_OPTIONS'
    alias la='ls -A $LS_OPTIONS'
    alias ll='ls -alF $LS_OPTIONS'
fi

# In Mint Cinnamon add:
if [ -x /usr/bin/dircolors ]; then
    test -r ~/.dircolors && eval "$(dircolors -b ~/.dircolors)" || eval "$(dircolors -b)"
    # Set up aliases for listing the contents of directories and environment
    alias egrep='egrep --color=auto'
```

```
    alias fgrep='fgrep —color=auto'
    alias dir='dir $LS_OPTIONS'
    alias vdir='vdir $LS_OPTIONS'
    alias l='ls -CF —color=auto'
    alias l.='ls -d .* —color=auto'
    alias la='ls -A —color=auto'
    alias li='ls -li —color=auto | sort -n | more'  # List files with their inode numbers
    alias ll='ls -alF $LS_OPTIONS'
    alias ls-l='ls -l —color=auto'
fi


# In openSUSE, add the following:
if [ -x /usr/bin/dircolors ]; then
    test -r ~/.dircolors && eval "$(dircolors -b ~/.dircolors)" || eval "$(dircolors -b)"
    alias li='ls -li —color=auto | sort -n | more'  # List files with their inode numbers
    alias l.='ls -d .* —color=auto'
    alias dir='dir $LS_OPTIONS'
    alias vdir='vdir $LS_OPTIONS'
fi


# In Ubuntu, add the following:
if [ -x /usr/bin/dircolors ]; then
    test -r ~/.dircolors && eval "$(dircolors -b ~/.dircolors)" || eval "$(dircolors -b)"
    # Set up aliases for listing the contents of directories and environment
    alias li='ls -li —color=auto | sort -n | more'  # List files with their inode numbers
    #alias vdir='vdir —color=auto' is available to uncomment in the .bashrc file
    alias l.='ls -d .* —color=auto'
    alias ls-l='ls -l —color=auto'
fi


# Windows command aliases for all Linux flavors:
alias cls='clear'
alias md='mkdir -p'
alias rd='rmdir'


# General purpose aliases for all Linux flavors:
alias env='env | sort'
alias mybeep='echo -en "\007"'     # the beep tool can also be installed
alias psg="ps -ef | grep -v grep | grep "     # Find a running process
alias ff="find . -type f -name "     # Find a file
alias mocd='mount /mnt/cdrom'
alias uncd='umount /mnt/cdrom'
# Find top 5 big files:
alias findbig="find . -type f -exec ls -s {} \; | sort -n -r | head -5"
alias cd..='cd ..'
alias ..='cd ..'      # Set by default in openSUSE
alias ...='cd ../..'       # Set by default in openSUSE


# Set by default in Fedora:
alias which='alias | /usr/bin/which --tty-only --read-alias --show-dot --show-tilde'
```

There are a few settings in BackTrack-KDE-GNOME, Mint-KDE & Ubuntu that we can quickly alter to make using a terminal window a little more user-friendly.   The **.bashrc** file views a color prompt as a distraction. Another way we can customize a terminal characteristics is using the tput options at https://www.gnu.org/software/termutils/manual/termutils-2.0/html_node/tput_5.html. You might prefer a color prompt and a color dir command by uncommenting the following:

```
# cd /etc/skel  &&  cp -ip .bashrc .bashrc.orig  &&  vi .bashrc
force_color_prompt=yes
alias dir='dir --color=auto'
alias vdir='vdir --color=auto'
```

NOTE	Upon installation, some flavors of Linux provide a .bashrc file for the 'sudoroot', 'suroot' and 'root' users. Changing the */etc/skel* will only affect new users unless you copy the *.bashrc* file to their home directories. It is not suggested you use the same *.bashrc* file for common users and root. You may want to customize things in the 'root' .bashrc such as making the prompt PS1 red, which is the default in many flavors of Linux.

The default Ubuntu prompt, **~username/.bashrc PS1**, is very good and even sets the terminal window title. A prompt used to be the pride of UNIX geeks everywhere. You may want to customize it to change or reveal other information that is not in the default prompt. The Linux Documentation Project, http://tldp.org shows you many ways in which you can customize your prompt at http://tldp.org/HOWTO/Bash-Prompt-HOWTO/c327.html.

When you look at the **PS1** prompt variable it may seem very complex. For example, the prompt assumes that we may set up a change root *chroot* configuration to change the root location for using tools such as FTP or SFTP. We will actually be doing that in a Chapter 9 to allow partners, vendors, friends and/or family to send and receive files securely to/from our server.

The **PS1** prompt setting, in Debian flavors of Linux like Ubuntu and Mint, includes the content of file **/etc/debian_chroot**, inside parentheses. This variable is initialized in **/etc/bash.bashrc** during terminal startup. Your default Mint and Ubuntu installations do not create the **/etc/debian_chroot** file, so having this in the prompt adds nothing. However, when we set up *chroots* and follow this convention to include a name for your chroot(s) at a location such as **/path/to/chroot/etc/debian_chroot**, our prompt will indicate which chroot you are logged in as. With virtualization, you may have the 32-bit and 64-bit versions of an OS installed on a 64-bit machine. Hence, a very easy way to identify which OS you are running is:

```
# root1  or  sudo su -
# cd /etc  &&  test ! -f debian_chroot && uname -i > debian_chroot  # In BackTrack, Mint,
Ubuntu
# cd /etc  &&  test ! -f fedora_chroot  &&  uname -i > fedora_chroot  # To add to Fedora
```

cd /etc && test ! -f opensuse_chroot && uname -i > opensuse_chroot # To add to openSUSE

In Fedora, openSUSE, and Mint Cinnamon, we can use the same useful options in the default Ubuntu and the Mint KDE **.bashrc** file. Examine your terminal configuration and add or change your .bashrc file with some the following suggested settings:

cd /etc/skel && cp -ip .bashrc .bashrc.orig && vi .bashrc

```
# set -x       # Uncomment for debugging
#
# If not running interactively, don't do anything
# In Fedora, place after /etc/bashrc is sourced
# [ -z "$PS1" ] && return

# If not running interactively, don't do anything
case $- in
    *i*) ;;
      *) return;;
esac

# man bash - to see more options
# ignorespace - lines which begin with a space character are not saved
#                in the history list. In Mint-KDE set by default
# ignoredups - lines matching the previous history entry are not saved
# ignoreboth - is shorthand for ignorespace and ignoredups
# In Fedora & Mint-KDE, HISTCONTROL=ignoredups is set by default
export HISTCONTROL=ignoreboth

# append to the history file, don't overwrite it
shopt -s histappend

# HISTSIZE - The number of commands to remember in the command history
# HISTFILESIZE - make sure the history file contains no more than
#                j HISTFILESIZE lines
# In Fedora, Ubuntu, HISTSIZE=1000 by default
export HISTSIZE=1500
export HISTFILESIZE=2000

# Add a few things to the "change directory" path to navigate directories faster
export CDPATH=/usr/share/doc

# check the window size after each command and, if necessary,
# update the values of LINES and COLUMNS.
shopt -s checkwinsize
```

```
# If set, the pattern "**" used in a pathname expansion context will
# match all files and zero or more directories and subdirectories.
#shopt -s globstar

# Make less command more friendly for non-text input files, see lesspipe(1)
[ -x /usr/bin/lesspipe ] && eval "$(SHELL=/bin/sh lesspipe)"


#-------------------------------------------------------------------------
# Returncode.
#-------------------------------------------------------------------------
function returncode
{
  returncode=$?
  if [ $returncode != 0 ]; then
    echo "[$returncode]"
  else
    echo ""
  fi
}


# set variable identifying the chroot you work in (used in the prompt below),
# delete the lines for other flavors of Linux.
if [ -z "$debian_chroot" ] && [ -r /etc/debian_chroot ]; then
if [ -z "$fedora_chroot" ] && [ -r /etc/fedora_chroot ]; then
if [ -z "$opensuse_chroot" ] && [ -r /etc/opensuse_chroot ]; then
    debian_chroot=$(cat /etc/debian_chroot)
    fedora_chroot=$(cat /etc/fedora_chroot)
    opensuse_chroot=$(cat /etc/opensuse_chroot)
fi


# The default prompt in most flavors of Linux is usually adequate.
# Below will set a fancy prompt (non-color, unless we know we
# "want" color)
#case "$TERM" in
#    xterm-color) color_prompt=yes;;
#esac
#
# There are a few tweaks you may want to consider such as uncommenting the
# following for a colored prompt in Ubuntu, if your terminal graphics have
# this has the capability; they may be turned off by default to not
# to distract the user: the focus in a terminal window should be on the
# output of commands, not on the prompt
#force_color_prompt=yes
#
#if [ -n "$force_color_prompt" ]; then
#    if [ -x /usr/bin/tput ] && tput setaf 1 >&/dev/null; then
#        # We have color support; assume it's compliant with Ecma-48
#        # (ISO/IEC-6429). (Lack of such support is extremely rare, and such
```

```
#        # a case would tend to support setf rather than setaf.)
#        color_prompt=yes
#    else
#        color_prompt=
#    fi
#fi
#
#if [ "$color_prompt" = yes ]; then
#  if [[ ${EUID} == 0 ]] ; then
#PS1='\[\033[0;31m\]$(returncode)\[\033[0;37m\]\[\033[0;35m\]${debian_chroot:+($debian_chro
ot)}\[\033[01;31m\]\h\[\033[01;34m\] \W \$\[\033[00m\] '

#PS1='\[\033[0;31m\]$(returncode)\[\033[0;37m\]\[\033[0;35m\]${fedora_chroot:+($fedora_chro
ot)}\[\033[01;31m\]\h\[\033[01;34m\] \W \$\[\033[00m\] '

#PS1='\[\033[0;31m\]$(returncode)\[\033[0;37m\]\[\033[0;35m\]${opensuse_chroot:+($opensuse_
chroot)}\[\033[01;31m\]\h\[\033[01;34m\] \W \$\[\033[00m\] '

#
# else
#PS1='\[\033[0;31m\]$(returncode)\[\033[0;37m\]\[\033[0;35m\]${debian_chroot:+($debian_chro
ot)}\[\033[0;35m\]\u@\h\[\033[0;37m\]:\[\033[0;36m\]\w >\[\033[0;00m\] '

#PS1='${debian_chroot:+($debian_chroot)}\[\033[01;32m\]\u@\h\[\033[00m\]:\[\033[01;34m\]\w\
[\033[00m\]\$ '

#PS1='${fedora_chroot:+($fedora_chroot)}\[\033[01;32m\]\u@\h\[\033[00m\]:\[\033[01;34m\]\w\
[\033[00m\]\$ '

#PS1='${opensuse_chroot:+($opensuse_chroot)}\[\033[01;32m\]\u@\h\[\033[00m\]:\[\033[01;34m\
]\w\[\033[00m\]\$ '
#  fi
#fi
#
#unset color_prompt force_color_prompt
#
# If you want a simpler prompt you could use:
#   PS1='${debian_chroot:+($debian_chroot)}\u@\h:\w\$ '
#   PS1='${fedora_chroot:+($fedora_chroot)}\u@\h:\w\$ '
#   PS1='${opensuse_chroot:+($opensuse_chroot)}\u@\h:\w\$ '
#   PS1='[\u@\h \W]\$'      # Default Fedora prompt, you may prefer prompt below:
#
#
# If this is an xterm set the title to user@host:dir
#case "$TERM" in
#xterm*|rxvt*)
#     PS1="\[\e]0;${debian_chroot:+($debian_chroot)}\u@\h: \w\a\]$PS1"
#     PS1="\[\e]0;${fedora_chroot:+($fedora_chroot)}\u@\h: \w\a\]$PS1"
```

```
#      PS1="\[\e]0;${opensuse_chroot:+($opensuse_chroot)}\u@\h: \w\a\]$PS1"
#      ;;
#*)
#      ;;
#esac


# Add an "alert" alias for long running commands, like so: # sleep 10; alert
alias alert='notify-send --urgency=low -i "$([ $? = 0 ] && echo terminal || echo error)"
"$(history|tail -n1|sed -e '\''s/^\s*[0-9]\+\s*//;s/[;&|]\s*alert$//'\'')"'


if [ -f ~/.bash_aliases ]; then
    . ~/.bash_aliases
fi


# enable programmable completion features (you don't need to enable
# this, if it's already enabled in /etc/bash.bashrc and /etc/profile
# sources /etc/bash.bashrc).
if ! shopt -oq posix; then
  if [ -f /usr/share/bash-completion/bash_completion ]; then
    . /usr/share/bash-completion/bash_completion
  elif [ -f /etc/bash_completion ]; then
    . /etc/bash_completion
  fi
fi


# Treat unset variables and parameters as an error when performing
# parameter expansion
# set -u      # Uncomment for debugging


# Set VIM as the default command line editor for your terminals,
# add the following to the bottom by typing <Shift G><Shift A>.
# Set vi mode in bash
set -o vi       # Change command line editing from bash to vi mode
export EDITOR=/usr/bin/vim       # Change the default command line editor to vim


# exit
$ cd && mv .bashrc .bashrc.orig && cp -ip /etc/skel/.bashrc .       # Copy the .bashrc file to
our current user home directory.
```

When we have a **.bashrc** and **.bash_aliases** setup the way we want it for our 'suroot' or 'sudoroot', and 'root' users, copy the **/etc/skel** files to those user home directories. You have to figure out what to uncomment in the **.bashrc** file above. For example, in Mint Cinnamon the default prompt was just fine. By editing the **/etc/skel** files any new users created will also adopt these useful aliases and environment changes.

```
$ cd && mv -i .bashrc .bashrc.orig && mv .bash_aliases .bash_aliases.orig
```

```
$ cp -ip /etc/skel/.bashrc . && cp -ip /etc/skel/.bash_aliases .
$ chmod 640 .bash*
$ su -    or,    sudo su -     # In Ubuntu
# cd && mv -i .bashrc .bashrc.orig && mv .bash_aliases .bash_aliases.orig
# cd && cp -ip /etc/skel/.bashrc . && cp -p /etc/skel/.bash_aliases .
# chmod 640 .bashrc .bashrc.orig .bash_aliases .bash_aliases.orig .profile
```

GParted – Manually Creating Partitions

If you have never installed an OS or created a VM, you might not be familiar with partitions. Partitioning a computer is a way of dividing up a hard drive, storage device or RAID for different purposes. These logically separated sections can then be accessed independently. There are no set rules on how to partition an OS and most modern OSs will partition the space you set aside for them automatically. For a Linux VM, you may want one or possibly two (/ or root, and swap). The swap partition can be used as virtual RAM when your OS runs out of usable RAM memory. However, as OSs advance, even that partition is not necessary anymore. A swapfile is an alternative and has the advantage of being easier to resize. Another reason to repartition a Linux OS is if you want to use a different file system type than the default one. Most Linux OSs are still using the *Ext4* file system format, which we will talk about soon, although, for years now, developers have been working on the B-Tree File System file system (Btrfs) as a replacement. Consequently, you may want to change the file system while installing Linux into a VM.

By default, Windows 7 creates a 100 MB System Reserved partition and allocates the rest of the space to volume C:\. The System Reserved partition houses the Boot Manager and the Boot Configuration Database; it also reserves space for the startup files required by BitLocker Drive Encryption feature covered in Chapter 5. (See: https://en.wikipedia.org/wiki/Disk_partitioning, https://wiki.archlinux.org/index.php/Partitioning)

One can see that there may be reasons to alter the default partitions, and Linux provides various tools for doing so. GParted, the GNOME Partition Editor is a free partition editor for graphically managing your disk partitions. GParted supports many file system types (btrfs, ext2 / ext3 / ext4, fat16 / fat32, hfs / hfs+, linux-swap, ntfs, reiserfs / reiser4, ufs, xfs). (See: http://gparted.sourceforge.net) Any Linux install in VirtualBox can be manually partitioned. However, VMware Player installs most Linux OSs without allowing the user to manually partition the VM. Mint can be manually partitioned in all three, so this tutorial of how to use GParted to create partitions was done using Mint Cinnamon.

Another partition manager to consider is GNU Parted which also allows you to create, destroy, resize, move, and copy hard disk partitions. GNU Parted can be used for creating space for new operating systems, reorganizing disk usage, and copying data to new hard disks. (See: http://www.gnu.org/software/parted)

Mint Debian defaulted to a small swap area for the VM. Depending on your computer's memory, the RAM allocated to the VM could be much larger than the default swap settings. The rule of thumb that Linux administrators used to follow was to make the size of the swap area match (or double) the RAM allocated to the VM. However, as RAM became cheap and abundant, this hard and fast rule no longer applies.

The GParted tool can be used to manually create partitions. If you plan to let the VM applications or Linux automatically handle this task, skip ahead to the sections on the install, update, and setup of the different flavors of Linux. If you are considering manually setting up your partitions, then also skip ahead and perform the install up to the point where the OS allows you to specify if you want to automatically partition your disks. Manually configuring the partition might allow you to allocate the disk space in your VM more logically than using the defaults.

Click on the <u>Edit partitions</u> button lower right > click on the partition <u>unallocated – unallocated</u> > click on the <u>Device</u> menu > select <u>Create Partition Table...</u> > a <u>WARNING: This will ERASE ALL DATA...</u> box will appear > click on <u>Advanced</u> or the <u>+</u> to expand the Advanced menu so you can <u>Select new partition table type:</u>

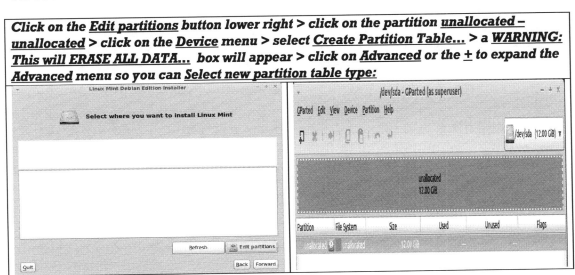

If you look at the screenshot to the right, you will see the GParted defaults to creating an MS-DOS partition table. Click on the ± sign next to the word <u>Advanced</u> and expand the window thus giving us the option to change. *Click on the down arrow and select <u>GPT</u> > select <u>Apply</u>.* Globally Unique Identifier Partition Table (GPT) http://en.wikipedia.org/wiki/GUID_Partition_Table has become the standard layout of the partition table replacing the outdated Master Boot Record (MBR) that dates back to the 1980s.

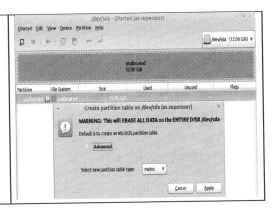

As of Windows 7, even Microsoft has begun adoption of GPT in their 64-bit OS. Most current operating systems support GPT. GPT provides redundancy for your OS boot sector and can improve performance on modern storage devices like solid-state drives that use larger sector sizes. Now we have to partition the disk by setting up individual partitions the old fashioned way. Depending on your virtual OSs purpose, setting up these partitions can be done many ways. A server running a Linux OS setup may include partitions like:

Swap	anything up to 2 times RAM size	/boot	20MB to 1 GB

/home	200MB to many GB	/var	100MB to many GB
/tmp	100MB to 20GB	/opt	100MB to many GB

For our purposes, we will just create two partitions (Swap and /). Separating out the /boot partition can cause trouble applying updates to the kernel if not enough space is allocated. We might want to do this on a non-virtual install. Some flavors of Linux, by default, only allocated 512 RAM to the VM, which should be increased to 1 to 2 GB depending on the RAM available in your computer. Contingent on the RAM allocated to the VM, we may want to raise the amount of swap. The danger with just using / as our second partition is that we could fill up all the disk space and lock up the OS, creating the worst-case scenario that we have to recreate the VM. First, create the swap partition. *Select __unallocated – unallocated__ > click on __Partition__ menu > select __New__ > next to __Create as:__ select __Primary Partition__ > for __New size (MiB):__ (e.g. specify 1025 if 1 GB of memory for VM, 2049 if 2 GB of memory for VM, 4097 if 4 GB of memory for VM) to allow enough space for Swap > change __File System:__ to __linux-swap__ > for the __Label:__ enter __swap__ > click on the __Add__ button.*

GParted can create a partition in many formats. For years, ***Ext4*** has been the most advanced file system format for most Linux OSs. (See: https://en.wikipedia.org/wiki/Ext4) It became widely adopted in 2010, and has proven very stable and reliable. Until recently, Ext4 was the best choice for the creation of new VMs, and may still be if stability is mandatory. *Btrfs* has made great strides, and some feel it should be the default Linux file system. *Btrfs* will eventually replace *Ext4*, which is still currently the default for most distributions.

Btrfs is the next generation file system for Linux with a range of features that are not available in other Linux File Systems (FS). Developed by Sun Microsystems for the Solaris Operating System, Oracle continued development after purchasing SUN. Btrfs 1.0 was finally packaged with the 2.6.9 Linux kernel in 2009 as an experimental choice for Linux users. According to Wikipedia "*Oracle Linux 5 and 6, Kernel Release 2 have moved Btrfs from experimental to production/supported.*" But then in June 2012, Chris Mason, the creator and one of the projects primary engineers, left Oracle for Fusion-IO. If we look at the changelog for *Btrfs*, this project is active and new versions are being released. (See: https://btrfs.wiki.kernel.org/index.php/Changelog).

The article, "How I Got Started with the Btrfs File System for Oracle Linux" by Margaret Bierman with Lenz Grimmer, published July 2012, states, "*My research into Btrfs revealed that it addresses long-standing deficiencies found in conventional file systems. Better yet, setting up and using a Btrfs file system is quick and easy, particularly if default configuration parameters are used. These defaults provide a reasonable amount of data protection and improved functionality— and little or no effort is required compared to the default file system. Many advanced features are in place to help improve data integrity and reliability, unify volume management, increase device utilization, and more. In our view, it is the best file system to use when deploying Oracle Linux platforms.*" (See http://www.oracle.com/technetwork/articles/servers-storage-admin/gettingstarted-btrfs-1695246.html). The File System is mature and more modern than *ext3* and *ext4*, and it can manage large storage systems. I expect *Btrfs* to become the default standard in future releases of Linux as it rapidly replaces ext4. However, for support and proven current stability you might want to stick with *ext4* until the Linux OS developers officially adopt *Btrfs*. (See: https://en.wikipedia.org/wiki/Btrfs, https://btrfs.wiki.kernel.org)

NOTE I had mixed results selecting Btrfs for Linux OSs. For example, using Btrfs in Mint-Debian-Cinnamon-201303 resulted in the error: FATAL: No bootable medium found! System halted. However, some flavors of Linux are now using Btrfs by default.

Select the remaining __unallocated-unallocated__ *space > click on the* __Partition__ *menu > select* __New__ *> the default will be to allocate all remaining space > Change* __File System:__ *to* __ext4__ *or* __Btrfs__ *> for* __Label:__ *type* __root__ *or* __/__ *> click on* __Add__ *> these operations are now pending so click on the* __Edit__ *menu at the top > select* __Apply All Operations__ *> when prompted* __Are you sure... ___ *click on* __Apply__.

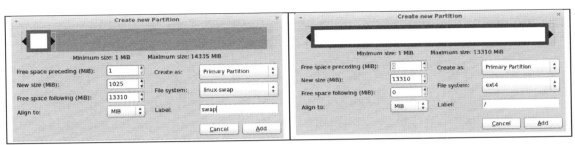

You should see a dialog box stating "__All operations successfully completed__" click on __Close__. To check your configuration *click on* __View__ *>* __Device Information__ and you should see something like:

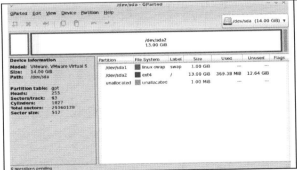

Now that the partitions are set up, *click on* __GParted__ *menu, arrow down to select* __Quit__ *> at the bottom click on the* __Refresh__ *button to see your partition setup > double click on* __swap__ *> select* __Mount point: swap__ *>* __Format as: swap, OK__ *> double click on the* __ext4__ *partition > select* __Mount point: /__ *>* __Format as: btrfs__ *or* __ext4, OK__ *> click on the* __Forward__ *button to continue with your VM installation*.

Kali/BackTrack – General Description – Install & Update in VMware Player &VirtualBox

BackTrack is/was an excellent penetration tool used by highly paid IT security professionals to test computer and network security for corporate and government data centers. A person skilled with these tools (university master's students) can make a very good living traveling to corporate and government computer data farms to try to break their security. However, as an SBO/HCU we often times don't have the deep pockets needed to hire these highly trained professionals to do this type of testing. Luckily, Kali/BackTrack will install into a Virtual environment so that we can experiment with it, and perhaps do some penetration testing on our own, or have an employee, friend, relative, or family member research how to use some of its features.

After seven years of development, the Offensive Security/Kali Linux/Backtrack teams decided to completely revamp their penetration testing tools and training. They are calling it the "next generation" in penetration testing tools. This release, which they are calling "Kali Linux," is a completely redeveloped distribution that is no longer a live CD, but an operating system. It is based on the GNOME desktop but if you want KDE or some other desktop Kali provides the Live Build a Custom Kali ISO guide. (See: http://docs.kali.org/downloading/live-build-a-custom-kali-iso) In the words of the Offensive Security developers, "*Kali Linux is the most advanced and versatile penetration testing distribution ever created. Kali is a more mature, secure, and enterprise-ready version of BackTrack Linux.*" Kali is based on Debian Linux, which we have discussed and stays current with the Debian repositories. (See: http://www.offensive-security.com, http://www.backtrack-linux.org/backtrack/kali-linux-has-been-released, http://www.kali.org, http://docs.kali.org, http://www.kali.org/downloads)

As with all downloads we have to verify the checksums of the ISO images before installing them. **In Windows click on _Start_ > _Run..._ > type _cmd_ > type _cd \Downloads\Linux\Kali_ > type _fsum /sha1 kali-linux-1.0.8-i386_, or _fciv -sha1 kali-linux-1.0.8-amd64.iso_:**

-
- kali-linux-1.0.9a-i386.iso: 89acef59694abc6858da681bb466355f6a31fdb6
- kali-linux-1.0.9a-amd64.iso: 2744d50f56c3d6332bc75e676f36aad3058d0aad

In Linux type $ sha1sum kali-linux-1.0.9-i386.iso
8964b2adf6dd2a61975b1e2b5867aba2c82f1e24 kali-linux-1.0.9-i386.iso

, http://docs.kali.org/downloading/download-official-kali-linux-images):

wget -q -O - http://archive.kali.org/archive-key.asc | gpg --import
or,
gpg --keyserver subkeys.pgp.net --recv-key
44C6513A8E4FB3D30875F758ED444FF07D8D0BF6

Once you have downloaded both SHA1SUMS and SHA1SUMS.gpg, you can verify the signature as follows:

gpg --verify SHA1SUMS.gpg SHA1SUMS
gpg: Signature made Thu Mar 7 21:26:40 2013 CET using RSA key ID 7D8D0BF6
gpg: Good signature from "Kali Linux Repository <devel@kali.org>"

The signature above can now be used to verity official Kali Linux Images.

When the Kali Linux Install screen appears select _Graphical Install_ and the _Select a language_ screen will appear, _Continue_ > _Select you location, Continue_ > _Configure the keyboard, Continue_ > the _Load installer components from CD_ followed by _Configure the Network_ screens will appear > for _Hostname:_ refer back to _Virtual Machine Name Standardization_; to determine you hostname, _Continue_ > when prompted for _Domain Name:_ Enter your SBO domain (e.g. thatcybersecurityguy.com), _Continue_ > enter your _Root password:, Continue_ > _Configure the Clock, Continue_ > _Partition disks, Continue_,

*Continue > for a VM select **All files in one partition (recommended for new users)**, Continue, **Continue**, Write the changes to disks? tick **Yes**, **Continue** > the Installing the system... dialog will appear > choose if you want to Use a network mirror? tick **Yes**, **Continue** > for proxy leave blank, **Continue** > when asked to Install the BRUB boot loaded... tick **Yes**, **Continue** > Installation complete, Continue.*

From the old BackTrack website, "*BackTrack is a Linux-based penetration testing arsenal that aids security professionals in the ability to perform assessments in a purely native environment dedicated to hacking. BackTrack is intended for all audiences from the most savvy security professionals to early newcomers to the information security field. BackTrack promotes a quick and easy way to find and update the largest database of security tools collection to-date. Our community of users range from skilled penetration testers in the information security field, government entities, information technology, security enthusiasts, and individuals new to the security community.*" Thus, as we can see, this suite of tools is something that we can try out to secure our computers and networks. Entire books have been written, and master's degrees are offered in Information Assurance/Penetration Testing. These degrees require years of study on the use of BackTrack's multitude of hacking software, which is beyond the scope of this book.

Go to http://www.backtrack-linux.org and download BackTrack 5 R3 that was released August 13, 2012. When done downloading, use the utilities we downloaded and installed in Chapter 5 to check the MD5 sum(s) of the ISO files. *In Windows click on **Start** > **Run...** > type **cmd** > type cd **\Downloads\Linux\BackTrack** > type fsum -md5 BT5R3-KDE-32, or fciv BT5R3-KDE-64; in Linux type # md5sum ISOFileName > should see:*

- BackTrack 5 R3 KDE 32-Bit: d324687fb891e695089745d461268576
- BackTrack 5 R3 KDE 64-Bit: 981b897b7fdf34fb1431ba84fe93249f
- BackTrack 5 R3 GNOME 32-Bit: bca6d3862c661b615a374d7ef61252c5
- BackTrack 5 R3 GNOME 64-Bit: 8cd98b693ce542b671edecaed48ab06d

BackTrack is not the only open source or donationware* available for testing network and device security. Two excellent websites for finding security tools to experiment with are https://www.techsupportalert.com/content/probably-best-free-security-list-world.htm and http://sectools.org, if you do want to research other tools. Many of these tools, like the popular Metasploit, come installed in BackTrack by default. From the Metasploit website about their tools, "*Metasploit software helps security and IT professionals identify security issues, verify vulnerability mitigations, and manage expert-driven security assessments, providing true security risk intelligence. Capabilities include smart exploitation, password auditing, web application scanning, and social engineering. Metasploit Community Edition simplifies network discovery and vulnerability verification for specific exploits, increasing the effectiveness of vulnerability scanners such as Nexpose - for free.*" (See http://metasploit.com or http://metasploit.org) Installing Metasploit is a somewhat complex process in other versions of Linux. If you want to try it in Fedora, reference https://fedoraproject.org/wiki/Metasploit, and in Ubuntu reference https://community.rapid7.com/docs/DOC-1296.

Tip BackTrack at http://www.backtrack-linux.org had both a VMware and an ISO version of their tool set. Consequently, you can create a virtual install of the software then be off and running at home if you want to experiment with some penetration testing tools for fun in a virtual install. To fully enable penetration testing from a BackTrack VM on your local network change the Network setting from NAT to Bridged.

To install BackTrack into deprecated Parallels refer back to Parallels-Creating Virtual Guest Operating Systems, for VMware Player refer back to VMware Player-Creating Virtual Guest Operating Systems), for VirtualBox refer back to VirtualBox-Creating Virtual Guest Operating Systems.

When BackTrack boots before the software is installed, select the default BackTrack Text – Default Boot Text Mode > when BackTrack comes up with the prompt type startx, (e.g. root@bt:~# startx).

When the back | track 5r3 screen appears double click on Install BackTrack icon in the upper left corner > on the Welcome screen select your language (e.g. English), click on the Forward button lower right > on the Where are you? screen select your location, Forward > select your Keyboard layout, Forward > on the Prepare disk space screen tick Erase and use the entire disk, Forward > on the Ready to install screen click on the Install button > an Installing system dialog box will pop up showing the Copying files... progress > when the Installation Complete dialog appears click on the Restart Now button.

In BackTrack5R3-GNOME after install prompted "Please remove installation media and close the tray (if any) then press ENTER:" > press ENTER and the VM will reboot.

When the bt login: prompt appears login as 'root':

bt login: root
Password: toor

Applying updates to BackTrack is a bit different than other operating systems based on Ubuntu. Apply updates at the login prompt, without starting the GUI and the OS again:

root@bt:~# apt-get update && apt-get upgrade -y
root@bt:~# shutdown -r now

In KDE on my VMware server installing BT5R3-KDE, a Removed Sound Devices Dialog appeared with two sound devices that were not installed on my laptop and server > click on Manage Devices button to select the correct sound device for your system.

The startx command will bring up BackTracks GUI where we will want to apply the updates again. Skip down to BackTrack/Kali/Mint/Ubuntu-VM Setup Steps after Install to continue setting up the VM. Then apply the updates again at the login prompt. BackTrack is now installed in VMware Player for you to learn about and test your SBO/HCU security weaknesses in your local network and computers.

Kali-Debian -- Install and Setup in VirtualBox & VMware Player

The install in VirtualBox and VMware Player was basically the same except that VMware Player recognized that Kali is based on Debian Linux. Don't forget to set the VM Network setting to *Bridged* not *NAT*. **Arrow down to select Install > press enter > select your Language, enter > select your country, enter > select you keymap, enter > the install will begin. Enter your hostname (e.g. kali109-deb32-gp, kali109-deb64-gp), Continue > you can probably leave the Domain name: blank, Continue > for Root password: enter something simple unless this is a traveling Internet device, Continue > Select your time zone:, enter > under Partition disks select Guided - use entire disk > go with the default under Select disk to partition: > since this is a VM go with the All files in one partition default, enter > press enter to Finish partitioning and write changes to disk, select Yes > the Kali system should install > under Use a network mirror? Yes > under HTTP proxy leave blank, Continue > Install the GRUB boot loader to the master boot record? Yes > Finish the installation, Continue**. The system should automatically reboot. You can log in as 'root' using the password from above. Skip down to BackTrack/Kali/Mint/Ubuntu-VM Setup Steps after Install to set up the VM and come back to perform the general configuration steps below.

In Kali, click on Applications, arrow down to System Tools > right to Preferences > down to System Settings. To adjust the sound settings, click on > Sound to bring up the Sound window > on the top next to Output volume, drag the volume bar to desired volume > click on the Input tab and adjust the Input volume: > on the Sound Effects tab set your Alert volume, click on the icon upper left > under Personal, click on Brightness and Lock and adjust accordingly > under Hardware, when I clicked on Printers there were no options to set up a printer. I was getting the following error under the Printers dialog:

On the left was the text *No printers available*, on the right frame was *Sorry! The system printing service doesn't seem to be available.* To install the CUPS printing services I had to add the following to the */etc/apt/sources.list* file, which we covered earlier for installing Kali software in other flavors of Linux:

deb http://http.kali.org/kali kali main non-free contrib

Then to get printing set up you need to install CUPS:

```
# apt-get install cups -y
```

Unfortunately, upon reboot the *cupsd* daemon did not start automatically. To configure the daemon to start automatically add it to the Debian system startup by selecting **Applications > System Tools > Preferences > Startup Applications and add the following**:

Name: CUPS
Command: /usr/init.d/cups start
Comment: System print service daemon

Now when you are in <u>System Settings</u> under <u>Hardware</u> click on <u>Printers</u> and you should be able to add your network printers (be sure they are powered on and connected to the network).

BackTrack -- GNOME/KDE -- Setup in VirtualBox & VMware Player

NOTE	In Backtrack when attempting to configure sound a dialog stating <u>Waiting for sound system to respond</u> displayed and never closed. To enable sound detection, *select **System** > highlight **Preferences** > arrow down to select Startup Applications > select the **Startup Programs** tab if not already selected > click on the **Add** button > in the **Add Startup Program** dialog, for **Name:** Pluseaudio daemon; **Command:** /usr/bin/pulseaudio; **Comment: Needed to have sound as root ID** > click on the **Add** button > **Close** > reboot the VM.*

*To adjust the sound settings in BackTrack-GNOME, click on **System** > **Preferences** > **Sound** to bring up the **Sound Preferences** window > on the top next to **Output volume**, drag the volume bar to desired volume > click on the **Input** tab and adjust the **Input volume:** > **Close**.*

*In BackTrack-GNOME, add the Firefox browser to the desktop and panel by clicking on the **Applications** menu upper left > highlight **Internet** > right click on **Firefox Web Browser** > click on **Add this launcher to panel** and **Add this launcher to desktop** > repeat this procedure for other useful tools and applications that are used regularly > when done, right click on the desktop > select **Clean Up by Name**.*

*In BackTrack-KDE, the sound was enabled by default and the volume could be adjusted by clicking the sound icon on launcher bar bottom right > click on the launcher icon lower left > right click on the tool > select **Add to Desktop** and/or **Add to Panel**.*

*In BackTrack-GNOME and KDE, applying updates from the default BackTrack repositories did not bring down the latest Firefox release. To upgrade, either download and apply their latest release from https://www.mozilla.org/en-US or run Firefox, click on **Help** > scroll down to select **About Firefox** > click on the **Check for Updates** button > click on the **Apply Updates** button.*

We can add other applications, tools and utilities by adding repositories to BackTrack. However, we must carefully consider any repository or software additions because any application, tool, or utility that is needed may introduce security holes in our penetration testing VM. Carefully consider any additional software that you install in a Backtrack VM. Refer down to <u>BackTrack/Kali/Mint/Ubuntu-VM Setup Steps after Install</u>.

Mint -- General Description

The user community's interest in Linux Mint soared in 2011-2014. Visit http://distrowatch.com and you will see how Linux Mint is now ranked as high as other popular Linux distributions. Some argue that Mint has usurped Ubuntu as the most popular Linux distribution. Where Ubuntu turned off their user community with the divisive Unity desktop in their 11.10, 12.04,

12.10, 13.04, 13.10 and 14.04 releases, Mint looked for alternatives to the GNOME 3 and Unity desktops. Both desktops have been controversial, and many users in the Linux community refuse to use either, opting for other desktop choices. Many users consider Mint an elegant and easy-to-use flavor of Linux. Mint offers their operating system on a variety of desktops, like Cinnamon, XFCE, KDE and MATE, which we have discussed in the Linux Desktops, Applications, Software, Packages, Utilities and Tools section of this chapter. Mint's support schedule mirrors Ubuntu because Mint is based on Ubuntu. Mint "Maya" 12.04 LTS will be supported until April 2017 and "Petra" 16, which was released December 2013, was supported until July 2014. Mint 17 "Qiana" is another Long Term support release maintained until 2019. The release notes say it fixes Issues with Skype, DVD Playback with VLC, EFI support, Bluetooth, solves freezes with some NVIDIA GeForce GPUs, booting with non-PAE CUPs and more. You can read about Mint and other versions at https://www.pcworld.com/article/2021461/three-new-features-coming-in-linux-mint-15.html. (See: http://linuxmint.com, http://www.linuxmint.com/download.php, https://en.wikipedia.org/wiki/Linux_Mint)

In addition to releasing a version of their OS based on the desktops above, they also released a MATE/Cinnamon based on Debian. Mint calls these releases Linux Mint Debian Edition (LMDE), which is a rolling distribution based on Debian Testing. By rolling distribution Mint says that LMDE constantly receives updates. Mint's website states, *LMDE is compatible with Debian, which isn't compatible with Ubuntu.* Mint's web page http://www.linuxmint.com/download_lmde.php lists all the pros and cons with using LMDE versus Ubuntu-based editions.

Mint also has another advantage over other Linux distributions. It is one of the few Linux distributions that include proprietary software, which does not add steps to getting the things that we may need. From their website, *we also owe a lot to all developers who have had good ideas and created great tools and who have been working to make software better. Some of them have released their source code as well and have thus granted us more freedom and more flexibility. Others released their software with proprietary licenses and no source code, and although this doesn't give us the freedom we would like, it still contributes to make software better. We like Software in general, Free Software even more, but we do not believe in boycotting Proprietary Software.* Mint is based on Debian and Ubuntu Linux so it has all the applications that run in Ubuntu. Mint's main edition provides full multimedia support out of the box, meaning that you can listen to MP3's, watch DVDs, and view web pages that require Flash technology right after install. Other versions of Linux cannot do this without special downloads because of licensing issues. Mint has multimedia codecs, Adobe Reader, and Google Earth. Mint's wise transition step from the unpopular GNOME 3 desktop makes Mint a great choice as our virtual OS for family members, shopping, and perhaps banking. Mint's user-friendly desktop is an excellent fit for users familiar with (used to) the Windows 7 desktop. We can still litter the desktop with icons, just like in Windows. Getting employees and family members to do all their Internet activity in a virtual OS should prove easier in Mint than in any other recent flavor of Linux that I have reviewed in this book.

Mint has also chosen to provide separate releases for supporting various desktops. By packaging the desktop with the release, Mint can optimize the install for that desktop. This takes the burden off the SBO/HCU to work our way through the installation process to determine the best setup for our Linux OS VMs. Prior to this strategy, it was difficult to get multiple desktops working together in the same Mint OS install. Other flavors of Linux are beginning to adopt this strategy because it can sometimes be difficult to get multiple desktops installed and blissfully working together. Looking at the Mint model, it is best to create a separate VM for each desktop in the other flavors of Linux, which will eat up disk space, but be a more stable solution. For more information on the various desktops available to Linux, refer back to <u>Linux Desktops, Applications, Software, Packages, Utilities and Tools</u>.

Mint comes with the VirtualBox Guest Additions (VBGA) pre-installed, but upon VM creation, you should consider reinstalling VBGA to make sure the OS is at the latest version. The VBGA allows the user to run the live session GNOME Shell and the Mint GNOME Shell Extensions (MGSE). MGSE is a desktop layer that is on top of GNOME 3, which makes it possible for the user to use GNOME 3 in a traditional way. Users who are used to Windows or the old GNOME 2 desktop should find this easier and more efficient to use than a pure GNOME 3 experience.

Mint 17.1 -- Cinnamon Install in VirtualBox & VMware Player

Go to <u>http://www.linuxmint.com/download.php</u> and download the latest Linux Mint release. When done, use the utilities that we downloaded and installed in <u>Chapter 5</u> to check the MD5 sum(s) of the ISO files. *In Windows click on <u>Start</u> > <u>Run...</u> > type <u>cmd</u> > type cd \Downloads\Linux\Mint > type fsum -md5 linuxmint-17.1-cinnamon-dvd-32bit, or fciv linuxmint-17.1-cinnamon-dvd-64bit; in Linux type # md5sum ISOFileName > should see:*

- Mint17.1-Cinnamon 32-bit: d1a9474f4f48c3a2220ddd1ff57f76b3
- Mint17.1-Cinnamon 64-bit: 0307ffcd5046c176599904193899426e

Once the ISO downloads have been checked we are now ready to install the OS into our VM. The installation of Mint after the VM is created in VirtualBox and VMware Player is identical. Below is an example install of Mint Cinnamon. *To install Mint refer back to <u>VMware Player-Creating Virtual Guest Operating Systems</u>), for VirtualBox refer back to <u>VirtualBox-Creating Virtual Guest Operating Systems</u>. Once the ISO is loaded and the Mint Install screen appears double click on the <u>Install Linux Mint</u> CD icon.*

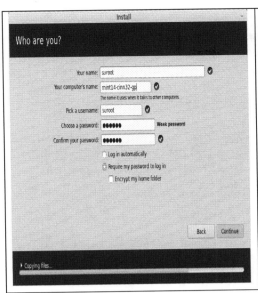

Work your way through the installation questions: select your language on the Welcome screen, Continue > on the Preparing to install Linux Mint screen, Continue again > on the Installation type screen select Erase disk and install Linux Mint, click on the Install Now button > on the Where are you? screen select or type the nearest large city in your timezone, Continue > on the Keyboard layout screen select your keyboard layout (e.g. English (US)), Continue > on Who are you? screen for Your name: type 'suroot'; for Your Computer's name: refer back to Virtual Machine Name Standardization; enter the same easy password used for all VMs. Do NOT select Log in automatically so we can configure the VM later as 'root', Continue > Mint will install the OS.

When the Installation Complete dialog box appears click the Restart Now button > the restart may prompt Please remove installation media and close the tray (if any) then press ENTER: hit the ENTER key, which will allow the restart to continue > upon reboot login in as user 'suroot'. Skip down to BackTrack/Kali/Mint/Ubuntu-VM Setup Steps after Install to setup the VM.

Mint 17.1 -- KDE/MATE/XFCE-Install in VirtualBox & VMware Player

Go to http://www.linuxmint.com/download.php and download the Linux Mint release you want, loaded with the desktop that you prefer. When done, use the utilities that we downloaded and installed in Chapter 5 to check the MD5 sum(s) of the ISO files. *In Windows click on Start > Run... > type cmd > type cd \Downloads\Linux\Mint > type fsum -md5 linuxmint-17-kde-dvd-32bit.iso, or fciv linuxmint-17-kde-dvd-64bit.iso; in Linux type # md5sum ISOFileName. You should see:*

- Mint17.1-KDE-32-bit: 3ffc18a5544fefd62dd14e21cce34fcb
- Mint17.1-KDE-64-bit: 33a571b1cf513045963ee624a35ddedf
- Mint17.1-MATE-32-bit: a8c7529d3bc0d3a4b1c03a9163cab1e8
- Mint17.1-MATE-64-bit: c37ca530d17bfdf6431e92c92baf8503

To install Mint in VMware Player, refer back to VMware Player-Creating Virtual Guest Operating Systems), for VirtualBox refer back to VirtualBox-Creating Virtual Guest Operating Systems.

Once the ISO is loaded and the Mint Install screen appears double click on the Install Linux Mint icon > on the Welcome screen select your language and click on the Continue button > on the Preparing to install Linux Mint screen click on Continue > on Mint-XFCE/MATE on the Installation type leave Erase disk and install Linux Mint ticked, Install Now > in KDE Mint on the Installation type screen under Disk Setup tick Guided - use entire disk, Install Now > on the Where are you? screen select the nearest *large city in your timezone, <u>Continue</u> > choose your <u>Keyboard layout</u>, <u>Continue</u> > on the <u>Who are you?</u> screen for <u>Your name:</u> 'suroot', Pick a username: 'suroot', Choose a password: something simple, for <u>Your computer's name:</u> Refer back to <u>Virtual Machine Name Standardization</u>, do NOT select <u>Log in automatically</u> in Mint-KDE so we can login and work as 'root', (root logins were not allowed in Mint 16 or 17), we will configure automatic logins as a less privileged user later > <u>Continue</u> and installation will begin.*

When the <u>Installation Complete</u> dialog box appears click the <u>Restart Now</u> button > the restart may prompt <u>Please remove installation media and close the tray (if any) then press ENTER</u>: or appear to hang, hit the <u>ENTER</u> key which will allow the restart to continue. After logging in skip down to <u>BackTrack/Kali/Mint/Ubuntu-VM Setup Steps after Install</u> to setup the VM.

Mint-Debian 201403 Mate or Cinnamon Install in VirtualBox & VMware Player

Mint is also offering what they call the Linux Mint Debian Edition (LMDE) distribution. This stands in contrast to the KDE or GNOME Ubuntu based OSs, in which the above was installed. Go to <u>http://www.linuxmint.com/download_lmde.php</u> and download the 32-bit or 64-bit release of linuxmint-201403 MATE and/or Cinnamon. When done, use the utilities that we downloaded and installed in <u>Chapter 5</u> to check the MD5 sum(s) of the ISO files. *In Windows click on <u>Start</u> > <u>Run...</u> > type <u>cmd</u> > type <u>cd \Downloads\Linux\Mint</u> > type fsum -md5 linuxmint-201403-mate-dvd-64bit.iso, or fciv linuxmint-201403-cinnamon-dvd-64bit.iso; in Linux type # md5sum ISOFileName. You should see:*

- linuxmint-201403-cinnamon-dvd-32bit: ba865cdb8defc2114713037f43429bf6
- linuxmint-201403-cinnamon-dvd-64bit: bace9a8f23c9b6e984a5894669946122
- linuxmint-201403-mate-dvd-32bit: fa20dba24e4d321ad616b6037c06a79f
- linuxmint-201403-mate-dvd-64bit: 6192a558df6db67a10bda4e34deef22e

To install into Parallels refer back to <u>Parallels-Creating Virtual Guest Operating Systems</u>, for VMware Player refer back to <u>VMware Player-Creating Virtual Guest Operating Systems</u>), for VirtualBox refer back to <u>VirtualBox-Creating Virtual Guest Operating Systems</u>.

When the initial Mint screen appears double click on the <u>Install Linux Mint</u> icon, you should see a <u>Granting Rights</u> box appear on the taskbar, give the system time for the <u>Language</u> screen to appear, select your language (e.g., <u>English (United States)</u>, click on the <u>Forward</u> button > on the <u>Choose your timezone</u> screen select your timezone (e.g., <u>America/Detroit</u>), <u>Forward</u>.	

On the <u>Keyboard layout</u> screen, click on the <u>Model</u> drop down and select your keyboard layout (you may have to surf to your keyboard manufacturer to find a suitable choice) (e.g., Logitech Cordless Desktop LX-300) > choose your <u>Layout</u> and <u>Variant</u>, <u>Forward</u>.

The Installation Tool will prompt you if you want the installer to create a set of partitions for you. If you want to manually specify your partitions, **select <u>No</u>** and refer back to <u>GParted – Manually Creating Partitions</u>. If you **selected <u>Yes</u>,** which automatically created them, you can still edit the partitions. The default settings created *swap* and an *ext4* partition. However, manually creating the partitions will enable you to allocate the partitions optimally. The default settings left a small amount of disk space unused and did not choose the advanced GPT boot format.

On the user information screen for <u>Your full name</u>, enter 'suroot' > <u>Your password</u>, enter the same simple password used for all VMs > for <u>Hostname</u> refer back to <u>Virtual Machine Name Standardization</u> > click on <u>Forward</u>, on the <u>Install GRUB</u> screen leave the boot loader as <u>/dev/sda</u> > click on <u>Forward</u> to install the boot loader in /dev/sda > review your settings and click on <u>Install</u>.

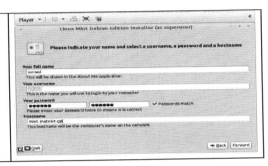

After the install an <u>Installation finished (as superuser)</u> dialog should appear, click on <u>Yes</u> to restart > in Mate and Cinnamon the VM had to be reset or restarted to get it to boot up > in VirtualBox click on <u>Machine</u>, arrow down to select <u>Reset</u> , in VMware click on <u>Player</u> , highlight <u>Power</u>, select <u>Restart Guest</u>, <u>Yes</u> > otherwise click on <u>OK</u> > select the <u>Menu</u> lower left > select <u>Quit</u>, <u>Shut Down</u> or <u>Restart</u> > if prompted <u>Please remove the disc...</u> hit <u>ENTER</u> to continue > upon startup the VM should boot up to show the <u>Welcome to Linux Mint</u> screen.

If, after applying updates there is no menu, right click on the desktop and select <u>Open in Terminal</u> > switch user to root $ su - > # apt-get dselect-upgrade -y > halt the VM # shutdown -h now adjust the VM settings and then restart.

| **WARNING** | In some versions of Mint Debian, trying to apply dist-updates to the distribution cleanly was not possible using the normal Ubuntu method of applying updates. Performing a dist-upgrade sometimes destabilized the VM. It is recommended that you do not attempt this, and just do an # apt-get upgrade -y, but if you must, you can try the directions below:

＃ apt-get dist-upgrade
`Errors were encountered while processing:`
`   /var/cache/apt/archives/gstreamer0. 10-plugins-bad_0. 10. 22. 3_amd64. deb`
`E:  Sub-process /usr/bin/dpkg returned an error code (1)`

The updates could be applied successfully using the dselect-upgrade command: |

	# apt-get dselect-upgrade -y # From the apt-get man page dselect-upgrade is used in conjunction with the traditional Debian packaging front-end, dselect. Using the option, dselect was sometimes able to remove the old packages and install new updated packages. Performing a # apt-get -f upgrade after a # apt-get dselect-upgrade -y stabilized the VM.

The restart may prompt <u>Please remove installation media and close the tray (if any) then press ENTER</u>: hit the <u>ENTER</u> key, which will allow the restart to continue > login in as '<u>suroot</u>'. Skip down to <u>BackTrack/Kali/Mint/Ubuntu-VM Setup Steps after Install</u> to setup the VM and come back to perform the general configuration steps below.

Mint-201403-mate-cinnamon-dvd Setup in VirtualBox & VMware Player

In Mate-Cinnamon, as '<u>suroot</u>' click on the <u>Menu</u> icon lower left > right click or drag and drop a few icons for frequently used applications, tools and utilities to the desktop and panel (e.g. <u>Calculator</u>, <u>Firefox Web Browser</u>, <u>File Browser</u>, <u>GNU Image Manipulation Editor</u>, <u>LibreOffice Calc</u>, <u>LibreOffice Writer</u>, <u>Terminal</u>, and so on).

In Mate-Cinnamon, click on the <u>Volume Control</u> icon lower right and raise the volume to your desired level.

Click on <u>Menu</u> > under <u>Applications</u> highlight <u>Preferences</u> > arrow right and select <u>Additional Drivers</u> > click on <u>Screensaver</u> and adjust the settings, <u>Close</u> > click on <u>Desktop Settings</u> and add <u>Trash</u> and <u>Network</u> icons to the desktop, <u>Close</u>.

Enable printing by clicking on <u>Menu</u> > under <u>Applications</u> highlight <u>Administration</u> > you may see a message stating <u>There are no printers configured yet.</u> Arrow right to select <u>Printing</u> > click on the down arrow below the Server menu and to the right of the +<u>Add</u> button > select <u>Printer</u> from the drop down > <u>Authenticate</u> as 'root' > click on <u>Network Printer</u> to expand the menu > if your printer is not displayed select <u>Find Network Printer</u> > Enter the IP address of your network printer (e.g. 192.168.0.104), click on the <u>Find</u> button to the right. When the tool is done searching, you should see your printer displayed under <u>Network Printer</u> on the left.

Select your printer on the left pane and click on <u>Forward</u> > select your make if not already selected, <u>Forward</u> > under <u>Choose Driver</u> choose the best driver if it not already displayed and selected, <u>Forward</u> > under <u>Describe Printer</u> change the description to whatever you want or accept the default, <u>Apply</u> > <u>Authenticate</u> as 'root' > the <u>Printing</u> dialog should appear with an icon displaying your printers short name.

NOTE	In older versions, *JetDirect would pop up with port number 9100 on the right if the <u>New Printer</u> tool finds your printer > click on <u>Forward</u> > if your printer is supported you can select it from the database > if not, copy the PPD file for your printer from Windows and select it > if you cannot find a PPD file for your printer click on <u>Select printer from database</u> > <u>Forward</u> > choose the Model (e.g. PCL 6/PCL XL Printer) > <u>Forward</u> > <u>Apply</u>.*

Ubuntu and Lubuntu 14.10/14.04 LTS – General Description

Ubuntu is a Debian based Linux OS that is considered very user friendly. According to Wiki, *"Ubuntu is the most popular desktop Linux distribution. Ubuntu holds and estimated global usage of more than 20 million users."* (See: https://en.wikipedia.org/wiki/Ubuntu_operating_system) Go to http://www.ubuntu.com and you can take a tour introducing you to the OS. Ubuntu also has excellent help and online documentation at https://help.ubuntu.com. Ubuntu dropped support for the "Natty Narwhal" 11.04 release of their OS 28 October 2012. Ubuntu "Precise Pangolin" 12.04 LTS will be supported until April 2017. Ubuntu 13.10 named "Saucy Salamander was released on 17 October 2013 and will be supported until July 2014. (See: https://wiki.ubuntu.com/Home, https://wiki.ubuntu.com/Releases, https://wiki.ubuntu.com/LTS, https://en.wikipedia.org/wiki/List_of_Ubuntu_releases) Ubuntu is now asking for a donation of $16 or less to expand its desktop, performance, hardware support and more. These are all things to consider as you install and need long term Linux solutions. We may see other Linux OSs adopt this strategy to fund their projects which is understandable.

Ubuntu also releases what they call "Long Term Support" releases of their OS about every two years. Starting with their 12.04 release, Ubuntu offers five years of support for both their Desktop and Server OSs for no extra fee. In April 2014 Ubuntu released Ubuntu 14.04 LTS, which will be supported until April 2017. These LTS releases make excellent choices for your financial VM or a SSH server, which we will discuss later.

There is also the Lubuntu Project. The website states, *"Lubuntu is a flavor of Ubuntu based on the Lightweight X11 Desktop Environment (LXDE), as its default GUI. The goal is to provide a very lightweight distribution, with all the advantages of the Ubuntu world (repositories, support, etc.). Lubuntu is targeted at "normal" PC and laptop users running on low-spec hardware."* (See: http://lubuntu.net). Even though Lubuntu calls itself lightweight it comes packed with useful tools and applications (e.g. Chromium, Openbox, Pidgen, and much more). Windows 7 users will like the LXDE desktop and find it intuitive. Lubuntu is an excellent OS to run on that old virus and spyware riddled Windows XP machine. (See: https://wiki.ubuntu.com/Lubuntu, https://help.ubuntu.com/community/Lubuntu). Visit https://help.ubuntu.com/community/Lubuntu/GetLubuntu to download the appropriate version for your PC. The next sections describe the specific steps to install and setup the last three releases of the Ubuntu OS.

Ubuntu -- Continued Install into VirtualBox & VMware Player

Go to http://www.ubuntu.com/download and download Ubuntu. When done, use the utilities that we downloaded and installed in Chapter 5 to check the MD5 sum(s) of the ISO files. *In Windows click on Start > Run... > type cmd > type cd \Downloads\Linux\Ubuntu > type fsum -md5 ubuntu-14.04.1-desktop-i386, or fciv ubuntu-14.04.1-desktop-amd64; in Linux type # md5sum ISOFileName. You should see:*

- ubuntu-14.10-desktop-amd64.iso: 08494b448aa5b1de963731c21344f803
- ubuntu-14.10-desktop-i386.iso: 4a3c4b8421af51c29c84fb6f4b3fe109
- ubuntu-14.10-server-amd64.iso: 91bd1cfba65417bfa04567e4f64b5c55

- ubuntu-14.04.1-desktop-i386: a4fc15313ef2a516bfbf83ce44281535
- ubuntu-14.04.1-desktop-amd64: 119cb63b48c9a18f31f417f09655efbd
- ubuntu-14.04.1-server-amd64: ca2531b8cd79ea5b778ede3a524779b9

All of the Ubuntu MD5 Hashes can be found at
https://help.ubuntu.com/community/UbuntuHashes. Once the ISO downloads have been
checked we are now ready to install the OS. The installation of Ubuntu in Parallels/VirtualBox
and VMware Player is different. VMware Player actually installs the OS while Parallels and
VirtualBox allows you to perform the OS installation steps.

*To install in VMware Player refer back to __VMware Player-Creating Virtual Guest__
__Operating Systems__), in VirtualBox refer back to __VirtualBox-Creating Virtual Guest__
__Operating Systems__. After the install, you may be prompted to __Disconnect or override a__
__CD-ROM lock__ > click on __Yes__.*

NOTE	Ubuntu could not render 3D graphics in VMware Player with the 4.0.x VMware Tools. When logging in, select the graphic and login as "Ubuntu 2D". This problem was fixed in early VMware Player 5.0.x releases but came back in the 6.0.x releases. If you encounter this problem, try adjusting the VM display settings by unchecking the Accelerate 3D graphics option in the settings.

*After automatic install in VMware Player upon reboot click on the __Restart Now__ button >
during installation in VirtualBox on the __Welcome__ screen select your language in the left
pane and click on the __Install Ubuntu__ button in the right pane > on the __Preparing to install__
__Ubuntu__ screen check __Download updates while installing__ and check __Install this third-__
__party software__, __Continue__ > on the __Installation type__ screen tick __Erase disk and install__
__Ubuntu__ if it is not already selected, click on the __Install Now__ button > on the __Where are__
__you?__ screen, select or type the name of the nearest big city in your timezone, __Continue__ >
on the __Keyboard layout__ screen select your language, __Continue__ > on the __Who are you?__
screen, for Your name: 'sudoroot', for __Your computer's name:__ refer back to __Virtual__
__Machine Name Standardization__, for the __Choose a password:__ field choose something
simple, consider ticking __Log in automatically__ for convenience, Ubuntu does not allow
ROOT GUI login by default, we will look at enabling root login later, click on __Continue__ >
on the __One account to log in to everything on Ubuntu__ screen click on the __Log in later__
button if you don't have an Ubuntu One account > when Ubuntu is done installing click
on the __Restart Now__ button > when prompted press __ENTER__, if the shutdown hangs in
VirtualBox click on __Machine__ menu upper left and scroll down to select __Reset__, when
prompted, click on the __Reset__ button.* The VM will reboot and the Unity GUI login page will
come up. Login as 'sudoroot' and continue the VM setup.

Ubuntu -- Root Login Setup

Ubuntu, by default, sets up the installation 'sudoroot' ID that we used above as part of the
'admin' group in the directory **/etc/group**. The file **/etc/sudoers** is configured to allow
anyone in the 'admin' group to run commands with super user privileges by using the sudo
command to become 'root' (super user in Linux). This is much the same as being
administrator in Windows.

Because we will need 'root' privileges for many of the things that we will be doing in setting up Ubuntu, consider enabling root login by just setting a root password. The web page https://help.ubuntu.com/community/RootSudo helps us enable root login. Years ago in Ubuntu 11.10 we could setup root login simply by changing the root password, $ sudo passwd root. *Then to log in, reboot the VM and as 'root' click on **Other...** at the login screen > enter **Username: root**, for **Password:** 'sudoroot' password*. However, to login as 'root' to set up the VM, this simple approach was no longer possible after the 12.04 release of Ubuntu, but by performing a few added steps we can enable 'root' login for these newer versions also. Depending on your version of Ubuntu, the steps vary slightly to enable 'root' login. In Ubuntu 14.04 and 13.10, to become 'root' we need to alter the *50-unity-greeter.conf* file. However, this file is located in two different directories depending on the OS version:

```
$ sudo su -
[sudo] password for sudoroot:
# passwd      # Must set a root password for login
# cd /usr/share/lightdm/lightdm.conf.d     # In Ubuntu 14.04, 14.10
# cd /etc/lightdm/lightdm.conf.d      # In Ubuntu 13.10
# cp -ip 50-unity-greeter.conf 50-unity-greeter.conf.orig
# echo "greeter-show-manual-login=true" >> 50-unity-greeter.conf
# shutdown -r now
```

In Ubuntu 13.04/12.04 we became 'root' and altered the lightdm.conf file:

```
# passwd
# cd /etc/lightdm/lightdm.conf.d  &&  cp -ip lightdm.conf lightdm.conf.orig
# echo "greeter-show-manual-login=true" >> lightdm.conf
# shutdown -r now
```

Upon reboot you will see a Login choice available that you can click on and type 'root' to login as 'root'. When we are done setting everything up as 'root', lock things back down again by disabling 'root' login. Login as 'sudoroot' and type $ sudo passwd -dl root. You might also want to disable logins again for users not presented by the GUI.

```
# cd /etc/lightdm  &&  cp -ip lightdm.conf.orig lightdm.conf   # In 13.04/12.04
# cd /etc/lightdm/lightdm.conf.d    # In 13.10
# cd /usr/share/lightdm/lightdm.conf.d     # In 14.04, 14.10
# cp -ip 50-unity-greeter.conf.orig 50-unity-greeter.conf
```

Another option is changing the **/etc/sudoers** file thus allowing login without entering a password for the 'admin' group to make setting everything up much easier. By default, Ubuntu created our specified 'sudoroot' user ID as part of the 'admin' group. Below, when we type *visudo*, it will bring up the default GNU Nano editor, which you may prefer, but personally, I change that to *vim*, which I find easier to use. Open up a terminal window and make the following changes to **/etc/sudoers**: (See: https://help.ubuntu.com/community/RootSudo)

```
$ sudo su -
[sudo] password for sudoroot:
```

```
# cd /etc && cp -ip sudoers sudoers.orig
# visudo      # surf to the bottom of the file and enter:
# Enable becoming root without a password for the admin group:
%admin ALL=NOPASSWD: ALL
:wq      # if using the Vim editor
```

If using the nano editor:
```
Hit <Ctrl-X-Y> and when prompted specify filename to write as /etc/sudoers···
OVERWRITE Y
```

If you want other users to have sudo root privileges to run commands add them to the 'sudo' group:

```
# useradd -G sudo userid.
```

In versions of Ubuntu before 13.10 we would have used the 'admin' group.

Ubuntu -- Timezone and Distribution Upgrade

VMware Player creates a virtual Ubuntu, all versions of the OS flawlessly and booted up to the GUI login prompt. VMware Tools installed automatically, which allows seamless integration with Windows 7 using your mouse and keyboard. The timezone may have to be changed from the installed default settings in VMware Player. In VirtualBox, the timezone was set during install. To change your timezone type:

```
$ date
Mon Oct 31 20:25:04 PDT 2011
$ sudo su -
# dpkg-reconfigure tzdata
Current default time zone: 'America/Detroit'
Local time is now:     Thu Jan 17 10:30:54 EST 2013.
Universal Time is now:  Thu Jan 17 15:30:54 UTC 2013.
```

The __Configuring tzdata__ window will pop up > on the __Geographic area:__ screen select your area (e.g. __America__) > tab down to select __Ok__, hit <enter> > on the __Time zone:__ screen select the nearest city in your time zone (e.g. __Detroit__)> tab down to select __Ok__ , hit <enter>.

If you have a server running Ubuntu and want to upgrade to the latest release (*Not recommended and should be avoided if possible, better to zero the hard drive and reload*):

```
# do-release-upgrade -d   # will check to see if upgrading to the latest release is possible
# do-release-upgrade      # will actually upgrade the OS, not recommended
```

With the advent of free virtualization for the SBO/HCU, doing a release-upgrade to a virtual OS should be done only as a last resort because of the risks involved. You could lose the work that you have done setting up packages, and the system could become unstable. Just like installing a fresh Windows OS is better on a new or zeroed hard disk, it is best to create a new virtual environment in the new version of the OS and slowly part ways with your old data, configuration, and package installs/changes in the previous version.

Ubuntu -- General Setup after Install in VirtualBox & VMware Player

Before we get into the general setup of Ubuntu, we have to address a few general security concerns. The Dash utility that comes installed in Ubuntu is beginning to do things that proprietary non-free operating systems have been doing for years, which is to scour the Internet without your knowledge that it is doing so. This is, once again, done in the guise of making an OS such as Ubuntu more convenient and a better user experience. In this author's view, any OS that does this is violating of your privacy. One argument in Ubuntu's favor is that this type of activity is easy to turn off. Nevertheless, in my view it should be off by default, and you should have to turn it on. Ubuntu has also opened up Dash to Amazon. When you do a search with Dash, it opens up a secure HTTPS connection to productsearch.ubuntu.com, and then sends along whatever you search for, along with your IP address. This allows Ubuntu to include Amazon ads in Dash. This also opens up another security hole. (See: https://www.eff.org/deeplinks/2012/10/privacy-ubuntu-1210-amazon-ads-and-data-leaks)

To set up the OS we will need to navigate to a few tools that are buried in the Unity GUI. We want to add these tools and utilities to the launcher to make things easy revising the settings. *To support their project Ubuntu added an icon to the Amazon website onto the Launcher, remove this by right clicking on the "a" icon and select Unlock from Launcher, if we want to visit Amazon we can use the browser to do so > add tools to the Ubuntu Launcher bar by clicking on Dash home in the upper left > type the name of the application in Search box (e.g. Calc, System Settings, Term, Software Updater, Thunderbird Mail, etc.) > drag and drop the application icons on to the Launcher bar.* Another method you can use if you do not know the name of the tool you want to add is *click on Dash home > at the bottom select the icon to the right of the house located on the far left > select Filter results in upper right corner > select Accessories in upper right > next to Installed click on See X more results > left click on icons such as Calculator, Terminal, etc. > under Filter results select System and look for System Settings and drag all of them over to the Launcher bar.*

Ubuntu changed its privacy statement to say that unless you opt-out they will send your keystrokes as a search term to third parties like Facebook, Twitter, BBC and Amazon. They do this to complement your search results online. Canonical and its third parties will collect your search terms to improve your search results.

apt-get purge unity-lens-shopping -y   # Remove Dash's integration with Amazon in 13.04

In Ubuntu 13.10/14.04 there is no shopping lens, as it comes with a feature called "Unity Smart Scopes", which uses a huge list of scopes to display results in Dash. Some of the scopes will give you shopping suggestions that you may want to disable, otherwise Dash will suggest merchandise from Amazon, EBay, Music Store, Popular Tracks Online, Skimlinks and Ubuntu Shop.

gsettings set com.canonical.Unity.Lenses disabled-scopes "['more_suggestions-amazon.scope', 'more_suggestions-u1ms.scope', 'more_suggestions-populartracks.scope', 'music-musicstore.scope', 'more_suggestions-ebay.scope', 'more_suggestions-ubuntushop.scope', 'more_suggestions-skimlinks.scope']"

Disable online search results and enable other privacy options options by clicking on the __System Settings__ icon on the __Launcher__ > under __Personal__ click on the __Security & Privacy__ icon > click on the __Search__ tab > next to __Include online search results__ select __Off__ > go through the __Privacy__ options and decide what you think should also be disabled (e.g. on the __Files__ tab under __Don't record activity for following type of files:__ consider unchecking __Instant Messaging__, __Website__, and __Email__ > under __all tabs__ consider turning off __Record Activity__ > under __Diagnostics__ uncheck __Send error reports to Canonical__). Click on the All Setting icon upper left and continue.

Click on the 🖼 *__System Settings__ icon > under __Personal__ select the __Brightness and Lock__ icon > adjust the __Turn screen off when inactive for:__ and __Lock screen after:__ settings, consider unchecking __Require my password when waking from suspend__ > click on the __All Settings__ button upper left to return to the main icon screen > to have sound for audio or video, you may have to adjust the sound settings, under __Hardware__ click on the __Sound__ icon > at the bottom middle adjust the __Output volume:__ > select the __Input__ tab and adjust the __Input volume:__ > select the __Sound Effects__ tab and adjust the __Alert volume:__ > to setup a working printer click on __All Settings__ button upper left > if your printer is not automatically detected under __Hardware__ click on the __Printers__ icon > if your printer is not automatically detected and listed under __Network Printer__ click on the __Add__ button > select __Network Printer__, __Find Network Printer__ > next to __Host:__ enter your printers IP address, click on the __Find__ button to the right, give Ubuntu time to detect your printer and hopeful find your driver, __Forward__ > under __Choose Driver__, __Forward__ > __Forward__ > __Apply__. If your printer is detected click on the printer shown under __Network Printer__, you should see the __Host:__ and __Port number:__ fields populated in the right pane, __Forward__ > the __Searching__ dialog will appear, under __Choose Driver__ go with the default, __Forward__ > the driver (e.g. gutenprint) will install, __Forward, Forward, Apply__.*

Ubuntu, like Windows, will automatically check for updates unless you turn this feature off. This can be annoying, as the OS prompts you to apply updates every time you log in. If you do turn this feature off, get in the habit of applying updates manually, often. I try to remember to apply them every time I log in. This is also a security hole as the OS polls the Internet.

In Unity, if you are not going to use the command line (recommended) to apply software updates drag the __Software Updater__ icon to the quick launch bar if it is not there already > click on it to run updates. To turn off automatic updates click on the __Settings...__ tab lower left > change __Automatically check for updates: Daily__ to __Never__. From now on you have to click on the __Check__ and __Install Updates__ buttons to apply updates.

In Unity with the Cinnamon desktop installed, to turn off automatic updates click on Menu lower left > select Preferences > in the right menu scroll down to select Software & Updates > click on the Updates tab > next to Automatically check for updates: change the setting to Never, Close.

Another simple approach that we will cover later is open a terminal window, become root, and apply updates manually from the command line every time you login:

```
# sudo su -
# apt-get update  &&  apt-get upgrade -y
```

It is not a bad idea to perform both these steps because sometimes the applying software updates from the GUI pulled down security updates that the command line did not.

When done setting up a VM, another thing that you can do to make using the VM more convenient is; *under System select the User Accounts icon > click on Unlock in the upper right corner > select the button to turn Automatic Login ON for the 'sudoroot' user > select Lock*. Since we use these environments for surfing/using the Internet, we may not be concerned with entering a password every time we log in. Adjust any other system settings that you may want to change.

Ubuntu -- Setup libdvdcss Repository

For many years the Medibuntu repository could be used to add useful Multimedia, Entertainment & Distractions. This repository contained packages that could not be included in the Ubuntu distribution for legal reasons. Patent and copyright laws in some countries prohibited using some software in Ubuntu. As of October 2013, The Medibuntu Project came to an end, and the Medibuntu repository is now unmaintained and offline. (See: http://www.medibuntu.org, https://help.ubuntu.com/community/Medibuntu, https://help.ubuntu.com/community/Repositories/Ubuntu, https://en.wikipedia.org/wiki/Medibuntu) If Medibuntu is installed in your flavor of Linux, you may see the following upon update:

W: Failed to fetch http://packages.medibuntu.org/dists/precise/free/i18n/Translation-en_US. Something wicked happened resolving 'packages.medibuntu.org:http' (-5 - No address associated with hostname)

If so type, # rm /etc/apt/sources.list.d/medibuntu.list to remove the Medibuntu repository. Or edit the /etc/apt/sources.list.d/official-package-repositories.list or the /etc/apt/sources.list file and remove the Medibuntu repository from either of those configuration files, depending on your flavor and version of Debian Linux. Add the latest *libdvdccs* repository by typing:

```
# apt-get install curl
# curl ftp://ftp.videolan.org/pub/debian/videolan-apt.asc | sudo apt-key add -
# echo "deb ftp://ftp.videolan.org/pub/debian/stable ./" | tee
/etc/apt/sources.list.d/libdvdcss.list
# apt-get update  &&  apt-get upgrade -y
```

(See: http://gauvain.pocentek.net/node/61, http://blogs.kde.org/2013/09/11/medibuntu-disappear-libdvdcss-now-direct-videolan)

Ubuntu 14.10/14.04 -- Getting the Old Look and Feel of Ubuntu 11.04 Back

There are multiple ways to get back to the old Ubuntu 11.04 look and feel. Below are three methods that you can use, such as install http://www.florian-diesch.de/software/classicmenu-indicator. From their website, "*ClassicMenu Indicator is a notification area applet (application indicator) for the top panel of Ubuntu's Unity desktop environment.*

It provides a simple way to get a classic GNOME-style application menu for those who prefer this over the Unity dash menu. As with the classic GNOME menu, it includes Wine games and applications if you have those installed." Perhaps we will see this style of menu packaged with future Ubuntu releases. There has been a lot of commentary online from users who were not happy with the Unity GUI changes. Preform the following steps as 'root' to get some of the old Ubuntu 11.04 menus back:

```
# add-apt-repository ppa:diesch/testing
# apt-get update && apt-get upgrade -y
# apt-get install classicmenu-indicator -y
# shutdown -r now
```

The Cinnamon desktop created for Mint can also be used in Ubuntu, but I had limited success with its 3D VM support. (See: https://launchpad.net/~gwendal-lebihan-dev/+archive/cinnamon-stable) To add Mint's Cinnamon desktop, add the following PPA and install Cinnamon. ***Reboot the VM, and when the login screen comes up click on the down arrow lower left and tick the Cinnamon desktop option and login.***

```
# add-apt-repository ppa:gwendal-lebihan-dev/cinnamon-stable
# apt-get update  &&  apt-get upgrade -y
# apt-get install cinnamon -y
# shutdown -r now
```

Once the desktop is added, reboot the VM and when the GUI login screen appears ***click on the icon next to your username and select the desktop (Cinnamon) you want to use, OK***.

The last option to consider would be to install the GNOME desktop if it did not come installed as a selection by default. Installing GNOME to get some of the old Ubuntu look and feel back is akin to using a sledge hammer to drive in a nail, but you may need the GNOME desktop for some reason.

	Adding any desktop to a Linux VM requires much more disk space and can destabilize the OS, requiring recreation of the VM.

*Click on **Ubuntu Software Center** on the launcher or click on **Dash home** > select **More Apps** > **Filter results** > select **System** > select **Ubuntu Software** icon to open up the Ubuntu Software Center > in the search box upper right type **GNOME** and select **The GNOME Desktop Environment, with extra components** > click on the **More Info** button > depending on the purpose of your VM, select the Add-ons that you will need.* You can also surf to http://www.gnome.org/getting-gnome to install the GNOME software from there. After rebooting, if you log in using GNOME classic, you will immediately notice the lack of a *system* selection on the menu, which used to be the default. Reference http://askubuntu.com/questions/58172/how-to-revert-to-gnome-classic to explore other options for changing/customizing the Ubuntu desktop.

Skip down to BackTrack/Kali/Mint/Ubuntu-VM Setup Steps after Install to setup the VM and then follow the next general setup steps.

Mint-Ubuntu – Finance Virtual Machine Creation

For security purposes, we only want a minimal set of tools and utilities installed for our Finance Linux VM. This environment and a minimal set of software is all that is necessary to conduct all of our financial Internet activity (e.g. banking, investing, and ecommerce). Refer to the General Setup directions to determine the flavor of Linux that you prefer to use as your finance VM and to configure it.

I had been using Quicken in Windows for years. As hardware and the application advances, Quicken users only have to upgrade (buy the latest Quicken release) every few years. This model is unlike other software vendors who require users to purchase a new license as often as each year. However, moving my family into using virtual OSs to surf the Internet has required me to look at some of the open source solutions that can be installed in a stripped down virtual OS install, which would prove safer for online banking. If you use Quicken and want to follow the advice of this book and use a VM, you could install Wine. Wine provides a Windows compatibility layer in Linux that contains alternative implementations of the DLLs for which Windows programs call. (See: https://en.wikipedia.org/wiki/Wine_(software))

WARNING **Tip**	Open source financial solutions can often support *Direct Connect* with your banking institution. OFX Direct Connect is a means of connecting to a financial institution and then syncing up the financial data in your local data file(s) with the last 60 days of transactions housed at your bank. All of this can be done with a few clicks of the mouse. I have never heard of a bank supporting Direct Connect with open source software; do you wonder why? If you have never set up Direct Connect with your banking institution, you may want to purchase Quicken and set it up with the help of your financial institution. They will freely help you to get things set up, which have to be configured on both sides of the transaction exchange, yours and theirs. Fields such as Username and Password often are not the same as your online login and password. Other fields such as Fipid, URL, Org and Fid can be figured out by open source financial software if your institution is

supported, which it probably is. If it is not, then using open source becomes difficult, as the technical support at your financial institution will not know what these values are. Once Quicken is set up, you can obtain these values.

If you have to call your bank to get Direct Connect set up or for support, TELL THEM THAT YOU NEED THE ACCOUNT SET UP FOR DIRECT CONNECT TO QUICKEN. You are not lying; you just did not tell them that you would also use that information to set up your open source solution. If you do not do this, you will confuse the technician that is on the phone or quite possibly be denied support at all. If the technician wants to walk you through the steps necessary to set up Quicken, explain that it is not a convenient time and you just want the information so that you can try to get things working later. Ask them if there is any other information that you may need beyond just a Username and Password, such as special URL.

There are many excellent choices for your financial software, and Wikipedia has an admirable comparison of accounting and personal finance software as a standalone or business financial solution. (See: https://en.wikipedia.org/wiki/Comparison_of_accounting_software) Our financial VM will contain a minimal install set of useful Linux applications. Create a finance VM and refer down to Backtrack/Kali/Mint/Ubuntu-VM Setup Steps after Install for detailed instructions on the steps that you may want perform in your finance VM. You will also need to refer down to Adding Less Privileged User IDs for Specific Purposes to Linux to create your finance VM user ID(s). Unlike other VMs you may want to disable some of the features in your finance VM that we installed or got working in other VMs. For instance, in addition to the steps that we took in securing your browser, you may want to disable some of the add-ons, such as Shockwave Flash, Windows Media Player Plug-in, etc. instead of disabling cookies that financial sites like to deposit and use; you could just set "Never remember history" and so on.

KMyMoney -- Installing, Configuring and Using in a KDE VM

For an actively updated personal finance application, I found KMyMoney to be an excellent choice for Windows and Linux. However, since it is designed as a personal finance manager, it does not provide the accounting functions that may be needed by a Small Business. However, if you do not need sophisticated functions such as payroll, you may find KMyMoney sufficient to meet your business needs. For example, it comes with budgeting and forecasting features as well as customizable reports that you can export into various formats, which can also be imported into other applications.

Mint Software Manager says KMyMoney operates similar to Quicken and the now deprecated Microsoft Money. It "*supports different account types, categorization of expenses, QIF import/export, multiple currencies and initial online banking support.*" It stores all of your financial data in a file that you create. You can have multiple files that house separate sets of accounts, but KMyMoney can only open one at a time. From the KMyMoney website you can download or view their outstanding 165 page manual, which will get you started using their software like finance professionals. (See: http://kmymoney2.sourceforge.net/index-gen.html) As with most open source software, you can download their software from their website or install it from the Linux repositories, although, it is much easier to use the repositories. (See:

http://kmymoney2.sourceforge.net/index-home.html,
https://en.wikipedia.org/wiki/KMyMoney)

apt-get install kmymoney -y

NOTE 	Suggested and recommended packages to support KMyMoney-KDE: # apt-get install aqbanking-tools gwenhywfar-tools ktoblzcheck ofx libaqbanking34-plugins libaqbanking34-plugins -y

It is difficult to improve on KMyMoney's manual, but since I use it for my finances I decided to include a brief tutorial. For our purposes, let us set up a checking account and have it download the transactions automatically. *Login as your 'finance' user ID and start out by setting up your desktop and panel icons > right click on the __Application Launcher Menu__ > select __Switch to Classic Menu Style__ > arrow up to highlight Office > arrow right and then right click on __KMyMoney (Personal Finance Manager)__ and add the icon to your desktop and panel.*

Double click on the icon to open up __KMyMoney__ and if this is your first run, the KMyMoney __New File Setup__ dialog should appear, __Next__, if not click on __Get started and setup my account__ on the __Start with one of the following activities...__ screen > enter your __Personal Data__, __Next__ > select your __Currency__, __Next__ > enter your checking account data, __Next__ > leave __Opening balance__ blank since we will automatically download that > select the groups of accounts that correspond to the ways in which you will use KMyMoney, I used __Base-Detail__, __Next__ > check __Configure preferences after finishing the wizard__, __Next__, > on the __New File Setup__ screen consider renaming the default because you may want to use a subdirectory and/or multiple files for different reasons (e.g., /home/<UserID>/finance/..., homefinance.kmy, sbofinance.kmy, parentsfinance.kmy, etc.), __Finish__ and set up preferences. We now have to set up automatic downloads to this account, which may require a call to your financial institution. *Click on the __Institutions__ icon on the left then right click on the account on the right > arrow down to select __Edit institution...__ where you can enter your __Institution Details__.*

Tip 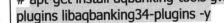	Go to your financial institution's web page, look for a link such as <u>Contact Us</u> and open up the <u>Contact & Support Center</u>. On this web page, you might find a lot of the information you need, for instance, phone, address and bank routing number. KMyMoney also asks for BIC Number, which is the Bank Identifier Code* (BIC), which can likely be left blank.

Click on the <u>Accounts</u> icon on the left to highlight it, then in the right pane right click on the account that you want to configure and arrow down to select <u>Edit account...</u> > the <u>Institution</u> tab can likely be left blank as the United States and Canada do not use International Bank Account Number* (IBAN) as account numbers. If you live in a country that does use IBAN, click on the <u>Institution</u> tab where you can, and enter the IBAN, which is necessary to automate cross-border transaction processing. (See: http://www.swift.com/dsp/resources/documents/IBAN_Registry.pdf) On the <u>Limits</u> tab, consider entering some limits so that KMyMoney will warn you when the account balance reaches those values.

Set up Personal Online Banking in KMyMoney

Click on the <u>Accounts</u> icon in the left frame > right click on the asset account on the right and arrow down to select menu item <u>Map to online account</u> > select <u>KMyMoney OFX</u>, which will display an extensive list of financial institutions from which you choose from > choose your financial institution, <u>Next</u> > KMyMoney ask you to password protect the KDE Wallet Service, which you may want to skip, <u>Cancel</u> > enter your banking institution <u>Username</u>, <u>Password</u>, (different from your browser Username & Password) and select <u>Identify as Quicken Windows 2011</u>, <u>Header Version</u> should be <u>102</u>, <u>Next</u> . If everything is correct, KMyMoney will connect and present you with a list of accounts that you can automatically download from your banking institution. We are now ready to update the account so *right click on the account under <u>Asset</u> and arrow down to select <u>Update account...</u> enter your banking institution's online account password, <u>OK</u>,* it will then download the last 60 days of account transactions.

GnuCash -- Installing, Configuring and Using in a GNOME VM

If you are Small Business, you may want to use GnuCash, which does run on many platforms, including Linux, MAC and Windows. Install GnuCash and all of its supporting applications before adding supporting utilities. GnuCash installs cleanly in the GNOME desktop, but in a KDE desktop, the suggested packages brought down many GNOME packages and will eventually bring down the GNOME desktop itself if you keep applying the suggested packages. If you are planning to use GnuCash, I suggest that you only use it in a GNOME Linux OS. If you visit http://wiki.gnucash.org/wiki/FAQ it explains that GnuCash uses specific GNOME libraries for the following: printing (gnomeprint), configuration storage (gconf), graphing (goffice), UI support (libgnomeui), HTML rendering (gtkhtml), and Help (yelp). GnuCash says that their software will run on a non-GNOME desktop, but since we are using a VM, there is no reason to introduce possible incompatibilities. Mint Cinnamon or Ubuntu LTS are good choices for your finance VM since they are supported until April 2017.

 **Tip**	Before you install from the repositories of whichever flavor of Linux you are using, consider downloading and installing from http://gnucash.org. After I installed from the Mint 16 repository, I clicked on GnuCash Help>About and saw that I was running version 2.4.13 when the project at the website was at 2.6.3. However, GnuCash developers recommend that we use the GnuCash version that comes with your distribution.

apt-get install gnucash -y   or,   # yum install -y gnucash   # zypper install -y gnucash
GunCash is only recommended for a limited VM install specifically for Finance. (See:
http://gnucash.org, http://wiki.gnucash.org/wiki/RedHat,
https://en.wikipedia.org/wiki/GnuCash, https://help.ubuntu.com/community/GnuCash)

GnuCash is an active, open source software solution for personal and small business financial accounting. You can track bank accounts and stocks, as well as income and expenses. As a quick and intuitive solution to use as a checkbook register, it is based on professional accounting principles to ensure balanced books and create accurate reports. Accountants love it because it does things like double-entry accounting, financial calculations, reports and graphs and much more for SBO's. The featured highlights include Stock/Bond/Mutual Fund Accounts, QIF/OFX/HCBI Import, Transaction Matching, Scheduled Transactions and Financial Calculations. The application comes with an excellent "Tutorial and Concepts Guide" to learn how to use this software. There is also a book that you can purchase by Ashok Ramachandran titled "Gnucash 2.4 Small Business Accounting" to guide you in the use of this open source solution to your SB needs. The publisher of the book allocates a percentage of the book sales back to the GnuCash project.

NOTE

Suggested packages to support GnuCash in Mint-Cinnamon:
apt-get install aqbanking-tools gnucash-docs guile-1.8-doc guile-1.8-doc-non-dfsg gwenhywfar-tools libchipcard-libgwenhywfar60-plugins libdbd-mysql libdbd-pgsql libdbd-sqlite3 libgwenhywfar60-dbg libhttp-daemon-perl libhtml-element-extended-perl libhtml-format-perl libhtml-form-perl ktoblzcheck ofx -y

Suggested packages to support GnuCash in Ubuntu:
apt-get install lsb-rpm lintian lzma dh-make debian-keyring g++-multilib g++-4.6-multilib gcc-4.6-doc libstdc++6-4.6-dbg libstdc++6-4.6-doc lsb libmail-box-perl elfutils rpm-i18n -y

When you create a new finance setup, GnuCash will create one file that you can share between computers or copy to other OSs. To house the GNU data file you may want to create a directory to do so. By default, GNUCash stores its configuration files in the */home/<finance user>/.gnucash* directory and whatever you name your data file will get the '.gnucash' extension added to it. However, only one person at a time should open the file to edit it at any given time. This book is about security and not about using individual open source applications, so we will only cover a few details to get you started configuring and setting up GnuCash. Skip down to creating less privileged users to create your 'finance' user ID, login as that user, and then select GnuCash from the application menu.

$ cd && mkdir gnucash

Upon startup, GnuCash is very different from Quicken, as it is account based. Launch GnuCash from the menu or command line and get started by creating a new account. *From the __Welcome to GnuCash!__ screen leave __Create a new set of accounts__ ticked, __OK__ or from the base screen select the __File__ menu, __New__ > __New file__ >the __New Account Hierarchy Setup__ assistant will appear, __Forward__ > the __Choose Currency__ screen will appear for you to select your currency, __Forward__ > on the __Choose accounts to create__ screen where __Common Accounts__ is checked by default, by using these options you can set up personal accounting solution categories or if you are a SBO check __Business Accounts,__ __Forward__ > on the __Setup selected accounts__ screen you can change the names of accounts and click on the accounts, such as the __Checking Account__ line to enter opening balances, __Forward__ > click on the __Opening Balance__ column and when a text box appears enter your opening balance, __Forward__. > on the __Finish Account Setup__ screen, __Apply__ > this will bring you back to the GnuCash main window showing a full set up of business accounts with the title __Unsaved Book - Accounts__ > when the __Save As...__ dialog opens, type the name of file and navigate to the folder where you want your data stored, click on Save As*. You have now created a default business account hierarchy with which your SB can experiment.

Jumping far ahead in the GunCash book or tutorial documentation, the first thing I wanted to do was connect/reconcile GnuCash with my business checking and savings accounts. Since GnuCash supports QIF/OFX/HBCI Import and does Transaction Matching, I wanted to do this electronically. Back when I used to use Quicken, the ability to download transactions from multiple credit union accounts saved me many hundreds of hours of work from having to enter all of this data manually. GnuCash offers online banking support but how to configure it without technical support was difficult.

Click on the Tools menu > select Online Banking Setup... > the Initial Online Banking Setup screen will appear > it will inform you of all sorts of information that it needs:

- *The bank code of your bank*
- *The user ID that identifies you to your bank*
- *The Internet address of your banks Online Banking server*
- *For HCBI Online Banking, information about the cryptographic public key of your bank (Ini-Letter) click on the Forward button > click on the Start AqBanking Wizard button to begin > The AqBanking Setup dialog will appear > click on the Create User button to bring up the New User Wizard, Next > select the format, for accounts that support Quicken leave OFX-DirectConnect backend ticked, Next, Run > the OFX DirectConnect Setup Wizard screen will appear, Next > click on the Select button to the right > on the Select a Bank screen enter your Bank Name, hopefully GnuCash will show your bank and fill in the bank's information automatically, OK, Next > for User Name, call your bank to find out what to use, in my case I used my online login; my User Id was my member number, and the Client UID I left blank, Next > for Emulated Application: I left it as Intuit Quicken Windows 2013, Application ID: QWIN, Application Version: 2200, Header Version: 102, Next > click on the Special Settings button and check Force SSLv3, OK, Next > hopefully you will see a Certificate Received dialog appear, Yes to accept it > click on the Retrieve Account List button which will prompt for a Password, that was my PIN number, OK.*

The Requesting account list dialog should appear and will show a list of accounts that can be managed via OFX. You should see Adding account... to bank... Operation finished, you can now close this window. When you close and finish everything GnuCash will ask you to Match Online Banking accounts with GnuCash accounts. *Since we are setting this up for the first time check the New? box to the right of each account > on the Select Account screen click on the New Account button > the New Account dialog will appear for you to enter all of your account information, for Account code: I entered the bank code, for Description: use something like Bank Joint Savings, select you currency, under Parent Account expand the menu Assets-Current Assets-Saving Account, OK. > if you have more accounts, navigate your way back to the Match Online Banking... screen and click on the remaining New? boxes to create additional accounts.*

From now on you can download transactions from your SB accounts by *clicking on the account you just set up > click on Online Actions > arrow right to select what you want to*

bring down from your account (e.g. Get Balance, Get Transactions..., and so on). If the menu is greyed out, try applying OS updates to the VM and rebooting.

KeePass – Installing and Using in a Linux VM

Using financial software usually requires many online accounts and passwords. The safest place to keep your passwords is on your core OS or a device that is not being exposed to the Internet. Alternatively, you can put them in a BoxCryptor folder and store that on encrypted on and encrypted sky drive and share it between your Internet devices (See: Chapter 5). Nonetheless, for convenience you may want to add your password file to the finance VM. KeePass Password Safe, which works well in Windows 7, can also be used in Linux. It is a handy and robust tool that can provide for all your virtual banking and ecommerce login needs. Not long ago, KeePassX was the only alternative to using KeePass in Linux. The application has evolved to include a Linux version of the software that is compatible with Windows.

 The install of KeePass Password Safe should never be done in a loaded General Purpose or anonymous (tor) surfing environment, which we will setup in the next chapter. Only consider installing it in our minimal finance VM.

Below are two options for using KeePass in Linux:

KeePassX's website states: "*Originally KeePassX was called KeePass/L for Linux since it was a port of Windows password manager* Keepass Password Safe.*" (See: http://www.keepassx.org) KeePassX has many of the same capabilities of KeePass and can be directly installed from Linux repositories. You can export passwords from KeePass 2.x (.kdbx) in Windows and then import them into KeePassX in Linux.

Method 1: KeePassX can be installed from the default Ubuntu repositories. KeePassX is a FREE password manager* which is very useful. It was originally ported from Windows KeePass2, and expanded upon for Linux. The password database is encrypted using the AES and Twofish algorithms.

KeePassX stores your password database in passfile.kdb form, which is not compatible with Windows 7 KeePass 2 passfile.kdbx file format. If you want to use the Windows 7 version of the passfile.kdbx in Ubuntu, you can export your passfile.kdbx to a KeePassX.kdb file and then import it into Ubuntu KeePassX.

apt-get install -y keepassx

Keepass2 also manages passwords securely and is an open source password manager* that is well maintained for Windows. From looking at the websites, it appears to be a better maintained project than KeePassX. It is somewhat disappointing that since 2009 it has not developed support for the Windows KeePass 2.x (.kxdb) format. Keepass 2 also allows you to store passwords in one secure encrypted database that can be accessed via one password. Written originally for Windows there are now multiple methods for running it under Linux (See http://KeePass.info, http://en.wikipedia.org/wiki/KeePass).

Method 2: KeePass2, which you can use on a *bootable Ubuntu USB drive* (see Chapter 10 about how to create a multiboot USB drive) and encrypt your USB data drive, is a solution that works in Mint, Ubuntu and Windows 7 on a passwordfile.kdbx file. You can drag and drop your latest password file into Linux from Windows, and back again, which is convenient. This provides seamless integration between Windows 7 and the latest flavors of Ubuntu-based Linux. Keepass2 did not used to be included in the Debian main archives. That changed with later releases of the OS. To try this solution rather than use KeePassX, type the following:

```
# apt-get install keepass2 keepass2-doc mono-dmcs xdotool libmono-i18n4.0-all libgnomeui-0 libgamin0 -y
```

In earlier versions of Mint and Ubuntu you can add the following PPA and install Keepass this way:

```
$ sudo su -
# apt-add-repository ppa:jtaylor/keepass
# apt-get update  &&  apt-get upgrade -y
# apt-get install keepass2
```

Backtrack/Kali/Mint/Ubuntu —VM Setup Steps after Install

1. Skip down to BackTrack/Kali/Mint/Ubuntu-Applying Software Updates to install all the latest updates. It is important to apply all updates prior to installing the Parallels, VMware Tools or VirtualBox Guest Additions because of kernel updates, and updates to the tools that the installation OS software uses to build the tools.
2. Parallel Tools needs to be installed in every OS. Refer back to Parallels-Manual Installation of Parallel Tools.
3. VMware Tools automatically installs in Fedora, openSUSE and Ubuntu, but not in Mint. The procedure to install/reinstall the tools is well documented by VMware Player however, this book attempts to streamline those directions a bit. The tools can be reinstalled or upgraded by referring back to VMware Player-Manual Installation of VMware Tools.
4. VirtualBox Guest Additions come preinstalled in most flavors of Mint but not in Ubuntu. To make sure the VM is at the latest version, or to reinstall, refer back to VirtualBox-Installing the VirtualBox Guest Additions.
5. Refer back to Firefox-Setup & Hardening your Browser Security to customize Firefox.
6. Some flavors of Linux do not come preconfigured with **.bashrc** file, or just have a primitive one. Ubuntu comes with an excellent default terminal window **.bashrc** configuration, which this book uses as template for other Linux OSs. To make life easier using a terminal window, refer back to Terminal Window-Customizing the Linux Command Line to Make Life Easy to customize the terminal window. This will make the command line experience easier and more productive for all users of your VM.
7. Because Mint is created and maintained in Japan, it comes preinstalled with a working flash player. Other flavors Linux require a flash player to be installed. Refer down to BackTrack/Kali/Mint/Ubuntu-Flash Player Installation to install a working flash player if it was not installed during VM creation.

8. If there are any general setup steps remaining for the VM, like in Ubuntu, refer back to complete those steps.
9. Skip down to <u>Adding Fonts to Linux</u>.
10. Skip down to <u>Tor Bundle-Install & Setup in any Linux OS as a Regular User</u> to enable the VM for convenient anonymous surfing (covered in the next chapter).
11. If using Cinnamon/GNOME desktop, skip down to <u>GNOME Desktop-Fedora-Mint General Configuration & Setup</u>; if using the KDE desktop skip down to <u>KDE Desktop-Fedora-Mint-openSUSE General Configuration & Setup</u>.
12. Skip down to <u>BackTrack/Kali/Mint/Ubuntu-Installing additional Applications, Tools & Utilities in Debian based Linux</u> to add software to the VM.
13. If you are going to have multiple user accounts, or just want to run the VM as a less privileged user than 'suroot' or 'sudoroot', skip down to <u>Adding Less Privileged User IDs for Specific Purposes to Linux</u>, where creating user accounts in Linux is described.

BackTrack/Kali/Mint/Ubuntu -- Applying Software Updates & Package Management

After an install of a Debian flavor of Linux, there are a few steps needed to bring all of your software up-to-date. Login as root and then perform the following steps to apply all of the latest software.

Update the Package Index: The *APT package index* is essentially a local database of available packages from the repositories as defined in the **/etc/apt/sources.list** file. It must be updated to enable you to search for the latest packages quickly and thoroughly. Halting the VM after an update is our opportunity to check and adjust the virtual machine settings.

```
# apt-get update && shutdown -h now
```

Upgrade Packages: Over time, updated versions of the packages that are currently installed on your computer may become available from the package repositories (for example, security updates). We have to instruct APT to contact all of the servers that it is configured to use, and to download any software that has been updated. A basic upgrade will never remove software or add new software. This makes it safe to use on a server where applying patches should never break things.

```
# apt-get upgrade -y && shutdown -r now
```

NOTE	If Mint asks to replace the configuration files, and if it has not been customized, do so by typing Y. If you are prompted to install GRUB by Mint-Debian, install it on the same partition that you did during the loading of the VM, most likely **/dev/sda**.

Upgrade dependencies: As open source development continues, we find that we cannot satisfy the dependencies of an update package using an upgrade. Software may need to be installed or removed to satisfy the dependencies of an updated package. This requires a distribution upgrade, which allows users to upgrade from one version of Debian Linux to a newer version. For servers, keeping regular upgrades separate from distribution upgrades is very important. For our guest VMs, much less so. Therefore, after a fresh install of the latest release of a Debian Linux OS, a **dist-upgrade** can be performed. However, sometimes applying a **dist-upgrade** can destabilize an OS, so consider just performing an upgrade.

```
# apt-get dist-upgrade -y && shutdown -r now     # In some disto's there where were no
updates available.
```

Sometimes, such as after applying software and updating packages, we find installs that satisfied dependencies that are no longer needed by the OS. In addition, there may be packages that were retrieved from repositories on an earlier update/upgrade that are no longer available in the repositories. It is a good idea to clean up these dangling references.

```
# apt-get autoclean -y     # Remove package files that can no longer be downloaded
# apt-get autoremove -y    # Remove obsolete packages
```

Some other package commands you may need:

apt-get clean	Same as autoclean, except it removes all packages from the package cache.
apt-get purge <package(s)>	Remove package(s) and their configuration files.
apt-get remove <package(s)>	Remove package(s) and leave their configuration files in system.
apt-get -f install	Attempt to correct any broken any broken dependencies.
dpkg --configure -a	Configure any packages which have been unpacked but not yet configured.
dpkg --list	List all install packages.

Mint/Ubuntu -- Flash Player Installation

While we don't need to install a flash player in Backtrack or Kali, in other flavors of Linux to keep your family happy and using the virtual environments it is mandatory that you have a working browser Flash Player. To view Flash files in Linux, **there are open source alternatives** to the proprietary Adobe Flash Player. The two mentioned on http://fedoraproject.org/wiki/ForbiddenItems page are Swfdec at http://swfdec.freedesktop.org/wiki/, and Gnash at http://www.gnu.org/software/gnash. After further reading on Wiki and about Swfdec and Gnash, coupled with reading their websites, Gnash seemed the better choice of the two, both being excellent open source alternatives to the proprietary Adobe Flash Player. (See: http://en.wikipedia.org/wiki/Swfdec#Players and http://en.wikipedia.org/wiki/Gnash)   Gnash is a GNU Flash movie player that supports most SWF v7 features and some SWF v8 and v9. It is available as both a standalone player and a browser plugin for Firefox (and all other Gecko based browsers), Chromium and Konqueror. Swfdec development has stopped for the most part and has not been updated since December 2009.

Despite limited resources, Gnash is keeping their software somewhat up-to-date. This is difficult when you compare their development budget to the deep pockets of a big corporation like Adobe. I tried Gnash in Ubuntu 32-bit and 64-bit installs and it worked very well in viewing YouTube videos. Therefore, Gnash is a good alternative to Adobe Flash, which is both easy to install and renders videos well in Firefox. This will allow you to stick with the open source philosophy and use Gnash in flavors of Linux that don't come with an Adobe Flash Player installed. For example, Mint comes with the Adobe flash player installed by default. (See: http://packages.ubuntu.com/search?keywords=gnash)

 If this VM is being used for anonymous web surfing, Tor (which we will discuss in Chapter 8) do NOT install a Flash Player.

Install FlashBlock on your Firefox and you won't even know websites use flash anymore (except for ads).

sudo add-apt-repository ppa:nilarimogard/webupd8
sudo apt-get update
sudo apt-get install freshplayerplugin
This will install pepper flash (google chrome's flash player) to firefox

To install Gnash from a terminal window type <Ctrl><Alt><T> # apt-get install gnash gnash-doc gnash-tools browser-plugin-gnash -y   # Some extra packages to consider are gnash-common contains common files and libraries and is installed as an extra package, gnash-cygnal is a Media Server, gnash-dbg contains Debug Symbols, gnash-ext-mysql is a MySQL extension, gnash-tools contains Command-line Tools, python-gtk-gnash contains Python binding, browser-plugin-gnash is a plugin for Mozilla and other derivatives.

# apt-get install klash   # GNU Shockwave Flash (SWF) player/viewer for KDE.
sudo add-apt-repository ppa:nilarimogard/webupd8
sudo apt-get update
sudo apt-get install freshplayerplugin
This will install pepper flash

From Wikipedia on Adobe Flash Player support, "*Since version 11 of Adobe Flash Player, released October 4, 2011, 64-bit and 32-bit builds for Windows, Mac and Linux have been released in sync. Previously, Adobe offered experimental 64-bit builds of Flash Player for Linux, from November 11, 2008 to June 15, 2010.*" I experimented with and documented many of those solutions. However, according to Wikipedia, "*after version 11.2, Flash Player for Linux will no longer be released by Adobe, but made available only as built into the Chrome browser.*" The Adobe agreement with Google is a plugin dedicated to Chrome that uses the Pepper Plugin API (PPAPI). The Adobe Flash Player for Linux was removed from the official repositories of Adobe. So having access to a working Flash player in Linux will be restricted to Google Chrome, if at all. (See: https://en.wikipedia.org/wiki/Adobe_Flash#64-bit_support)

Another alternative to Adobe Flash is the Lightspart project. This flash player is trying to support Adobe's newer Flash formats and AVM2 virtual machine. (See: http://lightspark.github.io)

apt-get install lightspark browser-plugin-lightspark   # or to be on bleeding edge:
add-apt-repository ppa:sparkers/daily && apt-get update
apt-get install lightspark browser-plugin-lightspark

	Historical Reference -- The History of 64-bit Flash Players and Why You Should Consider Open Source solutions.

Years ago, I was unable to find any decent, working, uncomplicated alternatives to the proprietary Adobe 64-bit Flash Player for 64-bit OSs. After viewing a multitude of how-to videos, I tried to view the suggested methods from Adobe, to no avail. Adobe eventually came out with an easily installed 64-bit release of Flash Player for Linux. Adobe Flash Player has worked in 32bit Linux OSs for years by installing the *flashplugin-nonfree* package. (See: https://help.ubuntu.com/community/RestrictedFormats/Flash, https://help.ubuntu.com/community/AMD64/FirefoxAndPlugins) Firefox uses the advanced Linux Sound Architecture plugin by default when you play a video. Advanced Linux Sound Architecture provides for automatic configuration of sound-card hardware, as well as other things. (See: http://en.wikipedia.org/wiki/Advanced_Linux_Sound_Architecture) For 32-bit flavors of Debian Linux, type the following:

apt-get install ubuntu-restricted-extras   # Not recommended for Mint, as this will remove the *mint-flashplugin* and the *mint-codecs*.

Some packages from multiverse are restricted by copyright in some countries. The Ubuntu-restricted-extras package brings down support for audio (Gstreamer plugins), Microsoft fonts, Java runtime, Flash plugin, and LAME. (See: http://www.ubuntu.com/ubuntu/licensing, https://help.ubuntu.com/community/RestrictedFormats/PlayingDVDs)

WARNING	Mint Linux comes with the *mint-flashplugin* and the *mint-codecs* package pre-installed. Installing the *Ubuntu-restricted-extras* or *flashplugin-nonfree* packages will remove the optimized Mint codecs and flash plugin.

apt-get install flashplugin-nonfree -y   # For Ubuntu and other flavors, and 32-bit flavors of Debian Linux to get the deprecated Adobe flash player.

Mint/Ubuntu – Installing Additional Drivers, Applications, Tools & Utilities in Debian-Based Linux

We can now load up our Debian based flavors of Linux with open source applications, which offer free capabilities that we would have to pay for in Windows. The list below is a subset of what is available for the Debian flavors of Linux. Only install the applications that you need from the list below. Also, carefully consider which desktop you are using. Many of the GNOME applications will work in KDE and vice-versa, but you may also pull down many redundant capabilities and possible incompatibilities. It is best to install the applications, tools and utilities that are either designed for both, or specifically for your desktop.

If you are turning over a Linux virtual environment to family members, you will want them spending time learning about the many useful Linux applications, tools, and utilities rather than spending all their time in social networks. Give them as many options to play with as possible, which will occupy them for many hours as they harmlessly-point-and-click away. All of this fun and interesting software can be installed using the GUI very easily, but as you keep creating VMs you will find that using the command line and cutting and pasting from this book is much easier. The commands below can also be scripted to quickly create a virtual OS with all of the software that our employees and family might want. The page https://help.ubuntu.com/community/SoundVideoDefault is a good read on some sound and video options that are available. If security is a concern for your Debian OS, the securing Debian How-to has many solutions. (See: http://www.debian.org/doc/manuals/securing-debian-howto)

If you want to use Linux as a robust gaming platform or use graphical software solutions you may want to try third-party drivers. To get them you will have to add third party repositories, called PPAs. A Personal Package Archive (PPA) is a web address with prebuilt applications and drivers for specific versions of Linux. These unofficial repositories create an avenue for software developers and users to create their own personal distribution mechanism for prebuilt packages and drivers that can then be easily installed in Mint and Ubuntu. If you are using a GeForce graphics card such as a GTX 600 or 700 series, you may want to try the latest driver available. The Ubuntu X/SWAT PPA contains updated version of the X.org drivers, libraries, etc. (See: http://www.nvidia.com/object/desktop.html, http://www.ubuntuupdates.org/ppa/ubuntu-x-swat) https://wiki.ubuntu.com/X/DriverBuilding)

```
# add-apt-repository ppa:ubuntu-x-swat/x-updates
# apt-get update  &&  apt-get upgrade
# apt-get install nvidia-current nvidia-settings
```

If you have an AMD Radeon card, you may want the latest open source driver from a community maintainer. Since Nvidia develops its own driver for Linux rather than releasing it as open source code, the AMD open source driver may not perform as well or run bleeding-edge games. Driver releases can lag behind the latest AMD hardware that arrives on the market. If that is the case, you can try their website to see if they are providing a proprietary driver for your card. The following PPA contains updated X (2D) and mesa (3D) free graphics drivers for Radeon, Intel and Nvidia hardware:

```
# add-apt-repository ppa:oibaf/graphics-drivers
# apt-get update  &&  apt-get upgrade -y  &&  apt-get dist-upgrade
```

Don't forget to reboot your VM after you update your drivers. If you run into trouble after installing drivers from these repositories, you can use the PPA-PURGE command to roll back the packages and disable a PPA. PPA-PURGE resets all packages pulled down from a PPA to their standard stable versions from the Ubuntu official repository.

```
# apt-get install ppa-purge
# ppa-purge <ppa:repository-name>/<subdirectory>
# apt-get update  &&  apt-get upgrade -y
```

If the solution above does not work, we can try downloading the latest driver for your AMD card from AMD website. (See: http://support.amd.com/en-us/kb-articles/Pages/latest-linux-beta-driver.aspx) On the web page it lists other packages that are needed to install and use the driver optimally. Make sure these are installed prior to installing the drivers along with the

Catalyst Control Center GPU management software. Note that since we did not use a PPA or Ubuntu repositories to install the driver, we won't get automatic updates of the drivers and software. If the PPA solution above meets your needs, stick with that solution.

```
# unzip amd-catalyst-13.11-beta-v9.4-linux-x86.x86_64.run.zip
# mv "amd-catalyst-13.11-beta V9.4-linux-x86.x86_64.run" amd-catalyst-13.11-beta-V9.4-
linux-x86.x86_64.run
# sh amd-catalyst-13.11-beta-V9.4-linux-x86.x86_64.run
# apt-get update  &&  apt-get upgrade  &&  shutdown -r now
```

You can now use the Kali repositories to download penetration testing and security auditing software from the Kali repositories. Just add the following to your */etc/apt/sources.list* file. (See: http://docs.kali.org/general-use/kali-linux-sources-list-repositories)

```
# cd /etc/apt && cp -ip sources.list sources.list.orig
# vi /etc/apt/sources.list     # Add the following to sources.list
deb http://http.kali.org/kali kali main non-free contrib
deb http://security.kali.org/kali-security kali/updates main contrib non-free
# apt-get update
```

Much of the following documentation and commentary was taken from the Software Manager in Linux Mint and Ubuntu, which are excellent tools for finding useful software. Many of the applications recommended for your VM have suggested packages, which may or may not be needed by the application. The suggested packages will also vary depending on what has been previously installed. In the days of 3 and 4 terabyte hard drives for home use, I recommend installing many of the suggested packages to alleviate problems using the applications. Login as, or become, root in BackTrack and Mint # su -, in Ubuntu # sudo su -.

In Mint, make sure that you have a version of *mintsources* later that 1.1.5 by typing:
apt version mintsources && apt-get install mintsources.

Try running Jockey before trying to install it. The GTK or KDE version of the software may already be installed by default; you don't want both.

apt-get install jockey-gtk -y for Ubuntu or, # apt-get install jockey-kde -y for Mint-KDE   # Jockey provides a user interface to examine and configure third-party drivers, such as the Nvidia, ATI and various Wireless LAN kernel modules.

apt-get install rkhunter -y && apt-get autoremove -y   # RKHunter is a tool for checking computers running Linux (clones) for the presence of rootkits and other black hat tools. Type # rkhunter --update to check if there is a later version of its text data files. Type # rkhunter --versioncheck to check if there is a later version of the tool available. Type # rkhunter --propupd to create the rkhunter.dat file after installing the OS and before installing any applications, tools or utilities. Type # rkhunter --check to examine the system any time after that. When done, examine the file # vim /var/log/rkhunter.log to see if everything was OK, if

so empty the file # > /var/log/rkhunter.log. Also examine and then empty the root mail file #
> /var/spool/mail/root. (See: http://rkhunter.sourceforge.net,
http://en.wikipedia.org/wiki/Rootkit).

<table>
<tr><td>

NOTE

</td><td>

Evince is a GNOME document viewer for multiple document formats. (See:
http://projects.gnome.org/evince) Ocular is the document viewer for KDE.
(See: http://okular.kde.org) Both support document viewing for many
document formats, including PDF, Postscript, djvu, tiff, dvi, XPS, SyncTex
support with gedit and comics books (cbr, cbz, cb7 and cbt). Evince and
Ocular are the open source alternative to Adobe Reader (not to be confused
with the Adobe Flash Player discussed previously). Most flavors of Linux come
with the Evince or Ocular viewers installed by default. In addition, Adobe also
does not appear to support 64-bit Linux OSs. You can run 32-bit Adobe in a
64-bit Linux OS, but that is not recommended. If for some reason your
requirements call for Adobe's 32-bit Proprietary Reader, visit their website and
download the Adobe Reader for Linux. (See: https://get.adobe.com/reader/)

$ sudo su -
# chmod 700 AdbeRdr9.5.5-1_i486linux_enu.bin
# ./AdbeRdr9.5.5-1_i486linux_enu.bin

</td></tr>
</table>

apt-get install abiword -y   # The AbiWord website describes this open source software as
"*an award winning, small, fast, featureful and crossplatform word processor.*" AbiWord also
boasts that it is tightly integrated with https://abicollab.net which will allow you collaborate
and write documents with your friends in real time. This is a fairly active project that is well
supported in Linux. The 3.0.1 release was December, 2014. (See: http://www.abiword.org)

Often times Aircrack, replaced by "iw", can be installed by typing # apt-get install aircrack-ng -
y. Unfortunately, in some flavors of Linux, it was not available in the repositories. Aircrack is
an 802.11 WEP and WPA-PSK keys cracking program that can recover keys once enough data
packets have been captured. Aircrack-ng is a set of tools for auditing wireless networks.
(See: http://aircrack-ng.org). It is a bit more complicated to get it installed from their
website. Below, it summarizes how to get it installed without adding the BackTrack
repositories. (See: http://www.aircrack-ng.org/doku.php?id=install_aircrack):

```
# apt-get install build-essential sqllite libssl-dev subversion
# mkdir Downloads && cd Downloads
# svn co http://trac.aircrack-ng.org/svn/trunk aircrack-ng
# cd aircrack-ng && make      # If everything compiles OK
# make install
# airodump-ng-oui-update
```

apt-get install iw   # Ubuntu/Mint are now recommend installing and using "iw" instead of
Aircrack. The "iw" tool is a new nl80211 based CLI configuration utility for wireless devices. It
is a powerful network tool that can be used for getting device capabilities, scanning, listening
to events, getting link status, adding and deleting interfaces, etc. (See:
http://wireless.kernel.org/en/users/Documentation/iw).

apt-get install alacarte -y   # Alacarte is a GNOME graphical menu editor that lets you edit, add and delete menu entries; it also allows you to create custom application launchers. Because Alacarte is a GNOME application, installing this in KDE will bring down many GNOME updates. (See: https://en.wikipedia.org/wiki/Alacarte, http://linux.softpedia.com/get/Desktop-Environment/Tools/Alacarte-14607.shtml)

apt-get install amarok -y   # Amarok is a KDE feature-rich media player that supports many formats, such as FLAC, Ogg, MP3, AAC, WAV, Windows Media Audio, Apple Lossless, WavPack, TTA and Musepack. Many Linux experts prefer this media player for music over most others. (See: http://amarok.kde.org)

apt-get install amule -y   # aMule stands for all-platform Mule and is a multi-platform, open source, peer-to-peer (P2P) file sharing application designed to connect to eDonkey and Kademlia networks. It is an excellent application for streaming a variety of different media to your computer. There are still plenty of file sharing networks and clients you can use to obtain free music, video and files like FrostWire. There is a LOT to aMule, such as the support of compressed transfers, support for secure ID, proxy* support, and much more. Suggested packages: # apt-get install amule-utils-gui amule-gnome-support libgnomeprintui2.2-0 -y. (See: http://www.amule.org, http://wiki.amule.org/wiki/Main_Page, https://wiki.archlinux.org/index.php/Amule, https://en.wikipedia.org/wiki/AMule).

apt-get install anjuta -y   # Anjuta is a GNOME development IDE with excellent support for the C and C++ languages. From the Anjuta website, "*Ajunta is a versatile software development studio featuring a number of advanced programming facilities including project management, application wizard, interactive debugger, source editor, version control, GUI designer, profiler and many more tools. It focuses on providing simple and usable user interface, yet powerful for efficient development.*" (See: http://www.anjuta.org)

NOTE	Mint Cinnamon suggested packages to support Anjuta: # apt-get install autoconf autoconf-archive autoconf-doc autogen libgtk-3-dev libgtkmm-3.0-dev glade gnu-standards intltool javascript-common libauthen-ntlm-perl libcrypt-ssleay-perl libgda-5.0-bin libgda-5.0-mysql libdata-dump-perl libgda-5.0-postgres libglib2.0-doc libtool libtool-doc valac-0.20 -y Ubuntu suggested packages to support Anjuta: # apt-get install libgtk-3-dev libgtkmm-3.0-dev glade autoconf2.13 autoconf-archive gnu-standards autoconf-doc gettext-doc libgda-5.0-bin libgda-5.0-mysql libgda-5.0-postgres libglib2.0-doc libdata-dump-perl javascript-common libtool-doc libcrypt-ssleay-perl gfortran libauthen-ntlm-perl -y

apt-get install audacious -y   # Audacious is a simple, small and fast audio player that supports many codecs and has advanced features. This is a very active open source project that is a descendant of XMMS. You can do things like create custom playlists, stream music from the Internet, tweak the sound with a graphical equalizer, and experiment with LSDSPA effects. (See: http://www.audacious-media-player.org)

apt-get install audacity -y   # Audacity is a cross-platform, digital, multi-track audio editor for easy recording, playing and editing of digital audio. It is available for Windows, Mac, Linux and other OSs. This is a very active project, with frequent new releases. (See: http://audacity.sourceforge.net)

NOTE  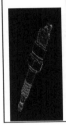	You can add packages from the "*Linux Audio Developer's Simple Plugin API (LADSPA)*". From their website, "*LADSPA is a standard that allows software audio processors and effects to be plugged into a wide range of audio synthesis are recording packages.*" (See: http://www.ladspa.org). wah-plugins – provides Wahwah effect for guitars or other instruments vco-plugins - LADSPA plugin sporting anti-aliased oscillators tap-plugins - Tom's Audio Processing LADSPA plugins swh-plugins - Steve Harris's LADSPA plugins rev-plugins - greverb-like ladspa plugin omins - a collection of LADSPA plugins aimed at modular synthesizers mcp-plugins - LADSPA plugins designed for Alsa Modular Synth ladspa-sdk - sample tools for linux-audio-dev plugin architecture invada-studio-plugins-ladspa - Invada Studio Plugins, a set of LADSPA audio plugins fil-plugins – Four-band parametric equalizer csladspa - LADSPA plugin for Csound cmt – Computer Music Toolkit, a collection of LADSPA plugins caps – C*Audio Plugin Suite, including a range of guitar amp emulations blop - limited wavetable-based oscillator plugins for LADSPA hosts blepvco - LADSPA, minBLEP-based, hard-sync-capable oscillator plugins autotalent – Real-time pitch correction plugin ambdec – is an ambisonics decoder amb-plugins - ambisonics LADPSA plugins

apt-get install avidemux mpeg2dec a52dec -y   # Avidemux is designed for multi-purpose video editing and processing, which can be used on almost all known operating systems and computer platforms. The website documents well how to configure and use the program. (See: http://www.avidemux.org/admWiki/doku.php)

apt-get install bum menu-l10n -y   # Boot-Up Manager (BUM) is a graphical tool to configure and manage system services in /etc/init.d, system runlevels by changing Start/Stop services priority. This is an alternative to using the update-rc.d command to create symbolic links in the /etc/rc?.d directories to control startup and stopping services. (See: https://help.ubuntu.com/community/BootServices, http://www.marzocca.net/linux/bum.html)

apt-get install rcconf   # Rcconf is an ncurses-based GUI tool that can be used via the command line. Rcconf works with System-V runlevel configuration for system services. It is a Text User Interface (TUI) frontend to using the update-rc.d command. NOTE: This install had the error "Use of uninitialized value $description_header" but seemed to run OK.

apt-get install sysv-rc-conf -y   # The sysv-rc-conf utility is an ncurses-based tool that gives the administrator control over all system services. Unlike other system service runlevel

config programs, sysv-rc-conf allows the administrator to configure services to start at any runlevel and not just your current one.

`# apt-get install cdrdao -y`   # needed to burn CDs using Banshee in Mint.
`# apt-get install banshee -y`   # Banshee is a versatile GNOME Multimedia Management and Playback application for all your music and videos. The Audio/Video player can encode/decode various formats and synchronize music with Apple iPods. (See: http://www.banshee.fm)

If you want to get Banshee on the bleeding edge you can visit and download their community maintained extensions. Years ago, these extensions were available in the Mint/Ubuntu repositories but appear to no longer be. (See: http://banshee.fm/download/extensions, https://gitorious.org/banshee-community-extensions)

`# apt-get install bleachbit menu-l10n -y`   # BleachBit is a system temporary file, cookie, Internet history, and a log-cleaner similar to CCleaner for Windows. BleachBit will also shred files to prevent file recovery and wipe free disk space to hide files deleted by other applications. BleachBit will wipe clean 90 applications, including almost every flash player and browser that will run in Linux. (See: http://bleachbit.sourceforge.net)

`# apt-get install bluefish bluefish-plugins weblint-perl php5-cli tidy tidy-doc -y`
Bluefish is a web design tool suitable for many programming and markup languages like HTML, PHP, Java, Perl, Python, C, and more that can be used to develop dynamic websites. It is suitable for many programming and markup languages and provides many features used to develop websites. There is a tutorial under **/usr/share/doc/bluefish-doc**. (See: http://bluefish.openoffice.nl/index.html, http://bfwiki.tellefsen.net/index.php/Installing_Bluefish)

`# apt-get install brasero -y`   # Brasero Disk Burner is a versatile GNOME, easy to use CD/DVD burning program. (See: http://projects.gnome.org/brasero)

`# apt-get install byobu -y`   # Byobu's website states it is, "*an Ubuntu's text-based window manager based on GNU Screen. Using Byobu you can quickly create and move between different windows over a single SSH connection or TTY terminal, monitor statistics about your system, detach and reattach to sessions later while your programs continue to run in the background.*" (See: http://launchpad.net/byobu).

`# apt-get install calibre -y`   # Calibre is meant to be a complete e-library solution. It includes library management, format conversion, news feeds to e-book conversion, as well as e-book reader sync features. Supported input formats are: MOBI, LIT, PRD, EPUB, ODT, HTML, CBR, CBZ, RTF, TXT, PDF and LRS. (See: http://calibre-ebook.com, http://calibre-ebook.com/demo)

NOTE 	Suggested packages to support Calibre: `# apt-get install imagemagick-doc autotrace cups-bsd curl enscript gimp gnuplot grads hp2xx html2ps javascript-common liblcms-utils libqt4-declarative-folderlistmodel libqt4-declarative-gestures libqt4-declarative-`

particles libqt4-declarative-shaders libqt4-dev libwmf-bin perl-tk python-psycopg2 python-mysqldb python-flup python-imaging-doc python-imaging-dbg python-lxml-dbg python-paste python-sqlite python-yaml python-qt4-dbg python-paste qt4-qmlviewer qt4-qtconfig radiance sane-utils texlive-binaries transfig ufraw-batch xhtml2ps -y

Suggested packages, *povray*, *povray-doc* and *povray-examples* had no installation candidate. Packages *lpr* and *lprng* had conflicts. Do not install *textlive-base*, but use *texlive-binaries* (above) instead.

apt-get install ccrypt -y   # Ccrypt and Mcrypt are replacements for the old crypt file encryption utility. They are utilities for encryption and decryption files and streams. Ccrypt's website is somewhat up-to-date, and the latest release of the tool was October, 2012. The Mint Software Manager reports that Mcrypt is buggy and recommends using OpenSSL, GnUTLs, and GunPG instead. (See: http://mcrypt.sourceforge.net, http://ccrypt.sourceforge.net)

apt-get install cheese gnome-video-effects-frei0r frei0r-plugins gstreamer1.0-tools -y   # Cheese is a versatile GNOME fully featured webcam application. You can take photos and make videos with special effects. (See: http://projects.gnome.org/cheese)

apt-get install chromium-browser -y && apt-get update   # Chrome is Google's browser, which according to Google is designed to be fast, streamlined, clean, simple, secure and has built in malware and phishing protection. The update refreshed the Google repositories. (See: https://www.google.com/chrome)

apt-get install clementine libchromaprint-tools python-acoustid -y   # Clementine is a multi-platform interface for searching and playing music. It is inspired by Amarok 1.4 and focuses on a fast and easy-to-use interface for searching and playing your music. (See: http://www.clementine-player.org)

apt-get install crack-md5 -y   # MD5 version of the crack password checking tool.

apt-get install cscope   # Interactive text screen C & C++ source browsing tool.
apt-get install cscope-el -y   # Only install if you use the emacs editor, this update is 93.6 MB.

apt-get install deluge libtorrent-rasterbar-dbg -y   # Deluge is a BitTorrent* client written in python/pygtk. It is a full featured*, multi-platform, multi-interface client-server model with a daemon process that handles all BitTorrent* activity. (See: http://www.deluge-torrent.org)

apt-get install devhelp libgtk2.0-doc -y   # Reference http://live.gnome.org/devhelp API documentation browser for GTK+ and GNOME.

apt-get install debian-policy   # Documentation **/usr/share/doc/debian-policy** on the system run levels and init.d scripts, among other things.

apt-get install di   # Disk information utility that shows everything that the Linux *df* command does and more.

apt-get install dia dia-shapes gsfonts-x11 -y   # Dia is a GNOME drawing program, much like Windows Visio, it can be used to draw many different kinds of diagrams. It currently has special objects to help draw entity relationship diagrams, UML diagrams, flowcharts, network diagrams, and many other diagrams. (See: http://projects.gnome.org/dia)

apt-get install diffuse   # Diffuse is a graphical tool for merging and comparing text files. (See: http://diffuse.sourceforge.net)

apt-get install dvdrip -y   # DVDRip is a full featured* DVD ripping program written in Perl. It has a feature-rich Gtk+ GUI to control the ripping and transcoding process. This project is somewhat dated, as the last release was May, 2010. (See: http://www.exit1.org/dvdrip, https://help.ubuntu.com/community/RestrictedFormats/RippingDVDs)

NOTE	Suggested packages to support dvdrip: # apt-get install dvdrip-doc graphicsmagick-dbg gxine libasync-interrupt-perl libev-perl libguard-perl libio-async-perl libjson-perl libjson-xs-perl libpoe-perl libtask-weaken-perl libintl-xs-perl libxine1-gnome rar vorbis-tools xvid4conf -y

apt-get install eclipse -y   # Eclipse is a tool platform and IDE compiler for Java. This is a very large download so only install this package if you plan to do JAVA development. (See: http://www.eclipse.org)

apt-get install empathy -y   # Empathy is a GNOME multi-protocol chat and call client. Empathy supports Google Talk (Jabber/XMPP), MSN, IRC, Salut, AIM, Facebook, Yahoo!, Gadu Gadu, Groupwise, ICQ and QQ. Empathy supported protocols depend on installed Telepathy Connection Manager Components. Supports all protocols supported by Pidgin. There are many other features such as file transfer, private and group chat, conversation logging, and much more. (See: http://live.gnome.org/Empathy)

NOTE	Suggested packages to support Empathy: # apt-get install apparmor apparmor-profiles apparmor-docs apparmor-utils telepathy-idle apparmor -y

apt-get install evolution -y   # Evolution is a GNOME-integrated mail, calendar, address book, to-do/task list and memo tool. Evolution is a fully operational open source substitute for Outlook that is packed with features. (See: http://projects.gnome.org/evolution).

WARNING ONLY If Exchange	Evolution, with its connecting exchange packages is a very large install. If you don't need to integrate Evolution with Microsoft Exchange, then **don't install** the suggested packages. Evolution is an excellent alternative to Microsoft Outlook, with a full suite of useful applications like Outlook, but if all you need is an email client, Thunderbird is an excellent choice. Suggested packages to support Evolution with exchange are: # apt-get install db5.1-util evolution-dbg evolution-plugins-experimental gsl-ref-

Support Is Needed	psdoc gsl-doc-pdf gsl-doc-info gsl-ref-html gv libmail-dkim-perl libdbi-perl libnet-ident-perl pyzor razor

yum install exaile -y   # Exaile is a music player similar to the popular KDE's Amarok, but it's based on GTK+ toolkit rather that Qt. Therefore, it's an excellent solution for GNOME users. It incorporates automatic fetching of album art, lyrics fetching, handling of large libraries, artist/album information via Wikipedia, last.fm support and options iPod support. (See: https://en.wikipedia.org/wiki/Exaile, http://www.softpedia.com/reviews/linux/Exaile-44202.shtml, http://www.exaile.org)

apt-get install fcrackzip   # From the Mint Software Manager, *"fcrackzip is a fast password cracker that is able to crack password protected zip files with brute force dictionary based attacks."*

For Ubuntu you may need to add this PPA:
add-apt-repository ppa:jon-severinsson/ffmpeg && apt-get update
apt-get install ffmpeg ffmpeg-doc winff winff-doc -y   # FFMpeg is a hyper-fast (real time) live audio and video encoder, which is needed to play various video format codecs, including MPEG-1 audio and video, MPEG-4, h263, ac3, asf, avi, real, mjpeg, and flash. (e.g. ffmpeg -i input-file.mp3 output-file.ogg) (See: http://ffmpeg.org, http://libav.org) Winff is a graphical video and audio batch converter using ffmpeg or avconv. (See: http://www.winff.org)

apt-get install filezilla -y   # FileZilla supports FTP, FTP over SSL/TLS (FTPS) and SSH File Transfer Protocol (SFTP). FileZilla is a cross-platform, multithreaded FTP, FTPS, and SFTP client that has an intuitive GUI interface. It is fast and reliable, easy to use, and has many useful features. (See: http://filezilla-project.org)

apt-get install firestarter -y   # Firestarter is a GNOME program to manage and observe firewalls. This could be installed in earlier versions of Ubuntu repositories but **was not available** in versions after Ubuntu 13.10 or Mint 16. It is a GUI frontend to setting up firewall rules using either the ipchains or iptables commands. When you install firestarter from a system package it will configure itself to automatically run as a system service. (See: http://www.fs-security.com/docs).

apt-get install gcalctool -y   # GNOME calculator package. (See: https://live.gnome.org/Calculator, https://en.wikipedia.org/wiki/Gcalctool)

apt-get install gecko-mediaplayer -y   # Gecko is a GNOME browser plugin that uses GNOME MPlayer to play media in browsers. If you plan to use the more advanced MPlayer2 fork, you might want to consider not installing this software. (See: https://sites.google.com/site/kdekorte2/gecko-mediaplayer)

apt-get install gftp -y   # gFTP is very dated GNOME project (11/30/2008) which is multi-threaded FTP client for the X Window System. The creator wants to hand this project off to someone willing to take over support. The five year old gFTP supports simultaneous downloads and file transfer queues to allow downloading of multiple files, resumption of interrupted file transfers, support for downloading entire directories/subdirectories, a bookmarks menu to allow quick connection to FTP sites, caching of remote directory listings,

local and remote chmod, drag and drop, a connection manager, and much more. (See: http://www.gftp.org)

apt-get install gimp gimp-help-en gimp-data-extras gimp-dcraw gimp-plugin-registry gmic gphoto2 gtkam gthumb bison-doc icc-profiles libtiff-opengl -y   # GIMP is the open source GNU Image Manipulation Program with advanced features for image editing, composition and image authoring. GIMP supports many image formats as a polished, user-friendly, image editor with professional tools. It lets you draw, paint and edit images with a lot of other features. (See: http://www.gimp.org)

apt-get install gmlive -y   # GMLive is a GNOME live video frontend for Mplayer. Do not install if you plan to use Mplayer2. (See: http://code.google.com/gmlive)

apt-get install gnote   # GNote is a GNOME note-taking application cloned from Tomboy; it is simple and easy to use. It is a good alternative to using Tomboy in GNOME or the more fully featured Microsoft OneNote in Windows 7. (See: http://live.gnome.org/Gnote, https://en.wikipedia.org/wiki/Gnote).

NOTE	Mint comes with a shockwave flash plugin installed called *mint-flashplugin*. In reading the Mint Forums, they say that the plugin is updated by Mint soon after Adobe releases a new version of Flash. However, if you are having problems using Flash, you can install the latest Adobe Flash plugin using # apt-get install flashplugin-nonfree. The installation of *flashplugin-nonfree* will remove *mint-flashplugin* and *mint-meta-codecs* packages. Other suggested packages to support flash plugin: # apt-get install -y konqueror-nsplugins msttcorefonts ttf-xfree86-nonfree xfs libnspr4-0d libnss3-1d

apt-get install crafty gnuchess phalanx xboard -y   # Craft is a chess-playing program that uses opening books and endgame databases. GNU Chess is a text-mode chess opponent. Phalanx is another smart chess-playing program. Xboard is a graphical interface for chess in all its major forms, which serves as a front-end to many of the chess services, including GNU Chess. (See: https://www.gnu.org/software/chess)

GnuCash is GNOME open source software for personal and small business financial accounting. You can track bank accounts and stocks, as well as income and expenses. As quick and intuitive to use as a checkbook register, it is based on professional accounting principles to ensure balanced books and accurate reports. Refer back to Finance Virtual Machine Creation to learn about GNUCash.

apt-get install gnutls-bin   # GnuTLS is a portable library that implements the Transport Layer Security (TLS 1.0, 1.1, 1.2) and Secure Sockets Layer (SSL 3.0) protocols. (See: http://www.gnutls.org)

apt-get install gnupg2 gnupg-doc xloadimage pinentry-doc pinentry-curses pinentry-qt4 pinentry-gtk2 -y   # GnuPG2 is a new modularized version of GnuPG supporting OpenPGP and S/MIME. (See: http://www.gnupg.org)

apt-get install googleearth   # GoogleEarth lets you observe satellite imagery, 3D buildings, 3D trees, terrain, Street View, planets and more. This is not recommended on a 64bit OS or a less powerful machine. (See: http://www.google.com/earth/index.html)

 NOTE The install of GoogleEarth suggests and uses many i386 packages, so I do not recommend installing it on a 64-bit OS. Installing GoogleEarth is a bit different than installing other software. The web page https://help.ubuntu.com/community/GoogleEarth describes in detail, multiple methods for installing GoogleEarth. I don't recommend installing GoogleEarth on older hardware because of its high demand for computer resources.

NOTE

Google Talk will allow you to use voice and video capabilities in your Google Chat properties (i.e Gmail, Google+, orkut). From within these services, you can have an actual conversation with someone, or even chat face-to-face over video. Visit Google.com/chat/video to get started. ***Click on the Install voice and video chat button > select your download package (e.g. 32 bit .deb (for Debian/Ubuntu) > click on the Install voice and video chat button > if you see the message "This type of file can harm your computer..." > click on the Keep button > you can then install the package using the Package Installer or follow the directions below.***

Save the file and use the command line:
cd ~suroot/Downloads
dpkg -i google-talkplugin_current_i386.deb
dpkg -i google-talkplugin_current_x86_64.deb
apt-get update && apt-get upgrade -y

apt-get install gparted -y   # GParted is the GNOME partition editor and is not needed in a VM. (See: http://gparted.sourceforge.net)

NOTE Suggested additional GParted packages:
apt-get install xfsprogs reiserfsprogs reiser4progs jfsutils kpartx dmraid gpart xfsdump attr quota -y

apt-get install gromit -y   # Gromit allows the user to make annotations on the screen. It is very useful to be able highlight things while making a presentation. (See: http://home.unix-ag.org/simon/gromit).

apt-get install gtkPod -y   # Gtkpod from Ubuntu Software Center it is a platform independent GUI for Apple's iPod using GTK3. It allows the user to upload songs and playlists to their iPod. It is similar to Apple's iTunes, and supports iPod, iPod nano, iPod shuffle, iPod photo, and iPod mini. (See: http://www.gtkpod.org, http://www.gtkpod.org/wiki/Home).

apt-get install guake   # Guake is a drop-down terminal for GNOME desktop. It is an alternative to the Terminator desktop. To me, Guake did not seem to me to be a better alternative to other terminal options. (See: http://guake.org)

apt-get install gwibber gwibber-service-flickr gwibber-service-statusnet gwibber-service-foursquare -y   # Gwibber is a GNOME open source microblogging client. It brings the most popular social networking web services to your desktop and gives you the ability to control how you communicate. (Identi.ca, StatusNet, Facebook, FriendFeed, Digg, Flickr, Qaiku). (See: http://gwibber.com)

apt-get install gxine gxineplugin -y   # Xine is a multi-platform, multimedia player that plays CDs, DVDs, and VCDs. It also decodes multimedia files such as AVI, MOV, WMV, and MP3 from local disk drives, and also displays multimedia. Gxine is the gtk+/GNOME user interface for xine video player. The suggested package realplayer has no installation candidate. (See: https://www.xine-project.org)

apt-get install hardinfo -y   # HardInfo is a hardware analysis, system benchmark and report generator. (See: https://help.ubuntu.com/community/HardInfo)

apt-get install imagemagick imagemagick-doc -y   # ImageMagick is a software suite to create, edit, and compose bitmap images. (See: http://imagemagick.org)

apt-get install graphicsmagick graphicsmagick-dbg -y   # GraphicsMagick is a fork from the ImageMagick project that puts a larger emphasis on stability. It can be used in parallel with ImageMagick. it provides a robust and efficient collection of tools and libraries that support reading, writing, and manipulating an image in over 88 major formats including important formats like DPX, GIF, JPEG, JPEG-2000, PNG, PDF, PNM, and TIFF. (See: http://www.graphicsmagick.org)

apt-get install inkscape -y   # Inkscape is a SVG based vector image manipulation program/graphics editor. Use Inkscape for creating text and graphics compositions, including business cards, book covers, fliers, and ads. Inkscape is similar in capabilities to Adobe Illustrator and CorelDRAW. Inkscape can also be used to create fonts. (See: http://www.inkscape.org)

NOTE

Suggested packages to support Inkscape:
apt-get install dia dia-gnome gsl-ref-psdoc gsl-doc-pdf gsl-doc-info gsl-ref-html libgnomevfs2-extra libsvg-perl libxml-xql-perl imagemagick-doc pstoedit python-coverage python-lxml-dbg python-numpy python-numpy-doc python-numpy-dbg python-nose python-dev gfortran python-renderpm-dbg python-egenix-mxtexttools python-egenix-mx-base-dbg python-egenix-mxtexttools-doc python-reportlab-doc python-uniconvertor-dbg -y
and so on, if further suggested packages are needed...

---

apt-get install john john-data -y   # John the Ripper is an active password cracking tool. Its primary purpose is to detect weak passwords. (See: http://www.openwall.com/john)

apt-get install k3b -y   # K3B provides KDE a graphical user interface to perform most CD/DVD burning tasks including creating an audio CD from a set of audio files or copying a CD/DVD, as well as more advanced tasks such as burning eMoviX CD/DVDs, for instance. It can also perform direct disc-to-disc copies. (See: http://www.k3b.org)

apt-get install k9copy   # Development on K9Copy for KDE ceased April 2011. It is still a useful tool but is becoming less so every day. It provides several methods for backing up a DVD. (See: http://k9copy.sourceforge.net/web/index.php/en)

apt-get install kaffeine -y   # Kaffeine is a KDE media player based on the Xine engine. (See: http://kaffeine.kde.org)

apt-get install kde-full -y   # You may want to try adding the KDE desktop to Ubuntu as an alternative to the Unity desktop. Bear in mind this requires much more disk space and may destabilize the OS requiring recreation of the VM. (See: http://kde.org)

KMyMoney is an excellent personal finance management tool that Mint Software Manager says operates similar to Quicken and the now deprecated Microsoft Money. It "*supports different account types, categorization of expenses, QIF import/export, multiple currencies and initial online banking support.*" Refer back to Finance Virtual Machine Creation to learn about KMyMoney. (See: http://kmymoney2.sourceforge.net/index-home.html)

apt-get install kolourpaint4   # KolourPaint is a KDE simple drawing and image editing application. It is simple to use for common tasks such as drawing simple graphics and touching-up photos.

apt-get install kompozer -y   # Kompozer is a dated project (latest stable release August 30, 2007) that is a full web authoring system, complete with a WYSIWYG HTML editor for easy web page production. It has many features that are similar to Macromedia Dreamweaver, but not as feature rich. (See: http://kompozer.sourceforge.net, http://www.kompozer.net).

apt-get install ktorrent -y   # KTorrent is a BitTorrent client for the KDE desktop which allows you to download files. (See: http://ktorrent.org)

apt-get install lame lame-doc -y   # Tool to learn about MP3 encoding that includes an MP3 encoding library.

apt-get install libdvdcss2 libdvdread4 libdvdnav4 lsdvd -y   # These packages include codecs that are needed to play DVDs. *Libdvdcss* is a cross-platform library designed for accessing DVDs (on-the-fly CSS decryption) like a block device without having to bother about the decryption. It allows applications to use the more advanced features of the DVD format. (See: http://www.videolan.org/developers/libdvdcss.html)

apt-get install w32codecs   # 32bit non-free-codecs for video formats
apt-get install w64codecs   # 64bit non-free-codecs for video formats

NOTE LibreOffice is a multi-platform, feature-rich suite of applications that can handle all your document production and data processing needs. The open source productivity suite includes: Writer-Word Processor, Calc-feature-rich Spreadsheet; Impress-create multimedia presentations; Draw-build diagrams and sketches; Math-simple equation editor for math, chemical, electrical and science calculations;

and Base-database front-end to the LibreOffice suite. These tools can perform most tasks that can be done using the Microsoft Office suite. The Writer tool has advanced to point of being able to ready the Microsoft Office DOCX format and render the documents almost flawlessly. (See: https://www.libreoffice.org) Suggested packages as additions to LibreOffice:

apt-get install libreoffice-pdfimport libreoffice-help-en-us unixodbc fonts-sil-gentium libreoffice-officebean libreoffice-report-builder odbc-postgresql openclipart-png openclipart-libreoffice postgresql pstoedit unixodbc unixodbc-bin -y

apt-get install hyphen-en-us mythes-en-us   # US English hyphenation patterns for Libreoffice and the English thesaurus.

apt-get install linphone -y   # Linphone is Internet phone or Voice Over IP (VOIP) software. Use Linphone to communicate freely with people over the Internet with voice, video, and text instant messaging. (See: http://www.linphone.org)

apt-get install lynis -y   # Lynis is an open source security and system auditing tool. Its primary goal is to help users with security auditing, system hardening, vulnerability scanning and penetration testing of Unix and Linux OSs. (See: https://en.wikipedia.org/wiki/Lynis, https://cisofy.com/lynis)

apt-get install lynx -y   # Lynx is a text-based web browser, which is useful for scripting and obtaining text information from websites. (See: https://en.wikipedia.org/wiki/Lynx_(web_browser), http://lynx.isc.org)

apt-get install marble marble-plugins -y   # Marble is a KDE generic geographical map widget and framework. Marble shows the earth as sphere but does not require hardware acceleration. It also includes a minimal set of geographical data so it can be used offline. (See: http://edu.ked.org)

apt-get install mawk -y   # Conforms to the POSIX 1003.2 and extends the capabilities of old *awk* tool, and is smaller and much faster than *gawk* utility. In Mint, *mawk* is installed by default.

apt-get install mc -y   # Midnight Commander is a Norton Commander clone for managing files and directories. It is a powerful file manager that uses a two-panel interface and a subshell for command execution. Also included is Virtual File System (VFS), which allows files on a remote system (e.g. FTP, SSH servers) and files inside archives to be manipulated like real files. (See: http://www.midnight-commander.org)

NOTE Suggested packages to support *mc*:
apt-get install arj catdvi dbview djvulibre-bin links lynx imagemagick imagemagick-doc odt2txt python-boto python-tz w3m -y

apt-get install meld -y   # Graphical tool to help use the *diff* command line tool to merge files or directories.

apt-get install minitube -y   # Minitube is a native YouTube client that focuses on a pleasing experience. It is not an attempt to clone the YouTube website. Type a keyword, Minitube gives you and endless video stream to view. (See: http://flavio.tordini.org/minitube)

apt-get install medusa -y   # Medusa is intended to be a speedy, massively parallel, modular, login brute-forcer. It supports many protocols including: AFP, CVS, FTP, HTTP, IMAP, rlogin, SSH, Subversion, and VNC to name a few. (See: http://sectools.org/tag/crackers).

apt-get install mgdiff -y   # MGDiff is a GUI front-end to the *diff* utility for comparing text files.

MPlayer is a GNOME GTK2/GTK3 interface that can play all your multimedia including audio, video, streams, CD, DVDs, and VCDs, etc. (See: https://code.google.com/p/gnome-mplayer)

apt-get install mplayer2 -y   # MPlayer2 is the next generation movie player that replaces mplayer. The developers claim it contains significant further development and supports a number of features not available in other Unix players. (See: http://mplayer2.org)

NOTE

Choose from MPlayer or MPlayer2. Installing MPlayer2 will remove MPlayer. The MPlayer2 project is a fork from the original MPlayer project that claims significant further development and support than other Linux players. If you want MPlayer instead:
apt-get install mplayer mplayer-doc smplayer smplayer-themes -y

---

apt-get install mmv -y   # Move/Copy/Append/Link Multiple Files by Wildcard Patterns.

apt-get install nautilus-actions -y   # Nautilus-Actions is an GNOME extension for Nautilus. It provides an easy way to add arbitrary actions to the file manager context menus. (See: http://www.grumz.net)

apt-get install nautilus-image-converter   # Add a "Resize Images..." menu item to the GNOME context menu of all images. This opens a dialog where you set the desired image size and file name. A click on "Resize" finally resizes the image(s) using ImageMagick's convert tool.

apt-get install nautilus-open-terminal -y   # The nautilus-open-terminal GNOME extension provides a right-click "Open Terminal" option for Nautilus users who prefer that option.

apt-get install nautilus-pastebin -y   # A Nautilus GNOME extension written in Python and allows users to upload text-only files to a pastebin service just by right-clicking on them. Users can also add their favorite service just by creating new presets.

Ncrack was not available in the Mint or Ubuntu repositories.

apt-get install nmap umit zenmap -y   # NMap is a multi-platform security auditor complete with network scanner and mapper, port scanner, OS/version detection and much more. *Umit* and *Zenmap* are graphical user interface front-ends to the nmap penetration tool. (See: http://nmap.org, http://www.umitproject.org, https://en.wikipedia.org/wiki/Zenmap#Graphical_interfaces)

NOTE	Suggested packages to support nmap, umit and zenmap: # apt-get install python-pysqlite2-doc python-pysqlite2-dbg -y

apt-get install oggconvert -y   # Oggconvert is a small and simple GNOME utility used to convert media files to the patent-free Vorbis, Theora, Dirac, and now VP8 formats. (See: http://oggconvert.tristanb.net, https://launchpad.net/oggconvert)

apt-get install ogmrip ogmrip-doc mkvtoolnix-gui -y   # OGMRip is an application for ripping and encoding DVDs into AVI, OGM, MP4 or Matroska files using lots of audio and video formats: Vorbis, MP3, PCM, AC3, DTS, AAC, MPEG-4 ASP, MPEG-4 AVC, and Theora. (See: http://ogmrip.sourceforge.net/en/manual.html, https://help.ubuntu.com/community/RestrictedFormats/RippingDVDs)

apt-get install openjdk-7-jdk -y   # OpenJDK is the open source implementation of the Oracle Java Platform, Standard Edition. JDK is a development environment for building applications, applets, and components using the Java programming language. (See: http://openjdk.java.net)

apt-get install openjdk-7-jre -y   # OpenJRE is the full Java runtime environment that is needed for executing Java GUI and Websmart programs. (See: http://home.java.net, http://www.oracle.com/technetwork/java/javase/downloads/index.html). There are many suggested fonts that will be covered later in Adding Fonts to Linux.

apt-get install opera && apt-get update   # Opera is a fast and secure Web Browser/Internet Suite, which was available in early Ubuntu repositories. (See: http://www.opera.com/browser) This install method will work in Mint.

NOTE 	Opera.com is a fully featured, compact, customizable, fast web browser with advanced browser HTML 5 and CSS 3 support. Opera is a good browser choice to boost surfing speed on older computers and slow Internet connections. The Opera browser is not installable from the default Ubuntu repositories for legal reasons (copyright, license, patent, etc). There are two ways we can add Opera browser. We can manually setup the Opera repository and GPG key to install and maintain Opera from that repository. (See: http://deb.opera.com, https://help.ubuntu.com/community/OperaBrowser) A method you might find easier is to visit the http://www.opera.com/download web page and download the latest version of the Opera browser. Install it by typing # dpkg -i ./opera_12.16.1860_i386.deb or # dpkg -i ./opera_12.16.1860_amd64.deb. The install will automatically add the Opera repository to **/etc/apt/sources.list.d**, so we will get future updates.

apt-get install p7zip-full p7zip-rar -y   # 7-Zip is a file archiver that archives with very high compression ratios. From the website, "*The program supports 7z, XZ, BZIP2, GZIP, TAR, ZIP, WIM, ARJ, CAB, CHM, CPIO, CramFS, DEB, DMG, FAT, HFS, ISO, LZH, LZMA, MBR, MSI, NSIS, NTFS, RAR, RPM, SquashFS, UDF, VHD, WIM, XAR, Z*". (See: http://7-zip.org, http://p7zip.sourceforge.net, http://sourceforge.net/projects/sevenzip)

apt-get install partitionmanager -y   # Partition Manager is the KDE Partition Manager. It manage disks, partitions, and file systems on the KDE desktop: create, resize, move, copy, back up, restore or delete partitions. (See: http://sourceforge.net/projects/partitionman, http://partitionman.sourceforge.net)

NOTE

Password Safe is an open source password manager similar to KeePass that you can use to maintain an encrypted database of passwords. (See: http://pwsafe.org) We will discuss Password Safe in detail in Chapter 11. There is a BETA release that you can download and try out at http://sourceforge.net/projects/passwordsafe/files. To install the software, try using # synaptic, which is a graphical tool that makes install Password Safe easy. Otherwise, click on the Name, Linux-BETA link > click on the Download passwordsafe-ubuntu-0.94BETA.i686.deb link and save the file to your Downloads directory. Then type the following as 'root':

cd ~suroot/Downloads   or   cd ~sudoroot/Downloads
dpkg -i ./passwordsafe-ubuntu-0.94BETA.amd64.deb
dpkg -i ./passwordsafe-ubuntu-0.94BETA.i686.deb

I encountered the following error attempting to install the package:
dpkg: dependency problems prevent configuration of passwordsafe:
 passwordsafe depends on libykpers-1-1 (>= 1.7.0-1); however:
  Package libykpers-1-1 is not installed.
dpkg: error processing package passwordsafe (--install):
 dependency problems - leaving unconfigured
To fix broken dependencies because this method did not work type:
apt-get -f install

apt-get install pdfshuffler -y   # PDF-Shuffler is a small application that allows the user to merge or split PDF documents. The user can also rotate, crop and rearrange pages. (See: http://pdfshuffler.sourceforge.net)

apt-get install phatch phatch-cli phatch-doc -y   # Phatch is a simple-to-use, cross-platform GUI Photo Batch Processor that handles all of the popular image formats and can duplicate sub-folder hierarchies. *Phatch* can batch re-size, rotate, apply perspective, shadows, rounded corners and more. (See: http://photobatch.stani.be, http://photobatch.wikidot.com)

apt-get install picasa -y   # Picasa is an image management application from Google. It is good for organizing, editing, and sharing digital photos. *Picasa* uses 109 MB of additional disk space, so it is a large installation. (See: http://picasa.google.com)

| NOTE | The install of Picasa suggests and uses many i386 packages, so I do not recommend installing it in a 64-bit OS. Picasa was not available for the Ubuntu distribution. |

apt-get install pidgin pidgin-libnotify -y   # Pidgin is a graphical multi-platform instant messaging client. It supports chat networks including AIM, Bonjour, Gadu-Gadu, Google Talk, Novell Groupwise, ICQ, IRC, Jabber/XMPP, MSN, MXit, MySpaceIM, SILC, SIMPLE, Sametime, XMPP, Yahoo! and Zephyr. *Pidgin* integrates with the system tray on Windows, GNOME 2, KDE 3, and KDE 4. It has been suggested by Kiplinger's magazine that Pidgin is not tracked by the NSA. (See: http://pidgin.im, http://www.pidgin.im/download/source)

apt-get install pinta -y   # Simple drawing/painting program which features: Adjustments (Auto Level, Black and White, Sepia, etc.), Effects (Motion blur, Glow, Wrap, etc.), Multiple layers, Unlimited undo/redo, Drawing tools (Paintbrush, Pencil, Shapts, etc). (See: http://pinta-project.com).

apt-get install rhythmbox-radio-browser -y   # Rhythmbox is a GNOME integrated music management system, organizer, audio player and ripper similar to Apple's iTunes, with support for iPods. (See: http://projects.gnome.org/rhythmbox).

| **NOTE** | Suggested packages to support rhythmbox-radio-browser:
apt-get install gnome-codec-install python-beaker python-mako-doc python-sqlalchemy python-pylibmc python-memcache python3-mako -y
and so on if other suggested packages are needed. Suggested packages rhythmbox-plugin-coherence and kstreamripper had no installation candidate. The gnome-codec_install contains a GTK+ based GStreamer codec. |

apt-get install scribus scribus-doc scribus-template -y   # Scribus is a large 70 MB install so only install if needed. Scribus is an open source desktop publishing (DTP) application capable of producing commercial grade output in PDF and Postscript as a professional publishing tool. It comes complete with page layout features, flexible formatting and typesetting, as well as the ability to prepare files for professional image setting equipment.   This application supports CMYK color, spot color, separations, and ICC color. (See: http://www.scribus.net, http://sourceforge.net/projects/scribus, http://en.wikipedia.org/wiki/Scribus)

| NOTE | SeaMonkey was unavailable in the Ubuntu, Mint GNOME-KDE and Debian repositories. It is an activily supported project and can be downloaded from the Sea Monkey project website. You can also add the http://ubuntuzilla.sourceforge.net repository, which has favorable ratings. Add the following to sources.list:

deb http://downloads.sourceforge.net/project/ubuntuzilla/mozilla/apt all main

or, run the following command if you are uncomfortable editing the file:
echo -e "\ndeb http://downloads.sourceforge.net/project/ubuntuzilla/mozilla/apt all main" \| tee -a /etc/apt/sources.list
Add the signing key to your keyring:
apt-key adv --recv-keys --keyserver keyserver.ubuntu.com C1289A29 |

```
# apt-get update
# apt-get install firefox-mozilla-build  thunderbird-mozilla-build  seamonkey-mozilla-
build
```

The Seamonkey Internet Suite is a set of Internet applications that contains a Mozilla based web browser, an HTML WYSIWYG editor, a Mail and News client, and an address book. (See: http://www.seamonkey-project.org) To install the downloaded software:
```
$ cd Downloads  &&  tar jxvf seamonkey-2.*.tar.bz2
```
Be sure to download the correct version for your OS. For example, if you attempt to run a 32-bit version of SeaMonkey in a 64-bit OS you may see: bash: ./seamonkey: No such file or directory. This means the application is looking for 32-bit dynamic libraries that don't exist.

```
# add-apt-repository ppa:savoirfairelinux && apt-get update
```
  # Only if SFLphone and its plugins are not in your flavor of Linux repositories.
```
# apt-get install sflphone-client-kde -y
```
   # For KDE desktops.
```
# apt-get install sflphone-gnome -y
```
   # For GNOME desktops. SFLphone is an excellent alternative to Microsoft-owned Skype for VOIP. It may not be monitored by the U.S. NSA as Skype is. This is a very active project, so this is a good VOIP solution. SFLphone states that they are an enterprise or individual solution that can handle several hundred calls a day. To use VOIP, you will need a webcam, speakers, and a microphone. For a video call, a high-speed Internet connection is also needed. (See: http://sflphone.org/download/stable-release)
```
# apt-get install sflphone-plugins -y
```
   # To install the GNOME-Evolution addressbook support.

```
# apt-get install shutter -y
```
   # Shutter is a GNOME feature-rich screenshot application used to take screenshots. (See: http://shutter-project.org)

> **NOTE**
>
> Suggested packages to support Shutter:
> ```
> # apt-get install libunicode-map8-perl libunicode-string-perl xml-twig-tools libnet-
> dbus-glib-perl -y
> ```

```
# apt-get install shotwell -y
```
   # Shotwell is a GNOME full featured* personal photo management application. You can import photos from a USB drive, disk or camera. Then organize and view them various ways, as well as export them to share with others. (See: http://yorba.org/shotwell)

```
# apt-get install skype -y
```
   # Skype is a free video call service that you can use to talk, send messages and share files with other Skype users. To use Skype, you will need a computer or mobile device with speakers and a microphone attached an optional webcam, and an Internet connection. For a video call you a high-speed Internet connection. Skype, if fairly up-to-date, supports Ubuntu with a 12.04 32bit releases of their product, but consider using SFLphone, the open source alternative to this proprietary and NSA spied upon software. (See: http://www.skype.com/intl/en-us/home)

| **WARNING**  | There are very serious privacy concerns with using Skype. Microsoft will not release information on how much data is being gathered about its 600 million users worldwide, or make a statement about the confidentiality of Skype conversations. If you read the Skype privacy statement, it leaves the door open for Microsoft to share just about everything you do using their tools. We also don't know if third parties intercept and listen in on Skype calls, but we now know that the U.S. government's NSA does so. Microsoft also needs to describe its relationship with Chinese mobile provider TOM Online and other third parties. The Electronic Frontier Foundation joined with other privacy groups and wrote a letter to Microsoft requesting to know how much data is shared with third parties, government agencies, and other organizations that Microsoft has not commented on. (See: http://www.skype.com/en/legal/privacy, https://www.eff.org/deeplinks/2013/01/its-time-transparency-reports-become-new-normal). |

apt-get install sound-juicer -y   # Sound Juicer is simple, clean and easy to use. Sound Juicer lets you extract the audio from CDs and convert them to audio files that your computer can play. This program also plays CDs and is simple, clean and easy to use. (See: http://www.burtonini.com/blog/computers/sound-juicer, http://library.gnome.org/users/sound-juicer/stable/sound-juicer.html)

| **NOTE** | Suggested packages to support gstreamer which sound-juicer uses:
apt-get install gstreamer0.10-plugins-bad gstreamer0.10-plugins-good gstreamer0.10-doc gstreamer0.10-plugins-bad-doc gstreamer0.10-plugins-good-doc -y |

Goto https://spideroak.com click on Downloads > under Linux OS 32 or 64 bit > click on Debian Based > select Save File > download spideroak_version_processor.deb. To install the package, type # cd ~sudoroot/Downloads && dpkg -i ./spideroak_version_processor.deb. This will enable the encrypted sharing of files between VMs and Windows over the cloud.

| WARNING | Stellarium renders 3D photo-realistic skies in real-time. It did not render the 3D graphics in VirtualBox Mint, and affected the 3D graphics. The menu to root was no longer available until the software was removed; it also did not work in a VirtualBox Ubuntu VM and had to be removed. (See: http://www.stellarium.org)
apt-get install stellarium -y # apt-get purge stellarium stellarium-data -y |

apt-get install synaptic -y   # Synaptic is a graphical package management program for the *apt* command line tool. It provides the same features as the apt-get command line utility with a GUI front-end based on Gtk+. (See: http://www.nongnu.org/synaptic)

| **NOTE** | Ubuntu suggested installing the dwww deborphan packages to support synaptic. Doing so will bring down the apache2 web server, which you probably do not want. Synaptic works fine without them. |

apt-get install sysinfo -y   # Sysinfo displays computer and system information. (See: https://sourceforge.net/projects/sysinfo)

apt-get install terminator -y   # Terminator is an alternate terminal manager to GNOME Terminal. *Terminator* is a cross-platform GPL terminal emulator with advanced features. It allows the user to arrange terminals in grids and manage multiple terminals in one window. Its features are more advanced and easier to use than the default terminals that come with most versions of Linux. It has a menu across the top that makes it customizable and easy to use with some added capabilities. The web page provides pre-built packages, which can be installed. (See: http://www.tenshu.net/p/terminator.html, http://software.jessies.org/terminator)

apt-get install thunderbird enigmail libdbusmenu-gtk4 -y   # Thunderbird is a full-featured* email client that is an excellent alternative to Windows Outlook or Live Mail. Enigmail is a security extension to Mozilla Thunderbird and Seamonkey that enables the user to send and receive signed and encrypted email. Thunderbird comes complete with easy email account setup, customizable options, spam filters, search tools, address book, phishing protection, privacy protection, and much more. (See: https://www.mozilla.org/en-US/thunderbird)

One calendar add-on to consider for Thunderbird is Thunderbird Lightning which integrates well with Thunderbird email. From the website, "Organize your schedule and life's important events in a calendar that's fully integrated with your Thunderbird or Seamonkey email. Manage multiple calendars, create your daily to do list, invite friends to events, and subscribe to public calendars. (See: https://www.mozilla.org/projects/calendar/lightning, https://addons.mozilla.org/en-US/thunderbird/addon/lightning)

Download and save the lightning--linux.xpi file to your hard disk > open up **Mozilla Thunderbird** and add the **Menu bar** to Thunderbird by right clicking at the top and check Menu bar > click on the **Tools** menu and select **Add-ons** > from the options button to the left of the add-on search field, select **Install Add-on From File...** > locate the downloaded add-on file, **Open** > click on **Install Now**, **Restart Now**.* The other option is to install Lightning from Thunderbird Add-ons collection.

apt-get install totem totem-mozilla -y   # Totem is a simple GNOME media player for the based on GStreamer. It features a playlist, a full-screen mode, seek and volume controls, as well as keyboard navigation. The *totem-mozilla* plugin will allow viewing movies in a Mozilla based browser with other codes and plugins installed. (See: http://www.gnome.org/projects/totem).

Ubuntu briefly ventured out into the cloud data music storage world. However, this marketplace proved too difficult for them to compete in. From the link below, "As of today, it will no longer be possible to purchase storage or music from the Ubuntu One store." (See: http://blog.canonical.com/2014/04/02/shutting-down-ubuntu-one-file-services)

apt-get install transmission transmission-cli -y   # Transmission is a cross-platform, fast, easy and free BitTorrent* Client. It boasts that is uses fewer resources than other clients. It features: native Mac, GTK+ and Qt GUI clients, remote control by Web and Terminal clients, Local Peer Discovery, Full encryption, DHT, uTP, PEX and Magnet Link support. The CLI package will install the command line version of Transmission. (See:

http://www.transmissionbt.com/,
http://en.wikipedia.org/wiki/Transmission_(BitTorrent_client))

apt-get install tree -y   # Tree is a tree-like directory listing program with dircolors support.

apt-get install tomboy tomboy-blogposter tasque -y   # Tomboy is a GNOME application which from the website "*is a desktop note-taking application for Linux, Unix, Windows, and Mac OS X. Simple and easy to use, but with potential to help you organize the ideas and information you deal with every day.*" It lets you organize your notes intelligently by allowing you to easily link ideas together easily with Wiki style interconnects. (See: http://projects.gnome.org/tomboy)

apt-get install unoconv -y   # Unoconv is a utility to convert between many documents and graphic formats supported by LibreOffice and OpenOffice. (See: http://dag.wieers.com/home-made/unoconv)

apt-get install unrar -y   # UnRAR Reference is a utility to extract and view the contents of archives created by the RAR archive tool. (See: http://www.rarlab.com/rar_add.htm)

apt-get install vlc videolan-doc browser-plugin-vlc -y   # VLC is a multimedia player and streamer. The project page for VLC (initially VideoLAN Client) describes VLC as a highly portable multimedia player for various audio and video formats, including MPEG-1, MPEG-2, MPEG-4, DivX, MP3, and OGG, as well as for Audio CDs, DVDs, VCDs, and other various streaming protocols. It also can be used as a server for unicast or multicast streams in IPv4 or IPv6 on a high-bandwidth network. The browser plugin adds support for formats to web browsers. (See: http://www.videolan.org/vlc, https://en.wikipedia.org/wiki/VLC_media_player)

apt-get install wdiff wdiff-doc dwdiff -y   # WDiff is a GUI front-end to to the command line tool *diff* for comparing text files. (See: http://www.gnu.org/software/wdiff)

apt-get install wine -y   # Wine is a compatibility layer for running Windows software on Linux. *Wine* allows unmodified Windows binaries to run on x86 and experimentally in x86_64 Linux OSs. It does this by translating Windows API calls into POSIX calls on demand. This allows Windows applications to be cleanly integrated into OSs like Linux, Mac OSX, BSD as well as other OSs. (See: http://www.winehq.org, http://wiki.winehq.org/Wine64)

NOTE

Wine brought down many i386 supporting packages. I don't recommend installing it from the default repositories in a 64-bit VM until the experiment 64-bit version is no longer experimental. The install of WINE also installed the Microsoft Fonts. If installing WINE in an i386 OS, consider adding the front-end PlayOnLinux. It permits easy installation of Windows Games and software in Linux.
apt-get install playonlinux
Suggested packages to support playonlinux:
apt-get install wx2.8-doc wx2.8-examples python-wxtools mksh pdksh editra
and so on, if other suggested packages are needed...

apt-get install xchat -y   # XChat is a GNOME, easy-to-use, graphical IRC Client for both Linux and Windows. It allows a user to join multiple IRC channels (chat rooms) at the same time, talk publicly, have private one-on-one conversations, etc. Even file transfers are possible. (See: http://www.xchat.org)

apt-get install vuze -y   # Vuze, previously known as Azureus, is a powerful multimedia BitTorrent* client for peer-to-peer file distribution. Vuze gives the user comprehensive entertainment search capabilities. Vuze comes with a 1080p Video Player, Device Playback (drag-and-drop to iPad, iPod, iPhone, Xbox, PS3 and TIVO), DVD Video and Data burner. (See: https://www.vuze.com, https://en.wikipedia.org/wiki/Vuze, http://azureus.sourceforge.net)

NOTE	Other suggested packages for Mint to support Vuze: # apt-get install liblog4j1.2-java-gcj libgnumail-java libmx4j-java libswt-gtk-3-java-gcj Other suggested packages for Ubuntu to support Vuze: # apt-get install -y liblog4j1.2-java-gcj libgnumail-java libmx4j-java libswt-gtk-3-java-gcj libbcel-java-doc libgcj12-dbg libgcj12-awt libgnumail-java-doc libservlet2.4-java jython libjetty-java libhessian-java

apt-get install wireshark wireshark-doc -y   # Wireshark is a network protocol and traffic analyzer. It lets you capture and interactively browse the traffic running on a computer network to troubleshoot network issues. (See: http://www.wireshark.org, https://en.wikipedia.org/wiki/Wireshark)

	Suggested packages to support Wireshark in Mint and Ubuntu: # apt-get install libcap-dev snmp-mibs-downloader manpages-dev -y

apt-get install xmms2 gxmms2 -y   # XMMS is an audio (Ogg Vorbis, CDs) player for the X Window System with an interface similar to Winamp's. XMMS supports playlists and streaming content and has a configurable interface as well. It is an audio framework, not a general multimedia player, and it runs a daemon independent of any graphics output. The supported audio formats are expandable via plugins. (See: http://wejp.k.vu/projects/xmms2, http://xmms2.org/wiki/Main_Page)

NOTE	To use XMMS2 is not as simple as point and click. The GUI front-end is primitive; the other media players may be a better choice but it is popular.

apt-get install zim -y   # Zim is a graphical text editor used to maintain a collection of Wiki pages. All data is stored in plain text files with Wiki formatting. Zim features the following: keeps an archive of notes, takes notes during meeting or lectures, organizes task lists, drafts blog entries and emails, as well as brainstorming. (See: http://zim-wiki.org)

Skip back to BackTrack/Kali/Mint/Ubuntu-Applying Software Updates to update and upgrade any package dependencies that may still be needed, and clean up the VM OS.

Fedora -- General Description

Fedora is another flavor of Linux that claims they have the "best, latest, and most robust" collection of free and open source software available. The project is supported by Red Hat and other donors. Fedora, the RPM based solution, is very popular, user-friendly, and comes packed with excellent solutions for engineers and scientists. Running Fedora would be an excellent way to introduce your family members or employees to a RPM solution before you decide to purchase Enterprise Linux from https://www.redhat.com. Information about Fedora can be found in many places; https://fedoraproject.org, https://fedoraproject.org/wiki/FAQ and https://en.wikipedia.org/wiki/Fedora_operating_system are a few of the sites to visit to learn about Fedora.

Consider using Fedora KDE desktop instead of the Fedora GNOME desktop. If you are a Windows 7 user, you might find it more intuitive and user-friendly. VirtualBox will allow you to choose the desktop you want during installation. If your computer is light on resources XFCE might be a better choice. Fedora is a high-quality OS for your selection as a General Purpose VM since it comes with a wide range of additional applications, tools and utilities for you to choose from for development, science, and education, some of which are not available in the other flavors of Linux.

WARNING	Linux Mint adopted the strategy of offering an optimized version of their OS prepackaged for each type of desktop. During the install of Fedora 17 in VirtualBox, you could choose both the GNOME and KDE desktops, but doing so could destabilize the VM as you configured it and added software. Later Fedora versions only allow you to pick a single desktop to install, which is wise. If you want to experiment with multiple desktops, create a separate VM for each one.

After following the VirtualBox directions to add the Guest Additions, the 3D acceleration of GNOME 3 was fairly stable even though VirtualBox states that 3D acceleration contains experimental hardware 3D support through OpenGL nad Direct 8/9 interfaces.

Fedora 18 and above allows terminal programs to use enhanced color capabilities, improved discovery of MDNS printers and devices, updates the GNOME desktop to the 3.6 release, and includes several language and programming environment updates. They also includes the new Samba 4 release that includes the first free and open source implementation for Active Directory protocols. For SBs there are multiple enhancements to storage management and new tools for storage areas network (SAN) and network-attached storage (NAS), and much more. Fedora releases are maintained until one month after the next two releases. For example, Fedora 21 was released 9 December, 2014 and will be maintained until one month after the release of Fedora 23. (See: https://fedoraproject.org/wiki/Changes, https://fedoraproject.org/wiki/Releases/21/FeatureList, https://fedoraproject.org/wiki/Fedora_Release_Life_Cycle, https://fedoraproject.org/wiki/End_of_life, https://fedoraproject.org/wiki/Releases/20/ChangeSet, https://fedoraproject.org/wiki/Releases/20/Schedule)

Fedora -- Install in VirtualBox & VMware Player

Go to https://fedoraproject.org/en/get-fedora and download the Fedora DVD you want to install. When done, use the utilities we downloaded and installed in Chapter 5 to check the SHA256 Hash or follow the Linux directions on Fedora's website to verify the checksum. The SHA256 sums are found at https://fedoraproject.org/en/verify. *In Windows click on Start > Run... > type cmd > type cd \Downloads\Linux\Fedora > type fsum -sha256 Fedora-Server-DVD-i386-21.iso; in Linux type # sha256sum ISOFileName > you should see:*

- Fedora-20-i386-DVD: 284ea30d dd50db1b 30cd5cd9 fae7495d ad8714ef 1e4428d6 9a8c8ce8 0e03b6a9
- Fedora-20-x86_64-DVD: f2eeed51 02b8890e 9e6f4b90 53717fe7 3031e699 c4b76dc7 028749ab 66e7f917
- Fedora-Live-Workstation-x86_64-21-5.iso: 4b8418fa 846f7dd0 0e982f39 51853e1a 4874a1fe 023415ae 27a5ee31 3fc98998
- Fedora-Server-DVD-i386-21.iso: 85e50a8a 93899652 2bf1605b 3578a2d6 680362c1 aa963d05 60d59c2e 4fc795ef
- Fedora-Server-DVD-x86_64-21.iso: a6a2e83b b409d6b8 ee3072ad 07faac0a 54d79c9e cbe3a40a f91b773e 2d843d8e
- Fedora-Live-KDE-i686-21-5.iso: 3a16ee37 c9795b60 04f31d29 4af28591 cea05ca9 7c92699f a725eec2 352fac71
- Fedora-Live-KDE-x86_64-21-5.iso: 8459bca9 e1005a0b b5ccba37 7f2908ed a75e3ec8 9ae87f2a 4a7b520f 673f3b02

If you downloaded Fedora to a Linux OS, you can be even more secure by using the following procedure to verify the checksum against the key. This procedure was taken and tweaked from the web link:

1. Download or copy the Fedora ISO file into a directory in an existing Fedora installation.
2. Go to https://getfedora.org and click on the distribution you are going to verify. Click on Download now, Download > click on the Validate! button > this will bring up the checksum and signature beginning with -----BEGIN PGP SIGNED MESSAGE----- which will need to be cut and pasted into a checksum file in the same directory as the ISO image file. Name the file after the ISO image file (e.g. Fedora-Live-Workstation-x86_64-21-5-CHECKSUM).
3. Import Fedora's GPG keys:

```
$ curl https://fedoraproject.org/static/fedora.gpg | gpg --import
gpg: directory `/home/suroot/.gnupg' created
gpg: new configuration file `/home/suroot/.gnupg/gpg.conf' created
gpg: WARNING: options in `/home/suroot/.gnupg/gpg.conf' are not yet active during
this run
gpg: keyring `/home/suroot/.gnupg/secring.gpg' created
gpg: keyring `/home/suroot/.gnupg/pubring.gpg' created
  % Total    % Received % Xferd  Average Speed   Time    Time     Time  Current
                                 Dload  Upload   Total   Spent    Left  Speed
100 27858  100 27858    0     0  35974      0 --:--:-- --:--:-- --:--:-- 35945
gpg: /home/suroot/.gnupg/trustdb.gpg: trustdb created
```

```
gpg: key 3AD31D0B: public key "Fedora-SPARC (15) <fedora@fedoraproject.org>" imported
gpg: key FB4B18E6: public key "Fedora (19) <fedora@fedoraproject.org>" imported
gpg: key BA094068: public key "Fedora Secondary (19) <fedora@fedoraproject.org>"
imported
gpg: key 246110C1: public key "Fedora (20) <fedora@fedoraproject.org>" imported
gpg: key EFE550F5: public key "Fedora Secondary (20) <fedora@fedoraproject.org>"
imported
gpg: key 95A43F54: public key "Fedora (21) <fedora@fedoraproject.org>" imported
gpg: key A0A7BADB: public key "Fedora Secondary (21) <fedora@fedoraproject.org>"
imported
gpg: key 8E1431D5: public key "Fedora (22) <fedora@fedoraproject.org>" imported
gpg: key A29CB19C: public key "Fedora Secondary (22) <fedora@fedoraproject.org>"
imported
gpg: key 0608B895: public key "EPEL (6) <epel@fedoraproject.org>" imported
gpg: key 352C64E5: public key "Fedora EPEL (7) <epel@fedoraproject.org>" imported
gpg: Total number processed: 11
gpg:                 imported: 11   (RSA: 11)
```

4. Verify that the CHECKSUM file is valid:
   $ gpg --verify-files *-CHECKSUM

```
gpg: Signature made Fri 05 Dec 2014 04:47:31 PM EST using RSA key ID 95A43F54
gpg: Good signature from "Fedora (21) <fedora@fedoraproject.org>"
gpg: WARNING: This key is not certified with a trusted signature!
gpg:           There is no indication that the signature belongs to the owner.
Primary key fingerprint: 6596 B8FB ABDA 5227 A9C5  B59E 89AD 4E87 95A4 3F54
```

5. Check to make sure the ISO file is valid:
   $ sha256sum -c *-CHECKSUM

```
Fedora-20-x86_64-DVD.iso: OK
```

The installation of Fedora in VirtualBox and VMware Player are different. VMware Player actually installs the OS, whereas VirtualBox allows you to perform the OS installation steps.

To install Fedora in Parallels refer back to _Parallels-Creating Virtual Guest Operating Systems_, in VMware Player refer back to _VMware Player-Creating Virtual Guest Operating Systems)_, in VirtualBox refer back to _VirtualBox-Creating Virtual Guest Operating Systems_. After the install you may be prompted to "Disconnect or override a CD-ROM lock > click on _Yes_.

Virtual Machine technology keeps evolving and over the years of writing this book I worked many weeks doing research and experimentation to discover workarounds to get virtual OSs installed. Now things are as simple as just installing the Linux OS in a VM, which will install most times without any complex problems to solve. If a new release of Linux will not install correctly in a VM solution, simply wait for the next release of your chosen virtual solution and see if that fixes the problem. As new releases of VMware Player and Fedora come out you may find varied success with the Easy Install of VMware Tools into the OS. If the tools did not install, follow the manual installation directions for VMware Tools to get the tools installed after applying updates. If Fedora does not boot up to the user sign-in screen, try unchecking Accelerate 3D graphics in the VM's Display settings. VMware Player now installs Fedora 20 and 21 without a hitch, and VMware Tools now installs automatically in Fedora OSs.

Fedora -- Continued Install after Reboot in VirtualBox & VMware Player

For whatever reason, Fedora drastically changed and reduced the installation options that we can use to configure their OS in Fedora 18 and later. The installation, after selecting language and keyboard, displayed the INSTALLATION SUMMARY screen. Clicking on the options that are available on the screen provided very few ways to customize the OS installation. For example, you could no longer do things like add additional repositories or load up the OS with many applications, utilities, and tools, except through some of the general selection options. These things have to be done after installing the operating system, which we will discuss how to do. This was a terrible mistake by Fedora developers and another "what were they thinking about" moment. Fedora also limits your desktop selection to only one desktop, which is actually a good thing, because having multiple desktops in the same VM could destabilize it. Fedora 21 limited things even more so the installation steps did not even need to be covered. Another good thing Fedora did was tailor the packages you can install for each desktop to whatever is available for that particular desktop. Before Fedora 18, users could combine desktops such as GNOME and KDE during the install process. But this generally did not work well because something written for GNOME was often not a good fit for KDE desktop and vice-versa.

On the <u>Welcome to Fedora 21</u> screen click on <u>Install to Hard Drive</u> button > on the <u>Welcome to Fedora 21.</u> screen, select your language, <u>Continue</u> > *on the **INSTALLATION SUMMARY** screen set your **LOCALIZATION**, in the upper right turn off **Network Time** unless you plan to setup Fedora to poll a NTP server, click on **Done** upper left > software selection was no longer possible > click on **Network & Hostname** and skip back to **Virtual Machine Name Standardization** change the VM hostname, **Begin Installation**.*

The install of Fedora 20 in VirtualBox selected <u>Test this media and Install Fedora</u> by default. The first time that you build the VM, you should leave this option selected; for future installs just select <u>Install Fedora</u>. *When Fedora boots up to the **<u>Welcome to Fedora 20</u>** screen, select your language; in 19 consider checking the **<u>Set keyboard to default layout for select language</u>** at the bottom, **<u>Continue</u>** > on the **INSTALLATION SUMMARY** screen set your **LOCALIZATION**, in the upper right turn off **<u>Network Time</u>** unless you plan to setup Fedora to poll a NTP server, click on **<u>Done</u>** upper left > under **SOFTWARE** click on SOFTWARE SELECTION and select the other software you want to install (e.g. **C Development Tools and Libraries**, **Development Tools**, **Epiphany Web Browser**, **Extra games for the GNOME Desktop**, **LibreOffice**), click on the **<u>Done</u>** button upper left > click on **NETWORK CONFIGURATION**, at the bottom for hostname refer back to <u>Virtual Machine Name Standardization</u>, if you have a special network configuration click on the **Configure...** button lower right, **<u>Done</u>** upper left, **Begin Installation**.*

*In 19, 20, and 21 select lower right > under **<u>USER SETTINGS</u>** click on **<u>ROOT PASSWORD</u>** to set the password, **<u>Done</u>** > click on **<u>USER CREATION</u>** and create user 'suroot', check **<u>Make this user administrator</u>** > when the install completes click on the **<u>Reboot</u>** button or **<u>Finish configuration</u>** lower right >.* In versions of VirtualBox prior to 4.3.6 and before Fedora 20, the reboot would bring up the installation screen and ask you to install the operating system all over again. To fix this you needed to power off the VM before the installation could begin again. If you encounter this, refer back to VirtualBox-Creating Virtual Guest Operating Systems for the work around to this problem.

After reboot there are a few more steps to finish installing Fedora 19, 20 and 21, which are almost identical, *on the __Welcome__ screen select your language, __Next__ > on the __Input Sources__ screen select you input source, __Next__ > on the __Online Accounts__ screen select __Add a cloud account__ and/or __Next__ > click on the __Start using Fedora__.*

Fedora 17 -- Historical Reference About Continued Install after Reboot in Oracle VirtualBox

The following reference is included in the hope that the Fedora team will someday consider reverting back to the old installation option which was far superior to the way later releases install. *Upon boot up of the VM OS to the installation screen, click on __Install or upgrade Fedora__, in Fedora 16 and below click on __Skip__ (we already verified the sum on the ISO file) > select your language, __Next__ > select the appropriate keyboard (e.g. __U.S. English__), __Next__ > leave the default __Basic Storage Devices__ ticked, __Next__ > on the __Storage Device Warning__ dialog select the __Yes, discard any data__ button > for hostname refer back to __Virtual Machine Name Standardization__. If you have a special network configuration, click on the __Configure Network__ button lower left, __Next__ > select the nearest large city in your time zone, __Next__ > for Password, enter something simple, when the __Weak Password__ dialog appears, click on the __Use Anyway__ button > for the installation type tick __Use All Space__, and in Fedora 15 and before at bottom check __Review and modify partitioning layout__, __Next__ > in later versions of Fedora the default was OK for VMs, __Next__.*

When the __Format Warning__ dialog appears after either of the steps above, click on the __Format__ button > when the __Confirm__ dialog appears click on the __Write Changes to Disk__ button > on the next screen leave __Install boot loader on /dev/sda__ checked, __Next__ > add additional repositories in Fedora 16 by checking __Fedora 16-x86 64__ > on the __Select network interface__ dialog select your network interface, click on the __OK__ button > when the __Network Connections__ dialog appears select __System p2p1__, Close > you should see a __Retrieving install information for Fedora-16-x86 64__ window appear. When the retrieval is done click on __Fedora 16 - x86 64 - Updates__ > on the __Select network Interface__ dialog click on the __OK__ button > in Fedora 17 checking the __Fedora 17-x86 64__ repository did not result in the network dialog appearing > click on the __Add additional software repositories__ button at the bottom and add the following repositories:

Repository name: <u>RPM Fusion Free</u> > Repository Type: <u>HTTP/FTP</u> > Repository URL > <u>http://mirrors.rpmfusion.org/free/fedora/16/i386</u> or <u>http://mirrors.rpmfusion.org/free/fedora/16/x86 64</u>. Check <u>URL is a mirror list</u> > <u>OK</u>. <u>http://mirrors.rpmfusion.org/free/fedora/17/i386</u> or <u>http://mirrors.rpmfusion.org/free/fedora/17/x86 64</u>. Check <u>URL is a mirror list</u> > <u>OK</u>	**Add Repository** Please provide the configuration information for this software repository. Repository name: RPM Fusion Free Repository type: HTTP/FTP Repository URL http://mirrors.rpmfusion.org/free/fedora/16/x86_64 ☑ URL is a mirror list ☐ Configure proxy Proxy URL (host:port) Proxy username Proxy password Cancel OK
Repository name: <u>RPM Fusion NonFree</u> > Repository Type: <u>HTTP/FTP</u> > Repository URL > <u>http://mirrors.rpmfusion.org/nonfree/fedora/16/i386</u> or <u>http://mirrors.rpmfusion.org/nonfree/fedora/16/x86 64</u>. Check <u>URL is a mirror list</u> > <u>OK</u>. <u>http://mirrors.rpmfusion.org/nonfree/fedora/17/i386</u> or <u>http://mirrors.rpmfusion.org/nonfree/fedora/17/x86 64</u>. Check <u>URL is a mirror list</u> > <u>OK</u>.	**Add Repository** Please provide the configuration information for this software repository. Repository name: RPM Fusion Nonfree Repository type: HTTP/FTP Repository URL p://mirrors.rpmfusion.org/nonfree/fedora/16/x86_64 ☑ URL is a mirror list ☐ Configure proxy Proxy URL (host:port) Proxy username Proxy password Cancel OK

*Tick the <u>**Customize Now**</u> button at the bottom and select <u>**Next**</u> to add additional software > under <u>**Desktop Environments**</u> consider using the <u>**Xfce**</u> or the <u>**KDE Software Compilation**</u> desktops as an alternative to GNOME (remember, if you install more than one desktop it can destabilize the VM). Under <u>**Applications**</u> select everything > under <u>**Base System**</u> select <u>**System Tools**</u> > under <u>**Content**</u> select <u>**Books and Guides**</u> > and whatever else you want for each selection on the left > for each category (Applications, Development, etc.) on the left pane > click on the <u>**Optional packages**</u> button at the bottom and add any other useful GNOME packages you may want:*

Desktop Environments	alacarte	Menu editor for GNOME
Desktop Environments	byzanz	A desktop recorder
Desktop Environments	gedit-plugins	Plugins for gedit
Desktop Environments	gnome-schedule	Graphical interface to *crontab* and the *at* command
Desktop Environments	gnote	Note-taking application
Desktop Environments	gonvert	Units conversion utility
Desktop Environments	nautilus-actions	Nautilus extension for customizing the context menu
Desktop Environments	nautilus-open-terminal	Nautilus extension for an open terminal shortcut
Desktop Environments	nautilus-search-tool	Nautilus extension to have "search files" on the popup menu

Desktop Environments	tomboy	Note-taking application
Base System	ntop	Network traffic probe similar to UNIX top command

Click on _Next_, which begins the installation > when done the _Congratulations..._ screen appears, select _Reboot_.

Installing KDE, LXDE and Xfce are other optional GUIs you can try if you don't like GNOME. Depending on the software you attempt to install, you may have to add more disk space if you are using fixed size VMs for performance. With the added GUIs and many of the packages selected, 20 GB was not enough space for the VM. Consider using multiple VMs with only one desktop installed for added stability (already discussed).

NOTE	Using the KDE, LXDE or Xfce are good GUI alternatives to the GNOME 3. You might prefer using the KDE desktop because of their support for adding icons and neat gadgets to the desktop. If your computer is light on powerful hardware or is an older laptop, you might want to consider using the "Lightweight X11 Desktop Environment" (LXDE), which is designed to be a fast-performing and energy-saving environment. (See: http://lxde.org, http://wiki.lxde.org/en/Category:LXDE, http://wiki.lxde.org/en/Fedora)

In Fedora 18/17 on the _Date and Time_ screen, in a VM do NOT check _Synchronize date and time over the network_, _Finish or Forward_ > under _Hardware Profile_ check your settings and click on _Finish_ > In Fedora 17 when the _Congratulations..._ screen appears, click on the _Reboot_, button lower right > when the dialog appears to reconsider sending your profile, it is recommended you select the _No, do not send_ button > this will bring up the login screen to login as 'suroot'.

NOTE	Windows 7 automatically synchronizes its clock with time.windows.com, so there is no need to have Fedora synchronizing to an external NTP server. Most updates were applied automatically, if you had added the repositories. However, be sure to run a # yum update to apply any of the updates that may have been missed during the installation.

In Fedora 17, I encountered the error, "Sorry! The system printing service doesn't seem to be available." This meant that the CUPS printer server was not installed. # yum install cups fixed this problem. Reboot the VM and add your printer.

Fedora -- General VM Configuration, Repository Setup, Applying Updates

The Yellowdog Updater Modified (YUM) tool is an interactive, automated update program that can be used for maintaining systems using the _RedHat Package Manager_ (RPM). The installation of most new programs can be performed by RPM (unless you compile it yourself). If life is good, then all you have to do is download the appropriate _.rpm_ file for the application you wish to install, and use RPM to install it on the system. The advantage of RPM (yes, it is an advantage!) is that it automatically checks for dependencies — libraries and other files that the program needs — before actually allowing you install it. RPM tells you that there is a dependency missing and refuses to install the program. YUM acts as a front-end to RPM by automatically downloading all of the necessary dependencies for you (assuming it can find them) and then installs each of the dependencies in the correct order, followed by your desired program. YUM does this by looking for programs and dependencies within central repositories (or through repository mirrors), such as Fedora Extras. Secondary repository sources can be added by creating an appropriate .repo file in **/etc/yum.repos.d**. The "Fedora 21 System Administrators Guide" section on "Configuring Yum and Yum Repositories" is a good Yum reference. (See: https://docs.fedoraproject.org/en-US/Fedora/21/html-single/System_Administrators_Guide/index.html#sec-Configuring_Yum_and_Yum_Repositories, http://www.rpm.org)

To adjust the System Settings add the <u>Settings</u> icon to the favorites menu > in the search box type <u>settings</u> > when the <u>Settings</u> icon appears, drag and drop it to the favorites menu on the left. Open up the System Settings and begin customizing Fedora. Note: after adjusting any settings *click on the <u>All Settings</u> button in the upper left to display all the GUI settings icons you can adjust to customize your computer setup.*

Adjust the sound settings by clicking on the sound icon in the upper right on the <u>Activities</u> bar and drag the volume to your desired volume > with the icon menu expanded click on <u>Sound Settings</u> to adjust other sound settings. The Sound dialog can also be brought up by clicking on the <u>Settings</u> icon > under <u>Hardware</u> click on the <u>Sound</u> icon. With the <u>Sound Effects</u> tab selected drag the <u>Output volume:</u> bar on top to the right to turn up the sound > do the same for the <u>Alert volume</u> > click on the <u>Input</u> tab and drag the <u>Input volume</u> to your desired level.

In Fedora 17/18 under <u>Personal</u> click on <u>Brightness and Lock</u> icon > adjust the <u>Turn screen off when inactive for:</u> and <u>Lock screen after:</u> settings. In Fedora 19/20 the <u>Brightness and Lock</u> icon was no longer available and the only option found was under <u>Personal</u> click on <u>Privacy</u> and turn off <u>Screen Lock</u> > click on <u>Usage & History</u> and <u>Purge Trash & Temporary Files</u> to turn these <u>On</u> and adjust the settings accordingly.

You can use CUPS by using your browser to open the link http://localhost:631 to add your printer to the VM. Fedora offers a system tool that can sometimes be easier to use. *Click on <u>Activities</u> > click on the <u>Settings</u> icon > under <u>Hardware</u> click on the <u>Printers</u> icon > if logged in as 'suroot' on the upper right click on the <u>Unlock</u> button and <u>Authenticate</u> with the 'root' password > click on the <u>Add New Printer</u> button in the center > the <u>Add a New Printer</u> dialog will appear and search for your printer > if the tool does not find your printer enter the IP address of your printer, <u>Add</u> > when <u>Add a New Printer</u> finds your printer click on <u>Add</u>, hopefully your printer will be found and added .*

In Fedora 17, I received the error message "FirewallD is not running. Network printer detection needs services mdns, ipp, ipp-client and samba-client enabled on firewall."
If you do see the error on the right, you can run # system-config-firewall to adjust your firewall settings.

- mDNS is the Multicast DNS service.
- ipp is the Network Printing Server
- ipp-client is the Network Printing Client

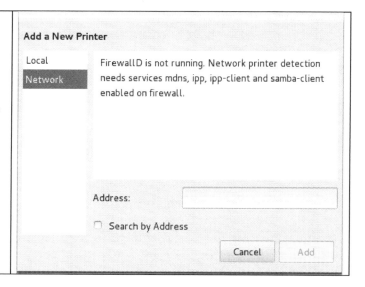

If the steps above did not work, you can use the *system configure printer* utility by installing it # yum install system-config-printer and then follow the procedure below:

*Open a terminal window and type # **system-config-printer** > click on the **Add** button > when the **Adjust Firewall** dialog appears, click on the **Adjust Firewall** button to:*

- *Allow all incoming IPP Browse packets*
- *Allow all incoming mDNS traffic*

*Under **Select Device** on the left, expand the **Network Printer** menu and select **Find Network Printer** > next to **Host:** type in the IP address of your Network Printer and, with the printer on, click on the **Find** button to the right, the **Port** text box should appear and be populated with **Port number: 9100**, which later changes to **Queue: PASSTHRU**, **Forward**. When the **Choose Driver** dialog appears select your print driver (or the **Generic (recommended))** driver, **Forward** > on the next screen leave PostScript (recommend) selected, **Forward** > on the **Describe Printer** screen enter a descriptive name for the printer, **Apply**.*

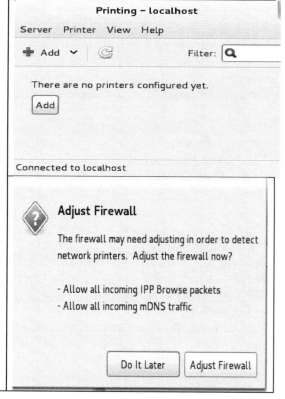

If security is not a concern, when you are done applying updates, configuring, and adding software to your VM, *you can enable the **Automatic Login** for a user by clicking on **System Settings** or **Settings** icon > under **System** select the **User Accounts** icon > click on the*

***Unlock** button on the upper right > under **Login Options** enable **Automatic Login**.* The next time you boot up you won't be prompted to enter a password.

In a Fedora 17, VirtualBox install, check to make sure the install updated all of the repositories correctly. In later versions of Fedora we have to manually add the RPM Fusion repositories that provide many software extras that the Fedora Project or Red Hat can't ship due to license concerns. In VMware Player the repositories could not be added during OS installation. In the Fedora of the past, there were a few other repositories such as Dribble, Freshrpms, and Livna but in newer versions of Fedora, those repositories were merged with RPM Fusion. (See: http://rpmfusion.org) ***In Fedora 17 you can also use the GUI to add the repositories after installation by clicking on Activities > select Applications > arrow down to select Other > click on the Software Settings icon > when the Software Update Preferences window appears click on the Software Sources tab > check the repositories you wish to add to your VM.*** In later Fedora versions, the Settings icon added to the Activities bar above did not offer an option to set up the RPMFusion repository, which is another mistake.

Fedora -- Using the Command Line to Add the RPM Fusion Repository

You also may find it easier to use the command line to do so after the VM has been created. The RPM website does not have detailed directions as to how to download the GPG keys to verify this important repository. Their directions recommend installing this repository without key verification, which is a security risk. Installing the keys will ensure that the packages you install came from RPM Fusion and not from another mirror or malicious website.

*To verify the RPM Fusion repositories surf to **http://rpmfusion.org/keys** > click on **Download** link next to the PGP key for your version of Fedora, which will display the attachment screen > click on **get** next to your version of Fedora and save the free and nonfree key files to the VM > become root and type the following:*

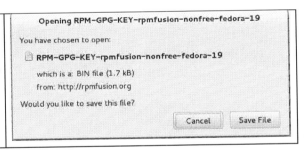

```
$ cd Downloads && su  or,  cd ~suroot/Downloads
# rpm --import ./RPM-GPG-KEY-rpmfusion-free-fedora-20
# rpm --import ./RPM-GPG-KEY-rpmfusion-nonfree-fedora-20
# yum update -y
```

Perform the following steps to enable access to both the free and nonfree repositories in Fedora (See: http://rpmfusion.org/Configuration):

```
# yum localinstall http://download1.rpmfusion.org/free/fedora/rpmfusion-free-release-$(rpm -E %fedora).noarch.rpm http://download1.rpmfusion.org/nonfree/fedora/rpmfusion-nonfree-release-$(rpm -E %fedora).noarch.rpm -y
# yum update -y
```

Prior to the generic command above the commands below could be used:

```
# yum localinstall http://download1.rpmfusion.org/free/fedora/rpmfusion-free-release-
18.noarch.rpm  http://download1.rpmfusion.org/nonfree/fedora/rpmfusion-nonfree-release-
18.noarch.rpm

# yum localinstall http://download1.rpmfusion.org/free/fedora/rpmfusion-free-release-
17.noarch.rpm  http://download1.rpmfusion.org/nonfree/fedora/rpmfusion-nonfree-release-
17.noarch.rpm

# yum localinstall http://download1.rpmfusion.org/free/fedora/rpmfusion-free-release-
16.noarch.rpm  http://download1.rpmfusion.org/nonfree/fedora/rpmfusion-nonfree-release-
16.noarch.rpm
```

I also found the following recommended procedure, which I don't recommend because of the key verification issue. I only list this as another option to consider:

```
# yum -y localinstall --nogpgcheck http://download1.rpmfusion.org/free/fedora/rpmfusion-
free-release-stable.noarch.rpm http://download1.rpmfusion.org/nonfree/fedora/rpmfusion-
nonfree-release-stable.noarch.rpm
```

Reference http://fedorasolved.org/post-install-solutions/yum-config for this dated 2011 alternative method to add the Fedora repositories:

```
# rpm -Uvh http://download1.rpmfusion.org/free/fedora/rpmfusion-free-release-
stable.noarch.rpm
# rpm -Uvh http://download1.rpmfusion.org/nonfree/fedora/rpmfusion-nonfree-release-
stable.noarch.rpm
# rpm -Uvh http://rpm.livna.org/livna-release.rpm
```

Make sure all of the new repositories are present, # cd /etc/yum.repos.d && ls, then apply all updates, if the updates repository was not selected during installation, by doing the following:

```
$ su -
# yum check-update      # To see what updates are available
# yum list updates     # Display a list of updated software if interested
# yum update -y && shutdown -r now     # Download  and install all updates
# yum upgrade && shutdown -r now    # Make sure system is fully up-to-date
# yum clean all    # Cleanup expire-cache, packages, headers, metadata*, dbcache rpmdb,
plugins
```

Fedora's default desktop environment is GNOME 3, which functions best with hardware acceleration. You may want to try alternative desktops if you have older graphics hardware or are having performance issues with LLVMpipe driver.

NOTE	In VirtualBox, another desktop such as Cinnamon, KDE, MATE, etc. can be specified during installation of the OS. With VMware Player, the KDE desktop can be added after the OS has been installed. The KDE desktop should be considered a welcome

alternative to GNOME 3. But now, there are separate releases in the various desktops for additional VMs, which may be a better solution. (See: https://fedoraproject.org/wiki/KDE)

```
# yum install @kde-desktop or yum groupinstall kde-desktop or yum groupinstall "KDE Plasma Workspaces"
# yum install -y switchdesk
# yum install -y system-switch-displaymanager
# system-switch-displaymanager kdm
# yum grouplist -v hidden | grep desktop      # To view available desktops.
# yum install @mate-desktop-environment     # To install MATE desktop
# yum install yumex -y     # Yum extender, is a graphical user interface (GUI) for
```
yum. Sometimes we need to browse through all of the programs that are present in a repository or to narrow down the list of programs by performing a search, Yumex allows you to do so.
```
$ yumex -n # Will allow you to view, enable and disable repositories as user 'suroot'.
```

Fedora – Guided Steps to Set Up Your OS

1. VMware Tools is installed automatically in Fedora. The procedure to install/reinstall the tools is well documented by VMware Player. Nonetheless, this book attempts to streamline those directions a bit. The tools can be installed or upgraded by referring back to VMware Player-Manual Installation of VMware Tools.
2. VirtualBox Guest Additions does not come preinstalled in Fedora by default. If you want to make sure you are at the latest version, or to reinstall them, skip back to VirtualBox -- Installing the VirtualBox Guest Additions to reinstall the software.   To fix this, refer back to Fedora -- VirtualBox Guest Additions.
3. If you decide to use Fedora KDE, refer down to KDE Desktop-Fedora-Mint-openSUSE General Configuration & Setup.
4. The Fedora .bashrc file was not very user-friendly, but we can tweak a few things. Refer back to Terminal Window -- Customizing the Linux Command Line to Make Life Easy to customize the terminal window. This will make the command line experience easier and more productive for all VM users.
5. Refer back to Firefox -- Setup & Hardening your Browser Security to customize Firefox.
6. Refer down to Fedora -- Flash Player Installation and Configuration to install a flash player.
7. Skip down to Adding Fonts to Linux.
8. If using GNOME, skip down to GNOME Desktop -- Fedora -- Mint General Configuration & Setup, if using the KDE desktop, skip down to KDE Desktop -- Fedora -- Mint-openSUSE General Configuration & Setup.
9. Refer down to Fedora -- Installing Additional Applications, Tools & Utilities to install all the tools, utilities and applications you may need in your VM.
10. If you are going to have multiple user accounts, or just want to run the VM as less privileged user than 'suroot' or 'sudoroot', refer down to Adding Less Privileged User IDs for Specific Purposes to Linux.
11. Skip down to Tor Bundle -- Install & Setup in any Linux OS as a Regular User to enable the VM for convenient and anonymous surfing (covered in the next chapter).

Fedora -- Flash Player Installation and Configuration

Because of licensing, Fedora does not come with a flash player preinstalled. Before you install the proprietary Adobe Flash player and plugin for Firefox, give the open source https://www.gnu.org/software/gnash solution a chance. It renders YouTube videos just fine, without the licensing concerns, as well as supports an impressive list of codecs. Adobe Flash has had many issues with security and privacy. Visit the web page https://en.wikipedia.org/wiki/Adobe_Flash and search for Flash client security to read about these issues. If you find Gnash adequate, the open source developers would appreciate a donation!

WARNING	If this Fedora VM is being used for anonymous web surfing Tor and others recommend against installing a Flash Player in a browser.

NOTE 	The web page https://fedoraproject.org/wiki/Flash also includes the procedure for using the open source flash player. (See: https://www.gnu.org/software/gnash) If you did not install Adobe Flash, Gnash will work as a desktop player, and as a plugin for Mozilla and Konqueror browsers. Fedora comes with the nspluginwrapper installed. The procedure has us uninstall the nspluginwrapper that is used to push plug-ins out-of-process. From http://nspluginwrapper.org/why.html, the reason to uninstall NSPluginwrapper is that modern browsers do a better job of supporting out-of-process plugins, and nspluginwrapper will add unnecessary overhead.

```
# yum install firefox -y     # Already installed in Fedora GNOME
# yum remove nspluginwrapper -y     # Not needed in Fedora GNOME
# yum install gnash gnash-plugin -y   # To install in Fedora GNOME and GNOME browsers
# yum install -k gnash-klash     # To install in KDE desktop Konqueror web browser
```

You can also use the proprietary Adobe Flash Player, "*Adobe Flash Player is a cross-platform, browser-based application runtime that provides uncompromised viewing of expressive applications, content, and videos across browsers and operating systems.*" In other Linux flavors a flash player sometimes comes installed by default, so try those first. (See: https://www.adobe.com/products/flashplayer.html)

If you have to have Adobe Flash, the FedoraProject.org/wiki/Forbidden_items page, which links to Fedoraproject.org/wiki/Flash, describes in detail how to install Adobe Flash Player in Fedora Linux 32-bit and 64-bit. *Browse to Get.Adobe.com/flashplayer > Adobe correctly identified the OS as Linux 64-bit, Firefox > click on Select version to download... box > select YUM for Linux (YUM) > click on Download now to download and install, or save the file and use the command line to install the software.*

For Fedora 32-bit:

```
$ su -
# rpm -ivh adobe-release-i386-1.0-1.noarch.rpm     # or,
```

```
# rpm -ivh http://linuxdownload.adobe.com/adobe-release/adobe-release-i386-1.0-
1.noarch.rpm
```

For Fedora 64-bit:

```
$ su -
# rpm -ivh adobe-release-x86_64-1.0-1.noarch.rpm        # or,
# rpm -ivh http://linuxdownload.adobe.com/adobe-release/adobe-release-x86_64-1.0-
1.noarch.rpm
```

Installing this RPM file will install the repository file adobe-linux-i386.repo or adobe-linux-x86_64.repo to **/etc/yum.repos.d** directory. You will get a warning about not having a key. From Fedora, *"the install copies the adobe General Public Key (GPG key) to /etc/pki/rpm-gpg/RPM-GPG-adobe-linux but does not import it."* To import the key, type:

```
# rpm --import /etc/pki/rpm-gpg/RPM-GPG-KEY-adobe-linux
# yum update
```

On 32-bit Fedora install the following, though some packages may already be installed and will be ignored; this is OK. From Fedora, *"after completing the Adobe repository configuration, you must run the following command to install the Flash plugin and ensure sound is enabled:"*

```
# yum install nspluginwrapper alsa-plugins-pulseaudio flash plugin
```

On 64 bit, all you need is the plugin:

```
# yum install -y flash-plugin
```

When you are done picking and installing your flash plugin of choice, type the following in the Firefox address bar: about:plugins to make sure your plugin is installed and functional.

Fedora -- Installing Additional Applications, Tools & Utilities

Many of the descriptions and reference locations were taken from the Fedora Package Manager Add/Remove Software application. The other information was taken from the various websites that are presented. We will use YUM to litter our VM with applications, tools, and utilities. Many of these application descriptions are redundant to what was described when we loaded up our Backtrack/Kali/Mint/Ubuntu VM with utilities, tools and applications with a few differences. Originally there was one generic section that described this software. But, by building VMs over and over again, it quickly became apparent that flipping back and forth in the book to read about each program and determine if it was wanted or needed would be time consuming and difficult.

```
# yum install rkhunter -y     # RKHunter is a tool for checking computers that are running
```
Linux (clones) for the presence of rootkits and other black hat tools. Type # rkhunter --update to check if there is a later version of its text data files. Type # rkhunter --versioncheck to check if there is a later version of the tool available. Type # rkhunter --propupd to create

the rkhunter.dat file after installing the OS and before installing any applications, tools or utilities. Type # rkhunter --check to examine the system any time after that. When done, examine the file # vim /var/log/rkhunter.log to see if everything was OK, if so empty the file # > /var/log/rkhunter.log. Also, examine and then empty the root mail file # > /var/spool/mail/root. (See: http://rkhunter.sourceforge.net, https://en.wikipedia.org/wiki/Rootkit)

yum install yum-fastestmirror -y   # Yum-fastelistmirror plugin sorts each repository's mirrorlist by connection speed prior to downloading packages and will choose the fastest mirror whenever yum is used. (See: http://fedorasolved.org/Members/zcat/yum-rpm-faq)

yum install yum-utils   # Yum utilities is a collection of utilities and plugins that provide additional flexibility when using yum. These utilities include package-cleanup, repoclosure, repomanage, repoquery, repo-rss, yum-builddep, and yumdownloader. Package-cleanup is very useful because it checks for unneeded packages and dependency problems; it will also remove old kernels from the system.

yum install abiword -y   # The AbiWord website describes this open source software as "an award winning, small, fast, featureful and crossplatform word processor." AbiWord also boasts that it is tightly integrated with https://abicollab.net which will allow you collaborate and write documents with your friends in real time. This is a fairly active project that is well supported in Linux. The 3.0.1 release was December, 2014. (See: http://www.abiword.org)

yum install aircrack-ng -y   # Aircrack is an 802.11 WEP and WPA-PSK keys cracking program that can recover keys once enough data packets have been captured. Aircrack-ng is a set of tools for auditing wireless networks. (See: http://aircrack-ng.org)

yum install alacarte -y   # Alacarte graphical menu editor lets you edit, add, and delete menu entries, as well as create custom application launchers in GNOME 3. (See: http://library.gnome.org/admin/system-admin-guide/stable/menustructure-0.html.en)

yum install amarok -y   # KDE-Amarok, feature-rich media player that supports many formats such as: FLAC, Ogg, MP3, AAC, WAV, Windows Media Audio, Apple Lossless, WavPack, TTA and Musepack. Many Linux experts prefer this media player for music over most others. (See: http://amarok.kde.org, http://amarok.kde.org/wiki/Download:Fedora)
yum install phonon-backend-gstreamer   # KDE-Phonon provides options from which to choose the multimedia framework that works best with Amarok. (See: http://phonon.kde.org, http://amarok.kde.org/wiki/Phonon)
yum update @sound-and-video -y   # KDE-(See: http://amarok.kde.org/wiki/MP3_on_Fedora_Core)

yum install amule -y   # aMule stands for all-platform Mule and is a multi-platform, open source, peer-to-peer (P2P) file sharing application designed to connect to eDonkey and Kademlia networks. It is an excellent application for streaming a variety of different media to your computer. There are still plenty of file sharing networks and clients you can use to obtain free music, video and files like FrostWire. There is a LOT to aMule, such as the support of compressed transfers, support for secure ID, proxy* support, and much more. (See:

http://www.amule.org, http://wiki.amule.org/wiki/Main_Page, https://wiki.archlinux.org/index.php/Amule, https://en.wikipedia.org/wiki/AMule)

yum install anjuta -y   # Anjuta is a GNOME development IDE with excellent support for the C and C++ languages. From the Ajuta website, "*Ajunta is a versatile software development studio featuring a number of advanced programming facilities including project management, application wizard, interactive debugger, source editor, version control, GUI designer, profiler and many more tools. It focuses on providing simple and usable user interface, yet powerful for efficient development.*" (See: http://www.anjuta.org)

yum install audacious audacious-libs audacious-plugins audacious-plugins-freeworld audacious-plugins-freeworld-aac audacious-plugins-freeworld-ffaudio audacious-plugins-freeworld-mp3 -y   # Audacious is a simple, small and fast audio player that supports many codecs. (See: http://www.audacious-media-player.org)

yum install audacity -y   # Audacity is a cross-platform, digital multi-track audio editor used for easy recording, playing and editing of digital audio. (See: http://audacity.sourceforge.net)

yum install avidemux -y   # Avidemux is a very good video editor. (See: http://www.avidemux.org/admWiki/doku.php)

yum install azureus -y   # Vuse, previously known as Azureus, is a powerful multimedia BitTorrent* client for peer-to-peer file distribution. Vuze provides the user with comprehensive entertainment search capabilities. Vuze comes with a 1080p Video Player, Device Playback (drag-and-drop to iPad, iPod, iPhone, Xbox, PS3 and TIVO), plus a DVD Video and Data burner. (See: https://www.vuze.com, https://en.wikipedia.org/wiki/Vuze, http://azureus.sourceforge.net)

Banshee, installed by default in the GNOME desktop, is a versatile Multimedia Management and Playback application for all of your music and videos. The Audio/Video player can encode/decode various formats and synchronize music with Apple iPods. (See: http://www.banshee.fm)

yum install cdrdao -y   # Needed to burn CDs using Banshee.
yum install banshee banshee-community-extensions -y   # Community Extensions is a repository and project for extensions to the Banshee media player. (See: http://gitorious.org/banshee-community-extensions).

yum install bleachbit -y   # BleachBit is an open source system temporary file, cookie, Internet history, log-cleaner, and is similar to CCleaner for Windows. BleachBit will also shred files to prevent file recovery and wipe free disk space to hide files deleted by other applications. BleachBit will wipe clean 90 applications, including almost every flash player and browser that will run in Linux. (See: http://bleachbit.sourceforge.net)

yum install bluefish tidy -y   # Bluefish is a web design tool that is suitable for many programming and markup languages as HTML, PHP, Java, Perl, Python, C, and more; it can

also be used to develop dynamic websites. The bluefish-doc documentation was not available in the Fedora repositories. There are few useful files at /usr/share/doc/bluefish-2.0.3. (See: http://bluefish.openoffice.nl/index.html, http://bfwiki.tellefsen.net/index.php/Installing_Bluefish, http://tidy.sourceforge.net)

Brasero Disc Burner is a versatile, easy-to-use CD/DVD burning program for the GNOME desktop, which is installed by default. (See: http://projects.gnome.org/brasero)

Boot-Up Manager (BUM) that is a graphical tool to configure and manage system services was not available in the Fedora repositories.

NOTE 	Reference https://www.google.com/chrome is Google's browser, which according to Google, is designed to be fast, is streamlined, clean, simple, and secure, with built in malware and phishing protection. Chromium is now releasing stable builds for Linux, which work with no problems. If you want Chromium, https://fedoraproject.org/wiki/Chromium will show you one way of obtaining it. You may find my method, shown below, easier and safer. Surf to https://www.google.com/linuxrepositories tells you how to add the Google's Linux packages which are signed with a GNU Privacy Guard (GPG) key. If we install a Google product with this GNU key, then the Google repository will be added automatically, but this does not verify the initial download of a Google product. The key is very easy to add prior to downloading a Google product. ***If you want Chrome, surf to https://www.google.com/chrome > select a language > click on the Download Google Chrome button > tick your download package (e.g. 32 bit .rpm (For Fedora/openSUSE)) > click on the Accept and Install button to accept the Google license agreement > tick Save File, OK to save the RPM file to the ~suroot/Downloads directory > then perform the following steps at the command line:*** # cd ~suroot/Downloads or, cd && mkdir Downloads && cd Downloads # wget https://dl-ssl.google.com/linux/linux_signing_key.pub # rpm --import linux_signing_key.pub Verify the key installation by running: # rpm -qi gpg-pubkey-7fac5991-* Download and verify the Google RPM package (can be done from the GUI): # rpm --checksig -v google-chrome-stable_current_i386.rpm # rpm --checksig -v google-chrome-stable_current_x86_64.rpm # yum install -y google-chrome-stable_current_i386.rpm # yum install -y google-chrome-stable_current_x86_64.rpm # yum update If you change directory # cd /etc/yum.repos.d you will see that the install added the file google-chrome.repo, so now the Chrome browser will update automatically. Fedora does not bundle Chrome because it is a proprietary product, which bundles other proprietary software such as Adobe Flash plugin.

yum install calibre -y   # Calibre is meant to be a complete e-library solution. It includes library management, format conversion, news feeds to e-book conversion, as well as e-book reader sync features. Supported input formats are: MOBI, LIT, PRD, EPUB, ODT, HTML, CBR, CBZ, RTF, TXT, PDF and LRS. (See: http://calibre-ebook.com)

Cheese is a versatile and fully-featured webcam application for the GNOME desktop, and in Fedora, is installed by default. You can take photos and make videos with special effects. (See: http://projects.gnome.org/cheese)

yum install -y ccrypt   # Ccrypt and Mcrypt are replacements for the old crypt file encryption utility. These are utilities for encryption and decryption files and streams. Ccrypt's website is somewhat up-to-date, and the latest release of the tool was October 2012. Mcrypt is reported to be buggy by the Mint Software Manager, and recommend using OpenSSL, GnuUTLs, and GunPG instead. (See: http://mcrypt.sourceforge.net, http://ccrypt.sourceforge.net)

yum install chmsee -y   # Chmsee is an HTML Help viewer for viewing .chm files. Chmsee can extract files to the $HOME/.chmsee directory, so cleanup may be necessary. Chmsee is an actively maintained project whose last update as of this writing was June 2013. Gnochm, which was a CHM file viewer for GNOME whose last update was 2007, was no longer available. Only install either if .chm file support is necessary. (See: http://code.google.com/p/chmsee, http://gnochm.sourceforge.net)

yum install cinnamon -y   # Install the Mint Cinnamon desktop and an alternative to GNOME. I tried this but had limited success getting it to render 3D graphics properly.

yum install clementine -y   # Clementine is a multi-platform interface used for searching and playing music. Inspired by Amarok 1.4, it focuses on a fast and easy-to-use interface used for searching and playing your music. (See: http://www.clementine-player.org)

yum install crack ncrack -y   # Ncrack is used as a high-speed network authentication cracking tool. It was built to help companies secure their networks by proactively testing all of their hosts and networking devices for poor passwords. (See: http://nmap.org/ncrack)

yum install deluge -y   # Deluge is a BitTorrent* client written in python/pygtk. It is a full-featured*, multi-platform, multi-interface client-server model with a daemon process that handles all BitTorrent* activity. (See: http://www.deluge-torrent.org)

yum install devhelp -y   # Devhelp is an API documentation browser for GTK+ and the GNOME desktop. (See: http://live.gnome.org/devhelp)

DI is a disk information utility that shows everything the *df* tool does and more; it was not available in the Fedora repositories.

yum install dia -y   # Dia is a GNOME drawing program, much like Windows Visio, it can be used to draw many different kinds of diagrams. It currently has special objects to help draw

entity relationship diagrams, UML diagrams, flowcharts, network diagrams, and many other diagrams. (See: http://projects.gnome.org/dia)

yum install diffuse -y   # Diffuse is a graphical tool for merging and comparing text files. (See: http://diffuse.sourceforge.net).

yum install dvdrip -y   # Dvd::rip is full featured* DVD ripping program written in Perl. It has a feature-rich Gtk+ GUI to control the ripping and transcoding process. The last project update was May 6, 2010. (See: http://www.exit1.org/dvdrip, https://help.ubuntu.com/community/RestrictedFormats/RippingDVDs)

yum install eclipse -y   # Eclipse is a tool platform and IDE compiler for Java. This is a very large download, so only install it if you plan to do JAVA development. Eclipse can be installed during OS installation. (See: http://www.eclipse.org)

Empathy is a GNOME multi-protocol chat and call client installed by default in Fedora. Empathy supports Google Talk (Jabber/XMPP), MSN, IRC, Salut, AIM, Facebook, Yahoo!, Gadu Gadu, Groupwise, ICQ and QQ, and also supports all protocols supported by Pidgin. Supported protocols depend on installed Telepathy Connection Manager Components. There are many other features like file transfer, private and group chat, conversation logging, and much more. (See: http://live.gnome.org/Empathy)

Evince is an open source alternative to Adobe Reader and is installed in Fedora by default. It supports document viewing for many document formats including PDF, Postscript, djvu, tiff, dvi, XPS, SyncTex support with gedit, and comics books (cbr, cbz, cb7 and cbt). (See: http://projects.gnome.org/evince)

The Enigmail security extension to Mozilla Thunderbird and Seamonkey that enables the user to send and receive signed and encrypted email was not available in the Fedora repositories. However, it can be downloaded and installed. Refer back to Thunderbird -- Using Enigmail to Encrypt Emails to install the plugin. (See: https://enigmail.net/home/index.php)

Evolution is an open source alternative to Microsoft Outlook, packed with features, and installed in Fedora by default. Evolution is an integrated mail, calendar, address book, to-do/task list and memo tools for the GNOME desktop. (See: http://projects.gnome.org/evolution).

yum install exaile -y   # Exaile is a music player similar to the popular KDE's Amarok, but it's based on GTK+ toolkit rather that Qt. Therefore, it's an excellent solution for GNOME users. It incorporates automatic fetching of album art, lyrics fetching, handling of large libraries, artist/album information via Wikipedia, last.fm support and options iPod support. (See: https://en.wikipedia.org/wiki/Exaile, http://www.softpedia.com/reviews/linux/Exaile-44202.shtml, http://www.exaile.org)

yum install ffmpeg ffmpeg-libs winff winff-doc -y   # FFmpeg is a hyper-fast (real time) live audio and video encoder. It is necessary in most Linux OSs to play various video format codecs, including MPEG-1 audio and video, MPEG-4, h263, ac3, asf, avi, real, mjpeg, and

flash. (e.g. ffmpeg -i input-file.mp3 output-file.ogg) (See: http://www.ffmpeg.org, http://libav.org) Winff is a graphical video and audio batch converter using ffmpeg or avconv. (See: http://www.winff.org)

yum install filezilla -y   # FileZilla supports FTP, FTP over SSL/TLS (FTPS) and SSH File Transfer Protocol (SFTP). FileZilla is a cross-platform, multithreaded FTP, FTPS, and SFTP client that has an intuitive GUI interface. It is fast and reliable, easy to use, and has many useful features. (See: http://filezilla-project.org)

yum install firefox -y   # Can bring down updates for the Firefox browser installed by default in Fedora.

If you love to play games, Fedora has many from which to choose. From the website, "*The included games span several genres, from first person shooters to real-time and turn based strategy games to puzzle games.*" (See: https://fedoraproject.org/wiki/Games_Spin)
yum install pychess gl-117 -y   # Chess game for GNOME, action flight simulator.

apt-get install gcalctool -y   # GNOME calculator package. (See: https://live.gnome.org/Calculator, https://en.wikipedia.org/wiki/Gcalctool)

yum install gecko-mediaplayer -y   # Gecko media player is a browser plugin that uses GNOME MPlayer to play media in browsers. (See: https://sites.google.com/site/kdekorte2/gecko-mediaplayer)

yum install gedit-plugins -y   # Gedit Plugins is a collection of plugins used to dynamically extend the capabilities and add advanced features to gedit for the GNOME desktop. (See: http://live.gnome.org/Gedit/Plugins, http://projects.gnome.org/gedit/plugins.html)

yum install gftp -y   # gFTP is very dated GNOME project (11/30/2008) that is a multi-threaded FTP client for the X Window System. The creator wants to hand this project off to someone willing to take over support. The five-year-old gFTP supports simultaneous downloads, file transfer queues to allow downloading of multiple files, resumption of interrupted file transfers, support for downloading entire directories/subdirectories, a bookmarks menu to allow quick connection to FTP sites, caching of remote directory listings, local and remote chmod, drag and drop, a connection manager, and much more. (See: http://www.gftp.org)

yum install gimp gimp-help gimp-data-extras gimp-help-browser -y   # GIMP is the open source GNU Image Manipulation Program with advanced features for image/picture editing, composition and image authoring. GIMP also supports many image formats as a polished, user-friendly image editor with professional tools, as well as lets you draw, paint, and edit images with a lot of other features. (See: http://www.gimp.org)

yum install gimp-lqr-plugin gimp-resynthesizer -y   # From the Liquid Rescale GIMP plugin web page, "*gimp-lqr is an open source frontend to the Liquid Rescale Library, which provides an implementation of the Seam Carving algorithm. The Seam Carving procedure aims at resizing pictures non uniformly while preserving their features, i.e. avoiding distortion of the important*

parts." It is a GIMP plug-in for texture synthesis. From the web page, "*Given a sample of a texture, it can create more of that texture. This can create more of a texture, remove objects from images, and create themed images.*" Its last release was April 2012. (See: http://liquidrescale.wikidot.com, http://logarithmic.net/pfh/resynthesizer)

yum install gnote -y   # Gnote is a desktop note-taking application cloned from Tomboy, which is simple and easy to use. It is a good alternative to using Tomboy in GNOME, or even the more fully-featured Microsoft OneNote in Windows 7. (See: http://live.gnome.org/Gnote, https://en.wikipedia.org/wiki/Gnote)

yum install gnome-tweak-tool -y   # GNOME Tweak Tool is a tool used to help adjust/tweak the advanced configuration settings like interface, fonts, themes, and other settings. (See: http://live.gnome.org/GnomeTweakTool)

GnuCash is GNOME open source software for personal and small business financial accounting. You can track bank accounts and stocks, as well as income and expenses. As quick and intuitive to use as a checkbook register, it is based on professional accounting principles to ensure balanced books and accurate reports. Refer back to <u>Finance Virtual Machine Creation</u>.

yum install gnutls* -y   # GNUtls is a portable library that implements the Transport Layer Security (TLS 1.0, 1.1, 1.2) and Secure Sockets Layer (SSL) 3.0 protocols. (See: http://www.gnutls.org)

GnuPG2, is a new modularized version of GnuPG supporting OpenPGP and S/MIME installed at this step. (See: http://www.gnupg.org)
yum install gnupg2-smime -y   # Add support for smart cards and S/MIME encryption and signing to the base GnuPG package.

NOTE	Google Talk will allow you to use voice and video capabilities in your Google Chat properties (i.e Gmail, Google+, orkut). From within these services, you can have an actual conversation with someone, or even have a face-to-face chat over video. Surf to http://www.google.com/chat/video/download.html to download and install the RPM file. # cd ~suroot/Downloads # yum install -y google-talkplugin_current_i386.rpm # yum install -y google-talkplugin_current_x86_64.rpm # yum update

NOTE	Google Earth is not recommended for install into a 64-bit OS. It would not launch at all in a VirtualBox Fedora 64-bit OS and gave the error message: googleearth-bin: /lib/ld-lsb.so.3: bad ELF interpreter: No such file or directory. Reference http://www.google.com/earth/index.html, did not appear to be available in the Fedora repositories. GoogleEarth lets you observe satellite imagery, 3D buildings, 3D trees, terrain, street view, planets and more. Surf to https://www.google.com/earth/download/ge/agree.html to download and install the RPM file.

```
# cd ~suroot/Downloads, or cd ~/Downloads
# yum install -y google-earth-stable_current_i386.rpm
# yum install -y google-earth-stable_current_x86_64.rpm
# yum update    # update the installed repository
```

yum install gparted -y   # GParted is the GNOME partition editor, and is not needed in a VM. (See: http://gparted.sourceforge.net)

NOTE GStreamer is a multimedia framework used by many media players, including Rhythmbox, Banshee, and Totem, among others. Licensing issues prevent Fedora from including support for non-free formats like MP3. Once GStreamer is installed there are support packages from third-party repositories that can be added depending on your country's laws. (See: http://fedoraunity.org/Members/jpmahowald/non-free-plugins-for-gstreamer).
yum install -y gstreamer gstreamer-plugins-good gstreamer-plugins-bad gstreamer-plugins-ugly gstreamer-ffmpeg

yum install gtkPod -y   # Gtkpos, from the Ubuntu Software Center, is a platform independent GUI for Apple's iPod using GTK3. It allows the user to upload songs and playlists to their iPod. It is similar to Apple's iTunes and supports iPod, iPod nano, iPod shuffle, iPod photo, and iPod mini. (See: http://www.gtkpod.org, http://www.gtkpod.org/wiki/Home)

yum install guake -y   # Guake is a drop-down terminal for the GNOME desktop and is an alternative to the Terminator and GNOME terminal. (See: http://guake.org)

yum install gwibber -y   # Gwibber is a GNOME open source microblogging client. It brings the most popular social networking web services to your desktop, plus gives you the ability to control how you communicate. Useful with: Identi.ca, StatusNet, Facebook, FriendFeed, Digg, Flickr, Qaiku. (See: http://gwibber.com/download)

yum install inkscape inkscape-docs inkscape-view openclipart -y   # Inkscape is an open source, SVG-based, vector image manipulation program/graphics editor. It is used for creating fonts, text and graphics compositions; including business cards, book covers, fliers and ads. Inkscape is similar in capabilities to Adobe Illustrator and CorelDRAW. (See: http://inkscape.org)

To get the latest version of the Java SE Runtime and SE Development Kit 7u7, or the Java SE Runtime Environment 7u7, go to the link below, accept the license agreement, and download the latest RPM files. The Java Development Kit includes the JRE, but installing both will update the installation database. If you are planning to do Java Development you should also download the NetBeans IDE. NetBeans is only supported on 32-bit OSs. If you download the latest version of Java, also download the latest version of Netbeans All. The disk space requirement is only 214 MB. (See: http://www.oracle.com/technetwork/java/javase/downloads/index.html)

\# yum install netbeans* -y   \# Use Netbeans to develop desktop, mobile and web applications with Java, PHP, C/C++ and more. (See: http://www.oracle.com/technetwork/java/javase/downloads/index.html, http://netbeans.org/index.html, http://netbeans.org/downloads/index.html)

The website http://java.com/en/download has the latest release, which may not be in the Fedora repositories. You can see which open version of Java is installed in Fedora by typing \# yum install java. Please note that updating to a version of Java that is outside of the Fedora repositories may be unstable.
\# cd ~suroot/Downloads
\# yum install -y jre-8u25-linux-i586.rpm && yum install -y jdk-8u25-linux-i586.rpm
\# yum install -y jre-8u25-liniux-x64.rpm && yum install -y jdk-8u25-linux-x64.rpm
\# chmod 700 jdk-8u25-nb-8_0_1-linux-i586.sh && ./jdk-8u25-nb*-i586.sh
\# chmod 700 jdk-8u25-nb-8_0_1-linux-x64.sh && ./jdk-8u25-nb*-x64.sh

NOTE	When the script above asks where to install Java NetBeans IDE, pick a system-wide location (e.g. /usr/local), thus making it available to all users. To do this, you must be logged in as root.

\# yum install john -y   \# John the Ripper is an active password cracking tool. Its primary purpose is to detect weak passwords. (See: http://www.openwall.com/john)

\# yum install kaffeine   \# Kaffeine is KDE media player with xine engine. It is a somewhat dated project, last updated 04/04/2011. (See: http://kaffeine.kde.org)

\# yum install keepassx   \# Consider only installing this into your financial VM.

NOTE   Years ago, KompoZer was an excellent web authoring system with a WYSIWYG editor. The last stable release was August 30, 2007. It is still a decent tool for simple websites, but should be considered deprecated unless there is another release.

To install KompoZer, surf to http://www.kompozer.net/download.php and click on the version of KompoZer for your language, and then download the latest release (something like kompozer-0.8b3.en-US.gcc4.2-i686.tar.gz).
$ cd Downloads   \# or wherever you put the file
$ tar zxvf komp*   \# to extract the files
$ cd kompozer   or,   cd ~suroot/Downloads/kompozer
$ nohup ./kompozer &

You can make kompozer available to other users by moving its directory to /opt, changing the ownership and adding its home directory to the system path. You can also drag the binary to the Launcher in the KDE desktop.

\# yum install k3b* -y   \# K3B provides a graphical user interface to perform most CD/DVD burning tasks, which includes creating an Audio CD from a set of audio files or copying a

CD/DVD, or even more advanced tasks to include burning eMoviX CD/DVDs. It can also perform direct disc-to-disc copies. (See: http://www.k3b.org)

yum install ktorrent -y   # KTorrent is a BitTorrent client for the KDE desktop which allows you to download files. (See: http://ktorrent.org)

yum install lame -y   # Lame is an MP3 encoder that handles MPEG-1, MPEG-2 and 2.5 layer III encoding. (See: http://lame.sourceforge.net)

yum install libdvdread libdvdnav lsdvd libdvdcss -y   # Install codecs in order to play DVDs. Libdvdcss is a cross-platform library designed for accessing DVDs (on-the-fly CSS decryption); it is similar to a block device without having to bother about the decryption. (See: http://www.videolan.org/developers/libdvdcss.html)

NOTE

Earlier versions of Fedora did not have LibreOffice installed by default. LibreOffice is a multi-platform, feature-rich suite of applications that can handle all of your document production and data processing needs. This open source productivity suite includes Writer-Word Processor, Calc-feature-rich Spreadsheet, Impress-create multimedia presentations, Draw-build diagrams and sketches, Math-simple equation editor for math, chemical, electrical and science calculations, and Base-database front-end to the LibreOffice suite. These tools can perform most of the tasks that can be done using the Microsoft Office suite, and can be kept up-to-date using the Fedora repositories. The Writer tool has advanced to the point of being able to ready the Microsoft Office DOCX format and render the documents almost flawlessly. Using the GUI is a quick and easy way to install LibreOffice. *Click on **Activities** > in Search, type **Software** > drag and drop it onto the quick launch bar, if it is not already there > click on it to run the software > next to the **Find** button in the upper left, type **libreoffice** and then click on **Find** > check the packages you want to install, **Apply Changes***. (See: https://www.libreoffice.org).

To run the latest version of the suite you may have to resort to using command line. Surf to https://www.libreoffice.org/download and select the LibreOffice*x86*.rpm and the LibreOffice*helppack*.rpm downloads, and then store them in the ~suroot/Download directory. You may have to change the language by selecting Change System, Version or Language at the top of the browser page. For example, LibreOffice defaulted to *en-GB*, and I wanted *en-US*. Installing the latest software will be a more complete and up-to-date package, but perhaps unstable (although I have never had problems). Follow the directions at https://www.libreoffice.org/get-help/install-howto/linux or mine below:

```
# cd ~suroot/Downloads
# tar zxvf LibreOffice_4.3.4_Linux_x86_rpm.tar.gz       # For 32-bit
# tar zxvf LibreOffice_4.3.4_Linux_x86-64_rpm.tar.gz       # For 64-bit
# tar zxvf LibreOffice_4.3.4_Linux_x86_rpm_helppack_en-US.tar.gz
# tar zxvf LibreOffice_4.3.4_Linux_x86-64_rpm_helppack_en-US.tar.gz
```

```
# cd LibreOffice_4.3.4.1_Linux_x86_rpm/RPMS  # for i386
# cd LibreOffice_4.3.4.1_Linux_x86-64_rpm/RPMS # for 64-bit
# yum install *.rpm -y
```
Continued install of LibreOffice into Fedora Linux:
```
# cd ~suroot/Downloads/LibreOffice_4.3.4.1_Linux_x86_rpm_helppack_en-US/RPMS # for i386
# cd ~suroot/Downloads/LibreOffice_4.3.4.1_Linux_x86-64_rpm_helppack_en-US/RPMS # for 64-bit
# yum install -y *.rpm
# cd  ~suroot/Downloads; rm -rf LibreO*     # Remove everything if disk space
is needed
```

Please note that updating from the RPM did update many items in YUM as installed, except for the main modules, which were still earlier versions. Things like applying updates may not detect these RPM's as installed. Yet, this is a superior way of keeping LibreOffice up-to-date in Fedora, even if you have to repeat this procedure from time to time.

yum install -y linphone   # Linphone is Internet phone or Voice Over IP (VOIP) software. Use Linphone to communicate freely with people over the Internet with voice, video, and text instant messaging. (See: http://www.linphone.org)

yum install -y lynis -y   # Lynis is an open source security and system auditing tool. Its primary goal is to help users with security auditing, system hardening, vulnerability scanning and penetration testing of Unix and Linux OSs. (See: https://en.wikipedia.org/wiki/Lynis, https://cisofy.com/lynis)

yum install lynx -y   # Lynx is a text-based web browser. A text-based browser is useful for scripting and obtaining text information from websites. (See: https://en.wikipedia.org/wiki/Lynx_(web_browser), http://lynx.isc.org)

yum install gnome-mplayer mplayer mplayer-doc mplayer-gui smplayer -y   # MPlayer is a GNOME movie player that plays many formats and has won various awards. There are several front-ends for this player in the vein of smplayer, gnome-mplayer and mplayer-gui that you can try. GNOME MPlayer is a GTK2/GTK3 interface for MPlayer. MPlayer can play all of your multimedia (audio, video, CD, DVDs, and VCDs, streams, etc.). There is also an MPlayer2 fork that claims to be an enhancement to MPlayer. MPlayer2 did not appear to be available in the Fedora repositories. (See: http://www.mplayerhq.hu, https://code.google.com/p/gnome-mplayer, http://www.mplayer2.org)

yum install Graphics* -y   # GraphicsMagick is a fork from the ImageMagick project that puts a larger emphasis on stability. It can also be used in parallel with ImageMagick. (See: http://www.graphicsmagick.org)

yum install inkscape -y   # From the Inkscape website, this tool "*is an open source vector graphics editor, with capabilities similar to Illustrator, CorelDraw, or Xara X, using the W3C standard Scalable Vector Graphics (SVG) file format. Inkscape supports many advanced SVG*

features (markers, clones, alpha blending, etc.) and great care is taken in designing a streamlined interface. It is very easy to edit nodes, perform complex path operations, trace bitmaps and much more." Inkscape is a very active project and kept current as of 3 February, 2013. (See: http://www.inkscape.org)

yum install mawk -y   # Conforms to the POSIX 1003.2 and extends capabilities of the *awk* command and is smaller and much faster than *gawk*. Gawk is the GNU implementation of the older *awk* command line utility. From the Fedora Add/Remove Software tool, "Awk interprets a special-purpose programming language to do quick and easy text pattern matching and reformatting jobs." Mawk is another interpreter for the AWK programming language. (See: http://invisible-island.net/mawk)

yum install mc -y   # Midnight Commander (MC) is a Norton Commander clone for managing files and directories. MC is a powerful file manager that uses a two-panel interface and a subshell for command execution. Also included is Virtual File System (VFS), which allows files on remote system (e.g. FTP, SSH servers) and files inside archives to be manipulated like real files. (See: http://www.midnight-commander.org)

yum install meld -y   # Meld is a graphical tool to *diff* and *merge* file or directories.

yum install medusa -y   # Medusa is intended to be a speedy, massively parallel, modular, login brute-forcer. It supports many protocols, including AFP, CVS, FTP, HTTP, IMAP, rlogin, SSH, Subversion, and VNC, just to name a few. (See: http://sectools.org/tag/crackers)

yum install minitube -y   # Minitube is a native YouTube desktop client. Type a keyword and Minitube provides many streaming videos to view. (See: http://flavio.tordini.org/minitube)

yum install mmv -y   # Move/Copy/Append/Link multiple files by wildcard patterns.

yum install nautilus-actions -y   # Nautilus-Actions is an extension for Nautilus, the GNOME file manager. It provides an easy way to add arbitrary actions to the file manager context menus. (See: http://www.grumz.net)

yum install nautilus-image-converter -y   # Nautilus Image Converter adds a "Resize Images..." menu item to the context menu of all images. This opens a dialog wherever you set the desired image size and file name. A click on "Resize" resizes the image(s) using ImageMagick's convert tool. (See: http://git.gnome.org/browse/nautilus-image-converter)

yum install nautilus-open-terminal -y   # The nautilus-open-terminal extension provides a right-click "Open Terminal" option for Nautilus users who prefer that option.

yum install nautilus-pastebin -y   # Nautilus extension is written in Python, and allows users to upload text-only files to a pastebin service just by right-clicking on them. Users can also add their favorite service by creating new presets. (See: https://launchpad.net/nautilus-pastebin)

yum install nmap nmap-frontend umit -y   # Nmap is a sophisticated network mapper. Umit and nmap-frontend are graphical user interface front-ends to the nmap penetration tool. (See: http://nmap.org, http://www.umitproject.org)

yum install oggconvert -y   # OggConvert is a small and simple GNOME utility to convert media files to the patent-free Vorbis, Theora, Dirac and now VP8 formats. (See: http://oggconvert.tristanb.net, https://launchpad.net/oggconvert)

yum install ogmrip mkvtoolnix-gui -y   # OGMRip is an application for ripping and encoding DVD into AVI, OGM, MP4 or Matroska files using lots of audio and video formats (Ogg Vorbis, MP3, PCM, AC3, DTS, AAC, MPEG-4 ASP, MPEG-4 AVC, and Theora). Installing ORMRip brings down MPlayer as a dependency. (See: http://ogmrip.sourceforge.net/en/manual.html, https://help.ubuntu.com/community/RestrictedFormats/RippingDVDs)

yum install p7zip p7zip-plugins -y   # 7Zip is a file archiver that archives with very high compression ratios. From the website, "*The program supports 7z, XZ, BZIP2, GZIP, TAR, ZIP, WIM, ARJ, CAB, CHM, CPIO, CramFS, DEB, DMG, FAT, HFS, ISO, LZH, LZMA, MBR, MSI, NSIS, NTFS, RAR, RPM, SquashFS, UDF, VHD, WIM, XAR, Z*". (See: http://7-zip.org, http://p7zip.sourceforge.net, http://sourceforge.net/projects/sevenzip)

NOTE	Password Safe is an open source password manager similar to KeePass that you can use to maintain an encrypted database of passwords. (See: http://pwsafe.org) We will discuss Password Safe in detail in Chapter 11. There is a BETA release that you can download and try out at http://sourceforge.net/projects/passwordsafe/files. Click on the Name, Linux-BETA link > the latest version (e.g. 0.94) > save the RPM file to your Downloads directory. Then type the following as 'root':
	# cd ~suroot/Downloads or cd ~sudoroot/Downloads # yum install pwsafe-0.94BETA-3.i686.rpm # yum install pwsafe-0.94BETA-3.x86_64.rpm

yum install pdfshuffler -y   # PDFShuffler is a small application that allows the user to merge or split PDF documents, as well as rotate, crop and rearrange pages. (See: http://pdfshuffler.sf.net)

yum install phatch nautilus-phatch -y   # Phatch is a simple to use cross-platform GUI Photo Batch Processor that handles all of the popular image formats and can duplicate (sub)folder hierarchies. Phatch can batch re-size, rotate, apply perspective, shadows, rounded corners and more. (See: http://photobatch.stani.be, http://photobatch.wikidot.com)

yum install pidgin -y   # Pidgin is a graphical multi-platform instant messaging client. You can log into multiple chat rooms and Pidgin will integrate them. It supports many chat networks such as AIM, Bonjour, Gadu-Gadu, Google Talk, Novell Groupwise Messenger, Gadu-Gadu, ICQ, IRC, Jabber/XMPP, MXit, MySpaceIM, Sametime, SILC, SIMPLE, Yahoo!, and

Zephyr. Skype is proprietary and does not allow open source to integrate with their product. It has been suggested that Pidgin is not tracked by the NSA. (See: http://pidgin.im, http://www.pidgin.im/download/source)

NOTE	There are many supporting packages for Pidgin that can be installed. ***Click on Activities > type "software" in the search box upper left type "pidgin".*** For example: # yum install pidgin-evolution pidgin-rhythmbox pidgin-docs -y

yum install pinta -y   # Simple drawing/painting program which features: Adjustments (Auto Level, Black and White, Sepia, etc.), Effects (Motion blur, Glow, Wrap, etc.), Multiple layers, Unlimited undo/redo, Drawing tools (Paintbrush, Pencil, Shapts, etc). (See: http://pinta-project.com).

yum install pulsecaster -y   # Plusecaster is a Voice-over-IP recorder that is used to store a conversation to a file and then publish later; it can also be used to record Skype calls. (See: https://fedorahosted.org/pulsecaster)

NOTE	Opera is a fully-featured, compact, customizable, and fast web browser with advanced browser HTML 5 and CSS 3 support. Opera is a good browser choice to boost surfing speed on older computers and slow Internet connections. The Opera browser is not installable from the repositories. ***Surf to Opera's website http://www.opera.com/computer > under Select distribution and vendor, select Fedora > leave the Choose package format as default package > under Download location go with the default value > click on the Free download button.*** Then install the browser from the RPM file with the following steps: # cd ~suroot/Downloads # yum install -y opera-12.16-1860.i386.rpm or yum install -y opera-12.16-1860.x86_64.rpm

yum install rhythmbox rhythmbox-equalizer -y   # Rhythmbox is a GNOME integrated music management system, organizer, and audio player and ripper, similar to Apple's iTunes, with support for iPods. RBEQ is a plugin equalizer for Rhythmbox, and RBEQ has 10 channels and ties directly into the GSreamer framework. (See: http://projects.gnome.org/rhythmbox, https://code.google.com/p/rbeq)

yum install scribus scribus-devel scribus-doc -y   # Scribus is a large 70 MB install so only install if needed. Scribus is an open source desktop publishing (DTP) application capable of producing commercial grade output in PDF and Postscript as a professional publishing tool. It comes complete with page layout features, flexible formatting, typesetting and the ability to prepare files for professional image setting equipment. This application supports CMYK color, spot color, separations, and ICC color. The scribus-devel package contains the header files for Scribus. (See: http://www.scribus.net, http://sourceforge.net/projects/scribus, http://en.wikipedia.org/wiki/Scribus)

yum install seamonkey -y   # Seamonkey Internet Suite is a set of Internet applications. It contains a Mozilla based web browser, an HTML WYSIWYG editor, a mail and news client, and an address book. (See: http://www.seamonkey-project.org)

<table>
<tr>
<td>

NOTE

</td>
<td>

SFLphone is an open source alternative to the Microsoft-owned Skype for VOIP. This is a very active project updated frequently. SFLphone express that they are an enterprise or individual solution that can handle several hundred calls a day. The Fedora repositories do not offer SFLphone as an installation alternative. SFLphone used to most actively support Debian flavors of Linux akin to Ubuntu and Mint. However, on the SFLphone's website they are now actively supporting Fedora also. (See: http://sflphone.org)

For Fedora 20:
yum install https://yum.savoirfairelinux.com/sflphone/f20/RPMS/x86_64/sflphone-release-1-5.noarch.rpm -y
yum update -y
yum install sflphone-gnome-video -y   # For the Video software,
yum install sflphone-gnome -y   # For the audio software, or,
yum install sflphone-kde -y   # If using the KDE Desktop
yum install sflphone-plugins -y

</td>
</tr>
</table>

Shotwell Photo Manager is a full-featured* personal photo management application for the GNOME desktop and is installed by default in Fedora. You can import photos from a USB drive, disk or camera, organize and view them various ways, and export them to share with others. (See: http://yorba.org/shotwell)

<table>
<tr>
<td>

NOTE

</td>
<td>

Before you install and use Skype refer back to BackTrack/Kali/Mint/Ubuntu-Installing additional Applications, Tools & Utilities in Debian based Linux to read about Skype privacy concerns. To install Microsoft Skype in Fedora to be able to use free video and voice calls, send instant messages, and share files with other Skype users, in Fedora *surf to http://www.skype.com/intl/en/get-skype/on-your-computer/linux > click on the Download now button > pick the latest version of Fedora offered > click on OK*. Open a terminal window and type the following:

yum install -y skype-4.2.0.11-fedora.i586.rpm

Skype did not update the **/etc/yum.repos.d** repository directory that would provide Fedora repository updates, but Google Chrome did. Skype for Fedora is very dated as the latest Microsoft Skype release was for Fedora 16 32bit. Skype is more active in supporting Ubuntu with a 12.04 release of their software.

</td>
</tr>
</table>

yum install sound-juicer -y   # Sound Juicer lets you extract the audio from CDs and convert them to audio files that your computer can play. This program also plays CDs, and is simple, clean, and easy to use. (See: http://www.burtonini.com/blog/computers/sound-juicer, http://library.gnome.org/users/sound-juicer/stable/sound-juicer.html)

yum install shutter -y   # Shutter is a GNOME feature-rich screenshot application, which is an alternative to Fedora's default, Take Screenshot. (See: http://shutter-project.org)

yum install terminator -y   # Terminator allows you to use multiple GNOME terminals in one window. It features the arranging of terminals in a grid, tabs, drag and drop re-ordering of terminals, many keyboard shortcuts, and more. (See: http://www.tenshu.net/terminator)

yum install thunderbird thunderbird-lightning -y   # Thunderbird is a full featured* email client that is an excellent alternative to Windows Outlook or Live Mail. It comes complete with easy email account setup, customizable options, spam filters, search tools, address book, phishing protection, privacy protection, and much more. Lightning is a calendar add-on that integrates with Thunderbird email. (See: https://www.mozilla.org/en-US/thunderbird, https://www.mozilla.org/projects/calendar/lightning)

yum install tomboy -y   # TomBoy "is a desktop note-taking application for Linux, Unix, Windows, and Mac OS X. Simple and easy to use, but with potential to help you organize the ideas and information you deal with every day." It lets you organize your notes intelligently by allowing you to easily link ideas together easily with Wiki-style interconnects. (See: http://projects.gnome.org/tomboy)

The Totem Movie Player is a simple media player for the GNOME desktop, based on GStreamer. It features a playlist, a full-screen mode, seek and volume controls, as well as keyboard navigation, and it comes installed in Fedora by default. There are many additions to Totem that you could consider installing. (See: http://projects.gnome.org/totem, https://en.wikipedia.org/wiki/Totem_(media_player))

yum install totem-mozplugin -y   # Totem-mozplugin will allow the viewing of movies in a Mozilla-based browser with other codes and plugins installed.
yum install totem-youtube -y   # Totem-youtube allows the browsing of YouTube videos in Totem, and watching them with other codecs installed. Not available in Fedora 20.

yum install transmission transmission-cli -y   # Transmission is a cross-platform, fast, easy and free BitTorrent* client that boasts it uses fewer resources than other clients. It features native Mac, GTK+ and Qt GUI clients, remote control by Web and Terminal clients, Local Peer Discovery, Full encryption, DHT, uTP, PEX and Magnet Link support. The CLI package will install the command line version of Transmission. (See: http://www.transmissionbt.com, http://en.wikipedia.org/wiki/Transmission_(BitTorrent_client))

yum install tree   # Tree is a recursive directory listing command that is installed in Fedora by default. (See: Mama.indstate.edu/users/ice/tree).

yum install unoconv -y   # Unoconv is a utility to convert between many document and graphic formats supported by LibreOffice and OpenOffice. (See: http://dag.wieers.com/home-made/unoconv)

yum install vlc mozilla-vlc phonon-backend-vlc -y   # VLC is a multimedia player and streamer. VLC (initially VideoLAN Client) is a highly portable multimedia player for various

audio and video formats, including MPEG-1, MPEG-2, MPEG-4, DivX, MP3, and OGG, as well as for Audio CDs, DVDs, VCDs, and various streaming protocols. It also can also be used as a server for unicast or multicast streams in IPv4 or IPv6 on a high-bandwidth network. (See: http://www.videolan.org/vlc, https://en.wikipedia.org/wiki/VLC_media_player)

yum install unrar -y   # UNRAR is a utility used to extract and view the contents of archives created by the RAR archiver. (See: http://www.rarlab.com/rar_archiver.htm)

yum install wdiff -y   # WDiff is a GUI front-end to *diff* for comparing text files. (See: https://www.gnu.org/software/wdiff)

yum install wine -y   # Wine is a compatibility layer used for running Windows software on Linux. Wine allows unmodified Windows binaries to run on x86 and experimentally in x86_64 Linux OSs. It does this by translating Windows API calls into POSIX calls on demand. This allows Windows' applications to be cleanly integrated into Linux, Mac OSX, & BSD and other OSs. (See: http://www.winehq.org, http://wiki.winehq.org/Wine64, http://fedoraproject.org/wiki/AndreasBierfert/Wine)

yum install wireshark -y   # Wireshark is network protocol and traffic analyzer. It lets you capture and interactively browse the traffic running on a computer network to be able troubleshoot network issues. (See: http://www.wireshark.org, https://en.wikipedia.org/wiki/Wireshark)

yum install -y xine xine-lib xine-lib-extras xine-lib-extras-freeworld xine-plugin xine-ui xine-ui-skins gxine   # Xine is multi-platform, multimedia player that plays CDs, DVDs, and VCDs. It also decodes multimedia files as AVI, MOV, WMV, and MP3 from local disk drives, and displays multimedia. It can be used to play back various media, decode multimedia files from local disk drives, and display multimedia streamed over the Internet. Gxine is the xine gtk+/GNOME user interface for xine. The suggested package realplayer has no installation candidate. (See: https://www.xine-project.org/home)

yum install xchat -y   # XChat is an easy to use GNOME graphical IRC chat client for both Linux and Windows. It allows a user to join multiple IRC channels (chat rooms) at the same time, talk publicly, have private one-on-one conversations, etc. Even file transfers are possible. (See: http://www.xchat.org)

yum install xbmc -y   # XBMC media center is a media center application for Linux. XBMC can play a spectrum of multimedia formats, featuring playlists, audio visualizations, slideshow, and weather forecast functions, together with third-party plugins. It also supports various kinds of remote controls. (See: http://xbmc.org)

yum install xmms xmms-mp3 -y   # XMMS is an audio (Ogg Vorbis, CDs) player for the X Window System with an interface similar to Winamp's. XMMS supports playlists and streaming content and has a configurable interface as well. It is an audio framework, not a general multimedia player, and it runs a daemon independent of any graphics output. The supported audio formats are expandable via plugins. (See: http://wejp.k.vu/projects/xmms2, http://xmms2.org/wiki/Main_Page)

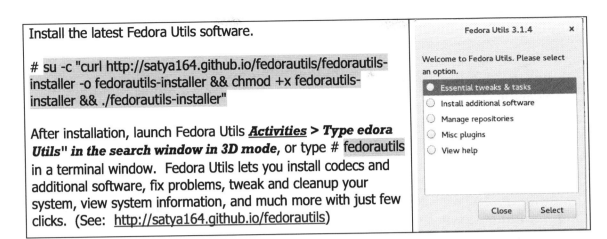

Install the latest Fedora Utils software.

su -c "curl http://satya164.github.io/fedorautils/fedorautils-installer -o fedorautils-installer && chmod +x fedorautils-installer && ./fedorautils-installer"

After installation, launch Fedora Utils ***Activities > Type edora Utils" in the search window in 3D mode***, or type # fedorautils in a terminal window. Fedora Utils lets you install codecs and additional software, fix problems, tweak and cleanup your system, view system information, and much more with just few clicks. (See: http://satya164.github.io/fedorautils)

The Zim graphical text editor is used to maintain a collection of Wiki pages and was not available in the default Fedora repositories. This tool stores all of the data in plain text files with wiki formatting and can be downloaded from their website. (See: http://zim-wiki.org)

yum clean all   # Clean all cached files and headers from any enabled repository. (See: http://yum.baseurl.org/wiki/YumCommands)

Fedora -- A Lesson in Starting and Stopping Services Automatically

In writing the Tor Chapter, with earlier versions of their software, the "tor" and "polipo" services had to be started manually:

service tor start
The command above only starts Tor; upon the next reboot Tor will need to be started again. Hence, research was needed to determine how to start the service upon VM startup. Many of the old methods shown below are now obsolete. They are documented here because there is lot of old web pages on the Internet detailing these solutions.

ntsysv
This is an old text-based application that allows you to configure which services are started at boot time for each runlevel. Non-xinetd services, such as *Tor cannot be started, stopped, or restarted using this program*.

chkconfig
This is a command line utility that used to allow you to turn services on and off for the different runlevels. Chkconfig suffers the same non-xinetd start and stop limitation as ntsysv. Using (# chkconfig --list) will only show SysV services only. For example:
 # chkconfig --level 5 tor - *did not start Tor at run level 5*. Try it, reboot, and you will see your service is not running.
You can get the Tor service Tor started at the current run level on reboot by using:
chkconfig tor on

After a reboot, the Tor service was running at startup:
```
# pgrep tor
716
```

The utility below was also useful if you want to install it and view the startup status of services in the same vein as Tor:

```
# yum install system-config-services
# system-config-services
```

Once installed, if you run the utility, it will show tor as "This unit is running". With further research, Fedora 15 and later versions use "systemd" as their system and service manager. This is a replacement for the old SysVinit and Upstart daemons. The daemon "systemd" project's objective is to take the maximum advantage offered by modern Linux kernels. The old tools for managing services in Fedora akin to *service, chkconfig, ntsysv, service, serviceconf, and system-config-services* are now obsolete, but most (if not all) of their functions can still be accomplished with "systemctl" command.

The "systemctl" command is now the primary tool to use. It combines the functionality of both *service* and *chkconfig* into a single tool that you can use to enable/disable services permanently or just for the current session. There is an excellent read on this at https://fedoraproject.org/wiki/Systemd. Below is a brief summary of the *systemctl* commands:

Activate a service immediately:
```
# systemctl start tor.service    and/or,    systemctl start polipo.service
```
Deactivate a service immediately:
```
# systemctl stop tor.service    and/or,    systemctl stop polipo.service
```
Restart a service:
```
# systemctl restart tor.service
```
Shows status of a service including whether it is running or not:
```
# systemctl status tor.service
```
Enables a service to be started upon boot up:
```
# systemctl enable tor.service
```
Disables a service to not start during boot up:
```
# systemctl disable tor.service
```
Check to see whether a service is already enabled or not:
```
# systemctl is-enabled tor.service; echo $?
```
0 indicates that it is enabled. 1 indicates that it is disabled

OpenSUSE – General Description

OpenSUSE is another flavor of Linux that is popular in Europe, especially in Germany and to a lesser degree in the United States. OpenSUSE comes with over 1,000 open source applications and the choice of four desktops, GNOME, KDE, Xfce and LXDE. It can function as both, a standalone desktop or as a server environment. Many businesses use openSUSE as their server of choice. OpenSUSE, by default, presents the KDE desktop, which has a different look and feel from the other flavors of Linux using GNOME or Xfce, and is covered in this book. From http://en.opensuse.org/Portal:12.1 "*openSUSE 12.1 ships the KDE Plasma Desktop 4.7 as default workspace and is the first major Linux distribution to ship the new KolorManager + Oyranos color management tools. Another major new addition is KPackageKit replacement Apper, simplifying installation and removal of applications.*" With KDE, we can litter the desktop and panel with icons. OpenSUSE-KDE presents a green icon, called the Kickoff Application Launcher (KAL), on the lower left, that acts a lot like the Windows Start icon. This is your doorway to the many applications that openSUSE comes with, as well as the ones that we will add later. This makes openSUSE very intuitive to a prior Windows user. Even though openSUSE is not used for exercises later in this book, you can easily substitute it to perform the exercises that are offered later. OpenSUSE 13.1 was released November 19, 2013 and has been selected as extended community maintenance release supported until a date to be announced. OpenSUSE 13.2 was released Nov, 2014. OpenSUSE releases operate on an eight-month release cycle, so we can expect the next release around July 2015. (See: http://www.opensuse.org/en, http://en.wikipedia.org/wiki/OpenSUSE, https://en.opensuse.org/Lifetime)

From the install, "*SUSE is committed to your success with Linux. In additions to openSUSE, SUSE also delivers an exciting suite of products designed to meet the needs of businesses large and small.*

The enterprise Linux products from SUSE include SUSE Linux Enterprise Server and SUSE Linux Enterprise Desktop. Our enterprise products are delivered with a seven-year maintenance guarantee and optional support programs. For more information on enterprise Linux from SUSE, visit http://www.suse.com."

OpenSUSE -- Install in VirtualBox & VMware Player

Go to http://software.opensuse.org/132/en and download the openSUSE DVD that you want to install. When done, use the utilities that we downloaded and installed in Chapter 5 to check the MD5 or SHA256 Hash. The MD5 and SHA-1 sums are found on the download page. *In Windows, click on Start > Run... > type cmd > click on OK > type cd \Downloads\Linux\openSUSE > type fsum -sha1 openSUSE-13.2-DVD-i586.iso; in Linux type # sha1sum ISOFileName > you should see:*

- openSUSE-13.2-DVD-i586 MD5: 43869f9b9b944adc1b210649d3730980
- openSUSE-13.2-DVD-i586 SHA-1: 2ec28606829d6408efc5a79b70d1da738fdc09de
- openSUSE-13.2-DVD-x86_64 MD5: 350b8cb014a4e342cc9a7cc9df891b99
- openSUSE-13.2-DVD-x86_64 SHA-1: a1bd237ccfb07939953a9681607c99c00bc78d5d

OpenSUSE also provides the GPG signature so that you can use that very accurate tool to verify the downloaded file. OpenSUSE suggests using http://en.opensuse.org/SDB:Metalink, which uses the http://www.downthemall.net Firefox extension.

To install openSUSE in Parallels refer back to Parallels-Creating Virtual Guest Operating Systems. Refer back to VirtualBox-Creating Virtual Guest Operating Systems to install openSUSE in VirtualBox. Refer back to VMware Player-Creating Virtual Guest Operating Systems) to install openSUSE in VMware Player.

OpenSUSE -- Continued Install after VM Reboot in VirtualBox

During installation openSUSE offers the user the option of selecting the B-Tree File System file system (Btrfs). Refer back to <u>GParted-Manually Creating Partitions</u> for a description of Btrfs. (See: <u>https://en.wikipedia.org/wiki/Btrfs</u>, <u>https://btrfs.wiki.kernel.org/index.php/Main_Page</u>)

 **NOTE**	Years ago Mint adopted the strategy of offering a separate distribution for each desktop. If you have the disk space, a better strategy would be to create a VM for each desktop rather than installing multiple desktops in the same VM and possibly having conflicting software. The only advantage of having multiple desktops is having all of the software available for both in multiple desktops.

In VirtualBox, once the VM is created, we have to work through the installation steps after agreeing to the License Agreement. *On the initial <u>openSUSE installer</u> screen select <u>Installation</u>, the <u>Loading Linux Kernal</u> dialog should appear > on the <u>Welcome</u> screen select your <u>Language</u> and <u>Keyboard Layout</u>, <u>Next</u> > openSUSE will probe the system and in 13.1 the <u>Installation Mode</u> screen will appear, leave <u>New Installation</u> ticked, check <u>Add Online Repositories Before Installation</u>, uncheck <u>Use Automatic Configuration</u>, <u>Next</u>.*

NOTE	Unchecking the <u>Use Automatic Configuration</u> will add installation steps and make the install a bit more complex. However, this will allow us to specify a hostname during the installation and pick which updates we want to apply during the installation. If you do not check <u>Add Online Repositories Before Installation</u> the steps below will change but the directions remain the same.

On the <u>Network Setup</u> screen leave <u>Yes, Run the Network Setup</u> ticked, <u>Next</u>, leave <u>Automatic Address Setup (via DHCP)</u>, <u>OK</u> > on the <u>List of Online Repositories</u> screen select the repositories you want (e.g. <u>Main Repository (OSS)</u>, <u>Main Repository (NON-OSS)</u>, <u>Main Update Repository</u>, <u>Update Repository (Non-Oss)</u>, <u>Next</u> > on the <u>Writing List of Online Repositories</u> screen give the repositories time to install > on the <u>License Agreement</u> screen, <u>Next</u> >

In 13.2 the <u>Installation Options</u> screen will appear check <u>Add Online Repositories Before Installation</u> > the <u>Suggested Partitioning</u> screen should appear, click on <u>Edit Proposal Settings</u> > uncheck <u>Propose Separate Home Partition</u> as this is a VM, leave <u>Btrfs</u> as the default OS, <u>OK</u>, <u>Next</u> > in both 13.1 and 13.2 on the <u>Clock and Time Zone</u> screen select your <u>Time Zone</u> by clicking on the nearest large city in your time zone (e.g. Michigan (Detroit)), consider whether you want <u>Date and Time NTP</u> configured. In a VM you may want to click on the <u>Change...</u> button in 13.1 and the <u>Other Settings...</u> button in 13.2, uncheck <u>Run NTP as daemon</u> and <u>Save NTP Configuration</u>, tick <u>Manually</u> to keep the VM synced up with the host OS, leave <u>Change the Time Now</u> checked, <u>Accept</u>, <u>Next</u>.

On the <u>Desktop Selection</u> screen, tick which desktop you prefer (openSUSE defaults to the <u>KDE Desktop</u> and is recommended), if you want both popular desktops we can add the *GNOME Desktop* later, *Next* > on the *Suggested Partitioning* screen check *Create LVM Based Proposal*, uncheck *Propose Separate Home Partition*, depending on its use and purpose in your VM, consider checking *Use Btrfs as Default File System*, which is rapidly becoming a better and more stable alternative to the dated ext4 file system, *Next* > on the *Create New User* screen, *User's Full Name:* 'suroot', *Username:* 'suroot', *Password:* something simple, check *Use this password for system administrator* and *Receive System Mail*; uncheck *Automatic Login*, we will configure that later, *Next* > if a warning dialog pops up about the password being too simple click on *Yes* > in 13.2 on the *Installation Settings* click on *Software* and follow the 13.1 directions below.

In 13.1 on the *Installation Settings* screen click on the *Change...* dropdown at the bottom of the window and arrow down/up to select *Software...* > on the *Software Selection and System Tasks* screen review and select the added software that you want to install (e.g. *AppArmor*, *Console Tools*, *Documentation*, (*GNOME Desktop* can destabilize VM), *Technical Writing*, *Base Development*, *C/C++ Development*, *Laptop* (if Laptop), *Perl Development*, *Python Development*, *Ruby Development*, *Web Development*, etc.) *OK* > *Accept* any license agreements > review your settings and click on the *Install* button twice > after installation configuration will begin.

On the *Hostname and Domain Name* screen, uncheck *Change Hostname via DHCP* to prevent the hostname from being set automatically by the DHCP client. It is important to have a stable hostname to be able to use tools such as FTP or SSH, and if you have to connect to different networks.

Check *Assign Hostname to Loopback IP*, which associates your hostname with 127.0.0.1 (loopback) IP address in /etc/hosts. This is useful if you want to have the hostname resolvable at all times, even without an active network. In all other cases, use it carefully, especially if this VM will provide some network services.

Upon reboot in earlier versions, select *Boot from Hard Disk*, the *Hostname and Domain Name* screen will appear, refer back to *Virtual Machine Name Standardization* to enter a hostname, *Next* > openSUSE should detect your *Network Configuration* setup earlier, *Next* > on the *Test Internet Connection* screen leave *Yes, Test Connection to the Internet Via...* ticked, *Next*, *Next* again > on the *Online Update* screen leave *Run Update* ticked, *Next* > this will run the *Internet Connection Test* and hopefully give you a *Test Result: Success*, *Next* > when the *Online Update* screen appears leave *Run Update* ticked, *Next* , click on the *Patch* menu, arrow down to select *Update if new version available*, *Accept*, leave the *Automatic Changes* checked, *Continue*, *Continue* (applying updates will take a while), *Next* > the *Release Notes* screen will appear, *Next* > the *Hardware Configuration* screen will appear, *Next* > the *Saving sound card...* screen will appear > on the *Installation Completed* screen click on the *Finish* button and the login screen will appear.

If your printer was not detected on the *Hardware Configuration* screen, click on *Change...* button lower center and select *Printer...* > click on the *Add* button lower left to retrieve your print driver information > if no connection was found, click on the *Connection Wizard* button upper right > under *Access Network Printer or Printserver Box via* select *TCP Port (AppSocket/JetDirect)* > under *IP Address* or *Host Name* enter your *printer's IP address, at the bottom select your printer's manufacturer, OK > under Find and Assign a Driver select the closest driver that matches your printer, at the bottom under Set Arbitrary Name type a name for your printer consisting of letters, numbers and underscores, click on OK then OK again > you should see Found existing configuration: your printer, listed now on the Hardware Configuration screen, Next. Your printer can all be added later using YaST.*

VirtualBox renders the 3D graphics correctly for openSUSE. GNOME and KDE offer different tool sets that can be used from both desktops, so having them both installed is worthwhile, but not as stable as having a single desktop which I recommend for a VM. VirtualBox with openSUSE is a superior solution to using Parallels or VMware Player with openSUSE under Windows.

If you missed the step above to add your printer during the installation in KDE, you can add it afterward. OpenSUSE offers "Yet another Setup Tool" (YaST) as your portal to configuring just about everything in an openSUSE OS. *Click on the KAL lower left hightlight Computer > arrow up to select YaST > click on Hardware in the left panel > click on the Printer icon > click on the Add button and follow the directions above.*

During the install in VirtualBox we can configure the standard and update repositories during installation. However, the install left the CD/DVD mount point configured in the openSUSE repository setup, which resulted in the following error when we attempt to apply updates:

```
File '/media.1/media' not found on medium 'cd:///?devices=/dev/disk/by-id/ata-
VBOX_CD-ROM_VB2-01700376,/dev/sr0'
```

```
Please insert medium [] #1 and type 'y' to continue or 'n' to cancel the operation.
[yes/no] (no):
```

Skip down to OpenSUSE-Repository Setup and Tools Update for directions on how to disable this IDE_CDROM repository. *Do not* add the additional nonstandard repositories until after updates have been applied.

OpenSUSE -- Setup in VMware Player after VM Creation

VMware Player installs VMware Tools automatically in openSUSE. If reinstallation or upgrading VMware Tools becomes necessary, install the following:

zypper install -y kernel-devel kernel-headers

then refer back to VMware Player-Manual Installation of VMware Tools for directions on how to install the tools.

Once openSUSE is installed, shutdown and alter the VM Settings if you have not already created the VM in KDE, click on Application Launcher > Leave > Shut Down.

If upon initial boot up of openSUSE the <u>Community Repositories</u> option is not available, simply reboot the VM, and the option to select <u>Community Repositories</u> will become visible. OpenSUSE, unlike some flavors of Linux, allows a user to login as 'root'. When the login screen comes up after reboot, *type <u>root</u> for the username, and enter the 'suroot' password you specified when building the VM*. This will log you in as 'root', which we will use to setup the VM. The alternative is to use $ su - as the 'suroot' user ID. The VMware Player installation picked up the printer configuration automatically.

During the install in VirtualBox, we can configure the standard and update repositories during the installation. The VMware Player automatic install does not do so. The Player left the VMware Tools mount point configured in the openSUSE repository setup, which results in the following error when we attempt to apply updates:

```
Failed to mount cd:///?devices=/dev/disk/by-id/ata-
VMware_Virtual_IDE_CDROM_Drive_10000000000000000001 on /var/adm/mount/AP_0xEn96sZ:
Mounting media failed (mount: no medium found on /dev/sr0)

Please insert medium [] #1 and type 'y' to continue or 'n' to cancel the operation.
[yes/no] (no):
```

Skip down to <u>OpenSUSE-Repository Setup and Tools Update</u> to disable this IDE_CDROM repository and add the standard and update repositories to openSUSE to apply updates. *Do not* add the additional nonstandard repositories until after the updates have been applied.

Upon reboot, openSUSE may display the dialog to the right. Clicking on <u>Yes</u> to go with KDE's recommendation worked fine. Check <u>Do not ask again for these devices</u> when you have proven the sound is working in your VM.	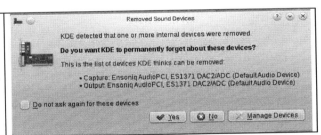

NOTE	Sometimes, after applying the updates, openSUSE was unable to obtain a NAT IP address. Type # ifconfig to view the network information. To fix this, *click on <u>KAL</u> > <u>Computer</u> > <u>YaST</u> > select <u>Network Devices</u> on the left > click on the <u>Network Settings</u> icon to the right > highlight your network connection > click on the <u>Edit</u> button > <u>Next</u> > <u>OK</u>.*

WARNING	Before 13.2 VMware Player did not give us the option of selecting the GNOME GUI during the OS installation. I attempted to install it after the OS had loaded and received many conflicts and downgrades for the packages. If you want to attempt it, reference http://www.gnome.org/getting-gnome, which will direct you to http://en.opensuse.org/openSUSE:GNOME_3.0 for the steps to install GNOME in openSUSE. *Click on the <u>Install</u> button for your CPU type of openSUSE > click on Open with <u>YaST 1-Click Install (default)</u> > be*

patient it took a long time to offer up the GNOME 3 Installation screen to appear > click Next a few times and install the GNOME 3 desktop.

OpenSUSE -- General VM Configuration, Applying Updates

If 'root' login is disabled from the GUI, change the following setting to allow 'root' logins *in GNOME 3D mode open a 'root' terminal window by selecting Activities > Applications > Accessories > GNOME Terminal*.

```
$ su -
# cd /etc/sysconfig
# cp -ip displaymanager displaymanager.orig
# vi displaymanager
DISPLAYMANAGER_ROOT_LOGIN_LOCAL="yes"
```

If you missed the step during installation to disable automatic login you can disable automatic login after installation in GNOME by *selecting Activities > System Tools > System Settings > User Accounts > Unlock and turn off Automatic Login*.

VMware Player did not allow us to specify a hostname when the VM was created. *In KDE, to run YaST select KAL lower left > arrow right to Computer > arrow up to select YaST > in YaST change the hostname by selecting Network Devices on the left panel > click on the Network Settings icon on the right panel under Network Devices > click on the Hostname/DNS tab at the top > make note of the current Hostname because we will search on that value for other files we need to change > under Hostname change the hostname to one of our Virtual Machine Name Standardization options, OK > open a terminal window and search for the old hostname using the following command:*

```
# find /etc -type f -exec grep -l "linux-s5kq" {} \;
/etc/postfix/main.cf
/etc/aliases.db
/etc/printcap     # is automatically generated by cupsd from /etc/cups/printers.conf
```

OpenSUSE 12.3+ correctly changes this file. In earlier versions the *main.cf* file had to be manually edited to change the *myhostname* parameter to the new "suse123-xx-xx.site" hostname set in YaST:

```
# cd /etc/postfix && cp -ip main.cf main.cf.orig && vim main.cf
myhostname= suse123-32-gp.site
```
Then update the /etc/aliases.db file by typing the following:
```
# newaliases     # Initialize the /etc/alias.db database
# shutdown -r now     # This will refresh the printcap file
```

Open a terminal window and type the following:
```
# zypper refresh
# zypper update -yl && shutdown -r now
```

```
# zypper dist-upgrade -l && shutdown -r now
```

WARNING 	VMs had to be rebuilt after adding the additional repositories when performing a distribution upgrade, which rendered them unstable. A dist-upgrade will work fine unless you have conflicting repositories, but I have found that just sticking with the stable upgrade releases is the best use of our time. There were also other problems in performing a dist-upgrade once additional software was added. As long as you apply these updates at the beginning of your VM setup with the standard openSUSE repositories, you should be fine. Do not do a dist-upgrade after applications, repositories, tools and utilities have been added to the VM.

NOTE
 	
	We talked about the GNOME controversy, asking "what were they thinking?" With VirtualBox, we have the option of installing both the KDE and GNOME desktops, which is the cleanest way to have both desktops in one VM, although *not recommended*. If you only installed GNOME and want to look at or switch to KDE, perform the following steps to do so:
	`# zypper install -ty pattern kde4 kde4_basis` # (See:
	http://en.opensuse.org/SDB:KDE_install to install KDE, select **KDE** under **Session Type** at the login manager.
	
	The install recommends and suggests adding the following packages:
	`# zypper install -y oxygen-gtk aria2 kalarm kcron kdeartwork4-decorations kdebase4-wallpapers kepas kfloppy kiosktool kjots krename ksystemlog ktimetracker moonlight-plugin qtcurve-gtk2 qtcurve-kde4 vym yakuake`
	
	`# cp -p displaymanager displaymanager.orig` # Backup the original configuration
	`# cd /etc/sysconfig && vi displaymanager` # Change the manager setting
	`# Original display manager setting for GNOME 3 as default:`
	`# DISPLAYMANAGER="gdm"`
	`# Display Manager setting for KDE as default:`
	`DISPLAYMANAGER="kdm4"` # :wq save the changes
	`# shutdown -r now` # to present the KDE Plasma Workshop
	
	In the Fedora tools we used switchdesk but the system-switch-displaymanager utilities were not available in the openSUSE repositories. Click on the lower left icon and select the KDE desktop. OpenSUSE should use KDE as the default for future logins.
	
	During the install, the following warnings may appear and can be ignored:
	
	`warning: group mysql does not exist - using root`
	`Warning: Do not know how to create missing GreeterUID user kdm`
	`Information: reading pre-existing kdmrc /usr/share/kde4/config/kdm/kdmrc (config version 2.4)`

1. VirtualBox Guest Additions came preinstalled in openSUSE by default. To make sure the VM is at the latest version, or to reinstall, refer back to <u>VirtualBox-Installing the VirtualBox Guest Additions</u>.

2. VMware Tools installed automatically in openSUSE. The procedure to install/reinstall the tools is well documented by <u>VMware Player</u>; however, this book attempts to streamline those directions a bit. The tools can be installed or upgraded by referring back to <u>VMware Player-Manual Installation of VMware Tools</u>.
3. If you decide to use openSUSE KDE, refer down to <u>KDE Desktop-Fedora-Mint-openSUSE General Configuration & Setup</u>.
4. OpenSUSE does not come with a very robust .bashrc file for user's terminal windows. Refer back to <u>Terminal Window-Customizing the Linux Command Line to Make Life Easy</u> to customize the terminal window. This will make the command line experience easier and more productive for all users of your VM.
5. Refer back to <u>Firefox-Setup & Hardening your Browser Security</u> to customize Firefox.
6. Skip down to <u>Adding Fonts to Linux</u>.
7. If you are going to have multiple user accounts, or just want to run the VM as a less privileged user than 'suroot' or 'sudoroot', refer down to <u>Adding Less Privileged User IDs for Specific Purposes to Linux</u>.
8. Skip down to <u>Tor Bundle-Install & Setup in any Linux OS as a Regular User</u> to enable the VM for convenient anonymous surfing (covered in the next chapter).

OpenSUSE -- Repository Setup & Tools Update

We must add additional repositories to openSUSE to apply updates and download additional useful applications. In VirtualBox, after a normal install, we get the basic repositories that include the updates repository. Other repositories can be easily added using YaST, or manually from the command line, which is described below. The GUI is the best way to add repositories quickly and easily. OpenSUSE has a good description of how to do this at <u>OpenSUSE.org/YaST_Online_Update</u>.

OpenSUSE's default repository is the VMware ISO file or the DVD drive. This repository will look something like:

```
cd:///?devices=/dev/disk/by-id/ata-
VMware_Virtual_IDE_CDROM_Drive_10000000000000000001'  or,
cd:///?devices=/dev/disk/by-id/ata-VBOX_CD-ROM_VB2-01700376. /dev/sr0
```

My initial inclination was use the GUI to delete the CD repository, but if you want the ability to burn openSUSE ISO to a DVD, or install software from a CD/DVD, it is best to just enable and/or disable this repository as needed.

The command line method is included here for servers, which may not have a GUI and scripts. After reboot, we must add a few repositories that will support your VMs purpose. *In GNOME 3D mode, click on <u>Activities</u> > <u>Applications</u> > <u>YaST</u> > under <u>Software</u> click on <u>Software Repositories</u>. In GNOME-fallback mode, click on the <u>Applications</u> menu > arrow down to select <u>System Tools</u> > arrow down to the bottom to select <u>YaST</u> > under Software click on the <u>Software Repositories</u> icon.*

In KDE, click on <u>KAL</u> lower left > arrow right to highlight <u>Computer</u> > arrow up to <u>YaST</u> > select <u>Software</u> on the left panel > click on <u>Software Repositories</u> icon on the right. From this point on the procedure remains the same for GNOME and KDE. *If the CD/DVD repository is selected by default > uncheck the Enabled box at the bottom left under Properties > click on the Add button lower left > arrow up to tick Community Repositories, Next > and tick the boxes next to the repositories that you need:*

As you can see above, we have to be careful about the repositories we add to openSUSE. In my experimentation the following steps proved to be stable. After installation in VirtualBox, the standard repositories installed and enabled in 13.2 were: openSUSE-13-2-Update-Non-OSS, openSUSE-13.2-Non-Oss, openSUSE-13.2-Oss, openSUSE-13.2-Update configured and enabled. The repositories openSUSE-13.2-Debug, openSUSE-13.2-Update-Debug, openSUSE-13.2-Update-Debug-Non-Oss, openSUSE-13.2-Source were configured but not enabled. Adding the standard enabled repositories to VMware Player also proved stable, and that is what I recommend as we apply updates.

Performing a # zypper dist-upgrade with these repositories enabled following the installation, proved to be stable; conversely, performing a dist-upgrade with other repositories can destabilize the OS. For example, performing a dist-upgrade with the Packman Repository resulted in KDE Daemon being unstable to start when both GUIs were installed in an earlier version of openSUSE. We can add a few other repositories to upgrade software and applications without a dist-upgrade:

openSUSE BuildService - Games	*openSUSE BuildService - Education*
openSUSE BuildService - LibreOffice	*openSUSE BuildService - Mozilla*
Packman Repository	*openSUSE BuildService – devel:languages:perl*
openSUSE BuildService - KDE:Extra	*libdvdcss repository*

The combination above proved to be stable just doing an update, but there are other repositories you can try to add if you need them. *Click on OK > Next to add the repositories > depending on what you selected, windows stating Import Untrused GnuPG Key may appear, if the Trust button is not visible, expand the window by clicking on the lower right corner and dragging until you see the Trust button and then click on it.*

Reference http://en.opensuse.org/KDE_repositories and http://en.opensuse.org/Additional_package_repositories to add a few additional repositories by URL. *Click on the Add button > tick Specify URL..., Next > under Repository Name: type Name of repository, under URL type http://link to repository).* When done, openSUSE will display all of the configured software repositories. *Click on the lower right Refresh combo box > select Refresh All Enabled > OK.*

Most of the time, using the command line will expedite building a VM, or may have to be used if no GUI is available, as on a server. OpenSUSE provides the Zypper command line tool for adding repositories, as well as installing and updating packages. Other repositories can also be added to openSUSE. For example, the Packman project repositories offer codecs and audio and video player applications; multimedia related applications and games. (See: http://en.opensuse.org/Portal:Zypper, http://en.opensuse.org/Package_repositories, http://en.opensuse.org/SDB:Add_package_repositories, http://packman.links2linux.org)

The syntax to add a repository from the command line is # zypper ar <URL> <alias>. To remove a repository # zypper rr <URL> and/or <alias>. To list the syntax used below, go to an existing openSUSE VM or OS and type # zypper lr and make note of the information. You can then add the repositories on the command line using something similar to the following commands:

```
$ sudo su -
Password:
# zypper lr -d     # List repositories and their descriptions
```

As openSUSE releases new versions of the OS, it is often difficult to find documentation on how to add new versions of the repositories via the command line. Create a VM and add repositories from the GUI, then look in the directory **/etc/zypp/repos.d** for the names of the repository files that can be used. Below are a few examples of using the command line to add openSUSE repositories:

```
# zypper ar -f -n 'openSUSE-13.2-Update' http://download.opensuse.org/update/13.2/ repo-update
# zypper ar -f -n 'openSUSE-13.2-Update-Non-Oss'
http://download.opensuse.org/update/13.2-non-oss/ repo-update-non-oss
# zypper update -yl     # apply all the latest updates, -l automatically agrees to third party license confirmation prompts
# shutdown -r now     # reboot to stop obsolete processes and start the new ones

# zypper ar -f -n 'openSUSE-13.2-Oss'
http://download.opensuse.org/distribution/13.2/repo/oss/ repo-oss
# zypper ar -f -n 'openSUSE-13.2-Non-Oss'
http://download.opensuse.org/distribution/13.2/repo/non-oss/ repo-non-oss

# zypper ar -f -n 'openSUSE BuildService – LibreOffice'
http://download.opensuse.org/repositories/LibreOffice:/4.3/openSUSE_13.2/

# zypper ar -f -n packman-essentials
http://packman.inode.at/suse/openSUSE_13.2/Essentials/ packman-essentials

# zypper ar -f -n packman-multimedia
http://packman.inode.at/suse/openSUSE_13.2/Multimedia/ packman-multimedia
```
The repository above, see: http://en.opensuse.org/Additional_package_repositories.

```
# zypper ar -f -n 'libdvdcss repository' http://opensuse-guide.org/repo/13.2/ opensuse-guide.org-repo

# zypper ar -f -n 'nVidia Graphics Drivers' ftp://download.nvidia.com/opensuse/13.2/
download.nvidia.com-opensuse
```

```
# zypper ar -f -n 'openSUSE BuildService - Education'
http://download.opensuse.org/repositories/Education/openSUSE_13.2/
download.opensuse.org-Education

# zypper ar -f -n 'openSUSE BuildService - Games'
http://download.opensuse.org/repositories/games/openSUSE_13.2/ download.opensuse.org-
games

# zypper ar -f -n 'openSUSE BuildService - Mozilla' http://download.opensuse.org/repos
itories/mozilla/openSUSE_13.2/ download.opensuse.org-mozilla

# zypper ar -f -n 'openSUSE BuildService - KDE:Extra'
http://download.opensuse.org/repositories/KDE:/Extra/openSUSE_13.2/
download.opensuse.org-Extra
```

```
# zypper lr -pu       # View the repositories
# zypper refresh      # To manually refresh the repositories
```

 **Tip**	Repositories need to be refreshed when they become out-of-date. This can be enabled to happen automatically by using the -f option: # zypper ar -f \<URL\> \<alias\> The disadvantage of doing this is that you are not in control and may find yourself waiting for a refresh to complete. While many Windows users like the automatic update features offered by Windows software manufacturers, this is a way of using them in openSUSE as well.

Now that the repositories are in place, apply all of the latest updates again and reboot:

```
# zypper update -yl && shutdown -r now      # repeat this step until all updates are installed
# shutdown -r now
# zypper clean      # Clean up the repositories.
```

OpenSUSE -- General Configuration for GNOME 3D and Fallback

In GNOME 3D, click on Activities > System Tools > System Settings. In GNOME-Fallback mode select the Applications menu upper left > arrow down to System Tools >select System Settings. From this point forward, the procedure remains the same for both. Under Hardware, select the Sound icon > and change the Alert volume and Output volume to your desired levels > click on the Input tab and adjust the Input Volume > click on All Settings in the upper left > under Personal, click on the Screen icon > adjust the Turn off after: and Lock screen after: settings > click on All Settings > click on the Printers icon > if no printer is configured, click on the Add New Printer button > select Network and next to Address: enter your Printer's IP address and check Search by Address > ignore the error messages and openSUSE eventually configures the correct printer.

OpenSUSE -- Install Additional Applications, Tools & Utilities

For an Ecommerce, Finance, or Investments VM, we only want to install the software below that is necessary. If you are strictly using the KDE desktop, consider only installing software meant for KDE, or both KDE and GNOME. Many of these install descriptions are redundant with what was previously described for the Debian and RPM flavors of Linux such as Fedora, Mint and Ubuntu. But to aid you in building an openSUSE VM, these descriptions are included with the software recommended for your OS because continually flipping back and forth through the pages of this book proved to be too cumbersome. Plus, some installs and descriptions differ slightly from previous installs. (See: Mint13-Ubuntu12.04-Finance Virtual Machine Creation, and the somewhat dated link, http://www.thomasguymer.co.uk/tutorials/opensuse-11-1-guide, which still has relevant information).

NOTE	Occasionally an install may have left the process, *packagekitd* running and you may have to kill it.

```
# ps -ef | grep -i pac
root     4306     1 56 11:17 ?          00:04:55 /usr/lib/packagekitd
# kill 4306
```

zypper install -y rkhunter   # RKHunter is a tool for checking computers running Linux clones for the presence of rootkits and other black hat tools. Type # rkhunter --update to check if there is a later version of its text data files. Type # rkhunter --versioncheck to check if there is a later version of the tool available. Type # rkhunter --propupd to create the rkhunter.dat file after installing the OS and before installing any applications, tools or utilities. Type # rkhunter --check to examine the system any time after that. When done, examine the file # vim /var/log/rkhunter.log to see if everything was OK; if so, empty the file # > /var/log/rkhunter.log. Also examine and then empty the root mail file # > /var/spool/mail/root. (See: http://rkhunter.sourceforge.net, http://en.wikipedia.org/wiki/Rootkit)

Before we install all our audio and video players, let's apply the codecs needed.
zypper install -y ffmpeg gstreamer-0_10-plugins-ffmpeg   # FFMpeg is a hyper-fast (real time) live audio and video encoder, which is needed to play various video format codecs including MPEG-1 audio and video, MPEG-4, h263, ac3, asf, avi, real, mjpeg, and flash. *As of version 13.1 this install had dependency problems*. (e.g. ffmpeg -i input-file.mp3 output-file.ogg) (See: http://www.ffmpeg.org, http://libav.org)

zypper install -y lame lame-mp3rtp lame-doc   # Lame is a MP3 encoder that handles MPEG-1, MPEG-2 and 2.5 layer III encoding. (See: http://lame.sourceforge.net)

zypper install -y libdvdread4 libdvdnav4 libdvdcss2 lsdvd   # Libdvdcss2 installs the Codecs needed to play DVDs. Libdvdcss2 is a cross-platform library designed for accessing DVDs (on-the-fly CSS decryption), similar to a block device without having to bother about the decryption. LSDVD is a tool used to display a directory housing video DVDs. (See: http://www.videolan.org/developers/libdvdcss.html)
zypper install -n libdvdplay0   # Libdvdplay0 is a portable abstraction for DVD menu support w/API for DVD block access.

zypper install libxine2-codecs k3b-codecs gstreamer-plugins-bad gstreamer-plugins-ugly gstreamer-plugins-ugly-orig-addon gstreamer-plugins-libav   # If media players such as VLC are not working in the KDE desktop after the above installations you can try installing all the codecs to the left to see if that fixes the problem.

yum install abiword -y   # The AbiWord website describes this open source software as "*an award winning, small, fast, featureful and crossplatform word processor.*" AbiWord also boasts that it is tightly integrated with https://abicollab.net which will allow you collaborate and write documents with your friends in real time. This is a fairly active project that is well supported in Linux. The 3.0.1 release was December, 2014. (See: http://www.abiword.org)

zypper install -y aircrack-ng   # Aircrack is an 802.11 WEP and WPA-PSK keys cracking program that can recover keys once enough data packets have been captured. Aircrack-ng is a set of tools for auditing wireless networks. (See: http://aircrack-ng.org)

zypper install -y alacarte   # Alacarte is a GNOME 3 graphical menu editor that lets you edit, add and delete menu entries, as well as create custom application launchers. (See: http://library.gnome.org/admin/system-admin-guide/stable/menustructure-0.html.en)

zypper install -y amarok kde3-amarok kde3-amarok-xine   # Amarok is a KDE feature-rich media player that supports many formats to include FLAC, Ogg, MP3, AAC, WAV, Windows Media Audio, Apple Lossless, WavPack, TTA and Musepack. Many Linux experts prefer this media player for music over most others. (See: http://amarok.kde.org, http://amarok.kde.org/wiki/Download:Fedora)

zypper install phonon-backend-gstreamer-0_10   # Phonon gives you options to choose the multimedia framework that works best with Amarok. (See: http://phonon.kde.org, http://amarok.kde.org/wiki/Phonon)

zypper install -y anjuta   # Anjuta is a GNOME development IDE with excellent support for the C and C++ languages. From the Ajunta website, "*Ajunta is a versatile software development studio featuring a number of advanced programming facilities including project management, application wizard, interactive debugger, source editor, version control, GUI designer, profiler and many more tools. It focuses on providing simple and usable user interface, yet powerful for efficient development.*" (See: http://www.anjuta.org)

zypper install -y amule   # aMule stands for all-platform Mule and is a multi-platform, open source, peer-to-peer (P2P) file sharing application designed to connect to eDonkey and Kademlia networks. It is an excellent application for streaming a variety of different media to your computer. There are still plenty of file sharing networks and clients you can use to obtain free music, video and files like FrostWire. There is a LOT to aMule, such as the support of compressed transfers, support for secure ID, proxy* support, and much more. (See: http://www.amule.org, http://wiki.amule.org/wiki/Main_Page, https://wiki.archlinux.org/index.php/Amule, https://en.wikipedia.org/wiki/AMule)

zypper install -y audacious +audacious-plugins   # Audacious is a simple, small and fast audio player that supports many codecs and has advanced features. This is a very active open

source project that is a descendant of XMMS. You can do things like create custom playlists, stream music from the Internet, tweak the sound with a graphical equalizer and experiment with LSDSPA effects. (See: http://www.audacious-media-player.org)

zypper install -y audacity   # Audacity is a cross-platform, digital, multi-track audio editor used for easy recording, playing and editing of digital audio. (See: http://audacity.sourceforge.net)

zypper install -y avidemux   # Avidemux is a very good open source program designed for multi-purpose video editing and processing that can be used in my OSs. (See: http://www.avidemux.org/admWiki/doku.php)

zypper install -y cdrdao banshee banshee-community-extensions-common   # Cdrdao needed to burn CDs using Banshee for GNOME. Banshee, installed by default in the GNOME desktop, is a versatile Multimedia Management and Playback application for all of your music and videos. The Audio/Video player can encode/decode various formats and synchronize music with Apple iPods. Banshee GNOME Community Extensions is a community maintained repository and project for extensions to the Banshee media player. These extensions were no longer available in the Mint/Ubuntu repositories but openSUSE seems to be keeping them available. (See: http://www.banshee.fm , http://banshee.fm/download/extensions, http://gitorious.org/banshee-community-extensions) Install in openSUSE KDE is questionable.

> **NOTE**
> Banshee http://banshee.fm/download/extensions has many extensions that are not installed by default. For example, below are a few that might prove useful.

zypper install -y banshee-extension-karaoke   # filter the singer's voice out of songs
zypper install -y banshee-extension-streamrecorder   # record Internet radio streams
zypper install -y banshee-extension-lyrics   # view song lyrics as they play
zypper install -y banshee-extension-liveradio   # find and listen to Internet radio stations
zypper install -y banshee-extension-radiostationfetcher   # fetch Internet radio stations

zypper install -y bleachbit   # BleachBit is a system-wide cookie, temporary file, Internet history, and log-cleaner, similar to CCleaner for Windows. BleachBit will also shred files to prevent file recovery and wipe free disk space to hide any files that were deleted by other applications. In addition, BleachBit will wipe clean 90 applications, including almost every flash player and browser that will run in Linux. (See: http://bleachbit.sourceforge.net)

zypper install -y bluefish bluefish-doc tidy tidy-doc   # Bluefish is a web design tool that is suitable for many programming and markup languages consisting of HTML, PHP, Java, Perl, Python, C, & more, which can be used to develop dynamic websites. There is a tutorial under /usr/share/doc/bluefish-doc. (See: http://bluefish.openoffice.nl/index.html, http://bfwiki.tellefsen.net/index.php/Installing_Bluefish, http://tidy.sourceforge.net)

zypper install -y brasero   # Brasero Disc Burner is a GNOME versatile, easy-to-use CD/DVD burning application. (See: http://projects.gnome.org/brasero)

Boot-Up Manager (BUM) that is a graphical tool to configure and manage system services was not available in the openSUSE repositories.

zypper install -y calibre   # Calibre is meant to be a complete e-library solution. It includes library management, format conversion, news feeds to e-book conversion as well as e-book reader sync features. Supported input formats are MOBI, LIT, PRD, EPUB, ODT, HTML, CBR, CBZ, RTF, TXT, PDF and LRS. (See: http://calibre-ebook.com)

zypper install -y cheese   # Cheese is a GNOME versatile and fully-featured webcam application. With this you can take photos and make videos with special effects. (See: http://projects.gnome.org/cheese)

<table>
<tr><td>

NOTE

</td><td>

Reference https://www.google.com/chrome is Google's browser, which according to Google, is designed to be fast, streamlined, clean, and simple, as well as secure, with built in malware and phishing protection. The install from the openSUSE repositories did not update Google Chrome to the latest version or add the Google Chrome Repository to */etc/zypp/repos.d* directory. Downloading and installing Google Chrome is a superior method to install Chrome as it did update /etc/zypp/repos.d. *From Google's website tick the package for 32 or 64 bit OpenSUSE, and then save the RPM file.*

cd ~suroot/Downloads, or cd ~/Downloads
zypper install -y google-chrome-stable_current_i386.rpm
zypper install -y google-chrome-stable_current_x86_64.rpm
zypper update   # update the installed repository

Or if you want to use the repositories:

zypper install -y chromium chromium-ffmpeg chromium-desktop-gnome   # To install Google Chrome in a GNOME desktop install.
zypper install -y chromium chromium-ffmpeg chromium-desktop-kde   # To install Google Chrome in a KDE desktop install. (See: https://www.google.com/intl/en/chrome/browser)

</td></tr>
</table>

zypper install -y chmsee kchmviewer   # These are HTML Help viewers for viewing .chm files. Chmsee can extract files to the *$HOME/.chmsee* directory, so cleanup may be necessary. Only install them if the .chm file support is necessary. Gnochm is a CHM file viewer for GNOME. (See: http://code.google.com/p/chmsee, http://gnochm.sourceforge.net)

If you have a working version of GNOME 3, openSUSE will allow you to install the Cinnamon desktop. (See: http://en.opensuse.org/openSUSE:GNOME_Cinnamon)
zypper install -y clementine   # Clementine is a multi-platform interface for searching and playing music. Inspired by Amarok 1.4, it focuses on a fast and easy-to-use interface for searching and playing your music. (See: http://www.clementine-player.org)

The 'crack' and 'ncrack' utilities did not appear to be available in the openSUSE repositories.

zypper install -y cscope   # An interactive and screen-oriented tool that allows the user to browse through C source code files for specified elements of code.

zypper install -y deluge   # Deluge is a BitTorrent* client written in python/pygtk. It is a full-featured*, multi-platform, multi-interface client-server model with a daemon process that handles all BitTorrent* activity. (See: http://www.deluge-torrent.org)

zypper install -y devhelp gedit-plugin-devhelp vim-plugin-devhelp   # Devhelp is an API documentation browser for GTK+ and GNOME. (See: http://live.gnome.org/devhelp).

DI is a disk information utility that shows everything the *df* tool does and more; it was not available in the openSUSE repositories. Try the following instead:
zypper install -y kdf   # KDF is the KDE disk space utility

zypper install -y dia   # Dia is a GNOME drawing program much like Windows Visio, it can be used to draw many different kinds of diagrams. It currently has special objects to help draw entity relationship diagrams, UML diagrams, flowcharts, network diagrams, and many other diagrams. (See: http://projects.gnome.org/dia)

The *diffuse* utility was not available in the openSUSE repositories, although the openSUSE *mgdiff* tool installed later is very similar.

zypper install -y dvdrip   # DVDRip is a full-featured* DVD ripping program that is written in Perl. It has a feature-rich Gtk+ GUI to control the ripping and transcoding process, among other options. (See: http://www.exit1.org/dvdrip, https://help.ubuntu.com/community/RestrictedFormats/RippingDVDs)

zypper install -y ecj   # Eclipse is a tool platform and IDE compiler for Java. This is a very large download, so only download it if you plan to do JAVA development. (See: http://www.eclipse.org)

zypper install -y emount   # Emount can mount, encrypt and manage disk image files and drives. (See: http://emount.sourceforge.net)

zypper install -y empathy   # Empathy is a GNOME multi-protocol chat and call client. Empathy supports Google Talk (Jabber/XMPP), MSN, IRC, Salut, AIM, Facebook, Yahoo!, Gadu Gadu, Groupwise, ICQ and QQ. It supports all protocols supported by Pidgin, although supported protocols depend on installed Telepathy Connection Manager Components. Empathy also has many other features including file transfer, private and group chat, conversation logging, and much more. (See: http://live.gnome.org/Empathy)

zypper install -y evince   # Evince is a GNOME document viewer for multiple document formats. It supports document viewing for many document formations including: PDF, Postscript, djvu, tiff, dvi, XPS, SyncTex support with gedit, and comics books (cbr, cbz, cb7 and cbt). Evince is the open source alternative to Adobe Reader. (See: http://projects.gnome.org/evince)

zypper install -y evolution pidgin-evolution evolution-plugin-rss   # Evolution is an GNOME integrated mail, calendar, address book, to-do/task list and memo tools. It's packed with features and is a fully operational open source substitute for Outlook. (See: http://projects.gnome.org/evolution)

Exaile was not available in the openSUSE repositories. It is a music player similar to the popular KDE's Amarok, but it's based on GTK+ toolkit rather that Qt. Therefore, it's an excellent solution for GNOME users. It incorporates automatic fetching of album art, lyrics fetching, handling of large libraries, artist/album information via Wikipedia, last.fm support and options iPod support. (See: https://en.wikipedia.org/wiki/Exaile , http://www.exaile.org) The 'fcrackzip' tool did not appear to be available in the openSUSE repositories.

zypper install -y filezilla   # FileZilla supports FTP, FTP over SSL/TLS (FTPS) and SSH File Transfer Protocol (SFTP). FileZilla is a cross-platform, multithreaded FTP, FTPS, and SFTP client that has an intuitive GUI interface. It is fast and reliable, easy to use, and has many useful features. (See: http://filezilla-project.org)

zypper install -y gcal   # Gcal is an older program for printing calendars. It features a user / group based schedule with sharing options and is capable of exporting information to a variety of formats. (See: http://gcal.sourceforge.net)

zypper install gcalctool   # GNOME calculator package. (See: https://live.gnome.org/Calculator, https://en.wikipedia.org/wiki/Gcalctool)
zypper install -y gcc47 gcc47-c++ gcc47-info gcc47-locale   # The GNU C & C++ Compilers, GNU info-pages cover both user-level and internals documentation.

zypper install -y gedit-plugins   # GEdit Plugins is a GNOME collection of plugins that is used to extend the capabilities of gedit. (See: http://live.gnome.org/Gedit/Plugins)

zypper install -y gftp gftp-common gftp-text   # gFTP is very dated GNOME project (11/30/2008) that is a multi-threaded FTP client for the X Window System. The creator wants to hand this project off to someone willing to take over support. The five-year-old gFTP supports simultaneous downloads, file transfer queues to allow downloading of multiple files, resumption of interrupted file transfers, support for downloading entire directories/subdirectories, a bookmarks menu to allow quick connection to FTP sites, caching of remote directory listings, local and remote chmod, drag and drop, a connection manager, and much more. (See: http://www.gftp.org)

GIMP is the open source GNU Image Manipulation Programs with advanced features for image editing, composition and image authoring. GIMP supports many image formats as a polished, user-friendly, image editor with professional tools. It lets you draw, paint, and edit images with a lot of other features. GIMP comes installed by default in openSUSE. (See: http://www.gimp.org, https://en.wikipedia.org/wiki/GIMP)

zypper install –y gnash-browser-plugin   # GNU Gnash is the GNU Flash movie player. supports most SWF v7 features and some SWF v8 and v9. (See: https://www.gnu.org/software/gnash)

zypper install -y gnome-themes gnome-themes-extras   # Gnome-themes is a GNOME theme manager. Include Ximian Industrial, extra and selected background images.

zypper install gnome-tweak-tool   # Installing the GNOME package gnome-tweak-tool would break some gstreamer dependencies, so do NOT automatically answer yes. GNOME Tweak Tool is used to help adjust/tweak the advanced configuration settings consisting of interface, fonts, themes, as well as some other settings. (See: http://live.gnome.org/GnomeTweakTool)

zypper install -y gnote   # Gnote is a GNOME desktop note-taking application cloned from Tomboy that is simple and easy to use. It is a good alternative to using Tomboy or the more fully-featured Microsoft OneNote in Windows 7. (See: http://live.gnome.org/Gnote, https://en.wikipedia.org/wiki/Gnote).

GnuCash is GNOME open source software for personal and small business financial accounting. You can track bank accounts and, stocks, as well as income and expenses. As quick and intuitive to use as a checkbook register, it is based on professional accounting principles to ensure balanced books and accurate reports. Refer back to Finance Virtual Machine Creation.

zypper install -ny brainparty crafty gnuchess phalanx xboard   # Brain Party is a puzzle-solving, brain-stretching game that comes with 36 minigames. Craft is a chess-playing program that uses opening books and endgame databases. GNU Chess is a text mode chess opponent. Phalanx is another smart chess-playing program. Xboard is a graphical interface for chess in all of its major forms, which serves as a front-end to many of the chess services, including GNU Chess. (See: https://www.gnu.org/software/chess)

zypper install -ny gnutls   # GnuTLS is a portable library that implements the Transport Layer Security (TLS 1.0, 1.1, 1.2) and Secure Sockets Layer (SSL) 3.0 protocols. (See: http://www.gnutls.org)

NOTE  	Google Earth is not recommended for install into a 64-bit OS. It would not launch at all in an openSUSE 64-bit OS and bore the error message: googleearth-bin: error while loading shared libraries: libGL.so.1: cannot open shared object file: No such file or directory. In VMware Player, it generated the error "Can't open /var/run/atd.pid to signal atd. No atd running?, though is it did work within the VMware Player VM. GoogleEarth did not appear to be available in the openSUSE repositories. GoogleEarth lets you observe satellite imagery, 3D buildings, 3D trees, terrain, street view, planets and more. Surf to https://www.google.com/earth/download/ge/agree.html to download and install the RPM file. (See: http://www.google.com/earth/index.html) # cd ~suroot/Downloads, or cd ~/Downloads # zypper install -y google-earth-stable_current_i386.rpm # zypper install -y google-earth-stable_current_x86_64.rpm # zypper update # update the installed repository

NOTE Google Talk will allow you to use voice and video capabilities in your Google Chat properties (i.e Gmail, Google+, orkut). From within these services, you can have an actual conversation with someone (seriously, aloud), or even chat face-to-face over video. Surf to http://www.google.com/chat/video/download.html download and install the RPM file.
cd ~suroot/Downloads
zypper install -y google-talkplugin_current_i386.rpm
zypper install -y google-talkplugin_current_x86_64.rpm
zypper update

Gromit allows the user to make annotations on the screen. It is very useful to be able to highlight things while making a presentation. It was not available in the openSUSE repositories. (See: http://home.unix-ag.org/simon/gromit)

zypper install -ny GraphicsMagick   # GraphicsMagick is a fork from the ImageMagick project that puts a larger emphasis on stability. It is a powerful image manipulation and translation utility and can also be used in parallel with ImageMagick. (See: http://www.graphicsmagick.org)

zypper install -y gtkPod   # Gtkpod from Ubuntu Software Center documentation is a platform independent GUI for Apple's iPod using GTK3. It allows the user to upload songs and playlists to their iPod and is similar to Apple's iTunes, supports iPod, iPod nano, iPod shuffle, iPod photo, and iPod mini. (See: http://www.gtkpod.org, http://www.gtkpod.org/wiki/Home)

zypper install -y guake   # Guake is a GNOME drop-down terminal and is an alternative to the default GNOME and Terminator terminals. (See: http://guake.org).

zypper install -y gwibber   # Gwibber is a GNOME open source microblogging client. It brings the most popular social networking web services to your desktop and gives you the ability to control how it is that you want to communicate, for instance Identi.ca, StatusNet, Facebook, FriendFeed, Digg, Flickr, or Qaiku. (See: http://gwibber.com/download)

zypper install -y inkscape   # Inkscape is an open source SVG based vector image manipulation program/graphics editor and is similar in capabilities to Adobe Illustrator and CorelDRAW. Use Inkscape for creating fonts, text and graphics compositions including business cards, book covers, fliers, and ads. (See: http://inkscape.org)

NOTE The openSUSE repositories did not have the latest Oracle Java Development Kit or Java Runtime Environments, although they can be obtained, downloaded and installed from
http://www.oracle.com/technetwork/java/javase/downloads/index.html.
Nonetheless, do this at your own risk as installing in this fashion sometimes has had problems unpacking the JAR files.
zypper install -y jre-7u17-linux-i586.rpm or, # rpm -ivh jre-7u17-linux-i586.rpm
zypper install -y jre-7u17-linux-x64.rpm or, rpm install -ivh jre-7u17-linux-x64.rpm

zypper install -y ipcalc xcalc   # IPcalc takes and IP address and netmask and calculates the resulting broadcast. Xcalc is a scientific calculator X11 client that can emulate a TI-30 or an HP-10C.

zypper install -y john   # John the Ripper is an active password cracking tool. John's primary purpose is to detect weak passwords. (See: http://www.openwall.com/john)

zypper install -y k3b or zypper install -y k3b-2.0.2-45.1.x86_64   # K3b is a KDE graphical user interface to perform most CD/DVD/Blu-ray burning tasks to include creating an Audio CD from a set of audio files or copying a CD/DVD, as well as more advanced tasks, such as burning eMoviX CD/DVDs. It can also perform direct disc-to-disc copies. (See: http://www.k3b.org)

zypper install -y k9copy   # K9copy provides several methods for backing up a DVD. (See: http://k9copy.sourceforge.net/web/index.php/en)

zypper install -y kaffeine kde3-kaffeine-gstreamer kde3-kaffeine-mozilla or zypper install -y kaffeine-1.2.2-27.3.x86_64 # Kaffeine is KDE media player with xine engine. (See: http://kaffeine.kde.org)

zypper install -y kde3-quanta   # Part of the KDE Web Development Suite, Quanta is a feature-rich HTML editor (native source and WYSIWIG) with lots of features such as an php debugger.

zypper install -y kdirstat   # Kdirstat (KDE Directory Statistics) is a graphical small utility program that sums up disk usage for directory trees, much like the Unix *du* command. It also comes with some cleanup facilities to reclaim disk space.

The keepassx password management tool was not available in the openSUSE repositories. It can be downloaded from http://www.keepassx.org. Refer to Chapter 11 on Identity Theft in which passwords are covered.

The KompoZer web authoring system was not available in the openSUSE repositories. This is probably because the latest stable release is from Aug 30, 2007, although there is a development release dated Feb 2, 2010. Considering the project has had over three years to turn this development release into something stable, this project may be dead. (See: Kompozer.net/download.php)

zypper install -y ktorrent   # OpenSUSE's description states, *"KTorrent is a BitTorrent application for KDE which allows you to download files using the BitTorrent protocol."* KTorrent is installed by default in KDE desktop. (See: http://ktorrent.org)

LibreOffice comes installed by default in openSUSE. LibreOffice is a multi-platform, feature-rich suite of applications that can handle all of your document production and data processing needs. The open source productivity suite includes a Writer-Word Processor, Calc-feature-rich Spreadsheet, Impress-create multimedia presentations, Draw-build diagrams and sketches, Math-simple equation editor for math, chemical, electrical and science calculations and a Base-database front-end to the LibreOffice suite. The Writer tool has advanced to point of being able to ready the Microsoft Office DOCX format and render the documents almost flawlessly. To read about these components to LibreOffice suite, visit https://www.libreoffice.org/features. These tools can perform most of the tasks that can be done using the Microsoft Office suite. (See: https://www.libreoffice.org)

zypper install -y openclipart-png openclipart-svg   # Libreoffice contains extra galleries to enrich documents with graphics arts.

zypper install -y linphone   # Linphone is Internet phone or Voice Over IP (VOIP) software. Use Linphone to communicate freely with people over the Internet with voice, video, and text instant messaging. (See: http://www.linphone.org)

zypper install -y lynis   # Lynis is an open source security and system auditing tool. Its primary goal is to help users with security auditing, system hardening, vulnerability scanning and penetration testing of Unix and Linux OSs. (See: https://en.wikipedia.org/wiki/Lynis, https://cisofy.com/lynis)

zypper install -y lynx pinfo   # Lynx is text-based browser that is useful for scripting and obtaining text information from websites. For example, from the command line, Lynx can be used to obtain the weather report for any area. Pinfo is a curses text-based, Lynx-style information browser that allows you to view man pages in color. (See: http://lynx.isc.org, https://en.wikipedia.org/wiki/Lynx_(web_browser)), http://www.cyberciti.biz/open-source/command-line-hacks/linux-command-pinfo-for-colorful-info-pages)

zypper install -y mawk   # Mawk conforms to the POSIX 1003.2 and extends capabilities of awk, which is smaller and much faster than gawk.

zypper install -y mc   # Midnight Commander is a Norton Commander clone used for managing files and directories. MC is a powerful file manager that uses a two panel interface and a subshell for command execution. Also included is Virtual Filesystem (VFS), which allows files on remote system (e.g. FTP, SSH servers) and files inside archives to be manipulated like real files. (See: http://www.midnight-commander.org)

zypper install -y mcrypt   # Ccrypt and Mcrypt are replacements for the old crypt file encryption utility. These are utilities for encryption and decryption files and streams. Ccrypt's website is somewhat up-to-date, as the latest release of the tool was October 2012, but was not available in the openSuse Repositories. The Mint Software Manager reports that Mcrypt is buggy and recommends using OpenSSL, GnuUTLs, and GunPG instead. (See: http://mcrypt.sourceforge.net, http://ccrypt.sourceforge.net)

Medusa is a speedy, massively parallel, modular, login brute-forcer, which did not appear to be available in openSUSE repositories, except as a 'server python platform'. (See: http://sectools.org/tag/crackers).

zypper install -y meld   # Meld is a graphical tool to *diff* and *merge* tools for files or directories.

zypper install -y mgdiff   # Mdiff is a graphical front-end to the *diff* command for comparing text files.

zypper install -y mplayer2   # MPlayer2 is a fork from the original MPlayer project that contains significant further developments and supports more features than other players. *Do not install MPlayer if you install MPlayer2.* MPlayer2 had dependency problems in openSUSE 13.1. (See: http://www.mplayer2.org).

zypper install -y mplayer kmplayer gecko-mediaplayer gnome-mplayer kmplayer mplayer-doc smplayer smplayer-themes   # MPlayer is a movie player that plays many formats and has won various awards. There are several frontends for the player that you can try, as in smplayer, gnome-mplayer and mplayer-gui. From https://code.google.com/p/gnome-mplayer is a GTK2/GTK3 interface for MPlayer. MPlayer can play all of your multimedia (audio, video, CD, DVDs, and VCDs, streams, etc.). (See: http://mplayerhq.hu/design7/news.html)

Minitube is a native YouTube desktop client. Type a keyword and Minitube provides many streaming videos for you to view. It did not appear to be available in the openSUSE repositories. The 32-bit binaries can be downloaded. (See: http://flavio.tordini.org/minitube).

zypper install -y mmv   # Move/Copy/Append/Link Multiple Files by Wildcard Patterns.

zypper install -y nmap ndiff nping zenmap   # NMap is a network mapper. Nmapsi4 is a Qt4-based GUI front-end to nmap. NDiff is a tool used to aid in the comparison of Nmap scans. NPing is a network packet generation tool. Zenmap is also a graphical user interface front-end to the Nmap penetration tool. (See: http://nmap.org, https://en.wikipedia.org/wiki/Zenmap#Graphical_interfaces)

While the openSUSE included the oggvideotools libraries, it was not clear which applications to install to use them, akin to oggconvert in other Linux OSs.

zypper install -y ogmrip ogmrip-dirac ogmrip-flac ogmrip-mpeg ogmrip-oggz ogmrip-profiles ogmrip-video-copy ogmtools mkvtoolnix   # OGMRip, with its accompanying packages, is a large installation for ripping and encoding DVDs into AVI, OGM, MP4 or Matroska files using lots of audio and video formats, including Vorbis, MP3, PCM, AC3, DTS, AAC, MPEG-4 ASP, MPEG-4 AVC, and Theora. *Installing ORMRip brought down **MPlayer** as a dependency which will conflict with MPlayer2.* (See: http://ogmrip.sourceforge.net/en/manual.html, https://help.ubuntu.com/community/RestrictedFormats/RippingDVDs)

zypper install -y opera opera-gtk opera-kde4   # Opera is a fully-featured, compact, and fast web browser with advanced browser HTML 5 and CSS 3 support. Opera was not found in the openSUSE 13.2 repositories. (See: http://www.opera.com/browser)

zypper install -y p7zip Q7Z kde4-Q7Z   # P7Zip is a file archiver with a high compression ratio. P7zip is a port of 7za.exe for POSIX systems where 7za.exe is the command line version of 7-zip. Q7Z is GUI front-end to p7zip, kde4-Q7Z in the KDE4 service menu for Q7Z. (See: P7zip.sourceforge.net , www.7-zip.org)

PDF-Shuffler is a small application that allows the user to merge or split PDF documents, as well as rotate, crop and rearrange pages. It was not available in the openSUSE repositories. (See: PDFShuffler.sourceforge.net)

zypper install -y pdftk   # From openSUSE application description, *"Pdftk is a simple tool for doing everyday things with PDF documents. You can Merge PDF Documents - Split PDF Pages into a New Document - Rotate PDF Documents or Pages - Decrypt Input as Necessary (Password Required) - Encrypt Output as Desired - Fill PDF Forms with X/FDF Date and/or Flatten Forms"* and more.

Pgcalc is a calculator that works in reversed polish notation mode. It recognizes real and complex numbers and allows vectors manipulations. There are over 120 recognized units of measure with the possibility to make easy conversions between consistent units. Pgcalc was not found in the openSUSE repositories.

Phatch is a simple to use cross-platform GUI Photo Batch Processor that handles all popular image formats, and can duplicate (sub)folder hierarchies. It can also batch re-size, rotate, apply perspective, shadows, rounded corners, and more. Phatch did not appear to be available in the openSUSE repositories. (See: Photobatch.stani.be, Photobatch.wikidot.com)

Picasa is an image management application from Google and is good for organizing editing, and sharing digital photos. Picasa did not appear to be available in the openSUSE repositories. (See: Picasa.google.com)

zypper install -y pidgin   # Pidgin is a graphical, multi-platform, instant messaging client. It supports various chat networks (AIM, Bonjour, Gadu-Gadu, Google Talk, Novell Groupwise, ICQ, IRC, Jabber/XMPP, MSN, MXit, MySpaceIM, SILC, SIMPLE, Sametime, XMPP, Yahoo!, and Zephyr). Pidgin integrates with the system tray on Windows, GNOME 2, KDE 3, and KDE 4. It has been suggested that Pidgin is not tracked by the NSA. Pidgin Rhythmbox does not appear to be available in the openSUSE repositories. (See: http://pidgin.im, http://www.pidgin.im/download/source)

#zypper install -y pinta   # Simple drawing/painting program which features: Adjustments (Auto Level, Black and White, Sepia, etc.), Effects (Motion blur, Glow, Wrap, etc.), Multiple layers, Unlimited undo/redo, Drawing tools (Paintbrush, Pencil, Shapts, etc). The install pulls down some other GNOME packages so it appears to best for the GNOME Desktop. (See: http://pinta-project.com).

Pulsecaster is a Voice-over-IP recorder used to store a conversation to a file and publish later. Pulsecaster was not available in the openSUSE repositories. (See: https://fedorahosted.org/pulsecaster)

zypper install -y rhythmbox   # Rhythmbox is a GNOME integrated music management system, organizer, and audio player, and ripper, similar to Apple's iTunes, with support for iPods. Rbeq is a 10 Band Equalizer for Rhythmbox. (See: http://projects.gnome.org/rhythmbox, https://code.google.com/p/rbeq)

zypper install -y scribus AdobeICCProfiles   # Scribus is a large 70 MB install so only install if needed. Scribus is an open source desktop publishing (DTP) application capable of producing commercial grade output in PDF and Postscript as a professional publishing tool. It comes complete with page layout features, flexible formatting and typesetting, as well as the ability to prepare files for professional image setting equipment. This application supports CMYK color, spot color, separations, and ICC color. (See: http://www.scribus.net, http://sourceforge.net/projects/scribus, http://en.wikipedia.org/wiki/Scribus)

zypper install -y seamonkey enigmail   # The Seamonkey Internet Suite is a set of Internet applications that contains a Mozilla-based web browser, an HTML WYSIWYG editor, a mail and news client, and an address book. Enigmail is a security extension to Mozilla Thunderbird and Seamonkey that enables the user to send and receive signed and encrypted email. (See: http://seamonkey-project.org, http://www.enigmail.net/home/index.php)

NOTE	SFLphone is an open source alternative to the Microsoft-owned Skype for VOIP. SFLphone states that they are an enterprise or individual solution that can handle several hundred calls a day. There does not appear to be a repository that houses SFLphone for openSUSE. The latest SFLphone RPM install offering is for openSUSE 11-3. However, they are keeping current with Ubuntu, Debian and Linux Mint, the latest release being January 14, 2014. This indicates that the developers are having a difficult time supporting the flavors, other than the Debian flavors of Linux. You can download the openSUSE from the openSUSE website, if you want to try it. I would suggest creating an Ubuntu VM and using SFLphone in that VM. (See: http://sflphone.org, https://software.opensuse.org/package/sflphone)

zypper install -y shotwell   # Shotwell Photo Manager is a GNOME full-featured,* personal photo management application installed by default in openSUSE desktop. You can import photos from a USB drive, disk or camera, organize and view them various ways, and export them to share with others. (See: http://yorba.org/shotwell)

NOTE 	In openSUSE, to install Skype to be able to use free video and voice calls, send instant messages and share files with other Skype users. Skype only had a 32-bit version available for openSUSE 12.1. This means Skype for openSUSE is over two years old in supporting a modern version of openSUSE. But if you want to try it, in openSUSE *surf to http://www.skype.com/intl/en/get-skype/on-your-computer/linux, click on the Download now button > once Skype is downloaded > click on Places > Downloads > double click on the skype*.rpm file > Install button*. Alternatively, you can use the command line and install an RPM package, if it exists, is valid, and isn't already installed: # zypper install -y skype-4.3.0.37-suse.i586.rpm. The problem with this form of installation is that you are responsible for any future updates to Skype. The Skype install did not update the /etc/yum.repos.d directory to provide automatic updates as Google Chrome did. You may also need the following to use Skype in openSUSE: # zypper install libqt4 libqt4-x11 libqt4-dbus-1 libsigc++2 libpng12-0

zypper install -y sound-juicer   # Sound Juicer lets you extract the audio from CDs and convert them to audio files that your computer can play. This program also plays CDs, and is simple, clean, and easy to use. (See: http://www.burtonini.com/blog/computers/sound-juicer, http://library.gnome.org/users/sound-juicer/stable/sound-juicer.html)

zypper install -y shutter   # Shutter is a GNOME feature-rich screenshot application.   It allows you to apply different effects to your screenshot and draw on it to highlight points. (See: http://shutter-project.org)

NOTE	OpenSUSE did not include the Terminator terminal window alternative in the common repositories. You can surf to http://software.jessies.org/terminator/#downloads, download the RPM file, and install it using # zypper install org.jessies.terminator.i386.rpm. However, there is a reason it was not included in the distribution; Terminator did not render the graphics very well in openSUSE or add a leap over the capabilities of the openSUSE default terminal Konsole.

zypper install -y MozillaThunderbird   # Thunderbird is a full-featured* email client that is an excellent alternative to Windows Outlook or Live Mail. Thunderbird comes complete with easy email account setup, customizable options, spam filters, search tools, address book, phishing protection, privacy protection, and much more. MozillaThunderbird had dependency problems in openSUSE 13.2 repositories. (See: http://www.mozilla.org/en-US/thunderbird)

Lightning is a calendar add-on that integrates with Thunderbird, although it does not appear to be available in the openSUSE repositories. Nevertheless, it can be downloaded from the Thunderbird website. (See: http://www.mozilla.org/projects/calendar/lightning)

zypper install -y tomboy   # From the Tomboy website, Tomboy "*is a desktop note-taking application for Linux, Unix, Windows, and Mac OS X. Simple and easy to use, but with potential to help you organize the ideas and information you deal with every day.*" It lets you organize your notes intelligently by allowing you to link ideas together easily with Wiki style interconnects. (See: http://projects.gnome.org/tomboy)

zypper install tor -y   # Installing Tor in openSUSE did not start the Tor daemon automatically. In addition, there was very little documentation that could be found on using Tor with openSUSE. Tor works best with the Ubuntu/Debian flavors of Linux. Refer down to Chapter 8 to learn about being anonymous on the Internet using Tor.

zypper install -y totem   # Totem Movie Player comes installed by default in openSUSE GNOME, and is a simple media player for the GNOME desktop based on GStreamer. It features a playlist, a full-screen mode, seek and volume controls, as well as keyboard navigation. There are many additions to Totem that you can consider installing. (See: http://projects.gnome.org/totem)

zypper install -y transmission   # Transmission is a cross-platform, fast, easy and free BitTorrent* Client. It boasts that it uses fewer resources than other clients, and it features native Mac, GTK+ and Qt GUI clients, remote control by Web and Terminal clients, Local Peer

Discovery, Full encryption, DHT, uTP, PEX and Magnet Link support. The CLI package, in the other flavors of Linux, will install the command line version of Transmission, but in the openSUSE repositories a command line version did not seem to be available. (See: http://www.transmissionbt.com/, http://en.wikipedia.org/wiki/Transmission_(BitTorrent_client))

zypper install -y tree   # Tree is a recursive directory listing command and dircolors support. (See: http://mama.indstate.edu/users/ice/tree)

zypper install -y unoconv   # Unoconv is a utility that is used to convert between many document and graphic formats that are supported by Libreoffice and OpenOffice. (See: http://dag.wieers.com/home-made/unoconv)

zypper install -y unrar   # UNrar is a utility used to extract and view the contents of archives that are created by the RAR archiver. (See: http://www.rarlab.com/rar_archiver.htm)

zypper install -y vlc vlc-qt vlc-aout-pulse vlc-codecs   # For a KDE desktop install.
zypper install -y vlc vlc-qt vlc-gnome vlc-mozillaplugin   # For GNOME desktop, VLC is a multimedia player and streamer. From their project page, VLC (initially VideoLAN Client) is a highly portable multimedia player for various audio and video formats, including MPEG-1, MPEG-2, MPEG-4, DivX, MP3, and OGG, as well as for Audio CDs, DVDs, VCDs, and various streaming protocols. Furthermore, it can be used as a server for unicast or multicast streams in IPv4 or IPv6 on a high-bandwidth network. (See: http://www.videolan.org/vlc, https://en.wikipedia.org/wiki/VLC_media_player)

zypper install -y phonon-backend-vlc   # Phonon VLC Backend is a cross-platform Multimedia Support Abstraction, which allows the play of multiple audio or video formats.

Vuze, previously known as Azureus, is a powerful multimedia BitTorrent* client for peer-to-peer file distribution. Vuze gives the user comprehensive entertainment search capabilities. Vuze comes with a 1080p Video Player, Device Playback (drag-and-drop to iPad, iPod, iPhone, Xbox, PS3 and TIVO), DVD Video and Data burner. Vuze was not available in the openSUSE repositories. (See: https://www.vuze.com, https://en.wikipedia.org/wiki/Vuze, http://azureus.sourceforge.net)

zypper install -y wdiff   # WDiff is a GUI front-end to diff for comparing text files. (See: GNU.org/software/wdiff)

zypper install -y wine   # Wine is a compatibility layer for running Windows software on Linux. Wine allows unmodified Windows binaries to run on x86 and experimentally in x86_64 Linux OSs. It does this by translating Windows API calls into POSIX calls on demand. This allows the Windows applications to integrate cleanly into, among others, Linux, Mac OSX, & BSD OSs. (See: http://www.winehq.org, http://wiki.winehq.org/Wine64)
zypper install -y w32codec-all   # win32 DLLs to decompress AVI/Quicktime movies.

zypper install -y wireshark   # Wireshark is network protocol and traffic analyzer. It lets you capture and interactively browse the traffic running on a computer network in order to troubleshoot network issues. (See: http://www.wireshark.org, https://en.wikipedia.org/wiki/Wireshark)

zypper install -y xine-ui   # Xine can be used to play back various media, decode multimedia files from local disk drives, and display multimedia that is streamed over the Internet. (See: https://www.xine-project.org/home)

zypper install -y xchat   # For the KDE Desktop.
zypper install -y xchat xchat-gnome   # XChat is an easy-to-use GNOME graphical IRC chat client for the X Window System. It allows a user to join multiple IRC channels (chat rooms) at the same time, talk publicly, have private one-on-one conversations, etc. Even file transfers are possible. (See: http://www.xchat.org)

zypper install -y xmms2   # XMMS is an audio (Ogg Vorbis, CDs) player for the X Window System with an interface similar to Winamp's. XMMS supports playlists and streaming content and has a configurable interface as well. It is an audio framework, not a general multimedia player, and it runs a daemon independent of any graphics output. The supported audio formats are expandable via plugins. (See: http://wejp.k.vu/projects/xmms2, http://xmms2.org/wiki/Main_Page)

The Zim graphical text editor is used to maintain a collection of Wiki pages and was not available in the default openSUSE repositories. This tool stores all of the data in plain text files with wiki formatting and can be downloaded from their website. (See: http://zim-wiki.org)

shutdown -r now   # Reboots and logs as user 'suroot'

GNOME Desktop -- Fedora-Mint General Configuration & Setup

In Mint-Cinnamon, add icons to the desktop and panel by selecting __Menu__ lower left > arrow up to select the applications you use most often (e.g. Firefox, Terminal, Calculator) > right click on them and select __Add to panel__ or __Add to desktop__. Select __Menu__ again > arrow up and right to highlight __System Tools__ > arrow right to select __System Settings__.

To adjust the sound settings, under __Hardware__ click on the __Sound__ icon > at the bottom adjust the __Output volume__ > with the __Sound Effects__ tab selected drag the __Alert volume:__ bar on top to the right to turn up the sound > click on the __Input__ tab and drag the __Input volume__ to your desired level > click on __All Settings__ in the upper left > under __Preferences__ click on the __Screensaver & Lock Settings__, __Brightness and Lock__ or __Screen Locker__ icon > examine the __Lock settings__ such as __Turn off after:__, __Lock screen after:__ or __Lock the computer...__ to see if the duration need be changed or unchecked. Depending on the VMs purpose and who will be using it, you may want to enable automatic login. *__Click on the All Settings__ button upper left > under __System__ or __Administration;__ click on __User Accounts__ or __Login Screen__ > select the account and next to __Automatic Login__ slide the bar to the right to turn ON the automatic login; or select the __Auto login__ tab and check __Enable__*

Automatice Login. The next time the system is booted it will not prompt for a username and password. If the VM is running on a laptop, ***click on All Settings > under Hardware click on the Power Management icon and adjust the settings accordingly***.

Depending on the distro, the printer and other settings may need to be configured. There should be a <u>Printers</u> icon under <u>System Setting</u> or <u>Hardware</u> but if this is not, open a terminal window and type # system-config-printer > ***click on the <u>Add</u> button > if an <u>Adjust Firewall</u> dialog appears, click on the <u>Adjust Firewall</u> button > expand <u>Network Printer</u> and if your network printer is displayed click on it > if not, select <u>Find Network Printer</u> > next to <u>Host:</u> type in the IP address of your Network Printer and with the printer on click on the <u>Find</u> button, <u>Forward</u> > a <u>Searching for drivers</u> dialog should appear > on the <u>Choose Driver</u> screen select your print driver (e.g. gutenprint), should see <u>Install driver gutenprint</u> dialog, <u>Forward</u> > Model & Driver, <u>Forward</u> > when done click on <u>Apply</u>***.

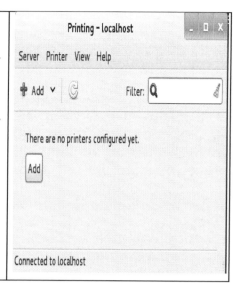

KDE Desktop – Fedora-Mint-openSUSE General Configuration & Setup

The general configuration and setup in the KDE desktop differs slightly depending on the flavor of Linux and the virtualization solution you are using. In spite of this, the steps were similar enough that they could be consolidated into one description for all three OSs.

Add the Firefox browser to the desktop by clicking on ***KAL > right click on Web Browser Firefox > click on Add to Desktop > do the same for File Manger (Dolphin)***. If Firefox is not already on the panel, add it to the panel. The directions later will require the use of a terminal window, so to add a terminal window ***click on KAL > right click on Terminal > click on Add to Panel or Add this launcher to panel > right click again on Terminal and select Add to Desktop > add other useful icons to the panel and desktop in the same manner***.

The KDE desktop comes with an excellent customization feature called Widgets. These can be added to the taskbar by ***right clicking on it > arrow up to Panel Options select Add Widgets... and double click on widgets you want to add > you can also add useful Widgets to the desktop by right clicking anywhere on the desktop > select Add Widgets... > drag and drop the widgets that you like onto the desktop, for instance the Analog Clock, Calculator, Dictionary, Weather Forecast whatever you find useful > select the Menu icon in the upper left corner > select To Desktop > select All Desktops***.

In openSUSE, set up the sound up by ***clicking on KAL > arrow over to Computer > select YaST > on the left pane select Hardware > the sound is not configured by default, so on the right pane arrow down to click on the Sound icon > select the Edit button to configure > select the option for the path that you want, in this case, the Quick automatic setup***,

Next > select OK > click on the Sound icon again > select the Other down arrow on the lower right > select Play Test Sound > if you are unhappy with the volume do the same thing and select Volume... > adjust the Master Volume and select Test repeatedly until you reach your desired volume > Adjust the other channels accordingly > OK.

In Fedora-KDE and Mint-KDE, turn up the volume by clicking on the sound icon on the lower right and raise the volume until you see Volume at 100%.

OpenSUSE, like most OSs, sets the screen server time interval annoyingly short. To lengthen the time before the screen blanks out in openSUSE, *in Application Launcher Style click on the KAL lower left > move up to click on Configure Desktop.*

In Mint-KDE to set the screen saver time, arrow over to Computer > arrow up to select System Settings > under the Hardware group click on the Display and Monitor icon > on the left select Screen Locker > consider unchecking Start automatically after: or adjusting this value to something more preferable > tick Screen Saver and select a screen saver (e.g. Clock in Mint, or Miscellaneous > Clock in openSUSE), Apply.

In openSUSE, the printer was discovered by default and no configuration was required. If you do have to set up your printer in openSUSE-KDE *click on KAL > select YaST > select Hardware on the left panel > click on the Printer icon > click on the Add button lower right > select the Connection Wizard button upper right > below Access Network Printer or Printserver Box via select TCP Port (AppSocket/JetDirect) > in the right panel under IP Address or Host Name enter your network printers IP Address, OK.*

Some versions of Mint-KDE did not detect my network printer. *In Mint-KDE click on KAL > select System Settings > under Hardware select Printers > click on the Click here to add a new printer button in the center > if your printer is listed under the Discovered Network Printers select it, Next > on Pick a Driver select the driver that matches or closely matches your printer, Next > enter a location and click on Finish.*

If your printer is not discovered select AppSocket/HP JetDirect, in the Host box on the right or under Other Network Printer, on the right pane enter the IP address of your network printer, Forward > on the Select printer from database screen select your printer manufacturer, Forward or Next > select the printer model (or the one closest) to your printer model, Forward > enter the Printer Name and Description, OK > check that the Make default box is enabled > click on the Print Test Page button > Apply. To verify this configuration in openSUSE, click on KAL > arrow over to Applications > arrow up to select System > arrow up to select Configuration > select Manage Printing > click on the Administration tab > select the Manage Printers button and you should see your printer. In Mint-KDE just repeat the steps above and verify that your printer is displayed under Local Printers.

Earlier versions of Mint-KDE did not automatically detect my network printer and after # apt-get upgrade yielded the error "The service 'Printer Configuration' does not provide an interface 'KCModule' with keyword 'system-config-printer-kde'/system-config-printer-kde.py..." when attempting to configure it. To fix this, simply surf to:

http://localhost:631/printers/

*Under **Administration** click on the **Add a Printer** button, for username enter **root** and for password enter the root password. While this error will not go away using the browser link above to configure your printer settings, it will allow your applications to print.*

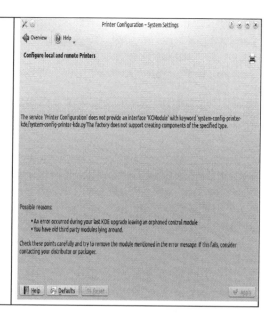

In order to run scripts or view directories on the desktop, change the Desktop Settings. *Right click on the Desktop > scroll down to select **Desktop Settings** > next to Layout: click on the down arrow > select **Folder View** > click on **OK**.* Any scripts, files or folders in the home/Desktop directory will become visible on the desktop; this is needed for future exercises where we will write a few simple scripts to use from the desktop. Consider switching to the Classic menu for quicker navigation. *Right click on **KAL** > arrow up to select **Switch to Classic Menu Style**.*

Once everything is setup and installed, it is convenient to set up the automatic login for a user ID on the system. The 'suroot' user ID has admin privileges so we should not use that ID on our finance VM. *Click on **KAL** > mouse to **Computer** > select **System Settings** > Under the **System Administration** group double click on the **MDM Login Manager** icon > select the **Security** tab > check **Enable Automatic Login** and select the user ID you want to have automatically login, **Close**.*

Adding Fonts to Linux

If you use OpenOffice or LibreOffice, you may need other fonts comparable to the Microsoft fonts that are installed in Windows so when you open documents they will look the same as in Windows Office. The Microsoft TrueType core fonts can be installed using the # apt-get install -y ttf-mscorefonts-installer package or by a multistep procedure in Fedora. This package is installed with the WINE package, if you had added that to Linux.

NOTE	The package ttf-liberation http://en.wikipedia.org/wiki/Liberation_fonts, which is installed by default, contains free variants of the TrueType Times, Arial, and Courier fonts. It is better to use the Liberation fonts, unless you specifically need to use proprietary Microsoft font's package.

Many other fonts can be added to Linux to enhance document production and viewing websites. Some of these TrueType fonts were part of the XFree86 distribution, but in most flavors of Linux, because of licensing terms, they are not installed by default.

The gsfonts-other package is additional fonts for the ghostscript interpreter, which includes Cyrillic, Kana, and fonts derived from the free Hershey fonts. (See: http://www.ghostscript.com)	t1-xfree86-nonfree - Non-free postscript type 1 fonts from xfree86 (IBM Courier, B&H Luxi Mono, B&H Luxi Sans, B&H Luxi Serif).
The fonts-comfortaa is a geometric, rounded, Sans Serif font. (See: http://aajohan.deviantart.com/art/Comfortaa-font-105395949)	The fonts-dustin package is TrueType fonts for using general purpose Sans Serif and Roman fonts. (See: http://www.dustismo.com)
The ttf-essays1743 is a TrueType font based on 1743 English translation of Montaigne's Essays. (See: http://www.thibault.org/fonts/essays)	The ttf-f500 font is similar to the one used in the Sony PlayStation video game "Wip3out".
The ttf-georgewilliams forts are free unicode TrueType fonts (Caslon, Caliban, & Cupola) by George Williams. (See: http://fontforge.sourceforge.net/sfds)	The ttf-isabella font is a cool free TrueType font. (See: http://www.thibault.org/fonts/isabella)
The ttf-larabie-deco, ttf-larabie-straight, ttf-larabie-uncommon are decorative and straight freeware* TrueType fonts from Ray Larabie. (See: http://www.larabiefonts.com)	The ttf-staypuft font is a comic Sans MS font good for art stuff. (See: http://www.thibault.org/fonts/staypuft)
The fonts-ubuntu-title package is good for making logos and it was used to create the lettering of the Ubuntu logo. (See: http://launchpad.net/ubuntutitle)	The ttf-xfree86-nonfree are TrueType fonts from xfree86. Fonts are B&H Luxi Mono, B&H Luxi Sans and B&H Luxi Serif.

In Debian flavors, as with Mint and Ubuntu:

```
# apt-get install gsfonts-other t1-xfree86-nonfree fonts-comfortaa fonts-dustin ttf-essays1743 ttf-georgewilliams ttf-isabella ttf-staypuft  fonts-ubuntu-title ttf-xfree86-nonfree -y
```

	There are many fonts for other languages, for example: sun-java6-fonts - Part of the Java JRE package. ttf-baekmuk - Korean TrueType fonts. ttf-unfonts ttf-unfonts-core ttf-unfont-extra - more Korean TrueType fonts. ttf-sazanami-gothic - Sanzanami gothic Japanese TrueType font. ttf-kochi* - more Japanese TrueType fonts, and so on...

In Fedora and openSUSE, enable Automatic Font Hinting, and Subpixel rendering (See: http://fedorasolved.org/Members/khaytsus/improve-fonts):

```
# cd /etc/fonts/conf.d
```

```
# ln -s /etc/fonts/conf.avail/10-autohint.conf /etc/fonts/conf.d/
# ln -s /etc/fonts/conf.avail/10-sub-pixel-rgb.conf /etc/fonts/conf.d/
```

Enable the Freetype Freeworld package from RPMFusion for which the FreeType Project says all bytecode patents have expired. (See: http://www.freetype.org/patents.html)
```
# yum install freetype-freeworld -y
```

Free Fonts in Fedora:
```
# yum install *inconsolata-font* google-droid*fonts* dejavu*fonts* liberation*fonts* bitstream-vera* -y
```

Non-Free Larabie fonts in RPMFusion, do not meet Fedora licensing guidelines:
```
# yum install larabie-uncommon-fonts larabie-straight-fonts larabie-fonts-common larabie-decorative-fonts -y
```

Download and install the Microsoft TrueType fonts from Microsoft's website. The spec file that someone created downloads the fonts and packages them into an RPM; procedure was taken from http://fedorasolved.org/Members/khaytsus/improve-fonts.

1. Download and create an RPM from the MS Fonts:

```
# yum install rpm-build ttmkfdir cabextract -y
# mkdir -p ~/rpmbuild/SOURCES
# wget http://fenris02.fedorapeople.org/msttcore-fonts-2.0-6.spec
# rpmbuild -bb msttcore-fonts-2.0-6.spec
```

2. Install the RPM:

```
# rpm -Uvh ~/rpmbuild/RPMS/noarch/msttcore-fonts-2.0-6.noarch.rpm
```

3. Read the TrueType fonts and create a suitable fonts.scale file for use with the X font server. Run fc-cache for the fonts to take effect.

```
# ttmkfdir /usr/share/fonts/msttcore
# fc-cache     # Needs to be run for the fonts to take effect
```

In openSUSE:

```
# zypper install -y fetchmsttfonts     # Running this retrieves and unpacks the freely available
```
MS TrueType fonts.

Adding Less Privileged User IDs for Specific Purposes to Linux

We have to carefully consider how we plan to set up our user IDs in our new Linux Virtual Machines. The chart below is meant to aid you in that task. Upon VM creation, two user IDs are created by default. In the examples in this chapter, they are ('root' & 'suroot') in most Linux OSs, and ('root' & 'sudoroot') in Ubuntu.

The 'root' ID in Linux has total access to everything in the Linux OS. This is VERY convenient, and Linux flavors that restrict your access to this ID are not in our best interest. When you need to perform functions that require root access, you should have the ability to log in as "root" and perform them. Making things more difficult does not solve the fundamental problem. The problem is that anything done as 'root' has to be carefully thought out by the systems administrator. Consequently, the OS developers are trying to protect people from themselves by making things more difficult to do as 'root'. Establishing rules and laws to protect us from ourselves is not an answer to anything. Two good analogies are the laws that require us to wear seatbelts in cars and helmets on motorcycles.

Story  	This is rare, but I am only alive because I was not wearing a seatbelt in two separate car accidents. In the first, I was driving, and in a frontal collision, it resulted with my head punching through the windshield, and me ending up partially on the hood of car. This was in the days before air bags. While I later had to pick glass out of my scalp, this was a far better alternative than the snapping of my neck that would have occurred from wearing a seatbelt. In the second accident, I was asleep in the back seat, lying down, as the roof was ripped off the car. The driver of the car I was in decided to see if a car could indeed punch through a house trailer; it can. If I had been sitting up I would have been decapitated. The fact that I am alive is testimony to the fact that wearing a seatbelt is not always in your best interest. Rules that are meant to protect us from ourselves are not always effective. They serve no purpose except to restrict our freedom and cost us valuable time and money. Frivolous laws only make money for governments in the guise of making us protect ourselves from ourselves.

Linux maintains a file called **/etc/group**, with fields that control what access a user has in the OS. Groups are used to grant and limit access to system resources to only those users that need them. The files and directories on the Linux system belong to these groups. Adding a user ID to these groups grants them more and more privileges on a Linux system. For example,

```
# cat /etc/group | grep suroot
adm:x:4:suroot
dialout:x:20:suroot
cdrom:x:24:suroot
plugdev:x:46:suroot
lpadmin:x:115:suroot
admin:x:117:suroot
sambashare:x:122:suroot
suroot:x:1000:
```

Subsequently, our 'suroot' ID has many privileges and would *not* be a good choice to use for conducting finance or using anonymous software like Tor. If you open your browser to the file file:///usr/share/doc/base-passwd/users-and-groups.html and/or https://wiki.ubuntu.com/Security/Privileges you can read about the purpose of each user and group type. The Fedora documentation Deployment Guide is also a good reference. (See: https://docs.fedoraproject.org/en-US/Fedora/15/html/Deployment_Guide/s1-users-groups-standard-users.html)

Suppose we want to set up a more privileged user? If we look in the **/etc/sudoers** file, or edit it with # visudo file, you will see:

Members of the admin group may gain root privileges
%admin ALL=(ALL) ALL

Accordingly, if we want another user ID to be able to become 'root' they would have to be a member of the 'admin' group. Let us discuss the options we will use creating User IDs for all the various Internet uses covered in this book.

useradd OPTIONS	DESCRIPTION
-c "COMMENT"	Generally a short description of the user account, often times used to provide the user's full name.
-m	Create the user's home directory if it does not exist. The files and directories contained in the skeleton directory (/etc/skel) (which can be defined with the -k option) will be copied to the home directory.
-g group	Set the primary group (as listed in the /etc/group file) that the new user will be in. Replace group with the group name to use. The default is to assign the user name as the group name.
-G grouplist	Add the new user to the supplied comma-separated list of groups.
-N	Turn off the default behavior of creating a new group that matches the name and user ID of the new user.
-s SHELL	The name of the user's login shell.
-s /usr/sbin/nologin	Specifying /usr/sbin/nologin as the user's shell name prevents login to a user ID. For port forwarding we don't want the user to be able to login. This would be a potential security hole to our server.

For example, if we wanted to create another 'sudoroot' user, we could use the command below, and if we are using a Desktop OS install, we would logout and log back in again to create a user profile, just like we do in Windows:

useradd -c "Admin User ID" -G adm,cdrom,sudo,dip,plugdev,lpadmin,sambashare -m adminuser -s /bin/bash

Additional IDs will need varying privileges based on what they will be used for. An ID setup for finance will vary from an ID for Tor, which we will use to surf the Internet anonymously and will be used to click on many questionable links presented by search engines. As such, we need to create a limited privileged user ID for conducting your various activates using the Internet. (See: https://help.ubuntu.com/12.10/serverguide/user-management.html) If your Linux OS is used by multiple users, we need to create separate user IDs for each user to separate financial transactions, anonymous activate, creating tunnels and more. Ubuntu provides the *adduser* http://manpages.ubuntu.com/manpages/natty/man8/adduser.8.html script, which many Linux users find a lot easier to use than the old useradd command. Once the user ID is created you will need to logout and login as that user. Below are two examples you can use to create your 'finance' user:

useradd -c "Finance User ID" -G audio,cdrom,fax,floppy,lpadmin,plugdev,scanner,video -m finance -s /bin/bash   # or if job scheduling or ssh capabilities are needed:
useradd -c "Finance User ID" -G audio,cdrom,crontab,fax,floppy,lpadmin,plugdev,scanner,ssh,video -m finance -s /bin/bash
passwd finance   # Not needed for automatic login, which you may want

If we want to search the Internet anonymously, we need a user ID with very limited privileges and minimal access.   Adding a 'tor' and/or 'anon' user ID using the *adduser* script in Ubuntu is as easy as typing # adduser tor and following the prompts, otherwise try the more complex *useradd* commands below in Mint and Ubuntu for anonymous Tor User IDs:

useradd -c "Tor Anonymous ID" -G audio,cdrom,crontab,fax,floppy,lpadmin,plugdev,video -m tor -s /bin/bash && passwd tor
useradd -c "Anon Anonymous ID" -G audio,cdrom,crontab,fax,floppy,lpadmin,plugdev,video -m anon -s /bin/bash && passwd tor

In Fedora the command is slightly different:
useradd -c "Tor Anonymous ID" -G audio,cdrom,floppy,video -m tor -s /bin/bash &&
passwd tor   # User ID for Tor VMs

When we are setting up SSH user IDs we also have to limit privileges and have minimal access. Below are a few examples of how you can setup SSH user IDs. Below we add a SSH Port Forwarding Only ID:

useradd -c "Port Forwarding Only SSH ID" sshdynlocal -s /usr/sbin/nologin   # User ID for Port Forwarding && passwd <username>

Add a fully empowered SSH user ID then logout and login as this User ID:
useradd -c "Partner Company" -m partnercompany -s /bin/bash
passwd partnercompany
Enter new UNIX password:
Retype new UNIX password:
passwd: password updated successfully

useradd -c "Partner Company SFTP Account" -m partnercompany -s /bin/bash # on SSH client && passwd partnercompany

Some flavors of Linux use the Debian Almquist Shell "dash" as the default user shell, reference https://wiki.ubuntu.com/DashAsBinSh; this was done for efficiency. Bash is excellent for interactive (command line) use, even though it is bulky and slow when compared to Dash.

After creating a user ID, you have to log out and log back in as that user ID so that all of the X Window directories and files are created for that user ID. With VMware Player, the 3D graphics had to be disabled before logging in as other user IDs.

```
# usermod -a -G tor anon     # Add existing user to a group
# usermod -g group user      # Change the primary group of a user
```

If you make a mistake, the user ID can be easily removed:

```
# userdel -r <User ID>
```

Using the Lynx Text-Based Browser

One of the tools we installed above is the Lynx text-based web browser. It was created back in 1992 and released in 1995 under the GNU Public License. It is excellent for use in character cell terminal windows. Browsing with Lynx is a bit different from using a traditional web browser. From Wiki, "*Browsing in Lynx consists of highlighting the chosen link using cursor keys, or having all links on a page numbered and entering the chosen link's number. Current versions support SSL and many HTML features. Tables are formatted using spaces, while frames are identified by name and can be explored as if they were separate pages. Lynx cannot inherently display various types of non-text content on the web, such as images and video, but it can launch external programs to handle it, such as an image viewer or a video player.*" (See http://en.wikipedia.org/wiki/Lynx_(web_browser), http://lynx.isc.org/lynx2.8.7/lynx2-8-7/lynx_help/Lynx_users_guide.html).

Lynx has many uses and advantages over a graphical browser, and the Wiki link above describes them very well. Lynx, being text-based, makes it less susceptible to attack than a graphical browser and can also be used in scripting to develop useful tools to use from a terminal. It is an excellent tool for hacking and gathering text-based information quickly. It handles cookies, has many options and you will not have to suffer with ads.

As discussed previously, your IP address can reveal so much about you when you surf the Internet. As we have discussed most websites you visit make a record of your IP address, among other things. If I were a hacker, I would use the information to quickly determine your county, state, and city. Let's do that; taken from http://www.commandlinefu.com/commands, create the following simple script in Linux:

```
#!/bin/bash
# set -x      # Uncomment for debugging
# Script name: getloc.sh
lynx -dump http://www.ip-adress.com/ip_tracer/?QRY=$1|grep address|egrep
'city|state|country'|awk '{print $3,$4,$5,$6,$7,$8}'|sed 's\ip address flag \\'|sed
's\My\\'
```

Then ping a URL to get the IP address:

```
$ ping www.newegg.com
PING www.newegg.com (216.52.208.185) 56(84) bytes of data.
$ ping www.walmart.com
PING e4373.b.akamaiedge.net (23.60.145.194) 56(84) bytes of data.
```

Now, let's run this simple one line script from above to determine where our victim is located. We are using a corporation in this example, but this could very well be your IP address.

```
$ ./getloc.sh 216.52.208.185
country: United States
state: California
city: Whittier
$ ./getloc.sh 23.60.145.194
country: United States
state: Massachusetts
city: Cambridge
```

If you scour the Internet, you will find many nifty scripts that use the Lynx browser to filter and use data off web pages. Below are few handy Lynx commands:

```
$ lynx -dump filename.htm     # Takes and HTML file and outputs the plain text from it so you
```
do things such as 'grep' for items.

```
$ lynx –accept_all_cookies –cmd_script=/<dir>/keystroke-file     # This is good for repeating
```
website actions such as logging in. Evidentally some websites give points to people who login daily. This command will read from the keystroke-file and perform those steps when run.
```
$ lynx -dump http://thatcybersecurityguy.com/favorites | awk '/http/{print $2} | sort -u'     #
```
Print all the links I have on my main favorites website page and remove any duplicates.
```
$ lynx -dump http://checkip.dyndns.org     # Show my ISP/DNS assignend IP address.
```

Windows – Vista/XP -- Install and Setup in VirtualBox and VMware Player

Setting up an XP VM is almost exactly the same in VirtualBox as it is in VMware Player. Having a virtual Windows Vista/XP environment is a wonderful testing center for software before installing it in a core Window 7 computer. If the software is not useful, or is inferior to other products, you have not corrupted your core OS. It is also a good way to run old software and for Windows users who don't what to experiment with Linux to setup applications such as Tor to surf the Internet.

Whether you are installing Vista or XP Microsoft limits the number of times you can activate a license. You do not want to waste a product key on an activation of a VM that you may have to burn if something goes wrong. Therefore, it is a good idea to do a test install first where you do not enter your product key and to uncheck the automatically activate in your VM install checkbox. When you do enter a product key, uncheck the automatic activation just in case you run into problems getting everything working in the VM. Microsoft will continually annoy you to activate OS, later giving you many opportunities to do so.

Although customizing Windows 7, Vista and XP differ, it does not make sense to go into too much detail about customizing soon-to-be deprecated unsupported OSs such as Vista and XP. Most Windows users are very familiar with the 14-year-old XP, and can handle that task on their own. The steps outlined in Chapter 6 on Windows 7 can be used as a guide for customizing and adding software. Automatic updates can be left off and applied manually on occasion since updates for XP are not being produced by Microsoft. Windows XP does have some underlying software in common with Vista and 7, and security updates are supported until April 8, 2014, so occasionally checking for updates is adequate. If antivirus protection is necessary for your VM, refer back to Chapter 6 for free options that are available. VirtualBox did not install the Guest Additions automatically; refer back to Windows Vista/XP-VirtualBox Guest Additions.

*In Vista, the **Install Windows** screen will appear where you can select **Language to Install:**, **Time and currency format:**, **Keyboard or input method:**, **Next** > click on the **Install now** button > consider not typing your Product key and unchecking **Automatically activate Windows with I'm online**, **Next** > accept the license terms and if you don't enter the **Product Key** pick the **Windows version** you are trying to install, **Next** > on **Which type of installation...** choose **Custom (advanced)** if it is not already selected > on **Where do you want to install Windows?** your VM disk should be selected, **Next** > windows will install and reboot to set up the VM.*

*Choose a user name and picture enter **admin** for a user name, since this is a VM you may not want a password, **Next** > for **Computer name:** refer back to **Virtual Machine Name Standardization** , **Next** > you can **Use recommended settings** and turn off automate updates later > select you **Time zone:**, **Next** > select your current location, **Start** > Vista will finish installing and configure itself > when the Welcome screen appears connect to the Internet and wait for Vista to download and install all updates, when complete reboot, once all updates are complete disable automatic updates.*

You can also now make use of that old XP license until Microsoft cuts you off completely, which we replaced with a new computer and installed the much more secure Windows 7/8 operating system on. (See: http://windows.microsoft.com/en-US/windows/products/windows-xp, https://en.wikipedia.org/wiki/Windows_XP) If you were using a 32-bit version of XP, then all your old games and software should run fine. However, if you installed the better-performing XP 64-bit, you may find that some 32-bit applications may have problems. As I stated, remember that every time you activate a virtual XP license, Microsoft will count that install, and you are limited in how many XP VMs you can create. In addition, it is not recommended that you install any other PAID software that requires registering or activation in an XP VM, as those installs will burn licenses also. Refer back to Chapter 6 for tons of open source, donationware*, and other free software you can use as an alternative.

*To install Windows XP in VMware Player refer back to **VMware Player-Creating Virtual Guest Operating Systems**), in VirtualBox refer back to **VirtualBox-Creating Virtual Guest Operating Systems**.*

When the <u>*Windows XP Professional Setup*</u> *screen appears, press* <u>*ENTER*</u> *to set up Windows now > press* <u>*F8*</u> *to agree to the* <u>*Windows Licensing Agreement*</u> *> press* <u>*ENTER-Install*</u> *to tell Windows to use all of the* <u>*Unpartitioned space*</u> *> use the default formatting method Windows selects (e.g.* <u>*Format the partition using the NTFS file system*</u>*) > after format,* <u>*Windows XP Professional Setup*</u> *will reboot and copy files to the Windows installation folders > Windows XP will prompt for a few items like* <u>*Regional and Language Options*</u>*,* <u>*Next>*</u> *> for* <u>*Name:*</u> *enter* <u>*admin*</u>*,* <u>*Organization:*</u> *Blank for HCU, for SBO enter company name,* <u>*Next>*</u> *> enter* <u>*Product Key:*</u>*,* <u>*Next>*</u> *> for* <u>*Computer name:*</u> *refer back to* <u>*Virtual Machine Name Standardization*</u> *(NOTE: The computer name has to be 15 characters or less), leave the* <u>*Administrator password:*</u> *blank unless multiple users will use this VM,* <u>*Next>*</u> *> adjust your* <u>*Date and Time Settings*</u>*,* <u>*Next>*</u> *> on the* <u>*Network Settings*</u> *screen leaving* <u>*Typical settings*</u> *ticked should work on most computers,* <u>*Next>*</u> *> enter a* <u>*WORKGROUP*</u> *or domain if you have one,* <u>*Next>*</u> *> the installation should complete and reboot.*

To work with an XP VM we need to adjust a few settings. The screen resolution defaults to the lowest setting. *Right click on the desktop, arrow down to select* <u>*Properties*</u> *> click on the* <u>*Desktop*</u> *tab, select* <u>*Customize Desktop*</u> *button > select the desktop icons that are useful and uncheck* <u>*Run Desktop Cleanup Wizard every 60 days*</u> *,* <u>*OK*</u> *> click on the* <u>*Settings*</u> *tab on the right > adjust the* <u>*Screen resolution*</u> *to the highest setting,* <u>*Apply*</u> *> if the Monitor Settings rendered the new resolution correctly,* <u>*Yes*</u> *to keep those settings, if not, next resolution down and so on >* <u>*OK*</u>*.*

If you are unable to install updates you may have to download Windows XP SP1 32/64 bit, then Windows XP SP2 32/64 bit before this old OS will allow you to apply updates. Apply all of the XP updates by clicking on <u>*Start*</u> *>* <u>*All Programs*</u> *> arrow up to click on* <u>*Windows Update*</u> *(if that does not work click on Microsoft Update, Start Now) > allow the Microsoft Windows* <u>*ActiveX control 'Windows Update'*</u> *to install > ignore the Security Warning and click on* <u>*Install*</u> *>* <u>*Install Now*</u> *> on the* <u>*Keep your computer up to date*</u> *click on* <u>*Express*</u> *>* <u>*Install Updates*</u> *> apply all Service Packs,* <u>*Next>*</u> *>* <u>*Restart Now*</u> *> continue this process until all high priority updates are applied. When the* <u>*Welcome to Internet Explorer 8*</u> *dialog appears,* <u>*Next*</u> *> do NOT turn on Suggested Sites,* <u>*Next*</u> *> tick* <u>*Use express settings*</u> *as you can adjust them later,* <u>*Finish*</u> *> when the* <u>*Your browser has been upgraded*</u> *screen appears install Microsoft Silverlight by clicking on* <u>*Click now to install*</u>*,* <u>*Run*</u> *> then* <u>*Run*</u> *again,* <u>*Install now*</u> *>* <u>*Enable Microsoft Update*</u>*,* <u>*Next>*</u> *>* <u>*Close*</u>*. Go back to* <u>*Window Update*</u> *and continue applying priority updates and restarting until they all have been applied.*

After all priority updates have been installed click on the <u>*Custom*</u> *button to apply optional updates > repeat this process until of the all optional* <u>*Software*</u> *and* <u>*Hardware*</u> *updates, as well as any additional high priority updates are applied*. Some updates don't require a reboot, but reboot anyway. This, often times, brings up additional updates.

Starting and Stopping Parallels & VMware Player and its Services to Keep Your Computer Finally Fast!

Background processes and services running on your core OS will drag down the performance of your computer. VMware Player and the deprecated Parallels run services in the background on your Windows 7 computer. VMware automatically starts VMware Authorization Service, VMware DHCP Service, VMware NAT Service, and VMware USB Arbitration Service, which is excessive for one application. The deprecated Parallels software started Parallels Networking Service and Parallels Virtualization Service as background services. Having only these services running does little to impact performance, but having many background processes will eventually have a significant impact on your computer's performance. As we install more and more applications, anything running in the background is bad. Both Parallels and VMware Player should offer the user the option of running these processes or being able to start them manually, when and if the user wants to use their applications. For security and performance concerns, it is important to investigate and stop anything from running in the background on your computer. These processes also stay active in the background LISTENING on ports that are security holes for a cracker or malicious software to exploit. *Click on __Start__ > __All Programs__ > select __Accessories__ > right click on __Command Prompt__ > select __Run as administrator__, Yes > type netstat -ab to see what programs are listening on what ports.*

I was able to run VMware Player and start my virtual machines with only the VMware Authorization Service running. I wanted to see if VMware Player would start the other services on its own, which it did not. You can view the services by *clicking on __Start__ > __Run...__ > and type __services.msc__* in the Windows __Run...__ prompt. Likewise, Parallels will not start its services automatically after they have been set to manual startup.

If you choose to use the script, you can create a shortcut to the script command file by right clicking on it and choosing __Send to Desktop (create shortcut)__ > then change the script icon to the VMware icon by right clicking on the shortcut > click on the __Change Icon...__ button at the bottom > browser to the C:\Program Files (x86)\VMware\VMware Player directory and choose the "vmplayer.exe" executable > click on __Open__ > __OK__ > __OK__. You can then remove the VMware Player icon from your desktop and only use the script to start and stop VMware.

Below are two simple CMD scripts that can be used to start and stop Parallels and VMware Player, and all their services. To be used, these CMD files have to be run as administrator. Just being logged into Windows 7 in as administrator account will not grant you the privilege to run the scripts. Consider using these command scripts if you do not want Parallels or VMware Player's vampire services running in background consuming precious computer resources.

```
@echo off
REM Written by Kirk Ellis
REM
REM These Parallels Workstation services should be set to manual to keep your computer
REM finally fast.
REM
REM Parallels Virtualization Service
REM Parallels Networking Service
REM
REM Parallels Virtualization Service enables you to run and manage Parallels virtual
```

```
REM machines.  If this service is stopped, you will not be able to use your virtual
REM machines.
REM
REM Provides the Host-Only and Shared types of networking for Parallels virtual machines.
REM If this service is stopped, your virtual machines will fail to connect to the network if
REM they are in the Host-Only or Shared networking modes.
REM
REM To set them to manual go to "Start," "Run...," type "services.msc." Scroll down to the
REM Parallels Workstation and Right Click on each one and select "Properties." Change the
REM "Startup type:" from "Automatic" to "Manual."
REM
REM This script must be "Run as administrator" even if the user running it is in the
REM administrator group. Otherwise the following error will result:
REM
REM          System error 5 has occurred. Access is denied.
REM
REM When attempting to start or stop the system services needed by Parallels Workstation.
REM
REM Running this script as administrator can be accomplished three ways:
REM
REM Way1: Create a shortcut on your desktop. Right click on the shortcut and select
REM        "Run as administrator."
REM
REM Way2: Create a shortcut on your desktop. Right click on the shortcut and select
REM        "Properties" then select the "Advanced..." button. Check the box "Run as
REM        administrator."
REM
REM Way3: Setup the command prompt to permanently run as administrator.
REM
REM        - Create a link from %SystemRoot%\system32\cmd.exe in the documents folder
REM          called cmd.lnk.
REM        - Right click on the shortcut and select "Properties," "Advanced...," then check
REM          the box always run as administrator. You must now remove the file
REM          %SystemRoot%\system32\cmd.exe
REM          from the index.
REM        - Right click on cmd.exe, scroll down to "Properties," click on Advanced,
REM          and uncheck "Index this file for faster searching".
REM        - Go to "Start," type in "Index options," Select "Indexing Options," "Advanced,"
REM          "Rebuild." NOTE: I did not try this but found this procedure documented at
REM          http://superuser.com. The shortcut solution is sufficient for me.
REM
REM Once the shortcut is set up drag it down to the taskbar.  Change the shortcut icon by
REM clicking the Change Icon... button.  Browse to the directory containing the Parallels
REM executable and select it.  Then change the icon to the prl_client_app.exe icon.
REM
REM Set the executable path for (Parallels) based on 32 bit or 64 bit machine running
REM script:
REM
if defined ProgramFiles(x86) (
  set parallelsdir="%ProgramFiles(x86)%\Parallels\Parallels Workstation\Application"
  set parallelspg="%ProgramFiles(x86)%\Parallels\Parallels
Workstation\Application\prl_client_app.exe"
  echo "Running script on 64 bit machine..."
```

```
) ELSE (
set parallelsdir="%ProgramFiles%\Parallels\Parallels Workstation\Application"
set parallelspg="%ProgramFiles%\Parallels\Parallels Workstation\Application\prl_client_app.exe"
echo "Running script on 32 bit machine..."
)

set /p start_or_halt="Enter (S) to Start, (H) to Halt Parallels Workstation: "
set answer=%start_or_halt%

if "%start_or_halt%"=="s" set answer="S"
if "%start_or_halt%"=="S" set answer="S"
if "%start_or_halt%"=="h" set answer="H"

if %answer%=="S" (
  echo Starting 'Parallels Networking Service'
  net start "Parallels Networking Service"
  echo Starting 'Parallels Virtualization Service'
  net start "Parallels Virtualization Service"
  echo Running Parallels executable at %parallelspg%
  %parallelspg%

  REM Just kill the command prompt window after Parallels starts.

  ) ELSE (

  REM %parallelspg% stop
  REM I don't like to FORCE anything to stop unless I have to. Read about
  REM taskkill at http://technet.microsoft.com/en-us/library/bb491009.aspx
  REM taskkill /f /im "prl_client.exe"
  echo Halting 'prl_client_app.exe'
  taskkill /im "prl_client_app.exe"

  echo Stopping 'Parallels Networking Service'
  net stop "Parallels Networking Service"
  echo Stopping 'Parallels Virtualization Service'
  net stop "Parallels Virtualization Service"
  )
pause
exit
```

```
@echo off
REM Written by Kirk Ellis.
REM
REM These VMware Player services should be set to manual to keep your computer
REM finally fast.
REM
REM - VMware Authorization Service (needed for power on)
REM - VMware DHCP Service
REM - VMware NAT Service
REM - VMware USB Arbitration Service
REM
```

```
REM To set them to manual, "Click on [Start] > [Run...] > type [services.msc]".
REM Scroll down to the VMware service, "Right Click on each one > select
REM [Properties]". Change the "Startup type: from [Automatic] to [Manual]".
REM
REM NOTE: This script must be "Run as administrator" even if the user running it
REM is in the administrator group. Otherwise the following error will result:
REM
REM      System error 5 has occurred. Access is denied.
REM
REM When attempting to start or stop the system services needed by VMware.
REM
REM Running this script as administrator can be accomplished three ways:
REM
REM Way1: Create a shortcut on your desktop. Right click on the shortcut >
REM        select [Run as administrator].
REM Way2: Create a shortcut on your desktop. Right click on the shortcut >
REM        select [Properties] > select the [Advanced...] button.
REM        Check the box [Run as administrator].
REM
REM Once the shortcut is set up drag it down to the taskbar. These services
REM are not started by the "VMware Player" but may be started by Workstation:
REM net start "VMware Registration Service"
REM net start "VMware Virtual Mount Manager Extended"
REM net stop "VMware Registration Service"
REM net stop "VMware Virtual Mount Manager Extended"
REM
REM Set the executable path for (VMware Player) based on 32 bit or 64 bit machine
REM running script:

if defined ProgramFiles(x86) (
  set vmwaredir="%ProgramFiles(x86)%\VMware\VMware Player"
  set vmwarepg="%ProgramFiles(x86)%\VMware\VMware Player\vmplayer"
  echo "Running script on 64 bit machine..."
  ) ELSE (
  set vmwaredir="%ProgramFiles%\VMware\VMware Player"
  set vmwarepg="%ProgramFiles%\VMware\VMware Player\vmplayer"
  echo "Running script on 32 bit machine..."
  )

set /p start_or_halt="Enter (S) to Start, (H) to Halt vmplayer: "
set answer=%start_or_halt%

if "%start_or_halt%"=="s" set answer="S"
if "%start_or_halt%"=="S" set answer="S"
if "%start_or_halt%"=="h" set answer="H"

echo Running vmplayer executable at %vmwarepg%

if %answer%=="S" (
  net start "VMware Authorization Service"
  net start "VMware DHCP Service"
  net start "VMware NAT Service"
  net start "VMware USB Arbitration Service"
```

```
%vmwarepg%

REM Kill the command prompt window after VMware Player starts.

) ELSE (

net stop "VMware USB Arbitration Service"
net stop "VMware NAT Service"
net stop "VMware DHCP Service"
net stop "VMware Authorization Service"

REM %vmwarepg% stop
REM I don't like to FORCE anything to stop unless I have to. Read about
REM taskkill at http://technet.microsoft.com/en-us/library/bb491009.aspx
REM  taskkill /f /im "vmplayer.exe"
taskkill /im "vmplayer.exe"
)
pause
exit
```

The future of Virtualizaion is bright for everyone:

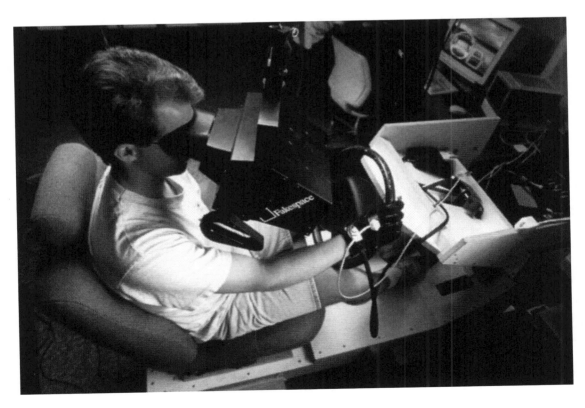

Anonymity and Privacy and Why You Need Both!

Chapter 8 — Prevent Corporations from Stalking You — How To Use the Tor Network, a Proxy, or JonDonym to Cloak Your Browser Activity (Surf Anonymously) in a Virtual OS

Before the invention of the Internet, anonymity and privacy (I consider them both synonymous) were not something to which earlier U.S. or western world citizens needed to give much thought. To invade a person's privacy, as prevented by the original U.S. Constitution and other post WWII western nations, required legal authority (warrants), expensive eavesdropping equipment and personnel, and legal considerations from their police and judicial government branches. There were checks and balances between competing branches of government as designed by our forefathers. U.S. citizens have grown up with these luxuries/rights/freedoms in their lives and have now taken them for granted. Our children no longer enjoy these God-given rights that were written into the U.S. Constitution over 238 years ago. Many U.S. soldiers' blood has been spilled throughout the centuries ensuring these rights, and we now are losing these freedoms, which I find very sad. I have already talked about how these luxuries in our lives are being eroded in the guise of national security, as in anti-terrorism legislation, like the Patriot Act, and failed government legislation, like SOPA and CISPA, which were narrowly defeated, as well as in the convenience of using digital Internet devices. These bills are continuously being reintroduced by a few select senators, so we have to examine who these Senators are being financed by to stay in office. (See https://en.wikipedia.org/wiki/Foreign_Intelligence_Surveillance_Act)

Still, the U.S. Constitution's privacy guarantees, even without this approved legislation, are being colossally eroded by modern technology. There is a lack of will from U.S. elected officials and the world's civilians/veterans to address what is taking place with the evolution and exploitation of our use of the infected Internet. Corporations, billionaires, and groups with deep pockets continue to expand their corporate/government invasion into our Internet privacy and our day-to-day lives beyond what the book "1984" presented.

It's not like we have only seen this future life in fiction, we recently experienced this non-fiction in our lives with the Soviet Union and Nazi Germany, where many millions were butchered and killed. How many times must we repeat these travesties over and over again in our human history for these lessons to be learned? The only difference is in that today's world, as technology advances, the common citizen cannot keep up with how their freedom is swiftly being taken away. We are seeing technology invented and laws passed with fewer and fewer restrictions on this mass-monitoring of communication technology. People around the world do not know that they must demand protection from their government's (and everyone else's) ever expanding power of eavesdropping on our Internet devices and our daily lives. Instead, we are all being coursed and even encouraged into having to use our Internet devices to survive. We are working more and more hours every day and being presented with less information about how the technological world around us is changing. This is happening while governments pass laws, and corporations with unlimited budgets are developing more and more sophisticated ways of monitoring our day-to-day activities. How far do we want to allow this type of surveillance to progress before taking a stand?

I understand that most of the world's people don't know about, or can't afford the time to learn about, how to fight this rapidly advancing invasion of their privacy and intellectual freedom. Most people are struggling to provide for their families by whatever means possible. However, we must all accept that this intrusion into our daily lives and Internet freedom is taking place without our full understanding of the data that is being collected. If we did understand what was happening and being recorded, there should/would be a public cry of outrage against what big government, corporations, cellphone, ISP, tablet, smartphone, search engines, scorned lovers, thieves, criminals and everyone else who is recording and what they are doing to invade your Internet privacy. These new technologies are being served up on a platter to everyone to make our lives easier, while the whole world is tracking everything we do, everywhere we go, everything we buy, everything we look at, and much more. Consequently, the question for this chapter becomes, *"**Anonymity, why do we need it? It has been argued that if you are an honest citizen, there is no need to be anonymous on the Internet.**"* After all, if you are a law-abiding citizen and if you feel you have nothing to hide, then why worry about who is watching what you do on the Internet?

We all love James Bond and seeing spies on television. But coming into the understanding that many surveillance resources (governments, corporations, crackers, criminals, hackers for fun, crackers for gain, neighbors, former government and corporate employees, scorned lovers, thieves, ***everyone***) are spying on your Internet and day-to-day activity should be very disturbing to you! Your smartphones signals show where you are and where you have been. Movies showing this to be true have little impact on their viewers (after all, this is entertainment and make-believe Hollywood stuff desensitizes viewers to the real world they are living in). Nevertheless, the true-life reality is that these devices show how long you spend in various bars or visiting places you might not want everyone to know you are visiting. Even turning these devices off is no longer a way to protect ourselves. Law enforcement and the government still track these devices, by law. In your Web browsers, tracking cookies among other things deposit themselves to track your Internet activity. Applications and add-ons that we install run processes in the background to track what we are doing and where we go on the Internet. Businesses, corporations and governments are continually coming up with ways to shadow our every move. Who knows how the data that they are collecting about us is being used, as there is no one to track the trackers. Our privacy has already been invaded in other ways.

For example, cameras are positioned everywhere on highways, neighborhood streets, banks, malls, businesses, almost everywhere, to record your day-to-day activity. If you are drinking a beer in your car (something my grandfather considered his God-given right to do after working in a factory all day and while on his way home from making shoes) can now result in substantial fines and litigation, as cameras record this type of activity. How far do we want to go with this policing and recording of everything that every person is doing? Many places of business and government watch behind one-way mirrors at what you see and do. In Kathy M. Kristof's excellent article from Kiplinger's in December 2011, http://www.kiplinger.com/magazine/archives/how-to-fight-privacy-pirates.html?topic_id=42, *"How to Fight Privacy Pirates"*, claims, *"The average consumer doesn't realize the extent to which information is being gathered," says John Simpson director of the privacy project at Consumer Watchdog, in Santa Monica, Cal. "Everywhere you go, the sites you visit and what you see are all being tracked."'* Another excellent article, by Brad Chacos, and was written for PCWorld, Nov 7, 2012 http://www.pcworld.com/article/2013534/how-and-why-to-surf-the-web-in-secret.html#tk.nl_secur points out, *"Simply visiting a website can allow its operators to figure out your general physical location, identify details about your device information, and install advertising cookies that can track your movements around the web."*

As previously discussed, if you have not read the book *1984*, written by George Orwell, you should. It is a very dark description of a possible future for totalitarian control of the human race in which technology enslaves the common man. In my youth, a police officer gave me a simple warning to go home when I had too much to drink; today I would be prosecuted to the full extent of the law, lose my job, and probably have to resort to criminal activity to survive. In another example, an officer caught some of my friends and myself at age 14 smoking marijuana. His response was to confiscate our pot, destroy all our pot-smoking paraphernalia, and send us home. Imagine what today's laws or police officers would do? If you think this view of the world is unrealistic, understand that according to Forbes, almost half of the world's wealth is now owned by less than one half of one percent of the world's population. (See: http://www.forbes.com/sites/laurashin/2014/01/23/the-85-richest-people-in-the-world-have-as-much-wealth-as-the-3-5-billion-poorest)

These examples show just how much the laws have changed in today's world. Now-a-days, these types of transgressions land our children in jail, at huge expense and consequence to their families and to their future, as these arrests are permanently recorded in computer databases (unless their families have the means to otherwise bribe the system). Some news organizations, such as *The Blaze* post these misdemeanors and crimes on web pages and keep them there for many years, where they can easily be found by search engines. It seems that we are being brainwashed into submitting to a system of intolerance, where there are no second chances. Our religions teach us the folly of this type of thinking and conduct, but we pay no attention to these teachings, and as a result, our children are becoming criminals before they have been given a chance to define their future. Since the United States incarcerates more of its youth than any other country, it has a large percentage of their population perpetually tied into a criminal justice system for most of their lives. This yields government officials/judges in U.S. courts huge profits. There is little hope for these now-labeled youthful criminal victims. Go online and view the statistics as to how many people we have in jail in the United States, and you will find that it is staggering. According to Wikipedia, The Unites States has the highest documented incarceration rate in the world. *"According to the U.S. Bureau of Justice Statistics (BJS), 2,266,800 adults were incarcerated in U.S. federal and state prisons, and county jails at year-end 2011 – about 0.7% of adults in the U.S. resident population. Additionally, 4,814,200 adults at year-end 2011 were on probation or on parole. In total, 6,977,700 adults were under correctional supervision (probation, parole, jail, or prison) in 2011 – about 2.9% of adults in the U.S. resident population. In addition, there were 70,792 juveniles in juvenile detention in 2010."* (See: https://en.wikipedia.org/wiki/Incarceration_in_the_United_States)

Western civilizations' society has dissolved into one of intolerance and persecution instead of one of reformation and forgiveness. Are we all becoming the very thing that we fought against in our country's past wars for freedom? Veterans everywhere need to be standing up against this threat to our freedom. There has been a very slow and methodical erosion of our youth's individual stupidity being corrected with just a warning, in favor of the state profiting from their minor transgressions. These transgressions that certainly don't need to be major crimes should be a slap on the wrist and a good scare, which used to suffice and should still. Many lapses in youthful judgment can prove fatal, but we should consider allowing these young men and women a chance at life instead of bankrupting their families and throwing their children into jail at taxpayer expense. Once you bleed their parents dry, the State (taxpayers) pays to keep them in jail. This is the real future of being tough on crime! Let's try to amend that type of thinking.

Instead of discerning "So what if some stranger or group wants to watch everything I do on the Internet? I've got nothing to hide, "we should be thinking about why our privacy is being invaded, and if nothing else, consider why that should be unacceptable. Surveillance is capturing more and more of our daily lives as technology advances and as we use the Internet in our daily lives. Even if you are not using the web to commit crimes or engage in nefarious activities, you still have a right to expect your interests, habits, correspondences, and purchases to remain between yourself and those with whom you choose to share it. More and more authorities/corporations/criminals/crackers/scorned lovers disagree with that thinking.

From Wikipedia, "*Espionage or spying involves a government or individual obtaining information that is considered <u>secret</u> or <u>confidential</u> without the permission of the holder of the information.*" (See: https://secure.wikimedia.org/wikipedia/en/wiki/Spying) Espionage, by definition, is inherently clandestine, otherwise the legitimate holder of the information would change plans or take other countermeasures once they know the information is compromised or has fallen into unauthorized hands. This *chilling mass monitoring* of our activities that is taking place should be viewed as a form of espionage, except for the fact that most of the world's population knows this monitoring is taking place, and that the Internet is being used as a source of gathering information with their mass permission. The common citizen is not totally at fault because the mass media reveals too little about this surveillance in the news and desensitizes the pubic in blockbuster films or TV shows depicting this activity. This complacency by the general public is similar to what the German citizens allowed to take place when the Nazis came to power, ultimately exterminating millions and bringing the world to war.

Where do we draw the line? The extent of this violation of our privacy is not being publicized or reported properly by the media and must be addressed in modern day, free-world laws that our veterans have fought for in the United States for over 237+ years. Veteran's organizations need to rise up to fight these threats, or our Internet and personal freedom will be lost forever. I'm very afraid that all of this sacrifice in blood for freedom may be lost in modern day technology that average citizens, and even some veterans, do not understand. This mass-monitoring of individual activity must be curtailed, otherwise the liberties that so many American veterans have fought for will be lost to these unchecked advancements in modern technology; this book is now here to address some of those concerns.

	Historical Reference – John Anthony Walker, Agent Number 1 for the KGB
Let's take a historic moment to look at John Anthony Walker who according to https://secure.wikimedia.org/wikipedia/en/wiki/John_Anthony_Walker was a Chief Warrant Officer and communications specialist. "*During his time as a Soviet spy, CWO Walker helped the Soviets decipher more than one million encrypted naval messages,* ||

organizing a spy operation that The New York Times reported in 1987 "is sometimes described as the most damaging Soviet spy ring in history." He was able to maintain a 17-year relationship with the Soviets and single handedly:

- compromised military communication systems
- nuclear submarine locations and procedures
- secret underwater microphone locations used to track Soviet submarines
- each and every American troop movement to Vietnam from 1971 to 1973
- planned sites for U.S. airstrikes against North Vietnam, which was passed along

One man selling information may have lost us a war if we had ever fought the Soviet Union, and certainly cost us many lives and spent munitions on empty targets in Vietnam; and he did it all for the low price of one million dollars. "It was the greatest case in KGB history," Vitaly Yurchenko, a KGB officer who defected for a brief time in 1985, told American intelligence officers. "We deciphered millions of your messages. If there had been a war, we would have won it."

From Wikipedia, "*In the June 2010 issue of Naval History Magazine, John Prados, a senior fellow with the National Security Archive in Washington, DC, pointed out that after Walker introduced himself to Soviet officials, North Korean forces seized the USS Pueblo (AGER-2). Prados added that North Korea subsequently shared information gleaned from the warship to the Soviets, enabling them to build replicas and gain access to the US naval communications system, which continued until the system was completely revamped in the late-1980s.*" This damage was done by giving information to the enemy!

Even after all the carnage he caused this country, John Anthony Walker arranged a plea agreement with federal prosecutors to testify against Jerry Whitworth in exchange for a reduced sentence for Walker's son, who was also involved in the spy ring.

I hope the above example helps you to understand that you have to be a more vigilant SBO/HCU in your use of the Internet. We all have to take measures to prevent someone from stealing information that could harm our business or families during our Internet use. You have to change your paradigm from one of "the Internet is a useful tool" to one that "the Internet is my enemy that I will use and not let it use me". Question how any information that you post or send on the Internet might prove harmful? Companies and governments will exploit your information. For example, consider that your health insurance provider was notified that you have been conducting research for cancer cures or studying mental health issues? Or, your smartphone or car GPS data could be given to your auto insurance company to determine your driving habits to help them deny payment of a claim. We all know that our employers watch everything we do on the Internet while we use it in the office, but what if they could now get information about where you go, what you do and how you use the Internet outside of work?

We know that companies are viewing the information that you voluntarily put on the Internet, such as in your Facebook page, but what if they are viewing the information that you did not volunteer? If you work for a financial institution, imagine how your employer would react if they discovered you were viewing sites about debt relief or visiting competitor's websites looking for another job? What happens if they are monitoring your smartphone to see how long you spend at casinos, local bars, or strip clubs, for example? Some hospitals now require workers to sign agreements stating that they do not smoke, or they are required by financial wrangling (higher priced health care) to submit to health screenings.

The possibilities for exploitation of your private life are endless, and privacy laws have either been stifled or ignored as technology has advanced. Everyone's personal information is becoming ever more freely available to corporations and governments as you purchase and use increasingly advanced technology that you really don't fully understand. More and more, we need these advanced devices in order to survive and make a living in today's world, but this book is about limiting the powerful entities from invading your privacy and individual freedom while still allowing you to use your electronic devices the way in which you need and want.

Develop a Split Personality While Using the Infected Internet

We have and will cover many things to keep you safe while using the Internet. But nothing is better than using the infected Internet to gather information against itself. This drops into the spy 101 book of how to operate in an Internet world gone wrong. In the post George Orwell 1984 book world, you have to assume that your employer and everyone else is monitoring your social network posts, Internet search activity, and everything else you are doing while using the Internet (at home and at work). Why not turn their monitoring to your benefit? Develop a persona that only posts Facebook, LinkedIn, and other social media commentary and images and conversations that you want them to read. Notice I did not say to present any false information that is considered deceitful and possibly criminal, just carefully guard what you and your "friends" put up on these sites. If your friends and associates will not go along with your requests, then dissociate yourself publically from them in emails, Facebook posts, and via any other social media. These people are too dangerous to be allowed into your public Internet life.

Develop a split personality that you want to present to all of the information gatherers so that you can use one personality in Internet anonymity and the other as a very public, traceable and cookie-ridden, common-user, public space. You still have to be very careful how you use each personality, and in the back of your mind, decide how that proves most beneficial to you, keeping in mind that everything you do is being monitored, tracked, recorded, and logged. Most people don't care about this mass-monitoring that is taking place, so face the fact that what you do makes your Internet activity less susceptible to crimes, such as identity theft, and will help keep you below the criminals radar. Open up your Internet activity in a very public VM to cookies, super cookies, temporary files, and everything else discussed in this book that the average user allows so as to not draw attention to your Internet activity. For example, there are benign activities that we want very much traceable during our use of the Internet. These activities should be performed in virtual environments that allow cookies, temporary files and other things not recommended in this book that we don't mind corporations, governments and everyone else tracking. Lead them to believe that you have no care for your privacy in mind as you blindly move about the Internet. Use this infected VM for all your frivolous Internet activity, allowing viruses and malware to attack this virtual environment and nuke it from time to time as new Linux OSs are released.

Why Do We Need Anonymization When Using the Internet?

Most telecommunications, corporations, Internet retail companies, search engines, and governments track (or try to track) all of your Internet activity. There are now over 580 tracking technologies and 200 different companies, including social networks, which follow all of your activity across the web. They are building up a detailed profile from what you click on, read, like, click, and buy, and they sell this to advertisers. This detailed profile about you reveals your interests, your relations, your business activities and your problems. They can include information about your physical and mental health, assets, income, personal interests, shopping habits, and much more. The information is also used to record your IP address, your current location or where you live, your ISP and how you are accessing them (mobile-DSL-modem), whom you have been talking to, what you type (search for), and more. From PCWorld, Nov 2011, in an article by Dan Tynan, ITworld, http://www.pcworld.com/article/243264/everything_you_always_wanted_to_know_about_web_tracking_but_were_too_paranoid_to_ask.html#tk.nl_spx_t_crawl, points out that, according to Evidon, over 800 companies drop tracking cookies on your PC. According to an article titled "*Milking Cookies: The FTC's $22.5 Million Settlement with Google*", written by Lesley Fair, Attorney, FTC, online targeted advertising and tracking user Internet activity is now a multi-billion dollar industry. From the article, "*In Google's case, the company uses the DoubleClick Advertising Cookie to collect info about a person's browsing activity and send targeted ads.*" In working on PCs, I can't even describe how many times I have used anti-malware software to eradicate the DoubleClick cookie. With billions at stake, companies are willing to violate laws and accept multi-million dollar fines to make multi-billions. (See: http://onguardonline.gov/blog/milking-cookies-ftcs-225-million-settlement-google).

Trackers don't know everything about you, but as they put the pieces of the puzzle together, they are learning more and more every day. For example, I did a lot of "**open surfing**" on Lymphoma Cancer after my first and second diagnosis of the disease; we all have needs for using the Internet. If you would have examined the data collected by these corporations, it would have been easy to discern the fact that I had cancer. At that time I was guilty of the **crime** I now call "***open web surfing***". Let me define what I call an "**open web surfer**" for your benefit, and maybe someday it shall be added to Webster's dictionary.

Definition **Open Surfing or an Open Web Surfer**	To open surf or do open surfing is what I call an ___open web surfer___. It is anyone, using any device connected to the Internet, who exposes their personal data, computer hardware and software information, location, browser type and header information, ISP and IP, and web surfing behavior to any entity (cracker, corporation, criminal, hacker, neighbor, thief, scorned lover, or government) also connected to the Internet. This material is then used to determine their interests, business activity, relations (friends, family and acquaintances), medical condition, and personal or family problems. It is also used by corporations to target advertising, make money selling that information, suggest paid web links and send spam email to open surfers thus wasting their valuable time. The information collected by corporations and other entities can be subpoenaed by governments everywhere to target citizens and suppress their freedom. It can also be used to compromise or hijack a device connected to Internet and exploit it.

There are many instances where we need the Internet to research topics of which we would not want friends, neighbors, co-workers, corporations, government, and everyone else to know.

- A working member of the family has an illness or mental condition and if that condition became general knowledge, it could affect their employment or ability to find employment. Corporations and the government have the tendency not to view a condition like depression or mental illness as a reason to take sick leave.
- You may not want to announce to the office that you have a treatable disease like cancer, AIDs, herpes, venereal disease, and so on. You may not want it public knowledge that you recently battled bed bugs, lice, or some other infestation in your home.
- You are a hunter who wants to research all the latest and greatest hunting innovations. Imagine how this type of research could be misinterpreted?
- You are taking medications and want to know how they interact with each other or with alcohol. Revealing the medications you are on reveals for what you are being treated. Checking to see how medications interact with alcohol could be misinterpreted as you have an alcohol problem.
- Chatting with known gays, criminals, crackers, hackers or others could cause you to be grouped in their categories of the populace, which you may not want, even though they may be your friends. Being openly gay was grounds for dismissal from the military not long ago and may become so again as political parties change office.
- The GPS in your vehicle can be used by insurance companies to price your car insurance by how you drive. Your employer, the government, or a cracker for blackmail could track your GPS to determine the places you frequent, which you might not want known.

There are many other instances in which you do not want data collected about your Internet activity, even when you are NOT doing anything malicious. You need your Internet privacy, which should be guaranteed by the United States Constitution and is NOT currently granted. The data that is collected about you is a gold mine for businesses storing this information and for exploitation to target their advertising, but it can become your worst nightmare when something like a data leak occurs. EFF reported that this happened in 2006 when AOL published the search queries of 650,000 AOL users. (See: http://w2.eff.org/Privacy/AOL) In another recent example, Sony suffered a data breach that exposed the credit card numbers of 12 million customers. In a later breach, crackers stole data about 77 million user accounts, revealing people's names, addresses, email addresses, birthdates, usernames, security questions, purchase history, and possibly credit card data. Sony has estimated its losses at $173 million. If after all this you think Sony invested in protecting its data think again! In December, 2014 we found out Sony's lack of cyber security allowed it to be hacked again when Sony staffers received and internal email from hackers threatening their families. The group who call itself Guardians of Peace (GOP) claimed credit for the hack. In the December 3, 2014 Wired magazine article titled, "Sony Got Hacked Hard: What We Know and Don't Know So Far" by Kim Zetter states that the information exposed from the hack reveals, *"Sony's top brass, a line-up of mostly white male executives, earn $1 million and more a year? Or that the company spent half a million this year in severance costs to terminate employees? Now we all do, since about 40 gigabytes of sensitive company data from computers belonging to Sony Pictures*

Entertainment were stolen and posted online." Imagine how much Information Technology talent that $173 million in losses combined with those million dollar executive salaries could have purchased in cyber security talent, which once again in hindsight would have been a much wiser use of Sony's capital expenditures.

The Sony continued catastrophes illustrate how your surfing activity might also be cracked. Picture what information your surfing activity reveals about you, facts you may not want everyone knowing (like my Internet investigation of lymphoma cancer four years ago). Envision what will happen, if the government subpoenaed your surfing activity. You might be guilty before being proven innocent, regardless of the real purpose of your surfing activities. The government believes the truth is out there; can you handle the truth?

As we have talked about, Google has entire server farms storing the search information on millions of "***open surfers***" worldwide. When you visit a web page, your browser submits a request for the data on that page and then returns it to your home PC. When you receive a web page like this **"out in the open"**, it exposes your IP address, the URL of the website, and the contents of the site, among other information to third parties. On March 1, 2012, Google unified the privacy policy across 60 of their service offerings. This enables Google to now share the data that they collect (your location, search history, preferences, and much more) about you across all of their services. In the article "'Liberate Your Archived Data from Google?" in the September, 2012 PCWorld by Christopher Null, he points out there is also a lot of voluntary data that Google collects and archives. Some of these are: Contacts, Gmail, Google Docs; photos, personal data in your Google+ Profile, links to entries you've shared on your Google+ Stream, your full Google Voice log including Google's transcripts, Google Talk chat history, Google Wallet and Checkout details, YouTube activity, Blogger posts, Calendar entries, Google Health data, Bookmarks, data related to your Android phone including your account information and your Android Market downloads, anything involving AdWords, Google Finance, and more. The idea is to improve your experience with Google so that they can target things such as advertising more effectively. Where are the privacy questions and why are users going along with this? Your alternative is to delete your Google accounts and stop using their tools, except for using the methods described in this chapter.

Christopher Null goes on to point out that Google is now voluntarily offering things like https://google.com/takeout, which will allow you to download and archive your data from various Google services. However, it is far from a comprehensive list. The link http://google.com/history will reveal your search history using Google. The Google engineers who coded Takeout, http://dataliberation.org offers detailed instructions on how to manually obtain your information from other Google services, but looking at what Google knows about you does not remove your data from their servers. You will have to go to each Google service that you have used and see which options are available for you to remove your data. Also, bear in mind that Google can refuse to remove your data, or just partially remove it.

When you visit Amazon.com, you will see advertisements based on what you have purchased and looked at on your previous visits. At sites such as http://www.ask.com, http://www.bing.com, http://www.dogpile.com, http://www.google.com, http://www.yahoo.com, and many other shopping sites you will see advertisements based on your past search engine activity. This is a form of Interactive Advertising done under the pretext that collecting and storing information about your visits and what you search and click on will enhance your web experience at their sites. The true facts are that this information is sold and marketed for profit. Google has often been in the news about these practices, but the others not so much. There is an open source alternative to the big-name search engines rich in features called https://duckduckgo.com. (See: https://secure.wikimedia.org/wikipedia/en/wiki/Interactive_advertising)

DuckDuckGo.com is a different sort of search engine that is trying to protect everyone's privacy. They do not track user's web activity, have trackers feeding other corporations, or collect personal information. If you use https://duckduckgo.com your activity to and from the search engine is encrypted when you click on the green magnifying glass to search on the text you have entered. What you visit and search on is not recorded. DuckDuckGo is a powerful web search tool with its own database. It also queries as many as 30 other search engines to supplement its results. Those search engines include Google, Bing, Yahoo, Wikipedia, Wolfram Alpha and others, which it uses to create short summaries and "O-click boxes," so that you don't have to click on the links, thus exposing yourself to those websites. Often times those summaries provide all of the information that you need. There is lot more to DuckDuckGo in its settings menu in which you can turn on Web of Trust (WOT) integration that will rate all of the links brought up by your latest search. Any link without a GREEN rating by WOT should be avoided. All searches will get the same unfiltered results, and your privacy will be respected. ***To get to the Settings and other options click on More on the lower right of your browser > arrow up to select Settings > next to Site icons consider setting All WOT + favicons (both)***.

There are also for-profit alternative search engines that will protect your privacy as well. Look at https://startpage.com and you will find that they remove all identifying information from your query and submit it anonymously to Google. People who go around saying Google this and Google that should instead be saying StartPage this and StartPage that. This front-end prevents Google and the U.S. government from tracking everything you search for when using Google. StartPage promotes itself as the world's most private search engine and backs it up with a heck of a privacy policy statement! The website states, "*StartPage is headquartered in The Netherlands, Europe. Any request or demand from any government (including the US) to deliver user data, will be thoroughly checked by our lawyers, and we will not comply unless the law which actually applies to us would undeniably require it from us. And even in that hypothetical situation, we would refer to the fact we have no personal user data to share.*

In the fourteen years we've been in business, we have never received such a request.

The only legitimate way that we see to make us start collecting personal information, is if there is a valid warrant or court order, obliging us to do so in relation to a specific user because that person is suspected to have committed a crime which is serious enough to warrant such a restriction of privacy.

Given the strong protection of the right to privacy in Europe, European governments cannot just start forcing service providers like us to implement a blanket spying program on their users. If that ever changed, we would fight this to the end." StartPage also provides a proxy service for viewing third party websites anonymously for added protection. (See: https://startpage.com/proxy/eng/help.html)

There is also StartPage's sister site https://ixquick.com, which also claims to be the world's most private search engine. The difference between StartPage and Ixquick is that Ixquick searches many popular search engines simultaneously and anonymously. Ixquick created StartPage and is also headquartered in The Netherlands, and their privacy policy is just as pointed and specific as StartPage. Ixquick seems to have many added search capabilities and may provide you a more extensive result than StartPage. Ixquick boldly states, *"No PRISM. No Surveillance. No Government Back Doors. You Have our Word on it. Ixquick and its sister search engine StartPage have in their 14-year history never provided a single byte of user data to the US government, or any other government or agency. Not under PRISM, nor under any other program in the US, nor under any program anywhere in the world."* If only that could be said in the United States, where Facebook, Microsoft, Google, Apple, Yahoo, YouTube, AOL and Skype share everything with the U.S. government! The PRISM program allows the NSA to collect emails, search queries, and other online activity of U.S. citizens and foreigners for the companies listed above through the previously discussed court-approved process authorized by the FISA Amendments Act of 2008.

Another option for you to consider is the Freenet project. This is a free, anonymous, and private Internet service within the highly exploited Internet we all now know and use. From their website, *"Freenet is free software which lets you anonymously share files, browse and publish "freesites" (websites accessible only through Freenet) and chat on forums, without fear of censorship. Freenet is decentralized to make it less vulnerable to attack, and if used in "darknet" mode, where users only connect to their friends, is very difficult to detect."* In their FAQ they describe how Freenet differs from Tor, *"Tor is a proxy network that lets you access the web anonymously, or use "hidden services", which are web servers (or other services) hidden behind the Tor tunnel network. Freenet is a separate network that runs over the Internet. You can only access Freenet content through Freenet: Freesites (websites on Freenet), in-Freenet chat forums (FMS, Sone, etc.), files shared within Freenet, in-Freenet email. Freenet is a distributed datastore, meaning there are no central servers at all (when used correctly), which stores content."* (See: https://freenetproject.org)

From a PCWorld, October 11, 2011 article titled "FAQ: Will Your ISP Protect Your Privacy?" by Alex Wawro, the answer is NO. From the article, *"Political activists using technology to stay organized should take care with what they share online. Earlier this week we learned that Google and Internet service provider Sonic.net were forced to hand over WikiLeaks volunteer Jacob Applebaum's Gmail account data, including the names and addresses of people he corresponded with (though not the actual content of his correspondence.)"* It gets worse as governments try to push through bill after bill disguised as something else to give them easier access to collect and gather more data about you. Take the Internet invasion bill H.R. 1981 introduced May 25, 2011 that was cloaked as the *Protecting Children from Internet Pornographers Act of 2011*. Alex Wawro goes on to say, *"That's why civil liberties groups in the European Union are railing against the Data Retention Directive, which requires all member states to retain private telecommunications data–including IP addresses and traffic logs–for up to two years and turn it over to police with a court order. A similar data retention law is being pushed through the U.S. Congress under the header H.R. 1981, rankling privacy advocates and jeopardizing your anonymity online."* (See: http://www.pcworld.com/article/241591/faq_will_your_isp_protect_your_privacy_.html#tk.nl spx_t_cbintro, https://en.wikipedia.org/wiki/Protecting_Children_from_Internet_Pornographers_Act_of_2011)

Every time you connect to the Internet, your Internet Service Provider assigns you a dynamic IP address that links you to your online activities, and at the very least, log the time, date, and link to every website you visit. Theoretically, these logs are anonymous since they are tied to your IP address rather than your name. However, since your ISP records which IP address is assigned to which subscriber, it's child's play for an investigator to figure out where you've been and who you've been talking to, if your ISP turns over or has those records cracked.

There is also the threat of "Deep Packet Inspection", as in the recently defeated bills like SOPA and the Protect IP Act, which would have required your ISP to start monitoring your online activity. Our politicians are constantly being lobbied to restrict and monitor our free use on the Internet. Both bills were defeated, but now we have H.R. 1981 to worry about, and who knows what will come in the future? Without strong rejection by the electorate of this and other cloaked legislation, there will soon be even more monitoring and logging of our Internet activity.

Your ISP will become legally obligated to prevent you from accessing restricted websites. To do this they will use deep packet inspection tools to watch your Internet activity. All Internet activity is made up of packets, like little nanobots running around electronically from device to device. Each packet contains information about itself as to what they are, whom they are from, and where they are going. Anyone engaging in deep packet inspection can scan, log, route or block those packets. With legislation like this, the government or your ISP can root through all of the information you exchange online, like your age, location and shopping records, as well as other personal data. Your ISP could profit by selling that data to advertising companies. Law enforcement can monitor and curtail your Net access without your knowledge. The exploitive possibilities are limitless, and there must be a public outcry to stop this. If you visit the website https://xerobank.com/personal/tour it lists some of the threats we face:

Surfing Habits & Email History	Online Banking & Retirement
Personal Files, Photos, etc.	Identity Theft
Business Communications	Sales & Marketing Research
Employee Monitoring	Website Restriction & Censorship
Behavioral & Financial Profiling	Religious & Sexual Targeting
Data Retention & Data-mining	Mass Surveillance of Citizens

Story 	Let's explore a story that I call the bouncing grenade! While serving in the Army Light Infantry, we were on a training exercise to learn about throwing live grenades into a live grenade range. To understand what this is, imagine a wall created with cinderblocks that sits a few feet above where you will be throwing the grenades downrange. There are also cinderblock walls to the left and the right to protect other soldiers who are also using the range. You stand about 4 to 6 feet below where the grenade will explode, making your throwing point safe. This whole exercise is meant to instill in young army or marines soldiers that throwing grenades around is perfectly safe for them and yet detrimental to the enemy. During this training exercise, there is a safety monitor nearby to capture and throw the grenade if anyone panics and/or drops the grenade, which sometimes happens. While training, I heard a panicked

shout of "LOOK OUT! GRENADE!" nearby and had no idea what was going on. I soon learned that some panicked soldier had tossed their grenade sideways. It was bouncing across the top of the cinderblock wall, and we all wondered which grenade throwing slot it was going to pick to drop into. As luck would have it, the grenade picked mine, but decided to fall on the opposite side of the wall from my throwing position. The instructor and I dove for cover not knowing if the cinderblock would prove sufficient to protect us from the explosion and debris. The range was designed to have the grenades explode as far away as they could be thrown, not right next to the wall. The grenade exploded, and shovelfuls of dirt rained down on our backs, demonstrating how close we had come to being shredded by shrapnel.

Your Internet activity is now that bouncing grenade waiting to blow up and destroy your life. You have to start thinking about how you are using the Internet and how it will be used against you. Sun Tzu, author of *The Art of War*, one of the most-read books in human history on how to conduct warfare, wrote "*Know your enemy and know yourself and you can fight a thousand battles without disaster.*" By now, you know the Internet is your enemy, and now you are learning about the threats you/we all face so you/we can someday win our battles.

What the Internet Search Engine Privacy/Spying Statements Tell You

Go visit the privacy/spying statement of any search engine and what you read will be a real ***eye opener***. For example, go to https://www.google.com/intl/en/policies/privacy, or http://www.dogpile.com/info.dogpl.t2.1/support/privacypolicy; the private statements point out what their server's record; *what you search for, your Web request, the date and time of your search, the links you click on, your IP, your browser type, browser language, and your browser configuration*, need I continue? They also compile any volunteer information that users may provide them. For example, Dogpile admits that, depending on what service/third party you use, they will collect first and last name, mailing address, email address, telephone number, age, gender, occupation, household income, credit card information, and more. They receive the information from surveys you fill out, contests you may enter, program registrations, and a lot more. I wanted to include some of the privacy statements in this book but I doubt any search provider would grant me permission, and I did not ask. I mentioned Dogpile above, but the others do the same.

Search engines record a lot about your Internet activity as you use their services. They profile and track your interests, behavior and relationships. They lure you in as a victim to be exploited by offering free services such as Search, Email, Apps, Docs, Wallet, Voice, an OS, DNS, Games, etc. These Internet services are offered up to enable them to gather profile and track user's use of the Internet so they can profit off this information. They do this with no regard for your privacy and users often have no way of removing this data from their data servers.

Use a Web Proxy or Web Proxy Server to Be More Anonymous

We will soon discuss how to set up and manage your own proxy, but perhaps that is more effort than you want to expend for anonymity on the Internet. Before we discuss anonymity software and products, you may just want to use a simple, free web proxy or web proxy server. There are many web proxies that appear and disappear on the Internet, and we have to be careful in how we use them. It is not an easy task to determine if they are somewhat legitimate or not. Luckily, there are websites that have done this research for us.

However, FREE web proxies have their drawbacks, such as slow data speeds, difficulty viewing videos and listening to music, they may inject advertising into their use, and you may find you cannot access some websites using them. In the March, 2013 issue of PCWorld, in the article "Surf the Web in Secret" by Brad Chacos, he states "*Anonymouse, Hide My Ass, and Proxify are long-standing and well trusted Web proxies, however, and each offers a paid subscriber service that nixes the speed and content complaints. Also, Proxy.org and PublicProxyServers.com maintain extensive, frequently updated lists of Web proxies.*"

You can visit http://anonymouse.org/anonwww.html and click on <u>Your Calling Card without Anonymouse</u>, and view the results. Anonymouse is another way for you to become anonymous on the Internet. Anonymouse and Hide My Ass can be used to send anonymous Email, or post anonymous entries in newsgroups. Both sites offer free, basic anonymous email services that also can be very advantageous if you don't want to train the recipient to unencrypt an encrypted email. To use the sites/services, you agree to never send spam or use them for any illegal purposes.

A web proxy can also observe what you are doing on the Internet, so you never want to do things such as banking or ecommerce while using them. (See: https://hidemyass.com/proxy, https://proxy.org, https://proxify.com, http://www.publicproxyservers.com). A paid proxy recommended by many computer professionals is FoxyProxy. (See: http://getfoxyproxy.org). We will soon discuss using a VPN to encrypt your Internet activity, but you should compare using a proxy versus a VPN by visiting http://getfoxyproxy.org/vpn/proxy-vs-vpn.html, which details the advantages and disadvantages of both approaches and determines which is best for you. In addition, my first blog entry at http://thatcybersecurityguy.blogspot.com teaches you how to set up a simple Windows 7 VPN, which you may want to use behind your local firewall.

A proxy server is a bit of a different animal than a web proxy and requires some browser configuration. You will have to enter the <u>Preferences</u> or <u>Options</u> section of your browser and configure it to connect to the proxy's IP address. Mr. Chacos also states that "*Hide My Ass and ProxyNova keep two of the best lists of active proxy servers, with each individual proxy's speed, uptime, country of origin, and level of anonymity clearly identified.*"

How the US Government Can Probably Track You Even If You Are Using Tor

From https://secure.wikimedia.org/wikipedia/en/wiki/USA_PATRIOT_Act on continuing the Patriot Act, "*On May 26, 2011, President Barack Obama signed a four-year extension of three key provisions in the USA PATRIOT Act: [2] roving wiretaps, searches of business records (the "library records provision"), and conducting surveillance of "lone wolves" — individuals suspected of terrorist-related activities not linked to terrorist groups.*" People viewed his second election as a possible scaling back of this continued monitoring, but his administration became a testament to solidify corporate and government surveillance of their citizens. Consequently, thanks to this invasion of privacy, agencies like the NSA still spend large sums of U.S. taxpayer dollars to stay abreast of tools like Tor, unlike much rest of the world and unscrupulous individuals without the billion dollar pockets, who probably cannot. After all, Tor is an invention of the US Navy.

I've have tried to explain this insidious attack on our Internet privacy, described above, to friends and family and the response is usually, "*let them track me... I'm not doing anything wrong on the Internet.*" One man, who wrote into a forum on a magazine that I will not name, said that while at a company crime prevention seminar, a government agent from a cybercrime unit said the Tor network, its users, and privacy activists were mostly crooks. He went on to say with pride that he has no concern if Big Brother is watching. I have news for him, even if he was using Tor, **Big Brother is watching**. If an agency like the NSA wants to track your Internet activity, in my experience, they can and will, *Tor or no Tor*. The NSA has infinite amounts of computing hardware compared to the average Internet device user. The Onion Router upon which Tor is based, was originally developed by the Navy (in fact, Naval Research Lab, one of the best jobs I ever had working on chaff testing) to hide the true origin of packets on an IP network. If the core of the Tor software was developed by the US Navy, what do you think about the government's ability to track users accessing Tor relays? (See: https://secure.wikimedia.org/wikipedia/en/wiki/Onion_routing)

Tor tends to get bad press, so allow me to cite one example of that. In the PCWorld article by Lucian Constantin, from Jan 30, 2014, titled "*Tor-enabled malware stole credit card data from PoS systems at dozens of retailers*", we are guided to think that this theft had something to do with the Tor network. The truth is the Tor network is almost completely irrelevant to this conversation and theft. If you bother to read the article you will discover that PoS terminals do not employ any sort to encryption techniques, are easily exploited, and the retailers have little interests in securing them. In fact, eighty percent of antimalware software would have detected the ChewBacca malware that was used to transfer the data. However, these companies are so callous about their customer's identity and credit card data that they do not run antimalware on their PoS devices. So the fact that the Tor network was used is almost irrelevant, but was included in the headline nonetheless. (See: http://www.pcworld.com/article/2093200/torenabled-malware-stole-credit-card-data-from-pos-systems-at-dozens-of-retailers.html#tk.nl_secur)

With that said, I don't want *big Corporations and the rest of the world (China's millions of crackers, for example) watching everything we do.* In article after article that I have read on Tor, I have found no evidence that the search engines or average corporations have developed ways to track what you are doing and surfing when using Tor. They can only exploit backdoors into other applications that leak information about your Internet activity, such as a Flash player. Does that mean they can't, or don't have teams dedicated to doing so? Yes they do! Many corporations are closely affiliated with the government and using Tor with virtualization should make your Internet activity more secure than much of the other lower-hanging fruit. My analogy for all this is, *do you want a stalker following you around (can you say paparazzi) recording everything you do all day?* To me, the corporations that are tracking your every mouse click are your paparazzi. Guess what, you are now a celebrity! *Tor is worth a try!* As with any software, it will have to be kept up to date in the hopes of keeping us anonymous, just as anti-malware software tries to keep us all safe.

I will emphasize again, **snoopers** and deceitful **crackers** use the "**open surfer**" information (once compromised) to hack into and steal your identity to target their scams. Greedy corporate and government employees have been known to compromise this information for profit. They sell this information for substantial sums of money and for far greater than what they are paid. As I mentioned previously, the US government can subpoena your web information from any business that tracks your Internet activity, anytime (can you say the George Bush/Obama Patriot Act, which is still in place?) In the worst cases, "**open surfing**" provides information to corporations, crackers/criminals and governments that can be used to cost you your life (in some countries), get you incarcerated, cost you many thousands of dollars in litigation, lose years in frustration getting back your identity, ruin your credit, and destroy your life as you know it. No technique is perfect, and some crackers/governments will have a work around to anything (the NSA for example). Nonetheless, you will be safe from most of the rest of the world, which is a lot more secure than "**open surfing**," thus exposing your home PC to every site that you visit on the Internet! Please read and learn about Tor's limitations at https://www.torproject.org/download/download.html.en#Warning before you accept this technique at hardening your security.

From the Tor website about the use of the Tor Browser, "*Tor does not protect all of your computer's Internet traffic when you run it. Tor only protects your applications that are properly configured to send their Internet traffic through Tor. To avoid problems with Tor configuration, we strongly recommend you use the Tor Browser Bundle. It is pre-configured to protect your privacy and anonymity on the web as long as you're browsing with the Tor Browser itself. Almost any other web browser configuration is likely to be unsafe to use with Tor.*" To get even better privacy you can integrate other applications with Tor, which we will cover shortly.

Tor – How It Works, Tor Drawbacks, Everything Done Using Tor Is Not Safe

Before we get into how Tor works, think back to all of those Hollywood movies where the government or bad guys are trying to trace a phone call or some sort of computer Internet activity. Somehow, the person being traced is always able to outsmart the legions of highly paid people at the top of their field, using state-of-the-art hardware and software that cost billions, but somehow can't find from where the hackers signal is originating from. Usually it is some geeky guy hammering on a keyboard with a supervisor who has no clue what he is doing, but is constantly badgering the geek for results. The geek mumbles under his breath "this guy is good; somehow he is staying one step ahead of our ability to trace him." The supervisor then snaps, "What was that, why can't you figure out where he is? I thought you said this trace software was foolproof!" The geek responds, "I can't get a lock on the signal because he is bouncing the signal off other servers." Can't you break through that?" the supervisor shouts. "I can, but it will take time" the geek yammers, wishing the supervisor would just go away and let him do his job.

Tor works in a similar fashion by not establishing a direct connection to Internet, but instead uses what is called a "Tor Server Relay". That relay is picked at random from a distributed network of Tor relays/servers all around the world, called onion routers. When the Tor software is started, it makes a request to the Tor network and says make a path/circuit for us to get to the Internet via the Tor relays. Relays will answer and one will be picked at random to be the first non-exit relay. Your Internet device and the first relay know only each other.

The first relay will then say, "I need a second non-exit relay; which is available?" A middle relay will respond and one will be picked at random, keys will be exchanged that only those two servers can communicate on your circuit, and now the first and second relays can communicate with each other. This process continues with middle relay as yet another new set of keys are generated to send and communicate with what is called the exit relay, which completes the circuit.

Now that your circuit to the Internet is set up, these intermediaries encrypt your traffic multiple times, to multiple key pairs, which helps defend against traffic analysis. All that the destination website sees is the address and information provided by the exit relay. This makes it very difficult for the destination server and trackers to trace back or record information about the original Internet page request. The requested information is then returned back to the originator in the same fashion. (See: https://ssd.eff.org/tech/tor, https://www.torproject.org/about/overview.html.en, https://blog.torproject.org)

I am only covering the open source use of Tor Network for your Internet searching and browsing to questionable sites. By questionable, I am referring to the links to web pages that a search engine may present when you are researching something benign, as when I was when looking for reviews on computer components for the computer build I proposed in Chapter 3, for example. Clicking on some of those links took me to places where I was not sure if malware existed. If a corporation can track your browser back to your computer, so can criminals and crackers. Tor will make that malicious activity more difficult even if you are using questionable web Tor relay sites.

- As Tor pointed out, and I want to say again, whatever you are doing using the Tor network data can be examined at the entrance and exit relays. Since anyone can run a Tor relay, any relay can examine traffic, and the entry and exit points. For example, if you are using Tor for your unencrypted email, assume you now have **greater** chance of someone reading your email than you did just sending it the old-fashioned way, from Mail Transfer Agent (MTA) to MTA. You can alleviate some of this risk by specifying relays using Vidalia, but even a trusted relay might be reading your clear text packets as they enter and depart.
- From https://ssd.eff.org/tech/tor "*If you aren't using encryption with the actual servers you're communicating with (for instance, if you're using HTTP rather than HTTPS), the operator of an "exit node" (the last Tor node in your path) could read all your communications, just the way your own ISP can if you don't use Tor. Since Tor chooses your path through the Tor network randomly, targeted attacks may still be difficult, but researchers have demonstrated that a malicious Tor exit node operator can capture a large amount of sensitive unencrypted traffic. Tor node operators are volunteers and there is no technical guarantee that individual exit node operators won't spy on users; anyone can set up a Tor exit node.*"
- Tor cannot guard against application-level attacks. If an application (malware) is broadcasting information, the attacker can still receive information about your system, which is why I recommend using virtual environments. If you have malware on your core computer broadcasting to a bot-net, key-logger, or criminal, then Tor is of no help.
- There are people/governments/corporations everywhere dedicating many hours of their time to circumventing Tor. According to http://en.wikipedia.org/wiki/Tor_(anonymity_network), a French research team made a

map of the Tor network nodes, managed to control one third of them and direct traffic to the nodes that they controlled. Thereby, they tracked all Tor activity that happened to go through their nodes.
- And let's not count out the NSA. They have safeguards in place to track your use of Tor with the Homeland Security Act https://en.wikipedia.org/wiki/Homeland_Security_Act that was pushed through by George Bush after 9-11, vastly expanding the NSA's Internet surveillance powers.

The old fashioned "cookie" that sites would drop on your computer used to just track you at a single site. However, today's super cookies track everywhere you go, as well as what you click on and view on the Internet. But even that was not enough for companies like Facebook and Google. Those little Facebook share icons featured on hundreds of sites used to send data back to Facebook only when you clicked on them. However, that was not invasive enough, and now they send data back to Facebook whether you click on them or not.

The Facebook privacy invasion continues as it collects data from millions of people, even those without Facebook accounts, creating what privacy advocates call "shadow profiles" of people around the world. This means that even if you delete your account, your phone number, or email, it will still be on the Facebook's servers if one of your friends has saved it in their address book and then gave Facebook permission to access it. There are no laws to stop this.

Now that you know your confidential information is being logged without your knowledge (you have given tacit permission whether you know it or not), let's take countermeasures to keep our information out of these clandestine hands! Virtualization was an additional security layer toward hardening your defenses and achieving Internet surfing privacy. Tor, acronym of "The Onion Router", will provide another hardening layer of security. (See: https://www.torproject.org/index.html.en, https://secure.wikimedia.org/wikipedia/en/wiki/Onion_routing) From the Mint Software Manager, "_Tor is a connection-based low-latency anonymous communication system which addresses many flaws in the original onion routing design._" Tor is open source software that helps users remain anonymous on the Internet.

From the July 2011 PCWorld article, "_Tor Network Cloaks Your Browsing from Prying Eyes_" by Alex Wawro, "_To maintain privacy while surfing the Web, you need to encrypt the data you exchange with websites and mask where that data is coming from. Enter the Tor Network, a free service maintained by the nonprofit Tor Project and a worldwide network of volunteers dedicated to keeping the Internet free and private._

Tor is completely free to access, and it's been used with great success by hackers, privacy enthusiasts, and political dissidents in Egypt and Iraq to elude government surveillance. " (See: http://pcworld.about.net/od/security2/Tor-Network-Cloaks-Your-Browsing-From-Prying-Eyes.htm, https://en.wikipedia.org/wiki/Anonymizer). There have been many articles written about Tor. (See: https://www.torproject.org/press/press)

WARNING	Setting up Tor in a VM offers up two points of possible Internet leaks, one from your core OS and the other from the VM. Many applications poll the Internet for updates and report back to their creators about your Internet activity. These leaks are exploited to defeat Tor, so open source developers have created total anonymity solutions, such as Whonix and TAILS, which we will soon cover.

Tor is not perfect and has a list of warnings at
https://www.torproject.org/download/download-easy.html.en#warning. You can also follow
along on Tor development by reading their blog at https://blog.torproject.org/blog. Nothing is
flawless at helping your home security (or in military security, as I know from 11 years of
service). Remember we are building *multiple lines* of defense/offense, unlike the "French
Maginot Line", which was a *single line* of defense. (See:
http://en.wikipedia.org/wiki/Maginot_Line) We have no idea of the technological advances
that have been made and have to do our best through due diligence. In my experience, by
employing these techniques, we are becoming a harder target, and the criminals and crackers
will go after the easier, soft targets. Most users connected to the Internet in the world today
don't employ these techniques. Think of your home; do you still have doors that criminals can
break a windowpane, reach in and turn the deadbolt? If so, you may want to rethink that
idea. Is your deadbolt in wood or steel? Could one slam of a sledgehammer break the
deadbolt out of the fragile wood in your doorframe? How secure do you want to be? We can
only do so much. If you want to consider a possible better alternative to Tor, consider
JonDonym.

JonDonym as an Alternative to Tor

Tor is not the only game in town if you want to be anonymous on the Internet. There is also
the JonDonym https://anonymous-proxy-servers.net/en, which may be a superior alternative
to using Tor. JonDonym (JonDo) has a paid and a free service. JonDo presents a very nice
comparison of all the various ways of trying to stay secure on the Internet, which includes
(JonDonym, Tor, VPN's*, and Proxies) at https://anonymous-proxy-
servers.net/en/benefits.html). JonDonym also provides an *Anonymity Test* at http://ip-
check.info/?lang=en. If you really want to know why you need this chapter, perform the
anonymity test on your computer and you will really see how corporations stalk and make a
record of everything you do on the Internet. JonDonym's website provides the most
impressive argument I have seen as to why we all need anonymity software. The first thing
that hit home for me was that I was not using Firefox in Privacy mode, which is something we
all should consider using when possible. JonDo also taught me to change other Firefox
browser settings, which I detailed earlier. To get a much more comprehensive look at what
you present about your Internet activity, refer down to Anonymity Testing and Final
Commentary.

In the Feb 1, 2012 PCWorld article http://find.pcworld.com/72449 titled "What Is Deep Packet
Inspection", by Alex Wawro "*But deep packet inspection has a dark side, and in the absence of
strict legal restrictions, your ISP is free to root through all the information you exchange online and
use it as they see fit. Personal data like your age, location, and shopping records can be logged
and sold in anonymized batches to advertising companies, and law enforcement agents can
monitor and curtail your Internet access without your knowledge. Without strict limitations to*

preserve user privacy, this sort of deep data filtering can significantly impair your ability to remain anonymous online." Let's hope that our government does not work further to erode our individual freedom, but if they do, the article goes on to explain the following about how the US could look like China.

"This level of surveillance is nothing new; Internet service providers in China already employ deep packet inspection software to scan for sensitive keywords and block access to sites like YouTube. Chinese citizens often employ foreign VPN services to access websites blocked by the Chinese government, and you can do the same. "If you want to prevent this sort of inspection, you could use someone else's network," says Steven Andrés, founder and CTO of Special Ops Security. "I imagine if Congress [ever] enacts SOPA into law, a number of VPN services will crop up in other countries.""

The web page https://anonymous-proxy-servers.net/en/law_enforcement.html details how governments have tried to force JonDonym to cooperate to reveal information about its users. However, this proved to not be possible because this requires the cooperation for all operators of a Mix cascade. JonDonym boldly promotes itself as the best anonymity solution available for our use on the infected Internet.

Another anonymity solution to consider is the Java Anonymous Proxy (JAP) at http://anon.inf.tu-dresden.de/index_en.html, which also remains free of charge. This software makes it possible to surf the Internet anonymously and unobservable. This is also an alternative to Tor. The website has an Anonymity Check link on the left pane that you can also use. JAP is a continuously redeveloped research project. Tor, being open source should be safe to use for anonymity, but with all of the revelations about the NSA, we can rest assured they are working to find, or have found, many Tor vulnerabilities. In addition, since the Naval Research Laboratory originally developed Tor, the NSA knows every detail about it. The JAP software download can also be found at http://www.softpedia.com/get/Internet/Servers/Proxy-Servers/JAP.shtml.

| WARNING  | In reading the Ubuntu Forums and other websites, I found a warning that JAP has a backdoor created to satisfy a German court of law. This warning is true, but in a press release for AN.ON they describe how restrictive the use of this backdoor is. *"Therefore, making the monitoring of access to a particular IP address related to criminal contents possible does not mean that all users of the service are monitored. Only in single cases and if all legal requirements are met, i.e. if there is a binding judicial instruction, the AN.ON service will record the access to a particular IP address which has been precisely defined by the judge."* (See: http://www.securityfocus.com/news/6779, https://www.datenschutzzentrum.de/material/themen/presse/anonip_e.htm) This press release dates back to 2003 so I do not know if this backdoor still exists. |

Tails – Live DVD or USB Install for Anonymity

The Amnesic Incognito Live System (TAILS) is a free live system that aims to preserve your privacy and anonymity based on Debian GNU/Linux.   It helps you to use the Internet anonymously and circumvent censorship almost anywhere you go and on any computer, leaving no trace, unless you explicitly ask. It is a complete operating system designed to be used from a DVD, USB stick, or SD card independently of the computer's original operating system. When TAILS is used as a live CD, your data is wiped when you power off your system, which means that you boot it from a disc or USB drive. TAILS also has what the developers call "persistence", which is a way to create a persistent volume using the TAILS Installer on a USB drive or SD card. When the persistent volume is created, you can store personal files, working documents, encryption keys, software packages and save program configurations. When you start TAILS where a persistent volume has been created, it gives you the choice whether to activate it or not, keeping with their "leave no trace" motto. TAILS comes with several built-in applications preconfigured with security in mind, including a web browser, instant messaging client, email client, office suite, image and sound editor, etc. (See: https://tails.boum.org)

When you boot up, it offers a neat Windows XP simulator so that anyone shoulder surfing in the vicinity will think you are using this outdated OS and will be easy to hack. The website http://www.idgconnect.com/abstract/3541/here-secure-nsa-crack-encryption says "*TAILS comes packed with numerous privacy and encryption tools baked in, including Tor, who allows you to browse the web (mostly) anonymously and access a Darknet of so-called "Hidden Services" that grant anonymity to both web servers and web browsers. Bruce Schneier—a longtime security guru who has actually read the documents detailing the NSA's encryption-busting methods— recommends using Tor and Hidden Services to thwart NSA surveillance.*"   You can install Tails in VM and/or add TAILS to a multiboot USB drive, which we cover in Chapter 10 and use it for an anonymity solution, especially when using hotspots.

Tails provides a signature file that you need to download with their ISO file. If you refer back to Chapter 5 on encryption we covered how to verify downloads using the Tails detailed directions for all software downloads. (See: https://tails.boum.org/download/index.en.html#verify)

Whonix – Anonymity OS Solution

Like Tails, Whonix is an OS based on the Tor anonymity network for you to consider. Whonix boasts that security and isolation are paramount, DNS leaks are impossible, and not even malware with root privileges can find your real IP. From the Whonix website, "*Whonix consists of two parts: One solely runs Tor and acts as a gateway, which we call Whonix-Gateway. The other, which we call Whonix-Workstation, is on a completely isolated network. Only connections through Tor are possible.*" To verify the Whonix download we will first need to first download and install gpg4win, which we discussed in detail in the encryption chapter.

Surf to https://www.whonix.org/wiki/Whonix_Signing_Key, right click on patrick Schleizer's (adrelanos') OpenPGP key patrick.asc file link and select Save Link as... to a file on your hard drive > open up Gpg4win Kleopatra and click the Import Certificates... button upper left > navigate to the file containing the public key and select it, Open > the Detailed results of importing C:\...\patrick.asc dialog should confirm that the certificate was processed and imported, OK. Right click on the key and arrow down to select

Certificate Details *to verify that fingerprint for the public key is Key fingerprint = 916B* *8D99 C38E AF5E 8ADC 7A2A 8D66 066A 2EEA CCDA,* *Close*. Based on the fingerprint we should certify the certificate. *Click on the* *patrick.asc* *key and select the* *Certificates* *menu > arrow down to* *Certify Certificate...* *> check the* *Patrick Schleizer* *<adrelanos@riseup.net> public key and check the box at the bottom* *I have verified the* *fingerprint,* *Next* *> on Step 2: Choose how to certify. Leave* *Certify only for myself* *ticked,* *Certify* *> enter your passphrase,* *Finish*.

We can now surf to https://www.whonix.org/wiki/Main_Page) and download the Whonix Gateway and Workstation VirtualBox OSs. Once they are downloaded, we can use the Whonix imported public key to verify the digital signature that Whonix provided for the files that we downloaded. On the Whonix download web page the cryptographic signature corresponding to the virtual machine image (.ova) is provided, so we can verify the (.ova) file. This file must be downloaded and stored in the same folder as the virtual machine image, using the same procedure we did above for their public key. *Using* *Kleopatra* *again click on* *File* *> arrow* *down to select* *Decrypt/Verify Files...* *> select the (.ova.asc) signature of the Open* *Virtualization Format Archive file that we are trying to verify,* *Open* *> on the* *Choose* *operations to be performed* *screen leave* *Input file is a detached signature* *checked and* *click on the* *Decrypt/Verify* *button > the* *Results* *screen will appear and verification may* *take a few minutes so be patient > assuming you have done everything correctly, the* *result will appear in* *GREEN* *and under* *All operations completed.* *you will see* *Whonix-* *Workstation-8.2.ova.asc: Signature is valid.,* *OK*. Close Kleopatra and copy the images to the directory, where all of your other VirtualBox VMs are located.

We can now import the images into VirtualBox by clicking on *File* *>* *Import Appliance...* *> on the* *Appliance to import* *screen navigate to Whonix file(s) to import (Whonix-* *Gateway-8.2.ova, Whonix-Workstation-8.2.ova),* *Open,* *Next* *> on the* *Appliance settings* *screen consider checking* *Reinitialize the MAC address of all network cards*. The Whonix MAC address is probably well known to crackers and governments trying to track your use of their anonymity solution, so changing the MAC address is probably a good idea, Import, Agree. Refer back to our virtualization chapter to tweak the virtualization settings for Whonix imported VMs. Run and update them by once again referring to the virtualization chapter. Run the Whonix-Gateway VM before running Whonix-Workstation, and if you did not, be sure to run the command whonixcheck again. The default user account is 'user', default root account 'root' and default password is 'changeme'.

Tor Bundle -- Install & Set Up in Any Linux OS as a Non-Root User

The Tor Bundle can be set up quickly and easily, as well as used by any user ID quickly and easily. Surf to their website at https://www.torproject.org/index.html.en and download the Tor bundle to your OS or USB drive. Expand the bundle and you can then run their software and surf the Internet anonymously. If all you need is an anonymous browser, downloading and unpacking the Tor bundle in a general purpose VM as an unprivileged user ID is an adequate solution. Nonetheless, remember that Tor is unsecure at the entrance and exit relays, so having a separate VM for anonymous surfing might be something you want to consider. Make sure that any Tor user ID you are using in your VM is limited only to the privileges which that user ID needs.

Historical Reference – How Tor has evolved over the years and how the December 2013 release changed things.

Tor used to provide the TorButton that you added to the latest version of Firefox. Firefox introduced an accelerated release schedule for their browser in 2012 that the Tor developers could not keep up with. The TorButton may work with your version of Firefox, and for years the Tor developers have recommend only using the Tor Browser Bundle (TBB). TBB includes a patched version of Firefox, Tor, Vidalia GUI, and the TorButton. (See: https://www.torproject.org/torbutton/index.html.en)

Use the Tor network to handle all Internet research so as not to draw unwanted attention to you. This environment should shut down cookies and temporary files using an unprivileged private ID to prevent data gathering. Create a special unprivileged 'tor' user ID that you can log in as to run the Tor bundle. Refer back to Adding Less Privileged User IDs for Specific Purposes to Linux to add a 'tor' user to your VM as 'root' where we discussed these types of user IDs and cover all of the options. *To install the Tor Bundle in Linux, login as a non-root user ID, surf to https://www.torproject.org, click on the Download Tor button > click on the Download Tor Browser Bundle button for your Linux OS (32-Bit or 64-Bit) > when prompted What should Firefox do with this this file? tick Save File, OK > depending on the OS, click on Home upper left > double click on the Downloads directory, or in some OSs that default to the Downloads directory > click on the Save button lower right > when the download is complete, open a terminal window > change to the Downloads directory (e.g. /home/suroot/Downloads or /home/sudoroot/Downloads) and perform the following steps:*

Historical Reference – The 2.x stable Tor Browser Bundle was officially deprecated December, 2013

In December 2013, Tor officially deprecated the 2.x stable series of their software. Prior to this development one could retrieve and expand the bundle using the following commands:
```
$ wget https://www.torproject.org/dist/torbrowser/linux/tor-browser-gnu-linux-i686-2.3.25-15-dev-en-US.tar.gz
$ wget https://www.torproject.org/dist/torbrowser/linux/tor-browser-gnu-linux-x86_64-2.3.25-15-dev-en-US.tar.gz
$ tar zxvf tor-browser-gnu-linux-i686-2.3.25-15-dev-en-US.tar.gz    # for 32-bit
$ tar zxvf tor-browser-gnu-linux-x86_64-2.3.25-15-dev-en-US.tar.gz    # for 64-bit
```

After December 2013, the browser bundle could only be retrieved from the Tor Package archive. The method is less circumspect than using a browser that leaks information:

```
$ cd Downloads    or,    cd /home/sudoroot/Downloads
$ rm -rf tor-browser_en-US
$ wget https://archive.torproject.org/tor-package-archive/torbrowser/4.0.2/tor-browser-linux32-4.0.2_en-US.tar.xz    # for 32-bit
$ wget https://archive.torproject.org/tor-package-archive/torbrowser/4.0.2/tor-browser-linux64-4.0.2_en-US.tar.xz    # for 64-bit
$ tar -Jxvf tor-browser-linux32-4.0.2_en-US.tar.xz    # for 32-bit
```

```
$ tar -Jxvf tor-browser-linux64-4.0.2_en-US.tar.xz      # for 64-bit
```

Refer back to Chapter 5 to verify the signature on the download, which is located just under the download button. (See: https://www.torproject.org/projects/torbrowser.html.en)

Once the bundle tor*.tar.gz is downloaded and installed the inclination is to just remove it. After all, the Tor browser default home page at https://check.torproject.org/?lang=en-US&small=1&uptodate=1 will let us know when an update is needed. But the bundle is fairly small and is good for reference. To remove it: # rm tor-browser-gnu*

Create a script named **tor.sh** in the **Desktop** directory with the following:

```
$ cd /home/suroot/Desktop      # In most Linux flavors
$ cd /home/sudoroot/Desktop      # In Ubuntu
# cd /home/tor
$ gvim tor.sh
#!/bin/bash
#------------------------------------------------------------------
# tor.sh
# Script to start the Tor browser from the desktop
#------------------------------------------------------------------
#set -x     # displays the script as it executes if debugging necessary
if [[ ! -d ../Downloads/tor-browser_en-US ]]; then
    echo "Fatal Error: /home/`whoami`/Downloads/tor-browser_en-US not found"
    sleep 5
    exit 1
fi

cd ../Downloads/tor-browser_en-US
sleep 5
nohup ./start-tor-browser > /dev/null 2>&1 &
sleep 5
$ chmod 750 tor.sh
```

If the script is not visible on the desktop, refer back to KDE Desktop-Fedora-Mint-openSUSE General Configuration & Setup to change the layout. Tor comes out with updates on a regular basis. In Linux there is no one click button to update Tor. When you startup Tor 3.5.x for the first time, the Tor Network Settings dialog appears, which will allow you to configure your Internet connection or just connect to the Tor network. If you are clear of obstacles, click on the Connect button and you will briefly see the Connecting to the Tor network dialog followed by the Congratulations! about:tor web page. You are now connected to the Tor network and the about:tor web page defaults to the private search engine https://startpage.com. To make sure that you are using the latest version of Tor, click on the Test Tor Network Setting link that will display the "Congratulations. Your browser is configured to use Tor." web page, which alerts you when Tor needs to be updated.

When you are alerted that Tor needs to be updated, the method to update it is almost identical to installing it. Click on the <u>Download Tor...</u> link on their home page, or surf to <u>https://www.torproject.org</u> and follow the download directions above. Once the Tor bundle is in the <u>Download</u> directory in Linux type:

$ rm -rf tor-browser_en-US   # To remove the old version of Tor

Then follow the directions above with the new version. I could find no easy way to set up the Tor bundle for multiple user IDs by using something such as */usr/local/bin*. There are safeguards built into the software that prevent this. The best option for an HCU/SBO would be to set up one 'tor' user ID and have everyone share it, or install the browser bundle under every user ID on the computer, which is more secure.

WARNING	Using the nuclear option above will destroy any customizations like Bookmarks, configuration, etc. that you have made to your Tor Browser (if any). Refer back to <u>Firefox-Backing up and Restoring Your Bookmarks</u> to see how to save and restore them when upgrading Tor.

If there is a need to run Tor as 'root', you can use the following to do so:
cp -ip tor-browser-gnu-linux* /tmp

```
# vi tor.sh
#!/bin/bash
#
xhost +local:
su - tor -c /home/tor/tor.sh
xhost -local:
# chmod 700 tor.sh
```

Then perform the following steps as user 'tor':
```
# su - tor
$ mkdir Downloads
$ cd Downloads
$ cp -p /tmp/ tor-browser-gnu-linux* .
$ tar zxvf tor-browser-gnu-linux*
$ cd && vi tor.sh
#!/bin/bash
cd ../Downloads/tor-browser_en-US
./start-tor-browser > /dev/null 2>&1
$ chmod 750 tor.sh
```

Double clicking on the **tor.sh** script will bring up Tor, Vidalia and Firefox with the Tor button enabled. The browser can also be opened using the OS's File Manager. Having the Tor Browser available allows us anonymous surfing from any Linux environment, quickly and easily. The only drawback is to keep Tor up to date, we will have to download the latest Tor bundle from time to time because it is not downloaded by applying system updates to Linux.

If you go into the TBB Preferences and look at the **Network > Settings** you will TBB is configured to use SOCKS Host: 127.0.0.1 on port 9150. This allows it to be used with an installed Tor daemon which listens on SOCKS Host: 127.0.0.1 port 9050.

```
# netstat --tcp --listening --programs --numeric
tcp    0    0 127.0.0.1:9050       0.0.0.0:*            LISTEN
tcp    0    0 127.0.0.1:9150       0.0.0.0:*            LISTEN
tcp    0    0 127.0.0.1:9151       0.0.0.0:*            LISTEN
tcp    0    0 127.0.0.1:8118       0.0.0.0:*            LISTEN
```

The last thing you can do is possibly tweak a few TBB, and later some VM Tor package settings. You can try these settings to see if the following speeds up Tor or TBB:

```
# cd ./Downloads/tor-browser_en-US/Data/Tor  &&  cp -ip torrc torrc.orig  &&  gvim /torrc

# Try for at most NUM seconds when building circuits. If the circuit isn't
# open in that time, give up on it. (Default: 1 minute).
CircuitBuildTimeout 5

# Send a padding cell every N seconds to keep firewalls from closing our
# connections while Tor is not in use.
KeepalivePeriod 60

# Force Tor to consider whether to build a new circuit every NUM seconds.
NewCircuitPeriod 15

# How many entry guards should we keep at a time?
NumEntryGuards 8
```

Windows 7/Vista/XP – How-to Install, Run and Set Up Tor

When you download the Tor software bundle you also get Vidalia. From the Tor website, *"Vidalia is a cross-platform graphical controller for the Tor software, built using the Qt framework. Vidalia lets you start and stop Tor, see how much bandwidth you are consuming, see how many circuits you currently have active, see where these circuits are connected on a global map, view messages from Tor about its progress and current state, and let you configure your Tor client, bridge, or relay with a simple interface. Included in Vidalia is an extensive help system which helps your understanding all of the options available to you."* (See: https://www.torproject.org/projects/vidalia.html.en) To use Tor in Windows, download the browser bundle from https://www.torproject.org and install it. When the Tor Network Setting dialog pops up, simply click on Connect or Configure and you are using Tor. The install in Window will create a folder on your desktop. If you open that folder and double click on the "Start Tor Browser" icon, you will bring up its version of Firefox with the TorButton installed.

- When you start Tor's Firefox browser, you will see the Tor button next to the URL bar.

- You can verify that the Tor button is installed and view the version by *clicking on Tools > arrow down to Add-ons > click on Extensions*.
- If you don't want Tor enabled every time you start up the Tor configured Firefox browser, *Click on the Tor button > arrow down to select Preferences... > at the bottom uncheck Disable Button and Hotkeys to prevent accidental toggle*. When you click the Tor Button again you will see the option Toggle Tor Status.
- If you click on the Test Tor Network Settings link it will take you to https://check.torproject.org/?lang=en_US and you will see a web page displaying, "*Congratulations. This browser is configured to use Tor.*" The web page will also display something like, "*Your IP address appears to be: 85.114.142.172*". This tells you your IP address is masked and you are surfing through a Tor server relay.
- The web page may also display an additional message stating, "***There is a security update available for the Tor Browser Bundle***." This means another TBB is available and needs to be downloaded.

Firefox — Hardening the Browser to Use with the Tor Daemon and Proxy

The Tor Firefox browser comes preconfigured to surf the Internet anonymously. Some websites, such as http://www.tigerdirect.com, may reject your Tor Firefox browser. Many of these websites redirect your browser and want to deposit invasive cookies. When you find such websites you have to ask yourself, do you really want to do business with someone that demands to invade your privacy or that may have other hidden agendas?

When visiting various anonymizing websites, they suggested some changes to the Tor browser configuration that you may or may not want to make. Another option we will soon explore is to install the Tor Linux package in a VM and set up the entire VM to use Tor. Then we can configure native browsers and other applications to use the Tor network. Setting up a Tor Firefox browser is a bit different from what we did back in Firefox-Setup & Hardening your Browser Security, which may give us better anonymity. TBB comes with some of the add-ons that we previously discussed that includes HTTPS-Everywhere and NoScript. We have to carefully consider any other add-ons to protect our privacy and make sure they have been properly vetted.

- *Under Edit in Linux or Tools in Windows > arrow down to select Preferences in Linux or Options in Windows > at the top, arrow over to select the Content icon > make sure Block pop-up windows is checked.*
- *Click on the Privacy icon > under History, next to Firefox will: change the setting to Use custom settings for history > check Always use private browsing mode > uncheck Accept cookies from sites*. It is not intuitive, but setting Firefox will: to Never Remember History still allowed cookies.

I briefly mentioned the website http://ip-check.info/description.php earlier, which can teach us some more advanced settings for the Firefox browser to gain better anonymity while surfing the Internet. When you run an Anonymity Test, it will reveal some things that you may want to experiment with and configure to ensure better anonymity. It also demonstrates why JonDonym, which is a paid alternative to Tor, may be a superior solution.

Turn off the browser to cache any third party content at all. This is somewhat advanced and you must be very careful! *Type __about:config__ in your Firefox address bar, scroll down to the __browser.cache.disk.enable:false__, __browser.cache.memory.enable:true__ entries. Double click on either if set to true to set it to false.*

browser.search.update.interval	default	integer	21600
browser.search.update.log	default	boolean	false
browser.send_pings	default	boolean	false
browser.send_pings.max_per_link	default	integer	1
browser.send_pings.require_same_host	default	boolean	false
browser.sessionhistory.max_entries	default	integer	50
browser.sessionhistory.max_total_viewers	default	integer	-1
browser.sessionhistory.optimize_eviction	default	boolean	true
browser.sessionstore.interval	default	integer	15000
browser.sessionstore.max_concurrent_tabs	default	integer	3
browser.sessionstore.max_resumed_crashes	default	integer	1
browser.sessionstore.max_tabs_undo	default	integer	10

Change the browser.sessionhistory.max_entries from 50 to 2. Double click and type __2__ in the Enter integer value dialog box, __OK__. If you are using the Socks proxy set network.proxy.socks_remote_dns=true.

Mint/Ubuntu -- Installing Tor Daemon and Supporting Software

As shown in Chapter 7 on using virtualization, there is multiple user-friendly and intuitive Linux Operating System solutions from which we can choose and use. We are now going to set up our virtual Linux Operating System to use Tor and surf the Internet anonymously. If you have not read Chapter 7, be sure to study all of the general steps to set up the various flavors of Linux, as well as review the secure Firefox Settings in Chapter 6. You should perform those steps prior to continuing with the installing and configuring of Tor in this chapter. The order in which these steps are run should not be altered.

Tor presents multiple methods for installing and using Tor beyond just downloading and using TBB. Back in the virtualization chapter, I proposed the creation of a separate VM for use with Tor. The reason for this will soon become apparent. TBB will work for any user ID under any OS without the need to complicate Tor's use by installing packages or configuring anything. It is an adequate solution for most users, and according to https://wiki.archlinux.org/index.php/Tor, the TBB is the only currently supported browser solution considered safe to use for anonymity.

Therefore, the question becomes, why install the Tor packages into a VM OS? What if you want to torify other applications to make sure that other things you do may be anonymous; how do you do that? TBB then becomes an inadequate solution to meet all of your needs. Suppose you want to SSH to your server behind a firewall anonymously? Or perhaps you want to make sure that something your VM is doing in the background is anonymous? How can you do that?

In addition to using the TBB we can have an entire Linux (Tor) VM in which to install the Tor packages and perhaps some other proxy* software to channel all of our Internet communication through the Tor SOCKS 9050 port to make the entire VM as anonymous for running everything in the VM as possible.   All we have to do is go into the OS Network Settings and configure the VM OS Network settings. We can then configure each VM's application settings to use Tor SOCKS port 9050. Any application that can communicate with SOCKS will then be using the Tor network. If you don't want to do that, we could just torify individual applications from the command line, scripts, and through configuration. In Chapter 9 we will cover setting up and using a command line SSH Tor solution. For example, to configure the SOCKS network setting in a Mint KDE VM to use the Tor daemon and a proxy:

Click on the <u>Launcher</u> > click on <u>Applications</u> > arrow up to select <u>Settings</u> > click on <u>System Settings</u> > under <u>Network and Connectivity</u> double click on <u>Network Settings</u> > under <u>Configure the proxy servers</u> used tick <u>Use manually specified proxy configuration:</u> > for <u>SOCKS Proxy: 127.0.0.1, Port: 1950, Apply</u>. We now have to instruct all applications on the VM to use the system SOCKS Proxy or configure them individually to use the Tor Proxy. Even with the system proxy setup this may not be helpful for most VM applications. Only the SOCKS network protocol can use the Tor Proxy, so to configure an application such as Firefox to use the Tor Proxy:

Open Firefox, click on <u>Edit</u> menu > arrow down to select <u>Preferences</u> > click on the <u>Advanced</u> icon > on the <u>Advanced</u> sub-tabs, click on the <u>Network</u> tab > click on the <u>Settings...</u> button > under <u>Configure Proxies to Access the Internet</u> tick Manual proxy configuration: next to SOCKS Host: type 127.0.0.1, Port: 1950. To make sure everything is working, skip down to <u>Anonymity Testing and Final Commentary</u> and check out your anonymity. Realize that by not using the TBB Firefox browser you are compromising your anonymity in other ways, such as having an active FLASH player in your browser.

The web page <u>https://www.torproject.org/download/download-unix.html.en</u> shows how to set up the Tor repositories for various operating systems. We can then install the latest Tor daemons and software for doing things such as setting up a relay or torifying other applications beyond just using the Firefox browser that comes with TBB. Much of the following how-to is taken from <u>https://www.torproject.org/docs/debian.html.en#ubuntu</u>, <u>https://www.torproject.org/docs/debian</u>, <u>https://Help.ubuntu.com/community/Tor</u>, <u>http://ubuntuguide.org/wiki/Tor</u>, <u>https://trac.torproject.org/projects/tor/wiki</u>, <u>https://wiki.archlinux.org/index.php/Tor</u> and updated/corrected/streamlined for applying these steps to Mint & Ubuntu.

WARNING	Tor's website warns, "*Do not use the packages in Ubuntu's universe. In the past they have not reliably been updated. That means you could be missing stability and security fixes. You'll need to set up our package repository before you can fetch Tor.*" In addition, the web pages detailing how to use the Tor package with other software is not updated often. Trying to torify some applications might be outdated, but you can study the Torify HOWTO for warnings and instructions about how to try.

If you want to ignore the warning above, you can just install the Tor packages from the default Ubuntu repositories. However, to ensure we have the latest important stability and security fixes, let us configure Mint or Ubuntu to use the Tor repository. To do that, Tor recommended using the commands below to determine the name of your distribution:

```
# lsb_release -c    or,    cat /etc/debian_version
```
- The next Debian release is codenamed (jessie)
- Debian 7.0 (wheezy) - current stable release
- Debian 6.0 is (squeeze) - obsolete stable release
- Mint 16 is (saucy)
- Ubuntu 13.10 is (saucy)

For Ubuntu/Debian you can visit
https://en.wikipedia.org/wiki/List_of_Ubuntu_releases#Table_of_versions or
http://www.debian.org/releases, which shows the codename and other information about
every Ubuntu/Debian release dating back to 2004. However, I found that visiting the web
page http://deb.torproject.org/torproject.org/dists and comparing this index to what we
viewed above would narrow things down, and we could quickly determine the proper
candidate.

Before we install the *tor* daemon, utilities and perhaps another proxy*, lets discuss some Tor
supporting packages. From http://linuxappfinder.com/package/tor-geoipdb and the Mint
Software Manager, "*The tor-geoipdb package provides a geoIP database for Tor, i.e. it maps IPv4
addresses to countries. Bridges (special Tor relays that aren't listed in the main Tor directory) use
this information to report which countries they get access from. This allows the Tor network
operators to learn if certain countries started blocking access to bridges.*" (See:
https://bridges.torproject.org) From the Tor Bridge Relay Help, another way to find Tor
Bridge Relay addresses to connect to is to send an email to bridges@torproject.org with the
line 'get bridges' by itself in the body of the message. This is only allowed from the gmail.com
or yahoo.com domains, so many companies, ISPs and the U.S. government will know that you
have requested this information. A better way might be to use an encrypted email service
such as Hushmail to request relay information from help@rt.torproject.org.

The Mint & Ubuntu installs of Tor also suggested adding the anon-proxy, mixmaster,
mixminion, polipo, privoxy, socat, or tor-arm package. However, if we review some of Tor's
documentation web pages they do not list some of these packages as support programs for
Tor. (See: https://trac.torproject.org/projects/tor/wiki/doc/TorifyHOWTO,
https://trac.torproject.org/projects/tor/wiki/doc/SupportPrograms) With further investigation
from the Ubuntu Software Center and the following websites we can find out what these
packages are:

- The *anon-proxy* can act as a local proxy* listening on port 4001 between your browser
  and the Internet, which is also what Polipo does. Using anon-proxy is another method
  of providing multiple layers of encryption to protect your Internet traffic. Its JAP client,
  who encrypts the messages several times, handles requests for web pages. The
  encrypted messages are sent through a chain of intermediate servers much the way Tor
  does (called Mixes) and are finally passed on to their final destination.
- From their website, "*Mixmaster is a type II remailer protocol and the most popular
  implementation of it. Remailers provide protection against traffic analysis and allow
  sending email anonymously or pseudonymously.*" (See:
  http://mixmaster.sourceforge.net) Mixmaster is a very dated project with the last
  signing release being in 2008.
- Mixminion is deprecated anonymous remailer client and a server for a Type III network.
  It is no longer supported but could serve as a basis for future development. (See:
  http://mixminion.net)
- From their website, "*Privoxy is a non-caching web proxy with advanced filtering capabilities
  for enhancing privacy, modifying web page data and HTTP headers, controlling access, and
  removing ads and other obnoxious Internet junk. Privoxy has a flexible configuration and
  can be customized to suit individual needs and tastes. It has application for both stand-*

alone systems and multi-user networks." (See: http://www.privoxy.org) Privoxy, the "Privacy Enhancing Proxy" is a fairly active project with excellent documentation that can be combined with Tor for better privacy protection.

- Socat (for Socket CAT) is a command line based utility that establishes two bidirectional byte streams and transfers data between them. A good comparison that UNIX or Linux users can understand is to think of socat as the "cat" command line, which as an alternative of listing the contents of a file to STDOUT instead transfers data between two locations. Data channels may be files, pipes, devices or sockets. Socat is an active project with excellent documentation, and there are many technical web pages that you can study to learn about this very useful tool. (See: http://www.dest-unreach.org/socat, http://www.dest-unreach.org/socat/doc/socat.html)
- The anonymizing relay monitor *tor-arm* is a terminal status monitor for Tor relays, useful for SSH connections. (See: https://www.atagar.com/arm) The monitor works much like the Linux *top* command, providing real time statistics such as bandwidth, cpu and memory usage, relay's current configuration, logged events, and connection details (ip, hostname, fingerprint, and consensus data).
- The *torsocks* utility is designed to allow use of most socks-friendly applications in a safe way with Tor. It is supposed to ensure that DNS requests are handled safely and will reject UDP traffic from the application you're using. From the manpage, *"torsocks is a wrapper between the torsocks library and the application what you would like to run socksified."* Torsocks is available for Linux, BSD and Mac OSX and will allow you to network applications such as "ssh" and "irssi" with the Tor network. (See: https://code.google.com/p/torsocks, https://trac.torproject.org/projects/tor/wiki/doc/torsocks, http://manpages.ubuntu.com/manpages/precise/man1/torsocks.1.html)

Before we add a Tor repository or make any changes to our Tor VM, refer back to BackTrack/Kali/Mint/Ubuntu-Applying Software Updates to apply all updates. For example, it was suggested by a few blogs and websites that we can use the following untrusted repository to install a Tor PPA to ensure getting the latest Tor package version (**do not do this!**):

```
# apt-add-repository ppa:ubun-tor/ppa
You are about to add the following PPA to your system:
 This ppa publishes the latest version of tor, vidalia, polipo and privoxy.

Up-to-date versions of polipo and privoxy are backported to previous release of
Ubuntu (currently: Oneiric, Natty, Maverick, Lucid, Karmic, Hardy).
 More info: https://launchpad.net/~ubun-tor/+archive/ppa
Press [ENTER] to continue or ctrl-c to cancel adding it
```

However, I could not find anything on Tor or Ubuntu's official web pages to suggest that using this repository was safe or recommended. Therefore, I followed and tweaked the directions from the Tor and Ubuntu web pages to add the repository. (See: https://www.torproject.org/docs/debian)

```
deb    http://deb.torproject.org/torproject.org <DISTRIBUTION> main
```

The codename of your distribution (e.g. saucy, quantal, precise, Jessie, lucid, wheezy, sid, etc.) is used after the URL. In Ubuntu and Mint create a new file **tor.list** for your Linux versions repository at:

```
# cd /etc/apt/sources.list.d  &&  vi tor.list
## --------------------
## TOR MINT/UBUNTU REPOSITORIES
## --------------------
# Add one of the following as the Tor Project repository to Ubuntu or Mint:
deb http://deb.torproject.org/torproject.org precise main # Ubuntu 12.04, Mint 13
deb http://deb.torproject.org/torproject.org quantal main # Ubuntu 12.10
deb http://deb.torproject.org/torproject.org saucy main # Ubuntu 13.10, Mint 16
```

In some earlier Debian flavors of Linux the configuration change above needed to be added to the bottom of */etc/apt/sources.list* file. This is what Tor's official directions recommended, but the solution above is cleaner. Backup and edit the */etc/apt/sources.list* file to add the Tor project software repository to *sources.list* to receive software updates from the Ubuntu software updates repositories as Tor provides them to Ubuntu:

```
# cd /etc/apt  &&  cp -ip sources.list  sources.list.orig
# vi sources.list     # In Vim <Shift-G> to go to the bottom of the file <Shift-A> to type
```

Then add the gpg key following Tor's directions, as we have to use a user ID that is capable of becoming 'root'. This key will be used to sign the packages, and we will add it by running the following commands at a command prompt. The gpg --keyserver command sets a preferred keyserver for the current user ID, so this command should be run for any ID intended to use torified applications or that will be used to update the systems apt-key. (NOTE: this should not be done as 'root' but as a privileged admin ID such as 'suroot' or 'sudoroot'). Type:

```
$ gpg --keyserver keys.gnupg.net --recv 886DDD89
gpg: directory `/home/suroot/.gnupg' created
gpg: new configuration file `/home/suroot/.gnupg/gpg.conf' created
gpg: WARNING: options in `/home/suroot/.gnupg/gpg.conf' are not yet active during
this run
gpg: keyring `/home/suroot/.gnupg/secring.gpg' created
gpg: keyring `/home/suroot/.gnupg/pubring.gpg' created
gpg: requesting key 886DDD89 from hkp server keys.gnupg.net
gpg: /home/suroot/.gnupg/trustdb.gpg: trustdb created
gpg: key 886DDD89: public key "deb.torproject.org archive signing key" imported
gpg: no ultimately trusted keys found
gpg: Total number processed: 1
gpg:               imported: 1  (RSA: 1)
```

The following command exports the downloaded Tor key that was added to user 'suroot' keyrings from the keyserver to STDOUT. That key is then piped to the 'root' user who will run the *apt-key* command, which is used to manage the list of keys used by Advanced Packaging Tool (APT) to authenticate packages. From the apt-key man page, "*Packages which have been authenticated using these keys will be considered trusted.*" The trusted APT database allows updates to be received from the Tor repository, authenticate them, and apply them as trusted without question. (See: https://en.wikipedia.org/wiki/Advanced_Packaging_Tool)

```
$ gpg --export A3C4F0F979CAA22CDBA8F512EE8CBC9E886DDD89 | sudo apt-key add -
[sudo] password for suroot:
OK
```

As we discussed, the codename shown by the *lsb_release* command above for the Tor repository may not be correct. If what you specify does not work, and this will be very obvious when you attempt a # apt-get update, you will see an error message such as the following:

```
W: Failed to fetch http://deb.torproject.org/torproject.org/dists/petra/main/binary-
amd64/Packages  404  Not Found [IP: 93.95.227.222 80]
```

When updates apply correctly go ahead and perform a # apt-get upgrade -y to make sure you have all of the latest stability and security fixes, then reboot shutdown -r now. Tor recommends installing the Debian package deb.torproject.org-keyring, which will keep the Tor signing key current:

apt-get install deb.torproject.org-keyring

We are finally ready to install the Tor daemon and some supporting software:

```
# apt-get install tor tor-arm tor-geoipdb torsocks -y
Suggested packages:
  mixmaster xul-ext-torbutton socat polipo privoxy apparmor-utils
Recommended packages:
  torsocks
```

When researching how to manage services in Ubuntu, many websites recommended using the following antiquated commands (# service --status-all, # initctl list), which did not reveal the status of the *polipo* or the *tor* service. The command # service --status-all showed *[?] polipo*, which means:

"+" means started	"-" means stopped	"?" means unknown status

Installing the Tor packages will start the *tor* daemon in the background to service torified applications:

```
# ps -ef | grep tor | grep -v grep
avahi        463      1   0 20:32 ?        00:00:00 avahi-daemon: running [mint16-kde64-tor.local]
118         1224      1   0 20:32 ?        00:00:01 /usr/bin/tor —defaults-torrc /usr/share/tor/tor-
service-defaults-torrc —hush
suroot      1609   1520   0 20:32 ?        00:00:00 /usr/bin/ssh-agent /usr/bin/gpg-agent —daemon —sh
—write-env-file=/home/suroot/.gnupg/gpg-agent-info-mint16-kde64-tor /usr/bin/dbus-launch —exit-
with-session /usr/bin/im-launch x-session-manager
suroot      1613   1520   0 20:32 ?        00:00:00 /usr/bin/gpg-agent —daemon —sh —write-env-
file=/home/suroot/.gnupg/gpg-agent-info-mint16-kde64-tor /usr/bin/dbus-launch —exit-with-session
/usr/bin/im-launch x-session-manager
```

Now that we have installed the Daemon we have to know how to configure, manage and use it. Below are a few commands you will need now and later in this chapter. Substitute *tor* in place of <service>:

/etc/init.d/<service> start	Start the <service>
/etc/init.d/<service> stop	Stop the <service>
/etc/init.d/<service> status	Show <service> status
/etc/init.d/<service> restart	Restart the <service>
runlevel	Get current runlevel
psg <service> 120 3956 1 5 15:37 ? 00:00:01 /usr/sbin/<service>	Set up as an alias in Chapter 6 to show information about a running process.
ss -aln	grep 9050 LISTEN 0 128 127.0.0.1:9050 *:*	Dump socket statistics that a service is listening to.

A good tool to use in Ubuntu for configuring/viewing services that will show and allow you to configure at which run levels Tor will start is the following:

```
# apt-get install sysv-rc-conf  -y  &&  sysv-rc-conf
```

We have talked about the advantages of installing Tor as a package as opposed to running it from the bundle, but here are few more reasons for doing so:

- TBB startup seemed to be faster having the Tor software installed and the daemon running in the background.
- TBB is experimenting with rotating ports. This can be changed in TBB Vidalia, *click on the **Settings** icon at the bottom >at the top click on **Advanced** > uncheck the box that says **Configure ControlPort automatically** > click **OK** and restart TBB*. The SOCKS* port when the bundle is running will then be on 9050.
- The *tor* system wide daemon also listens on port 9050 by default. This is important to torifying the VM network proxy* or other applications. For example, by installing the Tor package we now have a SOCKS5* proxy* that we can use for SSH anonymous Dynamic port forwarding, which we will discuss later. This is an added dimension to our Internet security and anonymity.
- We can now torify the applications in the VM by simply configuring individual applications to use the SOCKS5* port 9050 to access the Internet. For example, all we

have to do is point our installed Firefox browser at Tor SOCKS5* (not the TBB browser) at port 9050 and we are using the Tor network, so there is no need to download and install TBB for individual user IDs. As long as updates are applied to the VM, Firefox will use the latest repository version of Tor. If you do this, be sure to study the TBB browser settings and try to match them up to your Firefox browser settings.

Remember, we will have to configure each application to use the Tor's socks port. To torify other applications that support SOCKS* proxies, just point them at Tor's SOCKS* IP 127.0.0.1 and port 9050. However, applications that do not support SOCKS* will need a tool such as torsocks, socat, proxychains or another chained proxy such as Polipo or Privoxy, to forward other protocols that we will soon cover. (See: https://trac.torproject.org/projects/tor/wiki/doc/TorFAQ#SocksListenAddress, https://github.com/dgoulet/torsocks, http://www.dest-unreach.org/socat, http://proxychains.sourceforge.net)

We also have to make sure that applications we set up to use the Tor proxy do not have DNS leaks. To do this we can transparently torify the VM by routing all DNS traffic through Tor. This will prevent any application configured to use the Tor's SOCKS port from revealing our IP address by a direct connection to a DNS. Tor provides a built-in DNSPort, which is designed to operate as a limited DNS server. This may slow down our applications, but we will gain more anonymity.

We will combine this with using the *iptables* command, which is a powerful Linux firewall that allows us to configure chains and rules for the VM. By doing this, in conjunction with using TBB would also provide strong leak protection as our anonymous Tor VM, which may have applications venturing out into the infected Internet, thus revealing our IP address and other information. This is all VERY important in setting up an anonymous Tor VM.

We now need to edit the global *torrc* file. The *torrc* file contains the configuration instructions that instruct Tor on how to behave. For TBB that file is located at *Data/Tor/torrc*, or in our case, if you installed a core package or compiled Tor from other source locations, you will find the file at */usr/local/etc/tor/torrc*, */etc/tor/torrc* or */etc/torrc*. (See: https://wiki.archlinux.org/index.php/tor#HTTP_proxy, https://help.ubuntu.com/community/IptablesHowTo, https://trac.torproject.org/projects/tor/wiki/doc/TransparentProxy) The Tor Trac TransparentProxy page recommended adding the following configuration items to the *torrc* file:

```
# cd /etc/tor && cp -ip torrc torrc.orig && vi torrc
VirtualAddrNetwork 10.192.0.0/10
AutomapHostsOnResolve 1
TransPort 9040
DNSPort 53
```

From the # man torrc page:

VirtualAdd rNetwork	When Tor needs to assign a virtual (unused) address because of a MAPADDRESS command from the controller or the AutomapHostsOnResolve feature, Tor picks an unassigned address from this range. (Defaults: 127.192.0.0/10 and [FE80::]/10 respectively.) When providing proxy server service to a network of computers, using a tool like dns-proxy-tor, change the IPv4 network to "10.192.0.0/10" or "172.16.0.0/12" and change the IPv6 network to "[FC00]/7". The default VirtualAddrNetwork address ranges on a properly configured machine will route to the loopback or link-local interface. For local use, no change to the default VirtualAddrNetwork setting is needed.
AutomapH ostsOnRes olve	When this option is enabled and we get a request to resolve an address that ends with one of the suffixes in AutomapHostsSuffixes, we map an unused virtual address to that address and return the new virtual address. This is handy for making ".onion" addresses work with applications that resolve an address and then connect to it. (Default: 0)
TransPort	Open this port to listen for transparent proxy connections. Set this to 0 if you don't want to allow transparent proxy connections. Set the port to "auto" to have Tor pick a port for you. This directive can be specified multiple times to bind to multiple addresses/ports. See SOCKSPort for an explanation of isolation flags. TransPort requires OS support for transparent proxies, such as BSDs' pf or Linux's IPTables. If you're planning to use Tor as a transparent proxy for a network, you'll want to examine and change VirtualAddrNetwork from the default setting. You'll also want to set the TransListenAddress option for the network you'd like to proxy. (Default: 0)
DNSPort	If non-zero, open this port to listen for UDP DNS requests and resolve them anonymously. This port only handles A, AAAA, and PTR requests -- it doesn't handle arbitrary DNS request types. Set the port to "auto" to have Tor pick a port for you. This directive can be specified multiple times to bind to multiple addresses/ports. See SOCKSPort for an explanation of isolation flags. (Default: 0)

Reading the above sounds as if we need to set *TransListenAddress*, but it defaults to 127.0.0.1 and is deprecated. To make sure Tor is listening for transparent proxy connections, open a terminal by **right clicking on _Terminal_ icon on launcher and select _New Terminal_**, then to see if Tor is listening on socket 9050 type:

```
# ss -aln | grep 9050
0      128                      127. 0. 0. 1 :9050                        *:*

# netstat --tcp --listening --programs --numeric
tcp      0      0 127. 0. 0. 1 :9050      0. 0. 0. 0:*           LISTEN      1264/tor
tcp      0      0 127. 0. 0. 1 :9040      0. 0. 0. 0:*           LISTEN      1264/tor
```

According to the old 2010 web page, we have to update the *resolv.conf* file and set up an iptables NAT rule, # vi /etc/resolv.conf, then add the following:
```
nameserver  127. 0. 0. 1
```

However, these directions are somewhat outdated if your system uses the *resolvconf* utility. When you edit the */etc/resolv.conf* file you may see the instructions DO NOT EDIT THIS FILE BY HAND -- YOUR CHANGES WILL BE OVERWRITTEN. This means that you may be editing a symbolic link to a file that is actually located somewhere below the */etc/resolvconf* directory and in which hook scripts use the *resolvconf* utility to manage your nameserver information. These hook scripts furnish the *resolvconf* utility the nameserver information for your VM. You can delete the symbolic link and edit the file that will not be overwritten; this was the old way of configuring nameservers and perhaps the easiest solution for a simple Tor VM.

However, if we have a static IP, the more appropriate solution would be to use the Network Manager GUI or to edit the */etc/network/interfaces* file to have the *ifup* command push nameserver information to the *resolv.conf* file. This is necessary if you have multiple programs that need to dynamically modify the nameserver information. To add a nameserver, add the following line to the interfaces file within static IP <u>iface</u> stanza:

```
dns-nameserver 127.0.0.1
```

Then make sure that */etc/resolv.conf* is a symbolic link to */etc/resolvconf/run/resolv.conf* which it already should be. For dynamic IPs, which almost all VMs are, you will find that using the Network Manager GUI is the easiest solution. ***Open up System Settings > under Network and Connectivity* click on *Network Settings* > in older versions of Mint and Ubuntu click on the tab for the network connection you are specifying a DNS server for (e.g. *Wired* for a VM) > select your *Wired connection 1*, click on the *Edit...* button > next to *Method:* change this to *Automatic (DHCP) addresses only* > next to *DNS Servers:* enter 127.0.0.1.*** This will update the file */etc/NetworkManager/system-connections/Wired connections 1* to the 127.0.0.1 DNS. (See: https://wiki.debian.org/NetworkConfiguration#The_resolv.conf_configuration_file)

In later versions of Mint and Ubuntu, left click on the network icon lower right > click on the wrench and select *Edit Connections* > when the connection editor appears highlight your *Wired* Internet connection and click on *Edit* > select the *IPv4* tab and change the connection Method: to *Automatic (Only addresses)* > next to *DNS Servers:* enter 127.0.0.1, OK. # shutdown -r now

Next, we need to set up our iptables rules and save the original iptables firewall rules:
```
# mkdir /etc/iptables && cd /etc/iptables && iptables-save > iptables.rules.orig
# iptables -t nat -A OUTPUT -p tcp -d 10.192.0.0/10 -j REDIRECT --to-ports 9040
```

If using a 192.168.x.x network use:
```
# iptables -t nat -A OUTPUT -p tcp -d 192.168.0.0/16 -j REDIRECT --to-ports 9040
```

Looking at the command above we see the IP Address is represented at IP/10. The /10 specifies how many bits to use in the netmask. In an IPv4 address, there are 32 bits with which to work. So specifying /10 means that network portion of the IP address gets 10 bits and the hosts gets 22 bits, this is called the netmask. So the IP address above would be masked with: 11111111 11000000 00000000 00000000. If you refer back, we specified the VirtualAddrNetwork as 10.192.0.0/10. This means we took $2^7 + 2^6 = 128 + 64 = 192$. (See: http://www.comptechdoc.org/independent/networking/guide/netaddressing.html)

Save your Tor iptables firewall rules settings:
cd /etc/iptables && iptables-save > iptables.rules.tor && iptables -t nat --list-rules

Next we need to add this script to our system startup:
cd /etc/network/if-pre-up.d && vi iptablesload

```
#!/bin/sh
iptables-restore < /etc/iptables/iptables.rules.tor
exit 0
```

chmod 755 iptablesload

If you have no other iptables rules, you need no further configuration. However, the Ubuntu community help recommends adding the following script to */etc/network/if-post-down.d/iptablessave*:

```
#!/bin/sh
iptables-save -c > /etc/iptables/iptables.rules.tor
if [ -f /etc/iptables/iptables.downrules ]; then
    iptables-restore < /etc/iptables/iptables.downrules
fi
exit 0
```

chmod 755 /etc/network/if-post-down.d/iptablessave

Now we should configure the VM network settings to use the Tor proxy. The easiest way to do this is to use the Network Management GUI. In Mint or Ubuntu, find *System Settings* > under *Network and Connectivity* click on *Network Settings* > select *Network Connections* on the left menu > click on the *Add button on the right* > select *Proxy* on the left menu > tick *Use system proxy configuration* > next to *SOCKS Proxy:* enter *1950*.

There are other solutions presented on various Internet web pages on how to set up a VM to use Tor. For example, the wiki.archlinux.org web page above had a sophisticated iptables setup and detailed other methods you can try. I was unable to get their solution working, and I found this to be a very technical solution to present in this book. To use Tor or TBB, refer back to Adding Less Privileged User IDs for Specific Purposes to Linux to create a 'tor' or other anonymous user IDs. We should not be using the Tor network with privileged IDs. Also refer back to Ubuntu-General Set up after Install in VirtualBox & VMware Player to turn off automatic updates and set other privacy setting to plug those Tor leaks.

While the whole VM is not configured to use the Tor network, which makes leaks possible from applications not using the Tor SOCKS proxy*, we have locked things down pretty good. Plus, to make the VM usable, we may not want some applications, such as a non-TBB browser, configured to use the Tor proxy, and if we do, we may not want it configured the same as the TBB. If you do configure other browsers to use Tor, perform the Anonymity tests suggested in the coming section Anonymity Testing and Final Commentary.

Vidalia – Setting Up and Using It, Manage or Relay Tor TBB or Daemon

Vidalia was a cross-platform GUI controller for Tor, built using the Qt framework. It has been replaced by the Firefox extension TorLauncher, which provides similar functionality. **Startup TBB > click on Tools arrow down to select Add-ons > click on Extension in the left menu and you will see the TorLauncher**. Tor is still providing standalone Vidalia packages that can be used to view the status of Tor at a glance and monitor Tor's bandwidth usage. If you want to use Vidalia with TBB, it **must be started before the TBB has been launched**. Vidalia also makes it easy to contribute to the Tor network by helping you to set up and manage your own Tor relay. Vidalia runs on most platforms supported by Qt 4.2 or later, including Windows, Mac OS X, and Linux or other UNIX variants using the X11 Window system. (See: https://www.torproject.org/projects/vidalia.html.en, https://www.torproject.org/docs/debian-vidalia.html.en, https://www.torproject.org/dist/vidalia-bundles, https://www.torproject.org/docs/tor-doc-relay.html.en, https://www.torproject.org/docs/tor-relay-debian.html.en)

As Tor development advances Vidalia may become deprecated, but for now Tor recommends that you download the Vidalia packages from their download page for Windows and https://people.torproject.org/~erinn/vidalia-standalone-bundles for Linux. MacOS is under development and requires a little additional configuration. Another option that you can consider is installing Vidalia from the above Tor repositories that we configured above. First, refer back to Chapter 7 to create a few unprivileged Tor user IDs following the directions there, and then become 'root' and type:

apt-get install vidalia   # In Mint & Ubuntu, # yum install vidalia   # In Fedora

After Vidalia finishes installing, you will see a dialog box titled Configuring vidalia where you are prompted with Users to add to the debian-tor group: so add the 'anon' and 'tor' users previous added by ticking both users with the space bar, <Tab>, <Ok>, <Enter>. The install will also install some documentation for you to examine so that you can learn about using Vidalia with Tor, # cd /usr/share/doc/vidalia; # gunzip README.Debian.gz FAQ.gz. Refer back to how we downloaded, scripted and started TBB and do this as an 'anon' or 'tor' user, Connect. From /usr/share/doc/vadalia/README.Debian:

Currently, Vidalia speaks against using Tor directly through a local (Unix) socket. However, this is recommended, and is Debian's default configuration. You have to answer the *debconf* question at Vidalia's config/upgrade time with the proper user/list of users that you'll allow to connect/configure/monitor your local instance of Tor and, if the user/any of the users from the list below is currently logged in, they will have to restart their X session before starting Vidalia.

After TBB starts in Linux, open a terminal window and type $ nohup Vidalia & as one of the unprivileged Tor users to startup and use the software or use the following script:

```
$ vi vidalia.sh
nohup vidalia &
sleep 3
rm nohup.out
exit
$ chmod 750 vidalia.sh
```

The Vidalia Control Panel will appear and you are off and running to Stop Tor, Setup Relaying, View the Network, Use a New Identity or to use all of the other options.

Fedora – Installing Tor Daemon and Supporting Software

 This solution for using the Tor daemon became somewhat deprecated with the 19 and 20 version releases of their OS. With a bit of tweaking, further research and experimentation, or perhaps an update to the 2010 Tor documentation we can finish this project. However, this project is still valid to torifying the applications that run in your VM.

Refer back to Mint-Ubuntu-Installing the Tor Daemon and Supporting Software where we discuss the Tor VM, supporting software, repositories, and the reasons for using them. Below I present most of the steps necessary to set up Fedora in a similar manner. Refer back to Fedora-General VM Configuration, Repository Setup, Applying Updates to bring the Fedora VM up-to-date.

Installing the Tor packages into Fedora is very similar to Ubuntu/Mint, as in it is better to configure the Tor repository first, and then download the Tor packages from the latest version from those Tor repositories. If you were mistakenly using Tor from default repositories you may need regroup from a Tor install conflict from the non-Tor repositories by typing # yum remove tor tor-arm tor-core tor-systemd -y, and then reinstall these packages after setting up the Tor repository file. As previously discussed, we want the Tor package repository configured to make sure that Tor is at the latest security release. The YUM repository files for Fedora are housed in the /etc/yum.repos.d directory where we will create a file called torproject.repo:

cd /etc/yum.repos.d && vi torproject.repo

In Fedora 20/19, use the following repo file - substitute the word "DISTRIBUTION" with fc/20, fc/19 or el/6 according to your distribution. The following repo files were taken from https://www.torproject.org/docs/rpms.html.en:

```
[tor]
name=Tor experimental repo
```

```
enabled=1
baseurl=http://deb.torproject.org/torproject.org/rpm/DISTRIBUTION/$basearch/
gpgcheck=1
gpgkey=http://deb.torproject.org/torproject.org/rpm/RPM-GPG-KEY-torproject.org.asc

[tor-source]
name=Tor experimental source repo
enabled=1
autorefresh=0
baseurl=http://deb.torproject.org/torproject.org/rpm/DISTRIBUTION/SRPMS
gpgcheck=1
gpgkey=http://deb.torproject.org/torproject.org/rpm/RPM-GPG-KEY-torproject.org.asc
```

The key's fingerprint should be: 3B9E EEB9 7B1E 827B CF0A 0D96 8AF5 653C 5AC0 01F1
(for RPM-GPG-KEY-torproject.org.asc above, yum will ask about the fingerprint).

Once the repository is set up and updates applied, install the Tor software:

```
# yum install tor tor-arm -y && shutdown -r now
Retrieving key from http://deb.torproject.org/torproject.org/rpm/RPM-GPG-KEY-torproject.org.asc
Importing GPG key 0x5AC001F1:
Userid    : "torproject.org RPM signing key"
Fingerprint: 3b9e eeb9 7b1e 827b cf0a 0d96 8af5 653c 5ac0 01f1
From      : http://deb.torproject.org/torproject.org/rpm/RPM-GPG-KEY-torproject.org.asc
```

Rebooting and installing Tor from the Tor repositories should automatically start the *tor*
daemon. Type # psg tor if you configured your aliases as directed in the previous chapter. If
not, you can check this by typing # pgrep tor   or   # ps –ef | grep tor | grep –v grep.
Alternatively, type the following to show the status of the Tor service, including whether it is
running or not:

```
# systemctl status tor.service
tor.service - SYSV: Onion Router - A low-latency anonymous proxy
   Loaded: loaded (/etc/rc.d/init.d/tor)
   Active: inactive (dead)
```

```
# systemctl start tor.service
```
If Tor is not enabled, reboot the VM or type # systemctl enable tor.service and then start it
up. In Ubuntu/Mint, we used iptables to set up the following rule:

```
# iptables –t nat –A OUTPUT –p tcp –d 10.192.0.0/10 –j REDIRECT ––to-ports 9040
```

However, as of Fedora 19 their developers would prefer that we use the FirewallD utility to
manage their firewall rules. If the rule above is not set properly in their firewall configuration

when we configure the */etc/tor/torrc* file to the settings recommended back in 2010, the Tor daemon will fail to start with an error out because it could not bind to port 9040. Since FirewallD is a new utility, there are not a lot of examples on the Internet about how to set up rules to match the iptables command above and not conflict with other complex Fedora FirewallID firewall rules. Rather than spend many hours learning about this tool or blindly experimenting, I have found it is best to wait for these project's developers and network firewall experts to catch up with the ever-changing technology and post the solutions. For example, we could change the Fedora VM to use an IPTables configuration, but that will probably become obsolete in future releases of Fedora. When/if the Tor project or someone else posts another solution that we can use with FirewallID, I will post that up on my blog in the future at https://thatcybersecurityguy.blogspot.com. (See: https://fedorahosted.org/firewalld, https://fedoraproject.org/wiki/FirewallD) As we did in Ubuntu/Mint, we will now set up the VM global configuration to use the Tor Socks proxy.

Under _Activities_ type _System Settings_ > drag and drop it onto the quick launch bar > bring up the _System Settings_ by clicking on the icon > under _Hardware_ click on the _Network_ icon > select _Network proxy_ > on the _Method_ drop down select _Manual_ > beside _Socks Host_ enter _127.0.0.1_ and the port _9050_, Apply. This will configure the VM to use Tor SOCKS5* proxy*. To test this, configure and surf your non-Tor browser to https://check.torproject.org/?lang=en-US&small=1 to see if your non-tor browser is using Tor. This will reveal if other applications configured to the VM proxy were also using the system wide Tor's Network proxy*.

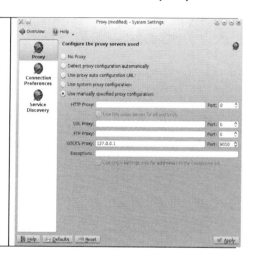

With a Tor VM we have to try to keep other applications from polling the Internet, which we call leaks. For example, **turn off automatic updates by bringing up System Settings > under _System Administration_ click on _Software Management_ > on the _Get, Remove and Update Software_ dialog click on the icon upper right and select _Settings_ > next to Check for new updates: change setting to _Never, Apply_.**

Eventually, a solution will evolve a solution such as the one presented for Mint and Ubuntu. To make that work with new FirewallID rules, you will need to update the */etc/resolv.conf* file. When we examine the */etc/resolv.conf* file we see something like:

```
# Generated by NetworkManager
nameserver 192.168.0.1
```

```
# cp -ip resolv.conf resolv.conf.orig
```

The Tor documentation suggests that we change this to 127.0.0.1. The easiest way to do this is by using the NetworkManager that comes with Fedora. **Left click on the network icon lower right > click on the wrench and select _Edit Connections_ > when the connection** *editor appears highlight your <u>Wired</u> Internet connection and click on <u>Edit</u> > select the* *<u>IPv4</u> tab and change the connection Method: to <u>Automatic (Only addresses)</u> > next to* *<u>DNS Servers:</u> enter <u>127.0.0.1</u>, <u>OK</u>.* # shutdown -r now and hopefully all we have left is to properly set up the Fedora firewall rules to get everything working. Refer down to <u>Anonymity Testing and Final Commentary</u> to perform some anonymity testing to see what you may still be leaking that can identify you on the web, such as DNS settings, since we did not finish that project.

Tor/Polipo/Privoxy Proxies – General Information

If you are like me, I had always thought of a proxy* as the evil middle man that companies/schools set up to limit access to the Internet and track everything that students/employees were doing using their browsers. So I was curious as to how implementing an individual proxy* in a Linux environment could possibly benefit anonymous web surfing. (See: https://en.wikipedia.org/wiki/Privoxy, https://en.wikipedia.org/wiki/Polipo, https://wiki.archlinux.org/index.php/Polipo, http://www.pps.univ-paris-diderot.fr/~jch/software/polipo)

Under a proxy* type of setup, when a client tries to access the Internet it is really asking the proxy* server to request the object (web pages, images, movies, etc.) from the Internet. This server can then act as a filter, both to and from the Internet, and it can *log all activity* both ways. A proxy is a very useful tool for finding employees or students who are using their computers or mobile devices in violation of business, school or home policies.

The Polipo proxy* was built with a focus on individual users or for use in small offices. It has limited capabilities for filtering, but its emphasis is actually on performance. It caches your Internet activity and communicates with web servers as optimally as possible. Polipo has some features that, its creator says, are unique among currently available proxies. From the Polipo web page http://www.pps.univ-paris-diderot.fr/~jch/software/polipo/polipo.html#Privoxy, it states some reasons to consider using Polipo with Tor:

- Polipo will use HTTP/1.1 pipelining if it believes that the remote server supports it, whether the incoming requests are pipelined or come in simultaneously on multiple connections (this is more than the simple usage of persistent connections, which is done by, for example, Squid).
- Polipo will cache the initial segment of an instance if the download has been interrupted, and, if necessary, complete it later using Range requests.
- Polipo will upgrade client requests to HTTP/1.1 even if they come in as HTTP/1.0, and up/downgrade server replies to the client's capabilities (this may involve conversion to or from the HTTP/1.1 chunked encoding).
- Polipo has complete support for IPv6 (except for scoped (link-local) addresses)
- Polipo can optionally use a technique known as Poor Man's Multiplexing to reduce latency even further.
- Since it can speak the SOCKS* protocol, Polipo can be used together with the Tor anonymizing network.

- Since it can speak both IPv4 and IPv6, Polipo can be used as a bridge between the IPv4 and IPv6 Internets to allow an IPv6-only host to access IPv4 servers, or vice versa.

Plus a few that the author did not list:

- Polipo can speak SOCKS5* protocol.   We will later use SSH Port Forwarding to connect to our home server through a firewall and surf the Internet using our home network. So SOCKS5* will become much more important.
- SOCKS5* can stop DNS leaks, which are used at the Tor exit relays to track your Internet activity. Tor has a brief read on this on this at https://www.torproject.org/docs/faq.
- Other SOCKS* aware applications can be pointed at Tor. They can route DNS requests through Tor, thus giving them the same anonymity at the exit relay as other Tor traffic. To explain, Tor **had** an Achilles heel. Tor used to allow DNS through the exit relay, which allowed someone monitoring a user's connection to determine which websites were being viewed. Tor has fixed that now, but if we combine Tor with Polipo, it may fix that for other applications as well. However, those applications will have to be configured to use the Polipo proxy*.
- Polipo can be used in place of ad-filtering, privacy-enhancing proxies such as Junkbuster, Privoxy or WWWOFFLE. Since Polipo has much more refined HTTP support, it doesn't impose the speed tax usually associated with such proxies.

In short, Polipo has a few techniques to make web browsing (seem) faster. This dated 2010 tool might be something that we should consider adding to our Tor setup, but is not recommend by Tor. One thing that you can try is to add Polipo and see if it improves your Anonymity Testing tests using the latest Firefox browser. In earlier versions of Tor, I did see an improvement on a few anonymity tests. Therefore, the following additions to your Tor VM may be worthwhile.

The Privoxy proxy is a well maintained project for enhancing privacy by modifying web page data and HTTP headers, controlling access, and removing ads and other Internet junk. Installing Privoxy will set up a very basic configuration that should enhance your privacy when using your Web browser. Using Privoxy will give you fine-tuned control over your Internet experience if you are willing to take the time to study their documentation. It is a highly configurable web proxy that can be set up as a firewall with a focus on privacy enhancement, and ad and junk elimination. There are many ways that Privoxy can be used to sanitize and customize your web browsing experience, such as blocking ads and banners, managing cookies, and provides many other ways to protect your privacy. (See: http://www.privoxy.org, http://www.privoxy.org/faq/index.html) From the Privoxy FAQ here are a few features:

- Good proxy* for multiple computers running multiple browsers as it can be set up to run as a server application for a LAN.
- Supports "Connection: keep-alive". Outgoing connections can be kept alive independently from the client.

- Supports tagging, that allows changing the behavior based on client and server headers.
- Can be run as an "intercepting" proxy, which obviates the need to configure browsers individually.
- Sophisticated actions and filters for manipulating both server and client headers.
- Integrated browser-based configuration and control utility at http://config.privoxy.org (shortcut: http://p.p/). Browser-based tracing of rule and filter effects. Remote toggling.
- Web page filtering (text replacements, removes banners based on size, invisible "web-bugs" and HTML annoyances, etc.)
- Modularized configuration that allows for standard settings and user settings to reside in separate files, so that installing updated actions' files won't overwrite individual user settings.
- Support for Perl Compatible Regular Expressions in the configuration files, and a more sophisticated and flexible configuration syntax.
- GIF de-animation.
- Bypass many click-tracking scripts (avoids script redirection).
- User-customizable HTML templates for most proxy-generated pages (e.g. "blocked" page).

There are compelling arguments for chaining the Polipo and/or Privoxy proxies with our Tor proxy that connects to the Tor network. We can also use the Privoxy proxy* and/or forward the Polipo proxy* to the Privoxy proxy*, which serves another function. As we have discussed, the two proxies have different goals in mind and merge together well. Unlike the Polipo proxy*, the Privoxy is not cached, so by combining the two we may get improved performance and improved privacy, which is why both are covered.

Fedora — Install and Chain the Polipo Proxy to the Tor Proxy

Years ago, the Polipo proxy* used to be included in the TBB. It was needed as a work around to a bug in Firefox that was fixed. However, as Tor has progressed, using Polipo was no longer required or even recommended for use with Tor. I tried chaining Polipo with the Tor proxy* and I found little evidence that the Polipo proxy* will speed up your browsing or offer benefits over the Tor SOCKS5* proxy* listening on 9050. The Tor proxy* is now automatically started when Tor is installed. The Polipo proxy* is not necessary if you can point your Internet application at Tor SOCKS (e.g. 127.0.0.1:9050). We have discussed the advantages and disadvantages of using Polipo, so you may want to try it to see if it improves your use of Tor or the Internet in a non-Tor VM.

```
$ su -
Password:
# yum install polipo
```

Package	Arch	Version	Repository	Size
Installing:				
polipo	x86_64	1.0.4.1-11.fc20	fedora	215 k

Start up the Polipo proxy* and you will see that the default configuration listens on port 8123:
```
# systemctl status polipo.service
polipo.service - A caching web proxy
   Loaded: loaded (/usr/lib/systemd/system/polipo.service; disabled)
   Active: inactive (dead)
     Docs: man:polipo(1)
           http://localhost:8123/
```

We want the daemon to start automatically on the next reboot. Years ago the Fedora OS switched to using the *systemctl* to enable/disable and start/stop services. (See: https://fedoraproject.org/wiki/Systemd) Refer back to Fedora-A Lesson in Starting and Stopping Services Automatically to learn a bit about handling services in Fedora. To show the status, enable, and start the Polipo service, type the following:

```
# systemctl status polipo.service
polipo.service is not a native service, redirecting to /sbin/chkconfig.
Executing /sbin/chkconfig polipo on
# systemctl enable polipo.service    # enable service startup on boot
ln -s '/usr/lib/systemd/system/polipo.service' '/etc/systemd/system/multi-
user.target.wants/polipo.service'
# systemctl start polipo.service
# netstat --tcp --listening --programs --numeric | grep polipo
tcp       0      0 127.0.0.1:8123      0.0.0.0:*           LISTEN      2138/polipo
# systemctl stop polipo.service
# cd /etc/polipo  &&  cp -ip config config.orig
```

The Polipo web page has all of the information about setting up Polipo at http://www.pps.univ-paris-diderot.fr/~jch/software/polipo/tor.html. To use Polipo in Fedora, uncomment the following in the default Polipo configuration file, which should enable Polipo to be chained with the Tor proxy*:

```
# Uncomment this if you want to use a parent SOCKS proxy:
socksParentProxy = "localhost:9050"
socksProxyType = socks5
```

From the Polipo manual, you will also want to disable the local configuration interface in order to protect yourself from browser vulnerabilities. Add this setting to the configuration file to use Tor with Polipo:
```
# Disable the local configuration interface
disableLocalInterface = true
```

```
# ss -aln | egrep -e 8123 -e 9050
tcp    LISTEN   0      128       127.0.0.1:9050              *:*
tcp    LISTEN   0      32        127.0.0.1:8123              *:*
# netstat --tcp --listening --programs --numeric | egrep -e polipo -e tor
tcp       0      0 127.0.0.1:8123      0.0.0.0:*           LISTEN      2318/polipo
```

```
tcp       0     0 127. 0. 0. 1 :9050        0. 0. 0. 0:*          LISTEN      995/tor
```

Now point your application and system proxy settings at the Polipo proxy. *Open up System Settings > under Hardware click on the Network Settings icon > click on Proxy on the left and tick Use manually specified proxy configuration: and enter the following:*

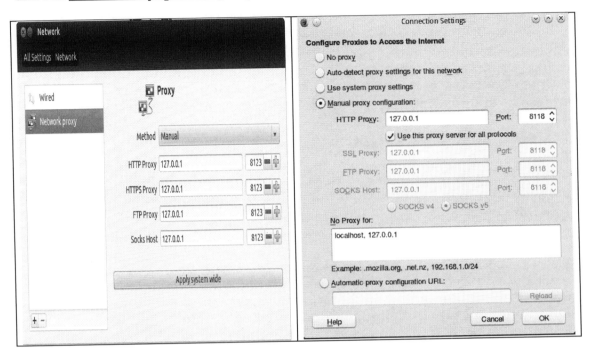

Fedora -- Other Polipo Proxy Configuration Settings to Consider

Tor has a legacy *polipo.conf* file that you can download and try in the */etc/polipo* directory. The link for the file can be found on the web page https://trac.torproject.org/projects/tor/wiki/doc/TorifyHOWTO/Polipo, where it says you can use "our old polipo *config* file" if you like. This file worked very well in older versions of Fedora and in Ubuntu/Mint, but in versions of Fedora later than 17, I found it best to edit and use the default Polipo *config* file. If you want to try the old Tor configuration file, you can download it using the following, which failed in Fedora 20:

```
# cd /etc/polipo  &&  wget
https://gitweb.torproject.org/torbrowser.git/blob_plain/1ffcd9dafb9dd76c3a29dd686e05a71a9
5599fb5:/build-scripts/config/polipo.conf
# cp -ip polipo.conf config  &&  mv polipo.conf polipo.tor.orig  &&  chmod 644 config
# systemctl start polipo.service
```

The default Polipo */etc/polipo/config* file uses port 8123. The downloaded Tor configuration */etc/polipo/polipo.conf* file has Polipo using port 8118. Port 8118 is the default for the Privoxy proxy, which we will soon cover. The web page http://www.pps.univ-paris-diderot.fr/~jch/software/polipo/faq.html, states that the default port should be 8123. In searching for an answer as to why Polipo was being configured to use port 8118, you can get

additional information at
https://trac.torproject.org/projects/tor/wiki/doc/TorifyHOWTO#TorifyingsoftwareHOWTO.
Add explanations such as this to the configuration file, to do so cut and paste the following to
the */etc/polipo/config* file commenting out proxyPort = 8118:

```
# In order to get the privacy enhancements of Privoxy and much (but not all)
# of the performance of Polipo, you should put Polipo upstream of Privoxy.
#
# In other words, you should:
#  - point your web browser at Privoxy (localhost:8118);
#  - point Privoxy at Polipo (put forward / localhost:8123 in the Privoxy
#    config file);
#  - Use no parent proxy in Polipo.
#
# Since we are not using Privoxy the port was changed to 8123.
proxyAddress = "127.0.0.1"
# proxyPort = 8118
proxyPort = 8123
```

We may also want to enable the *polipo.service* to start in the background **when run
manually**. The Polipo Manual states, "*If the configuration variable daemonise is set to true,
Polipo will run as a daemon: it will fork and detach from its controlling terminal (if any). The
variable daemonise defaults to false.*" If we set this option, it is useful to get Polipo to
automatically write its pid to a file. From the Polipo Manual, "*If the variable pidFile is defined, it
should be the name of a file where Polipo will write its pid. If the file already exists when it is
started, Polipo will refuse to run.*" For these reasons, you may want to add the following
settings to the */etc/polipo/config* file.

```
### Configuration from Fedora RPM
### ****************************
daemonise = true
pidFile = /var/run/polipo/polipo.pid
```

Next, examine the memory settings. From the Polipo manual, "*Unless set explicitly, both
chunkLowMark and chunkCriticalMark are computed automatically from chunkHighMark.*" If
using the default Polipo *config* file the old Tor configuration had this set to:

```
chunkHighMark = 67108864
```
This is higher than the recommended values in the Polipo default *config* file of:
```
# Uncomment this if you've got plenty of memory:
# chunkHighMark = 50331648
# objectHighMark = 16384
```

From https://en.wikipedia.org/wiki/Transparent_proxy#Transparent_proxy *"a transparent proxy intercepts normal communication at the network layer without requiring any special client configuration."* The Polipo FAQ says that it is transparent if you set the following in the *config* file:

```
maxAge = 0
maxExpiresAge = 0
```

shutdown -r now

From the Polipo manual, *"The variable logFile defaults to empty if daemonise is false, and to '/var/log/polipo' otherwise."* So there was no reason to uncomment the following:

```
# logFile = /var/log/polipo
```

Because the Polipo install puts the following entry in the */etc/logrotate.d* directory their log file will not grow unchecked, which is always a concern:

```
/var/log/polipo {
    create 0640 polipo polipo
    missingok
    notifempty
    delaycompress
    postrotate
        /sbin/chkconfig polipo && /sbin/service polipo reload 2>/dev/null >/dev/null || :
    endscript
}
```

From the Polipo manual, *"The on-disk cache consists in a file system subtree rooted at a location defined by the variable diskCacheRoot, by default "/var/cache/polipo. This directory should normally be writeable, readable and seek able by the user(s) running Polipo."*

 I found no evidence that using the cache with Polipo will significantly speed up browsing. The cache is also seen as a security compromise. The following is presented if you want to try the cache on your own.

The default Tor *polipo.conf* configuration disabled disk caching, whereas the Polipo *config* enabled this option. Using the Tor setting should be left disabled as in the Tor configuration, but Polipo brags about how using disk caching will speed up browser activity; if you want to try it:

```
# If diskCacheRoot is an empty string, no disk cache is used.
# Uncomment this if you want to disable the on-disk cache:
diskCacheRoot = ""
```

There was a difference between Fedora and Ubuntu, which was that I did not have to add the non-root user to the polipo group to get caching to work. You can check to see if disk caching is actually taking place by logging in as a user, surfing to a few websites and looking at the */var/cache/polipo* directory. Please be advised that the default Tor configuration also sets:

```
# Uncomment this if there's only one user using this instance of Polipo:
cacheIsShared = false
```

Hence, if you have more than one user you might want to stick with the Tor setting of having no disk cache.

Ubuntu/Mint – Install and Chain the Polipo Proxy to the Tor Proxy

Refer back to how we set up and configured Polipo in Fedora, as the steps in Ubuntu/Mint are very similar. Become 'root' and type:

```
# apt-get update && apt-get upgrade -y
# apt-get install polipo -y
# psg polipo
proxy     3901    1  0 15:37 ?        00:00:00 /usr/bin/polipo -c /etc/polipo/config
pidFile=/var/run/polipo/polipo.pid daemonise=true logFile=/var/log/polipo/polipo.log
forbiddenFile=/etc/polipo/forbidden
# /etc/init.d/polipo status
 * polipo is running
```

There were a few differences setting up Polipo between Fedora and Ubuntu, but not many. One difference was that *polipo* service from the Ubuntu started automatically as a daemon by just installing the package in Ubuntu. (See: https://help.ubuntu.com/community/Polipo) Set up the configuration file recommended by Tor:

```
# cd /etc/polipo && mv -i config config.orig
```

Retrieve the *polipo.conf* file for Tor below, which is the Tor recommended configuration file for the */etc/polipo* directory. (See: http://www.pps.univ-paris-diderot.fr/~jch/software/polipo/tor.html)

```
# wget
https://gitweb.torproject.org/torbrowser.git/blob_plain/1ffcd9dafb9dd76c3a29dd686e05a71a9
5599fb5:/build-scripts/config/polipo.conf
```

```
# cp -ip polipo.conf config && mv polipo.conf polipo.tor
# chmod 644 config      # Probably already set
# vi config
```

The configuration item in the file that allows Tor and Polipo to work together is:
```
# Uncomment this if you want to use a parent SOCKS proxy:
socksParentProxy = "localhost:9050"
socksProxyType = socks5
```

Restart the polipo daemon and make sure it is running:

```
# /etc/init.d/polipo restart
# /etc/init.d/polipo status     # or,    # ps -ef | grep polipo | grep -v grep   # or,
# pgrep polipo
868
```

The # sysv-rc-conf tool for configuring/viewing services in Ubuntu was installed in Tor section of this chapter. Using this tool you can see that the *polipo* service is configured to start at run levels 2-5.

As discussed, when configuring Fedora the default Tor configuration file had Polipo using port 8118. Add the following to the */etc/polipo/config* configuration file and change the port to Polipo's default port file:

```
# vi config
# In order to get the privacy enhancements of Privoxy and much (but not all)
# of the performance of Polipo, you should put Polipo upstream of Privoxy.
#
# In other words, you should:
#  - point your web browser at Privoxy (localhost:8118);
#  - point Privoxy at Polipo (put forward / localhost:8123 in the Privoxy
#    config file);
#  - Use no parent proxy in Polipo.
#
# Since we are not using Privoxy the port was changed to 8123.

proxyAddress = "127.0.0.1"
# proxyPort = 8118
proxyPort = 8123
```

As we discussed, when setting up Fedora, the default Tor configuration had the disk cache disabled. If you want to try to speed up browsing, consider trying the following:

```
# If diskCacheRoot is an empty string, no disk cache is used.
# Uncomment this if you want to disable the on-disk cache:
diskCacheRoot = ""
```

Change it to:

```
# diskCacheRoot = ""
```

Commenting this out enables disk caching. You will also have to enable the users to write to the cache directory:

```
# ll /var/cache
drwxr-x---. 115 polipo polipo 4096 Sep 12 21:43 polipo
# cd /var/cache && chmod 770 polipo && ll /var/cache
drwxrwx---. 115 polipo polipo 4096 Sep 12 21:43 polipo
```

Then add the users who need to use the proxy* to the proxy* group:

```
# usermod sudoroot -G proxy -a      # -a appends user to group, -G specifies group
# more /etc/group    # to view the changes
```

You can check later to see if disk caching is actually taking place by looking at the */var/cache/polipo* directory. Restart the daemon either by rebooting or manually by typing:

```
# cd /etc/init.d/polipo restart
```

Be advised that the default Tor configuration also sets:
```
# Uncomment this if there's only one user using this instance of Polipo:
cacheIsShared = false
```

Consequently, if you have more than one user, you might want to stick with the Tor setting of having no disk cache, or comment the above out and see if everything works OK for all of your users.

Privoxy — Install and Chain the Privoxy Proxy to the Tor Proxy

We can easily use the default Privoxy proxy* installation or chain multiple application Internet protocols to the Tor proxy. This is an excellent solution to torifying applications in a VM when combined with the Tor configuration above. Install the Tor and Privoxy daemons, then use the default Privoxy Tor settings that you will have to uncomment in their provided configuration file:

```
# apt-get install privoxy
# ps -ef | grep privoxy | grep -v grep
privoxy    4408    1  0 16:22 ?        00:00:00 /usr/sbin/privoxy --pidfile
/var/run/privoxy.pid --user privoxy /etc/privoxy/config
```

The install automatically started the daemon above. To chain the Privoxy ports to Tor SOCKS search the Privoxy config file for port 9050, from the *config* file: "To chain Privoxy and Tor, both running on the same system, you uncomment the following in the Privoxy config file:"

```
# cd /etc/privoxy && cp -ip config config.orig && vi config
forward-socks5   /    127.0.0.1:9050 .
```

```
# netstat --tcp --listening --programs --numeric
```

tcp	0	0 127.0.0.1:9050	0.0.0.0:*	LISTEN	1264/tor
tcp	0	0 127.0.0.1:9040	0.0.0.0:*	LISTEN	1262/tor
tcp	0	0 127.0.1.1:53	0.0.0.0:*	LISTEN	1011/dnsmasq
tcp	0	0 127.0.0.1:8118	0.0.0.0:*	LISTEN	3036/privoxy

As discussed previously, Privoxy listens by default on port 8118, so we will need to configure our VM Network proxy settings to use the Privoxy proxy. You might wonder, why have the Tor SOCKS proxy and what is the advantage of chaining Privoxy to Tor? Using Privoxy we can also forward the HTTP Proxy, HTTPS Proxy and FTP Proxy ports to the Tor SOCKS proxy* using the VM System Settings and applying them system wide. We still need to configure our Internet applications to use the system proxy,* so this is not the perfect solution. There are also other problems with those Internet applications, such as plug-ins that will leak information about our Internet use. For example, using a Firefox browser with a Flash plug-in enabled showed the following from JonDonym, "*Sorry, you are not using Tor correctly. An unknown IP address, possibly your own, was uncovered by FLASH.*"

Perform the tests in order to get more details about other potential anonymity problems. Since we have the Tor TransPort configured to handle DNS requests we have prevented DNS leaks, but there are other ways and ports that applications leak information to on the Internet. We must restart Privoxy so that it reads the new *config* file # /etc/init.d/privoxy restart

Using Privoxy with Tor gives you the ability to send all protocols to the Tor Proxy. You can test this by performing the anonymity testing in the next section, which will show how well this works using a non-TBB browser or other Internet application. Refer down to Anonymity Testing and Final Commentary to test everything out with a non-TBB browser.

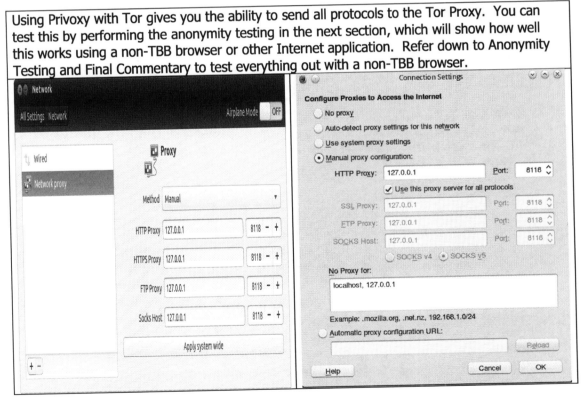

Another unique configuration you can use with Privoxy chained to the Tor daemon is to install the TBB and configure it to use Privoxy for all ports except the SOCKS Host. You will also

want to use the Firefox hardening techniques we discussed previously. My anonymity testing using this configuration was very good and unique.

Everything that has been presented on Tor is considered adequate for your protection. If you want to experiment with Privoxy I found the following web links, information from which you can experiment further:

http://sourceforge.net/projects/ijbswa/files/	https://help.ubuntu.com/community/Privoxy
https://trac.torproject.org/projects/tor/wiki/doc/PrivoxyConfig	https://wiki.archlinux.org/index.php/Privoxy
http://thestegemans.com/2011/06/03/blocking_ads_on_arch_linux_with_privoxy	http://www.privoxy.org/config/
http://www.privoxy.org/faq/	http://www.privoxy.org/faq/misc.html#TOR
http://www.macos.utah.edu/documentation/servers/privoxy.html	

Anonymity Testing and Final Commentary

This final testing will be a huge wakeup call to consider employing the techniques described in this chapter to help make you become more anonymous. Performing these checks/tests should be a shock when you see the amount of detail your computer is actually providing to governments, search engines, corporations, crackers, criminals and thieves who are watching and collecting details about your Internet activity. It is easy to test the various anonymity configurations outlined in this chapter, which hopefully you have set up. A few websites provide easy-to-use tools to check your setup.

- Visit http://privacy.net/analyze-your-Internet-connection, which checks your IP address and host name. It also examines Java, flash cookies, Silverlight cookies, browser plug-ins and much more. I really liked its analysis; it showed me:

    o My IP address
    o My host name from ISP
    o My local IP address from Java (this is a BIG hole in security)
    o How to adjust my Flash cookie settings
    o How to adjust my Microsoft Silverlight cookie settings
    o My browser type and operating system

- Go to the http://panopticlick.eff.org website and **click on the _TEST ME_ button** and you will see something like, "*Within our dataset of several million visitors, only one in 1,385 browsers have the same fingerprint as yours.*" I added the Polipo proxy* with disk caching and got the result, "*Within our dataset of several million visitors, only one in 1,383 browsers have the same fingerprint as yours.*" As you can see it did not improve my browser fingerprint by much.
- The BrowserSPY website http://browserspy.dk is a collection of tests that you can perform on your browser. It shows you in vivid detail just how much personal information your browser is revealing about yourself.

- Perform a ShieldsUp experiment at http://www.grc.com to test many things about which you might want to know. This is a free Internet security checkup and information service.
- Visit is http://www.hostip.info, which will show your IP Address, your country and city, as well as a map to your general location. This is a community database where people give up the location of their IP and allow it to be stored in the hostip database.
- Perform the Anonymity test at http://ip-check.info/?lang=en to see how you are doing with your anonymity setup! *__Click on Anonymity Test > Cancel button > START TEST!__*" and it will display all of the information that websites everywhere are collecting on you. On the Anonymity test web page, the only thing you should see in red are the fonts, which you might want to allow to be broadcast.
- You can also get a glimpse on how much is already known about your Internet presence by visiting http://www.peekyou.com, which will show your digital profile on the Internet. You may see things like your age, address, where you work, where you went to school, photo, contact information, photo of your home or former home, and more.
- Cruise to http://www.rapleaf.com, where you enter your email address, and you may see where you live, your age, household income, education level, homeownership status, personal interests, number of children in your family, and more.

With these steps, you have now hardened your Internet device from a tracking attack while doing all of your needed Internet search activity. By *needed* I mean doing research on whatever you are looking into using the search engines, visiting shopping websites, and clicking on links you are unsure about, as in the way I had to do my research to write this book. I clicked on many links that I had no idea where I was going. These steps also keep criminals, search engines, governments, etc. from easily tracking your Internet activity and recording all of your personal information! It is not foolproof, but by implementing these simple steps you are doing more than most other users out there and becoming a **HARD TARGET**. Who are criminals going after, you or the plentiful supply of soft targets out there? Now let's do even more to layer our defenses!

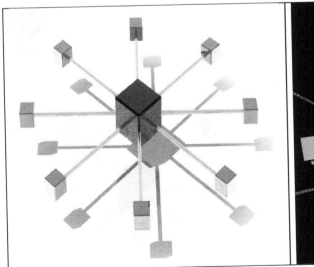
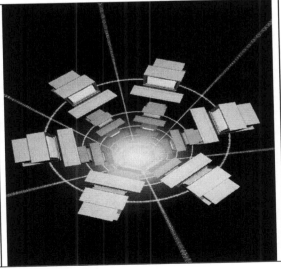

Chapter 9 -- Hardening Security Using Your Mobil Devices by Setting Up and Using an SSH Server on Your Remote Secure Network

We established a secure home base of operations in Chapter 2; we layered our defenses and now it is time to build an airstrip as Marine Major General Smith did so that we can advance on the enemy (venture out into the world and use the infected Internet from our mobile devices). When using the Internet, you have to consider yourself a scout behind enemy lines and pray that your method of communication with your home base does not become compromised. We have painstakingly, step-by-step, protected ourselves with known methods that are constantly improving (and being cracked), hoping to stay one step ahead of the enemy. You have to take the paranoid view that everyone connected to the Internet is seeking to do you harm. This is what we do in the military and this is the focal viewpoint of this book. If we don't do this, we will essentially suffer the same fate that the Confederate soldiers did at Gettysburg during Pickett's charge.

 Historical Reference -- The Charge of Pickett, Pettigrew, and Trimble was the climax of the Battle of Gettysburg (1863), the most disastrous infantry attack of the American Civil War, and largest infantry battle on the American continent ever!

Why Lee and Longstreet decided to take an inferior and less well-supplied Northern army to fight a superior force who would establish a well-fortified, entrenched defensive position will be a subject of speculation for all time. From Civil War Times "Shelby Foote makes the case for a Rebel offensive. A move into Pennsylvania "might or might not cause the withdrawal of [Ulysses] Grant from in front of Vicksburg, but at least it would remove the invaders from the soil of Virginia *during the vital harvest season*"–emphasis Allen Barra "while at best it could accomplish the fall of the northern capital and thus encourage the foreign intervention which Jefferson Davis long has seen as the key to victory of the superior forces of the Union."[2] So, we can see that the invasion of the North was a calculated but desperate gamble by the South who saw this as their only hope of winning the war. "When the fighting began on July 1, Maj. Gen. George Meade had 51 brigades of infantry and seven of cavalry, comprised of nearly 80,000 men, while General Lee, with J.E.B. Stuart's cavalry still away from the main body, had perhaps 50,000 men, 34 brigades of infantry and just one of cavalry. Thus the Federals began the fight with an 8-to-5 advantage."[2]

During the first two days of fighting, the Army of Northern Virginia was able to inflict heavier casualties on the Federals, but by the third day Lee's options were to retreat, or find the most vulnerable place in the Union defense and try an all-out assault, hoping that the Union lines would break. Given the mindset of that era, a retreat would have meant Lee and his Army would leave the field of battle in disgrace, having not to at least have tried to overrun the Union's defenses.

Lee chose the weakest point and massed his troops and cannon against it. However, even the weakest point in a defensive line can stand against superior numbers and firepower, if the position is unattainable. Lee's generals argued against this frontal assault on a position where the Union was on high ground and with a mile of open terrain for the South to cover before the enemy could be engaged in hand-to-hand combat. Longstreet argued vehemently against the attack, so much so that he bordered on insubordination. Longstreet is quoted in numerous sources as saying "No 15,000 men ever arrayed for battle could take that position."[3][5] From R.E. Lee, by Douglas Southall Freeman, Longstreet told Lee, "I have had my scouts out all night, and I find that you still have an excellent opportunity to more around to the right of Meade's army, and maneuver him into attacking us." Longstreet felt that if they threatened Washington D.C., Meade would have no choice but to move his army off the high ground to confront Lee's Army on the ground of their choosing. Longstreet believed so strongly about this that he had already given the order for his troop to move to the right. Ultimately, Lee overruled Longstreet who, riding away, is quoted as saying, ""Never was I so depressed as upon that day." Longstreet was listless and despairing after the argument and his eyes remained fixated upon the ground."[6]

The Union commanders were able to predict Lee's moves as well, so it seems his moves weren't very inventive or "secret". You could possibly pronounce this as a "last ditch" effort of a very desperate commander. Lee began the battle in Napoleonic style by arraying 160 cannons, which stretched for over two miles, to bombard the Union position on Cemetery Ridge. Against the Rebels stood 100 Union cannons. For two hours, the Confederates bombarded the Union lines and cannons, hoping to take them out and weaken their defenses. To imagine what this was like, this was the greatest concentration of artillery and the largest artillery barrage that has ever existed on the American continent. It could be heard 40 miles away in Harrisburg, Pennsylvania. In the heated exchange of cannon, the Union wisely held back cannon and shot in reserve, and eventually had to pull back the limited cannon that they were using, to let them cool because of overheating. (The Union version of the story was that the Union commanders silenced their guns to lure the Confederates into the infantry attack that they knew was coming.) Confederate Col. Edward P. Alexander mistook this lull and lack of cannon fire to mean that the barrage had destroyed most of the Union cannon, while in fact the bombardment had inflicted little damage to the Union cannon or their infantry. Lee had entrusted him as to when, or if, to order Pickett to begin the infantry attack.

At 3:00 PM the Rebel cannon stopped firing and 12,500 Rebel infantry, which stretched a mile long, began their assault as the Union brought up their rifle cannon that they had held in reserve, as well as the cannon that had now cooled down, to begin the slaughter. Civil War, Vol. II states "Pickett, saddened by the dreadful waste of life he foresaw, tears filling his eyes, stood in front of his three brigades and shouted, "Charge the enemy and remember Old Virginia!"[3] The Confederates began marching at 110 steps per minute across the mile long open field, which would end with a race uphill with what remained of their soldiers to reach Union lines. The Union began by using the 3-inch ordnance rifle cannon, invented just two years earlier, which was made with 4 ½ inch rod iron; the cannon had a 3-inch groove bore engineered for deadly accuracy. These cannons began tearing into the Rebel infantry with shells that exploded upon impact, as well as timed shells, which had been engineered to burst over top of the now exposed Confederate ranks raining down death from above. From Civil War, Vol. II "Union gunners feverishly fired shells into the huge columns... Men, it was said, "fell like ten pins."" About half way through the assault, the Rebels came into range of the smooth-style Napoleonic cannon, which made them continued target practice for Union artillery. When the Rebels reached 400 yards, the Union soldiers loaded the cannon with canister, which are tin cans packed with 28 iron balls. These shots mowed down 20 or more troops a time; entire companies of Rebel soldiers ceased to exist. The remaining troops fell under Union musket fire as they approached Union lines. In one hour, "Pickett's division lost 2,882 officers and men, killed, wounded and missing. That figure represented a staggering 62 percent casualty rate. Thirty-one of Pickett's majors were killed, wounded or missing. All three brigadier generals were casualties. Within Pettigrew's and Trimble's commands the losses were equally great. Some 3,585 officers and men were casualties, nearly 56 percent. Nearly all of Pettigrew's regiments returned without their field grade commanders. Marshall's (Pettigrew's) and Davis's brigades each lost a ghastly 74 percent. Some companies lost over 90 percent of their officers and men, while three companies–the University Greys of the 11th Mississippi, the Color Company of the 38th North Carolina Infantry and Company F of the 26th North Carolina were totally wiped out."[3]

Taken from "Statement as to Where the General Was During the Charge. Why the Attack Failed as told by Captain Robert A. Bright". "As the charge ended and the retreat has begun "General Robert E. Lee the Peerless, alone on Traveler, rode up and said, "General Pickett, place your division in rear of this hell and be ready to repel the advance of the enemy should they follow up their advantage." (I never heard General Lee call them the enemy before: it was always those or those people.) General Pickett, with his head on his breast said, "General Lee, I have no division now. Armistead is down, Garnett is down, and Kemper is mortally wounded." General Pickett never forgave Lee for the disaster wreaked upon his command in Pennsylvania. Pickett was the one officer who wrote a derogatory report about the battle, but apparently, either Lee ordered him to destroy it because it was "so bitter" or Lee himself tore up the letter and no copy of it has ever been found. The sources for these possible reports are Wert, Jeffry D., *Gettysburg: Day Three*, New York: Simon & Schuster, 2001. The other possibility that Lee tore it up himself is from Civil War, Vol. II, under JUSTICE FOR OUR DEAD IS ALL WE WANT, "The report of the role of his division in the battle of Gettysburg was destroyed on Lee's orders. It was too critical."[3] Pickett suffered most of the blame for this disaster and for nine years after his death, General Pickett's grave remained unmarked.

Lee's education and experience were such that he did not realize how advances in weapons technology made a frontal charge against a defensible position, a fool hardy endeavor. He certainly did not understand how the advances in cannon and cannon ammunition had changed how frontal assaults should be made. Many historians view this one-hour battle as the turning point of the war. The Southern army was defeated and Lee saw no way to continue the campaign. Through a confluence of misinformation, exhausted soldiers, weather and other factors, Lee was able to withdraw to Virginia with the 2/3rds of his remaining army intact. However, the South fought a defensive battle for the remainder of war, never again attacking the North. It can be argued that Pickett's charge was the quietus to the South's cause. A victory at Gettysburg was vital to the South's hopes for aid and would have demoralized the Northern troops and civilians. My belief is that Lee also hoped to destroy some of the North's infrastructure by laying waste to the cities and countryside before the North could regroup and counter attack. Lee had to know that with the North's manufacturing infrastructure and superior numbers, the South was destined to lose the war.

There was also no way for Lee to anticipate how the ever-advancing weapons technology would continue to change the field of battle. His Napoleonic form of attack proves he was a connoisseur of history. No one could have predicted how the coming rapid-fire weapons that the North would later produce, would hasten the war's conclusion. Still, he had to have known that the South's ability to out-mass-produce the North in weapons was not feasible. With or without this foolhardy charge, the South was doomed to lose the war without foreign aid. It is certain that this one hour of mass carnage hastened the demise of the South. Toward the end of war, Sherman's march showed what was possible if the South had won the day. Sherman destroyed the South's ability to wage war by destroying the South's agriculture, weapons manufacturing, transportation and infrastructure. Read about this epic battle at http://www.encyclopediavirginia.org/Pickett_s_Charge and Encyclopedia Virginia is an online publication at http://www.virginiafoundation.org.

I hope reading about this historical travesty helps you understand how advancing technology could possibly destroy your HCU/SBO Internet life. If you work for a business or corporation large enough to have an Information Technology (IT) department, those IT folks probably provide a Virtual Private Network (VPN*) setup to allow employees to connect to the corporate network. Employees with mobile devices or home computers that need access to the corporate or government network are given a set of directions drafted by their IT department's gurus that have them perform a few simple steps to get connected (to operate their Internet devices behind friendly corporate or government lines). Most large entities also make use of a security token. This token displays six digits that randomly rotate. In addition to the rotating token number, the user is usually assigned a four digit serial number that they have to enter along with the token number. This seemingly random number is actually based on a mathematical computation; when the user VPN*s into the network, the number on the token and PIN are verified against what the VPN* server is programmed to allow. This type of scheme can also be used for logging into websites. This is much more secure than just password authentication. If someone loses a token, access can be quickly revoked on the VPN* server. Plus an attacker in possession of the token would have to guess the correct four digit PIN number in three tries or less before the server locks out that VPN* account.

The security token works very well to keep unauthorized people from accessing their network, but what about when the employee is using their mobile device(s) outside the VPN*? For example, if it were a laptop, the employee probably got a vague lecture they did not pay attention to from an IT department professional about how they should be careful using unencrypted hotspots and such. Since the employee only knows how to access the business network using VPN* via client software such as Jupiter Networks and/or Citrix software, they are only protected while connected to their corporate network using corporate applications; this is usually through a web browser. Often they receive little or no instructions regarding the use of applications installed on their mobile device outside the VPN* connection. As a result, if they are connected to a hotspot, they may be using Internet applications outside the encrypted VPN* while connecting to these hotspots. By doing this they are exposing their business devices and their own personal Internet devices to crackers. Scammers are always working hard to fool customers which the Anti-Phishing Working Group (APWG) 2011 report describes. (See: http://apwg.org/reports/apwg_trends_report_h2_2011.pdf) In the report, Carl Leonard of Websense Security Labs issued this warning to consumers about using their mobile devices, "*A great many of us use our mobile phones to check our bank account balances using the plethora of applications available. We saw malware authors seeking to exploit this in 2011, and it could turn out to be an increasingly attractive attack vector in 2012 as tablets and smartphones are adopted not just for personal use but for corporate use also.*" (See: http://securitylabs.websense.com) Increasingly these devices are being used to conduct credit transactions with businesses which open up a whole new set of cracking possibilities. There is a lot more to these reports and new reports are constantly being released. (See: http://docs.apwg.org/reports/apwg_trends_report_q2_2012.pdf) Refer back to Introduction-A Review of the Usual Inadequate Methods for Securing your Internet Activity for a few examples of phone or email phishing attacks. Look at these statistics from the APWG report, *"Phishing attacks targeting consumers remain at high levels, with 20,000 to more than 32,000 unique phishing email campaigns documented each month through the half. Each campaign can involve hundreds of thousands or millions of emails sent to consumers. There are hundreds of phishing websites established online every day, luring any number of consumers to trouble and loss."* The report also is very informative about many other forms of attack.

I did not know the success rates of phishing attacks but after study, these attacks are proving to be very successful. Unfortunately, correlation numbers indicate that the elderly are much more likely to be targeted than the general population, reference http://www.symantec.com/avcenter/reference/phishing-stats.pdf titled *"Phishing Attacks In and Around April through September 2006"*, written by Zulfikar Ramzan of Symantec Security Response.

Another problem is that employees are working from home using their own personal computers to tunnel into business networks with no policing of these home systems. I have never heard of, or seen, the use of government sleuths or corporate IT department's specialists, rushing into the homes of employees to scan their home computer(s), or to educate them on the use of these devices used to VPN* into the networks of these billion dollar entities, searching for malware. Nor have I heard of them evaluating and properly configuring the home-provided networking equipment that employees use to VPN* into large entity networks. This seems like Cyber Security 101 to me. In October 2012, Leon Panetta called for a country-wide cyber security analysis as a major initiative to try to stop cyber-attacks on the United States. My suggestions above seem like a good step to getting his initiative started! We have to police the corporate and government provided devices that are exposed to the Internet, which connect to these sensitive VPN*s. Government, large entity employees, or SBO/HCU users, must become educated, or should be provided a secure means of using mobile devices outside the VPN* or using an SSH server, which does not violate their privacy. If that device becomes corrupt with malware, crackers might be watching what the user is doing and typing while performing their job. This could enable a cracker access behind firewalls exposing all their/your business data and infrastructure to the cracker's misdeeds.

| Story  | This chapter came about from a confluence of events. A close friend who was fed up with his old Windows XP machine asked me to dispose of it for him. It was still a decent piece of hardware, and I figured I could come up with some use for it. When doing volunteer work at a local private university where the master's students were being taught ethical hacking and using tools such as https://www.kali.org, I saw how easily crackers exploit weaknesses in computers and mobile technology that are connected to public hotspots. This was a wake-up-call to me since I was using the university's public network with my laptop. By doing so, I was exposing my laptop to many very smart, educated and innovative college hackers some of whom now work for NSA. Then a master's student showed me how he was using an encrypted SSH tunnel to his dorm server whenever he connected his iPhone or laptop to the university public Internet. These genius hackers were having fun breaking into each other's Internet equipment (see the movie *Real Genius*), wreaking havoc on each other for fun. It showed me that everyone connected to the university's open network needed to employ the same encryption techniques |

that these students were using. This friendly competition and constant pranking also encouraged them to learn what was necessary to protect their Internet equipment and eventually help everyone at the college who was connected to the Internet. We must encourage this sort of activity to become a more educated public. It occurred to me while working with those students that I could do the same sort of thing using my buddy's old PC to create an SSH tunnel. This would protect my laptop and my other Internet devices while doing volunteer work at the college, and later, using hotspots anywhere around the world. So I took that old PC my friend had given me, turned it into an SSH server running behind my home-protected firewall and local network. Now I will teach you how to do that and more.

If you are using a company or government VPN* connection, bear in mind that you are using their network to access the Internet. Assume that everything you do and type is being recorded. Your company's proxy* Filter as detailed by http://en.wikipedia.org/wiki/Proxy_filter#Content-filtering_web_proxies, will monitor and filter where you are surfing and what you are viewing on the Internet. That government, company or school proxy* will log and audit your Internet usage. Big business or school brother is watching everything you are doing, and big, big government brother can gain access to those databases and view all of your surfing history with minimal legal wrangling. In the August 2012 PCWorld article *"Employers to Increase Monitoring of Social Media Use?"* by Grant Gross, he states, *"New technologies and services permit expanded employee monitoring."* Companies are also, with the employee's permission, increasingly requesting to monitor social media activity on company and employee-owned devices. Most employees know this, and it is stated very clearly in large entity policy statements (which employees are required to read). So if an employee or student can't use the VPN* connection for personal Internet activity such as banking, shopping, or maybe visiting restricted websites, they must resort to open surfing at hotspots, thereby exposing their computers and mobile devices to attack. Their mistaken assumption is that it is better to expose their Internet devices to crackers, who may or may not be monitoring that hotspot, than to sit before a board on inquiry explaining why they violated policy regulations they were forced to read.

I strongly argue against this strategy and suggest that businesses and governments should offer up some other private encrypted options to employees. This will benefit everyone, allowing them to use their mobile devices for private use, much like how an SBO/HCU router can present a guest network to visitors. A corporation or government agency should set up a minimally monitored encrypted network for their employees to use with their mobile devices for personal purposes and guarantee their privacy. Most people have no clue how vulnerable their devices are to crackers on the Internet, and corporate and government employees need to be given FREE and unmonitored choices as alternatives to OPEN SURFING using hotspots. Then during off hours when personal Internet use is needed, these entities could protect them with encryption so they could safely shop, bank, or manage investments without those activities violating corporate or government policy. Their alternative is allowing the unsafe exposure of their corporate or government mobile devices to hotspots and crackers everywhere. Another option might be setting up a VPN* or SSH server that employees can plug into their home network and connect too remotely, creating an encrypted tunnel to their personal network.

Consider this example, how many of your salespeople, marketers, and average computer users are going to setup a safe SSH server at home by reading this book? I'm hoping a LOT, but the reality is they are focused on a different profession, don't really think about exposing their devices to crackers, and have minimal interest or time to study the art of cyber security. They will expose their Internet devices to hotspots against corporate / government / small business / or what should be home computer user policy. This could/will bring malware behind your firewalls with catastrophic results. You as an SBO/HCU can make the choice!

Hotspots everywhere are malware-infested danger zones to your business, corporation or government installation. If you use your mobile device on a public network, everything you are doing is open to cracking. Once a compromised device is behind our firewalls, many of the things that we do on our local Internet are now available to the enemy. Our anti-software knows nothing about these new threats and cannot stop this malware from spreading or disseminating information back to its creators. This malware can broadcast all of our activity and data to a cracker, possibly thousands of miles away. According to *60 Minutes*, in 2007 the U.S. had espionage Perl Harbor when some unknown entity broke into the Department of Defense, Department of State, Department of Commerce, probably the Department of Energy, probably NASA, all of the high tech agencies, all the military agencies, and downloaded terabytes of sensitive data. To put this in perspective, the library of congress, which has millions of volumes, is only about 12 terabytes so the U.S. probably lost the equivalent of a library of congress of government information to an unknown enemy. Where was the media outcry about this?

It did not end there; in November 2009 DOD acknowledged that someone got behind DOD firewalls downloading sensitive information for days before being detected. They were able to sit there behind those firewalls and watch everything DOD did. In essence, they became part of the American military command. It is believed they did this by planting malware-infected USB drives in Department of Defense (DOD) locations.[1] Unsuspecting government employees, thinking they had found a free goodie, plugged those USB drives into government hardware enabling the crackers to view and gain control of defense computers (the U.S. Central Command (CENTCOM network that was fighting two wars). This scheme planted malware-infected devices behind our government's firewalls, circumventing all their defenses. This happens because there is a disincentive culture within the U.S. government to admit when the incidents occur. For example, the Bush administration did not want to admit to the Obama administration that these incidents had occurred. As Jim Lewis, a Director at the Center for International Studies put it, "*Everyday a little bit more of our intellectual property, our innovative skills, our military technology, is stolen by somebody. It is like little drops and eventually we will drown but every day we don't notice.*"[1] This happens because good men and women cannot come forward to tell the public about these events.

Understand, there was no frontal assault or great cracker exploit that could be a "made for Hollywood" movie. The attackers merely devised a means of operating behind enemy (our friendly) lines to gain intelligence. We won't even get a good spy novel out of this catastrophe. Another good analogy would be pop culture's infatuation with vampires. The vampire solicits an invitation into your house, but cannot come in until invited. In the example above, the infected devices invited the cracker into our house with only our inadequate anti-software to save us. Because the malware was unknown at the time, our anti-software's front line of defense was overrun. The vampire was allowed in our house and was free to attack its victims. They sucked all the data out of our devices before the threat was discovered doing devastating damage to our business.

Many corporate and government employees reading this book should also consider what happens when they lose their job, get sick, retire, or venture out to start a business of their own. I hope that we have learned that most crackers are not all that sophisticated in their attacks. They use known software hacking techniques, which white hat hackers attempt to prevent by staying one step ahead of black hat crackers and expose gaps in our security by using the same tools the Grey and Black Hats use. For example, consider the corporate executive who has unlimited access to the corporate network. His laptop gets cracked at a hotspot with some new (and as yet undetectable) malware and he plugs that laptop into the corporate network behind the firewalls.

This chapter is meant to offer the SBO/HCU an open source and easy alternative to VPN* where we don't have an IT department to do it for us. We don't ever want to surf naked (without encryption) with any device running an Internet application from a hotspot.

WARNING 	If you use your mobile device on a public network without encryption, assume someone is watching everything you are doing on the Internet. If you are OK with that, then keep on using those public connections without security. Enjoy Identity Theft, the thousands it will cost you, and the time you will spend dealing with it! There are thousands of government intelligence employees, Mafia and crime organizations, which have been documented by multiple sources dedicated to breaking into your Internet devices to steal your data and to watch everything you do when connected to the Internet.

There are many options available to the SBO/HCU to keep ourselves safe anywhere there is a connection to the Internet that we can use. When you connect your computer to one of these hotspots, you are exposing yourself to crackers and therefore must use some sort of encrypted tunnel.

As I have shown and debased, the advice usually given is: keep your anti-software up-to-date, use a firewall, use encryption *with no explanation on how to do so*, and be sure to ask the establishment the SSID name so that you don't connect to a rogue access point. This last tip is valuable to this chapter, and you should do that. As stated in the introduction, anti-software is reactionary and should be considered a last line of defense. Setting up a comprehensive software firewall (Windows 7 comes preconfigured with a good one) is beyond the scope of this book. However, later in this chapter we are going to use Windows firewall to block some common ports and lock down things while you travel with your mobile Internet devices.

Tunnels -- How Can We Use Paid VPN Services to Keep Ourselves Secure at Hotspots Everywhere, and What Are They

We have talked about the VPN* options available to corporate and government workers, but as a small business or home gamer, we may not have things like a security token or a VPN* server setup behind our firewall. A VPN* can also keep you anonymous as you surf the Internet. However, be careful choosing your VPN* service provider by making sure they do not keep logs of all your Internet activity. Before we talk about the complexity of setting up SSH Server behind your hardware router firewall, let's examine some paid VPN* alternatives available to the SBO/HCU that will enable us to safely use hotspots. We must have some sort of tunnel to keep our mobile devices secure, so let's first talk about what a tunnel is.

It seems strange to refer to something in the computer world as a tunnel, but just like prisoners digging a tunnel out of a jail, or criminals digging a tunnel under the fence on the border, computer tunnels are designed to hide people from the authorities, crackers or spies. A software tunnel digs a hole into a secure protocol hiding an unsecure protocol within it. From http://en.wikipedia.org/wiki/Tunneling_protocol, which defines a tunnel as, "*Computer networks use a tunneling protocol when one network protocol (the delivery protocol) encapsulates a different payload protocol. By using tunneling one can (for example) carry a payload over an incompatible delivery-network, or provide a secure path through an untrusted network. Secure Shell (SSH) tunnel consists of an encrypted tunnel created through an SSH protocol connection. Users may set up SSH tunnels to transfer unencrypted traffic over a network through an encrypted channel. To set up an SSH tunnel, one configures an SSH client to forward a specified local port to a port on the remote machine. Once the SSH tunnel has been established, the user can connect to the specified local port to access the network service. The local port need not have the same port number as the remote port.*"

If you don't have a computer or virtual computer that you can set up behind a Remote Secure Network (RSN), then there are some paid options available to you. An RSN is a company, small business or home network that is secure behind a hardware firewall, which is usually a secure router. A Remote Secure Network Server (RSNS) is a company, small business or home computer server that has a router connected to the modem, which an ISP has assigned an IP address and is forwarding requests on certain ports to the server.

If you don't have a computer behind your firewall that can act as a server, there are companies who can provide secure connections to the Internet through encrypted tunnels. There are some drawbacks to this approach but it is better than open surfing using a hotspot. Let's examine some of the drawbacks to using a paid service:

- Expense. The services usually charge a monthly fee, which varies greatly depending on your SBO/HCU needs.
- If you decide to host your website or blog with them, it could result in added expense and less control and security over what you present and post.
- Since your entire Internet traffic is traveling through your paid service, you have to trust in the fact that they are not capturing where you surf to and what you type. Be sure to study their privacy statement. Even with that privacy statement, the government can easily obtain your data without a warrant.

Some of the advantages of using you own RSNS are:

- An RSNS can be very versatile. For example, a server can be setup to allow businesses, friends, and family to use a user ID that you set up for them to send and receive files that you may need to exchange securely. This is much safer than exchanging files via email, which could leave a copy of your files on various email servers for crackers to view and attack.

- You can experiment with setting up your server to host a website or blog and present it to the world using your own domain at little or no expense.
- Your server can act as a backup device on which to keep important files that you may only want on an "as needed" basis for your mobile device. This way if your mobile device is lost or stolen, the damage done exposing your data is minimal.

In the PCWorld June 3, 2010 article titled "*How to Set Up a Secure Web Tunnel*" by Steven Andres, http://www.pcworld.com/businesscenter/article/197725/how_to_set_up_a_secure_web_tunnel .html, Mr. Andres gives us two paid solutions for tunneling. One solution is by using http://www.hostgator.com, which is a Web Hosting service that costs about $5.00 a month to setup a secure SSH tunnel to the Internet from anywhere. The HostGator "Hatchling plan" also offers you Single Domain, UNLIMITED Disk Space, UNLIMITED Bandwidth, and Shared SSL Certificate for your website. You can use their free software to build your own website and host it. If you are a small business this may be a good deal, but if you are just an individual, your ISP probably offers enough disk space for you to host your own website. You can use HostGator for SSH access http://support.hostgator.com/articles/getting-started/how-do-i-get-and-use-ssh-access. The PCWorld article also recommended using free Hotspot Shield software. (See: http://anchorfree.com) Hotspot Shield is a no-cost VPN* service from AnchorFree that you can use to be secure at hotspots. The free version comes loaded with bloatware* advertising that you must uncheck when installing. Once you enable the software and service, it encrypts all of your traffic and transmits it through a tunnel to the Hotspot Shield data center and then out to Internet. For users of Hotspot Shield outside the United States the creators claim that "*Hotspot allows you to view US websites that are usually restricted to people who don't live in the US.*" (See: http://hotspot-shield.en.softonic.com, http://find.pcworld.com/70053, http://www.bestvpnserver.com) If you wish to learn more about the possibility of creating your own VPN* server, reference https://help.ubuntu.com/12.04/serverguide/openvpn.html, https://help.ubuntu.com/community/OpenVPN, and paid solution https://openvpn.net.

Another solution to keep you safe while surfing the Internet is by using a free proxy*. The website http://www.proxy4free.com has a free rated proxy* list that allows you to bypass firewalls and content filters to get to blocked websites, also hiding your IP address. This is better than open surfing with your core or virtual OS, but not as thorough as using an encrypted tunnel.

In the Feb 1, 2012 PCWorld article titled "*What Is Deep Packet Inspection*", http://find.pcworld.com/72449 by Alex Wawro, he lists two more VPN* services such as http://www.hidemynet.com and http://www.witopia.net as alternatives. These services claim that they not only encrypt your web traffic, but will also keep your IP address secret, thus giving you anonymity on the Internet. The Witopia support https://www.witopia.net/support/why does an excellent job describing why we need anonymity and encryption when using the Internet, which we covered in the anonymity chapter.

In the July 2012 article titled "*Private Wi-Fi Encrypts Airborne Data*,"
http://find.pcworld.com/72897 Jon L. Jacobi talks about Private Communications,
http://www.privatewifi.com. For $10 a month, or $85 a year, the company states that they
will provide a VPN* service after their client software is installed. From the article, "*Once you
have installed the client, you may activate or deactivate the VPN–secure connection—as you wish.
Private Wi-Fi's server at the other end completes the VPN tunnel.*" Consequently, if you are at a
hotspot, all traffic between you and the server will be encrypted, thus ensuring that someone
monitoring your Internet traffic will only see gibberish.

You can also configure your router and a computer behind your firewall to accept incoming
VPN connections. In Windows 7 and 8 it is very easy to configure a VPN client or set up a VPN
server. If you have a hardware router firewall, you will have to forward port 1723 to the
Windows VPN server IP address. You will also have to make sure that PPTP and or VPN pass-
through options are enabled. (See: http://go.pcworld.com/vpns,
http://go.pcworld.com/vpn7,
http://www.pcworld.com/article/223044/vpns_for_beginners_to_experts.html) To learn how
to setup and establish a Windows VPN connection to a computer behind your firewall, see my
blog at http://www.thatcybersecurityguy.com.

> NSA and GCHQ pay vast sums of money to corporations that provide paid
> VPN services to have backdoors into your encrypted sessions. VPN is known
> to be an encryption standard that has been compromised.

VPN* tunnels offer a complete application-level solution to encrypt all your Internet activity,
SSH does not. With that being said, SSH is progressing and is still an excellent open source
solution for most SBO/HCUs. As a small business myself, I find using SSH is adequate to
meeting all of my needs, and I hope yours as well.

OpenSSH Server for Your SB/HC — What Hardware Is Needed?

When reading periodicals, books, and listening to computer talk radio shows, you will hear
over and over again how connecting to a public wireless networks is perilous. I hear or see
this warning stated repeatedly, suggesting not to use them at all, and there is certainly no
advice on how use them safely. As everyone knows, many coffee shops, airports, hotels,
restaurants, schools, libraries, friend's houses, cellphones, etc. offer public wireless access
points that don't require passwords and don't use encryption; or they might be using
breakable WEP encryption discussed in Chapter 2.

SSH is another protocol for encrypting traffic on the Internet and can serve as a wrapper
around arbitrary TCP traffic. "*You can cloak unencrypted services like telnet, POP3, IMAP, or
HTTP inside SSH, securely transporting these unencrypted protocols.*"[6] Any TCP/IP protocol can
be concealed and carried by an SSH session. SSH is an excellent solution to using hotspots
everywhere and is not presented by the mainstream media or their talk show hosts.

Another way of stating this comes from the "Linux+ Complete Study Guide," written by
Roderick W. Smith, "*SSH has the ability to extend its encryption capabilities to other protocols, but
doing so requires extra configuration. The way this is done is known as tunneling. The server*

computer runs two server programs: a server for the tunneled protocol and an SSH server. The client computer also runs two clients: one for the tunneled protocol; and one for SSH. The SSH client also listens for connections for the tunneled protocol; it's effectively both a client and a server. When the SSH client receives a connection from the tunneled protocols' client, the result is that the tunneled protocol's connection is encrypted using SSH, tunneled to the SSH server, and then directed to the target server. Thus, data passes over the network in encrypted form, even if the target protocol doesn't support encryption." Another good read on SSH Tunnels can be found on Provo, Utah's Brigham Young Universities Computer Science wiki, found at https://docs.cs.byu.edu/wiki/SSH_Tunnels. An SSH tunnel is a secure connection between two systems that allows regular data to be transmitted between them wrapped in strong encryption.

You know that old Junker computer that was running Windows XP that you have not recycled and properly disposed of at Best Buy yet? You will now learn how to turn that computer into a home server for you to use from anywhere in the world. This will give you a FREE SSH server (of course you are paying for the electricity to keep it on 24/7) that you can use as an encryption tunnel, and I will show you how to use it to secure your remote Internet activity. This means that you can use your Internet devices via your remote secure network (RSN) from hotspots everywhere.

 No encryption protocol/tunnel/public-private key pair technique or scheme has been shown to be secure against eavesdroppers with unlimited computational power, but an SSH tunnel should be secure against the normal computing power found in most areas where public access to the Internet is available.

The method we are going to set up is an RSN-SSH server using Ubuntu or Mint desktop (you can use any flavor of Linux) for remote access from you mobile device (laptop, tablet, smartphone, etc.). An Ubuntu Server without a GUI would be the best choice for a SB because it is less venerable to attack, but it would prove difficult to set up if you or one of your employees is not a Linux guru. It is designed for security with no GUI, which is more secure then setting up a home SSH server with a GUI. Universities and corporations would find this solution most useful. To keep things simpler, I chose to outline my solutions for the HCU/SBO audience, and present a GUI solution. We are going to use the old Junker PC to handle our remote Internet activity, so why not have the convenience of a GUI? It is also nice having a GUI so you can use the SSH server for many other things, like partner accounts with which to exchange data. Once your server is set up we will use our RSNS to safely conduct all of our Internet activity and data transfer from hotspots anywhere in the world.

Unless you expect a ton of activity on your RSNS, you will want a small footprint in the power budget for a computer that will be left running 24/7. That old PC with low power consumption, when compared to modern power hungry computers, is likely a good choice. The 7-year-old Dell computer with cheap hardware that my friend wanted to dispose of, with my addition of an 80GB hard drive, was my choice. It is now my home SSH server and works great. This old computer is obviously no powerhouse but it is adequate as an SSH or VPN* server. I recommend using the latest, long-maintenance version of Ubuntu or Linux Mint KDE/Cinnamon. I wanted a flavor of Linux that has a small footprint and is a very popular and well-maintained OS. If your computer is a bit older or less powerful, consider using a lightweight OS such as Lubuntu. (See: http://lubuntu.net) Older PCs often don't have a DVD drive and Ubuntu, or Lubuntu, are designed to install from a CD. Most every flavor of Linux offers a CD version of their OS to install from, which is convenient for installing an OS on ancient hardware. Ubuntu has stated that it has long term support for version 14.04 and Mint for version 17 of their OSs, which you want for your SSH server. We have to rebuild VMs often enough without having to worry about rebuilding an SSH server, which is more difficult.

Zero the Hard Drives and Install the Ubuntu OS on Your Server

The first thing I do when I rebuild any computer with a new operating System is zero the hard drive. Linux distributions offer a distribution upgrade option but that is never as clean as a fresh install. Refer back to Chapter 3 where we cover various tools that can zero a hard drive.

I had a bit of trouble getting that old PC to recognize a modern CD. The first thing that I did was flash the BIOS up to latest version. The procedure to do this is different from computer to computer and you can look up how to do it at your manufacturer's website. I present a little more detail about how to do that in Chapter 2. The second thing I had to do was press F12 to select the boot menu and tell my Dell computer to formally boot from the CD. Installing Ubuntu onto your server is a bit different from doing it into a virtual environment as we did before. First, you will have to burn a bootable copy of the downloaded OS ISO file to CD. This is simple in Windows 7. ***Double click on the ISO file and the Windows Disc Image Burner window should appear > check the box beside Verify disk after burning at the bottom left > Insert a blank disc > click on the Burn button on the bottom to write the image to your DVD or CD media***. This server is about allowing our remote devices to use the Internet securely; if you plan to have valuable data on it, lock it down thoroughly with a software firewall in addition to your hardware firewall. We opened a port to this server in Chapter 2, which bypasses the protection provided by our hardware firewall. We covered the steps to building a virtual OS in multiple OSs in Chapter 7, which can also be used to build your SSH server.

WARNING	Remember the user ID created by the OSs installation are privileged. We will need to create less privileged user IDs to connect to the server for better security. In addition, the hostname will need be something different from what was recommended for a VM. Since the server is secure behind our firewall you can make the hostname something informative (e.g. ubuntu1404-ssh or ubuntu1404-dimension2350) to identify it. Then lock down the firewall so as to not allow host discovery on the local network.

Refer back to Chapter 2 where I discussed how to set up an Address Reservation for your server. The router will always assign the same IP address to our SSH server. This way if we reload an OS in the future, the IP address won't change via DHCP. The router knows the MAC address to reserve for your server hardware, so the OS is irrelevant.

Unless you set up a static IP during installation of your OS, your Linux SSH server OS is using DHCP. This means that even with an assigned IP address, your SSH server will poll for an IP address. This is a minor security hole, so consider setting up your SSH server as a static IP. Using the Ubuntu GUI is very easy to do and is covered later.

Backing up Important System Files

The important configuration files that we may alter later differ slightly from Linux distribution to distribution. Below are a few important files that are found in most flavors of Linux. The configuration changes we will make are, basically, the same. You can use the GUI tools, which require no knowledge as to the files location. Nonetheless, you should try to learn which underlying files will be affected by configuration changes made using the GUI, and back them up beforehand. It is important to have original files for later reference.

```
# cd /etc/network && cp -ip interfaces interfaces.orig
# cd /etc/dhcp && cp -ip dhclient.conf dhclient.conf.orig
# cd /etc
# cp -ip passwd passwd.orig
# cp -ip group group.orig
# cp -ip shadow shadow.orig
# cp -ip resolv.conf resolv.conf.orig
# cp -ip nsswitch.conf nsswitch.cong.orig
# cp -ip hosts host.orig
# cp -ip sysctl.conf sysctl.conf.orig
# cp -ip hostname hostname.orig
# cd /etc/xdg/autostart && cp -ip nm-applet.desktop nm-applet.desktop.orig
# cd /etc/init && cp -ip network-manager.conf network-manager.conf.orig
# cd /etc/NetworkManager && cp -ip NetworkManager.conf NetworkManager.conf.orig
```

In Red Hat and Fedora add:

```
# cd /etc/sysconfig/network-scripts
# cp -pi ifcfg-eth0 ifcfg-eth0.orig
# cp -pi gateway gateway.orig
```

Unchanging/Static IP – Setting It up in Ubuntu Desktop

To tunnel to your home computer using mobile devices outside your home you must have a RSNS IP address that does not change. Chapter 2 describes how to do this for our Linux server by setting up an *Address Reservation*. When you specify a reserved IP address for a PC on the LAN, that PC will always receive the same IP address each time it accesses the DHCP server. Reserved IP addresses should be assigned to servers that require permanent IP settings. The router does this by MAC Address and Device Name, so a simple address reservation configured in the **LAN Setup** in your home router solves the home roving IP (changing address) problem. Upon initial boot, make note of your server's DHCP address and make an **Address Reservation** for that IP in the router. Your server can just be left as DHCP and your router will always assign the same IP based on the MAC address. If you decide that you want a static route, I recommend the simple solution of configuring the SSH server as a static IP and leaving the router as an Address Reservation rather that complicating things by setting up the router as a static route.

A static route in a router is there to configure information that the router cannot learn automatically through other means. For example, when Routing Information Protocol (RIP) is disabled on the LAN, you may need to teach the router about devices connected to the network, something that might prove confusing or difficult for some SBO/HCUs.

NOTE	Dynamic Routing uses RIP to exchange routing information with other routers in a network. The router dynamically learns routes on all its configured interfaces.

There are a few reasons for setting up the SSH server as a static IP.

1. Having the SSH server poll the router for an IP address every time it boots is a security hole (layers of security).
2. Having a static server IP is more efficient in computer resource. No exchange of address information is necessary between the router and the SSH server.
3. If your router hardware fails, your server will end up with a new IP until you configure the new router.
4. It is easy to do using the GUI's in Linux OSs using multiple methods.

The minimum information that we need to configure a Static IP are IP Address, Subnet Mask, Gateway Address, and the DNS Server Address. In Ubuntu LTS, there is an icon in the upper right of the taskbar with two arrows pointing up and down. If you *right or left click on the arrows > arrow down to select* _Connection Information_ it will show you all of the network information that you need to configure things manually. Before making any changes to the server's network configuration, make note of this information in a text file such as network_info.txt.

Click on the arrows again > arrow down to select _Edit Connections..._ *> click on your network connection which will be something comparable to* _Wired connection 1_ *> click on the* _Edit..._ *button to the right > select the* _IPv4 Settings_ *tab > change the* _Method:_ *from* _Automatic (DHCP)_ *to* _Manual_ *> click on the* _Add_ *button to add the IP, Netmask (e.g. 255.255.255.0), Gateway (e.g. 192.168.1.1) > click on the DNS servers: box and type your DNS (router IP) gathered from the* _Connection Information_ *> select* _Save...._.

Another method is to *select* _System Settings_ *> under* _Hardware_ *click on* _Network_ *icon > make note of the Connection Information > click on the* _Options_ *button > select* _IPv4 Settings_ *tab > and so on, same as above*. This will update the _/etc/NetworkManager/NetworkManager.conf_ to a manual IP and create a connection file, which should be backed up.

```
# cd /etc/NetworkManager/system-connections
# cp -ip "Wired connection 1" Wiredconnection1.orig
```

NOTE | If your router fails, or if you purchase a new router, it may assign a DHCP address to your servers behind your firewall if you are using address reservations in your router. Since you have set up a STATIC IP ADDRESS in your server, it will not notify your router that it needs a new address. You will have to change your server to request a DHCP address so the router knows to assign the address reservation to that device. Then change the server back to a static IP for security.

Tip | Sometimes we want to boot a computer and not have it connect to a network. One way of doing this is for Ubuntu to become 'root' and type the following:
```
# mv /etc/init/network-manager.conf /etc/init/network-manager.conf.disabled
# mv /etc/xdg/autostart/nm-applet.desktop /etc/xdg/autostart/nm-applet.desktop.disabled
# shutdown -r now
```

To enable networking again:
```
# mv /etc/init/network-manager.conf.disabled /etc/init/network-manager.conf
# mv /etc/xdg/autostart/nm-applet.desktop.disabled /etc/xdg/autostart/nm-applet.desktop
# shutdown -r now
```

Some networking commands that you can use in Linux:

Display network information: # ifconfig or, ifconfig -a # ifconfig eth0	Take down network interface ech0: # ifconfig ech0 down or, ifdown eth0
Bring up network interface eth0 # ifconfig ech0 up or, ifup eth0	Display the routing table: # /sbin/route or, /sbin/route -n
Add a new gateway: # route add default gw 192.166.1.1	Display current active Internet connections (servers and established connections): # netstat -nat
Display open ports: # netstat -tulp or, netstat -tulpn	Display network interface statistics: # netstat -i
Display output for active/established connections only: # netstat -e or, netstat -te # netstat -tue	Test network connectivity: # ping router or, ping 192.168.1.24 # ping google.com

OpenSSH Server – Installation and Configuration

The software that you need for an SSH server is not installed in most Linux OSs by default. We need the open source OpenSSH software to make this all work. The Ubuntu server guide at https://help.ubuntu.com/12.10/serverguide/openssh-server.html gives you a few configuration ideas and references on how to setup your SSH server.

OpenSSH is the result of a donationware* project http://www.openssh.org, aka http://www.openssh.com, aka http://openbsd.org.my/openssh. If you find using their SSH encrypted connectivity tools useful, please consider donating to their project.

The link https://help.ubuntu.com/community/SSH is your portal to Ubuntu help on installing, configuring and using SSH on your home server. The https://help.ubuntu.com/12.04/serverguide/openssh-server.html is the Ubuntu SSH server guide page. From the server web page, "*OpenSSH is a freely available version of the Secure Shell (SSH) protocol family of tools for remotely controlling a computer or transferring files between computers. The OpenSSH server component, sshd, listens continuously for client connections from any of the client tools. When a connection request occurs, sshd sets up the correct connection depending on the type of client tool connecting. For example, if the remote computer is connecting with the SSH client application, the OpenSSH server sets up a remote control session after authentication.*" The openssh-blacklist package contains a list of all blacklisted OpenSSH RSA and DSA keys. The openssh-blacklist-extra package contains a list of non-default blacklisted OpenSSH RSA and DSA keys. You can read about why you want these extra packages at https://wiki.debian.org/SSLkeys. They are important in keeping you safe from connecting to a device with a compromised key. The install of openssh-server also recommends http://pizzashack.org/rssh, which you can read about at their website. From the author's website, "*RSSH is a restricted shell for use with OpenSSH, allowing only scp and/or sftp.*"

After installing Ubuntu desktop on that old Dell computer, applying updates and then after reboot logging in again, it would hang requiring another reboot over, and over again; if this happens, log in as Ubuntu 2D. You can do so by clicking the icon on the right shown below and selecting Ubuntu 2D. Then, if desired, log back in as Ubuntu 3D.

The install of openssh-server suggested packages molly-guard and monkeysphere. The molly-guard package installs a front-end to the existing shutdown/reboot/halt/poweroff commands. The shell script that is installed prompts the user to enter the name of host that the server administrator (you) wants to shutdown. Another script checks to see if there are open SSH connections to the server. So if the SSH server is going to service more than one person or if you have multiple SSH servers, then you may want the molly-guard package. The monkeysphere package, http://web.monkeysphere.info, allows for Public Key Infrastructure (PKI) for key certification. PKI is useful if you are a small business or power user and have many other business and/or power users that need to connect to your SSH server(s) or use them for a protected encryption tunnel. Under SSH without monkeysphere, when a new user that you had set up logs in for the first time, the SSH server and client exchange keys and your server provides a fingerprint that the client user is supposed to verify (e.g. makes a phone call to the server administrator and reads the fingerprint digits). Once the client types "yes", the server's public key is stored on the client in the ~/.ssh/known_host file.

From the man page: # man sshd   # on ~/.ssh/known_hosts

"Lists the public keys (DSA/ECDSA/RSA) that can be used for logging in as this user. The content of the file is not highly sensitive, but the recommended permissions are read/write for the user, and not accessible by others."

Vice versa, the client's public key needs to be copied to the server account and stored in the servers *~/.ssh/authorized_keys* file. From the man page: # man sshd   # on ~/.ssh/authorized_keys

"Lists the public keys (DSA/ECDSA/RSA) that can be used for logging in as this user. The content of the file is not highly sensitive, but the recommended permissions are read/write for the user, and not accessible by others."

We will discuss copying and setting up this key exchange later, in much detail. However, if the server changes its private/public keys for any reason, then all the *~/.ssh/known_hosts* files on your clients will have to be edited to delete all references to your SSH server's changed public key. If your server is their only connection, they can just delete the *known_hosts* file. Consequently, if you lose control of your key and/or need to revoke it, this will prove to be a very difficult and confusing task for everyone. Without PKI, someone would have to comb through every account that needs to connect to your SSH server and perform this task. Trying to instruct your partners on how to do this is a distraction you and they don't need. The same holds true to add or revoke the ability of a user or business to authenticate across your entire infrastructure. So depending on your sophistication and needs, you have to consider how you want to set all this up. I'm sure you know how large entities do it.

OpenPGP provides PKI servers where you can add and revoke keys the monkeysphere will check for you on any client or server running the monkeysphere software. Update any PKI server and your change is propagated throughout the keyserver network. There is no longer the need for your public key to be stored locally on your server's and client's accounts. From http://web.monkeysphere.info/why/#index1h2, *"It works like this: Person A trusts Person B. Person B verifies Person C's identity. Then, Person A can verify Person C's identity because of their trust of Person B."* Two examples of keyservers where you can register your public key are the Ubuntu SKS OpenPGP Keyserver http://keyserver.ubuntu.com:11371 and the SKS OpenPGP Keyserver http://pool.sks-keyservers.net:11371. Port 11371 is the official OpenPGP HTTP key server port. I only introduced these abilities to let you know that they exist; it is beyond the scope of this book to setup a PKI infrastructure within the target audience of the average SBO/HCU. I'm assuming that most SBO/HCUs are not interested in the big entity stuff that could have been presented. My audience does not have a huge, well-paid IT staff to dedicate to things like this. Install secure shell server plus assorted security packages:

```
# apt-get install -y openssh-server
# apt-get install -y openssh-server openssh-blacklist openssh-blacklist-extra
# ps -ef | grep -v grep | grep sshd
```

In Fedora to see what SSH software is installed type:
```
# rpm -qa | grep ssh
```

To install OpenSSH server in Fedora (if not already installed by default):

```
# yum install openssh-server
```

The command(s) above may not bring down the latest version of SSH server. If you want to try the latest version of the software, you can view the web page http://openssh.com/portable.html, which has the latest software for you to install in your flavor of Linux.

```
# cd Downloads
# wget http://ftp.openbsd.org/pub/OpenBSD/OpenSSH/portable/openssh-6.3p1.tar.gz
# cd openssh-6.3p1  &&  ./configure  &&  make  &&  make install
```

This will install the Open SSH binaries in the */usr/local/bin*, configuration files in */usr/local/etc*, and the server files in */usr/local/sbin*. See the "INSTALL" file for further installation instructions.

```
# service sshd restart      # Restart the daemon
```

To test SSH try connecting to the localhost by IP address:
```
# ssh $(ifconfig | grep 'inet addr:'| grep -v '127.0.0.1' | cut -d: -f2 | awk '{ print $1 }')
```

In Ubuntu, the install not only installed OpenSSH, it also started the daemon. All system-wide SSH server configuration is housed in the directory */etc/ssh*. Briefly they are:

/etc/ssh/sshd_config - OpenSSH sshd daemon configuration file.
/etc/ssh/ssh_config - OpenSSH client configuration file.
~/.ssh - Partner/client user SSH configuration directory.
/etc/ssh/ssh_host_<keytype>_key - Private SSH server key, which must be guarded.
/etc/ssh/ssh_host_<keytype>_key.pub - Public SSH server key copied to client ~/.ssh/known_hosts files when they connect to the SSH server.
/etc/nologin - If this file is present, OpenSSH will not allow anything but 'root' login and will display whatever text is in the file.

Before we make changes to any of these files, let's back them up (notice a recurring theme):

```
# cd /etc/ssh && cp -ip ssh_config ssh_config.orig
# cp -ip sshd_config sshd_config.orig
```

Installing our SSH server did many things behind the scenes.   To prevent spoofing attacks against our SSH server, the install generated *ssh_host_<algorithm>_key* files for three supported encryption techniques. These keys are used to allow a client to verify that it has connected to the correct server. As long as you keep your server keys protected, no client connecting to your server will ever be subject to a spoofing attack.

```
# cp -ip ssh_host_rsa_key ssh_host_rsa_key.orig      # Server private RSA key
# cp -ip ssh_host_rsa_key.pub ssh_host_rsa_key.pub.orig      # Server public RSA key
```

And so on for the rest of the files. We briefly introduced the concept of a fingerprint that we have to use to verify our client/server connection. Let's record those fingerprints for our server so that when clients call we can reference them quickly.

cd /etc/ssh && ssh-keygen -lf ssh_host_dsa_key.pub > fingerprints.txt   # Which adds:
2048 74:e8:79:d9:26:13:65:79:d0:5d:c6:07:2e:ea:42:70   root@ubuntu1404-sshvpn (RSA)

ssh-keygen -lf ssh_host_dsa_key.pub >> fingerprints.txt   # Which adds:
1024 7e:e1:ae:b3:c7:78:c2:c8:1b:89:6b:a9:b3:31:98:c0   root@ubuntu1404-sshvpn (DSA)

To get help on the configuration settings view the man page: # man sshd_config   # To read about the sshd_config settings

There are some things we could change to make remote Internet surfing more secure or even help us get around firewalls. For example, for added security and unconventional use, we could add or change the default connection port that sshd uses. The default port is 22, so we could change it to something like port 22222. This might get us around a hotspot, college or network administrator who is blocking port 22, but what if they are blocking unconventional ports? Often the answer is to have your SSH server listen on a port that is not usually blocked, such as port 80 (HTTP) or port 443 (HTTPS). Most every hotspot, place of business or college have to leave HTTPS port 80 and 443 open, but we can broaden our thinking because sshd can be configured to listen on multiple ports.

To forward additional alternate ports requires configuring your router to forward multiple ports to your SSH server. You can have access to your SSH server from almost everywhere by having it listen on multiple ports. Refer back to Chapter 2 where we describe how to forward router ports to your SSH server. We allow this on the SSH server by adding the following to the */etc/ssh/sshd_config* configuration file:

```
#Port 22      # Consider disabling this port for added security
Port 443      # Port that is usually open, that is easily used in most cases
Port 22222     # Example port to use in hard core situations
```

Remember that once you make configuration changes you should restart the sshd daemon or reboot your server # service ssh restart.

When you try to connect to a port on a SSH server for which everything is not setup properly you will see the following message:

```
ssh: connect to host <yourdomainname>.dyndns.<extension> port 443: Connection
refused
```

Another important setting to make note of is:
X11Forwarding yes
The default setting is "yes" in the */etc/ssh/sshd_config* file in Ubuntu. This setting enables us to use our remote applications on an encrypted tunnel using "dynamic" port forwarding, which we will soon discuss.

SSH Client -- Obtaining, Installing and Setting Up Software on Our Mobile Devices to Access Our Secure SSH Server Remotely

It may have seemed like a long road getting here, but now the SBO/HCU SSH server is ready to use to access the Internet securely using our mobile devices. You can log into your router and record the IP address of your cable modem and use an SSH client to connect to your home server. Instead, I'm hoping that you studied Chapter 2 to learn how to set up a *Dynamic DNS* domain that will keep your network accessible 24/7. Your ISP provides a DHCP IP address to your modem that will change every few months. Depending on which OS you are using on your remote device there are various SSH client options from which to pick. In Linux and on the MAC, an SSH client comes installed by default. If for some reason you need to download it in Ubuntu and Mint # apt-get install openssh-client and Fedora # yum install openssh-client will install the necessary client software.

In Windows 7, it is not quite so simple. Windows does not come with an SSH client by default (it should). Consequently, we have to resort to open source or donationware* software to achieve our goal of having Windows 7 communicate with an SSH server. There are a few other options, which can be found, such as http://www.putty.org. PuTTY comes with command line utilities and a GUI and is used extensively by corporations. Most people are not comfortable with the command line, but I find the Windows 7 command line easier to use than the PuTTY GUI, so I will cover both. In using the command line we can automate things by using scripting, which have distinct advantages over using the GUI, as we have to often click on the same things over and over again. I will show you a few scripts later, which you can type verbatim and use on your mobile device.

One argument for using PuTTY is that, as of the publish date of this book, the OpenSSH project for Windows has not come out with a new SSH client release since 2004. However, the http://sshwindows.sourceforge.net web page says that the project is under new development and will eventually have an updated release based on OpenSSH 5.1p1 release. All you have to do to install this very old release, which I recommend against, is download it from http://sourceforge.net/projects/sshwindows/files/OpenSSHforWindows-Release, double click on the compressed file to expand it, go to the directory (e.g. C:\Downloads\OpenSSH\setupssh381-20040709.zip) and run the executable setupssh.exe.

Rather than use a **very old** SSH Windows implementation you should consider using PuTTY (at least until the SSH client re-development is complete). Go to http://www.chiark.greenend.org.uk/~sgtatham/putty/download.html and download the putty-0.63-installer.exe, which includes everything you need to use PuTTY as a GUI or from the command line. PuTTY's latest release Aug 6, 2013 of version 0.63 shows that the authors are staying current. Just double click on the installer to install the software. If PuTTY does not create a desktop icon *click on Start > All Programs > select PuTTY > right click on PuTTY > arrow up to select Send to > select Desktop (create shortcut). Then if you want it on your taskbar drag and drop it there*. To make using PuTTY or SSH from the command line convenient and easy we need to add their executable directory to the Windows 7 System PATH environment variable. PuTTY does not add the location of its executable files to the System PATH during installation. If someone else installed PuTTY on your computer, or if it came preinstalled, make sure that it is not already in your System PATH before making the following delicate changes to your computer.

We need PuTTY in the System PATH to invoke it from the data directories on the computer or mobile device to/from which we will transfer files. If you are not sure if PuTTY is in your system path, test your computer by opening a command prompt and click on **_Start_** > **_All Programs_** > **_Accessories_** > **_arrow down to select Command Prompt_**. At the command prompt that appears, type the following:

C:\Users\<UserID>>plink -V
plink: Release 0.63

If typing plink -V does not display the release version (as shown above), **then the PuTTY directory is not in your Windows 7 System Path**. Refer back to <u>Chapter 5-Windows 7--Adding Tools and Utilities to the System PATH</u>.

 **NOTE**	Typing plink by itself will list all of the options available when using the plink command. Adding PuTTY to the system path is for convenience and later use of the PuTTY utilities. You can also use the full path to the plink executable from the command prompt if you don't want to alter your system path. For a 64-bit OS: C:\Users\<UserID>>\"Program Files (x86)"\PuTTY\plink -V For a 32-bit OS: C:\Users\<UserID>>\"Program Files"\PuTTY\plink -V

The path you will add will be one of the following depending on which Windows 7 OS (32-bit or 64-bit) and the SSH application you are using:

For 32-bit SSH software	; C:\Program Files\OpenSSH\bin
For 64-bit SSH software	; C:\Program Files (x86)\OpenSSH\bin
For PuTTY on a 32-bit Windows OS	; C:\Program Files\PuTTY
For PuTTY on a 64-bit Windows OS	; C:\Program Files (x86)\PuTTY

To actually use an SSH tunnel from a hotspot will require at lease three devices and hopefully, also a hardware firewall router, which would make four:

1. An Internet device (laptop, smartphone, tablet, etc.)
2. An intermediate device (cable, DSL or phone modem) with a public IP or domain name connected to the Internet
3. An private RSNS based inside your business or home
4. A router providing a hardware firewall to the local private network and is forwarding activity on your SSH port(s) to your SSH server

We are now ready to use our SSH client to connect to our SSH server and venture out into the world safely using the Internet with our SBO/HCU setup.

Dynamic SSH Domain – Connect to Your Private Network from Anywhere by Creating an Unchanging Domain

Before we actually discuss establishing connections or transferring files between our SSH client and server, let's examine an additional step that you should consider before traveling abroad. While traveling, we need 24/7 access to our RSNS. Back in <u>Chapter 2</u> we covered setting up a domain for our home router at the <u>http://dyn.com</u> website. A quick refresher on how this all works is appropriate at this point:

1. Start an SSH connection from your remote device to the intermediate device (your home modem/router) with a public IP address that was provided by your ISP to your remote network modem, which passes that IP address along to your home router, which in turn keeps your domain at <u>http://dyn.com</u> updated. In <u>Chapter 2</u> we set up our router to update <u>http://dyn.com</u> whenever our ISP changes our secure network modem's DHCP IP address. You don't have to set up a domain; you can log into your secure network router and write down the IP address every time it changes. However, it would be very inconvenient to be on an important trip somewhere and be cut off from using your secure remote network to keep your mobile devices safe and backup/retrieve your files.
2. Being able to provide our partners an unchanging domain is very important.   It would be a major inconvenience to everyone if we had to contact them with a new IP address every few months.
3. We told our router to listen for SSH traffic on some port (22 by default), and send it through (forward) it to a specific port on our privately addressed SSH remote/server computer.
4. On our remote device, we want to use some application to access the Internet, and instruct that application to use a forwarded port that is tunneled to our home router listening on port 22, which in turn will forward that to our home server. Thus, when you connect an application on your mobile device to a local port, it will in reality forward it to your home secure server listening behind your RSN.

Using Software Firewalls to Harden Security and Block Ports

Before we can use our SSH server we have to open up a port (hole) in our hardware firewall to allow access to it through our router. What we mean by *port* on a computer is kind of curious. A good definition comes from <u>https://en.wikipedia.org/wiki/Computer_port_(hardware)</u> that describes a port as a "*gate, entrance or door*". That is exactly what an open *port* is to your Internet device. Before we learn how to protect our mobile devices by tunneling or blocking our ports we have to learn which ports (doors) our devices have open, and which applications are using them and why. There is a comprehensive list of ports at <u>https://secure.wikimedia.org/wikipedia/en/wiki/List_of_TCP_and_UDP_port_numbers</u>.

On all of your Internet devices, you should do a port analysis and question why they are being served up to the Internet to access your computer. Every open port is a potential security threat that you need to investigate and possibly close. An easy way to do this is by using the netstat command, which works in both Windows and Linux. You can use the information the netstat command to determine what those ports are being used for. (See: <u>https://secure.wikimedia.org/wikipedia/en/wiki/List_of_TCP_and_UDP_port_numbers</u>) Wiki does not list all ports, and application ports are constantly changing, but this web page is a good starting point in our open port examination.

In Windows 7 click on __Start__ > arrow right to select __Run...__ > type __cmd__ to open a command prompt. Then use the following command to observe all of the ports that your device is serving up to the Internet:

C:\...\netstat -ano | more   # Observe the ports

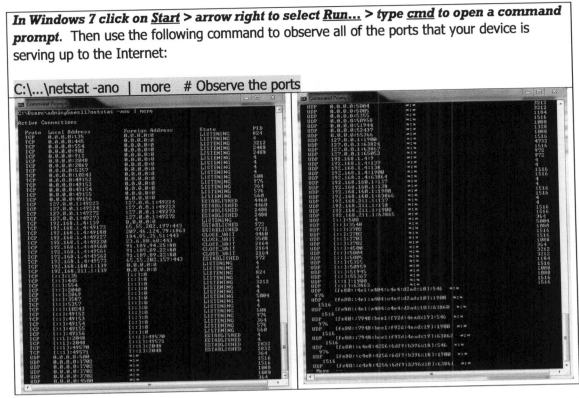

-a	Displays all connections and listening ports.
-n	Displays addresses and port numbers in numerical form.
-o	Displays the owning process ID associated with each connection.
?	Show the other options to consider using.

When you see all of the open ports, it is an outrage consumers are not protesting all of these unnecessary open connections to the Internet, any one of which could be malware running in the background, serving up information about everything you are doing. Even the legitimate ports are supplying information about who-knows-what, which current laws allow. These ports show everything that you are doing while using the Internet and are also open holes that crackers can attack. Many companies' applications cloak this activity in the guise of providing automatic updates, some of which we stopped in Chapter 5. These are updates that could easily be initiated by the Internet user and should not be kicked off by a process running in the background on your device, doing who knows what. These vampire processes suck down computer resources and are constantly polling the Internet, providing information to the company that produced them. We are continuously learning about security holes in these applications that are being exploited and patched, as well as being used to learn about your day-to-day activities.

Many commands in Linux now have short and long-hand notation. I prefer the short, but below is an example of both. Once the ports are forwarded by your hardware router to your SSH server, you need to make sure they are indeed connected to your SSH server. For example, if your router were forwarding port 8080, you would see:

```
# netstat -tln     # or,
# netstat --tcp --listening --programs --numeric
tcp      0      0 127.0.0.1:18080        0.0.0.0:*              LISTEN      5885/ssh

# netstat --tcp --listening --programs
tcp      0      0 localhost:http-alt     *:*                    LISTEN      6192/ssh
```

[--tcp|-t]	Display only TCP connections.
[--numeric|-n]	Show numerical addresses instead of trying to determine symbolic host, port or user names.
[--listening|-l]	Show only listening sockets.
[--program|-p]	Show the PID and name of the program to which each socket belongs.
man netstat	To see all the other options that are available.

Make note of your open ports and block them with a few simple software firewall rules. In Chapter 2 we placed a hardware firewall between our local network and the Internet. This hardware router firewall protects us from devices on the Internet trying to get into our network, but it did not protect us from our own devices that are connected to our local network venturing out onto the Internet. Consider that statement for a moment. We are secure from people breaking in, but not secure from malware or bloatware* venturing out. We may have let a stranger into our house behind our security system, and now that program is broadcasting information across the Internet to someone interested in what we are typing and doing on our computer. This malware can get installed many ways, and Phishing attacks are among the most prevalent.

The website http://www.antiphishing.org houses the "Phishing Activity Trends Report, 1st Quarter 2013" which states, "*Most phishing occurs on hacked or compromised Web servers. The United States continued to be the top country hosting phishing sites during the first quarter of 2013. This is mainly due to the fact that a large percentage of the world's Websites and domain names are hosted in the United States.*

During the first three months of 2013. PandaLabs collected more than 6.5 million malware samples. Trojans are still the most common, accounting for three out of four cases. An average of 31 percent of computers worldwide were infected with malware in 1Q 2013." (See: http://press.pandasecurity.com/wp-content/uploads/2013/02/PandaLabs-Annual-Report-2012.pdf) Hence, the potential exists for 31% of all computers worldwide to connect to local networks behind hardware firewalls, which will attempt to infect other local private network devices and send information over the Internet to crackers. I hope you find that as staggering a number as I do!

To protect devices connected to our local area network, we need a software firewall in addition to our hardware firewall. So what is a software firewall? A software firewall is another layer of protection for your Internet device(s) that applies rules to incoming and outgoing information and either blocks or allows that information to and from your device(s). Windows 7 Software Firewall comes preconfigured with many rules to protect your Internet device. However, to employ the techniques described in this chapter; it requires that you consider defining some additional rules. Opening up and using Windows Firewall to create rules, block, or open ports is very straightforward.

Open the Windows __Control Panel__ > make sure __View by:__ upper right has __Large__ or __Small__ icons selected > click on __Windows Firewall__ > on the left click on __Advanced settings__ > the __Windows Firewall with Advanced Security__ window will appear > on the left under __Windows Firewall with Advanced Security on Local Computer__ click on __Inbound Rules__ > or scroll the center window down to __View and create firewall rules__ > click on __Inbound Rules__ > on the right click on __New Rule...__ to start blocking ports > then on the left click on __Outbound Rules__ and do the same thing to block outbound ports.

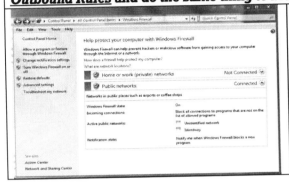

When the __Rule Type__ dialog pops up tick __Port__, __Next >__ > on the Protocol and Ports screen tick __TCP__ and for Specific local ports: enter 1-21, 23-1024, 43173-49573 to block the ports shown by netstat, __Next >__ > on the __Action__ dialog tick __Block the connection__, __Next >__ > on the __Profile__ dialog under __When does this rule apply?__ we just want the __Public__ box checked on our mobile devices, but for testing your tunnels also check __Domain__ and __Private__, __Next >__ > on the __Name__ dialog call the rule something like "__Block Inbound TCP Ports 1-21, 23-1024, 49173-49573__", for the description you can enter something like "__Don't allow this mobile device to use any TCP port that is not tunneled__", __Finish__.

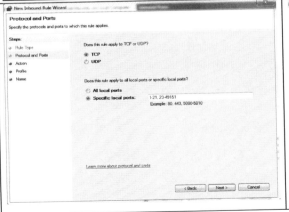
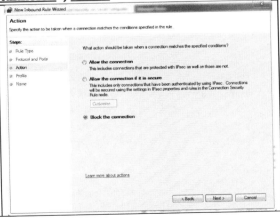

Now whenever your mobile device is connected to a public Internet connection no application can communicate with the Internet except via your tunnel(s). If we are using virtualization with NAT, this will also block the ports of your VM.

If you are running Linux as your core OS, we can easily block ports using the iptables command. We also want to do this on our private network to prove that our port forwarding tunnels are working. Below is an example of blocking a few important ports, except 22, which is our tunnel.

```
# Script for removing and defining software firewall rules
#
# Before defining firewall filtering rules in Linux we should remove any existing
# rules from their chains.  Otherwise, any new rules that are defined will be added
# to the end of existing rules.  This can override firewall behavior that we want
# enabled.  To do this we use iptables —flush as our first command.  However,
# without an argument, the flush option flushes only the filter table. The NAT
# and MANGLE tables may also need to be specifically flushed.  However, if there are
# no NAT or MANGLE rules defined do not flush those tables because that will load
# them.  This would be inefficient. Use the following to determine if they are present:

iptables —L —t nat     # In more recent flavors of Linux there are loaded by default
iptables —L —t mangle

iptables —flush
iptables —delete-chain   # Delete all chains that are not in default filter and NAT table
# iptables  —t nat —flush
# iptables  —table nat —delete-chain
# iptables  —t mangle —flush

iptables —A INPUT —p tcp —dport 1:21 —j DROP
iptables —A INPUT —p tcp —dport 23:79 —j DROP
#iptables —A INPUT —p tcp —dport 80 —j DROP
iptables —A INPUT —p tcp —dport 81:442 —j DROP
#iptables —A INPUT —p tcp —dport 443 —j DROP
iptables —A INPUT —p tcp —dport 444:1024 —j DROP
iptables —A INPUT —p tcp —dport 49173:49573 —j DROP

iptables —A OUTPUT —p tcp —dport 1:21 —j DROP
iptables —A OUTPUT —p tcp —dport 23:79 —j DROP
#iptables —A OUTPUT —p tcp —dport 80 —j DROP
iptables —A OUTPUT —p tcp —dport 81:442 —j DROP
#iptables —A OUTPUT —p tcp —dport 443 —j DROP
iptables —A OUTPUT —p tcp —dport 444:1024 —j DROP
iptables —A OUTPUT —p tcp —dport 49173:49573 —j DROP

iptables —L     # Display the Filtering Rules

# If you want to reestablish your basic Linux OS without rules type:

iptables —flush
```

Linux SSH Client -- Establishing the First Client Connection with Our Linux SSH Server & the Copy of Our Client Public Key to the SSH Server

Before we have our partners exchange files or use their Linux SSH client to connect to our Linux SSH server, have them check to see if one option in the client configuration file, /etc/ssh/ssh_client file, is set. When our partner connects to our SSH server, a file named $HOME/.ssh/known_hosts will be created in their Linux client users' account. If not properly configured, this file can provide valuable information about our SSH server to a cracker if our partners connection (client) mobile device is compromised. We have to assume that our partners have not read this book and are not employing all of the techniques that you are now using to protect yourself and your business. In your directions to them, have them make sure they are hashing their known_hosts file. The known_hosts file in older versions of SSH contains an unencrypted list of hosts to which the SSH user account connects. Having this set on their client computer will help protect your SSH server when/if their security is compromised. This setting is the default in modern-day versions of Linux, but without this setting a hacker has a road map to attack your SSH server(s). Have your partner examine the content of the /etc/ssh_config file to see if:

```
HashKnownHosts yes
```

is set. We should also have our partner check which version of the SSH client that they are using. If it is earlier than what is shown below, have them ask their Linux administrator to upgrade their flavor of Linux or SSH client.

```
$ ssh -V
OpenSSH_5.9p1 Debian-5ubuntu1, OpenSSL 1.0.1 14 Mar 2012
```

We can use telnet to knock on our partner's SSH server client account, which is also a cracker's way of gathering information about your SSH server:

```
$ telnet yourdomainname.dyndns.org 22Trying 24.192.100.40...
Connected to yourdomainname.dyndns.org.
Escape character is '^]'.
SSH-2.0-OpenSSH_5.9p1 Debian-5ubuntu1.1
```

At http://openssh.org the 6.3 release of SSH can be downloaded. We also want to instruct our partner to create the same username as we setup for them on our SSH server. By default, SSH assumes the same username when connecting to our SSH server. If your client wants to connect to your SSH server as a different user ID, they will need to type:

```
$ ssh -l <SSHServerID> yourdomainname.dyndns.extension
```

Before we talk about connecting an SSH client to our SSH server or using things such as port forwarding via SSH or PuTTY installed earlier in Windows, let's discuss what happens when we establish our first client connection with our SSH server. When you connect for the first time to an SSH server, you will see something like:

```
# ssh <username>@yourdomainname.dyndns.<extension>
The authenticity of host '<yourdomainname>.dyndns.<extension> (IP Address)' can't be
established.
ECDSA key fingerprint is d4:66:f9:b8:7c:1a:dd:f5:ef:25:1a:9a:49:7c:d9:1c.
Are you sure you want to continue connecting (yes/no)?  yes
Warning: Permanently added '<yourdomainname>.dyndns.<extension>,<IP Address>'
(ECDSA) to the list of known hosts.
```

If you are saying "HUH?" then you are not alone. What just happened? Was there something that you were supposed to do? What does all this information from SSH mean? The first thing to discuss is the fingerprint, and then we will move on the exchange of the public key that just took place. This all seems very complex, but it really is very simple.

Say for example, you just met someone at a secure location and shook hands. Now that you have met each other, you can exchange information securely by always meeting in person at the same secure place. Another example is imagining you are working for the CIA running a spy, and they will only use you as a drop for their stolen information. They refuse to deal with anyone else out of concern for their safety. Similarly, using SSH with key exchange, there can be no middleman in the swap of information between your server and client because of key verification. If ever someone/something comes between your secure means of exchanging information, then SSH will ask for a new fingerprint and a new exchange of public key. If this exchange was unexpected, then this would be a RED FLAG to your client that somehow your exchange of information had been compromised. You would have to figure out what has happened to what used to be a secure and verified means of exchanging information. Specifically, let's look at what just took place between the client and the SSH server. The server's public key */etc/ssh/ssh_host_ecdsa_key.pub* contains a string like:

```
ecdsa-sha2-nistp256
AAAAE2VjZHNhLXNoYTItbmlzdHAyNTYAAAAIbmlzdHAyNTYAAABBBBDDOIaG+NnewEbWrUHxRKj3RvkfsyPKT
6ZkOv4vnt+/MiH2wi7yOZOINafO6HXwieLIr7sSz/2A73KELOHK3OUg=
```

SSH client just got copied down to the user account *~/.ssh/known_hosts* file on your Linux computer or VM. So now when you reconnect your client to the SSH server, a handshake can be done to make sure that a "man-in-the-middle attack" is no longer possible. The public key above matches up with the private key on the SSH Server. Unless either key is changed you will never again be prompted for a fingerprint. You will always know that you are connecting to the correct SSH server. Speaking of the importance of exchanging information, below is a comical example from my past that shows how the lack of, and then the establishing of communication can cost and save lives.

Story	The call came down, engineer's up. The infantry's advance had halted because of some concertina wire, again. The life of a combat engineer really sucks. You ride around the track vehicle in the dessert, sweating profusely, with temperatures reaching in excess of 120 degrees inside the armored vehicle in the desert. Whoever designed and manufactured the track vehicle of the 1980's gave no thought to the health and welfare of the soldiers housed inside. The diesel fumes

(carbon dioxide) from the vehicle's engine exhaust vent that is located on the front of the track would blow back into area housing the soldiers, making them sick. We would breathe these toxic fumes for many hours each day before being asked to engage in combat.

Suddenly the track would stop, and then we all were expected to do our job as quickly as possible. We all stumbled out of the track wearing heavy flak jackets and helmets and sometimes carrying over a hundred pounds of explosives and gear to ignite them. The track drivers were instructed to stop well behind the infantry and out of harm's way, so we would have to hump it for a thousand yards, add to that the desert heat, which was over 110+ degrees at ground level, to reach the wire after breathing diesel fume exhaust for hours; we felt sick, exhausted, and dehydrated. We humped our weapons, flak gear and as many 13-pound sections of Bangalore torpedoes as we could carry to the wire. When we got to our destination we were all disoriented, disheartened, and way too exhausted to worry about a possible enemy shooting at us. At this point, if there were an enemy shooting, being killed might not be such a bad thing. As it was, we sweat and laid in the Bangalore's, and then the Sergeant ordered everyone back except him and me (I had the radio). About 10 minutes later, the engineers behind us blew the breach and then we started back ourselves. Shortly after we started hiking back to the front lines, I noticed puffs of desert sand popping up all around us. The troops behind us had been ordered to open fire on our position. The Sergeant was right beside me so I quickly tackled him and rolled us both into a ditch. I then unclipped the mike of my radio and shouted into it "RED FLAG... I say again RED FLAG", which was the signal for all divisions to halt all activity and to quit live fire. This was the "RED FLAG" radio signal we had been briefed on to use in a dire emergency when life was in danger. We were instructed that it would halt the division's wide exercise until conditions were safe again to continue. Much to my dismay, it was ignored and the mock battle continued. I eventually tied a cloth to my M-16 rifle barrel and waved it back and forth from the safety of the ditch. Eventually the cloth was seen, and I heard a soldier in the distant Tennessee infantry ranks shout in a southern accent, "Hey, I think there are a couple of guys up there." The live fire on our position ceased, and we slowly rose up from the ditch and walked the long way back to our track, carrying all of our gear in the 110 degree heat. I thought the Sergeant would give them hell, but all he and I did was walk back to the track, with him mumbling a lot of foul language. I think he was just too exhausted to expend the energy that it would take to cuss someone out; not even a thank you to me for saving his life was given, but I knew he owed me one!

As we talked about the SSH, the client made a copy the server's public key in the client user's *~/.ssh/known_hosts* file. Verification of the fingerprint should be made by a phone call. However, suppose that multiple users on your client's computers need to connect to and use your SSH server. Do we really want multiple calls from every user to check their fingerprint individually? A better plan is to provide your partner's computer administrator with your SSH server public key(s) so that they can propagate them globally to all their user's SSH client computers. Most small businesses deal with large corporations who employ legions of IT professionals who can do this. These large entities probably only have a few, extremely expensive, high-powered server(s) with many users.   Their corporate administrator can take your public key and add it to their Linux client computer's */etc/ssh/ssh_known_hosts* file so that all users on those Linux computers can connect to your SSH server without being asked for key fingerprint verification, confusing them and troubling your small business with a flood of phone calls. All you have to do is confirm that fingerprint one time with that large corporation's IT guru/administrator and then have them do all the work.

The easiest way that I have found to do this is, briefly instruct your large entity partner administrator on how to set up a client account to connect to your SSH server (e.g. client and server account names should be the same). Then have them connect to your SSH server and verify the account's SSH fingerprint over the telephone. If you are dealing with a large corporation, very limited directions should be necessary for them to do this. When they connect, your large corporation IT professional should know that a */home/<UserID>/.ssh/known_hosts* file will be created in their newly created <UserID> SSH user directory. If this corporate administrator does not know this, then **be very afraid**. You are dealing with a corporation that has cut or outsourced their IT services, which could make your data exchange very unsecure. You should seek out a different corporate partner with which to do business. This is very basic IT knowledge to a large entity, which should have highly paid computer professionals, not foreign-outsourced, low-paid workers handling this type of data exchange.

Let's outline this process for you and your SBO/HCU partners in case you are not dealing with a large entity with deep pockets, or are with one that has poor IT management. Below is the command to have them connect to your SSH server.

```
$ ssh <UserID>@<YourDomainName>.dyndns.<extension>
```

As we saw above this will create the */home/<UserID>/.ssh/known_hosts* that houses your SSH server's public key file.

```
$ exit      # exit your connection with the SSH server
$ su -      # become root
# cat /home/<UserID>/.ssh/known_hosts >> /etc/ssh_known_hosts
```

Once this connection has been established between you and your client, the command above will concatenate your public key to their computer's global *known_hosts* file. All users on that client host will no longer be prompted for a fingerprint to login to your SSH server.

Macintosh SSH Client—Establishing the First Client Connection with Our Linux SSH Server & the Copy of Our Client Public Key to Server

On your Macintosh, open a terminal window by *arrowing up to select the __Application__ menu > when it expands arrow down to select __Utilities__ > upon selection of __Utilities__ arrow over to select the __Terminal__ menu item to open a terminal window > once the terminal window is open type __ssh –V__ and you should see the version information, for example:*

```
OpenSSH_5.2p1, OpenSSL 0.9.8r 8 Feb 2011
```

Once the terminal window is open, the description of how to establish your first connection to a SSH server is identical to a Linux SSH Client. Refer back to Linux SSH Client-Establishing the first Client Connection with our Linux SSH Server for a detailed discussion of what takes place when we connect to an SSH server for the first time. Below is the command to type to connect to the SSH server for the first time:

$ ssh <UserID>@<yourdomainname>.dyndns.<extension>

Explain that when they connect to your SSH server for the first time, they will see something like:

```
The authenticity of host '<yourdomainname>.dyndns.<extension> (IP Address)' can't be
established.
ECDSA key fingerprint is d4:66:f9:b8:7c:1a:dd:f5:ef:25:1a:9a:49:7c:d9:1c.
Are you sure you want to continue connecting (yes/no)?  yes
Warning: Permanently added '<yourdomainname>.dyndns.<extension>,<IP Address>'
(ECDSA) to the list of known hosts.
```

As we talked about establishing the first connection with a Linux SSH client, the Macintosh just made a copy the server's public key in the client user's ~/.ssh/known_hosts file. The fingerprint above should be verified by a phone call to eliminate the possibility of a man-in-the-middle attack. We have to make sure that our Macintosh user is indeed connected to our SSH server. Review the section on Linux for further explanation on connecting to an SSH server for the first time.

Windows PuTTY Client -- Establishing the First Client Connection to a Linux SSH Server & the Copy of Our Client Public Key to the Server

There are two ways that we can establish our first connection with our SSH server. The easiest way is to create an account on the SSH server, so have our partner double click on their desktop PuTTY icon to open the PuTTY GUI and have them configure and save a PuTTY session to the Windows Registry. Refer back to SSH client-Obtaining, Installing and Setting up Software on our Mobile Device to Access our Secure SSH Server Remotely to install the PuTTY software on your Windows PC.

Once PuTTY is installed, there are a few options that we can have our client configure to make things easier. *In the PuTTY configuration window under Host Name (or IP address) enter the address to the SSH server (e.g. <yourdomainname.dyndns.org>) > under Connection Type: tick SSH > under Saves Sessions enter a name for your session (e.g. ssh<ServerUserID>).*

NOTE Help your client understand that <yourdomainname.dyndns.org> is an alias for your modem's DHCP IP address assigned by your ISP. Your router is then forwarding connections made to <yourdomainname.dyndns.org> to your SSH server behind your hardware firewall router. Explain to your partner that this address is not a URL

| | that they can use their browser to surf to; I had one of my partners get confused about this. The above address looks much like a URL in which to surf. |

This is all the information needed to connect and login to our SSH server, but there are still a few other options to consider setting.

Click on __Window__ > __Behaviour__ > and __Below Window title:__ enter a title for their PuTTY terminals > click on __Connection__ > check __Enable TCP keepalives__ (__SO_KEEPALIVE option__) if our partner will remain connected for extended periods of time (like using port forwarding) > Under __Connection__ > __Data__ our client can enter a default user name for login.

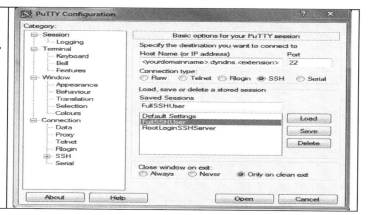

Once these settings are set, it is not intuitive on how to save them to our Windows registry entry. __Under __Category:__ at the top, click on __Session__ > arrow down and right to select the __Save__ button.__

Upon connecting the first time, you will see a security alert pop up, which we will discuss soon. __Click on __Yes.____ This is the fingerprint discussed earlier in establishing Linux SSH connections that must be verified with your SSH server provider. This will copy the public key to your Windows client registry.

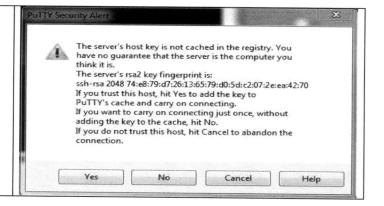

Future first connections to new accounts from the client will look like:

```
Using username 'sshuserID'
sshuserID@<yourdomainname.dyndns.<extension>'s password:
You are required to change your password immediately (root enforced)
Welcome to Ubuntu 12.04.1 LTS (GNU/Linux 3.2.0-30-generic-pae i686)
```

We will see all this again using the "PLINK" PuTTY command line utility, which we are now going to discuss.

Windows PuTTY -- Using the Command Line to Establish the First SSH Connection

Hopefully, by now you have added a desktop and/or taskbar icon to run the Windows Command Prompt. If you have not, **open up a *Windows 7 command prompt by clicking on Start > All Programs > select Accessories > right click on the Command Prompt to bring up the right click menu > arrow down to Send to > arrow over to Desktop (create shortcut) > double click on the Command Prompt desktop icon to open up a Command Prompt,** or just keep selecting the Command Prompt using the Start menu.

We are now going to use the command line to setup our client/server SSH key relationship, which you may find easier. Type the following into your command prompt to get connected to your partner's SSH server for the first time. Use your SSH server IP address or substitute your SSH server ID for <sshuser>, your SSH server domain name for <yourdomainname>, and your SSH server domain extension for <extension>:

C:\Users\<userID>>plink -ssh -l sshuser <yourdomainname>.dyndns.<extension>

The first time you use PuTTY's (plink) to connect to your partner's SSH server, you should see something like the following:

```
The server's host key is not cached in the registry. You have no guarantee that the
server is the computer you think it is.
The server's rsa2 key fingerprint is:
ssh-rsa 2048 74:e8:79:d7:26:13:65:79:d0:5d:c2:07:2e:ea:42:70
If you trust this host, enter "y" to add the key to PuTTY's cache and carry on
connecting.
If you want to carry on connecting just once, without adding the key to the cache,
enter "n".  If you do not trust this host, press Return to abandon the connection.
Store key in cache? (y/n) y
Using username "sshuser".
sshuser@<yourdomainname>.dyndns.<extension>'s password:
You are required to change your password immediately (root enforced)
Welcome to Ubuntu 12.04.1 LTS (GNU/Linux 3.2.0-30-generic-pae i686)

 * Documentation:  https://help.ubuntu.com/

0 packages can be updated.
0 updates are security updates.

The programs included with the Ubuntu system are free software; the exact
distribution terms for each program are described in the individual files in
/usr/share/doc/*/copyright.

Ubuntu comes with ABSOLUTELY NO WARRANTY, to the extent permitted by applicable law.
```

```
WARNING: Your password has expired.
You must change your password now and login again!
Changing password for <sshuser>.
(current) UNIX password:
Enter new UNIX password:
Retype new UNIX password:
passwd: password updated successfully
```

NOTE 	Sometimes, when following these directions, my partners got the error:
	`passwd:  Authentication token manipulation error`
	`passwd:  password unchanged`
	
	Notice above that Linux states "You must change your password now and login again!" and prompts for the "(current) UNIX password:" first. So you have to type the administrator-defined login password on the client **TWICE** to actually change your password on the SSH server to one that you will define.

Record your new password in a safe place. For future connections to the SSH server you will use the password that you setup above until we copy our client public key to the SSH server. We will go over how to do that using PuTTY's tools in Windows 7 later. The warning "*You have no guarantee that the server is the computer you think it is*", is meant to scare the heck out of the Windows user so that they know something important just took place. It means that your partner is supposed to contact you (the SSH server owner) with the fingerprint information that identifies your unique host key to make sure they are indeed connected to your server. This prevents a middleman (spoofing) attack.

PuTTY will record the host public key in the Windows registry so it can warn your client if the SSH server they are connecting to is ever switched. When your partner connects to your server the first time, PuTTY has no way of knowing if your client is connected to the correct server or a spoofed* server. That is what the warning above is meant to convey to your partner. It is your client's decision to decide whether to trust the SSH server or not. It is also your client's responsibility to contact you with the fingerprint to make sure they are indeed connecting to your SSH server. Once the SSH server public key has been copied to your client device, test your connection to the SSH server by typing the following into the Windows 7 Command Prompt:

```
C:\Users\<userID>>plink -ssh -l sshuser <yourdomainname>.dyndns.<extension>
Using username "sshuser"
sshuser@<yourdomainname>.dyndns.<extension>'s password:
Welcome to Ubuntu 12.04.1 LTS (GNU/Linux 3.2.0-30-generic-pae i686)

 * Documentation:  https://help.ubuntu.com/


0 packages can be updated.
0 updates are security updates.
```

```
Last login: Fri Sep  7 12:05:49 2012 from d192-24-28-40.try.wideopenwest.com
←]0;sshuser@ubuntu1204-sshvpn: ~←[01;32msshuser@ubuntu1204-sshvpn←[00m:←[01;34
m~←[00m$
```

You should note above that the Windows <u>Command Prompt</u> is not rendering the graphics from Linux properly on this Windows computer. This means that the SSH server administrator has copied in a *.bashrc* environment establishment file to your Linux server account. This is OK for a Linux SSH client to Linux SSH server connection, but may not work well using plink in a Windows command prompt. If you know that your partner is going to use Windows with plink to connect to your server, you or your client can modify the Linux SSH server *.bashrc*, or simply move it out of the way and login again to fix the Windows prompt.

```
# cd ~sshuser; mv .bashrc .bashrc.linux     # as root
$ mv .bashrc .bashrc.linux      # as the client after login
```

The exchange of keys with PuTTY is not a simple as with Linux. PuTTY chooses to store all of its data (saved sessions, SSH host keys, etc.) in the Windows registry. To most of us, the Windows 7 registry is a forbidden place where most average Windows users are afraid to venture. I have never read a book that fully demystifies the Windows registry, and the computer periodicals that I subscribe to offer little insight into the registry other than how to tweak a key here and there. I would prefer that PuTTY store its information in files located on the hard drive and not the registry, but that is the developer's choice. Subsequently, we will have to get into a little bit of registry education. PuTTY stores most of its information in the registry location:

```
HKEY_CURRENT_USER\Software\SimonTatham\PuTTY
```

The SSH keys that are more important to this SSH client discussion are stored at:

```
HKEY_CURRENT_USER\Software\SimonTatham\PuTTY\SshHostKeys
```

If our clients connect to our server using PuTTY, and we have to create a new account for them because of a compromised mobile device, you will have to instruct them on how to delete these keys from their Windows registry. If you or a client is using PuTTY, I encourage you to go to http://www.chiark.greenend.org.uk/~sgtatham/putty/docs.html and read the PuTTY manual. It is an excellent read on their donationware* product. To clean up all connections and keys, or to start all over getting connected to our SSH server, type the following as a PuTTY user from the CMD prompt:

```
C:\path\<UserID>\putty -cleanup
```

This is the nuclear option and will delete all sessions, keys and random files that PuTTY has generated for the currently logged in Windows user. If all you want to delete is a specific key in Windows 7, ***click on Start > Run... > type regedit and use the registry editor to navigate to HKEY_CURRENT_USER\Software\SimonTatham\PuTTY\SshHostKeys***. In that registry location, you can delete specific public keys that are no longer valid.

 **NOTE** When the client establishes a connection with our SSH server, the SSH server's public key was copied down to the SSH client's local directory. This means that our client will no longer be prompted for a fingerprint because a relationship has been established. Then when the client connects to the SSH server, it has to verify who we are with a passphrase (password). What is now needed is to exchange our client public-generated SSH key with the SSH server so that the server can verify us in the same manner without a passphrase. We will cover how to do this soon.

Dynamic Port Forwarding — Establishing a Dynamic SSH Tunnel Using the Command Line to Secure Our Browser Activity at Hotspots

From https://help.ubuntu.com/community/SSH/OpenSSH/PortForwarding: *"There are three types of port forwarding with SSH:*

- **Local port forwarding (LPF):** *connections from the SSH client are forwarded via the SSH server, then to a destination server*
- **Remote port forwarding (RPF):** *connections from the SSH server are forwarded via the SSH client, then to a destination server*
- **Dynamic port forwarding (DPF):** *connections from various programs are forwarded via the SSH client, then via the SSH server, and finally to several destination servers "*

Local Port Forwarding (LPF) will be discussed later and Remote Port Forwarding which is less common will not be covered at all. Remote Port Forwarding allows you to connect your SSH server to another computer/server on your company's intranet. Dynamic Port Forwarding is a method by which a remote SSH server will interpret what protocol a client is requesting through an SSH tunnel, and then service that request. We will cover DPF first because I feel it is the easiest to use and setup. It is also the most powerful because of its ability to use a SOCK5* proxy*, bypassing higher level proxies.

Dynamic SSH will turn our SSH into a SOCKS* proxy* server for your request. DPF can also be specified in the client configuration file. There is a very complete read on what a proxy is and what the SOCKS and SOCKS5 protocols are in the Glossary. Another way of viewing the SOCKS5 protocol comes from http://en.wikipedia.org/wiki/SOCKS, *"Bill wishes to communicate with Jane over the Internet, but a firewall exists on his network between them and Bill is not authorized to communicate through it himself. Therefore, he connects to the SOCKS5 proxy on his local network and sends to it information about the connection he wishes to make to Jane on the remote network. The SOCKS proxy opens a connection through the firewall and facilitates the communication between Bill and Jane."*

 In Linux, any port below 1024 is reserved for system use. To tunnel ports below 1024 requires *root* privilege. Windows 7 allows anyone to bind to any open port. So any port can be forwarded by any user.

Dynamic port forwarding is similar to the way that X Windows https://en.wikipedia.org/wiki/X11 works in Linux. For example, if you have an X client and an X server, the X client (our mobile device) that is running our client application and can be anywhere; it makes a request to an X server, which serves up the GUI, and can be on the same computer or exist on a faraway server. The server listens for requests from the client and then provides whatever is requested, which can be web pages from our Remote Secure Network Server (RSNS).

To access our secure server remotely we will need to setup a user ID that has limited privileges on our server. The 'sudouser' installation user ID that we use to become 'root' or to run root commands is not an ID that should be exposed to remote Internet connections. You can use the GUI to create a user ID or do it from the command line.

Using the GUI, *click on **System Settings** > **User Accounts** icon > **Unlock** button upper right > the **+** sign lower left > keep Account Type **Standard** > enter the account information*.

Refer back to <u>Adding Less Privileged User IDs for Specific Purposes</u> to Linux to examine what you might want for your port forwarding SSH user ID. Because of the *-s /usr/sbin/nologin* option we used if someone tries to login to the account using the following without the -N SSH option, they will get the following:

```
C:\Users\<UserId>>ssh -l sshdynlocal -D 18080 domainname.dyndns.org
sshdynlocal@domainname.dyndns.org's password:
Could not chdir to home directory /home/sshdynlocal: No such file or directory
This account is currently not available.
Connection to domainname.dyndns.org closed.
```

The user ID can be up to 32 characters long. Choose something easily remembered unless you plan to put scripts (recommended) on your mobile device(s) or laptop(s) to perform the connection for you. This will be the user ID that we will use to connect to our SSH server.

To use DPF to establish an SSH connection to your RSNS, *click on **Start** > **Run...** > type **cmd** and open a command prompt*.

PuTTY, which has remained current with updates and new releases, comes with the plink utility (discussed previously). For Windows, PuTTY's plink utility is an excellent SSH solution.

```
C:\...\plink -ssh -2 -N -P 22 -l username yourdomainname.dyndns.<extension> -D 18080
```

-2	force the use of version 2.x protocol
-D port	Dynamic SOCKS-based port to forward
-l username	connect to the server with the specified username

-N	don't start a shell/command (SSH-2 only)
-P port	connect to the specified port
-ssh	force the use of the SSH protocol when connecting

Linux comes with an updated SSH client installed. In Windows, you can install Cygwin, and have an OpenSSH client available using Cygwin, but consider using a virtual Linux OS with OpenSSH, which might make much more sense. (See: http://cygwin.com) Syntax in Linux:

```
# ssh -D localaddress:localport <dyndnsname, hostname, or IP>
```

If you don't specify a <local address/IP>, then SSH will bind to "localhost" or IP address 127.0.0.1. Type the following if you are using the OpenSSH client:

```
$ ssh -fN -D 18080 <ServerUser>@<DomainName, HostName or IP>      or,
$ ssh -fN -l <ServerUser> -D 18080 <ServerUser>@<DomainName, HostName or ServerIP>
```

-D port	Specifies a local (your mobile device) "dynamic" application-level port to forward to your home SSH server. This only works for TCP and UDP protocols.
-f	Only for Linux. Requests ssh to go to background just before command execution.
-l user	User ID being used to connect to the server.
-N	Do not execute a remote command i.e. just forward ports.

In Linux, once a password is supplied, the *ssh* command will go to background. You can verify your SSH connections by typing:

```
$ netstat -ano     # Observe the ports to see your dynamic connection
```

Normally when we make a browser request to the Internet over a public network, that request goes out unencrypted for crackers to view our activity. The command above has established an encrypted "dynamic" tunnel to our home SSH server that we will teach our Internet applications to take advantage of, but be careful choosing your port so as not to conflict with another application. The rule used to be anything above 1024, but in today's world, there are many ports in use above 1024.

| **NOTE** | In Linux, if you want the client machine to listen to a privileged port below 1024, SSH must be run as 'root'. This is often convenient to keep from having to reconfigure applications to new ports. With the ease in which we can create Virtual Machines connecting as 'root' in a VM, it is not a big security threat (except to the VM). In Windows with PuTTY's plink command, or using the 2004 version of SSH client, we can put together a command script and run it on any port. |

Depending on the network you are using (your local community college for example), the network administrator may be blocking or monitoring ports, especially those below 1024. This works by telling your mobile device to allocate a socket to listen to port (in our case 18080) on the local side bound to our remote home server DYN domain or IP address. Whenever a connection is made to this port using our mobile device application, the connection is forwarded over our SSH tunnel secure channel to our HCU/SBO SSH server rather than using the public network to service requests to the Internet. In other words, when our browser makes a connection to this port, the connection uses our secure encrypted SSH channel. Our home server will interpret the application (HTTP-80/HTTPS-443) protocol to determine which port to use to service our mobile devices' request. This can allow communication with the Internet through restricted firewalls.

 	The first time you connect the SSH client in Windows it will create a file called *C:\Users\username\.ssh\known_hosts*, which contains the SSH server's public key. If you build a new server, or create a new user ID, you will have to delete or rebuild this file on your mobile device to get connected to your new server using the same DYN address as new user ID unless you are using Public Key Infrastructure (PKI). As discussed previously, PuTTY will create the equivalent of the *known_hosts* file in the Windows registry.
NOTE	The terminal window with the connection to your home computer account needs to stay connected for DPF to work. If DPF is needed for long periods of time refer down to <u>SSH KeepAlive to Keep Your Session Active</u>. Once you close the terminal your tunnel will be lost and you can no longer surf the web using this SSH encrypted method.

The command above established a tunnel to your home server using port 18080. From now on, SSH listens dynamically on port 18080 for a mobile device application to use it.

Dynamic Port Forwarding – Establishing a Dynamic SSH Tunnel Using the Windows PuTTy GUI to Secure Our Browser Activity at Hotspots

The setup in the PuTTY GUI is exactly the same as what we accomplished from the command line. When sessions are configured, the PuTTY GUI will save sessions in the Windows registry. We are going to use a "dynamic" GUI connection to our RSNS rather using than SSH client or PLINK.EXE. *In the **Putty** > **SSH** > **Tunnels** Panel there is a Radio button called Dynamic.* Selecting this option instructs PuTTY SSH to use the -D [bind_address:]port option we used previously from the command line with PLINK.

The PuTTY manual at <u>http://www.chiark.greenend.org.uk/~sgtatham/putty/docs.html</u> states, *"The Session configuration panel contains the basic options you need to specify in order to open a session at all, and also allows you to save your settings to be reloaded later."* From the command line, we forwarded port 18080 dynamically to out RSNS. To be consistent, let's do the same using the PuTTY GUI.

The Host Name is the host or IP address to which you are connecting. The <u>Saved Sessions</u> are whatever you want to call them. Both must be filled in when you save the entry for later use. *Call the session something descriptive like "SSHTunnel18080Dynamic." **The Host Name with be your domain name setup at <u>http://dyn.com</u> (e.g. yourdomainname.dyndns.org) of our SSH server > for port specify SSH port 22 > under Connection type: tick <u>SSH</u>. Click on the <u>Connection-SSH</u> option > check <u>Don't start a shell or command at all</u> > > for the <u>Preferred SSH protocol version:</u> tick <u>2 only</u>.***

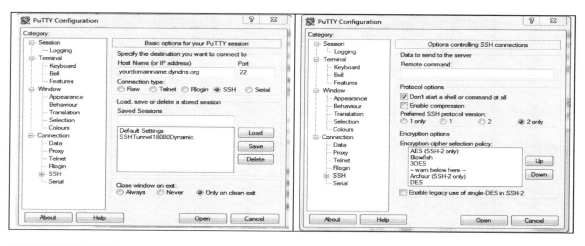

Select the + sign next to SSH to expand the menu and arrow down to select <u>Tunnels</u> >
next to <u>Source port</u> enter the local port we are going to tunnel (e.g. <u>18080</u>) > for
<u>Destination</u> tick <u>Dynamic</u> > go back to the left <u>Category:</u> menu and at the top click on
<u>Session</u> > select the <u>Save</u> button on right to save the connection information to the
registry > when done click on the <u>Open</u> button to tunnel the port 18080 to our RSNS.
Later on we will be forwarding other ports. To know which session is being used click on
<u>Window</u> > select <u>Behavior</u> and under <u>Window title:</u> enter something like (<u>SSH 18080
Dynamic SOCKS5 Tunnel, or SSH Tunnel All Ports</u>).

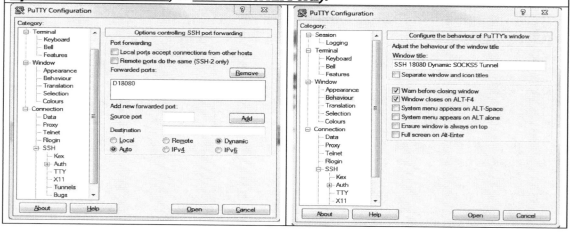

To maximize security, there is no reason to open up a remote shell on your
host computer, giving the user terminal access to their account. If someone
hacks your username and password, all you want them to see is blackness.

The next step is to set up our mobile applications like Firefox, Internet Explorer, and Hotmail
to use the tunnel so we can use the web encrypted, **free from most prying eyes**.

Firefox/Internet Explorer and Hotmail SOCKS5 Configuration for Our Dynamic Tunnel

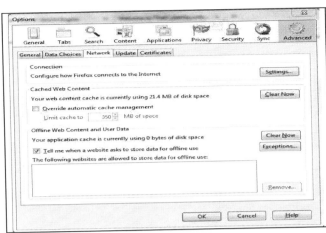

Open up the Firefox browser and in Linux > click on Edit menu item > arrow down to select Preferences; or in Windows 7 select Tools > arrow down to select Options > click on the Advanced icon on the far right > select the Network tab > under Connection click on the Settings... button. This will bring up the Connection Settings where we will direct Firefox to use our SOCKS* proxy to facilitate communication via our encrypted SSH tunnel to our RSNS.

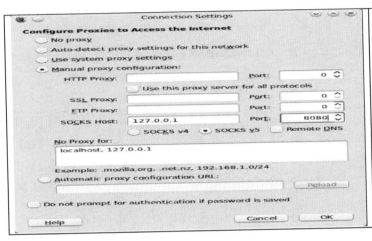

Click on the Manual proxy configuration: and for SOCKS Host: enter localhost or 127.0.0.1 > for Port enter 18080 or 8080 > SOCKS should have SOCKS v5 ticked > note any other entries in the HTTP proxy and remove them > OK. Firefox will now communicate with our client SOCKS* proxy* on a local port which will forward our browser requests to our RSNS SOCKS* proxy*.

Whether our browser connects via port 80 or secure port 443, our dynamic tunnel to the RSNS will interpret the protocol being used and forward all communication to the Internet using the RSN and your remote modem. (See: https://secure.wikimedia.org/wikipedia/en/wiki/Hypertext_Transfer_Protocol, https://secure.wikimedia.org/wikipedia/en/wiki/HTTPS) The target/URL requested will then pass back through RSNS SOCKS* proxy*, who will send the packets across the SSH tunnel to our local SOCKS* proxy*, and ultimately to our local application (browser). From now on we are surfing the Internet encrypted via the SOCKS5* protocol. Our hotspot is merely a conduit to our encrypted tunnel RSNS rather than surfing openly for crackers to observe. When you want to use Firefox at home without a tunnel *click on the No proxy and the top* button and go back to surfing the old open way.

Windows wisely has the proxy* settings centralized and points its Internet applications to these central settings. Setting these proxy* settings enables both Windows Live Hotmail and Internet Explorer to use our SSH tunnel. *Select Start > Control Panel > if View by: Large or Small icons > select Internet Options > this will bring up the Internet Properties dialog or, open Internet Explorer > select Tools > arrow down to the button to select Internet Options and follow the same procedure > select the Connections tab on the top right.*

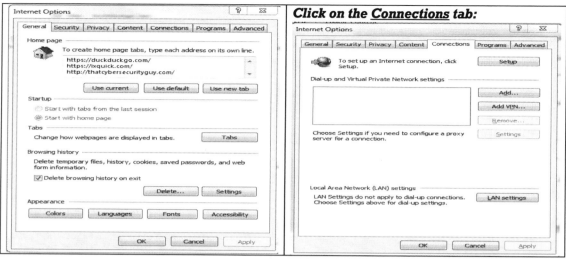

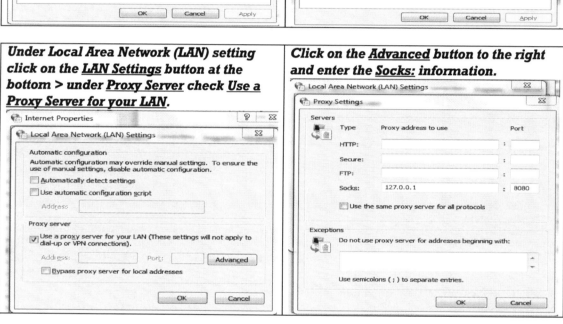

Local Port Forwarding – To Secure Internet Applications that Can't use SOCKS

Local Port Forwarding (LPF) redirects one port on the client to one port on the server. We are reaching out across the Internet to seize a port on our RSNS running behind our proxy* server or our secure firewall and make it local to our mobile device through an encrypted SSH tunnel. That parent that is blocking your favorite game ports cannot stop your SSH tunnel. The college proxy* can no longer monitor what you are doing on your mobile device, and that work firewall can be bypassed allowing you to shop online. A knowledgeable network administrator in these arts can catch you using an SSH tunnel from work; it is probably a violation of company policy and could get you fired. However, from my experience most corporate and government network administrators are overworked, overwhelmed and underpaid with monitoring and keeping these monstrous networks up and running. The constant downsizing to maximize profits has this type of high-paid talent resourced to their max, and their staff is kept to a less educated and lower paid minimum level. They are constantly jumping from fire to fire with thousands of devices to monitor and have little time to examine your tunnels through the corporate networks to your home server. With that said, automatic tools are getting better and better at monitoring this type of activity and reporting back to the network professionals (who have less and less knowledge of what is really taking place or how to understand this type of monitoring), so this this data is often ignored due to time constraints and other priorities. I am not suggesting that an employee use LPF as a form of criminal activity or as a way to bypass a firewall, but I do suggest to government, corporations, and small businesses everywhere that you get what you pay for. If you want security that will protect your business from thousands, millions, or billions of dollars in losses using the Internet, then you will have to invest in quality talent and not over work them. Using SSH tunnels to harden your security while accessing the Internet from hotspots, colleges or from countries that limit your Internet freedom is good way to protect your mobile device.

How LPF works is, we configure a local (client) application to use a local port that we will forward to a port on our RSNS server. We then use that tunnel to attach another protocol like IMAP, HTTP, TCP, IP, FTP, POP3 that are commonly used to access the Internet. In Electronic Warfare, we call this burying a signal within a carrier wave. We are allowing several protocols to share a common transmission medium, in this case our SSH tunnel.

The true value of LPF comes in when we are using hotspots. Previously, we learned how to determine which ports our mobile device or computer is serving up to the Internet. What we want to do now is either block those ports or create a simple script to tunnel all those ports (protocols) and web addresses to our RSNS. The simplest method to do that is to create a command file in Windows or a script in Linux to tunnel the important ports and addresses we will need when using hotspots. All we have to do is launch that script and then all of our Internet traffic is using our encrypted tunnel, thus protecting our mobile device from crackers who are also using that hotspot. We can even add on the dynamic ports to the script, thereby making all our browser activity, and other applications configured to use those browser ports, transparent as well.

Local port forwarding may seem to be the long way around to doing anything, but it is very useful when it works. It does not require setting up a proxy* and can be used very easily. It was suggested by sources I have referenced that we can use LPF to visit specific websites using another local port; I tried this and had very limited success. Forwarding websites did not work well unless port 80 and 443 were open in the firewall. Many corporations, SBOs and almost all hotspots have these ports open, so using this technique to forward a URL may work for you.

For example, suppose you are at work or a hotspot and you want to access a website using a web browser without prying eyes, or suppose you want to use a benign search engine site such as https://duckduckgo.com, which is forbidden for some reason. Try forwarding any local port not blocked in the following fashion to your favorite website in Windows. To enter this click on *Start* > *Run...* > *type cmd*:

```
C:\...\plink -ssh -2 -N -P 22 -l sshuserid -L 127.0.0.1:18080:duckduckgo.com:80
yourdyndomain.dyndns.(com, org, etc.)
```

```
C:\...\plink -ssh -2 -N -P 22222 -l sshuserid -L 127.0.0.1:80:walmart.com:80 -L
127.0.0.1:443:butzel.com:443 yourdomain.dyndns.(com, org, etc.)
```

or as an example in Linux:

```
$ ssh -N -l sshuserid -L 127.0.0.1:18080:duckduckgo.com:443 yourdomain.dyndns.(com, org,
etc)
```

```
$ ssh -N -l root -L 127.0.0.1:18080:butzel.com:80 -L 127.0.0.1:443:walmart.com:443
yourdomain.dyndns.(com, org, etc.)
```

The "-L 127.0.0.1:18080:websitedomain:80" specifies that the client computer is listening on port 18080, which is to forwarded to the specified SSH server and port on the remote side. Forwarding a different port to 80 or 443 on the server with this technique had limited success. The 127.0.0.1 can be omitted, but it reinforces exactly what the command is doing. It is taking the localhost (laptop, smartphone, etc.) host port and forwarding it to port 80 or 443 on your RSNS. You can then surf your local (client) device's browser to "localhost or 127.0.0.1", which will land you on a domain web page through your RSNS tunnel. At a higher education institution or a hotspot with a proxy*, LPF using this technique might prove useful. You can try doing this for any domain.

I had very limited success using the technique from my SSH client using hotspots. While I could surf to and use walmart.com using localhost:18080, I had to leave ports 80 and 443 open to do so. Surfing to newegg.com would redirect localhost:18080 to http://www.newegg.com. Surfing to http://www.butzel.com, a law firm, would not work at all; perhaps you will have greater success using this technique.

Specifying web pages like the one below, which is my website collection of links to the Internet, was rejected by my SSH client in Linux as a bad local forwarding specification:

```
$ ssh -N -l <sshuser> -L 18080:thatcybersecurityguy.com:80 yourdomain.dyndns.org
400 - Bad Request
```

Back in the section on DPF we briefly described some of the SSH client options being used. Let's go into more detail on some of the options that we want to use with LPF. Most of this information taken from the manual page # man ssh, which is available in Linux from the command line. It is included here for reference.

Client Option	ssh Client Option Description
-2	Forces ssh to try protocol version 2 only.
-4	Forces ssh to use IPv4 addresses only.
-6	Forces ssh to use IPv6 addresses only.
-f (only works in Linux)	Requests ssh to go to background just before command execution. This is useful if ssh is going to ask for passwords or passphrases, but the user wants it in the background. This implies -n. The recommended ways to start X11 programs at a remote site are with something like ssh -f host xterm.

	If the ExitOnForwardFailure configuration option is set to "yes", then a client started with -f will wait for all remote port forwards to be successfully established before placing itself in the background.
-L [bind_address:]port:host:host port	Specifies that the given port on the local (client) host is to be forwarded to the given host and port on the remote side. This works by allocating a socket to listen to <u>port</u> on the local side, optionally bound to the specified <u>bind_address</u>. Whenever a connection is made to this port, the connection is forwarded over the secure channel, and a connection is made to <u>host</u> port <u>hostport</u> from the remote machine. Port forwarding's can also be specified in the configuration file. IPv6 addresses can be specified by enclosing the address in square brackets. Only the superuser can forward privileged ports (1-1024). By default, the local port is bound in accordance with the GatewayPorts setting. However, an explicit <u>bind_address</u> may be used to bind the connection to a specific address. The <u>bind_address</u> of "localhost" indicates that the listening port be bound for local use only, while an empty address or '*' indicates that the port should be available from all interfaces.
-l login_name	Specifies the user to log in as on the remote machine. This also may be specified on a per-host basis in the configuration file.
-N	Do not execute a remote command. This is just useful for forwarding ports (protocol version 2 only).
-n	Redirects stdin from */dev/null* (actually, prevents reading from stdin). This must be used when ssh is run in the background. A common trick is to use this to run X11 programs on a remote machine. For example, ssh -n shadows.cs.hut.fi emacs & will start an emacs on shadows.cs.hut.fi, and the X11 connection will be automatically forwarded over an encrypted channel. The ssh client program will be put in the background. (This does not work if ssh needs to ask for a password or passphrase; see also the -f option.)
-p <u>port</u>	Port to connect to on the remote host. This can be specified on a per-host basis in the configuration file.
-v	Verbose mode. Causes ssh client to print debugging messages about its progress. This is helpful in debugging connection, authentication, and configuration problems. Multiple -v options increase the verbosity. The maximum logging level is 3.

A good 2006 read on bypassing firewalls and proxies can be found at http://polishlinux.org/apps/ssh-tunneling-to-bypass-corporate-firewalls. Even though this information is old, it was useful in describing local port forwarding. Later we will discuss much more useful forms of Local Port Forwarding for other applications on our mobile device, such as email clients.

Using X11 Forwarding from Your SSH Server to Your Client

X11 forwarding is another form of port forwarding for presenting graphical information. (See: https://en.wikipedia.org/wiki/X11 and https://en.wikipedia.org/wiki/X_Window_System) It is less secure than the other port forwarding techniques, but it is a great way of running applications remotely without having to do a lot of configuration. Unlike forwarding other protocols, SSH comes with built-in support for forwarding the X protocol. X is cross-platform, which means it can run on multiple operating systems, multiple processors, and multiple hardware platforms; this makes it a versatile, widely supported GUI.

UNIX and now Linux developers have been evolving the X protocol and GUI client/server software for many years. Designers have continued to improve X, and it is a good graphical solution. With X, you can run a program on your remote SSH server and export the GUI (display) back to the X server running on your client. To state this a different way so this does not get confusing, your client is running an X server and your SSH server is running the X application (e.g. Firefox, Thunderbird, Kwrite), so SSH sends all X11 graphics back to you through the encrypted tunnel you opened. Therefore, even though you are running the application remotely, it appears as if you are running it locally. Consequently, your mobile device is displaying what the server application is doing on your remote SSH server, which resides behind your SB/HC firewall. From your laptop's perspective, it appears as if the application is running locally, but you are getting the graphical display, mouse and keyboard of the remote SSH server that you are connected to. SSH X11 forwarding is not as safe and secure as port forwarding as it occurs at the application level and not the network level of the OSI model. However, now we have another use for our RSNS SSH server that is still pretty secure and useful. Another security concern is that we don't want to load up our SSH server with lots of applications that may have their own agendas. This is especially true if that SSH server is being used to exchange sensitive data with our partners.

We can connect to a hotspot, school or work network, open an X11 forwarded tunnel into our SSH server, run a browser or email application, and use our HCU/SBO network to handle all of our Internet activity. This keeps us somewhat safe and bypasses some firewalls and proxies again. This technique is also handy for a SBO/employee who may need to login remotely to troubleshoot some problem on the network or server within your company.

Just like HTTP for browsing the web, the X protocol was not designed with security in mind. So forwarding X requires a level of trust between the client and server. This could prove dangerous if you trust a compromised server; because a cracker could hijack your X session, take over your Internet device, watch your keystrokes, and attack your devices with your privileges. As a result, we have to be very careful to whom we grant X11 access. From the man page on sshd_config, "*Additionally, the authentication spoofing and authentication data verification and substitution occur on the client side. The security risk of using X11 forwarding is that the client's X11 display server may be exposed to attack when the SSH client requests forwarding (see the warnings for ForwardX11 in ssh_config(5)).*" Taken from http://www.openbsd.org/cgi-bin/man.cgi?query=sshd_config&sektion=5&arch=&apropos=0&manpath=OpenBSD+Current:

| X11DisplayOffset | Specifies the first display number available for sshd(8)'s X11 forwarding. This prevents sshd from interfering with real X11 servers. The default is 10. |
| X11Forwarding | Specifies whether X11 forwarding is permitted. The argument must be "yes" or "no". The default is "no". When X11 forwarding is enabled, there may be additional exposure to the server and to client displays if the sshd(8) proxy display is configured to listen on the wildcard address (see X11UseLocalhost below), though this is not the default. Additionally, the |

	authentication spoofing and authentication data verification and substitution occur on the client side. The security risk of using X11 forwarding is that the client's X11 display server may be exposed to attack when the SSH client requests forwarding (see the warnings for ForwardX11 in ssh_config(5)). A system administrator may have a stance in which they want to protect clients that may ultimately expose themselves to attack by unwittingly requesting X11 forwarding, which can warrant a "no" setting. Note that disabling X11 forwarding does not prevent users from forwarding X11 traffic, as users can always install their own forwarders. X11 forwarding is automatically disabled if UseLogin is enabled.
X11UseLocalhost	Specifies whether sshd(8) should bind the X11 forwarding server to the loopback address or to the wildcard address. By default, sshd binds the forwarding server to the loopback address and sets the hostname part of the DISPLAY environment variable to "localhost". This prevents remote hosts from connecting to the proxy display. However, some older X11 clients may not function with this configuration. X11UseLocalhost may be set to "no" to specify that the forwarding server should be bound to the wildcard address. The argument must be "yes" or "no". The default is "yes".
X11Forwarding yes	If on an SSH server X11 forwarding is not enabled (enabled is the default in most cases on the SSH server), change the following option in the /etc/ssh/sshd_config file to "yes".

The best way to do X forwarding from your client is by using the command line. This is a better method rather than opening up your client to X attacks by configuring a global option for all of the users in the SSH client /etc/ssh_config file. We can just establish an X11 connection with our SSH server by typing:

```
$ ssh -X <userID>@<yourdomainname>.dyndns.<extension>
```

and then run our favorite GUI programs on the command line such as:

```
$ firefox &     or,     thunderbird &
```

The "&" tells these applications to run in the background thus freeing up the terminal window to run other software. These applications will use the resources of your SSH server and the hotspot Internet connection. If your hotspot has limited throughput, then using X11 forwarding may appear slow. Consider using a Long Term Support (LTS) version of Linux as your SSH server, which Ubuntu and Mint support. There are many programs such as Firefox or Thunderbird that come in the basic release of the OS. Subsequently, and with some exceptions, there is little need to load it up with many other applications that may not work. In addition, even though we can run Internet applications on our SSH server, we should do so only on the rare occasion that it is totally necessary. For example, we probably want a fully functional version of LibreOffice to edit remote documents, though when I ran earlier versions of LibreOffice, I got the following error:

```
Please ensure that a JVM and the package libreoffice-java-common are installed.
```

Back in the chapter on virtualization, I covered how to download or install LibreOffice in the various flavors of Linux. We want LibreOffice fully functional on our server so we can edit documents remotely for convenience. If you are using Fedora, the recommended method is to download LibreOffice from https://www.libreoffice.org/download and install it using YUM. In Ubuntu, just apply the first round of suggested additions to LibreOffice. If you download LibreOffice to your SSH client, you can use the following to copy the files to your SSH server as root:

```
# scp LibO* <mydomainname>.dyndns.org:/root/Downloads
```

We can also do this more securely by kicking off individual applications on our SSH server. Below are some examples of applications that you can run on your remote server with X11 forwarding:

```
$ ssh -fTXC <UserID>@<yourdomainname>.dyndns.<extention> (firefox,
libreoffice, libreoffice --calc, libreoffice --draw, libreoffice --impress,
libreoffice --math, libreoffice --web, libreoffice --writer, thunderbird, wireshark,
xcalc, xclock, xedit, xeyes, xterm)
```

Using this technique worked very well in Fedora, Mint Cinnamon, Mint KDE, Ubuntu and other flavors of Linux. However, after applying updates and installing software on some VMs, X11 forwarding would no longer work when connecting to my Ubuntu SSH server. You may have to experiment to see what may break X11 forwarding to your VM if you need it for your mobile devices. Most of the options above have been covered, but let's talk about them again.

-C	Requests compression of all data (including stdin, stdout, stderr, and data for forwarded X11 and TCP connections).
-f (only works in Linux)	Requests SSH to go to background just before command execution. This is useful if SSH is going to ask for passwords or passphrases, but the user wants it in the background. This implies -n. The recommended ways to start X11 programs at a remote site are with something like ssh -f host xterm. If the ExitOnForwardFailure configuration option is set to "yes", then a client that started with -f will wait for all remote port forwards to be successfully established before placing itself in the background.
-T	Disable pseudo-tty allocation.
-X	Enables X11 forwarding. This can also be specified on a per-host basis in a configuration file.
-Y	I call this the nuclear option. Enables trusted X11 forwarding. Trusted X11 forwarding's are not subjected to the X11 SECURITY extension controls.

On the client side, we can use the command line or specify the "ForwardX11 yes" option in the /etc/ssh/ssh_config file. Setting this option is our most secure form of X11 global forwarding. Most applications should work with this more secure form of X11 forwarding. However, setting this option globally is not recommended because X11 forwarding can also be done using the command line. Why open up a global client security hole when it is not necessary?

The somewhat secure command line version above will open up a Firefox browser and many other applications that are running on your SSH server through an encrypted SSH tunnel and render the graphics on your remote Internet device. Depending on your server's power and connection speed, this may slow things down a bit, but it is a fairly secure solution. This enables you to run applications that you don't need to have installed on your client. In the old days, this was the way things were done; we used powerful servers to run our applications and kept our primitive client devices free just to render the graphics. Imagine a world where, if your employee's laptop is stolen, the only thing we have to do is delete their SSH server public key and there is no threat to the computers behind our firewall since there was no data on their mobile device to be compromised. Why can't we compromise and somewhat return to this model, be more secure while traveling, and save money on our remote devices?

Suppose we need an application that uses X library functions that are not in the secure subset; that application will crash using this technique. To get these applications to work we have to resort to something called Trusted X11 Forwarding. Using the trusted form will allow applications to run the full set of X functions, but opens up your local system to attack. This is much less secure than secure X11 forwarding and many computer professionals feel it should never be used. *"Trusted X11 permits all X functions. An intruder on the SSH server can capture everything on your local screen and your every keystroke. Be really, really sure you trust every single remote server you might ever log into before permitting this level to trust globally. And once you're absolutely certain - don't do it."*[6] Even doing this from the command line is not usually necessary. There are a few troubleshooting steps to try first:

1. Login on your client and type la or ls -la; when you see the .Xauthority file, delete it. You can also try deleting this file on your SSH server account. Reboot or logout on either, login again, and it will be recreated (backup first). This will sometimes solve problems with X11 forwarding.
2. Try resetting your host key relationship if you have not copied your public key to the SSH server. Type rm -rf .ssh from the $HOME directory. This will force the SSH server to reset your *$HOME/.ssh/known_hosts* file.
3. The last, worst option is to use Trusted X11 forwarding.

An update, upgrade or configuration item sometimes breaks X11 -X forwarding and sometimes "-Y" (trusted forwarding will work). Nevertheless, if at all possible, try not to open up this security hole; simply rebuild your VM or OS and most likely everything will work again. I realize that this nuclear option is not always available, but when setting up Linux OSs for users, make plans to be able to do this. For convenience, we can also enable this option globally by specifying "ForwardX11Trusted yes" option in the */etc/ssh/ssh_config* file, but consider using the command line, which does not open up this global security hole.

```
$ ssh -Y <username>@<remote/ssh server or domain>
```

In Windows, we can use PuTTY to do X11 forwarding but Windows does not come with an X server by default. There are many X options to choose from for Windows, like Cygwin/X, Xming, WeirdX, Mocha X Server, and proprietary products like Xmanager, Exceed, eXcursion

(Hewlett-Packard), MKS X/Server, Reflection X, X-Win32 and Xming (current version). With the ability to virtualize a Linux OS on top of Windows in a guest OS, I chose not to present a Windows X server. I feel using virtualization with a modern Linux OS is a more secure and far easier solution.

GNOME Secure Shell Tunnel Manager -- Graphical Tool to Manage Tunnels in Linux

The GNOME Desktop provides a front-end graphical tool to configure and manage secure shell tunneled port redirects. The GNOME Secure Shell Tunnel Manager (GSTM) does not come installed by default. To install it, become 'root' and type the following:

apt-get install gstm -y

Now we can login as our Linux tunnel user ID and start gSTM from the graphical menu or from the command line by typing # gstm, which will bring up the SSH Tunnel Manager. *Click on the **Add** button and type a name for your tunnel (e.g. **dSTMSSHUserDynTun**), which will bring up the **Tunnel configuration** screen > enter Host: (e.g. **yourdomainname.dyndns.com**), **Login:** (e.g. **gstmssh**), **Port:** defaults to **22**, check **Autostart** if we want this tunnel every time we log in as this user, **Privkey: (optional)** warrants further explanation, click on the **Add** button. When you click on OK this will open up a tunnel to your SSH server.*

To fill in the Privkey: field, refer down to the section on SSH Public/Private Key Establishment Between an SSH Client & SSH Server to learn how to set this up. Briefly, we will generate a key pair using $ ssh-keygen -b 4096 and then use the $ ssh-copy-id <UserID>@yourdomainname.dyndns.com command to install your public key on the SSH server. Depending on how your SSH server administrator setup your account, you may have to login and establish your password before you can use a script like *ssh-copy-id*. If you see the warning:

WARNING: Your password has expired.
Password change required but no TTY available.

Login using $ ssh <UserID>@yourdomainname.dyndns.com and setup your connection password then run *ssh-copy-id*. If you see:
Permission denied, please try again.

Make sure that you typed the correct SSH user ID for the server to which you are connecting. To copy the private key into gSTM $ cd ~/.ssh and cut and paste the contents of the file id_rsa between "-----BEGIN RSA PRIVATE KEY-----" and "----END RSA PRIVATE KEY-----" into the Privkey: (optional) field in GSTM. When you establish the tunnel, you will see a green dot indicating that the tunnel is established. Using a public/private key combination makes the whole tunnel process extremely convenient and easily automated.

Below is a sample configuration that you can set up for your tunnel. This configuration will create a dynamic tunnel on port 8080 for your client, which you can have started automatically.

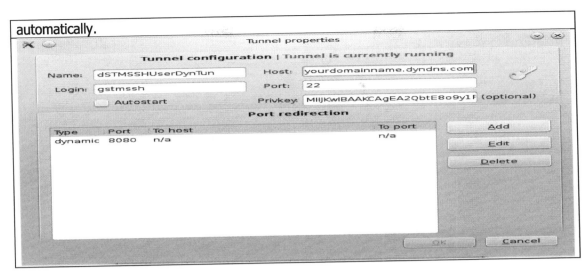

GSTM is a very simplistic tool without much versatility, but it is very simple to use, and you can quickly establish many automatically activated tunnels as well.

Securing Windows Live OneDrive and Other Internet Applications on Your Mobile Device while on the Road to Keep Them from Automatically Connecting to a Public Network

If you use any sort of sky drive or Internet application, you don't want your mobile device using hotspots to automatically send unencrypted files, information and data back and forth over the Internet. Imagine if a cracker captured my laptop, sending my eight years' worth of work on this book over a public Internet hotspot. To write this book I used the now deprecated Windows Live Mesh, https://en.wikipedia.org/wiki/Windows_Live_Core, and later SpiderOak, to keep my various computers synchronized up to latest version of this book and my research. Mesh was discontinued on February 13, 2013, so I had to consider other alternatives. Microsoft now offers what they call their OneDrive service. With Mesh, turning off communication with the Internet was not transparent, and the only solution found by this author was by blocking the Mesh ports, something an HCU/SBO may not know how to do. The truth is, for applications like the deprecated Mesh, this should have been as simple as a double click on the icon and selecting something like stop synchronizing.

I did not investigate to see if this problem continued with the new Windows OneDrive as I switched to SpiderOak, which keeps my data encrypted. Some other applications are deceptive by offering up GUI options that make you think that you are turning off all processes that are running in the background, but upon further investigation, you will find that the processes or services are still running.

Another good example is to look at the free LightScribe tools that you can download and use to burn images on to LightScribe CDs and DVDs. ***Running the <u>LightScribe Control Panel</u> will allow you to uncheck the <u>Display notification messages</u> and <u>Run this program when I log on to Windows</u>***. However, if you examine the services running on your computer, you will discover that the <u>LightScribe Direct Disc Labeling Service</u> is still running in the background on your computer doing who knows what.

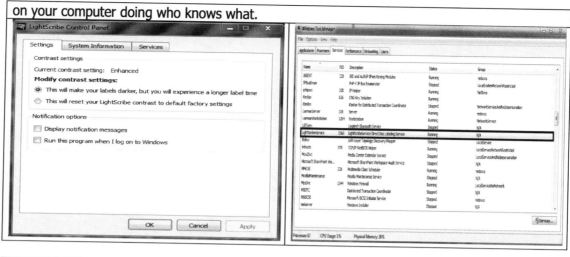

There are many other examples of applications that hang around in the background after turning off options that should disable all background activity. Adobe and Oracle offer <u>Control Panel</u> options where you can turn off automatic updates; however, doing so left the Adobe Updater service and the Java™ Update Scheduler, "jusched.exe" still running in the background. You can use a tool such as CCleaner to disable the processes from running the background.

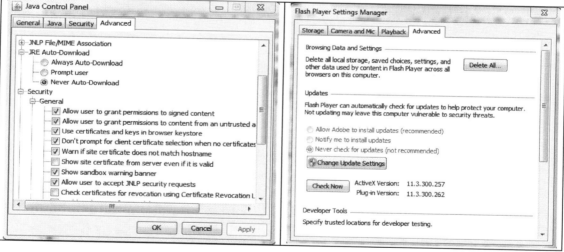

Please note that these examples are a small subset of overall problems. There are many more processes and questionable services running in the background. An excellent tool by Mark Russinovich and Bryce Cogswell for viewing everything starting up in the Windows background is the <u>autoruns</u> application, which can be downloaded and used from <u>http://technet.microsoft.com/en-us/sysinternals/bb963902.aspx</u>. By using this tool, combined with Windows Task Manager, it was easy to determine that the old Windows Live Mesh background processes were MOE.exe and WLSync.exe. *We could get the same information by clicking on __Start__ > arrow over to __Run__ > type __msconfig__ > and select the __Startup__ tab.* You could stop Mesh from starting by scrolling down to the Startup Item <u>Windows Live Mesh</u> and unchecking it. Although, if you later double click on the Windows Live Mesh icon or want to use Mesh, you would have to do this over and over again.

 **Historical Reference – The Deprecated Mesh Application in Windows 7.**

In my case, as soon as I ran Window Live Mesh again, it would create a new startup entry in addition to the unchecked entry. No matter how many times I restarted the computer I would see one unchecked and one checked <u>Windows Live Mesh</u> entry. To get things back to normal I checked both Windows Live Mesh entries in the startup menu and restarted. This cleaned things up for using Mesh. Given this example, it is easy to see that stopping applications one by one from communicating with the Internet is the *long way* around to protecting our mobile devices and beyond anyone's time to investigate and read about. We have to question why corporations are making this process so difficult.

If you want to use an OneDrive, you should consider tunneling the ports and protocol that your OneDrive uses. This can be done by using an SSH tunnel as we did with our web browser and will soon do with our email ports. Discovering which ports an OneDrive is using is not simple. Searching the Internet and Microsoft's support pages only provided the obsolete Mesh ports from 2008 in the range of 30000 to 40000 as a possibility. Running C:\...\netstat -ano at the command prompt showed no ports open in this range. Running C:\...\netstat -b as administrator revealed the Mesh ports were 49570 and 49571, before Microsoft replaced it with SkyDrive and then OneDrive. ***You do this by clicking on <u>Start</u> > <u>All Programs</u> > <u>Accessories</u> > right click on <u>Command Prompt</u> > and select <u>Run as administrator</u>.***

Another layer of security for your mobile device is to lock down your applications' public use of the Internet using your software firewall. ***Click on <u>Start</u> > <u>Control Panel</u> > <u>Windows Firewall</u> > on the left panel click on <u>Allow a program or feature through Windows Firewall</u> > click on the <u>Change settings</u> button, top right > scroll down to applications such as <u>Microsoft SkyDrive</u> , <u>Windows Live Messenger</u>, and uncheck the <u>Public</u> check box > <u>OK</u>.*** This is supposed to prevent those applications from using public hotspot Internet connections.

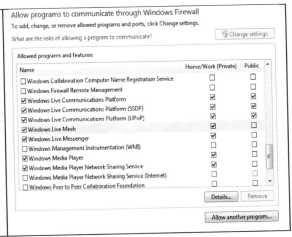

 **Tip** — Anytime you have process running in the background that you don't need you should investigate how to remove the application completely. This is the only way to ensure that it does not have multiple ways of starting up and reviving itself. For example, Windows Live Mesh and Windows Live Messenger had a tenacious way of hanging around until Windows Live 2011 was completely uninstalled.

NOTE — When installing Windows Essentials 2012, it said that it would uninstall their deprecated Mesh product and install the SkyDrive software. Upon review of the firewall rules, it still had Mesh in the firewall rules and had

 the public port for Mesh open. Check the private box and make sure Windows Live Mesh is unchecked under Name.

Uninstalling Mesh, Microsoft had a rule that still allowed public connections to the removed Mesh application. These rules need to be enabled to block these ports. *Click on Start > Control Panel > Windows Firewall > on the left panel Advanced settings > on the left panel select Inbound Rules > scroll down to select the Windows Live Mesh rules > on the right panel click on Enable Rule > for Action select Block.*

If you still have the deprecated Microsoft Mesh installed, you can also block Mesh by *clicking on the Windows Live Mesh rule > on the right click on Properties > at the bottom tick Block the connection. Windows Live Messenger was also deprecated as of March 2013. If you have firewall rules, block Windows Live Messenger as well.* If you needed to have any other applications that you want to work using ports while traveling, you can use Local Port Forwarding to tunnel those ports. Refer back to the section on SSH Clients to add PuTTY to the system path if you have not already done so. We will be putting together a comprehensive LPF tunnel script so that if you only need to use OneDrive while on the road, the coming port tunnel will work just fine. We could also use the command line, which is what we need for scripting a CMD file. The command below is used to tunnel the Mesh ports:

```
C:\...\plink.exe -ssh -2 -P 22 -N -l sshdynlocal youdyndnsdomainname.dyndns.org -L
127.0.0.1:49570:127.0.0.1:49570 -L 127.0.0.1:49571:127.0.0.1:49571
```

WARNING	As physics majors know, scientific methods require multiple independent verifications of this tunneling method. To do that would require blocking the Mesh ports and tunneling other ports. There is/was no apparent way to reconfigure Mesh to use other ports. The only choice was to tunnel the original Mesh ports, which meant that I could not definitively limit the actual ports that were tunneled successfully or determine if my mobile device was still serving up those ports to the hotspot. Tunneling the Mesh ports appeared to be successful, and by experimenting with tunneling other ports later, I concluded that this technique was working as documented by the open source application developers with their SSH software.

Thunderbird – Setting Up Gmail in a Linux VM

All Internet activity on any device connected to the Internet should be conducted virtually, especially when viewing your email. Email is one of the top providers of serving up malware to your computer. If you read your email in a virtual environment, you will keep your core OS safe from many threats on the Internet.

Linux comes packaged with excellent email client software for reading your email. They are very easy to set up and use. This book only covers the popular Thunderbird application. *In Ubuntu click on Dash Home upper left > in the Search box type Thunderbird > drag and drop the Thunderbird*  *icon onto the quick launch bar on the left > click the Thunderbird icon to launch the application. In Mint click on the start menu lower left >*

arrow up to highlight the __Internet__ icon > arrow right to highlight and right click on the __Thunderbird Mail__ icon > click on __Add to panel__ and/or __Add to Desktop__ and/or __Add to favorites__.

Create a new email by clicking on __File__ > __New__ > arrow down to select Get a New Mail Account... > if this is not a new email address click on __Skip this and use my existing email__ > the __Mail Account Setup__ screen will appear, (enter __Your name:__, __Email address:__, and __Password:__), click on the __Continue__ button > Thunderbird is very good at automatic configuration and it configured everything needed to access my Gmail account > click on the __Create Account__ button and everything was then setup to use my email.	

With email set up in a VM, we can now automate the securing of our mobile device using Local Port Forwarding (LPF), which is our ticket to allow Internet applications to use hotspots securely, everywhere.

Thunderbird & Windows Live Mail – Setting up Gmail to Use an SSH Tunnel

Gmail uses outgoing SSL (SMTP) port 465 and its Incoming SSL (IMAP) port 993 to communicate with its server. This email communication is already encrypted, so tunneling these ports using LPF is another layer of hardening our security. It is also a method of viewing your email if you need to bypass a firewall or proxy*. Suppose you work for corporation X and they block ports 465 and 993. You can set up your laptop to use virtualization, install a Linux VM, and run that on the corporate network with your Gmail account preconfigured. To make all of this work, we have to make some configuration changes to Gmail and script an SSH tunnel to our SSH server.

In Thunderbird click on __Edit__ > arrow down to select __Account Settings...__ > click on __Server Settings__ > change the Server Name: from __imap.googlemail.com__ to __localhost__, change the port to something that is not blocked by your firewall.

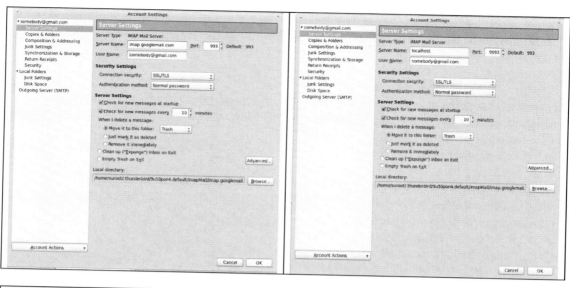

Click on _Outgoing Server (SMTP)_ on the bottom > click on the _Edit..._ button > change the _Server Name:_ from _smtp.googlemail.com_ to _localhost_, change the port to something not blocked by your firewall.

Back in the section on software firewalls, we learned how to block ports on our Internet device. Refer back to that section and enable your port blocking rules so we can test Thunderbird Gmail using our new ports and localhost configuration. Use the following script or command line from your VM or Linux OS to create an SSH tunnel to your home server:

```
$ ssh -N -l sshdynlocal youdyndnsdomainname.dyndns.org -L
127.0.0.1:4465:smtp.googlemail.com:465 127.0.0.1:9993:imap.googlemail.com:993
```

| **NOTE** | Tunneling the ports on your core OS using Putty's plink tool will not work for the VMs installed on your computer. Each VM would have to be individually tunneled from the VM OS. |

If you are using Windows as your VM or have to tunnel from a Windows core OS, the same technique can be used to get your Gmail.

From Windows Live Mail, click on the down arrow upper left > arrow down to __Options__ > arrow up to select __Email accounts...__ > select your Gmail account and click on the __Properties__ button on the right > select the __Servers__ tab and change __Incoming mail (IMAP):__ from __imap.gmail.com__ to __localhost__ > change the __Outgoing mail (SMTP):__ from __smtp.gmail.com__ to __localhost__.

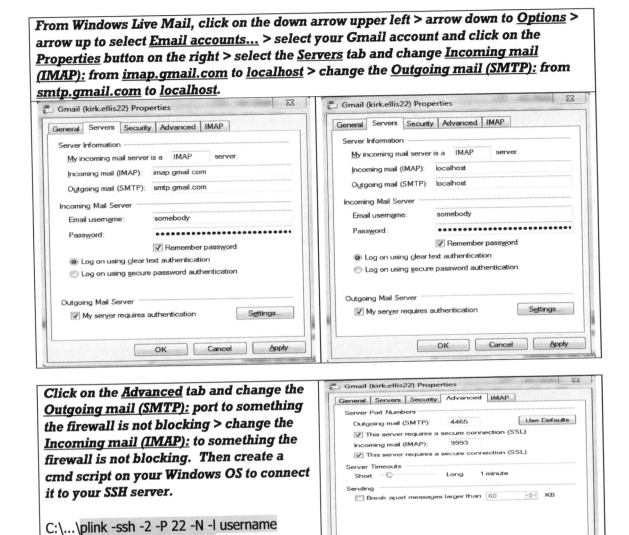

Click on the __Advanced__ tab and change the __Outgoing mail (SMTP):__ port to something the firewall is not blocking > change the __Incoming mail (IMAP):__ to something the firewall is not blocking. Then create a cmd script on your Windows OS to connect it to your SSH server.

C:\...\plink -ssh -2 -P 22 -N -l username
yourdomainname.dyndns.org
127.0.0.1:4465:smtp.gmail.com:465 -L
127.0.0.1:9933:imap.gmail.com:993 -L

As you can see, setting up tunnels and using port forwarding requires changes to the configurations of most Internet applications. Think again about what we are doing; much like tunneling web page's addresses, we are tunneling email's outgoing and incoming server IP/HTTP addresses. We are setting our mobile device to use a local optional port and forward it to the remote HTTP address and port. If we have a laptop and we want to use hotspots, we can setup a VM with all our applications and script the connection to our home SSH server. Originally, I was going to propose a separate SSH VM in the virtualization chapter, which you can still do, but why not just setup a General Purpose VM to use as your tunnel VM OS? For most of us getting our email and browser to work using our tunnels is sufficient. If you do not have to bypass a firewall, sometimes tunneling the normal ports will work. For example:

```
C:\...\plink -ssh -2 -P 22 -N -l username yourdomainname.dyndns.org -L
993:imap.gmail.com:993 -L 465:smtp.gmail.com:465 -D 18080
```

Using an SSH Tunnel to Forward Email Ports and Use Dynamic Port Forwarding for the Web Browser to Keep Your Laptop Secure while on the Road

To keep your mobile device secure while traveling refer back to <u>Using Software Firewalls to Harden Security and Block Ports</u>. If there are services that you don't need while on the road, enabling software firewall rules is by far the quickest and easiest way to keep your laptop secure. However, if you need those services, we don't want these services on our mobile device accessing the Internet except through our encrypted SSH tunnel. Below is a command script that will accomplish that goal if you need to use hotspots with services that you don't want to block.

Most Internet mail is unencrypted. An email service such as Hotmail, which does not use HTTPS, is very open to snooping. Google's Gmail, which uses HTTPS throughout the Webmail session, is more secure for your correspondence. Or course, as we talked about, using an encrypted email service that does not exploit your information is better yet!
If you are not going to block the ports on your laptop, you have to discover and tunnel every email application and browser port to your home SSH server so you can get email, surf the web, and do everything in Windows from anywhere, totally secure. Below is an example SSH script for doing just that once your SSH Server is set up:

```
echo off
REM
REM Download OpenSSH for Windows from http://sshwindows.sourceforge.net or
REM use Putty's PLINK.EXE from
REM http://www.chiark.greenend.org.uk/~sgtatham/putty/download.html
REM
REM This sets up a tunnel for Windows 7 Browsers:
REM
REM Tools > Internet Options > Connections Tab > LAN Settings button
REM Click on "Use a proxy server for your LAN" check box.
REM Click on "Advanced" button.
REM
REM Enter 127.0.0.1 in the SOCKS5 box. Port 18080.
REM
REM This sets up a tunnel for all email ports:
REM
REM Forwarded port TCP UDP Description Status
REM
REM 22  TCP UDP Secure Shell (SSH) used for secure logins, file transfers (scp,
REM   sftp) and port forwarding - Official
```

```
REM 25  TCP    Simple Mail Transfer Protocol (SMTP) used for email routing
REM     between mail servers - Official
REM 80  TCP UDP Hypertext Transfer Protocol (HTTP) - Official
REM 110 TCP UDP Post Office Protocol v3 (POP3) - Official
REM 143 TCP UDP Internet Message Access Protocol (IMAP) management of email
REM     messages - Official
REM 220 TCP UDP Internet Message Access Protocol (IMAP), version 3 - Official
REM 443 TCP  HTTPS (Hypertext Transfer Protocol over SSL/TLS) - Official
REM 465 TCP  SMTP over SSL - Unofficial
REM 587 TCP  email message submission[18] (SMTP) - Official
REM 993 TCP UDP Internet Message Access Protocol over SSL (IMAPS) - Official
REM 995 TCP UDP Post Office Protocol 3 over TLS/SSL (POP3S) - Official
REM

if defined ProgramFiles(x86) (
  set sshdir="%ProgramFiles(x86)%\OpenSSH\bin"
  set sshpg="%ProgramFiles(x86)%\OpenSSH\bin\ssh"
  echo Running script on 64 bit machine..."
) ELSE (
  set sshdir="%ProgramFiles%\OpenSSH\bin"
  set sshpg="%ProgramFiles%\OpenSSH\bin\ssh"
  echo Running script on 32 bit machine...
)

set strSSHServer=yourdomainname.dyndns.(com, org, edu, etc.)

%sshpg% -N -l username -L 25:%strSSHServer%:25 -L 110:%strSSHServer%:110 -L
143:%strSSHServer%:143 -L 220:%strSSHServer%:220 -L 587:%strSSHServer%:587 -L
993:%strSSHServer%:993 -L 995:%strSSHServer%:995 -D 18080 %strSSHServer%

pause
exit 0
```

Another option is to use PuTTY's plink client software. Below is the scripting for using PuTTY's plink binary:

```
set plinkdir="%ProgramFiles(x86)%\PuTTY"
set plinkpg="%ProgramFiles(x86)%\PuTTY\plink"
set strSSHServer=yourdomainname.dyndns.(com, org, edu, etc.)

%plinkpg% -ssh -2 -P 22 -N -l sshdynlocal -L 25:%strSSHServer%:25 -L
110:%strSSHServer%:110 -L 143:%strSSHServer%:143 -L 220:%strSSHServer%:220 -L
587:%strSSHServer%:587 -L 993:%strSSHServer%:993 -L 995:%strSSHServer%:995 -L
49570:127.0.0.1:49570 -L 49571:127.0.0.1:49571 -D 18080 yourusername@%strSSHServer%
```

```
pause
exit 0
```

SSH Server – Secure Connections & File Transfer Using SSH Public & Private Keys

You never again have to send unsecure email attachments to friends, customers, partners, or relatives. Emails and their attachments bounce from email server to email server where copies of them can be made for later review by crackers. Many people assume that encrypting a document to a password, which Microsoft Word allows you to do, is sufficient for document security. However, crackers can make a copy of that attachment and then spend infinite amounts of time finding the password or breaking the encryption on that document. Let me repeat this, NO KNOWN FORM OF ENCRYPTION IS SECURE FROM INFINITE amounts of computer power. Consequently, the cracker can just run some cracking software, thus attacking your document(s) and walk away; that software will attack your document(s) 24/7 for as long as it takes. This is why you want a direct link with your business partners, so you can exchange data without these middlemen potentially breaking your security, of which many HCU/SBOs have none.

You need a secure SSH server so that your customers, clients, relatives, etc. can send and receive files to/from you securely. We have already talked about the benefits of the tunneling that your HCU/SBO SSH server provides, but suppose you have a need to exchange data files with your partners securely. Depending on the level of trust between you and your partners, there are various ways we can set up our HCU/SBO SSH server to do this and use it as an inexpensive tunneling device as well. This old PC is becoming more and more valuable behind our secure hardware firewall and into our local network. For example, we may just want to setup a simple SSH public/private key relationship to allow for the exchange of files with trusted partners. To make things easy for everyone, we won't make our partners enter a password every time they log in or jump through hoops to exchange data.

WARNING	The SSH passphrase is an added layer of security that you should consider having your partners use. If somehow your partner's mobile device is compromised, the crackers will be in possession of their private key. Without a passphrase this gives them unrestricted access to your SSH server unless you alter their account on your server. If you do require a passphrase, and even though the cracker has your partner's private key, they will also have to figure out the passphrase in order to attack your SSH server. This will give you more time to lock things down so all the cracker has is a new toy. I hope you can see that this is much more secure than just using password authentication. However, requiring a passphrase makes things such as automating file transfers and other functions between the client and the server, more difficult. If automation is

	not needed or required, have your partners enter a passphrase.

There are options that will allow scripting when using a passphrase. We will discuss that in the next section. When we login to an SSH Server that requires a passphrase, we will see:

```
sshagent@ubuntu:~$ ssh sshagent@<yourdomainname.dyndns.<extension>
Enter passphrase for key '/home/sshagent/.ssh/id_rsa':
```

You might be asking yourself if all this effort in setting up and using an SBO/HCU SSH server is worth the effort, but consider the alternative. Do you want your employees, partners or family members exposing your/their data to questionable corporations (paid middle men) who may not have everyone's best interests at heart? In addition these cloud corporations, like the Internet search engines, can be subpoenaed by the government (or may have other agendas) to reveal every bit of data you have ever housed or passed through their servers. Moreover, we would have to trust in their security measures, which are being cracked regularly. I'm not suggesting that anything we put there was/is illegal, or that these cloud computing entities don't have our best interests for our home or business in mind, but you must diligently study their privacy policy, data retention policies, encryption techniques, and revelation policies to their affiliates and their governments, as these privacy protections suggested on their websites can change as rapidly as political climates change. Every day, it appears our constitution is being rewritten by the courts, Congress or whichever administration is in office. If you don't know all the facts which suggest using cloud computing for your business may not be in your best interests, know that there are many. No one can keep up with how things keep changing! My opinion is that we need to minimize this easy invasion of our privacy by not housing our data out on/in the cloud. We can manage the exchange of our data in-house to make sure it is not being compromised by a cloud-computing third party. I am presenting encrypted solutions to house your data locally, so you should consider using them first.

To keep it simple and make it easy for our partners, we can set up an SSH server to allow them to be able to reset or change the assigned administrator password used to initially log in with, which is insecure, to one that we can provide as something they will maintain. Since we have 'root' access on our server, we have no need to know their password setup, and once all of our partner relationships are established we should consider disabling password entry into our SSH server, which I will show you how to do later. As we set out to improve the use of our SSH server beyond tunnels let's consider what our requirements are. I drafted a simple set of requirements that we will steadily make more complex as this chapter progresses; this is akin to how the software development takes place at large entities. I present this example to demonstrate how, as an HCU/SBO, you cannot allow this type of creep to affect your expenses. Everyone's needs are different, and while this book can't cover every situation, I believe that this and the following sections of this book will be enough for you to adapt them to your circumstances.

In the IT world, when we start a project in which we are supposed to produce a product or outcome, we have to draft a document that is known as a Requirements Definition. This step is often (usually) not done and the lack of this formal definition results in project creep, which creates a lot of agony for IT professionals and expense for the large entities for whom they are working. After the Requirements Definition, the next step in any project is to create a straw man prototype, which is meant to be thrown away completely, but this has never happened in my 28 years' experience in the large entity world. Wanting quick results, once large corporations and government management see these prototypes they do not permit the developers to start over from scratch, which in college theory was always supposed to happen. By proceeding with the development of a flawed straw man prototype, these projects take far longer to compete than would normally have been necessary to complete. This is because these prototypes are riddled with flaws and have had corners cut, just to present a concept; they have no foundation. This is similar to building a house of plywood and two-by-fours and never pouring a foundation, much like Hollywood or a play does for screen sets. What we, as computer professionals, present is smoke and mirrors to show a proof of concept, not a basis from which to proceed with the project. Nevertheless, large entities want to run with these prototypes and can absorb these extra costs easily. Therefore, government and corporate contract companies, knowing that this is not in their customer's best interest, instruct their staff to proceed with these misguided prototypes work and milk their deep-pocketed paying customers for many extra hours of paid work. In government contracting, for the executives of those companies that are inside the Washington Beltway, this makes them tons of money and prolongs these projects far beyond what would have been required had the uninformed politicians been instructed in a very basic understanding of how a computer software project progresses. So let's examine that requirements creep, because as an HCU/SBO, you cannot afford to make this mistake. If you hire someone and they show you a straw man, allow them to start over from scratch!

Story	While maintaining a Computer Integrated Manufacturing system at a large corporation, I was tasked with helping to find an off-the-shelf computer messaging bus that would replace a custom message bus that manufacturing devices used to communicate. I maintained the custom socket-based message bus that various computers and manufacturing devices used to communicate with each other. I was part of a team that evaluated 12 communication-based products. We had vendors jumping through hoops for over a year in this large corporate business in which the smaller, startup IT companies had even customized their software to meet our needs. Our large team of corporate computer scientists finally presented a "top twelve" list to corporate management, demonstrating the pros and cons of the off-the-shelf products. At the expense of many vendor and employee hours of labor, we had working prototypes for the top two. Then a salesman came in from Digital Corporation and pitched their product to a high-level manager (I can name them because Digital Corp. is now out of business and I won't be sued). Digital's solution was number 12, at the bottom of our evaluation list, and we found it was not a viable technical solution that would meet our needs. However, this one-day presentation, lunch and dinner (and probably a nice backdoor exchange of funds), resulted in the purchase of over one million dollars of Digital's product, which was piled into a closet near my office and later thrown away in the garbage. To my knowledge, no repercussions resulted from this ineptitude or corruption, but for me this was this was a revelation in corporate greed and corruption.

Of course, I said nothing because I wanted to keep my job for a few more years,

but as fate would have it cutbacks q would not compensate my contract company the $110 rate it was charging the company for my time. I offered to work for that same car company as an employee for $35 an hour, but my signed contract would not allow that. It took many years of life and nearly dying of cancer to understand these things. These contract companies are often times owned by these companies' executives' friends and relatives. So charging huge salaries to the contract companies is a boon for everyone in their system of influence. All I wanted was a better salary, which would have committed me to greater loyalty to the large entities for which I was working. You have to understand in today's world, these corporate contract companies are owned by the family members/relatives/or business partners that the executives of the company know. Having worked for both, and being easily disposed of by both, this high-paid contractor system now makes much more sense to me. However, at that time in the past, this car company did not see an IT department as part of their core business and was seeking to outsource 70% of its IT labor (as much as possible to be exported and imported to/from overseas). Six months after my contract company had laid me off, I was rehired as a UNIX guru, and at that time knew nothing about Windows and my contract company was a Windows shop. I was later brought back in with another high paid contract company as a UNIX administrator at the same company. This whole outsource strategy eventually backfired on the car company. Imagine for yourself that these multi-million dollar paid executives could not see this coming, where 70% of their IT staff were/are under paid, had access to all their data, which could be given to criminals and competitors for money, they also had no loyalty to their company and cared nothing about their business. These ill-advised US corporations only had only a few honest workers left of which would leave on a dime for other, more lucrative employment (especially after that same company paid to train them on many things essential to their business, but were also essential to their competitors). Who could have understood this obvious out-flux of talent that would take place?

One would think it would be obvious that these assets are necessary to protect their confidential data and should not be contracted out to foreign nationals or the lowest, unscrupulous bidder. Information Technology is not something that we should ship overseas, which is exactly what keeps happening in US corporations. For example, as a contractor I received $26,000 in paid training, which I very much appreciated, and tried desperately to become an employee at the corporation for whom I was working. They would not hire me as an employee, so my only choice was to market those skills outside the business to the highest bidder, which kept going up in price. In the organizations I have worked for and been replaced in, the applications I worked on made me privy to everyone's social security numbers, birth dates, salaries of corporate executives, and all other data maintained by these organizations. Over a ten-year period, my example car company eventually converted back to a 70-30 employee/contractor relationship, although we all now know the history of the car companies as well as many big corporations. It was a great job working for the same car company; I was working there until my military service dragged me down to Keesler Air Force Base for Electronic Warfare Training. One last thought on this topic, once my

> military service was complete I went to work for another American car company parts manufacturer. In this company, I was privy to the confidential information of everyone employed by the company. I was eventually replaced by three low-paid foreign nationals, who were brought in on a green card; they were also granted access to that information. I tend to think that low-paid personnel, not from this country, who have not served this country in war, will not have the same regard for that confidential information that I had. Your personal data in corporate America is not safe given these measures.

To catch a glimmer of the IT world that I know, during my 28-year IT career in all the various organizations that I have worked for and are detailed at the start of this book, I have never been asked to advise a corporate executive or high-level government official on how to improve their IT systems or security. The distance between IT professionals and extremely highly paid executives and the actual troops doing the front line work is a line that is rarely crossed. In contrast to this, high ranking officers in the military will occasionally converse with their troops for their ideas and feedback.

Story  	This also happens in the military. Let's take the example of the High Mobility Multipurpose Wheeled Vehicle (HMMWV), reference https://en.wikipedia.org/wiki/Humvee. During the time that I was serving in the Army as an MP, I was tasked with driving and protecting the company commander. Our unit had many HMMWVs but only a few Ford Broncos, so to keep my commander safe I always chose the Bronco. It was a GREAT vehicle; it was narrow, durable, and could travel anywhere. During these military exercises no one ever captured my company commander, due to the fact that his crazy driver (me) would take that Bronco places the HMMWVs could not go (many times scaring the hell out of him). In hindsight, I did risk our lives in some crazy driving that I probably should not have done in an exercise situation, but I treated those exercises as the real thing. If I had lost my commander to the make-believe enemy, I would have felt that I had failed in my mission. The design of the HMMWV was ludicrous for combat. It was too wide; while driving them through construction zones, our troops were constantly breaking off the mirrors. It had a vinyl doors and was not armored in any way, so the soldiers that were inside could be easily killed by small arms fire. The turret on top had no protection, so the troops that were on top trying to kill the enemy were vulnerable to any enemy fire. Lastly, the vehicles batteries were mounted under the passenger seat and in the desert when those batteries reached high temperatures, they emitted toxic fumes. If any high-level military officer or even the contract companies profiting from these vehicles ever questioned the common soldier, we would have told them they were crazy. Many American soldiers are now dead because of this type of stupidity. Whatever government official signed off on this should be in jail for the lives lost!

In the civilian world, I also have *never* seen this type of interaction. I have never met with, or ever recall having seen a high-level executive fired for wasting money or failing in their direction of expensive projects in any large organization for whom I have worked. It was similar during Operation Iraqi Freedom; I never met or saw my Air Force First Sergeant; I cannot even tell you his name. (This is not true in the Army or Marine Corps). Although, as an HCU/SBO, if it is unclear in what we are trying to accomplish, then there are many rabbit holes we could travel down before we have a usable tool, the expense of which is unacceptable.

In this instance the following is ***Requirements Definition 1***, which we will later build upon: Each company / partner / family member / friend shall have a separate account on our SSH server. They will generate a DSA, ECDSA or RSA key pair from their remote device (computer, laptop, mobile device, bootable USB drive, etc.) to transfer data files to/from our SSH server that is either running virtually or as a stand-alone server behind our private network's hardware firewall. Communication or the exchange of data shall solely be accomplished using the SSH protocol. The exchange between devices shall be encrypted with the private/public key pair, which allows the secure exchange of data to and from our SSH server, for our business/home to later process later. After the initial key pair setup that has been completed by our partners, no password shall be required to log into the server. If there is ever any question that your partner's private key has been compromised, the process below will be repeated to render any compromised keys invalid.

If you have not already done so, refer back to the section on installing OpenSSH Server to install the software. First, let's cover how to setup an SSH file transfer without the complications of a heightened security setup. If this is an SSH server for personal use, or one where we trust everyone using it, there is no need to add things like a CHROOT to our setup. Since there may be many user accounts to create, let's use a simple script to create our user accounts. The users will have to log in with a password the first time they login via *scp, sftp, or ssh* to the server and set up their private/public key relationship so we will make sure they change their common password upon login. This can be accomplished by using the *chage* command. The *chage* command is used to set the password expiration rules for the user. Let's get started setting up our SSH server for correspondence with our partners.

This following simple script, run as 'root' on our SSH Linux Server, can be used to create User IDs:

```
#!/bin/bash
#set -x      # Uncomment to debug script
# Script name createkeyserversshuser.sh.   SSH Server User addition script.
# $1  -  User ID being created.
# $2  -  Comment about the user ID contained in double quotes.

Usage ()
(
    echo "Usage:"
    echo "$0 <User Account>" "\"<User's full name or comment>\""
)
```

```
if [ "$#" -lt 2 ]
then
    Usage
    exit
fi


useradd -c "$2" -m $1 -s /bin/bash
mkdir /home/$1/.ssh && chown $1:$1 /home/$1/.ssh
chmod -R 700 /home/$1
passwd $1
chage -d 0 $1
chage -l $1
```

Refer back to <u>Adding Less Privileged User IDs for Specific Purposes to Linux</u> to understand what this simple script is doing.

```
# su - partnercompany
$ mkdir .ssh
$ chmod -R 700 $HOME
```

The chmod -R 700 $HOME is a little added security. Before we get into exchanging keys and such, let's briefly discuss what the script above did as the bare minimum we need to exchange files securely with our business partners. It created an account with your partner that they will need to connect to with the following information you need to provide them with:

- IP address or domain name of your SSH server
- Temporary username you created for them
- Temporary password you set up for them to change upon connection and login

There is one thing that may confuse them upon their initial SSH connection, which prompts with:

```
$ ssh tempuser@24.192.40.20
WARNING: Your password has expired.
You must change your password now and login again!
Changing password for tempuser.
(current) UNIX password: (put temp password here and bold it in your directions)
Enter new UNIX password:
Retype new UNIX password:
passwd: password updated successfully
Connection to 24.192.40.20 closed.


$ ssh tempuser@24.192.40.20
tempuser@24.192.40.20's password:
```

`Welcome to Ubuntu 12.04.4 LTS (GNU/Linux 3.2.0-30-generic-pae i686)`

I have found that often times people will enter what they want for their new password rather than the temporary password you provided them at this step. If they do that, they will not be able to set up their account and set their new password requiring you to recreate the account and explain this to them. It is best to put this in your directions initially so as avoid this unnecessary added work. Check the SSHD daemon configuration file **/etc/ssh/sshd_config** to make sure that the following options are set by default:

`LoginGraceTime 120`	From the man page, "*The server disconnects after this time if the user has not successfully logged in. If the value is 0, there is no time limit. The default is 120 seconds.*"
`PermitRootLogin yes`	From the man page, " *Specifies whether root can log in using ssh(1). The argument must be "yes", "without-password", "forced-commands-only", or "no". The default is "yes".*" Once everything is set up, we should set this option to "no" to disable root login to our SSH server.
`Protocol 2`	The OpenSSH daemon supports the legacy version 1 protocol and the much more secure version 2. The default is to use protocol 2 only. Protocol 2 supports DSA, ECDSA and RSA keys. The web page http://www.snailbook.com/faq/ssh-1-vs-2.auto.html documents the differences in a tabular format very well.
`StrictModes yes`	The *StrictModes* directive above instructs our server sshd daemon, documented at http://openssh.org/faq.html#3.14 to make sure the user account is not set up to be too permissive.

To make things easy, we want our partners to manage their own passwords. We have no interest in what they set their passwords to, and we may turn off password identification once all of our partners have logged in and set up their accounts. From the *chage* man page the options we used are as follows:

`-d 0`	Sets the number of days from January 1st, 1970 since the password was last changed. Setting this option to zero will force a password change upon first login.
`-l`	Shows the account aging information to make sure we set it correctly.

One of our requirements is to allow our partners to be able to log in and transfer files without having to enter a password. Our clients will have to generate a key pair and copy the public key to our server. All we have to do is provide each partner with a cheat sheet or script so that our partners can set this up themselves. The government and large corporations have personnel who know how to do this.

Before we get into generating key pairs, we want to examine what the differences are in the types of encryption, what is recommended, and what are the SSH's limitations in generating keys. To make a key pair more difficult to crack, increasing the number of bits in the key pair will help. The -b option in the ssh-keygen will allow us to specify the number of bits in the key to create. However, the SSH client man page states, "*DSA keys must be exactly 1024 bits as specified by FIPS 186-2.*" This is a serious limitation. The National Institute of Standards and Technology's (NIST) publication 800-57 early recommendation for key management, http://csrc.nist.gov/publications/PubsSPs.html#800-57-part1 stated that any key generated after 2010 should be at least 2048 bits for both DSA and RSA keys. This was later revised to 3072-bit in July 2012. Below is what happens when we attempt to make a DSA key more secure with SSH:

```
# ssh-keygen -t dsa -b 2048
DSA keys must be 1024 bits
```

If you wish to study the differences between the algorithms, the Wiki pages https://en.wikipedia.org/wiki/Digital_Signature_Algorithm and https://en.wikipedia.org/wiki/RSA_(algorithm) provide a good read on both types of keys.

SSH Public/Private Key Establishment Between an SSH Client & SSH Server

The simplest form of SSH server connection is just to have our partner connect and allow our public key to be copied down to their Linux user account ~/.ssh/known_hosts file. Below is a very simple client user creation script, which runs as 'root' and will create their client account:

```
#!/bin/bash
#set -x      # Uncomment to debug script
# Script name createempoweredclientsshuser.sh.   SSH Server User addition script.

Usage ()
(
    echo "Usage:"
    echo "$0 <User Account>" "\"<User's full name or comment>\""
)

if [ "$#" -lt 2 ]
then
    Usage
    exit
fi

useradd -c "$2" -m $1 -s /bin/bash
mkdir /home/$1/.ssh && chown $1:$1 /home/$1/.ssh
chmod -R 700 /home/$1
passwd $1
```

The above script above will work fine for a fully empowered SSH client/server user, which may be perfect for an HCU, but maybe not so great for an SBO. This is the bare minimum in SSH security that we can set up and is far superior to using email or File Transfer Protocol (FTP), but we can make things much more secure. Later in the chapter we will discuss how to do things like a change root (CHROOT), which jails our partner's access to our SSH server. We will also discuss CHROOT using SFTP to severely restrict our partner's access to our SSH server. We have already talked about what happens when our partner connects to our SSH server for the first time.

First, let's examine step-by-step how to manually set up an SSH user account and exchange keys. This will enable us to use the *ssh, scp,* and *sftp* commands without having to retype the same password repeatedly when logging in:

1. To make things easy, have your partner create an account named the same as what you created on your SSH server. Refer back to Adding Less Privileged User IDs for Specific Purposes to Linux for directions on how to do so.

```
# su - partnercompany
```

NOTE SSH keys only need to be generated once by the client. Do not generate them again unless you lose your SSH keys. If you plan to use other mobile clients to connect to this account on your SSH server, skip to Step 4 and copy your generated keys to your other mobile devices. If a mobile device or private key is lost, stolen, or the SSH server requires a new key, the easiest method to re-establish the client-server private/public key relationship is to remove the client/server user accounts and recreate them, after backing up your files:
```
# userdel -r <UserID>     # The -r option removes all files owned by <UserID>
```

2. Type the following to generate and backup the SSH key:

NOTE Accept the default key file location by pressing <Enter>. Consider leaving the passphrase blank; if you do enter a passphrase you will be prompted for that information each time in the future whenever you wish to copy files or log in to the SSH server. Our client can press <Enter> (twice) to assign a *blank* passphrase. This is a security hole, and there are options available to our partners that will automate entering a passphrase for scripting. If our partner is not using scripts to automate processes or logging into our server often, they should enter a passphrase. That way, if their device is stolen, our SSH server password security remains secure.

```
$ ssh-keygen -b 4096 -C "$(whoami)@$(hostname)-$(date -I)"     # Even using ultra secure
8192 bits is OK
ssh-keygen -b 4096
Generating public/private rsa key pair.
Enter file in which to save the key (/home/testuser/.ssh/id_rsa):  <enter>
Created directory '/home/testuser/.ssh'.
Enter passphrase (empty for no passphrase):  <enter>
Enter same passphrase again: <enter>
Your identification has been saved in /home/testuser/.ssh/id_rsa.
Your public key has been saved in /home/testuser/.ssh/id_rsa.pub.
The key fingerprint is:
44:32:f5:40:66:d4:61:e5:32:f8:de:86:6e:31:ba:c3 testuser@mint13-cinnamon32-gp
```

```
The key's randomart image is:
+--[ RSA 4096]----+
|      o+0. oo.   |
|       * =..     |
|        o + .    |
|         . . o   |
|          S .    |
|           . oo  |
|           . .ooo|
|          E...   |
|           .+.   |
+-----------------+
```

The command above created a public/private key pair in your ~/.ssh directory called *id_rsa* and *id_rsa.pub*. These can become very important files, so back them up before sharing them with any clients or SSH servers.

```
$ cd ~/.ssh
$ cp -ip id_rsa id_rsa.orig && cp -ip id_rsa.pub id_rsa.pub.orig
```

Or, if you have to use DSA:

```
$ ssh-keygen -t dsa -C "$(whoami)@$(hostname)-$(date -I)"
Generating public/private dsa key pair.
Enter file in which to save the key (/home/<UserID>/.ssh/id_dsa):
Created directory '/home/<UserID>/.ssh'.
Enter passphrase (empty for no passphrase):  <Enter>
Enter same passphrase again:  <Enter>
Your identification has been saved in /home/<UserID>/.ssh/id_dsa.
Your public key has been saved in /home/<UserID>/.ssh/id_dsa.pub.
The key fingerprint is:
08:af:77:1a:55:fa:17:22:ad:d1:52:00:a2:a7:f3:9e <UserID>@ubuntu
The key's randomart image is:
+--[ DSA 1024]----+
|    . ...        |
|   . .   .       |
| . o     o       |
|  o o . *        |
| o   o S + .     |
|  o . . * . .    |
|   o o o . .     |
|   . o +   .     |
|    E .          |
+-----------------+
```

```
$ cd ~/.ssh
$ cp -ip id_dsa id_dsa.orig  &&  cp -ip id_dsa.pub id_dsa.pub.orig
```

3. SSH default settings require you to secure the permissions of your authentication keys by closing permissions to the *.ssh* directory, and the private authentication files. The default behavior of *ssh-keygen* is to do this for you except for the fact that the public key on the client is left open to READ access. For a little added security, do the following:

```
$ chmod 700 $HOME  &&  chmod -R 700 $HOME/.ssh
```

4. There are multiple methods that we can use to get our public key to our SSH server user account. We will start with the more complex ways and work our way to the easiest. If this will be the only public authorization key that will be copied to this SSH server account, the following procedure will accomplish the task:

```
$ ssh <UserID>@<ServerIP>    # To change the password
The authenticity of host '<ServerIP> (<ServerIP>)' can't be established.
ECDSA key fingerprint is 66:93:29:ed:25:ff:0a:bd:62:df:0c:f5:93:8c:27:45.
Are you sure you want to continue connecting (yes/no)? yes
Warning: Permanently added '<ServerIP>' (ECDSA) to the list of known hosts.
<UserID>@<ServierIP> password:


You are required to change your password immediately (root enforced)
Welcome to Linux Mint 13 Maya (GNU/Linux 3.2.0-26-generic i686)


Welcome to Linux Mint
 * Documentation:  http://www.linuxmint.com
Last login: Mon Jul 16 03:40:05 2012 from <ClientIP>
WARNING: Your password has expired.
You must change your password now and login again!
Changing password for <UserID>.
(current) UNIX password:
Enter new UNIX password:
Retype new UNIX password:
passwd: password updated successfully
Connection to <ServerIP> closed.
```

```
$ ssh <UserID>@<ServerIP> 'mkdir /home/<UserID>/.ssh'    # If not done by the SSH
Server administrator.
<UserID>@ServerIP password:
```

```
$ scp id_rsa.pub <UserID>@<ServerIP>:/home/<UserID>/.ssh/authorized_keys
<UserID>@<ServerIP>'s password:
id_rsa.pub                         100%   619      0.6KB/s    00:00
$ ssh <UserID@<ServerIP> 'cp -ip /home/<UserID>/.ssh/authorized_keys
/home/<UserID>/.ssh/authorized_keys.orig'
```

However, suppose we want more than one public/private key combination to be able to connect to the same account. In that case we will need to concatenate the key to the SSH server's authorized keys. This will allow multiple private keys from multiple clients to connect to our SSH server. We want to do this because a cracker gaining access to an account on one of our partner's machines would not jeopardize our other partners' connections. This becomes much more significant to devices in our own business where one broken passphrase or private key could gain a cracker access to many devices using the same. The previous procedure would overwrite the file. We can use the following commands to accomplish that:

```
$ cd ~/.ssh
$ cp -ip id_dsa id_dsa.orig && cp -ip id_dsa.pub id_dsa.pub.orig
$ ssh <UserID>@<ServerIP>     # To change the password
The authenticity of host '<ServerIP> (<ServerIP>)' can't be established.
ECDSA key fingerprint is 66:93:29:ed:25:ff:0a:bd:62:df:0c:f5:93:8c:27:45.
Are you sure you want to continue connecting (yes/no)? yes
Warning: Permanently added '<ServerIP>' (ECDSA) to the list of known hosts.
<UserID>@<ServerIP>'s password:

You are required to change your password immediately (root enforced)
Welcome to Linux Mint 13 Maya (GNU/Linux 3.2.0-26-generic i686)

Welcome to Linux Mint
 * Documentation:  http://www.linuxmint.com
Last login: Mon Jul 16 03:40:05 2012 from <ClientIP>
WARNING: Your password has expired.
You must change your password now and login again!
Changing password for testuser2.
(current) UNIX password:
Enter new UNIX password:
Retype new UNIX password:
passwd: password updated successfully
Connection to <ServerIP> closed.


$ scp id_dsa.pub <UserID@<ServerIP>:/tmp
$ ssh <UserID>@<ServerIP> 'cat /tmp/id_dsa.pub >>
/home/<UserID>/.ssh/authorized_keys'
<UserID>@<ServerIP>'s password:
$ ssh <UserID@<ServerIP> 'cp -ip /home/<UserID>/.ssh/authorized_keys
/home/<UserID>/.ssh/authorized_keys.orig'
```

Type the following to remove the public key from the temporary directory:

```
$ ssh <UserID>@<ServerIP> 'rm /tmp/id_dsa.pub'
```

Or better yet, use one of the following:

```
$ cd ~/.ssh && cat id_rsa.pub | ssh <UserID>@<ServerIP> 'sh -c "cat -
>>~/.ssh/authorized_keys"'
$ cat .ssh/id_rsa.pub | ssh <UserID>@<ServerIP> "cat >>~/.ssh/authorized_keys"
```

A much easier scripted alternative than either of the previous two options is to use the *ssh-copy-id* command. The *ssh-copy-id* command will install your public key in your account on a remote SSH server. If the key is an RSA key:

```
$ ssh-copy-id <UserID>@<ServerIP>
```

For a DSA key:

```
$ ssh-copy-id -i ~<UserID>/.ssh/id_dsa.pub <UserID>@<ServerIP>
```

Then backup the copied key on the SSH server:

```
$ ssh <UserID@<ServerIP> 'cp -ip /home/<UserID>/.ssh/authorized_keys
/home/<UserID>/.ssh/authorized_keys.orig'
```

| **NOTE**  | You will notice that the *ssh-copy-id* command will create the file */home/<UserID>/.ssh/authorized_keys* on the SSH server if it does not already exist. If it does exist, "ssh-copy-id" will append to the file. In earlier versions of OpenSSH, the *authorized_key2* file was used. The release announcement for version 3 on web page http://marc.info/?l=openssh-unix-dev&m=100508718416162&w=2 explains:

The files
   /etc/ssh_known_hosts2
   ~/.ssh/known_hosts2
   ~/.ssh/authorized_keys2
are now obsolete, you can use
   /etc/ssh_known_hosts
   ~/.ssh/known_hosts
   ~/.ssh/authorized_keys

For backward compatibility ~/.ssh/authorized_keys2 can still be used for authentication, and hostkeys are still read from the known_hosts2. However, those deprecated files are considered 'readonly'. Future releases of OpenSSH are likely not to read these files. |

5. In order for the 'sshd' daemon on the SSH server to accept the *authorized_keys* file you created, your server directories and authentication files must have secure permissions. If SSH server admin did not secure those files and directories, type the following:

```
$ ssh <UserID>@<ServerIP> 'chmod 700 $HOME'
$ ssh <UserID>@<ServerIP> 'chmod 700 $HOME/.ssh'
$ ssh <UserID>@<ServerIP> 'chmod 600 $HOME/.ssh/authorized_keys'
```

It is important to note that once this is working, it will work regardless of how many times the IP address changes on your mobile device. IP address has nothing to do with this form of authentication. If you decide to change your passphrase at a later date:

```
$ ssh-keygen -f ~/.ssh/id_rsa -p
```

SSH Agent, Specific Purpose Keys, Using *authorized_keys* to Restrict Access

When your partners connect to your SSH server for the first time, they are presented with a key fingerprint. This fingerprint is the identifying marker for your partners to know that they are indeed connected to your SSH server. In a middleman attack crackers can spoof your SSH server and fool your partners into thinking that they are connecting to your server unless you have your partners check the fingerprint. Adding a fingerprint comparison step to your partners' directions will eliminate spoofing attacks and ensure the safe exchange of data. So in the directions/scripts that you provide to your partners you must provide them the fingerprint to your SSH server and instruct them to compare that value presented above as "ECDSA key fingerprint is 66:93:29:ed:25:ff:0a:bd:62:df:0c:f5:93:8c:27:45". This is how your partners will know that they are connecting to your server and not a spoofed* site. "How do you do that?" you may ask. Executing the following commands on your SSH server will give you the fingerprints to provide to your partners. In my case, OpenSSH defaulted to using the ECDSA key. Other flavors of Linux may use your RSA or DSA key instead. Log in as 'root' and do the following to concatenate your fingerprint(s) to your *partnerdirections.txt* file:

```
# cd /etc/ssh
# ssh-keygen -lf ssh_host_dsa_key.pub >> $HOME/partnerdirections.txt
# ssh-keygen -lf ssh_host_rsa_key.pub >> $HOME/partnerdirections.txt
# ssh-keygen -lf ssh_host_ecdsa_key.pub >> $HOME/partnerdirections.txt
```

OpenSSH also provides the *ssh-agent* command, which will hold your passphrase in the RAM memory of the process in which it was run. For example, typing $ ssh-agent /bin/bash will load a bash terminal and allow login without a password to an SSH server. If we load an agent:

```
sshagent@ubuntu:~$ ssh-agent /bin/bash
sshagent@ubuntu:~$ ssh-add
Enter passphrase for /home/sshagent/.ssh/id_rsa:
Identity added: /home/sshagent/.ssh/id_rsa (/home/sshagent/.ssh/id_rsa)
sshagent@ubuntu:~$ ssh sshagent@<yourdomainname>.dyndns.<extension>
Welcome to Ubuntu 12.04.1 LTS (GNU/Linux 3.2.0-30-generic-pae i686)
Last login: Fri Sep 28 23:17:43 2012 from···
```

Or, just type the following on the command line:

`$ ssh-agent sh -c 'ssh-add < /dev/null && bash'`

The command above will perform three tasks: start the *ssh-agent* background process, add your default identity, which prompts you for your passphrase and lastly, spawns a bash shell to allow connection without a password to the SSH server. Having no password or using the *ssh-agent* method covered above will enable you to use the current bash shell to *ssh* and *scp* to the SSH server without having to type a passphrase every time you perform a command. I hope you can see the benefit of using *ssh-agent* rather than have a blank passphrase to make scripting easier. Both methods will make running scripts possible, but *ssh-agent* achieves the same results with added password security.

If you wish to study the details about how this works (See: http://unixwiz.net/techtips/ssh-agent-forwarding.html), this is an excellent read on using SSH agents. In Debian flavors of Linux, we can install *keychain* # apt-get install keychain, which is an OpenSSH key manager (See: https://help.ubuntu.com/community/QuickTips). We can then add *keychain* to the terminal window startup *${HOME}/.bashrc* or */etc/bash.bashrc* file. The great thing about keychain, taken from the Ubuntu Software Center description of the tool, is "*it saves the ssh-agent environment variables to ~/.keychain/\$\{HOSTNAME}\}-sh, so that subsequent logins and non-interactive shells such as cron jobs can source the file and make passwordless ssh connections.*" This will become very important in using scripts that automate processes on our SSH server. After you install keychain add the following to the *${HOME}/.bashrc* or the */etc/bash.bashrc* file:

```
keychain id_rsa
. ~/keychain/`uname -n`-sh
```

Then the next time you open up a terminal window for that SSH client user ID, you will see:

```
root@ubuntu:~# su - sshagent
 * keychain 2.7.1 ~ http://www.funtoo.org
 * Starting ssh-agent...
 * Adding 1 ssh key(s): /home/sshagent/.ssh/id_rsa
Enter passphrase for /home/sshagent/.ssh/id_rsa: <passphrase>
 * ssh-add: Identities added: /home/sshagent/.ssh/id_rsa
```

Future logins to your SSH server will be automated. This book is meant to be a step-by-step cyber security instruction manual, not a technical reference on SSH and its agents. I only wanted to introduce the concept of SSH agents; we have to move on to address the purpose of this book, which is to make you secure while using the Internet.

| **WARNING** | The downside to using SSH Agent is if you have a cracker or unscrupulous administrator with 'root' access to your Internet device. A 'root' user can impersonate the client user and gain access to all their remote connections, thus granting them access to all that remote data. As we have previously discussed, about half of the computers in the world have been cracked, so |

	we have to wonder how many underpaid, unscrupulous administrators work at companies worldwide, so who is watching the watcher?

If we don't want to use an agent, we can generate a key that is meant to have a specific purpose or to handle a situation.

1. Suppose you or your partner need to automate some ssh/scp process to perform a task on the remote host. To automate everything, you don't want to have to enter a passphrase, deal with agents or work with a key manager.
2. You or your partner want to perform some specific task on a SSH server but don't want to append a privileged key to the *authorized_keys* file. Appending a privileged key to this file would grant the SSH account the freedom to do anything they want, not just the tasks we want to allow them to do.

In this example we will create another user account on our SSH client and generate a new key. This account is meant to have limited access to our SSH server and is to be used with a specific purpose in mind.

```
$ ssh-keygen -b 4096 -f ~/.ssh/scpkey -C "Key for SCP only" -N " -q
```

This will create the *scpkey* and *scpkey.pub* key pair in the *~/.ssh* directory. Since we are going to alter the public key, lets backup both keys, edit it, and copy it to */tmp*:

```
$ cd ~/.ssh && cp -ip scpkey scpkey.orig && cp -ip scpkey.pub scpkey.pub.orig
$ vi scpkey.pub  && cp scpkey.pub /tmp
```

There are many configuration items that we can add to our new public key to restrict access to our SSH server. At the beginning of the key we can add keywords such as the keyword from="string"; this restricts the use of the key on that line to sessions that originate from hosts that match "string", for example: from=trusted.dyndns.org, *.partnerdomain.org, partner????host.dyndns.org, !rejecthost.dyndns.org.

The hostname specified needs to be the hostname reported when the IP (network) address of the connecting machine is looked up in our local DNS. Therefore, you may not find this option useful except restricting machines behind our local firewall. The * wildcard matches one or more characters, while the ? wildcard matches a single character. If you want to exclude the connecting hostname, you can prefix it by '!' so that it is rejected. Below is an example *scpkey.pub* file after editing:

```
# comments such as SCP public key file
# This key fingerprint is: 79:a4:94:5b:b8:b8:0a:55:09:f7:0e:d3:ee:ea:e9:3d
#
from="yourdomain. dyndns. org", no-port-forwarding, no-pty, no-X11-forwarding, noagent-
forwarding ssh-rsa
lAAAAB3NzaClyc2EAAAADAQDies/3eAld/pNzcJoWYLawqq6T9vbJN8sLVbJhFP40X06fz0iUKoXtKxg5N···
== sshuser@mint15-kde32-gp
```

Next, from a privileged SSH client or server account, we want to back up our remote *~/.ssh/authorized_keys* file before we append our specific purpose key for another account user.

```
$ ssh <UserID@<ServerIP> 'cp -ip /home/<UserID>/.ssh/authorized_keys
/home/<UserID>/.ssh/authorized_keys.bak1'
```

Now we need to append this key to our remote SSH server user's *~/.ssh/authorized_keys* file. To make all this work we need to use a client account with privileged access to our SSH server user ID to append the new key.

```
$ ssh-copy-id -i /tmp/scpkey.pub <UserID>@<ServerIP>
```

With everything set up we should now be able to transfer files using our limited SSH public key. If you experience problems, look at the file permissions in your *~/.ssh* directory. When you perform a directory listing you may see:

```
-rw------- 1 sshuser sshuser 1675 Sep 30 00:21 scpkey
-rw-r--r-- 1 sshuser sshuser  403 Sep 30 00:21 scpkey.pub
```

A key file being writable by anyone other than the user or a private key file being readable by anyone other than the user will cause SSH to fail.

Another option we can use is to generate a key and modify it to perform a specific command on our partner's SSH server, such as something as simple as to show whether our partner has outbound files that we need to process. We could have a fully empowered key attached to a command specific key so that they could use both.

```
$ ssh-keygen -b 4096 -f ~/.ssh/lskey -C "Key for LS only" -N " -q
command="echo For user `/usr/bin/whoami` on `/bin/hostname` files to process are `ls
~/partnercompany/out`",no-port-forwarding,no-X11-forwarding,no-agent-forwarding,no-
pty ssh-rsa...
```

```
$ ssh sshuser@yourdomainname.dyndns.org
PTY allocation request failed on channel 0
For user sshuser on ubuntu1204-sshvpn files to process are out1.asc out1.gpg out2
out2.asc out3 out3.asc out4.asc outfile
Connection to yourdomainname.dyndns.org closed.
```

If you remove the *no-pty*, you will no longer get the PTY allocation message above. I hope you can see the potential of single purpose keys. There are other options you can use in the *authorized_keys* file that you may want to investigate. (See: http://www.openbsd.org/cgi-bin/man.cgi?query=sshd&sektion=8, http://www.eng.cam.ac.uk/help/jpmg/ssh/authorized_keys_howto.html) We can enable our partners to do anything on our SSH server through scripting or command execution.

You could also use *sshpass* # apt-get install sshpass, which is a non-interactive SSH password provider to deliver the passphrase to your SSH scripts. Depending on how you use *sshpass* it could be less secure than using keychain, but if you use an anonymous pipe and keep the password encrypted in a file that the script encrypts and decrypts on the fly, this would be difficult to crack.

Before we continue discussing SSH clients, we should probably think about making things easier for our partners. Imagine trying to explain all this agent stuff to your partners, who may live many miles away, and might not be very savvy with computers or know how to perform all the steps above so that you can exchange data and files with them. This knowledge provides convenience, but only makes them less secure. Below is the script that we can send to our partner(s) as directions on how to set up their SSH clients as 'root' on their SSH client Linux computers. I hope that this will make things easier for them.

```bash
#!/bin/bash
# set -x      # Uncomment for debugging script
# Script name createsshclientuser.sh.   SSH Client User addition script.

fUserSSH=/home/$1/ssh.sh
echo User script ${fUserSSH} being created.

Usage ()
(
    echo "Usage:"
    echo "$0 <User Account>" "\"<User's full name>\"" "<SSH Server IP>" "<Key Type
(rsa or dsa)>"
)

if [ "$#" -lt 4 ]
then
    Usage
    exit
fi

useradd -c "$2" -m $1 -s /bin/bash
passwd $1

/bin/bash << EOF2
cat << 'EOF' > ${fUserSSH}
#!/bin/bash
# set -x      # Uncomment for debugging user account script
echo "Accept the default key file location by pressing <Enter>.   Then"
echo "press <Enter> again (twice) to assign a blank passphrase.   (If"
```

```
echo "you enter a passpwill be prompted for that passphrase"
echo "and won't be able to log in without it.)"

if [[ $4 == "dsa" ]]; then
    ssh-keygen -t dsa -C "$(whoami)@$(hostname)-$(date -I)"
else    # For a RSA key use the following:
    # For a RSA key use either of the following:
    ssh-keygen -b 4096 -C "$(whoami)@$(hostname)-$(date -I)"
    # ssh-keygen -b 8196 -C "$(whoami)@$(hostname)-$(date -I)" # For MAX security
fi


chmod 700 ~$1 && chmod 700 ~$1/.ssh
cd ~/.ssh


cp -ip id_$4 id_$4.orig && cp -ip id_$4.pub id_$4.pub.orig
echo "Private key ~/.ssh/$4 and Public key ~/.ssh/id_$4.pub have been backed up"


echo "When you connect to the SSH Server for the first time:"
echo "The authenticity of host '<ServerIP> (<ServerIP>)' can't be established."
echo "ECDSA key fingerprint is 66:93:29:ed:25:ff:0a:bd:62:df:0c:f5:93:8c:27:45."
echo "Be sure to compare this fingerprint to the fingerprint provided to you"
echo "for our SSH server in the directions on setting up a SSH connection."


ssh $1@$3       # Needed only if a password reset in required by the server


# Alternative method to using ssh-copy-id:
# scp id_$4.pub $1@$3:/tmp
# ssh $1@$3 '/bin/cat /tmp/id_$4.pub >> /home/$1/.ssh/authorized_keys'
# ssh $1@$3 'rm /tmp/id_$4.pub'


# Use the easiest method to copy the key to the server:
if [[ $4 == "dsa" ]]; then
    ssh-copy-id -i ~$1/.ssh/id_$4.pub $1@$3
    echo "$4 key ~$1/.ssh/id_$4 has been copied to $1@$3"
else
    # Use the following for an RSA key:
    ssh-copy-id $1@$3
    echo "$4 key ~$1/.ssh/id_$4 has been copied to $1@$3"
fi


# Backup the authorized_keys file on the server
ssh $1@$3 'cp -ip /home/$1/.ssh/authorized_keys /home/$1/.ssh/authorized_keys.orig'


EOF
```

```
EOF2

chown $1:$1 ${fUserSSH}
chmod 700 ${fUserSSH}

su $1 -c ${fUserSSH}
rm ${fUserSSH}


# chmod 700 createsshclientuser.sh
# ./createsshclientuser.sh <userID> "User full name or description" domainname-or-IP
keytype
```

If your partner's connections will remain static for long periods of time, as previously discussed, we should consider disabling password authentication in the */etc/ssh/sshd_config* file. Taken from http://www.openbsd.org/cgi-bin/man.cgi?query=sshd_config&sektion=5&arch=&apropos=0&manpath=OpenBSD+Current:

PasswordAuthentication no	The default behavior of SSHD is to allow password authentication. Once all your partners have established accounts we can edit the */etc/sshd_config* file and uncomment PasswordAuthentication no to make sure no one but our partners can connect to our SSH server.
PermitEmptyPasswords no	When password authentication is allowed, it specifies whether the server allows login to accounts with empty password strings. The default is "no".

By disabling the "PasswordAuthentication" option, and even if a password is stolen or shared, only the public/private key pair will still work. If someone tries to connect another mobile device to a partner's account, they will get *Permission denied (publickey). Couldn't read packet: Connection reset by peer.* Changing the "PermitEmptyPasswords" option was not necessary since the password is not empty. This approach does not protect against the event that a USB drive or Private Key is shared or stolen from one of your partners. However, if they read this book they would have had that USB drive encrypted and having it stolen would not be a security breach unless the cracker is very good at breaking encryption; but they probably have not, so one of our requirements is to have them periodically repeat this process on an agreed upon basis. Sharing a private key is akin to sharing a password and SSH has no defense against that except changing our handshake every now and then.

PuTTY -- SSH File Transfer Using a Fully Empowered Windows Client

Refer back to Establishing the first SSH connection between a Windows a PuTTY SSH client and our SSH server. Even though we have shown how easy it is to run a Linux guest OS on a Windows 7 OS, there will be instances where our partners must use Windows 7 to communicate and exchange data with our SSH server. To do so is somewhat less straightforward than using a Linux guest OS. We have already covered some of the ground necessary to make that possible. So now we need to teach them the final steps to make the exchange of data possible. Plus, sometimes the guest OS running virtually on our partners computers may be Windows.

I find setting and transferring files in Linux far easier than using Windows with PuTTY, but this chapter would not be complete without covering both options. To read more about everything that we are going to discuss, refer to PuTTY's documentation at http://www.chiark.greenend.org.uk/~sgtatham/putty/docs.html.

We looked at using *plink* from a Windows Command Prompt so that we can now teach our partners how to transfer files with our SSH server. We are methodically breaking down the process step-by-step to enable the maximum use of our SSH server by our employees, our partners, and ourselves, all of which have different needs for our SSH server.

NOTE	The following directions can be difficult for Windows users who are used to using their GUI. The use of a command line is something alien to them. I am trying to strike a balance in this book by not over-simplifying things, but at the same time presenting what is necessary to help the broadest audience possible. If you can open and use Windows Explorer, you can master the following steps.

Open up a Windows command prompt and type:

```
C:\Users\<UserID>\pscp -V      # or pscp -V to see all the command line options available
pscp:  Release 0.63
```

If the command is not found, refer back to establishing your first connection to our SSH server so you can alter your system path. The first step is to have our partner try to send a file. When our partner opens up a Windows Command Prompt, it defaults to their Windows home directory C:\Users\<UserID>\. In that directory are all of the places that they are used to visiting through using the Window Explorer GUI utility (not to be confused with Windows Internet Explorer browser).

| NOTE | If your partner cannot use the Windows Explorer tool to navigate to files and directories on their Window 7 computer, then they or you need to consider hiring an outside consultant to help them establish a connection with your SSH server. This basic skill is necessary for transferring files back and forth.

Sometimes our partner does not understand that they are using Windows Explorer to navigate to their files and directories/folders. I had never noticed before, but Windows Explorer does not have a title at the top showing "Windows Explorer". When you click on **Help > About Windows**, it only tells you which version of Windows you are running. Consequently this confusion, which seems very basic, was a dividing rod between me and getting a few of my partner(s) to understand my directions. I could not figure out how my business partners were finding their files and folders after the exchange of many emails. The directions below seemed impossible for them to follow, and we both did not understand why. I finally found the correct question and asked one partner to detail how they were getting to their folders and documents. *I was told to select the **Start*** |
|------|------|

> *button on the lower left > on the right arrow up to select <u>Documents</u> > from there they could get to all their documents on their computer.* Our whole disconnect was my partner did not understand that what they opened *is* the Windows Explorer tool. So given these types of experiences, I am trying to balance the level of granularity that this book covers to help the most people.

Another thing I encountered when teaching my partners how to navigate to their files is their love of shortcuts on the desktop. Shortcuts were discussed back in the Windows 7 chapter, but I was surprised at my partner's lack of depth of understanding in the configuring of and using shortcuts. So another method to help them navigate to the files to transfer is *right click on the desktop shortcut that they created > arrow down to select <u>Properties</u> > click on the <u>Shortcut</u> tab > and then in <u>Target:</u> box copy the path and then paste that path into the command prompt.*

NOTE

Windows is historically based on DOS, which was the original Microsoft Operating System and what started the company. Much of the command line syntax in DOS was borrowed from UNIX with enough minor alterations to keep Microsoft from being sued. Windows 7 allows for the use of spaces in the naming of folders and files. Nevertheless, given Windows origins and the continued popularity of Linux, I recommend against having spaces in the names of your folders or filenames. Not doing so will make the use of the command line and Windows Explorer easier. Spaces in the path can become very confusing to Windows users who are trying to use a Command Prompt that is very unfamiliar to them. Sometimes those paths have to have double quotes around them making things even more confusing. Some people may find the following directions very basic in a book on cyber security, while others may appreciate these details. I have tried to strike a balance.

Get your partner to navigate <u>Windows Explorer</u> to where the files to transfer are located. Then open a command prompt in another window. *Pressing <Alt+D> or clicking on the navigation window will change the top of Windows Explorer to the actual path that your partner could type at a command prompt. It will also highlight the actual path so that it can be copied. Right click on the top of <u>Windows Explorer</u> to the right of the highlighted path > select <u>Copy address as text</u> > right click in the bar to the right of highlighted path and arrow down to select <u>Copy</u>.* This will copy the path to your partner's files to the clipboard. *In the command prompt window > on the command line type* cd *followed by a space > right click in the command prompt window and arrow down to select <u>Paste</u> to paste the path to the files directory into the command prompt window > hit enter.* This will change the command prompt directory to where the files to transfer are located. *Another way of doing this is, in the upper left of the prompt window, to the left of the words <u>Command Prompt</u> there is a tiny icon that looks like the command prompt window > click on the icon then arrow down to expand the <u>Edit</u> menu > arrow right and down to select <u>Paste</u>.* This will also paste the path to your partner's files in the command prompt window.

If the directions above don't work in getting your partner to the directory in which the files to transfer are located on their PC, have them send you a screenshot reflecting what Windows Explorer is showing when they are in the correct directory. This way, you can help them use the command line that they are unfamiliar with to get to the file(s) that need to be transferred back and forth.

One of my Windows partners was very confused when using the command line. After exchanging many emails, I had them send a screenshot showing the Windows Explorer directory where their file(s) to be transferred, were located. I then sent them the exact command line syntax to help them change to the directory where their files were located. This enabled them to transfer the files that we needed to exchange between their client computer and my SSH server. Showing them things, like typing dir /w only confused things; the dir /w is the command line tool to show a directory listing that shows what is in the current working directory on their computer. In the example to the right, the command line directions to change to this directory would read:

C:\...\UserID>\cd C:\Program Files (x86)\PuTTY

This would change the prompt to:

C:\Program Files (x86)\PuTTY>

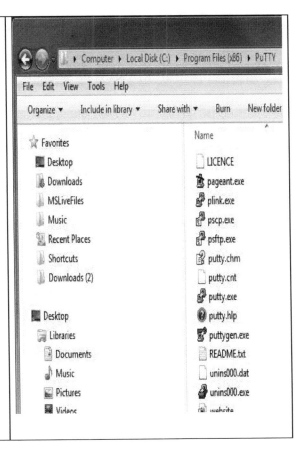

Once your partner opens a command prompt, give them the following additional directions:

C:\Users\<UserID>\dir /w

As previously stated, the dir /w command will show your partners the files that are in their home directory, as well as the directories they can navigate to for files that they may want to send to your SSH server. This can confuse things but with the directions above, it helps clarify things. It shows your partners how to use the command line to get to other places on their computer. If it does not, have them send you another Windows Explorer screenshot and give them the exact syntax again. Repeat this process until using the command line becomes clear and easy. Sending screenshots back and forth of something they are unfamiliar with, such as using the command line, is a waste of time. You have to give them the exact steps and hope they eventually garner an understanding of what is taking place on the command line. This is not their field of expertise but these are intelligent people and they will figure it out when presented in the correct fashion. The text names that are seen flashing across the command prompt using dir /w in the command line window will eventually become familiar to what they are used to seeing using the Windows Explorer GUI. The *Documents* directory is most likely the directory where the documents and directories are housed for them to send and receive data.

```
C:\Users\<UserID>\cd  Documents
C:\Users\<UserID\Documents\dir /w
```

Above is an example of helping your partners to find the document(s) that they need to transfer. We have no way of knowing the actual directory where those documents are stored on their hard drive. The above example may not be enough information to help them find the directory where their files are stored when using the Command Prompt. Once again you will need a Windows Explorer screenshot to show them where their documents are. Once your partners find their documents using the command line, they can use the following commands to send and receive files to/from your SSH server. To send a file, our partners need to type:

```
C:\Users\<UserID>\pscp  <filename>
<YourSSHServerID>@<YourDomainName>.dyndns.<extension>:<filename>
<YourSSHServerID>@<YourDomainName>. dyndns. <extension>'s  password:
<filename>          | xxxx kB | xxxx kB/s | ETA: 00:00:00 100%
```

Or, if this is easier,

```
C:\Users\<UserID>\pscp  <filename>
<YourSSHServerID>@<YourDomainName>.dyndns.<extension>:.
```

To get a file from our partners as 'root' type:

```
C:\Users\<UserID>\pscp <YourSSHServerID>@<yourdomainname>.dyndns.<extension>:
/home/<username>/<filename>
YourSSHServerID>@<yourdomainname>. dyndns. <extension>'s  password:
<filename>          | xxxx kB | xxxx kB/s | ETA: 00:00:00 | 100%
```

Or, if this is easier for your partners and 'root' type:

```
C:\Users\<UserID>\pscp
<YourSSHServerID>@<yourdomainname>.dyndns.<extension>:<filename>  .
```

The next step in exchanging data with our partners is having them exchange keys with our SSH server. This will enable our clients to automate processes via scripts and log into our SSH server without having to type a password every time. This was very easy to do in Linux because all we had to do was provide them with a script to run, which automated everything, but with PuTTY, the key exchange is a little more complex. Scripting in Windows is not as intuitive or as easy to do as it is in Linux. We have already gone over setting up a public/private key relationship in Linux, so all I will cover in Windows is how to generate and exchange keys using PuTTY. **PuTTYgen** is the tool that we will need to generate our key pair in Windows 7. In setting up an SSH-Client in Linux we talked about the types of key pairs that we can generate and the security levels we want, so we will just use the best available in

PuTTY, which is an RSA key for use with the SSH-2 protocol. Once again, we will use the command line to kick off the PuTTYgen program:

C:\Users\<UserID>**puttygen**

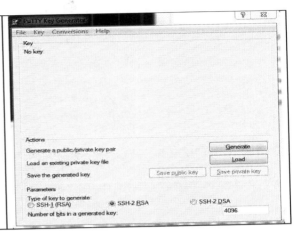

This will bring up the PuTTYgen utility, which we will use to generate our key relationship. PuTTY defaults to the US government recommendation of using 2048 for the "Number or bits in a generated key:". I recommend using 4096, which should keep you secure for a few more years. Using my limited computing power, specifying 4096 had little or no effect on connection speed with my SSH Server. Changing this setting, no matter what computer hardware you are using, will have limited consequences.

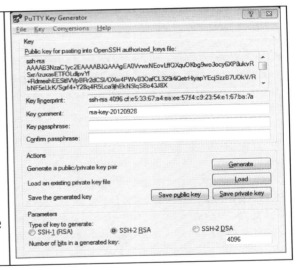

Click on the Generate button and start moving the mouse around to generate randomness in your key. This is supposed to make duplicating the keys impossible. Who can wave a mouse in exactly the same fashion? It is kind of genius when you think about it. Even if a cracker had a video camera viewing your computer screen they could not duplicate your public and private keys. The only way to compromise your security is if someone has stolen or broken into your mobile device to obtain your private key. To the right is what the screen looks like after you generate your PuTTY key without a passphrase.

You should record this screenshot for your records. You can always reload the private key and this information will be generated from that key. In this case, we are not going to enter a passphrase so click on Save public key and Save private key buttons.

Save these keys in a place that is important so that you will remember. Both will be needed for file transfer with our SSH server. ***Save the public key in a file named "authorized_keys" for transfer to our OpenSSH server > click on Save public key to the Save private key button to create the private key in the same directory. The default in Windows is C:\Users\<UserID>. Name the private file something like "putty<userID>privatesshkey", which will automatically get the ".ppk" extension.***

The establishment of a public/private key relationship with our Linux OpenSSH server is more complex than using Linux. It is better to use a virtual Linux OS for SSH connections but some of our partners will need to use Windows, which we hope is not their core OS thereby exposing it to attack. A Virtual OS sandbox using NAT would better protect our, as well as their, SSH security. When using an SSH client in Linux, all we had to do was copy the public key to our SSH server to */home/<UserID>/.ssh/authorized_keys* file. Before we modify our PuTTY generated key, let's view what a Linux SSH client generated public key looks like:

```
ssh-rsa AAAB3NzaC1yc2EAAAADAQABAAACAQDuFd7g6PVUx7CvoVMiciWdqenaMVOjz+8/FDf+qkYl
6GvlVya26ysCy86Ws911XtPVhxrE9iZz0xzSXDK59Kj+RILwYPGOGOFKIEH/1L3MiWTDOPGsQ5YURrZA65zW
Du+4WaV1yAjy1TT3tdwWScxuGJejZsfBKjZEhva1U6pX4gcNkwD92Vhj7ahWO20blimB+oQAt6P6JE7uqYIX
umtPibfvUd25mnLQaaAYCd8w6gQf01cXSivM98JrFbf4LY6TBoLqYLJ6ZByOU86yXallWcGoJtbuwRVfkivO
T70Ygjywftl+S7bLVRXd+4xCDjkxKS2zHzmKhSWOnNN7r6UljlYun0IU2VJyoT31QaQvV6XY/By3bxO7sXK7
k7dwC7spRxqNHdVrfkLCNR9yKUap+op6E1flTOmqQiCCppcvxuClaweBdUhyDIP8LAcDy2LBXy+QXoymfEuE
txu8ltxCf+UHOGXh67RdDEg6Tp8HJxMputN1zHAZmBcZKEBDGnplMvBASMrHU5xOvCWl9lWJMjM/TpvVotql
hXg7lKtQ6vOHLyYrX2gkVpNwHTiTy3xphlFXNQQXHn1ltliA6dgkGekc/sOpDT/TeQ5Gnsq2tV145uqp8GCc
VBGi+UAhCZn51YcYFDRcsUwtHslE/TFfYi5daoAKSxlAwA8klyliFQ== testuser@mint13-kde32-gp
```

Now let's look at what a PuTTY generated public key looks like:

```
---- BEGIN SSH2 PUBLIC KEY ----
Comment: "rsa-key-20120928"
AAAAB3NzaC1yc2EAAAABJQAAAIEAl7U/7syOJTaxiQ13nFDOOd8A4mrMGGxkdekp
twi2OQd1bVNzcD9yHcSvw2tl12TIV3DqfoAoDRip4595mqKmFBwzQpGEepnSQNZn
ognzrbsuU4Qdnn3x0Ev4g+UHG9u3poONSJ74vqa6mNwVzcAp+yFCawTiuA9WWuto
VOcOzd8=
---- END SSH2 PUBLIC KEY ----
```

Notice that at the top of the PuTTY Key Generator screenshot above under Key is the text "Public key for pasting into OpenSSH authorized_keys file:", which is the actual public key we need to transfer or store on our SSH server. Open a text editor and cut and paste this key to a text file before closing the PuTTY Key Generator; but suppose we closed the Key Generator window without saving the OpenSSH *authorized_keys* version of the key?

If we forgot to save the OpenSSH key, we can generate a new key or just load the private key. Perhaps we are on a machine that does not have PuTTY installed and we want to send a PuTTY public key to an OpenSSH server. We can modify the PuTTY public key to turn it into an OpenSSH key before we transfer it to our SSH Server, or afterward. I am comfortable using Vim as my text editor of choice, so I edited the key after transfer. Open a <u>Command Prompt</u>, which will default to Windows user home directory, then perform the following to copy your public key to the SSH server:

```
C:\Users\<UserID>\pscp authorized_keys
fullsshuser@<yourdomainname>.dyndns.<extension>:.ssh/authorized_keys
fullsshuser@<yourdomainname>. dyndns. <extension>'s password:
authorized_keys     | 0 kB |    0.8 kB/s | ETA:  00:00:00 | 100%
```

If you transferred an OpenSSH *authorized_keys* file, your task is complete. If we transferred a PuTTY public key file to our SSH server, there are a few modifications that must be made:
1. Open up your favorite text editor on your SSH server (e.g. Vim).
2. Delete the first two lines and last line in the public-key file.
3. Join the remaining lines into one single line, by using the Shift-J command shortcut.
4. Trim the space between any lines that has been joined by a CTRL shortcut.
5. Insert the **ssh-rsa** keyword (with one trailing space) in front of the single line. In the end your key should look like:

```
ssh-rsa
AAAB3NzaC1yc2EAAAABJQAAAgEAOVvwxNEovLffQXquOKbg9wo3ocy6XP8ukvRSxr/izuxasETFOLdlpvYf+
RdmeshEESitlVVpBRr2dCSI/OXw4PWvB3OafCL329i4iQetrHiyapYEcjSzzB7UOkV/RbNF5eLkK/Sgrf4+Y
28q4R5Lca9jhEkNSlqSBo43J8X+dswJVAyOsnDoMs8+kwTi8ZMidKyuyK1MgXmCRmv5h6gYHVRmZZokezvxx
PjoluDedxmb93qQXsdd/UUQMzFV1ABq8EQNcgx+AMOy8O1JD4AAOd364THpO5O4WlPy+JneiLhiTjWyDQ7+N
Yj8JCsnSnTE5xh7Hxqisy00mtr4fG1gmXq9RS4AgzCE4/1HX5hptsbPJoeh23TP5oKqgnY8JAyrPFT3sx8pP
vYFUJAFJODjJOxkeFHxGWRxI1TWK4IPB2/OQpm4MIFPtlYxciysdW1o8L7T8s9KcPN9DEHMfbyphlkS+vjrj
4loIOcQnndilpiwWmo76PjDGhgZQCp2KZoAyjy2oZy2Rk66+FSfZzyAJcMaZG49ZWoO8+bFNj5un7qWOYfuy
gqNCgkMgh2cOMiw7fxnZ2ajSOEB7fEUi+5x1kvsWNGe8yMqR5RB5DMNJ29y9Mw1lVsi2OT21pLtS3nhFCbfD
en3WWDLTEg5W1CvKKZAru/nYMBGpOjPRsz13uM=
```

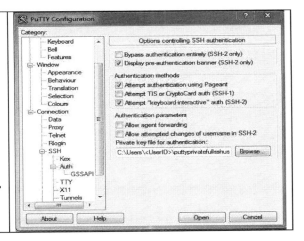

From now on when you open a *Putty configuration* window > select your *Saved Session* > click on *Load* > select the *Open* button at the bottom and you will be automatically logged into the SSH Server >the next time we transfer a file to or from the SSH server we will no longer have to enter a password.

As with *ssh-agent* discussed previously, PuTTY provides the *pageant.exe* tool for storing private keys in RAM memory. Earlier, we discussed how not having a passphrase is a security risk, (See: http://unixwiz.net/techtips/putty-openssh.html), which is an excellent read on using PuTTY, agents and keys. Consequently, if our partner created their key pairs with a passphrase, the directions above will make things much more convenient for them. *Navigate Windows Explorer to C:\Program Files (x86)\PuTTY\pageant.exe > right click on the file > arrow down to select Send to > arrow right to select Desktop (create shortcut) > arrow down to the lower right and open the system tray > right click on the Pageant icon > arrow up to select Add Key and add your private key > once the key is added, click on*

***View Keys* to see your key.** The next time our clients start work, all they have to do is double click on this shortcut, enter their passphrase(s), and all their SSH sessions will connect automatically until Windows is rebooted.

Linux/MAC -- SSH Client & Windows PuTTY Cheat Sheets

We have already discussed establishing a key exchange between our SSH Client and SSH Server. To enable my clients to retrieve and send files, I found myself constantly cutting and pasting the exact commands they needed to type. Then one client suggested that I develop a Cheat Sheet to send him that would outline everything he needed to type in a terminal and what it did. So I put together the table below to aid him in the use of my SSH server. I send this table to all of my SSH clients.

Linux and Macintosh OS's terminal window commands, userid= , serverdomain= , ext=	
ls or ls -al	List directory contents in the current working directory on the client.
pwd	Print the name of your current directory on the client.
mv "file name.ext" filename.ext	Rename/move a file with a space in the name on the client to a new name without a space.
cp "file name.ext" filename.ext	Copy/duplicate a file with a space in the name on the client to a new name without a space.
ssh-keygen -b 4096	Only run once to generate client SSH keys.
cd ~/.ssh	Change Directory to the client SSH key directory created by *ssh-keygen*.
cp -ip id_rsa id_rsa.orig && cp -ip id_rsa.pub id_rsa.pub.orig	Only run once to back up the client RSA generated keys in the *~/.ssh* directory.
scp id_rsa.pub userid@serverdomain.dyndns.ext:.ssh /authorized_keys	Only run once to copy the client public RSA key generated by *ssh-keygen* to the SSH server *$HOME/.ssh* directory.
ssh userid@serverdomain.dyndns.ext 'cp -ip .ssh/authorized_keys .ssh/authorized_keys.orig && ls .ssh'	Only run once to backup/copy/duplicate the *auhorized_keys* file on the SSH server from the SSH client and list the files.
cd Desktop/SSHFileDirectory or, cd "Dir With Spaces or - special characters"	Change Directory from the user home directory to the **Desktop** and/or the directory where the SSH files to be transferred are.
ssh userid@serverdomain.dyndns.ext	Connect and log in to your account on the SSH server.
ssh userid@serverdomain.dyndns.ext 'ls'	Get a directory listing from the SSH server home directory without logging in.
scp filename.ext userid@serverdomain.dyndns.ext:.	Copy one file *to* the SSH server users home directory. Don't forget the ":." at the end.
scp userid@serverdomain.dyndns.ext:file name.ext .	Copy one file *from* the SSH server to the current client directory.
scp filename1.ext filename2.ext userid@serverdomain.dyndns.ext:.	Copy two or more files to the SSH server user home directory.
scp *	Copy all files in the current client directory to the

userid@serverdomain.dyndns.ext:.	users home directory on the SSH server.
scp *.docx userid@serverdomain.dyndns.ext:.	Copy all files with the extension .docx to the users home directory on the SSH server.
scp root@serverdomain.dyndns.org:/home/userid/sshin/* .	Copy all files that a user has transferred to our SSH server to the current working directory.
mkdir sshout && ssh userid@serverdomain.dyndns.org 'mkdir sshin'	Make the directories to send and receive files to/from the SSH server and client, very useful for recursive folder copies.
scp * userid@serverdomain.dyndns.ext:./sshin	Copy all files in the current client directory to the users $HOME/sshin directory on the SSH server.
scp userid@serverdomain.dyndns.ext:./sshout/* .	Copy all files from the SSH server $HOME/sshout directory to the current directory on the SSH client.
scp -r sshout userid@serverdomain.dyndns.ext:.	Copy the client directory sshout and all its contents/files to the SSH server user home directory.
scp -r userid@serverdomain.dyndns.ext:sshin .	Copy the server directory sshin and all its contents/files to the current SSH client directory.
rm -rf sshout # or, rm -rf sshin	Remove the sshout or sshin directory and all contents/files.

PuTTY is not added to the Windows 7 system path by default. If typing any of the commands below shows: 'command' is not recognized as an internal or external command... refer back to SSH client-Obtaining, Installing and Setting up Software on our Mobile Devices to Access our Secure SSH Server Remotely.

Windows 7 OS & PuTTY terminal window commands, , userid= , serverdomain= , ext=	
dir or dir/w	List directory contents on the client in the current working directory.
cd "C:\dir with space\user id" or, cd C:\dirwithoutspace\userid	Change directory to where the files are located to operate upon.
move "file with space.txt" filename.txt move filewithoutspace.ext filename.ext	Rename/move a file on the client to a new name without a space.
copy "file with space.ext" filename.ext copy filewithougspace.ext filename.ext	Copy/duplicate a file on the client to a new name without a space.
cd Desktop/SSHFileDirectory or, cd "Dir With Spaces or - special characters"	Change Directory from the user home directory, to the **Desktop** and/or the directory where the SSH files to be transferred are.
puttygen	Bring up the PuTTY Key Generator.
plink	Show all command line options for PuTTY command-line connection utility.
plink -V	Print version information about plink (e.g. pscp: Release 0.63)
plink userid@serverdomain.dyndns.ext	Connect and log in to your account on the SSH

	server.
plink userid@serverdomain.dyndns.ext 'ls'	Get a directory listing from the SSH server home directory without logging in.
pscp	Show all command line options for PuTTY Secure Copy client.
pscp -V # or	Print version information about pscp (e.g. pscp: Release 0.63)
pscp authorized_keys userid@domainname.dyndns.ext:.ssh/authorized_keys	Only run once to copy the client public RSA key generated by *puttygen* to the SSH server *$HOME/.ssh* directory.
pscp filename.ext userid@serverdomain.dyndns.ext:.	Copy one file *to* the SSH server users home directory.
pscp filename1.ext filename2.ext userid@serverdomain.dyndns.ext:.	Copy two or more files to the SSH server user home directory.
pscp *.docx userid@serverdomain.dyndns.ext:.	Copy all files with the extension .docx to the users home directory on the SSH server.
pscp * userid@serverdomain.dyndns.ext:./sshin	Copy all files in the current client directory to the users *$HOME/sshin* directory on the SSH server.ls
pscp userid@serverdomain.dyndns.ext:./sshout/ * .	Copy all files from the SSH server *$HOME/sshout* directory to the current directory on the SSH client.
pscp -r sshout userid@serverdomain.dyndns.ext:./sshin	Copy the client directory *sshout* and all its contents/files *to* the SSH server user home directory *sshin*.
pscp -r userid@serverdomain.dyndns.ext:sshout .	Copy the server directory *sshin* and all its contents/files to the current SSH client directory.
putty	Bring up the PuTTY Configuration GUI.
pscp root@serverdomain.dyndns.ext:/home/userid/sshout/* .	As owner 'root' of the SSH server copy all file in a partners directory to the current working directory on the Windows 7 machine.
pscp root@serverdomain.dyndns.ext:/home/userid/sshin/* .	Copy all files that a user has transferred to our SSH server to the current working directory.

SSH KeepAlive to Keep Your Session Active

If you are working remotely connected to your SSH server, you never know how your day may progress. Say, for example, you have connected to your SB/HC server and get called to a meeting, or you have to leave the office for an extended duration. Assuming your mobile device is in a secure location, you may not want your connection to your SSH server to cease. SSH comes with an option called TCPKeepAlive enabled by default that sends packets back and forth across your connection to keep you session alive. This is probably adequate for most SSH sessions but it has a few advantages and drawbacks.

Advantages:

- Without TCPKeepAlive enabled, the server would have no way of determining if the client crashed or the connection was severed. The server would become what is known in the Linux world as a zombie and continue to service a severed connection. This would consume SSH server resources, and after it occurs enough times, will require a reboot. With this option enabled, the server will detect when the client is no longer connected and shutdown processes servicing that connection accordingly.

Disadvantages:

- A TCPKeepAlive is spoofable. It is part of the TCP protocol and is not sent through the SSH encrypted protocol. It is sent at the Transport Layer of the OSI model, so it is not as secure as using SSH-ClientAlive packets. We will refer to these as SSH-Encrypted-KeepAlives, which can be used in addition to TCPKeepAlives, or as an alternative.
- The router or OS behind an SBO/HCO network may have their own rules on how long to keep a TCP session active with TCPKeepAlives. For example, if you are running you SSH server as Virtual Machine, the NAT rules may sever your connection.
- TCPKeepAlives are not very configurable, where-as SSH-Encrypted-KeepAlives are.

We can setup how our SSH server and mobile device interact very precisely using SSH-Encrypted-KeepAlives. There are two options on both the client and the server that can be used to enable and control how we do this. On the server side in the */etc/sshd_config* file set:

```
ClientAliveInterval 900      # Number of seconds before an I-am-alive message is sent
ClientAliveCountMax 16       # Number of times before the server severs the connection
```

On the client side in the /etc/ssh_config file set:

```
ServerAliveInterval 900      # Number of seconds before an I-am-alive message is sent
ServerAliveCountMax 16       # Number of times before the server severs the connection
```

SSH-Encrypted-KeepAlives operate across your encrypted tunnel. If using TCPKeepAlives are not keeping your connection open for extended periods of time, set up SSH-Encrypted-KeepAlives.

NOTE	If your router or SSH OS tear down your TCP connection to your SSH server, you will lose your SSH tunnel. You may have to figure out what is happening at the Transport Layer to keep your connection active for extended periods.

Setting Up a Fixed CHROOT to Secure a Linux SSH SFTP Server for File Transfer Using Public/Private Keys

Regrettably, our example large entities requirements creep that was discussed earlier has happened again. This is beneficial to our SB, as the open source community has made alternate solutions available to us. In this book, I wanted to present various SSH solutions for you to choose from and have some fun describing the corporate and government worlds of Information Technology (IT). I'm hoping you are finding this book somewhat entertaining as well as informative on how government and corporations work. With the infinite amounts of cash that large entities have at their disposal, the IT manager has called another meeting of all the people involved in the previous SSH project.

The IT staff was happy that the SSH project requirements were met and then had moved on to other things. Unfortunately, security concerns came to management's attention in that the transfer of files and data between their organization and partners had a few security holes.

1) Once a partner is logged into the SSH server, the server is open to limited attack.
2) Our partners could mistakenly set permissions on files that could compromise that data to other partners or employees that use the SSH server.

This was discovered by an incredibly expensive security audit conducted by well-paid contract penetration testers. They were unleashed to hack the computers and networks behind the corporate firewalls. A better alternative would have been, after completion of the SSH project, for management to sit down with their IT staff and discuss what could have been done to improve security. Often times the IT staff knows about possible security holes and would suggest repairing them. I'm sorry to say that upper management and IT staff rarely, if ever, meet.

 **Story**	I have always wondered if this could be the old bait and switch. These holes may be left open intentionally. If you present a witch hunter with a witch to burn, then the auditors are less inclined to dig deeper for security holes to present to government officials and management. If the auditors continued to poke around, they might find nothing, but with further digging they might turn over a rock rather than a pebble that would cost a lot more to fix. Leaving open these obvious security holes present security professionals (auditors) with holes they are trained to find. They go home knowing they ran the usual software that would find the usual mistakes that the corporations offered up in the usual manner. This makes everyone looking in from the outside happy.

Now we move on **_Requirements Definition 2,_** which is similar to RD1. The Requirements Definition remains the same as RD1, except we will add the following:

Communication or the exchange of data shall be solely accomplished using the SSH protocol via Secure File Transfer Protocol (SFTP). The server *sftp* connections shall be made completely secure (from hacking) by what is known as a *chroot* to a server subdirectory that will render all files on the SSH server invisible to our partners.

In other words, each partner account will be excluded access to any directory or data on the SSH server except the directories to/from which our partners use to exchange files and data. Our partners will only be allowed SFTP (no ssh or scp) access to our SSH server, which only allows for the transfer of files. The account and directory that we allow our partners to use to exchange files and data with our SSH server will be put in a jail cell that where they can see nothing else that exists on the SSH server except their home directory and the files there. We don't want our clients to have access to other files on the server, so where they *sftp* their files to/from should be all they will see when logged in. This way, even if their private key is compromised, the cracker has a limited hole in our defenses that can be exploited. In addition, by limiting them to only SFTP access to only allow file transfer, no login or shell functions are available. We are layering our defenses again, the mantra of this book!

Let's break down the tasks into what is needed. The */etc/ssh/sshd_config* file will have to be configured to allow only *sftp* connections. The man pages at http://www.openbsd.org/cgi-bin/man.cgi?query=sshd config&sektion=5 reveal how to do that. We need to think about/create the groups and organize our SSH server(s) users and groups.

Performing a change root (CHROOT) to another directory will limit the user's visibility to a Linux/UNIX computer that user is logged into. It essentially changes the user's *root* directory so that anything higher in the directory hierarchy is invisible and completely inaccessible. For example, your SB may contract out your payroll to ADP or have your employee benefits with Prudential; you need to exchange data with them that has to be kept secure and separate between each of your business partners. This means granting them access to your SSH server but not to the other directories and other data that exists on your server. It is not cost effective to set up a separate SSH server for each of them.

Sounds ambitious, so let's get started. My original plan to fulfill these requirements was to only allow sftp transfers in passive mode, which is a more secure way of using FTP to transfer files. Good descriptions of Active verses Passive FTP can be found at http://dant.net.ru/wiki/info/networking/ftpmodes or http://en.wikipedia.org/wiki/File_Transfer_Protocol. From Wiki, "*In passive mode FTP the client initiates both connections to the server, solving the problem of firewalls filtering the incoming data port connection to the client from the server.*" After further research, I did not find anything indicating *passive* transfers were possible or recommended with sftp. Let's add two groups to our SSH server that we will use to then lock things down and use scripts to automate things later.

```
# groupadd partners
# groupadd sftponly
```

In researching all of this, there were many incomplete and old articles on the Internet about setting up a *chroot* to another directory when a user performs a *sftp* to an SSH server. You have to configure OpenSSH to use its internal SFTP subsystem. Then add a few configuration lines to have it do a *chroot* to a fixed location. Later we will discuss doing a *chroot* to a variable user location, which locks things down even further. I will distinguish between what worked and what did not so you do not go down these same rabbit holes should you decide to pursue other options. To get started we have to examine the Subsystem configuration item in the */etc/ssh/sshd_config*.

From the man page, The Subsystem "*configures an external subsystem (e.g. file transfer daemon).*" The first argument is the subsystem name, the second argument is the command (with optional arguments) to execute when the subsystem name is requested.

```
# cd /etc/ssh && vi sshd_config
```

Go to the bottom of the configuration file. Comment out the line:

```
#Subsystem sftp /usr/lib/openssh/sftp-server
```

Replace it with:

```
Subsystem sftp internal-sftp
```

Changing "/usr/lib/openssh/sftp-server" to "internal-sftp" will implement an in-process "sftp" server. In other words, we are configuring OpenSSH to use its internal SFTP subsystem. Otherwise when we attempt to connect to our SSH server with a CHROOT account we will get:

```
subsystem request for sftp by user testuser
debug1: subsystem: cannot stat /usr/lib/openssh/sftp-server: No such file or
directory
debug1: subsystem: exec() /usr/lib/openssh/sftp-server
debug1: Received SIGCHLD.
```

The man page states, "*This may simplify configurations using ChrootDirectory to force a different filesystem root on clients.*" It does!

NOTE	Performing a CHROOT into an SSH server is much like Sandboxing an application. We are jailing our partner(s) in an area of our SSH server that has no access to other directories, files or executables on our SSH server.

The configuration item that we will use to keep each partner in their own jail cell is *ChrootDirectory*. If our goal was to just jail the users and protect our SSH server files above the directory /home the following would work. Specifying */home* as a fixed configuration will work for a single user, or if all our SSH server users are SFTP only. The default *$HOME* directory for Linux users is */home/<UserID>*. The *ChrootDirectory /home* will house our SFTP user IDs in the usual location with the slight modification of adding the directory */home/home*. We can then create our SFTP User IDs the standard way and move them under */home/home* directory.   However, if we plan to have other users on our SSH server in the standard /home directory, we will want to house our SFTP users in a directory below */home* like */home/chroot*. This change to a lower directory in the hierarchy insulates our SFTP users from our regular users and privileged SSH server users.

```
Match group sftponly
     ChrootDirectory /home      # or,
     ChrootDirectory /home/chroot
#    PasswordAuthentication no      # Enable when all SFTP users are setup
     X11Forwarding no
     AllowTcpForwarding no
     ForceCommand internal-sftp
```

Before we start creating the user IDs, let's examine what the man page for OpenSSH says about the changes just made to the bottom of the */etc/ssh/sshd_config* configuration file. The

Match group sftponly configuration item tells sshd to override everything previously specified, and for the group *sftponly* to implement the new security protocols. All members of the *sftponly* group will only be allowed to connect to our SSH server using the OpenSSH *sftp* client using an encrypted connection. All we now need to do now is modify or create accounts for all of our partners to be members of the *sftponly* group. This will force them to only be able to transfer files between our HC/SB SSH server using encryption and jail (better than sandbox) their access to our SSH server.

To understand the options we are using, a good description was taken from the documentation at http://www.openbsd.org/cgi-bin/man.cgi?query=sshd_config&sektion=5&arch=&apropos=0&manpath=OpenBSD+Current:

AllowTcpForwarding	Specifies whether TCP forwarding is permitted. The default is "yes". Note that disabling TCP forwarding does not improve security unless users are also denied shell access, as they can always install their own forwarders.
ChrootDirectory	Specifies the pathname of a directory to chroot(2) to after authentication. All components of the pathname must be root-owned directories that are not writable by any other user or group. After the chroot, sshd(8) changes the working directory to the user's home directory.
ForceCommand	Forces the execution of the command specified by ForceCommand, ignoring any command supplied by the client and ~/.ssh/rc, if present. The command is invoked by using the user's login shell with the -c option. This applies to shell, command, or subsystem execution. It is most useful inside a Match block. The command originally supplied by the client is available in the SSH_ORIGINAL_COMMAND environment variable. Specifying a command of "internal-sftp" will force the use of an in-process sftp server that requires no support files when used with ChrootDirectory.
Match	Introduces a conditional block. If all of the criteria on the Match line are satisfied, the keywords on the following lines override those set in the global section of the config file, until either another Match line or the end of the file. (see man ssh_config(5) for further information).
X11Forwarding	Specifies whether X11 forwarding is permitted. The argument must be "yes" or "no". The default is "no". When X11 forwarding is enabled, there may be additional exposure to the server and to client displays if the sshd(8) proxy display is configured to listen on the wildcard address (see X11UseLocalhost below), though this is not the default. Additionally, the authentication spoofing and authentication data verification and substitution occur on the client side. The security risk of using X11 forwarding is that the client's X11 display server may be exposed to attack when the SSH client requests forwarding (see the warnings for ForwardX11 in ssh_config(5)). A system administrator may have a stance in which they want to protect clients that may expose themselves to attack by

	unwittingly requesting X11 forwarding, which can warrant a "no" setting. Note that disabling X11 forwarding does not prevent users from forwarding X11 traffic, as users can always install their own forwarders. X11 forwarding is automatically disabled if UseLogin is enabled

Save the file and restart the *sshd* daemon to apply the changes:

```
# cd /etc/init.d && ./ssh restart    # The old way
# service ssh restart     # The new way
```

Tip
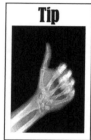
	Something that came in very handy for troubleshooting were the debug options of the SSHD server process. The debug options of the SSH server *sshd* process can be used to troubleshoot any daemon problems by stopping the background daemon and starting it again in the foreground of a terminal window:
	
	`# service ssh stop     # Stop the SSH daemon`
	`# psg sshd     # Make sure the daemon is stopped`
	`# /usr/sbin/sshd -d -d -d     # Each additional -d increases logging.`

So our server script to create our SFTP Server User IDs becomes:

```
#!/bin/bash
# Script name createfixedsftpserveruser.sh.   SSH Server User addition script.
# Use: ./createsftpserveruser.sh <UserID> "User Description" <home|chroot>
# set -x     # Uncomment to debug this script

Usage ()
(
    echo "Usage:"
    echo "$0 <User Account>" "\"<User's full name>\"" "<home|chroot>"
)


proc_root_check ()
{
    # Make sure script is being run by root
    if [ "$(id -u)" != "0" ]; then
        echo "ERROR: This script must be run as root!"
        exit
    else
        echo "INFO: Script running as root."
    fi
}
```

```
if [[ "$#" -lt 3 ]]; then
    Usage
    exit
fi


proc_root_check

# Create the user account and set the permissions:
useradd -c "$2" -g partners -G partners,sftponly $1 -m -N -s /usr/sbin/nologin
chmod 700 /home/$1
rm -rf /home/$1/.* 2>/dev/null     # Delete the dot files from /etc/skel
mkdir /home/$1/.ssh
mkdir /home/$1/in  &&  mkdir /home/$1/out


chown -R $1:partners /home/$1
chmod -R 700 /home/$1


# Move the home directory to our chroot and create link to it to make
# access to <UserID> same as other users.  This is convenient for
# root scripting.  Check to see which jail we are using:
if [[ $3 == "home" ]]; then
    if [[ ! -d /home/home ]]; then
        mkdir /home/home
    fi
    mv /home/$1 /home/home
    ln -s /home/home/$1 /home/$1
elif [[ $3 == "chroot" ]]; then
    # If /home/chroot is preferred for better security:
    if [[ ! -d /home/chroot/home ]]; then
        mkdir -p /home/chroot/home
    fi
    mv /home/$1 /home/chroot/home
    ln -s /home/chroot/home/$1 /home/$1
else
    userdel -r $1
    if [[ $3 == "home" ]]; then
        rm /home/$1
        rm -r /home/home/$1
    elif [[ $3 == "chroot" ]]; then
        rm /home/chroot/$1
        rm -r /home/chroot/$1
    fi
    Usage
    exit
```

```
fi

passwd $1
# chage -d 0 $1  &&  chage -l $1     # Will not work for SFTP only user's
```

```
# vim createfixedsftpserveruser.sh      # Cut and paste above
# chmod 700 createfixedsftpserveruser.sh
# ./createfixedsftpserveruser.sh <UserID> "User Full Name" home|chroot
```

Refer back to <u>Adding Less Privileged User IDs for Specific Purposes to Linux</u> to understand the *useradd* options utilized. In the example script above we added the user ID to two groups and did not allow the default behavior of creating a group ID the same as the user ID. The group 'sftponly' is our "match" in the SSHD configuration file */etc/ssh/sshd_config* to jail this user as a SFTP only User ID. We added the 'partners' group so that a non-SFTP user, who is also a member of the 'partners' group can consolidate all of the files transferred to our SSH server. Otherwise, this function would have to perform by the privileged 'root' user ID.

Trying to have a SFTP only user reset an expired passwd set by *chage* will result in a *Connection closed* error, and our partners will not be able to login. Therefore, we commented that line out, and we had to set up and provide our SFTP only partners their initial password to log in to their account. It is up to our partners to manually send their public key to our SSH server. We may also want to jail our SFTP users separately from our regular or fully empowered SSH server users. To do that, we would use something such as ChrootDirectory /home/chroot to create the SFTP chroot directory below the */home* directory. The script above allows for both options depending on your needs. We specified the "-m" option to the "useradd" command above so that the user's home directory was created. However, this option also copied in the dot files from directory */etc/skel* that had to be deleted for a SFTP user. Moreover, because we are only allowing SFTP connections, we don't allow an interactive login to the account by specifying the *-s /use/sbin/nologin* option, making our SSH server more secure. Everything else remains the same as in the previous requirements definition.

To remove a user from our SSH server using the following script:

```
#!/bin/bash
# Script name removesftpserveruser.sh.   SSH Server User delection script.
# Script will work for fixed or variable SFTP user IDs.
# set -x     # Uncomment to debug this script

Usage()
(
    echo "Usage:"
    echo "$0 <User Account>" "<home|chroot|var>"
)

if [[ "$#" -lt 2 ]]; then
```

```
    Usage
    exit
fi


userdel $1      # Remove the Userfrom the /etc login files

if [[ $2 == "home" ]]; then
    rm /home/$1      # Remove the symbolic link
    rm -rf /home/home/$1
elif [[ $2 == "chroot" ]]; then
    rm /home/$1      # Remove the symbolic link
    rm -rf /home/chroot/home/$1
elif [[ $2 == "var" ]]; then
    rm -rf /home/$1
else
    Usage
    exit
fi
```

The symbolic link in the fixed directory configuration above seemed unnecessary at first, but without it passwordless authentication is not possible in *home/home* or */home/chroot/home*. The SSH server will prompt for a password regardless of the fact that you may have copied the public key to the server in the user's *~/.ssh* directory. It is also unfortunate that using SFTP is a bit more complex for our partners. SFTP does not provide an easy way to script entering a password and sending their client public key to our SSH server. The only thing we can do for our clients is to give a partner a script to create their user ID(s) and generate their keys. However, they will have to log in manually and follow our directions to send their public key to our SSH sever for passwordless login. The client user creation script outlined for SFTP SSH file transfer now becomes:

```
#!/bin/bash
# set -x      # Uncomment to debug script
# Script name createsftpclientuser.sh.   SSH Client User addition script.
# This script works for both fixed and variable SFTP users.
# To delete our client user simply type:
# userdel -r <User ID>

fUserSSH=/home/$1/ssh.sh
echo User script ${fUserSSH} being created.

Usage ()
(
    echo "Usage:"
    echo "$0 <User Account>" "\"<User's full name>\"" "<SSH Server IP>" "<Key Type
(rsa or dsa)>"
```

```bash
)

if [ "$#" -lt 4 ]
then
    Usage
    exit
fi


useradd -c "$2" -m $1 -s /bin/bash
passwd $1


/bin/bash << EOF2
cat << 'EOF' > ${fUserSSH}
#!/bin/bash
# set -x       # Uncomment to debug script
echo "Accept the default key file location by pressing <Enter>.  Then"
echo "press <Enter> again (twice) to assign a blank passphrase.  (If"
echo "you enter a passphrase, you will be prompted for that passphrase"
echo "and won't be able to log in without it.  This will not allow the"
echo "automation for file transfer)"

if [[ $4 == "dsa" ]]; then
    ssh-keygen -t dsa -C "$(whoami)@$(hostname)-$(date -I)"
else     # For a RSA key use the following:
    # For a RSA key use either of the following:
    ssh-keygen -b 4096 -C "$(whoami)@$(hostname)-$(date -I)"
    # ssh-keygen -b 8196 -C "$(whoami)@$(hostname)-$(date -I)"
fi


chmod 700 ~$1 && chmod 700 ~$1/.ssh
cd ~/.ssh


cp -ip id_$4 id_$4.orig && cp -ip id_$4.pub id_$4.pub.orig
echo "Public key ~/.ssh/id_$4.pub and private key ~/.ssh/$4 have been backed up"

echo "When you connect to the SSH Server for the first time:"
echo "The authenticity of host '<ServerIP> (<ServerIP>)' can't be established."
echo "ECDSA key fingerprint is 66:93:29:ed:25:ff:0a:bd:62:df:0c:f5:93:8c:27:45."
echo "Be sure to compare this fingerprint to the fingerprint provided to you"
echo "for our SSH server in the directions on setting up a SSH connection."
echo
echo "We are now connecting to the SSH server.  Once connected, to enable"
echo "passwordless authentication you now need to transfer your public key just"
echo "generated to the SSH server.  Follow these commands to do so:"
```

```
# echo "lcd .ssh"      # Already done above
echo
echo "cd .ssh"
echo "put id_rsa.pub authorized_keys"
echo "put id_rsa.pub authorized_keys.orig"
echo "exit"
echo

sftp $1@$3      # Connect to SSH server so we can transfer the public key

EOF
EOF2

chown $1:$1 ${fUserSSH}
chmod 700 ${fUserSSH}

su $1 -c ${fUserSSH}
rm ${fUserSSH}
```

Once this is set up, if your users attempt to connect with any other method than sftp without the ForceCommand option specified, you will see:

```
$ ssh hometestuser@192.168.1.5
testuser1@ubuntu:~$ ssh testuser1@192.168.1.5
Welcome to Linux Mint 13 Maya (GNU/Linux 3.2.0-30-generic i686)


Welcome to Linux Mint
 * Documentation: http://www.linuxmint.com
/usr/sbin/nologin: No such file or directory
Connection to 192.168.1.5 closed.
```

The *ForceCommand* option under *Match group sftponly* disables all types of connections except for *sftp* users in the *sftponly* group. If your partner attempts something like $ scp <file> <userid>@<ServerIP>:<file> they will get the message:

```
This service allows sftp connections only.
Connection to 192.168.1.5 closed.
```

```
# vim createfixedsftpclientuser.sh      # Cut and Paste above
# chmod 700 createfixedsftpclientuser.sh
# ./createfixedsftpclientuser.sh <UserID> "User Full Name" <Server IP> rsa|dsa
```

To actually use the client account as described above, edit the */ssh/sshd_config* file:

```
ChrootDirectory /home
# service ssh restart      # On the SSH Server
```

Then on the Client:
```
# ./createfixedsftpclientuser.sh hometestuser "Home SSH Fixed Test User" home
# su - hometestuser
$ sftp hometestuser@192.168.1.5
```

```
ChrootDirectory /home/chroot
# service ssh restart     # On the SSH Server
```

Then on the Client:
```
# ./createfixedsftpclientuser.sh chroottestuser "Chroot SSH Fixed Test User" chroot
# su - chroottestuser
$ sftp chroottestuser@192.168.1.5
```

We are steadily layering our security, so I'm presenting different options for you from which to choose. If we look back at our requirements definition 2 it says that *the server sftp connections shall be made completely secure (from hacking) by what is known as a chroot to a server subdirectory that will render all files on the server invisible to our partners.*

Using */home/chroot* accomplishes that except for the fact that our partners can change directory # cd / to the root directory, which will show the other partner's accounts. This is perfectly fine because the directory permissions that were set by our script will keep the other partners from viewing or copying each other's files; but do we want our partners to know who our other partners are? Our partners are in jail in their one cell, but have not been cut off from the general prison population.

Setting up a Variable CHROOT to Secure a Linux SSH SFTP Server for File Transfer Using Public/Private Keys

Once again, requirements have changed. Somehow, one of our partners opened up the permissions on their directories and files and another partner was able to view some sensitive data. That partner brought this to our management's attention and another IT meeting was called to address this security breach. Many potential solutions were discussed, and rather than house all partners in one jail cell where permissions keep them apart, it was decided that we would completely separate each partner into their own CHROOT. This will completely separate them from each other and lock things down further by putting each partner in solitary confinement, making our SSH server even more secure. This means that our CHROOT jails need to vary based on our partners <UserIDs>.

So now we move on **Requirements Definition 3,** which is very similar to RD1-RD2, but with the following notable exception.

The server *sftp* connections shall be made completely secure (from hacking) by what is known as a *chroot* to a server subdirectory that will render all files and accounts on the server invisible to our partners except for what is in their own *sftp* $HOME directory.

This differs slightly from *Requirement Definition 2* in that our partners will no longer be able to "sftp> cd /" and see what other accounts exist on our SSH server. All that they will see are their own files and directories, and nothing else on the server. The OpenSSH *sshd* daemon has the following variable configuration options:

ChrootDirectory /home/dir%%/chroot	Is replaced by a literal '%' in case a path looks like /home/dir%/chroot.
ChrootDirectory %h	Is replaced by the user's home directory of the user being authenticated, as specified in the /etc/passwd file. This will jail all users in their home directory /home/<UserID>.
ChrootDirectory /home/%u	Is replaced by the username of the user /home/<UserID>.

As wonderful as having these options are, using these options can be confusing. The man page for *sshd_config* states, "*All components of the pathname must be root-owned directories that are not writable by any other user or group. After the chroot, sshd(8) changes the working directory to the user's home directory.*" This means OpenSSH requires that the root directory of a CHROOT be owned by the superuser 'root'. So when we create user IDs we will have to change their home directory ownership to 'root'. This is counterintuitive because a directory owned by 'root' is inaccessible by any other user on a Linux system, so the second restriction has to read *literally*. Searching the Internet held no answer to this riddle and would yield many hours of frustration were you not reading this book. The server */etc/ssh/sshd_config* configuration for fixed location SFTP CHROOT server remains the same as for a variable location with the following exceptions in the */etc/ssh/sshd_config* file:

```
Match group sftponly
    ChrootDirectory /home/%u      # or,
    ChrootDirectory %h
```

Save the file and restart the *sshd* daemon to apply the changes # service ssh restart.

In trying to get all of this working, I went down many blind alleys. This was very frustrating since I had a fixed location solution that was working fine; I was tempted to leave a variable solution out of the book. There were many web pages, man pages, and books that I referenced to solve this riddle, but none had the step-by-step examples that I needed to satisfy this new requirements definition. All that was stated in those references was that this was possible and that these options existed. A few examples of things you might try, as I did, that will fail are:

```
# chown root:root /home/<UserID>      # Will fail
# chmod 777 /home/<UserID>      # Will fail with bad ownership
# chmod 770 /home/<UserID>      # Will fail with bad ownership
# usermod -d / <UserID>      # Will fail
# chown testuser /home/<UserID>      # Will fail with bad ownership
# chmod 700 /home/<UserID>      # Will allow you to connect but permission is denied
# chmod 740 /home/<UserID>      # Will allow you to connect but permission is denied
# mkdir /chroot/home && mount --bind /home /chroot/home      # Will fail
```

And so on... I only detail the list above to show how there are many blind alleys that we can go down in setting up a variable SSH CHROOT following old advice. The latest version of OpenSSH is very strict about allowing access to accounts on an SSH server, as it should be and **as the developers intended it!** Unless the directory permissions, ownership, groups, and configuration are set up correctly, SSHD will **wisely** not allow a connection, giving an error resembling "`bad ownership or modes for chroot directory "/home/<UserID>`" error". Recall that with a fixed location, when a partner SFTPs to our server, they will land in a server directory such as */home/chroot/home/<UserID>*. This means that the partner's home directory can have different ownership and permissions than our actual SSH server */home/chroot* directory. Using a variable CHROOT that is set up correctly will work in much same fashion. The words on the *sshd_config* man page "*not writable by any other user or group*" now come into play in the changes that are necessary to meet RD3. To understand the following, let's briefly examine how the file permissions work in Linux.

Linux has three specific permissions on file and directory systems that apply to each class. Let's discuss the two that you need to set for a directory. The read permission, when set for a directory, grants the ability to read the names of files in a directory. Execute permission is needed to allow a user to "cd" into a directory. Execute-only permission allows a user to access the files in a directory as long as the user knows the names of the files in the directory and then the user is allowed to read the files. To allow our variable CHROOT to work we have to set both permissions. We also have to set the group to a specific group to which our variable CHROOT user belongs. Let's revisit our server user creation script and modify it for our new variable CHROOT, meeting our new requirements.

```
#!/bin/bash
# Script name createvarsftpserveruser.sh.   SSH Server Variable SFTP User addition
script.
# set -x     # Uncomment to debug this script

Usage()
(
    echo "Usage:"
    echo "$0 <UserID> \"User Description\""
)

if [[ "$#" -lt 2 ]]; then
    Usage
    exit
fi


# Create the user account and set the permissions and group needed by SSHD:
useradd -c "$2" -g partners -G partners,sftponly $1 -m -N -s /usr/sbin/nologin
chmod 750 /home/$1  &&  chown root:sftponly /home/$1
rm -rf /home/$1/.* 2>/dev/null
```

```
# Create the sub-directory structure needed for a variable CHROOT by our client:
mkdir /home/$1/.ssh && chown $1:sftponly /home/$1/.ssh && chmod 700 /home/$1/.ssh
mkdir -p /home/$1/home/$1/in  && mkdir /home/$1/home/$1/out
chown root:sftponly /home/$1/home && chmod 750 /home/$1/home


chown -R $1:partners /home/$1/home/$1
chmod -R 770 /home/$1/home/$1


passwd $1
# chage -d 0 $1  &&  chage -l     # Will not work with SFTP only user IDs


# vim createvarsftpserveruser.sh
# chmod 700 createvarsftpserveruser.sh
# ./createvarftpserveruser.sh <UserID> "User Full Name"
```

From the SSHD ChrootDirectory description above, it specified that the path we *chroot* to must be root-owned and not writable by any other user or group. This means that everything in the path is:

- owned by root
- not group or otherwise writable

The defaults for system directories in the usual Linux user's path are:

```
# ll /
drwxr-xr-x  4 root root   4096 <date time> ./
drwxr-xr-x  4 root root   4096 <date time> ../
drwxr-xr-x  4 root root   4096 <date time> home/
```

Therefore, nothing in the default path needs to be changed. I have already discussed how we do not want all the partner files stored in an unconventional location as */var/chroot/home*. This would prove difficult to support if we have to hire an outside consultant. In the past I have worked with administrators that have set things up in weird ways (can you say job security) and then they left the company; I had a dickens of a time figuring out what they did. So our question becomes how to keep our partner accounts under */home* and easily administered. The standard path setup in the */etc/passwd* is */home/<UserID>*. We want to use the Linux OS's standard path within our chroot. This way, if we chroot somewhere on the system, we will see something like *<chroothome>/home/<UserID>*, which anyone familiar with Linux will understand. Refer back to Setting up a Fixed CHROOT to use that client user creation script. Everything else remains the same.

```
# su - testvaruser
$ sftp testvaruser@192.168.1.5
```

If you wish to do some additional reading on SSH, (See: https://help.ubuntu.com/community/SSH/OpenSSH/Configuring)

To remove a CHROOT user is not as simple as the traditional method we covered above:

```
# userdel -r <UserID>
userdel: /home/<UserID> not owned by <UserID>, not removing
```

So refer back to our removesftpserveruser.sh script covered in the previous section. The last thing to set up is our application administrator accounts. These users will not be included in the *sftponly* group so they can "sftp, scp, ssh" to the server without difficulty. I wanted to set up their accounts so that they could change their password upon login, but once again got "connection closed" when I did a "# chage -d 0 $1". Consequently, they will have to either guard their password or set up the public/private key pair and disable Password Authentication in the configuration file's main body. The last step will be automating encrypting and decryption files from/to our partners. To do this we will use the Linux *cron* process to consolidate all the files into a location that our application administrators know of so they can quickly copy/view the files. If we put everybody in the partner's group, the admins have permission to do what they want with the partner's files. This will be covered soon. The public/private key pair login can also be accomplished from Windows 7. (See: http://www.linux-sxs.org/networking/openssh.putty.html)

Setting up CHROOT Secure Linux SSH Server for SSH Login Using Public/Private Keys

Our corporate requirements drift has continued. Now management wants to allow a few of our partners the ability to login and use a restricted subset of our SSH's servers capabilities. Management wants to use this same server to keep their employees secure using hotspots everywhere in the world and to use it as an SFTP only server. We are creating an ever more complex SSH server setup with many options for our partners.

So now we move on ***Requirements Definition 4***, which is similar to RD1-RD2-RD3, but allows our partners to log in to our SSH server, so let's change it to the following:
An area on our SSH server shall be configured to allow a limited group of privileged partners the use of some commands and utilities within a CHROOT. Communication or the exchange of data with our SSH server shall be made completely secure (from hacking) by using the *chroot* command to a server subdirectory that will render all command and utilities on the SSH server invisible, except what we choose to set up for our partners to use. Other less privileged partners will be restricted to SFTP only access to our server. Other more privileged partners and administrators will be allowed non-CHROOT SSH access to our SSH server.

Most of these requirements have already been met. We can create a User ID to allow a partner or administrator non-CHROOT access to our SSH server simply by making sure they are not a member of a CHROOT 'match' group. We covered how to set up those user IDs with Requirements Definition 1. The SFTP setup we covered in RD2 and RD3, so now we are going to setup CHROOT users with SSH login and a limited set of utilities.

Enabling CHROOT SSH login with limited capabilities is much more complicated than just allowing a fully empowered SSH login or setting up a partner for SFTP only. This is because we must set up a chroot environment as a mini OS with all programs/tools/utilities (e.g. /bin/bash, /bin/cp, etc.) that our partners will need to use. This means that we must create a minimal OS set up within the CHROOT OS directory on our SSH server by copying in all the devices, binaries, libraries, links, and anything else that these users need to login and use in their CHROOT jail. While this could be done for each user in a Variable CHROOT, it makes more sense to create a fixed CHROOT and only set this up once. Then we can add users who will all have the same capabilities on our SSH server.

This can be a very time consuming and somewhat complicated task where many steps may be involved. There has been work done on this in the open source community that could help. Regrettably, I could find no modern, straightforward approach to setting up a minimal CHROOT OS environment, so I will present my own, somewhat complicated solution, which can be scripted. I wanted to only give my partners the minimal access and capabilities they needed using my SSH server and not the capabilities some of these other scripted or programmed solutions provided.

We have to modify the */etc/ssh/sshd_config* file to allow for this type of access.

```
# cd /etc/ssh && vim sshd_config
```

So the bottom of our config file now becomes:
```
Match group partners
    ChrootDirectory /home/chroot
    AllowTcpForwarding yes


Match group sftponly
    ChrootDirectory %h
#    ChrootDirectory /home/%u
#    ChrootDirectory /home
#    ChrootDirectory /home/chroot
    X11Forwarding no
    AllowTcpForwarding no
    ForceCommand internal-sftp
```

There are websites that you can visit, which offer other ideas such as http://www.fuschlberger.net/programs/ssh-scp-sftp-chroot-jail, which has an April 2008 script for creating a CHROOT jail. This script is an excellent starting point and expands on the minimal CHROOT setup below that I present. The website http://olivier.sessink.nl/jailkit offers a set of executable binaries for creating CHROOT solutions. To examine and/or use the make_chroot_jail.sh script, type the following:

```
# apt-get install debianutils coreutils
# cd /usr/local/sbin
# wget http://www.fuschlberger.net/programs/ssh-scp-sftp-chroot-jail/make_chroot_jail.sh
# chmod 700 /usr/local/sbin/make_chroot_jail.sh
# vim /usr/local/sbin/make_chroot_jail.sh
```

Before we discuss the steps needed to set up our new SSH server CHROOT, we need to discuss briefly which device files are in Linux. Rather than get into a lengthy discussion, let's look at the old way of doing things in Linux. The *mknod* command can be used create device files. If we were doing so for a CHROOT, the process would be:

```
# cd /dev; ls -al | egrep -e null -e urandom -e zero
```

Looking at the output above we would make note of the major and minor numbers and then use the *mknod* command to create these character special files.

```
# cd /home/chroot && mkdir dev
# mknod dev/null c 1 3 && dev/urandom c 1 9 && mknod dev/zero c 1 5
# chmod 0666 dev/{null,zero,urandom}
```

OPTIONS	DESCRIPTION
mknod c	Create a character (unbuffered) special file. A character devices communication is based on serial communication character by character. Serial ports are an example of a character device.
mknod c 1	The 1 is called the devices major number. This number tells the Linux kernel how to handle the device. It is the offset into the kernel's device driver table, which tells the kernel what kind of a device this is (e.g. a hard disk, serial terminal, etc.)
mknod c 1 5	The 5 is called the devices minor number. This number tells the kernel the special characteristics of the device to be accessed. (e.g. a second hard disk or a second COM port will have different minor numbers)

If you wish to learn more about Linux device files visit https://en.wikipedia.org/wiki/Device_file, https://en.wikipedia.org/wiki/Makedev#Node_creation, https://en.wikipedia.org/wiki/Udev or http://www.linux.com/news/hardware/peripherals/180950-udev. With older versions of Linux running old kernels, the */dev* directory contained a static set of devices. As the types of devices that we could connect to in Linux OSs exploded, this 8-bit scheme for assigning major/minor numbers was quickly becoming exhausted. Therefore, Linux developers created the udev daemon to assign dynamic major/minor numbers. One way we can setup a CHROOT /dev directory with all the device files needed is by using the old MAKEDEV script. Type # man MAKEDEV to see all the devices that can be created. Below is what we can use to set up a minimal set of devices for our CHROOT environment. Create the directories and devices:

```
# cd /home/chroot && mkdir dev && cd dev && mkdir pts && mkdir proc
# MAKEDEV std
```

Above is an example MAKEDEV command that created the minimal set of devices that will allow you to connect to your SSH server. You can experiment by doing things like removing some of these devices if they are security concerns. For example, removing the kernel random number source device "urandom" had no effect on my ability to login. When you login you will get the error message:

```
/dev/pts/2: No such file or directory
```

That is because the */dev/pts* device files are dynamic. They are created as connections are made to the SSH server, so we have to somehow make them dynamic under our CHROOT so that when users connect, the */dev/pts* devices are available. This is done by using the # mount --bind command. The # mount --bind command remounts part of the non-CHROOT directory hierarchy under our CHROOT so that CHROOT users have access to those files and folders. Using # mount --bind in a liberal manner can make setting up a CHROOT very easy but will give partners logging in much more access to our SSH server, which we may be trying to limit. We want to provide the bare minimum first and then selectively pick and choose what we want to give our partners access to and what we do not. A good read on binding directories can be found at http://www.tldp.org/HOWTO/Chroot-BIND-HOWTO-2.html. Below shows how to manually bind/mount and unbind/unmount the */dev/pts/2* devices to correct the error above.

To get all of this set up, consider running the "sshd" daemon in debug mode:

```
# service ssh stop     # Stop the SSH daemon
# psg sshd     # Make sure the daemon is stopped
# /usr/sbin/sshd -d -d -d     # Each additional -d increases logging.
```

```
# mount --bind /dev/pts /home/chroot/dev/pts     # mount pts under CHROOT
# umount /home/chroot/dev/pts     # unmounts pts under CHROOT
```

Looking at the example above it is easy to see that we can easily accomplish setting up our device files just by mounting them rather than creating them:

```
# mount --bind /dev /home/chroot/dev && mount --bind /dev/pts /home/chroot/dev/pts
```

The problem with this approach is that this will give anyone logging in access to all of the devices that are connected to our SSH server. If this is OK for your HCU/SBO security, then just mounting the devices is a superior solution. However, we need to make all of these solutions permanent by adding them to the system startup. Otherwise, whenever we reboot we will lose these mount points. A good read on this can be found at http://wiki.debian.org/chroot and http://www.debian.org/doc/manuals/securing-debian-howto/ap-chroot-ssh-env.en.html.

```
# cd /etc && cp -p fstab fstab.orig && vim fstab
```

Add the following bind mount points to the */etc/fstab* file for */home/chroot* logins:

```
/dev /home/chroot/dev auto bind 0 0
/proc /home/chroot/proc auto bind 0 0
```

The */proc* mount point was not needed to login, but is meant to be an example of a mount point that some binaries may need. Because the SSH server is booting up, we cannot mount the `/dev/pts /home/chroot/dev/pts auto bind 0 0` during boot up in the usual *fstab* fashion. If we add this device to the */etc/fstab* file, we will get the following error during startup:

```
The disk drive for /home/chroot/dev/pts is not ready or not present.
Continue to wait, or Press S to skip mounting or M for manual recovery
```

To get *pts* mounted during startup we will have to add this mount to the system startup and shutdown. This one requirement complicates the setup of SSH server by adding the requirement of a creating and configuring an OS startup script. The Linux developers have tried to make this easier than it used to be in UNIX, where we had to manually create links and figure out run order. They have also standardized and documented how a start/stop script should be written. To mount this device directory add the following script to the */etc/init.d* directory:

```
# cd /etc/init.d && vi mountdevpts.sh
#!/bin/sh
### BEGIN INIT INFO
# Provides:            CHROOT pts mount
# Required-Start:      N/A
# Required-Stop:       N/A
# Should-Start:        N/A
# Should-Stop:         N/A
# X-Start-Before:      N/A
# X-Stop-After:        N/A
# Default-Start:       2 3 4 5
# Default-Stop:        0 1 6
# X-Interactive:       true
# Short-Description: Mount or un-mount /dev/pts under CHROOT
# Description:         This file should be used to construct scripts to be
#                      placed in /etc/init.d.
### END INIT INFO

which mount >/dev/null 2>&1 || exit 0
which umount >/dev/null 2>&1 || exit 0
[ -f /etc/default/chrootvars ] && . /etc/default/chrootvars

# Load the VERBOSE setting and other rcS variables
. /lib/init/vars.sh

# Define LSB log_* functions.
# Depend on lsb-base (>= 3.0-6) to ensure that this file is present.
. /lib/lsb/init-functions

case $1 in
    start|restart|force-reload)
```

```
        [ "$VERBOSE" != no ] && log_action_msg "Mounting /dev/pts under
${strCHroot}/dev/pts"
        [ -d ${strCHroot}/dev/pts ] || mkdir -p ${strCHroot}/dev/pts
        mount --bind ${strCHroot}/dev/pts
        [ "$VERBOSE" != no ] && log_end_msg $?
        ;;
    stop)
        [ "$VERBOSE" != no ] && log_action_msg "Unmounting ${strCHroot}/dev/pts"
        umount ${strCHroot}/dev/pts
        [ "$VERBOSE" != no ] && log_end_msg $?
        ;;
    status)
        mount | grep "${strCHroot}" | grep pts
        [ $? = "0" ] || echo "${strCHroot}/dev/pts is not mounted"
        ;;
    *)
        echo "Usage $0 {start|stop|status|restart|force-reload}" >&2
        exit 3
        ;;
esac

exit 0
```

At the top of the script we source file **/etc/default/mountdevpts** that looks like:

```
# Default fixed chroot path for SSH privileged users
strCHroot=/home/chroot
```

This may seem like overkill to have a one line configuration file, but this is the standard for Linux, and we may expand on the variables needed during system startup and shutdown. Once this script is created we have to add it to the SSH server startup and shutdown. The commands below will make this script:

```
# cd /etc/init.d && chmod 755 mountdevpts.sh && chown root:root mountdevpts.sh
# update-rc.d mountdevpts.sh defaults 98 02
```

Reboot your SSH server and make sure everything is set up and mounted properly. We previously used the *createfixedsftpserveruser.sh* to create user IDs. We could modify that script to match our new requirements or just make a few adjustments after it has been run. Rather than present a slightly modified script, let's just make a few adjustments after it has been run. Then do the following to modify your SSH server user ID:

```
# usermod -s /bin/bash      # This will enable the user to login
# groupadd <GroupID>        # If you want to use a new group
```

usermod -G <GroupID>   # This will remove the user from all groups but <GroupID> and assign them to their new group

The most important thing is to make sure is that the user ID is no longer a member of the 'sftponly' group. The script added the user to the 'sftponly' & 'partners' groups. The steps above will override that and allow our SSH server user to login to our CHROOT under the <GroupID> we set as the 'partner' group. Below is a minimal example setup that gives our SSH partners access to a few commands, utilities, and programs they may need after their privileged SSH CHROOT log in:

```
# cd /home/<UserID>/home
# mkdir -p {bin,dev,etc,lib,lib/i386-linux-gnu,usr/bin}
# cp -p /bin/bash bin/ && cp -p /bin/grep .
# cp -p /lib/ld-linux.so.2 lib/
# cp -p /lib/i386-linux-gnu/libc.so.6 lib/i386-linux-gnu/libc.so.6 lib/
```

```
# mkdir -p /chroot/home/sshprivuser
$ cd /home/chroot/etc
$ cp -p /etc/ld.so.cache . && cp -p /etc/ld.so.conf .
$ cp -p /etc/nsswitch.conf . && cp -p /etc/hosts .
```

```
# cd /home/chroot/bin
# cp /bin/bash . && cp -p /bin/cat .
# cp -p /bin/ls . && cp -p /usr/bin/grep .
# ldd bash
        linux-gate.so.1 =>   (0x00466000)
        libtinfo.so.5 => /lib/i386-linux-gnu/libtinfo.so.5  (0x001d6000)
        libdl.so.2 => /lib/i386-linux-gnu/libdl.so.2  (0x00270000)
        libc.so.6 => /lib/i386-linux-gnu/libc.so.6  (0x00aad000)
        /lib/ld-linux.so.2  (0x007a6000)
```

```
# cd /home/chroot/lib
# cp -p /lib/linux-gate.so.1 . && cp -p /lib/ld-linux.so.2 .
# cd /home/chroot/lib/i386-linux-gnu
# cp -p /lib/i386-linux-gnu/libtinfo.so.5 . && cp -p /lib/i386-linux-gnu/libdl.so.2 .
# cp -p /lib/i386-linux-gnu/libc.so.6 .
```

```
$ ldd ls
        linux-gate.so.1 =>   (0x00c44000)
        libselinux.so.1 => /lib/i386-linux-gnu/libselinux.so.1  (0x00a84000)
        librt.so.1 => /lib/i386-linux-gnu/librt.so.1  (0x00435000)
        libacl.so.1 => /lib/i386-linux-gnu/libacl.so.1  (0x00bb2000)
        libc.so.6 => /lib/i386-linux-gnu/libc.so.6  (0x00d00000)
        libdl.so.2 => /lib/i386-linux-gnu/libdl.so.2  (0x001ca000)
        /lib/ld-linux.so.2  (0x008a7000)
        libpthread.so.0 => /lib/i386-linux-gnu/libpthread.so.0  (0x00a54000)
```

```
libattr.so.1 => /lib/i386-linux-gnu/libattr.so.1 (0x00110000)
```

```
# cd /home/chroot/lib/i386-linux-gnu
# cp -p /lib/i386-linux-gnu/libselinux.so.1 . && cp -p /lib/i386-linux-gnu/librt.so.1 .
# cp -p /lib/i386-linux-gnu/libacl.so.1 . && cp -p /lib/i386-linux-gnu/libdl.so.2 .
# cp -p /lib/i386-linux-gnu/libpthread.so.0 . && cp -p /lib/i386-linux-gnu/libattr.so.1 .
```

We can continue to repeat this process for other programs and utilities until our partners have everything they need to use on our SSH server. However, if we perform a # ldd vim we will see a long list of libraries we would have to copy into the CHROOT.

Then manually copy each file from the lib directory to your jail. This would be a very time consuming process, especially if there is a lot of shared libraries for the binaries you want in the CHROOT. If the use of utilities like this are needed in the CHROOT, we may just want to open up the SSH server security further by mounting the library directories from the host OS:

```
# mkdir -p /home/chroot/lib/i386-linux-gnu
# mkdir -p /home/chroot/usr/lib/i386-linux-gnu
# mount --bind /lib /home/chroot/lib
# mount --bind /usr/lib /home/chroot/usr/lib
```

This also has the added benefit of keeping the libraries up-to-date as we apply updates to our SSH server. I came across a useful script called *l2chroot*, which automatically finds the libraries and copies them to your chroot jail. This script examines which libraries are linked to a binary and will copy them to your CHROOT library directories. Put this script in the */home/chroot/bin* directory and edit the following:

```
# cd /home/chroot/bin && wget -O l2chroot http://www.cyberciti.biz/files/lighttpd/l2chroot.txt
# chmod +x l2chroot && vi l2chroot
[ -f /etc/default/chrootvars ] && . /etc/default/chrootvars
# Change the BASE variable used by script to SSH server CHROOT
BASE=${strCHroot}
```

We can then copy in commands such as:
```
# cd /home/chroot/bin && cp -p /usr/bin/vim . && l2chroot vim
```

The *l2chroot* script will copy in all of the libraries used by Vim to the corrected CHROOT library jail directories. This makes adding the utilities and tools that our clients need to have available very easy. We no longer have to open up a security hole by mounting all the libraries on the SSH server into the CHROOT. The website http://www.cyberciti.biz/tips/linux-unix-bsd-openssh-server-best-practices.html is a good read on other security options that you may want to consider for your SSH server.

Automating the Consolidation of Data on Our SSH Server

A multi-thousand-million-billion dollar business likely has many partners with whom to exchange data. As we have shown above, we likely had to set up multiple partner (possibly jailed) accounts. Data we are exchanging with one partner should be kept separate from another partner. This makes knowing when we have data present or viewing data scattered about on our SSH server difficult. More than likely, as an SBO/HCU we don't have an employee that we can pay, who is dedicated to looking for this data, consolidating it, and physically logging in to send and retrieve data to/from our partners. We have to focus our resources on our core business and simplify things by moving our data to a central location.

Because our SSH tunnel is encrypted, to save time, and for convenience, many of our files may be exchanged unencrypted. Sometimes the partners we work with will have a difficult time just sending you a file; more or less teaching them how to encrypt a file to a public/private key pair, may prove very difficult, no matter how simple you think you have made the directions given to them. God gifted us all with different skill sets and your partner(s) may have a master's degree in their field of study, but may find setting up an SSH client to send, or retrieve a file from your SSH server very difficult. Depending on the sensitivity of the data that we are exchanging, we may want to allow them to send us files unencrypted, which is less than ideal but much better than using encrypted files over email. Since our SSH connection is encrypted, exchanging data with our partner in this fashion is much more secure than doing so in an email, where we run the danger of crackers making a copy of our emails and attachments. This would give them infinite amounts of time read our emails and be able to break any encryption we might have been using on those attachments.

So now corporate wants us to move on to **_Requirements Definition 5_**, which is similar to RD1-RD2-RD3-RD4, but adds a consolidation of data feature.

All partner accounts will be swept automatically for incoming files, which will be archived and then copied to a safe/central place on the SSH server for processing. Directories housing outgoing files to our partners shall be automated and swept in much the same fashion and sending that data to our partners.

Below is a simple script that automates the moving of files to a central directory that our partners send to our SSH server. On my website http://thatcybersecurityguy.com, I have/will be posting more in-depth and detailed scripting projects to help you automate encrypting and decrypting files sent and received from your SSH server processes as you request them. I will continue to add many detailed solutions in C, C++, C#, POSIX and other computing languages that you request. I didn't spend 28 years in this business to only present the very basic solutions that are presented in this book. This old dinosaur (as I have been described) has many things that might prove useful to you or your business. Computer Science has evolved, but I think you will find my blog and website very beneficial. I wanted to offer an additional something extra to my readers beyond what other computer books provide. If you have an employee or you are proficient in computer languages or Linux Bash scripting, then visit my website and you will find things such as scripts that will help you automate many things for your home or business.

- Script and test in increments to allow for debugging in steps.
- Type # bash -x script.sh or # bash -vx script.sh, this will help you debug unmatched ", ', {, or [, which are tough errors to track down or use _set -x_ or _set -xv_ from within the script as shown below.

- If you want to receive email from your script, a mail client may have to be installed. To use mail and mailx utilities from scripts you may have to install those by typing # apt-get install mailutils. If you need a nice GUI mail client, refer back to Windows or Virtualization chapters to get Thunderbird installed.

```
#!/bin/bash
# SCCS File %P%
# %Z%  %M%:  %Q% Version %I%.
# Made on %G% at %U%.
#
# set -x     # Uncomment to debug getopts portion of script
#==============================================================
# {Description}
#
# Sweep the SSH partner accounts specified on the command line or in the
# default configuration for incoming files which will be archived and then
# copied to a safe/central place on the SSH server for processing.
#
# The script uses Hungarian Notation prefixes as developed by Microsoft:
#
# strVar - string variable
# bVar   - Boolean variable
# iVar   - integer variable
# procRoutine - Procedure that has no return value
# funcRoutine - Function that returns a value
#==============================================================
# Declare static CONSTANT variables.  They are declared here in the
# header for ease of change.
#
BREAK="----------------------------------------------------------------"
typeset -x strBaseName="`basename ${0}`"    # Get name of running script
typeset -x strHost=`hostname`    # Name of the host script is running on
typeset -x strLogsDir=/root/logs        # Name of the logs directory
typeset -x strLogFile=${strLogsDir}/sshlog.txt
#
#==============================================================
# Declare static variables
#
typeset -x strFilesToProcess    # List of file(s) being processed
typeset -x strArchiveFiles      # Name(s) of the file(s) to be archived
typeset -x strUserID            # UserID to change the moved files(s) owner to
typeset -x strGroupID           # GroupID to change the moved files(s) group to
typeset -x strSSHUserID         # SSHUserID being processed
typeset -x strSSHGroupID        # SSHGroupID being processed
typeset -x strAddToFN           # String to add to Prefix or Suffix of archive
```

```
#=================================================================
# Declare Boolean and character command line static variables:
typeset -x strEmailList=root      # Application owners to be notified
typeset -x bDebug=/bin/false              # -d Debug command line arg
typeset -x strInSSHDir=/home/suroot/indir  # -i Incoming command line arg
typeset -x strTargetDir=/root/sshdir      # -t Target command line arg


#=================================================================
# Send an Email with subject $1 and Email addresses $2.  The current log
# file is concatenated into the Email.  To use mailx below you may need to:
# apt-get install mailutils  # View http://mailutils.org/ or
# http://packages.ubuntu.com/precise/mail/maildir-utils for details.
#=================================================================
procSendEmail()
{
if ${bDebug}; then
    set -x
    echo "Entering procSendEmail" >> ${strLogFile}
fi
    strSub=$1
    strMList=$2
    strTmpMailFile=/tmp/mailfile.tmp

    date +"%d%b%y(date +%H)$(date +%M)" > ${strTmpMailFile}
    cat ${strLogFile} >> ${strTmpMailFile}

# If you are using the advanced Thunderbird email client you can try the
# following to send an email using the following syntax:

# thunderbird -compose "to=foo@bar.com,bar@foo.com,subject='Some Subject',body=' $(cat
file.txt)',attachment=file:///home/admin/tip.txt'"

    mailx -s "${strHost}-${strSub}" ${strMList} < ${strLogFile}
    rm -f ${strTmpMailFile}
}


#=================================================================
# Severity codes in $1 are as follows:
#  - 1 means log a warning and continue processing
#  - 2 means log a Fatal Error and exit 1
#  - 3 means log a Fatal Error, send an email and exit 2
#=================================================================
procLogAbort()
{
    typeset -i iSeverity=$1
    strMsg="$2"

    if [[ ${iSeverity} -eq 3 ]]; then
```

```
            echo "Fatal Error: ${strMsg}, aborting..." | tee -a ${strLogFile}
            echo "Finished processing of ${strInSSHDir} on `date`" >> ${strLogFile}
            procSendEmail "Fatal Error: ${strMsg}" ${strEmailList}
            exit 1
    elif [[ ${iSeverity} -eq 2 ]]; then
            echo "Fatal Error: ${strMsg}, aborting..." | tee -a ${strLogFile}
            echo "Finished processing on `date`" >> ${strLogFile}
            exit 1
    else
            echo "Warning: ${strMsg}" | tee -a ${strLogFile}
    fi
}


#===================================================================
# Display script usage help.
#===================================================================
Usage ()
{
    echo "Usage:"
    echo " $0"
    echo "    -d                      Enable debug logging"
    echo "    -g <Group ID>           Group ID to set file(s) group to"
    echo "    -G <SSH Group ID>       SSH Group ID being process to use"
    echo "    -l <Log file Dir>       Log file directory"
    echo "    -i <Incoming SSH Dir>   Incoming SSH files directory"
    echo "    -t <Target SSH Dir>     Consolidation directory for Incomming SSH files"
    echo "    -u <User ID>            User ID to set file(s) ownership to"
    echo "    -U <SSH User ID>        SSH User ID being processed to use"
}


#===================================================================
# Get and process the command line arguments.
#===================================================================
while getopts di:l:g:G:ht:u:U: option
do
    case $option in
        d)
            bDebug=/bin/true
            ;;
        i)
            strInSSHDir=$OPTARG
            echo "Processing files in ${strInSSHDir}"
            ;;
        l)
            strLogDir=$OPTARG
            echo "Log files to house in directory ${strLogDir}"
            ;;
        g)
```

```
                strGroupID=$OPTARG
                echo "Moved files new Group ID will be '${strGroupID}'"
                ;;
         h)
                Usage
                exit
                ;;
         G)
                strSSHGroupID=$OPTARG
                echo "The Group ID '${strSSHGroupID}' being processed"
                ;;
         t)
                strTargetDir=$OPTARG
                echo "Targeet directory for files ${strTargetDir}"
                ;;
         u)
                strUserID=$OPTARG
                echo "Moved files new Owner ID will be '${strUserID}'"
                ;;
         U)
                strSSHUserID=$OPTARG
                echo "The User ID '${strSSHUserID}' being processed"
                ;;
         *)
                Usage
                procLogAbort 2 "Invalid command line argument '$option' specified..."
                ;;
      esac
done


#=================================================================
# Log variable values for debugging or history.
#=================================================================
procLogVars()
{
if ${bDebug}; then
    set -x
    echo "Entering procLogVars" >> ${strLogFile}
fi

    echo "Incomming dir being processed---> ${strInSSHDir}"   >> ${strLogFile}
    echo "Target dir for SSH files--------> ${strTargetDir}"  >> ${strLogFile}
    echo "Email list to notify on errors--> ${strEmailList}"  >> ${strLogFile}
    if [[ -n ${strUserID} ]]; then
    echo "User ID to change ownership to--> ${strUserID}"     >> ${strLogFile}
    fi
    if [[ -n ${strUserID} ]]; then
    echo "Group ID to change ownership to-> ${strGroupID}"    >> ${strLogFile}
```

```
        fi
        echo "SSH User ID being processed-----> ${strSSHUserID}"  >> ${strLogFile}
        echo "SSH Group ID being processed----> ${strSSHGroupID}"  >> ${strLogFile}
        echo "${strBaseName} Logging Directory> ${strLogsDir}"     >> ${strLogFile}
}


#=======================================================================
# If the file exists then
# - Move filename.2 to filename.3 and so on...
# - Move filename.1 to filename.2
# - Move filename.0 to filename.1
# - Move filename    to filename.0
#=======================================================================
function funcStash
{
if ${bDebug}; then
     set -x
     echo "Entering funcStash" >> ${strLogFile}
fi

if [[ ! -f ${1} ]] # If file does not exist or is not a regular file
then
     return 1 # Ignore request to stash file and return non-zero value
fi


typeset -i j k=10
until [[ $k -eq -1 ]]; do
     j=$k+1
     if [[ -f ${1}.${k} ]]; then # File exist and is a regular file
     if [[ -s ${1}.${k} ]]; then # File exist and has size greater than zero
         mv -f ${1}.${k} ${1}.${j} 1>>${strLogFile} 2>&1
     else
         rm -f ${1}.${k} 1>>${strLogFile} 2>&1    # Remove zero byte files
     fi
     fi
     k=$k-1
  done

  if [[ -s ${1} ]]; then # File exist and has size greater than zero
     chmod 660 ${1} 1>>${strLogFile} 2>&1
     mv -f ${1} ${1}.0 1>>${strLogFile} 2>&1
  else
     rm -f ${1} 1>>${strLogFile} 2>&1       # Remove zero byte files
  fi

  return 0 # Return 0 to show normal successful completion of stash
  }
```

```
#=================================================================
# Move file specified in parameter 1 to the file specified in parameter 2.
#=================================================================
procMoveFile()
{
if ${bDebug}; then
    set -x
    echo "Entering procMoveFile()" >> ${strLogFile}
fi
    typeset strFromFile=$1
    typeset strToFile=$2

strBreak="_____"

    if [ ! -f ${strFromFile} ]; then
        echo "Attempt to move a file that does not exist!" >> ${strLogFile}
        procLogAbort 3 "File `pwd`/${strFromFile} not found"
    fi
    if ${bDebug}; then
        echo "mv -f ${strFromFile} ${strToFile}" >> ${strLogFile}
    fi
    mv -f ${strFromFile} ${strToFile} 1>>${strLogFile} 2>&1
    if [[ $? -ne 0 ]]; then          # Check the return status
        echo ${strBreak} >> ${strLogFile}
        echo "ls -lF listing of directory `pwd`" >> ${strLogFile}
        ls -lF >> ${strLogFile}
        echo ${strBreak} >> ${strLogFile}
        procLogAbort 3 "'mv -f ${strFromFile} ${strToFile}' failed with status $?."
    fi
    if [[ ${strUserID} != "" ]]; then
        if [[ ${strGroupID} != "" ]]; then
            chown ${strUserID}:${strGroupID} ${strToFile} 1>>${strLogFile} 2>&1
        else
            chown ${strUserID}:${strUserID} ${strToFile} 1>>${strLogFile} 2>&1
        fi
    fi
}


#=================================================================
# Archive the files in variable "strArchiveFiles" in the current directory
# to ./archive.
#
# - If parameter $1 is the word "stash" then we roll the previous archive to
#   a <file>.1, <file>.2, <file>.3, or <file>.4 suffix by calling "funcStash".
#
# - If parameter $2 is the format for appending the current date and sometimes
#   time to the archive filename.  (e.g. "%y%m%d%H %M").
#
```

```
# - If parameter $3 is the word "remove" then the file is removed after it
#   has been archived.
#
# - If parameter $4 is the word "prefix" then what ever is in static variable
#   "strAddToFN" is appended to the beginning of the archived file.
# - If parameter $4 is the word "suffix" then what ever is in static variable
#   "strAddToFN" is appended to the end of the archived file prior to the
#   extension.

# - If parameter $5 is anything other than the word "noowner" then what ever
#   is in $5 becomes the owner of the file.

# - If parameter $6 is anything other than the word "nogroup" then what ever
#   is in $6 becomes the group of the file.
#
# All archived files are compressed.
#
# NOTE: The current working directory is considered housed in the
#       static variable "strInSSHDir".
#       The directory "${strInSSHDir}/archive" will be created if it does
#       not exist.
# NOTE: PGP binary encrypted files are already compressed.  No gzip is done
#       on any file with a ".pgp" extension.
#================================================================
procArchiveFiles()
{
if ${bDebug}; then
    set -x
    echo "Entering procArchiveFiles()" >> ${strLogFile}
    printf "Files to archive\n${strArchiveFiles}\n" >> ${strLogFile}
fi
    typeset -i iRet=0
    typeset -i isGPGFile=0
    typeset -i isASCFile=0
    typeset -i isGZFile=0
    strStash=$1
    strDate=$2
    strRemove=$3
    strFix=$4
    strOwner=$5
    strGroup=$6

    if [ ! -d ${strInSSHDir}/archive ]; then
        mkdir ${strInSSHDir}/archive 1>>${strLogFile} 2>&1
        chmod 770 ${strInSSHDirDir}/archive 1>>${strLogFile} 2>&1
        chown ${strSSHUserID}:${strSSHGroupID} ${strInSSHDir}/archive 1>>${strLogFile} 2>&1
        iRet=$?
        if [[ iRet -ne 0 ]]; then # chmod failed
```

```
                procLogAbort 2 "chown on ${strSSHUserID}:${strSSHGroupID} failed."
                id >> ${strLogFile}
                ls -lF . >> ${strLogFile}
        fi
    fi


    cd ${strInSSHDir}
    for j in ${strArchiveFiles}
    do
        if [[ ! -f ${j} ]]; then
            procLogAbort 3 "Archive attempt on ${j} failed, file does not exist"
        fi

        echo "Archiving `ls -lF ${j}`" >> ${strLogFile}

        isASCFile=`echo ${j} | grep ".asc" | wc -l`
        isGZFile=`echo ${j} | grep ".gz" | wc -l`
        isGPGFile=`echo ${j} | grep ".gpg" | wc -l`
        if [[ ${strFix} = "prefix" ]]; then
            strTargFile=archive/${strAddToFN}${j}
        elif [[ ${strFix} = "suffix" ]]; then
            if [[ $isASCFile -eq 1 ]]; then
                strBase=$(basename ${j} .asc)
                strTargFile=archive/${strBase}${strAddToFN}.asc
            elif [[ ${isGZFile} -eq 1 ]]; then
                strBase=$(basename ${j} .gz)
                strTargFile=archive/${strBase}${strAddToFN}.gz
            elif [[ ${isGPGFile} -eq 1 ]]; then
                strBase=$(basename ${j} .gpg)
                strTargFile=archive/${strBase}${strAddToFN}.gpg
            else
                strTargFile=archive/${j}${strAddToFN}
            fi
        else
            strTargFile=archive/${j}
        fi

        # What we do is archive the file as is and then compress and rename
        # that compressed file.
        cp -p ${j} ${strTargFile} 1>>${strLogFile} 2>&1
        iRet=$? # File has been archived, see if we need to change archive name
        if [[ iRet -ne 0 ]]; then # cp -p failed
            procLogAbort 1 "cp -p on ${strSSHInDir}/${strTargFile} failed."
            id >> ${strLogFile}
            ls -lF . >> ${strLogFile}
        fi

        strFileOwn=`ls -o ${strTargFile} | awk '{print $3}'`
```

```
        if [[ ${strFileOwn} = ${strSSHUserID} ]]; then
                chmod 660 ${strTargFile} 1>>${strLogFile} 2>&1
        else
                echo "Warning: File ${strTargFile} is owned by '${strFileOwn}' and not SSH user
'${strSSHUserID}'." | tee -a ${strLogFile}
        fi

        # GPG binary encryption does its own compression so we do not gzip
        # the file, or the file might already be gzip'ed.
        if [[ ${isGPGFile} -eq 0 && ${isGZFile} -eq 0 ]]; then
                gzip -f ${strTargFile} 1>>${strLogFile} 2>&1
                iRet=$?
                if [[ iRet -ne 0 ]]     # Check to make sure gzip did not fail
                then # Compression failed
                        procLogAbort 1 "gzip compression failed on ${strInSSHDir}/${strTargFile}."
>> ${strLogFile}
                fi
        fi # The file has been compressed, but we cannot add the .gz extension

        if [[ ${strDate} != "nodate" ]]; then # Check to add date in filename
                if [[ ${isGPGFile} -eq 1 ]]; then # Is a compressed .gpg file
                        strBase=$(basename ${j} .gpg)
                        procMoveFile ${strTargFile} archive/${strBase}.$(date +${strDate}).gpg
                        strTargFile=archive/${strBase}.$(date +${strDate}).gpg
                elif [[ ${isASCFile} -eq 1 ]]; then # Is a compressed .asc.gz file
                        strBase=$(basename ${j} .asc)
                        procMoveFile ${strTargFile}.gz archive/${strBase}.$(date
 +${strDate}).asc.gz
                        strTargFile=archive/${strBase}.$(date +${strDate}).asc.gz
                elif [[ ${isGZFile} -eq 1 ]]; then # Is an existing .gz file
                        strBase=$(basename ${j} .gz)
                        procMoveFile ${strTargFile} archive/${strBase}.$(date +${strDate}).gz
                        strTargFile=archive/${strBase}.$(date +${strDate}).gz
                elif [[ -s ${strTargFile}.gz ]]; then # Is a newly created gz file
                        procMoveFile ${strTargFile}.gz ${strTargFile}.$(date +${strDate}).gz
                        strTargFile=${strTargFile}.$(date +${strDate}).gz
                else # Not compressed, not a .asc, not a .gpg, just rename/mv file
                        procMoveFile ${strTargFile} ${strTargFile}.$(date +${strDate})
                        strTargFile=${strTargFile}.$(date +${strDate})
                fi
        fi

        if [[ ${strStash} = "stash" ]]; then
                if [[ ${isGPGFile} -eq 1 || $isGZFile -eq 1 ]]; then
                        funcStash ${strTargFile}
                        strTargFile=${strTargFile}.0
                elif [[ ${isASCFile} -eq 1 || -s ${strTargFile}.gz ]]; then
                        funcStash ${strTargFile}.gz
```

```
                    strTargFile=${strTargFile}.gz.0
              else
                    funcStash ${strTargFile}
                    strTargFile=${strTargFile}.0
              fi
        fi

        echo "${j} archived to `ls -lF ${strTargFile}`" >> ${strLogFile}

        if [[ ${strGroup} != nogroup ]]; then    # Change the archive file group
              chgrp ${strGroup} ${strTargFile}
        fi

        if [[ ${strOwner} != noowner ]]; then    # Change the archive file owner
              chown ${strOwner} ${strTargFile}
        fi

        if [[ ${strRemove} = "remove" ]]; then      # Remove original file
              echo Removing ${j} >> ${strLogFile}
              rm -f ${j} 1>>${strLogFile} 2>&1
              iRet=$?
              if [[ iRet -ne 0 ]]
              then # rm -f failed
                    procLogAbort 1 "rm -f ${strInSSHDir}/${j} failed."
                    id >> ${strLogFile}
                    ls -lF . >> ${strLogFile}
              fi
        fi
        printf "\n" >> ${strLogFile}
    done
}


#=============================================================================
# Main procedure to guide the processing of incoming SSH files.
#=============================================================================
procProcessInSSHFiles ()
{
if ${bDebug}; then
    set -x
    echo "Entering procProcessInSSHFiles()" >> ${strLogFile}
fi
    typeset -i iRet=0

    if [[ ! -d ${strInSSHDir} ]]; then
        procLogAbort 3 "In SSH Directory ${strInSSHDir} does not exist"
    fi
    cd ${strInSSHDir}  1>>${strLogFile} 2>&1
    iRet=$?
```

```
    if [[ iRet -ne 0 ]]
    then # cd failed
        procLogAbort 2 "cd ${strInSSHDir} failed."
        id >> ${strLogFile}
        ls -lF . >> ${strLogFile}
    fi

#    strFilesToProcess=`find . -maxdepth 1 -type f \(! -iname ".*"\)`
#    strFilesToProcess=`ls -l | awk 'NR!=1 && !/^d/ {print $NF}'`
    strFilesToProcess=`ls -l | awk '/^-/ {print $NF}'`
    strArchiveFiles=${strFilesToProcess}

    if [[ "" = "${strFilesToProcess}" ]]; then
        echo "No Files to process in ${strInSSHDir}" >> ${strLogFile}
    else
        if ${bDebug}; then
            printf "Processing files:\n${strFilesToProcess}\n" >> ${strLogFile}
        fi
        procArchiveFiles stash nodate keep nofix noowner nogroup
#        procArchiveFiles nostash "%y%m%d$(date +%H)$(date +%M)" keep nofix noowner nogroup
#        procArchiveFiles nostash "%y%m%d$(date +%H)$(date +%M)" keep prefix noowner
nogroup
#        procArchiveFiles nostash "%y%m%d$(date +%H)$(date +%M)" keep suffix noowner
nogroup
        for i in ${strFilesToProcess}
        do
            procMoveFile ${i} ${strTargetDir}/${i}
        done
    fi
}


#================================================================
#                        MAIN PROGRAM
#================================================================
#
# Check to see if number of parameters is correct if defaults are not accpeted.
# This may be needed in the future.
#
# if [[ "$#" -eq 0 ]]; then
#        Usage
#        procLogAbort 2 "No Argument specified..."
# fi

if ${bDebug}; then
    set -x
    echo "Entering Main Program" >> ${strLogFile}
fi
```

```
# Initialize static variables:
if [[ -z ${strSSHUserID} ]]; then
    strSSHUserID=`ls -od ${strInSSHDir} | awk '{print $3}'` 1>>${strLogFile} 2>&1
fi
if [[ -z ${strSSHGroupID} ]]; then
    strSSHGroupID=`cat /etc/passwd | grep ${strSSHUserID} | cut -d: -f4` 1>>${strLogFile}
2>&1
    strSSHGroupID=`grep ${strSSHUserID} /etc/passwd | cut -d: -f4` 1>>${strLogFile} 2>&1
fi


procLogVars
procProcessInSSHFiles
echo "Finished processing of ${strInSSHDir} on `date`" >> ${strLogFile}
procSendEmail "Processing complete on ${strInSSHDir}" ${strEmailList}
funcStash ${strLogFile}    # Stash the previous log or initialize a new log
```

The script above is meant to be an example to adapt from this IT professional and that can be used to run on our SSH server to consolidate data files received, archive, and roll files. The archive procedure is the most complex portion of the script and had to be limited. Let's discuss why I chose to present this somewhat complex archive example procedure in this chapter. While handling all incoming and outgoing files at a large corporation, there were issues that I often encountered when dealing with our corporate and government partners.

- Partners would often claim that they sent data that was actually not sent. Unless I kept an archive of everything received on the server, I had no way to prove that we did not receive the data.
- My user community would sometimes claim that they never got the data after our server had deposited files on our server for processing. Consequently, log files became the key to finding the fate of the processing that took place on those files.
- You will find that every partner has different requirements for exchanging the data files. Sometimes the files they send will be named the same thing, over and over again. Sometimes the filename will be unique and have a date-time stamp embedded in the name. Sometimes the data will be encrypted, and/or compressed. One technique I found useful was archiving the partners' files deposited on the server to an archive directory under their SSH home directory. This way my partners could log in and determine for themselves if/when/what had been sent and received. Allowing them to do this on their own can save you many hours of work. The more that you can empower them without broadening their access, thus compromising security, the better life will be for you.
- My users all have different requirements for their data. Sometimes they want to keep every file they have received for weeks, months, or years, and sometimes they only want a few copies for reference. Sometimes they want a date-time stamp or demand some other weird naming convention.

In the next section, things get more complex as to what your business may demand. The truth is that just sending data back and forth over an encrypted connection is not secure enough; large corporations and government have learned this. From what I have seen, the average SBO/HCU has not. I'm trying to teach the SBO/HCU the lessons learned by their corporations and representative government before it is too late. We must continue to layer our security and continue to employ techniques that large entities use, which this book teaches. These security techniques may prove adequate and are superior to anything you are using today. They allow you a somewhat secure means of exchanging data with your partners. To truly secure your data you need to add file level encryption, refer back to <u>Chapter 5</u>, in addition to using a secure connection file transfer. Once again, we have to think in layers of security.

Automating the Encryption and Exchange of Data between Our Partners and Our SSH Server

While working for a larger corporation, I handled all the encryption/decryption and transferring of files to and from our partners. At that time, there were many partners and many different ways of transferring and retrieving files. The complexity, length and scope of this type of scripting are beyond what I could present in this book. I can/will have scripts available through links on my blog and website at <u>http://thatcybersecurityguy.blogspot.com</u> | <u>http://thatcybersecurityguy.com</u> that will fulfill the following requirements definition (should my readers request it). If requested, and as they come available, you will be notified via my blog and Twitter @thatcybersecguy. The Requirements Definition below states:

> So now corporate wants us to move on to **Requirements Definition 6**, which is an addition to our previous requirements RD1-RD2-RD3-RD4-RD5.
>
> All data exchanged with our partners will be encrypted to a GPG public/private key pair. For the exchange of public keys, our files are encrypted to between us and our partner and shall be verified by fingerprint (discussed in <u>Chapter 5</u>). The accounts/connection between our partner and us will also be encrypted to a public/private key pair (discussed earlier in this chapter). The partner accounts will be swept automatically for incoming files, which shall be decrypted and moved to a safe, central place on our SSH server for processing. The same process shall be used for outgoing files, except that they will be encrypted to our partner's public key and sent to our partners where they dictate the format of files we send.

While I have scripts for satisfying this requirement, they are better presented later, if readers demand it. It would require many pages to present this solution, and you might find it useful. I present this final requirement to show how large corporations and government operate, as well as to give you some ideas on what you might want in future correspondence, which you are entitled to through the purchase of this book.

Enabling Anonymous SSH Connections Using TOR

While OpenSSH will encrypt our traffic between our mobile device and our SSH server, it will not obfuscate the SSH server to which you connect. Talented network administrators can and will track you down using this technology behind their firewalls. However, suppose you want to use hotspots in foreign counties where anonymity is needed? You would need to combine the anonymity of Tor with your SSH connection. There are multiple ways of doing this, and you will have to decide which setup works best for you. For example, you could install Tor on your SSH server and then forward application ports to the Tor software running on your server. There is an excellent read on how to do this at https://trac.torproject.org/projects/tor/wiki/doc/SshPortForwardedTor. However, to keep our secure SSH server as clean and safe as possible we may not want a Tor daemon running in the background. The Tor service will establish a source-routed path by communicating with a set of random nodes, and the daemon will listen on in port 9050. This opens a minor security hole that could be exploited in some unknown fashion. In the virtualization chapter it was suggested that you to install a guest OS on your mobile device that is dedicated to being set up and used with Tor. In that guest OS we installed the Tor packages and configured the Tor repository to keep them updated:

```
# cd /etc/apt/sources.list.d  &&  vi tor.list
```

Since SSH encrypts our activity between the mobile device and the SSH server, the password or login should be secure even if the Tor entry and/or exit relay are watching our activity. However, perhaps you are a reporter operating within dictatorial governments' borders. To be more secure you should establish a public/private key relationship between your mobile devices' "anon" or "tor" account and your SSH servers' "anon" or "tor" account. That way even if someone is packet sniffing your activity at the Tor entry and exit relay, you do not have to enter authentication information. This is where the beauty of SSH public/private key relationships really comes in handy. You can also refer back in this chapter for how-to about "CHROOT and key" your anonymous SSH server account as a further layer of security.

If you are an SBO, you can consider setting up multiple accounts for your employees' mobile devices. For example, you may want a file transfer account and a dynamic port forwarding account with minimal privileges for use with Tor and simple SSH port forwarding. To keep things simple, name the account the same thing on the client as it is on the server. If you don't need to obfuscate your SSH server connection, a quick solution would be to use local port forwarding:

```
$ ssh -L 9050:127.0.0.1:9050 anon@sshhost.dyndns.org
Last login: Sun May  5 23:48:16 2013 from d192-24-28-40.try.isp-provider.com
```

Then all activity using Tor port 9050 will be SSH encrypted and sent to your SSH server. This is also very easy to set up in PuTTY for Windows, which we covered earlier. Once this is done, configure your Internet options, application or browser to use the SOCKS5 Proxy at IP 127.0.0.1, Port 9050 and you will be tunneled anonymously to your SSH server. However, this configuration is not enough to keep you anonymous, as your browser may still request the local DNS for the IP-address of the web page you requested. If you are tunneling through a firewall, this would be a red flag to any network administrator, informing them of the web pages that you are requesting. You have to tell your browser or application to request everything through SOCKS. *In Firefox type* __about:config__ *> scroll down to the setting* __network.proxy.socks_remote_dns__ *> if the "value" is not set to "true" right click on it and select* __Toggle__ *to set it to* __true__ *from* __false__. Nevertheless, this approach does not camouflage the SSH connection to our SSH server. You will notice when you connect to you SSH server it still identifies the mobile device that you are using to connect to the Internet.

There are multiple approaches we can use to obfuscate our SSH connection to our server using Tor. The web page https://trac.torproject.org/projects/tor/wiki/doc/TorifyHOWTO/ssh details a few methods for using the command line to establish an SSH connection using Tor. The first is using 'netcat' with the 'ProxyCommand' option. OpenSSH has a configuration parameter called VerifyHostKeyDNS that will try to resolve the hostname before the ProxyCommand is issued. The default value is 'no' but adding this to your alias is an added assurance of security, especially if you don't administer the OS. Edit your ~/.bashrc file to add the following alias:

```
$ vi ~/.bashrc
alias ssh-tor='ssh -o "ProxyCommand nc -X 5 -x 127.0.0.1:9050 %h %p" -o
VerifyHostKeyDNS=no'
```

The command above warrants some explanation, and I hope the table below will help you understand what this does.

ssh -o	Is used to pass options to the SSH client that could be set in the configuration file. They usually have no separate command-line flag.
ProxyCommand	Specifies the command to use to connect to our SSH server. The '%h' parameter will be substituted with the host name to connect to. The '%p' parameter is the port to use. See: man ssh_config.
nc	Netcat is a TCP/UDP utility that can do anything. It can open a TCP connection, send UDP packets, listen on arbitrary TCP and UDP ports, do port scanning, and deal with both IPv4 and IPv6. See: man nc.
nc -X 5	Requests netcat to use the SOCKS v5 protocol, which is the default.
nc -x 127.0.0.1:9050	Requests netcat connect to 127.0.0.1 using the Tor proxy at port 9050.

Then when we use the following command to connect to our SSH server:

```
# ssh-tor anon@sshserver.dyndns.org
Last login: Sun May 5 23:43:10 2013 from foto.ro1.torservers.net
```

We can now see that the SSH server does not recognize how our remote device is connecting as it shows the domain of exit Tor relay that is actually connecting to our SSH server. This verifies that our SSH server connection is anonymous; but how do we use this with the applications on our client? Refer back to our discussion about port forwarding, and use your imagination as to how you want to use this. For example, to use an anonymous SSH connection with Dynamic Port Forwarding, simply type:

```
$ ssh-tor anon@sshserver.dyndns.org -D 18080 -N
```

Now you can set up applications such as your mobile device browser to use an anonymous SOCKS5 proxy on port 18080 connected to your SSH server. There are other methods to accomplish this goal that you can also consider. Torify is a wrapper that attempts to wrap your application in the best Tor solution. For example, 'torsocks' or 'tsocks' is called by 'torify' if that is best solution on your system. Torify, when used with torsocks, should not leak DNS information and may be more anonymous than our previous solution. It also only works with TCP, which limits attack vectors. (See: https://wiki.torproject.org/noreply/TheOnionRouter/TorifyHOWTO). We use 'torify' in much the same way as the solution above:

```
$ vi .bash_rc
alias ssh-torify='torify ssh'
```

```
$ ssh-torify anon@sshserver.dyndns.org -D 18080 -N
```

Or perhaps you want all connections from your 'anon' or 'tor' user ID to be anonymous without remembering things like aliases. Edit the file *~/.ssh/config* and add the following:

```
$ cd ~/.ssh && vi config
host sshserver.dyndns.org
    user anon
    port 22
    ProxyCommand nc -X 5 -x 127.0.0.1:9050 %h %p
```

From now on when you type $ ssh anon@sshserver.dyndns.org -D 18080 -N it will be torified. There are other Tor configurations with which you can experiment. I was able to find a few dated references from which you may be able to extrapolate. (See: http://www.debianadmin.com/anonymous-ssh-sessions-with-tor.html, http://www.howtoforge.com/anonymous-ssh-sessions-with-tor, https://trac.torproject.org/projects/tor/wiki/doc/OpenbsdChrootedTor)

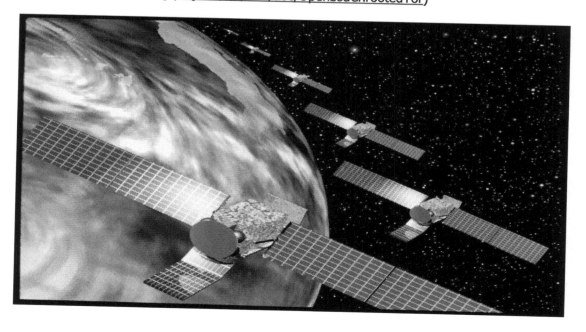

Multiboot USB Drive, Your Multipass

Chapter 10 – Setting up a Multiboot USB Drive, HAK5 at YouTube Calls it Your Multipass, One USB Key to Rule Them All. How to Encrypt and Use a USB Data Drive from a Multiboot USB Drive!

Many travelers don't want to lug around expensive laptops through airports and smartphones are filling that void. Smartphones continue to get smarter and much more advanced. These devices are expensive and very much valued by the criminal community. Even so, their coverage is not global, as my wife fusses about when I backpack and camp in remote places on the planet. We also may not want to risk these devices being lost or stolen while traveling. Stories abound of instances where thefts happen, as in when drivers with their windows down get punched in the face as the thief grabs their smartphone and takes off running. I suggest that when you are traveling abroad to questionable destinations, you leave the expensive smartphone at home and purchase what the cops and criminals call *throw away or burner phones*. For your privacy protection, pay cash for the phone. As we now know, your government(s) can track all cellphones, and if you become a person of interest, any phone you use is not safe. However, changing phones often is a good way to have a few unrecorded phone conversations before "the man" connects the dots, and using a cheap throw away phone will keep your identity safe for a few days. You can buy one of these phones for a nominal cost at a store, such as Walmart, and then renew the phone plan when you travel. However, you will have to investigate whether the network it uses is supported in the areas of the world in which you are traveling. Hence, we arrive at an additional solution to consider, which would be to carry a portable computer and all of our data with you safely, but without exposing our high technology equipment or data. How do we do this you may ask?

The answer is a Multipass USB drive combined with a second USB data drive. As technology has progressed the two have been combined, but I suggest you keep them separate. We often see USB drives depicted in the movies when the actors plug them in the USB port and hack the computer or use them to copy data to in some covert fashion. Years ago, loading up a multiboot USB was an arduous task that required a lot of experimentation and permutations to get applications working together. The art of creating and using a multiboot USB drive was the purview of geeks and a source of pride among computer experts. With many boot options available for a USB drive, the number of combinations and conflicts became too large to determine. Some programs could co-exist together and others could not. What order they were installed in determined how they could coexist together. For example, to have 9 options to boot to is 9 factorial or 362,880 possible combinations. To fix this the open source community has once again produced solutions that almost automate the creation of a Multipass. Years ago, when I got the idea to write this book, creating a multiboot USB was an entirely long and difficult chapter of this book that was difficult to understand.

Conversely, now there is an abundance of software that can be easily installed and run from a bootable USB drive. These tools are the "who's who" of the hacking world. Even so, using a Multipass is not as good as Virtualization. Software installed on a USB drive is not updatable, except on a scripted basis, until the next release and the install of that software update becomes available. This presents work on your part, scripting solutions after boot up if there are bug fixes, updates or software that you need to perform the tasks that you want.

The http://www.pendrivelinux.com website has put together most of the latest and greatest open source options to create on a Multipass. Their amazing YUMI USB creator, which is my favorite tool, can be downloaded at http://www.pendrivelinux.com/yumi-multiboot-usb-creator. When you run YUMI it shows you all of the OSs, utilities and tools that you can install on your Multipass. YUMI literally builds the Multipass for you.

Once the software that you want to use is downloaded, the YUMI tool makes loading up the USB drive with bootable OSs, tools and utilities very easy. Pick the programs that you want and install them one by one testing the USB Multipass once they are all installed. You then will have a set of bootable tools to use anywhere in the world on any computer.

In these days of cheap USB drives, you should purchase at least a 32 GB or larger USB drive if you want to LOAD it up with boot options (multiple tools and utilities). It is time to recycle the old 2-32 GB USB drives that are not going to cut it in today's world, unless you only want a few boot options. YUMI will format your USB drive as FAT32 or you can do it yourself using Windows Explorer.

Make sure your computer has USB boot support in the BIOS. Cheap or old computers may not, so if you are creating the USB to use on a known computer, double check first. In addition, booting from USBs may have been disabled on computers in corporations or government offices, but there are ways around that, as in opening up the computer and changing the jumper settings on the motherboard. This may get you fired, but this book is about achieving Internet privacy! If you purchased your computers in the last few years, they probably will have USB boot support. If your computer does not support booting from a USB drive, try flashing your BIOS up to the latest release, see Chapter 3, and see if that enables booting from your USB drive. *On my laptop, upon boot, the <ESC> key is used to bring up the Startup Menu > hit the <F9> key to bring up the Boot Device Options > select the USB drive from which to boot.*

You have to determine which tools you want on your Multipass. YUMI supports many bootable options and most flavors of Linux, some of which we discussed in Chapter 7. Depending on the size of your USB drive, we have to come up with a plan on how to lay it out. YUMI is a brilliant tool that has links to the websites that you can go to download anything you want on your Multipass. It is best to let YUMI do everything. Format your USB drive to FAT32 and then let YUMI do the same thing upon your first installation of software. This will establish the MBR necessary for everything to work correctly. Below is a sample list of some of the things YUMI presents as additional tools that you may find useful.

OSs, Tools and Utilities to Install on Your MultiPass

- Download Acronis Antimalware CD at http://kb.acronis.com/content/18647. We can boot from this CD and scan the computer for malware.
- Download AVG Rescue CD (Antivirus Scanner) at http://www.avg.com/us-en/avg-rescue-cd-download. Read about it at http://www.avg.com/us-en/avg-rescue-cd. From AVG's web page, "*AVG Rescue CD is a comprehensive toolkit that will repair system crashes and return systems to a state where they can operate at full capacity, thanks to deep-rooted infections having been removed and file systems repaired.*"

- Download Avira Antivirus Rescue CD (Antivirus Scanner) at https://www.avira.com/en/download/product/avira-rescue-system.
- Download Bitdefender Rescue CD (Antivirus Scanner) at http://www.bitdefender.com or http://download.bitdefender.com/rescue_cd. MD5SUM for bitdefender-rescue-cd.iso: 2332abf04a8fe923a491987eb97e30cc
- Download BackTrack 5 R3 Final at http://www.backtrack-linux.org or http://www.backtrack-linux.org/downloads. From their website, "*BackTrack is the highest rated and acclaimed Linux security distribution to date. BackTrack is a Linux-based penetration testing arsenal that aids security professionals in the ability to perform assessments in a purely native environment dedicated to hacking.*" BackTrack has a VMware Image release that can also be downloaded in addition to the ISO file. Backtrack has been replaced by Kali Linux, which can also be added to a Multiboot USB drive and used instead. (See: http://www.kali.org)
- Download Clonezilla at http://clonezilla.org. This is the open source "Norton Ghost" or "True Image" and a lot more. From their website, "*It helps you to do system deployment, bare metal backup and recovery. Two types of Clonezilla are available, Clonezilla live and Clonezilla SE (server edition). Clonezilla live is suitable for single machine backup and restore. While Clonezilla SE is for massive deployment, it can clone many (40 plus!) computers simultaneously. Clonezilla saves and restores only used blocks in the hard disk. This increases the clone efficiency. At the NCHC's Classroom C, Clonezilla SE was used to clone 41 computers simultaneously. It took only about 10 minutes to clone a 5.6 GBytes system image to all 41 computers via multicasting!*"
- Dban can be found at http://www.dban.org. From their website, "*Darik's Boot and Nuke ("DBAN") is a self-contained boot disk that securely wipes the hard disks of most computers. DBAN will automatically and completely delete the contents of any hard disk that it can detect, which makes it an appropriate utility for bulk or emergency data destruction.*" You can also use Partition Wizard, Seagate's or Western Digital's utilities, which can be downloaded from their websites.
- Download Debian Live Project at http://www.debian.org/CD/live. Debian Live is a version of Debian Linux that can be booted from various media. (See: http://www.debian.org , https://en.wikipedia.org/wiki/Debian)
- Download Fedora Live, covered in Chapter 7, at http://fedoraproject.org.
- Download FreeDOS at http://www.freedos.org or for YUMI at http://www.finnix.org/Balder. Balder is based on FreeDOS and is a more developed DOS solution. From their website, "*FreeDOS is a free DOS-compatible operating system for IBM-PC compatible systems. FreeDOS is made of up many different, separate programs that act as "packages" to the overall FreeDOS Project.*"
- Download GParted which is a free partition editor for graphically managing your disks. (See: http://gparted.org, http://gparted.sourceforge.net)
- Download HDT - Hardware Detection Tool at http://hdt-project.org. This comes in handy when you're talking to customer support or working on someone else's computer. Most people don't know what hardware they are using.
- Download Kali Linux, developed by Offensive Security who describes their OS as "The most advanced penetration testing distribution, ever". Kali Linux is an OS that replaces the Backtrack live CD. (See: http://www.kali.org)
- Download Kaspersky Rescue Disk 10 kav_rescue_10.iso at http://support.kaspersky.com/viruses/rescuedisk/main or http://support.kaspersky.com/viruses/rescuedisk. From their website, "*Kaspersky*

Rescue Disk 10 is designed to scan and disinfect x86 and x64-compatible computers that have been infected. The application should be used when the infection is so severe that it is impossible to disinfect the computer using antivirus applications or malware removal utilities (such as Kaspersky Virus Removal Tool) running under the operating system. In this case, disinfection is more efficient because malware programs do not gain control when the operating system is being loaded. In the emergency repair mode, you can only start objects scan tasks, update databases roll back updates and view statistics." The latest release was June 01, 2010 and Kaspersky does not support or error fix the rescue CD software but the do update the virus definitions database.

- Download Memtest86+ at http://www.memtest.org. From their website, "*Based on the well-known original memtest86 written by Chris Brady, memtest86+ is a port by some members of the x86-secret team, now working at www.canardpc.com. Our goal is to provide an up-to-date and completely reliable version of this software tool aimed at memory failures detection.*"
- Download Linux Mint, covered in Chapter 7, at http://www.linuxmint.com/download.php.
- Download Offline NT Password & Registry Editor at http://pogostick.net/~pnh/ntpasswd. From their website,
  - ➤ This is a utility to reset the password of any user that has a valid (local) account on your Windows NT/2k/XP/Vista/Win7 etc. system.
  - ➤ You do not need to know the old password to set a new one.
  - ➤ It works offline, that is, you have to shutdown your computer and boot off a CD or USB disk to do the password reset.
  - ➤ Will detect and offer to unlock locked or disabled out user accounts!
  - ➤ There is also a registry editor and other registry utilities that works under Linux/Unix, and can be used for other things than password editing.
  - ➤ cd140201.zip md5sum: f274127bf8be9a7ed48b563fd951ae9e
  - ➤ usb140201.zip md5sum: a60dbb91016d93ec5f11e64650394afb
- Download ophcrack at http://ophcrack.sourceforge.net. From their website, "*Ophcrack is a free Windows password cracker based on rainbow tables. It is a very efficient implementation of rainbow tables done by the inventors of the method. It comes with a Graphical User Interface and runs on multiple platforms.*"
- Download the Panda SafeDisk CD tool http://www.pandasecurity.com/usa/homeusers/support/card/?id=80152. From their website "*allows you to scan and disinfect your computer from a virus-free environment.*"
- Download Parted Magic at http://partedmagic.com for $4.99. From the website, "*Parted Magic OS employs core programs of GParted and Parted to handle partitioning tasks with ease, while featuring other useful software (e.g. Partimage, TestDisk, Truecrypt, Clonezilla, G4L, SuperGrubDisk, ddrescue, etc...) and an excellent set of info to benefit the user.*"
- Download Partition Wizard at http://partitionwizard.com or http://www.partitionwizard.com/download.html. From their website, "*MiniTool Partition Wizard is an easy-to-use partition manager software with comprehensive functions. It offers partition management for Windows server 2000/2003/2008/2008 R2 and Windows 2000/XP/Vista/7/8. MiniTool Partition Wizard fully supports the latest Windows Operating System: Windows 8. MiniTool Partition Wizard also supports hard disks with GPT partitions. As a partition manager, MiniTool Partition Wizard has the capability to Resize and Move, Merge, Extend, Split, Copy, Create, Delete and Format, Convert, Explore, Hide and Unhide*

server and non-server partitions and much more." Excellent tool for zeroing and sanitizing hard disks.

- Download PING "Partimage Is Not Ghost" at http://ping.windowsdream.com to backup and restore partitions. Internet reviews say this is an excellent tool for backing up and restoring partitions. The open source project boasts that it has better features than Symantec Ghost has. Another thing the project says is that it can back up your BIOS as well. Downloading the software required registration, which I was unwilling to do.
- Redo Backup and Recovery at http://redobackup.org. From their website, "*Redo Backup and Recovery is so simple that anyone can use it. It is the easiest, most complete disaster recovery solution available. It allows bare-metal restore. Bare metal restore means that even if your hard drive melts or gets completely erased by a virus, you can have a completely-functional system back up and running in as little as 10 minutes. All your documents and settings will be restored to the exact same state they were in when the last snapshot was taken. Redo Backup and Recovery is a live CD, so it does not matter if you use Windows or Linux. You can use the same tool to backup and restore every machine. And because it is open source released under the GPL, it is completely free for personal and commercial use.*"
- Download System RescueCd at http://www.sysresccd.org. From their website, "*SystemRescueCd is a Linux system rescue disk available as a bootable CD-ROM or USB stick for administrating or repairing your system and data after a crash. It aims to provide an easy way to carry out admin tasks on your computer, such as creating and editing the hard disk partitions. It comes with a lot of Linux software such as system tools (parted, partimage, fstools, ...) and basic tools (editors, midnight commander, network tools).*"
- Download Trinity Rescue Kit at http://trinityhome.org. From their website, "*This is a free Linux distribution that aims specifically at the recovery and repair operations on Windows machines, but is equally usable for Linux recovery issues.*"
- Download Tails (Anonymous Browsing), a.k.a. The (Amnesic) Incognito Live System, at https://tails.boum.org, a Linux distribution built with security and anonymity in mind. Refer back to the anonymity chapter for a more detailed description.
- For a flavor of Linux that requires less computer resources try Lubuntu at http://lubuntu.net.
- If you favor the KDE desktop, try http://www.kubuntu.org, which is a very active project keeping up with Ubuntu releases.
- Download openSUSE Linux, covered in Chapter 7, at http://www.opensuse.org/en.
- Download Ubuntu Linux, covered in Chapter 7, at http://www.ubuntu.com.
- Download Ultimate Boot CD at http://www.ultimatebootcd.com. In July 2013, the Ultimate Boot CD website had multiple mirrors listed at http://www.ultimatebootcd.com/download.html from which to download the 5.3.0 version. When the 5.3.0 version is downloaded be sure to check the [SHA-256] 05b8bbae27377c332b046025a3dd6b3b969328f0cf6c9d953816bd4e3ba4b4c2 checksum of the file as there are many questionable copies of UBCD floating around. The CD is a store of useful software for BIOS, CPU, Boot Management, Data Recovery, Hard Disk Information & Management, Hard Disk Diagnostics, Hard Disk Cloning, Hard Disk Low-Level Editing, Hard Disk Wiping, Hard Disk Installation, Partition Management, Memory, Peripherals, and System Tools. The website has links to much of the software that is on the CD where you can read about all of the tools.

Above is a list of the "who's-who" that you may want on your Multipass. The best way to get started creating it is, after downloading everything, put together a spreadsheet of the software that you want, along with the size in bytes, and in alphabetical order. With that spreadsheet we can move software in and out to maximize the potential of our multiboot USB drive. Below is an example configuration that you may consider for a USB drive.

Product Name	Filename	Date Updated	Bytes in KB
Acronis Antimalware CD	AcronisAntimalwareScanCD.iso	1.19.2015	341,648
AVG Rescue CD	avg_arl_cdi_all_120_141126a8645.iso	1.19.2015	135,192
Avira Antivirus Rescue CD	rescue_system.iso	1.19.2015	632,580
BackTrack 5 R3 Final	BT5R3-KDE-32.iso (See Kali)	1.19.2015	3,247,672
BitDefender Rescue CD	bitdefender-rescue-cd.iso	1.19.2015	619,520
Clonezilla Disk Imaging & Cloning 32bit	clonezilla-live-2.2.4-12-i686-pae.iso	1.19.2015	150,528
Clonezilla Disk Imaging & Cloning 64bit	clonezilla-live-2.2.4-12-amd64.iso	1.19.2015	151,552
Darik's Boot And Nuke (DBAN)	dban-2.2.8_i586.iso	1.19.2015	15,144
Debian Live GNOME 32bit	debian-live-7.7.0-i386-gnome-desktop.iso	1.1.2015	1,318,032
Debian Live KDE 32bit	debian-live-7.7.0-i386-kde-desktop.iso	1.19.2015	1,357,216
Debian Live GNOME 64bit	debian-live-7.7.0-amd64-gnome-desktop.iso	1.19.2015	1,230,592
Debian Live KDE 64bit	debian-live-7.7.0-amd64-kde-desktop.iso	1.19.2015	1,267,968
Fedora Live GNOME 32bit	Fedora-Live-Desktop-i686-20-1.iso	1.19.2015	944,128
Fedora Live KDE 32bit	Fedora-Live-KDE-i686-20-1.iso	1.19.2015	917,504
Fedora Live GNOME 32bit	Fedora-Live-Workstation-i686-21-5.iso	1.19.2015	1,305,600
Fedora Live GNOME 64bit	Fedora-Live-Workstation-x86_64-21-5.iso	1.19.2015	1,437,696
Fedora Live KDE 32bit	Fedora-Live-KDE-i686-21-5	1.19.2015	959,488
Finnix Balder FreeDOS	balder10.img	1.19.2015	1,440
GParted Partition Editor	gparted-live-0.20.0-2-i486.iso	1.19.2015	224,256
Hardware Detection Tool	hdt-0.5.2.iso	1.19.2015	1,308
Kali Linux	kali-linux-1.0.9a-i386.iso	1.19.2015	3,073,536
Kali Linux	kali-linux-1.0.9-amd64.iso	1.19.2015	2,981,808
Kaspersky Rescue Disk 10	kav_rescue_10.iso	1.19.2015	386,912
Kubuntu 14.04.1 (KDE Ubuntu 32-bit)	kubuntu-14.04.1-desktop-i386.iso	1.19.2015	1,048,576
Kubuntu 14.04.1 (KDE Ubuntu 64-bit)	kubuntu-14.04.1-desktop-amd64.iso	1.19.2015	1,053,520
Kubuntu 14.10 (KDE Ubuntu 32-bit)	kubuntu-14.10-desktop-i386.iso	1.19.2015	1,158,720
Kubuntu 14.10 (KDE Ubuntu 64-bit)	kubuntu-14.10-desktop-amd64.iso	1.19.2015	1,135,680
Linux Mint 17/32 Cinnamon LTS	linuxmint-17.1-cinnamon-dvd-32bit.iso	1.19.2015	1,379,328
Linux Mint 17/64 Cinnamon LTS	linuxmint-17.1-cinnamon-dvd-64bit.iso	1.19.2015	1,513,296
Linux Mint 17/32 KDE LTS	linuxmint-17-kde-dvd-32bit.iso	1.19.2015	1,363,968
Linux Mint 17/64 KDE LTS	linuxmint-17-kde-dvd-64bit.iso	1.19.2015	1,495,552
Linux Mint 17/32 MATE LTS	Linuxmint-17.1-mate-32bit.iso	1.19.2015	1,461,248
Linux Mint 17/64 MATE LTS	Linuxmint-17.1-mate-64bit.iso	1.19.2015	1,594,656
Lubuntu 14.04.1 (Lightweight Ubuntu)	lubuntu-14.04.1-desktop-i386.iso	1.19.2015	712,704
Lubuntu 14.04.1 (Lightweight Ubuntu)	lubuntu-14.04.1-desktop-amd64.iso	1.19.2015	722,944
Lubuntu-14.10-32(Lightweight Ubuntu)	lubuntu-14.10-desktop-amd64.iso	1.19.2015	718,848
Lubuntu-14.10-64(Lightweight Ubuntu)	lubuntu-14.10-desktop-amd64.iso	1.19.2015	721,920
Memtest86+	memtest86+-5.01.iso.gz	1.19.2015	58
Offline NT Password & Registry Editor	cd140201.zip	1.19.2015	16,932
OpenSUSE Linux 13.2 i586	openSUSE-13.2-DVD-i586.iso	1.19.2015	4,515,840
OpenSUSE Linux 13.2 x86_64	openSUSE-13.2-DVD-x86_64	1.19.2015	4,569,088
ophcrack	ophcrack-vista-livecd-3.6.0.iso	1.19.2015	664,576
Panda SafeCD	PandaSafeCD.iso	1.19.2015	165,786
Partition Wizard	pwhe8.1.iso	1.19.2015	42,492

System RescueCd	systemrescuecd-x86-4.4.1.iso	1.19.2015	403,586
Redo Backup and Recovery	redobackup-livecd-1.0.4.iso	1.19.2015	255,352
Tails Amnesic Incognito Live System	tails-i386-1.2.2.iso	1.19.2015	929,522
Trinity Rescue Kit	trinity-rescue-kit.3.4-build-372.iso	1.19.2015	154,692
Ubuntu Linux LTS 32bit	ubuntu-14.04.1-desktop-i386.iso	1.19.2015	1,034,944
Ubuntu Linux LTS 64bit	ubuntu-14.04.1-desktop-amd64.iso	1.19.2015	1,004,544
Ubuntu Linux 12.10 32bit	ubuntu-14.10-desktop-i386.iso	1.19.2015	1,158,720
Ubuntu Linux 12.10 64bit	ubuntu-14.10-desktop-amd64.iso	1.19.2015	1,135,680
Total Bytes			54,834,092

Story

After creating my Multipass, my first experiment was at my local library. My original idea was to plug the Multipass into the library computer, boot a flavor of Linux off the USB drive, then SSH to my home server to surf the Internet. That way I would not be subject to any surveillance setup on the computers' or libraries network. All of my activity would be encrypted through the SSH tunnel. Imagine if you will, a strange man crawling around under the tables plugging something into computer after computer, and then rebooting them. I was surprised no one called me out. When a woman sat down directly across from me... well you get the picture. Lucky she had pants on (not a dress) and there was no scream. Access to the BIOS required a password and booting from a USB drive was disabled or not possible in their old computers. So this experiment was a failure.

All of the library computers were still running XP, so perhaps I was not yet defeated. I also noticed that I could boot the computers into Safe Mode using Networking. Additionally, when I inserted my USB drive, the automated media play screen sometimes popped up before I was even logged in. I could have attempted to install WUBI (See: https://en.wikipedia.org/wiki/Wubi_(Ubuntu)) to attempt to use Ubuntu in Windows, but that would have been doing harm, so I did not try it. All hope was not lost on my original plan, but you may find booting a USB is not possible on many public computers.

Portable Applications You May Want to Add to Your USB Data Drive

In addition to a multitude of bootable USB OSs, tools and utilities, there are also portable applications you may want on your USB drive. In order to easily use these solutions from the multiple boot options above, consider putting them on your data drive. That way they are easily accessed from your MultiPass, no matter what OS you boot into:

- Autoruns Portable is a tool to find and stop all of the bloatware that is starting in the background on your computer. Windows in notoriously bad at making it easy to determine what is starting up automatically in the background thus dragging your computer's performance down and providing a security threat. Autoruns provides a one-stop shop where you can simply uncheck a program you don't want to run and it will no longer start in the background. (See: http://portableapps.com/apps/utilities/autoruns-portable)
- Apache OpenOffice portables are unofficial third-party ports of this popular productivity suite that you can run on your USB drive. These downloads allow execution of their

office applications without installation. (See:
http://www.openoffice.org/porting/index.html)

- Google Chrome Portable is an excellent mobile browser that you can download and place on your bootable USB drive. Chrome Portable comes with sandboxing security features as well as Safe Browsing functionality--which guards against malicious sites and downloads. If you are working on an infected system and need to download a tool or utility, you can boot up to a USB OS and use Chrome Portable to surf the Internet. (See: http://portableapps.com/apps/Internet/google_chrome_portable)
- Clamwin Portable is a Windows GUI for the Clam open source antivirus software. If you are troubleshooting a computer and you need an anti-virus solution, you can try using Clam to scan the system from your data drive. (See: http://portableapps.com/apps/security/clamwin_portable)
- Eraser Portable is a program for making sure that a file is really and truly gone. When you delete a file in Windows, it is still recoverable using certain utilities. However, suppose you have sensitive documents that you want to be sure no one can ever recover. Eraser Portable claims that it securely erases files and directories on standard IDE and SATA hard drives. It uses patterns that overwrite data several times using methods such as the National Industrial Security Operating DOD Manual. Eraser Portable cannot securely erase files on Solid State and USB drives. (See: http://portableapps.com/apps/security/eraser-portable)
- FileAssassin Portable is a program for deleting files that Windows or malware doesn't want you to delete. FileAssassin claims it can eradicate any type of locked file from your computer. If you have ever seen messages such as "A file is locked by another user, access to a file is denied; the source or destination file may be in use" or Windows refuses to delete the file for some other reason, FileAssassin may delete that file. The portable version is located on bottom right under the Spanish version. (See: http://www.malwarebytes.org/products/fileassassin)
- Foxit Reader Portable is a secure PDF document viewer and creator that is a fast, small in size and rich in features. Foxit can read, create, sign, and annotate PDF documents as well as fill out PDF forms. (See: http://portableapps.com/apps/office/foxit_reader_portable)
- Kaspersky TDSKiller is a utility that you can use to find and remove rootkits. If you have a computer that is exhibiting strange behavior such as annoying popups, bogus error messages or hijacking your browser and sending it to bogus web pages (some malicious), Kaspersky TDSKiller is a specifically designed portable application to target known and difficult to find rootkits that other security software misses. (See: http://support.kaspersky.com/5350)
- KeePass PassWord Safe Portable is a tool no traveler should do without. We discussed KeePass in Chapters 6, 7 and will again in detail, in Chapter 11. KeePass encrypts your passwords to an encrypted file and when used properly, guards against keyloggers* getting your passwords. (See: http://keepass.info/download.html)
- LibreOffice Portable is a full-featured portable version of LibreOffice that includes a word processor, spreadsheet, presentation tool, drawing package and database that is officially supported by the LibreOffice Document Foundation. (See: https://www.libreoffice.org/download/portable)

- Notepad++ Portable is a text editor that will allow you to use Notepad++ without having to install the software. (See: http://portableapps.com/apps/development/notepadpp_portable)
- Password Safe is the open source twin of KeePass. It is also covered in Chapter 11. (See: http://pwsafe.org, http://passwordsafe.sourceforge.net)
- Revo Uninstaller Portable is a utility for removing installed applications that you never wanted or no longer need. We discussed Revo back in Chapter 6 as a tool that does a thorough job of removing everything associated with install programs and better than Windows or a standard uninstaller that comes with the application. (See: http://www.revouninstaller.com/revo_uninstaller_free_download.html)
- SpyBot Search & Destroy was discussed back in Chapter 6. This software has been around for years and was originally the "go to" application for spotting and destroying spyware. The definitions have been kept up-to-date, but the application languished a few years. However, SpyBot came out with a new release and is now an excellent 2014 solution to your spyware problems. (See: http://portableapps.com/apps/security/spybot_portable)
- Thunderbird Portable is an email client to use with your email service provider. You can take your email, address book and account settings with you on your USB drive to anywhere in the world. Be sure to add in Enigmail to encrypt and sign your email. (See: http://portableapps.com/apps/internet/thunderbird_portable), http://enigmail.mozdev.org/home/index.php.html)
- Tor Bundle Anonymizer is portable application to use on your USB drive. Refer back to Chapter 8. (See: https://www.torproject.org/index.html.en)
- VLC Media Player Portable is a multimedia player for various audio and video formats which includes MPEG-1, MPEG-2, MPEG-4, DivX, XviD, WMV, mp3, ogg as well as DVDs, VCDs, and various streaming protocols. (See: http://portableapps.com/apps/music_video/vlc_portable)
- WinPatrolToGo is a portable version of WinPatrol that can analyze all the programs that startup in the background on your computer and presents them in an organized fashion. It shows hidden files, IE Helpers, Scheduled Tasks and more. If you work on computers or help friends and family with computer problems WinPatrolToGo can come in handy. (See: http://www.winpatroltogo.com)

Setting up a Secure USB Drive and a Bootable USB Drive for Travel

Booting any OS, Tool or Utility off of a Multipass is the same as booting off of a Live CD. Anything you setup or copy into your Linux OS will be lost when you shutdown. Try it. Boot into a Multipass OS, copy a bunch of files from your data USB drive to your Ubuntu desktop, and then reboot... no more files. In addition, any work you did adjusting the volume, fixing your display, connecting to a network or any other system settings will be lost. Another disadvantage is that some Linux OSs such as Ubuntu Unity, do not automatically mount the Multipass, whereas Mint-KDE does. You can get it mounted in Ubuntu by unplugging and plugging the USB in after the OS has loaded. The web page https://help.ubuntu.com/community/Mount/USB presents other options if you want to experiment with getting the Multipass mounted without unplugging it. Rather than take that approach, carry a second USB data drive. If we have a dedicated USB data drive we can encrypt the whole drive; that way all of our data is secure.

Another argument against unplugging the Multipass and plugging it back in to get to your data files were that things really got flakey if I did not. For example, files copied could be opened but the Ubuntu OS would lose its menus or have other problems. When you think about this; mounting the drive that you booted your OS from into the OS that is loaded into the computer's RAM that you are running it on, is a BAD idea. This is like running an OS off of a hard drive and then mounting that hard drive in the OS you are running. If you find this confusing, just follow my recommendation and don't do it. Buy a second USB drive for your data and then when you are running Ubuntu or other OS/utility off a bootable USB, insert the second USB drive when you want to copy files in and out.

When we use the Multipass to boot off, our data USB can house all of our scripts, applications and data. If all you want is an encrypted USB drive then you can use Microsoft's BitLocker to encrypt the drive or just encrypt a folder on the USB drive. To encrypt a folder, format the USB drive in NTFS, create a folder on the USB drive, *right click on the new folder > choose **Properties** > Click on the **Advanced** button in the Attributes section > check the **Encrypt contents to secure data** box > Click **OK** and click **OK**.* The folder will appear in green indicating that it is encrypted and then viewable only by your user account on the computer that created it. You can then copy EFS Files and Certificates to allow other computers to use the folder, but that is complex. (See: http://technet.microsoft.com/en-us/library/cc722147(WS.10).aspx)

Another less complex option to consider is the purchase of a Secure USB Drive that uses hardware-based encryption. Hardware-based encryption has advantages over software encryption as in the ability to lock down if the wrong password is entered too many times. When I first investigated them, their cost, performance and capacity did not keep up with unsecure flash drives; all that changed in 2013 as USB 3.0 drives came to market. If you are going to purchase a secure USB drive you should choose one that is certified to Level 3 of the government's FIPS 14-2 security standard. According to a July 2012 PCWorld article titled "Your Data Safely in Your Pocket" by Jon L. Jacobi, the Apricorn Aegis Secure Key http://www.apricorn.com/products/hardware-encrypted-drives/aegis-secure-key.html was under review for Level 3 certification and the Imation Defender F200 http://www.imation.com/en-US is certified Level 3. Kingston http://www.kingston.com/en/usb/encrypted_security also had Level 3 drives.

In May of 2012, there were little or no secure USB 3.0 drives on the market (See: http://find.pcworld.com/72933)   This article by Jon L. Jacobi, titled "The Best Encrypted Flash Drives" only reviewed encrypted USB 2.0 options, which had more disadvantages than advantages to using unencrypted USB 3.0 drives. However, USB manufacturers began releasing the 3.0 models in late 2012. If you cannot afford an encrypted flash drive, then you can purchase a much cheaper unencrypted USB 3.0 drive and use software encryption.

The Lacie XtremeKey USB 3.0 is an amazing USB drive that you can purchase. This drive sports AES 256-bit encryption and up to 230MB/s transfers speeds. The manufacturer says that the drive can withstand being submerged in 200 meters of water and is heat, cold, shock, pressure, and drop resistant. This might be an understatement because after visiting websites and reading about other tests done on the drive, it appears that it not only can withstand being set on fire for 10 minutes, be run over by a 10 ton truck, take a dip in a pool, travel with a deep water diver, but it can also survive a drop of 33 feet, be frozen in a glass or water overnight, travel to the Artic, or be put in an office toaster for about 10 minutes reaching temperatures of 389 degrees Fahrenheit. This appears to be the backup solution for a traveler who is active and wants peace of mind in having secure data available, no matter where they go. It is backed by a three-year warranty and sells for $85 for the 32GB version and $140 for the 64GB version. (See: http://www.lacie.com/products/product.htm?id=10612#a5)

However, you may not want the added expense of a hardware encrypted USB drive. Perhaps using the software encryption technology covered in Chapter 5 is adequate for your business needs. If so, consider purchasing an unencrypted USB 3.0 drive for sometimes less than half the price of a hardware encrypted USB drive.

Savings 	To write the book I needed unencrypted USB drives to practice software encryption on. Initially I had an adequate supply of 2.0 drives but I lost one, two died and the others I had to give to partners I did not want to attempt to teach how to use my SSH server to exchange files. So I traveled to Costco to purchase a USB 3.0 flash drive. Amazingly, in September 2013 Costco only offered USB 2.0 flash drives for sale. I tracked down the electronic Costco employee working that department and asked where the USB 3.0 drives were. He did not know what a USB 3.0 drive was and told me the 2.0 drives were flying of the shelves with no one asking about 3.0 devices. I tried to explain that these 2.0 devices had been around since the year 2000, and USB 3.0 since 2008, and that there was even a new 3.1 USB standard that manufactures have made devices for. Why on earth would anyone waste money on a USB 2.0 device? They should remove these devices from their store! Unfortunately my tirade fell on deaf ears, and I was very disappointed in Costco for pushing this outdated cheap technology on unsuspecting customers. For a few dollars more than what Costco was charging for their 2.0 drives, I picked up a USB 3.0 drive at Amazon.

If you choose to travel with an unsecure USB drive, there are a few things to consider:

1. One article I read summed up deleting files from a USB drive. Where you see the word *delete*, think instead of the word *hide* instead. Hiding a file or performing a Quick Format on a USB drive will leave all files that were there easily recoverable. Anyone using FAT data recovery or repair tools can easily bring those files back to the light.
2. Make sure you are in possession of your USB data drive at all times. It only takes a few minutes for a competitor, corporate espionage, or thief to copy all the files (encrypted or not) off of your USB drive, leaving you none the wiser. They can then spend infinite amounts of time performing an offline attack. Any encryption is breakable using things such as rainbow tables and encryption breaking software. Plus, most users have weak encryption passwords for the USB drives that can allow them to be broken by brute force.
3. Using really cheap USB drives can pose a risk to your data. The old adage you get what you pay for is true with USB drives. A flash drive is like a circuit board with millions of miniature switches in the surface chips. Quality USB drives have good switches that can last many years of perhaps your life-time. Cheap drives may have

broken switches and more and more of them will break over time. If you see the storage capacity of your USB drive diminishing, buy a new, quality drive before your data becomes corrupted.

4. Some operating systems allow programs to autorun off of a USB drive. Windows 7 turned this off, but I have seen many businesses and organizations still using XP. However, Microsoft still allows the Autoplay feature to function, which is a security hazard. Malware leverage these automatic features by using an autorun.inf file in the root device directory to try and install itself on every computer the infected media is attached to. ***Click on Start > Control Panel > click on the Autoplay icon > uncheck Use AutoPlay for all media devices***.

Refer back to Chapter 5 to learn about the various GUI and command line options for encrypting files and folders on your USB drive. These tools can also be used for encrypting files to send/transfer over the Internet. We want to layer our security by encrypting important files that we will store on encrypted USB drive. If we encrypt both the files and the USB drive, we achieve *double encryption* of important data files. Assume any cracker that comes into possession of a stolen USB drive is skilled at breaking encryption. They may have algorithms and computing power that could eventually break the encryption on a lost or stolen USB drive. What we want to do is buy ourselves time before that encryption is broken, which will allow us time to do things like change passwords, anticipate the effects of compromised data, and hopefully, prevent them from ever getting to our online accounts.   It will make you smile to imagine the cracker's frustration when they break through your first level of USB drive encryption only to discover that really important files are doubly encrypted and they have to begin the process all over again.

The Time Has Come to Thwart Identity Theft!

Don't Get Cracked. Take These Preventive Measures!

Chapter 11 – Before You Are Cracked! There Are Many Preventive Measures You Can Take to Thwart Identity Theft!

This chapter came about because I grew tired of reading and hearing the same old common sense steps that we can all take to protect our identity. These conversations talk about solutions without the mandatory HOW-TO-DO instructions that always seem to be missing from the interviews and discussions. Western media presents so-called experts who tell us about these problems but offer little information about what we can do to prevent them. Many of these supposed pundits claim to be authorities on the subject of cyber security, but really know very little about it. Their ideas are touted by the media they work for who know even less. Plus, I was worried that once this book was published my family and friends might become targets by many malicious entities who might not appreciate the value of what I am presenting in this book to help everyone to avoid Identity Theft. After all, this is a multi-billion dollar business, which our governments, corporations and criminals depend on.

This is akin to telling the truth about the drug trade, which so many people depend on and will kill for. Go to https://krebsonsecurity.com and see how criminal organizations have been Brian Krebs worst enemy due to his work on keeping you and me safe using the Internet. I'm worried this type of cracking may happen on my website, and in my personal life once this book is published. You might ask why I might invite this invasion into my family's life while I have enjoyed living in relative anonymity, but all I can say is, it comes out of my continued need to service mankind after military service. I want to see us all rise above our petty quests for power and wealth that the super wealthy seem to want, and do what is moral and correct for our planet and fellow citizens.

Paying a for-profit company to protect my family's and your identities while I am writing a book about cyber security did not seem an appropriate solution to present in this book, so I spent years researching this topic. After all, if I could not present solutions doing research on my own, you would have to ask what business did I have writing a book about identity thief for the average SBO/HCU? I had to present ways that we all could accomplish this task without paid services or our paid-for government and for profit corporations that provide limited information to you about how to prevent this crime. Understand these businesses are often cracked, which then provide your information to criminal organizations with minimal consequences. As we have previously discussed, most for-profit entities and local, state or federal, western governments reject the idea of personal privacy protection even when it is required by their state or federal government's constitutions. These governments, corporations, charities, social media, and medical databases have been cracked, in part, due to their lack of understanding of cyber security. This is because there are minute repercussions to the entities involved, but there are severe consequences for individuals whose personal information was stored in their databases.

Governments publicize the fact that they **ask** corporations to implement cyber security, which is often ignored, given minimal resources, or is addressed by untrained corporate personal to implement. The Internet and news media abound with articles on Identity Theft and breaches in security, but few people seem to realize this is an epidemic, and they need litigation to protect themselves from it. The PCWorld article "Identity Theft on the Rise," from January 20, 2010 by M. E. Kabay, NetworkWorld states, "*Almost 10 million American learned they were* *victims of identity fraud in 2008, up from 8.1 million victims in 2007.*" A later PCWorld article titled "What You Need to Know about Identity Theft" by Lisa Gerstner states that number has increased to 12.6 million in 2012. This was a rise of more than one million from the numbers recorded in 2011. Subsequently, we can see that this trend continues to increase year after year. The Identity Theft Prevention and Survival website states that "*Identity-Theft is the fastest growing crime in America; 9.9 MILLION victims were reported last year, according to a Federal Trade Commission survey.*" The quotation does not give the year, but the web page is dated 2010. (See: http://www.identitytheft.org) The website goes on to point out that all a criminal needs to take your identity is your Social Security number, birth date and some other minor identifying information, such as your address, phone number or whatever else they can find out about you. Then with a forged driver's license, they can pose as you to apply for credit, open accounts and do all sorts of unsavory things. From the 2007 FTC report http://www.ftc.gov/bcp/edu/pubs/consumer/idtheft/idt06.pdf, "*The FTC estimates that as many as 10 million Americans have their identities stolen each year.*" (See: http://www.consumer.ftc.gov/topics/privacy-identity) A good resource from the government is http://www.idtheft.gov, which has information about how criminals obtain your identity, what your rights are, how to report Identity Theft, and much more.

As we have also previously discussed, the Internet and general marketing of your personal data is now a for-profit business that is on amphetamines. Your name, address, zip code, birth date and any other potentially damaging and personal information have become a marketing commodity that is sold everywhere, unless you **try very hard** to put a stop to this activity, which is often not possible. You might come to think that this is a hopeless cause, but with due diligence you can make a difference in establishing your privacy and protecting your identity on the Internet. While writing this book, I felt many times that this task was hopeless, but then I would think about all of the people around the world blindly using their PCs, laptops, tablets, smartphones and other mobile devices, with everyone spying on them and I knew that this book would help them become much more difficult targets than they currently were. We all have to ask ourselves why our governments and corporations are spying on us and seem to allow this Internet spying activity to take place by everyone and why it is so difficult to stop.

This is a battle that we all need to undertake at the ballot box and demand attention to. Ask yourself, when was the last time a politician was asked in a debate or by a media commentator what they think their nation needs to do to prevent Identity Theft? How about asking them a question on what cyber security is, or what they would do to educate the general public about the threats they face using the infected Internet? Better yet, wouldn't it be nice if the media asked the politician what he or she would do to protect individual privacy on the Internet? These important issues have been absent from the media and public political debate, and I hope this book corrects that omission. These significant issues have been lost in the public debate as litigation battles abound on many other issues, such as abortion, drug use, gay marriage, drunken driving, cellphone texting while driving, gun control, wearing your seatbelt, protecting the American flag, wearing a motorcycle helmet, deficit spending, and a host of other problems that keep distracting us from the crucial issues of Identity Theft and spying on your Internet activity. Ask any person who has had their identity stolen and they will tell you that this needs to be a national priority in their country's political and privacy agenda.

Our media and politicians keep stating over and over again, how cyber security and/or Identity Theft are a national priority, but give us few, if any, details about the steps that are being taken to help protect their citizens against these threats. These topics only get lip service at government websites and by media commentators, who either don't know or choose to present little information about these important topics. Their lack of knowledge is obvious because what they suggest rarely gets to the core/root of the problem or even provides much detail on the steps that you should take to protect yourself. This chapter is meant to address these inadequacies and oversights, which should encourage you to lobby for litigation to protect your privacy and your identity. The U.S. government, the media, and corporations reveal insufficient information that will help the average SBO/HCU protect their identity, and they certainly don't sufficiently report on how widespread this problem is or how big a threat this is to our personal, as well as their nation's security.

 **Story**	My parents liked to brag how they did not use the Internet or allow anyone into their sphere of existence while I was writing this book. However, after using the Internet tools that you will discover soon, I could learn everything about them including relative history, their address, and so much more. Just because you don't use the Internet does not mean it cannot report everything it knows about you! Big Data is out there and easy to access as privacy laws are relatively non-existent for U.S. citizens.

You have come to the understanding that anyone working for any entity could possibly be up for sale to the highest bidder. The easiest ways for the bad guys to get your personal information is to coerce or install a worker to steal employees' or customers' information from a corporation or government for whom they work. These incidents are quickly covered up for fear that if the public ever knew how prevalent this problem was, they would correctly fear that using the Internet or computers for anything is very risky. They would understand that laws are needed to penalize criminals who take advantage of this lack of security but these laws rarely exist. Let's examine the recent examples where whistleblowers were labeled as traitors by the U.S. government for revealing the information they easily stole.

The U.S. fully funds the NSA while it lets their nation's infrastructure and corporations to continuously cut IT budgets and hire foreign workers as low-paid IT talent. These foreign workers manage much of the U.S.'s contracted, most sensitive data and its IT infrastructure, as well as to do jobs, such as clean their facilities after hours. Can anyone possibly be surprised to find out that some of these foreigners came or were sent to the U.S. to steal information from the government and corporations for whom they are working? How about some of the foreign university students that are being educated about the latest U.S. IT technology, who often times provide software and intelligence to corporations and government? Common sense beyond greed and worship of the almighty dollar would reveal:

1. They are not U.S. citizens, so they may care little for the U.S. or other western nations.
2. Their governments may be coercing or rewarding them to steal intellectual and individual personal data.
3. Some foreign workers on green cards make less than ½ of the salary of their educated U.S. counterparts that they are replacing (quickly altering the landscape). In my case,

at a U.S. corporation, it took three foreign nationals to replace my work, which is not self-aggrandizement. It was a little ironic that the corporation laid me off too quickly before I could teach them how to do my job, which I would have done willingly. I have always believed that I will always move on to bigger, and better things, which is why I will help anyone who is replacing me. There is no such thing as job security in today's world; there is only the technological advancement of your mind to protect your future!

4. There are foreign workers who are given the "key" to all the U.S. corporate data, which could be used to make them many hundreds of thousands of dollars if they could make a hard copy, copy it to a disk, USB, hard drives, or steal it by any other digital means possible and smuggle it out of the corporation or government agency for whom they are working. Corporate and government management have little knowledge of these technologies and rarely, if ever, consult their computer geeks as to how to prevent this theft. Perhaps that is changing, but if you listen to the news it does not appear so.

5. Some of them are backed by criminal foreign Identity Theft rings that are intent on obtaining corporate or government secrets, as well as their customers' and employees' personal information. This type of data is often freely available when you are working for a corporate or government entity.

Simple Prevention Measures to Save You the Cost of Paid Services

If you have not noticed, I use each chapter of this book to shamelessly promote more advanced security techniques, which we are constantly layering to protect ourselves. This is because I am sick of the simple, regurgitated security and identity theft measures preached by some colleges, continuing education classes, other books, blogs, as well as media and magazine articles. We quickly went through them in the introduction of this book to demonstrate how inadequate they are to the task at hand in our use of the infected Internet. Remember the adage, **"once online, it will be there for all time."** Our Internet world has degenerated into one that everything we do follows us for the remainder of our lives. There seems to be no forgiveness, redemption or reformation. This needs to change, but until it does, refrain from posting pictures, non-neutral commentary, politically charged statements, observations about the company you work for and so on. Do not post or store anything online that you don't want the whole world to see. Posting anything controversial, even though it may be true and beneficial to the company or government agency, can cause you to lose you your job, and follow you the rest of your life. Employees are often fired by their companies and/or their governments for posting truthful information online that needs to be brought to everyone's attention about wasteful and incorrect practices. This can occur even if it is in their company's best interest. The Internet world has become backwards as to the way it should be.

Also remember the axiom from Benjamin Franklin, **"An ounce of prevention is worth a pound of cure"**. Identity theft is not a simple matter to correct. You will spend much more time clearing up your stolen identity than working your way through this chapter. To briefly summarize the threats presented by other authoritative sources: your security can be compromised by a missing CD, shoulder surfing, losing a laptop, someone stealing your laptop or smartphone, losing a USB drive, not shredding a document (stealing trash), faxes, copying, interception of your information, instant messages, print jobs, removable storage, digital cameras, PDAs, wallets, purses, credit cards, bank cards, check books, Social Security cards, un-shredded trash, not sanitizing a hard drive, hardware theft, fire, revealing your private information to a company or to someone on the Internet, clicking on an email attachment or link, surfing to a malicious website, and the list goes on. If we all don't know these simple things by now, we certainly should! Media experts and talk radio shows seem to regurgitate these simple steps constantly as if they are presenting new and informative information to you. This is all very common sense stuff, and if we are not thinking about protecting ourselves from this mayhem (love those Allstate Insurance commercials), we certainly should be.

There are monitoring programs that you can pay for to monitor when ID theft takes place. However, from the September 2013 Kiplinger's article titled "Hire an Identity Bodyguard" by Lisa Gerstner, she states "*In a 2009 study, the Consumer Federation of America found that ID-theft programs exaggerated what they could deliver to customers and failed to provide clear information on their Websites.*" These services focus mostly on notifying their customers when suspicious activity occurs that may indicate identity theft. They automate notifying your creditors and provide advice and assistance after your identity has been stolen. If you travel, their agents can help you replace lost or stolen credit cards, IDs, etc. However, I have found my credit unions more than sufficient to performing these tasks for free, with a little extra work on my part checking my accounts online a few times a week. If you want to use one of these paid services, I suggest using one that will dig into areas that you would or could not monitor yourself. For example, the Kiplinger's article suggests using "*TrustedID's IDEssentials program ($15 a month, or $125 a year) included monitoring of your health-insurance policy of black-market sites in can your policy number if for sale; it also scans the sites for your Social Security and credit card numbers. The Identity Guard Platinum plan (recently $19 a month) also surveys the black market, and it checks public records to see whether someone has used your personal information to say, get a driver's license. In addition, the service offers antivirus protection and software for your computer that encrypts keystrokes.*" They also offer a Platinum plan for a few dollars more that will monitor your children's Social Security numbers. From the article, "*AARP members can use a special TrustedID service for $110 a year, a discount of $15.*" (See: http://articles.chicagotribune.com/2013-08-14/business/sns-201308011730--tms--kplngmpctnkm-a20130814-20130814_1_credit-card-credit-reports-credit-karma)

Before you consider using a paid ID Theft service, think about how you are harassed in every facet of your life now. I don't know about you, but my time is constantly consumed shredding snail mail that I care nothing about, investigating suspicious bills that I receive, increases in billing amounts that I did not understand, emails that I have to investigate, and so on. Do you really want to add a paid ID theft service to that mix that you may not have time to respond to anyway? Consider how many false alarms might they present you with that may waste your valuable time? At the same time, if you are in the public eye and don't have time to investigate these events on your own, these services may be worth your while, especially employing a knowledgeable black arts service to protect your identity!

Story	My wife and I live in a decent suburb near Detroit. With all the crime around us, my wife insisted we put in a monitored security system. One day I was working in the backyard as the police strolled through my gate to question who I was and what I was doing. I explained I was building a vanity for the bathroom, but I wonder what they thought of the open beer I had sitting on ground. They really

grilled me as the alarm was going off, which was loud and somehow I had not heard it. After I proved I was the owner of the house they finally left. In another instance, our house was vinyl sided by contractors who cut our phone wire. We had some visiting relatives set the alarm off, but amazingly my security service never called or sent out the police to investigate. I wondered about this, so I called the security company. Turns out that when the phone wire was cut, our security service could no longer monitor our house. I came to understand that any good burglar who knew their trade would cut the phone line into our house, which gave them access to rob us of all our belongings! So the monitoring service I was paying to protect my house was worthless. I asked them about wireless services, but those added services sold for about twice the price I was paying.

Think about your use of these paid services and what you want or expect out of them. They may leave you wanting and may be an expense you can do without.

How bad is Identity Theft?

We all know that Identity Theft is ruinous, and most of us know someone who has experienced it, but do we really know what they went through in correcting it? Believe me, it was a horrible and time-consuming experience for them. All victims now know that what they heard from the media and other corporate and government sources contained inadequate information to prevent it from happening or how they should deal with it once it has happened. However, after all this carnage, they have found no avenue to convey their outrage against this huge waste of their time and impact on their finances and violation to their reputation. Some call into talk radio to describe their experiences, but these conversations seem to be lost as most of us assume it could not happen to our family. In 2013, more than 13 million people fell victim to identity thieves, with some $18 billion stolen, reports financial consultant Javelin Strategy & Research. Javelin found this problem to be worse, as identity thieves have moved beyond simple credit card theft to paying utilities by piggybacking on victims' utility accounts, running up charges on mobile phone accounts, and penetrating other Internet accounts such as Amazon, eBay, and PayPal. In the United States, individual Identity fraud incidents occur every three seconds. (See: https://www.javelinstrategy.com/brochure/276)

Pray that your family never experiences an event like this in their lives. Knowing this is a serious problem, the question we must ask ourselves is, what should we do to prevent the same thing from happening to our families or businesses? Hollywood makes light of this crime in entertaining movies, but the truth is that your household can/will be wrecked by this crime. Think about what you have seen and heard as to what your friends or competitors went through when trying to clear their names to get their lives back after an identity theft. Watching movies and hearing these stories seems to have a negligible effect on the average person's thinking. We also need to investigate how these tragedies happen and work to prevent them. We must come to understand that this is a topic important to all of us as HCUs/SBOs. We also need to come to the realization that because this topic is so important, we must spend a few minutes of our lives educating ourselves on how to prevent ID theft, as well as holding our elected officials' feet to the fire on this important problem.

Identity Theft means that someone is impersonating you, almost always for malicious intent, profit/theft, or espionage. I was curious as to what the formal definition would be, so I investigated. The United States Post Office FAQ defines Identity theft as "*acquiring key pieces of someone's identifying information, such as name, address, birth date, Social Security number or mother's maiden name, in order to impersonate them. The information enables the thief to commit numerous forms of fraud which may include taking over a victim's financial accounts, opening new bank accounts in a victim's name, purchasing automobiles, applying for loans, credit cards and Social Security benefits, renting apartments or establishing utility or phone services.*" From https://en.wikipedia.org/wiki/Identity_theft, "*Identity theft is a form of stealing someone's identity in which someone pretends to be someone else by assuming that person's identity, typically in order to access resources or obtain credit and other benefits in that person's name. The victim of identity theft (here meaning the person whose identity has been assumed by the identity thief) can suffer adverse consequences if they are held accountable for the perpetrator's actions. Identity theft occurs when someone uses another's personally identifying information, like their name, Social Security or identifying number, or credit card number, without their permission, to commit fraud or other crimes.*" Consider for a moment the definitions above. All the thief needs is your name, address, birth date, Social Security number, and mother's maiden name, and suddenly they can wreak havoc in your life with this freely available information provided by big data, and for nominal fees much more detailed information about you.

| **Story**
 | As a person living on a fifth of my former income while writing a book on cyber security, my taxes became so complex that after having one tax company, who reported my taxes incorrectly thus costing me hundreds of dollars, I had to hire another much more highly paid tax company to fix what the first company reported. However, my new highly paid "Master Tax Advisor" asked me to send our birth dates to her in an unencrypted email. I asked if her HIGHLY PAID office had any sort of encrypted email service or use of encryption keys, and the response was that if I was that concerned to just stop by the office and physically give them the information, which I did. What I hope is you see is a pattern of how corporations who deal in personal information have not trained their upper level "Master Advisors" in rudimentary privacy safeguards. Imagine what their less trained staff is revealing about their tax customers, and we have to wonder how many of those underpaid underlings have more highly paid identity theft hidden agendas! I hope you can now see why identity theft is so rampant. |

The goal of this chapter is help you understand how this information is easily obtainable and point out a comprehensive list of counter measures that you must perform to prevent someone who has this information from exploiting it. Cleaning up from a case of Identity Theft is a stressful, chaotic and very time-consuming process. Not to mention the embarrassment and damage that must be rectified to your good name and credit.

Some common scams that we are wary of are where scammers post a pretend job ad and gather your personal information. They send their victims' upbeat emails phishing for personal information and request payment for supposed services rendered. Be wary of foreclosure or debt relief offers. The scammer offers false promises of debt forgiveness or to save your home from foreclosure in exchange for money. Sometimes scammers pretend to represent organizations pretending to offer you financial help you with some ailment or other problem.

Be sure to double-check any solicitations you receive for personal information in return for financial help.

Identity Thieves — Who Are They and How Do They Do It? Could Be Anyone You Know!

The government says that "*According to law enforcement agencies, identity thieves often have no prior criminal background and sometimes have pre-existing relationships with the victims. Indeed, identity thieves have been known to prey on people they know, including coworkers, senior citizens for whom they are serving as caretakers, and even family members. Some identity thieves rely on techniques of minimal sophistication, such as stealing mail from homeowners' mailboxes or trash containing financial documents. In some jurisdictions, identity theft by illegal immigrants has resulted in passport, employment, and Social Security fraud. Occasionally, small clusters of individuals with no significant criminal records work together in a loosely knit fashion to obtain personal information and even to create false or fraudulent documents.*"

However, before you purchase a PAID Identity Theft plan, contact your credit union(s), bank(s) and ISP to see what free, if any, Identity Theft protection tools they may offer. Many smaller banks and credit unions offer free ID theft protection. Those tools include things such as credit bureau checks and alerts at no additional cost. Also consider the cost of ID theft before paying as much as $10 to $15 dollars a month for protection. According to an article by David Daw in the October 2011 PCWorld issue, titled "Free ID Theft Protection Deals" "*Consider your odds of being a victim: In 2009 and estimated 11.1 million people in the United States were subject to ID theft, losing an average of $4841 according to a study by Javelin Strategy and Research. Those victims ended up paying only $373 on average (banks subsumed the rest).*" However, this minor monetary loss is nothing compared the amount of time and effort it will take from you to restore your identity, not to mention the damage done to your credibility, credit, reputation and more, which can take years.

How do ID thieves steal an identity? As we have already stated, it starts with a few tidbits of your personal identifying information, such as your name and Social Security number, credit card numbers, driver's license number, or financial account information. For identity thieves, this information is **gold**. Visit the website http://www.spokeo.com and you will see how identity thieves gather information about you. The website showed my name and age, my wife's name and age, our middle initials, current and previous address, email address, the value of my home, square footage and lot size, a description of my home, my family tree and so on. The website selling your information is even so bold as to state "*Your purchase is confidential. Kirk Ellis will not be notified of your purchase.*" Skilled identity thieves use a variety of methods to get hold of your information, and below are some of the mainstream things that you can find on any website as advice as to what you need to worry about:

Dumpster Diving They rummage through trash looking for bills, statements or other paper with your personal information on it.

Skimming They steal credit/debit card numbers by using a special storage device when processing your card.

Phishing Individuals call your phone then send spam email or present pop-up messages as you visit websites on your Internet devices to entice you into revealing your personal information. They sometimes do this by pretending to be a financial institution or company that you conduct business with. Phishing can be done as scammers pretend or pose to be debt collection agencies, offer up phony prizes and lotteries, say they will provide mortgage foreclosure relief, conduct phony check scams, offer auto related help, and say they have work-from-home opportunities.

Changing Your Address Mail stolen from your mailbox can be used to divert your billing statements to another location by completing something as simple as a change of address form.

Story	A relative of mine went to a local department store and was talked into signing up for a credit card. The employee at the department store changed the address on their application to the thief's address. The thief then charged thousands to the credit card and was never caught. Creditors came after my relative and it took months to prove that they were a victim of fraud.

Old-Fashioned Stealing They steal wallets and purses, mail, including bank and credit card statements, pre-approved credit offers and new checks or tax information. They steal personnel records, or bribe employees who have access.

Pretexting They use false pretenses to obtain your personal information from financial institutions, telephone companies, and other sources.

Espionage A very pervasive problem that is not mentioned often, except in a few news articles or on NPR, that points out how loose cyber security by corporate, government, social networks, banks and other websites have been cracked, thus obtaining millions of peoples personal information. This is by far our biggest threat to Identity theft. Unfortunately, you have to share your personal information with them. My suggestion is to share the minimum information that is required for you to conduct business with them. When possible, give bogus information if it does not violate the law.

Fraud The countries Indonesia, Vietnam, Egypt, Morocco, Algeria, Pakistan, Libya, Lebanon, Palestine, Cameroon, Nigeria, Ghana, Congo and Benin have all been blacklisted by some proxies due to online fraud. If you conduct business with those countries, be very careful.

When you look at the cover of this book, you see a menacing looking woman peering over the shoulder of my computer user. This is because of numerous encounters of spurned computer-literate loved ones striking back at their former mate. This is also another common form or identity theft you need to look out for. They do this to make their former mates' and their new lover's lives a living hell.

As you can see we need to go beyond the conventional type of thinking you hear about. There are other spy techniques that the main stream media and government websites do not seem to want to mention. We see these technologies used in movies all the time, but as individuals or SBOs we don't seem to make the connection as to how they might affect us personally and our everyday lives. There are GPS tracking, hidden listening devices, and hidden cameras, but somehow these devices don't come up in the conversation that is in other books about cyber security or on popular radio talk shows. This computer/Internet/spy device technology has advanced so far as to be something every HCU/SBO needs to take very seriously. Every cyber security website, article or book should include some details about this invasion that is taking place into our privacy. This book attempts to amend that omission in their writings.

Visit Your Local Spy Store, Hidden Cameras, Bug Detection and More

Back in the introduction, I briefly mentioned something to look out for was *Shoulder Surfing*. A shoulder surfer can do something as simple as watch you enter your PIN at an ATM, or employ something as advanced as a hidden camera. We often hear about this technique from mainstream media, though with little or no information on how to prevent it. Nevertheless, take comfort in the fact that there are low cost methods that you can purchase to protect your family or business from attack. When I entered the local "Spy Store" there was many devices on the shelves that looked like common things that you might have around the house, such as a few books, smoke detectors, a box of tissues, and so on. I explained to the store technician that I was writing a book on cyber security and that I was curious about all the ways people can spy on each other. The spy store guy was amazing; he started rattling off about this and that, but I could only follow along on a small percentage of what he was talking about.

I vowed on the spot to come back and take more detailed notes with pencil and pad in hand (at that time I was still in the dark ages as young people tell me, with no smartphone to record the conversation). He was a treasure chest of spy technology, and I was envious of his job. I wanted so much to play with and learn about all the devices and gizmos he knew so much about. I had no clue how far-reaching and invasive this technology has become or how cheap it is. Soon I had to redirect our conversation to topics specific to this book. The first thing that I was curious about was how to detect hidden cameras. The "Spy expert" handed me the *SpyFinder Personal Hidden Camera Locator* and suggested I have a look around the store. It was amazing; there were hidden cameras everywhere in the store that were disguised as common things you would find in any home or office. The books, fire alarms, a tissue box, brief cases, smoke detectors, almost everything was in reality, hidden cameras. To write about a thing means I have to purchase and use it. To justify the purchase to my wife, I explained, "How many creepy stories have we heard about hidden cameras in people's homes, hotel rooms, bathrooms, or other locations that have been inadvertently discovered? Now we can travel with peace of mind, and scan for hidden cameras, which is good thing!" Of course, all I got was her evil eyes depicted on the inside of my book cover. Plus, money talks, and if I did not buy something, how was I going to get more information? Eventually she took the camera locater to her work to see if there were any hidden cameras in a new set of lockers that had been installed in the women's bathroom that she found suspicious, so I felt vindicated.

The above story may sound paranoid until you learn how prevalent these hidden cameras have become in our everyday lives. In the December 2011 issue of Kiplinger's magazine, in an article titled "How to Fight Privacy Pirates" by Kathy M. Kristof, she points out that "*brick-and-mortar retailers are increasingly employing "digital signs" that appear to show videos or news but actually function as cameras, capturing your image-what you view, how you behave, what catches your interest, says Dixon. You can't even get away from computerized spies when you jump in the car. General Motor subsidiary OnStar just told customers that it will be tracking their every move starting in December. And it will be monitoring customers even after they cancel the service. (Customers can call OnStar to deactivated data collection.)"* (The Dixon quotation above was identified in the article as Pam Dixon, executive director of the World Privacy Forum). In a CNN special by Morgan Spurlock, Inside Man posted May 1, 2014 titled, "How many cameras watch you every day?", he says that the average New Yorker is videoed 350 times a day. Standing on a street corner as he pointed out cameras, he also stated that that there are around 20 to 25 cameras within 50 feet of any New York City street corner.

The reality is, how many videos show up on the Internet of unsuspecting victims filmed in private acts? This may violate laws, but the damage is done. Is it a bad idea to scan your hotel room for hidden cameras or bugs in any place you may visit? Are you being paranoid by doing so? **I think not**. In fact, I was showing off the SpyFinder to my racquetball buddies, and we actually discovered two hidden cameras in the health club where we play. Having the finder has made me realize how pervasive this technology is. It is one thing to read about and state these facts based on references; it is another to find and see these cameras for yourself with the counter-technology you can purchase and use. This book is about teaching you to find and see these things for yourself (not just reading about it, hearing a conference speaker lecture about it, or listen to a college professor or supposed "media expert" stating on the radio or TV that these things exist, with no explanation on how to counter this technology).

Story	My wife and I enjoy TV series that show the reality of how much these technologies have advanced. Viewers see this and may not understand how real this supposed make-believe technology is. At the same time, TV shows allow experienced operatives to be spied upon by this technology that is somewhat possible, but not likely. On TV, these operatives are never shown to be taking measures to sweep their houses, hotel rooms or sometimes their visitors for hidden cameras or listening devices. I mean, come on TV writers, you can do better!

Detecting Hidden Cameras and Finding Surveillance Bugs

The SpyFinder hidden camera detector/locator is very easy to use and only costs between $85 to $100 dollars. I purchased mine retail from the spy store so I could get local technical support, which I will never regret. If you visit a few websites, they describe it as the most reliable and easy-to-use technology on the market for finding hidden cameras. From the manual, SpyFinder allows the user to *"locate hidden cameras by using an array of ultra-bright LEDs in a patented optical configuration. The SpyFinder works on a variety of camera types including video CCTV cameras, digital cameras, auto focus cameras, camcorders, and spy/pinhole-type cameras."* The way it works is as simple as pressing a button on the side, looking through a lens, and then the camera(s) light up as a blinking red dot. This reflection coming from the camera lens reveals its location, which you will have to inspect closely. You have now become James Bond, which is an empowering feeling.

However, you have to be careful as you can get hidden positives from this device. From the manual, *"Some objects within an area being scanned will generate false positive signals. These are caused by items that will reflect the light from the SpyFinder unit. Curved surfaces that are reflective are the most common source of false positives. (e.g. door knobs or other rounded reflective surfaces."*

Story	An SBO thought that an employee was stealing from him so he went to his local spy store and purchased a hidden camera. Within a week of observing the employee, the SBO found out that the employee was indeed stealing from him. It is unknown how much was stolen, but it was many thousands more than what a SpyFinder would cost. Had the thief had a SpyFinder, they may have discovered the hidden camera, thus avoiding going to jail. This technology goes both ways.

Possessing something like a SpyFinder might be worth having, just to give you peace of mind to examine your home, your hotel room while traveling, or at work in your cube. At any job we have to assume we are being observed in everything we do. It would be nice to know for sure there is not a hidden camera located in your cube, which would mean that you, personally, are under investigation. Discovering that fact may give you time to find another job before having the stigma of *fired* on your record for all time!

It is easy to understand how a cracker, scorned lover, SBO, or government with deep pockets could install and pay for an expensive hidden camera. But how can the average person do so? The spy technician showed me an independent system that uses the Verizon network. It costs $15,000 dollars, which would be cost prohibitive to the average person. So I redirected the conversation to low-cost solutions. He then explained that cameras costing a few hundred dollars or less (disguised as a smoke detector, book, tissue box and many other things) could be easily installed and piggy backed on the SBO/HCU's wireless network. That way, a cracker could use the Internet to view and record everything that the camera was setup to view.

We talked about other low-cost solutions and who would be purchasing them. Deep down I believe that purveyors of this type of equipment know that much of what they sell goes for illegal or misguided motives. The technician seemed to want to bare his soul and explain everything that he had surmised about the people purchasing their equipment. I think he found it refreshing to be talking to someone who wanted to write about this type of technology, and not exploit it. In no way do I want to stop or ban the sale of this type of equipment, but I do want to help you understand how easy it is to obtain and its prevalence in our lives.

Let's examine the hot-selling **"Cell Phone Recon"** product and see where it might invade our privacy. According to the technician, this is the favorite product of parents and suspecting husbands and wives everywhere. It allows them to track their spouses or children's where-a-bouts by an application installed on their cellphone. Even more, it can monitor Global System for Mobile Communications (GSM) text messages and call logs as well as emails sent and received. The application will not allow the installer to hear or record call conversations. In addition, it is used extensively by small businesses to find stolen or lost cellphones and to monitor employees. Once the application is installed, the cellphone user will not know the application, although the phone does have to be on and connected to the Internet to transmit its data. These uses seem benign, but take into consideration that other entities may also be exploiting this technology to track the use of these devices. They have been granted this permission by the Bush administration and allowed to continue to do so under the Obama administration. Where do we draw the line on this type of spying? Parents love the ability to spy on their children, but in doing so, are they allowing backdoors for spies to also track them as well? (See: http://www.cellphonerecon.com) Another thing to consider before employing this technology is, what happens to the data that is collected, and what is CellPhoneRecon's privacy policy? The website states that users have access to the data for one month and then it is archived. It is disturbing that CellPhoneRecon uses the word *archive* and not *delete* for the fate of your data, and I could not find a privacy policy stated on their website.

How about **"Spy Cobra Deluxe"** (SCD), which is an undetectable Windows PC monitoring tool that can capture all activity on a PC? It can be used by parents, employers or private investigators. The application will install itself in 15 seconds by plugging in the SCD portable USB flash drive into the PC. The firewall may prompt the installer to allow access to the Internet and as soon as the installer says "yes," the user will never know it is running in the background. Antivirus software will not identify this software once it is installed. SCD will provide the person monitoring that PC's keystrokes, take screenshots, remember all websites visited, detect encrypted password keys, monitor both sides of IM conversations, check the sender and recipient of every email sent or received, and even provide key word detection. This information can be emailed to you, or you can just stick the SCD USB drive back into the PC at a later time to quickly and easily download the saved information onto the Flash Drive. It is easy to imagine the potential for the abuse of this technology. Suppose you allow someone into your house, and they manage to get physical access to your computer and you take your eye off of them for 15 seconds; or you are an SBO with a disgruntled or dishonest employee; imagine the havoc they could reap on your business if they got this application installed on an important PC. (See: http://spycobra.com) If you recall back in the introduction, I talked about how slipping USB drives behind the U.S. government's firewalls allowed crackers to steal terabytes of sensitive government information.

I investigated how something like SpyCobra might be detected and/or removed and found a program called Malwarebytes that has an Anti-Rootkit BETA tool to do such a thing; some other websites recommended trying the GMER rootkit removal tool. There are other rootkit options that the website TechNibble lists for you to consider as well. You could also shut down your system, boot up the antivirus CD software that we loaded onto our Multipass, and see if it can detect SpyCobra. (See: http://www.gmer.net, https://en.wikipedia.org/wiki/GMER, http://support.kaspersky.com/faq/?qid=208283363 , http://www.technibble.com/rootkit-detection-and-removal-tools)

The next thing we got into was how to detect bugs (listening devices) and how they work. Bugs can be found in air filters, alarm clocks, books, coat hangers, a computer mouse, DVR box, power strips, small electronics, a watch with a cellphone, just about anywhere and anything. But take comfort in the fact that to really have an effective long-term bug it needs a power source, so this limits the placement of bugs in a home or office. Running a bug off batteries is only effective over a short period of time. This technique would be very successful to record a corporate meeting or target something specific, but for long-term surveillance, this is not a very effective technique. The movies rarely point this out. In addition, the surveillance listening to a bug would need to be positioned nearby for a non-Internet bug to work. You would have to be considered a high-value government target to warrant this type of scrutiny. However, if the bug is tied into your Internet equipment, it can be surveyed from anywhere in the world and for long periods of time. So if someone wants to bug you, they will connect the bug to a power source in your business or home, most likely tied into your Internet equipment.

Many bugs are easily detectable by purchasing a radio frequency detector. The inexpensive detectors that we can afford, such as the DD2020 Personal RF Detector, can operate in the 1MHz - 6GHz range. From the manual, "*The DD2020 personal radio frequency detector is a pocket-sized, portable test instrument designed to locate stuck transmitters and bugging devices in any home, office, or automobile.*" It comes with multiple modes that you can use to detect RF signals that may be broadcasting from your home or small business. The device is very easy to use; all you have to do is adjust it to the lowest possible gain (the indicator bars go out) and start sweeping everything. The red bars will go crazy if they detect something transmitting. Of course, you will have to turn off things like wireless routers in your house, and you could also receive false positives from neighboring homes. The best way to determine if you have a bug is to take everything that is in the area where you are receiving a false positive, move it to an area where you are not, and then sweep it. If the signal is still active, you have a bug.

WARNING	If you think you are safe from bugs because you are not 007, think again. I swept a hotel room at an Indian casino where I was staying and found a phone broadcasting an RF signal even with the receiver in place. I did not take the phone apart to see if it was bugged, but I unplugged the phone connection just in case. These devices may transmit RF signals with the receiver in place, but they should not, for fear there could be a bug housed in the device. They should only transmit when the phone is undocked.

Speaking of bugs, they come in many shapes and sizes. In any place we find ourselves it is imperative that we recon the area for potential threats. Otherwise we risk our health, privacy, livelihood, and ultimately our very lives.

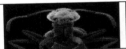 ## Historical Reference – Bedding Down with Mojave Desert Ants; They Bite and Will Make you Sick!

My platoon and I bedded down for the night by lying on the desert ground and burrowing a nice comfortable position into the sand. Early on in the night I groggily realized that something was biting me, so I stumbled over the track and curled up to sleep on the hard metal back door. My buddy Dillion, another Marine in my platoon, was already asleep there. It was a rough night sleeping on something more uncomfortable than concrete, but at least whatever it was that was biting me had gone away. The next morning I awoke to the sound of a medevac helicopter landing and watched as two Marines from another platoon were being loaded into the chopper. I could not fathom what was going on. Turns out, we had bedded down near an ant hill and the ants had chewed on everyone during the night, making a real bad meal out of two of the guys. They were really sick, and I never did find out what happened to them. Somehow I got some of the blame as certain guys accused me of spitting out my toothpaste too close to the sleeping area. The truth is I spit out my toothpaste further away than they did. They were just mad about the fact that I woke up when no one else did and had not awakened them as to the danger, and had slept on uncomfortable steel rather than in the biting soft sand. You might wonder how anyone could sleep through being eaten by ants, but when you have survived fighting in 140 degree heat, wearing and carrying over a hundred pounds of gear all day, you sleep like a log. In my case, it was a miracle that I woke up all. The next morning, I was found sleeping on the track door with only a few ant bites. Most of the guys had been bitten more than a few times and were upset that Dillon and I had gotten off so easy after violating orders. Of course that begs the question, why were troops forbidden from sleeping on the equipment? Which ignorant commander had given that order? The equipment is there to aid in a soldier's survival and comfort and should be used to its fullest capacity.

The story above is meant to teach a lesson on how important it is to recon your area or accommodations wherever you travel. Your million dollar small business may be the target of some unscrupulous individuals. Technology has advanced so much that you have to employ some countermeasures in the places you visit, just in case. People have been killed for a few thousand dollars or less, and your small business is a ripe melon to be picked.

Invisible Ink -- Using and Creating

Another stealthy technique that you can employ is to use a UV black light pen (invisible ink). You can mark something that you suspect is being stolen from your SB and see if it turns up at a local pawn shop or merchant. These special inks are only visible under UV light. There are some other unconventional uses for UV ink, as in marking your personal property with an identifier, such as your house number and zip code, and if it is stolen, the police can then easily identify it as your property and return it to you, you could use it to pass secret messages, or college students can use it for highlighting and then get a better price for selling a used book, clubs use it to identify people over 21, amusement parks use it to identify paid patrons leaving and coming back into the park, and so on.

If you want to use something a little less common and is a more covert ink, you should consider infrared inks. They also cannot be seen by the human eye nor can they be seen with ultraviolet lights. These inks absorb light at one frequency and emit light at another; you have to wear special contact lenses or glasses to see these inks. Gamblers use them to mark cards by wearing the special glasses, so in a poker game they can see the marks on the cards to know what the other players have in their hands. These types of inks are also good for surreptitious authentication technology to protect products or passwords. I hope you are seeing that these technologies are not beyond you. These are simple measures we can take to protect our individual privacy. If you want to purchase invisible ink online, or a pen, simply visit Amazon and do a search on "invisible ink".

If you don't want to pay for invisible ink, there are many recipes that you can use to create your own. This becomes especially true if you are worried about "the man*" knowing that you are using invisible ink to pass messages to others. In the article "A Recipe for Invisible Ink" by Kristie Macrakis, who wrote the book *Prisoners, Lovers & Spies: The Story of Invisible Ink from Herodotus to al-Qaeda*, she whipped up the following:

"Heat 2 cups of water to boiling in a small saucepan. Mix 2 heaping teaspoons of a starch (like oatmeal) in 1/3 shot glass of cold water, and stir to make a slurry.

Once the water in the saucepan is boiling, carefully add the white starch slurry, stirring and continuing to boil for two minutes to make a good solution. The starch solution will thicken as it cools. A message can be written with a fine paintbrush or a Q-tip. For a finer line, snip one end from the Q-tip and use the cut end.
Once dried, the writing is developed with a dilute iodine solution. Always wear gloves and glasses to protect skin and eyes. Simply brush medicinal iodine tincture (or povidone) on the paper or apply it with an eye dropper. The paper will also pick up iodine initially—but without the starch, most of the iodine will leave the paper within a few hours, really contrasting the blue starch writing."

In another article by Anne Marie Helmenstine, Ph. D, titled "How to Make Invisible Ink - Baking Soda" she outlines the following procedure:

1. There are at least two methods to use baking soda as an invisible ink. Mix equal parts water and baking soda.
2. Use a cotton swab, toothpick, or paintbrush to write a message onto white paper, using the baking soda solution as 'ink'.
3. Allow the ink to dry. One way to read the message is to hold the paper up to a heat source, such as a light bulb. The baking soda will cause the writing in the paper to turn brown.
4. A second method to read the message is to paint over the paper with purple grape juice. The message will appear in a different color.

Tip 	✓ If you are using the heating method, avoid igniting the paper; don't use a halogen bulb. ✓ Baking soda and grape juice react with each other in an acid-base reaction, producing a color change in the paper. ✓ The baking soda mixture can also be used more diluted, with one part baking soda to two parts water. ✓ Grape juice concentrate results in a more visible color change than regular grape juice.

What You Need: baking soda, paper, water, hair dryer (heat source), paintbrush or swab, measuring cup, purple grape juice (opt.). She also details additional methods using corn starch and lemon juice. (See: http://chemistry.about.com/cs/howtos/ht/invisibleink1.htm, http://chemistry.about.com/cs/howtos/ht/invisibleink2.htm, http://chemistry.about.com/cs/howtos/ht/invisibleink3.htm)

Password — The Weak Link in Securing Information and Remains as the Default Method of Authentication

In the PCWorld October 13, 2010 article titled *"Surprise! Passwords Are (Still) Weak Link in Security Chain"* by Tony Bradley, it points out that passwords are still the weak link in the security chain. One would think that in the days of laptops with fingerprint scanners and other advanced technology, the dated username and password authentication would be something that was deprecated. Yet, according to the article, the username and password are still the default method of accessing secure accounts and information. (See: http://www.pcworld.com/article/207718/surprise_passwords_are_still_weak_link_in_security_c hain.html) The article refers to a Webroot survey that found that users continue to follow poor password practices. From the article the survey found:

- "*4 in 10 respondents shared passwords with at least one person in the past year.*
- *Nearly as many people use the same password to log into multiple websites, which could expose their information on each of the sites if one of them becomes compromised.*
- *Almost half of all users never use special characters (e.g. ! ? & #) in their passwords, a simple technique that makes it more difficult for criminals to guess passwords.*
- *2 in 10 have used a significant date, such as a birth date, or a pet's name as a password– information that's often publicly visible on social networks.*
- *86 percent do not check for a secure connection when accessing sensitive information when using unfamiliar computers.*
- *14 percent never change their banking password.*
- *20 percent have used a significant date in a password.*
- *And 30 percent remember their passwords by writing them down and hiding them somewhere like a desk drawer,*" where, I'd like to add, someone in the nighttime cleaning crew or a fellow employee can easily obtain them.

See also http://www.macworld.com/article/1168035/security_in_the_icloud_age.html for a good read on passwords. The security software development company Splashdata, that sells their SplashID Safe line of password management applications, has released their annual top 25 list of the most common account passwords used on the Internet. This list enlightens and entertains, to say the least. In the order from most to least used, that list is password, 123456, 12345678, abc123, qwerty, monkey, letmein, dragon, 111111, baseball, iloveyou, trustno1, 1234567, sunshine, master, 123123, welcome, shadow, ashley, football, jesus, michael, ninja, mustang, and password1. (See: http://www.splashdata.com/press/PR121023.htm) You might think "Naw that cannot be!" as I did, but in my IT career I have witnessed this personally.

Any password recovery tool, for example Cain & Able, can crack passwords like the ones above in less than 15 seconds. If you are not familiar with Cain and Able, it is a brute-force password cracking program for Microsoft Windows. Brute Force includes Dictionary Attacks, which tries words from a dictionary list. Optimized Brute Force Attacks tries character combinations of dictionary words. Brute Force Attacks tries random combinations of characters of varying lengths, are techniques used to crack these simple passwords. Cain & Able can also sniff networks using various techniques to crack those passwords as well. Brute Force Attacks goes through every possible combination of legal characters in a sequence to crack a password. These tools have other capabilities built in to aid administrators in securing their users network password files and other authentication mechanisms. (See: http://www.oxid.it/cain.html)

Additionally, password guessing does occur. In the movies it occurs in a desperate minute of need as the actor guesses the password, which is totally unrealistic. Still, on more than one occasion, I have visited friends and found their children using their neighbor's wireless networks. I never let out their secret to their parents, but the password to their neighbor's network password was that easy to guess. Refer back to Chapter 10 to see how easy it is to load up a USB drive with easy-to-use password-cracking software.

Story I helped a corporate employee get logged into to their work applications. They needed to get their computer set up to telecommute (work from home). To set them up I had to log in with their work password, which was promptly changed after they watched everything I did. I was shocked at the simplicity of the password and asked them how long they had been using that password. The answer amazed and horrified me; that person had been using that password for years. The person I was helping worked for a large corporation and had access to tons of personal information in an industry that should have had better security.

Given the simplicity of the password list above, it indicates a total lack regard for cyber security by unsuspecting Internet users. I have personally witnessed this phenomenon in companies that do not audit their password files or set up proper rules for their employees to enter a password. The IT administrators were clearly not checking the network passwords their users were using, even after long periods of time. If they had, they would have long since identified these holes in their security and forced their users to correct it. This puts all of our personal information housed in these corporations' databases at risk. If that information is hacked and it is discovered, it could cost millions in litigation for that breach in security and possibly put them out of business. It would cost them much more than they would have paid for a security audit or some qualified IT professionals that could secure all facets of their computer systems. The days of contracting out everything to computer service companies should come to an end.

An additional tool you can add to your accounts is something called "two-factor authentication" (2FA), which most of the big technology companies such as Apple, Dropbox, Facebook, Google, Microsoft, and Twitter now offer. What 2FA does is add an extra step to your login process, thus protecting your account if your username and password are compromised. However, having this added requirement of two out of three types of credentials before accessing an account can prove to be annoying, especially if you delete cookies and temporary files from your Internet device(s) often. To make things easier on users, upon first login, companies will store the second ID PIN/password/pattern on the Internet device so that users don't have to enter the second factor ID every time they login. This opens up those tidbits of login information to attack by crackers. You can preserve these cookies with some added work using a tool such as CCleaner, which is worth the effort if your Internet devices are secure.

Password — Examples of Corporations Hacked for Their Password Databases and Your Personal Information

From a Kiplinger's article written by Lisa Gerstner in the April 2012 issue, "*Accounts of security breaches at retailers and other businesses have become an ongoing saga. In a recent installment, Zappos.com said in January that hackers had tapped its database of more than 24 million users. Customers' credit card information remained safe, but email and billing addresses, phone numbers, and encrypted passwords may have been exposed.*"

In an article by PCWorld, March 5, 2013 by Tony Bradley, "*Evernote revealed over the weekend that it was the victim of a data breach, emailing users and posting a notice on its Website that attackers had gained access to usernames, email addresses, and encrypted passwords associated with Evernote accounts. As a precaution, Evernote forced all 50 million users to reset their passwords."* Consequently, we can see how the password scheme of authentication is outdated. This example also stresses how you must use different passwords for every Internet site your visit. We will cover that seemingly herculean task soon, thus proving it can be done and is manageable. Given these types of constant security breaches, the next section details a few simple password rules that should be followed.

A password breach is the path to gathering more information about your credit information or report, and ultimately your identity. This occurs because the security questions asked by the credit reporting agencies tend to mirror the security questions of breached websites. In the news recently it was reported that detailed credit information was posted online about some very prominent people ranging from Paris Hilton to Michelle Obama. (See: http://www.bloomberg.com/news/2013-03-12/equifax-transunion-say-hackers-stole-celebrity-reports.html) We will soon talk about "Zombie Accounts" that are also places that can be mined for security question answers and other personal information. The local library, websites online, search engines, etc. are all gathering places for answers to your security questions or credit report. Having a multitude of strong passwords is important, as we will discuss next, but it is only a single vital step in protecting your identity.

Many users record their user passwords in the browsers for convenience. When a cracker or someone you trust gets access to your Internet device, it is often child's play to gain access to your browser-stored passwords which you maintain to automatically login to websites. Let's explore the example of Firefox; *click three horizontal lines icon upper right and choose Options > click on the Security tab and click the Saved Passwords... button > you'll see a list of website addresses and usernames > click the Show Passwords button lower right to see your passwords.* Imagine if a snoop got hold of this list. Firefox offers you the ability to set up a master password to control all these logins, but how many users really do this or know this option exists?

Password – Management Tools, Rules and Websites

We hear from a variety of sources on how important the password is to our security, but usually without advice on guidelines, generation methods or even the means to store them properly. Below are a few rules that you need to follow with online passwords:

1. If you change your password, make note of your previous password. It is rarely needed, except in the instance where something happens when changing the password or perhaps in the case where your company maintains a database of all your previous passwords.
2. Never use the same password to login to multiple online sites, because if a cracker is able to decode or obtain your password to one site, they cannot use it to exploit your other accounts. I have heard it suggested that you could get by with a single password for similar types of sites, such as one password for banking and one for shopping. I strongly suggest otherwise, just in case that password is somehow compromised.
3. Your email account password should be a very secure password and never be redundant. Confirmations and warnings of your online activity are sent to your

registered email account(s). A cracker can cloak their online activity (like draining your bank accounts), if they have access to your registered email account(s).

4. Use a strong password. Password strength refers to the ability of a cracker to guess, discover (physically or remotely via monitoring), or be cracked using an attack algorithm. A weak password would be one that could be easily cracked, such as the name of pet or a dictionary word. A strong password is one that would be difficult or impossible to crack. Password generators are a good way to create a random mix of uppercase and lowercase letters, as well as numbers and symbols, which would constitute a strong password. Use a combination of letters, numbers and characters (such as ! or @) and again, change them often. Avoid using birthdates or repeating numbers for your PINs.

5. After generating a password, change a few characters in the password. You don't know the underlying mathematical algorithm that the website or application used to generate that password (unless you created it). If a cracker ever compromises or obtains the algorithm or reverse engineers the tool that you used to generate your passwords, they might be able to generate the same password(s). This is very unlikely, but the possibility still exists.

6. For a website that you are logging into, use the maximum length that is allowed for a password. For example, Hotmail appears to allow 16 characters and Google 50 characters. At my ISP, the max length was 20 characters, but I had to use 19 to get the website to accept the password change.

7. If you have to write down a password, consider using invisible ink that we discussed previously. Keep in mind that written paper lists, or unencrypted files with your passwords and PIN numbers are "keys to the castle" if a thief finds them.

It is easy for a business to help their employees choose strong passwords. It is as simple as having their employees to go to a reputable website to test the strength of their password when they are being required to change it; once again, change a character or two after testing it. (Remember my adage: Typed online, there for all time). (See: https://www.microsoft.com/security/pc-security/password-checker.aspx, http://www.strongpasswordgenerator.org, http://www.pctools.com/guides/password) I really don't trust that any passwords generated online is not recorded or possibly captured by a yet unknown, nefarious means. As an alternative, a business could provide a local tool such as KeePass Password Safe or the open source Password Safe tool, both of which we will discuss soon, to enable their employees to generate their network password, thus keeping the less secure encrypted password database on their home/business computer. (See: http://keepass.info, http://pwsafe.org)

There is a dark side to a strong password. We mentioned the fact that employees can write down their password and keep it in an unsafe place, such as their desk drawer. They do this for a variety of reasons; these passwords are difficult to remember, some companies require changing them often, employees believe that because they work in a secure area no one can rifle through their desk, and it is embarrassing and time consuming to call IT to have their password reset. Consequently, while some companies enforce strong passwords and make employees change them often, there is often a lack of effort or understanding by management that they need training and help managing these complex passwords and other confidential files. At one company, I had over 10 passwords to various applications and websites, which

I'm sad to say I was forced to store in a simple text file on my desktop PC. When I inquired about installing encryption software on my PC to encrypt sensitive files such as my text password file, I was told no such software was approved for employee use. The corporate policy only allowed approved software on company computer equipment. It does not have to be this way, which I hope the next section will make abundantly clear.

While I don't condone this, one method that you can use to manage your passwords is at an online website. With one master password you have online access to all of your passwords via computers, laptops and mobile devices to services that provide mobile access on iPhone, BlackBerry, Android and Windows Phone, or use Agilebits which is available for Apple and Android mobile devices. (See: https://agilebits.com/onepassword/overview, http://luxsci.com/blog/how-secure-are-password-protected-files.html, https://lastpass.com/, http://www.roboform.com) There is also Passpack, the #1 recommended by June 2010 PCWorld, which has free personal use. (See: http://passpack.com/en/home) It also generates secure passwords and has an automatic login feature.

However, just like the dark side to remembering strong passwords, using cloud-based password management services is very dangerous--especially if that service can access or promotes that they can recover your passwords. If the service promises that it can turn over your passwords to a next kin or recover a forgotten password, then they have access to your passwords and can be hacked! If a hack such as this occurs, imagine the nightmare race you would have to change all of your online passwords before the hacker can raid your accounts. A few other reasons not to use cloud based storage of passwords: 1) If you don't have access to the Internet then you don't have access to all of your latest passwords. 2) Storing passwords on the infected Internet in any form is very dangerous. 3) You might be forced to use an open hotspot to login and get access to your passwords.

Password – KeePass and Password Safe Encrypted Password Databases

We previously introduced KeePass, which is a free, open source password manager* that operates as a local database of passwords. (See: http://keepass.info) The KeePass database uses the AES and Twofish encryption algorithms and can be accessed via a single password. It generates secure passwords so you can easily maintain a different password for every online account. There is also an "Auto Type" feature that will type your username and password for you. If convenience is important you, house your KeePass at an encrypted cloud sync, such as SpiderOak. Using an encrypted cloud disk will achieve double encryption, which should be very secure. This way you will always have a local and a sky copy of your encrypted password file available to all of your Internet devices. To get started using KeePass, just open it up and point it to where you want your encrypted password file stored.

KeePass saves me loads of time over my old manual-encrypted, text-based password file from which I used to cut and paste. The KeePass database is encrypted and requires a password making it a good choice for your laptop. If you add GPG encryption or Boxcryptor, which we talked about in Chapter 5, you will have double encryption that will frustrate crackers. KeePass also works in Linux, so you could access your password file from a multiboot USB drive.

1. Double click on the URL in the database entry, which takes you right where you need to be. This eliminates possibly mistyping the URL and inadvertently visiting a phishing site. It also eliminates the need for surfing to a web page on my site, or cutting and pasting the URL; both are methods I used before using KeePass.
2. Drag and drop the username and password, which makes logging in fast for all of your websites. It also has features for setting up AUTO key strokes and macros, with which I have not yet experimented. No more cutting and pasting.
3. The encrypted database requires a password to log in, so you only have to remember one password to log in and keep your passwords secure. This is much better than having a text file/word document sitting wide open on your home computer.
4. It has a field for notes so you can store things such as website questions, account numbers, etc. and other important information you or your spouse may need to get to and use important online accounts. For example, they may not know the name of your first girlfriend/boyfriend. From my own experience, when I was in the hospital my spouse was managing things, and she needed this information!

WARNING	As much as I love using KeePass I have not vetted this software solution and question its need to startup in the background on a Windows 7 computer the KeePass 2 PreLoad process. Perhaps Domink Reichl will someday help me fully understand the need for this process to constantly be running in the background. Use ***CCleaner > Tools > Startup*** to disable this process.

There is also the open source solution Password Safe. (See: http://pwsafe.org, http://passwordsafe.sourceforge.net) It can also be used in Windows and has over four million downloads. It is very similar to KeePass in that it maintains an encrypted database so that you only have to remember one master password to use it. Since this is open source, it is very unlikely this tool has any hidden agendas or back doors. The software takes many precautions to protect your master password and database. This reliable solution includes; never storing the master password in the clear, keeping sensitive memory from swapping to disk, file integrity checks, and more. (See: http://passwordsafe.sourceforge.net/readmore.shtml)

When you install Password Safe on the Installation Type screen it asks if you want to use the Registry or choose Disk-on-Key , which does not. ***To keep the password manager as portable as possible on the Installation Type screen, choose Disk-on-Key so that we can use it on our USB Drive, Next> > on the Choose Components screen be sure to uncheck Start automatically, Next> > Install. You can now run Password Safe from the Desktop or from the Start menu > click on the New... button to create a password database > type in your password Safe Combination:, OK > you can now start adding password entries by clicking on the Add New Entry icon > fill out the basic fields, OK.*** When you right click on your new password entry we can automate just about everything to log in to our online accounts. For example the Browse to URL + Autotype feature worked well with most logins.

Don't Let Your Tax Return Result in Identity Theft, Cause an Audit Disaster or Defraud You

NOTE	The following two sections have been reviewed by an H&R Block Master Tax Advisor for accuracy. To achieve master tax advisor status, an H&R Block tax professional has to pass a 14-level certification program. H&R tax professionals must complete 15 hours of continuing education annually. (See: http://newsroom.hrblock.com/about)

If you have more than a simple W-2 and a mortgage, the United States tax code can become incredibly complex very quickly. The January 5, 2011 Forbes article by Janet Novack titled *"Tax Waste: 6.1 Billion Hours Spent Complying with Federal Tax Code"*, has some amazing statistics about the U.S. tax code. In 2001, the monstrous U.S. tax code was a mind blowing 1.3 million words. Since the U.S. tax code is constantly tweaked and changed every year, it has mushroomed into 3.8 million words as of February 1, 2010, and is increasing, so we can only imagine what it now is in 2015. This has resulted in about 60% of taxpayers paying CPAs, enrolled agents, and tax preparation services, while another 29% use software that touts itself as up-to-date with the latest tax codes. The average median U.S. taxpayer was paying about $258 for tax preparation in 2007 according to an IRS study, up from $220 in 2001. I found no statistics on how many hours Americans spend to abide by state and local tax laws, but the number of federal hours is the equivalent of giving three million U.S. workers full time jobs years round. What is even more outrageous about the U.S. tax system is that taxpayers are responsible for the information on their tax returns even though they pay so-called tax professionals to examine, provide advice on, and prepare their tax returns. This inspires some preparers to promise the world and stretch the bounds of what is legally conceivable in every possible way, expanding the even more complex tax codes that their U.S. Congress votes in, thus exhausting the U.S. IRS who are also incapable of dealing with this crazy tax system nightmare. Your odds of being audited are varied, and depend on the type of return and forms you file, as well as the amount of income that you make. If you report less than $200,000 in income and don't have to attach Schedules C or E to your tax return, you only have a 0.4% chance of being audited. (See: http://www.forbes.com/sites/anthonynitti/2013/03/25/what-are-your-odds-of-being-audited-by-the-irs, http://www.forbes.com/sites/janetnovack/2011/01/05/tax-waste-6-1-billion-hours-spent-complying-with-federal-tax-code)

Story  	If you ask a friend, neighbors, colleague or supervisor, who might help you find someone to help you with your taxes, which is what some tax writer articles suggest, you may get some interesting recommendations. In one instance, a neighbor steered me to a CPA who yielded quite a surprise when I arrived at his office. The building was in a rundown, shabby looking golf store with arrows leading me to a room in the back. The back room looked like a dusty hoarder room, and there were two men sitting in chairs that were behind two desks with piles of paper upon them and a chair in front, upon which they motioned for me to sit. I sat down and nervously felt like I was meeting a crime syndicate boss. I handed them my tax return information, and an hour later I was ushered out the door with them telling me that we were done. The whole experience left me feeling dirty and insecure that my taxes were done completely correctly, as I felt that tax saving deductions had likely been missed in the brief question and answer exchange. A later review by an H&R Block "Master Tax Advisor" found nothing wrong with that tax return, so my fears were unfounded.

There are many consequences of this out-of-control tax system that Americans should consider lobbying their Congress to change:

- In 2011, the IRS identified over 1.1 million incidents of identity theft that affected the U.S. tax system. (See: http://www.treasury.gov/tigta/congress/congress_05082012.pdf)
- Increased numbers of Americans are cheating on their taxes and an underfunded IRS is having an increasingly difficult time catching them.
- More and more mistakes are being made by tax preparers and taxpayers, which an overwhelmed IRS may or may not detect.
- Tax preparation expenditures continue to increase on median income earners as the U.S. tax code expands.
- Special interests constantly lobby Congress to keep them from reforming the U.S. tax code and distract them from working on other important issues that the American people need addressed.
- Identity theft using tax form information is rising rapidly as Americans turn to outside agencies, companies and preparers.
- Because the IRS is overwhelmed and underfunded with a 3.8 million word tax code, it is very difficult to reach to answer tax questions. American's not only have to pay their taxes, but they also have to pay someone to answer questions about their taxes.
- No matter how much U.S. taxpayers pay tax professionals, the IRS will hold the taxpayers culpable for what is on their tax return, which is outrageous. In any other business, if you pay someone for a service, they are at least partially responsible for the accuracy, quality and follow-up for their possibly shoddy work.
- We are living in a digital world where people are all too willing to give away their information. This puts your tax information at risk.

SAVINGS 	I hope you can see how the American people are tasked with an impossible tax system and how their underfunded IRS has the undertaking of trying to enforce this impossible mission. Please think carefully as to who profits from this incredibly complex system of taxation and give careful consideration to whom benefits from this. They are tax preparers, CPAs, accountants and other individuals who wish to waste our time on these frivolous matters. I do not disrespect these professions but see them being used for some other mission to distract you from other more important matters. These are noble professions that have to exist but been exaggerated by a system whose creators consume billions of dollars at expense to the U.S. economy and at a sacrifice to U.S. infrastructure such has roads and bridges. The U.S military needs these dollars to defend their citizens in buildup and expenditures; the public needs mass transit, green energy, food production and so on that makes this tax system incredibly stupid and complex.

Young Americans even blame themselves for the problems that our complex U.S. tax code causes. One young man pointed out to me that if you cheat on an exam and/or have someone else write your paper for you, do you put their name on it or yours? Therefore, you are culpable even if you hire someone to do your taxes and sign your name; you are attesting to the fact that everything in the return is accurate. This point would be valid except for the fact that the tax laws have ***3.8 million words of complexity***, requiring us to hire someone to navigate this maze. As law-abiding citizens working 60+ hours a week, we must somehow try to offload this responsibility, thinking that legality is part of that mix, about which most Americans assume and are incorrect about.

Story	In 2012, book expenses piled up, my emergency fund savings was running out and I wanted to use them to try to offset what we owed in taxes. I also procrastinated in hiring a Jackson Hewitt tax office until April 1st, 2013, which put us in a mad scramble to get our taxes done by the 15th. After much despair we ended up retrieving and mailing out that tax return on April 15, so this is not a mistake I will ever repeat again.

In 2012, book expenses piled up, my emergency fund savings was running out and I wanted to use them to try to offset what we owed in taxes. I also procrastinated in hiring a Jackson Hewitt tax office until April 1st, 2013, which put us in a mad scramble to get our taxes done by the 15th. After much despair we ended up retrieving and mailing out that tax return on April 15, so this is not a mistake I will ever repeat again.

Later, in October of 2013, I had some complex tax questions that I needed answered so I went to the Jackson Hewitt tax office only to find it closed. I called the Jackson Hewitt headquarters and was informed that after tax season most of their satellite **franchise** offices close. The closest location that I could go to for possible tax help was an hour away in Troy, MI. Turns out Jackson Hewitt offices are independently owned franchises that are only open during tax season and then close for the rest of the year, with no guarantee that tax franchise will even exist or open back up the next year. Since I was trying to start a book publishing business, this was totally unacceptable, so I hired H&R Block that had permanent year round tax offices and thought I was done; *but the story continues...*

In February 2014, I brought in my 2013 taxes to H&R Block and began asking all sorts of small business tax questions. I never realized that tax preparation businesses employ personal with different levels of expertise and certifications, but in hindsight, this only makes sense. Most accounting and tax-preparation firms will obviously assign new customers to their less-experienced and less-educated staff first. Then a letter arrived in the mail from Social Security Disability stating that I had made $10,050 in 2012 as a Sole Proprietorship, which was news to me, since I had not even published my book yet. All I had during that year was expenses for editing, artwork, purchasing ISBNs and so on. I naively thought that all tax preparers had to pass the same certifications and tests, but that is not true, as my taxes were quickly forwarded to an H&R Block "Master Tax Advisor/Preparer" to

rescue me from this disaster. After filing an amendment to my 2012 tax return showing I was not the profitable Sole Proprietorship Jackson Hewitt had painted me as, I received a letter later in July 2014 informing me I owed an additional $980 for the disability had I received and some IRA income we earned during 2012. If you understand IRA's income you earn in them is not taxable until you take distribution from them. I quickly rushed that letter to my Master Tax Advisor who spent five days and four hours on the phone with the IRS to straighten this chaos out for free. To their credit when you pay H&R Block once to file a tax return they back up their work. I rushed her tax amendment, to my previous tax amendment, to the post office to report on my $22,000 in net disability income that was stated incorrectly by the incompetent Jackson Hewitt tax franchise.

Then in August of 2014, because of the storm my incorrectly 2012 prepared tax

return caused, Social Security Disability wanted an additional pound of flesh putting me under a medical review. They gave me 15 days to write letters, visit doctors' offices and try to amass a flurry of paperwork to respond requiring me to work night and day. The Continuing Disability Review Report alone had 13 pages of hand written paperwork to fill out. Then on August 18, 2014 I received a threatening letter from the IRS stating that the IRS would let me know what action they planned to take against this poor disabled veteran making $22,000 in disability income in 60 days or less. In the letter they suggested I pay what I owe or face interest on unpaid tax from the due date of my 2012 return so I quickly rushed this letter to my Master Tax Advisor. This disaster was very frustrating because I was within months of finishing this book and had to put it aside for an entire month that cost me additional weeks of research to bring dated material in the book up-to-date. **The moral of the story is to always review and understand your entire return before signing and mailing it to the IRS, avoid Jackson Hewitt and hire an H&R Block master tax preparer or CPA backed up by guarantees.**

Consequently, as a disabled veteran receiving a Social Security Disability income that is 1/5 of what I used to make and working feverishly to start up a small business, we paid almost $700 to file and later amend our 2012 taxes, twice. This is all very upside down as when I was employed, I paid about 1/5 of that amount, while making four times as much. Let's do the math and have a good laugh, making about $22,000 in net disability a year my family paid about $700 of that yearly salary and spent about 50 hours of our time to file and try to understand two amendments to my disabled veteran's tax return. Social Security Disability spent eight hours to review my case and put together the package to mail to me about income I never made and then review the amended tax return and other paperwork I sent them to correct this error in their computers. My weary H&R Block Master Tax Advisor correcting what Jackson Hewitt reported (and is not liable for) probably spent an additional 30 hours writing letters and preparing not one but eventually two amendments to this tax return, waiting on hold for two and a half hours to talk to the IRS, and was then transferred from one IRS agent after another just to address precisely what the IRS wanted. This probably resulted in four hours of IRS government time plus an additional 16 hours to review and process the two amended tax returns and update their computers. Since this brought my case to light, Social Security quickly spent four hours looking at my case and sending me a medical review packet for me to respond to in 15 days or less. This medical review cost me an about 150 hours of work to fill out the 13 pages of hand written questions and gather the information they requested. I also had to travel to and ask that my doctors write letters as I gathered records from various hospitals and doctors' offices, which cost their supporting staff at least eighteen hours to produce. SSD then probably spent 12 hours to review and process the paperwork I put together at their request. Then my H&R Block Master Tax Advisor and I spent four hours emailing and reviewing the threatening letter from the IRS. SSD then reviewed massive amount of paperwork sent from all my many doctors' offices and said I was denied SSD because I could work. I never said I could not but to make a living wage on a part time salary as I am was

limited is another thing. I then traveled the SSD office taking a day to appeal and explain to them they had not reviewed all the paperwork they needed to review... and the saga continues! If everyone was making $25 an hour and as we add up the hours described above we have 300 hours of effort multiplied by $25, which equals $7,500 of effort spent on a poor disabled veteran's family tax return making almost a poverty wage. I wonder what Warren Buffet's or Bill Gate's taxes are like?

I eventually sued that Jackson Hewitt franchise office in small claims court on December 22, 2014, which will cost me an extraordinary amount of time and effort for a nominal reward. You might ask why I would even take on this battle on while fighting SSD, IRS, the VA, "The Hartford" and still trying to launch my book and future small business. My wife has certainly questioned the wisdom of this venture but the reason is fourfold:

1. My wife took our amended H&R Block return to that franchise Jackson Hewitt office showing them how they had terribly messed up my 2012 tax return and asked for a refund. They said they would review our case and get back to us. Who upon review said they did nothing wrong except to not report our IRA withdrawals correctly. They would not admit that they incorrectly presented my family as a profitable Sole Proprietorship causing an s$$t storm beyond imagination nor refund us in anyway. Months later after filing my second H&R block amendment to our 2012 tax return I called that Jackson Hewitt franchise Livonia, Michigan office and gave them the opportunity to make things right. The conversation when like this, "*Hello... Hi my name is Kirk Ellis and I am calling to discuss getting a refund on what we paid you to prepare my 2012 tax return... I am familiar with your case and for the record we don't give refunds... you may want to reconsider that statement if you will allow me to describe the chaos that tax return caused my family... I am not interested in that and we will not consider a refund... very well then, I will see you in court.*" I could not make that threat and not act upon it. Believe me; it just came out in the gist of the conversation as I had the thought about that course of action in the back of my mind for months.

2. Then, later as my friend Tom Mcginn told me, "*If you lie down and allow bad people who refuse to make things right for their incompetence or fraud, we only encourage that type of behavior from them in the future. Someone has to stand up and sacrifice themselves to show these people that they will not profit from their activities in the future.*" I contacted Jackson Hewitt corporate HQ and all they would say was deal with their franchise disassociating themselves from this crisis. They totally disconnected themselves from this ongoing saga, which reflects how little they care for their customers or what activities and nefarious acts their franchises engage in. I found this activity appalling and encourage no one to do business with a firm that will not reprimand their franchises or hold them to any righteous standard.

3. For my third reason, I want to recount from my favorite speech in Star Trek from Juan-Luc Picard, "*I will not sacrifice the Enterprise. We've made too many compromises already; too many retreats. They invade our space and we fall back. They assimilate entire worlds and we fall back. Not again. The line*

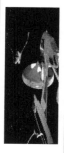

must be drawn here! This far, no further! And *I* will make them pay for what they've done!" Later Captain Picard narrated from Moby Dick, "And he piled upon the whale's white hump, the sum of all the rage and hate felt by his whole race. If his chest had been a cannon, he would have shot his heart upon it." This was how I felt about Jackson Hewitt to my wife's dismay.

4. I knew this would make a wonderful story to add to this book as it all played out! It even gave me the opportunity to send a registered letter to the Jackson Hewitt HQ letting them know I painted their franchise in a derogatory fashion because they would not help me in any way dealing with one of their out of control franchises. Believe me I saved all those emails/letters and eventually filed a lawsuit against the franchise.

Given the above stories and information, you can see that you never want to make the same mistakes we have. As the "Master Tax Preparer" worked on the last four years of our tax returns, I started researching tax preparers, tax preparer fraud, tax preparer identity theft and who the IRS targets. I quickly learned that the IRS and Social Security target small businesses, which we can see includes sole proprietorships making $10,050 in revenue, which is how my inept Jackson Hewitt tax franchise had presented me. It was even worse, as the IRS is skeptical of any business that looks like a hobby, which is how my writing a book was viewed. Any deductions for my book should really have waited until my first book rolled off the press, which my 2011 tax attorney advised, **if only I had listened!**

Story

Many years ago I was doing well as a single young man who was renting a house and making plenty of money while working for a large corporation. I don't remember exactly how I was hooked up with this particular tax preparer, but I contracted her to do my taxes. My taxes at that time were very simple, as I date myself stating there were no Internet or computer tax programs around such as Turbo Tax to easily produce the tax return by myself. All I knew was that my parents had paid someone to do their taxes all of their lives, and I should probably do so as well. I went into shock when I saw my tax preparer's fee, which was over $800 dollars. She based her fee on a percentage of my refund, which she felt she deserved because I was an idiot who had vastly overpaid my taxes. I did not even get any advice on how I should increase my deductions in the coming years instead of giving this gift to the IRS. The moral of this story is to never, ever employ a tax preparer who bases their fee percentage on the amount of your tax refund, unless you run your taxes through tax software, find you owe tons of money and want to challenge your tax service to come up with some innovative ideas, for which you may eventually be audited. Then they may save you thousands... but be careful...

The stories above are examples of the problems that every American citizen suffers and are taught to believe "I should have known and researched that." However, as we are continually harassed with frivolous snail mail, spam financial email, and are pursued by many other financial and supposed investment vectors and institutions involved in our lives, how can we possibly properly vent something considered as trivial as a tax preparer or protect our retirement, finances or other ways as we are continually exploited? You have to understand that you are not seeking and asking the proper fundamental questions about this crazy system of complex taxation and your complex financial system.

The U.S. tax system is an albatross designed to allow an audit of almost anyone in the United States should the need arise by the U.S. government to harass you. How else can we possibly explain a tax system where we pay tax professionals and there are no laws to say these people are responsible for their work? There is also another horror that comes from this out-of-control system of taxation, and that is tax-related identity theft.

Many Americans believe that if they wait until the last minute to file their taxes, their chance of being audited is less. I have found no evidence that this is true, and please bear in mind that the IRS issues refunds within 10 to 21 days of receiving a request for a refund. Therefore, filing your tax return early may mean that you beat the criminals to your tax refund. If you are due a tax refund, then that is something for you to think about correcting, as any financial planner will tell you is something that you should not do. If you are getting money back, then you gave the U.S. government a tax-free loan, and they have your refund ready and waiting for an identity thief to steal. This is money you could have put to work in some other manner. Think of it this way, if you owe taxes at the end of the year, and someone files a fraudulent return in your name and gets money back, imagine the attention you will get when you file your "IRS Identity Theft Affidavit", Form 14039, telling the IRS you owe them money! This problem has become so rampant that the IRS issues billions of dollars in fraudulent refunds paying identity thieves well for their labor. Because of the way that the U.S. handles and process tax returns, the IRS now employs 3,000 full-time employees whose sole task is to work on fraud cases.

Your tax return can also be your first indication that your identity has been stolen. Since the IRS uses your SSN to file, track, and check the accuracy of your return, an unexpected notice from the IRS could alert you that your SSN has been stolen. All an identity thief needs is your name, SSN, a new address and a bank account number.   Identity thieves can use your SSN to file for a tax refund before you do, get a job that will report income to the IRS in your name that will show up as unreported income, or conduct other crimes in your name that will result in many hours of your time to clear up, and may even require you have to obtain a new Social Security Number. This will result in you having to file a police report, complete mountains of paperwork, and delay getting your return for up to a year or more. Unfortunately, a victim of this fraud may see reductions in their state or federal benefits, which could really affect an elderly household dependent on those benefits.

WARNING 	Even after April 15th tax season has passed scammers continue to harass try to solicit cash from unsuspecting people. The IRS still uses snail mail to notify you of tax problems you need to address. Understand that if you receive an unsolicited email or phone call that appears to be from either the IRS or an organization closely linked to the IRS, such as the Electronic Federal Tax Payment System (EFTPS), report it by sending it to phishing@irs.gov. The IRS does not initiate contact with taxpayers by email to request personal or financial information. This includes any type of electronic communication, such as text messages and social media channels.

What to Look for in a U.S. Tax Preparer

The first thing to find out is does your tax preparer have a valid PTIN registered with the IRS for the current year. (See: http://www.irs.gov/Tax-Professionals/PTIN-Requirements-for-Tax-Return-Preparers) A PTIN costs $63.00 and can be obtained in about 15 minutes. It requires the applicants SSN, personal information, business information, previous year's tax return, felony convictions, and tax obligations. The fact that your tax preparer has to provide this information gives you a relative degree of certainty they may not steal your identity. Make sure your tax preparer puts their PTIN on your tax return, but if you do not verify it, this means very little to the IRS who will hold you responsible for everything on your return. Therefore, the question becomes how do U.S. taxpayers verify the PTIN that their tax preparer provides them that the IRS and web page after web page suggests they do? The only way I found to verify this information was to visit "The National Directory of Registered Tax Return Preparers & Tax Professionals," which my Master Tax Preparer verified is your go-to source. (See: http://www.ptindirectory.com)

To do your SBO taxes you need an enrolled agent, certified public accountant or a tax attorney to do your taxes. All of them are required to recertify each year with continuing education credits to maintain their designation as tax preparers, which means they are up to date on the latest tax law changes. If you are making a million dollars or more you probably should consider a tax attorney, which will prove costly, but as a small-time SBO, an enrolled agent or CPA should prove adequate. However, once you choose your tax preparer, dig a little deeper and find out how long they have been in the business and how many other SBOs they have represented in their career. Also inquire as to how many professional organizations they belong to. These credentials are somewhat bogus, but they do verify their commitment to the tax professional business. You can ask for references, which are a good idea, but those can be forged; vet them as best you can and understand that if you make a mistake, it is not your fault. You government, by design, has set up an impossible maze for you to navigate, and all you can do is the best you can!

As a U.S. citizen, get a feel for your new tax preparer quickly and early. Ask yourself, are they returning your calls or responding to your email promptly, can they communicate effectively, are they difficult to contact, do they appear to be overburdened with clients and make you wait for long periods of time, especially on scheduled visits, do they seem knowledgeable about others in your business and can cite experiences doing other tax returns, and lastly, are they available to be contacted year round and consider everything else mentioned above?

72 Steps You Need to Perform to Protect Your Identity

The list below has been gathered from many resources, organizations, books, magazines, websites and blogs, and is a comprehensive list of steps that you can take to protect your identity. I tried to place the steps in order of importance, leaving the reminder, common-sense stuff that you hear often from other sources as the last steps.

1) Protect all bank, credit card, lending, utility, and institution accounts by calling the institutions you deal with and setting up a voice password. If someone gets your personal information they can take over your accounts by posing as you with a few simple, easily found personal details about you, **unless your accounts are voice password protected.** Adding this one security step will protect your accounts from changes and not

allow access to your account for the institution to give out your personal information with the routine questions such as in what city were you born? What was your mother's maiden name? What is your birthday? Any poor ID thief can easily obtain this type of personal information about anyone. Therefore, when the ID theft guru calls with your personal information ready, unless they can give the correct voice password, it was all for naught, and they will move on to easier/greener pastures. Caution - Don't ever forget this voice password as it will prove very difficult to get voice access back to your accounts! Change your voice password from time to time.

2) Obfuscate your answers to security questions where possible. Create a set of answers to security questions that websites use to identify you and then allow you to reset your account password. Identity thieves can easily obtain information about you such as your birth date, mother's maiden name, father's middle name, what city your high school is in, etc. They can also make good guesses about things like the city in which you met your spouse if you ever had a residence there. If you don't want to use fictitious words where you may have to look up your answers, use something easily remembered such as your grandfather's or grandmother's middle name in place of "what is your father's/mother's middle/maiden name." Where possible, enter a birth date other than your own. For example, your online shopping, Car Company, Netflix, Google, PlayStation, Yahoo, AOL, and ISP support websites do not need to know your birth date! Be sure to make note of the birth date that you enter in your password database.

3) Configure online or by phone (much more difficult), for all your accounts to send email and phone notifications when unusual events occur as in large withdrawals. Most (if not all) banks, credit unions, brokerages, credit card companies, insurance companies, etc. allow you to setup automatic triggers for notifications. Ensure that your personal information is correct so they can contact you. This is also a good time to check beneficiary information as well. However, you have to be careful how you set this up. For example, one of my credit unions would call and leave a message for me to call them back and would make me verify each and every charge on the account for charges as little as $600. One time when my family was on vacation, they went so far as to freeze my account. It was very embarrassing when my wife and I could not pay our restaurant bill because my card was not accepted. While I applaud their vigilance, these calls wasted a lot of my time until I put a stop to them. Specify to your bank or credit union that simple email or a voice mail message on these events will suffice.

4) If you have no near term plans for credit (loan, new car, card), place/maintain a fraud alert on your credit reports. A fraud alert will guard against any new credit or bank accounts from being opened in your name. By using the credit agency's automated system, setting the alert is easy and only takes a minute to do. The system will prompt you for your SSN and numeric address. The fraud alert will last 90 days. Put a recurring event on your online calendar to call back every 90 days to keep the alert active. One call to any of the three credit agencies will place the fraud alert at all three. You will receive confirmation in the mail that the alert has been set up.

	URL	Request a CR copy	Fraud Units
Equifax	http://www.equifax.com	800-685-1111	800-525-6285 or FA 888-766-0008
Experian	http://www.experian.com	888-397-3742	888-397-3742
TransUnion	http://www.transunion.com	800-888-4213	800-680-7289

5) The federal Fair Credit Reporting Act (FCRA, 15 USC 1681) and some states' laws require credit reporting companies to delete any consumer's name and address from mailing lists if the consumer so chooses. Identity thieves use these lists, to identify you and retrieve these credit mail offers from your mailbox, without your knowledge, for their own use. Many renters and home owners who sell their properties find out that after they have moved to another address the snail mail they leave coming to their former mailbox becomes their worst nightmare. Before this happens, mail back any postage paid envelope offers (making the company pay the postage) and ask repeatedly that you be removed from all mailing and distribution lists. Go to https://www.optoutprescreen.com to opt-out of receiving pre-screened credit card offers. Otherwise, call (888) 5OPTOUT (888.567.8688), which is a single number you can call to opt-out of Innovis and the three major credit bureaus.

Equifax Options, Marketing Decision Systems
By phone: (888) 567-8688
By mail:
Equifax Credit Information Services, Inc.
P.O. Box 740241
Atlanta, GA 30374

Experian Marketing Lists
By phone: (402) 458 5247
By mail:
Experian Consumer Services
901 West Bond Street
Lincoln, NE 68521

TransUnion
By phone: (888) 567-8688
By mail:
TransUnion Name Removal Option
P.O. Box 505
Woodlyn, PA 19094

Include the following information with your request: First, middle, and last names (including Jr., Sr., III), current address, previous address (if you've moved within the last six months), Social Security number, date of birth, and signature. Doing this will not eliminate, but will reduce the number of pre-approved credit card offers with which you are harassed.

6) Before you spend money to monitor your credit or to get your credit score, consider doing it yourself. Use the law that requires the major credit reporting companies to give you a free copy of your credit report annually. Don't be fooled by look-alike sites that promise free reports if you subscribe to their credit monitoring services. Since there are three credit-reporting companies, you can ask for one credit report every four months thus monitoring your credit on your own. Getting the first credit report might prove somewhat difficult as the credit companies may ask questions that you don't have the answer to. For

example, I moved around a lot as a renter, and one of the questions was for one of those addresses that I have long since forgotten. However, once you have the first credit report in your hands, you can use that to answer those difficult questions in the future. For FREE copies of all your credit reports annually, visit https://www.annualcreditreport.com or order by phone by calling 877-322-8228 annually. Scan the report for any unfamiliar information, such as accounts that you don't remember opening, or accounts that show as open that have been closed. If you find something that is incorrect, simply write the credit company a letter asking that they correct your information. Calling them is a waste of your time as you work through the call labyrinth to get someone on the phone. The company cannot correct your information on the spot and will have to investigate your claims before correcting it in their databases. If you find fraud, put a freeze on your credit right away and contact the credit companies immediately.

WARNING	To get these reports you must enter sensitive information that is a treasure trove to phishing Identity Thieves. There are many scammer websites with similar URLs that try to look like the real thing. As such, you should enter the URL directly into your browsers address bar, double check what you typed for the link, and never rely on a link presented by a search engine.

7) Another option is to get free credit report updates from free online services. Credit Sesame and Credit Karma are two online services that will send you updates if there is something they deem suspicious appearing in your credit report. Credit Sesame monitors your Experian report daily and will send you an email alert. Credit Karma works with Transunion to do the same thing. This type of monitoring gives you the ability to instantly catch an identity thief or something you may have neglected, such as a delinquent bill or erroneous accusation from a creditor or customer. (See: http://www.creditsesame.com, https://www.creditkarma.com).

8) If all you are interested in is your credit score, you can sign up for a free account at http://www.credit.com that gives you two measures of your credit score. They also rate you on how you are doing in five key areas that make up your credit score so that you know where to focus your time to improve your credit rating. A FICO score about 720 is considered good for applying for a loan, which you can obtain at http://www.myfico.com. Discovercard now also offers your credit score. When I checked with Discover I saw "Kirk, your FICO Credit Score is 784" and a message saying "Your credit report shows one or more accounts with missed payments", which was news to me. With these details and copies of my free credit reports I could fight back on these key factors affecting my credit score without paying anyone.

9) Register with the National "Do Not Call Registry" to keep your information away from telemarketers. Visit http://www.donotcall.gov or call 888-382-1222. While this is supposed to keep telemarketers at bay, it is not well enforced by the federal government. If you are being pestered, your only course of action is to report whoever is calling and hope the government may take action, if you want to keep your phone number. The *National Do Not Call Registry will **NOT** call you* to provide an opportunity to sign up; this is a phishing scam that you must not respond to.

10) Surf to PwnedList https://pwnedlist.com; this is a tool that allows the average person to check if their accounts have been compromised. You can also use a SHA-512 hash of your email/username as input. This website provided a simple one-click service to help the

average user verify if their accounts have been compromised as a part of a corporate data breach, a malicious piece of software sneaking around on their computers, or any other form of security compromise.

11) Go to http://www.aboutads.info to opt-out of advertising cookies. This is a volunteer program in which 90% of the Web's behaviorally targeted advertisers have joined.

12) Remove yourself from ALL free catalog lists. Companies that send you free catalogs often share your information with other companies, organization and charities. This may not be easy and may require a long phone call with the company who keeps sending you catalogs. Sometimes when we move or a child moves out our current address keeps receiving their catalogs. The inclination may be to just throw them in the trash, hopefully after shredding our address, and forget about it. However, that catalog company may give out your address information. Remember every piece of information an Identity Thief can obtain about you is of value.

13) Wherever possible, remove yourself from online databases, called data brokers. These data miners are not transparent, and Congress is just now beginning to inquire into the data that they are collecting and selling, such as race or religious data, ethnicity, social network or mobile activity, and much more. For example, it was revealed that law enforcement agencies requested subscriber data from wireless companies 1.3 million times in 2012. Companies are purchasing this data and making inferences that may not be accurate or flattering. Data miners could take your online presence with Tweets, Facebook posts, comments, purchases, searches and Web surfing records to produce sources for your hire-ability, marketability, likelihood of filing an insurance claim, political and religious leanings and more. The profile that they build also includes information gleaned from your assets, income, loyalty cards, physical and mental health, shopping habits, personal interests, and much more. Your online presence is information that corporations can use and in many ways that you may not want. Online databases, such as Epsilon, did not seem to provide a means to remove your data from their databases, which by law should be required and is not.

As I market my book, I often hear a lack of concern from people that I talk to about the data that is being collected and sold about them. I try to explain that this data can be inaccurate and affect such things as eligibility determinations. I try to describe how this data may have important repercussions in their lives, such as how they can be made out to be someone whom they are not. There is also the concern that the data may reveal sensitive issues such as financial problems, a medical condition, sexual orientation or race and this information is traded and/or sold, it could be used against them. Examples of data brokers' lists include "Mid-Life Strugglers," "Living on Loans," and "Retiring on Empty", so we can see how the lists that you may land on can affect you.

As we can see, opting out of data collection is a complex and difficult process and is sometimes impossible by design. As consumers, we have no insight or control over how this data is traded and/or sold. The World Privacy Forum has a complied list of opt-outs but in August 2014, when I tried to visit the website it sent me to malicious website, which installed malware on my computer. I revisited the site in December 2014, and the site was back up. (See: http://www.worldprivacyforum.org/2013/12/data-brokers-opt-out, http://www.worldprivacyforum.org/2013/08/consumer-tips-top-ten-opt-outs)

The following are a few examples of the big online databases and instructions on how to remove your data. If you decide to write them be sure to include your name and address in your letter. Some of the following was taken from "Ask Kim" at USA today. Direct links to these sites can be found at http://www.komando.com/columns/index.aspx?id=2229.

Acxiom Corporation, 601 East Third Street, Little Rock, AR 72201 (See: http://www.acxiom.com, https://en.wikipedia.org/wiki/Acxiom):
Acxiom provides data to websites, businesses and law enforcement officials. Its products fall into two categories: marketing and reference. Reference data is culled from public records. It also includes financial information and Social Security numbers. This information is only provided to businesses and law enforcement. You can't opt-out. However, you can opt-out of its marketing database. The marketing database does not include credit information or Social Security numbers. (See: http://www.acxiom.com/usoptoutrequestform). You can also request an opt-out form via telephone, 888-322-9466 / 501-342-7799, or by email. Since other businesses use Acxiom's data, this also removes data from some other sites.

Direct Marketing Association (See: http://thedma.org, https://www.dmachoice.org/register.php):
Many marketers use the Direct Marketing Association's (DMA) preferences. You can submit removal requests for mailing, telemarketing and email lists. You'll find removal forms on the DMAChoice website and snail mail form carries a $1 fee. This won't remove your information from all marketing databases, but DMA members are required to adhere to the lists. The registration protecting you from junk mail will end after three-years, requiring you to send in another request.

Epsilon (See: http://www.epsilon.com):
Epsilon houses data on 130 million households or 250 million consumers in the U.S. This data is sold to companies worldwide to allow them to market their products in "real-time" to people everywhere. If you visit their Consumer Preference Center at http://www.epsilon.com/consumer-preference-center, you can opt-out of various things. For example, to opt-out your email from their database, just click on the link and enter your email address. Other things to opt-out of are not quite that easy, but you should investigate them. To block Internet Banner Advertising, it will require a cookie to be installed on your device in the browser of your choice. If you switch browsers or clean your cookies, your opt-out preference will not be maintained.

Intelius (See: http://www.intelius.com):
Like US Search, Intelius sells background reports to anyone. Reports include your birth date, court records and address history. In order for Intelius to opt-out your public information from being viewable on the Intelius website, it requires faxed proof of identity, which can be a state issued ID card or driver's license. If you are faxing a copy of your driver's license, obscure the photo and the driver's license number. They only need to see your name, address and date of birth. Allow 2 to 3 weeks for them to process your request. Fax your information to their customer service department at 425-974-6194. If you are not comfortable faxing them your information, you can send them a notarized form proving your identity and they will remove your public information.

555-1212.com (See: http://555-1212.com):
Marketers use 555-1212.com to find addresses and phone numbers of potential leads. You can remove your information from its database via an online form. Removal requires minimal information, but you must provide your name as it appears in the site's listing. This may be difficult, as you can't view your listing. You must also provide a phone number and email address.

R.L. Polk & Company now IHS Automotive, (See: https://www.ihs.com/btp/polk.html , https://www.ihs.com/Legal/privacy-pi.html), Polk used to allow you to opt-out of their data gathering but IHS may not. Reviewing their privacy policies, all I found was the ability to unsubscribe from their email list. IHS does say IHS will not sell, disclose or rent personal information for direct marketing purposes. Polk provided consumer information to the automotive industry so we have to assume IHS is continuing that business model.

US Search (See: http://www.ussearch.com):
US Search frequently shows up in online searches. Many online phone directories also link to it. US Search sells background reports to anyone, but you can remove your records from most of its search results. You must send your request via postal mail, though to do this US Search requires your name, birth date and Social Security number. Additionally, it wants your addresses going back 15 years. You should also supply any aliases, including your maiden name.

WhitePages.com (See: http://www.whitepages.com):
WhitePages.com is an online directory that is available to anyone. It lists your name and address in its search results. You can remove your information via an online form. Your name, city and State are required, along with a reason for removal. You can select General Privacy Concerns as your reason.

14) Abine is a company that works to remove your public profile from data brokers, social media and other sites. Their DeleteMe service for $129 for one person or $220 for two will help you opt-out of data sites such as Spokeo, PeopleFinders, Intelius and many other data brokers. For the complete list that they will protect you from, which is quite extensive, visit https://abine.com/deleteme/iframe.html. You can also install their free DoNotTrackPlus (DNT+) add-on that Abine claims blocks more than 600 trackers as well as allowing web pages to load up to 4 times faster. They also offer a Masked Emails service that allows you to decide who gets to contact you. Their blog is also an interesting read and is full of tips on privacy and identity theft. The next two ID theft items demonstrate how difficult it is to remove your data from these data brokers, but you can do these things on your own if you cannot afford Abine. (See: https://abine.com, https://abine.com/deleteme/landing.php, https://abine.com/dntdetail.php, https://abine.com/optouts.php)

15) Remove yourself from Spokeo: Go to http://www.spokeo.com using TOR and type your full name in the search box, along with the city and state where you currently live, click on "Search." Spokeo will generate results from what you searched on and you will have to find your listings. Note that you may have more than one listing. Copy the URL of your listing from your browsers web address bar by highlighting the URL, right click and select "copy" from the menu. Each page generated will display personal information about you

and offer "Full Results" for a price. Go to Spokeo's opt out page www.spokeo.com/optout in another browser window or tab and fill out the specified fields:

    a. Paste the URL of your listing in the "Profile URL" text box.
    b. Enter the email address that Spokeo shows on your profile listing in the "Email" text box.
    c. Enter the code in the show on the web page in the "Enter Code" text box.
    d. Click on the "Remove This Listing" text box.

Spokeo will warn you that it aggregates publicly available information from third-party sources. What this means is that they gather data that you freely post about yourself from social networking sites and then sell it to everybody. There is also a suggestion to search for other listings about yourself that you might also want to remove. To get yourself removed from Spokeo you have to log into whatever email address you provided and click on "click here" to confirm removal. Spokeo will come up with a web page showing "This directory listing has been removed." Give Spokeo 24 hours to make sure your information is indeed removed. Note that Spokeo only allows five removal requests per email address so you may want to use a service such as http://www.fakemailgenerator.com to have Spokeo remove your information. Also since there are no laws protecting you, Spokeo could be using this as a tactic to obtain your email address.

16) Remove yourself from 123People: Go to https://www.123people.com and visit their opt-out page at http://www.123people.com/page/people-manager and type in your Salutation, First Name, Last Name, Email, Search Country, Language and click on the Submit button. Once again, consider using TOR and a service such as http://www.fakemailgenerator.com to mask your email address. You will be sent a link to click on pertaining to your person where you will be taken back to their website to click on the trash cans to remove yourself from their databases. You may have to click around advancing through people with your name until you find your record. Click on the trash cans next to your information, check the verify box and privacy boxes then click on the Send button. This will submit a request to remove your data within 48 hours. You should see "Opted Out The request to block your records is being process, and should be finished within the hour in rare cases, ...".

17) Your domain can reveal valuable information about you. Visit http://www.whois.com/whois/thatcybersecurityguy.com and see what I am talking about. You should also do a search on your own domain at http://www.whois.com to make sure you own it and see when it will expire. Support my efforts to establish a Digital Fourth Amendment so we can suppress this type of information sharing.

| **Tip/Story**  | I investigated turning off this type of information sharing my domain hosting service was providing to the public and found out that for a mere $12 a year I could keep my personal domain information private. The other alternative was to set up my domain address as a post office box, which was also possible. Because I am a public small business I chose the latter to keep my home address private and still give my customers a PO Box address at which they can contact me. The question we all have to ask is, why does it cost us money to keep our information private instead of the opposite, where web hosting companies make money helping identity thieves keep our personal information public? |

18) When you receive offers in the mail with postage paid envelopes, stuff them with what was sent to you, and include a note asking to remove you from all mailing and distribution lists. They already have your address! You can also call or go on-line, and ask to be removed. The Internet can be used to browse their products.

19) Consider carefully the information you provide on entries to win a car, shopping spree, a vacations, and so on. For example, you should not reveal information such as your age, birthday or income range.

20) Assume that anything you do on social networks is public by default. Most social media sites have privacy settings, so there are a few things that you can do. At Facebook, turn OFF tag suggestions, turn on tag and profile review, disable apps that you don't use or might suspect, and only share with close friends. For example, if you share with friends of friends, it has been reported that 150,000 people on average can view your info.

21) Go to various search engines and search for your name and contact information using Tor. This will tell you if your personal information is available publicly online. There is a lot more out there besides your search results, which may be listed across the black bar on the top of your search engine's window. This is also very important to do to find out if there is any negative press about you that needs to address. Employers use this technique to inquire about prospective candidates.

22) When you receive First-class mail, you can return this mail to the sender at their expense. On the envelope write "refused: return to sender" and see how quick they remove you from their mailing list. (See: http://www.obviously.com/junkmail)

23) Bulk mail is a bit different. There is not much you can do about this. However, if they have the clause "address correction requested" written on the label, you can circle "address correction requested" and send it back just like First-class mail.

24) We are often asked to fill out a warranty registration card, which you *should not do*. If you choose to do so, write in VERY LARGE LETTERS, "**Please do not sell my name or address**". Companies often take your card information and market or sell that information. Warranty cards are just personal information collection services. They collect information on your habits and income and then provide this information to direct mail targeting companies. Filling out these cards are not required in most situations. You just have to have a receipt. Avoid sending them!

25) We all want to donate money to a worthy cause, but doing so can open your family up to numerous solicitations and even harassment. Some charities that I have donated to in the past junked mailed (harassed) me so often I had to write them a letter to get my name removed from their mailing lists. What was worse, they shared my information with other organizations and charities who also starting soliciting donations and harassing my family.

26) Secure your sensitive documents in a locked, fireproof safe. Never leave sensitive documents lying around the house, in your office, hotel room or car.

27) As retailers try to entice you into deals with store credit cards, turn them down. The 10% discount you are going to get for signing up is not worth the headache or cost of having another vulnerable line of credit. You will have to monitor this account and deal with all the snail mail that this account will generate as they distribute and sell your information. Your credit rating (score) may suffer as a result of establishing too much credit. Many of the cards carry interest rates of 20% or more if you can't or forget to pay off your balance each month. These types of accounts are easy targets for Identity Thieves. You also may get slammed, which is what Sam's Club did to our Sam's Club line of credit. For example, in 2011, Sam's Club had a promotion to sign up for their "plus" membership for about the

same price as their "advantage" $40 membership. The catch was that we had to sign up for a store credit card. This seemed to be OK until, in 2012, Sam's Club slammed our account with a charge of $100 to *automatically renew* our "plus" membership. It took me hours on the phone to cancel our membership and get this charge removed from our Sam's Club account. Below are a few other examples:

The Target Redcard has an annual percentage rate of 22.9%, will give a 5% discount on purchases in stores and at Target.com, plus you get free shipping with no minimum purchase amount. (See: http://www.target.com)
The Kohl's card has an annual percentage rate of 21.9%, qualify for periodic discounts of 15% to 30%.
The True Earning card has no annual fee with a Costco membership, 0% for six months, and then rises to 15.24%. Card holders get 3% back on gas purchases up to $4,000 per year, 1% thereafter, 2% on dining and eligible travel and 1% on other purchases.

27. Walgreens was sued by customers who were not happy that their private prescription information was sold to data-mining companies. Under U.S. laws and technological complexes your best bet is not to share your personal information with these types of U.S. corporations. Once again, outdated U.S. laws will not protect their citizens' privacy rights.

28) Where possible, when eating out, pay your bill yourself at the front desk or use cash. Never allow your photo ID and/or credit card out of your sight. If the business will not allow you to pay yourself, consider taking your business elsewhere or just paying cash. If you use a credit card and your server checks your ID, make sure they hand it back to you at the table (don't let them take it out of your sight). Once a credit card has been out of your sight, check that account often.

29) **Shred, shred, shred to frustrate dumpster-diving Identity Thieves!** Account numbers, Social Security numbers, your address or other personal information are ripe for theft from documents that you put in the trash. Buy a *heavy duty crosscut* (not a straight cut) shredder that can destroy credit cards, data CDs and DVDs, as well as paper. A shredder of this type can be obtained for approximately $60 - $70. Place it wherever you open your mail or toss your trash. Shred all bank statements, insurance forms, bills, checks, credit applications, credit card receipts and statements, old credit card or ATM receipts and mortgages when they are paid off. Identify and shred medical statements, physician statements, and prescription bottle labels that can't be used for taxes. Shred expired charge cards, mailers, personal papers, junk mail solicitations with your address, floppy disks, CD/DVDs - anything containing personal, financial or investment information. Crosscut shredders slice paper into small confetti-like squares by cutting both lengthwise and crosswise. This shredded paper makes a good base for getting a nice campfire started. Go to http://www.consumersearch.com/paper-shredders/best-paper-shredders for some good shredder reviews.

Story	It is one thing to recommend these steps, but altogether another to hear witness of Identity Theft first-hand. At a restaurant, I went to the front desk to pay my bill, explaining that I did not want my credit card or ID out of my sight. It was also an opportunity to shamelessly promote this book. The owner said that she completely understood and rang up our bill, all the while telling us her Identity Theft story. She had ordered a product from Sears, and after taking it out of the

box, her mother set the box out front for trash pickup. She did this without removing her daughter's personal information printed on the box. Before she could correct this mistake by her trusting mother in a world gone mad, the box disappeared. At the end of the month, when she got her store credit card bill from Sear's, there was over $3,000 in charges on the account. The thieves printed up a fake ID with her name and address, traveled to Sear's and gave a sob story about how they forgot their card. The clerk, eager to make a sale, quickly divulged the store credit account information and charged the purchases. After all, he had checked for ID, which appeared legit. It took her over a year to clear this up.

30) To minimize shredding, use electronic billing, which prevents someone from stealing your bills from your mailbox. If you do not use electronic billing, pay attention to the billing cycles on your accounts. If a bill doesn't arrive on time, it could mean that someone has changed the billing address.

31) Purchase and use a home or business postal mailbox that can be locked or use a post office (PO) box. Put outgoing mail in the post office collection boxes (the big blue ones) or at the post office, rather than in an unsecured mailbox at home. Checks paying bills that were stolen from a home mailbox can easily have the recipient's name and amount paid changed using an acid wash. If you do not install a mailbox that locks, remove mail promptly from the unlocked home mailboxes that makes it easy to steal mail. Send all your magazines, newsletters, charities and organization periodicals that you support or belong to your PO Box. The information you house with them such as your address, credit card information, personal questionnaires they want to fill out, and etc. is of value to Identity Thieves. If an ID thief gets your PO Box information, you can easily switch PO boxes, but switching your address is another matter entirely. Where possible, cancel subscriptions and tell organizations you do not want their periodicals and newsletters, and go online to read their articles.

32) If you need a new set of checks from your local bank or credit union and don't have a PO Box, have them delivered to your local branch office - not to your home address.

33) When you go out of town, notify your postal carrier so they can hold your mail. This can be done by placing a simple note in your mailbox, or ask a neighbor to pick up your mail while you are gone. Stolen snail mail is a treasure trove for Identity Thieves. Mail sitting for days in a mailbox piling up is an open invitation to identity and house thieves.

34) Be wary of suspicious snail mail. Your name and home address are very easy to obtain by cybercriminals who may then use that information to send you scam mail via the postal service. If you receive anything asking for money or personal information, verify it with the company or institution that they may be mimicking.

35) If you are asked by a business, charity, doctor's office, financial institution, school, social service, governmental office, veteran service, workplace or some other institution for your personal information, ask why they need it, how they safeguard or shred it, and what is the minimum amount of information they need. For example, social services may try to gather your information before determining if they can help you or not. Find out what the salary and other minimum requirements are for them to help you before giving them your personal information. Operate upon the assumption that all of these entities give little thought to protecting your personal information and know nothing about cyber security.

The low-paid data gathering person sitting across from you typing all your personal information into their malware infested computer has been instructed to gather it with no thought as to why they are doing so. We must focus attention on the problem of these entities gathering personal information they do not need and cannot use to help you.

Story 	I walked into a Pizza Hut and ordered a pizza. The young girl taking my order asked for my name and phone number. I told her I did not want to give her either. She the demanded my phone number and told me she could not take my order if I did not give her my phone number. I told her she was not getting my phone number and that I would take my business elsewhere. She relented and said any phone number would do. So I told her fine, how about 555-555-5555. She finally went with the corporate policy and entered her Pizza Hut's number into the computer. This confused things in their ordering system, but I eventually got my pizza. You have to stand your ground on giving out this type of information that corporations and businesses are trying to gather about you!

Story 	My mother was seeking a legal consultation to discuss some things. I found a social organization that said they provided free legal consultation services for seniors. She called the number and they grilled her for every piece of personal information she would reveal about herself and my father. Early on during the inquisition the woman asked my mother about the pensions and Social Security benefits they were receiving. When they asked for her Social Security number she woke up and refused to give it to them. They told her they could not give her aid without her SSN. She refused again, and then woman on the phone informed her she made too much money per month for them to help her. One would have thought this woman would have informed my mom early on about how the pensions my father and she were receiving disqualified them from the program but they continued questioning to get all their personal information. My mother shouted back at the women, "why didn't you let me know that in the first place!" I apologized to my mother for giving her that number, about which you can imagine I rightfully received and earful. I called the police to report this phishing expedition who said that until I could show a crime had been committed there was nothing they could do. It should be a crime to gather personal information before making sure someone qualifies for your services! As a result of this carnage, we put a fraud alert on my parents' credit, and I visited the organization in question and requested my mother's information be deleted from their database. Who knows if it ever was.
WARNING	While helping my parents and working with rehabilitation services for myself, I noticed their computers were still running XP. These government organizations request all of your personal information to supposedly help you or your loved ones. At the social services office the computer took an extraordinary amount of time to boot up and quickly crapped out. The social worker had to go retrieve her laptop. I told her that the long boot time indicated her computer was infested with malware and that by running XP someone was watching her every keystroke while that computer was connected to the Internet. I even explained that I was writing a book on cyber security. The care factor was minimal, and

she just continued to ask for and enter my mom's personal information in those infected computers. Governments give lip server to cyber security and practice it in military and intelligence organizations, but government social services do nothing to protect your identity! Don't give them your personal information unless it is absolutely necessary, and make sure you know how they will help. All we got out of the visit was a few pamphlets to study.

36) Maintain a separate password for all of your online login sites. If that is too much to remember, separate you banking password from your shopping password and so on. Make your passwords and PIN numbers hard to guess and change them periodically. Pros can guess or use software to identify/break many passwords and PIN numbers. Refer back to previous sections of this chapter where we talk about password management tools and how they are still weak links in security.

37) Encrypt files with sensitive information on your Internet devices such as your notebook, laptop and home computer. (See Chapter 5)

38) It should be illegal, but once an online account is created, it is either difficult or impossible to get it deleted. In the April, 2013 issue of PCWorld in an article titled "Prevent 'Zombie Accounts' From Haunting You" by Tony Bradley, it states that "*Paul Henry, security and forensic analyst for security firm Lumension, cautions that deactivating an account and removing sensitive data is easier said than done. "Look at sites like Facebook–you have to work to remove your data. Even if you delete your information, it will still be around for at least 30 days. And if you then log back in within that 30-day window, they'll keep your information forever, even if you re-delete."*" You information can linger for many years without your attention or knowledge that it still exists. PCWorld used the title "Zombie Accounts" for these languishing corporate online sources of personal information. For example, my family tried out an Internet communication product, which did not work out for our use. The people that we had called when we used the device to communicate complained about how we sounded. So I took it back to store where I had purchased it for a refund. I then called that company to get the account deleted that I had to set up when trying out their product. The support person that I had on the line told me it was not possible to delete an account once it had been created. If you encounter this at the online sites you use, rarely use, or have just used once or twice, change/cloak all of your personal information (Name, Address, Phone, Credit Card, etc.) to BOGUS values like (111 Bogus Avenue, Bogus, NC, 55555) to prevent the site from sharing or compromising your information. Don't be surprised if you see your cloaked personal information show up on your credit reports as these companies all share your information. In my case, my credit report show I lived at 10 Bogus Avenue once upon a time, which made me smile! Then ask them to deactivate the account since they would not delete it.

In another example, we changed cellphone plans, and I wanted our former cellphone company to remove our online account. The customer service representative that I got on the phone did not know how to remove the account, but assured me that the account would be deleted in 90 days. I logged into the account to obfuscate our personal information and was unable to do so. Personal information fields were locked and unchangeable. If you run into this, make sure the account is indeed removed after 90 days.

Tip

Keep a database of every online account that you cannot delete. When we switched from an expensive cellphone provider to a plan with no contract and more capabilities, the path of least resistance was to change our phone numbers. I asked my wife to use our password database to change all of our accounts online to the new phone number. I forgot that the database contained information on all my "Zombie Accounts" as well and she wasted a lot of time updating those accounts. I explained to her that I could not figure out how to delete them, so I kept my login information to change all my personal information in them to bogus values. Moreover, in the event of ID Theft, I may need to know how to log into them to stop a thief from switching and reopening the account for nefarious deeds. I also tried a second experiment for this book. I had financed and paid off an automobile loan years ago, so I had not logged into that account since. When I logged in, sure enough, all my finance history and personal information were there for the taking. The account was still active, for who knows what reason. I could find no options that would allow me to delete the account, so I decided to request via internal email that Honda do this. As I learned later, this is also an opportunity to check the title of your vehicle to see whose name is on the title, which I did not do. If it is your finance company you will need to request a letter from them stating that they no longer have a lien on your vehicle. You will then have to take that letter to your Division of Motor Vehicles (DMV) or Secretary of State (SOS) to get a title that shows you as the owner. I logged in to the account and sent an internal email to their customer service department stating:

"My car has been paid off for quite some time. Please delete my online account as it has no further relevance except for storing and marketing my personal information. I will establish a new account if I purchase a new car product in the future. Account information and VIN as follows: Account:, Product:, VIN:. I also need a letter stating that you no longer have a lien on my car. Please send the letter to..." I finally found a link to discontinue management of my account. This did not disable my ability to log in, but it did disable access to all of my account information, which I hoped that if the site were cracked it would limit a cracker's access as well. One more Zombie account taken care of, partially.

I sent them a second email stating: I have paid off my loan. Please remove the zombie account <account name>.

The result was the car company ignored my request to delete the account. I then called them to see if I could get the account deleted that way. The customer service representative had me add a finance account and then remove that account. This seemed to finally and completely remove the account.

Years later, I wanted to sell my car and noticed that the title I had still had Honda Financial as a lien holder. I traveled to my SOS, reading my American Legion magazine all the way through waiting over two hours, to fix the title, and SOS informed me that Honda had never informed them the car was mine. Honda quickly corrected this after I called them, but this should never have been a necessary waste of my time.

Another option is to consider using online Internet sites that will help you delete your online accounts. One of the best I know is Account Killer at http://www.accountkiller.com/en who provide instructions on how to remove your account or public profile from many websites. They even have a blacklist that will show you websites that will not allow you to remove your account at all.

39) As with Zombie Accounts, we also have to worry about Zombie Services. Sometimes just canceling services, such as OnStar, is not enough to protect your privacy. People are allowing OnStar and other telematics devices to monitor vehicle performance, provide diagnostics of vehicle systems and GPS data to these companies. However, what happens when a driver stops paying for these services? One would expect the monitoring to cease, but this information is so valuable that these companies continue to collect data about the driver. This happens because terminating the service and deactivating the device are considered two separate processes. This important information is clearly stated in privacy policies that car owners rarely read. In addition, the data that is collected could be obtained very easily by insurance companies and governments and then used against you in other ways. Willingly providing this information to insurance companies for discounts is dangerous as well. Make sure you carefully read and understand the insurances companies' privacy policy before sharing you driving habits with them.

40) In the same vein as the last entry, delete old email and voice mail records. When I was in the hospital with cancer, I set up a Google Voice account so I had a one number that notified all my devices. With Google Voice you can have one number call multiple phones and send you an email transcript of the voice messages. This was very handy when I would be out of touch with friends and family for days or weeks at a time, in and out of hospitals and very sick at home and not able to check my messages. Life since then has been very busy writing this book. Imagine my shock when I logged into Google to see every voice message I had, archived there in my account from 2010 to 2013. Some of them were very personal. I discovered that there was no easy way to delete them, so I spent hours deleting those messages 10 at a time. This is an example of how corporations are storing your information and when hacked, subpoenaed or as we now know just commanded to will reveal many years' worth of information about you. As we now know many of these companies freely share all this information about you with the U.S. government. Most times we don't even know how long this information lingers after we delete it, but I have read that in a few instances only for 30 days at some corporations. However, U.S. NSA has an infinite storage capacity, so it could reside indefinitely on their storage devices.

41) Consider a service such as OpenDNS or other DNS provider to protect your home computers from phishing sites. (See: Chapter 4)

42) Consider using the DMAchoice online tool http://www.dmachoice.org to help you manage your mail. DMAchoice will also remove the names of deceased individuals from commercial marketing lists. Before using DMAchoice, be sure to read their privacy policy https://www.dmachoice.org/static/privacy_policy.php, which admits that they deposit cookies onto your hard drive and collect clickstream data. You also have to register with the site, something else on which you should contemplate.

43) This may seem like common sense but we are still tempted to share our personal information on social media sites. For example, we want information on our

http://www.linkedin.com account to connect us with SBO and employment opportunities. However, sharing information such as your phone number, email address, unfavorable pictures or birthday is something Identity Thieves can use to piece together your puzzle. There is no hard and fast rule as to what you can share, so perform a litmus test on everything you post at social media sites, such as is the information you are posting easily obtainable? For example, if you published a book or an article, these are things you might want to post. Do you have easily obtainable skeletons in your closet that warrants explanation? If you cannot explain these obtainable items in a favorable light, then post no explanation at all! Leave it up to whomever is researching you to find out about these things. The Internet is a two-way street; you may be able to take a sorted past and turn yourself into an upstanding citizen or vice versa, which may not help your case.

44) Speaking of social media, the Facebook Places, Foursquare check-ins, & Twitter may be giving out your location while you are using your smartphone unless you turn off these things. There are some third-party apps that can access your public social network then use and advertise your location and public information around the world. This is especially dangerous to our youth and should be legislatively stopped. We have already debated those topics in the Introduction and Chapter 1 of this book.

45) If you are posting to a forum, social network, news article, or online group consider using a pseudonym and Tor. Any comments you post will exist for all time and may come back to haunt you. You may think your post is benign and could survive being on the cover of a magazine, but it may offend a future employer or business partner. Avoid sites such as Facebook for instance, that require your full legal name to sign up and post.

46) Consider signing up at http://www.catalogchoice.org for a FREE service to reduce unwanted mail and to get your name off mailing lists for catalogs that you don't even want. To sign up, your name and email address are all that are required.

47) If you didn't initiate a phone call, never give out your personal information. If asked for information such as account or Social Security numbers or other personal information, hang up and contact the calling institution at a number you trust. Be sure you understand how your personal information will be used, how it will be protected, if it is really necessary for this transaction, and what the consequences will be if you chose to withhold this information.

48) Use separate accounts or credit cards to protect your family's main bill paying bank accounts from risk. Create an account/credit card with a low balance/credit limit just for your family's online purchases. Give family members separate debit and/or credit cards for other purchases on accounts/credit cards with the same low balance and limits.

49) When you order new credit cards in the mail, or your previous ones have expired, watch the calendar to make sure that you get the card within the appropriate time. If it is not received by a certain date, call the credit card grantor immediately and find out if the card was sent. Find out if a change of address was filed if you don't receive the card or a billing statement. As stated above, send them to your PO Box if you have one.

50) Be vigilant about checking for unexpected entries on your various statements (credit card, bank/credit union, 401K, IRA, etc.). Login online regularly or use your favorite financial software (http://www.gnucash.org, https://www.mint.com, https://quicken.intuit.com, etc.) to automate downloading or to view your account transactions. Once things are automated in a virtual OS, a few clicks of the mouse will reveal all of your latest account activity. Make a habit of doing this each day you use your computer. Never wait until the end of the month or quarter to review your statements because the clock is always ticking

and your financial institutions can hold you liable for the damages if you don't catch the fraud in time. If you find something unexpected, contact the institution immediately by phone or email. If you can't solve the problem you may have to resort to a formal dispute with your card issuer/institution in writing and within 60 days. Send your complaint via certified mail to the address for billing inquiries—not the one for payments—and include your name, account number, address, an explanation of the error, plus copies of the bill, receipts and any other supporting documents. The lender must acknowledge your complaint within 30 days, remove the charge until the issue is resolved, and clear up the dispute within two billing cycles or 90 days.

51) Simplify, simplify, simplify. If you have multiple checking, savings, credit cards, IRAs, or utilities, consider consolidating. Accounts you keep open at credit unions in case you move back to an area, or think you may work in an area where you did before will start charging you inactivity fees when not in use. Cancel all credit cards that you do not use or have not used in the last six months. Thieves look for these unmonitored and unused lines of credit. Research companies and find the best package offering bundles for TV, Internet, phone, and cellphone in one bill. When shopping for a broker, bank, mortgage, etc., see my website on Internet links, as there are many links to sites that will aid your research.

52) Dispose of your old laptop, PC or hard drive safely and environmentally. Before disposing or donating your computer, be sure all personal information has been wiped from your hard drive. ***Simply erasing and reformatting the hard drive isn't enough***; refer back to Chapter 3, which details how to properly dispose of your old computer hardware. If that won't work for you, you can pay any number of companies to erase all data from hard disks using Department of Defense recommended methods, or destroy the hard drive completely. Visit http://pcdisposal.com, http://redemtech.com, http://www.retire-it.com for companies that provide such services. If you can't wipe the drive, look into degaussing it with the companies above. Even a hammered drive is recoverable.

53) Empty your wallet of all extra credit cards and Social Security numbers, etc. Do not carry any identifiers you do not need on your person or in your car. Don't carry your birth certificate, Social Security card, or passport, unless necessary. Make a copy of your Medicare card and black out all but the last four digits on the copy. Store your passport, Social Security card, extra credit cards, library cards, etc. when not planning to use them. Use the hotel safe when traveling. If you have a safety deposit box store them there.

Story	While on corporate travel to Brazil we stopped off in Rio on the way back. My co-workers wallet was quickly stolen while we were on the beach, and I learned then just how many pick pockets there were. So I locked my wallet in the hotel room safe (which I was informed later might not be safe). While on the way to the beach later, a group of attractive females made a beeline toward me and swiftly surrounded me in a flirtatious manner. The few dollar bills that were in my pocket rapidly disappeared in a very skillful manner and then they quickly moved on. The moral of this story is that losing a few dollars is nothing compared to what might have happened if it had been a credit card or some sort of identification.

54) Keep a photocopy of the contents of your wallet, copying both sides of each license, credit card, etc. You will then know what you had in your wallet and all of the account and phone numbers to call and cancel should it get lost or stolen. Keep the photocopy in a safe place.

If you travel a lot or carry important business credit cards, consider a paid service such as Alex's Lost Wallet Protector, which costs $40 per year or $100 for three years. This service will assist you in replacing your passport, and in some states even your driver's license. There is also Discover's Wallet Protection that costs $4 a month or $40 per year. (See: http://lwpenroll.americanexpress.com, http://www.discover.com/wallet)

If you don't have a paid service, you will need to take a day off of work or out of your vacation to deal with the theft. Time is of the essence when your wallet is lost or stolen. You must *immediately* report your lost or stolen debit cards to your banks and credit unions, then your credit cards, followed by filing a police report. If you don't report your debit card missing within 2 days, you could get hit with up to $500 in charges. Credit cards are a bit more forgiving as you are only liable for up to $50, which is often waived. You must report your lost or stolen credit card within 30 days, but it is wise to call right away. Contact your department of motor vehicles ASAP to let them know that someone may attempt to use your license to get a new one with a new number to create a new identity.

Canceling your credit or bank cards are NOT enough. Thieves can use your driver's license or other IDs to open instant credit in your name. Call the credit agencies and place a *fraud alert* or a *freeze* on all your credit. A FREEZE is different from a fraud alert in that it will lock down any NEW credit that would be thieves are trying to get issued in your name. PCWorld calls this "The Nuclear Option". From https://www.pcworld.com/article/145077-5/identitytheft_protection_what_services_can_you_trust.html "*with a freeze (which you can set up yourself for a small fee), credit bureaus won't release your report at all. TrustedID.com can set up a freeze for you for $15 plus any credit bureau fees, but you must mail it a power of attorney form. Or you can do it yourself via certified mail. The rules and fees vary depending on where you live, but the cost is usually $10 per bureau. (Consumers Union has a guide to each state's laws.).*" The article compares the various Identity Theft Protection services that are available.

When you place a security freeze on your file, you will be provided a personal identification number or password to use if you choose to remove the security freeze from your file or authorize the temporary release of your credit report for a specific person or period after the security freeze is in place. To provide that authorization, you must contact the reporting agency and provide all the following:

- Sufficient identification to verify your identity.
- Your personal identification number or password provided by the credit reporting company.
- A statement that you choose to remove the security freeze from your file or that you authorize the reporting agency to temporarily release your consumer report. If you authorize the temporary release of your consumer report, you must name the person who is to receive your consumer report or the period for which your consumer report must be available.

If you are actively seeking credit, you should understand that the procedures involved in lifting a security freeze may slow your own applications for credit. You should plan ahead and lift a freeze, either completely if you are shopping around, or specifically for a certain creditor, a few days before actually applying for new credit.

If you simply do a fraud alert on your accounts (the bureau you contact will notify the other two), the alert lasts 90 days and gets you a free credit report from each agency so you can monitor whether the perpetrator is also trying to masquerade as you. With a police report, you can extend the alert up to seven years and get two free reports from each bureau annually.

55) If traveling abroad, also carry a photocopy of your passport in a safe place. Lost passports and credit cards must be reported immediately. Where to report:

Credit/Debit Card: Company that issued the card within 24 hours. Waiting longer can have you liable for any credit issued in your name.
Driver's License: The government/state agency that issued the license.
Passport: The government agency that issued the passport. If traveling out of the country, report the theft to your country's embassy.
Social Security Card or National ID Number: The government agency that issued the SSN or National ID Number.

56) Reputable institutions never send emails requesting confidential personal or account information. Relay your personal information only by phone or by logging in on their secure website.

57) Never send unencrypted personal or account information in emails or email replies. Email bounces from server to server across the Internet where unscrupulous servers can make copies for identity/information thieves. Governments can also make a record of all your emails to search through.

58) Beware of links to phony *phishing* websites in email or otherwise, which act like the real URLs of the reputable institutions you deal with online. Unscrupulous thieves have commandeered domain names that closely resemble the URLs of frequently visited/important sites. Mistyping a letter or two in the URL can send you to these sites. These sites will try to load spyware, viruses, etc. They will also closely mimic (called a Trojan horse) the real site in the hopes of getting you to type your account name and password, while behind the scenes making copies of them. Make sure you are where you think you are on the Internet by looking at the URL and clicking on the little lock in the lower corner. If you're not sure, double click on the lock and view the site security certificate.

59) Avoid accidentally browsing to phishing sites by cutting and pasting URLs from a maintained file, use bookmarks, or put your personal links somewhere accessible on the Internet, like a personal website. Some ISPs and companies provide free space and a URL for you to post personal web pages. All you need is a web page editor and a way, such as using FileZilla to FTP (transfer) the files.

60) Use caution when opening emails and their attachments. Never click on links in an email (from banks, institutions, friends or otherwise). Type the secure site's address into your

browser, bookmark it, or use a website of safe links that you have set up. If the sending address is unfamiliar to you, consider deleting the email unopened.

61) Lock up your laptop. Lock it away or secure it with a cable. Use the hotel safe when you travel. Don't leave your laptop in your office, car or hotel room unattended. How do I obtain a security cable? Purchase a laptop security cable at a local retailer on-line. Some companies that offer laptop cables include Belkin, Kensington, PC Guardian, and Targus.

62) Keep your home PC or laptop secure. Be sure to protect your home machine with the fingerprint identification and a password. For your network, use a hardware router firewall and back it up with a software firewall on each Internet device, covered in Chapter 2. Set up parental controls if allowing children on the computer.

63) If an Internet device (e.g. phone, laptop or tablet) is lost or stolen, contact your carrier immediately. Type up a description of the device with identifying features such as make, model, color, etc. and file a police report for your missing technology. Visit your local pawnshops and offer a reward if someone sells your device to them. Be prepared to reimburse the pawnshop for the cost of purchasing your device plus your reward. If your phone uses a SIM card, make sure that your wireless carrier has deactivated or locked it. That move will prevent other people from simply pulling the SIM card out of your locked device, inserting it into their own, and then racking up minutes on your account.

64) If you do not need to use your credit card at US Government offices, do not sign the back of your credit cards. If you will never need to use the card at a US Government office put "PHOTO ID REQUIRED" instead. If unsure, leave the back of the card blank. To make a credit card payment at US Government offices, as in the post office, the card must have a signature on the back, which I admit is counterintuitive.

65) If you do not use online transfers or bill paying (recommended) to pay credit card bills, DO NOT put the complete account number on the "For" line of the check. Instead, just put the last four numbers. You don't want people that are handling the check processing to have access to your full account number. The credit card company knows the rest of your account number.

66) Put your work phone number on your personal checks rather than your home phone. If you have a PO Box, use that instead of your home address. If you do not have a PO Box, consider using your work address. Never have personal information like birth date, SSN, or driver's license number printed on your checks. If it is needed, you can hand write it onto the check.

67) Contact the U.S. Postal Service if you do not receive mail for a few days in a row. You want to confirm that your mail has not been diverted to an ID Thief's address because they filled out a change of address form in your name.

68) Protect your home from burglary. Thieves robbing your home are often times, looking for more than just your valuables. Personal information can also be used or sold for a profit by those burglars. Installing an alarm system, buying windowless steel reinforced doors, glass blocking easily accessible lower windows, and installing surveillance equipment will deter criminals into going after easier targets in your neighborhood. Make sure your deadbolt extends deep into a sturdy door frame so the burglar cannot easily kick in the door. Consider a secondary, one-sided deadbolt that can only be extended from the inside for protection from home invasion.

69) The government site http://onguardonline.gov has a lot of good general information on protecting kids online, avoiding scams, securing your computer and more.

70) Think you've been a victim of identity theft? See my help below:

If you believe you have been a victim of identity theft, take immediate steps to correct your records. Be sure to document every phone call and keep copies of every letter or email. Follow up all discussions in writing and use "certified mail, return receipt requested" to send your copies – never originals. Locate details on four important steps that the Federal Trade Commission advises you to take right now at
http://www.ftc.gov/bcp/edu/microsites/idtheft/consumers/defend.html

71) If you have a check stolen or misused:

1) Close the account and ask your financial institution to notify the appropriate check verification service.
2) File a report with your local police or the police in the community where the identity theft took place. Keep a copy of the report or at least get the report number.
3) TeleCheck is a risk analysis service for checks that thousands of retailers and financial institutions use. Their Electronic Check Acceptance service converts a check into an electronic transaction at the point of sale. They also try to help victims of check fraud. Contact TeleCheck at 800-710-9898 to report your fraud or lost / stolen checks. TeleCheck will need one of the following: a notarized Affidavit of Forgery; a notarized Identity Theft Affidavit or a police report, filed, with assigned case/incident number. (See: http://www.firstdata.com/telecheck/index.htm)
4) Order up a ChexSystems report at: https://www.consumerdebit.com/consumerinfo/us/en/chexsystems/report/index.htm.
5) Call Shared Check Authorization Network SCAN at 800-262-7771 to find out if the identity thief has been passing bad checks in your name.
6) File a complaint with the FTC. Visit http://www.ftc.gov/bcp/edu/microsites/idtheft or call the FTC's Identity Theft Hotline, toll-free: 1-877-ID-THEFT (438-4338); TTY: 1-866-653-4261; or write Identity Theft Clearinghouse, Federal Trade Commission, 600 Pennsylvania Avenue, NW, Washington, DC 20580. Be sure to call the Hotline to update your complaint if you have any additional information or problems.

Child Identity Theft Information and Prevention

The previous section was all about protecting your identity but what about your children's identity? Many of us have never given much thought or heard much about this rising problem. If we had by the media it might not be dismissed as we think things such as my child does not even have a credit card, bank account, or credit history, and pays cash for everything. Parents are more worried about childhood bullying, bad grades, vacations, field trips and a host of other things to consider adding *child identity theft* to the mix. However, while bad grades may affect your child's future, someone stealing their identity can have a much more profound effect on their prospects.

In the summer 2013 USAA magazine article titled "Meet the New Target of Identity Theft" by Hillary Chura, she revealed some startling statistics. She says that "*In a December 2012 report, the nonprofit Identity Theft Assistance Center determined that:*

- *One in 40 households with children under 18 experienced child identity fraud.*

- *Child identity fraud is more difficult to detect and resolve than adult identity fraud.*
- *Social Security numbers are the most commonly used piece of information by cyber thieves.*

"Children's Social Security number are a clean slate," says Tom Shaw, vice president of enterprise financial crimes management at USAA."

Thieves that obtain a child's SSN and use that information to create false identities, false paperwork such as passports, drivers licenses, etc. Once the false identity is in place they can open bank accounts, obtain credit cards, commit fraud, obtain employment, government benefits and medical care, and even establish a credit history, all in the name of your child.

Because parents are not looking out for this type of activity, this illegal activity can go undetected for years. Parents rarely check to see of their children have a credit trail, file, or report at the credit monitoring companies or pay a fee to the three credit reporting bureaus to watch their child's credit. The article by Hillary Chura states, "*In a 2011 study of 42,232 U.S. children - the largest of its kind - CyLab found that 10.2 percent of the children's Social Security numbers were used by someone else. Of the 4,311 numbers breached, the report found, 76 percent was attributed to fraud and 24 percent to file contamination.*" If a parent did find a credit record for their child, they should put a credit freeze, as discussed above, on their child's credit.

The impact of this scam is that a child victim of ID theft may find out they cannot use their SSN because it is in use by someone else. This could prevent them from obtaining credit, loans, and even impact their ability to obtain a job or secure a place to live. One family was even subpoenaed to pay taxes on income earned by the Identity Thief. Common sense dictates that the less your child's SSN is given out or used, the less chance it has of being stolen. When a school, sports team, nonprofit organization, charity, pediatrician or anyone wants your child's SSN, try to avoid it at all costs. Badger them as to why they want it, and ask if some other piece of information could be used instead.

Many of the steps we discussed above to prevent your identity from being stolen also apply to your children with a few additions and other things to consider. You will have to make an effort to teach your children cyber security, for example how to be safe on the Internet and how *not to* give out their personal information. Some organizations, charities, government offices, etc. have not made the practice of cyber security a priority to their staff. Ask your working friends and family about their cyber security training and you will see what I mean by that statement. For example, cyber security was not practiced by healthcare staff during my frequent visits to various medical facilities. I overheard staff asking for personal information in the presence of others who could eavesdrop. I also witnessed patients filling out the forms in clear view of other customers and then placing the forms on the counter where anyone could walk by and view them. In your case, find a private place to fill out the forms and make sure you place them in the staff's hands. If you are asked for personal information, request a private audience with that person.

I was also surprised to learn that some coaches ask for children's birth certificates and/or Social Security cards. While I can see the need for them to examine this type of information, I suggest you resist allowing them to take possession of these important documents. If they absolutely refuse and will not allow your child to participate in their activity, place the documents in a sealed envelope and write your name on the outside. This will make sure a skilled thief does not somehow get into the sealed envelope, or to track the theft of these documents. Also, initial or use one of the invisible inks discussed above to mark each document. If the place where these documents are stored gets violated, you may be able to track the criminal if the documents ever turn up. Also, make sure you ask where these documents will be stored and examine that place to determine how secure it is. If the coach will not allow you to inspect that location, strongly consider enrolling your child in some other activity.

Social Security Number Advice

Start guarding your Social Security Number as much as possible. There are many instances where you call an entity such as a bank, credit union or insurance company who ask for your member ID number. As an alternative if you do not know your number you can enter your Social Security number, NEVER DO THAT! There are multiple entities that record and store your phone call such as your ISP, your cell phone company, your cell phone OS provider, the institution you are calling, a possible cracker and your government. Any one of these is a possible source for someone malicious to get your Social Security Number. The only instances where you are required to reveal your SSN, which should only be done in person, are:

- Income tax records
- Medical records
- Credit bureau reports
- College records
- Loan applications
- Vehicle registrations

You can and should refuse to provide your SSN in the following situations:

- As driver's license number (in most states)
- On personal checks
- As discussed, over the phone
- On club memberships or to participate in activities or sports
- On address labels
- As identification for store purchases/refunds
- As a form of identification for anything

What to Do if Your Identity is Stolen

While it was difficult to obtain information beyond an elementary education on how to prevent Identity Theft, there is an abundance of information about what to do once your identity is stolen. There are many for-profit companies and organizations that will help you climb out of ID theft, which will prove costly. Below are a few brief steps and websites that you can visit to regain your identity:

1. Visit attorney Mari Frank's website http://www.idtheftcenter.org, which promotes materials (books) on Identity Theft and how to recover from it. You can quickly learn what has been stolen and from whom. The list is quite extensive. Volunteers there can walk you through the process of restoring your identity.
2. File a report with your local police or the police where the theft took place and get a copy of that report.
3. Contact all creditors, utilities, and financial institutions about fraudulent accounts and follow up each conversation with a registered letter that includes a copy of the police report.
4. File a complaint with the FTC at the Identity Theft Hotline, toll-free at 877-438-4338.
5. Ask your creditors if they will accept the FTC's ID Theft Affidavit. You can get one when you call the Identity Theft Hotline of at http://www.consumer.gov/idtheft . The affidavit allows consumers to report ID Theft information to several companies simultaneously.
6. If it appears someone is using your SSN, contact the SSA to verify your reported earnings and your name by calling 800-772-1213. Also check your social security statements closely.

|  **Tip**

 | In writing this book, especially this chapter about Identity Theft, I looked at my inbox often and despaired. My inbox stretched from inches to feet thick and then back again. A one-page article from a magazine could result in many hours of work and research. To make sure I kept my circulation going, I placed my trash can and shredder on the other side of house as a reward for processing an informative magazine article or just a piece or two of scribbled notes. When done writing about that topic I would rise up and walk that paperwork to the receptacle for exercise and to enjoy the satisfaction of knowing I had finished something.

This gave me inspiration to deal with the barrage of day-to-day nonsense that we all cannot ignore. It also inspired me to finish a book that most of my social network, friends and relatives felt would never be finished because of its technical ever-changing nature. I was asked often, "How do you think that you can stay on top of the technology you are writing about? Your work will be obsolete before your book can ever be published!" My answer was that I would work on it every moment that I could. The fun for me in all this criticism was that I had to stay on the leading edge of technology and news as they raced past while writing this book. This experience was both wonderful and horrible as it played out. The truth was, as technology raced on, I found my book rewrites became less and less difficult, thus reaffirming my belief that this book was possible to complete. I also used every social moment to promote the book, which appeared to be wanted and needed by people I met, thus reaffirming its need and possible future. |

Other useful links to follow privacy and identity theft issues online are:

https://www.abine.com/blog	http://www.idtheftawareness.com
https://www.privacyrights.org	http://www.privacyrights.org/fs/fs4-junk.htm
http://www.staysafeonline.org	

Chapter 12 -- All About Smartphones/Stupidphones and Why You Should Be Concerned

Smartphones are everywhere these days, and they have become the device of choice for many of us to connect to and use the Internet. As I move though chapter after chapter, expunging your need for Internet privacy and laws to protect you, perhaps this final chapter is the most important one that you will read. For some people, their computer is collecting dust as their smartphones take over their day-to-day lives. However, Internet users need to understand that a smartphone is just a hand held computer that runs an operating system and it is subject to the same attacks that we have discussed for computers and laptops. It is a device that is designed and engineered to be spied upon and exploited by law. They should be called *stupidphones* as they are the most hacked, most easily corruptible and most exploited device ever created in the history of the world to violate individual privacy. The scary thing is the world's public has adopted this technology with no objection as to how their privacy and personal information is now being invaded.

It is estimated that 90 percent of the Americans now own or regularly use a cellphone and 58 percent have a sophisticated smartphone that they have no idea how to secure. Smartphones are the most quickly adopted technology ever, and according to the United Nations, over seven billion people worldwide now use these mobile devices.

In an article in Semper-Fi magazine, July 1, 2012 by Richard Blum, CTO, MCLHQ he states, "*Smartphones are the new "in" targets for virus and malware creators.*" From PCWorld, January 2013, "Malware Attacks Target Home Network" by John P. Mello Jr. "*Kindsight also reported that it saw a 165 percent increase in the number of Android malware samples during the quarter. While software aimed at removing aggressive adware from mobile devices exists, the report said, its effectiveness remains to be seen. Because ad-funded Android apps are distributed from the Google Play App Store, that lends considerable legitimacy, the report said.*" In the December 2012 PCWorld article by John P. Mello Jr., he reports that on the Android platform, "*In Q2 alone, one cyber security firm discovered almost 15,000 new malware-laced apps.*" According to USA Today seven percent of smartphone users were victims of identity theft, which is a higher rate than the general public.

Some of the things that we have discussed to protect our computers are not possible using a smartphone. If we are going to connect our smartphone to the Internet, running security software, such as antivirus, should be mandatory. There are anti-malware apps for smartphones but they are not installed by default and Apple goes so far as to claim that an unrooted iPhone is secure without any sort of anti-malware running, which has been debunked by crackers' success in hacking them. (See: https://play.google.com/store/apps/details?id=com.antivirus, http://news.softpedia.com/news/iPhone-iPad-Finally-Get-Antivirus-App-211088.shtml) Just like your computer, once the malware is installed on your phone, a cracker or government can read all of your text messages, view your contacts, listen in on your phone conversations, or make using your phone no longer possible. In the previous chapter on Identity Theft, we talked about the *Cell Phone Recon* product, which should open your eyes as to what malware installed on your smartphone can accomplish. Years ago when computers were first connecting to the Internet, security was almost non-existent. Unsophisticated malware could easily crack those early technological PCs and OSs. However, as hardware, OSs and security software evolved, so did the crackers. We are **at war** with the Internet, and every move or advance that is made for better security it is countered by the enemy. We are being overrun by technology that many of us know nothing about. For example, consider the tip that you should not allow your smartphone to get too hot or too cold. The safe operating zone is between 32 and 95 degrees Fahrenheit. As I think about heat destroying a smartphone let me distract, and hopefully entertain you with a story about an M-60 tank and me sleeping to show how extremely hot temperatures can be a bad thing for a soldier also.

Story	I have found that when wearing a green uniform in ground level temperatures of 140 degrees in the Mojave, you can sleep through anything. Your clothing, if left idle, will burn the skin when you start moving. One day after lunch while I was taking a nap, the guys thought it would be funny to convince the M-60 tank guys into moving a tank over the top of me. You might think, "how would that be possible?", but with all the noise that you are used to from diesel engines, explosions, and gun fire, having a tank rolling over the top of you is just more noise and vibration around you as you are sleeping. The heat sucks all the energy out of you no matter how much water you drink. I have always been a deep sleeper so I awoke to the terrifying sight of a tank rolling over me and freaked out. The tanks turret had long since passed over me and my body was entering the underbelly of the tank. Coming out of a deep slumber to this spectacle was terrifying; while freaking out I rolled like hell to keep forward and above the tank's tracks. There was not much danger because the tank drivers were rolling the tank VERY slowly over me. This gave me plenty of time to get out from underneath it, which is not as dangerous as it sounds. There was little danger of me being flattened under the tracks, but still, this memory is burned into my brain forever. It is a joke I will never forget, but one I valued as a funny experience in my life. My fellow Marines howled in amusement at my expense and after I calmed down, I laughed as well. These types of outlets have to be allowed for our soldiers, not prosecuted, as occurs in today's world.
	The moral of the story above is you must never operate your stupidphone after leaving it in a hot car or having left it to bake the hot sunlight.

Like the early computer technology, smartphones are still in their infancy and we are making the same security mistakes that were made with the early PCs, except on a much grander scale. We are discovering major security holes in these devices that now dwarf what our PCs used to and perhaps continue to reveal. Not only that, we are racing forward with these new technologies that allow smartphones to scan bar codes for pricing and websites, act as a credit card, provide your personal information to get a transaction approved, perform online banking, handle all of our email and text messages, and so much more. We have hardly secured the last advance in technology before the next leap occurs that changes all our lives. No one seems to be questioning if we need to step back, breathe the free air, and not enslave ourselves to a technology that we don't really understand, is cracked constantly, and easily exploited to reveal too much private information about us. More and more we are all enticed and forced for our survival to spy on each other and use these infected devices. This is a trend we need to scale back in our need for individual privacy and survival.

When connecting a smartphone to a hotspot, using encryption is very important but not touted as necessary by these device and network providers. Since we are all learning about the security holes in using smartphones, we have to be much more careful using them now than when we were blindly using them in the past, as we were when using our laptops and PCs. Unlike when PCs came into vogue in the Internet's infancy, in today's world there are well-established, sophisticated devices, utilities, and tools that can be used to track and attack all of our shiny, new smartphone Internet devices. As a result, **major security holes** exist and there are many more exploits that can be used and quickly deployed and used by crackers and governments than what existed 15 years ago. When companies now reveal these exploits after the fact, crackers have already attacked and gathered all your personal information. What you have to wonder about is how surprising it is that you are provided so little education by your government, or how little information or education now exists on how using these insecure and complex Internet devices that corporations force us to use are easily cracked constantly. I hope you find this as disturbing as I do.

As previously discussed in my military experience, a Marine is taught to understand everything they need to know about the weapons and tactics that they use to kill the enemy. We were never handed a weapon that we knew nothing about (except maybe in combat) and told to learn about it and use it on our own. At boot camp, we were quizzed constantly about our weapon's facts and must never hesitate with our answers. Therefore, I found the lack of public, college, or adult continuing education about how to secure a smartphone, tablet or other mobile device astounding. One would think smartphones would be a class topic that would be on the radar of colleges and universities everywhere. Governments, Universities and colleges should be educating every smartphone/tablet user as to how to protect their devices.

In writing this book, I personally scoured adult continuing education and college catalogs for classes on how to secure or learn anything about how to use or secure my smartphone and found, once again, nothing. I surveyed everyone I came across who owned a smartphone or tablet about what they were using to secure them and found nothing but blank stares and little understanding about why I was concerned about this technology. They all knew nothing about securing these devices, and they all blindly assumed that because of the underlying complexity of their smartphone that they used daily for everything in their lives to survive, that security was built in and could be taken for granted. I tried to then explain that I wanted to know what apps they are using for things such as anti-malware; encrypted communication for chat rooms, email or phone conversations; personal smartphone security such as tunneling, anonymizing, tracking or any other security measures that they were taking to use and secure their smartphone use.

When my original questioning approach did not work, I asked my smartphone-using relatives and friends if they knew anyone whom I could pay to teach me about these devices and was once again met with blank stares. This pointed out to me the vast chasm that exists between what crackers, governments, and corporations know and collect about what the common smartphone user allows to be disseminated about them, and what the common user is blindly allowing to take place. I now had a mission to show how these devices are Orwellian. In the February 2014 release of Semper-Fi Magazine in an article written by Richard Blum, he states

"Google bought Boston Dynamics, and then went out to take away a method of choosing privacy settings on Android phones the same day."

The result of all this is that malware infesting PCs and laptops may eventually be dwarfed by malware infesting the proliferation of mobile devices around the world. We can view the Influenza Epidemic of 1918, which was toward the end of the World War I (known as the Great War), as much like the current situation with infected PC's. In the end, we won the war, but only to turn around and lose more human life to a vicious bug that went global and resulted in more life lost than soldiers saw fighting the war.

However, during our current World War on malware we have already lost half of all Internet PC users, who are still infected, to malware and exploitation. Shouldn't this be viewed in the loss column? Smartphone exploitation could be considered far worse than the great plague in its numbers and scope. So are now we are gearing up to fight World War III without learning the lessons of World War II or the Great War (World War I).

It is estimated that 20 to 40 million people lost their lives during the Great War. During World War II there were over 60 million people lost, which was an estimated 2.5% of the world's population at that time. So the question now is, since close to half of the world's Internet population is infected with malware, are we going to turn around and lose an even greater war by offering up a new round of Internet devices for the enemy to infect? Are we going to condemn ourselves to an even worse technical war in which we again lose half the world's Internet devices to the enemy? Smartphones are the latest malware target and as this new technology is produced we have to ask ourselves, are the manufacturers of this technology just as unprepared for this malware onslaught as were the PC manufacturers of the late 1990s? The producers of this technology certainly seem to be seeking to exploit, log and monitor our use of them in ways that we should be very concerned about.

Furthermore, using smartphones to pay for purchases appears to be a disaster waiting to happen. In the stores we visit, (the cash register clerks are not trained nor do they have any understanding of the technology that they are employing on your device, which is not their fault) these devices read and process a transaction from your phone. It is a foregone conclusion that crackers are working to devise methods to do the same thing to steal money from your accounts. We already know they know how to do this when we swipe machines using our credit cards, and if those can be massively compromised on a monumental scale, tapping into a wireless signal to steal a transaction should prove to be an even easier target.

In April 2013, there were two possible methods for using mobile wallets. One involved downloading an app to your smartphone and linking that app to a bank or credit service. You then make payments by tapping a button on your phone or make the phone display a code for the cashier to scan. The other method used a near-field communication (NFC) equipped phone and a mobile app. You could then use your mobile phone to pay from the account of your choosing by tapping the phone on an NFC payment terminal. Obviously, corporations are encouraging smartphone users to use these apps, as they have store loyalty-cards and reward accounts for using these apps to redeem discounts, organize coupons, movie tickets or even pull up a digital boarding pass. The following are some methods of payment just now starting to be used:

- Google Wallet is now available for near-field communication (NFC) enabled phones. The Google Wallet application stores and supports all of your credit and debit cards online. After setting up your wallet account, all you have to do is download the free app and install it on your Internet device. Google Wallet is password-protected and you can disable your wallet account from anywhere at any time. Google Wallet supports the Sprint and Virgin Mobile phones, including the Samsung Galaxy S3, Samsung Galaxy Nexus, LG Viper, LG Optimus Elite, and HTC EVO 4G. (See: http://www.google.com/wallet).
- LevelUp, for the Android iOS, claim that paying with LevelUp is almost the same as swiping a card, but is faster and more secure. Use the service to download the LevelUp app, and then link a credit or debit card to get a LevelUp code, bring that code up on the screen of the phone and then swipe that code to pay. By using the code you earn rewards to spend with new vendors and savings for repeat visits. There are only a few participating vendors, so options are limited. (See: https://www.thelevelup.com).
- PayPal, for the Android iOS, offers a free wallet app that allows you to send money, track your balance, or choose how to pay a small transaction. Like LevelUp, you can link your bank, debit and credit card to your PayPal account, and then select PayPal when you are at the register. Rather than scan a code, you enter your mobile number and PIN, or swipe your PayPal card that was sent to you in the mail. PayPal is working with vendors to get it accepted anywhere you shop--online, on your phone, and at the registers in stores. (See: https://www.paypal.com/webapps/mpp/mobile-apps).
- Apple PassBook, included in iOS 6 and 7, is a digital way of storing things that used to be paper-based documents, such as movie tickets, loyalty-cards, gift cards, boarding passes and more. Open the passbook and tap the pass you need; the Aztec, PDF417 or QR barcode is then scanned to book a flight, earn loyalty points, or redeem a coupon and more. (See: https://www.apple.com/ios/whats-new/#passbook).

If your phone is lost or stolen, you will need some means of disabling it so that these apps cannot be used. You will probably want to sign up with a service that can disable your phone remotely.

Unlike my chapter on computer hardware, I could not cover expensive smartphone hardware. I could not afford the popular Samsung Galaxy S4/S5 or the Apple iPhone6/7, so I went with the budget Walmart T-Mobile Family plan, and I purchased two $300 Samsung Galaxy S-II phones that will work with the T-Mobile, AT&T and Sprint networks. I did not want a two-year contract and the $75 a month fee for unlimited everything, less than what we were paying Verizon per month for less options, should rapidly cover the cost of these new phones. Prior to this, my wife and I were paying Verizon $89 a month for voice only technology, and if I am going to be selling books about cyber security, it appears that text messaging and unlimited Internet access are mandatory.

| Story | You have to be very careful dealing with a cellphone provider. My wife and I have had two very bad experiences with sales representatives taking advantage of us, which I hate to admit, by whom we were victimized. In the first instance, my father-in-law was dying, and I wanted a temporary, extra cellphone for my mother-in-law to allow her to stay in touch with us. The sales rep gave us the |

new phone at a very nominal cost and a few signatures, which I thought was very nice of him. However, we later found out that he roped us into a new two-year contract for that phone. AT&T would not cancel that contract until its expiration two years later. To cancel that contract or even discontinue that extra cellphone would have cost us many hundreds of dollars. We had been duped, and I went along with this manipulation because I saw no legal recourse. After all, I did sign the contract without first reading and understanding the fine print, which is something you should never do! When the contract ended, we quickly switched to Verizon Wireless hoping for a better relationship. While with Verizon, my wife's phone died, so I went in to get a new phone from the sales representative. We looked at all of the alternatives, and then after picking out a phone, I unknowingly signed an agreement and was, once again, duped into another two-year agreement for my wife to have a new phone that we needed for her work. The moral of the story is, buyer beware, because these sales reps will not bring these things to your attention and are encouraged to make a sale at all costs!

Smartphones are also a disaster waiting to happen for you, as under current law, officers may search a person under arrest, checking pockets and looking through a wallet, car, house or purse, and in most cases, obtain everything on your smartphone with a warrant. Even if you are not guilty of the crime that they have accused you of, there may be a crime your smartphone implicates you of, and could possibly affect others.

The Movies Are Real-Everyone Is Tracking Your Smartphone

If you are not troubled by everything revealed in this book thus far, you should be, as this saga continues. Everything you do while carrying your smartphone (stupidphone) is a potential target by the NSA, retail stores, friends, relatives, neighbors, enemies, thieves, criminals, and scorned lovers who can and will track everything you do in life and can examine your whereabouts at any time they want. For example, your stupidphone will switch to using Wi-Fi whenever a signal is present, thus saving your mobile phone carrier network from having to service your phone activity. There are two problems with this as one, your phone will connect to unsecured networks (secure networks require a password). Crackers may be lurking on those networks and will attack your phones vulnerabilities and if found, exploit them. The other problem with this is, that retailers and others are using the Wi-Fi signals emitted from your phone to gather real-time data about everywhere you go, what you pause to look at, how much time you spend somewhere, what route you took, which departments you visited, how often you linger and more. This eavesdropping is much more prevalent than you might think and retailers say little about the tracking they are doing.

Retailers say that this does not violate your privacy since all they record is the MAC address of your smartphone, but it is very easy to tie that address back to the actual owner. When we combine this tracking with store cameras, facial recognition technology and more, this invasion into our privacy becomes much more specific. They say they use this data to improve store layout, schedule staff efficiently and shorten lines.

Retailers are creating profiles about customers based on when their stupidphones enter their stores until when they leave the premises. They can infer lifestyle interests by recording how long you linger at certain displays, what aisles you spend time in, visit certain locations in their stores and they trace these patterns storing years of data about you. You can try to limit this tracking by visiting http://smartstoreprivacy.org but only a handful of companies have agreed to comply. The better solution is to turn off your stupidphone or disable Wi-Fi and Bluetooth while shopping. There is some hope for privacy seekers from this invasion for iPhone users as iOS 8 says they will have privacy-friendly feature that broadcasts randomized MAC addresses.

If companies can do this it should come as no big surprise that the NSA can also track your smartphone. In an article published on September 8, 2013 by CBS News titled "Report: NSA can track your smartphone" states "*BERLIN German news weekly Der Spiegel reports that the U.S. National Security Agency can access users' data on all major smartphones.*

The magazine cites internal documents from the NSA and its British counterpart GCHQ in which the agencies describe setting up dedicated teams to crack protective measures on iPhones, BlackBerry and Android devices... This data includes contacts, call lists, SMS traffic, notes and location data... The NSA has bypassed or cracked much of the digital encryption used by businesses and everyday Web users, according to reports Thursday in The New York Times, Britain's Guardian newspaper and the nonprofit news website ProPublica. The reports describe how the NSA invested billions of dollars since 2000 to make nearly everyone's secrets available for government consumption.

In doing so, the NSA built powerful supercomputers to break encryption codes and partnered with unnamed technology companies to insert "back doors" into their software, the reports said." (See: http://www.cbsnews.com/news/report-nsa-can-track-your-smartphone) The article indicated that this might be yet another revelation by the privacy hero, Edward Snowden.

In later articles from the BBC and Washington Post, it was revealed that this surveillance goes much further as the NSA is collecting some five billion records a day on the location of mobile phones around the world. This information is added to a gigantic database that shows the locations of "at least hundreds of millions of cellphones" worldwide, a stunning revelation that suggests the NSA's eavesdropping agency has created a previously unthinkable mass surveillance and tracking tool capable of creating a map of where you go, who you know and what you do. These huge databases are capable of mapping movement and relationships in ways that are unprecedented in human history. The BBC article from 5 December 2014, revealed, "*the analysis is so detailed that it can be used to thwart attempts to hide from scrutiny by people who use disposable phones or only use a handset briefly before switching it off. The vast majority of the information gathered is said to come from taps installed on mobile phone networks and used the basic location-information that networks log as people move around. Analyzing this data helps the NSA work out which devices is regularly in close proximity and, by implication, exposes a potential connection between the owners of those handsets.*"

What is shocking is how the NSA and GCHQ could build such huge apparatuses without any outcry from U.S. or British citizens, or even a public debate. These databases do not target persons of interest as much as they gobble up data about huge numbers of innocent people. They are tracking political beliefs, contacts, relationships and Internet histories. One can quickly see how this data gathering is ripe for government exploitation and invades the privacy of citizens worldwide. These stories are yet another revelation of the whistleblower Edward Snowden, who pointed out that we all must consider how this data could be abused.

It is very alarming as to how far the U.S. and U.K. citizens are willing to allow this invasion into everyone's privacy. These assaults on personal liberty are taking place without much of a fight or argument. The U.S. government has used this data to reveal intimate and private information about the individuals not agreeing with the views that they hold. Here are few more facts and things for you to consider as you use this technology. The data stored on most smartphones can paint a complete picture about everything you do while carrying and using these devices. Your call history, voicemails, text messages, photographs and videos, apps, web browsing, Google searches, passwords, what you read or listen to, your location during every day of your life, and more were all available by a simple subpoena from anyone in authority until the June 25, 2014 Supreme Court ruling. In an unprecedented victory for privacy advocates, the U.S. Supreme Court unanimously ruled that police may not search the cell phones of criminal suspects without a warrant. The court cited that smartphones and other electronic devices were not in the same category as wallets, briefcases, and vehicles, which are subject to limited examination by law enforcement. The court ruled in this fashion because of the enormous amounts of personal information that users store on them. This ruling is not related to the massive surveillance and metadata gathering program still in operation by the National Security Agency. (See: http://www.cnn.com/2014/06/25/justice/supreme-court-cell-phones/index.html)

There is also the problem that smartphone apps are also tracking users' locations, according to new research. For example, the handy illuminating app Brightest Flashlight, the popular app Angry Birds and others collect data about users' location smartphone device IDs. It was reported by recently on the CNN Morgan Spurlock show that 45% of apps track your location. (See: https://www.aclu.org/blog/technology-and-liberty-criminal-law-reform-immigrants-rights/new-document-sheds-light, http://www.bbc.co.uk/news/technology-25231757, http://www.washingtonpost.com/world/national-security/nsa-tracking-cellphone-locations-worldwide-snowden-documents-show/2013/12/04/5492873a-5cf2-11e3-bc56-c6ca94801fac_story.html, http://www.bbc.co.uk/news/technology-25118156, http://www.nydailynews.com/news/national/angry-birds-flashlight-apps-track-location-article-1.1241250)

Your correspondences, such as year-old emails, can be tracked with the use of these devices, which are stored on the NSA and corporate servers for many years.

- NSA is researching or may be able to tap into your smartphone to control the computers in your vehicle.
- NSA and the FBI can override the webcam in your computers or smartphones, thus activating them when they are connected to the Internet or cellphone towers.
- Companies now use caller ID to track and record your calls to match up your personal information stored in their databases.
- As cookies are being blocked using your smartphones browser, companies now look at the individual signature of your device so that they can track its use. A company can tell how often you visit their site and where you go using their site.

One thing I thought you could do to avoid this invasion into your privacy was to purchase a drop phone with prepaid minutes for cash. If you are not a person of interest, this may protect you from corporate and cracker invasions into your privacy. Governments can track these devices as soon as they connect to the infected Internet if you are person of interest, thus linking them back to you even when you pay cash for them, but it is nice to have an alternative communication device handy that you can turn off quickly. For example, perhaps you are about to become a public figure and don't what to give out your personal cell phone number, such as with my launch of ThatCyberSecurityGuy. Maybe you want to set up a public Facebook or email account that requires your cellphone number to send your text message to finish the enrollment process. They will obviously provide that cellphone number too many other U.S. corporations and government agencies, so perhaps you don't want that with your personal phone number.

| **Story**  | I traveled to a Walmart store in Lynchburg, Virginia to purchase another cell phone so I could set up my business Facebook and Yahoo email accounts. Given what we have learned in this book, I was not about to give them my personal cellphone number. This action does not grant me much more privacy, but it sure felt like I was being clandestine. I boldly walked up the Walmart employee and stated loudly that I needed a BURNER PHONE. The poor guy had no idea what I was talking about, and after repeating my request a few times, I spelled it out for him. Unbelievably he did not know what a burner phone was, so I asked all too loudly, "Don't you ever have any drug dealers come in here purchasing phones?" This really set him back, so I explained I was from Detroit, and the term "burner phone" is common language. However, I quickly realized that I had overstepped the boundaries of what I should shout out in a southern town Walmart and explained to everyone that I was not a drug dealer and needed the phone for my upcoming cyber security business, which was met with skeptical eyes from my many spectators. I was laughing about this whole incident on my way back to my parents' house to help them and continue putting the finishing touches on a few first *ThatCyberSecurityGuy* blog entries. |

To register my new Tracfone I had to reveal personal information about myself as well use a personal phone so it would be easy to trace my use of this phone back to me personally. I'm sure there are ways around this that criminal and crackers know, and perhaps one day I will write about that topic in subsequent releases of this book. My view of using a drop phone for personal privacy was abused in the NBC news exclusive interview between Brian Williams and Edward Snowden titled "Inside the Mind of Edward Snowden". (See: http://www.nbcnews.com/feature/edward-snowden-interview)

In the interview, Snowden said the following about drop phones in an exchange with Brian Williams, "*I want to ask you about this device, this is not my iPhone, this is what drug dealers resort to, this is called a burner, it's the one I brought over to cover the Olympics because our IT people told me that the Russians are so good at infiltration, how good, and how good are the Americans, and what can the NSA do if they wanted to get into my life?*" Snowden, "*So First off that is probably the most expensive burner I have ever seen. But I guess we are at the upmarket drug dealer here...*" Williams, "*It is turned off its inert.*" Snowden, "*The NSA, the Russian intelligence service, the Chinese intelligence service, any intelligence service in the world who has significance funding and a real technological research team can own that phone the minute it connects to their network... as soon as you turn it on it can be theirs, they can turn it into a microphone, they can take pictures from it, they can take the data off of it, but it's important to understand that these things are typically done on a targeted basis. It is only done when people using this phone are considered suspicious. If they think it is being held by a drug dealer, think it is being used by a terrorist; or if you're an intelligence service, they think the person who came into the country is a spy and has got something they need to know."*

Having examined everything above the question becomes how can you carry and use a device which, whether on or off, tracks and records everything you do in life? During my long walks I came up with an idea of putting these spy devices in a lead box when not in use so that no signal could get in or out. I thought along with selling my book I would make a fortune off of my new idea for privacy. However, I did a search on the Internet to see if others had the same notion and found that there are products that say will do this. I have not tested these products nor have I found independent reviews showing that they work but I think we should all have them to put our stupidphones in if they actually work. (See: http://www.solrus.com/sentry.html)

Ex-Partner's Pictures and Data Posted Online, Cellphone Users Beware!

If you do a search for something such as "ex-lover picture websites", you will find all sorts of unsavory websites that exploit the pictures that cellphone users take of themselves and their lovers. Once these pictures are posted online, there is little or no hope for the victim to ever remove them from our infected Internet. Worldwide laws have not yet evolved to deal with this type of digital crime. These popular websites get hundreds of user-submitted pictures every day. These websites do not care if the pictures are stolen or who submits them. They even go so far as to categorize the photos as "New user submission, Self-shot pictures, Hacked exes', Ex-Girlfriend's video, etc." The Feb. 4, 2013 McAfee survey titled "Lovers Beware: Scorned Exes May Share Intimate Data And Images Online" states, *"McAfee has found that 13% of adults have had their personal content leaked to others without their permission. Additionally, 1 in 10 ex-partners have threatened that they would expose risqué photos of their ex online. According to the study, these threats have been carried out nearly 60% of the time."* (See: http://www.mcafee.com/us/about/news/2013/q1/20130204-01.aspx) Sometimes the posting of revenge pictures, text messages, and email has resulted in suicide, which also needs to be addressed in worldwide legal systems. There are many differing opinions on this issue, as we must protect the First Amendment; but that needs to be balanced with the necessity of creating a Digital Fourth Amendment to protect U.S. citizens' privacy.

Since data on cellphones is considered public by governments and corporations, many people feel that pictures taken and exchanged using cellphones are fair game to be posted by anyone and anywhere on the Internet. They see nothing wrong with taking something that was meant to be private and making it public by posting it on the Internet. These unauthorized disclosures of cellphone data and pictures are rarely punished under current privacy laws. This is a double standard, since from http://www.attorneylawyerdirectory.org/law/62-privacy-laws.html, *"the introduction of the Human Rights Act 1998 incorporated into English law the European Convention on Human Rights. Article 8.1 of the ECHR provided an explicit right to respect for a private life for the first time within English law. The Convention also requires the judiciary to "have regard" to the Convention in raising the common law."* There are other legal precedents, for example:

- U.S. citizens can file a HIPAA privacy complaint with the federal Department of Health and Human Services if your health information privacy rights are violated.
- U.S. companies have asked the court system to identify the authors of anonymous defamatory messages.
- The Children's Online Privacy Protection Act of 1998 requires website operators to maintain privacy policies, grants parents the power to regulate the information that their children can glean from websites and grants regulatory power to the FTC.
- A lawyer could be disbarred if they expose a guilty client to the public or police.
- Whistleblowers who post governmental or corporate data are hunted down and prosecuted to the fullest extent of American law or have to choose to live in exile.
- If a priest takes a confession and then directly violates the seal of confession, he will automatically be excommunicated from the church.
- The U.S. Supreme Court ruled that attaching a GPS tracking device to a suspect's vehicle requires a warrant.
- Media outlets can be charged with liability if they blatantly publish material that they know to be false and that information cause's harm to a person's reputation.

Consequently, we can see that there are instances for protecting privacy under the law, and we should hold everyone accountable to these very same standards that have existed for centuries before the invention of the infected Internet. (See: http://law2.umkc.edu/faculty/projects/ftrials/conlaw/rightofprivacy.html) However, today's sad reality is that you have to assume that any picture taken using your cellphone is public property and probably will end up on the Internet. It is hard for a public that is used to not having any privacy to sympathize with victims who they feel willingly provided this public information to their friends or lovers, until they find themselves as the victim of this crime. This information should have privacy protection, but that does not seem to exist in today's digital world. Nonetheless, there are obvious exceptions that need to be addressed to the "everything on our cellphone is public rule" stated above.

Think about the instances in where others take pictures without your permission and share or post them online. We also have to wonder about how people who don't want this information being public can get it removed. There is no mechanism to do so, and some of these website owners will extort money to remove the data and/or pictures and then may even repost it saying someone else posted it on their website. We all have to accept the fact that once posted on the Internet it is there for all time. Take down one website and another website owner who copied your pictures from somewhere else in the world will repost it. Even trying to keep your digital data and photos private provides no protection from crackers. If your cellphone is stolen or hacked, your information, pictures and data can still end up on the Internet. Deleting pictures and data does not remove them from your cellphone, as this data is easily recovered from your SIM card, which you should destroy. You must also pray that your data was never shared with a cloud service provider, many of whom have been often hacked for your personal cellphone data and retain it in their databases for years.

Another worry is Cyber Stalking, in which a majority of Americans are engaged. According to the same McAfee survey, "When armed with their partner's passwords, a majority of Americans snoop and check out their partners' emails, bank accounts and social media pages. More than 56% of people surveyed have admitted to checking their significant others' social media pages and *bank accounts and nearly half (49%) log in to scan their partners' emails. The survey also revealed that slightly more people (48%) track their ex-partner on Facebook more than they do their current partner (44%). More than two out of five 18-24 year olds have admitted to even tracking their partner's ex on Facebook and/or Twitter, compared to the 28% national average that snoops on their partner's ex."*

When reading this, we can see that as we engage in digital relationships we need some sort of legal framework that forces our partners to respect our privacy. We need a digital prenuptial agreement that states that anything shared digitally with our partner cannot be posted on the Internet without consequences. This gets back to my demand for a Digital Fourth Amendment to the U.S. Constitution and to implement Internet usage laws that are now needed worldwide!

Getting Started with Your Smartphone

Taking on the task of purchasing a smartphone and setting up a network plan is a daunting task. Even our young do not give proper consideration to the costs and contracts they sign to use this technology. Choosing your plan and deciding on the options that you need is maze that most of us don't have the time work our way through. Over the years that I have spent writing this book, I knew I would have to join the 21st century, choose an all-inclusive text and web smartphone plan, and purchase and learn how to use a complex smartphone. It proved difficult finding a contract that I was comfortable with and included an advanced smartphone that I wanted to write about, given my family's very limited budget. Therefore, during the last eight years, my wife and I used voice-only AT&T and Verizon plans with some very old LG phones. Our smartphone friends wondered why we did not upgrade, given the advanced nature of this book. My feeling on this subject was that while writing a book on cyber security I was much more secure using a low-tech cellphone. I was also not ready to research and write about these high-tech smartphones. Until I could afford to take the time to plunge in and research smartphones, why bother to upgrade to them and have to learn about the use of this technology? They would be of limited benefit to our personal lives and communication with our very limited social network.

This is a question that we all must ask ourselves before bringing this added complexity and expense in to invade our private lives. If your job or life does not require the use of these devices, use the cheap prepaid alternatives at local retail stores, such as Walmart. The cheap models reveal less information about you, and you are not tied into a contract that may cost you thousands rather than hundreds of dollars. Because I was busy writing, it took until June 2013 before I could begin experimenting with a smartphone and learning about this technology to write this chapter. However, I knew this book could never be complete without adding something about smartphones to this cyber security conversation. Being viewed as a 50+-year-old dinosaur by our younger smartphone counterparts, it has been difficult for me learn about and adopt this technology. However, because of these complications, I have been able to add to my writing to make things easier for everyone.

To keep this book on the leading edge of technology has been costly and painful. Not knowing our future as my wife retires, I could not tie my family into an expensive cellular company contract using lavish smartphones for the next two years. I watched the Walmart T-

Mobile Family Plans and the StraightTalk AT&T no contract plans for quite some time. For years, the phones that could be used with these plans were of old design, which the manufacturers were just trying to get rid of. Luckily for my family, Walmart made a big purchase of the last remaining Samsung Galaxy S-II phones. While I am not a fan of Google because of their constant tracking of all Internet activity, their technology is sound. Accepting this technology, I knew that everything my wife and I did on the phones would be tracked by Google and the NSA, but for this book, I reluctantly made the plunge. I purchased the Samsung Galaxy SII with the T-Mobile Family Plan at Walmart because:

- It is a good phone with a track record, even though I knew Samsung would discontinue it. Walmart being Walmart, they picked them up cheap and were marketing them for $300 apiece. In June 2013, this was one-half the price of Samsung Galaxy S III, which was not that much more advanced in features.
- The Galaxy S II would work with the AT&T, Sprint, and the T-Mobile towers. So if I needed move around or hated the service, I could try other providers.
- This is a month-to-month contract, so we could cancel at any time.

I present this so you know what you need to think about purchasing one of these plans. You can try to keep this phone somewhat private by purchasing a cheap phone and log that phone number with places such as Facebook, LinkedIn, etc.

Smartphones are all the rage, and I see people using them everywhere, but as we discussed, nobody can tell me how to make them secure. In my financial magazines I see wasted words that tell the reader that the data kept on your smartphone can exceed what is on your PC and is valuable to criminals. **No kidding**? But these article writers obviously do not know what to do and list the same common sense steps over and over again that we covered in the Introduction. The difference is that instead of email, the crackers are using text messages, and instead of calling it a phishing attack, we are calling text phishing a *smishing** attack. However, this type of attack may be more effective against a smartphone as we now have QR codes (bar codes that direct you to a website when scanned by your phone) and URL shortening services, such as tinyurl.com, and bit.ly, that make it harder to identify malicious links and websites. There is also a phishing over the phone attack called *vishing**. The criminal calls the intended victim pretending to be from a trusted bank or another institution, such as the local court system calling about jury duty, in hopes of garnering personal information.

Once you tie yourself into a smartphone iOS, you are also tied into the data collecting corporation supporting it. To take advantage of all the features that will make your life very public and convenient you have to open accounts and share email, conversations, recordings, etc., with that corporation. Even though I find this distressing, I had no choice but to do this to write this book. I set up a Google Voice account that fit well with my Android iOS phone and started exploring the options. There were many things I could use if I wanted totally ignore my privacy, which under certain circumstances we may want to do.

Google Voice (GV) will allow you to maintain multiple phone numbers with one GV phone number. This works very well for business cards and converting from one phone number to another if you change cellphone carriers. If you need to record your calls, pressing 4 will record incoming (but not outgoing) calls. You are not violating anyone's privacy because when you press 4, the Google Lady will announce, "This call is now being recorded" so that all parties can hear it. This is very handy if you are being stalked, receive an important call about a purchase, or want to record directions from technical support for reference later. When you finish your call, you'll find the recording in the Google Voice app's Inbox, where you can listen to it.

To set this up do this, travel to the Google Voice site and sign up. (See: https://www.google.com/voice) You'll be walked through the process of creating an account and assigning it to your phone. Once you have that account, travel to the Google Voice site once again and enable the call recording feature:

1. Click the gear icon upper right and select Settings.
2. Click the Calls tab.
3. Select the checkbox near the bottom next to Call Options.

Secure and Protect Your Smartphone

Secure your smartphone by setting a lock-screen PIN or password. Using a lock-screen only keeps someone from using your phone; it does not secure your data. If a cracker gets ahold of your smartphone it is a simple matter to get at the data by connecting that phone to a computer's USB port. Therefore, if your smartphone supports encryption, that feature should be turned on to thwart criminals from easily retrieving your data.

There are also security apps that you can install on your smartphone that have antivirus to block the emerging threat of mobile malware. These security apps will allow you to log on to their websites so as to locate your smartphone by having your phone make a location noise, or lock the device if you don't have a PIN or password set and be able to perform the nuclear option of wiping your data if all hope is lost. For example, Android users can download and use the free app Android Lost; the iPhone comes with Find my Phone, which must be activated, and Windows Phone owners can log in to their Microsoft accounts and to use their Find my Phone feature. There are other companies in the mobile anti-software game; some other products that you can examine are Bitdefender Mobile Security and Antivirus "PC Mag Editor Choice", TrustGo Antivirus and Mobile, Trend Micro Mobile Security & Antivirus among others. (See: http://go.pcworld.com/avastmobile, http://www.avgmobile.com, http://www.bitdefender.com/solutions/mobile-security-android.html, http://www.trendmicro.com/us/home/products/mobile-solutions/index.html, http://www.trustgo.com/en)

We also have to have common sense using these devices and do things such as log out of apps, especially banking apps, when we are not using them. Properly vet an unfamiliar app by searching the web for reviews which may tell you it is legitimate. If there are updates, install them as quickly as possible as they sometimes plug security holes.

Destroying the data on your smartphone will not protect it from forensic analysis. It is easy for a skilled technician to pull the data off a defunct or wiped phone. If law enforcement and the NSA can get at this data, it is not a big jump to imagine that skilled crackers can also. Conversely, if you encrypt the data to a cryptographic key, it scrambles all of the data on the phone, thus making recovering the data much more difficult or impossible. ***Open up your Android phone Settings menu > scroll down to select Security > under Encryption select Encrypt device***. Be advised that encrypting your phone is an inconvenience that you may not want to endure, as you will have to enter your encryption PIN/password to open the device every time you power it on in the future.

Tip	The encryption process can take thirty minutes or more, so don't start this process without the phone connected to a power source and a fully charged battery. As we have learned, there are likely backdoors built into this encryption technology as demanded by governments. If the NSA or GCHQ have backdoors, it is likely that other governments and crackers do also.

Lockout Security and Antivirus is another product to scan apps and links. Lockout claims they have the largest mobile threat dataset that they use to protect your device from malware, scan every app to ensure its safe and to block malicious websites. It also protects your privacy by allowing you to see which apps access your private info, or it can wipe your data so that no one can access it and helps prevent encounters with phishing scams. There is also a feature in the Lookout Security & Antivirus for Android called Lock Cam, which will snap a picture using the phone's front camera if someone makes three unsuccessful attempts to unlock the phone. The app will then email that picture to you with a warning about the attempted intrusion. Lockout does a pretty good job of protecting your privacy and giving you options to choose what you share with them. However, this mobile app is invasive, and you should read the privacy policy before signing up. (See: https://www.lookout.com, https://www.lookout.com/legal/privacy-policy)

Don't go in for the cheap plastic covers; buy a good cover, such as the Otter Box Defender or Cygnett Urban Shield. (See: http://us.cygnett.com) For longer battery life, check out the Sony Cycle Energy. (See: http://store.sony.com) The Sony Cycle Energy is an external battery that's a half-inch thick and shaped like a phone. Consider disabling remote connectivity, as some mobile devices are equipped with wireless technologies, such as Bluetooth, that can be used to connect to other devices or computers. You should disable these features when they are not in use to protect your device and save your battery.

From their website, "KoolSpan's TrustChip is designed to address security challenges affecting the broad array of connected devices, platforms and servers, including but not limited to mobile devices. TrustChip® is your mobile phone encryption engine. It simplifies the mobile security challenge with compatibility across multiple platforms and offers accessibility to any app via its developer kit. TrustChip mobile device security is fully manageable and is hardened with a 32-bit crypto processor at its core." (See: http://www.koolspan.com/trust-chip)

TextSecure is an open source SMS/MMS application for Android, which can encrypt your text messages. Upon startup, the app will prompt you to enter a passphrase and then will copy all of your text messages to a new encrypted database on your phone as protection from anyone attempting to access them. The app not only protects and encrypts text messages kept on your phone, but also when you send them. Consequently, if you lose or have your phone stolen, the person in possession of your phone will be unable to read your text messages.

TextSecure will prevent anyone from being able to read your messages, but it does not obfuscate the fact that you are sending messages or to whom you are sending them. To get started you will have to perform a one-time key exchange with all of your TextSecure contacts. This is akin to how SSH works, which we covered earlier. Once the key exchange is complete TextSecure will show you a padlock in the top-left corner. If you recall, back in the SSH chapter we discussed a fingerprint that needed to be verified. TextSecure works much the same way by providing you and your recipient with a set of characters. To make sure that you have the correct recipient will require a phone call to make sure that you are both viewing the same set of characters. From then on, whenever you see the padlock, you will be sending TextSecure messages to everyone with whom you need to correspond. (See: https://securityinabox.org/en/textsecure_main, https://www.whispersystems.org)

For the Android, iPhone, Mac, Linux and PCs there is the "Chat Secure" that promises free, unlimited, private, secure messaging with your friends on a variety of platforms such as Facebook Chat, Google Talk, Hangouts, Jabber, Dukgo & more. This open source project provides an encrypted chat client that supports Off-the-Record (OTR) encryption over Extensible Messaging and Presence Protocol (XMPP). OTR is a cryptographic protocol the promises strong encryption for instant messaging conversations. From Wiki, "XMMP is a communication protocol for message-oriented middleware back on Extensible Markup Language (XML)." Chat Secure is a very active project with regular updates. (See: https://chatsecure.org, https://en.wikipedia.org/wiki/Off-the-Record_Messaging, https://en.wikipedia.org/wiki/Xmpp)

Another Android open source app to consider is RedPhone, which allows you to encrypt your phone calls end-to-end. The app uses your normal phone number and can encrypt your voice calls to any person to whom you are calling that has RedPhone installed. Even though your call is encrypted end-to-end, RedPhone promises that you will not even know you are using encryption. RedPhone also promises to use Wi-Fi and data when they are available, instead of your smartphone's plan voice minutes. The software uses encrypted SMS messages to establish a connection with the recipient's cellphone, which is transparent to the user. (See: https://whispersystems.org, http://www.techrepublic.com/blog/it-security/encrypt-calls-on-your-android-device-with-redphone/5300)

On July 29, 2014, Whisper Systems released their Signal app, which is free, worldwide, encrypted voice calls for iPhone, and fully compatible with RedPhone for Android. According to their blog, "*Signal uses your existing number, doesn't require a password, and leverages privacy-preserving contact discovery to immediately display which of your contacts are reachable with Signal. Under the hood, it uses ZRTP, a well-tested protocol for secure voice communication.*" The Signal development team is promising expanded support for text communication, which will be compatible with TextSecure for Android. After that is accomplished, the developers plan to combine TextSecure and RedPhone for Android into a unified Signal app. (See: https://whispersystems.org/blog/signal, http://www.forbes.com/sites/davelewis/2014/07/29/encrypt-calls-on-your-iphone)

On October 8, 2014, NPR reported that Apple's new iOS 8 OS for iPhone and iPad tablets will feature encryption software that will be totally secure, even from Apple. Before Edward Snowden, I doubt that any company would've used encryption as a selling point because users equate encryption with complexity. Post Snowden it is now a thought on many peoples' minds. Apple CEO Tim Cook even stated, "People have a right to privacy, and I think that's going to be a very key topic over the next year or so." I very much doubt this encryption feature will ever see the light and I feel sure the U.S. government will either pay for or require Apple to provide backdoors.

On the other side of the argument, FBI Director James Comey told reporters that he does not understand why companies would "market something expressly to allow people to place themselves beyond the law." Really? The flaw in that argument is the implication that everyone who values their privacy should be considered "beyond the law." Hopefully, this will be the first step in stopping the whole world from freely spying on everyone's Internet devices. Ronald Hosko, former assistant director of the FBI Criminal Investigative Division says Apple is "*offering the consumer a virtual fortress from law enforcement.*" (See: http://www.npr.org/blogs/alltechconsidered/2014/10/08/354598527/apple-says-ios-encryption-protects-privacy-fbi-raises-crime-fears)

Extend Your Smartphone's Battery Life

There are some obvious things that you can do to extend your battery's life, such as dimming the screen and adjusting the screen timeout, but these settings can be annoying. Having the screen timeout constantly may not be the best way to save battery life. Below are a few other things for you to consider:

- You may not know it, but using Bluetooth and Wi-Fi consume battery life. When you are not using these features, turn them off.
- For security, and to save battery life, disable syncing services when not in use. Go into the Accounts section of Settings and turn off syncing for the services that you are not using.
- You may not be familiar with Airplane mode, but turning this on will disable the wireless features including cellular data, Wi-Fi, Bluetooth, GPS, and other location features.
- Turning off location services will save a lot of power.
- Turn off vibrate as vibrating uses a lot more power that playing a ringtone.

Most smartphones come with a cable that will plug into a USB 2.0 port to recharge the phone. However, this is very inefficient as a USB 2.0 port can only deliver up to 500 milliamps of juice to the phone. If you compare that to a typical AC wall charger that supplies 900-1000mA, it becomes obvious that you want an AC charger in your office. However, if you travel, you may have to use your laptop. In that case, make sure the laptop you purchase has USB 3.0 ports, which can deliver 900mA to charge your smartphone.

Turn off Geotagging in Your Smartphone Digital Camera; Don't Let Them Track You!

In new devices Geotagging features are integrated and sometimes on by default. The phone or camera that you take a digital picture with and post can reveal information that you may not want to be public knowledge. The Exchangeable Image File (EXIF) format is a standard for storing digital pictures on your devices as compressed JPEG or as TIFF image files. In each digital image the device taking the picture has data such as aperture, auxiliary lenses used, exposure compensation*, F-number, focal length, metering mode*, if a flash was used, ISO number*, date and time the image was taken, resolution, shutter speed, and white balance. This information can be used by a printer do things such as better color matching to enhance a printed image. This seems harmless enough, but modern digital devices also use a process known as Geotagging, which stores the latitude and longitude data in the images EXIF data. This information mates the image with the specific geographic location in which it was taken. There is also a unique identifier embedded in the image that allows the photo to be traced back to your device.

From these images, scraping scripts or mapping services such as Google Earth can figure out the latitude and longitude data, street address, city, and state of an image posted online. So strangers know where you took your pictures and can develop a profile, down to your address, Facebook account, and other items about which you may not want them to know about. So be sure and turn off Geotagging so that not everyone knows where you took those pictures or are carrying your cellphone, or better yet, don't post them online.

What You Need to Know about Cellphone Tracking & Encryption

Your iPhone/Android/RIM Blackberry/cellphone also broadcasts your location for anyone to see. Fortunately, you can go into the settings and toggle the location services. I had an old LG Env phone and was surprised to find the "***Settings >Tools > Location***" option. It was set to "911 only", which means that even though corporations are not supposed to be watching my location, the police and homeland security could still track my location, no matter where I went. There is a lot of conflicting information about whether or not your device can be tracked when powered off or if the GPS has been disabled. For example, there was an FBI case that utilized a "roving bug" to activate a powered off Genovese crime family's cellphone microphone for listening purposes.

The Wall Street Journal reports that the FBI can now remotely activate the microphones in Android smartphones and laptop computers to record conversations. The only way to stop this type of spying activity would be to disconnect power and remove the cellphone or laptop battery. The really disturbing news is that the FBI does not even need to get a warrant to obtain this type of information. However, this is not rocket science or magic, and when a cellphone is being used as a bug it is transmitting, so it can be detected with simple bug detection devices described in Chapter 11. If those are not available, pay attention to the electronics around you; if your cellphone is transmitting or you have some other device transmitting you may hear constant buzzing in nearby speakers that will get louder as you approach them. These devices routinely communicate with their towers when they are on so a certain amount of periodic buzzing that is only pinpointing is recording your phones location.

However, a continuous buzz is a sure-fire sign something on your body is transmitting a signal. A radio tuned to an AM station might be your best bet to use as a bug detection device if you cannot afford to buy the real thing. (See: http://www.zdnet.com/news/fbi-taps-cell-phone-mic-as-eavesdropping-tool/150467 , http://bgr.com/2013/08/02/fbi-android-microphone-hack, http://online.wsj.com/news/articles/SB10001424127887323997004578641993388259674, http://thehackernews.com/2013/08/Android-hacking-spying-tool-surveillance-FBI-virus-backdoor.html, http://www.theblaze.com/stories/2013/08/02/report-fbi-can-remotely-turn-on-phone-microphones-for-spying)

GPS comes standard in smartphones, and when this feature is turned on your location is tracked and logged constantly with exact location data. However, there is abundant evidence that your smartphone's location can be tracked even when it is off. The other method of tracking your location is called triangulation, which takes three cellphone towers to approximate the location of your cellphone. Cellphone towers constantly ping your cellphone to provide service so your whereabouts while carrying the phone are easily traceable. With triangulation, the exactness of your location depends on the density of the cell towers in your area. You might wonder why companies gather and pay to store this information; it is what they exist for, which is profit. The U.S. government pays provider services vast amounts of their citizens' taxpayer dollars to retain and provide data about its citizens' use of their cellphones. (See: http://www.pcmag.com/article2/0,2817,2404494,00.asp)

U.S. courts have ruled that tracking cellphone GPS locations is like intercepting a phone call or tailing someone on a sidewalk or street. This data does not need a warrant, and the U.S. government can track those citizens' locations as they use this equipment at any given time. In court cases where this data has been used, it has been argued that this violates the U.S. Fourth Amendment, but U.S. judges disagreed with that appeal. Judges have ruled that U.S. citizens using smartphones that revealed GPS data do not have a "reasonable expectation of privacy," and therefore can be tracked at will by law enforcement. This means that any U.S. law enforcement technically capable of this type of surveillance is free to do so, with little or no checks and balances. Once again they are missing the point, which is that people around the world do NOT want corporations tracking their cellphones, but there are no laws or opt-out methods for doing so. (See: https://ssd.eff.org/wire/protect/cell-tracking, http://www.wikihow.com/GPS-Track-a-Cell-Phone, http://www.motherjones.com/mojo/2012/08/court-warrant-cellphone-gps-data)

There are corporate products that you can purchase to encrypt your cellphone conversations that may work against crackers, but evidence abounds that they will not protect you against governments worldwide. You can assume that if governments can crack this encryption or have backdoors, many crackers can also. The Washington Post article dated December 13, 2013, titled "By cracking cellphone code, NSA has capacity for decoding private conversations" by Craig Timberg and Ashkan Soltani states "*The cellphone encryption technology used most widely across the world can be easily defeated by the National Security Agency, an internal document shows, giving the agency the means to decode most of the billions of calls and texts that travel over public airwaves every day.*

While the military and law enforcement agencies long have been able to hack into individual cellphones, the NSA's capability appears to be far more sweeping because of the agency's global signals collection operation. The agency's ability to crack encryption used by the majority of cellphones in the world offers it wide-ranging powers to listen in on private conversations.

U.S. law prohibits the NSA from collecting the content of conversations between Americans without a court order. But experts say that if the NSA has developed the capacity to easily decode encrypted cellphone conversations, then other nations likely can do the same through their own intelligence services, potentially to Americans' calls, as well."

The article points out that encryption experts have complained for years that the most commonly used A5/1 cellphone encryption technology used by corporations is easy to hack and have urged them to upgrade to newer systems. Most companies and security conscious SBOs have not done so, as they did not know they needed to do so. Governments conceal these vulnerabilities in their cyber security conversations, thus subjecting their country's SBO/HCU to espionage everywhere in the world. (See: http://www.washingtonpost.com/business/technology/by-cracking-cellphone-code-nsa-has-capacity-for-decoding-private-conversations/2013/12/13/e119b598-612f-11e3-bf45-61f69f54fc5f_story.html)

To address the cellphone spying craze, in February 2014, a new Switzerland-based company launched an innovative cellphone product that they call "blackphone". From their website back then, *"Blackphone is the first integrated smartphone from the best privacy minds in the industry."* They called this *"best-of-breed hardware with all the skills and experience necessary to offer PrivatOS, an Android™ based operating system without the usual compromises."* Blackphone now gives you the ability to decide what you publish, want to share, and gives you the capability of keeping your phone use entirely to yourself. The phone was developed by leading computer industry privacy advocates, which includes Phil Zimmermann, creator of PGP; Javier Aguera, co-founder of Geeksphone; Jon Callas, co-founder of PGP Inc. and CTO of Silent Circle; Rodrigo Silva-Ramos, co-founder of Geeksphone; and Mike Janke, CEO of Silent Circle and former US Navy SEAL.

Blackphone has now developed a security-oriented version of the Android OS that they call PrivatOS. This PrivatOS gives you the ability to make and receive secure phone calls, exchange secure texts, transfer and store files, and video chat privately. Blackphone is an alternative to the rest of the cellphone industry that spies on everything you do by ensuring privacy and control of your communications without the sacrifice of other high-end smartphone features that you have come to expect. It uses the Silent Circle suite that provides end-to-end encryption. This will work with other phones that are not a blackphone, but they will have to have the Silent Circle apps and subscription. (See: http://www.npr.org/blogs/alltechconsidered/2014/02/28/283523473/a-smartphone-that-tries-to-slip-you-off-the-grid, https://www.blackphone.ch, https://www.silentcircle.com/technology)

You Can Use an SSH Tunnel on Your Android Phone

Cellphones are much more complex to secure using security tools such as an SSH Tunnel. They seem to be designed to reveal everything you do while using them to corporations and governments, with only very complex privacy solutions. Since a cellphone is essentially a small hand-held computer, I investigated how to tunnel an Android SSH cellphone to your SBO/HCU SSH server.

The Android OS is based on Linux, which we covered in <u>Chapter 7</u>. In that chapter we discussed the 'root' user and how to perform administrative tasks. In my research, it appears that we have to establish 'root' access to a cellphone before we can use it to establish an SSH tunnel to our SSH server. In the cellphone world this is called rooting the device. However, unlike becoming 'root' in a Linux OS, the cellphone manufacturers do not want to allow users this capability or power.

- Rooting a cellphone can void a warranty if discovered, but a phone can be 'unrooted' so that a manufacturer does not know it has been 'rooted'.
- Applications such as Google Wallet may have vulnerabilities on 'rooted' devices that might allow other apps access to your PIN and other wallet information.
- Users not familiar with Linux who have 'rooted' a cellphone have been known to "brick" it. The word "brick" is cellphone slang meaning that a user who did know what they were doing somehow managed to break the device, rendering it unusable. In addition, 'rooting' a cellphone is also referred to as "jailbreaking" a cellphone.

One would think that cellphone manufacturers would include directions in their manuals as to how to 'root' a phone so that security applications could be used to globally tunnel your phone, but that is not the case. Cellphone users have to scour the web to download applications and perform risky procedures to get root access to their phone. Most users are not tech-savvy enough to accomplish this task, as users have to be careful following directions from various questionable website pages. If you are in China or a western user wanting better privacy, you can use the SSHTunnel app, which uses a DNS proxy to solve the DNS Pollution problem found in China. (See: <u>http://www.howtogeek.com/115297/how-to-root-your-android-why-you-might-want-to</u>, <u>http://www.howtogeek.com/121698/how-to-route-all-your-android-traffic-through-a-secure-tunnel</u>, <u>https://code.google.com/p/sshtunnel</u>, <u>https://play.google.com/store/apps/details?id=org.sshtunnel</u>, <u>http://darkk.net.ru/redsocks</u>) Rather than risk destroying your phone and warranty, you may just want to tunnel certain applications on your smartphone. We can do this by using apps that you can download from <u>https://play.google.com/store/apps?hl=en</u> by typing SSH in the Search box.
Another less complex option that has DNS leaks for using SSH on your Android phone is ConnectBot, which is an SSH client that allows you to connect to SSH servers. (See: <u>https://code.google.com/p/connectbot</u>, <u>https://play.google.com/store/apps/details?id=com.madgag.ssh.agent</u> <u>http://thecustomizewindows.com/2012/07/best-ssh-tunnel-apps-for-android/</u> <u>http://handheld.softpedia.com/get/Network/SSH-Tunnel-122711.shtml</u>)

About the Author Continued – This Author's Survival Story in War, from Cancer, and Life. Never Give Up! Never Surrender!

From <u>About the Author</u> at the beginning of the book you might be wondering why/how I could go from such an extensive resume with *supposedly* lucrative job opportunities to writing this book. The answer is, partly by circumstance and partly in response to the need that I have seen to keep our Internet use private and safe from prying eyes. Most war veterans hope to get an opportunity in life to do something greater than our prior service to our countries service that may benefit our country, and perhaps, even all of humanity. These are noble goals are why some veterans enlist, fight for freedom, and hope that future generations will benefit from our service and sacrifice. In today's world of greed, corruption and political benefit, this type of behavior and these traits are eccentric, but they really do exist in some people. I think that when veterans find themselves no longer relevant after returning home from war they must find new meaning to their lives. Otherwise, how can we explain the extremely high suicide rates among U.S. soldiers verses the general U.S. population. My life's experiences and questionable future health resulting from my service are such that all I wanted to do was pass on my experiences and knowledge before I die so I wrote this book to find relevance in today's infected Internet world. My dream is that one day my book will help keep future generations of people everywhere protected from the dangerous and wonderful advances made in technology that they do not understand from exploiting their privacy. They need to come to the understanding that using something that has become as invasive as the infected Internet and smartphone technology is against their best interests. I wanted to use my knowledge and experience to help the SBO/HCU compete/prevent the surveillance invasion that corporations and governments are now engaged in monitoring everyone's Internet use.

Let me tell you a little about myself so that you know I do not state my credentials idly, but merely to state the facts and gain your confidence about the solutions that I present in this book. Not only am I only a veteran who has fought in war and experienced the fear of being shot at, but I am also a two-time cancer survivor who has, in the last nine years, gone through three rounds of chemotherapy treatment, a peripheral stem cell transplant, three major surgeries, and ten minor surgical procedures. I have offered my body to medical clinical trials twice to further science so that others may live. As a result, I have nothing to lose by writing this book, as my body and stamina have suffered. I have often offered my diminished body and talents to the U.S. government and corporations, to try to once again make a decent living, become respected again, make a living and were rejected repeatedly by these entities. I completely understand their assessment that I am damaged goods and would have made the same call myself before my two bouts with cancer and surviving war. Everything in today's world is about the bottom line, and someone admitting they are damaged goods with special needs during an interview cannot be allowed back into the corporate or U.S. nation's work framework unless they wish to make minimum wage. This token poverty wage is what everyone advertises as they say they pretend to help disabled veterans.

Performing the daily walks that my doctors require, educated me on how limited my stamina and body had become as I worked my way back to health on a daily basis. I learned about the years-long disability side of the fence to life's existence that many of us experience after serving in wars, which our governments and corporations reject. After all this carnage, the Veteran's Administration gives me a 0% disability rating, even though I can no longer be on call 24/7 or work the 12-hour shifts that my previous IT job demanded. I can now participate in somewhat rigorous sports but with amazing consequences afterward such as 13 hours of rest to recover for a few hours of tennis or racquetball. With the help of the Disabled American Veterans organization, I battled with the Veteran's Administration for two and one half years trying to get them to understand that the radiation exposure that I received while serving in Kuwait during the Operation Iraqi Freedom war was what caused my lymphoma cancer. Finally, I did manage to get access to health care at the VA, albeit at a 0% disability rating with no access to vocational training to get me back into the job market.

Unlike many veterans still fighting these battles, I was very lucky in the fact that a few very prominent physicians at the top of their medical fields attested to the fact that lymphoma cancer, with no family heredity history, is almost always caused by an external catalyst. In letters submitted to the VA after exposure to the radiation in Kuwait, they stated that it would take three to seven years before lymphoma would appear. In my case, five years after the war, my lymph nodes suddenly swelled, and a local surgeon diagnosed my condition immediately. Imagine my shock when I went to see him on what I thought was a routine visit. He took one look at me and asked his staff, "When can we get Mr. Ellis scheduled for surgery?" Within one week of that pronouncement, my life changed forever. That man saved my life, over my objections, and I became a lab rat of the medical system. There were many horrors afterwards that were worse than being in war for which I am now paying.

This is the fight that U.S. veterans face when attempting to receive any sort of health care, which I find disheartening. The 0% disability rating that I received from the VA gave me no means or access to educational or vocational training, which would have helped me get back to work, and nothing in the way of financial compensation, which is fine. I never wanted or asked for a handout from the U.S. federal government, only to get training in a new skill, given my disability limitations, where I might work 40 or fewer hours a week, which was denied. *I hope this helps you to understand my undertaking and writing of this book*. This left me with no avenue which I could pursue to update my IT skills or attain training in another career path. Any applications or resumes I sent out were ignored as my skill set had become dated by six years trying to survive my cancer caused by the Iraq war.

This whole situation seemed contradictory to me, as I thought I was serving a country that honored its veterans. I would have gladly donated/dedicated my time to any government agency, or The Hartford Corporation from which I was receiving disability payments, to help me build up my resume, advance my career or continue my service to our country, all of which were denied.

After all this carnage, I came out of it a shell of the confident man I had been, and I needed some sort of bridge to seek gainful employment to get me going again. I even suggested this course of action to them many times. My efforts to elicit their help were repeatedly rejected, or met with reams of paperwork; many times this was due to liability concerns. Ultimately, The Hartford cut off payments in May 2013, requiring additional paperwork over and over again, which I tried to provide to them about my cancer's long-term conditions from harsh chemotherapy treatment. The U.S. insurance companies constantly came back demanding more and more records from doctor's offices and from the VA. I provided them with everything as to my condition from 2011 to 2014 that was relevant to my current condition.

When I gave them that paperwork months later they demanded a capacity evaluation of my functionality and gave me 14 days to provide it to avoid any delays in processing. If you follow the news you now know that it can take months for a veteran who meets their difficult qualifying criteria, to see a VA doctor and many more months to see a specialist. What I mean by that statement is that VA doctors have their plates full and do an amazing job servicing veterans and don't need their time wasted by answering frivolous requests from insurance companies which they constantly demand. This shell game is how insurance companies deny benefits to U.S. veterans and U.S. citizens, which the government allows them to do in the name of capitalistic profit.

Because of my prior illness, employers felt they could not use my services, **even for FREE!** If something happened, I might sue, (which means our legal system is also broken), or if I needed health care benefits because my cancer came back, it could reflect on the cost of their insurance premiums, which might go up. Ultimately, The Hartford outright rejected paying me the long-term disability payments that I had been promised and had paid into for so many years. The Hartford continually kept badgering my doctors for documentation on my condition when evidence abounds about the effects of three rounds of high-dose chemotherapy, 13 surgical procedures (two major) and a stem cell transplant on the human body. Since this information is abundantly available, I felt guilty even forwarding this type of paperwork on to my busy VA doctors and Oakwood hospital doctors, which this corporation constantly demanded. How U.S. corporations are permitted to deny benefits to their customers that are under this type of duress is amazing and how much VA doctor's time are they wasting with these frivolous requests? It is no wonder the VA cannot service veterans' health needs as they are constantly harassed by U.S. insurance companies.

On the other hand, as a hopeful for-profit small business, I completely understand these insurance companies' thinking because for me to be alive, many hundreds of thousands of dollars have been spent by my former insurance companies to keep me alive. **Americans as a society need to somehow rethink this for profit-lawyer and for-profit insurance company system**. It is not the insurance company's fault that they are set up to reject every claim and make profit for their shareholders. These companies should all be non-profit, strictly regulated, and setup to benefit their policy holders. I hope you can see the flaws in the U.S. capitalist insurance system, which also holds true for health insurance.

After my stem cell transplant and being sick for six years, I worked with various underfunded Michigan state institutions to try to find a job, which proved problematic given my extended time off from any form of gainful employment. Finding corporate or government work proved to be impossible given my physical limitations which they would not acknowledge. I tried to volunteer my time to various Michigan state agencies to rebuild my resume and was once again rejected.

Today's sad job market is all about cutting personnel and increasing hours. Volunteers with questionable health are rejected from this gap, which is a trend that the U.S., as a nation, needs to stand against as these excesses mount. I quickly realized that this was a work environment in which I could not compete, perform, or even volunteer in. Therefore, I decided, on my own, that there had to be some sort of consideration made for a disabled veteran's limitations, which in today's U.S. corporate or government world they give lip service to, **but in reality do not really help or give employment to**. We see many pretend TV advertisements that make the average U.S. citizen feel good about the fact that veterans are being taken care of by the charities they are giving to, but the fact of the matter is, that is far from the advertised truth. Some of these organizations solicit donated dollars and give nothing back to the veterans they pretend to represent. Consequently, you need to be very careful to whom you donate. That statement stands for other charities also. If you visit http://thatcybersecurityguy/favorites you will see charities that do a good job making your donations count.

Rehabilitation services guided me to jobs making, at most, $7 to $10 an hour, which is a very humbling experience considering my previous salaries of $50 to $120 an hour, plus overtime, and provided benefits prior to my illness. Lawyers I tried to hire to help me with this book wanted upwards of $240 an hour, which I found out when consulting with them on my now $22,000 net year impoverished disability salary; of course, living on my disability income, I had to turn them down. There was no sympathy from these lawyers, wanting to charge me, as a disabled veteran, $427 for less than two hours of work; do the math, and that work amounts to 47 hours on a $9 an hour salary! As a former "have" person, and now becoming a disabled "have-not" person, this was God humanizing me on how wrong I was in my former view of the unemployed world and their supposed lack of motivation to support their families. Before these experiences, my view was that the unemployed were people who lacked the motivation to look hard for a job as they benefited from my tax dollars, which I heard about on right-wing radio. I was a Republican/Libertarian in every sense of the word. However, now standing on the other side of the fence with my new reality, I quickly came to the understanding that this country has degenerated into the "haves" and the "have not's." The left and right wing have been pitted against each other, and both sides are wrong. Some people getting benefits from taxpayer dollars are veterans that fought for their country, who really need them, which right-wingers are standing against. At the same time, left-wingers fight for illegal aliens who came into our country to get these same benefits, which in my opinion, they do not deserve. It is no wonder that this country is polarized against itself. We have to ask ourselves, are these situations created by someone's design or are these nightmares of our own design?

In another instance, I took a class from a lawyer on how to self-publish my book. Afterwards, I asked for some simple advice and he wanted to charge me $93 an hour, which, given the lawyer rates above, he considered a bargain for his services. Of course, these privileged people have no clue as to how common disabled Americans live, so I ignored his rate and continued to work on writing this book. I had to spend every waking hour learning how to produce this book on my own and self-publish this work. My budget was such, as you now know, that his rates were completely unreasonable to my efforts to produce this book. Once again, I present these difficulties to show that the world we live in is crazy, as we have people expecting hundreds of dollars per hour as their God-given right, and then there are those of us who are just getting by on a poverty wage. Why is that?

I have always been accustomed to staying busy and active, so it was difficult for me to be out of work and not have something to put my mind to while undergoing the chemotherapy treatments, a stem cell transplant, and the many surgeries I endured. It is awful being a lab rat in the medical system for years at a time. In the aftermath of all this butchery, there have been many distractions, like the months/years of time I spent gaining access to Social Security

Disability (SSD) and VA health care. For a whole year I fought SSD while I also battled the VA, eight hours a day, sometimes seven days a week. The paperwork was enormous, and with tons of back and forth correspondence. The files I maintained grew to be inches thick, and after winning SSD, the VA battle took an additional two years. The VA requested my medical records many times (and seemed to lose them often) before they finally admitted that they had what they needed and granted me access to their facilities for healthcare. It then took an additional eight months of paperwork (and more medical records) to get an appointment to see a VA hematologist.

Continuously, I was billed and then cut off from access to VA cancer care, which I had proved they should provide, so I did not understand this denial of health care. As it turns out, they had erroneously entered my condition into their computer as a *benign tumor.* This was far from the truth of having *non-Hodgkin's lymphoma cancer caused by radiation exposure during the Iraq War.* It took me an additional nine months to get this error discovered and corrected in their computers, resulting in much more expense, hours on the phone after every visit, and days driving back and forth to the VA, which was an hour away. Finally, this was all cleared up when I visited the regional VA office in Detroit and then took the paperwork that they had given me to the Ann Arbor, Michigan VA. Getting the erroneously inputted computer information in my medical records corrected took many more months of work which, had I been employed, would have proven impossible (during this time I searched continuously for an answer, which also prolonged the writing of this book). The VA system seems to be designed to deny veterans' health care by assuming that they will never amass the time or the will to fight this massive government bureaucracy.

If you listen in to National Public Radio, or even some mainstream news agencies, you will hear about such things as the $800 million that the U.S. government gifted to a very questionable Egyptian government, which was later overthrown by a military coup. Let's see what that sum of money could have done for the U.S. unemployed veterans and citizens who could have been put to work for an honest $10 an hour wage. Let's examine that $800 million and put it in perspective: $800 million would purchase 80,000,000 hours of work for the unemployed in this country. The average year of work in the U.S. is about 52 weeks minus 2 day weekends, minus 10 days' vacation, minus 5 days sick leave. 365 - 104 - 10 -5 = 246 days X 40 hour work weeks = 9840 hours required by people working, divide that by 80,000,000 hours and we get the ability to happily employ 8,130 Americans for a year! Please notice I did not even include the cost of the NSA data center that we talked about that is storing data on the whole world. Am I the only one crunching these numbers? Where is the outrage about this in the USA? This is third grade math, but no one is talking about this in the U.S. media, and American citizens seem to accept this without any objection. Why is that?

Harassment by my Long Term Disability provider, as previously discussed, was continuous as well. I begged them for aid with this book, possible training/education, and help looking for a job. Instead, over and over again, I had to provide useless updates and explain how gainful employment was denied. I even explained that since they were helping my family with disability payments, I could benefit their company with IT work. I wanted to use my IT skills to work for the government, or any corporation or charitable organization they might know of, so that I could upgrade my resume. During these battles/distractions, I continued to do projects, research, and writing of my own, in my IT field, to write this book. These protestations were all rejected, and for those reasons, and many more I presented you with *"The Internet is Infected. Our World Needs The Ultimate Cyber Security Guide for Small Business & Home Computing."*

After all these battles it only seemed appropriate that our U.S. Social Security Disability Administration scheduled me for a medical review on Veteran's Day, November 11, 2014 at 9:40 AM after I had celebrated the Marine Corps birthday with my Marine comrades on November 10, which had to be cut short. This was another example of how I was thanked for my service and I expressed my injured sentiment to the medical review staff who could not understand what I have been through. I told them for a private company to even be open on Veterans Day to do medical reviews of anyone disrepected the living U.S. veterans everywhere and what they fought for. I was promptly informed that SSD scheduled and required this appointment not the other way around as they would rather have Turkey Day or someone's birthday off. Understand that these SSD employees enjoying a vacation day had no problem scheduling this medical review of a U.S. soldier who fought in the Iraqi Freedom war. I don't even think they even considered how this disrepects U.S. veterans everywhere. I should be dead from radiation exposure and have watched so many others die. After my anger management classes at the VA I could only smile as I sent this book to my printer hoping it might change the world and someday embarrass them.

I decided early on, that rather than beat my head against a wall of wasted applications and resumes that would be rejected; I would embark on this quest of writing *the ultimate book*, using my broad computer knowledge and military experience to help people everywhere. During the time I have spent writing this book, and because of my former resume, I was approached by a few recruiters who were, at first, interested in my skills. However, after describing my limitations and years out of work, they would not even present my resume or introduce me to the employers that they represented. They did not consider what I brought to the table worth their time or effort. The phone was outright hung up on me numerous times by recruiters. With my cancer in remission, I also approached former colleagues and people that I still knew in the IT field, because networking, as I was informed by job agencies, was the only way to find gainful employment. However, to quickly show how useless this pursuit was, we need a quick story.

Story	Sometimes the relationships that we build while doing the things that we enjoy open up opportunities that allow us to make a living wage (called NETWORKING, which is now the rage and mandatory to finding a job). Networking is the technique that modern day employment firms suggest we use to find skilled workers (me) a job. For many years, while gainfully working, and prior to my bouts with cancer, I enjoyed various sports at health clubs, played on golf course leagues, and hobnobbed with many influential people. I had many powerful friends and acquaintances there, with whom I had hoped to find support in looking for a job. Many of the individuals that I had competed against in sports worked for various small businesses and corporate IT departments. I figured that they would put in a good word for me, which some did. However, one acquaintance finally expressed a sentiment that I found amusing, disturbing, and common as his proclamation ultimately became part of my foundation for writing this book. His opinion spurred me along in my efforts at volunteer work and furthering my personal pursuit of

education to make a living wage with the publication of this book. The opinion that he expressed was; *"Kirk has not worked for a corporation, government or the military for six years while battling cancer. No one in his right mind would consider his book current with technology; or look at any resume or job application that he might apply for. Obviously Kirk's skills are so far out of date that he is no longer relevant."* This statement and type of thinking, this attitude, and this individual's expressed sentiments continually spurred me on/drove me on to write this book and never give up on this project. I knew I had to prove him wrong! My motto became **"Never Give Up! Never Surrender!"**

I admit, being disabled, with the next round of cancer as a death sentence, has not been an easy road to follow, and I pray that anyone reading this book never has to go down this path in their life. I decided to take classes and get certified in *Linux+*, and purchased and read many books and periodicals. I now bring my 28 years of corporate, military, government and private IT experience, knowledge and talents to the page in order to help the SBO and the average HCU. Some local universities, charitable organizations, friends, family, neighbors, and others have accepted my offered help, which has proven advantageous in my research for this book. These volunteer projects that I have worked on have led to my own personal projects on how to be safe and secure while computing at home and on the road. Using resources from my former career, on my very limited disability income I have purchased many thousands of dollars' worth of computer equipment for setting up a home lab and bought many periodicals and books to keep this book on the leading edge of technology. My wife has questioned these expenses many times. My experience in working for the large entities described earlier has helped me determine what I was trying to accomplish. The things that I discovered while doing research and projects on a volunteer basis has also taught me about how technology has changed while I was very sick. This provided me with many opportunities to test out new software and solutions that did not exist years ago. The results of what I have learned are included in this book to benefit readers with my own tried-and-true methods for securing small business and personal home networks, computers and mobile devices in 2014.

It is my hope that this book will be successful and I promise that profits will go to help people like the individuals described below in the following historical reference, which I will now present. My heart broke as he poured out his story to me years ago and all I could do was try to explain my work on this book. In the end, I had to get up from the table as his cries echoed behind me and travel back to my free campsite in the U.S. National Forest. All of my disability resources have been expended on this book and paying my family's bills. This has been the only choice available given my family's very limited resources. I desperately want to see my future self, making a living wage, and hopefully, someday, helping other veterans and charities as they have helped my family.

Historical Reference – What a Veteran Looking for Health Care Taught Me!

While editing my book in Manistee, Michigan at the American Legion hall, a veteran suddenly sat down opposite me. The poor man had gone through an extraordinarily difficult time trying to get any sort of health care from the VA or any doctor in the area to help him. He looked very ill of health and told me that no one would come to his aid. Because I was working at my laptop, he mistakenly viewed me as his last hope to get to see a doctor. I think he thought I was an officer of that Legion Post. He demanded that I advocate on his behalf, or he would die. I tried to explain that I was just a poor man writing a book on cyber security, but he got very animated and ignored my protestations to dismiss him. He demanded that I write about his plight in my book, so I am now honoring his request. I assume he is dead by now, denied any sort of access to medical care. Manistee Michigan is many miles away from a VA facility, and his wife was working, which meant his household made too much money for him to get access to VA health care. The VA will not give health care to veterans that do not have a documented service connected illness, or are not living in poverty and avoid the homeless. At that time, with my limited resources, I could do nothing to help him, but this book is now here to tell his story. My hope is that his probable death and that conversation will now have some meaning. Perhaps someday U.S. citizens everywhere who have the power to change these things will read this book and take action. Veterans don't need millions of dollars spent on monuments, parades, conventions, roads and bridges dedicated to them, medals or awards; they need health care, housing, education and a civilian living job wage after fighting wars that protected U.S. citizens back home. Veterans should not be tossed aside and deregulated as individuals but honored and integrated back into society with living wage jobs or helped to start Small Businesses.

Factoid 	In the September 2014 American Legion article, BETRAYED, by Ken Olsen, subtitled "*In West Los Angeles, VA is leasing property to private businesses as mentally disabled veteran languish in the streets*" we have the following numbers:

58,063	Homeless veteran in the United States as of 2013
4,000	Estimated number of new homeless veterans each year
50 %	Veterans with psychiatric problems
45 %	Veterans with substance-abuse problems when entering treatment programs which many time washes them out of further help

Glossary

This glossary is targeted to the broadest possible audience, which means defining most technical terms in the context in which they were used. In the many books that I have read I rarely refer to their glossary. There is nothing more annoying than constantly flipping back and forth in a book to understand what the author is talking about. I tried to strike a balance between an HCU/SBO and an educated IT professional; all of whom I hope enjoyed reading this book.

Address Reservation	You will find an Address Reservation defined as, "The assignment of a static (fixed) address to a device on a TCP/IP network" but it is a little more than that when it comes to routers. The advantage of an Address Reservation over a Static IP address is that an Address Reservation allows other devices on your network to continue receiving DHCP IP addresses. You are setting up an IP address within Dynamic Host Configuration Protocol (DHCP). If your router supports the use of both at the same time then there is no difference between the two. However, there are a few advantages to an Address Reservation, such as being able to have a client re-register with the server rather than having to restart it. (See: Support.microsoft.com/kb/170062).
Bank Identifier Code 	A BIC is a code used to identify a bank institution in order to facilitate processing of some domestic, but typically international financial transactions. It is also used to facilitate the automated processing of payments. BIC codes are managed by the Society for Worldwide Interbank Financial Telecommunications (SWIFT) and consist of eight or eleven characters. Many BIC codes can be found by doing a light search at SWIFT. To find your bank's SWIFT code, examine your bank's receiving international wire transfer instructions, which should include their SWIFT code. (See: https://www2.swift.com/directories, http://www.experianidentityandfraud.com/industry-hub/bank-identifier-code,-bic-code-(bic)-an-introduction.html)
Bloatware **Or** **Software** **Bloat**	1. Poorly designed and written applications that have suffered from poor project management. This results in poor coding practices, which leads to unnecessary features, many bugs, conflicts, and extensive use of computer resources dragging down performance. 2. Myriad applications pre-installed on a PC by the vendor. Many PC manufacturers are paid by software vendors to pre-install lite versions of their products on the PCs they sell. In addition, some of these applications load at startup, wasting computer resources. They also present a potential conflict with other installed/beneficial applications. For a fee, retailers offer to rid the new PC of bloatware for their customers, perpetuating the practice for everyone's profit.
Anti-Software	Anti-software is the software that we all use to search for viruses, spyware and clean temporary files off our computers. These products differ in their function(s) and can be separate products tailored for the specific purpose they are built to fix. Generally, we never want to run more than one product (e.g. antivirus, anti-spyware, cleanup software) that serves the same purpose, at the

	same time. Conflicts can develop crippling applications and may disable our computer OS.
Black Hat Hacker	This is what this book refers to as a *Cracker*. Hacker is a term of respect for someone who is talented and incredibly smart. A Black Hat Hacker uses their hacking talents almost exclusively for malicious purposes.
BitTorrent	BitTorrent is a protocol that allows client software to quickly download high-quality digital content such as games, music and video. The protocol was developed to handle the situation where thousands of users are clamoring to download the same file. This punished the hosting service or server with soaring bandwidth problems and costs. Therefore, developers devised a means to allow users that download something to provide their upload capacity to others, thus each new participant provides demand and supply. This yields limitless scalability for nearly a fixed cost. (See: https://en.wikipedia.org/wiki/BitTorrent, http://www.bittorrent.org/introduction.html)
Boolean Variables	Any variable, from the domain of Boolean algebra, having one of only two values. In computer languages, a Boolean variable can be used to hold the integer values 0 or 1, or the C++ literals true and false, which are implicitly promoted to the integers 0 and 1 whenever an arithmetic value is necessary. The Boolean type is unsigned and has the lowest ranking in its category of standard unsigned integer types. In simple assignments, if the left operand is a Boolean type, then the right operand must be either an arithmetic type or a pointer. An object declared as a Boolean type uses 1 byte of storage space, which is large enough to hold the values 0 or 1.
Brute-Force Attack	A Brute-Force attack is a password cracking program that uses exhaustive effort and advanced computing power to go through many combinations of predefined known usual passwords and then uses combinations of characters in sequences to crack a password.
Creepware	This is the nickname that the media has assigned to malware such as Blackshades that can hijack computers remotely and turn on computer webcams, access hard drives, and capture keystrokes to steal passwords -- without the victim ever knowing it.
Cyber espionage	The use of computer networks to gain illicit access to confidential information, typically that held by a government or other organization.
Donationware	From Wiki, "*Donationware is a licensing model that supplies fully operational unrestricted software to the user and requests an optional donation be paid to the programmer or a third-party beneficiary (usually a non-profit).*" Donationware projects depend on the users and sometimes organizations to fund their projects. This software comes fully operational and the authors hope that anyone finding their work useful will pony up a few dollars to fund future development. (See: https://en.wikipedia.org/wiki/Donationware)
Espionage Act Of 1917	While World War I was raging Woodrow Wilson decided that the U.S. government needed a new law that could be viewed as violating the original U.S. Constitution. He wanted a new ability to prosecute American citizens against what the law called "the insidious methods of internal hostile activities." The act superseded previous legislation and with future amendments enabled

	the U.S. government to suppress whistleblowers from revealing anything they saw wrong with U.S. government policies. The act is still cited by many civil libertarians as a law that went too far in its restrictions on freedom of speech. (See: https://en.wikipedia.org/wiki/Espionage_Act_of_1917, http://www.u-s-history.com/pages/h1344.html, http://legal-dictionary.thefreedictionary.com/Espionage+Act+of+1917)
Exposure Compensation	Exposure Compensation is adjusting the picture exposure measured by light meter. Usually, the range of adjustment goes from +2 to -2 EV in 1/3 steps. In other words, the camera is allowing more or less light in.
Freeware 	Freeware is software that is freely available but comes with some caveats. It can be shareware or closed source software and can have restricted usage rights. The software is sometimes provided with limited capabilities to entice the user to purchase the fully operable product. Freeware can run processes in the background that sometimes poll or send information about your Internet use. SBOs should not use freeware unless they study the license restrictions closely. (See: https://en.wikipedia.org/wiki/Freeware).
Full Featured	Defined by various websites as "Hardware or software that provides capabilities and functions comparable to the most advanced models or programs of that category."
Grey Hat Hacker 	A Grey Hat Hacker is someone who in politics would be considered a moderate. He sits the fence between a Black Hat cracker and a White Hat hacker. A Grey Hat sometimes uses his skills to act illegally in either a good or ill way. For example, a Grey Hat may illegally gain access to a network or website to prove that they need to improve their security. Also Grey Hats have been known to disclose vulnerabilities to who they hacked, the general public, or even to sell the information to White or Black Hat hackers.
International Bank Account Number	Each country has an International Bank Account Number (IBAN) which facilitates the automation of cross-border transaction processing. It is an ISO 13616 standard for numbering bank accounts. IBAN numbers are managed by the Society for Worldwide Interbank Financial Telecommunications (SWIFT) and consist of a two-letter ISO 3166-1 country code, followed by two check digits and up to thirty alphanumeric characters for Basic Bank Account Number (BBAN) which has a fixed length per country. (See: http://www.swift.com/dsp/resources/documents/IBAN_Registry.pdf, https://en.wikipedia.org/wiki/International_Bank_Account_Number)
ISO Number	ISO Number refers to film speed, which determines how sensitive the image sensor or film is to light; the lower the number, the slower the speed, the higher the number, the faster the speed.
Keylogger 	A keylogger is software or hardware that records (logs) your keystrokes, usually covertly, as you type so that the unsuspecting person can be monitored. (See: http://www.keyloggers.com, https://en.wikipedia.org/wiki/Keystroke_logging).
Logic Bomb 	A logic bomb is much like a land mine. It lies inactive until the event that its programmer designed into their program logic triggers to become active and perform its malicious deeds. The most common activator for a logic bomb is a date. The logic bomb checks the computers system date and does nothing until a pre-programmed date and time is reached. (See: https://en.wikipedia.org/wiki/Logic_bomb)

Metadata	Metadata is simply data about data; it describes an item's content. For example, a digital picture that you post on the web may contain the location of the picture taken, how large the picture is, the color depth, the image resolution, when of the picture taken and more. (See: https://en.wikipedia.org/wiki/Metadata).
Metering Mode	The ability of a camera to calculate the optimal exposure from the existing light conditions. In a fraction of a second the camera determines the subject, focuses the lens, determines amount of light available, and calculates the correct shutter and F-stop. In photographic terms this is called "metering" the scene.
Modulation	Modulation is the addition of intelligence to a carrier signal that is a high-frequency periodic waveform. The modulating signal attached to the carrier contains the information being transmitted. Typically, the carrier signal is a sinusoid waveform, but according to Wikipedia, a square wave pulse train may also be used. (See: En.wikipedia.org/wiki/Modulation, En.wikipedia.org/wiki/Waveform).
Password Manager	A password manager is a program that is used to keep and manage passwords in an encrypted database. Access to the database is granted by remembering and entering a single password.
Payola 	Payola is a combination of the words "pay" and "Victrola" that represented the huge problem that we saw in the music industry during the 1960s. It is the practice of companies receiving money to promote some products over others. In individual terms, this is bribery. Payola has been banned for radio, telegraphs, communication satellites, and cable TV by Title 47 of the United States Code. However, online publications suffer no legal ramifications for accepting payola. (See: http://www.dailytech.com/Pay+to+Play+Uncovering+Online+Payola/article7510.htm)
Plutocracy or Plutarchy	It is a society or system of government ruled by a very small minority of extremely wealthy people. Centuries ago this meant that a small minority of wealthy citizens ruled a country. However, in today's global world, it is believed a small monitory of very wealthy individuals rule the world, fund and own western government politicians. (See: https://en.wikipedia.org/wiki/Plutocracy, http://www.huffingtonpost.com/tag/plutocracy)
Proxy 	A proxy is a server-like program, receiving requests from clients, forwarding those requests to the real server on behalf of the user, and returning the response as it arrives. A web proxy is an application or service that sits between your browser or other Internet applications and the Internet. It is a "go-between" that can filter cache, block, speed up, and protect you from the Internet. Clients make Internet requests, and instead of connecting to web servers directly, they make Internet requests to the proxy. The proxy then handles the requested objects (web pages, images, videos, etc.) on the client's behalf and forwards they back to the client. (See: https://en.wikipedia.org/wiki/Proxy_server) A third-party proxy can come in handy when there is a firewall or some other mechanism that blocks known ports from accessing the Internet.

Rootkit	A rootkit is malicious malware that hides its presence on a computer system, including in boot records. It penetrates a system and effectively hides its malicious function making it difficult to detect and eradicate.
Security State	A security state is an existing state or social structure designed to protect the existing social structure and territorial integrity and independence of the state from subversive activities by the intelligence and other special services of hostile states, as well as from enemies of the existing order inside the country, many times circumventing all privacy and individual freedom.
SOCKS And SOCKS5 Proxies  	From Wikipedia, "*SOCKet Secure (SOCKS) is an Internet protocol that routes network packets between a client and server through a proxy server. SOCKS5 additionally provides authentication so only authorized users may access a server. Another use of SOCKS is as a circumvention tool, allowing traffic to bypass Internet filtering to access content otherwise blocked by governments, workplaces, schools and country specific web services. SOCKS is an Internet protocol that facilitates the routing of network packets between client–server applications via a proxy server.*" (See: https://en.wikipedia.org/wiki/SOCKS,  http://www.faqs.org/rfcs/rfc1928.html) The SOCKS* Internet protocol allows for the transparent proxying of applications. The SOCKS* client protocol operates at the session layer of the OSI model, which is lower than the HTTP protocol that operates at the application layer. (See: https://en.wikipedia.org/wiki/OSI_model) This allows it to establish a socket connection and bypass the usual application layer proxy* server. The SOCKS* protocol facilitates communication on behalf of a client application to a server application. For the application server, the SOCKS* proxy* is the client. SOCKS* protocol is actually made up of two components. The SOCKS* server is implemented at the application layer while the SOCKS* client operates at the session layer (which is below the Presentation (SSL) and Application (HTTP) layers of the OSI model). The SOCKS5* protocol is application independent, supports both the IPv6 and IPv4 protocols and both the TCP and UDP protocols used by most Internet applications. Transparent proxying, referred to above means that the presence of the proxy* is invisible to the user.
Smishing Attack	Smishing uses cellphone text messages to bait you into divulging personal information. For example, you might receive a text message requesting that you call an unfamiliar phone number, or that you go to a URL to enter information, or a message that prompts you to download software to your phone. If you access the URL in the Smishing text message or download any software to your device (PC or mobile device), you may unintentionally install malware on the device.
Spoofed	Spoof is formally defined as a "Forgery of goods or documents". As this applies to computers, it is an activity where something like email header and address are made to look like they originated from one source, but really came from another. Spoofing can also mimic things such as a website, an IP or MAC address or more. (See: https://wiki.archlinux.org/index.php/MAC_Address_Spoofing)
The Man	The Man is the head of "the establishment" put in place to bring us down. Though nobody has physically seen "the man," he is assumed to be a

	male Caucasian between the ages of 25-40 and is rumored to have a substantial amount of acquired wealth, presumably acquired by exploiting those whom his "establishment" is "keeping down." In the context of the book, this can be the NSA, FBI, or some other government agency being commanded by a plutocracy*. The words oligarchy or Aristocracy could also be used. Its use is meant it to be all-encompassing and imply conspiracy theory thoughts.
Virtual Private Network (VPN) 	From Wikipedia, "*A virtual private network (VPN) extends a private network and the resources contained in the network across public networks like the Internet. It enables a host computer to send and receive data across shared or public networks as if it were a private network with all the functionality, security and management policies of the private network. This is done by establishing a virtual point-to-point connection through the use of dedicated connections, encryption, or a combination of the two.*" You can view a VPN as virtual version of a secure local physical network housed behind a firewall that you are accessing across the Internet. In the data leaked by Edward Snowden, it indicated that the U.S. NSA has broken VPN encryption technology as a secure means of communication. (See: https://en.wikipedia.org/wiki/Virtual_private_network, http://go.pcworld.com/vpns). VPN's are used extensively by large corporations and are the realm of network guru's to set up and manage. There is a variety of authentication techniques for VPN and the SecurID (commonly referred to as a Key Fob) and used extensively for VPN. The RSA SecurID generates an authentication code every 60 seconds via a built-in clock to a factory-encoded random key. They are an added measure of protection that corporations and governments use.
Vishing	This is phishing attack over the phone -- the "v" stands for voice. The attacker calls the intended victim claiming to represent their bank or another institution they trust or are known to interact with. The criminal will try to get personal information such as Social Security number, birth date, etc. which can be used to steal the victim's identity.
White Hat Hacker	A White Hat is a hacker interested in learning about ways to help an SBO/HCU understand that their network(s) or computer(s) are not secure. They do this by using ethical hacking and penetration testing techniques. All vulnerabilities found are documented and presented to business owners or are published.

Appendix 1, Citations

Citation style taken from http://www.chicagomanualofstyle.org/tools_citationguide.html:

1. 60 Minutes, Season 42, Episode 7, *How safe are our computer systems?*, (aired November 8, 2009), titled *Sabotaging the System, Agassi*, URL: http://www.tv.com/shows/60-minutes/watch/november-8-2009-sabotaging-the-system-agassi-1307992.
2. Allen Barra, "One Mile of Open Ground. Was Pickett's Charge Lee's best chance for winning Gettysburg?", *Civil War Times Est. 1962, August 2012*, pp. 32-35 found at VA History Society Library, 428 North Boulevard, Richmond, VA 23220. 804-358-4901.
3. Kent Masterson Brown, "Pickett's Charge and Numerous Counterchanges", *Virginia Country's Civil War, F-221-V819 v.1-5, taken from Vol. II.*, pp. 36-41, 54 found at VA History Society Library, 428 North Boulevard, Richmond, VA 23220. 804-358-4901.
4. Science Museum of Virginia, Richmond, VA.
5. Douglas Southhall Freeman, "It Is All My Fault", *R. E. LEE A BIOGRAPHY, Volume III, Chapter VIII,* , pp. 107-134. E467.1 L4 F831 v.3 found at VA History Society Library, 428 North Boulevard, Richmond, VA 23220. 804-358-4901.
6. Michael W. Lucas, *SSH Mastery, OpenSSH, PuTTY, Tunnels and Keys* (Tilted Windmill Press, January 2012).
7. Patrick Engebretson, *The Basics of Hacking and Penetration Testing, Ethical Hacking and Penetration Testing Made Easy* (Syngress Press an imprint of Elsevier Inc. 2011).
8. Roderick W. Smith, *CompTIA Linux+ Complete Study Guide : Exams LX0-101 and LX0-102 -- First edition* (Wiley Publishing, Inc. Indianapolis, Indiana, 2010).
9. Dafydd Stuttard and Marcus Pinto, *The Web Applications Hacker's Handbook, Finding and Exploiting Security Flaws Second Edition* (John Wiley & Sons Publishing, Inc., Indianapolis, Indiana, 2011)
10. Christopher Negua and Eric Foster-Johnson, *Fedora 11 and Red Hat Enterprise Linux Bible* (Wiley Publishing, Inc. Indianapolis, Indiana, 2009).
11. Stuart McClure, CNE, CCSE; Joel Scambray, CISSP; George Kurtz, CISSP, CISA, *Hacking 7 Exposed, Network Security Secrets & Solutions, Seventh Edition* (McGraw-Hill Companies 2012).
12. Jeremy Faircloth, technical editor Neil Fryer, *Penetration Tester's Open Source Toolkit, Third Edition* , (Syngress Press an imprint of Elsevier Inc. 2011).
13. Matthew Helmke, Andrew Hudson and Paul Hudson; *Ubuntu Unleashed : 2011 Edition Covering 10.10 and 11.04* (Pearson Education, Inc., 2011).
14. Roger Whittaker and Justin Davies, *OpenSUSE 11.0 and SUSE Linux Enterprise Server Bible* (Wiley Publishing, Inc., Indianapolis, Indiana, 2008).
15. Nancy Curtis, *Security+ a CompTIA Certification (Windows Server 2003)*, (Element K Content LLC 2006).
16. Dan Poynter, *Self-Publishing Manual, How to Write, Print and Sell Your Own Book Sixteenth Edition* (Para Publishing, Santa Barbara 1979 through 2010).
17. Dan Poynter, *Self-Publishing Manual Volume II, How to Write, Print and Sell Your Own Book Employing the Latest Technologies and the Newest Techniques* (Para Publishing, Santa Barbara 2009, 2010).
18. Many educational images in this book were taken from Britannica ImageQuest, Inc., 331 North LaSalle Street, Chicago, Illnois 60654, Phone: 312-347-7000.

Appendix 2: A Brief Linux Vim Editor Cheat Sheet

Command Mode	Accepts commands usually entered as a single letter like below:
a-A-i-I-o-O-R	Enters Insert Mode to enter text
esc	Return to Command Mode from Insert Mode
~	swap case of character under the cursor and move to next character
ctx	enter Insert Mode and change till the letter x on current line
cw	change text from cursor position to end of word
dtx	delect till x on current line
d	delete selected text
dd	deletes one line
ddp	switch the current line with the next line
a	enter Insert Mode and insert text after the current cursor position
A	enter **Insert Mode** and move the cursor to end of line
b	moves cursor to the beginning of a word
B	moves cursor to the beginning of a white-space delimited word
e	moves cursor to the end of a word
D	delete from cursor till end of line
E	moves cursor to the end of a white-space delimited word
gg	move cursor to beginning of file
shift+g or G	move cursor to end of file
gD	move to first (intelligent) instance of word under cursor. When programming or scripting it takes you to the definition or the declaration of the function or variable
h l k j	move cursor left, right one character; one line up, down one line
H	moves cursor to the first line of the screen
i a	enter Insert Mode and insert text before, after the cursor
shift+i or I	enter Insert Mode and insert a text string at the beginning of the current line
J	join the link below cursor with current line
shift+K or K	display the man page for word under cursor if it exists
L	moves cursor to the last line of the screen
M	moves cursor to the middle line of the screen
o	enter Insert Mode and open a line below current postion in file
shift+o or O	enter Insert Mode and open a line above your current postion in file
p	paste lines from the buffer below current position in file
P	paste lines from the buffer above current position in file
r	replaces a character
shift+r or R	enter Insert Mode with the system configured to overwrite existing text
u	undo's the most recent command
U	undo the last undo command
w	advance one word
W	advance one word (includes "words" that may include special characters (excluding 'space')

x	remove character under the cursor. Like delete in insert mode
shift+x or X	remove character before cursor. Like backspace in insert mode
y$	copy from cursor to end of linn
yl	copies a certain number of characters into the buffer. For example, 4yl would copy the first four characters after the cursor
yy or Y	copy line to buffer that cursor is on
ZZ	save file and quit. Same as typing :wq
0	moves cursor to the beginning of the current line
.	repeat the last command executed
$	moves cursor to the end of the current line
^	moves cursor to the beginning of current line
%	jumps between match pairs of () {} [] <>. With the match-it addon, it will jump between matching pairs in an HTML file
"ty	copy selected text and paste in register t (any lower case character)
"td	delect selected text and paste in register t (any lower case)
"tp	paste what is present in register t at current cursor position
Ctrl+(a/A)	Increments the number under the cursor
Ctrl+(b/B)	scrolls up almost a full screen
Ctrl+(d/D)	scrolls down 1/2 screen
Ctrl+(e/E)	scrolls screen down one line at a time
Ctrl+(f/F)	scrolls screen down almost a full screen
Ctrl+(u/U)	scrolls screen up 1/2 screen
Ctrl+(x/X)	Decrements the number under the cursor
Ctrl+(y/Y)	scrolls screen up one line at a time
Ex mode	**Enter Ex Mode by typing a : in command mode to enter an Ex Mode command like below:**
:g/text/p	will display all lines that contain the text string "text"
:g/text/d	will delete all lines that contain string "text"
:g!/text/d	will delete all lines that do NOT contain string "text"
%s/word1/word2/gc	substitutes word2 for word1 globally with confirmation
:,$s/search/replace/gc	search from current line to end of file and confirm changes each time
:![command]	will issue the shell command specified. (e.g. :!bash - will open up a command line shell, 'exit' brings you back to Vim)
:r ![command]	will read the output of the subsequent shell command and write the output to the currently open file in vi
:reg	display what is in the registers
:reg f	shows the content of register 'f'
:sh	can be used to issue several Linux commands in succession without exiting the vi editor. This will create a subshell from which a user can issue multiple commands without exiting the current file. CTRL-D will return to the file.
:q :q!	quit and confirm, quit and discard changes
:w :wq	save file and continue editing, save file and quit
:/text	searches forward for "text"

:?text	searches backward for "text"
n	go the next instance of "text" in the file
N	go to the previous instance of "text in the file
#	search backwards for the word under the cursor
*	search forward for the word under the cursor

The Vim documentation page lists many references, books, turtorials and guides on using Vim. (See: http://vim.wikia.com/wiki/Vim_documentation, to get Vim (See: http://www.washington.edu/computing/unix/vi.html, http://www.vim.org) A few other web pages that are expecially useful are University of Washington "How to Use the vi Editor", the Vim Reference Card and the Vim quick reference card. (See: Washington.edu/computing/unix/vi.html, http://utools.com/vimrefcard.pdf, http://ls10-www.cd.uni-dortmund.de/~menge/vimquick.pdf) They provide more detail than the CheetSheet above.

Index